Handbook of Cognitive Linguistics
HSK 39

Handbooks of Linguistics and Communication Science

Handbücher zur
Sprach- und Kommunikationswissenschaft

Honorary Editor
Herbert Ernst Wiegand

Volume 39

De Gruyter Mouton

Handbook of Cognitive Linguistics

Edited by
Ewa Dąbrowska
Dagmar Divjak

De Gruyter Mouton

ISBN 978-3-11-029184-1
e-ISBN (PDF) 978-3-11-029202-2
e-ISBN (EPUB) 978-3-11-039380-4
ISSN 1861-5090

Library of Congress Cataloging-in-Publication Data

A CIP catalog record for this book has been applied for at the Library of Congress.

Bibliographic information published by the Deutsche Nationalbibliothek

The Deutsche Nationalbibliothek lists this publication in the Deutsche Nationalbibliografie; detailed bibliographic data are available on the Internet at http://dnb.dnb.de.

© 2015 Walter de Gruyter GmbH, Berlin/Boston

Typesetting: Meta Systems Publishing & Printservices GmbH, Wustermark
Printing and binding: Hubert & Co. GmbH & Co. KG, Göttingen
Cover design: Martin Zech, Bremen
♾ Printed on acid-free paper

Printed in Germany

www.degruyter.com

To Barney, Knut, Oskar and Poppy

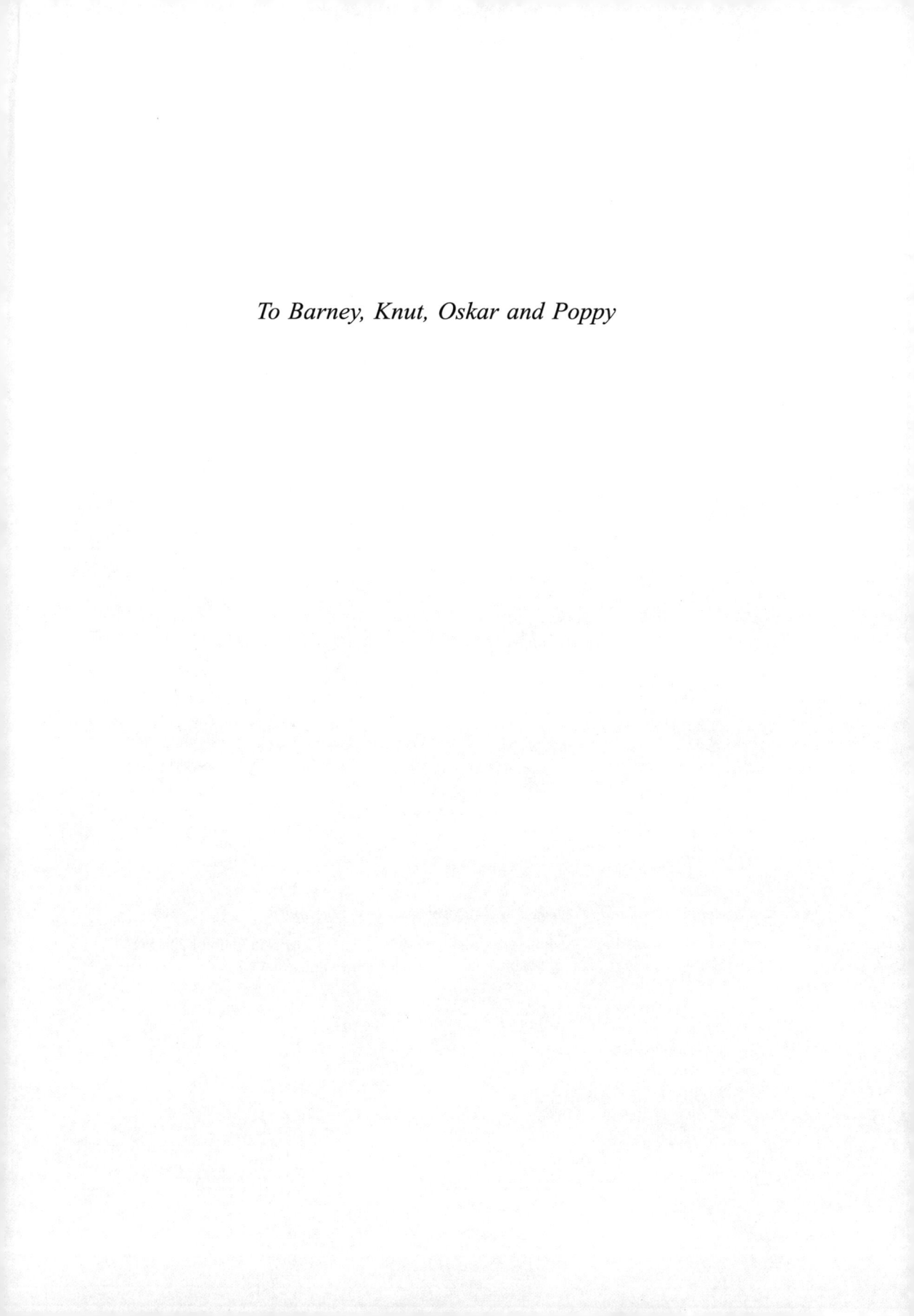

Contents

Introduction 1

I. The cognitive foundations of language

1. Embodiment · Benjamin Bergen 10
2. Attention and salience · Russell S. Tomlin and Andriy Myachykov 31
3. Frequency and entrenchment · Dagmar Divjak and Catherine L. Caldwell-Harris 53
4. Categorization (without categories) · Michael Ramscar and Robert Port ... 75
5. Abstraction, storage and naive discriminative learning · R. Harald Baayen and Michael Ramscar 100
6. Construal · Ronald W. Langacker 120
7. Metonymy · Antonio Barcelona 143
8. Metaphor · Raymond W. Gibbs 167
9. Representing Meaning · Laura J. Speed, David P. Vinson and Gabriella Vigliocco 190
10. Blending in language and communication · Mark Turner 211
11. Grammar and cooperative communication · Arie Verhagen 232

II. Overviews

12. Phonology · Geoffrey S. Nathan 253
13. Lexical semantics · Dirk Geeraerts 273
14. Usage-based construction grammar · Holger Diessel 296
15. Discourse · Christopher Hart 322
16. Historical linguistics · Martin Hilpert 346
17. Variationist linguistics · Dirk Geeraerts · Gitte Kristiansen 366
18. First language acquisition · Danielle Matthews · Grzegorz Krajewski 389
19. Second language acquisition · Nick C. Ellis · Stefanie Wulff 409
20. Poetics · Peter Stockwell 432

III. Central topics

21. Semantic typology · Maria Koptjevskaja-Tamm 453
22. Polysemy · Stefan Th. Gries 472
23. Space · Kenny R. Coventry 490
24. Time · Vyvyan Evans 509
25. Motion · Luna Filipović and Iraide Ibarretxe-Antuñano 527
26. Fictive motion · Teenie Matlock · Till Bergmann 546
27. Prototype effects in grammar · John R. Taylor 562
28. Argument structure constructions · Devin M. Casenhiser and Giulia M. L. Bencini 579

29. Default nonliteral interpretations The case of negation as a low-salience marker · Rachel Giora 594
30. Tense, aspect and mood · Laura A. Janda 616
31. Grammaticalization · Johan van der Auwera, Daniël Van Olmen and Denies Du Mon 634
32. Individual differences in grammatical knowledge · Ewa Dąbrowska 650
33. Signed languages · Sherman Wilcox 668
34. Emergentism · Brian MacWhinney 689

Indexes

Authors index 707
Subject index 711

Introduction

1. What is Cognitive Linguistics?
2. Some history
3. About the handbook
4. The future
5. References

1. What is Cognitive Linguistics?

Cognitive Linguistics is an approach to language study based on the assumptions that our linguistic abilities are firmly rooted in our general cognitive abilities, that meaning is essentially conceptualization, and that grammar is shaped by usage. In the early days, this was quite a bold claim to make, and it was diametrically opposed to the then-dominant generative framework. Nowadays, a growing number of linguists from different backgrounds share these assumptions and unite under the umbrella of Cognitive Linguistics. What draws the various strands of Cognitive Linguistics together is the Cognitive Commitment (Lakoff 1990: 40): all cognitive linguists are, or should be, committed to providing a characterization of the general principles of language that is informed by and accords with what is known about the mind and brain from other disciplines. It is this commitment that makes cognitive linguistics cognitive, and thus an approach which is fundamentally interdisciplinary in nature.

Following from the Cognitive Commitment, there are a number of assumptions that underlie the work of cognitive linguists. First, cognitive linguists share a usage-based view of language: grammar is shaped by usage, so in order to understand how languages are structured, how they have developed historically and how they are acquired by individual learners, we need to study how they are used. Second, cognitive linguists aim to show that speakers can build up language systems from usage by means of general cognitive abilities, such as perception, attention, memory, categorization and abstraction. These core general cognitive abilities are mainly studied outside of the discipline of linguistics, within the Cognitive Sciences. Third, cognitive linguists believe that language exists in order to convey meaning; all elements of language are meaningful, including grammatical constructions (cf. Langacker's conception of "grammar as image", Langacker 1979, 1991). Meaning, for cognitive linguists, involves conceptualization (see Langacker this volume and Speed, Vinson and Vigliocco this volume), is embodied (Bergen 2012 and this volume) and encompasses both dictionary and encyclopaedic information.

2. Some history

Cognitive linguistics has its origins in the late 1970s, when a number of linguists became increasingly dissatisfied with the then-prevailing generative paradigm with its focus on an autonomous formal grammar, and began to develop alternative approaches which emphasize function and meaning and the relationship between language and general cognitive processes (see, for example, Langacker 1979; Lakoff 1977; Talmy 1978). These early attempts began to combine into a more coherent and self-conscious movement about ten years later, with the publication in 1987 of George Lakoff's *Women, Fire and Dangerous Things* and Ron Langacker's *Foundations of Cognitive Grammar,* and, in the following year, of *Topics in Cognitive Linguistics,* an influential collection of articles edited by Brygida Rudzka-Ostyn. The next year, 1989, can be regarded as the official birth date of the movement. In the spring of this year, René Dirven organized a symposium in Duisburg at which the International Cognitive Linguistics Association (ICLA) was established. It was also decided to create a new journal, *Cognitive Linguistics,* and a monograph series entitled *Cognitive Linguistics Research*; both are published by De Gruyter Mouton. The Duisburg Symposium was retrospectively renamed the First International Cognitive Linguistics Conference.

Much of the early work in CL focussed on topics that were particularly problematic for generative approaches – prototype effects, radial categories, metaphor and metonymy, and the meaning of grammatical elements which were traditionally regarded as meaningless; but as the approach grew in strength, it expanded into virtually every area of linguistic organization. Several distinct strands emerged, including cognitive grammar, construction grammar, mental space and blending theory, neural theory of language, as well as a large body of more descriptive corpus-based work united under the banner of "usage-based" linguistics.

Today, there are several book series and at least fourteen journals devoted largely or entirely to CL (including *Cognitive Linguistics, Language and Cognition, Review of Cognitive Linguistics, CogniTextes, International Journal of Cognitive Linguistics, Constructions and Frames* and *Voprosy kognitivnoj lingvistiki*). The International Cognitive Linguistics Assocation [http://www.cognitivelinguistics.org/] has over 300 individual members and nearly 500 linguists attend the biennial International Cognitive Linguistics Conference. Sixteen regional and national organizations are affiliated with the ICLA. More and more universities offer courses in CL at undergraduate and postgraduate level; and there is growing interest from related disciplines, in particular, first and second language acquisition, adult psycholinguistics, and clinical linguistics, but also psychology, philosophy, and computer science.

3. About the handbook

The aim of this *Handbook* is to provide state-of-the-art overviews of the numerous subfields of cognitive linguistics written by leading international experts which will be useful for established researchers and novices alike. It is an interdisciplinary project with contributions from linguists, psycholinguists, psychologists, and computational modelling experts and emphasises the most recent developments in the field, in particular, the shift towards more empirically-based research. In this way, it will, we hope, help to shape the field, encouraging interdisciplinary and methodologically rigorous research which incorporates insights from all the cognitive sciences.

The handbook consists of 34 chapters, divided into three parts. Part 1: The cognitive foundations of language discusses the cognitive processes and abilities which underlie language, including embodiment (Bergen), attention and salience (Tomlin and Myachykov), entrenchment and its relationship to frequency (Divjak and Caldwell-Harris), categorization (Ramscar), analogy, schematization and naïve discriminative learning (Baayen and Ramscar), construal (Langacker), metonymy (Barcelona), metaphor (Gibbs), blending (Turner), conceptualization (Speed, Vinson and Vigliocco) and collaborative communication (Verhagen).

Part 2: Overviews consists of comprehensive surveys of the major subfields within the discipline. There are chapters on the basic areas of linguistic organization, i.e., phonology (Nathan), lexical semantics (Geeraerts) and construction grammar (Diessel), as well as chapters examining language use in a wider context: language variation and change (Kristiansen and Geeraerts, Hilpert), first and second language acquisition (Matthews and Krajewski, Ellis and Wulff), and discourse, including literary discourse (Hart, Stockwell).

Part 3: Central topics consists of shorter chapters on specific topics that illustrate the breadth of cognitive linguistic research. Most of these chapters deal with linguistic phenomena that have played a major role in the development of cognitive linguistic research. These include topics such as polysemy (Gries), semantic typology (Koptjevskaja-Tamm), space (Coventry), time (Evans), motion (Filipović and Ibarretxe-Antuñano), fictive motion (Matlock and Bergmann), tense, mood and aspect (Janda), grammaticalization (van der Auwera, Van Olmen and Du Mon), signed languages (Wilcox), argument structure constructions (Casenhiser), and prototype effects in grammar (Taylor). We have also incorporated some additional chapters on themes that are coming to the fore within Cognitive Linguistics: individual differences (Dąbrowska), emergence (MacWhinney), and default non-salient interpretations (Giora).

It becomes clear from this enumeration that the list is not exhaustive: there are many more topics that currently attract a considerable amount of attention, but have not been included for various reasons. Topics that were on our wish-list but did not materialize were, among others, those dealing with spoken language, gesture and multimodality (but see the handbook by Müller et al. 2014), chapters dealing with computational modelling, with case and with linguistic relativity, and chapters focusing on cognition in cognate areas, such as bilingual or translation cognition, to name but a few.

4. The future

The *Handbook* is intended to be a summary of the most important achievements of contemporary cognitive linguistic research but also a volume that looks forward and helps to shape the field in the years to come. For this reason, we conclude this introduction with some comments on what we think the future will bring.

4.1. Hypothesis testing and the use of behavioural and statistical methods

In the early stages (Lakoff 1987; Langacker 1987; Talmy 1978; Goldberg 1995), Cognitive Linguistics was very much an armchair discipline. Practitioners relied on introspection and reflected on linguistic examples, some of which were real and some of which had been constructed. These early analyses of important linguistic phenomena laid the theoretical foundations for much of the discipline. Since then, Cognitive Linguistics has undergone a significant shift towards a more empirical approach. This shift towards empiricism was driven by two main forces.

First, it was recognized from early on (e.g., Langacker 1988) that grammars are shaped by use, and therefore that to understand how grammars develop (in both the historical sense and the sense of individual speakers acquiring their language(s)) we must look at real usage. This lead to linguists working with corpora – large collections of authentic linguistic data. Methods and tools which were already widely used in usage-based lexicography were adopted in cognitive semantics and other areas and new methods were developed. Nowadays, a large body of cognitive linguistic research relies on corpus data; it distinguishes itself from traditional English corpus linguistics in that it considers corpora as tools and corpus linguistics as a methodology, not as a theory or discipline (Renouf 2005).

Secondly, as the body of cognitive-inspired analyses grew, we began to get competing accounts of the same phenomena. For instance, there is an on-going debate about whether it is the main clause or the subordinate clause verb which is the most prominent element in sentences containing a complement clause (such as *I know that she left*). Langacker (1991) adopts the traditional analysis, according to which the main clause verb is the profile determinant, pointing out that the sentence designates "the process of knowing, not of leaving" (436). Other linguists (e.g., Thompson 2002; Verhagen 2005) have argued that the subordinate verb should be regarded as the profile determinant, since (in the vast majority of cases, at least in conversation) it is the subordinate clause which constitutes the speaker's "interactional agenda", while the so-called "main clause" functions merely conveys "the speaker's epistemic, evidential or evaluative stance towards the issue or claim at hand" (Thompson 2002: 134). For instance, in the following excerpt, the main thrust of A's contribution is to indicate that whatever is being discussed is "cool", and B's and C's contributions show that this is how they interpret A's utterance.

A: I think it's cool.
B: It's cool.
C: It's great.
    (Thompson 2002: 132)

Langacker (2008: 419) acknowledges this argument, and proposes that we need to distinguish between different kinds of prominence. But how? There is a growing awareness that unless we develop reliable ways of measuring such differences, debates between linguists will be reduced to assertions that one's own intuitions are better than another analyst's. Cognitive linguists need to develop theories that make testable predictions, test these predictions and use the results to revise the theory if necessary, thus completing the empirical cycle.

Some researchers who took this step have adopted experimental methods from psychology (e.g., Ambridge and Goldberg 2008; Bencini and Goldberg 2000; Boyd and Goldberg 2011; Dąbrowska 2008, 2013; Gibbs and Colston 1995; Wheeler and Bergen 2010). While the earlier studies used mostly off-line judgement tasks, cognitive linguists are now increasingly relying on more sophisticated techniques, including on-line reaction time measurements and brain imaging. Many others (e.g., Arppe 2008; Divjak 2010; Geeraerts 1994; Gries 2003; Hilpert 2008; Lemmens 1998) applied sophisticated statistical methods to corpus data. In fact, the increasing reliance on quantitative methods (Geeraerts 2006: 17) has led some to declare that Cognitive Linguistics has taken "a quantitative turn" (Janda 2013: 1). A third line of research aims to combine both approaches and validates corpus-based findings experimentally (for book-length treatments, see Divjak and Gries 2012; Gries and Divjak 2012; Klavan 2012; many more studies have appeared as journal articles).

A question which many cognitive linguists are asking themselves now is: how far do we need to go? Do we all need to become statisticians, psychologists, neurologists? Ideally the answer to this question may be yes, but it seems hardly feasible, and is unlikely to happen in the foreseeable future. Instead, we can collaborate with experts from these fields. This type of interdisciplinarity presupposes a basic knowledge and understanding of cognate disciplines and a convergence in research methodology. It is this type of convergence that we aim to encourage with this handbook. The empirical trend is clearly on the increase and, it is to be hoped, will continue to gather momentum: human language is just too complex to understand by using traditional introspective methods (cf. Geeraerts 2010).

One way to achieve this goal more quickly would be to get linguists to archive their data and code used for analysis publicly. Some journals, including *Cognitive Linguistics*, already offer their authors the possibility to publish supplementary materials, including data and code, online. Transparency does not guarantee integrity, but it is certainly a step in the right direction as it makes it possible for other researchers to check, re-analyze, or re-intepret existing data and published findings.

A recently launched initiative, TrolLing [opendata.uit.no], takes this example of good practice to the next level by making available an independent platform for publicly archiving data and code, free of charge, to linguists of any theoretical persuasion. Sharing data helps with quality control at the submission and publication stage but also allows researchers to make progress more quickly by making negative results available and by making it possible to pool data, thus saving valuable time and resources.

4.2. Interdisciplinarity

Much of the early theorizing in cognitive linguistics was inspired by research in cognitive psychology, in particular, Eleanor Rosch's work on prototypes and basic level categories (Rosch 1973). While later work continued to draw on these findings, most cognitive linguistic researchers did not engage with more recent developments in psychology. This is evident in many of the chapters in the *Oxford Handbook of Cognitive Linguistics* (Geeraerts and Cuyckens 2007). For instance, Lewandowska-Tomaszczyk's (2007) excellent chapter on polysemy, prototypes, and basic level categories discusses the work of early pioneers like Rosch and Berlin, but not more recent reappraisals (Murphy 2002), work on exemplar theory (Nosofsky 1988, 1992), perceptual symbol systems (Barsalou 1999) or the relevant research in neuroscience (see Ramscar's chapter for a discussion of some of this work). Lewandowska-Tomaszczyk can hardly be blamed for this – the chapter provides a fair summary and assessment of CL work in the last two decades of the twentieth century – but one does feel that this work should be more strongly grounded in psychological research. Likewise, Talmy's chapter on attentional phenomena in the same volume (Talmy 2007), while providing an extremely useful framework for analysing salience in language, does not engage with psychological research on attention at all.

Even at the time the *Oxford Handbook* was published, there was a considerable amount of work which attempted to incorporate insights from more recent research in cognitive psychology and other cognitive science disciplines – work by scholars such as Lakoff, Levinson, Bowerman, Tomasello, Lieven, Bergen, Gibbs, and many others. Some of this work was already discussed in it; and much more has been published since then. Anyone will agree that in order to understand a phenomenon as complex as human language, it is necessary to combine insights from many disciplines, and so interdisciplinary work will continue to gather momentum. We hope that the chapters in this handbook – in particular, the "foundations" chapters – will assist this process.

4.3. The social turn

As explained at the beginning of this introduction, the most important feature uniting the various approaches of cognitive linguistics is a commitment to providing an account of language which is psychologically realistic. Because of this commitment, cognitive linguists have tended to account for linguistic structure by appealing to cognitive factors: languages are the way they are because humans are the way they are. However, properties of language can also be explained by appealing to its main functions, namely, communication and maintaining social cohesion. The two explanations are not, of course, mutually exclusive, but complementary, since human cognition is inherently social (Tomasello 1999). Although cognitive linguists have always recognized this, it is only relatively recently that researchers have begun to integrate the cognitive and social perspective into a single theoretical framework. In fact, in recent years, so many researchers have become interested in this area that we can speak of a genuine "social turn" (see, for example, Croft 2009; Geeraerts 2010; Geeraerts et al. 2010; Geeraerts and Kristiansen this volume; Harder 2010; Verhagen 2005, this volume). This development has involved research in three main areas: the role of joint attention and intention reading in language acquisition and use (Matthews and Krajewski this volume and Verhagen this volume), studies investigating how meaning is created by speakers engaged in social interaction (e.g., Du Bois 2014; Du Bois and Giora 2014), and the growing recognition that linguistic knowledge is socially distributed (Cowley 2011; see also Dąbrowska this volume). This trend will no doubt continue to flourish: fully integrating the cognitive and social perspective is probably the greatest challenge facing cognitive linguistics today.

5. References

Ambridge, Ben and Adele E.Goldberg
    2008   The island status of clausal complements: evidence in favor of an information structure explanation. *Cognitive Linguistics* 19: 357–389.

Arppe, Antti
   2008   Univariate, bivariate and multivariate methods in corpus-based lexicography – a study of synonymy. Publications of the Department of General Linguistics, University of Helsinki, No. 44. URN: http://urn.fi/URN:ISBN:978-952-10-5175-3.
Barsalou, Lawrence W.
   1999   Perceptual symbol systems. *Behavioral and Brain Sciences* 22: 577–609.
Bencini, Giulia M. L. and Adele E. Goldberg
   2000   The contribution of argument structure constructions to sentence meaning. *Journal of Memory and Language* 43: 640–651.
Bergen, Benjamin K.
   2012   *Louder than Words: The New Science of How the Mind Makes Meaning.* New York: Basic Books.
Boyd, Jeremy K. and Adele E. Goldberg
   2011   Learning what NOT to say: the role of statistical preemption and categorization in a-adjective production. *Language* 87(1): 55–83.
Cowley, Stephen J. (ed.)
   2011   *Distributed Language.* Amsterdam: John Benjamins.
Croft, William
   2009   Toward a social cognitive linguistics. In: V. Evans and S. Pourcel (eds.), *New Directions in Cognitive Linguistics*, 395–420. Amsterdam: John Benjamins.
Dąbrowska, Ewa
   2008   The effects of frequency and neighbourhood density on adult speakers' productivity with Polish case inflections: An empirical test of usage-based approaches to morphology. *Journal of Memory and Language* 58: 931–951.
Dąbrowska, Ewa
   2013   Functional constraints, usage, and mental grammars: A study of speakers' intuitions about questions with long-distance dependencies. *Cognitive Linguistics* 24: 633–665.
Divjak, Dagmar
   2010   *Structuring the Lexicon: A Clustered Model for Near-Synonymy.* (Cognitive Linguistics Research 43). Berlin: De Gruyter.
Divjak, Dagmar and Stefan Th. Gries
   2012   *Frequency Effects in Language Representation.* Volume 2. (Trends in Linguistics. Studies and Monographs. 244.2) Berlin: De Gruyter.
Du Bois, John A.
   2014   Towards a dialogic syntax. *Cognitive Linguistics* 25: 359–410.
Du Bois, John A. and Rachel Giora
   2014   Towards a dialogic syntax. *Cognitive Linguistics* 25: 351–358.
Geeraerts, Dirk
   2006   Introduction. A rough guide to Cognitive Linguistics. In: D. Geeraerts (ed.), *Cognitive Linguistics: Basic Readings,* 1–28. Berlin/New York: Mouton de Gruyter.
Geeraerts, Dirk
   2010   Recontextualizing Grammar: Underlying trends in thirty years of Cognitive Linguistics. In: E. Tabakowska, M. Choinski and L. Wiraszka (eds.), *Cognitive Linguistics in Action: From Theory to Application and Back*, 71–102. Berlin: De Gruyter Mouton.
Geeraerts, Dirk
   2010   *Theories of Lexical Semantics.* Oxford: Oxford University Press.
Geeraerts, Dirk and Hubert Cuyckens (eds.)
   2007   *The Oxford Handbook of Cognitive Linguistics.* Oxford: Oxford University Press.
Geeraerts, Dirk, Stefan Grondelaers and Peter Bakema
   1994   *The Structure of Lexical Variation: Meaning, Naming, and Context.* (Cognitive Linguistics Research 59.) Berlin: Mouton de Gruyter.

Geeraerts, Dirk, Gitte Kristiansen and Yves Peirsman (eds.)
  2010   *Advances in Cognitive Sociolinguistics*. Berlin: Mouton de Gruyter.
Gibbs, Raymond W. and Herbert L. Colston
  1995   The cognitive psychological reality of image schemas and their transformations. *Cognitive Linguistics* 6: 347–378.
Goldberg, Adele E.
  1995   *Constructions. A Construction Grammar Approach to Argument Structure*. Chicago: University of Chicago Press.
Gries, Stefan Th.
  2003   *Multifactorial Analysis in Corpus Linguistics: A Study of Particle Placement*. London and New York: Continuum Press.
Gries, Stefan Th. and Dagmar Divjak
  2012   *Frequency Effects in Language Learning and Processing.* Volume 1. (Trends in Linguistics. Studies and Monographs. 244.1) Berlin: De Gruyter Mouton.
Harder, Peter
  2010   *Meaning in Mind and Society: A Functional Contribution to the Social Turn in Cognitive Linguistics*. Berlin: Mouton de Gruyter.
Hilpert, Martin
  2008   *Germanic Future Constructions A Usage-based Approach to Language Change*. Amsterdam/Philadelphia: John Benjamins.
Janda, Laura A. (ed.)
  2013   *Cognitive Linguistics: The Quantitative Turn. The Essential Reader.* Berlin: De Gruyter Mouton.
Klavan, Jane
  2012   Evidence in linguistics: corpus-linguistic and experimental methods for studying grammatical synonymy. Dissertationes linguisticae Universitatis Tartuensis 15 (http://hdl.handle.net/10062/27865).
Lakoff, George
  1977   Linguistic gestalts. *Chicago Linguistic Society* 13: 236–287.
Lakoff, George
  1987   *Women, Fire and Dangerous Things. What Categories Reveal about the Mind*. Chicago: Chicago University Press.
Lakoff, George
  1990   The invariance hypothesis. Is abstract reason based on image-schemas? *Cognitive Linguistics* 1: 39–74.
Langacker, Ronald W.
  1979   Grammar as image. *Linguistic Notes from La Jolla* 6: 88–126.
Langacker, Ronald W.
  1987   *Foundations of Cognitive Grammar.* Volume 1: *Theoretical Prerequisites*. Stanford: Stanford University Press.
Langacker, Ronald W.
  1988   A usage-based model. In: B. Rudzka-Ostyn (ed.), *Topics in Cognitive Linguistics*, 127–161. Amsterdam: John Benjamins.
Langacker, Ronald W.
  1991   *Concept, Image and Symbol: The Cognitive Basis of Grammar*. Berlin: Mouton de Gruyter.
Langacker, Ronald W.
  2008   *Cognitive Grammar: A Basic Introduction*. Oxford: Oxford University Press.
Lemmens, Maarten
  1998   *Lexical Perspectives on Transitivity and Ergativity.* (Current Issues in Linguistic Theory 166.) Amsterdam: Benjamins.

Lewandowska-Tomaszczyk, Barbara
   2007   Polysemy, prototypes and radial categories. In: D. Geeraerts and H. Cuyckens (eds.), *The Oxford Handbook of Cognitive Linguistics*, 139–169. Oxford: Oxford University Press.

Müller, Cornelia, Alan Cienki, Ellen Fricke, Silva Ladewig, David McNeill and Sedinha Tessendorf/Jana Bressem (eds.)
   2014   *Body − Language − Communication. An International Handbook on Multimodality in Human Interaction.* [Handbücher zur Sprach- und Kommunikationswissenschaft / Handbooks of Linguistics and Communication Science (HSK) 38/1 and 2]. Berlin: De Gruyter Mouton.

Murphy, Gregory L.
   2002   *The Big Book of Concepts.* Cambridge: MIT Press.

Nosofsky, Robert M.
   1988   Similarity, frequency and category representations. *Journal of Experimental Psychology: Learning, Memory and Cognition* 14: 54–65.

Nosofsky, Robert M.
   1992   Exemplars, prototypes and similarity rules. In: A. F. Healy, S. M. Kosslyn and R. M. Shiffrin (eds.), *From Learning Theory to Connectionist Theory: Essays in Honor of W.K. Estes* Vol. 1, 149–168. Hillsdale: Erlbaum.

Renouf, Antoinette
   2005   Corpus Linguistics: past and present. In: W. Naixing, L. Wenzhong, and P. Jianzhong (eds.), *Corpora in Use: In Honour of Professor Yang Huizhong.* [English version downloaded from http://rdues.bcu.ac.uk/publ/Past_and_Present.pdf. – last accessed 26.1.2015]

Rosch, Eleanor
   1973   On the internal structure of perceptual and semantic categories. In: T. E. Moore (Ed.), *Cognitive Development and the Acquisition of Language*, 111–144. New York: Academic Press.

Rudzka-Ostyn, Brygida (ed.)
   1988   *Topics in Cognitive Linguistics.* Amsterdam: John Benjamins.

Talmy, Leonard
   1978   The relation of grammar to cognition – a synopsis. *Proceedings of TINLAP* 2: 14–24.

Talmy, Leonard
   2007   Attention phenomena. In: D. Geeraerts and H. Cuyckens (eds.), *The Oxford Handbook of Cognitive Linguistics*, 264–293. Oxford: Oxford University Press.

Thompson, Sandra
   2002   "Object complements and conversation". Towards a realistic account. *Studies in Language* 26: 125–164.

Tomasello, Michael
   1999   *The Cultural Origins of Human Cognition.* Cambridge: Harvard University Press.

TrolLing
   No date   The Tromsø Repository of Language and Linguistics. [URL: opendata.uit.no]

Verhagen, Arie
   2005   *Constructions of Intersubjectivity: Discourse, Syntax and Cognition.* Oxford: Oxford University Press.

Wheeler, Kathryn and Benjamin K. Bergen
   2010   Meaning in the palm of your hand. In: S. Rice and J. Newman (eds.), *Empirical and Experimental Methods in Cognitive/Functional Research*, 303–316. Stanford: CSLI.

Ewa Dąbrowska
Dagmar Divjak

I. The Cognitive foundations of language

1. Embodiment

1. Mind and body
2. A brief history of embodiment
3. The analytical phase
4. Process
5. Functional role
6. The future of embodiment in cognitive linguistics
7. References

1. Mind and body

There is a long history in philosophy of asking what the relationship is between the mind and the body. This question is as relevant to language as to any cognitive function, since language is at once a mental and a corporeal phenomenon. But perhaps this issue becomes even more relevant for language, a higher cognitive function that arguably distinguishes humans from other animals.

In general, the body appears to matter to the mind in a variety of ways. The concepts we have and the meanings we convey through language are not unrelated to the experiences we have moving our bodies or perceiving the world. But this leaves ample room for uncertainty. Exactly what impact do our bodies have? Are they important for how we learn new language and concepts? Or perhaps we use our bodies in an online fashion to make sense of even conventional language and concepts. Either or both of these may be true not only for things that are transparently related to bodily experiences, like motor actions and visual events, but also for concepts that are abstract in that their relation to the body is more tenuous – things denoted by words like *justice* or *truth*.

Since the 1980s, the idea that the body matters to the mind has been known as *embodiment* (Rosch and Lloyd 1978; Johnson 1987; Varela et al. 1991; Gibbs 2005; for an early precursor, see Merleau-Ponty 1945). This has been a central, orienting concept in cognitive linguistics research since its inception. But as big concepts often do, embodiment means different things to different researchers and its use has changed over time. This chapter begins by outlining the historical conceptions of embodiment in cognitive science. It then describes some of the ways that embodiment has been used in cognitive linguistics, and ends by anticipating the directions that linguistic embodiment research is currently moving in.

2. A brief history of embodiment

2.1. Dualism, monism, and everything in between

In principle, there are different ways the mind could relate to the body, and many of these possibilities have their own champions, arguments, and literatures. The strongest imaginable positions stand in contrast to one another. It could be on the one hand that there is no meaningful relation between the mind and body; the *dualist* position holds that the mind is of qualitatively unique stuff, irreducible to the material realm where the body lives. Or on the other hand, it could be that the mind and body are really one and the same; the strongest *monist* position argues that everything we want to know about the mind can be reduced to physics and explained away in material terms (this proposition therefore sometimes goes under the banner of *eliminative materialism*).

The vast majority of work in cognitive science, and cognitive linguistics as a sub-discipline, resides somewhere between these two extremes. At the time of the writing of this chapter, it's overwhelmingly clear that the body matters in profound ways to how the mind works. In the most banal way, for instance, having an intact, working brain is a pre-requisite to human cognition. Things without brains, like brooms and rocks, do not think, and they do not have language. Somewhat more informatively, the limits and nature of the brain's computational capacity shape what the mind can achieve; human language for instance requires a human brain – an elephant brain will not suffice.

Yet at the same time, it's clear, at least for the purpose of conducting meaningful and useful science, that we would be ill-served to throw out everything we want to know about the mind in an effort to reduce it to other, lower, physical levels of explanation. Even if we believed that in principle everything about human language could be reduced to the biology, chemistry, and ultimately the physics of individuals and the world (and many researchers do hold this non-eliminative materialist position) it currently appears that it is still useful to have a higher level of enquiry that addresses the mind and mental constructs. This is a level at which we can ask questions, formulate theories, and seek answers about how the mind works. For example, even if, ultimately, cognitive-level concepts like CONCEPT or WORD are merely epiphenomenal – even if they can be explained away in terms of underlying biochemistry and physics, it still makes sense for us, at least for the time being, to use the constructs of concepts and words in our science. That's because we're interested in how people learn words, how we figure out what they mean, how their meanings relate to concepts, and so on.

So it's a tacit assumption in most (but not all) of cognitive science that the parts and processes proper to what we think of as the mind need to be explained, and that the brain and body are one possible source of explanation. And because the brain and body seem deeply related to cognition, much of the work in cognitive science asks questions about the extent to which and the ways in which the particularities of the body, including the brain, affect the functioning and properties of the mind, or even, on some accounts constitute the mind themselves. This is the issue of *embodiment*.

2.2. Embodiment in cognitive science

There are roughly as many definitions of *embodiment* as there are people who use the word. I say "roughly" because many people who use the word seem to use it in multiple ways, while others may not have a particularly well formed idea of what they intend it to mean. In general, *embodiment* seems to be used to mean something about how the mind relates to the body. But this relation can come in many guises, and embodiment can signify any of the following things (see Wilson 2002; Ziemke 2003; and Ziemke et al. 2007 for much more thorough reviews):

- There are properties of the mind that can only be explained by reference to the brain or body
- The mind is not just generalized software, but is software than can be run on only one type of hardware, namely the brain
- Individual differences in brain and body produce individual differences in the mind
- For the mind to function, the organism must have a body, including but not limited to a brain (so a brain in a vat wouldn't have the same properties as a brain in a body)
- An individual's experience (presumably in his/her brain and body) are critical to the individual's mind
- The mind is not limited to brain functioning, but also extends to the use of other parts of the body (so that cognition isn't just between the ears)
- The mind is not limited to brain and body functioning, but also extends to the environment in which a person is situated, including other individuals or artifacts.

The version of embodiment that is most prevalent in the cognitive linguistics literature is this particular one:

> the structures used to put together our conceptual systems grow out of bodily experience and make sense in terms of it; moreover, the core of our conceptual systems is directly grounded in perception, body movement, and experience of a physical and social nature. (Lakoff 1987: xiv)

There's a lot built into this definition. But there are two key types of embodiment that it hints at. The first argues that the concepts or cognitive machinery we use for various cognitive behaviors, like reasoning, using language, and so on are built, presumably over the course of the development of an individual, from experiences that the individual has, which may be perceptual, motor, or affective in nature. This shapes the properties of those components of the cognitive system. This <u>developmental</u> notion of embodiment is more clearly distinguished in Lakoff and Johnson (1999).

> The claim that the mind is embodied is, therefore, far more than the simple-minded claim that the body is needed if we are to think. [...] Our claim is, rather, that the very properties of concepts are created as a result of the way the brain and body are structured and the way they function in interpersonal relations and in the physical world. (Lakoff and Johnson 1999: 37)

A second possibility is that the links between concepts on the one hand and the perceptual, motor, and affective experiences the individual has had are not lost over the course of development – they continue to play a role in ("grounding" or "making sense of") the use of concepts. This second, <u>online</u> position is described as follows:

> In an embodied mind, it is conceivable that the same neural system engaged in *per*ception (or in bodily movement) plays a central role in *con*ception. That is, the very mechanisms responsible for perception, movements, and object manipulation could be responsible for conceptualization and reasoning. (Lakoff and Johnson 1999: 38)

Although they seem superficially similar, these two possible relations between language and perception or action come with distinct causal and mechanistic claims. Each requires different sorts of evidence and if true has different consequences for what aspects of cognition embodiment is important to, and in what ways. I'll tease some of these differences apart in the next three sections, which cover three major phases of embodiment research in Cognitive Linguistics.

3. The analytical phase

Cognitive Linguistics has used the notion of embodiment to explain facts about language since its inception. There have been three distinct phases in the application of the idea of embodiment to empirical work on language and cognition. The first, discussed in this section, was *analytical* in that it involved linguists – inspired by work in cognitive psychology – looking for evidence of how the conceptual resources that underlie language use might be embodied through analysis of language. Work in this stage produced results that did not speak much to mechanisms, and as a result were equally compatible with the developmental and online types of embodiment. The second phase, discussed in the next section, is the *process* phase, which involved refinement of the online version of embodiment in a way that has generated a new theoretical framework, and inspired a substantial body of empirical work. And the third phase, which the field is currently moving into, is discussed in section 5. This is the *function* phase, in which researchers are refining their tools in an effort to determine exactly what embodiment does for specific aspects of language use and other cognitive operations.

3.1. Inspiration from cognitive psychology

The earliest self-consciously cognitive linguistic efforts were inspired by neighboring cognitive psychology and cognitive anthropology results suggesting a variety of ways in which language was not independent of the body. For instance, Eleanor Rosch's work on category structure provided evidence that the way we split up the world linguistically depends on the way we interact with it. This is perhaps most obvious in her work on basic level categorization (Rosch et al. 1976). She found that the words people are most likely to use in neutral contexts to describe things (e.g., *tree* for urban North Americans, as opposed to the more specific *pine* or more general *life form*) collect a whole host of properties. Like *tree*, these Basic Level terms tend to be short, learned early, faster to access, among other features. Critically, the taxonomical level that tends to be Basic appears to be dependent on human bodily interactions with the world. The basic level for objects appears to be best explained as the highest level of categorization that shares a common mental image and interactional affordances.

Another line of Rosch's work, on prototypicality, was similarly inspirational to early cognitive linguistics in terms of its contributions to the idea of embodiment (Rosch 1978). Rosch found that not all members of categories are equivalent in terms of people's mental representations. Americans treat robins as better examples of the category bird than they do ostriches, not only when explicitly asked to judge, but also when their reaction time to decide whether each category member is in fact a category member is measured. And there are even asymmetrical effects of prototypicality in reasoning – people are more likely to infer that a property of robins is true of ostriches than the reverse. Again, protoypicality seems to suggest that mental categories are embodied since they depend on our interactions with the world – the prototypical bird varies as a function of exposure, so people with different life histories have different mental categories.

Results like Rosch's inspired cognitive linguists to look, using the tools of analytical linguistics, for places where linguistic distributions appeared to depend on embodied knowledge. There have been five major lines of work to pursue this goal, each of which is addressed in turn below.

3.2. Embodied syntax

One of the central features of human language is that it displays structure at multiple levels (phonological, morphological, syntactic) that goes beyond mere sequence. Humans seem particularly well equipped to learn and use language with all its complexities, and many other animals do not. Consequently, it becomes very interesting to ask what the human capacity for complex linguistic structure is like. Linguistics in the second half of the 20th century was particularly oriented towards syntax, so a great deal of work during this period focused on the nature of the human cognitive capacity for structure at this level.

Beginning in the 1960s, the mainstream Generative (or Chomskian) approach to language posited that syntax is an informationally encapsulated module of the mind to be explained solely on the basis of internal computational principles. This product of a philosophical orientation towards neo-Cartesian dualism led many linguists to reject the possibility that the idiosyncratic and physically constrained working of the brain, the body, or experience could be relevant to the pinnacle capacity of human minds: abstract syntax.

But early cognitive linguists, as well as functionalists, attempted to demonstrate ways in which syntactic knowledge is sensitive to the body and bodily experience – in particular, ways in which meaning actually matters to syntactic form. This was seen as a type of embodiment, since the goals, intentions, knowledge, and beliefs of the individual can't help but be shaped by individual experience, and to the extent that they in turn affect grammar, that would mean that grammar depends on individual world experiences.

A good deal of the argument hinges on what, exactly, constitutes syntactic knowledge per se. At the time, much of the field held up grammaticality judgments as a valid measure of what language users know, and so early Cognitive Linguistics work aimed to determine whether these judgments reflected knowledge that couldn't be syntax-internal, but had to do with the meaning the language user wanted to convey. Consider, for instance, an utterance like *Rupert sneezed me the peanuts*. Determining whether this string of words forms a grammatical sentence or not depends entirely on how plausible the comprehender thinks it is that Rupert could transfer peanuts to someone through sneezing. It might become more plausible if we know that Rupert is not a person but rather an elephant, for example. When meaning intrudes on grammaticality, it is impossible to characterize syntax as a strictly autonomous system (for the full version of this argument, see Goldberg 1995).[1]

---

[1] Some linguists deal with this issue by making a distinction between grammaticality (a theory-internal construct) and acceptability (the judgments language users make), and acknowledge that the latter can be influenced by semantic plausibility but reject this possibility for the former (Chomsky 1965).

Other work in Cognitive Linguistics tried to derive the form of syntactic constructions directly or indirectly from the (embodied) functions people put them to. The idea here was that if the principles that govern syntactic structure can be shown to be syntax-external, then again individual world experiences, as channeled through the body, matter to linguistic knowledge. One well known example is the case of deictic there-constructions, as in *There's the restaurant we were looking for* (Lakoff 1987). Deictic there-constructions behave differently from any other constructions in the language. They start with a deictic demonstrative *there* instead of a subject, have a restricted range of verbs they can use (basically just the copula, and not in the past tense), and the verb is followed by an apparent subject that has a range of restrictions on it. Lakoff (1987) argues that this unique syntactic patterning is due to the unique function it has: linguistically pointing things out in the situated context of use. To the extent that conventional linguistic patterns can be explained as consequences of the functions they're put to, this means that syntax is again not encapsulated from the experiences a language user has had using that expression for embodied communication.

Complementary lines of work on Cognitive Grammar (Langacker 1987, 2002) and Construction Grammar (Goldberg 1995) advance two related ways that embodiment could have an impact on language. The first is the idea that the operations that an individual performs while using language have two facets – one part applies to the form, aggregating and ordering a string, but a second part operates in parallel over its meaning. Researchers in these traditions point to (sometimes subtle) differences in meaning, function, or use across different syntactic forms that may or may not have been previously analyzed as notational or surface variants of one another. For instance, the English double-object construction (as in *The mayor tossed his secretary the keys*) appears to bear a slightly different meaning from the English caused-motion construction (*The mayor tossed the keys to his secretary*), but this is best illuminated by the cases in which only the caused-motion is licit (*The mayor tossed his keys to the floor*) and the double-object version is not (**The mayor tossed the floor his keys*). In its strongest form, the hypothesis that any difference in form entails a corresponding difference in meaning is the Non-Synonymy Principle (Goldberg 1995), and it remains controversial, not in the least because there are different ways to define what synonymy and meaning mean. But to the extent that form and meaning constraints operate in parallel to constrain what is and what is not a licit utterance in a language, it's again impossible to hold syntax apart as a function immune from the body's effects.

The second way in which Cognitive Grammar in particular contributes to embodiment is through the importance placed on individual experience; the idea that language is learned bottom-up, such that individuals interacting with language (presumably in their bodies with their brains in the world) memorize and then schematize over useful and salient linguistic patterns. This is the idea of a usage-based model, which follows in the next section.

3.3. Usage-based models

As indicated by the cognitive psychology work that inspired early embodiment theory in cognitive linguistics, individual world experience might impinge on linguistic knowledge. At the time when Cognitive Linguistics started to coalesce, Linguistics displayed a prevailing research focus (based on the Generative tradition) on universal aspects of linguistic knowledge (both across languages and across speakers of the same language) and on the categorical nature of linguistic knowledge, including categorical and grammatical knowledge (Harris 1995). The idea that individual experience – language use – might affect language knowledge, while not necessarily in opposition to the mainstream, generative view, certainly placed emphasis differently. Indeed, this was very much the argument given by generativists, like Fritz Newmeyer, who in a presidential address to the LSA famously argued that "grammar is grammar and usage is usage" (Newmeyer 2003). Certainly, no-one would argue that people's knowledge is identical to what they say. The fact that I misspell the word *the* as 'teh' 25 % of the time when typing quickly doesn't entail that I think that the word is actually spelled 'teh' with probability 0.25. And the same is true of speech errors, disfluencies, and so on. However, the observation that people make and notice errors in production is not tantamount to endorsing a global distinction between knowledge and use, or competence and performance.

This intuition led many Cognitive Linguistics researchers to look to see whether aspects of language use affect undisputedly central representational aspects of language (see Divjak and Caldwell-Harris this volume). Are phonemes expressed in the same way in the same context, or does the frequency of the particular word they occur in affect the degree to which they will be reduced (Bybee and Scheibman 1999; Gahl and Garnsey 2004)? Does the frequency with which verbs occur in certain argument structure patterns predict how language comprehenders process those verbs in those argument structure constructions, and the perceived grammaticality of those verbs in those constructions (Ellis 2002; Gries et al. 2005)? These are questions about how use – typically operationalized in terms of frequency – affects linguistic knowledge.

There isn't much debate any longer about how valid usage-based theories of language are, in large part because the point has been made. Much of the work now done in psycholinguistics takes for granted that knowledge about frequency, both the raw frequency of particular linguistic units or the strength of their tendency to co-occur with others, plays a role in the millisecond-by-millisecond processing of language. That is, it's (nearly) universally accepted in psycholinguistics that people's knowledge of language includes knowledge based on frequency and probability. This has in large part made the debate about use and knowledge irrelevant. People have knowledge of use. And it's clear that if one's theory of language knowledge can only include things that can't be based on use, then this will cause one to define usage-based knowledge as qualitatively different from "core" language knowledge. But this is a debate about labeling and turf, not a real debate about the facts at hand. Use matters. And this means that this particular prong of embodiment work has come back with an answer in the affirmative. Yes, the experiences an individual language user has in the world matter to their linguistic knowledge (Dąbrowska this volume).

One particularly productive dimension of this usage-based approach has been in studies of early language development (Matthews this volume). What happens over the course of a child's first several years of life, and how – if at all – does the body matter to what children learn, how, and when? Perhaps the most complete account of how children acquire language from an embodied perspective is provided in Tomasello (2009), who argues that children build language from the ground up, on the basis of their situated experiences with language in use. Critical in this account is an ability that humans have (perhaps uniquely) to read the intentions of others – this is what allows the child to understand what a word refers to or what is intended with a speech act. Intention reading, on Tomasello's account, depends in no small way on bodily interactions, including monitoring, following, and directing attention of others through eye gaze and through bodily gestures.

3.4. Image schemas

A core issue for cognitive linguistics is the nature of the mental representations that underlie meaning. Are they abstract and detached from embodied experiences? A sort of Language of Thought or Mentalese? Or are they fine-grained sensorimotor representations? One idea that has emerged in the cognitive linguistic literature falls between these alternatives, and proposes a kind of mental representation called *image schemas*. The basic notion of an image schema, as articulated by Johnson, is "[…] a recurring dynamic pattern of our perceptual interactions and motor programs that gives coherence and structure to our experience" (1987: xiv).

The idea is that recurring interactional experiences we have in our bodies serve to ground linguistic meaning, as well as conceptualization, reasoning, and so on. As a result, image schemas are thought have certain features (see Hampe and Grady 2005). For one, they are generalized over many similar experiences, and are thus schematic (for instance, there wouldn't be an image schema for a specific container but might be one for a container in general). And although they are schematic, they're still believed to preserve both structural and perceptuomotor aspects of the specific experiences they schematize over. So an image schema for a container, for instance, would specify the schematic relations between the inside, outside, portal, and boundary, all while doing so in a representational modality that preserves the continuous, perception-, action-, or affect-specific content that it derives from – visual details about what a container looks or feels like to interact with. Because image schemas are thought to preserve aspects of the experiences that they're related to, they are characterized as grounded in those experiences. And because they are structured and schematic, they are believed to be usable for the normal sorts of things that concepts are used for, such as interfacing across cognitive systems, combining with one another, and being used in a displaced fashion.

The idea of image schemas has been influential in cognitive linguistics not least because of their perceived potential to explain distributional facts about language. To continue with the container example, there appear to be many words and grammatical structures that impose schematic constraints on how they can compose. For instance, the preposition *in* seems to evoke a schematic notion of containment such that the prepositional object can (at least in the concrete sense of *in*) be anything that can be construed as an instance of a container, from a garbage can to a galaxy. Image schemas are used to account for what *in* specifies its combinatorial affordances to be (it instantiates a container image schema and requires an object that can be a container). But because they're taken as intrinsically grounded (the container schema is bound to the experiences of containers that it's based on), image schemas are also taken as serving the function of grounding the meaning of words and their combinations.

3.5. Polysemy

Embodiment has also had an impact on the Cognitive Linguistic study of polysemy – understanding why words have which multiple meanings (see Gries this volume). Why are both the organ at the end of a human leg as well as the end of a bed called *foot*? Why does *hot* refer to both heat and spiciness? Why does the front of a clock share the name *face* with the front of an animal's head?

By the embodiment hypothesis, cases of polysemy like these might be explained by interventions of the human body on word meaning – interventions of different types in the three cases, each of which is merely a representative example of a much larger set of similar cases (Lakoff 1987). For instance, the foot of a bed is systematically co-located with human feet, and a process of metonymy might account for the extension of the word from the body to something body-adjacent (Barcelona this volume). The same process might account for the *head* of a bed. As for the case of *hot*, this word might refer not only to heat but also to spiciness because, given our bodies, the two experiences feel somewhat similar. Other examples of similarity in felt experience as potential mediator for polysemy include *over*, which although it prototypically refers to something that is located above another object in the vertical axis, can also refer to the relation where something merely covers a second object from view, even if they are arranged along a horizontal axis (as a picture can be placed *over* a hole in a wall to conceal it). And finally, we might use the word *face* for either a part of a clock or a part of a body because the former looks like the latter – humans for instance have a roundish thing centered at the top of their bodies, just as do clocks, especially analog ones. Words for body parts might get extended to things that look similar in other cases, like the *eye* of a hurricane or a potato, or the *shoulder* of a mountain.

Early Cognitive Linguistics was populated by many studies, exploring exactly these types of polysemy, trying to come to terms with the range and frequency of patterns like these within and across languages (Brugman 1981; Lindner 1983; Lakoff 1987; Tyler and Evans 2001; Bergen and Plauché 2005; among others). The upshot of this work is that there appear to be systematic relations among word senses, many of which plausibly relate to the body, including those exemplified above. As Gibbs and Colston (1995) point out however, without confirmation from other types of evidence, like psycholinguistic experimentation, this work presents only part of the story.

3.6. Metaphor

But likely the most widely recognized and influential place where embodiment has played a role in Cognitive Linguistics is metaphor (Gibbs this volume). It's not hard to believe that the body should matter to language about perception and action is structured. But it would be more surprising and revealing if we were to find that the body also matters to how language used to talk about abstract concepts like morality and transfinite numbers. That is what an embodied theory of metaphor would claim.

If the ability for abstract thought in general is grounded in our experiences in our bodies, then this would have important consequences. For one, in practical terms, it would be impossible to study any human cognitive endeavor without taking into consideration its bodily grounding, whether it be economic or political decision making or logical or mathematical inference. (Indeed, this has been a large part of George Lakoff and his colleagues' research program, applying embodied cognitive science to philosophy [Lakoff and Johnson 1999], math [Lakoff and Núñez 2000], and politics [Lakoff 1996]). Second, in terms of the question of the relation of the mind to the body, it would suggest that the body matters even to the least likely of mental capacities – if any human capacity is immune to embodied influence, then certainly it would be abstract thought. And third, in terms of the organization of the mind, embodiment of abstract concepts would suggest massive reuse of and interconnection among the various brain systems we have evolved, and would argue against any sort of strict modularity. At its core, the embodied metaphor story is a story about how we come to think and talk about abstract concepts, basing our understanding on concrete perceptual, motor, and affective experiences.

Certain parts of the literature on metaphor highlight aspects of embodiment. For one, it has often been observed that the body and bodily experiences are frequently taken as source domains, sometimes systematically across languages, and sometimes not (Kövecses 2002). Moreover, the preferred explanation for why bodily experiences come to act as sources for abstract targets is that the two systematically co-occur in early experience – perhaps because we co-experience affection and warmth, warmth, which can be concretely felt by the body, comes to relate to and subsequently structure and stand for affection. If this is true, then the body would play an integral role in the formation of metaphor.

But as noted by Grady (1997) there are exceptions. We have metaphors like THEORIES ARE BUILDINGS or SOCIETY IS A FABRIC, in which the source, though assuredly more concrete than the target, is nevertheless not particularly related to early bodily experience, and certainly not systematically co-occurring with the target. Perhaps, Grady has suggested, there are different sorts of metaphor. Some, so-called *primary metaphors*, are embodied in the way suggested above for AFFECTION IS WARMTH. Others, like THEORIES ARE BUILDINGS, are grounded indirectly through the combination of multiple primary metaphors.

How can we tell exactly how embodied metaphorical language and thought is? Work on polysemy, including ways in which the body has been hypothesized to matter through metaphor, metonymy, and so on, has been extremely influential in the growth of prominence of Cognitive Linguistics research. At the same time however, there are limits to what it can reveal about embodiment, perhaps best articulated through an example. The word *see* describes both vision and comprehension, and there are systematicities in which words have which pairs of such meanings. But how and when does the body matter to these patterns? That is, in exactly what way is embodiment intervening? It's possible that in the minds of contemporary adult English users, there is a functional connection between understanding and vision such that when they use the word *see* in the understanding sense, they are also activating knowledge about vision. But distributional linguistic evidence by itself is not compatible uniquely with this possibility. Gibbs et al. (1997) nicely articulate a range of possible degrees of metaphorical embodiment (see also Boroditsky 2000). Perhaps adult language users access vision only when reflecting consciously on polysemy patterns, as linguists do, but not when normally using language. Perhaps embodiment plays a role in the development of adult language and concepts, but fades away once a system is learned. This is the idea that metaphor helps people learn about abstract concepts by bootstrapping them off of more concrete ones, but that these connections are severed once developing minds have learned that seeing is not in fact understanding. And a more extreme version is also possible – perhaps embodiment only matters as a force in language change; on this account metaphors are cognitively "dead" and embodiment that might have mattered at the time of creation or adoption of novel senses for words is no longer relevant in either developing or adult language users once those changes have been propagated throughout a language community.

And to complicate things even more the same degree of embodiment need not necessarily apply to all users of a language or to all units within a language. So it could be that dead metaphors exist alongside ones that are fully alive, cognitively. And linguistic analysis by itself can't discriminate which language is embodied in which way for which people.

To deal with this limitation, different sorts of evidence have brought to bear on how active a role embodiment plays in what functions.

- Some evidence comes from novel uses of metaphor or metonymy to produce new uses for words that aren't already polysemous. For instance, if metaphorical mappings are still active in the minds of language users, then this should manifest in systematic interpretations of extensions of source domain language to target domains. A metaphor like UNDERSTANDING IS SEEING has a large number of lexical items with a foot in each domain, like *see, clear, cloudy*, and so on. But researchers have pointed out at times that completely novel extensions, while unconventional, are readily interpretable (Lakoff 1993). For instance, the intended meaning of *I'd need a scanning electron microscope to see your point* is probably not lost on many English speakers. Novel extensions like this naturally follow the same structural patterns of existing conventional polysemy patterns (understanding is still seeing, things that are hard to understand are hard to see, and so on). And they are interpreted exactly in these terms. So this might constitute evidence that the bodily systems for visual perception matter to our ability to understand language about comprehension.
- Studies of cognitive development have asked whether embodiment plays a role in the acquisition of concepts. For instance, it could be that learning about understanding involves passing through knowledge about vision. Corpus work shows that, for this case in particular, children begin producing the word *see* in situations that involve both sight and comprehension before they begin to also use the word for cases of comprehension in which sight is not relevant (Johnson 1999). This evidence is consistent with the idea that embodiment operates in the development of concepts and acquisition of language.
- Studies of semantic change have shown that words change meanings over time in directions predicted by synchronic metaphor, in the direction from more concrete to more abstract. For instance, words for vision gain additional meanings over time to denote knowledge as well (like the English word *see* has) (Sweetser 1991).

Again, however, although analysis of language patterns is revealing, it is ultimately unable to ascertain whether embodiment has an online function in language use. And because this is a particularly appealing version of embodiment, this has been one major direction of recent theory and investigation, one that has required more contact with experimental psychology and psycholinguistics.

4. Process

Lakoff and Johnson's proposal for online embodiment is that "the same neural system engaged in *per*ception (or in bodily movement) plays a central role in *con*ception" (1999: 38). Clearly this has been an influential idea. But stated in these broad terms, it's hard to derive specific claims about what mechanisms of the brain and mind are used to what end during the performance of exactly what cognitive tasks, and exactly with what timecourse. To become useful in explaining how people use language, this idea needs to be fleshed out in a theory of exactly how, when, and why which systems would be used during what linguistic and other cognitive functions. In the late 1990s, several research groups converged on a shared idea about how language use might be embodied, online, using systems that perform primary functions for perception, action, or affect. The idea was a simple one: perhaps the language user constructs denotational meaning in his or her mind by activating perceptual, motor, and affective systems to create or recreate the experience of the described scene. This is the *embodied simulation hypothesis* (Bergen 2012; see also Speed et al. this volume).

The embodied simulation hypothesis has been fleshed out in different ways (Barsalou 1999; Narayanan 1997; Glenberg and Kaschak 2002; Zwaan 2004; Feldman and Narayanan 2004; Gallese and Lakoff 2005; Feldman 2006; Bergen and Chang 2005, 2013; Bergen 2012). Some models are implemented computationally, making claims about exactly what processes lead what embodied mechanisms to be brought online at what time (like Embodied Construction Grammar [Bergen and Chang 2005, 2013; Feldman 2006]). Others describe hypothesized mechanisms in verbal terms, but in terms detailed enough to draw out predictions about timecourse of use of mechanisms and degree of detail (Kaschak and Glenberg 2000; Zwaan 2004; Barsalou et al. 2008)

Because these models make nuanced claims about cognitive processes, the appropriate tools for testing them are more properly drawn from the experimental methods of cognitive psychology and psycholinguistics, tools that afford measurements of cognitive operations over time in the online production or processing of language. Much of the work starting in the early 2000s asked people to perform both a linguistic task and a perceptual or motor task, in some order. The premise was that if perceiving some stimulus or performing some action used brain systems that were also recruited by language about similar percepts or actions, then the two tasks should interact. Typically, these studies measure reaction times. For instance, Glenberg and Kaschak (2002) had people read sentences describing motion towards or away from the body (like *You are closing/opening the drawer*) and then press a button to indicate whether they made sense or not, which was placed either close to or farther away from the experiment participants' own bodies. They found that people were faster to initiate their movement when the direction they had to move their hand in was the same as the direction of motion implied by the sentence. In another study focusing on vision, Zwaan et al. (2002) had people read sentences about objects that implied them to have a particular shape, like an egg in a pan versus a fridge. The participants then saw an image that depicted the object in the same implied shape or a different one, and had to judge whether it had been mentioned in the previous sentence or not. Though the answer to these critical sentences was always 'yes', reactions times differed – again, people were faster when the shape implied by the sentence and depicted by the image matched.

Another early line of work exploited brain imaging, mostly functional Magnetic Resonance Imaging (fMRI). The basic idea was that if understanding language about actions or perceivable events uses brain systems for action or perception in an online fashion, then known motor or perceptual regions should become differentially active when people were processing relevant language. A number of studies found precisely this. For instance, Tettamanti et al. (2005) presented people with sentences about hand, foot, or mouth actions while they laid in an fMRI scanner. They found that parts of the motor strip – the part of the brain that sends electrical signals to skeletal muscles – lit up in a body-part-specific way. The part of the motor strip that controls leg actions was more active when people were processing leg action sentences, and so on.

And these findings extend, albeit in a somewhat more complicated way, to language not about perceivable eventualities and performable actions, but also to language about abstract concepts that are only metaphorically related to perception and action. For instance, Glenberg and Kaschak's original work on action-sentence compatibility effects showed the same strength of effect when people were processing language not only about concrete motion, but also about abstract transfers (for instance, *You dedicated the song to Dan* versus *Dan dedicated the song to you* [Glenberg and Kaschak 2002]). What's more, Wilson and Gibbs (2007) found that performing a source-domain action primes comprehension of metaphorical language using that source domain. For instance, making a fist leads to faster subsequent comprehension of *grasp a concept*, and swallowing leads to faster comprehension of *swallow an idea*. There is also brain imaging work showing that even when processing metaphorical language, the perceptual and motor systems in comprehenders' brains light up in ways corresponding to language about the source domain. For instance, Boulenger et al. (2009) found that foot-controlling parts of the motor system become active when people are processing metaphorical language using foot actions as a source domain (like *Pablo kicked the habit*), while hand-controlling parts light up during processing of metaphorical language using hand actions as source domain concepts (like *John grasped the concept*).

Consequently, as a first-order issue, there is now a sizeable stable of experimental findings showing that language interacts with perception and action in an online fashion. This is especially true of language about perceptual or motor content, but extends at least in a number of studies to metaphorical language or language about abstract concepts.

However, fleshing out predictions of online embodiment to make concrete experimental predictions has also resulted in a great deal of nuance in the actual findings.

Some experiments find facilitation effects between language on the one hand and perception or action on the other (Zwaan et al. 2002; Glenberg and Kaschak 2002). Others find interference (Richardson et al. 2003; Bergen et al. 2007). And this has spawned a good deal of thought about exactly what factors lead effects to occur in what direction and what this all says about how systems for perception and action are in fact used during language production and processing (Kaschak et al. 2005; Bergen 2007).

Other work has shown that embodiment effects sometimes are and sometimes are not detected. This is especially true with metaphorical language, where for instance, some brain imaging studies have found perceptual or motor areas lighting up during processing of metaphorical language using perception or motor control as source domains (Boulenger et al. 2009) while others have not (Aziz-Zadeh and Damasio 2008). The situation is similar with literal language about perceivable or performance events, where the detectability of an embodiment signature appears to depend on subtle features of the linguistic signal, including grammatical aspect (Bergen and Wheeler 2010) and person (Sato and Bergen 2013). Moreover, it's known people can process meaning more or less deeply, and it's possible that while deep processing is associated with embodiment effects, superficial processing uses different strategies (as suggested by Barsalou et al. 2008).

It's important to note that not just motor systems of the brain but also bodily effectors might be engaged in real time processes of meaning-making. The most obvious uses are in iconic gesture (Hostetter and Alibali 2008) and signs (Taub 2001; Wilcox this volume). When a gesture or sign iconically models or represents an action or the shape, orientation, or motion of an object, it may be serving as an embodied analogue representation. A topic of current discussion is whether and to what extent these uses of the body play a role in meaning-making, beyond other linguistic signs and gestures.

5. Functional role

There's now little doubt that hearing or reading language about perceptible entities and events can result in measurable activity in the brain systems responsible for perception, and the same goes for language about action and the brain's motor systems. But these findings don't answer a more important question: what exactly is the use of perceptual and motor systems good for? What does it do? This is the question of the functional role of online embodiment. And it remains unanswered.

When we move, as the field has, from viewing language statically and analytically to considering language use as an online process, we're confronted with the question of mechanism. What is the best characterization we can come to of how language users produce or process language in real time? What are the component parts of that system? What exactly do they contribute to the outcome – the behavioral results we can measure and the subjective consequences, for example, experiences of successful comprehension?

There are many proposed possible functions that the online use of perception and actions systems could play in language use. The jury is still out, but some proposals include:

- Lexical access: In language comprehension, figuring out what word was intended might be facilitated by performing embodied simulation of the hypothesized sense, or by simulation of the described content preceding that word. In language production, selecting the right word representation might be mediated by accessing perceptual and motor knowledge about the referent of that word.
- Representational substrate: Denotational meaning might be represented in perceptual/motor terms. That is, what we think of as a message to be formulated in language production or to be decoded in comprehension in fact is a perceptual or motor simulation. To the extent that simulations performed by speaker and hearer are similar, they can be said to have similar representational content.
- Inference: An unquantified but surely important portion of language comprehension is performing inferences to flesh out unstated properties. Some of this inference-drawing may use perceptual or motor simulation – perhaps when you read that *Tristan spent all night at the pub and has a headache this morning*, you fill your preferred causal explanation (drinking alcohol? too loud in the pub?) through a process of

simulating what the scene would be like, based on but not limited to the explicitly articulated details.
- Contextual specification: Words have varied and underspecified denotational ranges. Perhaps embodiment plays an online role in fleshing out the details in a given context – perhaps a given utterance has fundamentally the same denotational meaning regardless of context of use, but varies in its context-specific interpretation by dint of how comprehenders bring their perceptual/motor systems to bear in any given instance (Mahon and Caramazza 2008). For example, perhaps when presented with *The chicken is sick*, people activate different perceptual and motor knowledge about chickens than they do when presented with *The chicken is delicious*.
- None. Perhaps what appears in experiments to be signatures of embodiment is in fact nothing more than the product of spreading activation based on associative learning that doesn't actually play a functional role in language use. It's possible that people have come to associate words like *jump* with perceptual and motor experiences that tend to co-occur with producing or perceiving that word. Just as a dinner bell might lead automatically to salivation, so *jump* might lead automatically to motor or perceptual traces of jumping. But this does not mean that the motor or perceptual systems play any functional role in language use. It could well be that comprehension and production proceed perfectly well without these associations.

This, then, is the current state of the house that embodiment built. We know that perceptual, motor, and affective systems are activated in a content-specific way during language use. But we don't know what that activation does, mechanistically, for language users. And this is where the attention of embodiment researchers is beginning to turn.

One promising way to investigate function is through knock-out effects. If some cognitive function, say some aspect of language use, relies in a functional way on a piece of brain circuitry, then when that piece of brain is unavailable, either permanently or temporarily, then the cognitive function should be impaired. That's basically the logic of dissociation studies, where damage to a particular brain region knocks out certain cognitive capacities but not others. Applied to embodiment, this logic goes like this: if certain aspects of language use, like those listed above, are in fact functionally dependent on the use of systems for perception or action, then the loss of these brain systems should make it harder, or even impossible, for people to perform these specific language functions.

There are different ways to knock out a piece of brain tissue in general. The most decisive method is what neuroscientists working with animal models often do – to excise tissue in a careful and localized way. The problem is that only humans have human language and removing brain tissue is not possible with human subjects. So other, less invasive but necessarily coarser means are necessary. One is to take naturally occurring cases of brain damage, and triangulate a particular region that happens to be an overlapping region damaged across patients. The challenges of this neuropsychological approach to dissociations are well known – it's rare to find patients with localized damage to a region of interest, in addition to the fact that the brain's plasticity after trauma means that the patient's brain will have been reorganizing itself since the insult. Another approach is to use transcranial magnetic stimulation (TMS), which induces a transient magnetic field from the outside of the skull that interrupts activity in a narrow, local part of cortex for a brief moment. But there remain concerns about TMS, both in terms of unknown long-term effects on subjects exposed to it, as well as uncertainty about its underlying physical mechanism. And finally, there are behavioral measures, like adaptation. Neurons can be fatigued by continuous presentation of some stimulus, which leads them to respond less strongly after adaptation than before.

Each of these approaches has seen some use in the function-of-embodiment literature. For instance, Damasio and Tranel (1993) found that patients who suffer damage to the left temporal cortex, where the shapes and other visual properties of objects are represented, often also lose access to nouns. At the same time patients who suffer from lesions to the left frontal cortex, an area dedicated to motor control, tend to have difficulties with verbs. Work using TMS has shown similar results. Shapiro and colleagues (2001) applied TMS to motor areas, and found that this impaired performance on verb production but not on noun production. And finally, there has been some work using behavioral manipulations to fatigue certain brain circuitry. Glenberg et al. (2008) fatigued people's motor systems controlling hand motion in a particular direction, away or towards the body by having them move hundreds of beans in one direction or the other. Then they had them make judgments about sentences describing motion in the same direction or a different direction. They found that when the motor system had been fatigued with action in a particular direction, it took people longer to make judgments about sentences describing motion in the same direction. In sum, a variety of techniques are now being brought to bear on the question of whether embodiment plays a role in online language use, and if so, what role (Speed et al. this volume). But with only a handful of studies pursuing this question so far, the field remains wide open.

6. The future of embodiment in cognitive linguistics

Embodiment as a blanket approach seems to have less substance now than perhaps it had thirty years ago. In part this is because it has been a victim of its own success. The ideas expressed under the banner of embodiment have caught on, so that, in a way only sociologists of science can explain, embodiment has become a hot topic. Everything, it seems, is embodied. Which means that calling research or findings embodied has become less specific and less informative. In addition, the battles that were waged under the banner of embodiment have for the most part been won. It's now inconceivable to most cognitive scientists that language, including syntax, could be informationally encapsulated, or that language wouldn't use other systems, including of the brain and body, or that individual experience wouldn't matter. These are, for the most part, taken as proven hypotheses. So there would appear to be little work left for embodiment as a general concept to do.

But the future of embodiment depends on what we consider it to be. Is it a single answer to a single question? (Is the mind embodied? Yes.) Or is it a class of questions about how the mind might relate to the body? If the latter, then we have barely scratched the surface. And to the extent that we're still asking questions about how language is shaped by the body, we're asking questions about the embodiment of mind. Here are some examples of embodiment-related questions that have persisting potential impact:

– When and how are abstract concepts (including those pertaining to math, time, and so on) embodied? To what extent does embodiment of abstract concepts change through development and depend on the use to which they're being put?

- What are the limits of online perceptual/motor embodiment and what's happening in those cases that seem to indicate disembodied processing?
- What's the functional role of these systems?
- What's the developmental role?

Moving forward, two trends that have already struck elsewhere in the embodiment literature will likely find purchase in Cognitive Linguistics as well (aside from an orientation towards function, as discussed in the last section, which appears to be leading in current embodiment work on language). The first is the situated component of embodiment. It's not merely the case that we have bodies that might be relevant to the functioning of the mind, but that those bodies are embedded in environments, which they interact with continuously. Situatedness can be relevant to language in a variety of ways. The way we use language is not independent of the situations of use; deixis, reference, gesture, and so on, which are already topics under cognitive linguistic scrutiny, might be well served by a careful look at how the situated nature of linguistic cognition affects the form and processing of language.

The second relevant trend is one that's somewhat more philosophically radical; the idea that it's not merely the brain that performs cognitive operations, but that other parts of the body are also, at times, organs of cognition (Clark and Chalmers 1998; Menary 2006). When people use their fingers to count out days of the week, for instance, external parts of their bodies are part of the physical structure that is performing cognitive operations. To the extent that people's bodies are engaged to perform cognitive functions during the production, comprehension, or learning of language, aren't parts of the organism other than the brain also the material substrate of the mind? And what's more, to the extent that parts of the material world, like writing for instance, serve similar functions, can they also constitute part of the substructure of cognition. To the extent that they are, then it's not merely that language is embodied in the brain; it's embodied in bodies and the material world around them, which, in concert, enact cognition (Hutchins 1995).

There's no longer any question that the body matters to the mind. The continuing question of embodiment is exactly how.

7. References

Aziz-Zadeh, Lisa and Antonio Damasio
   2008   Embodied semantics for actions: Findings from functional brain imaging. *Journal of Physiology (Paris)* 102: 35–39.

Barcelona, Antonio
   this volume   7. Metonomy. Berlin/Boston: De Gruyter Mouton.

Barsalou, Lawrence W.
   1999   Perceptual symbol systems. *Behavioral and Brain Sciences* 22: 577–609.

Barsalou, Lawrence W., Ava Santos, W. Kyle Simmons and Christine Wilson
   2008   Language and simulation in conceptual processing. In: M. De Vega, A.M. Glenberg, and A. Graesser (eds.), *Symbols, Embodiment, and Meaning*, 245–283. Oxford: Oxford University Press.

Bergen, Benjamin
   2007   Experimental methods for simulation semantics. In: M. Gonzalez-Marquez, I. Mittelberg, S. Coulson, and M. J. Spivey (eds.), *Methods in Cognitive Linguistics,* 277–301. Amsterdam: John Benjamins.

Bergen, Benjamin
   2012   *Louder Than Words: The New Science of How the Mind Makes Meaning*. New York: Basic Books.
Bergen, Benjamin and Nancy Chang
   2005   Embodied construction grammar in simulation-based language understanding. In: J.-O. Östman and M. Fried (eds.), *Construction Grammars: Cognitive Grounding and Theoretical Extensions*, 147–190. Amsterdam: Benjamins.
Bergen, Benjamin and Nancy Chang
   2013   Embodied construction grammar. In: T. Hoffmann and G. Trousdale (eds.), *Oxford Handbook of Construction Grammar*. Oxford: Oxford University Press.
Bergen, Benjamin, Shane Lindsay, Teenie Matlock, and Srinivas Narayanan
   2007   Spatial and linguistic aspects of visual imagery in sentence comprehension. *Cognitive Science* 31: 733–764.
Bergen, Benjamin and Madelaine C. Plauché
   2005   The convergent evolution of radial constructions: French and English deictics and existentials. *Cognitive Linguistics* 16(1): 1–42.
Bergen, Benjamin and Kathryn Wheeler
   2010   Grammatical aspect and mental simulation. *Brain and Language,* 112: 150–158.
Boroditsky, Lera
   2000   Metaphoric structuring: Understanding time through spatial metaphors. *Cognition* 75: 1–28.
Boulenger, Véronique, Olaf Hauk, and Friedemann Pulvermueller
   2009   Grasping ideas with the motor system: Semantic somatotopy in idiom comprehension. *Cerebral Cortex* 19: 1905–1914.
Brugman, Claudia
   1981   *The Story of Over: Polysemy, Semantics, and the Structure of the Lexicon*. New York: Garland.
Bybee, Joan and Joanne Scheibman
   1999   The effect of usage on degrees of constituency: the reduction of don't in English. *Linguistics* 37(4): 575–596.
Chomsky, Noam
   1965   *Aspects of the Theory of Syntax*. Cambridge: MIT Press.
Clark, Andy and David Chalmers
   1998   The extended mind. *Analysis* 58(1): 7–19.
Damasio, Antonio and Daniel Tranel
   1993   Nouns and verbs are retrieved with differently distributed neural systems. *Proceedings of the National Academy of Sciences (USA)* 90: 4957–4960.
Dąbrowska, Ewa
   this volume   32. Individual differences. Berlin/Boston: De Gruyter Mouton.
Divjak, Dagmar and Catherine Caldwell-Harris
   this volume   3. Frequency and entrenchment. Berlin/Boston: De Gruyter Mouton.
Ellis, Nick
   2002   Frequency effects in language processing. *Studies in Second Language Acquisition*, 24(2), 143–188.
Feldman, Jerome
   2006   *From Molecule to Metaphor: A Neural Theory of Language*. Cambridge: MIT Press.
Feldman, Jerome and Srinivas Narayanan
   2004   Embodied meaning in a neural theory of language. *Brain and Language* 89: 385–392.
Gahl, Susanne and Susan Garnsey
   2004   Knowledge of grammar, knowledge of usage: Syntactic probabilities affect pronunciation variation. *Language* 80: 748–775.

Gallese, Vittorio and George Lakoff
   2005   The brain's concepts: The role of the sensory-motor system in conceptual knowledge. *Cognitive Neuropsychology* 22: 455–479.
Gibbs Jr., Raymond W.
   2005   *Embodiment and Cognitive Science*. Cambridge: Cambridge University Press.
Gibbs Jr., Raymond W.
   this volume   8. Metaphor. Berlin/Boston: De Gruyter Mouton.
Gibbs Jr., Raymond. W., Josephine Bogdanovich, Jeffrey Sykes, and Dale Barr
   1997   Metaphor in idiom comprehension. *Journal of Memory and Language* 37(2): 141–154.
Gibbs Jr., Raymond W. and Herbert Colston
   1995   The cognitive psychological reality of image schemas and their transformations. *Cognitive Linguistics* 6: 347–378.
Glenberg, Arthur M. and Michael P. Kaschak
   2002   Grounding language in action. *Psychonomic Bulletin and Review* 9(3): 558–565.
Glenberg, Arthur. M., Marc Sato, and Luigi Cattaneo
   2008   Use-induced motor plasticity affects the processing of abstract and concrete language. *Current Biology* 18: R290–R291.
Goldberg, Adele E.
   1995   *Constructions: A Construction Grammar Approach to Argument Structure*. Chicago: Chicago University Press.
Grady, Joseph E.
   1997   Theories are buildings revisited. *Cognitive Linguistics* 8: 267–290.
Gries, Stefan Th.
   this volume   22. Polysemy. Berlin/Boston: De Gruyter Mouton.
Gries, Stefan, Beate Hampe, and Doris Schonefeld
   2005   Converging evidence: Bringing together experimental and corpus data on the association of verbs and constructions. *Cognitive Linguistics* 16(4): 635.
Hampe, Beate and Joseph Grady (eds.)
   2005   *From Perception to Meaning: Image Schemas in Cognitive Linguistics*. Berlin: Mouton de Gruyter.
Harris, Randy
   1995   *The Linguistics Wars*. New York: Oxford University Press, USA.
Hostetter, Autumn B., and Martha W. Alibali
   2008   Visible embodiment: Gestures as simulated action. *Psychonomic Bulletin and Review* 15(3): 495–514.
Hutchins, Edwin
   1995   *Cognition in the Wild*. Cambridge: MIT Press.
Johnson, Christopher
   1999   Metaphor vs. conflation in the acquisition of polysemy: The case of *see*. In: M. K. Hiraga, C. Sinha and S. Wilcox (eds.), *Amsterdam Studies in the Theory and History of Linguistic Science* Series 4, 155–170. Amsterdam/Philadelphia: John Benjamins
Johnson, Mark
   1987   *The Body in the Mind: The Bodily Basis of Meaning, Imagination, and Reason*. Chicago: University of Chicago Press.
Kaschak, Michael P. and Arthur M. Glenberg
   2000   Constructing meaning: The role of affordances and grammatical constructions in sentence comprehension. *Journal of Memory and Language* 43: 508–529.
Kaschak, Michael P., Carol J. Madden, David J. Therriault, Richard H. Yaxley, Mark E. Aveyard, Adrienne A. Blanchard, and Rolf A. Zwaan
   2005   Perception of motion affects language processing. *Cognition* 94: B79–B89.
Kövecses, Zoltán
   2002   *Metaphor: A Practical Introduction*. Oxford: Oxford University Press.

Lakoff, George
  1987 *Women, Fire, and Dangerous Things*. Chicago: University of Chicago Press.
Lakoff, George
  1993 The contemporary theory of metaphor. *Metaphor and Thought* 2: 202–251.
Lakoff, George
  1996 *Moral Politics: What Conservatives Know that Liberals Don't*. Chicago: University of Chicago Press.
Lakoff, George and Mark Johnson
  1999 *Philosophy in the Flesh*. New York: Basic Books.
Lakoff, George and Rafael Núñez
  2000 *Where Mathematics Comes From: How the Embodied Mind Brings Mathematics into Being*. New York: Basic Books.
Langacker, Ronald
  1987 *The Foundations of Cognitive Grammar:* Volume I: *Theoretical Prerequisites* Stanford: Stanford University Press.
Langacker, Ronald
  2002 *Concept, Image, and Symbol*. Berlin: Mouton de Gruyter.
Lindner, Susan. J.
  1983 *A Lexico-semantic Analysis of English Verb Particle Constructions with "out" and "up"*. Bloomington: Indiana University Linguistics Club.
Mahon, Bradford Z. and Alfonso Caramazza
  2008 A critical look at the embodied cognition hypothesis and a new proposal for grounding conceptual content. *Journal of Physiology-Paris* 102: 59–70.
Matthews, Danielle and Grzegorz Krajewski
  this volume 18. First language acquisition. Berlin/Boston: De Gruyter Mouton.
Merleau-Ponty, Maurice
  1945 *Phénoménologie de la Perception*. Paris: Éditions Gallimard.
Menary, Richard
  2006 Attacking The Bounds of Cognition. *Philosophical Psychology* 19(3): 329–344.
Narayanan, Srinivas
  1997 *KARMA: Knowledge-based active representations for metaphor and aspect*. University of California, Berkeley Doctoral dissertation.
Newmeyer, Frederick
  2003 Grammar is grammar and usage is usage. *Language* 79(4): 682–707.
Richardson, Daniel C., Michael J. Spivey, Lawrence W. Barsalou, and Ken McRae
  2003 Spatial representations activated during real-time comprehension of verbs. *Cognitive Science* 27: 767–780.
Rosch, Eleanor.
  1978 Principles of categorization. In: E. Rosch and B. B. Lloyd (eds.), *Cognition and Categorization*, 27–48. Hillsdale: Erlbaum.
Rosch, Eleanor and Barbara B. Lloyd (eds.)
  1978 *Cognition and Categorization*. Hillsdale: Erlbaum.
Rosch, Eleanor, Carolyn B. Mervis, Wayne Gray, David Johnson, and Penny Boyes-Braem
  1976 Basic objects in natural categories. *Cognitive Psychology* 8: 382–439
Sato, Manami and Benjamin Bergen
  2013 The case of the missing pronouns: Does mentally simulated perspective play a functional role in the comprehension of person? *Cognition* 127(3): 361–374.
Shapiro, Kevin A., Alvaro Pascual-Leone, Felix M. Mottaghy, Massimo Gangitano, and Alfonoso Caramazza
  2001 Grammatical distinctions in the left frontal cortex. *Journal of Cognitive Neuroscience* 13(6): 713–720.

Speed, Laura, David P. Vinson and Gabriella Vigliocco
  this volume 9. Representing meaning. Berlin/Boston: De Gruyter Mouton
Sweetser, Eve
  1991 *From Etymology to Pragmatics: Metaphorical and Cultural Aspects of Semantic Structure*. Cambridge: Cambridge University Press.
Taub, Sarah F.
  2001 *Language from the Body: Iconicity and Metaphor in American Sign Language*. Cambridge: Cambridge University Press.
Tettamanti, Marco, Giovanni Buccino, Maria Cristina Saccuman, Vittorio Gallese, Massimo Danna, Paola Scifo, Ferruccio Fazio, Giacomo Rizzolatti, Stefano F. Cappa, and Daniela Perani
  2005 Listening to action-related sentences activates fronto-parietal motor circuits. *Journal of Cognitive Neuroscience* 17: 273–281.
Tomasello, Michael
  2009 *Constructing a Language: A Usage-based Theory of Language Acquisition*. Cambridge: Harvard University Press.
Tyler, Andrea, and Vyvyan Evans
  2001 Reconsidering prepositional polysemy networks: The case of over. *Language* 77(4): 724–765.
Varela, Francisco J., Eleanor Rosch, and Evan Thompson
  1991 *The Embodied Mind: Cognitive Science and Human Experience*. Cambridge: MIT Press.
Wilcox, Sherman
  this volume 33. Signed language. Berlin/Boston: De Gruyter Mouton.
Wilson, Margaret
  2002 Six views of embodied cognition. *Psychonomic Bulletin and Review*, 9: 625–636.
Wilson, Nicole L., and Raymond W. Gibbs, Jr.
  2007 Real and imagined body movement primes metaphor comprehension. *Cognitive Science* 31: 721–731.
Ziemke, Tom
  2003 What's that thing called embodiment? *Proceedings of the 25th Annual Meeting of the Cognitive Science Society.* 1305–1310. Hillsdale: Lawrence Erlbaum.
Ziemke, Tom, Jordan Zlatev, and Roslyn Frank (eds.)
  2007 *Embodiment* (Vol. 1). Berlin/New York: Mouton de Gruyter.
Zwaan, Rolf A.
  2004 The immersed experiencer: Toward an embodied theory of language comprehension. In: B. H. Ross (ed.), *The Psychology of Learning and Motivatio* Volume 43, 35–62). New York: Academic Press.
Zwaan, Rolf A., Robert A. Stanfield, and Richard H. Yaxley
  2002 Language comprehenders mentally represent the shapes of objects. *Psychological Science* 13: 168–171.

Benjamin Bergen, San Diego (USA)

2. Attention and salience

1. Introduction
2. Theoretical considerations
3. Empirical research
4. Conclusions
5. References

1. Introduction

Our sentences about the world are organized to properly convey the constantly changing visual environment. This skill develops early in life. When fully developed, it entails constant, regular, and automatic mappings from elements of a visual scene onto sentence constituents and the grammatical relations between them. The visual system contributes initially to this process by providing perceptual information for conceptual and linguistic analysis but the perceptual information that enters the language production system is not organized indiscriminately. The attentional system filters information for processing based on its noticeability, importance, or relevance. This process allows representing salience parameters in linguistic output. Individual languages' grammars have specific devices responsible for this representation.

Consider, for example, an event in which a cowboy is punching a boxer. This event can be described in multiple ways including the following:

a) *The cowboy is punching the boxer.*
b) *The boxer is/gets punched by the cowboy.*
c) *It's the boxer that the cowboy is punching.*

Although these do not exhaust the structural alternatives in English that can be used to describe the event, they portray three distinct structural possibilities:

a) An active clause with *the cowboy* as syntactic subject in initial position[1] with *the boxer* as object in final position.
b) A passive clause with *the boxer* as syntactic subject in initial position and *the cowboy* part of an adverbial in final position.
c) A cleft sentence with *the boxer* the pre-posed object of the complement clause with *the cowboy* as subject.

There are important theoretical questions to consider for these cases and their relation to the conceptualizations of the event described above.

1. How do speakers select among the alternative structures when describing the event? Are the resulting choices holistic (e.g., active or passive) or incremental (e.g., assign a referent to subject or initial position with corresponding cascading resolution of other grammatical matters)?

---

[1] Please note that subject and initial position are not the same structural category, nor is one defined by the other. There is no such thing in the grammar of English as "subject position".

2. What relationship holds between event perception and the way speaker describes it?
3. Are the mapping principles universal; that is, do different languages map the perceived event onto comparable linguistic categories?

We assume that selecting among the structural alternatives is biased by how the event is perceived and conceptualized. From that viewpoint, the examples (a) and (b) highlight the relative importance or salience of one referent over the other. Theoretically, this difference can be operationalized via pragmatic categories like *topic*, *theme*, or *focus* (Tomlin et al. 2010), or Figure-Ground relations (Talmy 2000a, 2000b, 2007; Langacker 1987, 1991), or a degree of perceptual salience of the event itself (Prentice 1967; Tannenbaum and Williams 1968; Turner and Rommetveit 1968; Osgood and Bock 1977; Flores d'Arcais 1987; Sridhar 1988).

Many theorists subscribe to the idea that *attentional processes* bias the initial event conceptualization and that the resulting conceptual map is then translated into linguistic output as the event is described. However, linguistic and psychological traditions tend to focus somewhat differently on the interplay between attention and language. These differences, often inadequately articulated, have drawn the foci of investigation in somewhat distinct directions. The psychological literature tends to focus primarily on the role of attention in changing the information flow during language production (e.g., the role of priming) while the linguistic literature puts focus on the factors that lead to the selection of *particular* linguistic forms and on typological or cross-linguistic comparisons.

In the next section, we discuss the processes underlying event conceptualization; the interplay between conceptual and linguistic representations in language production, with the specific focus on the grammar organization within utterance formulation; and a set of more detailed questions about the role of attention in sentence generation. This is followed by a review and discussion of the principal research in attention and language with an emphasis on sentence production.

2. Theoretical considerations

The over-arching question driving research on attention and language is deceptively simple: How are attentional processes implicated in the language faculty, including production and comprehension? The question is, in fact, rather complex with at least three fundamental questions making distinctive contributions to advancing the over-arching question of the role of attention in language production and comprehension. The pursuit of these questions motivates our understanding of the grammatical operations involved during visually situated sentence production.

1. How is attention deployed during events conceptualization?
2. Do speakers and hearers exploit attentional processes in their communicative efforts? For example, do speakers organize their utterances to reflect allocation of attentional resources to components of conceptual representations? Similarly, do speakers seek to manipulate the listeners' attentional state in response to their linguistic input?
3. How do languages grammaticalize hypothetical correspondences between the aspects of attentional performance and the corresponding linguistic categories?

2. Attention and salience

In a way, the first question motivates the other two, and there is a widespread and deep literature addressing this first question. A full review of this question falls outside the scope of this chapter; however, we see work on event perception and representation as an essential prerequisite for our understanding of the interface between attention and language faculty, beginning as early as Yarbus (1967) and running through a number of important scholars including Newtson (Newtson 1973; Newtson and Engquist 1976; Newtson et al. 1977) and the Gibsonian tradition (Shaw and Pittinger 1978). Within linguistics the numerous contributions of Talmy (1988a, 1988b, 2000a, 2000b, 2007) and others (Langacker 1987, 1991) seek to reverse engineer aspects of conceptual representation and the possible deployment of attention within them.

The second question has been the province of a great deal of psychological research. These efforts embrace, mostly implicitly, the long-held distinction between the grammar, the knowledge of the language itself, and the parser, the operating system that is employed when the grammar is utilized. One of the important questions is how does the order of encountering components of a conceptual representation affect the order of their mention in language?

The third question evolved with an extended tradition of discourse studies stretching from Weil's (1887) comparative study of ancient Greek and Latin with their modern counterparts, through the Prague School (Dahl 1974; Daneš 1974, 1987; Firbas 1974, 1987a, 1987b; Hăjicová 1984), and on to contemporary work by Halliday (Halliday 1976), Chafe (Chafe 1974, 1979, 1980, 1994, 1998), Givón (Givón 1983, 1988), Lambrecht (Lambrecht 1994), Gundel (Gundel 1988a, 188b), Prince (Prince 1981, 1985), Vallduvi (Vallduvi 1992), Bates and MacWhinney (MacWhinney 1977; MacWhinney and Bates 1978) and many others (see Tomlin et al. 2010 for a review). The role of attentional processes in language processing is interesting primarily to the extent it plays a role in the coding relations of the functional grammar. Further, when linguists address a comparative question, they do not presume that each language must do what English does. Generalizations about language arise from empirical study of typologically diverse languages, and no amount of success with English alone permits generalizations about language overall.

A good deal of psycholinguistic research on attention and grammar is directed at understanding of how perceptual salience and the distribution of attention among competing referents biases the ordering of elements and the assignment of corresponding grammatical roles in a visually situated spoken sentence. Not surprisingly, this tradition provides most of the empirical evidence about the interplay between attention and grammar during language processing. The next section provides a comprehensive summary of these empirical findings and a discussion of their theoretical importance.

However, before we discuss this empirical evidence we need to outline the theoretical framework for a grammar and language processing. One of the most popular models of sentence production (Levelt 1989) includes a conceptualizer dedicated to mapping a conceptual representation onto a pre-verbal message, where the pre-verbal message is semantically complete and annotated for pragmatic roles like *topic*, *focus*, and *given information*. The pre-verbal message serves as input to an utterance formulator, which includes operation of the lexicon and the structural grammar, leading to a grammatical representation fully detailed for lexical, grammatical, and phonological information. Finally, the articulator operates on this input resulting in spoken (or written) linguistic output. Levelt's model serves well for our purposes with two modifications. Although the formulation of the preverbal message is quite detailed in terms of macro- and microplanning, we believe it is useful to think of the pre-verbal message simply as the conceptual representation of the currently perceived event with no need for a supervening layer of semantic representation. Also, we see the grammar of Levelt's model as a *functional* grammar in which structure-independent semantic and pragmatic relations are mapped onto syntactic relations and structures. While there are certainly generalizable characteristics to these inventories, it is nonetheless an empirical question what constitutes for any given language its particular inventory of semantic and pragmatic relations, its particular inventory of syntactic relations and structures, and the particular details of how the former is mapped into the latter (Tomlin 1985, 1994).

There are four mapping possibilities. It is possible that there *is no relationship* between a given syntactic form and semantic or pragmatic function. This is the null hypothesis for other kinds of interaction. It is possible that the linguistic form does interact with semantic or pragmatic function, either to *syntactically code* the function or *pragmatically signal* it. A syntactic form syntactically codes a given function if, and only if, the presence of the function in the message requires the speaker automatically and invariably to use the specific syntactic form, and the hearer, upon hearing the specific linguistic form, automatically and invariably recovers the associated function. A syntactic form pragmatically signals a function if the presence of the form permits the hearer to infer a particular function in a given context, but there is no automatic production requirement on the speaker. Finally, it is possible that the syntactic form correlates highly with some semantic or pragmatic function but still does not interact with it systematically. Such an *afunctional correlation* occurs when an additional semantic or pragmatic function intervenes between the examined form and function, unnoticed or not analyzed by the linguist.

The principal difficulties facing functional analysis center on determining whether linguistic data reveal a significant correlation between form and function and, if there is one, whether the correlation is one exploited by speaker and hearer during discourse interactions. It is best to think of syntactic coding and pragmatic signalling as stronger and weaker kinds of rule-like behavior, where the degree of such a behavior is tied to automaticity of mapping and derived from the frequency of use. A good example of syntactic coding is found in English subject-verb agreement, with the conventional mapping in American English of grammatical plural onto plural verb agreement (*The legislature convenes again in August* vs. *The legislatures convene again in August*). A clear case of pragmatic signalling is seen in the use of the English conjunction *and*, which gets used to convey both temporal sequence and causality, though neither can be said to constitute a definitive rule for its use. It is common to describe these rule-like behaviors in terms of *grammaticalization*, the extent to which a language deploys concrete structural forms to manifest some semantic or pragmatic function.

It should not be assumed that the details of mappings between semantics/pragmatics and syntactic relations and syntactic structures are universal or that the analysis of English and similar European languages is adequate to formulate generalizations about the interplay of attention with grammar. There is in fact considerable variability in how languages manage semantic and pragmatic functions, and this problem cannot be set aside for long in the pursuit of understanding how attention interacts with grammar. The logic of cross-linguistic issues is better approached outside of a discussion of attention. The cross-linguistic or typological variability that languages display in possible functional mappings can be succinctly demonstrated by considering TIME. A given event is located in time with respect to the moment the speaker describes it either in the past, the present or the future. The grammar of English maps just two of these onto linguistic form (tenses): past tense (*-ed*) and present tense (*-s*) or zero. English deals with future time through an extensive inventory of periphrastic future constructions (*be about to* V, *be going to* V, *will* V) or adverbials (Quirk et al. 1985). The semantics of present and past time are grammaticalized in English onto two tenses; the semantics of future time is *not* grammaticalized in English but is managed through periphrastic means only. Many languages – Bahasa Indonesia or Mandarin for example – have no syntactic codings of time whatever but rely exclusively on adverbials of time or on context to manage events in time for purposes of discourse. Further, while it is common in linguistics and psycholinguistics to do so, there is no *a priori* reason to suppose that time must be divided universally into just three parts.

3. Empirical research

The psychological literature provides (1) structural (2) developmental and (3) behavioral reasons to conclude that linguistic performance may rely upon allocation of attentional resources. The structural argument includes evidence that the human brain is flexibly organized so that the same cortical region often supports a variety of mental operations. For example, neuroimaging studies in reading identify brain areas involved in chunking visual letters into words, associating letters with sounds, and providing entry into a distributed lexicon of semantics. Chunking visual letters into words takes place in a posterior visually specific area of the left fusiform gyrus (McCandliss et al. 2003). In the right hemisphere similar areas are involved in the perception and individuation of faces (Kanwisher et al. 1997). While these areas were first thought to be word and face specific, more recent conceptualizations argue that they are related more to process of chunking of visual elements or individuation of complex forms which can be performed on other inputs (Gauthier et al. 1999). This same principle of localized mental operations over domain specific representations may explain why Broca's area seems important for forms of non-speech motor activity (e.g., Pulvermuller and Fadiga 2010). For example, structural ERP research has shown a large area of activation in the anterior cingulate gyrus during lexical search (Abdulaev and Posner 1998; Raichle et al. 1994). The same area is known to be involved in conflict resolution and executive attention (Fan et al. 2002; Posner and Petersen 1990; Petersen and Posner 2012). An fMRI study (Newman et al. 2001) revealed that syntactic violations elicit significantly greater activation in superior frontal cortex – the area largely involved in attentional control. ERP studies of syntactic violations confirm existence of two electrophysiological brain signatures of syntactic processing: an early left anterior negativity (LAN) and/or a late positive wave with a peak at 600 ms (P600) (Hagoort et al. 1993). Hahne and Friederici (1999) hypothesized that the LAN is a highly automated process whereas the P600 involves more attention. They tested this hypothesis in a study manipulating the proportion of correct sentences and sentences with structural violations in them. Syntactically incorrect sentences appeared in a low (20% violation) or a high (80% violation) proportion conditions. Both conditions led to the elicitation of the LAN effect while only low proportion of incorrect sentences resulted in P600. These results support the idea that LAN is an automated first-pass sentence parsing mechanism accompanying syntactic processing while the P600 component is a second-pass parsing that requires a deliberate deployment of executive attention. Together these findings demonstrate that the brain localizes *processes* or mental operations not particular *representations* (either linguistic or non-linguistic). Sharing processing regions may lead to sharing resources between domain-specific and domain-general operations computed in the same area.

Developmental research provides more reasons to hypothesize that attention and language are intimately linked (Matthews and Krajewski this volume). A number of studies suggest that attentional amplification of visual input is actively used by caretakers during the early stages of language development. Consistent pairing of attentional focus to real-world objects and events with the corresponding names and structures helps the infant build firm associations between the perceived world and the language about it. Experiments show for example that both individual and joint gazes of infants and caretakers can serve as indicators of current learning processes such as matching names to their referent objects (Baldwin 1995; Carpenter et al. 1998; Dominey and Dodane 2004; Estigarribia and Clark 2007). The establishment of the attention-language interface is a starting point in the development of a more complex linking system, one mapping event semantics onto sentence structure. Surprisingly, the rudiments of this system are in place already by 2–3 years of age. Research has shown that children regularly scan visual referents of transient events following the way they are described in auditorily perceived sentences (Arunachalam and Waxman 2010; Yuan and Fisher 2009). In this learning process the associations between event semantics and syntax are regulated by directing the child's attention to the structurally relevant elements of the described scene. The ability to successfully represent the perceptual details in the syntactic structure has been recently reported for children as young as 3–4 years old (Ibbotson et al. 2013). Some theorists (e.g., Mandler 1992) proposed that after initial visual analysis perceptual information in the child's mind becomes represented in a form of image schemas that support development of more abstract conceptual representations and derived thematic and structural relationships. Overall, the role of attentional control in language development suggests an early and a potentially strong coupling between the distribution of attention in the environment and the organization of the language about this environment.

The link between attending to objects and acting on them remains strong in adults. People tend to look at objects in their actions regardless of whether they linguistically describe their actions on these objects or not (Ballard et al. 1997). Understanding of linguistic processing as a subsystem of other behavioral tasks suggests that a similar link can be expected between attending to objects and naming them in a sentence. Indeed, some theoretical proposals claim that perceptual regularities are represented in the syntactic system. For example, Landau and Jackendoff (1993; also Jackendoff 1996) suggested that representing objects in the human mind (*what*) and locations (*where*) maps directly onto the distinction between nouns and prepositions.

3.1. Attention and syntactic choice

One aspect of visual attention important for linguistic research is its selective nature (Langacker this volume; Bock and Ferreira 2014). The surrounding world contains excessive perceptual information available for processing; attention facilitates selection of the information most relevant to making behavioral decisions (e.g., Chun and Wolfe 2001). This selectivity is central to many definitions of attention. For example, Corbetta (1998: 831) notes that "Attention defines the mental ability to select stimuli, responses, memories, or thoughts that are behaviorally relevant among the many others that are behaviorally irrelevant". Selection among stimuli leads to selection between competing responses (Fan et al. 2002). From this point of view linguistic behavior is not an exception as speakers often need to select between different names in order to refer to the same entity and they need to select among different syntactic alternatives when describing the same event.

The control of visual attention in experimental tasks is often achieved through a cueing paradigm (Posner, 1980). A cue here is something that determines a stimulus's salience. It can be an independent marker "pointing" to the stimulus (e.g., an arrow) or it can be a feature of the stimulus itself (e.g., a stimulus' size or luminance). Cues can be exogenous or endogenous, and they can be explicit or implicit; their presence can result in either overt or covert deployment of attention (Posner and Raichle 1994). Exogenous cues are external to the perceiver's mind. Endogenous cues originate from within the perceiver's mind and are guided by internally generated plans and/or intentions. An explicit cue is a clearly noticeable and, therefore, consciously processed marker (e.g., an arrow pointing toward a location on the screen presented long enough to be noticed and looked at. An implicit cue directs attention in a more subtle manner; it is usually presented for duration shorter than would be necessary for conscious processing (e.g., 50 msec.). An implicit cue is typically unnoticed but its display is sufficient for attracting attention and directing the gaze toward a cued location. Eye-movements do not necessarily accompany attentional shifts although they typically follow the allocation of attention (Fischer 1998). This property underlies the difference between overt and covert deployment of attention. An overt attentional shift occurs when the eyes move to align the visual focus with the attended object. A covert shift directs the focus of attention outside of the visual focus making the two foci dissociable (Posner 1980).

3.1.1. Referential priming

The potential of salient referents to occupy prominent sentential roles was reported in the early research that used variants of a *referential priming* paradigm. A participant previews a visual referent for some time before the target event involving this referent appears on the screen. The experimental instruction may differ from sentence verification to sentence description but the general prediction remains the same: The information about the referent extracted during the preview will facilitate its accommodation in the produced sentence. Thus, this *primed* referent may be more likely to become the starting point or (in English at least) the subject of a sentence describing the target event. Similarly, the perceiver in a sentence verification study may be faster to verify the target sentence as correctly describing the target event when this sentence starts with the primed referent or places it as its subject.

One of the earliest studies (Prentice 1967) investigated how attentional focus on the referent established by referent preview affects elicitation of active and passive voice

English sentences. Participants described pictures of simple transitive events involving two characters – Agent and Patient (e.g., *a fireman kicking a cat*) – after previewing one of them. In half of the trials participants previewed eventual Agents and in the other half eventual Patients. Target sentences were analysed for the Agent-Patient ordering. When the previewed referent was the Agent, participants were more likely to produce active voice sentences (e.g., *The fireman is kicking a cat*); when the previewed referent was the Patient they were more likely to produce passive voice sentences (e.g., *The cat is being kicked by the fireman*). Hence, the speakers were primed to place the previewed referent first and make it the sentential subject. The cueing effect was not equally strong in the Agent-preview and the Patient-preview trials: while Agent-cued trials resulted in almost 100 % active-voice sentences the Patient-cued trials elicited about 40–50 % passive-voice sentences. This shows how canonicality (i.e., preference for active voice in English) can act as a factual constraint on the degree to which perceptual processes may affect linguistic choices.

A recent study (Myachykov et al. 2012) investigated how informative (referent preview) and uninformative (pointer to referent's location) visual cues affect syntactic choice in English transitive sentence production. Two types of cues were used: (1) a pointer to the subsequent referent's location or (2) a picture of the corresponding referent (i.e., referent preview) in the same location. Crucially, while the first cue simply directs the speaker's attention to the referent's location, the second cue additionally reveals the referent's identity. Cueing the Agent or the Patient prior to presenting the target event reliably predicted the likelihood of selecting this referent as the sentential subject and triggered the associated choice between active and passive voice. However there was no difference in the magnitude of the general cueing effect between the informative (preview) and uninformative cueing conditions (location pointer). This suggests that attentionally driven syntactic choice relies on a direct and automatic mapping from attention to sentence and that this mechanism is independent of the degree of the referent's conceptual accessibility provided by referent preview.

3.1.2. Perceptual priming

Results of the referential priming studies prompted the development of theoretical accounts which related attentional processing to sentence organization. For example, Osgood and Bock (1977) suggested that the referent's salience (or *vividness*) may predict its positioning in a sentence with the most prominent referents assuming the most prominent positions. But what is the most prominent position in a sentence? The importance of sentential starting points was pointed out by MacWhinney (1977) who suggested that the salient referent tends to occupy the initial position in a sentence thus triggering structural organization of the sentence. The *starting point* however does not always have to correspond to the most prominent grammatical role (subject) in the sentence although in English this is almost always the case.

Contrasting with this positional view, Tomlin (1995, 1997) suggested that salient referents tend to occupy the most prominent syntactic role, e.g., syntactic subject, thus offering *the grammatical-role* hypothesis for perceptually driven syntactic choice. Initially this idea was tested in a study using a very strong variant of a *perceptual priming* paradigm known as the "FishFilm" (Tomlin, 1995). In a typical perceptual priming experiment speakers describe visually perceived events while their attention is directed to one of the event's referents by a cue unrelated to (and uninformative about) the cued referent. In its essence, therefore, the perceptual priming paradigm is a psycholinguistic adaptation of a visual cueing paradigm (Posner, 1980). In Tomlin's study, participants observed and described an animated interaction between two fish in which one fish always ended up eating the other. In half of the trials an explicit visual cue (arrow pointer) was presented above the Agent fish and in the other half of trials above the Patient fish. The results demonstrated that in virtually 100 % of the Agent-cued trials participants produced an active voice sentence (e.g., *The red fish ate the blue fish*). When the cue was on the Patient participants nearly always produced a passive voice sentence (e.g., *The blue fish was eaten by the red fish*). Tomlin concluded that attentional cueing promotes the assignment of the Subject-role (to either the Agent or the Patient) in an English transitive sentence thereby triggering the choice between active and passive voice.

Although Tomlin's results were very persuasive the FishFilm paradigm itself received significant methodological criticism (e.g., Bock et al. 2004). The most critical points were (1) the repetitive use of the same event without filler materials (2) the explicit nature of the visual cue (and related experimental instructions) and (3) the joint presentation of the cue and its target. Obviously in real life visual salience is more subtle; hence a more tacit manipulation of the attentional focus may be necessary to further substantiate the role of perceptual priming on syntactic choice. Gleitman and colleagues (Gleitman et al. 2007) conducted a study that avoided the methodological problems of the FishFilm paradigm. In this study participants observed and described interactions between two referents portrayed in still pictures. Speakers' attention was directed to the location of one of the referents by means a visual cue (a black square). The cue appeared on the screen *before* the target picture in the place of one of the subsequently presented referents. The cue was presented for only 65 msec. and participants remained largely unaware of its presence. This *implicit* cueing procedure was nevertheless successful in directing attention to the cued area of the screen (as revealed by eye-movement data) and subsequently to one of the referents (e.g., Agent or Patient). The use of filler materials minimized the probability of using event-specific linguistic strategies. In addition to the active/passive alternation the experiment included picture materials for a variety of other syntactic choices including symmetrical predicates (e.g., *X meets Y / Y meets X / X and Y meet*), verbs of perspective (e.g., *X chases Y / Y flees X*), and conjoined noun-phrases (e.g., *X and Y... / Y and X...*). Gleitman et al's syntactic alternation results largely confirmed Tomlin's findings yet their effects were much weaker due to the far more subtle perceptual cueing manipulation: Speakers were 10 % more likely to produce passive voice sentences when the cue attracted their attention to the Patient location. In the remaining 90 % of the Patient-cued trials speakers still produced the canonical active voice structure.

Indeed this result (as well as Tomlin's original findings) does not differentiate between a *positional* versus a *grammatical-role* account of perceptual cueing effects mainly because in English transitive sentences the syntactic subject is virtually always confounded with the sentential starting point. However, the symmetrical predicate data in Gleitman et al. (2007) provide some interesting new insights in this respect. When describing a symmetrical event speakers may choose among various canonical active voice options e.g.,: (1) *The man kissed the woman* (2) *The woman kissed the man* (3) *The man and woman kissed* and (4) *The woman and the man kissed*. Structural variants (1) and (2) rely on a canonical SVO-frame and the choice between them may reflect both positional (starting point) and grammatical-role (Subject) preferences for the most salient referent. The choice between structures (3) and (4) involves only positional mappings as the two referents are part of the same conjoined noun phrase (CNP) in Subject position. The participants in Gleitman et al. (2007) produced all four possible alternatives. Moreover they tended to assign the visually cued referent to an early position in the sentence i.e., to the Subject-position when choosing an SVO-frame (1 or 2) and to the first element when choosing a CNP-frame (3 or 4). Most interestingly the perceptual cueing effect was stronger when participants used an SVO-frame (31 %) than when they used a CNP-frame (23 %). This could suggest a *hybrid* system of attention-driven syntactic choice either with a stronger bias toward the grammatical-role assignment component or with additive effects of perceptual cueing on both linear positioning and grammatical-role assignment.

Perceptual priming studies using other structures came to similar conclusions. For example Forrest (1996) explored the visually cued production of locative sentences in English. As in Gleitman et al. (2007) speakers' attentional focus was attracted not to the cued referent itself but to its location prior to the target event presentation. The experimental materials were simple line drawings of locative events, for example a picture of *A star left of a heart*. Prior to target display presentation an explicit visual cue appeared in the location of either the star or the heart. As a result speakers tended to produce sentences like *A star is left of a heart* when the star's location was cued and *A heart is right of a star* when the heart's location was cued.

Together these results provide important evidence about the extent of the perceptual priming effect on syntactic choice in English. First, they demonstrate that the referent's salience alone can successfully predict syntactic choice in a variety of syntactic structures. Second, they suggest that the strength of the perceptual priming effect depends on the power of the cue (e.g., its explicitness) and the strength of the association between the cue and the referent. However, distinct features of English grammar, namely the tendency to confound the Subject role with the sentential starting point, make it difficult to distinguish between positional and the grammatical-role accounts of perceptually driven syntactic choice. The data from Gleitman et al. (2007) hint at the existence of a hybrid system of perceptually driven syntactic choice in which perceptual cueing affects both grammatical-role assignment *and* positioning of a constituent in a sentence. Research on languages with flexible word order may help to address this question more directly.

The studies reviewed thus far used English as the target language – an SVO language with a highly constrained word order. For example, in describing a transitive event the speaker of English primarily selects between the active voice and the passive-voice SV(O) options.[2] Hence the grammatical subject in English usually coincides with the sentential starting point. This feature makes it difficult to distinguish between assignment of the grammatical roles and linear ordering of constituents. Other languages allow for a more flexible organization of sentences. Three recent studies analyzed perceptually

---

[2] There is an order-only alternative possible, so-called topicalization, but this is not used for these descriptions.

primed syntactic choice in Russian (Myachykov and Tomlin 2008), Finnish (Myachykov et al. 2011), and Korean (Hwang and Kaiser 2009) sentence production. Unlike English these three languages permit flexible word ordering making at least some permutations of Subject, Verb, and Object grammatical. Russian and Finnish, like English, are SVO languages but, unlike English, they permit both Object-initial and Verb-initial constructions and thus allow a wider range of topicalization constructions. Korean is an SOV language that permits placement of subject and object before the verb (which always follows its arguments). Although topicalization is possible in these languages it is not freely licensed. For example, factors related to discourse context (e.g., contrast of given/new information) were shown to predict ordering of sentential constituents in Russian (Comrie 1987, 1989; Yokoyama 1986), Finnish (Kaiser and Trueswell 2004; Vilkuna 1989), and Korean (Choi 1999; Jackson 2008). The same, however, is true for English (e.g., Chafe 1976; Downing and Noonan 1995; Givón 1992; Halliday 1967; *inter alia*). More importantly, the role of discourse-level factors does not preclude the possibility that speakers of these other languages also accommodate referential salience in syntactic choice. The lack of corresponding evidence makes perceptual priming research in flexible word order languages very useful. Importantly, voice-based alternations are also possible in these three languages but they are greatly dispreferred and less frequent (e.g., Siewierska 1988; Vilkuna 1989; Zemskaja 1979) than in English (e.g., Svartvik 1966). In a perceptual priming task, speakers of flexible word order languages could map the salient referent either onto the subject or onto the sentential starting point without subject-role assignment. Such languages provide an optimal test-bed for independent predictions from the linear ordering and the grammatical-role accounts of perceptually driven syntactic choice.

Myachykov and Tomlin (2008) analyzed Russian transitive sentence production using the FishFilm paradigm (see Tomlin 1995). They hypothesized that if the visually cued referent becomes the sentential subject Russian speakers, like their English speaking counterparts, should be more likely to alternate between active and passive voice when describing FishFilm events. Alternatively, they may choose to use topicalization which in the Patient-cued condition would result in an increased percentage of Object-initial active voice structures. This would support a linear-ordering account of perceptual priming effect on syntactic choice. The results supported the latter view: Russian speakers produced 20 % more Object-initial (OVS or OSV) active voice structures (plus ca. 2 % passive voice sentences) when the perceptual cue was on the Patient. This perceptual priming effect is noticeably smaller than in Tomlin's (1995) study with English speakers who produced passive voice sentences in nearly 100 % of the Patient-cued trials. This is especially noteworthy given the fact that Myachykov and Tomlin (2008) employed exactly the same manipulations as Tomlin (1995).

Myachykov et al. (2011) compared perceptual priming effects between English and Finnish. Similarly to Gleitman et al. (2007) participants described pictures of transitive events after their attention was directed to the location of either the Agent or the Patient by an implicit (70 ms) visual cue. The data from the English participants replicated earlier findings (Gleitman et al. 2007): there was a reliable main effect of Cue Location with participants producing 94 % active voice sentences in the Agent-cued trials and 74 % active voice sentences in the Patient-cued trials. One difference between the form of the passive voice in Russian and in Finnish is that the passive voice in Finnish is not only infrequent but also always realized without a by-phrase (Kaiser and Vihman 2006).

Hence it may be difficult to induce passivization in a study using events that always involved two protagonists. Topicalization however is equally possible in Finnish and in Russian. Therefore, one could expect a reduced yet noticeable effect of perceptual priming in Finnish through topicalization similar to Russian. However, there was no reliable word order alternation in Finnish although the cueing manipulation was equally effective (as revealed in saccades to the cued locations). Virtually the same result was observed in Hwang and Kaiser (2009) who used an implicit cueing paradigm in a study with Korean: participants described transitive events (e.g., dog biting policeman) after their attention was directed to either the Agent or the Patient via the presentation of an implicit visual cue. Similar to the results of Myachykov et al. (2009) the cueing manipulation was successful (in terms of attracting initial fixations); however this did not lead to any perceptual priming effect affecting syntactic choice.

Together these results suggest the existence of language-specific differences in how visual cueing affects syntactic choice. The exact nature of these differences is not yet clear. It is possible that the largely dispreferred status of the passive voice in languages like Russian and Finnish makes mapping of a salient Patient referent onto the Subject role problematic. The same explanation is offered by Hwang and Kaiser who proposed that Korean has a strong bias toward actives with canonical word-order (SOV) and that passives in Korean are more marked than in English. However, it is important to remember that the decrease in the cue power was responsible for the decrease of the overall perceptual priming effect observed in Gleitman et al. (2007) as compared to Tomlin (1995). At the same time a FishFilm experiment with Russian (Myachykov and Tomlin 2008) also revealed a reliable yet greatly decreased perceptual priming effect compared to Tomlin (1995). Put together these studies suggest that in flexible word-order languages the extent of perceptual priming is consistently weaker than in the fixed word-order languages. An important question is why is this so? We propose that the grammatical-role assignment mechanism operates as the primary syntactic device responsible for representing the speaker's attentional focus while linear ordering of the constituents is only employed when the grammatical-role assignment mechanism is not easily available. In English transitive sentence production, the two routes coincide making the overall perceptual priming effect stronger. In languages like Russian and Finnish only the linear-ordering route is available (because of the unavailability of the passive); hence there is a much weaker effect in Russian (Myachykov and Tomlin 2008) and respectively null effects in Finnish (Myachykov et al. 2009) and Korean (Hwang and Kaiser 2009). Supporting the grammatical-role assignment view a recent FishFilm study using a VOS-language (Malagasy) demonstrated that speakers of Malagasy consistently assign the cued referent to the final Subject role (Rasolofo 2006). This provides further support for the dominance of the grammatical-role mechanism over the linear-ordering one: availability of structures that allow for direct mapping between the salient referent and the Subject makes the importance of linear ordering for the accommodation of referential salience in syntactic choice irrelevant.

The assignment of the grammatical roles in a spoken sentence and the resulting syntactic choice do not depend solely on the salience characteristics of the described event. Other factors such as prior activation of lexical and syntactic units affect the likelihood of selecting one structure over another too. One could naturally assume that the final choice of structure is a product of many interacting forces and little is known about how perceptual priming interacts with other priming parameters known to influence the speaker's choice of syntax, including both *lexical* (Bock and Irwin 1980) and *syntactic* priming (Bock 1986).

Similarly to perceptual priming, lexical priming (e.g., recent exposure to the word designating the referent) has been shown to increase the likelihood of the primed referent becoming the sentential starting point and/or its subject. This can be achieved by priming referent-related nouns (Bates and Devescovi 1989; Bock and Irwin 1980; Ferreira and Yoshita 2003; Flores D'Arcais 1975; Osgood and Bock 1977; Prat-Sala and Branigan 2000) or verbs related to the event portrayed in the target trial (Melinger and Dobel 2005). In addition, syntactic priming refers to a tendency to repeat the whole syntactic configurations of structures that the speaker has previously encountered or produced (for recent reviews cf. Branigan 2007; Ferreira and Bock 2006; Pickering and Ferreira 2008). Some accounts of syntactic priming claim that the tendency to repeat syntax from sentence to sentence has a strong lexical component (e.g., Pickering and Branigan 1998); other accounts claim that syntax is reproduced without necessary reference to either conceptual or lexical information (e.g., Bock and Loebell 1990; Bock et al. 1992; Desmet and Declercq 2006; Scheepers 2003).

Independent of these theoretical differences any interactive properties of the distinct priming effects established at different production stages remain largely unknown. This has motivated the experiments reported in Myachykov, Garrod, and Scheepers (2012). These experiments investigated syntactic choice in English transitive sentence production by combining priming manipulations at both linguistic and non-linguistic levels. In each of the three reported experiments, participants described visual events after receiving combinations of the following priming manipulations: (1) perceptual priming, (2) lexical (verb match), and (3) syntactic priming. Across all three experiments there were clear and robust perceptual priming effects even in the presence of concurrent linguistic manipulations (syntactic priming and verb match) (Bock et al. 2004; Kuchinsky and Bock 2010). These findings provide further evidence that perceptual information about the referents (e.g., referential salience) plays an integral and distinct role during the assignment of syntactic roles alongside available lexical and syntactic information. Importantly, the simultaneously observed syntactic priming effect *did not* interact with the perceptual priming effect suggesting that interactions between priming effects are constrained by a *neighborhood* principle, according to which only immediately *neighboring* processing stages (e.g., message and lemma; lemma and syntax) can interact with one another in determining syntactic choice while non-neighboring stages (message and syntax) cannot. The ubiquitous presence and comparable magnitude of the perceptual and the syntactic priming effects hint at the existence of a dual-path mapping mechanism akin to Chang (2002). According to dual-path mapping non-linguistic effects (such as perceptual salience) and linguistic effects (such as syntactic and lexical accessibility) can affect subject assignment independently and in parallel, each producing its individual biases.

One important additional finding was that the perceptual priming effect interacted with the verb-match effect. The visual cueing effect (the increase in the proportion of passive-voice responses in the Patient-cued condition) remained relatively unaffected by the verb match manipulation. This may indicate that speakers have a general tendency to use salient patients as subjects of their sentences (and correspondingly select a passive-voice frame) regardless of the co-presence of linguistic cues competing for the same choice. The verb match effect in this scenario would result from a relatively higher activation of the otherwise dispreferred passive voice frame when the prime verb matches the target event (cf. Melinger and Dobel 2005 who found that isolated verbs can indeed prime syntactic frames). Importantly this passive promoting verb match effect was only observed when the visual cue was on the agent or in the situation when the visual cue did not simultaneously compete for the choice of passive. One possibility is that matching prime verbs can only make the passive voice alternative to the canonical active more available in absence of a visual cue competing for the same choice: In the Agent-cued condition (supporting active voice) the verb cue is informative as it provides a cue toward the alternative (passive voice); in the Patient-cued condition (supporting passive voice) the verb cue is uninformative as it supports the same response as the Patient-cue itself. If this interpretation is correct then it follows that lexical information (whether the prime verb matches the target event or not) is considered only after perceptual information (visual cueing) has already been integrated into the grammatical encoding process. Thus perceptual information would take priority over lexical information (at least in the current experimental setup where the visual cue was always delivered most recently i.e., immediately before the target event). This theoretical scenario entails an interesting prediction, namely that it should be possible to register an independent transitive verb-match effect (more passive voice target descriptions after presenting a matching prime verb) in the absence of any visual cues to either Agent or Patient.

Still, the exact mechanism of the integration of non-linguistic and linguistic information during sentence production is not totally clear. We assume, as Bock and Levelt (1994) argue, that sentence production begins with the creation of a message – a conceptual representation of the event to be encoded linguistically. Accessibility of non-linguistic information about the referents extracted at this stage can vary (Bock and Warren 1985). As a result the speaker may be biased to process the more salient referents ahead of the less salient ones. If such preferential processing continues all the way to grammatical encoding and overt articulation, it is likely that the salient referent is encoded in a sentence before other referents. In English this may lead to the salient referent mapping onto the subject. Our data confirmed this hypothesis. Participants were more likely to assign the subject role to the Agent and choose the corresponding active-voice frame when the Agent was cued, and they were likewise more likely to assign the subject to the Patient and select the corresponding passive-voice frame when the cue was on the Patient. Importantly, the visual cueing used in these experiments did not provide participants with any information that might reveal the referent's identity or its semantic properties. Hence, simply directing visual attention to the location of the referent is enough to affect speakers' likelihood of producing an active or a passive voice sentence (cf. Gleitman et al. 2007; Myachykov et al. 2012; Tomlin 1995, 1997).

4. Conclusions

This chapter reviewed evidence for a regular link between visual attention and syntactic organization in discourse. A number of reviewed studies demonstrate how speakers regularly alternate between structural alternatives as a function of their attentional focus on one of the referents of the described events. The persistence of such an attentionally driven assignment of syntactic roles confirms that in English the attentionally detected referent tends to map onto the prominent syntactic relation (i.e., subject) in a produced sentence. However, the exact mapping from attention to syntax in different languages is far from certain. One possibility is that different languages' grammars provide speakers with *different* means of grammatically encoding perceptual properties of the described world. Another possibility is that the link between attentional focus and the choice of syntax via the assignment of subject *is* more or less universal in that speakers always *try* to map the salient referent onto subject. However, the accessibility of alternatives (e.g., active vs. passive) is not always equal across languages. When a direct mapping is much less accessible (e.g., passive in Russian), the attempt to map the visually focused referent onto subject needs to be discontinued. In this case, a "second-best" mapping may be used – one that *is not* syntactically coded in the language's grammar. One example is Russian speakers' tendency to resort to topicalization instead of activating the theoretically available passive when they attempt to preferentially position the salient patient in their transitive sentences. This assignment through topicalization, however, is secondary to a more preferred and automated direct mapping mechanism; hence, its use is associated with slower sentence production rates and inflated eye movement measurements, such as eye-voice spans (see Myachykov 2007). We propose that the grammatical role assignment mechanism and the positional assignment mechanism form a hierarchical dual-path system that allows grammatical representation of the perceptually salient referent in a sentence. This system is hierarchical in two ways. First, while the grammatical role mapping mechanism is a common but language-specific mapping based on syntactic coding, the positional mapping is, in principle, available regardless of the existence of the corresponding grammatical role mapping mechanism. It is undoubtedly easier to freely arrange the constituents in a language that licenses topicalization grammatically, e.g., via case marking, but it is still quite impossible to use "semi-legal" positioning devices like dislocations in languages that do not normally permit topicalization. Second, these two mapping mechanisms are hierarchically related in that in languages like English grammatical role assignment dominates over positional assignment. For example, speakers try to activate structural alternatives that permit direct mapping from attentional focus to subject before they (1) abandon this attempt in favour of a more dominant structure that requires remapping (e.g., the use of active voice in Patient-salient situations) or (2) using topicalization as the second-best mapping alternative.

All this does not generally mean that *subjecthood* only reflects attentional focus on a referent. What it means is that when attentional focus needs to be represented, the speaker tries to do it by assigning the subject role to the most salient referent in the scene. The problem is that the corresponding structural contrast may not always be available, as in languages like Russian and Finnish, because passives are rare or largely dispreferred. When the grammatical role assignment mechanism is not easily available the speaker looks for an alternative. In flexible word-order languages this alternative is topicalization. As a result a linear-ordering mechanism is used to accommodate referential salience in terms of word order but with detrimental effects on the speed of processing and the strength of the overall perceptual priming effect.

5. References

Abdullaev, Yalchin and Michael Posner
   1998   Event-related brain potential imaging of semantic encoding during processing single words. *Neuroimage* 7: 1–13.

Arunachalam, Sudha and Sandra Waxman
   2010   Meaning from syntax: evidence from 2-year-olds. *Cognition* 14(3): 442–446.

Baldwin, Dare
    1995   Understanding the link between joint attention and language. In: C. Moore and P. Dunham (eds.), *Joint Attention: Its Origins and Role in Development*, 131–158. Hillsdale: Lawrence Erlbaum Associates.

Ballard, Dana; Mary Hayhoe; and Polly Pook
    1997   Deictic codes for the embodiment of cognition, *Behavioral and Brain Sciences* 20: 723–742.

Bates, Elizabeth and Antonella Devescovi
    1989   Crosslinguistic studies of sentence production. In: B. MacWhinney and E. Bates (eds.), *The Crosslinguistic Study of Sentence Processing*, 225–256. Cambridge: Cambridge University Press.

Bock, Kathryn
    1986   Syntactic persistence in language production. *Cognitive Psychology* 18: 355–387.

Bock, Kathryn and Victor Ferreira
    2014   Syntactically speaking. In: M. Goldrick, V. Ferreira, and M. Miozzo, (eds.), *The Oxford Handbook of Sentence Production*, 21–46. New York: Oxford University Press.

Bock, Kathryn and David Irwin
    1980   Syntactic effects of information availability in sentence production. *Journal of Verbal Learning and Verbal Behavior* 19: 467–484.

Bock, Kathryn, David Irwin, and Douglas Davidson
    2004   Putting first things first. In: J. Henderson and F. Ferreira, (eds.), *The Integration of Language, Vision, And Action: Eye Movements And the Visual World*, 249–278. New York: Psychology Press.

Bock, Kathryn and Willem J. M. Levelt
    1994   Language production: grammatical encoding. In: M. Gernsbacher (ed.), *Handbook of Psycholinguistics*, 945–984. New York: Academic Press.

Bock, Kathryn and Helga Loebell
    1990   Framing sentences. *Cognition* 35: 1–39.

Bock, Kathryn, Helga Loebell; and Randel Morey
    1992   From conceptual roles to structural relations: bridging the syntactic cleft. *Psychological Review* 99: 150–171.

Bock, Kathryn and Richard Warren
    1985   Conceptual accessibility and structural structure in sentence formulation *Cognition* 21: 47–67.

Branigan, Holly
    2007   Syntactic priming. *Language and Linguistics Compass* 1(1/2): 1–16.

Carpenter, Malinda, Katherine Nagell, and Michael Tomasello
    1998   Social cognition, joint attention, and communicative competence from 9 to 15 months of age. *Monographs of the Society of Research in Child Development* 63(4): 1–143.

Chafe, Wallace
    1974   Language and consciousness. *Language* 50: 111–133.

Chafe, Wallace
    1976   Givenness, contrastiveness, definiteness, subjects, topics, and points of view. In: C. Li (ed.), *Subject and Topic*, 25–56. New York: Academic Press.

Chafe, Wallace
    1979   The flow of thought and the flow of language. In: T. Givón (ed.), *Discourse and Syntax*, 159–181. New York: Academic Press.

Chafe, Wallace
    1980   The deployment of consciousness in the production of narrative. In: W. Chafe (ed.), *The Pear Stories: Cognitive, Cultural, and Linguistic Aspects of Narrative Production*, 9–50. Norwood: Ablex.

Chafe, Wallace
- 1994 *Discourse, Consciousness, and Time: The Flow and Displacement of Conscious Experience in Speaking and Writing.* Chicago: University of Chicago Press.

Chafe, Wallace
- 1998 Language and the flow of thought. In: M. Tomasello (ed.), *The New Psychology of Language: Cognitive and Functional Approaches to Language Structure,* 93–111. Mahwah: Lawrence Erlbaum.

Chang, Franklin
- 2002 Symbolically speaking: a connectionist model of sentence production. *Cognitive Science* 26: 609–651.

Choi, Hye-Won
- 1999 *Optimizing Structure in Context.* Stanford: CSLI.

Chun, Marvin and Jeremy Wolfe
- 2001 Visual attention. In: E. B. Goldstein (ed.), *Blackwell Handbook of Perception,* 272–310. Oxford: Blackwell.

Comrie, Bernard
- 1987 *The World's Major Languages.* London: Croom Helm.

Comrie, Bernard
- 1989 *Language Universals and Linguistic Typology.* Chicago: University of Chicago Press.

Corbetta, Maurizio
- 1998 Frontoparietal cortical networks for directing attention and the eye to visual locations: Identical, independent, or overlapping neural systems? *Proceedings of the National Academy of Sciences* 95(3): 831–838.

Dahl, Östen
- 1974 Topic-comment structure in a generative grammar with a semantic base. In: F. Daneš (ed.), *Papers on Functional Sentence Perspective,* 75–80. The Hague: Mouton.

Daneš, František
- 1974 Functional sentence perspective and the organization of the text. In: F. Daneš (ed.), *Papers on Functional Sentence Perspective,* 106–28. The Hague: Mouton.

Daneš, František
- 1987 On Prague school functionalism in linguistics. In: R. Dirven and V. Fried (eds.), *Functionalism in Linguistics,* 3–37. Amsterdam: John Benjamins.

Desmet, Timothy and Mieke Declercq
- 2006 Cross-linguistic priming of syntactic hierarchical configuration information. *Journal of Memory and Language* 54: 610–632.

Dominey, Peter and Christelle Dodane
- 2004 Indeterminacy in language acquisition: the role of child-directed speech and joint attention. *Journal of Neurolinguistics* 17: 121–145.

Downing, Pamela and Michael Noonan
- 1995 *Word Order in Discourse.* Vol. 30 of Typological Studies in Language. Amsterdam/Philadelphia: John Benjamins.

Estigarribia, Bruno and Eve Clark
- 2007 Getting and maintaining attention in talk to young children. *Journal of Child Language* 34: 799–814.

Fan, Jin, Bruce McCandliss, Tobias Sommer, Amir Raz, and Michael Posner
- 2002 Testing the efficiency and independence of attentional network. *Journal of Cognitive Neuroscience* 3(14): 340–347.

Ferreira, Victor and Kathryn Bock
- 2006 The functions of syntactic priming. *Language and Cognitive Processes* 21(7/8): 1011–1029.

Ferreira, Victor and Hiromi Yoshita
    2003   Given-new ordering effects on the production of scrambled sentences in Japanese. *Journal of Psycholinguistic Research* 32(6): 669–692.
Firbas, Jan
    1974   Some aspects of the Czechoslovak approach to problems of functional sentence perspective. In: F. Daneš (ed.), *Papers on Functional Sentence Perspective*, 11–37. The Hague: Mouton.
Firbas, Jan
    1987a   On the delimitation of theme in functional sentence perspective. In: R. Dirven and V. Fried (eds.), *Functionalism in Linguistics*, 137–156. Amsterdam: John Benjamins.
Firbas, Jan
    1987b   On two starting points of communication. In: R. Steele and T. Threadgold (eds.), *Language Topics: Essays in Honour of Michael Halliday*, volume 1, 23–46. Amsterdam: John Benjamins.
Fischer, Burkhart
    1998   Attention in saccades. In: R. D. Wright (ed.), *Visual Attention*, 289–305. New York: Oxford University Press.
Flores d'Arcais, Giovanni B.
    1975   Some perceptual determinants of sentence construction. In: G. B. Flores d'Arcais (ed.), *Studies in Perception: Festschrift for Fabio Metelli*: 344–373. Aldo Martello-Giunti.
Flores d'Arcais, Giovanni B.
    1987   Perceptual factors and word order in event descriptions. In: G. Kempen (ed.), *Natural Language Generation: New Results in Artificial Intelligence, Psychology, and Linguistics*, 441–451. Dordrecht: Martinus Nijhoff.
Forrest, Linda
    1996   Discourse goals and attentional processes in sentence production: the dynamic construal of events. In: A. Goldberg (ed.), *Conceptual Structure, Discourse, and Language*, 149–162. Stanford: CSLI Publications.
Gauthier, Isabel, Michael Tarr, Adam Anderson, Pawel Skudlarski, and John Gore
    1999   Activation of the middle fusiform 'face area' increases with expertise in recognizing novel objects. *Nature Neuroscience* 2: 568–573.
Givón, T.
    1983   *Topic Continuity in Discourse A Quantitative Cross-Language Study*. Amsterdam/Philadelphia: John Benjamins.
Givón, T.
    1988   The pragmatics of word order: predictability, importance, and attention. In: M. Hammond, E. A. Moravcsik and J. Wirth (eds.), *Studies in Syntactic Typology*, 243–284. Amsterdam: John Benjamins.
Givón, T.
    1992   The grammar of referential coherence as mental processing instructions. *Linguistics* 30: 5–55.
Gleitman, Lila, David January, Rebecca Nappa, and John Trueswell
    2007   On the give-and-take between event apprehension and utterance formulation. *Journal of Memory and Language* 57: 544–569.
Gundel, Jeanette
    1988a   Universals of topic-comment structure. In: M. Hammond, E. Moravcsik and J. Wirth (eds.), *Studies in Syntactic Typology*, 209–239. Amsterdam: John Benjamins.
Gundel, Jeanette
    1988b   *The Role of Topic and Comment in Linguistic Theory*. New York: Garland.
Hagoort, Peter Colin Brown, and Jolanda Groothusen
    1993   The syntactic positive shift as an ERP measure of syntactic processing. *Language and Cognitive Processes* 8: 439–484.

Hahne, Anja and Angela Friederici
   1999   Electrophysiological evidence for two steps in syntactic analysis: early automatic and late controlled processes. *Journal of Cognitive Neuroscience* 11(2): 194–205.
Hăjicová, Eva
   1984   Topic and focus. In: P. Sgall (ed.), *Contributions to Functional Syntax, Semantics, and Language Comprehension*, 189–202. Amsterdam: John Benjamins.
Halliday, M.A.K.
   1967   Notes on transitivity and theme in English (part 2) *Journal of Linguistics* 3: 199–244.
Halliday, M.A.K.
   1976   Theme and information in the English clause. In: G. Kress (ed.), *Halliday: System and Function in Language*, 174–188. London: Oxford University Press.
Hwang, Heeju and Elsi Kaiser
   2009   The effects of lexical vs. perceptual primes on sentence production in Korean: An online investigation of event apprehension and sentence formulation. 22nd CUNY conference on sentence processing. Davis, CA.
Ibbotson, Paul, Elena Lieven, and Michael Tomasello
   2013   The attention-grammar interface: Eye-gaze cues structural choice in children and adults. *Cognitive Linguistics* 24(3): 457–481.
Jackendoff, Ray
   1996   The architecture of the linguistic-spatial interface. In: P. Bloom, M. Peterson, L. Nadel, and M. Garrett (eds.), *Language and Space*, 1–30. Cambridge: MIT Press.
Jackson, Kyuseek Hwang
   2008   The effect of information structure on Korean scrambling. Ph.D. dissertation. Department of Linguistics, University of Hawaii.
Kaiser, Elsi and John Trueswell
   2004   The role of discourse context in the processing of a flexible word-order language. *Cognition* 94: 113–147.
Kaiser, Elsi and Virve-Anneli Vihman
   2006   Invisible arguments: Effects of demotion in Estonian and Finnish. In: T. Solstad and B. Lyngfelt (eds.), *Demoting the Agent: Passive and Other Voice-Related Phenomena*, 111–141. Amsterdam: John Benjamins.
Kanwisher, Nancy, Josh McDermott, and Marvin Chun
   1997   The fusiform face area: A module in extrastriate visual cortex specialized for face perception. *Journal of Neuroscience* 17: 4302–4311.
Kuchinsky, Stephanie and Kathryn Bock
   2010   From seeing to saying: Perceiving, planning, producing. 23rd CUNY Sentence Processing Conference. New York.
Lambrecht, Knud
   1994   *Information Structure and Sentence Form*. Cambridge: Cambridge University Press.
Landau, Barbara and Ray Jackendoff
   1993   "What" and "where" in spatial language and spatial cognition. *Behavioral and Brain Sciences* 16: 217–265.
Langacker, Ronald W.
   1987   *Foundations of Cognitive Grammar*, vol. 1: *Theoretical Perspectives*. Stanford: Stanford University Press.
Langacker, Ronald W.
   1991   *Foundations of Cognitive Grammar*, vol. 2: *Descriptive Application*. Stanford: Stanford University Press.
Langacker, Ronald W.
   this volume   6. Construal. Berlin/Boston: De Gruyter Mouton.
Levelt, Willem J.M.
   1989   *Speaking*. Cambridge: MIT Press.
MacWhinney, Brian
   1977   Starting points. *Language* 53(1): 152–168.

MacWhinney, Brian and Elizabeth Bates
1978   Sentential devices for conveying givenness and newness: A cross-cultural developmental study. *Journal of Verbal Learning and Verbal Behavior* 17: 539–558.
Mandler, Jean
1992   How to build a baby: II. Conceptual primitives. *Psychological Review* 99(4): 587–604.
Matthews, Danielle and Grzegorz Krajewski
this volume   18. First language acquisition. Berlin/Boston: De Gruyter Mouton.
McCandliss, Bruce, Lauren Cohen, and Stanislas Dehaene
2003   The visual word form area: Expertise for reading in the fusiform gyrus. *Trends in Cognitive Sciences* 7: 293–299.
Melinger, Alissa and Christian Dobel
2005   Lexically-driven syntactic priming. *Cognition* 98: B11–B20.
Myachykov, Andriy
2007   Integrating perceptual, semantic, and syntactic information in sentence production. Ph.D. dissertation, University of Glasgow.
Myachykov, Andriy, Simon Garrod, and Christoph Scheepers
2010   Perceptual priming of syntactic choice during English and Finnish sentence production. In: R. K. Mishra and N. Srinivasan (eds.), *Language and Cognition: State of the Art,* 53–71. Munich: Lincom Europa
Myachykov, Andriy, Simon Garrod, and Christoph Scheepers
2012   Determinants of syntactic choice in visually-situated sentence production. *Acta Psychologica* 141(3): 304–315.
Myachykov, Andriy, Dominic Thompson, Simon Garrod, and Christoph Scheepers
2012   Referential and visual cues to syntactic choice in sentence production. *Frontiers in Psychology* 2: 396.
Myachykov, Andriy and Russell Tomlin
2008   Perceptual priming and syntactic choice in Russian sentence production. *Journal of Cognitive Science* 9(1): 31–48.
Newman, Aaron, Roumyana Pancheva, Kaori Ozawa, Helen Neville, and Michael Ullman
2001   An event-related fMRI study of syntactic and semantic violations. *Journal of Psycholinguistic Research* 30(3): 339–364.
Newtson, Darren
1973   Attribution and the unit of perception of ongoing behavior. *Journal of Personality and Social Psychology* 28: 28–38.
Newtson, Darren and Gretchen Engquist
1976   The perceptual organization of ongoing behavior. *Journal of Experimental Social Psychology* 12: 436–450.
Newtson, Darren Gretchen Engquist, and Joyce Bois
1977   The objective basis of behavior units. *Journal of Personality and Social Psychology* 35: 847–862.
Osgood, Charles and Kathryn Bock
1977   Salience and sentencing: Some production principles. In: S. Rosenberg (ed.), *Sentence Production: Developments in Research and Theory,* 89–140. Hillsdale: Erlbaum.
Petersen, Steven and Michael Posner
2012   The attention system of the human brain: 20 years after. *Annual Review of Neuroscience* 35: 73–89.
Pickering, Martin and Holly Branigan
1998   The representation of verbs: Evidence from syntactic persistence in language production. *Journal of Memory and Language* 39: 633–651.
Pickering, Martin and Victor Ferreira
2008   Syntactic priming: A critical review. *Psychological Bulletin* 134(3): 427–459.

Posner, Michael
 1980   Orienting of attention. *Quarterly Journal of Experimental Psychology* 32: 3–25.
Posner, Michael and Steven Petersen
 1990   The attention system of the human brain. *Annual Review of Neuroscience* 13: 25–42.
Posner, Michael and Marcus Raichle
 1994   *Images of Mind.* New York: Scientific American Library.
Prat-Sala, Merce and Holly Branigan
 2000   Discourse constraints on syntactic processing in language production: A cross-linguistic study in English and Spanish. *Journal of Memory and Language* 42: 168–182.
Prentice, Joan
 1967   Effects of cuing actor vs. cuing object on word order in sentence production. *Psychonomic Science* 8: 163–164.
Prince, Ellen
 1981   Towards a taxonomy of given-new information. In: P. Cole (ed.), *Radical Pragmatics*, 223–256. New York: Academic Press.
Prince, Ellen
 1985   Topicalization and left-dislocation. *Annals of the New York Academy of Sciences* 433: 213–225.
Pulvermüller, Friedemann and Luciano Fadiga
 2010   Active perception: sensorimotor circuits as a cortical basis for language. *Nature Reviews Neuroscience* 11(5): 351–360.
Quirk, Randolph, Stanley Greenbaum, Geoffrey Leech, and Jan Svartvik
 1985   *A Comprehensive Grammar of the English Language.* London: Longman.
Raichle, Marcus, Julie Fiez, Tom Videen, Ann-Mary McCleod, Jose Pardo, Peter Fox, and Steven Petersen
 1994   Practice-related changes in the human brain: functional anatomy during non-motor learning. *Cerebral Cortex* 4: 8–26.
Rasolofo, Andoveloniaina
 2006   Malagasy transitive clause types and their functions. Ph.D. dissertation. Department of Linguistics, University of Oregon.
Scheepers, Christoph
 2003   Syntactic priming of relative clause attachments: persistence of structural configuration in sentence production. *Cognition* 89: 179–205.
Shaw, Robert E. and John Pittenger
 1978   Perceiving change. In: H. Pick, Jr. and E. Saltzman (eds.), *Modes of Perceiving and Processing Information*, 187–204. Hillsdale: Erlbaum.
Siewierska, Anna
 1988   The passive in Slavic. In: M. Shibatani (ed.), *Passive and Voice*, 243–289. Amsterdam: John Benjamins.
Sridhar, Shikaripur N.
 1988   *Cognition and Sentence Production: A Cross-Linguistic Study.* New York: Springer-Verlag.
Svartvik, Jan
 1966   *On Voice in the English Verb.* The Hague/Paris: Mouton and Co.
Talmy, Leonard
 1988a   Force dynamics in language and cognition. *Cognitive Science* 12: 49–100.
Talmy, Leonard
 1988b   The relation of grammar to cognition. In: B. Rudzka-Ostyn (ed.), *Topics in Cognitive Linguistics*, 165–205. Amsterdam: Benjamins.
Talmy, Leonard
 2000a   *Toward a Cognitive Semantics,* Volume 1: *Concept Structuring Systems.* Cambridge: MIT Press.

Talmy, Leonard
   2000b   *Toward a Cognitive Semantics,* Volume 2: *Typology and Process in Concept Structuring.* Cambridge: MIT Press.
Talmy, Leonard
   2007   Attention phenomena. In: D. Geeraerts and H. Cuyckens (eds.), *The Oxford Handbook of Cognitive Linguistics,* 264–293. London: Oxford University Press.
Tannenbaum, Percy and Frederic Williams
   1968   Generation of active and passive sentences as a function of subject and object focus. *Journal of Verbal Learning and Verbal Behavior* 7: 246–250.
Tomlin, Russell
   1985   Foreground-background information and the syntax of subordination. *Text* 5: 85–122.
Tomlin, Russell
   1994   Functional grammars, pedagogical grammars, and communicative language teaching. In: T. Odlin (ed.), *Perspectives on Pedagogical Grammar,* 140–178. London: Cambridge University Press.
Tomlin, Russell
   1995   Focal attention, voice, and word order. In: P. Downing and M. Noonan (eds.) *Word Order in Discourse,* 517–552. Amsterdam: John Benjamins.
Tomlin, Russell
   1997   Mapping conceptual representations into linguistic representations: The role of attention in grammar. In: J. Nuyts and E. Pederson (eds.), *Language and Conceptualization,* 162–189. Cambridge: Cambridge University Press.
Tomlin, Russell, Linda Forrest, Ming Ming Pu, and Myung Hee Kim
   1997   Discourse semantics. In: T. van Dijk (ed.), *Discourse as Structure and Process,* 63–111. London: Sage.
Tomlin, Russell, Linda Forrest, Ming Ming Pu, and Myung Hee Kim
   2010   Discourse semantics. In: T. A. van Dijk (ed.), *Discourse Studies: A Multidisciplinary Introduction,* 78–137. London: Sage.
Turner, Elizabeth Ann and Ragnar Rommetveit
   1968   Focus of attention in recall of active and passive sentences. *Journal of Verbal Learning and Verbal Behavior* 7: 543–548.
Vallduvi, Enric
   1992   *The Informational Component.* New York: Garland.
Vilkuna, Maria
   1989   *Free Word Order in Finnish.* Helsinki: Suomalaisen Kirjallisuuden Seura.
Weil, Henri
   1887   *The Order of Words in the Ancient Languages Compared with That of the Modern Languages.* Trans. C. W. Super. Boston: Ginn.
Yarbus, A.L.
   1967   *Eye Movements and Vision.* NY: Plenum Press.
Yokoyama, Olga
   1986   *Discourse and Word Order.* Amsterdam/Philadelphia: Benjamins.
Yuan, Sylvia and Fisher, Cynthia
   2009   "Really? She Blicked the Baby?": Two-year-olds learn combinatorial facts about verbs by listening. *Psychological Science* 20: 619–626.
Zemskaja, Elena
   1979   *Russkaja razgovornaja reč': lingvističeskij analiz i problemy obučenija* [Russian colloquial speech: A linguistic analysis and teaching difficulties]. Moskva: Russkij Jazyk.

Russell S. Tomlin, Eugene (USA)
Andriy Myachykov, Northumbria University (UK)

3. Frequency and entrenchment

1. What is frequency?
2. What is entrenchment?
3. Continuing controversies and open questions
4. References

After half a century of self-imposed exile from the cognitive scene, cognitive linguists are putting language back on stage: language is no longer considered a highly specialized and largely autonomous cognitive module, needing special treatment. Instead, cognitive linguists endorse a sophisticated view of learning and memory-based processing. Key to this is the assumption that frequency-sensitive learning results in mental representations optimized for a particular environment. Human beings appear to extract frequency information automatically from their environment (see review in Ellis 2002). Both infants and adults use statistical properties of linguistic input to discover structure, including sound patterns, words and the beginnings of grammar (Saffran et al. 1996). This allows children to learn and adults to refine a probabilistic grammar grounded in our language experience (Diessel 2007; MacWhinney 1998; Saffran 2003).

Whether frequency-sensitive learning really constrains theories of the language faculty remains controversial, however (for an overview of the debate to date, see Lieven 2010; Ambridge and Lieven 2011; Evans 2014; Matthews and Krajewski this volume), and there is a lack of understanding as far as the mechanics are concerned. As recently as 2010, Schmid (2010: 125) concluded his chapter on the relation between frequency in the text and entrenchment in the mind by saying that "so far we have understood neither the nature of frequency itself nor its relation to entrenchment, let alone come up with a convincing way of capturing either one of them or the relation between them in quantitative terms".

We are less pessimistic. In the current chapter we survey new perspectives on frequency and show how and when frequency-sensitive learning may result in mental representations or memories that vary in robustness and efficiency.[1] Perspectives from both experimental psychology and cognitive linguistics are integrated, with the aim of providing a review that will facilitate future research. We start with the origins of the interest in frequency in cognitive psychology and its interpretation and application in linguistics (section 1). We then present how the concept of entrenchment has been interpreted in theoretical linguistics, and review the cognitive and neural mechanisms supporting language structures that vary in entrenchment (section 2). In section 3 we discuss new directions, controversial issues and open questions.

---

[1] In order to present a coherent narrative in the space available, we have had to omit many relevant papers in the corpus- psycho- and neuro-linguistic traditions. We hope that readers with backgrounds in these areas will understand that these omissions are consequences of the space limitations imposed, and that readers who are new to these approaches can use the references that we have supplied to find the many interesting studies that we could not cover here. We thank Hans-Jörg Schmid and two further anonymous reviewers of our chapter for their thoughtful comments and suggestions for improvement.

1. What is frequency?

In experimental psychology, frequency is a practical term that was, and still is, used to capture how frequently a stimulus (such as a word or a phrase) is encountered and processed in the environment.[2] Within psycholinguistics and cognitive linguistics, frequency most often refers to the number of times a particular chunk of language (such as a phoneme, word, or phrase) occurs in a specified environment. Frequency is typically used in a relative sense, to categorize some stimuli as being more or less prevalent in the environment than other stimuli.

Frequencies can be obtained in a variety of ways. Some approaches yield subjective results, e.g., asking speakers to estimate frequency of use for a range of language stimuli on a Likert scale from, for example, never encountered to encountered several times a day (Balota et al. 2001). Other approaches yield objective results and rely on counting occurrence of types of stimuli using computer-readable databases or corpora (see also section 1.4). Historically, most corpora have been drawn from printed text, given the difficulty of transcribing spoken conversations (e.g., Francis and Kucera 1982; Davies 2010), yet many written and spoken corpora now exist in diverse languages (see http://tiny.cc/corpora for an overview).[3]

We first describe the standard ways in which frequency is measured in linguistics. We then provide an overview of frequency effects, i.e., how human beings react differently to higher frequency stimuli compared to lower frequency stimuli. Finally, we draw attention to a range of measures that can help shed light on how frequency effects are rooted in basic brain mechanisms; these measures have been developed within corpus-based and computational approaches but have not (yet) made it into mainstream Cognitive Linguistics.

1.1. Type versus token frequency

Research on frequency in linguistics was given an impetus by the pioneering work of Joan Bybee and collaborators who distinguished between type and token frequencies. The distinction between type and token frequency is important because these two types of frequencies play different roles in the productivity of linguistic structures (Bybee and Thompson 2000).

---

[2] Because frequency is known to exert a strong influence on processing speed, psycholinguists need to avoid the "confound of frequency" and thus routinely match their experimental items for frequency when comparing reaction times to different categories of words or other language structures.

[3] A creative approach to obtaining a large corpus based on spoken language is SUBTL, a large database of frequency norms based on a corpus of subtitles from TV and films (Brysbaert and New 2009). Subjective frequency measures are known to correlate moderately to highly with counts from corpora (Balota et al. 2001; Caldwell-Harris et al. 2012). Using frequency counts based on a large database of subtitles from TV and films results in higher correlations with processing times than do frequencies from texts (Brysbaert and New 2009). This substantiates the intuition that how words occur in dialogue is a more representative measure of their entrenchment than is their frequency of occurrence in written text.

Token frequency refers to how often a particular form appears in the input, e.g., all instances of the past tense form of *read*, but excluding the present tense form (even though it is spelled identically). Type frequency refers to the number of distinct items that are used in or within the structure of interest "whether it is a word-level construction for inflection or a syntactic construction specifying the relation among words" (Ellis 2002: 166). An example is the number of verbs that create their past-tense by changing an *-ow* form to *-ew*, as in *throw* → *threw*, *blow* → *blew*, *grow* → *grew*.

Token frequency facilitates learning via repetition. The more often a particular token is experienced, the easier it becomes to access and use (Bybee and Hopper 2001). Because it comes with ease of access and use, token frequency can be a conservative force that protects high-frequency structures from analogical leveling.

In contrast to the effects of high type frequency, high token frequency promotes the entrenchment or conservation of irregular forms and idioms; the irregular forms survive because they are high in frequency, which means they are encountered and processed more often (although an irregular form can also survive because it is highly similar to a high frequency item, e.g., *behold, forsake*). Type frequency can also guide learners to create a category out of a type (Bybee 1995; Bybee and Hopper 2001). According to Bybee and Thompson (2000), there are three reasons for this:

a) the more lexical items that are heard in a certain position in a construction, the less likely it is that the construction is associated with a particular lexical item and the more likely it is that a general category is formed over the items that occur in that position
b) the more items the category must cover, the more general are its criterial features and the more likely it is to extend to new items
c) high type frequency ensures that a construction is used frequently, thus strengthening its representational schema and making it more accessible for further use with new items.

1.2. How can frequency influence processing?

The study of frequency effects has its origin in the seminal psychological research of Cattell (1886). Cattell was the first to demonstrate the word frequency effect, i.e., that higher frequency words are recognized more quickly than lower frequency words. Since the development of the information processing paradigm in psychology in the 1960s–1980s, it has become accepted that frequency is among the most robust predictors of human performance in general (Hasher and Zacks 1984; Howes and Solomon 1951). Human beings are also surprisingly good at providing frequency estimates for a range of language stimuli, suggesting that accumulating frequency information occurs automatically (Hasher and Zacks 1984; Jurafsky 1996; Saffran 2003).

Frequency effects have been found in virtually every subdomain of language that has been studied. Comprehensive reviews of frequency and its effects on first and second language learning, representation and change now exist (Sedlmeier and Betsch 2002; Ellis 2002; Diessel 2007; Blumenthal-Drame 2012; Gries and Divjak 2012; Divjak and Gries 2012; Hilpert this volume). Given these reviews, we will focus on providing a taxonomy of types of frequency effects, to set the stage for explaining these effects as the result of frequency-sensitive learning.

1.2.1. Types of frequency effects

It has been most common to study frequency effects using single isolated words, and indeed, the (single) word frequency effect is one of the most robust findings in experimental psychology (Monsell 1991). Frequency effects have also been found for phonemes, morphemes and multi-word expressions, and have been attested for items across the low to high frequency range although less research exists on the former (but see Bannard and Matthews 2008; Caldwell-Harris et al. 2012; Snider and Arnon 2012; Divjak under revision for recent work on these effects in low frequency structures). Although most of our citations below concern the (single) word frequency effect, note that usage-based linguists propose single-system models and predict frequency effects for all linguistic units: simple and complex, lexical and grammatical.

Frequency effects have been demonstrated for at least four types of behavior:

> *Faster and easier processing.* Using the paradigm of perceptual identification, high frequency words are identified more quickly than low frequency words (Whaley 1978; Monsell 1991). In natural reading using eye-tracking, readers' eye fixations are usually shorter for more frequent words, suggesting greater ease at obtaining the meaning and integrating it with sentence context (Rayner and Duffy 1986).
>
> *More accurate processing.* Retrieving high frequency items is less subject to error than retrieving low frequency items (Balota et al. 2012; Howes and Solomon 1951; MacKay 1982). When participants are asked to name visually displayed words, a common error is to produce the high-frequency orthographic neighbor of a low frequency target word, as in the case of uttering '*blue*' for the target '*blur*' (Grainger 1990). Analogous errors are made in spoken word tasks.
>
> *Resistance to noise.* In visual displays containing ink blots or obscured letters, high frequency words are more accurately detected (McClelland and Rumelhart 1981). In the spoken domain, high frequency words are recognized more accurately when embedded in noise (Pollack et al. 1959).
>
> *Resilience to brain damage and aging.* As semantic dementia progresses from mild to severe, patients have increasing difficulty naming low frequency objects, such as rare animals and items of furniture (Rogers and McClelland 2004). Naming of specific attributes of objects is impaired before naming of more general attributes.

In addition to the behavioral effects of frequency listed above, the neural signatures that accompany language processing vary for high and low frequency stimuli. Event-related potentials (ERPs) measure brain electrical activity that is time-locked to presentation of a word or other linguistic stimulus. A great deal is now known about how wave forms vary for lexical attributes such as word concreteness, word class, semantic ambiguity, and word frequency (Van Petten 1993). Bigram/trigram frequencies appear to influence the ERP wave form as early as 90 ms after the word is displayed (using single word presentations; Hauk et al. 2006). Lexical (word) frequency has its effect slightly later, at 110 ms post-stimulus onset (Lee and Federmeier 2012). Lexical status, operationalized in these studies as the word/pseudo word distinction, does not influence wave forms until 160 ms, simultaneously with the effects of semantic coherence of a word's morphological family. Researchers have inferred that words that are high in frequency also tend to be orthographically regular and contain frequent sub-lexical units. The word frequency effect at 110 ms is thus best understood as reflecting sensitivity to orthographic and possibly morphological regularities. In addition, different types of information are believed to be organized in cascades with interactive feedback (Hauk et al. 2006; Rogers and McClelland 2004). We will return to ERP findings later when discussing the role of context in frequency and entrenchment.

1.2.2. Are frequency effects causal?

The frequency with which words occur is strongly correlated with other characteristics (Cutler 1981). Highly frequent words tend to be short in length, concrete rather than abstract, easily imaginable, and have early age-of-acquisition (Whaley 1978). Word frequency also correlates positively with many lexical attributes that have been quantified from corpora, such as orthographic neighborhood density, syntactic family size, noun-verb ratio and number of meanings (Balota et al. 2012; Baayen 2010; Cutler 1981).

Researchers have long suspected that these correlated factors, rather than the extent to which people have been exposed to words, may contribute to the processing advantage found. To determine how increased usage itself may be responsible for frequency effects, researchers have tried to identify people who could reasonably be expected to have different usage histories. One method has been to compare the lexical processing by persons from different occupations or social groups. In a lexical decision study using nurses, law students and engineers, each group responded more quickly to words relevant to their area of expertise (Gardner et al. 1987). This finding at the word-level was replicated for phrases. Religious Jews have faster processing of religious phrases than secular Jews (Caldwell-Harris et al. 2012). These findings establish that at least part of the frequency effect is due to language users' actual experience with those words and phrases.

1.3. Is it contextual diversity that causes "frequency" effects?

The standard meaning of frequency, and the one we assumed above, is the frequency with which a stimulus is repeated in the environment. This can be called frequency$_{rep}$. Over the last decade, evidence has accumulated that factors which are highly correlated with frequency$_{rep}$ are more strongly correlated with behavioral outcomes than frequency$_{rep}$ itself. One of these factors is the typical context of occurrence of words (Adelman et al. 2006; Brysbaert and New 2009; McDonald and Shillcock 2001).

The discovery of the powerful effect of "contextual diversity" (CD) emerged from data-mining large corpora to extract frequency counts and other values associated with words. Because many words are part of multi-word utterances, researchers sought to understand how much of lexical learning is contextual in nature. McDonald and Shillcock (2001) used principle component analysis over vectors to measure target words' contexts, while Adelman et al. (2006) simply used the number of passages or documents in which words occurred. Even when using this very crude way to operationalize "context", contextual diversity (CD) predicted more variance in lexical decision and naming latencies than did frequency$_{rep}$, suggesting that CD is the psychologically more relevant variable.

Research on explanations for frequency effects turned another corner with Jones et al. (2012) claim that what really facilitates lexical processing is semantic diversity. Like Adelman et al. (2006), they counted the number of distinct documents in which a word occurred but defined the similarity of any pair of documents as a function of the proportion of overlapping words in those two documents. A word's semantic distinctiveness was defined as the mean dissimilarity over all of the documents in which it occurred. When used to predict lexical decision and naming times from the Balota et al. (2007) English lexicon database, semantic distinctiveness predicted more variance in response times than word frequency and contextual distinctiveness.

1.4. Contextualized frequency measures

As discussed, psycholinguists have spent decades focusing on word form (token) frequency, and only in the last years have explored alternatives to frequency$_{rep}$ such as contextual diversity. In contrast, among corpus linguists, context has always been a salient issue, and linguists have worked on capturing context in more sophisticated ways. In the section below, we discuss measuring phrase frequency, conditional probabilities, and relational measures from the perspective of corpus linguistics.

Work on lexicography rarely used counts of the occurrence of an individual word form in isolation. This is because words may express different meanings depending on the context. Classical concordances return a list of usage examples of the item of interest and count its number of occurrences. Words are thus typically examined in their phrasal or sentential context. Indeed, collocations, i.e., words that are regularly used together giving rise to an association, and colligations, where a lexical item is linked to a grammatical one, are important concepts in corpus linguistics (McEnery and Hardie 2012: 122–123). Raw frequencies do not provide a reliable way of distinguishing collocates objectively from frequent non-collocates. The combination of *the* and *review* will be rather frequent due to the frequency of *the*, but *the review* is not a collocation; *peer review*, on the other hand, is. To address this issue collocation scores were calculated that compare expected to observed frequencies to establish whether the observed frequency of co-occurrence is greater than what one would expect to find by chance given the frequencies with which each of the words that form the pair occur. Readers familiar with corpus linguistics will have encountered the terms Mutual Information (MI), T-score (Church and Hanks 1990) and Log-likelihood ratio score (or G2, developed by Dunning 1993). The number of association measures available within computational corpus linguistics has grown rapidly over the last decades and we refer to Evert (2005) and Pecina (2009) for exhaustive inventories.

Within linguistics, these mathematically complex measures that capture the strength of association between two items have been perceived to be "so technical that even linguists who had applied them with some success admitted they were not able to see behind the formulas and to interpret the actual linguistic significance" (Schmid 2010: 107). This led Schmid to create conceptually simpler collostructional measures, attraction and reliance (Schmid 2000: 54). Schmid's measures were designed to capture the interaction between nouns and constructions (rather than the association between two words). They take into consideration the linguistic relation between a so-called node and its collocate, be it another word or a construction, but do not compare observed with expected frequencies. Attraction and reliance were therefore soon supplemented by a set of collostruction techniques (Stefanowitsch and Gries 2003) that pair respect for the relation between a node and its collocate(s) with significance testing. Whether or not statistical significance testing is a desirable property of association measures remains a topic of debate (Schmid and Kuchenhoff 2013; Gries 2013; Divjak under review; Levshina under review).

Corpus linguists have also developed measures of contextual diversity, using the label "dispersion". Dispersion quantifies the homogeneity of the distribution of a word in a corpus (Lyne 1985). Gries (2008, 2010) provides an overview of dispersion measures, including those that penalize words for not occurring uniformly across a corpus. Behavioral data in this area is scarce, but Baayen (2010) shows that dispersion (defined as number of texts in which a word appears) is the second best single predictor of response latencies, after frequency-as-repetition but before contextual diversity (defined as percentage of films containing the word). Although frequency emerges as the best single predictor, frequency of occurrence, in the sense of pure repetition, is not a particularly important predictor in itself, but is instead highly correlated with a number of other factors. It is also interesting to note that dispersion appears to be highly correlated with word frequency (r = 0.82 reported by McDonald and Shillcock 2001; see also Baayen 2010).

Computational psycholinguists have argued that conditional probabilities (defined as the likelihood to encounter a word given it context, for example)[4] are more appropriate than frequencies for explaining language processing in general. Jurafsky (1996) showed that a probabilistic model differs in its predictions from the frequency-based models traditional in psycholinguistics, with true probabilities essential for a cognitive model of sentence processing (cf. Saffran et al. 1996 who showed that infants use transitional probabilities to segment speech and detect word boundaries). The usefulness of probabilities has been well-known within information-theory, where measures such as entropy and surprisal have been developed. Entropy is a measure of the unpredictability of information content: something that is predictable has low entropy, whereas something that is unpredictably has high entropy. In a similar vein, the surprise ratio, also called "suprisal" (Barlow 1990), measures how unexpected a sequence is, given the probabilities of its components.[5] Suprisal has been used in psycholinguistic models (Hale 2001; Levy

---

[4] Relative frequencies are conditional probabilities calculated on the basis of one sample only and can be treated as conditional probabilities given a sufficient level of faith in the representativeness of the sample.

[5] Hale (2001) showed that the difficulty of a word is proportional to its surprisal (its negative log-probability) in the context within which it appears.

2008; Jaeger 2010; Fernandez Monsalve et al. 2012) and in computational emergentist models (e.g., ADIOS, see Solan et al. 2005).

Contextualized frequency yields better predictions than isolated frequencies, even for low frequency words, and this can be expected: the brain makes use of learned contextual regularities. Seminal studies from the 1970s, such as Biederman et al. (1973), demonstrated already that objects are recognized faster and more accurately when accompanied by contextual information. Although for most research purposes, frequency$_{rep}$ should still be adequate for statistically equating stimuli, it is useful to be aware of alternative measures, since they help address the question of how frequency effects are obtained and are rooted in basic brain mechanisms, a topic addressed later in this chapter.

2. What is entrenchment?

Entrenchment was introduced to Cognitive Linguistics as a theoretical construct by Langacker (1987). Langacker used the term entrenchment to explain how linguistic structures are created and shaped through use. A key objective of cognitive linguistics is to determine whether and how the structure of language can result from patterns of usage. It was thus an important step in the foundational writings by cognitive linguists to discuss how linguistic patterns are mentally encoded, and how these representations vary with usage. In this section, we review what cognitive linguists mean by entrenchment and connect their theoretical ideas with contemporary views of learning and memory.

2.1. Cognitive linguists' characterizations of entrenchment

In his seminal book, *Foundations of Cognitive Grammar*, Langacker (1987: 59) made the case for a

> "continuous scale of entrenchment in cognitive organization. Every use of a structure has a positive impact on its degree of entrenchment, whereas extended periods of disuse have a negative impact. With repeated use, a novel structure becomes progressively entrenched, to the point of becoming a unit; moreover, units are variably entrenched depending on the frequency of their occurrence."

Langacker's definition of entrenchment focuses on the role of entrenchment for representation, looking at the storage and organization of structures in our mental inventory. Langacker's characterization of entrenchment is noteworthy on two accounts: it states explicitly that 1) increasing frequency of occurrence deepens entrenchment and that 2) increasing entrenchment can lead to qualitative differences in representation, as when a frequently co-occurring sequence becomes a unit in memory. In other words, it suggests that an increase in frequency deepens entrenchment, and that at a certain point entrenchment may lead to unitization.

Bybee's (2007: 324; cf. also 2007: 10, 279) characterization also emphasizes how repeated use leads to unitization, but she additionally refers to the processing characteristics of automatization and increased fluency or fluidity: "Each token of use of a word or sequence of words strengthens its representation and makes it more easily accessed.

3. Frequency and entrenchment

In addition, each instance of use further automates and increases the fluency of the sequence, leading to fusion of the units". Important in this second definition is the addition that a number of separate entities can fuse into one larger unit, a phenomenon known as fusion or chunking. Chunk status implies that the unit can be retrieved from mental storage as a whole rather than by accessing the individual component parts and parsing them on the basis of rules or schemas (see also De Smet and Cuyckens 2007: 188).

Blumenthal-Drame (2012: 68 f.) developed a working definition of entrenchment for her neuroimaging study of multimorphemic words. For this, she drew on concepts of gradedness, fluency, and unitization:[6]

> "[h]igher token frequencies in usage will correlate with a gradual increase in ease of processing, more precisely enhanced fluidity in composition or parsing. At some point, this process will lead to a new, holistic representation. After this point, facilitation – more precisely, ease of retrieval ... – will still continue to increase as a function of frequency."

Blumenthal-Drame (2012) argued that, crucially, these continuous properties seem to be related to processing, that is to changes in the use of stored entities, rather than the inventory of stored entities, as they imply that the process of fusing separate entities becomes easier and more fluid. She concluded that "entrenchment must be seen as a multi-layered phenomenon which is modulated by several stimulus variables and which affects different inter-related yet relatively independent processing dimensions at the same time" (Blumenthal-Drame 2012: 193).

Croft and Cruse (2004: 292) had already stressed the idea that with increasing use, structures continue to accrue representational strength and increase in automaticity, stating that "entrenchment comes in degrees, even beyond the minimum threshold required for independent storage".

From this brief survey, the family resemblance structure among the various characterizations of entrenchment becomes apparent. What these characterizations have in common is the belief that entrenchment refers to a process of strengthening memory representations. This may result in a general reduction in processing effort (automatization), gestalt formation ("unitization" à la Langacker) and/or chunking accompanied by formal reduction ("fusion" à la Bybee).[7]

Trying to define entrenchment in theory alone does not seem useful, however, and we now turn to some empirical work on the topic. Within usage-based linguistics proper, most empirical work on entrenchment has been carried out by acquisitionists. A classic question in language acquisition is how children construct grammatical categories and rules when adults rarely correct childrens' grammatical errors, an issue related to poverty of the stimulus arguments (Pullum and Scholz 2002). According to Braine and Brooks (1995), attending to frequently occurring constructions can mitigate the lack of negative evidence. They propose the "entrenchment hypothesis": repeated presentations of a verb in particular constructions (e.g., *The rabbit disappeared*) cause the child to probabilisti-

---

[6] There is some terminological proliferation in the entrenchment literature, with several terms pointing in the same direction, i.e., fluency, processing ease, automatization and routinization. We have opted for the term "fluency" to capture both ease in producing and comprehending speech.
[7] There are also linguists who see entrenchment as a cognitive process to be distinguished from the societal process of conventionalization (Schmid 2010; Mukherjee 2005).

cally infer that the verb cannot be used in non-attested constructions (e.g., *The magician disappeared the rabbit*). Learning from positive evidence will create verb-argument structures which have a strength proportional to how often a verb has been heard with that argument structure (this line of inquiry is taken further by work on statistical preemption, see Goldberg 2011; Boyd and Goldberg 2011; Casenhiser and Bencini this volume; see Ambridge et al. (2013: 49–55) for a comparison of entrenchment with preemption).

An implication of this view is that when an argument structure has been learned to a stable level of entrenchment, it will pre-empt alternatives, unless they have been independently witnessed. A second implication is that overgeneralizations will be less common, and will subjectively feel less acceptable for high frequency verbs than for semantically-matched lower frequency verbs. For example, *The magician vanished the rabbit* feels slightly more acceptable than *The magician disappeared the rabbit*, since this inference from absence is stronger for the higher-frequency verb *disappeared*. Ambridge (2013) confirmed that children were more accepting of low frequency verbs being used in novel high frequency constructions, than of high frequency verbs being used in alternative constructions. For alternating ones, such as the dative and locative constructions, the effects were less pervasive (see Ambridge and Lieven 2011: 252–254). This leaves open the question of how speakers deal with newly witnessed or rarely attested alternatives: since they have been independently witnessed they should no longer be pre-empted on a strict entrenchment account.

Like other researchers, Braine and Brooks (1995: 368) did not take a stance on the precise quantitative relation between representational strength and frequency of usage. They merely note that with age there appears to be an increase in flexibility in switching between sentence constructions to meet conversational demands (e.g., to have particular arguments as subject or as object). Our contribution here will therefore be to draw insights about learning and memory from cognitive psychology, so that cognitive psychology can underpin Cognitive Linguistics.

2.2. Entrenchment: what learning does to the brain

To be maximally helpful to linguists who want to draw on insights from cognitive science and learning, we suggest a working definition of the relation between frequency and entrenchment. Frequency facilitates language processing because the available mental representations have been shaped by frequency-sensitive learning. As such, they are prepared to process stimuli that vary widely in their probability of occurrence in the environment (Elman 1993; Saffran et al. 1996). From a cognitive science perspective, mental representations can be considered stable attractors in the brain's dynamic neural networks (MacWhinney 1998). These dynamic patterns vary along a continuum of strength of representation.

2.2.1. The neurocognitive basis of entrenchment

How are "strong" representations (or "deep attractors") mentally represented differently from weaker representations? There are several ways to conceive of representational strength, as has been done via modeling in artificial neural networks (Rogers and

McClelland 2004). Strength of representations can correspond to heavily weighted connections from some input features to processing units inside the networks' architecture. There can also be large numbers of connections, and more redundant connections. Weighted connections between processing units are functionally akin to neurons' dendrites and axons. Specific links between processing units that frequently match inputs to their expected outputs are strengthened, inspired by the Hebbian learning principle (Hebb 1949) in neuroscience that "neurons that fire together wire together".

It may seem odd to equate entrenched linguistic forms with something as prosaic as "memory". But entrenched forms must be memories (Bar 2011; Daelemans and Van den Bosch 2005). Memories capture information that has been encoded and can influence future processing; there is no requirement for memories to be conscious or to be recallable. This is clear from the classic distinction between declarative and procedural memories, also termed explicit and implicit memory. Declarative memories are those for which we have conscious recognition, including episodic memories. For language stimuli, we may be able to consciously recall autobiographical episodes when a specific word or phrase was used. Or we can have recognition memory – and be able to reliably confirm that a phrase such as "about which" is familiar and we have likely used it thousands of times. We can also confirm that the phrase "which about" is not familiar and indeed we may never have used it; it is highly unlikely to exist as an entrenched unit (Caldwell-Harris et al. 2012).

2.2.2. Is there a threshold number of occurrences required for entrenchment?

The cognitive science perspective provides a framework for thinking about some of the outstanding questions in the relationship between frequency and entrenchment. It is commonly assumed that a stimulus sequence needs to be encountered a certain number of times before it becomes unitized (i.e., encoded as such in memory). According to this view, once complex stimuli are encoded as units, their mental representations grow in strength as a function of experience. This common view lacks empirical support (Gurevich et al. 2010). Researchers have not been able to find evidence of what might be a frequency threshold for multimorphemic or multiword utterances. Alegre and Gordon (1999) have proposed a threshold of 6 occurrences per million words for inflected forms, but frequency effects have been observed well below that threshold (Baayen et al. 1997; Baayen et al. 2007; Blumenthal-Drame 2012; Arnon and Snider 2010; Caldwell-Harris et al. 2012, Divjak under revision), and are found for all frequency ranges for morphologically simple controls (Alegre and Gordon 1999).

A second counterargument is logical. If a single exposure is below the threshold where a counter begins accruing evidence, then the counter of exposures remains set to 0, and logically no experience can accrue (Gurevich et al. 2010). It may be more fruitful to assume that evidence accrues from the first exposure, but that speakers cannot formulate reliable hypotheses until sufficient evidence has accumulated: Divjak (under revision) finds frequency effects for rare lexico-syntactic combinations in Polish (< .66 pmw) but shows that these effects are driven by words that themselves occur at least 6 times pmw. Erker and Guy (2012) propose to think of frequency as a gate-keeper or potentiator: some constraints on subject personal pronoun use in Spanish are activated or amplified by high frequency. This is expected on a probabilistic approach to language, and can also be explained by what we know from memory research, in particular from research on how information is transferred from immediate working memory to long term memory.

2.2.3. The role of procedural and declarative memory systems

Memory for specific episodes is believed to be part of the declarative memory system, mediated by the hippocampus and medial temporal structures (Cohen and Squire 1980). The declarative memory system performs one-trial learning, but such information is subject to rapid decay. Recurring events are learned via the procedural system, mediated by neocortical structures (Gupta 2012). Here, slow learning allows information to be incrementally integrated into long term memory structures, where they have rich associations with many patterns, facilitating generalization and abstraction.

Connectionist models have been used to describe how human languages draw on both the procedural and declarative systems for learning (Gupta 2012; Rogers and McClelland 2004). The procedural system is most efficient at encoding systematic mappings using distributed representations. In distributed representations, multiple patterns are stored across the same set of processing units, allowing for extraction of regularities. Novel patterns can be rapidly learned via minor changes to the weighted connections in the network, but these minor changes will typically be overwritten again as soon as new patterns come in.

Learning unique arbitrary mappings, such as the link between word forms and meanings, can be done if sparse or localist representations are used, since the patterns won't interfere with each other. It has been proposed that hippocampal structures use sparse representational structures to implement arbitrary associations, including episodic and short-term memories (Rogers and McClelland 2004). Arbitrary associations can be permanently learned only with considerable exposure/training. Theorists propose that with continued rehearsal and learning, these associations are gradually displaced from the fast-learning hippocampal system and integrated into the neocortical procedural system.

Learning lexical items, morphological patterns and syntactic constructions is complex and relies on the integration of these two brain systems (see Gupta 2012 for a review). Learning a new morphological variant can usually be handled by the procedural system because it involves minor adjustments to established sound-to-motor patterns. Novel mappings, such as learning to pronounce a foreign word or learning someone's name, require creating new pathways between inputs and outputs, and thus may be initially stored as part of episodic memory. If that novel information is never encountered again, the weighted connections that represent it will be overwritten as new patterns are encountered. But if that stimulus is repeatedly encountered, each exposure provides another training trial in which it can be integrated into long-term memory structures in the neocortex.

2.2.4. Encoding in context

Appreciation is growing that language processing has more in common with memory retrieval than has previously been assumed (Adelman et al., 2006; see also the computational linguistic project called memory based learning [MBL], Daelemans and Bosch 2005).

The brain mechanisms that underlie entrenchment specify a major role for repeated experience, whether it is overt experience in the environment, or mental rehearsal during silent rumination. The best recall is for material that has been encountered at varying times and locations (i.e., in separated contexts).[8] To explain why words with high contextual diversity are recognized more quickly, Adelman et al (2006) turned to research on the advantage of spaced exposures for long-lasting learning (Anderson and Schooler 1991). Exposures that are widely spaced in time and occur in different contexts have the strongest impact on learning. The reason is that repeated stimuli that re-occur immediately may be processed as if they were a single episode, because of the phenomenon of repetition suppression (Grill-Spector et al. 2006). When a word (or other stimulus) is presented twice in rapid succession, the second occurrence is considered "primed" – it is more easily processed compared to following an unrelated stimulus (Lee and Federmeir 2012). But this ease-of-recognition brings with it reduced neural activation. This repetition suppression plausibly results in less opportunity for strengthening connections, meaning that less learning (and less entrenchment) occurs for items that are encountered repeatedly in a short period of time. Not surprisingly, people have the poorest recall for "massed practice", meaning training on items that are encountered within a defined time period, or in a single, predictable context, as is typical of classroom academic learning. High frequency$_{rep}$ thus does not in and of itself ensure integration into long term memory structures.

Another relevant line of thought comes from the perspective of "rational analysis of memory", which posits that it is adaptive from an evolutionary perspective to only encode items which are likely to reoccur in the future (Anderson and Schooler 1991). Indeed, a view from evolutionary and cognitive psychology is that the purpose of memory is not to remember past events, but to have mental resources to guide future action (Bar 2011). The greater the diversity of environments in which something has occurred in the past, the more probable is it to reoccur in the future. Simple frequency$_{rep}$ therefore strengthens an item's representation less than if the item was experienced in a different context.

Effects of contextual diversity appear to arise naturally in a learning model that includes context. Baayen (2010) found that contextual diversity is an emergent property of a computational model originally developed to explain morphological processing, the naive discriminative reader (NDR; see also Baayen this volume). In the NDR model lexical meanings are learned from contextually rich input.[9] These are letter bigrams and trigams drawn from a window of four words rather than from words in isolation. The activation of a meaning on a given trial is obtained by summing the weights from the active letters and letter pairs to that meaning. The NDR model correctly predicted a range of morphological phenomena and showed contextual diversity effects. The contextual diversity accounted for substantially more variance in word recognition efficiency

---

[8] This is the same finding as from the educational literature, where cramming for a test yields less enduring learning than do spaced study periods (Carpenter et al. 2012).
[9] The NDR model shares some features with connectionist models, using an error-driving learning algorithm to map from inputs (representations of letters) to outputs (representations of meanings). It differs from connectionist models by using straightforward symbolic representations for letters, letter pairs and meanings. It only uses one forward pass of activation, with weights set on links computed from corpus-derived co-occurrence matrices.

than did word frequency. Another success of the model was that it also predicted phrase frequency effects (Baayen and Hendrix 2011), which are known to be quite robust (Arnon and Snider 2010). Other computational models, such as the memory based learning approach (Daelemans and Bosch 2005) have likewise reported that token frequencies of linguistic patterns do not enhance classification accuracy.

3. Continuing controversies and open questions

In this final section, we highlight a few of the controversies and open questions concerning frequency and entrenchment within Cognitive Linguists. In our view, entrenchment is best thought of as the procedure that gives rise to mental representations through frequency sensitive learning. These mental representations are effectively memories, and thus concepts from current work on memory apply. Taking a broader cognitive science perspective also has the advantage of offering new points of view for two commonly asked questions about the relationship between frequency and entrenchment.

3.1. What can be entrenched?

A frequently asked question is: what can be entrenched? Single words, complex phrases, lexical items, abstract schemas? If entrenched expressions are mental representations of language forms which are either implicit or explicit memories, then, yes, all of these can be entrenched. The more difficult question is whether entrenchment necessarily implies chunking and chunk storage

It has been common practice to view frequency effects as proof of the existence of mental representations. If frequency effects were found for a specific morpheme sequence, then researchers felt justified in viewing that morpheme sequence to be mentally represented as a discrete unit. For example, Blumenthal-Drame concluded from her study of the processing of multimorphemic words that "[...] the effects of token frequency at different levels of language description attest to the necessity of positing full storage of tokens, irrespective of whether they are complex or simple" (2012: 193; cf. also Bannard and Matthews 2008; Arnon and Snider 2010).

Recent computational modeling casts doubts on the wisdom of these assumptions. Baayen's (2010; 2011) naive discriminative learner model contained no representations corresponding to whole words or phrases, only letter unigrams and bigrams (see also Baayen this volume). The model nevertheless showed frequency effects for multi-word units. Based on this demonstration, Baayen (2011) argued that specific morpheme sequences (including multiword expressions) show frequency effects: the model develops its own representations that are frequency sensitive, as a by-product of learning form-to-meaning mappings that vary in frequency.

3.2. Can we resolve the tension between storage and computation?

Another take on this problem comes from the discussion about the relationship between storage and computation. It continues to be debated whether frequency effects are observed because a frequent multimorphemic word or multiword expression is stored as a unit or whether its pieces are more rapidly assembled.

Blumenthal-Drame argued that "[...] highly independent representations will be holistically retrieved rather than analytically processed" (2012: 187). Tremblay et al. (2011: 595) provided evidence for holistic storage but noted at the same time that behavioral research may not be able to distinguish between holistic retrieval and speeded online computation. Other researchers have suggested that the tension between storage and computation is unnecessary. Shaoul proposed that "this graded effect of probability [...] is a side-effect of the emergent nature of n-gram processing" (2012: 171).

In other words, the neural patterns which mediate language processing contain expectations of how patterns will be completed. Any given syllable encountered in a speech stream activates expectations for a subset of all possible syllables based on prior processing (Elman 1993; Baayen and Hendrix 2011). Expectations are activated quickly and effortlessly, as if the predicted sequence was stored separately as a ready-made unit (see Baayen this volume). This view of expectation generation and processing rather than chunk storage is consistent with the workings of a probabilistic grammar. Given this, and the fact that frequency effects have been observed where they were not expected (section 3.1), we would not subscribe to the view that frequency effects are evidence of or reliable diagnostics of unit storage.

3.3. Which frequency measure is ideal for predicting entrenchment?

A key question that has received attention only recently (Divjak 2008; Wiechmann 2008; Gries 2013; Schmid and Kuchenhoff 2013; Divjak under revision; Levshina under review) is which frequency measure or family of measures is best suited to predict entrenchment? Do different frequency measures correlate with different incarnations of entrenchment (as summarized in section 2.1)? Issues that are currently debated in assessments of the usefulness of existing frequency measures include the uni- or bi-directionality of the measure, and the inclusion of contingency information and the relevance of statistical null-hypothesis testing.

Although earlier experimental work supports association measures (Gries et al. 2005; Ellis and Ferreira-Junior 2009; Ellis and Simpson-Vlach 2009; Colleman and Bernolet 2012), research contrasting association measures and conditional probabilities (Divjak 2008, under revision; Levshina under review; Wiechmann 2008; Blumenthal-Drame 2012; Shaoul 2012) shows that conditional probabilities are the favored predictors for a range of linguistic behaviors. Wiechmann (2008), for example, surveyed a wide range of association measures and tested their predictivity using data from eye-tracking during sentence comprehension. The best measure at predicting reading behavior was minimum sensitivity. This measure selects the best of the two available conditional probabilities, i.e., P(verb|construction) and P(construction|verb).

Recent studies have compared uni-directional probability measures to bi-directional measures; while the former calculate, for example, P(verb|construction) or how likely the verb is given the construction; the latter would supplement this information with a calculation of how likely the construction is given the verb and compute both P(verb|construction) and P(construction|verb). Divjak (2008, under revision) obtained sentence acceptability ratings on dispreferred and often low frequency Polish combinations of verbs and constructions. Levshina (under review) used gap filling and sentence production tasks on the Russian ditransitive. Both these studies surveyed a number of association measures, including conditional probabilities, and found that uni-directional probability measures explained behavioral performance at least as well as bi-directional measures. In a similar vain, Blumenthal-Drame (2012) studied the processing of complex word forms in English, using a variety of tasks and both reaction time as well as fMRI measurements. Her conclusion was that (log) relative frequencies (the ratio between surface ([root + affix] and base [root] frequencies) predict entrenchment best. Moreover, none of the probability-based measures that outperformed the others on the tasks described above related observed to expected frequencies in order to perform null-hypothesis statistical significance testing. The information gained from relating observed to expected frequencies the way this is done in statistics may have low psychological relevance to speakers.

3.4. The importance of context

Seminal studies from the 1970s, such as Biederman et al (1973), demonstrated that objects are recognized faster and more accurately when accompanied by contextual information. This translates straightforwardly to language, and linguists have indeed focused on frequency effects in language units varying in size from phonological to morphological and syntactic contexts. Even disciplines that have been preoccupied with frequency counts, such as corpus linguistics, have borne this principle in mind. Indeed, core concepts in corpus linguistics are collocations, i.e., words that are regularly used together giving rise to an association, and colligations, where a lexical item is linked to a grammatical one. It therefore comes as a surprise to linguists that psychologists interested in language have long focused on words in isolation. Yet behavioral evidence is accumulating that supports linguists' intuitions. One example comes from ERP studies of word processing in sentence context. The magnitude of the N400 component (meaning a negative voltage occurring 400 ms after presentation of a word) indicates difficulty integrating a word with its sentence context. Very large N400s occur for words that are anomalous in their sentence context. N400 wave forms are influenced by word frequency, being largest for very low frequency words. This suggests that contextual integration is most difficult for rare words. However, this frequency effect is strongest at the beginning of a sentence and diminishes for successive words in a semantically congruent sentence (but not a scrambled sentence; van Petten 1993). In van Petten's (1993) study, by the 5th word of a sentence, the N400 frequency effect had disappeared. This suggests that when sufficient context has been encountered, low frequency words are no more difficult to integrate into their context than are high frequency words.

3.5. Is frequency the most important factor for creating entrenched representations?

Following work in the cognitive sciences, we suggest that the answer to this question be "no". Frequency is an important contributor, but the relevance of a stimulus for learners' goals may be more important than frequency per se. Entrenchment can occur without repetition frequency, since robust memories can be formed with single-trial learning. A language example is fast mapping, whereby children and adults infer the meaning of a word from context (Carey and Bartlett 1978). But a strong mental representation will be formed from a single instance only in special cases, such as those associated with intense emotions. Future work on frequency that draws on insights from research on learning, memory and attention and contrasts frequency with salience will no doubt shed light on this question.

4. References

Adelman, James S., Gordan D. A. Brown and Jose F. Quesada
   2006   Contextual diversity, not word frequency, determines word-naming and lexical decision times. *Psychological Science* 17:814–823.

Alegre, Maria and Peter Gordon
   1999   Frequency effects and the representational status of regular inflections. *Journal of Memory and Language* 40: 41–61.

Ambridge, Ben
   2013   How do children restrict their linguistic generalizations: An un-grammaticality judgment study. *Cognition* 125: 49–63.

Ambridge, Ben and E. Lieven
   2011   *Child Language Acquisition. Contrasting Theoretical Approaches.* Cambridge: Cambridge University Press.

Ambridge, Ben, Julian M. Pine, Caroline F. Rowland, Franklin Chang and Amy Bidgood
   2013   The retreat from overgeneralization in child language acquisition: Word learning, morphology and verb argument structure. *Wiley Interdisciplinary Reviews: Cognitive Science* 4: 47–62.

Anderson, John R. and Lael J. Schooler
   1991   Reflections of the environment in memory. *Psychological Science* 2: 396–408.

Arnon, Inbal and Neal Snider
   2010   More than words: Frequency effects for multi-word phrases. *Journal of Memory and Language* 62: 67–82.

Baayen, R. Harald
   2010   Demythologizing the word frequency effect: A discriminative learning perspective. *The Mental Lexicon* 5: 436–461.

Baayen, R. Harald
   2011   Corpus linguistics and naive discriminative learning. *Brazilian Journal of Applied Linguistics* 11: 295–328.

Baayen, R. Harald, Ton Dijkstra and Robert Schreuder
   1997   Singulars and plurals in Dutch: Evidence for a parallel dual-route model. *Journal of Memory and Language* 37: 94–117.

Baayen, R. Harald and Peter Hendrix
   2011   Sidestepping the combinatorial explosion: Towards a processing model based on discriminative learning. In LSA workshop *Empirically examining parsimony and redundancy in usage-based models.*

Baayen, R. Harald
   this volume   5. Analogy and schematization. Berlin/Boston: De Gruyter Mouton.

Baayen, R. Harald, Lee H. Wurm and Joanna Aycock
   2007   Lexical dynamics for low-frequency complex words. A regression study across tasks and modalities. *The Mental Lexicon* 2(3): 419–463

Balota, David A., Maura Pilotti and Michael J. Cortese
   2001   Subjective frequency estimates for 2,938 monosyllabic words. *Memory and Cognition* 29: 639–647.
Balota, David A., Melvin J. Yap, Michael J. Cortese and Keith A. Hutchison, Michael J. Cortese, Brett Kessler, Bjorn Loftis, James H. Neely, Douglas L. Nelson, Greg B. Simpson and Rebecca Treiman
   2007   The English lexicon project. *Behavior Research Methods* 39: 445–459.
Balota, David A., Melvin J. Yap, Keith A. Hutchison and Michael J. Cortese
   2012   Megastudies: Large scale analysis of lexical processes. In: J. S. Adelman (ed.), *Visual Word Recognition* Vol 1. London: Psychology Press.
Bannard, Colin and Danielle Matthews
   2008   Stored word sequences in language learning the effect of familiarity on children's repetition of four-word combinations. *Psychological Science* 19(3): 241–248.
Bar, Moshe (ed.)
   2011   *Predictions in the Brain. Using our Past to Generate a Future.* Oxford: Oxford University Press.
Barlow, Horace B.
   1990   Conditions for versatile learning, Helmholtz's unconscious inference and the task of perception. *Vision Research* 30: 1561–1571.
Biederman, Irving, Arnold L. Glass and E. Webb Stacy
   1973   Searching for objects in real-world scenes. *Journal of Experimental Psychology* 97: 22–27.
Blumenthal-Drame, Alice
   2012   *Entrenchment in Usage-Based Theories. What Corpus Data Do and Do Not Reveal About The Mind.* Berlin: De Gruyter.
Boyd Jeremy K. and Adele E. Goldberg
   2011   Learning what not to say: the role of statistical preemption and categorization in "a"-adjective production. *Language* 81 (1): 1–29.
Braine, M. D. S. and Brooks, P. J.
   1995   Verb argument structure and the problem of avoiding an overgeneral grammar. In M. Tomasello and W. E. Merriman (eds.), *Beyond Names for Things: Young Children's Acquisition of Verbs*, 353–376. Hillsdale: Erlbaum
Brysbaert, Marc and Boris New
   2009   Moving beyond Kučera and Francis: A critical evaluation of current word frequency norms and the introduction of a new and improved word frequency measure for American English. *Behavior Research Methods* 41: 977–990.
Bybee, Joan
   1995   Regular morphology and the lexicon. *Language and Cognitive Processes* 10: 425–455.
Bybee, Joan
   2007   *Frequency of Use and the Organization of Language.* Oxford: Oxford University Press.
Bybee, Joan and Paul Hopper (eds.)
   2001   *Frequency and the Emergence of Linguistic Structure.* Amsterdam: John Benjamins.
Bybee, Joan and Sandra Thompson
   2000   Three frequency effects in syntax. *Berkeley Linguistics Society* 23: 378–388.
Caldwell-Harris, Catherine L., Jonathan Berant and Edelman Shimon
   2012   Entrenchment of phrases with perceptual identification, familiarity ratings and corpus frequency statistics. In: D. Divjak and S. T. Gries (eds.), *Frequency Effects in Language Representation.* Volume 2, 165–194. Berlin: Mouton de Gruyter.
Carey, Susan and Elsa Bartlett
   1978   Acquiring a single new word. *Papers and Reports on Child Language Development* 15: 17–29.

Carpenter, Shana K., Nicholas J. Cepeda, Dough Rohrer, Sean H.K. Kang and Harold Pashler
   2012   Using spacing to enhance diverse forms of learning: Review of recent research and implications for instruction. *Educational Researcher* 24: 369–378.

Casenhiser, Devin and Giulia Bencini
   this volume   28. Argument structure constructions. Berlin/Boston: De Gruyter Mouton.

Cattell, James M.
   1886   The time it takes to see and name objects. *Mind* 41: 63–65.

Church, Kenneth W. and Patrick Hanks
   1990   Word association norms, mutual information and lexicography. *Computational Linguistics* 16: 22–29.

Cohen, Neal J. and Larry R. Squire
   1980   Preserved learning and retention of pattern analyzing skill in amnesia: Dissociation of knowing how and knowing that. *Science* 210: 207–210.

Colleman, Timothy and Bernolet, Sarah
   2012   Alternation biases in corpora vs. picture description experiments: DO-biased and PD-biased verbs in the Dutch dative alternation. In: D. Divjak and S. T. Gries (eds.), *Frequency Effects in Language Representation*. Volume 2, 87–125. Berlin: Mouton de Gruyter.

Croft, William and Cruse, Alan
   2004   *Cognitive Linguistics*. Cambridge: Cambridge University Press.

Cutler, Anne
   1981   Making up materials is a confounded nuisance, or: Will we be able to run any psycholinguistic experiments at all in 1990? *Cognition* 10: 65–70.

Daelemans, Walter and Antal Van den Bosch
   2005   *Memory-Based Language Processing*. Cambridge: Cambridge University Press.

Davies, Mark
   2010   Corpus of Contemporary American English. Available from http://www.americancorpus.org/

De Smet, Hendrik and Hubert Cuyckens
   2007   Diachronic aspects of complementation: Constructions, entrenchment and the matching-problem. In: C. M. Cain and G. Russom (eds.), *Studies in the History of the English Language* III: *Managing Chaos: Strategies for Identifying Change in English*, 1–37. Berlin: Mouton de Gruyter.

Diessel, Holger
   2007   Frequency effects in language acquisition, language use, and diachronic change. *New Ideas in Psychology* 25: 108–127.

Divjak, Dagmar
   2008   On (in)frequency and (un)acceptability. In: B. Lewandowska-Tomaszczyk (ed.), *Corpus Linguistics, Computer Tools and Applications – State of the Art*, 1–21. Frankfurt: Peter Lang.

Divjak, Dagmar
   under revision   Pattern transparency and conditional probabilities affect acceptability of verbs in low frequent syntactic alternants.

Divjak, Dagmar and Stefan Th. Gries (eds.)
   2012   *Frequency Effects in Language Representation* Volume 2. Berlin: De Gruyter.

Dunning, Ted
   1993   Accurate methods for the statistics of surprise and coincidence. *Computational Linguistics* 19(1): 61–74.

Ellis, Nick C.
   2002   Frequency effects in language processing: a review with implications for theories of implicit and explicit language acquisition. *Studies in Second Language Acquisition* 24: 143–188.

Ellis, Nick C. and Fernando Ferreira-Junior
   2009   Constructions and their acquisition: Islands and the distinctiveness of their occupancy. *Annual Review of Cognitive Linguistics* 7: 188–221.

Ellis, Nick C. and Rita Simpson-Vlach
   2009   Formulaic language in native speakers: Triangulating psycholinguistics, corpus linguistics, and education. *Corpus Linguistics and Linguistic Theory* 5: 61–78.

Elman, Jeffrey L.
   1993   Learning and development in neural networks: The importance of starting small. *Cognition* 48(1): 71–99.

Erker Daniel and Gregory R. Guy
   2012   The role of lexical frequency in syntactic variability: Variable subject personal pronoun expression in Spanish. Language 88(3): 526–557.

Evans, Vyvyan
   2014   *The Language Myth: Why language is not an instinct.* Cambridge: Cambridge University Press.

Evert, Stefan
   2005   The statistics of word co-occurrences: Word pairs and collocations. Ph.D. Dissertation, Institut für maschinelle Sprachverarbeitung, University of Stuttgart. Retrieved from http://www.stefan-evert.de/PUB/Evert2004phd.pdf

Fernandez Monsalve, Irene, Stefan L. Frank and Gabriella Vigliocco
   2012   Lexical surprisal as a general predictor of reading time. *Proceedings of the 13th Conference of the European Chapter of the Association for Computational Linguistics*, 398–408. Avignon: Association for Computational Linguistics.

Francis, W. Nelson, and Henry Kucera
   1982   *Frequency Analysis of English Usage: Lexicon and Grammar.* Boston: Houghton-Mifflin.

Gardner, Michael K., E. Z. Rothkopf, Richard Lapan and Toby Lafferty
   1987   The word frequency effect in lexical decision: Finding a frequency-based component. *Memory and Cognition* 151: 24–28.

Goldberg, Adele E.
   2011   Corpus evidence of the viability of statistical preemption. *Cognitive Linguistics* 22(1): 131–154.

Grainger, Jonathan
   1990   Word frequency and neighborhood frequency effects in lexical decision and naming. *Journal of Memory and Language* 29: 228–244.

Gries, Stefan Th.
   2008   Dispersions and adjusted frequencies in corpora. *International Journal of Corpus Linguistics* 13: 403–437.

Gries, Stefan Th.
   2010   Dispersions and adjusted frequencies in corpora: further explorations. In: S. Th. Gries, S. Wulff and M. Davies (eds.), *Corpus Linguistic Applications: Current Studies, New Direction*s, 197–212. Amsterdam: Rodopi.

Gries, Stefan Th.
   2013   50-something years of work on collocations: what is or should be next. *International Journal of Corpus Linguistics* 18(1) 137–165.

Gries, Stefan Th. and Dagmar Divjak (eds.)
   2012   *Frequency Effects in Language Learning and Processing* Volume 1. Berlin: De Gruyter.

Gries, Stefan Th., Beate Hampe and Doris Schönefeld
   2005   Converging evidence: Bringing together experimental and corpus data on the association of verbs and constructions. *Cognitive Linguistics* 16(4): 635–676.

Grill-Spector, Kalanit, Richard Henson and Alex Martin
　2006　Repetition and the brain: neural models of stimulus-specific effects. *Trends in Cognitive Sciences* 10: 14–23.
Gupta, Prahlad
　2012　Word learning as the confluence of memory mechanisms: Computational and neural evidence. In: M. Faust (Ed.), *Handbook of the Neuropsychology of Language,* Volume 1, 146–163. Oxford: Wiley.
Gurevich, Olya, Matt Johnson and Adele E. Goldberg
　2010　Incidental verbatim memory for language. *Language and Cognition* 2(1): 45–78.
Hale, John
　2001　A probabilistic early parser as a psycholinguistic model. In *Proceedings of the second meeting of the North American Chapter of the Association for Computational Linguistics on Language technologies,* 1–8. Stroudsburg: Association for Computational Linguistics.
Hasher, Lynn and Rose T. Zacks
　1984　Automatic processing of fundamental information: The case of frequency of occurrence. *American Psychologist* 39: 1372.
Hauk, Olaf, Matthew H. Davis, M. Ford, Friedemann Pulvermüller and William D. Marslen-Wilson
　2006　The time course of visual word recognition as revealed by linear regression analysis of ERP data. *Neuroimage* 30: 1383–1400.
Hebb, Donald O.
　1949　*The Organization of Behavior.* New York: Wiley and Sons.
Hills, Thomas T., Michael N. Jones and Peter M. Todd
　2012　Optimal foraging in semantic memory. *Psychological Review* 119: 431–440.
Hilpert, Martin
　this volume　16. Historical linguistics. Berlin/Boston: De Gruyter Mouton.
Howes, Davis H. and Richard L. Solomon
　1951　Visual duration threshold as a function of word-probability. *Journal of Experimental Psychology* 416: 401–410.
Jaeger, T. Florian
　2010　Redundancy and Reduction: Speakers Manage Information Density. *Cognitive Psychology* 61(1): 23–62.
Jones, Michael N., Johns, Brendan T. and Gabriel Recchia
　2012　The role of semantic diversity in lexical organization. *Canadian Journal of Experimental Psychology* 66: 115–124.
Jurafsky, Dan
　1996　A probabilistic model of lexical and syntactic access and disambiguation. *Cognitive Science* 20: 137–194.
Langacker, Ronald W.
　1987　*Foundations of Cognitive Grammar,* Volume I, *Theoretical Prerequisites.* Stanford: Stanford University Press.
Lee, Chia-Lin and Federmeier, Kara D.
　2012　In a word: ERPs reveal important lexical variables for visual word processing. In: M. Faust (Ed.), *The Handbook of the Neuropsychology of Language,* Volume 1, 184–208. Oxford: Wiley-Blackwell.
Levshina, Natalia
　(under review)　Associations between constructions and collexemes revisited: convergent evidence of divergent knowledge.
Levy, Roger
　2008　Expectation-based syntactic comprehension. *Cognition* 106: 1126–1177.
Lieven, Elena
　2010　Input and first language acquisition: Evaluating the role of frequency. *Lingua* 120: 2546–2556.

Lyne, Anthony A.
   1985   Dispersion. In: *The Vocabulary of French Business Correspondence*, 101–124. Geneva/Paris: Slatkine-Champion.

MacKay, Donald G.
   1982   The problems of flexibility, fluency, and speed accuracy trade-off in skilled behavior. *Psychological Review* 89: 483–506.

MacWhinney, Brian
   1998   Models of the emergence of language. *Annual Review of Psychology* 49: 199–227.

Matthews, Danielle and Grzegorz Krajewski
   this volume   18. First language acquisition. Berlin/Boston: De Gruyter Mouton.

McClelland, James L. and David E. Rumelhart
   1981   An interactive activation model of context effects in letter perception: Part 1. An account of basic findings. *Psychological Review* 88: 375–407.

McDonald, Scott A. and Richard Shillcock
   2001   Rethinking the word frequency effect. The neglected role of distributional information in lexical processing. *Language and Speech* 44(3): 295–323.

McEnery, Tony and Andrew Hardie
   2012   *Corpus Linguistics: Method, Theory and Practice*. Cambridge: Cambridge University Press.

Monsell, Stephen
   1991   The nature and locus of word frequency effects in reading. In: D. Besner and G. W. Humphreys (eds.), *Basic Processes in Reading: Visual Word Recognition*, 148–197. Hillsdale: Lawrence Erlbaum.

Mukherjee, Joybrato
   2005   *English Ditransitive Verbs: Aspects of Theory, Description and a Usage-Based Model* (Language and Computers 53). Amsterdam/New York: Rodopi.

Pecina, Pavel
   2009   Lexical association measures: Collocation extraction. *Studies in Computational and Theoretical Linguistics* 44(1/2): 137–158.

Pollack, Irwin, Herbert Rubenstein and Louis Decker
   1959   Intelligibility of known and unknown message sets. *The Journal of the Acoustical Society of America* 31: 273–279.

Pullum, Geoffrey K., and Barbara C. Scholz
   2002   Empirical assessment of stimulus poverty arguments. *The Linguistic Review* 18: 9–50.

Rayner, Keith and Susan A. Duffy
   1986   Lexical complexity and fixation times in reading: Effects of word frequency, verb complexity and lexical ambiguity. *Memory and Cognition* 14: 191–201.

Rogers, Timothy T. and James L. McClelland
   2004   *Semantic Cognition: A Parallel Distributed Processing Approach*. Cambridge: MIT Press.

Saffran, Jenny R.
   2003   Statistical language learning: Mechanisms and constraints. *Current Directions in Psychological Science* 12: 110–114.

Saffran, Jenny R., Richard N. Aslin, Elissa L. Newport
   1996   Statistical learning by 8-month-old infants. *Science* 274: 1926–1928.

Schmid, Hans-Jörg
   2000   *English Abstract Nouns as Conceptual Shells. From Corpus to Cognition*. Berlin/New York: Mouton de Gruyter.

Schmid, Hans-Jörg
   2010   Does frequency in text really instantiate entrenchment in the cognitive system? In: D. Glynn and K. Fischer (eds.), *Quantitative Methods in Cognitive Semantics: Corpus-Driven Approaches*, 101–133. Berlin: Walter de Gruyter.

Schmid, Hans-Jörg and Helmut Küchenhoff
    2013   Collostructional analysis and other ways of measuring lexicogrammatical attraction: Theoretical premises, practical problems and cognitive underpinnings. *Cognitive Linguistics* 24(3): 531–577.
Sedlmeier, Peter, and Tilmann Betsch (eds.)
    2002   *Frequency Processing and Cognition*. London: Oxford University Press.
Shaoul, Cyrus
    2012   The processing of lexical sequences. PhD Dissertation. University of Alberta, Edmonton. http://hdl.handle.net/10402/era.26026
Snider, Neal and Inbar Arnon
    2012   A unified lexicon and grammar? Compositional and non-compositional phrases in the lexicon. In: D. Divjak and S. Gries (eds.), *Frequency Effects in Language Representation* Volume 2, 127–164. Berlin: Mouton de Gruyter.
Solan, Zach, David Horn, Eytan Ruppin and Shimon Edelman
    2005   Unsupervised learning of natural languages. *Proceedings of the National Academy of Sciences* 102: 11629–11634.
Stefanowitsch, Anatol and Stefan Th. Gries
    2003   Collostructions: Investigating the interaction of words and constructions. *International Journal of Corpus Linguistics* 82: 209–243.
Tremblay, Antoine, Bruce Derwing, Gary Libben and Chris Westbury
    2011   Processing advantages of lexical bundles: Evidence from self-paced reading and sentence recall tasks. *Language Learning* 61: 569–613.
Van Petten, Cyma
    1993   A comparison of lexical and sentence-level context effects and their temporal parameters. *Language and Cognitive Processes* 8: 485–532.
Whaley, C. P.
    1978   Word-nonword classification time. *Journal of Verbal Learning and Verbal Behavior* 17: 143–154.
Wiechmann, Daniel
    2008   On the computation of collostruction strength. *Corpus Linguistics and Linguistic Theory* 42: 253–290.

Dagmar Divjak, The University of Sheffield (United Kingdom)
Catherine L. Caldwell-Harris, Boston University (USA)

4. Categorization (without categories)

1. Introduction
2. Concepts, categories and categorization
3. Computational models of categorization
4. The neural bases of categorization
5. Concepts, contrasts and communication
6. Summary
7. References

1. Introduction

Cognitive linguists view language as a social artifact shaped by learning and cultural transmission, and emphasize the role of *categorization* in shaping our linguistic capacities (Lakoff 1987; Taylor 2003). This has resulted in something of a division of labor, as linguists seek to explain the role of categorization in shaping the functional properties of language, while psychologists seek to uncover the cognitive bases of categorization itself.

These endeavors share many assumptions and questions: how do people decide that an aspect of a scene should be labeled (in English) *a mountain* or *tree*? How do they determine that an instance of speech contains the sound [ɒ] that distinguishes *water* from *waiter*? And both approaches assume that the fact that people use words like *water* and *waiter* indicates they have access to the *concepts waiter, water,* and *[ɒ]*. These concepts are discrete mental units that (somehow) specify their content, and can be combined with other concepts to create thoughts, utterances and sentences.

Although this assumption makes some intuitive sense, it not clear that English speakers' use of the word *tree* does warrant the assumption that each speaker possesses a coherent, unified representation of the concept *tree*, or that trees form a coherent class of natural objects (Wittgenstein 1953; Quine 1960). Moreover, the struggles that are evident when categorization researchers seek to define the object of their study suggest that these assumptions may be unwarranted:

> The concept of concepts is difficult to define, but no one doubts that concepts are fundamental to mental life and human communication. Cognitive scientists generally agree that a concept is a mental representation that picks out a set of entities, or a category. That is, concepts refer, and what they refer to are categories. (Rips et al. 2013: 177)

However, because *reference* and *representation* are as ill defined as *concept*, describing concepts as mental representations that refer to classes of entities in the world simply exchanges one poorly defined term for another. This problem led Wittgenstein (1953) and Quine (1960) to reject the idea of concepts as discrete constructs, and emphasize instead the way that words function in systems, and the way that meanings result from the way words are *used* in these systems.

This distinction – between concepts as discrete mental tokens, and concepts as emergent aspects of systems – is usually glossed over in the literature, but its implications for language, both for semantics and for linguistic categories themselves, are far-reaching. To establish which characterization better describes the results of many years of empirical study, this chapter reviews the results of this work, along with the many computational models that have been developed to account for them, and recent work seeking to match these models to neural structures in the brain.

The findings of these lines of work make it clear that our minds do not learn inventories of discrete, stand-alone concepts. Instead, human conceptual capabilities are systematic: they are the product of a rich capacity to discriminate and learn *systems* of alternative responses (behaviors, affordances, words, etc.) and to use them in context. From this perspective English speakers do not acquire discrete concepts of *tree* or *friend*, but rather they learn a system of linguistic contrasts, and they learn how to discriminate when to use the words *tree* (rather than *bush, oak* or *shrub*) or *friend* (rather than *buddy* or *pal*) in order to satisfy their communicative goals. We conclude this review by briefly describing what this implies for future directions of research in cognitive linguistics.

2. Concepts, categories and categorization

2.1. Concepts and labels

It seems clear that the existence of individual nouns need not entail the existence of corresponding individuated cognitive representational entities yet speakers tend to talk about *concepts* as if they are discrete, countable things. Thus dictionaries characterize *concepts* as "directly intuited objects of thought" or "ideas of things formed by mentally combining their characteristics" (passing the buck of defining *concept* onto *idea* and *object of thought*). This practice extends to the categorization literature, which focuses on either discrete, artificially defined concepts, or the nature of frequent linguistic items like *tree*.

From this circumscribed perspective, researchers seek to explain how cognitive representations of concepts can be described in terms of relations between *features* (and where a *category* is the set of instances that exemplify a *concept*). To work, this approach requires clear definitions of what concepts and features are, and this, as noted above, is problematical: if the only thing that unifies the category of *games* is the fact that we call them games – i.e., they share the feature of being called *game* in English – then a definition of the concept *game* will add no more to our understanding of concepts than saying that *games* are whatever English speakers call *games*. Further, as Wittgenstein (1953) observed, if we take the common English word *game*, then *baseball* is a game, whether played by children for fun or by professionals for their livelihood; *polo* and *hopscotch* are games, as are *scrabble, solitaire,* and *monopoly*; yet *stockbroking* is not usually called a game, nor are *proofreading* nor *cavalry-charges* (military *maneuvers* are called games in peacetime but not wartime). And although many local similarities can be seen between different games, there are equally many local similarities between games and non-games (Goodman 1972), such that it appears that the only things that joins *games* together while ruling out *non-games* is the fact that some things are conventionally called *games* while others are not (Ramscar and Hahn 1998).

The circular relationship between labels and concepts is not restricted to abstract words like *game*: the English word *tree* does not correspond to a coherent class of objects, even leaving aside uses like *tree diagram*. Biologically, pine trees are *gymnosperms* (conifers), whereas oak trees are *angiosperms* (flowering plants). Oaks share an evolutionary lineage with cacti, daisies and roses; pines belong to a more primitive genus (Lusk 2011). *Vegetable* is a similar pseudo-natural kind: English *tomatoes* are vegetables, but most other edible fruits are not (Malt et al, 2010). And while even natural concepts (in the colloquial sense of the word concept) seem arbitrary because they lack defining features, defining features in turn raises problems that are disturbingly similar to those posed by concepts: What are they? Do features themselves merely reflect labels, etc. (Ramscar et al. 2010b; Port 2010; Port and Leary 2005)?

To illustrate the subtle problems these issues pose when it comes to forming a clear understanding of the role of concepts in categorization, consider a rare attempt to clearly define the terms concept and category from the literature: Goldstone and Kersten (2009) describe concepts as mental representation of individuals or classes that specify *what* is being represented and how to categorize it. They then note that if a concept is a mental representation of a class, and a category a set of entities that are appropriately categorized together by that concept, this leaves the question of whether concepts determine categories or categories determine concepts open:

> If one assumes the primacy of external categories of entities, then one will tend to view concept learning as the enterprise of inductively creating mental structures that predict these categories. [...] If one assumes the primacy of internal mental concepts, then one tends to view external categories as the end product of applying these internal concepts to observed entities. An extreme version of this approach is to argue that the external world does not inherently consist of rocks, dogs, and tables; these are mental concepts that organize an otherwise unstructured external world. (Goldstone and Kersten 2003: 600).

However, the basis for these distinctions is dubious: It is demonstrably the case that the world does *not* inherently consist of rocks, dogs, and tables. *Dog* and *table* are English words (i.e., culturally defined labels), and there is little evidence to support the idea that natural partitions in the universe are constrained by the vocabulary of English. Indeed, as *tree* and *vegetable* illustrate, there is little reason to believe the English lexicon maps onto reality in a privileged way at all; *trees* are simply what English speakers call trees.

So what is a concept, and how do categories relate to concepts? The answer is that in practical terms, regardless of what researchers take the relationship between words and reality to be, concepts are determined by the ways things are labeled. A rock is an instance of *rock* if English speakers would call it a rock, and when researchers talk about two items as instances of a concept they simply mean that the items can be spoken about using the same linguistic symbol (and, as Gahl 2008 shows, even apparent homophones are symbolically distinct).

This point even extends to the artificially defined concepts used in experiments, because the features used in their definitions are themselves linguistic concepts like red, square, etc. Indeed, even where concepts are only implicitly labeled in a study's procedure – for example in pigeon experiments, or in abstract discrimination tasks – the relevant stimulus dimensions will have been explicitly labeled at some point in its design (e.g., Zentall et al. 2014; Billman and Knutson 1996).

In other words, irrespective of whether researchers believe in the primacy of the word or the primacy of the world, in practice they study concepts that are determined by labels. For clarity, in the rest of this review the word *concept* will be used to describe a specific relationship between a group of items: that they share a label, typically a word (or phrase, discriminable symbol, etc.).[1] We will use *concept learning* to describe the way the relationship between a set of items and a label is learned: That is, the process by which people learn whatever it is that enables them to respond to new items in a manner appropriate to a label. *Category* will be used to describe a set of items with a common label (including new items that could be considered to be members of that category in an appropriate context), and *categorization* will be used to describe the

---

[1] This does not means that people only learn in reference to labels, or that they only acquire "conceptual knowledge" that can be labeled. Rather, for obvious reasons, there is little discussion of completely non-verbalizable content in the categorization literature.

various things people are asked to do with category members, i.e., sort them, label them, make inferences about them, etc.

2.2. One label; Two ideas

Many of the confusions that abound in discussions of categorization research arise out of the fact that it comprises two distinct lines of study:

1. *Concept learning* experiments originating in the associative paradigms that dominated early psychology, and which focus on classification and response discrimination tasks, usually employing artificial concepts;
2. Studies of *the structure of natural language concepts* that measure people's behavior as they respond to uses of words and phrases.

Because these two approaches employ the same terminology, but embody very different methodological approaches, potential for confusion abounds in the literature, especially when, as is common, results from studies of artificial concepts are discussed in the same breath as natural concepts.

2.3. Concept learning: from rules and definitions to prototypes and exemplars

Studies of *concept learning* typically examine people's ability to discriminate the appropriate dimensions of stimuli and learn to match them to discrete responses (Hull 1920; Smoke 1932). Researchers examine questions such as whether associations increase gradually or are better characterized in all-or-none terms (Trabasso and Bower 1968) and whether learning conjunctive dimensions (e.g., *blue* AND *triangular*) is easier than disjunctive dimensions (e.g., *blue* OR *triangular*; Bruner et al. 1956; Shepard et al. 1961).

Because artificial concepts are defined by feature-combinations, researchers often equate concept learning with acquiring a rule defining some kind of membership criterion (e.g., *"rule-based" concepts*; Smoke 1932): concepts are descriptions of the appropriate dimension(s) for class inclusion and categorization is a process in which item features are matched to rules across an inventory of concepts. Rule-based concept learning thus resembles early speculations about word meanings, e.g., Frege's (1892) distinction between the *intensions* and *extensions* of concepts (which is still widely used in linguistic analyses today): A concept's intension is the set of attributes defining its members, while its extension comprises its actual members.

Thus the intension of *bachelor* might include characteristics such as male, unmarried and adult, making its extension the set of male, unmarried adults in the world, which would mean that both the Pope and an unmarried man cohabiting with the same partner for 25 years are bachelors. One can, of course, amend the intension of bachelor to exclude Popes and cohabitees to fix this, but what is important to note here is a critical *difference* between natural language and artificial concepts: the latter are whatever a researcher defines them to be, whereas definitions for natural language concepts can only be imputed.

It follows that, theoretically, the question of **whether** there is an appropriate conceptual definition for bachelor at all is equally as valid as **what** the conceptual definition of bachelor is. Or, to put it another way, although the definitional status of artificial concepts can be taken for granted, valid definitions for natural concepts might not actually exist (Wittgenstein 1953). Intriguingly, this latter notion is supported by the results of artificial concept learning studies themselves: Findings from numerous experiments indicate that people don't actually learn to represent rules or feature specifications for carefully defined concepts even when they encounter them (Sakamoto and Love 2004).[2]

For example, Posner and Keele (1970) showed that people are better at classifying previously unseen *typical* artificial category exemplars than less typical exemplars they have actually seen in training. Along with numerous other similar findings, this result suggests that people learn *prototypical* information about item-categories, such that even well defined concepts are not learned as definitions.

Other findings muddy the waters still further. When typicality differences are controlled for, participants *are* better at categorizing items seen in training than new items (Nosofsky 1992; Smith and Minda 2000). Similarly, less typical new items similar to items seen in training are categorized more accurately and quickly than typical new items that are not (Medin and Schaffer 1978). These results suggest that participants learn details about the specific items they are exposed to (i.e., exemplars) rather than abstracting rule-based representation or pure prototypes.

On the other hand, concept learning does result in some abstraction: Posner and Keele (1967) showed that although participants retain information about the letters *a* and *A* for a couple seconds, these initial encodings give way to representations in which *a* and *A* are stored as exemplars of a more abstract (case-invariant) letter name. Similarly although participants adjusting the length of a reference line to that of a Müller-Lyer stimulus which is either in view or in memory exhibit a pattern of bias consistent with the Müller-Lyer effect in both cases, the adjustments made from memory are further biased towards the average line length presented in the experiment (Crawford et al. 2000).

What people learn about concepts is further influenced by the tasks they perform in experiments (Love 2002). Learning in inference tasks (answering questions like, "This is a mammal. Does it have fur?") highlights dimensions that are typical rather than diagnostic of concepts (which in this case would involve milk-producing glands). By contrast, classification tasks ("This has milk-producing glands. Is it a mammal?") promote learning of the diagnostic information that discriminates between categories (Yamauchi et al. 2002).

Finally, Brooks et al. (1991) have shown how specific exemplars play a role in experts' use of well-defined concepts. For example, doctors often base diagnoses on recent cases, rather than more general abstractions, suggesting that expertise involves the acquisition of knowledge about relevant exemplars, as well as rules.

This body of results is incompatible with the idea that concepts are defined in memory by stable feature sets, or that such things are even plausible as theoretical postulates

---

[2] Since "features" in artificial concepts are natural concepts at another level of abstraction, these findings are not entirely surprising.

(Ramscar et al. 2013d, 2014). Even where people learn clearly specified concepts, they learn both more and less than a definitional account might imply, and what they learn is influenced by the tasks they perform during learning, by context, and by the process of learning itself (Arnon and Ramscar 2012; Ramscar et al. 2013d).

2.4. The structure of natural language concepts and the basic level

The other line of categorization research examines the knowledge associated with the words used in languages (Rosch and Mervis 1975; Rosch et al. 1976). Rosch and colleagues argued that everyday concepts are not structured in ways that reduce to definitions based on necessary and sufficient features. Although a given feature might be common to many items corresponding to a word's usage (e.g., *birds fly*), it might not be common to all (*penguins*) and it might also be common to items labeled using other words (*insects*). Rosch et al. proposed that natural concepts have a *family resemblance* structure, and that category membership (labeling) depends on similarities between members of a category.

An idea that naturally follows from this suggestion is that there are better and worse examples of a concept: Category members that share more properties with other members should better exemplify a concept than those sharing fewer properties. And studies confirm that people believe canaries are better examples of *birds* than *penguins* (Rosch and Mervis 1975), and that these goodness judgments correlate with the number of features that a given example shares with other examples.

Rosch et al. (1976) argue that the distribution of features among concepts results in natural clusters that maximize within-category similarity and minimize between-category similarity. They termed these basic-level concepts. Examples would be *dog* (as opposed to *dachshund,* or *pet*) and *house* (as opposed to *duplex*, or *mansion*). Rosch et al suggest that basic-level categories are (a) preferred by adults in naming objects in tasks that contrast various levels of abstraction (b) used more in child directed speech, (c) learned first by children, and (d) are associated with the fastest categorization reaction times.

Although Rosch et al. repeatedly show that people are more likely to use basic level words than those at other levels in their abstraction hierarchy, they paradoxically maintain this is *not* because basic level words are more frequent (presenting evidence from small written corpora in support of this idea). However, it is worth noting first that Rosch et al. acknowledge that "basic level" categories can be influenced by culture and expertise (thus, for a real-estate agent, *colonial* may be a basic-level concept), and second, that word frequency effects are ultimately conditioned on an individual's experience, not corpus statistics (Ramscar et al. 2014). Further, the basic level labels studied by Rosch et al. are high frequency English nouns. Because of this, it is unclear whether basic level categories should be seen as offering insight into the structure of the world, personal and cultural structures, or interactions between the two (Malt et al. 2010).

Work in this tradition poses another problem for discrete theories of concepts because it provides evidence that some – if not all – natural language categories lack clear boundaries. Labov (1973) showed that there is a great deal of variability in the way people use terms such as *cup*, *bowl*, etc., with different labels being assigned to the same containers both between speakers and within speakers depending upon the linguistic context. If people are asked to look at a picture of an object whose shape is half way between a (tea) *cup* and a (soup) *bowl* and told that it contains mashed potatoes, they tend to consider the object to be a *bowl*. But if the ambiguous object contains hot coffee, it tends to be considered a *cup*. Similarly, in a study of exemplar-category pairs (e.g., *apple-fruit* or *chair-furniture*) McCloskey and Glucksberg (1978) found not only substantial between- and within-participant disagreement on category membership (measured over successive test-sessions) but also that levels of disagreement correlate with independently derived typicality ratings: McCloskey and Glucksberg's participants were certain that *chair* belonged to the category *furniture*, and that *cucumber* did not. However, there was much disagreement as to whether a *bookend* belonged to the category *furniture*, with many participants differing in their judgments from one session to the next.

Categorization in one domain can also be influenced by information from another. For example, thinking about space can influence subsequent temporal categorization judgments: the question *Next Wednesday's meeting has been moved forward two days: what day is the meeting on now?* is more likely to be answered with Friday than Monday by people who have been encouraged to think about moving towards a physical destination rather than staying in one place (Boroditsky and Ramscar 2002; Evans this volume). Rating the sensibility of fictive motion sentences (e.g., *Seven trees ran along the driveway* vs. *There were seven trees along the driveway*) also produces a similar, predictable influence on temporal categorization (Ramscar et al. 2010a). However, although time and space seem to be systematically linked, the basis of this linkage ultimately appears be lexical: the patterns of priming observed in these experiments are highly consistent with patterns of lexical co-occurrence in English (Ramscar et al. 2010a).

Finally, we should note that Rosch (1978) argued that it would be a mistake to assume that the discovery of prototype effects indicated that word meanings are themselves represented by prototypes. Yet the idea that concepts *can* be assumed to have prototypical representations has since been proposed in various guises: as *frames* (e.g., Fillmore 1982); as *Idealized Cognitive Models* (ICMs, Lakoff 1987); as *image schemas* (Johnson 1987); and *domains* (Lakoff 1993). It is thus worth stressing that none of these suggestions make it clear what is or is not part of a specific frame, ICM, or domain, or indeed how concepts are actually represented in terms of these constructs. Thus despite the fact that these suggestions are often referred to as theories of representation, they are more akin to the phenomenological descriptions that Rosch suggested prototypes actually are than theories of conceptual representation (Cienki 2007; these points also apply to *ad hoc categories*, Barsalou 1983).

2.5. Two traditions – one conclusion

Results from both lines of categorization research support the conclusion that words are *not* associated with invariant context-independent definitions. Even the learning of well-defined concepts appears to be sensitive to a range of contextual factors, such that people learn context-sensitive representations of even rule-based artificial concepts. It appears that natural language concepts do not have stable structures within or between individual speakers in a community (Ramscar et al. 2013d), and that people's use of words (and phrases) reflects conventions that probabilistically govern language use in context. That is, while it is clear that people learn and use conceptual knowledge in systematic ways, the results reviewed here offer little support for the idea that this behavior relies on or reflects their possession of discrete representations of concepts.

3. Computational models of categorization

Numerous computational models have been proposed to account for the empirical results discussed above, allowing theoretical proposals about conceptual representations to be evaluated by formal simulations of behavior. The development of categorization models has been a particular feature of the artificial concept learning literature, in part because the controlled nature of artificial stimuli is more amenable to formalization than the study of everyday concepts based on social convention. However, one of the earliest and most influential computational models of categorization (Collins and Quillian 1969) is an outlier in that it sought to formally characterize everyday semantic knowledge.

3.1. Hierarchical semantic networks

The Collins and Quillian model proposes that word use reflects a hierarchical network in which stimulus properties are stored in memory according to their generality or specificity in relation to a set of related concepts. This postulates, for example, a taxonomic representation of animal knowledge where properties general to all animals such as *breathing* are stored at the top of the hierarchy with the concept *animal*. Properties generally true of fish are stored at the *fish* node, and general bird properties are stored at the *bird* node. Properties distinctive to individual sub-kinds (e.g., *robin*) are stored with the specific concept nodes they characterize (e.g., the property *red-breasted*). In this model, category membership can then be defined in terms of the positions of nodes in the hierarchical network. Many properties of each category can be read off from its position. Thus the node for *salmon* does not directly store the information that salmon are *animals*, since that fact is specified by the hierarchical connection between the *salmon*, *fish* and *animal* nodes.

However the Collins and Quillian model is not a straightforward inheritance model as these are commonly understood in computer science: this is because sub-kinds on lower nodes do not always inherit all the properties of higher nodes. For example, *can fly* is associated with the *bird* node – because flying is usually a distinctive property of birds – and exceptions to this feature (i.e., *penguin*) are stored at a sub-kind node for *does not fly*. Thus while it is often reported that increases in network distance between concepts and properties successfully predict the time it takes people take to verify that concepts have a given property (e.g., people verify that a *canary* is *yellow* faster than that it *has feathers*), given the lack of any principles specifying exactly *where* in the hierarchy a given feature is represented positively or negatively, it is more accurate to say that Collins and Quillian's intuitions about the relationship between the various words used for nodes and features correlated well with the behavior of their participants.

(Nb. to some extent this criticism applies to *all* models that describe formal relationships between sets of arbitrary conceptual features defined by modelers.)

3.2. Prototype models

Prototype models are characterized as seeking to formalize concept representations in which degree of fit to the category is evaluated for the purposes of categorization. A *prototype* represents information about all relevant dimensions of the items in a stimulus set with the information represented as some kind of average value across all exemplars. In a prototype model, a novel item is classified as a member of the category whose prototype it is most similar to (e.g., Hampton 1995). The values used to define the prototype for each category are updated when new examples are encountered. These models thus seek to capture the critical structure of a category, without having to encode every detail of every item that a participant has seen.

Prototype models were developed to try to create accounts of discrete concepts that could nevertheless explain people's sensitivity to the degree to which features correlate across the exemplars of a concept. In a prototype model, similarity can be viewed in geometric terms – the closer together items are in feature-space, the more similar they are. Thus more typical category members will be closer in space to the prototype, and less typical category members will more distant. Prototype models account well for findings relating to graded typicality, and offer a formal account of why new exemplars that are very prototypical are likely to be judged as being the better examples of a given category than items farther from the prototype.

However, these models fail to account for other findings in the literature. For example, prototype models do not store information about the frequency of specific exemplars, yet it is clear that people are sensitive to this information (Kruschke 1996). Moreover, the averaging process at the heart of prototype representations can yield anomalous results: If the members of a disjunctive category comprise either large black vertical lines or small white horizontal lines, then averaging across both dimensions produces a medium-sized grey diagonal line. This would fail to represent any of the relevant dimensions of the items associated with the concept appropriately, and measurements of similarity between this prototype and the actual set of members would not provide a good estimate of category membership.

Neither of these problems immediately falsify prototype models: there is no in-principle reason why exemplar frequency could not be incorporated into a prototype representation. Nor is there any reason why multiple prototypes could not be used to represent categories that are not linearly separable (although this might be hard to implement in a principled way). However, a more serious problem for prototype models is that they do not easily accommodate people's ability to recognize specific exemplars of concepts. For example, people asked to listen for the recurrence of a word in a lengthy, spoken wordlist do better when repeated words are presented by the same voice rather than a different one (Palmeri et al. 1993), suggesting that people store more auditory speech detail than linguists often suppose, and that models that store category summaries discard too much information about the speech signal to provide an adequate account of people's behavior.

3.3. Exemplar models

In an *exemplar model* (e.g, Nosofsky 1991, 1992) every example of a concept is stored in memory in all its detail. Novel items are classified by their similarity to previously learned exemplars, and category membership is determined by a weighted voting system in which a new item is assigned to the category for which the summed pairwise similarities are greatest (Kruschke 1992).

Interestingly, because of the way this voting process works, exemplar models are able to account for the typicality effects that led to the development of prototype models. This is because more typical exemplars, which, of course, lie near the center of the feature space of a category (the prototype), share more similarities with other exemplars than less typical items. Because the number of votes an item receives is a function of these similarities, a typical new item receives greater support than a less typical item.

Exemplar models have been tremendously influential, and yet what is perhaps their most important feature is usually least remarked upon in the literature: exemplar models do not contain, or even attempt to define, unitary representations for concepts. Instead, they typically contain a system of exemplars that is related to a system of labels, and a methodology for incorporating new items into this system and for dynamically generating labels for unlabeled items.

3.4. Systems models

Prototype models are often criticized for throwing away too much information, whereas exemplar models challenge our intuitions through the promiscuity of their assumptions about storage and processing. What is clear is that depending upon the context in which a concept is learned, or the goal of the learner, more or less information is discarded in learning. Moreover, the processes that appear to be involved in learning and storage inevitably result in encodings in which some stimulus dimensions are ignored in order to increase the discriminability of encoded items (Kruschke 2001; Ramscar et al. 2010b).

However, while it is unclear that a "pure" exemplar model even makes theoretical sense, simply because identifying exemplar is itself an act of classification at a different level of abstraction (Ramscar et al. 2010b), what is interesting about exemplar models is that they seek to capture people's behavior in tasks rather than seeking to define concepts: They treat categorization as in inherently systematic process relying on multiple exemplar representations, and yet they successfully account for many empirical phenomena (Nosofsky 1990).

The shift towards trying to model systematic behaviors rather than defining representations has led to models that employ multiple representations to find the middle ground between maximal abstraction (with minimal storage, e.g., prototypes) and minimal abstraction (with maximal storage, e.g., "pure" exemplar models). For example, the RATIONAL model of categorization (Anderson 1991) neither stores every exemplar nor does it rely entirely on prototypes. Instead, the model creates hybrid representations in which a new item may either be used to update an existing cluster of similar examples (as in a prototype model) or, if unique enough, may initiate a new cluster. Which choice is made is a function of the probability that the new item belongs to an existing cluster.

When this probability is below a given threshold, a new cluster is created. If above the threshold, the existing cluster that it is most similar is updated to reflect the new exemplar. RATIONAL is thus capable of acquiring clusters that function like rules, or sets of clusters that function like exemplars, depending on the categories being learned.

Other systems apply explicitly different mechanisms (rules initially; exemplars later) at different stages of concept learning (Johansen and Palmeri 2002), while in others (e.g., ATRIUM: Erickson and Kruschke 1998; COVIS: Ashby et al. 1998), the contributions of rule-based and exemplar learning are flexible, and depend more on the learning context, or the context in which categorization decisions are made.

Whereas most models seek to learn the representational system that best segregates a training set, a more recent clustering model, SUSTAIN (Love et al. 2004) was developed to account for the fact that people learn different information about items according to their context and goals. In unsupervised learning, when a learner has no specific goal in mind, SUSTAIN adds clusters much as RATIONAL would, in order to minimize classification error. However, if a learner is, say, inferring the properties of an item as part of a task, this goal can influence what is learned about the items. SUSTAIN is thus able to capture the differences in learning that occur in different task environments.

Depending on the conceptual structure being learned, and whether a goal is present or not, the structure of the clusters SUSTAIN learns for any given label can functionally resemble either rule-based, prototype or exemplar models. What is important to note is that the internal structure of these representations are highly sensitive to the context provided by the presence (or absence) of goals. Depending on context, different information will be represented in the clusters and different information discarded in learning or used in categorization. The success of the SUSTAIN model when it comes to fitting a wide range of behavioral phenomena suggests that people may learn different representations when learning concepts in inference and classification tasks and thus contributes further evidence that human category learning involves multiple processes, and that what is learned depends on a learners' goals and prior experience (Mack et al. 2013).

4. The neural bases of categorization

Results from cognitive neuroscience research support the findings reviewed so far in that they indicate there is no single neural circuit for concept learning (Seger and Miller 2010; Davis et al 2014), and suggest that categorization is best understood in relation to the overall architecture of the brain's perceptual- and motor- learning and memory systems. (Understanding the relevant neural architecture also requires an understanding of brain anatomy and physiology that few linguists currently have, so while this section may be challenging, we hope readers will appreciate its relevance to our understanding of concepts.)

4.1. Perceptual concepts

Numerous neural structures are involved in the discrimination of classes of visual stimuli, and even systems usually considered to be primarily engaged in perceptual processing exhibit evidence of tuning in response to categorization tasks: Different neuronal assemblies in the inferior temporal cortex (ITC) respond selectively to different category types, such as complex shapes (Logothetis and Scheinberg 1996) or faces (Kanwisher et al. 1997). Studies of trained monkeys have shown that individual neurons in the ITC show selectivity for, say, trees or fish, and these neurons are relatively insensitive to variance within these categories (Vogels 2008).

Human patients with impaired higher order memory systems (e.g., medial temporal lobe lesions) or Parkinson's disease (which impairs corticostriatal learning) retain their ability to implicitly learn prototype patterns presented in a series of random dot displays in a classification task (each pattern is labeled either "A" or "not A"; Bozoki et al. 2006). In contrast, imaging studies show that neuronal assemblies in the extrastriate visual cortex (roughly, Brodmann Area 18/19 or visual area V2) deactivate selectively when dot patterns that conform to a previously learned prototype are presented (Koenig et al. 2008), and patient studies have found that performance on this task is impaired in Alzheimer's disease, which often damages this area (Zaki et al. 2003).

However, although extrastriate assemblies appear to learn perceptual prototypes (whether this represents long-term potentiation or short-term adaptation is an open issue), learning and representing the range of discriminations manifest in visual categorization clearly involves a range of functional systems, with different brain regions involved in learning in different contexts (Seger and Miller 2010).

4.2. Higher-level concept learning

The prefrontal cortex (PFC) plays a key role in rule-based learning (Monchi et al. 2001), however, its contribution to the learning *process* is best described as supervising input to other learning systems in the striatum and MTL (Ramscar and Gitcho 2007; Thompson-Schill et al. 2009) both by maintaining representations of explicit goals and by allocating attentional resources (Miller and Cohen 2001).

This characterization is supported by imaging studies of rule-based learning (Konishi et al. 1999; Monchi et al. 2001; Smith et al. 1998) and behavioral experiments showing that tasks that disrupt working memory or attention (known PFC functions) drastically impair performance on rule-based learning tasks (Waldron and Ashby 2001; Zeithamova and Maddox 2006). It is worth noting in this context that rule-based concept learning is very different from linguistic convention learning, where there is evidence that limiting PFC involvement actually benefits learning (Ramscar and Yarlett 2007; Ramscar et al. 2013a).

The actual learning systems most connected with the PFC, and which serve to discriminate the stimulus dimensions that encode concepts for long-term retention are located in the corticostriatal and medial temporal lobe regions (Seger and Miller 2010). The striatum (comprising the caudate, putamen, and nucleus accumbens, *Nacc*) implements an error-sensitive learning system that discriminatively strengthens and weakens associations between stimulus dimensions and behavioral responses and predicted outcomes in learning (Schultz 2006). In contrast to the perceptual regions described earlier, this system appears to learn the predictive, discriminatory codes that support future categorization behavior. However, the exact level at which striatal learning serves to encode concepts is open to question.

One reason why the role of striatal learning in categorization is hard to pin down is that the medial temporal lobe (MTL) also supports learning that is sensitive to prediction error (Davis et al. 2012a, 2012b; see Ramscar et al. 2010b for a tutorial), and also serves an encoding function. As with the striatal system, it is not clear *exactly* what part the MTL plays in concept learning or at what level of abstraction it encodes (indeed, it is not even clear whether this question is appropriate without reference to a learner's prior experience and goals). Some theories have proposed that the MTL learning system approximates an exemplar-model (Ashby and Maddox 2005); however evidence has been presented to suggest that the MTL stores representations of both rules (Nomura et al. 2007) and prototypes (Reber et al. 1998).[3]

It is of course possible that the striatal system might learn one form of conceptual representation, and the MTL another (Bornstein and Daw 2012). However, in reality it is unlikely that the function of *either* system corresponds exactly to any of the models reviewed above. As Kruschke (2008: 269) observes in this regard, "[a] representational assumption for a model does not necessarily imply that the mind makes a formal representation[...] Only a formal model requires a formal description." The brain's actual representational formats should not be expected to correspond to the ones researchers use to model behavior. Similarly, it is unlikely that the functions of brain regions map neatly to functions posited by researchers, such that perception is a function of one system, and learning and categorization others. Indeed, Bussey and Saksida (2007) propose that local brain functions are based on a hierarchy determined by the levels of stimulus representations that systems process, rather than traditional cognitive functions like language or memory.

From this perspective, regional functions are differentiated by the levels of stimulus complexity they process (Cowell et al. 2010a, 2010b), and the striatum and MTL are not qualitatively different learning systems, but rather they learn and encode stimulus representations at different levels of abstraction (e.g., features, objects, contexts, etc.). Depending on the experience of the speaker and the context, learning might be focused in the MTL *or* in the striatum, and the degree each region is engaged in specific categorization behavior will depend on the experience of the individual and the behavioral context (Davis et al. 2012a, 2012b).

4.3. Categorization in the brain

Many neural systems contribute to the behaviors we call categorization: There is no categorization area, but rather, consistent with the predictions of systems models such as SUSTAIN, the degree to which brain regions engage in categorization depends on a task, its context and prior learning.

---

[3] To confuse matters further, some researchers deny the MTL plays any role in category learning (Ashby et al 1998). However, this claim also conflicts with any broad definition of categorization, simply because perirhinal cortex – part of the MTL – appears critical to object recognition, and in particular, the discrimination of objects into old and new sets (Winters et al. 2004). Since old/new discrimination is thought of as an important categorization behavior, this debate helps illustrate how categorization is often poorly defined and circumscribed in the literature.

5. Concepts, contrasts and communication

From a linguistic perspective, the general lesson to be drawn from this review is that despite theorists' intuitions about concepts as abstract mental tokens suitable for binding to phrase, word, or morpheme-sized phonetic patterns, this conception of concepts is not supported by research results. Rather, the literature shows:

1. Category assignments vary with context. An item can be an exemplar of one category in one context, and another category in another context.
2. Even when people learn concepts with clear and consistent definitions, the representations they acquire diverge from these definitions.
3. When people list the properties of natural concepts, they may produce convergent sets of features that characterize these concepts, but these generally do not adequately define or discriminate between concepts.
4. The tasks people perform when learning to categorize has a strong effect on the representations they acquire.
5. Depending on the task and context in which people perform categorization tasks it appears that a variety of brain regions are differentially engaged in the behaviors we call categorization.

It seems clear that in the course of learning the relationships between a set of items and a label, people do not abstract a discrete concept that specifies these relationships. Instead, categorization can engage almost any aspect of a person's knowledge, depending on their experience, the context and the task. These conclusions are supported by modeling efforts which show how conceptual behaviors are best accounted for by systems in which behavioral outcomes do not imply explicit knowledge representations (Baayen et al. 2013) and in which consistent conceptual behavior emerges without the use of the discrete representations our intuitive understanding of the word concept implies (Love et al. 2004). These conclusions are further supported by neuroscience findings revealing the equally varied and complex relationship between categorization behaviors and neural processes.

5.1. Learning, discrimination and language

If, as seems clear, concepts are not mental tokens, then explaining the role of words in communication is likely to depend on our understanding the processes governing word use. Providing a detailed account of the processes that support the learning and use of language is beyond the scope of this review (indeed, we do not pretend that we have a comprehensive account). However, one implication of these results is easy to state and is clearly important to understanding of language: it is clear to us that concept learning is a *discriminative process*. In explaining what this means, and why it is important, we will try to sketch out some of its implications for our understanding of human communication.

We noted above that the brain regions that support learning about lexical "concepts" implement *error-driven learning processes* (Schultz 2006). Most psychologists and linguists labor under the erroneous belief that learning is a combinatorial process in which correlations lead to simple associations forming between stimuli (Rescorla 1988). However, the error-driven learning processes that have been shown to govern what we call associative learning are *discriminative* (Ramscar et al. 2013c). That is, they reapportion attentional and representational resources to minimize future *predictive* uncertainty (Rescorla and Wagner 1972; Sutton and Barto 1998).

Importantly, although linguistic meaning is rarely couched in these terms, it is clear that that uncertainty reduction lies at the heart of communication: Virtually every linguistic act – even saying, "Hello!" – is intended to reduce a listener's uncertainty, whether about the world, about the thoughts and feelings of a speaker, or a speaker's sincerity, etc. Error-driven learning tunes the representation of relevant features of the environment by incrementally discriminating against uninformative cues (those that do not improve predictions) and reinforcing informative cues (those that do tend to support successful predictions) in response to events as they unfold (Ramscar et al. 2010b). It generates predictive representations that serve to minimize uncertainty in discriminating between sets of possible outcomes (i.e., about what a speaker might mean in a given context, or what verbal gesture might be uttered next).

These representations are formed by a process of learning to *ignore* – i.e., discriminate against cues that are not informative for the discrimination being learned. If learners learn the relationships between utterances in context and specific words by this process, it implies that they will learn about the contexts in which a word can be expected to occur or be appropriately used. This learning will occur as a result of speakers' attempts to predict the next segment, syllable or word that an interlocutor uses.

This in turn suggests that the relationship between categories (a domain with a huge array of dimensions) and labels (a domain with a relatively small number of phonetic dimensions) is subject to an important constraint. A naïve view of labels is that they serve to encode or otherwise map onto meanings, such that that they support the retrieval of underlying semantic categories. For example, it is usually supposed that a phonological pattern like *dog* serves as a pointer or a link to the concept of dog. However, the evidence we have reviewed indicates that learners acquire a variety of representations comprising information at numerous of levels of abstraction relating to a word like *dog*, and mapping a low-dimensional space of labels onto this set of high-dimensional representations in a determinate way is not possible (Ramscar et al. 2010b).

Linguists have assumed since Saussure that the relationship between words and meanings is bidirectional (suggested by the up and down arrows in Saussure's model for a *linguistic sign* connecting a graphic image of a tree – the meaning – with the orthographic Latin word *arbor*). The array of evidence indicating that conceptual learning processes are error-driven makes clear that this relationship must actually be unidirectional. Error-driven learning processes encourage the acquisition of representations in which word meanings – and other words in the context – are part of a high-dimensional predictive code that allows word identities to be discriminated and uncertainty about communicative intentions to be reduced. They are completely unsuited to acquiring representations in which words directly encode meanings such that Meanings predict Signals *and* Signals predict Meanings (Ramscar et al. 2010b).

It is interesting to consider representational proposals such as *frames*, *ICMs*, *image schemas*, and *domains* in this light. When these proposals are conceived of as theories of representation, it is assumed that at some level, something that resembles a frame (or ICM, image schema or domain) *corresponds* to a similar level of linguistic construction (or feature), such that at an appropriate level of granularity, the frame (ICM, image schema or domain) *represents* the meaning of a construction or feature (i.e., these structures are thought to facilitate the process of going from the signal to the meaning). We noted above that none of these proposals has been described with the specificity required to explain how this actually works, and it is likely that the problems of mapping spaces of different dimensionalities this would entail means that it is impossible to do so (Ramscar et al. 2010b). (Although these proposals fail to meet the criteria for theories of representation, they may still be useful phenomenological descriptions of some aspects of the knowledge encoded in discriminative linguistic and conceptual systems; Rosch 1978.)

5.2. The concept of information

The predictive, discriminative codes that error-driven learning processes generate share many properties with the codes that *information theory* specifies for artificial communication systems (Shannon 1948). It is thus worth highlighting that artificial information systems are not merely digital in the commonly understood sense that they make use of binary codes of ones and zeros, but also in the more interesting sense that in information theory, the "information" communicated in systems is broken down into a system of discrete, discriminable states that can be encoded by various combinations of ones and zeros.

Shannon (1948: 379) defines artificial communication as the process of:

> reproducing at one point either exactly or approximately a message selected at another point. Frequently the messages have meaning; that is they refer to or are correlated according to some system with certain physical or conceptual entities. *These semantic aspects of communication are irrelevant to the engineering problem.* [Our emphasis]

Artificial communication systems encode discriminable messages in a common *source code* (which defines a system for contrasting between messages) and a receiver makes use of this code in order to discriminate (select) the actual message that has been sent in a signal from other possible signals. There is no meaning in this signal itself, but rather in the context of the source code, the zeros and ones that each message comprises serve to incrementally reduce uncertainty about the actual message being received.

Although it may seem counterintuitive, the findings we have reviewed indicate that the way in which we learn new conceptual distinctions is best characterized as a process that increases either the number of words and phrases that our minds are able to discriminate or the range of contexts across which known words and phrases can be discriminated (Ramscar et al. 2010b). Thus, for example, Ramscar et al. (2013d) show that changes in people's ability to learn the paired association of arbitrary words across the lifespan can be accurately predicted if the process is modeled discriminatively. People's ability to learn frequently co-occurring pairs, like *lock* and *door* differs little with age, whereas word pairs like *jury* and *eagle* become increasingly difficult to learn. Because the latter co-occur extremely rarely, discriminative learning causes them to become *negatively* associated in a system predicting lexical events. However, since both words are relatively infrequent, it takes many years of language experience for speakers to learn to this relationship well enough to exploit the negative expectation of *eagle* given *jury* in everyday language use. Negative associations not only help explain why learning pairs like *jury* and *eagle* gets more difficult the older a speaker as compared to pairs like *lock* and *door*, they allow discriminative learning models (Rescorla and Wagner 1972) to quantitatively predict the changes in their learnability across the lifespan with remarkable accuracy (Ramscar et al. 2013d).

From a discriminative perspective, language learning can be characterized as acquiring and mastering a predictive code for a system of lexical and phrasal contrasts. Language production can then be seen as the process of using this system to construct a message that best represents a speaker's intended meaning. A linguistic *signal* can be thought of as all of the conventional audible and visible behaviors of a speaking person (or, in written language, orthographic and other visual cues). Because the listener possesses a system of conventionalized knowledge relating semantic cues to signals that is similar to the one the speaker uses to construct her *message*, he is able to anticipate (that is, at least partially predict) the speaker's intended meaning by reconstructing the message from the signal itself. Other aspects of the message will be contained in the differences between what the speaker says and the learner predicts, and these differences will result in learning; an essential aspect of linguistic communication.

There is much consensus among cognitive linguists that intention reading – social prediction – is an important component of word learning (Tomasello 2003, 2008). The perspective we describe – which is a function of the way people learn to relate words to the world (Ramscar et al. 2013b) – simply extends intention reading to language processing more generally. Comprehension arises out of what listeners know – which enables them to predict a speaker – and what listeners *learn* from the speaker: identifying the words and constructions that a speaker actually says leads to learning about why a speaker made the choices they did.

Just as the source code lies at the heart of artificial communication systems, *linguistic codes* are the heart of language. The linguistic code is the entire conventionalized inventory of phones, words, idioms, expressions, collocations and constructions shared by a community of speakers and listeners that enable them to communicate. Importantly, rather than something that is explicitly encoded in the words of a message, meaning is merely implicit in the common linguistic code. The conventionalized, *systematic* relations that hold probabilistically between all the linguistic signals as well as between the signals and the world enable listeners to incrementally reduce uncertainty about the messages speakers send in context (Ramscar et al. 2010b; 2013c). In a linguistic signal – that is, in an utterance or piece of text – the occurrence of a word does not serve as a pointer to a concept, but rather in the context of the signal and the message, the word serves to reduce the listener's uncertainty about the speaker's intent. As is the case with an artificial communication system, the meaning is never "in" the signal. Instead the signal serves to reduce uncertainty in the listener's head about the actual intended meaning in the speaker's message (Ramscar and Baayen 2013).

5.3. Meaning and learning

Characterizing human communication in this way highlights a very obvious difference between human and artificial communication systems: Human communicators learn as they go, whereas most artificial systems don't. Thus whereas the goal of an artificial communication system is to send a signal that is predictable with $p = 1$, messages in human communication are rarely, if ever, intended to be perfectly predictable simply because they are *intended* to evoke or even highlight a listener's uncertainty about some aspect of what a speaker intends.

A number of researchers working on language have concluded that language understanding includes a process of making moment-to-moment predictions about what is coming next when listening to speech (Altmann and Mirkovic 2009; Kutas and Federmeier 2007). However this kind of moment-to-moment prediction has usually been seen as *assisting* the comprehension of linguistic signals that encode meanings in the traditional concept-by-concept ways that categorization research was expected to illuminate. Our review suggests this research can offer no such illumination simply because words do not *encode* meanings. Rather, because prediction drives learning, and because the function of learning is uncertainty reduction, prediction lies at the heart of linguistic communication. Seen from this perspective, moment-to-moment prediction in language does not merely help in the processing of language, but rather, because prediction drives learning, it is a critical part of the process that makes linguistic communication meaningful (Ramscar and Baayen 2013).

We end by acknowledging that although the view of communication we have sketched out manages to avoid many of the problems involved in appealing to illusory mechanisms like concepts, it paints a picture of language that is very different from traditional ideas, and that likely clashes with many researchers' beliefs about what language is. On the other hand, this perspective is still consistent with the impetus behind much work in cognitive linguistics in that its assumptions are shared with theories of learning and cognitive processing on multiple levels. And it is highly compatible with the findings of the research reviewed here.

6. Summary

Despite the way categorization researchers often describe their object of study, the detailed results of their work show that the representation of conceptual knowledge does not involve a neat story about inventories of individuated conceptual tokens. Rather, these results show that conceptual knowledge is as bound by context as language is itself (Malt 2013). Looking beyond naïve, intuitive conceptions of concepts, it is clear that cognitive linguists have much to learn from researchers' increasing understanding of the processes that give rise to systematic categorization behavior. We have sketched one way in which the insights that have arisen out of research into concepts and categories is likely to have an impact on our understanding of language. It will be fascinating to see what develops out of a richer synthesis of these lines of enquiry in the future.

7. References

Altmann, Gerry and Jelena Mirković
   2009   Incrementality and prediction in human sentence processing. *Cognitive Science* 33: 1–27.

Anderson, John R.
  1991   The adaptive nature of human categorization. *Psychological Review* 98: 409–429.
Arnon, Inbal and Michael Ramscar
  2012   Granularity and the acquisition of grammatical gender: How order of acquisition affects what gets learned. *Cognition* 122(3): 292–305
Ashby, Gregory, Leola Alfonso-Reese, And Turken and Elliott Waldron
  1998   A neuropsychological theory of multiple systems in category learning. *Psychological Review* 105(3): 442–481.
Ashby, Gregory, and Todd Maddox
  2005   Human category learning. *Annual Review of Psychology* 56: 149–178.
Baayen, Harald, Peter Hendrix and Michael Ramscar
  2013   Sidestepping the combinatorial explosion: Towards a processing model based on discriminative learning. *Language and Speech* 56(3): 329–347.
Barsalou, Lawrence
  1983   Ad hoc categories. *Memory and Cognition* 11(3): 211–227.
Billman, Dorrit, and James Knutson
  1996   Unsupervised concept learning and value systematicity: A complex whole aids learning the parts. *Journal of Experimental Psychology: Learning, Memory, and Cognition* 22: 458–475.
Bornstein, Aaron and Nathaniel D. Daw
  2012   Dissociating hippocampal and striatal contributions to sequential prediction learning. *European Journal of Neuroscience* 35(7): 1011–1023.
Boroditsky, Lera and Michael Ramscar
  2002   The roles of body and mind in abstract thought. *Psychological Science* 13(2): 185–189.
Bozokia, Andrea, Murray Grossman and Edward Smith
  2006   Can patients with Alzheimer's disease learn a category implicitly? *Neuropsychologia* 44(5): 816–827.
Brooks, Lee, Geoffrey Norman and Scott Allen
  1991   Role of specific similarity in a medical diagnostic task. *Journal of Experimental Psychology: General* 120(3): 278
Bruner, Jerome, Jacqueline Goodnow and George Austin
  1956   *A Study of Thinking*. New York: John Wiley and Sons, Inc.
Bussey, Tim and Lisa Saksida
  2007   Memory, perception, and the ventral visual-perirhinal-hippocampal stream: Thinking outside of the boxes. *Hippocampus* 17: 898–908.
Cienki, Alan
  2007   Frames, Idealized Cognitive Models and domains. *The Oxford Handbook of Cognitive Linguistics*, 170–187. Oxford: Oxford University Press.
Collins, Allan and Ross Quillian
  1969   Retrieval time from semantic memory. *Journal of Verbal Learning and Verbal Behavior* 8(2): 240–247.
Cowell, Rosemary, Tim Bussey and Lisa Saksida
  2010a   Components of recognition memory: Dissociable cognitive processes or just differences in representational complexity? *Hippocampus* 20(11): 1245–262.
Cowell, Rosemary, Tim Bussey and Lisa Saksida
  2010b   Functional dissociations within the ventral object processing pathway: Cognitive modules or a hierarchical continuum? *Journal of Cognitive Neuroscience* 22: 2460–2479.
Crawford, Elizabeth, Janellen Huttenlocher, and Peder Hans Engebretson
  2000   Category effects on estimates of stimuli: Perception or reconstruction? *Psychological Science* 11(4): 280–284.

Davis, Tyler, Bradley Love and Alison Preston
  2012a   Learning the exception to the rule: Model-based fMRI reveals specialized representations for surprising category members. *Cerebral Cortex* 22(2): 260–273.
Davis, Tyler, Bradley Love and Alison Preston
  2012b   Striatal and hippocampal entropy and recognition signals in category learning: Simultaneous processes revealed by model-based fMRI. *Journal of Experimental Psychology: Learning, Memory, and Cognition* 38: 821–839.
Davis, Tyler, Gui Xue, Bradley Love, Alison Preston and Russell Poldrack
  2014   Global neural pattern similarity as a common basis for categorization and recognition memory. *Journal of Neuroscience* 34(22): 7472–7484.
Erickson, Michael and John Kruschke
  1998   Rules and exemplars in category learning. *Journal of Experimental Psychology: General* 127(2): 107–140.
Evans, Vyvyan
  this volume   24. Time. Berlin/Boston: De Gruyter Mouton.
Fillmore Charles
  1982   Frame semantics. In: Linguistic Society of Korea (ed.), *Linguistics in the Morning Calm*, 111–137. Seoul: Hanshin.
Frege, Gottlob
  1892   Über Sinn und Bedeutung. *Zeitschrift für Philosophie und philosophische Kritik* 100: 25–50.
Gahl, Suzanne
  2008   "Thyme" and "Time" are not homophones. The effect of lemma frequency on word durations in spontaneous speech. *Language* 84: 474–496
Goldstone, Robert and Alan Kersten
  2003   Concepts and categories. In: A. F. Healy and R. W. Proctor (eds.), *Comprehensive Handbook of Psychology*, Volume 4:00 *Experimental Psychology*, 591–621. New York: Wiley.
Goodman, Nelson
  1972   Seven strictures on similarity. In: N. Goodman (ed.), *Problems and Projects*. New York: The Bobbs-Merrill Co.
Hampton, James
  1995   Testing the prototype theory of concepts. *Journal of Memory and Language* 34(5): 686–708.
Hull, Clarke
  1920   Quantitative aspects of the evolution of concepts. *Psychological Monographs* XXVIII(1.123): 1–86.
Johansen, Mark and Thomas Palmeri
  2002   Are there representational shifts during category learning? *Cognitive Psychology* 45(4): 482–553.
Johnson, Mark
  1987   *The Body in the Mind: The Bodily Basis of Meaning, Imagination, and Reason*. Chicago: University of Chicago Press
Kanwisher, Nancy, Josh McDermott and Marvin Chun
  1997   The fusiform face area: a module in human extrastriate cortex specialized for face perception. *The Journal of Neuroscience* 17(11): 4302–4311.
Koenig, Phyllis, Edward Smith, Vanessa Troiani, Chivon Anderson, Peachie Moore and Murray Grossman
  2008   Medial temporal lobe involvement in an implicit memory task: Evidence of collaborating implicit and explicit memory systems from and Alzheimer's disease. *Cerebral Cortex* 18: 2831–2843.

Konishi, S., M. Kawazu, I. Uchida, H. Kikyo, I. Asakura, and Y. Miyashita
 1999 Contribution of working memory to transient activation in human inferior prefrontal cortex during performance of the Wisconsin Card Sorting Test. *Cerebral Cortex* 9(7): 745–753.
Kruschke, John
 1992 ALCOVE: An exemplar-based connectionist model of category learning. *Psychological Review* 99: 22–44.
Kruschke, John
 1996 Base rates in category learning. *Journal of Experimental Psychology: Learning, Memory and Cognition* 22: 3–26
Kruschke, John
 2001 Toward a unified model of attention in associative learning. *Journal of Mathematical Psychology* 45(6): 812–863.
Kruschke, John
 2008 Models of categorization. *The Cambridge Handbook of Computational Psychology*, 267–301. Cambridge: Cambridge University Press.
Kutas, Martha, and Kara Federmeier
 2007 Event-related brain potential (ERP) studies of sentence processing. In: G. Gaskell (ed.), *Oxford Handbook of Psycholinguistics*, 385–406. Oxford: Oxford University Press.
Labov, William
 1973 The boundaries of words and their meanings. In: C.-J. N. Bailey and R. W. Shuy (eds.), *New Ways of Analyzing Variation in English*, 340–373. Washington, D.C.: Georgetown University Press.
Lakoff, George
 1987 *Women, Fire, and Dangerous Things: What Categories Reveal About the Mind.* Chicago: University of Chicago Press.
Lakoff, George
 1993 The contemporary theory of metaphor. *Metaphor and Thought* 2: 202–251.
Logothetis, Nikos and David Sheinberg
 1996 Visual object recognition. *Annual Review of Neuroscience* 19(1): 577–621.
Love, Bradley
 2002 Comparing supervised and unsupervised category learning. *Psychonomic Bulletin and Review* 9: 829–835.
Love, Bradley, Douglas Medin and Todd Gureckis
 2004 SUSTAIN: A network model of category learning. *Psychological Review* 111(2): 309–332.
Lusk, Christopher
 2011 Conifer–angiosperm interactions: Physiological ecology and life history. *Smithsonian Contributions to Botany* 95: 158–164.
McCloskey, Michael and Sam Glucksberg
 1978 Natural categories: Well defined or fuzzy sets? *Memory and Cognition* 6(4): 462–472.
Mack, Michael, Alison Preston and Bradley Love
 2013 Decoding the brain's algorithm for categorization from its neural implementation. *Current Biology* 23: 2023–2027.
Malt, Barbara
 2013 Context sensitivity and insensitivity in object naming. *Language and Cognition* 5: 81–97.
Malt, Barbara, Silvia Gennari and Mutsumi Imai
 2010 Lexicalization patterns and the world-to-words mapping. In: B. Malt and P. Wolff (eds.), *Words and the Mind: How Words Encode Human Experience,* 29–57. Oxford: Oxford University Press

4. Categorization (without categories) 97

Medin, Douglas and Marguerite Schaffer
    1978   Context theory of classification learning. *Psychological Review* 85(3): 207–238.

Miller, Earl and Jonathan Cohen
    2001   An integrative theory of prefrontal cortex function. *Annual Review of Neuroscience* 24(1): 167–202.

Monchi, Oury, Michael Petrides, Valentina Petre, Keith Worsley and Alain Dagher
    2001   Wisconsin card sorting revisited: Distinct neural circuits participating in different stages of the task identified by event-related functional magnetic resonance imaging. *Journal of Neuroscience* 21: 7733–7741.

Nomura, Emi, Todd Maddox, Vincent Filoteo, David Ing, Darren Gitelman, Todd Parrish, Marchsel Mesulam and Paul Reber
    2007   Neural correlates of rule-based and information-integration visual category learning. *Cerebral Cortex* 17(1): 37–43.

Nosofsky, Robert
    1991   Tests of an exemplar model for relating perceptual classification and recognition memory. *Journal of Experimental Psychology: Human Perception and Performance* 17: 3–27

Nosofsky, Robert
    1992   Similarity scaling and cognitive process models. *Annual Review of Psychology* 43(1): 25–53.

Palmeri, Thomas, Stephen Goldinger and David Pisoni
    1993   Episodic encoding of voice attributes and recognition memory for spoken words. *Journal of Experimental Psychology: Learning, Memory, and Cognition* 19(2): 309–328.

Port, Robert
    2010   Language is a social institution: Why phonemes and words do not have explicit psychological form. E*cological Psychology* 22: 304–326.

Port, Robert and Adam Leary
    2005   Against formal phonology. *Language* 81: 927–964

Posner, Michael, and Steven Keele
    1967   Decay of visual information from a single letter. *Science* 158: 137–139.

Posner, Michael, and Steven Keele
    1970   Retention of abstract ideas. *Journal of Experimental Psychology* 83(2): 304–308.

Quine, Willard Van Orman
    1960   *Word and Object*. Cambridge: MIT Press.

Ramscar, Michael and Harald Baayen
    2013   Production, comprehension and synthesis: A communicative perspective on language. *Frontiers in Language Sciences* 4: 233.

Ramscar, Michael, Melody Dye, Jessica Gustafson and Joseph Klein
    2013a   Dual routes to cognitive flexibility: Learning and response conflict resolution in the dimensional change card sort task. *Child Development* 84(4): 1308–1323.

Ramscar, Michael, Melody Dye and Joseph Klein
    2013b   Children value informativity over logic in word learning. *Psychological Science* 24(6): 1017–1023.

Ramscar, Michael, Melody Dye and Stewart McCauley
    2013c   Error and expectation in language learning: The curious absence of 'mouses' in adult speech. *Language* 89(4): 760–793.

Ramscar, Michael and Nichole Gitcho
    2007   Developmental change and the nature of learning in childhood. *Trends In Cognitive Science* 11(7): 274–279.

Ramscar, Michael, and Ulrike Hahn
    1998   What family resemblances are not: The continuing relevance of Wittgenstein to the study of concepts and categories. *Proceedings of the 20th Annual Conference of the Cognitive Science Society,* University of Wisconsin – Madison.

Ramscar, Michael, Peter Hendrix, Bradley Love and Harald Baayen
   2013d   Learning is not decline: The mental lexicon as a window into cognition across the lifespan. *The Mental Lexicon* 8(3): 450–481.
Ramscar, Michael, Peter Hendrix, Cyrus Shaoul, Petar Milin and Harald Baayen
   2014   The myth of cognitive decline: Non-linear dynamics of lifelong learning. *Topics in Cognitive Science* 6: 5–42.
Ramscar, Michael, Teenie Matlock and Melody Dye
   2010a   Running down the clock: The role of expectation in our understanding of time and motion. *Language and Cognitive Processes* 25(5): 589–615.
Ramscar, Michael and Daniel Yarlett
   2007   Linguistic self-correction in the absence of feedback: A new approach to the logical problem of language acquisition. *Cognitive Science* 31: 927–960.
Ramscar, Michael, Daniel Yarlett, Melody Dye, Katie Denny and Kirsten Thorpe
   2010b   The effects of feature-label-order and their implications for symbolic learning. *Cognitive Science* 34(6): 909–957.
Reber, Paul, Craig Stark and Larry Squire
   1998   Contrasting cortical activity associated with category memory and recognition memory. *Learning and Memory* 5(6): 420–428.
Rescorla, Robert
   1988   Pavlovian conditioning: It's not what you think it is. *American Psychologist* 43: 151–160.
Rescorla, Robert and Allan Wagner
   1972   A theory of Pavlovian conditioning: Variations in the effectiveness of reinforcement and nonreinforcement. In: A. H. Black and W. F. Prokasy (eds.), *Classical Conditioning II: Current Research and Theory*, 64–99. New York: Crofts.
Rips, Lance, Edward Smith and Douglas Medin
   2013   Concepts and categories: Memory, meaning, and metaphysics. In: K. J. Holyoak and R. G. Morrison (eds.), *The Oxford Handbook of Thinking and Reasoning*, 177–209. Oxford: Oxford University Press.
Rosch, Eleanor
   1978   Principles of categorization. In: E. Rosch and B. B. Lloyd (eds.), *Cognition and Categorization*, 27–48. Hillsdale: Erlbaum.
Rosch, Eleanor, and Carolyn Mervis
   1975   Family resemblances: Studies in the internal structure of categories. *Cognitive Psychology* 7(4): 573–605.
Rosch, Eleanor, Carolyn Mervis, Wayne Gray, David Johnson and Penny Boyes-Braem
   1976   Basic objects in natural categories. *Cognitive Psychology* 8(3): 382–439.
Sakamoto, Yasuaki and Bradley Love
   2004   Schematic influences on category learning and recognition memory. *Journal of Experimental Psychology: General* 33: 534–553
Schultz, Wolfram
   2006   Behavioral theories and the neurophysiology of reward. *Annual Review of Psychology* 57: 87–115.
Seger, Carol and Earl Miller
   2010   Category learning in the brain. *Annual Review of Neuroscience* 33: 203–219.
Shannon, Claude
   1948   A mathematical theory of communication. *Bell Systems Technical Journal* 27(3): 379–423.
Shepard, Roger, Carl Hovland and Herbert Jenkins
   1961   Learning and memorization of classifications. *Psychological Monographs* 75: 13.

Smith, David and Paul Minda
 2000   30 categorization results in search of a model. *Journal of Experimental Psychology: Learning, Memory, and Cognition* 26(1): 3–27.
Smith, Edward E., Andrea L. Patalano, and John Jonides
 1998   Alternative strategies of categorization. *Cognition* 65(2): 167–196.
Smoke, Kenneth
 1932   An objective study of concepts formation. *Psychological Monographs* XLII(191): 1–46.
Sutton, Richard, and Andrew Barto
 1998   *Reinforcement Learning.* Cambridge: MIT Press
Taylor, John
 2003   *Linguistic Categorization.* Oxford: Oxford University Press.
Tomasello, Michael
 2003   *Constructing a Language: A Usage-Based Theory of Language Acquisition.* Cambridge: Harvard University Press.
Tomasello, Michael
 2008   *Origins of Human Communication.* Cambridge: MIT Press.
Thompson-Schill, Sharon, Michael Ramscar and Evangelia Chrysikou
 2009   Cognition without control: when a little frontal lobe goes a long way. *Current Directions in Psychological Science* 8(5): 259–263.
Vogels, Rufin
 2008   Categorization of complex visual images by rhesus monkeys. Part 2:00 single-cell study. *European Journal of Neuroscience* 11(4): 1239–1255.
Waldron, Elliott, and Gregory Ashby
 2001   The effects of concurrent task interference on category learning: Evidence for multiple category learning systems. *Psychonomic Bulletin and Review* 8(1): 168–176.
Winters Boyer, Suzanne Forwood, Rosemary Cowell, Lisa Saksida and Tim Bussey
 2004   Double dissociation between the effects of peri-postrhinal cortex and hippocampal lesions on tests of object recognition and spatial memory: Heterogeneity of function within the temporal lobe. *Journal of Neuroscience* 24: 5901–5908.
Wittgenstein, Ludwig
 1953   *Philosophical Investigations.* London: Blackwell.
Yamauchi, Takashi, Bradley Love, and Arthur Markman
 2002   Learning non-linearly separable categories by inference and classification. *Journal of Experimental Psychology: Learning, Memory, and Cognition* 28: 585–593
Zaki, Safa, Robert Nosofsky, Nenette Jessup and Frederick Unverzagt
 2003   Categorization and recognition performance of a memory-impaired group. *Journal of the International Neuropsychological Society* 9(3): 394–406.
Zeithamova, Dagmar, and Todd Maddox
 2006   Dual-task interference in perceptual category learning. *Memory and Cognition* 34(2): 387–398.
Zentall, Thomas, Edward Wasserman and Peter Urcuioli
 2014   Associative concept learning in animals. *Journal of the Experimental Analysis of Behavior* 101(1): 130–151.

Michael Ramscar, Tuebingen (Germany)
Robert Port, Bloomington, (USA)

5. Abstraction, storage and naive discriminative learning

1. Introduction
2. Abstraction
3. Analogy
4. Hybrid models
5. Discrimination
6. Concluding remarks
7. References

1. Introduction

The English sentence *you want milk* can be uttered in a variety of circumstances, such as a mother about to feed her baby (answer: *bweeeh*), a father asking a toddler whether she would like a glass of milk (answer: *yes please*), or an air hostess serving black tea in economy class (answer: *sure*). Furthermore, similar sentences (*you want coffee, you want water, would you like coffee, would you like a cup of coffee*) can also be produced and understood appropriately across a wide variety of contexts. What are the cognitive principles that allow us to produce and understand these and a great many other different sentences across an even greater kaleidoscope of contexts and situations?

In this chapter, we discuss three very different approaches that have sought to answer this fundamental question about the workings of language. We begin with the oldest one, the structuralist tradition and its formalist offshoots, which posits that rules obtained by a process of abstraction are essential to understanding language. The second approach argues that generalizations are achieved not through abstraction, but by analogical reasoning over large numbers of instances of language use stored in memory. Finally, the third takes the perspective that to understand language and linguistic productivity, it is essential to take into account well-established basic principles of discrimination learning.

2. Abstraction

In traditional abstractionist approaches to language, it is assumed that the contexts in which a question such as *you want milk* can be uttered are so varied that the properties characterizing these contexts must be powerless as predictors of a given utterance. Accordingly, a child learning language is thought to face the problem of abstracting away from all the irrelevant contextual information in order to identify a level of elemental representations that capture abstract commonalities in instances of usage.

The common core of the set of utterances of *you want milk* is thus identified as roughly an abstract tri-partite knowledge structure comprising the phonological elements ($[[(ju)_w(wɒnt)_w(mɪlk)_s]]$) a syntactic structure comprising the elements ($[_{NP}$ you$[_{VP}$ want $[_{NP}$ milk$]]]$) and a semantic structure comprising the elements DESIRE(YOU, MILK).

It is then assumed that rules link the volitional agent element in the semantic structure to the subject element of the syntactic structure, while other rules specify that the pronoun element *you* is the string of phonemic elements [ju]. Typically, in order to keep the knowledge base as lean as possible, only the most elementary units (phonemes, morphemes, semantic primitives) and the rules for combining these units into well-formed sequences are stored in memory. Thus, the semantic structure DESIRE(YOU, MILK) would not be available in memory as such. Instead, only a more abstract structure, DESIRE(X, Y) would be stored, where X is a symbolic placeholder for any volitional agent able or imagined to be able to have desires, and Y any object, person, state, or event that is desired, or can be imagined to be desirable.

To further cut down memory requirements, and to make the relationships between words and utterances as transparent as possible, inheritance hierarchies (a formalism developed in the context of object-oriented programming languages) have been adopted in this context (see, e.g., Steels and De Beule 2006, for fluid construction grammar). Thus, instead of having to store different kinds of milk (*cow milk, goat's milk, sheep milk, mother milk, camel milk, coffee milk, coconut milk, ...*) and all their properties as separate lexical entries, one can set up one entry for the most typical kind of milk (e.g., the cow milk as bought in the supermarket),

> MILK: [type: thing;
> properties: concrete, inanimate, imageable, fluid, ...;
> function: to be consumed by drinking;
> color: white;
> source: cows],

and keep the entries for the other kinds of milk lean by having them inherit all the properties defined in the entry for milk except for where otherwise specified:

> CAMEL MILK:
> MILK [source: female camels].

When a mother offers milk to her child, while uttering *you want milk*, the semantic structure of the utterance may thus be characterized by lexical conceptual structures (Jackendoff 1990) such as

> OFFER(MOTHER, CHILD, MILK)
> ASK(MOTHER, CHILD, IS-TRUE(CHILD(DESIRE, MILK))).

These structures are, however, themselves the outcome of the application of more abstract semantic structures

> OFFER(X, Y, Z)
> ASK(X,Y, IS-TRUE(DESIRE, Y, Z)))

which also cover utterances such as *you want to play* and *you want to sleep*.

Several proposals have been made as to how such abstract structures (and the elements that they combine) might be identified or acquired. One class of theories holds that the language learner is genetically endowed with a set of abstract rules, constraints or primitives. This innate knowledge of an underlying universal abstract grammar relieves the learner of having to figure out the basic principles of human grammars, since these basics can be assumed to already be in place. Accordingly, the learner's task is reduced to solving simpler problems such as figuring out the proper word order in English for three-argument verbs in the light of innate knowledge such as verbs can have three arguments, word order can be fixed, etc.

However, innate rules and constraints by themselves have no explanatory value. Moreover, a half a century of research has not lead to any solid, generally accepted results that confirm that the basic principles of formal (computer) languages developed in the second half of the twentieth century are part of the human race's genetic endowment.

It should be noted, however, that not all rule-based theories of abstract linguistic structure make an explicit commitment to innate linguistic knowledge: in constraint-based approaches (see, e.g., Dressler 1985; Prince and Smolensky 2008), constraints can be argued to have functional motivations (see, e.g., Boersma 1998; Boersma and Hayes 2001). In phonology, for instance, voiceless realizations might be dispreferred due to voiced segments, as voiced segments require more articulatory effort, and hence more energy, than voiceless segments. In syntax, constraints might also be functionally grounded. For the dative alternation, for instance, a functional rationale motivating the observed preferences for particular constituent orders would be to provide a consistent and predictable flow of information, with given referents preceding non-given referents, pronouns preceding non-pronouns, definites preceding indefinites, and shorter constituents preceding longer constituents (Bresnan et al. 2007). However, even for constraints with reasonably plausible functional motivations, it is unclear how these constraints are learned. The problem here is that what is a hard constraint in one language, can be a soft constraint in another, and not a constraint at all in yet a third language. Skeptics of functional explanations will argue that functionally motivated constraints are unhelpful because it is not clear under what circumstances they are more, or less, in force.

Would it be possible to induce rules without invoking innate principles or presumed functional constraints? At least one proposal – the minimum generalization learning algorithm of Albright and Hayes (2003) – seeks to do exactly this in the domain of morphology. The algorithm gradually learns more abstract rules by iteratively comparing pairs of forms. Each comparison identifies what a pair of forms have in common, and wherever possible creates a more abstract rule on the basis of shared features.

For instance, transposed to syntax, given the utterances *you want milk* and *you want juice*, the minimum generalization learning algorithm would derive the structure

OFFER(MOTHER, CHILD, Z)
ASK(MOTHER, CHILD, IS-TRUE(DESIRE(CHILD,Z))
Z [type: thing;
properties: concrete, inanimate, imageable, fluid, ...;
function: to be consumed by drinking]

by deletion of the feature-value pairs [source:cow] and [source:fruit] in the respective semantic structures of the individual sentences.

For the pair of utterances *you want to play* and *you want to eat*, the shared abstract structure would be

OFFER(MOTHER, CHILD, Z)
ASK(MOTHER, CHILD, IS-TRUE(DESIRE(CHILD, Z)))
Z [type: event;
properties: volitional agent, social activity, ...;
agent: the child].

When in turn these structures are compared for further abstraction, all that remains is

OFFER(MOTHER, CHILD, Z)
ASK(MOTHER, CHILD, IS-TRUE(DESIRE(CHILD, Z)))

In turn, when the utterances are used with different interlocutors, this will undergo a further abstraction to

OFFER(X, Y, Z)
ASK(X, Y, IS-TRUE((DESIRE, Y, Z)))

A salient property of abstractionist theories is that although the rules and constructions are deduced from a systematic and comprehensive scan of any and all of the utterances in a language, the utterances themselves are discarded once the rules and constructions have been properly inferred. From the perspective of language processing, this raises several questions: First, if the original utterances are required for rule deduction, and hence have to be available in memory, why would they be discarded once the rules have been discovered?

Second, rule deduction requires a comprehensive set of utterances, but in real life, utterances become available one by one over time. We must thus assume that at some point in late childhood, after rule deduction is complete and the language has been learned, that the traces of past experience with the language can therefore be erased from a learner's memory. Yet this kind of fundamental discontinuity in the learning process seems at odds with recent evidence that language learning is a process that continues throughout one's lifetime (see, e.g., Ramscar et al. 2014, 2013d).

Third, the number of utterances that need to be stored in memory for rule deduction may be prohibitively large. Corpus surveys have revealed that there are hundreds of millions of sequences of just four words in English. Yet while some studies have reported frequency effects for sequences of words (Bannard and Matthews 2008; Arnon and Snider 2010; Tremblay and Baayen 2010), which have been argued to support the existence of representations of multi-word sequences in the mental lexicon (or mental construction), Shaoul et al. (2013) observed that knowledge about word sequences appears to be restricted to sequences no longer than four, perhaps five, words. Accordingly, it is unlikely that syntactic rules, especially those for complex sentences with main and subordinate clauses, could arise by a process of abstraction from a large set of stored full sentences, as the evidence suggests that the brain doesn't retain a rich set of memory traces for long complex sentences, but only for shorter sequences of words.

Abstractionist approaches presuppose that language is best understood as a formal calculus. A strength this provides is that it puts at their disposal all of the technology developed over many decades in computer science, and it is worth noting that most computationally implemented theories of various different aspects of linguistic cognition, whatever the very different schools of thought they come from, make use of abstractionist decompositional frameworks, as do most formal linguistic theories. Although the lexical conceptual structures of Jackendoff (1990) and Lieber (2004) look very different from the schemata of Langacker (1987) and Dąbrowska (2004a), these differences concern the aspects of human experience that the different theories seeks to formalize, and the particular flavor of formalization adopted; all of these approaches share the conviction that abstraction is at the heart of the language engine. Thus, for example, if we consider conceptual blending (for details, see the chapter by Turner in this volume), and the production of metaphorical expressions such as *Elephants were the tanks of Hannibal's army*, Veale et al. (2000) propose a computationally implemented model that generates conceptual blends from knowledge structures for elephants, tanks, classical and modern warfare, Hannibal, etc., in conjunction with an abstract rule that searches for n-tuples of knowledge structures across domains (e.g., Roman warfare and Modern warfare). On the basis of their features, n-tuples of knowledge structures in one domain can be matched to another. Given matching features (such as elephants being the strongest and most dangerous units in ancient warfare, and tanks being the strongest and most dangerous units in modern warfare), the algorithm can blend *elephants were the strongest units of Hannibal's army* with *tanks are the strongest units of a modern army* to create *elephants were the tanks of Hannibal's army*. In doing so, the algorithm abstracts away from the specific details of examples, and searches for correspondences across knowledge domains.

The tools of computer science provide the language engineer with valuable control over how a given computational operationalization will function. A further advantage they provide is that, in principle, computational implementations can be evaluated precisely against empirical data. However, this technology also has its share of disadvantages. First, the representations and rules employed by these formalisms typically require extensive, labor-intensive hand-crafting.

Second, and more importantly, it would appear that language itself is fundamentally contextual. A sentence such as *She cut her finger with a knife* typically suggests that the finger was not completely severed from the hand, whereas the sentence *These lumberjacks cut trees for a living* typically means that any trees involved were cut down and severed from their roots. The interpretation of the verb in *Outlines of animals were cut out of paper* is different yet again. Here, the verb indicates creation by means of cutting.

It is important to note here that the contexts in which words such as *cut* are encountered generate expectations that arise surprisingly early in the comprehension processing record (see, e.g., Elman 2009, for a review). Moreover, these expectations arise much earlier than one would expect given theories that assume an initial stage of abstract, purely form-based processing. Thus while it is of course true that within the abstractionist enterprise, one can distinguish between different senses of *cut* (WordNet distinguishes 41; see also Geeraerts this volume), each with its own semantic structure, with sufficiently narrowly defined features to make a sense fit only in very specific contexts, this still doesn't solve the problem posed by these early expectations, because it appears that they depend on exactly those subjects – she, lumberjacks, and outlines of animals – that these theories seek to abstract away from. Accordingly, while one might consider specifying in the lexical representation for lumberjack that this is a person whose profession it is to cut down trees, it stretches belief that outlines of animals (a lexical entry used by Google as a caption for images of outlines of animals [as of October 20, 2014]) would have an entry in the mental lexicon specifying that these are cutable.

Paradigmatic effects in language processing pose yet further problems for traditional abstractionist theories, because the paradigmatic dimensions of language are difficult to capture in abstractionist frameworks. Consider prepositional phrases in English, such as *with the onion, over the onion, in the onion, ...* . When abstraction is taken as the basis of generalization, then a structure such as [$_{PP}$ P [$_{NP}$ the [$_N$ N]]] captures crucial aspects of the abstract knowledge of prepositional phrases, in conjunction with the set of prepositions and the set of nouns in the lexicon. As far as language processing is concerned, all prior experiences with actual prepositional phrases (*with the onion, over the onion, in the onion ...*) are lost from memory. The abstractionist grammar reduces a rich slice of experience to a prepositional symbol, freely replaceable without reference to context by a single instance from the set of prepositions, followed by a definite determiner, in turn is followed by a noun symbol that is again selected without reference to context, from the set of nouns.

However, it would appear that different words make use of different prepositions in very different ways. To judge from both behavioral (Baayen et al. 2011) and electrophysiological (Hendrix and Baayen to appear) evidence, these paradigmatic differences influence, and indeed serve to co-determine lexical processing: Nouns that make use of prepositions in ways that are very different from the way an average noun uses its prepositions show very different characteristic profiles in processing. A measure capturing how well the use of prepositions by a specific noun corresponds to how prepositions are used in general is the Kulback-Leibler divergence, also known as relative entropy:

$$\text{relative entropy}(p, q) = \Sigma_i \, (p_i \log_2 (p_i / q_i)),$$

where p and q refer to the probability distributions of prepositional use given a specific noun, and the corresponding unconditional probability distribution of prepositions across all nouns . It turns out that when the relative entropy for a noun is large, i.e., when the noun makes atypical use of prepositions, response latencies to the noun, even when presented in isolation in the visual lexical decision task, are longer. Furthermore, in measures of speech production (gauged by a picture naming paradigm) relative entropy turns out to be an effective statistical predictor of the brain's electrophysiological response (Hendrix and Baayen to appear). Crucially, the effect of relative entropy arises irrespective of whether nouns are presented in isolation, or whether nouns are presented in the context of a particular preposition. What matters is how much a noun's use of prepositions differs from prototypical prepositional use in English. This paradigmatic effect poses a fundamental challenge to abstractionist theories, precisely because the point of assuming that learners create an abstract representation of "the" prepositional phrase is because it is assumed that language processing fundamentally relies on abstract representations. It is assumed that, for the purposes of processing, learners may as well have amnesia about how any given noun is actually used. Yet the way that speakers actually use nouns and prepositions indicates that not only do learners acquire and retain contextual information, but also that this contextual information plays a critical role in their processing of language.

3. Analogy

In traditional grammar, analogy was generally used to denote an incidental similarity-based extension of patterns that are not supported by more general rules. In some recent theories, however, analogy is seen as a much more foundational process of which rules are a special, typically more productive, case (see, e.g., Langacker 1987; Pothos 2005).

In morphology, Matthews (1974) and Blevins (2003) developed a framework known as Word and Paradigm Morphology, in which words, rather than morphemes and exponents, are the basic units in the lexicon. The theory posits that proportional analogy (*hand : hands = tree : trees*) drives the production and comprehension of novel forms, and explicit algorithms for capturing the core idea of analogy-driven prediction have been developed within the context of a class of computational approaches commonly referred to as exemplar models (see also Ramscar and Port this volume).

Exemplar models start from the assumption that learners acquire and store an extensive inventory of instances of language use (typically referred to as exemplars) in memory. Instead of seeking to account for the productivity of language through abstract rules operating over hand-tailored representations, exemplar models base their predictions about novel forms on these stored exemplars, in combination with a general, domain a-specific similarity-driven algorithm. One of the earliest linguistic exemplar models was Skousen's (1989) analogical model of language (AML), which grounds the analogical process in probability theory (Skousen 2002, 2000). The AML algorithm searches for sets of exemplars with characteristics that consistently support a particular outcome. An outcome can be a construction, a phonetic feature, etc., such as voicing alternation (Ernestus and Baayen 2003), or the choice between rival affixes (Arndt-Lappe in press). The output of this search process is a subset of consistent exemplars, the analogical set, in which the different outcomes are ranked by the number of exemplars supporting them, with the best-supported, highest-ranked outcome being considered the most likely outcome.

Skousen's AML model is computationally expensive, which makes the processing of data with many features difficult. Memory based learning (MBL), a framework developed by Daelemans and Van den Bosch (2005) sidesteps this computational problem. As in AML, the algorithm searches for a set of nearest neighbors, from which it selects the exemplar with the best support in the nearest neighbor set as its choice of outcome. In the very simplest set-up, the nearest neighbors are those instances in memory that share most features with a given case for which an appropriate outcome class has to be determined. This simplest set-up is not very useful, however, because in the presence of many irrelevant predictors, classification accuracy can plummet. By weighting features for their relevance for a given choice problem, accuracy can be improved dramatically while keeping computational costs down. By way of example, consider the choice of the plural allomorph in English, which is [iz] following sibilants, [s] following voiceless consonants, and [z] elsewhere. Knowledge of a word's final consonant nearly eliminates uncertainty about the appropriate allomorph, whereas knowledge of the initial consonant of the word is completely uninformative. Since manner of articulation and voicing of the final consonant are informative features, they can be assigned large weights, whereas manner and voicing for initial consonants can be assigned low weights. The values of these weights can be estimated straightforwardly from the data, for instance, by considering to what extent knowledge of the value of a feature reduces one's uncertainty about the class outcome. The extent to which uncertainty is reduced then becomes the weight for the importance of that feature.

One important message that has come from the literature on memory based learning is that forgetting is harmful (Daelemans et al. 1999): The larger the set of exemplars MBL is provided with, the better it is able to approximate human performance. This points to a conclusion that is exactly the opposite of that of abstractionist models, which seek to keep the knowledge base as lean as possible. However, in principle at least, these differences are not so large as they would seem. As Keuleers (2008) points out, abstraction, in the form of minimum generalization (MGL) learning, and memory based learning (under certain parameter configurations) are all but indistinguishable mathematically. However, whereas minimum generalization learning first deduces rules, then forgets about exemplars, and uses rules at run-time (greedy learning), memory-based learning simply stores exemplars, and runs its similarity-based algorithm at runtime (lazy learning).

Another similarity between MGL and MBL is that a new model is required for each individual problem set within a domain of inquiry. For instance, when modeling phonological form, one model will handle past tenses, another model the choice between the allomorphy of nominalizations in -*ion*, and yet a third model the allomorphy of the plural suffix. Thus, both approaches work with different rules (or schemas) for different phenomena, and differ only as to how these rules/schemas are implemented under the hood.

Exemplar models such as AML and MBL offer several advantages over abstractionist approaches. First, because analogical rules are executed at run-time, new exemplars in the instance base will automatically lead to an update in prediction performance. In MGL, by contrast, once the rule system has been deduced, it remains fixed and cannot be updated for principled reasons. (Technically, of course, the rules can be recalculated for an updated set of exemplars, but doing so implies that the exemplars are held in reserve, and are not erased from memory.) Another important advantage of AML and MBL is that getting the algorithms to work for a given data set requires very little handcrafting: the algorithms discover themselves which features are important.

Of course, these models also have disadvantages. First, compared to handcrafted abstractionist systems developed over many years and fine-tuned to all kinds of exceptions, AML and MBL can show a lack of precision. Second, it remains to be seen how plausible it is to assume that each and any exemplar is stored in memory. As we noted above, hundreds of millions of four-word sequences would have to be stored in an English mental lexicon. When it comes to languages with highly productive inflectional systems, millions of forms will have to be stored, just at the word level. Furthermore, the rampant variability in the speech signal makes it highly unlikely that each pronunciation variant of every word ever heard would be stored in memory (indeed, this last point highlights a problem posed by the idea of an exemplar itself, namely that of deciding at which level of abstraction something is to be considered a type or a token of an exemplar; see Ramscar and Port this volume).

4. Hybrid models

Hybrid models hold that schemata (or rules) and exemplars exist side by side. For instance, Langacker (2010: 109) argues for a hybrid approach when he states that, "structure emerges from usage, is immanent in usage, and is influenced by usage on an ongoing basis". The co-existence of rules and exemplars (see also Langacker 1987; Dąbrowska 2004b) implies a system that contains a great deal of redundancy, such that, for instance, in comprehension, an interpretation can be arrived at either by retrieving the appropriate holistic exemplar, or by application of a rule or schema to the relevant exemplars of smaller units. For morphological processing, Baayen et al. (1997) made a similar argument for the existence of whole-word representations for complex words, side by side with a parsing mechanism operating on the morphemic constituents of these words.

The redundancy offered by hybrid models is generally taken to make the processing system more robust. For instance, when one processing route fails to complete, another processing route may still be effective. In horse race models, which make the assumption that processing routes run independently and in parallel, a process of statistical facilitation can take place: If processing time is determined by the first route to win the race, and if the distributions of the completion times of the different routes overlap, then, across many trials, the average processing time of the combined routes will be shorter than the average processing time of the fastest route by itself (Baayen et al. 1997).

It should be noted, however that, in embracing both abstractionist and exemplar based approaches, hybrid models inherit many of the problems of both. Because they incorporate exemplars, hybrid models also posit large, high-entropy exemplar spaces. As we noted above, these pose deep practical and conceptual problems. For example, while it might be argued that not all exemplars are stored, but only large numbers of exemplars, this raises the question of under what circumstances exemplars are, or are not, stored. Positing a frequency threshold for storage runs into logical difficulties, because any new exemplar will start with an initial frequency of 1, far below the threshold, and hence will never be stored.

From abstractionist models, hybrid models inherit the problem of selecting the correct analysis from the multitude of possible analyses (Bod 1998, 2006; Baayen and Schreuder 2000). When schemata are assumed to be in operation at multiple levels of abstraction, how does the system know which level of abstraction is the appropriate one? How is competition between more concrete and more abstract schemata resolved?

5. Discrimination

It is clear that abstractionist approaches, exemplar models and hybrid models offer many insights into language production, comprehension and processing. However, as we noted above, when it comes to explaining how people learn to productively use language, and what they learn in order to do so, each approach has its weak points. Thus while we agree with Langacker's (2010) suggestion that usage shapes the grammar on an ongoing basis (Ramscar and Baayen 2013), we believe that in order to answer questions about the way people learn to use language, or the way that usage shapes the grammars people learn, it is essential to begin with learning theory, and the process(es) of learning itself.

Modern learning theory begins with Ivan Pavlov and his famous observations about bells and dog-food. Pavlov first noticed that his dogs salivated in the presence of the technician who usually fed them. He then devised an experiment in which he rang a bell before he presented the dogs with food. After a few repetitions, the dogs started to salivate in response to the bell, anticipating the food they expected to see (Pavlov, 1927). Pavlov's initial results led to a straightforward theory of learning that seems obvious and feels intuitively right: If a cue is present, and an outcome follows, an animal notices the co-occurrence and subsequently learns to associate the two.

It turns out, however, that this simple associative view of learning provides a one-sided and misleading perspective on the actual learning process and its consequences. For example, a dog trained to expect food when a bell is rung, can later be given training in which a light is flashed simultaneously with the bell. After repeated exposure to bell and light, followed by food, only a light is flashed. Will the dog drool? Surprisingly, the answer is no: the dog doesn't drool. Even though the light consistently co-occurred with the food in training, the dog does not learn to associate it with the food, a phenomenon known as blocking.

The problem for, e.g., memory-based learning is that this theory would pick out the light as an informative cue for food. After all, whenever the light is present, food is present. Since there is no uncertainty about the food given the light, the model predicts that the light should be an excellent cue, and that this cue should build strong expectations for food, contrary to fact.

The learning equations that Rescorla developed together with Wagner (Rescorla and Wagner, 1972), however, perfectly capture this finding. The reason that the light never becomes an effective cue for food is that the bell is already a perfectly predictive cue for the food. Because there are no situations in which the light predicts food but the bell does not, the light does not add any new information: it is not predictive of the food over and above the bell. As this and many similar experiments have revealed, associative learning is sensitive to the informativity of co-occurrences, rather than their mere existence.

Learning theory (Rescorla 1988) not only predicts a substantial body of findings in the animal and human behavior (Miller et al. 1995; Siegel and Allan 1996) but it has also recently been found to predict many aspects of first language acquisition as well as implicit linguistic learning in adults (see, e.g., Ramscar and Yarlett 2007; Ramscar and Gitcho 2007; Ramscar et al. 2010, 2013c, 2014). Learning theory specifies how the association weights from the cues in the environment (such as a bell and a flashing light in the case of Pavlov's dog) to an outcome (e.g., food) should be modified over time. The basic insights are, first, that if a cue is not present, association weights from that cue to outcomes are left untouched. For instance, whiskers are visual cues to various animals, such as cats, rabbits, rats, and mice. If there are no whiskers to be seen, then the weights on the links between whiskers and cats, rabbits, rats, and mice, are left unchanged, even though these animals might be present (as when they are observed from the back). When whiskers are seen, and a cat is present but no rabbits, rats, or mice, then the weight from whiskers to cat is increased. At the same time, the weights from whiskers to rabbits, rats, and mice are decreased, even though these animals have whiskers. This is a crucial element of modern theory that sets it apart from its associationist, even behaviorist, predecessors (Rescorla 1988). Learning is sensitive not only to associations forming when cues and outcomes co-occur. Learning is also sensitive to the success and failure of the implicit predictions that prior experiences relating cues to outcomes generate. Whiskers do not only predict cats, but also rabbits and other rodents. When these predictions turn out to be false, the weights that connect whiskers to the animals that were mispredicted to be present will be tuned down. As a result of this, outcomes

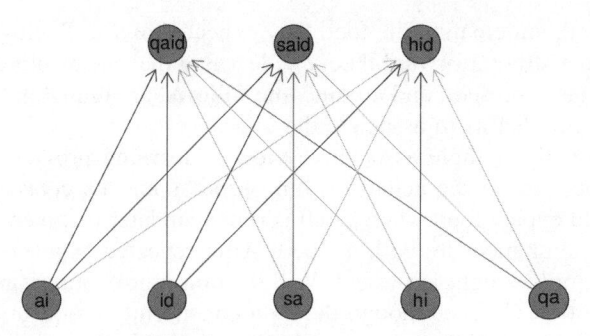

Fig. 5.1: A Rescorla-Wagner network with five digraphs as cues, and three lexemes as outcomes

(cats, rabbits, mice, rats) compete for the cues, while at the same time, cues compete for outcomes.

Baayen et al. (2011) used the Rescorla-Wagner equations to build a computational model for the reading of words, as gauged by the visual lexical decision task. The basic structure of the model is very simple, and is exemplified by Figure 5.1. The bottom layer of the network has nodes representing letter pairs (digraphs). The top layer of the network specifies lexemes, in the sense of Aronoff (1994), that is, as lexical nodes that are the symbols linking to rich form information (such as letter digraphs) on the one hand, and rich world knowledge (not shown in Figure 5.1) on the other hand. A system of lexemes is a set of symbolic focal points that serves to mediate and discriminate both between linguistic forms and our experiences of the world. Lexemes are, in themselves, neither forms nor meanings, but rather they systematically aggregate the form and meaning contrasts that a speaker hearer has learned to discriminate, and potentially communicate, at any given time.

Of course, this raises the question how the elements of form (n-graphs, n-phones) and the elements of experience (the lexemes) themselves are learned. Here, we assume that these units are simply available to the learner. Any computational implementation has to work with units that are primitives to that implementation, but which themselves have arisen as the outcome of other learning and classification processes, or the same processes at another level of abstraction. In this latter vein, one process that might give rise to these units is unsupervised category learning (see, e.g., Love et al. 2004, for a computational implementation, and also Ramscar and Port this volume).

The first word in Figure 5.1, the legal scrabble word *qaid* ('tribal chieftain'), has one letter pair, *qa*, that uniquely distinguishes it from the two other lexemes. The Rescorla-Wagner equations predict that this cue is strongly associated with *qaid*, and negatively associated with *said* and *hid*. Conversely, the letter pair *id* occurs in all three words, and as a result it is not very useful for discriminating between the three lexemes. As a consequence, the weights on its connections are all small. The total support that cues in the input provide for a lexeme, its activation, is obtained by summation over the weights on the connections from these cues (for *qaid*, the cues *qa, ai,* and *id*) to the outcome (the lexeme of *qaid*). This activation represents the learnability of the lexemes given the cues.

The naive discriminative learner model of Baayen et al. (2011) takes this simple network architecture and applies it rigorously to word triplets in the British National

5. Abstraction, storage and naive discriminative learning

Corpus. For each word triplet, all the letter diphones in the three words were collected. These served as cues. From the same words, all "content" lexemes and "grammatical" lexemes (number, tense, person, etc.) were collected and served as outcomes. The Rescorla-Wagner equations were then used to adjust the weights from the digraph cues to the lexeme outcomes. For any given word in the corpus, its activation was obtained by summing the weights from its orthographic cues to its lexemes. For words with multiple lexemes, such as a plural or a compound, the activations of its lexemes were summed. (In the actual implementation, a mathematical shortcut, due to Danks [2003], was used for estimating the weights.) It turns out that these activation weights are excellent predictors of lexical decision latencies: words with longer responses are the words with lower activations, i.e., the words that cannot be learned that well given their orthographic properties. The activation weights turn out to mirror a wide range of effects reported in the experimental literature, such as the word frequency effect, orthographic neighborhood effects, morphological family size effects, constituent frequency effects, and paradigmatic entropy effects (including the abovementioned prepositional relative entropy effect). What is especially interesting is that the model covers the full range of morphological effects, without having any representations for words, morphemes, exponents, or allomorphs.

In this approach, both the morphology and the syntax are implicit in the distribution of cues and outcomes, which jointly shape a network that is continuously updated with usage. Since morphology and syntax are implicit in the usage, we also refer to the discriminative approach as implicit morphology and implicit grammar. Interestingly, this approach to language dovetails well with the mathematical theory of communication developed by Shannon (1948).

When a photograph is sent over a cable from a camera to a laptop, it is not the case that the objects in the photograph (say a rose on a table, next to which is a chair), are somehow "encoded" and sent down the wire one by one (first the chair, and than the rose plus table). To the contrary, the picture is transformed into a binary stream that is optimized for the transmission channel as well as protected against data loss by error-correcting code. The laptop is able to reconstruct the picture, not by applying a grammar to "extract" the picture from the signal, but by making use of the same coding scheme that the camera used in order to select the appropriate distribution of pixel colors over the canvas, thereby discriminating the appropriate pattern of pixel colors from the possible distributions of pixel colors that the coding scheme allows for.

To make this more concrete, consider a coding scheme devised to transmit for experiences: the experience of a fountain, the experience of a fountain pen, the experience of an orange, and the experience of orange juice. Assume a code, shared by encoder and decoder, specifying that the four experiences can be signaled using the digit strings 00, 01, 10, and 11 respectively. When seeking to communicate the experience of a fountain pen, the speaker will encode 01, and thanks to the shared code, the listener will decode 01, and select the appropriate experience (a fountain pen) that the code discriminates from her total set of possible experiences. There is no need whatsoever to consider whether the individual ones and zeros compositionally contribute to the experiences transmitted.

Thus we can view language-as-form (ink on paper, pixels on a computer screen, the speech signal, gestures) as a signal that serves to discriminate between complex experiences of the world. The success of the signal hinges on interlocutors sharing the code for encoding and decoding the signal (see also Wieling et al. 2014). The same (or at least, a highly similar) code that allows the speaker to discriminate between past experiences in memory and encode a discriminated experience in the language signal, is then used by the listener to discriminate between her past experiences.

Discrimination is important here, as speakers will seldom share the same experiences. Consider, for example, a speaker mentioning a larch tree. The interlocutor may not know what exactly a larch tree is, because she never realized the differences between larches, spruces, and pine trees. Nevertheless, the communicative event may be relatively successful in the sense that the listener was able to reduce the set of potential past experiences to her experiences of trees. She might request further clarification of what a larch tree is, or, not having any interest in biology, she might just be satisfied that some (to her irrelevant) subspecies of trees is at issue. Thus implicit grammar views the language signal as separating encoded relevant experiences from the larger set of a listener's irrelevant experiences.

Thus far, we have discussed comprehension. What about speech production? The model we are developing (see also Baayen and Blevins 2014), proposes a two-layered knowledge structure, consisting of a directed graph specifying the order between production outcomes on the one hand, and of Recorla-Wagner networks associated with the vertices in the network on the other hand. Figure 5.2 presents such a knowledge structure for the sentences *John passed away*, *John kicked the bucket*, *John died*, *John passed the*

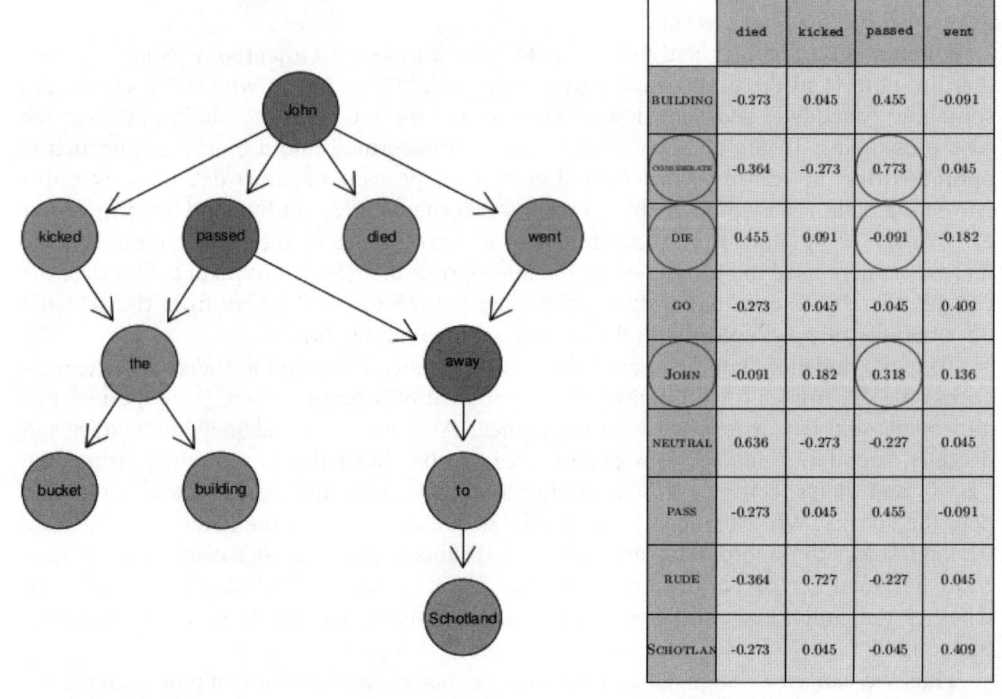

	died	kicked	passed	went
BUILDING	-0.273	0.045	0.455	-0.091
CONSIDERATE	-0.364	-0.273	0.773	0.045
DIE	0.455	0.091	-0.091	-0.182
GO	-0.273	0.045	-0.045	0.409
JOHN	-0.091	0.182	0.318	0.136
NEUTRAL	0.636	-0.273	-0.227	0.045
PASS	-0.273	0.045	0.455	-0.091
RUDE	-0.364	0.727	-0.227	0.045
SCHOTLAN	-0.273	0.045	-0.045	0.409

Fig. 5.2: An example of a directed word graph and the Rescorla-Wagner control network at the node John.

5. Abstraction, storage and naive discriminative learning 113

building, and *John went away to Scotland*. The left panel presents the directed graph specifying the potential paths defined by these sentences, and the right panel summarizes the connection strengths between lexemic cues (rows) and word outcomes (columns) in tabular form. These connection strengths are obtained with the Rescorla-Wagner equations applied to all sentences containing *John* (for detailed discussion of these equations, see Ramscar et al. 2010 and Baayen et al. 2011).

All sentences in this simple example begin with *John*, hence this is the top node. Given *John*, the possible continuations are *kicked*, *passed*, *died*, and *went*. When the speaker has the intention of communicating in a considerate way that John died (indicated by the lexemes *John*, *die*, *considerate*, highlighted in the table of weights), then the word *passed* has a total activation of 1 (the sum of the highlighted weights in the passed column), whereas the other continuations have activations of zero. Thus, sentences emerge as paths through the directed graph, where each choice where to go next is governed by the accumulated knowledge discriminating between the different options, guided by past experience of which lexemes predict which word outcomes.

Knowledge structures such as those illustrated in Figure 5.2 can be formulated for sequences of words, but also for sequences of diphones or demi-syllables. It is currently an open question whether separate structures above and below the word are really necessary. What is important is that the digraphs provide a very economical storage format. In a word graph, any word form is represented by a single vertex. In a diphone graph, any diphone is present only once. This is a large step away from standard conceptions of the mental lexicon informed by the dictionary metaphor, in which a letter or diphone pair is represented many times, at least once for each entry. The directed graph also sidesteps the problem of having to assume distinct exemplars for sequences of demi-syllables or sequences of words. In the present example, for instance, an opaque idiom (*kick the bucket*), a semi-transparent idiom (*to pass away*), and a literal expression (*die*) are represented economically with dynamical control from the Rescorla-Wagner networks.

From the discriminative perspective, questions as to how opaque and semi-transparent idioms are "stored" in the mental dictionary, decomposed, or not decomposed, simply do not arise because words are now part of a signal for which traditional questions of compositionality are simply not relevant. Thus, in implicit grammar, rules, schemata, constructions, inheritance hierarchies, multiple entries of homonyms in dictionary lists, and all other constructs based on formal grammars are unnecessary.

These constructs may provide high-level descriptions of aspects of language that may be insightful for the analyst reflecting on language, but in the discriminative approach, they are not taken to imply a corresponding cognitive reality.

The knowledge structures of implicit grammar do not permit redundancy, in the sense that different sets of representations, and different rules for achieving the same result, would co-exist. The theory acknowledges that the linguistic signal is rich, and that the experiences we encode in the signal are richer by many orders of magnitude (see Ramscar et al. 2010 for a discussion of the problems this dimensional mismatch poses to any traditionally combinatorial theory). But redundancy in the sense of having multiple ways in which to achieve exactly the same goal is ruled out. The directed graph and the Rescorla-Wagner networks define one unique most-probable path for the expression of a given message.

Research on child language acquisition (e.g., Bannard and Matthews 2008; Tomasello 2009) has shown that children are conservative learners who stay very close to known exemplars, and initially do not use constructions productively. One explanation holds that initially, children work with large unanalyzed holistic chunks, which they learn, over time, to break down into smaller chunks, with as end product the abstract schemata of the adult speaker (Dąbrowska 2004b; Dąbrowska and Lieven 2005; Borensztajn et al. 2009; Beekhuizen et al. 2014). Implicit grammar offers a very different – and currently still speculative – perspective on the acquisition process (Arnon and Ramscar 2012).

Consider a child inquiring about what activity her interlocutor is engaged in. Typically, an English-speaking child in North America or the U.K. will have ample experience with such questions, which often arise in the context of reading a picture book (*What's the bear doing? It's eating honey!*). However, with very little command over her vocal apparatus, in the initial stage of speech production, the full message (a question about the event an actor is engaged in) has to be expressed by the child in a single word, e.g., *Mommy?*. However, single-word expressions will often not be effective, as *Mommy?* could also be short-hand for what adults would express as *Mommy, where are you?* or *Mommy, I'm hungry*. From a learning perspective, the word uttered (*Mommy*), and the lexemes in the message (question, event, Mommy) constitute the cues in a learning event with the success of the communicative event as outcome. Over the course of learning during the one-word stage, the lexemes question, event, agent will acquire low or even negative weights to communicative success. Only Mommy will acquire substantial positive weights, thanks to the single-word utterances being successful for attracting attention.

By the end of the one-word stage, the child has a production graph with only vertices and no edges. Once the child succeeds in uttering sentences with more than one word (*What's Mommy doing*), thanks to increasing motor control over the articulators, the chances of successful communication rise dramatically. This will prompt the reuse of multi-word sequences, and the construction of edges between the vertices in the graph, together with the Rescorla-Wagner networks that discriminate between where to go next in the graph given the child's communicative intentions. The first path in the graph will be re-used often, consolidating both the edges between the vertices in the directed graph, as well as the associated Rescorla-Wagner control networks, which, in terms of what the child actually produces, will enable the child to demonstrate increasing fluency with multiword productions.

In this approach to learning, the empirical phenomenon of children proceeding in their production from a prefab such as *What's Mommy doing?* to utterances of the form *What's X V-ing?*, analysed in cognitive grammar as schematization, in implicit grammar does not involve any abstraction. What is at stake, instead, is learning to think for speaking (Slobin 1996). During the one-word stage, children gradually learn that many aspects of the experiences they want to express cannot be packed into a single word. Once they have accumulated enough articulatory experience to launch word sequences, they can develop their production graph and the associated control networks. As this graph is expanded, syntactic productivity, which is already nascent in small worlds such as shown in Figure 5.2, will increase exponentially.

It is worth noting that the process of chunking in acquisition, with the child as a miniature linguist trying to find units at varies hierarchical levels in the speech signal, is also is at odds with the ACT-R theory of cognition, according to which chunking evolves in the opposite direction, starting with the small chunks that are all that can be

5. Abstraction, storage and naive discriminative learning 115

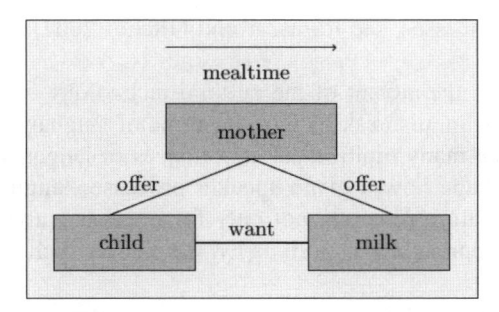

OFFER(MOTHER, CHILD, Z)
ASK(MOTHER, CHILD, IS-TRUE(CHILD(DESIRE, Z)))

$$z \begin{bmatrix} \text{type:} & \text{thing} \\ \text{properties:} & \text{concrete, inanimate, imageable, fluid, \ldots} \\ \text{function:} & \text{to be consumed by drinking} \end{bmatrix}$$

Fig. 5.3: Semantic representations in the style of cognitive grammar (after Dąbrowska (2004: 221) and Jackendoff's lexical conceptual structures.

handled initially, and that only with experience over time can be aggregated into the greater chunks representing the automatization of cognitive skills (Anderson 2007).

Theoretical frameworks have developed different notational schemes for describing the semantics of utterances such as you want milk, as illustrated in Figure 5.3 for cognitive grammar (top) and lexical conceptual structures (bottom) in the style of Jackendoff (1990). From the perspective of implicit grammar, the knowledge summarized in such representations is valuable and insightful, but too dependent on a multitude of interpretational conventions to be immediately implementable in a discriminative learning model. What needs to be done is to unpack such descriptions into a set of basic descriptors that can function as lexemes in comprehension and production models. For instance, OFFER(MOTHER, CHILD, MILK) has to be unpacked into lexemes not only for *offer*, *mother, child,* and *milk*, but also for the mother as the initiator of the offering, the milk as the thing offered, etc. In other words, the insights expressed by the different frameworks can and should be made available to the learning algorithms in the form of lexemic units. How exactly these units conspire within the memory system defined by the directed graph and its control networks is determined by how they are used in the language community and the learning algorithms of the brain.

Implicit grammar is a new computational theory, and it is still under development. We have illustrated that this theory makes it possible to reflect on language and cognition from a very different perspective. Computational simulations for comprehension indicate that the model scales up to corpora with many billions of words. For speech production, simulations of the production of complex words promise low error rates (Baayen and Blevins 2014), but whether the same holds for sentence and discourse production remains to be shown.

Implicit grammar grounds language in discrimination learning. There is, of course, much more to language and cognition than implicit discriminative learning. For discussion of the role of higher-order cognitive processes in resolving processing conflicts and integrating implicit learning with speakers' goals, and also the importance of the late development of these higher-order processes, see Ramscar and Gitcho (2007); Ramscar et al. (2013a, 2013b).

A further complication is that with the advent of the cultural technology of writing, literate speakers bring extensive meta-linguistic skills into the arena of language use and language processing. How exactly the many multimodal experiences of language use at both implicit and conscious levels shape how a given speaker processes language is a serious computational challenge for future research, not only for implicit grammar, but also for abstractionist and exemplar approaches, as well as hybrid models such as cognitive grammar.

6. Concluding remarks

When comparing different algorithms, it is important to keep in mind, irrespective of whether they come from abstractionist, exemplar-based, or discriminative theories, that they tend to perform with similar precision. For instance, Ernestus and Baayen (2003) compared AML, stochastic optimality theory, and two classifiers from the statistical literature, among others, and observed very similar performance. Keuleers (2008) showed equivalent performance for memory-based learning and minimum generalization learning for past-tense formation in English. Baayen et al. (2013) compared two statistical techniques with naive discrimination learning, and again observed similar performance. This state of affairs indicates that the typical data sets that have fuelled debates over rules, schemas, and analogy, tend to have a quantitative structure that can be well-approximated from very different theoretical perspectives. Therefore, the value of different approaches to language, language use, and language processes will have to be evaluated by means of the simplicity of computational implementations, the neuro-biological support for these implementations, and the extent to which the models generate concrete, falsifiable predictions regarding unseen data. That is, the extent to which it is the models themselves that generate insight, rather than models merely embodying the insights of their makers.

7. References

Albright, Adam and Bruce Hayes
   2003   Rules vs. analogy in English past tenses: A computational/experimental study. *Cognition* 90: 119–161.

Anderson, John R.
   2007   *How Can the Human Mind Occur in the Physical Universe?* Oxford: Oxford University Press.

Arndt-Lappe, Sabine
   in press   Analogy in suffix rivalry: the case of English *ity* and *ness*. *English Language and Linguistics*.

Arnon, Inbal and Michael Ramscar
   2012   Granularity and the acquisition of grammatical gender: How order-of-acquisition affects what gets learned. *Cognition* 122(3): 292–305.

Arnon, Inbal and Neal Snider
 2010 More than words: Frequency effects for multi-word phrases. *Journal of Memory and Language* 62(1): 67–82.
Aronoff, Mark
 1994 *Morphology by Itself: Stems and Inflectional Classes.* Cambridge: MIT Press.
Baayen, R. Harald and James Blevins
 2014 Implicit morphology. Manuscript, University of Tuebingen.
Baayen, R. Harald, Ton Dijkstra and Robert Schreuder
 1997 Singulars and plurals in Dutch: Evidence for a parallel dual route model. *Journal of Memory and Language* 36: 94–117.
Baayen, R. Harald, Laura Janda, Tore Nesset, Anna Endresen and Anastasia Makarova
 2013 Making choices in Russian: Pros and cons of statistical methods for rival forms. *Russian Linguistics* 37: 253–291.
Baayen, R. Harald, Petar Milin, Dusica Filipovic Durdevic, Peter Hendrix and Marco Marelli
 2011 An amorphous model for morphological processing in visual comprehension based on naive discriminative learning. *Psychological Review* 118: 438–482.
Baayen, R. Harald and Robert Schreuder
 2000 Towards a psycholinguistic computational model for morphological parsing. *Philosophical Transactions of the Royal Society* (Series A: Mathematical, Physical and Engineering Sciences) 358: 1–13.
Bannard, Colin and Danielle Matthews
 2008 Stored word sequences in language learning: The effect of familiarity on children's repetition of four-word combinations. *Psychological Science* 19: 241–248.
Beekhuizen, Barend, Rens Bod, Afsaneh Fazly, Suzanne Stevenson and Arie Verhagen
 2014 A usage-based model of early grammatical development. *Proceedings of the 2014 ACL workshop on cognitive modeling and computational linguistics,* 46–54. Baltimore, Maryland USA, June 26th, 2014. Association for Computational Linguistics.
Blevins, James
 2003 Stems and paradigms. *Language* 79: 737–767.
Bod, Rens
 1998 *Beyond Grammar: An Experience-based Theory of Language.* Stanford: CSLI.
Bod, Rens
 2006 Exemplar-based syntax: How to get productivity from examples. *The Linguistic Review* 23(3): 291–320.
Boersma, Paul
 1998 *Functional Phonology.* The Hague: Holland Academic Graphics.
Boersma, Paul and Bruce Hayes
 2001 Empirical tests of the gradual learning algorithm. *Linguistic Inquiry* 32: 45–86.
Borensztajn, Gideon, Willem Zuidema and Rens Bod
 2009 Children's grammars grow more abstract with age – evidence from an automatic procedure for identifying the productive units of language. *Topics in Cognitive Science* 1(1): 175–188.
Bresnan, Joan, Anna Cueni, Tatiana Nikitina and R. Harald Baayen
 2007 Predicting the dative alternation. In: G. Bouma, I. Kraemer, and J. Zwarts (eds.), *Cognitive Foundations of Interpretation,* 69–94. Amsterdam: Royal Netherlands Academy of Arts and Sciences.
Dąbrowska, Ewa
 2004a *Language, Mind and Brain. Some Psychological and Neurological Constraints on Theories of Grammar.* Edinburgh: Edinburgh University Press.
Dąbrowska, Ewa
 2004b Rules or schemas? Evidence from Polish. *Language and Cognitive Processes* 19: 225–271.

Dąbrowska, Ewa and Elena Lieven
   2005   Towards a lexically specific grammar of children's question constructions. *Cognitive Linguistics* 16(3): 437–474.
Daelemans, Walter and Antal van den Bosch
   2005   *Memory-based Language Processing*. Cambridge: Cambridge University Press.
Daelemans, Walter, Antal van den Bosch and Jakub Zavrel
   1999   Forgetting exceptions is harmful in language learning. *Machine Learning* 34: 11–41.
Danks, David
   2003   Equilibria of the Rescorla-Wagner model. *Journal of Mathematical Psychology* 47(2): 109–121.
Dressler, Wolfgang
   1985   On the predictiveness of natural morphology. *Journal of Linguistics* 21: 321–337.
Elman, Jeff
   2009   On the meaning of words and dinosaur bones: Lexical knowledge without a lexicon. *Cognitive Science* 33: 1–36.
Ernestus, Mirjam and R. Harald Baayen
   2003   Predicting the unpredictable: Interpreting neutralized segments in Dutch. *Language* 79: 5–38.
Hendrix, Peter and R. Harald Baayen
   to appear   Distinct ERP signatures of word frequency, phrase frequency, and prototypicality in speech production. *Journal of Experimental Psychology: Learning, Memory and Cognition*.
Jackendoff, Ray
   1990   *Semantic Structures*. Cambridge: MIT Press.
Keuleers, Emmanuel
   2008   *Memory-based Learning of Inflectional Morphology*. Antwerp: University of Antwerp.
Langacker, Ronald
   1987   *Foundations of Cognitive Grammar.* Volume 1: *Theoretical Prerequisites*. Stanford: Stanford University Press.
Langacker, Ronald
   2010   How not to disagree: The emergence of structure from usage. In: K. Boye and E. Engberg-Pedersen (eds.), *Language Usage and Language Structure* (Trends in linguistics: studies and monographs 213), 107–143. Berlin/New York: Mouton de Gruyter.
Lieber, Rochelle
   2004   *Morphology and Lexical Semantics*. Cambridge: Cambridge University Press.
Love, Bradley, Douglas Medin and Todd Gureckis
   2004   Sustain: a network model of category learning. *Psychological Review* 111(2): 309.
Matthews, Peter
   1974   *Morphology. An introduction to the Theory of Word Structure*. Cambridge: Cambridge University Press.
Miller, Ralph, Robert Barnet and Nicholas Grahame
   1995   Assessment of the Rescorla-Wagner model. *Psychological Bulletin* 117(3): 363
Pavlov, Ivan
   1927   *Conditioned Reflexes: An Investigation of the Physiological Activity of the Cerebral Cortex* (trans. G. V. Anrep). Oxford: Oxford University Press.
Pothos, Emmanuel
   2005   The rules versus similarity distinction. *Behavioral and Brain Sciences* 28(01): 1–14.
Prince, Alan and Paul Smolensky
   2008   *Optimality Theory: Constraint Interaction in Generative Grammar.* Hoboken: John Wiley and Sons.

Ramscar, Michael and R. Harald Baayen
   2013   Production, comprehension and synthesis: A communicative perspective on language. *Frontiers in Psychology* 4: 233.
Ramscar, Michael, Melody Dye, Jessica Gustafson and Joseph Klein
   2013a   Dual routes to cognitive flexibility: Learning and response conflict resolution in the dimensional change card sort task. *Child Development* 84(4): 1308–1323.
Ramscar, Michael, Melody Dye and Joseph Klein
   2013b   Children value informativity over logic in word learning. *Psychological Science* 24(6): 1017–1023.
Ramscar, Michael, Melody Dye and Stewart McCauley
   2013c   Error and expectation in language learning: The curious absence of mouses in adult speech. *Language* 89(4): 760–793.
Ramscar, Michael and Nichole Gitcho
   2007   Developmental change and the nature of learning in childhood. *Trends in Cognitive Science* 11(7): 274–279.
Ramscar, Michael, Peter Hendrix, Bradley Love and R. Harald Baayen
   2013d   Learning is not decline: The mental lexicon as a window into cognition across the lifespan. *The Mental Lexicon* 8: 450–481.
Ramscar, Michael, Peter Hendrix, Cyrus Shaoul, Petar Milin and R. Harald Baayen
   2014   Nonlinear dynamics of lifelong learning: The myth of cognitive decline. *Topics in Cognitive Science* 6: 5–42.
Ramscar, Michael and Robert Port
   this volume   4. Categorization (without categories). Berlin/Boston: De Gruyter Mouton.
Ramscar, Michael and Daniel Yarlett
   2007   Linguistic self-correction in the absence of feedback: A new approach to the logical problem of language acquisition. *Cognitive Science* 31(6): 927–960.
Ramscar, Michael, Daniel Yarlett, Melody Dye, Katie Denny and Kirsten Thorpe
   2010   The effects of feature-label-order and their implications for symbolic learning. *Cognitive Science* 34(6): 909–957.
Rescorla, Robert
   1988   Pavlovian conditioning. It's not what you think it is. *American Psychologist* 43(3): 151–160.
Rescorla, Robert and Allan Wagner
   1972   A theory of Pavlovian conditioning: Variations in the effectiveness of reinforcement and nonreinforcement. In: A. H. Black and W. F. Prokasy (eds.), *Classical Conditioning* II, 64–99. New York: Appleton-Century-Crofts.
Shannon, Claude
   1948   A mathematical theory of communication. *Bell System Technical Journal* 27: 379–423.
Shaoul, Cyrus, Chris Westbury, and R. Harald Baayen
   2013   The subjective frequency of word n-grams. *Psihologija* 46(4): 497–537.
Siegel, Shepard, and Lorraine Allan
   1996   The widespread influence of the Rescorla-Wagner model. *Psychonomic Bulletin and Review* 3(3): 314–321.
Skousen, Royal
   1989   *Analogical Modeling of Language*. Dordrecht: Kluwer.
Skousen, Royal
   2000   Analogical modeling and quantum computing. Los Alamos National Laboratory
Skousen, Royal
   2002   *Analogical Modeling*. Amsterdam: Benjamins.
Slobin, Dan
   1996   From 'thought to language' to 'thinking for speaking'. In: J. Gumperz and S. Levinson (eds.), *Rethinking Linguistic Relativity*, 70–96. Cambridge: Cambridge University Press.

Steels, Luc. and Joachim De Beule
　　2006　　A (very) brief introduction to fluid construction grammar. *Proceedings of the Third Workshop on Scalable Natural Language Understanding*, 73–80. New York, June 8th, 2006. Association for Computational Linguistics.
Tomasello, Michael
　　2009　　*Constructing a Language: A Usage-based Theory of Language Acquisition*. Cambridge: Harvard University Press.
Tremblay, Antoine and R. Harald Baayen
　　2010　　Holistic processing of regular four-word sequences: A behavioral and ERP study of the effects of structure, frequency, and probability on immediate free recall. In: D. Wood (ed.), *Perspectives on Formulaic Language: Acquisition and communication*, 151–173. London: Continuum.
Turner, Mark
　　this volume　　Blending in language and communication. Berlin/Boston: De Gruyter Mouton.
Veale, Tony, Diarmuid O'Donoghue and Mark Keane
　　2000　　Computation and blending. *Cognitive Linguistics* 11(3/4): 253–282.
Wieling, Martijn, John Nerbonne, Jelke Bloem, Charlotte Gooskens, Wilbert Heeringa and R. Harald Baayen
　　2014　　A cognitively grounded measure of pronunciation distance. *PloS One* 9(1): e75734.

R. Harald Baayen and Michael Ramscar, Tübingen (Germany)

6. Construal

1. Nature
2. Dimensions
3. Validation
4. References

1. Nature

Construal is our ability to conceive and portray the same situation in alternate ways. In cognitive linguistics, the term indicates an array of conceptual factors (such as *prominence*) shown to be relevant for lexical and semantic description. It underscores the role of conception in linguistic meaning, something denied even in semantics textbooks of the modern era (e.g., Palmer 1981: § 2.2).

An expression's meaning depends on both the conceptual *content* invoked and how that content is construed. Content is roughly comparable to truth conditions, a state of affairs, or the objective situation described; in a conceptualist semantics, it amounts to the neutral apprehension of a situation, conceived in its own terms. But since the world does not just imprint itself on our brains, conception is never really neutral – it consists in mental activity, being shaped by the previous experience, capabilities, and current state of the conceptualizer. Thus every conception and every linguistic expression construes the content invoked in a certain manner.

Content and construal are equally important aspects of the processing activity that constitutes linguistic meaning. They cannot be neatly separated (indeed, the selection of content is itself an aspect of construal). The rationale for distinguishing them is that the apprehension of a situation is more than just a representation of its elements. While content and construal are ultimately indissociable, the distinction draws attention to the flexibility of conception and the variability of expression even in regard to the same objective circumstances.

If cognition resides in neurological activity, it presents itself to us as mental experience. In principle we want to understand how the former gives rise to the latter, and certain dimensions of construal (e.g., *dynamicity*) can hardly be discussed without invoking processing factors. But in practical terms, the usual strategy is to start with conceptual experience as manifested in linguistic meaning and revealed through linguistic analysis. Working along these lines, cognitive linguists have noted that aspects of construal needed for describing language are analogous to basic aspects of visual perception. Talmy (1996) thus coined the term *ception* to cover both *per*ception and *con*ception. In Cognitive Grammar both are referred to as *viewing* (Langacker 1987: § 3.3, 1993a, 2008a: 261). Their extensive parallelism reflects the primacy of vision and the grounding of cognition in perceptual and motor interaction. It is not presumed that conception is exclusively visuospatial in origin. In fact, the dimensions of construal all have manifestations in other sensory modalities.

Construal encompasses numerous interrelated factors. While natural groupings can be observed, no one classificatory scheme captures all the relationships or does justice to a single factor. For instance, *immediate scope* – the general locus of attention – can equally well be discussed under the rubric of the *perspective* taken on a scene, the *selection* of conceptual content, or the relative *prominence* of conceived entities. The adoption of any particular classification is thus a matter of expository convenience. Rather than a definitive list or taxonomy, the objective of this chapter is to characterize construal factors with reasonable precision and investigate their linguistic manifestations.

2. Dimensions

The many aspects of construal will be considered under five broad headings: *perspective*, *selection*, *prominence*, *dynamicity*, and *imagination*. Like the factors they subsume, they overlap and all come into play in a given expression.

2.1. Perspective

Fundamental to conception is the asymmetry between its *subject* and its *object*. The subject (S) is the locus of neural activity through which it engages some facet of the world, the object (O). Activity mediated by receptor organs constitutes perceptual experience. The neural control of effective activity (instigation, proprioception, guidance) constitutes motor experience. As we construct our mental world, reaching progressively

(a) Conceptual Engagement (b) Mutual Apprehension (c) Intersubjectivity (d) Linguistic Interaction

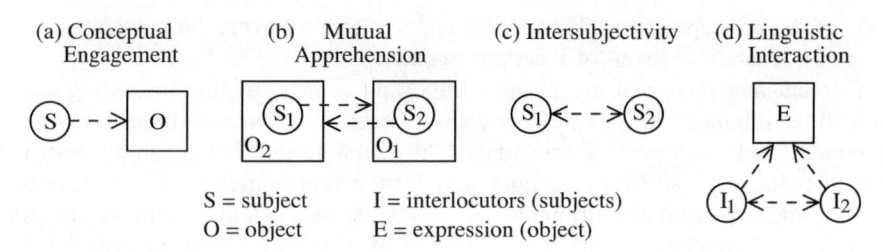

S = subject
O = object
I = interlocutors (subjects)
E = expression (object)

Fig. 6.1: Subject and object of conception

(a) Viewing Asymmetry (b) Canonical Expression (c) *I* (d) *you*

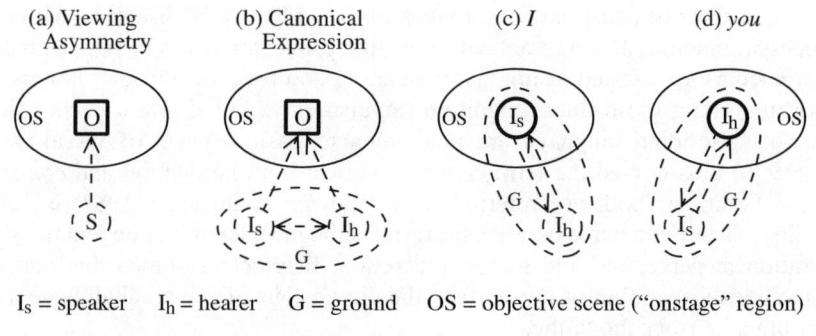

I_s = speaker I_h = hearer   G = ground   OS = objective scene ("onstage" region)

Fig. 6.2: "Onstage" vs. "offstage" elements

higher levels of abstraction and complexity, an increasing proportion of our experience is related only indirectly to perceptual and motor activity. But even when the object engaged is mentally constructed, it is still apprehended by a conceptualizing subject.

In an instance of conceptual engagement, the subject is by definition active (the locus of neural activity and experience), while the object (as such) merely functions as the target. Being social creatures, we recognize the existence of other conceptualizers, who engage us as objects just as we engage them. And through our further capacity for simulating another subject's experience, we achieve the intersubjective awareness crucial for cognitive development, language acquisition, and linguistic interaction. Canonical language use involves conceptual engagement in each of two dimensions. Along one axis the interlocutors engage one another, intersubjective awareness being one component of their interaction. Contributing to this awareness is their joint apprehension, along the other axis, of the expression's form and meaning.

Whereas the subject is *active*, the object is *salient* in the subject's experience. The subject apprehends the object but – *qua* subject – is not itself apprehended. So in contrast to the bird's-eye view of Figure 6.1(a), where S and O are equally prominent, the subject's actual experience is more akin to Figure 6.2(a), where only O has any salience. Metaphorically, we can speak of S being the offstage viewer and O the onstage entity being viewed. Status in regard to this asymmetry is one facet of an element's construal: S is construed *subjectively*, and O *objectively* (Langacker 2006).

This viewing asymmetry is reflected linguistically in the fact that the interlocutors – the joint subjects of conception – are always implicated in expressions even though they are commonly left implicit. In the canonical ("unmarked") case of third-person state-

6. Construal

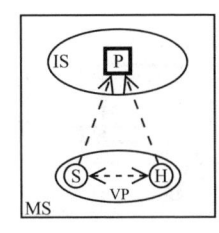

S = speaker
H = hearer
VP = vantage point
MS = maximal scope of conception
IS = immediate scope (onstage region)
P = profile (focus of attention)

Fig. 6.3: Canonical viewing arrangement

ments, e.g., *She bought an iPad*, the interlocutors and their interaction are external to the *objective scene*, i.e., the situation described. These offstage entities are nonetheless essential to the expression's meaning, defining the deictic center and providing the basis for person, tense, and illocutionary force. They constitute the *ground*.

The semantic import of the ground is more evident in expressions that depart from the canon, e.g., with speech acts other than simple statement. A very common departure is for the situation described to include some portion of the ground. Most obviously, a pronoun like *I* or *you* makes an interlocutor explicit, in which case it functions not only as a subject of conception but also as the object – both directly (for the other interlocutor) and indirectly (via simulation of the other's experience) (Langacker 2007). Performatives (e.g., *I order you [to stop]*) represent the extreme case of overlap, where the objective scene and the speaker-hearer interaction coincide (Austin 1962; Langacker 2008a: 469–470).

In addition to its salient onstage elements, an expression's meaning includes a *viewing arrangement*. Its canonical form is sketched in Figure 6.3, which introduces two additional perspectival factors: *vantage point* and *scope*. A vantage point is the location from which a situation is apprehended. In the canonical arrangement, the interlocutors are together in space as well as time, viewing the objective scene from the same vantage point offstage. Scope pertains to conceptual content: the extent of the content invoked and degrees of centrality imposed by viewing. The *maximal scope* is all the content that figures in an expression's meaning, even if only peripherally. Within that, the *immediate scope* is the portion being attended to (the onstage region). And within the immediate scope, the expression's *profile* is maximally prominent as the specific *focus* of attention. These notions have counterparts in vision: the maximal field of view is everything visible from a certain vantage point; within that is the region being looked at (the stage); and in that region a particular element stands out as the focus of attention. For language we are mainly concerned with their general conceptual analogs.

Analogs of spatial vantage point can be recognized for time and for other domains, e.g., a kinship network, where one's position determines who to address with terms like *father*, *uncle*, or *grandma*. Expressions differ as to how centrally vantage point figures in their meaning. For some it is peripheral in that the same description applies from any vantage point: Denver can be described as a *city*, or as being *in Colorado*, from any location. At the other extreme are cases where vantage point is crucial. It is only its relation to a temporal vantage point that distinguishes *yesterday* from any other day. Whether something is *on the left* or *on the right* depends on both vantage point and the related factor of *orientation*. This too has non-spatial analogs. What distinguishes *yester-*

(a) *yesterday* (b) *tomorrow* (c) *the next day*

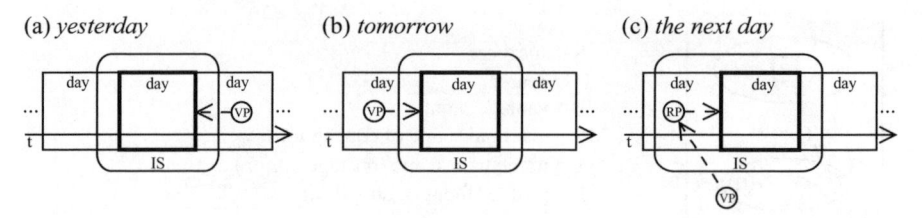

Fig. 6.4: Temporal vantage point and reference point

day from *tomorrow* is whether the viewer focuses attention on the adjacent day while oriented toward the past or toward the future.

Multiple viewers and vantage points figure in all but the simplest expressions (Langacker 2008a: § 12.3.2). The interlocutors recognize other viewers (including each other) and to some extent simulate their experience. Their actual position in the ground therefore functions not only as the default-case vantage point, but also as point of departure for invoking and simulating others. Expressions vary in the extent to which viewing is invoked and the strength of its association with the ground. For example, *tomorrow* consistently invokes the actual ground (except in special discourse modes). Normally a successor day is specified periphrastically with a non-deictic locution: *She delivered her lecture and left {the next day / *tomorrow}*. As shown in Figure 6.4(c), such locutions invoke an onstage temporal *reference point* (RP) whose relationship to the day in question is apprehended from an external vantage point.

The notions vantage point and reference point are distinct but closely related. By definition, a vantage point is the location from which a situation is apprehended (hence offstage for the viewer in question), whereas a reference point is part of that situation, invoked in order to mentally access an onstage target (Langacker 1993b). In *Bill's father*, for example, Bill functions as reference point for the target *father*, with the interlocutors as viewers. Given the overall objective of relating the target to the viewer, it is natural and efficient for the viewer itself to be invoked as the basis for computing the relationship. There is then no separate or explicit reference point, the offstage viewer assuming its role: to indicate her own male parent, the speaker need only say *father*. Alternatively, the speaker can go onstage, describing the relationship from the standpoint of an external viewer: *my father*. The same options are available for spatial reference points: *She lives across the hall from Bill* (with Bill onstage as RP) vs. *She lives across the hall from me* (with the speaker onstage as RP) vs. *She lives across the hall* (described from the speaker's offstage VP).

As for construal in general, the same perspectival factors are important for both lexicon and grammar. Consider immediate scope: the array of conceptual content attended to as the direct basis for apprehending an expression's profile (focus of attention), hence the immediate context for this purpose. While the boundary may be fuzzy, the immediate scope is limited in extent. For example, a kinship network extends indefinitely, but the lexeme *father* directly invokes just a small portion (what we call the *immediate family*), and *uncle* a slightly larger one. The lexical import of immediate scope is clearly evident in whole-part hierarchies, notably with body-part expressions, e.g., *body* > *leg* > *foot* > *toe*. Although a toe is part of the body, the direct basis for its characterization is the conception of a foot, which in turn is characterized directly in relation to a leg.

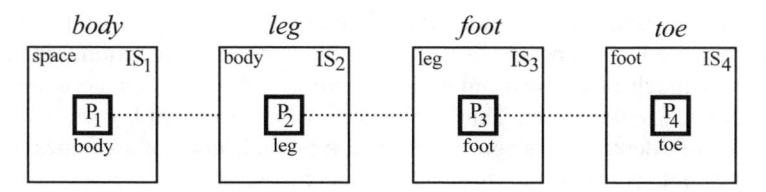

body	leg	foot	toe
space IS$_1$ / P$_1$ / body	body IS$_2$ / P$_2$ / leg	leg IS$_3$ / P$_3$ / foot	foot IS$_4$ / P$_4$ / toe

Fig. 6.5: Immediate scope relations

The lexical meanings are thus related as in Figure 6.5, where the profile of each expression functions as immediate scope for the next. Precisely analogous relationships function grammatically in a general compounding pattern, whereby $N_1 + N_2$ describes an immediate part of N_1. Responsible for a large number of lexicalized expressions (e.g., *fingertip, asshole, windowpane, car seat*), it also sanctions novel combinations (*toetip, nosehole, doorpane, truck seat*).

The progression *body > leg > foot > toe* illustrates another perspectival factor, the distinction (always relative) between a *global view* of a situation and a *local view* subsuming only part of it. This correlates with *scale*: *head, torso, arm*, and *leg* designate large-scale components of the body, evident in a global conception; *thigh, knee, calf, ankle*, and *foot* refer to smaller-scale components, more salient in a local view comprising just the leg.

Additional perspectival factors involve departures from the canonical viewing arrangement. As already noted, it is common for the ground and immediate scope to overlap, some facet of the ground being put onstage as an explicit object of description. Departing more drastically from the canon are cases where the interlocutors are separated in space – as in speaking by phone – or even time. Consider the following message on an answering machine: *I'm not here today. Try calling again tomorrow.* In canonical circumstances, *I'm not here* is contradictory (by definition, *here* is where I am). But the speaker is describing things from the temporal vantage point of an imagined later caller, when she expects to be elsewhere. *Today* and *tomorrow* are likewise relative to the time of calling.

Such examples make the obvious point that the presupposed viewing arrangement determines what it makes sense to say and how to say it. Normally, for instance, it makes no sense for towns to be described as *frequent*. But it is perfectly natural to say *The towns are getting less frequent* when the viewers are moving rather than stationary – another common departure from the canon.

2.2. Selection

Selection stems from the disparity between the vast complexity of our mental world and the severe limits on our processing capacity. It is therefore fundamental: if we had to describe everything, we could never describe anything. It is also ubiquitous, as everything expressed stands out against the backdrop of indefinitely much that is not expressed. Content selected for expression is never autonomous or self-contained, but embedded in an elaborate *conceptual substrate* comprising presupposed and associated knowledge (Langacker 2008a). Linguistic coding serves not to remove it from this substrate, but to activate it and make it accessible.

Every expression omits much more than it explicitly conveys. For the most part omission is not a matter of specific intent but a by-product of attention: since we can attend to only so much at a given moment, everything else is either peripheral to our awareness or outside it altogether. Thus the degrees of centrality in Figure 6.3 – organization into focus of attention, onstage region, and maximal scope of awareness – are not only perspectival but represent the most basic aspect of selection.

When a situation has been chosen for description, additional selective factors come into play. One is the level of *specificity* (or its converse, *schematicity*) at which the onstage content is characterized. It is a matter of "resolution" or "granularity": whether the situation is described in fine-grained detail or only in coarse-grained terms. This aspect of construal is manifested lexically in hierarchies such as *thing > creature > person > female > girl*, where each expression is schematic relative to the one that follows. Of course, specificity can also be achieved periphrastically, through longer descriptions (e.g., *young human female* for *girl*). Degree of specificity is one of the grounds for distinguishing lexicon and grammar (cf. Talmy 1988; Boye and Harder 2012). By and large, elements toward the grammatical end of the spectrum are quite schematic, their main import residing in the construal imposed on lexical content. For instance, progressive *-ing* is perspectival, its meaning residing in the immediate temporal scope imposed on the event designated by a verb stem (excluding its endpoints). A grammatical construction (e.g., *V + -ing*) is schematic vis-à-vis the specific content of instantiating expressions (*working, examining*, etc.); it is simply their reinforced commonality, hence immanent in them.

Another factor is the choice of *profile*, the focus of attention within the immediate scope. Although profiling is a kind of prominence, its selective aspect merits separate discussion. A key point is that meaning comprises considerably more than explicitly coded content, even in regard to the objective scene. Overtly mentioned elements are neither free-standing nor exhaustive of the situation described, but are embedded in a substrate providing the basis for a coherent interpretation. Reference to a single element may then be sufficient to evoke the entire conceptual complex. When multiple elements are capable of doing so, the speaker selects a particular element for explicit mention, so that it functions as point of access to the remainder. We speak of *metonymy* in cases where an entity accessed only secondarily, via this point of reference, is nonetheless pivotal for some evident purpose.

Metonymy reflects the general strategy of focusing entities that are salient or easily accessible, relying on the substrate for essential content left implicit. It thereby achieves both processing ease and coding efficiency. While conversing in a parking lot, *I'm over there* provides a natural, compact alternative to *My car is parked over there*. But it is not just a matter of efficiency, as the former frames the situation in terms of the speaker's experience and projected movement. It represents an alternative construal which has the advantage of conferring linguistic prominence on items of greater intrinsic interest.

Metonymic construal is pervasive in lexicon and grammar (Kövecses and Radden 1998; Panther and Radden 2004; Panther et al. 2009; Barcelona this volume). Non-explicit content is commonly invoked for grammatical composition. The verb *park*, for instance, profiles a telic event of brief duration: *She parked the car in a jiffy*. But since the car is expected to stay there for a while, *park* can also occur with adverbials specifying the duration of a stable situation: *You can park here for two hours*. Through conventionalization, this shift in focus produces a new lexical sense, so that *park* can mean either '**put** (and keep) in place' or '(put and) **keep** in place'. Alternative profiling is a major source of lexical polysemy (Gries this volume). In a car you can *roll down the window* (the glass pane), and if the door is broken you can *crawl out through the window* (the opening). Relational expressions are commonly polysemic in regard to the choice of focused participant, e.g., *hear a **car*** vs. *hear the **sound** of a car*. Respectively, these view the profiled relationship in terms of the element with greater cognitive salience vs. the one that figures in it more directly (Langacker 1990: ch. 7).

2.3. Prominence

Many kinds of prominence need to be differentiated for linguistic purposes (Tomlin and Myachykov this volume). We can first distinguish between inherent prominence and that conferred by linguistic means. Included in the former are the privileged cognitive statuses of space and vision, as well as salience asymmetries such as concrete vs. abstract, human vs. non-human, whole vs. part. Linguistic prominence has both phonological and semantic components. For phonology, obvious examples are accent and degrees of sonority. Relevant for construal are various types of semantic prominence and their manifestations in lexicon and grammar.

In sorting these out, it is useful to begin with the fundamental asymmetry between the subject and the object of conception. By nature it is a prominence asymmetry: being the onstage focus of attention, the object is highly salient, whereas the subject (when functioning exclusively as such) has no salience whatever, for it is not itself conceived. Attention is not the only source of prominence, however. The focus of attention is salient *within* the conception, as part of the conceptual experience. But we also speak of salience in regard to factors responsible for shaping that experience. Frequent, well-entrenched linguistic units are salient in the sense of being easily activated. Prototypes are prominent within their categories. Conceptual archetypes motivate basic aspects of language structure. Inhering in the subject's cognitive organization, these sorts of prominence are offstage and not per se apprehended, but are matters of *accessibility* and *degree of influence* in the shaping of onstage content.

Both onstage prominence (salience within a conception) and offstage prominence (accessibility/influence in shaping a conception) involve a central element and others that are more peripheral. Characterized as the onstage focus of attention, an expression's profile is central within the conception evoked as its meaning. The profile stands out as salient within the immediate scope (the content directly relevant to its apprehension), which defines the onstage region. But since meanings are never self-contained, the onstage conception recruits or elicits others, which in turn invoke still others, as shown for *toe* in Figure 6.6. The focused element is thus embedded in a substrate that extends indefinitely with diminishing levels of salience.

The offstage region centers on the subject of conception. As the very locus of experience (and the activity constituting it), the subject could not be more accessible and influential in shaping the apprehension of onstage content. Organized around it are several other kinds of offstage elements with varying degrees of prominence. Still quite central, in the sense of inhering in the subject, are the mental resources exploited in conception: a vast array of established structures (including linguistic units) whose differential

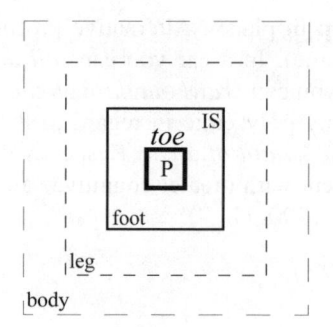

Fig. 6.6: Degrees of onstage prominence

salience consists in their ease and likelihood of activation. More extrinsic to the subject are the ground and the discourse context. Being primarily responsible for constructing an expression, the speaker is central to the ground: her own experience is real and immediate, the hearer's being accessible only via mental simulation. However, both interlocutors function as subjects, and each simulates the other's experience, so jointly they comprise a higher-level subject engaged in intersubjectively apprehending the ground and the wider context. An important facet of the context is the ongoing discourse. Along the discursive axis, the expression currently being processed is onstage by virtue of being attended to. When the next one comes along it is pushed offstage, becoming a shared resource employed by the interlocutors in processing the new one. Its offstage salience depends on recency: the most recent expression is generally the most accessible and has the greatest influence in shaping the new one.

Distinguishing onstage and offstage prominence resolves the conundrum of the speaker and the ground being both non-salient (usually not even mentioned) and highly prominent (in that everything revolves around them): it is just a matter of their onstage salience being minimized, and their offstage salience maximized, in the canonical viewing arrangement. Owing to their offstage salience, an implicit vantage point is normally identified with that of the speaker or the ground, as in *She lives across the hall*. The semantic contrast with *She lives across the hall from me* – less canonical because the speaker is construed objectively – nicely illustrates the distinction between offstage and onstage prominence. Further illustration is provided by discourse topics. When first introduced, a topic is made explicit as a salient onstage element (*She has **a good job** ...*). Once established, a topic is often left implicit but is still invoked, due to its offstage salience, as the basis for interpreting what follows (*... There's no pressure, and the benefits are excellent*).

To be mentioned explicitly is to be *profiled* by some expression. An essential factor in onstage prominence, profiling is the intersubjective focusing of attention induced by symbolization: through the directive force of symbolic expression, the interlocutors momentarily attend to the same entity in the objective scene. An expression's profile is thus its *conceptual referent* – the entity it designates or refers to within the array of content invoked (the *base*).

As described in Cognitive Grammar, expressions can profile either *things* or *relationships* (both abstractly defined). A few examples of the former are sketched in Figure 6.7. (As standard notational conventions, the profile is shown in bold, with circles often

6. Construal   129

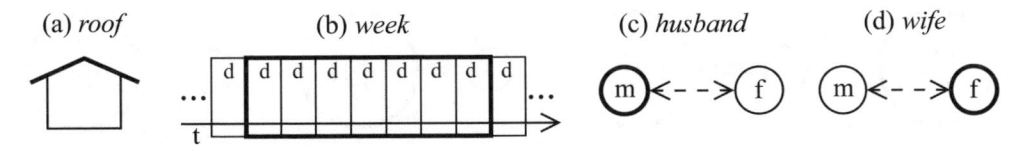

(a) *roof*   (b) *week*   (c) *husband*   (d) *wife*

Fig. 6.7: Examples of profiled things

used for things, and lines or arrows for relationships.) *Roof* evokes as its base the conception of a house or building, within which it profiles the covering part on top. *Week* designates any sequence of seven consecutive days. *Husband* and *wife* profile the male and female participants in a relationship of marriage. Observe that these latter expressions have the same essential content, referring to different elements within the same conceptual base. Their semantic opposition can only be ascribed to the difference in profiling.

Some examples of profiled relationships are sketched in Figure 6.8. *Tall* situates a thing on a scale of height. *Above* and *below* locate two things in relation to one another along the vertical axis. While they commonly endure, these relationships are fully manifested at a single point in time (hence observable in a photograph). By contrast, other expressions construe the profiled relationship as evolving along the temporal axis, so that a span of time is required for its full manifestation. Thus *fall* tracks through time the changing location of a single thing along the vertical axis.

Profiling is pivotal to a basic proposal of Cognitive Grammar which linguists are strongly inclined to resist (Hudson 1992; cf. Langacker 2013): that basic grammatical categories are susceptible to general conceptual characterization (Langacker 2008a: ch. 4). Very roughly, it is claimed that a noun profiles a thing, a verb profiles a "process" – a relationship tracked through time – while adjectives, adverbs, and prepositions profile non-processual relationships. The validity of this claim is not at issue here. It is however evident that an expression's category specifically reflects its profile, not its overall (or even its most important) conceptual content. For example, *husband* and *wife* are nouns because they profile things, even though the essential content is a relationship in which they participate.

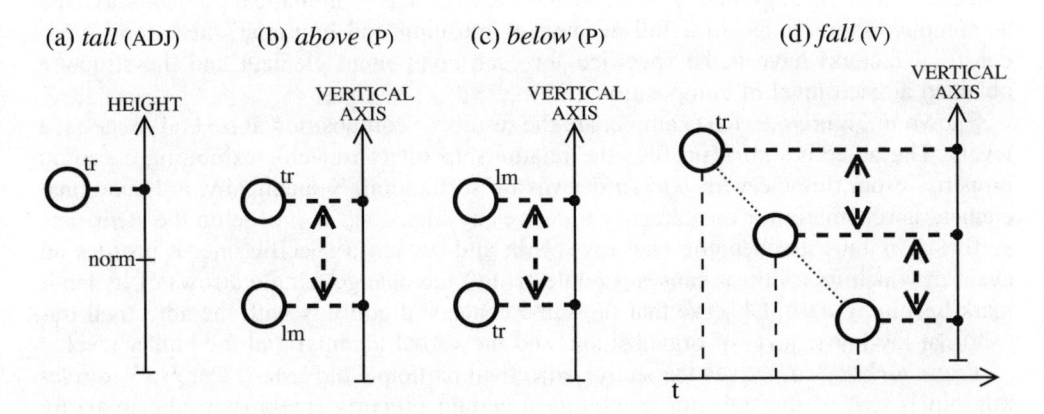

(a) *tall* (ADJ)   (b) *above* (P)   (c) *below* (P)   (d) *fall* (V)

Fig. 6.8: Examples of profiled relationships

dark	>	darken	>	darkened	>	darkened room
ADJ		V		PRTC (ADJ)		N

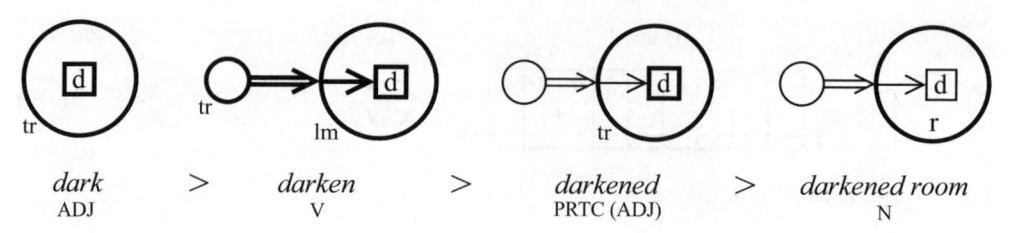

Fig. 6.9: Profiling and focal participants at successive levels of organization

Profiling is the focusing of attention through symbolic reference. Expressions that profile relationships involve an additional sort of focal prominence pertaining to participants. A relationship is *conceptually dependent* on its participants, i.e., they are inherent in its conception. Within a profiled relationship, a single participant is usually made salient as the one being assessed in regard to location, properties, or activity. This primary focal participant is called the *trajector* (tr). There is often a secondary focal participant, called a *landmark* (lm), with a salient role in assessing the trajector. The relationship profiled by an adjective (like *tall*) or an intransitive verb (*fall*) has just one focused participant, which is thus the trajector, whereas prepositions and transitive verbs have both a trajector and a landmark. As with profiling, trajector/landmark alignment may be solely responsible for a difference in meaning. For example, *above* and *below* have the same content and profile the same spatial relationship; the semantic distinction is just a matter of whether trajector status (as the participant being located) is conferred on the higher or the lower participant.

Like profiling, trajector/landmark alignment is necessary for semantic description but also has an important role in grammar. As proposed in Cognitive Grammar, it figures in the conceptual characterization of basic categories: what distinguishes adjectives and adverbs is whether their trajector is a thing or a relationship; prepositions are neutral in this respect (so prepositional phrases can function in either capacity) but differ by having a thing as their landmark. It is further proposed that trajector and landmark provide a general conceptual basis for the grammatical notions subject and object (Langacker 2008a: § 11.2). While these claims are controversial, it is evident that profiling and trajector/landmark alignment pertain to both lexical and grammatical elements as well as complex expressions. In a full account of meaning and grammar, these (and other construal factors) have to be specified for each component element and the structure obtained at each level of composition.

Shown in Figure 6.9, for example, are the results of composition at several successive levels. The adjective *dark* profiles the relationship of its trajector exhibiting a certain property. From this the verb *darken* derives by suffixation. Semantically, a derivational element is schematic for the category it derives by imposing its profile on the stem. The suffix *-en* is thus a schematic causative verb, and *darken* a specific one: it profiles an event in which its trajector causes (double arrow) the change (single arrow) of its landmark becoming dark. Observe that the same conceived entity is both the adjectival trajector, at the lower level of organization, and the verbal landmark, at the higher level.

From *darken*, *-ed* derives the stative-adjectival participle *darkened*. The profiled relationship is that of the trajector exhibiting a certain property (making it adjectival) by virtue of having undergone a change of state (unprofiled at this level). Thus *dark* and *darkened* profile the same relationship, with the same trajector, but differ in meaning because the latter specifically portrays this as resulting from the process *darken*. Finally, in *darkened room* the adjectival participle combines with a noun, which specifies its schematic trajector and imposes its nominal profile on the composite expression. *Room* is the *head* in the sense of determining the profile – hence the grammatical category – of the whole: *darkened room* functions as a complex noun (not an adjective).

2.4. Dynamicity

Language and conception are things that *happen*. Consisting in patterns of activity, they unfold through *time*, and the specific way in which they do so – their *time course* – is essential. Despite its inherent seriality, the processing involved does not reduce to a single linear sequence. It runs concurrently in different dimensions, at different levels of organization, and on different time scales (from the coordination of articulatory gestures to global discourse planning). It is organized hierarchically when elements that on one time scale are accessed sequentially, in separate processing windows, function as a single element in a window on a larger time scale. Additional departures from strict linearity are recall, anticipation, backtracking, and the interruption of one processing task by another.

Time has different linguistic roles. A fundamental distinction pertains to the subject vs. the object of conception. *Processing time* (T) inheres in the subject's activity: it is time as the medium of conception, through which processing occurs. Processing of even the smallest element has some duration, however brief. Conception occurs through time regardless of whether time per se figures in its content. To the extent that it does, it assumes the role of *conceived time* (t): time as an object of conception.

A conception unfolds through processing time in a certain manner, even in a non-linguistic task where conceived time is not a factor (e.g., observing the objects in a static array). On a small enough time scale, its elements are activated in some sequence, each with some duration, and need not all be active at any one instant. The *path of access* defined by this ordering is one facet (however minor) of the mental experience. Thus different paths of access to the same conceptual content constitute alternate ways of construing it.

As an aspect of linguistic meaning, sequential access has varied sources and functions. A very general source is symbolization. Because sounds evoke the associated meanings (and conversely), the order of symbolic elements induces the corresponding order of conception as one facet of the overall processing activity. The semantic effect of different orders may be quite minimal (even vacuous) in terms of the situation described. But it is never wholly negligible: the conceptions evoked by *X Y* and *Y X* are less than fully identical if only due to their components being accessed in different sequences.

As a matter of processing efficiency, the order of presentation tends to follow *natural paths* of mental access, such as causal chains, paths of motion, event sequences, established associations, and rankings for salience or other properties. While it need not (and cannot) align with all such paths, one that does mesh with the order of expression is reinforced by this iconicity. A sequence of elements that could represent a natural ordering thus invites the inference that it does: *She went to Denver, Boston, and Miami* suggests that Denver was the first stop, Miami the last. To varying degrees the alignment of expression with a natural path is established as part of the conventional import of particular constructions. For instance, a conventional pattern of English specifies location by "zooming in" to smaller and smaller areas: *It's in the garage, in the cabinet, on the top shelf, behind some paint cans.* Established to a lesser degree is the alternative of "zooming out" to larger and larger areas: *It's behind some paint cans, on the top shelf, in the cabinet, in the garage.* With either construction one follows a natural path of access obtained by successively contracting or expanding the immediate spatial scope. The two paths represent alternate construals of the same situation. The example shows that a natural path aligned with the order of expression need not be based on conceived time. Nor does order of expression have to be used iconically: like segmental content, it can participate in essentially arbitrary symbolic pairings (e.g., to mark grammatical relationships).

Within a symbolized conception, time (t) has a number of different roles with varying degrees of centrality. It may be effectively absent, as in the minimal apprehension of an object (*cup*), property (*blue*), or configuration (*above*). But time is too fundamental to be easily avoided altogether. It enters the picture with the evocation of events, even as part of background knowledge (e.g., the use of a cup for drinking). Its role is less peripheral with a verb or a clause, which profiles a relationship specifically viewed as evolving through time, either a bounded event (*fall*) or a state of indefinite duration (*resemble*). More central is its role as the domain in which a profiled relationship is manifested; for example, time is the domain for *before* and *after* in the same way that space is for *above* and *below*. Finally, time itself – or some instantiation of time – can itself be the profiled entity: *time, period, week* (cf. Evans 2004, this volume).

Though essential for a verb or a clause, conceived time is not itself the focus of attention, nor even the most central domain. The focus is the profiled relationship, which is usually spatial or at least non-temporal. Time figures at a higher level of conceptual organization, where the profiled relationship is followed in its temporal evolution. This is shown for *fall* in Figure 6.10: through time (t), the mover occupies a series of successively lower positions along the vertical axis. Their distribution through time is crucial:

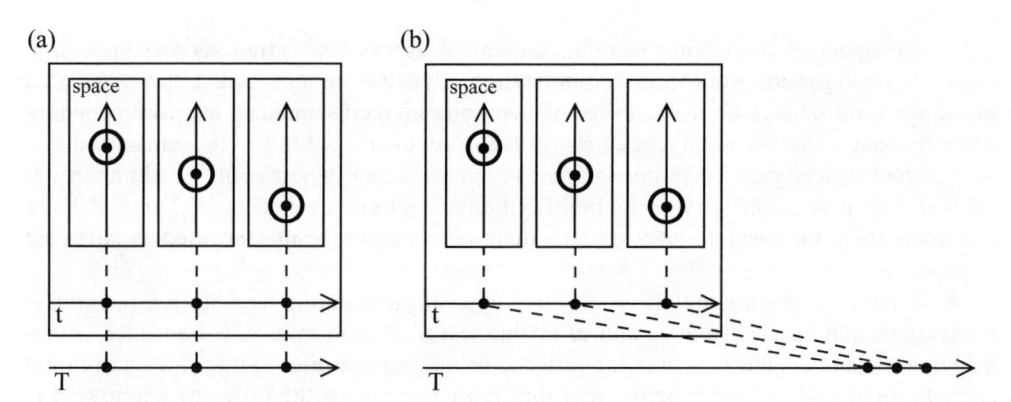

Fig. 6.10: Sequential scanning

6. Construal   133

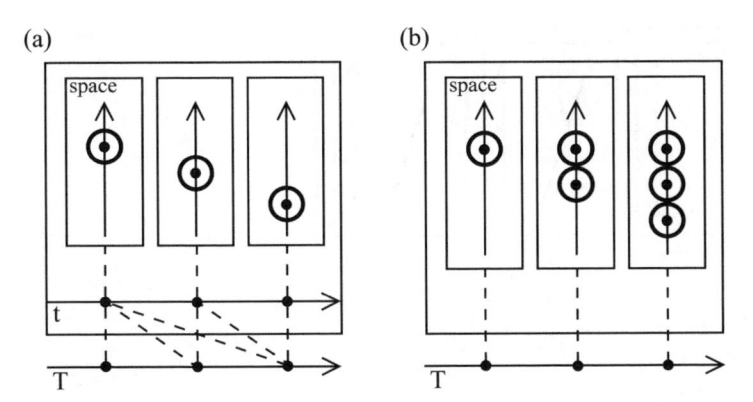

Fig. 6.11: Summation

without it, nothing would distinguish *fall* from *rise*. This inherent dimension of organization constitutes a natural path of mental access. It is thus proposed in Cognitive Grammar that the temporal phases of a verbal process are accessed ("scanned") sequentially as one aspect of its apprehension, so that conceived time correlates with processing time (T). This accords with a general hypothesis that any conception of ordering or directionality resides in sequenced mental activity at some level of processing (Langacker 1990: ch. 5).

When an event is directly observed, its apprehension coincides with its occurrence: its temporal phases are accessed serially, each being fully activated just when it is manifested. In this case conceived time and processing time are effectively equivalent, as in Figure 6.10(a). Usually, though, an event's occurrence and its apprehension in describing it linguistically are non-coincident, as shown in (b). In this case conceived and processing time clearly need to be distinguished. Occurrence and conception being independent, they normally differ in duration. There is however a correspondence, as the event's characterization requires that its phases be accessed (through T) in the sequence of their manifestation (through t). This sequential scanning of the event constitutes a mental simulation of its observation (Langacker 2008b).

Importantly, our apprehension of events is not exclusively sequential. We can also view them holistically through *summation*, represented by the additional dashed lines in Figure 6.11(a). These indicate that a temporal phase of the event, once activated at a given point in T, remains active as subsequent phases are processed. The resulting conceptual experience is sketched in Figure 6.11(b): each successive configuration is superimposed on those already active, until they are all active simultaneously, as in a multiple-exposure photograph. This increasingly complex configuration is solely a product of conception (in T), not taken to be an objective occurrence, so t is omitted from the diagram. Summation may well coexist with sequential scanning, perhaps emerging as a by-product. In any case, it comes to the fore when a verb's inherent sequentiality is overridden at higher levels of grammatical organization. It is claimed in Cognitive Grammar that holistic construal is one factor in the formation of infinitives (*to fall*), participles (*falling, fallen*), and derived nouns (*[a] fall*), which are therefore non-processual despite their verbal origin (Langacker 1991).

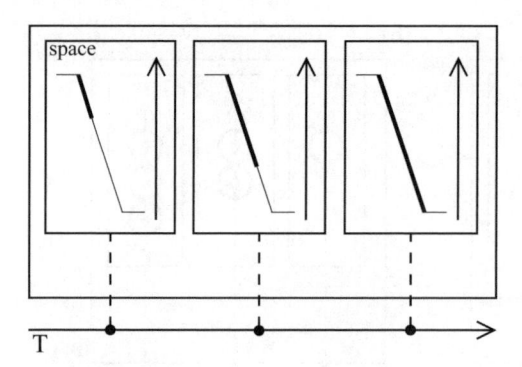

Fig. 6.12: Fictive motion

Summation can also be applied to static scenes. The result is *fictive motion* (Langacker 1990: ch. 5; Talmy 1996; Matsumoto 1996; Matlock 2004; Matlock and Bergmann this volume), where a motion verb occurs even though, objectively, nothing moves. Such expressions, e.g., *The cliff falls steeply to the valley floor*, describe the shape of entities having sufficient spatial extension to occupy all the points along a path at one time (t). The motion involved is subjective: the conceptualizer scans mentally along this path, building up a more and more elaborate structure, until arriving at a full conception of its shape. As shown in Figure 6.12, the conceptual experience is that of the cliff "growing" downward through processing time (with *rise*, of course, it grows upward instead).

Fictive motion is one of many linguistic phenomena effecting the dynamic construal of static situations. To cite just one more case, certain adverbs whose basic sense pertains to conceived time can instead be interpreted with respect to processing time. For example, *already* normally indicates that something happens earlier than expected: *It's already getting dark*. But it is also used in regard to stable circumstances: *Forget about algebra and calculus – arithmetic is already beyond me*. The import of *already* is quite comparable in this use. The main difference is that the event it concerns – what happens earlier than expected – is not an objective occurrence (in t) but consists in mental processing (through T). The expression invokes a scale on which mathematical subjects are ranked for difficulty. It indicates that, in scanning upward along this scale, a subject too difficult for the speaker is encountered sooner than might be anticipated.

A final point is that sequential access (through T) constitutes the essential semantic import of various grammatical notions. Prime examples are topic, anaphoric, and (at the most schematic level) possessive relationships, which share the essential feature of invoking one conceived entity as a *reference point* affording mental access to another (Langacker 2008a: §14.1). For instance, a topic relation has no objective content – it is not per se a facet of the situation described. Instead it pertains to how the onstage content is accessed and apprehended: by evoking associated knowledge, a topic allows the comment clause to be properly interpreted. Because it represents a natural path of mental access, the progression from topic to comment tends to align with the order of presentation: *Your daughter, she's very talented*. But natural paths do not always co-align, nor does language processing reduce to a single linear sequence. So while it may be less efficient, the non-congruent order is often possible: *She's very talented, your daughter*.

In this case apprehension of the topic-comment relationship, instead of coinciding with phonological expression, has to be effected post hoc (a kind of backtracking).

2.5. Imagination

All cognition is imaginative in the sense that the world as we experience it (including what we accept as the "real world") is mentally constructed. Far from being a passive mirror of reality, the mind consists in non-determinate processing activity which inherently imposes some construal on whatever is apprehended. In labeling certain conceptions as "fictive", "virtual", or "imaginative", we presuppose a contrast with others that are not. While this is a relative matter, with no clear line of demarcation, certain kinds of experience – notably the direct observation of physical objects and events – clearly have a privileged status. From this *baseline* we build up our mental world through many levels of conceptual elaboration. It is suggested that baseline and imaginative conceptions rely on the same basic mental capacities: *extensionality, integration, disengagement*, and *abstraction*.

By *extensionality* is meant the capacity for entertaining multiple entities as part of a single experience (in the same "representational space" or "processing window"). They are then subject to mental operations which serve to connect them and thereby effect their conceptual *integration*. In a temporal processing window, for example, a series of syllables is perceived as a word by virtue of prosodic grouping and phonetic integration. Two objects appearing in the visual field are connected by operations (assessments of distance, orientation, etc.) comprising a spatial relationship. And in processing windows of various sizes, simpler symbolic structures are integrated – semantically and phonologically – to form composite expressions. Plausibly analyzed as higher-level analogs of these capacities are some pervasive and fundamental imaginative phenomena: *mental spaces*, *metaphor*, and *blending* (Fauconnier 1985; Lakoff and Johnson 1980; Fauconnier and Turner 2002; Turner this volume).

Mental spaces are separate conceptual "working areas", each hosting a limited array of content which has its own status and function within the global conception that encompasses them. They are largely imaginative, representing myriad departures from baseline reality: fictional worlds; hypothetical situations; abstracted generalizations; projected future occurrences; the thoughts, beliefs, and desires of other conceptualizers; and so on. Spaces are connected through natural paths of access and correspondences between their elements. For example, *If Bill had a watch he would break it* defines an access path leading from the speaker's conception of reality, to the counterfactual situation of Bill having a watch, and then to the imagined event – predictable from this situation – of his breaking it. These spaces are further connected by correspondences. Bill is an element of all three spaces: accepted by the speaker as a real individual, he is also identified as the person who has a watch and who breaks it. The watch is only fictive, being introduced as part of the counterfactual situation, but figures as well in the predicted consequence.

Within each space, elements are connected by correspondences effecting their conceptual integration. In the counterfactual situation, for instance, Bill is identified with *have*'s trajector, and the watch with its landmark. But the same is true at a higher level of organization, where the spaces are connected to form a space configuration. Apprehen-

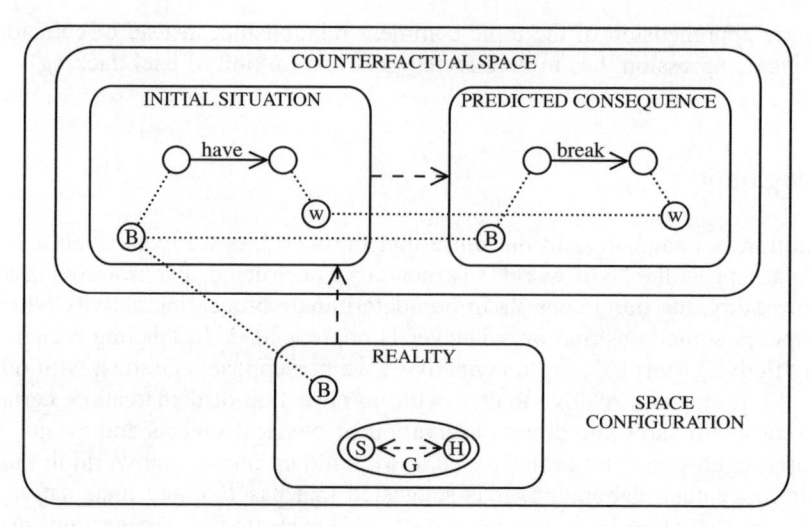

Fig. 6.13: A mental space configuration

sion of this higher-order structure requires a more inclusive representational space (a processing window on a larger time scale) with sufficient extensionality for connections to be established. For the example in question, the overall space configuration is sketched in Figure 6.13, where boxes delimit mental spaces, and dashed arrows indicate a path of mental access. While conceptual integration is naturally looser at this higher level, the configuration is a coherent structure in its own right: the initial situation and predicted occurrence are subspaces within the overarching counterfactual space, which (despite some overlap) is distinct from the speaker's conception of reality.

Metaphor and blending represent particular kinds of mental space configurations. In metaphor (Gibbs this volume), the *source* and *target domains* are spaces connected by mappings between their elements. As the terms suggest, the space configuration involves a functional asymmetry with inherent directionality: whereas the target is the actual object of description, it is mentally accessed via the source, which offers a structural analogy (perceived or imposed) for its apprehension (Gentner 1983; Lakoff 1990). Co-activation of the source and target produces a new conception with features of both: that of the target as structured by the source. Metaphor can thus be viewed as a case of blending. Defined more broadly, blending consists in selected elements from two *input spaces* being projected as elements of another space (the *blend*) with its own structure and emergent properties. A blend is always imaginative at least in the sense of being distinct from both inputs, e.g., brunch is not quite the same as either breakfast or lunch. Likewise, a corporation construed metaphorically as a person is not equivalent to either one.

The role of these phenomena in constructing our mental world could hardly be exaggerated. Equally important are the related capacities of disengagement and abstraction. We can speak of *disengagement* when processing activity that originates in a certain context is later carried out independently of that context. A prime example is sensory and motor *imagery*, consisting in the partial autonomous occurrence of activity responsible for perception and motor action (Shepard 1978; Kosslyn 1980). This is an important component of lexical meaning (e.g., *bell* invokes an auditory image, *grasp* a motor image). More generally, disengagement manifests as *mental simulation* (Bergen 2012), the presumed basis of numerous essential phenomena. Among these are recall (the simulation of a previous experience), the projection of future events, the ability to adopt a non-actual vantage point, as well as to apprehend the experience of other conceptualizers. Disengagement is also the crucial factor in fictive motion (e.g., *the cliff falls steeply*). In apprehending actual motion, the conceptualizer scans mentally through both space and conceived time. As shown in Figures 6.11 and 6.12, fictive motion results when the spatial scanning is disengaged from the latter, applying instead to the conception of a static shape.

Abstraction refers to the loss of information inherent in the formation of any kind of mental representation. A memory, concept, or semantic structure is necessarily impoverished relative to the full, rich, specific detail of the original experience it is based on. An abstracted structure can be impoverished in regard to either its internal characterization or its place within a more inclusive context. A typical lexeme, e.g., *bird*, is quite limited in both respects. On the one hand, its characterization abstracts away from the specific features distinguishing different kinds of birds. Even terms for particular species and varieties (e.g., *ruby-throated hummingbird*) are schematic vis-à-vis the fine-grained conception of actual instances. On the other hand, a lexeme represents a *type* rather than an *instance* of that type. The type conception symbolized by *bird* abstracts away from the external circumstances allowing instances to be differentiated and identified (e.g., *this bird* vs. *that bird*).

As described in Cognitive Grammar, a type is *instantiated* by being anchored to a distinguishing location in a certain domain – time in the case of verbs, space for typical nouns (Langacker 1991: § 2.2.1). Conversely, a type is obtained from instances by abstracting away from their locations and focusing on their common characterization. Types are thus imaginative, being transcendent with respect to baseline experience (the direct observation of objects and events). But instances can also be imaginative, representing various kinds and degrees of departure from the baseline.

In direct observation, a distinguishing location is known and an instance can be identified by pointing: *this [☞] watch*. More commonly, though, an instance is simply imagined as having a distinct location (at a given moment) without the speaker actually knowing where it is. Thus it either remains unidentified (*a watch*) or is identified in some other manner, e.g., being accessed via a reference point (*Bill's watch*). For the interlocutors, who abstract away from any particular location, the instance "floats unattached" within some range. A more drastic departure from the baseline consists in the referent being confined to a special mental space distinct from reality (e.g., *if Bill had a watch*), making it imaginative in the strong sense of being a *virtual* (or *fictive*) instance of the type. Virtual instances are also employed in making generalizations. For example, *Each boy wore a watch* generalizes over a certain range of actual occurrences by invoking and describing a virtual one conceived as being *representative* of them. The imagined instances of *boy*, *wear*, and *watch* float unattached within that range, as in Figure 6.14, being neither identified with nor distinct from any particular one. With a fully general statement the range is unrestricted (e.g., *A watch is a timepiece*).

Among the virtual entities invoked linguistically are imagined scenarios that remain implicit but are evident from their overt symptoms. There are many traces of fictive speech interactions (Pascual 2006). In speaking of *his can-do spirit*, for instance, we

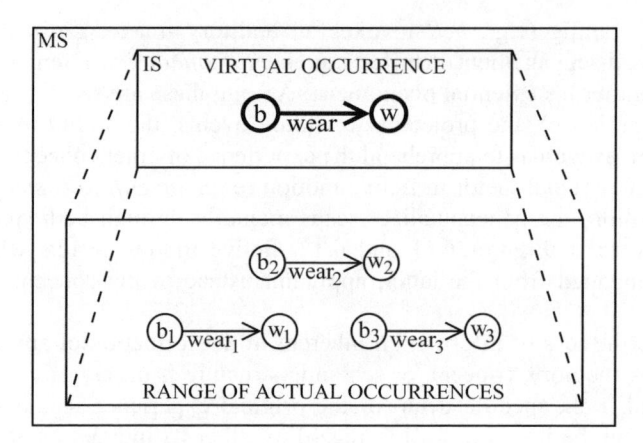

Fig. 6.14: Generalization by means of virtual instances

conjure up a scenario in which he always says *can do* when charged with a task. Also common are scenarios involving spatial motion, e.g., *It's pretty through the canyon*, where *through the canyon* invokes an otherwise implicit event of travel, and *it's pretty* describes the view at any moment of this imagined journey. A fictive motion scenario accounts as well for the apparent use of frequency adverbs as nominal quantifiers. On one interpretation, *A lawyer is usually devious* is equivalent to *Most lawyers are devious* in terms of what it says about the world. Yet they construe this circumstance rather differently. *Usually* does not mean *most* – it still pertains to the frequency of events. These events, however, are only fictive, part of an imagined scenario of traveling through the world, encountering lawyers, and ascertaining their properties. In the context of this scenario, it is *usually* the case that the lawyer examined proves to be devious.

3. Validation

An account of construal is based primarily on linguistic analysis and description. The notions proposed are motivated by their role in cogently and explicitly describing varied kinds of expressions (including their meanings). A limited set of descriptive constructs, each required for the characterization of specific phenomena, prove to have broad applicability, both within a language and cross-linguistically. Hence they are not adopted a priori or by appealing to intuition, but have a principled empirical basis (Dodge and Lakoff 2005: 58).

More specifically, a particular descriptive notion is supported by the convergence of three considerations: (i) it is needed for semantic description; (ii) it has psychological plausibility; and (iii) it plays a role in grammar (Langacker 1999: ch. 2). It is worth going through a few examples:

- SPECIFICITY/SCHEMATICITY: (i) This is a well-known dimension of semantic organization (*do* > *look at* > *examine* > *scrutinize*). (ii) It amounts to nothing more than resolution (granularity). (iii) Grammatical elements (*do*, *be*, *-ing*) are more schematic

than typical lexemes; constructions are schematizations of instantiating expressions (*be Ving* > *be working*).
- PROFILE: (i) The choice of profile distinguishes the meanings of expressions with the same content (*husband* vs. *wife* [Figure 6.7], *darken* vs. *darkened* [Figure 6.9]). (ii) Profiling is just the focusing of attention through symbolic expression. (iii) An expression's profile determines its grammatical category (despite their relational content, *husband* and *wife* are nouns).
- TRAJECTOR/LANDMARK: (i) These distinguish the meanings of relational expressions with the same content and profiling (*above* vs. *below* [Figure 6.8]). (ii) They are akin to figure/ground organization (Talmy 1978). (iii) They provide the basis for the grammatical notions subject and object.
- IMMEDIATE SCOPE: (i) This is evident in whole-part hierarchies (*body* > *leg* > *foot* > *toe* [Figure 6.5]); imposition of an immediate temporal scope accounts for the "internal perspective" on events characteristic of progressives (*be working*). (ii) This notion reflects the fact that we can attend to only so much at a given moment. (iii) It is needed to describe the $N_1 + N_2$ compounding pattern for partonomies (*fingertip*, *windowpane*, but not *armtip, *housepane).

Once proposed and supported on linguistic grounds, such notions are subject to validation and refinement by independent empirical means. Coming up with testable predictions is not an easy matter given the subtlety of the factors involved, the complexity of language processing, and the limitations of available methods. Validation is however possible in principle and increasingly in practice. Certain factors are amenable to corpus investigation. For example, if the dynamic construal induced by order of presentation does indeed tend to co-align with and reinforce a natural path of mental access, the congruent pattern *from X to Y* is expected be more frequent than the non-congruent *to Y from X*. The non-congruent order should also be harder to process, which can be tested experimentally. Though not intended as such, research by Tomlin (1995) and Forrest (1996) nicely illustrates the potential for experiments aimed at a specific construal factor. They tested whether focusing attention on one participant in a relationship would influence the choice of subject in a sentence describing it. The results were striking: when time constraints did not allow attention to wander, the focused participant was coded as subject with great consistency. This is evidence for the claim that a subject expresses the trajector, characterized as the primary focal participant in a profiled relationship.

Fictive motion has been extensively studied experimentally and shown to be grounded in the conception of actual motion (Matlock 2001, 2004; Matlock et al. 2004; Matlock and Bergmann this volume). Metaphor has likewise been the target of experimental work demonstrating its grounding in bodily experience (Gibbs 1990, this volume; Gibbs et al. 2004). More broadly, a large amount of research indicates that the mental simulation of sensory and motor experience has an important role in higher-level cognition. In particular, experimental and neural imaging evidence show that sensorimotor activity and its apprehension via language overlap in terms of processing resources and neural substrates (Bergen et al. 2007; Svensson et al. 2007; Taylor and Zwaan 2009; Bergen 2012, this volume).

Another source of validation is the computational modeling of language processing. While the empirical support this offers is indirect, it is at least suggestive when particular descriptive notions, e.g., trajector and landmark (Petitot 2011; Regier 1996), prove efficacious for modeling purposes. Ultimately, an account of construal should mesh with a comprehensive computational model, encompassing multiple levels of processing (from linguistic to neurological), as envisaged in the Neural Theory of Language and Embodied Construction Grammar (Lakoff and Johnson 1999: Appendix; Feldman 2006; Feldman et al. 2010). The two are mutually constraining. On the one hand, accommodating the many aspects of construal poses a major challenge for the model. On the other hand, construal notions can be validated by showing that they follow from general features of the model. Achieving this synthesis would be a major step toward the fundamental goal of understanding, in specific terms, how neurological activity gives rise to language and experience.

4. References

Austin, John L.
   1962   *How to Do Things with Words*. Cambridge: Harvard University Press.
Barcelona, Antonio
   this volume   Metonymy. Berlin/Boston: De Gruyter Mouton.
Bergen, Benjamin K.
   2012   *Louder Than Words: The New Science of How the Mind Makes Meaning*. New York: Basic Books.
Bergen, Benjamin K.
   this volume   Embodiment. Berlin/Boston: De Gruyter Mouton.
Bergen, Benjamin K., Shane Lindsay, Teenie Matlock and Srini Narayanan
   2007   Spatial and linguistic aspects of visual imagery in sentence comprehension. *Cognitive Science* 31: 733–764.
Boye, Kasper and Peter Harder
   2012   A usage-based theory of grammatical status and grammaticalization. *Language* 88: 1–44.
Dodge, Ellen and George Lakoff
   2005   Image schemas: From linguistic analysis to neural grounding. In: B. Hampe (ed.), *From Perception to Meaning: Image Schemas in Cognitive Linguistics*, 57–91. (Cognitive Linguistics Research 29.) Berlin/New York: Mouton de Gruyter.
Evans, Vyvyan
   2004   *The Structure of Time: Language, Meaning and Temporal Cognition*. (Human Cognitive Processing 12.) Amsterdam/Philadelphia: John Benjamins.
Evans, Vyvyan
   this volume   Time. Berlin/Boston: De Gruyter Mouton.
Fauconnier, Gilles
   1985   *Mental Spaces: Aspects of Meaning Construction in Natural Language*. Cambridge: MIT Press.
Fauconnier, Gilles and Mark Turner
   2002   *The Way We Think: Conceptual Blending and the Mind's Hidden Complexities*. New York: Basic Books.
Feldman, Jerome
   2006   *From Molecule to Metaphor: A Neural Theory of Language*. Cambridge: MIT Press.
Feldman, Jerome, Ellen Dodge and John Bryant
   2010   Embodied Construction Grammar. In: B. Heine and H. Narrog (eds.), *The Oxford Handbook of Linguistic Analysis*, 111–137. Oxford/New York: Oxford University Press.

Forrest, Linda B.
  1996   Discourse goals and attentional processes in sentence production: The dynamic construal of events. In: A. E. Goldberg (ed.), *Conceptual Structure, Discourse and Language*, 149–161. Stanford: CSLI Publications.
Gentner, Dedre
  1983   Structure mapping: A theoretical framework for analogy. *Cognitive Science* 7: 155–170.
Gibbs, Raymond W., Jr.
  1990   Psycholinguistic studies on the conceptual basis of idiomaticity. *Cognitive Linguistics* 1: 417–451.
Gibbs, Raymond W., Jr.
  this volume   Metaphor. Berlin/Boston: De Gruyter Mouton.
Gibbs, Raymond W., Jr., Paula Lenz Costa Lima and Edson Francozo
  2004   Metaphor is grounded in embodied experience. *Journal of Pragmatics* 36: 1189–1210.
Gries, Stefan Th.
  this volume   Polysemy. Berlin/Boston: De Gruyter Mouton.
Hudson, Richard A.
  1992   Review of Ronald W. Langacker: Concept, Image and Symbol: The Cognitive Basis of Grammar. *Journal of Linguistics* 28: 506–509.
Kosslyn, Stephen Michael
  1980   *Image and Mind*. Cambridge: Harvard University Press.
Kövecses, Zoltán and Günter Radden
  1998   Metonymy: Developing a cognitive linguistic view. *Cognitive Linguistics* 9: 37–77.
Lakoff, George
  1990   The invariance hypothesis: Is abstract reason based on image-schemas? *Cognitive Linguistics* 1: 39–74.
Lakoff, George and Mark Johnson
  1980   *Metaphors We Live By*. Chicago/London: University of Chicago Press.
Lakoff, George and Mark Johnson
  1999   *Philosophy in the Flesh: The Embodied Mind and Its Challenge to Western Thought*. New York: Basic Books.
Langacker, Ronald W.
  1987   *Foundations of Cognitive Grammar*, Volume 1: *Theoretical Prerequisites*. Stanford: Stanford University Press.
Langacker, Ronald W.
  1990   *Concept, Image and Symbol: The Cognitive Basis of Grammar*. (Cognitive Linguistics Research 1.) Berlin/New York: Mouton de Gruyter.
Langacker, Ronald W.
  1991   *Foundations of Cognitive Grammar*, Volume 2: *Descriptive Application*. Stanford: Stanford University Press.
Langacker, Ronald W.
  1993a   Universals of construal. *Proceedings of the Annual Meeting of the Berkeley Linguistics Society* 19: 447–463.
Langacker, Ronald W.
  1993b   Reference-point constructions. *Cognitive Linguistics* 4: 1–38.
Langacker, Ronald W.
  1999   *Grammar and Conceptualization*. (Cognitive Linguistics Research 14.) Berlin/New York: Mouton de Gruyter.
Langacker, Ronald W.
  2006   Subjectification, grammaticization, and conceptual archetypes. In: A. Athanasiadou, C. Canakis and B. Cornillie (eds.), *Subjectification: Various Paths to Subjectivity*, 17–40. (Cognitive Linguistics Research 31.) Berlin/New York: Mouton de Gruyter.

Langacker, Ronald W.
   2007   Constructing the meanings of personal pronouns. In: G. Radden, K. Köpcke, T. Berg and P. Siemund (eds.), *Aspects of Meaning Construction*, 171–187. Amsterdam/Philadelphia: John Benjamins.
Langacker, Ronald W.
   2008a   *Cognitive Grammar: A Basic Introduction.* New York: Oxford University Press.
Langacker, Ronald W.
   2008b   Sequential and summary scanning: A reply. *Cognitive Linguistics* 19: 571–584.
Langacker, Ronald W.
   2013   On grammatical categories. *Foreign Studies* 1(4): 1–23.
Matlock, Teenie
   2001   How real is fictive motion? PhD dissertation, University of California, Santa Cruz.
Matlock, Teenie
   2004   Fictive motion as cognitive simulation. *Memory and Cognition* 32: 1389–1400.
Matlock, Teenie and Till Bergmann
   this volume   Fictive motion. Berlin/Boston: De Gruyter Mouton
Matlock, Teenie, Michael Ramscar and Lera Boroditsky
   2004   The experiential basis of motion language. In: A. Soares da Silva, A. Torres and M. Gonçalves (eds.), *Linguagem, Cultura e Cognição: Estudios de Linguística Cognitiva*, Volume 2, 43–57. Coimbra: Almedina.
Matsumoto, Yo
   1996   Subjective motion and English and Japanese verbs. *Cognitive Linguistics* 7: 183–226.
Palmer, Frank R.
   1981   *Semantics.* 2nd edition. Cambridge: Cambridge University Press.
Panther, Klaus-Uwe and Günter Radden (eds.)
   2004   *Metonymy in Language and Thought.* (Human Cognitive Processing 4.) Amsterdam/Philadelphia: John Benjamins.
Panther, Klaus-Uwe, Linda L. Thornburg and Antonio Barcelona (eds.)
   2009   *Metonymy and Metaphor in Grammar.* (Human Cognitive Processing 25.) Amsterdam/Philadelphia: John Benjamins.
Pascual, Esther
   2006   Fictive interaction within the sentence: A communicative type of fictivity in grammar. *Cognitive Linguistics* 17: 245–267.
Petitot, Jean
   2011   *Cognitive Morphodynamics: Dynamical Morphological Models of Constituency in Perception and Syntax.* (European Semiotics 11.) Bern: Peter Lang.
Regier, Terry
   1996   *The Human Semantic Potential: Spatial Language and Constrained Connectionism.* Cambridge: MIT Press.
Shepard, Roger N.
   1978   The mental image. *American Psychologist* 33: 125–137.
Svensson, Henrik, Jessica Lindblom and Tom Ziemke
   2007   Making sense of embodied cognition: Simulation theories of shared neural mechanisms for sensorimotor and cognitive processes. In: T. Ziemke, J. Zlatev and R. M. Frank (eds.), *Body, Language and Mind*, Volume 1, *Embodiment*, 241–269. (Cognitive Linguistics Research 35.1.) Berlin/New York: Mouton de Gruyter.
Talmy, Leonard
   1978   Figure and ground in complex sentences. In: J. H. Greenberg (ed.), *Universals of Human Language*, Volume 4, *Syntax*, 625–649. Stanford: Stanford University Press.
Talmy, Leonard
   1988   The relation of grammar to cognition. In: B. Rudzka-Ostyn (ed.), *Topics in Cognitive Linguistics*, 165–205. (Current Issues in Linguistic Theory 50.) Amsterdam/Philadelphia: John Benjamins.

Talmy, Leonard
   1996   Fictive motion in language and "ception". In: P. Bloom, M. A. Peterson, L. Nadel and M. F. Garrett (eds.), *Language and Space*, 211–276. Cambridge: MIT Press.

Taylor, Lawrence J. and Rolf A. Zwaan
   2009   Action in cognition: The case of language. *Language and Cognition* 1: 45–58.

Tomlin, Russell S.
   1995   Focal attention, voice, and word order. In: P. Downing and M. Noonan (eds.), *Word Order in Discourse*, 517–554. (Typological Studies in Language 30.) Amsterdam/Philadelphia: John Benjamins.

Tomlin, Russell S. and Andriy Myachykov
   this volume   Attention and salience. Berlin/Boston: De Gruyter Mouton.

Turner, Mark
   this volume   Blending. Berlin/Boston: De Gruyter Mouton.

Ronald W. Langacker, San Diego (USA)

7. Metonymy[1]

1. Introduction. The notion of metonymy
2. Types of metonymy
3. The ubiquity of metonymy. Metonymy in cognition, especially in metaphor
4. Metonymy in grammar: The polysemy of derivational morphemes
5. Metonymy in lexical meaning
6. Metonymy in morphosyntactic processes: recategorization, compounding and abbreviation
7. Metonymy in clausal grammar
8. Metonymy in discourse
9. Research methods
10. Conclusions
11. References

1. Introduction. The notion of metonymy

To many cognitive linguists, conceptual metonymy is a fundamental cognitive tool in cognition and language. Langacker (this volume) regards it as a type of construal. Lakoff (1987: 113–114, 154, Chapter 5) regarded it as one of the mechanisms involved in the creation of cognitive models, together with conceptual metaphor, our "framing ability" and our image-schematic ability (Lakoff, however, seems to regard metaphor as a more important cognitive phenomenon).

---

[1] I am grateful to Günter Radden and two anonymous reviewers for their insightful comments on an earlier draft of this chapter. Any remaining inaccuracies are my sole responsibility. The present paper has been supported in part with the financial aid granted by the Spanish government to project FFI2012–36523 (see Blanco et al. in press).

This chapter is organized around four major themes: The *notion of metonymy* (which is the topic of the rest of the present section), the *typology of metonymy* (section 2), the *ubiquity of metonymy*, which the bulk of the chapter (sections 3–8) is devoted to[2], and *research methods* in the study of metonymy (section 9). The brief final section (10) contains a general comment on the chapter.

Before providing a "technical" definition of conceptual metonymy a few examples should help us introduce the notion informally:

(1) *"That's really his name, Marshall Brain, and he is* a brain *and he has a wonderful way of describing how everything works, how stuff works, everything from a computer to DNA."* (Spoken)

(2) *"The White House says the travel and tourism industry represented 2.7 percent of gross domestic product and 7.5 million jobs in 2010."* (Written)

(3) *"A friend of mine has a r1 and he painted his* flat *black and it looks a purpleish brown color now."* (Written)

(Examples (1) and (2) have been taken from the Corpus of Contemporary American English and (3) resulted from a Google search on March 12, 2014.)

In (1) the speaker seems to mean that Marshall is an intelligent person. A body part typically associated with intelligence in our encyclopedic knowledge evokes a certain type of person; this type of conceptual shift is known in cognitive linguistics (CL) as a PART FOR WHOLE metonymy (Lakoff and Johnson 1980: 36) and in traditional rhetoric as *synecdoche*. Example (2) means that the U. S. President's staff (or perhaps the President himself) made the statement reported. Here a location is used to evoke one or more entities located in it. Both the location and the "located" are two elements or "parts" of a type of spatial relation (the "locational" relation); therefore the conceptual shift from location to located is seen by some cognitive linguists (e.g., Radden and Kövecses 1999: 41–42) as a PART FOR PART metonymy. Finally, the normal understanding of (3) is not that the man painted the *whole* of his flat (including the floor, the door handles, the taps, washbasins, etc.) but only the ceiling and walls and perhaps another element such as the doors. A whole entity (in this case, a physical entity like a flat) is used to evoke its (normally) most relevant part(s) with respect to the action of painting; this type of conceptual shift is usually known as a WHOLE FOR PART metonymy.[3]

Like metaphor (see Gibbs this volume), metonymy is claimed in CL to be a *conceptual* process (Lakoff and Johnson 1980: 36; Lakoff 1987: Chapter 5, *inter alia*). That is, for CL metonymy is not simply a figure of speech, in the spirit of traditional rhetoric, or a mere "contextual effect", as claimed by certain relevance theorists (Papafragou 1996). CL regards it as an essentially conceptual process, which is reflected in various types of semiotic modes, particularly human language (both oral and sign language), but also gesture, art (music, painting, sculpture), etc.

---

[2] For a more detailed survey of research on the role of metonymy in cognition, grammar and discourse, see Barcelona (2011b), on which sections 3–9 are based.

[3] Examples (1) and (2) are metonymically more complex (e.g. (1) is also due to WHOLE (brain) FOR PART (salient property "(seat of) intelligence") but I have decided to mention only their more salient metoymy in this initial presentation of the notion.

Despite the universal agreement within CL on the conceptual nature of metonymy, not all the other properties of metonymy suggested by the initial proponents of the cognitive theory of metonymy, namely Lakoff and Johnson (1980: Chapter 8) and Lakoff and Turner (1989: 100–108) have been accepted by all cognitive linguists. Metonymy is characterized by these scholars as a process occurring within the same domain, whereby one conceptual entity, the source, "stands for" and is projected ("mapped"), with a primarily referential purpose, onto another conceptual entity, the target. This is what could be called the "initial cognitive definition of metonymy" (ICD). The ICD includes both uncontroversial and controversial additional properties of metonymy.

Among the uncontroversial properties we find these:

- Metonymy involves two conceptual entities which are *closely associated in experience* (Lakoff and Johnson 1980: 35); that is, metonymy is experientially grounded and it involves elements which are experientially (hence conceptually) contiguous (unlike metaphor). In (1)–(3) above the metonymy involves entities which are conceptually contiguous, like people and their body parts, locations and people or institutions located in them, or houses and their relevant parts.
- Metonymy often provides a conceptual perspective on the target, as in *We have some good heads for the project*, where *good heads* is used to refer to a group of people who are conceptualized in terms of their intelligence (Lakoff and Johnson 1980: 74). This property is implicit in the above definition, since the projection of the source (HEAD as the seat of intelligence in the example) imposes a perspective on the target (PEOPLE) (see Barcelona 2011a: 13–14).

All the other properties included in the ICD, which were at first accepted by many cognitive linguists (including myself), are either decidedly controversial or in need of further clarification:

- Referentiality. Some cognitive linguists seem to consider metonymy to be *necessarily* a referential device (the metonymies in (2) and (3) are referential, since they operate in referential noun phrases), while most others also recognize the existence of non-referential metonymies, like that in (1), which operates in a predicational, i.e., non-referential, noun phrase. The pioneers of the cognitive theory of metonymy, Lakoff and Johnson (1980: 74), however, had simply suggested that metonymy had a *primarily* referential function, and in Lakoff's (1987) study of cognitive models, non-referential metonymies are explicitly recognized.
- The nature of the "conceptual entities": Is metonymy a relationship between "entities" or a relationship between "domains"?
- The nature of the so-called "stand-for" relationship and of the "projection" or "mapping": What does the mapping consist of? Is it unidirectional (source to target) or also bidirectional (target to source)?

And the most controversial of all of these properties:

- The "same domain" property as a way of distinguishing metaphor from metonymy, that is, the claim that metonymy operates within the same conceptual domain, whereas metaphor connects two different conceptual domains.

In an attempt to take a stand on these and other problematic issues, some other direct or indirect definitions of metonymy were later provided in CL. One of them is Croft 2002

(1993), who characterized metonymy as the "highlighting" of a domain within a domain matrix, borrowing the latter notion from Langacker (1987: Chapter 4). Another, highly influential definition is Kövecses and Radden's (1998: 39; see also Radden and Kövecses 1999: 21): "Metonymy is a cognitive process in which one conceptual entity, the vehicle, provides mental access to another conceptual entity, the target, within the same domain, or ICM".

These and similar definitions, however, raise a further set of problematic issues, among others:

- What is the difference between "domain highlighting" and "mental access to a conceptual entity"? Do they result in the mental "activation" of the target? What does this activation consist of?
- Is *any* type of "highlighting", "mental access" or "activation" metonymic? In particular, since the notion of "mental access" is borrowed by Kövecses and Radden from Langacker (1993, 1999: 199, 363, 2009), who claims that what he calls a "reference point" provides mental access to a conceptual target, what is the exact difference between metonymy and reference point phenomena? This issue affects, in particular, the activation of certain parts from their corresponding wholes, as in *I read a book*, where the semantic content of the book is activated. Panther and Thornburg (2007: 241–242) have suggested that the connection between metonymic source and target is "contingent" (i.e., not conceptually necessary), which would exclude entailment relations from metonymy like the entailment of a superordinate concept by a hyponymic one; the problem with this view is that it would rule out MEMBER FOR CATEGORY metonymies such as the use of *aspirin* (Panther and Thornburg's example [2007: 241]) to designate any pain-relieving tablet (Kövecses and Radden 1998: 53), and cases like the one in 2.1.2 (d) below.
- Is there any essential difference between metonymy and other phenomena such as active-zone/profile discrepancy (Langacker 1999: 33–35, 67, 2009), "modulation" and "facets" (Cruse 2000; Dirven 2002; Croft and Cruse 2004), or even anaphora (Langacker 1999: 234–245 and Chapter 9), which also involve the "mental access" from one conceptual entity to another conceptual entity?
- Finally, another problematic issue is to determine the set of factors determining the conventionality of linguistic metonymy (Taylor 1995: 122–123; Kövecses and Radden 1998: 62–74; Radden and Kövecses 1999: 44–54).

Given the limitation of space I will not be able to discuss all of these issues in this chapter. The reader is referred to Barcelona (2002a, 2003a and 2011a), Geeraerts and Peirsman (2011), Panther and Thornburg (2007), Paradis (2004, 2011), Ruiz de Mendoza (2011) and to the other contributions in Benczes et al. (2011), for detailed discussions of these and other problematic issues. I will simply offer my own attempt at a broad unitary definition of metonymy (adapted from Barcelona 2011a). It is not essentially different from other well-known definitions within CL (those by Lakoff and Turner 1989; Kövecses and Radden 1998; or Panther and Thornburg 2003b, 2007), and may well be regarded as a synthesis of them all, with some additional ingredients:

> Metonymy is an asymmetric mapping of a conceptual entity, the source, onto another conceptual entity, the target. Source and target are in the same frame

and their roles are linked by a pragmatic function, so that the target is mentally activated.

This definition alone is not sufficient to solve all the problematic issues enunciated above, but it does provide an answer to most of them, especially the distinction between metaphor and metonymy.[4] The other issues (in particular the distinction between metonymy and other phenomena of activation or mental access) involve supplementing a unitary definition like this with a prototype-based approach to the notion of metonymy (section 2).

Let me now briefly discuss the above definition, especially its technical terms (more extensive discussions of the grounds for this definition are presented in Barcelona 2002a, 2003a, and 2011a).

As stated above, metonymy does not only have a referential function, hence the definition does not include referentiality as an essential property.

Let us now discuss the nature of the "mapping" or "conceptual projection" in metonymy. Lakoff and Turner (1989: 103–104) claim that metonymy is a mapping occurring between entities in the same conceptual domain, whereas metaphor is a mapping occurring across two different conceptual domains. Unlike metaphor, which symmetrically and systematically projects part of the conceptual structure of the source onto that of the target (Lakoff 1993), metonymy is "asymmetric". In the metaphor LIFE IS A JOURNEY, the beginning of the journey is mapped onto the beginning of life, the obstacles in the journey onto life's difficulties, etc. Metonymically linked elements do not normally exhibit any degree of structural similarity or equivalence. Wholes do not exhibit a similar abstract structure to that of their parts, and when the mapping relates two parts of the same ICM (e.g., the PRODUCER and the PRODUCT in the PRODUCTION ICM, as in *I bought a Stradivarius*), those parts are seldom, if ever, similar, and never equivalent functionally (the PRODUCER in that ICM is not functionally equivalent to the PRODUCT).

"Frame" is preferable to the term "domain", used by Lakoff and Turner (1989: 103) to designate the conceptual structure *within* which metonymic mappings are supposed to occur. The term "frame" designates an entrenched, knowledge-rich model of a recurrent, well-delineated area of experience (Fillmore 1985). That is actually the type of conceptual structure within which metonymy occurs. Frames are equivalent to one of the types of Lakoff's (1987) "Idealized Cognitive Models" (ICMs), namely "propositional ICMs". The terms "domain", "ICM" and "frame" are often used interchangeably but they should probably be distinguished. The reason is that "domain" is ambiguous: It can be used both in a "taxonomic" sense and in a "functional" sense. "Taxonomic domains" represent the classification and sub-classification of broad areas of experience, such as PHYSICAL ENTITIES, which include LIVING BEINGS and INERT PHYSICAL ENTITIES, etc. in our encyclopedic knowledge (Radden and Dirven 2007: 9–12). What I have called "functional domains" elsewhere (Barcelona 2002a, 2003a, 2011a) organize our detailed knowledge about more specific areas of experience; this term is thus synonymous to "frame" and "(propositional) ICM".[5]

---

[4] The issue of the exact distinction from metaphor is more complex, however, as it involves other aspects that cannot be discussed here (Barcelona 2002a, 2011a). A recent proposal sees metonymy and metaphor as the two extremes of a multidimensional continuum (Barnden 2010).

[5] It must be said, however, that Lakoff and Turner's (1989: 79–80) notion of "conceptual domain" seems to be equivalent to their notion of conceptual "schema" and to Lakoff's notion of

The relevant frames in metonymy are those that assign a *role* to source and target. Frames can be fairly specific or relatively generic. In example (1), the relevant frame is the HUMAN BEING frame, which represents speakers' detailed encyclopedic knowledge about human beings (their bodies and body parts, physiology, emotions, interaction, life cycle, etc.). The relevant frame in example (2) seems to be the (SPATIAL) LOCATION frame, which represents encyclopedic knowledge about the spatial location of entities (the basic properties of locations, the types of locations, the types of located entities, the relation between location and located and the constraints on that relation, etc.). And the relevant frame in (3) is the BUILDING frame (more exactly, its FLAT sub-frame); the relevant frame is different from that in (2) because the roles involved in (3) are related mainly to speakers' knowledge of the physical structure of buildings, whereas the role of the building in (2) is related exclusively to its locational connection with other entities.[6] An alternative, more specific relevant frame for (2) is the UNITED STATES POLITICAL INSTITUTIONS frame, which anyway assigns the same LOCATION-LOCATED roles to source and target.

The reason why we claim that metonymy operates within frames (see also Radden and Dirven 2007: 12–15; Radden and Kövecses 1999: 19–21) is that if we claimed, along with the initial cognitive definition (ICD), that metonymy occurs within one "domain", given the ambiguity of this term, we might be forced to regard as metonymic many mappings which are normally regarded as metaphorical, like the one operating in

(4) *Marshall is a bulldozer*

(meaning that he is an overbearing person, perhaps a bully), since both inert physical objects and human beings are included in the domain of physical entities (Barcelona 2002a). However, in (4) the knowledge that inert objects and living beings are included in that "taxonomic domain" is not relevant for the metaphorical mapping of BULLDOZER onto OVERBEARING PERSON. What is relevant is the fact that people and bulldozers, though different types of physical entities, are construed as sharing a certain number of properties, particularly the ability to overcome any counterforce, physical (bulldozer) or psychosocial (overbearing person). In other words, although people and machines can be taxonomically included in the same domain, they are not presented in (4) as included in the same frame. Therefore, if metonymy is claimed to operate within one frame/ propositional ICM whereas metaphor is claimed to operate across two different frames, the mapping in (4) can be described as metaphorical. And the mapping in (2) can be

---

"category", both of which are in turn similar to that of a (complex) "frame" or "propositional ICM", since all of them are supposed to be conceptual representations of relatively rich knowledge about a field of experience. The same applies to Langacker's (1987) notion of "domain matrix." The metonymic source and target "conceptual entities" can be argued in turn to constitute relatively complex domains in either sense (for details, see Barcelona 2011a); hence the frequent use of the terms "source domain" and "target domain" in metonymy.

[6] Of course, one could claim that part of our knowledge of the BUILDING frame is that buildings are at least potentially locations for other physical entities. By the same token, our knowledge of the LOCATION frame includes the types of locations, buildings among them. But these are in principle different frames. As is well known, frames, like all cognitive models, tend to be interrelated.

regarded as metonymic since the projection of an inert physical entity, a building, onto one or more people occurs within the SPATIAL LOCATION frame.

The inclusion of source and target within the same frame is a necessary, but not a sufficient condition for metonymicity. Source and target must, furthermore, be linked by what Fauconnier (1997) called a "pragmatic function". A "pragmatic function" is a privileged conceptual link in our long-term memory between the roles of metonymic source and target within the corresponding frame: CAUSE-EFFECT, PRODUCER-PRODUCT, AGENT-ACTION, CONDITION-RESULT, AGENT-INSTRUMENT, THING-REPRESENTATION, etc. (see section 2). This privileged link is an essential condition for the mental activation of target by source. The nose and the mouth are included in the HUMAN PERSON frame, where their roles are not connected by a pragmatic function; therefore neither normally acts as a metonymic source for the other (Kövecses and Radden 1998: 48–49). However, the pragmatic function SALIENT BODY PART-PERSON allows the mouth to act as a metonymic source for the whole person, as in *He only earns four hundred pounds a month and, with five* mouths *to feed, he finds this very hard*. As can be seen the classic "contiguity" criterion for metonymicity is not really reliable.

2. Types of metonymy

To my knowledge, there does not exist in CL a universally accepted typology of general, high-level conceptual metonymies operating in English or in other languages, let alone one of metonymies operating cross-linguistically.[7] Metonymies can be classified on the basis of several criteria. We present below some of those criteria and a sample of the resulting typologies.

2.1. Types in terms of pragmatic function

The most important of these criteria is the type of *pragmatic function* (see section 1) linking source and target within the relevant frame. In fact, most of the typologies in the literature apply this criterion, whether or not their proponents use the term "pragmatic function" to designate it; the other criteria described below (2.2–2.3) depend on this one. Unfortunately, there does not seem to exist a commonly accepted list of pragmatic functions. Below I offer a few common examples of metonymies classified in terms of this criterion and drawn at random, for illustrative purposes only, from those repeatedly mentioned in the literature (see in particular Fass 1997; Kövecses and Radden 1998; and Peirsman and Geeraerts 2006). They are, at the highest level, roughly grouped into the WHOLE-PART, PART-WHOLE and PART-PART generic types.

---

[7] I lead a small research project on metonymy funded by the Spanish government (FFI2012-36523) aimed at the creation of a detailed database of metonymy in English (see Blanco et al in press for its description and initial results). The present paper has been supported in part with the financial aid granted to that project.

2.1.1. WHOLE FOR PART metonymies

a) GEOGRAPHICAL UNIT FOR SALIENT PART, as in *America* used to refer to the United States.
b) ENTITY FOR RELEVANT PART(S), as in example (3), where "flat" activates its relevant parts i.e., its "active zone" (Langacker 1999) with respect to the action of painting.
c) CATEGORY FOR MEMBER, as in *The use of the pill has reduced the birth rate in many countries,* where "pill" activates "contraceptive pill" (Kövecses and Radden 1998: 53). On the corresponding reverse metonymy, see 2.1.2 d.

2.1.2. PART FOR WHOLE metonymies

a) SUB-EVENT FOR COMPLEX EVENT, as in *They stood at the altar,* where a sub-event of a wedding ceremony activates the whole complex event (Kövecses and Radden 1998: 52).
b) SALIENT PROPERTY FOR PERSON CATEGORY, as in *She is a beauty,* where these roles are respectively filled by "beauty" and "beautiful person".
c) SALIENT BODY PART FOR PERSON CATEGORY, as in example (1), where the brain activates "intelligent people".
d) MEMBER FOR CATEGORY, as in *That young man may become a new Aristotle* (said of someone who is a highly talented philosopher), where "Aristotle", an ideal instance of the GREAT PHILOSOPHER category, stands for that category (see section 6).

2.1.3. PART FOR PART metonymies

a) LOCATION FOR LOCATED, as in (2) above, where these roles are respectively filled by the White House and the U. S. President's staff (or perhaps the President himself).
b) PRODUCER FOR PRODUCT, as in *I'll have a Heineken,* where the beer maker stands for the beer itself. A special subtype is AUTHOR FOR WORK, as in *Proust is tough to read* (Croft [1993] 2002), where the novelist activates his literary work.
c) EFFECT FOR CAUSE, as in *You are my joy,* where the emotion of joy activates the person causing it, or as in *The car screeched to a halt* where a certain sound activates the motion causing it (Kövecses and Radden 1998: 56).
d) CONTROLLER FOR CONTROLLED, as *I am parked out there,* where the driver (*I*) activates the vehicle (s)he drives, i.e., controls; and its reverse metonymy, CONTROLLED FOR CONTROLLER, as in *That Mercedes is a bastard,* where the car is used to refer to its driver.
e) CONTAINER FOR CONTENT, as in *He drank a couple of cups,* where the cups activate their liquid content.
f) POSSESSED FOR POSSESSOR, as in *The fur coat left the meeting with a smile,* where the fur coat activates its possessor.
g) INSTRUMENT FOR ACTION, as in *The pen is mightier than the sword,* where pens and swords are instruments for the actions which they respectively evoke, i.e., communication (linguistic action) and reasoning, on the one hand, and violence and war on the other hand. On other metonymies arising within the "Action ICM" (ACTION FOR AGENT, AGENT FOR ACTION, etc.), see Kövecses and Radden (1998: 54–55).

I have followed Kövecses and Radden (1998: 54) in their classification of the metonymies in 2.1.3 as PART FOR PART, because, as they convincingly argue, the source and target roles connected by the corresponding pragmatic functions are conceptual elements within an ICM, i.e., "parts" of it. The relevant ICM is, furthermore an event or in general a relational ICM (action, causation, possession, containment, etc.), which is less clearly delineated than the "things"[8] corresponding to the wholes, including abstract wholes, in WHOLE FOR PART and PART FOR WHOLE metonymies.

As noted by many linguists, a large number of metonymies have their reverse, i.e., a metonymy with source and target reversed. For lack of space only two examples have been presented (in 2.1.1c and 2.1.3d). Reversibility, however, should not be confused with bidirectionality, i.e., the mapping does not take place in both directions simultaneously and is very different in each case (for details, see Barcelona 2011a: 15).

2.2. Types in terms of generality

Most of the metonymy types resulting from the pragmatic function criterion can be arranged into *hierarchies*, at whose top, i.e., its highest level of generality, we find the traditional basic typology WHOLE FOR PART, PART FOR WHOLE and PART FOR PART.[9] The metonymy lists in 2.1.1, 2.1.2, and 2.1.3 constitute partial hierarchies consisting of a *generic* and a subordinate level represented by each of the metonymies in the list. But the hierarchies are more complex. In sentence (1), we can just describe the metonymy at the *generic* level (PART FOR WHOLE), or describe it at increasingly more specific levels, that is, at a *high level* (SALIENT BODY PART FOR PERSON CATEGORY) or at a *low level* (BRAIN FOR INTELLIGENT PERSON). On a detailed discussion of the problems with metonymic hierarchies see Blanco et al (in press).

2.3. Types in terms of prototypicality

This is not a traditional classification. However, two recent complementary proposals in CL (Barcelona 2002a, 2003a, 2011a and Peirsman and Geeraerts 2006) suggest the existence of degrees of prototypicality in metonymy; see also Dirven (2002). Therefore, prototypicality can be added as an additional typological criterion. Both proposals are very complex and I can only present an oversimplification here.

Barcelona (2002a, 2003a, 2011a) characterizes "prototypical" metonymies as referential metonymies with an individual entity or a group (not a class or category) of individual entities as target, like those in examples (2) and (3). These are the metonymies usually studied in traditional rhetoric and semantics. A lower degree of prototypicality is exhibited by the metonymies he calls "(simply) typical", which are those whose target is a

---

[8] In Langacker's (1987: 183–213) technical use of this term in Cognitive Grammar.
[9] Ruiz de Mendoza (2000) and Geeraerts and Peirsman (2011) reduce generic level metonymies to WHOLE FOR PART and PART FOR WHOLE.

"secondary domain" (Langacker 1987: 165, 222),[10] within the source of WHOLE (source) FOR PART (target) metonymies or is not included in the source, as in all PART (source) FOR WHOLE (target) and PART (source) FOR PART (target) metonymies; these metonymies, furthermore, are either not referential, as in example (1), or they are used to refer to a type, class or category of entities, as in

(5)   *A good student should read extensively,*

where the generic reference of the subject noun phrase is motivated by the metonymy INSTANCE FOR TYPE (Radden, 2009: 207). Finally, the metonymies called "purely schematic" are WHOLE FOR PART metonymies whose target is a "minimally primary" or "minimally secondary" subdomain within the source, that is, deeply included in it; an example is *This book is highly instructive* (ENTITY [BOOK] FOR RELEVANT PART [SEMANTIC CONTENT]). These metonymies are very close to literality, as the semantic shift is very subtle and not immediately perceived by speakers, for which reason their status as metonymies is controversial in CL (the various positions on this issue are discussed by Barcelona 2011a; Ruiz de Mendoza 2000; Croft [1993] 2002; Paradis 2004 and 2011; and Geeraerts and Peirsman 2011, among others). The advantage of the broad, unitary definition of metonymy proposed in section 1 is that it stresses the common cognitive properties of a wide variety of phenomena. Its disadvantage is that it can include "purely schematic" metonymies, which given their marginality within the category, are not accepted as metonymic by all cognitive linguists. This is why that definition is supplemented with the above prototype-based set of definitions. Most of the research reported on from section 3 onwards applies only to uncontroversial instances of metonymy (i.e., "typical" and "prototypical" metonymies).

To Peirsman and Geeraerts (2006), the most highly prototypical metonymies are those operating in the spatial and material domains, particularly in cases where two physical entities reach the maximum degree on the two continua of spatial contiguity they propose: "strength of contact" and "boundedness". This degree is reached in their "material whole-part" relationship expressed by examples (1) (person-brain) and (3) (the walls and doors of a flat). Prototypicality is progressively weakened with lower degrees of boundedness of source or target, as in the metonymy (MATERIAL CONSTITUTING AN OBJECT FOR THAT OBJECT) extending the (unbounded) "substance" sense of *glass* to its (bounded) "object" sense; both senses are represented in *A good glass is made of glass*. The degree of prototypicality is also progressively lower as the strength of contact between source and target diminishes in the spatial and material domains, as in metonymies involving CONTAINER and CONTENT (as in *I drank a glass*), LOCATION and LOCATED (example 2 above) or mere "adjacency" (as in the noun *board* designating a group of people meeting at a council-table). On the whole the metonymies operating in these domains exhibit this gradient of prototypicality in terms of strength of contact, from highest to lowest: material and spatial, temporal, actions-events-processes (AGENT FOR ACTION, etc.), and "assemblies and collections" (CATEGORY FOR MEMBER, etc.).

---

[10] A "primary" domain is one which is obligatorily activated when understanding the meaning of a symbolic unit (i.e., a morpheme, a lexeme or any other grammatical construction), e.g. PHYSICAL OBJECT in *book*. We might then say that a "secondary" domain (a term not used by Langacker) is not (or less) obligatorily activated, e.g. LIBRARY in *book*. Both notions are scalar.

3. The ubiquity of metonymy. Metonymy in cognition, especially in metaphor

Most of the sections of the chapter (3–9) are devoted to reporting on important recent CL research illustrating the ubiquity of metonymy in cognition and language (Bierwiaczonek 2013 is a recent survey): Metonymy in cognition (this section), grammar (sections 4–7) and discourse (section 8). Lack of space prevents us from discussing the role of metonymy in phonology (Barcelona 2002b; Radden 2005) and the applications of metonymy research to work on second language acquisition (Littlemore 2009: Ch. 6; Holme 2009: 101–102, 117–120; Barcelona 2010), to computational linguistics (Fass 1997), or to work on multimodal communication (Forceville and Urios Aparisi 2009).

There are three areas in cognition where metonymy has been found to be particularly relevant: Cognitive models (Lakoff 1987: Chapter 5; Feyaerts 1999; Gibbs 1994, 2007a, on relevant psycholinguistic research), blending (Turner this volume; Turner and Fauconnier 2000; Radden 2009), and metaphor. (On the neural embodiment of metonymy, see Bierwiaczonek 2013: Ch. 6.)

I only have space to comment on metonymy in metaphor (Barcelona 2000a, 2000b, 2011a; Goossens [1990] 2002]; Goossens et al 1995; Radden [2000] 2002; and Taylor 1995: 138–141). A great many metaphors have been argued to be *conceptually* based on metonymy, i.e., to be conceptually possible thanks to it. In my opinion there are two major types of metonymic motivation of metaphor. The first type consists in the *generalization* or *decontextualization* of a metonymy. The metonymy HEIGHT (UP) FOR QUANTITY (MORE) is due to the frequent experiential association of HEIGHT and QUANTITY in POURING or HEAPING frames/scenarios, as in *The water level in the dam is too high. We should release some of it.* When HEIGHT is mapped onto QUANTITY in a context where HEIGHT is no longer really involved, the mapping is metaphorical (MORE IS UP), as in *The high cost of living/Skyrocketing prices* (Radden 2000, 2002). In the second type, which can be called *correlation-abstraction* (Barcelona 2000b, 2011a; see also Rudzka-Ostyn 1995), metaphors like DEVIANT COLORS ARE DEVIANT SOUNDS, as in *That's a loud color*, are made conceptually possible by the metonymic mapping of the salient EFFECT of deviant sounds and colors (IRRESISTIBLE ATTRACTION OF ATTENTION), onto its CAUSE (those sensory stimuli themselves), thereby highlighting the abstract similarity between these sounds and colors and motivating the aforesaid metaphor.

4. Metonymy in grammar: The polysemy of derivational morphemes

This is the first of a series of sections (4–7) surveying the role of metonymy in grammatical structure and meaning. That survey is quite selective for lack of space and does not include the role of metonymy in generic NPs (Radden 2005, 2009) and in the tense-aspect-mood system of English verbs (Brdar 2007; Panther and Thornburg 1998; Janda this volume). Langacker (1999: 67) says that though "usually regarded as a semantic phenomenon, metonymy turns out to be central and essential to grammar". For a general survey of the role of metonymy in grammar see Brdar (2007), Ruiz de Mendoza and

Pérez Hernández (2001), Ruiz de Mendoza and Otal Campo (2002), Panther et al. (2009), and within the latter volume, Langacker (2009).

Most derivational morphemes are polysemous, often due to metaphor and/or metonymy. Some of the relevant research on this issue is Barcelona (2005: 320–1, 2009a, in preparation) on the nominal suffixal morpheme {ful}, as in *a bottleful* or *a cupful*; Panther and Thornburg (2002) on the complex polysemy of the nominal suffixal morpheme {er}; Palmer et al (2009) on the Tagalog prefix {ka}; and Radden (2005), on the suffixal morpheme {able}.

One example is the metonymic motivation of a non-central sense of {able} (Radden 2005: 18–19). The central sense of the morpheme is illustrated by the phrase *a movable piano*; this central sense can be paraphrased as "can be VERB-ed" and the phrase *A movable piano* can thus be paraphrased as "a piano that can be moved", where "movability" is an inherent property of the piano. But in *drinkable water*, "drinkable" does not simply denote an inherent property of water, i.e., "can be drunk" abstractly, but also its relevance for humans, that is "can be drunk by humans", "safe to drink" (Radden 2005: 18). The semantic extension is motivated by GENERIC FOR SPECIFIC (or CATEGORY FOR MEMBER).

5. Metonymy in lexical meaning

Like morphemes, words are grammatical constructions, i.e., conventional form-meaning pairs (Goldberg 2006). Metonymy has traditionally been claimed to be a lexical phenomenon. Most of the examples of metonymy offered in rhetoric and semantics handbooks are lexical metonymies, many of them polysemy-creating metonymies like those motivating the "manual worker" or "sailor" senses of *hand*, or the "smelling ability" sense of *nose* (as in *this dog has a good nose*). Further examples of lexical polysemy motivated by metonymy were given in 2.1.1 (c), 2.1.2 (b, c), 2.1.3 (c *-joy-*, e, g *-pen, sword*). These metonymies are well-known in historical linguistics, rhetoric and lexical semantics (Geeraerts this volume; Hilpert this volume). Additional examples of metonymies operating on lexemes are discussed in section 6 and Bierwiaczonek 2013: Ch. 5.

Lexical metonymies are not necessarily restricted to nouns. The metonymy (CONTROLLER FOR CONTROLLED) in *I am parked out over there* (Nunberg 1995) affects the reference of the pronoun *I* (the speaker's car). Lexical metonymies are very often involved in reference. But referential metonymies are not exclusively lexical phenomena (Barcelona 2011b), since they affect the referential value of a noun *phrase* (even though that value often crucially depends on a metonymy-based lexical sense of the phrasal head), as in *the buses* (i.e., the bus drivers) *are on strike* (Lakoff and Johnson 1980: 38), where the underlying metonymy is called by Radden and Kövecses (1999: 40) CONTROLLED FOR CONTROLLER.

The success of referential metonymies in directing attention to the intended referent often requires inference, hence discourse-pragmatic inferencing (section 8) is often involved (Warren 1999: 123).

6. Metonymy in morphosyntactic processes: recategorization, compounding and abbreviation

The shift in lexical sense or in reference effected by metonymy often brings about a change in the morphosyntactic class of the respective lexeme (recategorization). Compounds are intrinsically metonymic, as they code a complex meaning by highlighting some of its facets (see Bierwiaczwonek 2013: Ch. 3) Abbreviation seems to be often motivated by metonymy.

Grammatical recategorization can be relatively transient or permanent (i.e., fully conventionalized). Both types are discussed below.

Stative predicates are often transiently recategorized as dynamic predicates. The metonymy EFFECT FOR CAUSE motivates this shift, as in *He asked her to be his wife* (paraphraseable as "He asked her to act in such a way so as to become his wife"). *Be someone's wife* profiles a *controllable* (Ruiz de Mendoza and Pérez Hernández 2001; Ruiz de Mendoza and Otal 2002), *resultant* (Panther and Thornburg 2000) state, which constitutes a metonymic source for its implicit causal action (i.e., to act in such a way so as to ...). Compare with *non-controllable, non-resultant states*: **He asked her to be tall*.

English proper nouns are often transiently converted into common nouns. One of the many metonymy-motivated examples of this conversion is *John has five authentic Picassos* (AUTHOR FOR (PIECE OF) WORK). Two special cases are paragons and partitive restrictive modification. On the metonymic motivation of "partitive restrictive modification" (Greenbaum and Quirk 1990: 88), as in *The young Joyce already showed signs of the genius that was to be fulfilled in Ulysses*, see Barcelona (2003c, 2003d, 2009b), Brdar (2007) and Brdar and Brdar-Szabó (2007). The use of names as *paragons* (Barcelona 2003c, 2003d, 2004; Brdar 2007; Brdar and Brdar-Szabó 2007; Pang 2006) is motivated in part by the activation of a class of individuals by one of its ideal members (IDEAL MEMBER FOR CLASS), as in *That graduate student is an Aristotle, There aren't any real Aristotles today*. This metonymy directly licenses the transient grammatical recategorization of a proper name as a common count noun (which takes plural, determiners and restrictive modifiers). This recategorization may become permanent: *lolita* (after Nabokov's character), as in *My 13 year old daughter is starting to act like a lolita*.

Permanent grammatical recategorization includes metonymy-motivated instances of conversion (Martsa 2013 for a general survey) and some instances of affixal derivation.

Mass-count noun conversion is analyzed by Brdar (2007), Ruiz de Mendoza and Pérez Hernández (2001), Ruiz de Mendoza and Otal (2002), and Kövecses and Radden (1998). An example of count-mass conversion motivated by MATERIAL FOR OBJECT MADE OF THAT MATERIAL is *We did not always eat turkey for Christmas dinner* (Brdar 2007), and one of mass-count conversion motivated by OBJECT FOR MATERIAL CONSTITUTING THE OBJECT is *To have won one gold medal and two silvers in those Games was historic* (Brdar 2007).

Noun-verb conversion is dealt with by Dirven (1999), Ruiz de Mendoza and Pérez Hernández (2001), and Ruiz de Mendoza and Otal (2002). Dirven (1999: 275–287) identified three metonymies involved in the process: INSTRUMENT FOR ACTION, as in *He was angling* (from noun *angle* 'fishing rod'); GOAL FOR MOTION, as in *The plane was forced to land in Cairo* (see also Kövecses and Radden 1998: 55, 60); CLASS MEMBERSHIP FOR DESCRIPTION (according to Dirven) or AGENT FOR ACTION (according to Barcelona 2002a), as in *Mary nursed the sick soldiers*.

On the metonymic motivation of adjective-noun conversion like the conversion of the adjective *interstate* (as in *interstate freeway*) into the noun *interstate* 'interstate highway' (as in *an/the interstate*), see Barcelona (2009a, in preparation).

On the metonymic motivation of certain instances of *affixal* derivation, see Panther and Thornburg (2002), on certain *-er* nouns; Szawerna (2007); Palmer et al (2009); and section 4. One of Panther and Thornburg's examples of *-er* nouns is *cliffhanger* 'suspenseful event', in which the metonymy EXPERIENCER FOR EVENT EXPERIENCED, motivates the shift from the agentive to the eventive sense of the {er} morpheme, whereas CAUSE (THE ACTIVITY OF CLIFFHANGING) FOR EFFECT (SUSPENSE),[11] motivates the shift in the meaning of the lexical base.

On compounding, see Radden (2005), Barcelona (2008, 2009a, in preparation), Benczes (2006, 2011), Geeraerts (2002), and Kosecki (2007). Radden (2005: 19–20) observes that endocentric (or hyponymic) compounds are intrinsically metonymic, as they typically activate all the properties of a category from a salient property (SALIENT PROPERTY FOR A BUNDLE OF PROPERTIES). This is particularly clear crosslinguistically: English *hiking boots* (function highlighted) vs. Spanish *botas de montaña* (literally 'boots of mountain'; location highlighted); see also Radden and Panther (2004: 5–8), on *screwdriver* and its crosslinguistic equivalents. Exocentric compounds, like Spanish verb-object compounds (*matamoscas*, lit. 'kills flies', i.e., 'fly spray') and *bahuvrihi* compounds (a special type of exocentric compounds) such as *highbrow* 'intellectual', *blockhead*, or *featherweight* are also based on the metonymy called by Barcelona (2008) CHARACTERISTIC PROPERTY FOR CATEGORY.

Finally, a few words on abbreviation due to formal metonymy. If one assumes that the set of basic forms[12] of a grammatical construction constitutes a conceptual frame, then metonymy can operate in it (Barcelona 2005, 2007a, 2009a, in preparation; Bierwiaczonek 2007, 2013: Ch. 2; Radden 2005: 17). Constructional forms partially motivated by metonymy include certain lexical abbreviations (like *gas* from *gasoline*) and certain types of ellipsis, as in '*Do you walk to work*' '*Yes, [I walk to work] every day*'; the metonymy at work is SALIENT PART OF FORM FOR WHOLE FORM. On factors determining the salience of the parts retained see Barcelona (in preparation).

7. Metonymy in clausal grammar

I can just comment very briefly on some examples of research in this area.

Ziegeler (2007) argues that analyses in terms of "nominal coercion", as in *She had a beer* (Michaelis 2004), "complement coercion" and "subject coercion" (Pustejovsky 1995) should be replaced by analyses in terms of metonymy. Her alternative proposals to Pustejovsky's are very similar to Langacker's work on *active zones* (Langacker 1999, 2009) and to work by Brdar (2007), Ruiz de Mendoza and Pérez Hernández (2001), and Ruiz de Mendoza and Otal (2002). Take *George began the book* (BOOK FOR RELATION [X READ / WRITE / BIND / ILLUSTRATE ... BOOK]) and '*What could we buy for Mary's birthday?*' '*A book would be a great idea*', where *book* activates "buying a book" (BOOK FOR RELATION [X BUY BOOK]).

---

[11] One of the effects of cliffhanging is creating suspense.
[12] That is, the uninflected full (i.e., non-abbreviated) form of lexemes and the full (i.e., non-elliptical or non-defective) form of syntactic constructions.

An example of work on metonymy and *valency extension/reduction* and *transitivity* (Brdar 2007; Ruiz de Mendoza and Pérez Hernández 2001; Ruiz de Mendoza and Otal 2002; Ruiz de Mendoza and Mairal 2007; Barcelona 2009a, Barcelona in preparation) is *This bread* cuts *easily*, motivated by the metonymic chain PROCESS FOR ACTION FOR RESULT (Ruiz de Mendoza and Mairal 2007: 45–47).

On metonymy and anaphora see Langacker (1999: 234–245 and Chapter 9, 2009) and Ruiz de Mendoza and Díez Velasco (2004). Metonymy is involved in anaphora resolution, especially in "indirect anaphora" (Emmott 1999), which lacks an explicit antecedent, as in *He speaks excellent French even though he's never lived there*, where the antecedent of *there* is the metonymic target of *French* (LOCATED [LANGUAGE] FOR LOCATION [FRANCE]).

CL research on metonymy in clausal grammar also includes modality (see, among others, Ruiz de Mendoza and Pérez Hernández 2001; Pérez Hernández 2007) and epistemic conditional constructions (Barcelona 2006, 2009a, in preparation).

8. Metonymy in discourse

Research on the role of metonymy in pragmatic inferencing and discourse (pioneered among others by Lakoff 1987: 78–79) has explored the role of metonymy in:

- Grammaticalization (Barcelona 2009a, in preparation; Hilpert 2007; Heine et al. 1991; Hopper and Traugott 1993; Traugott and Dasher 2002).
- Indirect speech acts (Brdar-Szabó 2009; Panther and Thornburg 1998, 2003a; Thornburg and Panther 1997; Bierwiaczwonek 2013: Ch. 4).
- Implicature and "explicature" (Barcelona 2002b, 2003b, 2005, 2007a, 2007b, 2009a, in preparation; Panther and Thornburg 2003a, 2007: 248–249; Ruiz de Mendoza and Pérez Hernández 2003; Ruiz de Mendoza and Peña 2005b: 274).
- Other areas, such as speakers' attitudes (especially euphemism), art (including film, and drama), literature, iconicity, sign language, aphasia, etc. (Gibbs 1994: 319–358; Barcelona 2013; Ciepiela 2007; Dzeren-Glówacka 2007; Kuzniak 2007; Kwiatkowska 2007; Littlemore 2009: 115–115, 2015; Pluciennik 2007; P. Wilcox 2004; S. Wilcox this volume).

On metonymy and anaphora, see section 7.

I can only offer examples of metonymy in *indirect speech acts* and *implicature*.

Thornburg and Panther (1997) assume that speakers operate on the basis of Speech Act Scenarios like the Scenario for Directive Speech Acts (S = Speaker, H = Hearer, A = Action requested):

(i)   the BEFORE: (a) H can do A
                   (b) S wants H to do A
(ii) the CORE: (a) S puts H under an obligation to do A
                   (b) the immediate RESULT: H is under an obligation to do A (H must/should do A)
(iii) the AFTER: H will do A

PART FOR WHOLE metonymies motivate indirect requests, as in "I need your help. *I would like you to send a message to my mom*" (part i-b activates the whole scenario).

An example of the metonymic guidance of *implicature* is this parliamentary anecdote:

Opposition MP, on the Prime Minister (P. M.): *But what can we expect, after all, of a man who wears silk underpants?*

PM: *Oh, I would have never thought the Right Honorable's wife could be so indiscreet!*

Barcelona (2003b) showed that it is possible to argue that all the implicatures invited by this exchange are guided by metonymy. Among those invited by the PM's repartee are these (with the chained metonymies guiding their derivation):[13] (a) "The MP's wife knows that the PM wears silk underpants because she has seen him undress" (FACT [knowing the underwear he uses] FOR SALIENT CONVENTIONAL EXPLANATION [seeing him undress]; (b) "She is on "intimate terms" with the PM" (FACT [seeing him undress] FOR SALIENT EXPLANATION [being on "intimate terms" with him]).

9. Research methods

Most research on metonymy so far has used "traditional" methods, i.e., collecting a number of more or less contextualized examples and studying them on the basis of introspection with occasional consultation of corpora, dictionaries and informants.

Gibbs (2007b) suggests that, even if cognitive linguists do not have to carry out psychological experiments, they should at least present their claims in a manner amenable to empirical testing. As regards metonymy research, one of the ways to do this is to devise explicit methods to identify linguistic metonymies and investigate their functioning in language, as in Barcelona (2002a), Dirven (2002) and the Pragglejazz Group (2007), whose complex Metaphor Identification Procedure (MIP), later refined as MIP-VU (Steen et al. 2010), has been adapted to metonymy identification (e.g., Zhang et al. 2011). Another complementary way is to study the distribution and variation of metonymy in various types of grammatical structures and discourse types by applying corpus analysis techniques (Markert and Nissim 2003; Stefanowitsch and Gries 2008), usually coupled with statistical and other quantitative methods (Glynn and Fischer 2010). An excellent application of these methods is Zhang (2013). These methods are extremely useful to rigorously characterize "visible" conceptual metonymies, i.e., those manifested in linguistic (especially lexical) meaning or form.

But testing the cognitive "reality" of *conceptual* metonymies, both the visible ones and the "invisible" ones, e.g., those underlying metaphors (section 3) and guiding implicatures (section 8), requires psycholinguistic experiments. Unfortunately, there is very little research in this direction, mainly due to the difficulties in designing the corresponding experiments (Gibbs 2007a). However, this research suggests that conceptual metonymy is regularly active in discourse comprehension (Gibbs 1994: 319–358, especially 329–330, 358; Frisson and Pickering 1999).

---

[13] This is an oversimplification of a much more complex analysis.

10. Conclusions

A rich amount of information has been offered on the role of metonymy in grammar and discourse. Metonymy is ubiquitous because it is a *conceptual mechanism* and a *natural inferencing schema* (Panther 2005) and this explains why we regularly find the same types of conceptual metonymies (EFFECT FOR CAUSE, PART FOR WHOLE, RESULT FOR CONDITION, ENTITY FOR SALIENT PROPERTY, etc.) at different linguistic levels and in very different expressive and communicative modes.

As tasks for future research, the following could be highlighted (see also Panther and Thornburg 2007):

– The compilation of a generally accepted detailed typology of metonymy which would include information for each metonymy on the relevant metonymic hierarchy/ies, the linguistic domains/ranks where it operates, the factors triggering or constraining it, its patterns of chaining and interaction with other metonymies and with metaphor and blending, and a unification of the terminology used to designate the types of metonymy (Blanco et al, in press).
– More research on the attitudinal uses of metonymy in discourse (Littlemore 2015).
– More research on the main types of metonymy in pragmatic inferencing.
– Developing a standard methodology in data collection and analysis.
– More psycholinguistic research on the psychological reality of metonymy.
– More studies to investigate crosslinguistic differences in the use of metonymy in such areas as advertising, art, second language acquisition, etc.

11. References

Barcelona, Antonio (ed.)
   2000a *Metaphor and Metonymy at the Crossroads. A Cognitive Perspective*. Berlin/New York: Mouton de Gruyter.

Barcelona, Antonio
   2000b On the plausibility of claiming a metonymic motivation for conceptual metaphor. In: A. Barcelona (ed.), *Metaphor and Metonymy at the Crossroads. A Cognitive Perspective*, 31–58. Berlin/New York: Mouton de Gruyter.

Barcelona, Antonio
   2002a Clarifying and applying the notions of metaphor and metonymy within cognitive linguistics: An update. In: R. Dirven and R. Pörings (eds.), *Metaphor and Metonymy in Comparison and Contrast*, 207–277. Berlin: Mouton de Gruyter.

Barcelona, Antonio
   2002b On the ubiquity and multiple-level operation of metonymy. In: B. Lewandowska-Tomaszczyk and K. Turewicz (eds.), *Cognitive Linguistics Today* (Łódź Studies in Language), 207–224. Frankfurt a. M.: Peter Lang.

Barcelona, Antonio
   2003a Metonymy in cognitive linguistics. An analysis and a few modest proposals. In: H. Cuyckens, K.-U. Panther and T. Berg (eds.), *Motivation in Language: Studies in Honor of Günter Radden*, 223–255. Amsterdam: John Benjamins.

Barcelona, Antonio
   2003b The case for a metonymic basis of pragmatic inferencing: Evidence from jokes and funny anecdotes. In: K.-U. Panther and L. Thornburg. *Metonymy and Pragmatic Inferencing*, 81–102. Amsterdam/Philadelphia: John Benjamins.

Barcelona, Antonio
2003c La gramática de los nombres propios: un viaje con retorno (por buenos motivos). In: M. White, H. Herrera and C. Alonso (eds.), *La Lingüística Cognitiva en España en el cambio de Siglo* (II), *Metáfora y Metonimia* [Cognitive linguistics in Spain at the turn of the century (II), Metaphor and metonymy], 7–30. Madrid: Universidad Autónoma de Madrid.

Barcelona, Antonio
2003d Names: A metonymic return ticket. *Jezikoslovlje* 4(1): 11–41.

Barcelona, Antonio
2004 Metonymy behind grammar: The motivation of the seemingly "irregular" grammatical behavior of English paragon names. In: G. Radden and K.-U. Panther (eds.), *Studies in Linguistics Motivation,* 357–374. Amsterdam: John Benjamins.

Barcelona, Antonio
2005 The multilevel operation of metonymy in grammar and discourse with particular attention to metonymic chains. In: F.J. Ruiz de Mendoza Ibáñez and S. Peña Cervel (eds.), *Cognitive Linguistics: Internal Dynamics and Interdisciplinary Interaction,* 313–352. Berlin/New York: Mouton de Gruyter.

Barcelona, Antonio
2006 On the conceptual motivation of epistemic conditionals: Metonymy or metaphor? In R. Benczes and S. Csabi (eds.), *The Metaphors of Sixty. Papers Presented on the Occasion of the 60th Birthday of Zoltán Kövecses,* 39–47. Budapest: Eötvos Loránd University, Department of American Studies, School of English and American Studies.

Barcelona, Antonio
2007a The multilevel role of metonymy in grammar and discourse: A case study. In: K. Kosecki (ed.), *Perspectives on Metonymy. Proceedings of the International Conference "Perspectives on Metonymy",* 103–131. Frankfurt a. M.: Peter Lang.

Barcelona, Antonio
2007b The role of metonymy in meaning at discourse level: A case study. In: G. Radden, Günter, K.-M. Köpcke, T. Berg and P. Siemund (eds.), *Aspects of Meaning Construction,* 51–75. Amsterdam: John Benjamins.

Barcelona, Antonio
2008 The interaction of metonymy and metaphor in the meaning and form of 'bahuvrihi' compounds. *Annual Review of Cognitive Linguistics* 6: 208–281.

Barcelona, Antonio
2009a Motivation of construction meaning and form: The roles of metonymy and inference. In: K.-U. Panther, L. Thornburg and A. Barcelona (eds.), *Metonymy and Metaphor in Grammar,* 363–401. Amsterdam/Philadelphia: John Benjamins.

Barcelona, Antonio
2009b Partitive restrictive modification of names in English: Arguments for their metonymic motivation. *Quaderns de Filologia de la Universitat de València. Estudis Lingüístics* 14: 33–56.

Barcelona, Antonio
2010 Metonymic inferencing and second language acquisition. In: J. Littlemore and C. Juchem-Grundmann (eds.), *Applied Cognitive Linguistics in Second Language Learning and Teaching. AILA Review,* Volume 23, 134–154. Amsterdam: John Benjamins.

Barcelona, Antonio
2011a Reviewing the properties and prototype structure of metonymy. In: R. Benczes, A. Barcelona and F.-J. Ruiz de Mendoza Ibáñez (eds.), *Defining Metonymy in Cognitive Linguistics. Towards a Consensus View,* 7–57. Amsterdam: John Benjamins.

Barcelona, Antonio
2011b Metonymy is not just a lexical phenomenon. In: C. Alm-Arvius, N.-L. Johannesson and D. C. Minugh (eds.) Selected Papers from the 2008 Stockholm Metaphor Festival, 3–42 (http://www2.english.su.se/nlj/metfest_08/Barcelona_08.pdf).

Barcelona, Antonio
2013   Metonymy-guided inferences in creative thinking (humour, theology, art). In: R. Monroy Casas (ed.), *Homenaje Francisco Gutiérrez Díez*, 39–58. Murcia: Universidad de Murcia.

Barcelona, Antonio
In preparation   On the pervasive role of metonymy in constructional meaning and structure in discourse comprehension: An empirical study from a cognitive-linguistic perspective (Provisional title).

Barnden, John A.
2010   Metaphor and metonymy: Making their connections more slippery. *Cognitive Linguistics* 21(1): 1–34.

Benczes, Réka
2006   *Creative Compounding in English. The Semantics of Metaphorical and Metonymical Noun-Noun Combinations.* Amsterdam: John Benjamins.

Benczes, Réka
2011   Putting the notion of 'domain' back into metonymy. In: R. Benczes, A. Barcelona and F.-J. Ruiz de Mendoza Ibáñez, *Defining Metonymy in Cognitive Linguistics. Towards a Consensus View,* 197–215. Amsterdam: John Benjamins.

Benczes, Réka, Antonio Barcelona and Francisco-José Ruiz de Mendoza Ibáñez (eds.)
2011   *Defining Metonymy in Cognitive Linguistics. Towards a Consensus View.* Amsterdam: John Benjamins.

Bierwiaczonek, Boguslaw
2007   On formal metonymy. In: K. Kosecki (ed.), *Perspectives on Metonymy. Proceedings of the International Conference "Perspectives on Metonymy",* 43–67. Frankfurt a.M: Peter Lang.

Bierwiaczonek, Boguslaw
2013   *Metonymy in Language, Thought and Brain.* Sheffield: Equinox.

Blanco Carrión, Olga, Antonio Barcelona, Pilar Guerrero Medina, Mª del Carmen Guarddon Anelo, Isabel Hernández Gomáriz, Carmen Portero Muñoz and Ana Laura Rodríguez Redondo
In press   Applying the entry model in a detailed database of metonymy: A discussion of the problems involved. *Linguistics Applied* 6, thematic isssue *The Character and Use of Figurative Language.*

Brdar, Mario
2007   *Metonymy in Grammar. Towards Motivating Extensions of Grammatical Categories and Constructions.* Osijek: Faculty of Philosophy, Josip Juraj Strossmayer University.

Brdar-Szabó, Rita
2009   Metonymy in Indirect Directives: Stand-alone Conditionals in English, German, Hungarian, and Croatian. In: K.-U. Panther, L. Thornburg and A. Barcelona (eds.), *Metonymy and Metaphor in Grammar,* 323–336. Amsterdam/Philadelphia: John Benjamins.

Brdar, Mario and Rita Brdar-Szabó
2007   When Zidane is not simply Zidane, and Bill Gates is not just Bill Gates: Some thoughts on the construction of metaphtonymic meanings. In: G. Radden, K.-M. Köpcke, T. Berg and P. Siemund (eds.), *Aspects of Meaning Construction,* 125–142. Amsterdam: John Benjamins.

Ciepiela, Kamila
2007   Metonymy in aphasia. In: K. Kosecki (ed.), *Perspectives on Metonymy. Proceedings of the International Conference "Perspectives on Metonymy",* 199–208. Frankfurt a.M: Peter Lang.

Croft, William
[1993] 2002   The role of domains in the interpretation of metaphors and metonymies. *Cognitive Linguistics* 4(4): 335–371.

Croft, William and David Alan Cruse
2004   *Cognitive Linguistics.* New York: Cambridge University Press.
Cruse, David Alan
2000   *Meaning in Language.* Oxford: Oxford University Press.
Dirven, René
1999   Conversion as a conceptual metonymy of event schemata. In: G. Radden and K.-U. Panther (eds.), *Metonymy in Language and Thought,* 275–287. Amsterdam / Philadelphia: John Benjamins.
Dirven, René
2002   Metonymy and metaphor: Different strategies of conceptualisation. In: R. Dirven and R. Pörings (eds.), *Metaphor and Metonymy in Comparison and Contrast,* 75–112. Berlin: Mouton de Gruyter.
Dzeren-Główacka, Silwia
2007   Beating up intelligence. Metonymy in Terry Pratchett's novels. K. Kosecki (ed.), *Perspectives on Metonymy. Proceedings of the International Conference "Perspectives on Metonymy",* 335–348. Frankfurt a.M: Peter Lang.
Emmott, Catherine
1999   Embodied in a constructed world: Narrative processing, knowledge representation, and indirect anaphora. In: K. van Hoek, A. A. Kibrik and L. Noordman (eds.), *Discourse Studies in Cognitive Linguistics,* 5–27. Amsterdam: John Benjamins.
Fass, Dan C.
1997   *Processing Metonymy and Metaphor* (Contemporary Studies in Cognitive Science and Technology, Vol. 1). Westport: Ablex Publishing.
Fauconnier, Gilles
1997   *Mappings in Thought and Language.* Cambridge: Cambridge University Press.
Feyaerts, Kurt
1999   Metonymic hierarchies. The conceptualization of stupidity in German idiomatic expressions. In: K.-U. Panther and G. Radden (eds.), *Metonymy in Language and Thought,* 309–334. Amsterdam/Philadelphia: John Benjamins.
Fillmore, Charles
1985   Frames and the semantics of understanding. *Quaderni di Semantica* 6(2): 222–254.
Forceville, Charles and Eduardo Urios-Aparisi (eds.)
2009   *Multimodal Metaphor.* Berlin: Mouton de Gruyter.
Frisson, Steven and Martin Pickering
1999   The processing of metonymy: Evidence from eye-movements. *Journal of Experimental Psychology: Learning, Memory and Cognition* 25: 1366–1383.
Geeraerts, Dirk
2002   The interaction of metaphor and metonymy in composite expressions. In: R. Dirven and R. Pörings (eds.), *Metaphor and Metonymy in Comparison and Contrast,* 435–465. Berlin/New York: Mouton de Gruyter.
Geeraerts, Dirk
this volume   13. Lexical semantics. Berlin/Boston: De Gruyter Mouton
Geeraerts, Dirk and Yves Peirsman
2011   Zones, Facets and Prototype-based Metonymy. In: R. Benczes, A. Barcelona and F.-J. Ruiz de Mendoza Ibáñez (eds.), *Defining Metonymy in Cognitive Linguistics. Towards a Consensus View,* 88–102. Amsterdam: John Benjamins.
Gibbs, Raymond W, Jr.
1994   *The Poetics of Mind. Figurative Thought, Language and Understanding.* Cambridge: Cambridge University Press.
Gibbs, Raymond W, Jr.
2007a   Experimental tests of figurative meaning construction. In: G. Radden, K.-M. Köpcke, T. Berg and P. Siemund (eds.), *Aspects of Meaning Construction,* 19–32. Amsterdam: John Benjamins.

Gibbs, Raymond W, Jr.
2007b   Why cognitive linguists should care more about empirical methods. In: M. González-Márquez, I. Mittelberg, S. Coulson and M. Spivey (eds.), *Methods in Cognitive Linguistics*, 1–16. Amsterdam: John Benjamins.
Gibbs, Raymond W, Jr.
this volume   8. Metaphor. Berlin/Boston: De Gruyter Mouton
Glynn, Dylan and Kerstin Fischer (eds.)
2010   *Quantitative Methods in Cognitive Semantics: Corpus-Driven Approaches*. Berlin: Mouton De Gruyter.
Goldberg, Adele
2006   *Constructions at Work. The nature of Generalization in Language*. Oxford: Oxford University Press.
Goossens, Louis
[1990] 2002   Metaphtonymy: The interaction of metaphor and metonymy in expressions for linguistic action. *Cognitive Linguistics* 1(3): 323–340.
Goossens, Louis, Paul Pauwels, Brygida Rudzka-Ostyn, Anne-Marie Simon-Vanderbergen, and Johan Vanparys
1995   *By Word of Mouth. Metaphor, Metonymy and Linguistic Action in a Cognitive Perspective*. Amsterdam/Philadelphia: John Benjamins.
Greenbaum, Sidney and Randolph Quirk
1990   *The Student's Grammar of the English Language*. London: Longman.
Heine, Bernd, Ulrike Claudi and Friederike Hünnemeyer
1991   *Grammaticalization. A Conceptual Framework*. Chicago.: University of Chicago Press.
Hilpert, Martin
2007   Chained metonymies in lexicon and grammar: A cross-linguistic perspective on body terms. In: G. Radden, K.-M. Köpcke, T. Berg and P. Siemund (eds.), *Aspects of Meaning Construction*, 77–98. Amsterdam: John Benjamins.
Hilpert, Martin
this volume   16. Historical linguistics. Berlin/Boston: De Gruyter Mouton
Holme, Randal
2009   *Cognitive Linguistics and Language Teaching*. Basingstoke: Palgrave Macmillan.
Hopper Paul and Elizabeth Closs-Traugott
1993   *Grammaticalization*. Cambridge: Cambridge University Press.
Janda, Laura
this volume   30. Tense, aspect and mood. Berlin/Boston: De Gruyter Mouton
Kosecki, Krzyscztof
2007   Some remarks on metonymy in compounding. In: K. Kosecki (ed.), *Perspectives on Metonymy. Proceedings of the International Conference "Perspectives on Metonymy"*, 241–251. Frankfurt a.M: Peter Lang.
Kövecses, Zoltán and Günter Radden
1998   Metonymy: Developing a cognitive linguistic view. *Cognitive Linguistics* 9(1): 37–77.
Kuzniak, Marek
2007   Part-whole relations in the selected epigrams by J. Staudynger. In: K. Kosecki (ed.), *Perspectives on Metonymy. Proceedings of the International Conference "Perspectives on Metonymy"*, 323–333. Frankfurt a.M: Peter Lang.
Kwiatkowska, Alina
2007   'Pre-linguistic and non-linguistic metonymy'. In: K. Kosecki (ed.), *Perspectives on Metonymy. Proceedings of the International Conference "Perspectives on Metonymy"*, 297–307. Frankfurt a.M: Peter Lang.
Lakoff, George
1987   *Women, Fire and Dangerous Things. What Categories Reveal About the Mind*. Chicago: University of Chicago Press.

Lakoff, George
   1993   The contemporary theory of metaphor. In: A. Ortony (ed.), *Metaphor and Thought* (2nd edition), 202–251. Cambridge: Cambridge University Press.

Lakoff, George and Mark Johnson
   1980   *Metaphors We Live By*. Chicago: University of Chicago Press.

Lakoff, George and Mark Turner
   1989   *More than Cool Reason: A Field Guide to Poetic Metaphor*. Chicago: University of Chicago Press.

Langacker, Ronald W.
   1987   *Foundations of Cognitive Grammar*. Vol 1: *Theoretical Prerequisites*. Stanford: Stanford University Press.

Langacker, Ronald W.
   1993   Reference-point constructions. *Cognitive Linguistics* 4: 1–38.

Langacker, Ronald W.
   1999   *Grammar and Conceptualization*. Berlin/New York: Mouton de Gruyter.

Langacker, Ronald W.
   this volume   6. Construal.Berlin/Boston: De Gruyter Mouton

Langacker, Ronald W.
   2009   Metonymic grammar. In: K.-U. Panther, L. Thornburg and A. Barcelona (eds.), *Metonymy and Metaphor in Grammar*, 45–71. Amsterdam/Philadelphia: John Benjamins.

Littlemore, Jeannette
   2009   *Applying Cognitive Linguistics to Second Language Learning and Teaching*. Basingstoke: Palgrave Macmillan.

Littlemore, Jeannette
   2015   *Metonymy: Hidden Shortcuts in Language, Thought and Communication*. Cambridge: Cambridge University Press.

Markert, Katja and Malvina Nissim
   2003   Corpus-based metonymy analysis. *Metaphor and Symbol* 18(3): 175–188.

Martsa, Sándor
   2013   *Conversion in English: A Cognitive Semantic Approach*. Newcastle-upon-Tyne: Cambridge Scholars Publishing.

Michaelis, Laura
   2004   Type shifting in construction grammar: An integrated approach to aspectual coercion. *Cognitive Linguistics* 15: 1–67.

Nunberg, Geoffrey
   1995   Transfers of meaning. *Journal of Semantics* 12: 109–132.

Palmer, Gary, Russell S. Rader, and Art D. Clarito
   2009   The metonymic basis of a 'semantic partial': Tagalog lexical constructions with *ka-*. In: K.-U. Panther, L. Thornburg and A. Barcelona (eds.), *Metonymy and Metaphor in Grammar*, 111–144. Amsterdam/Philadelphia: John Benjamins.

Pang, Kam-Yiu
   2006   A partitioned-narrative model of the self: Its linguistic manifestations, entailments, and ramifications. Ph.D. Dissertation. University of Otago, New Zealand.

Panther, Klaus-Uwe
   2005   The role of conceptual metonymy in meaning construction. In: F. J. Ruiz de Mendoza Ibáñez and S. Peña Cervel (eds.), *Cognitive Linguistics: Internal Dynamics and Interdisciplinary Interaction*, 353–386. Berlin/New York: Mouton de Gruyter.

Panther, Klaus-Uwe and Linda Thornburg
   1998   A cognitive approach to inferencing in conversation. *Journal of Pragmatics* 30: 755–769.

Panther, Klaus-Uwe and Linda Thornburg
  2000   The EFFECT FOR CAUSE metonymy in English grammar. In: A. Barcelona (ed.), *Metaphor and Metonymy at the Crossroads. A Cognitive Perspective*, 215–231. Berlin/New York: Mouton de Gruyter.
Panther, Klaus-Uwe and Linda Thornburg
  2002   The roles of metaphor and metonymy in English *-er* nominal. In: R. Dirven and R. Pörings (eds.), *Metaphor and Metonymy in Comparison and Contrast*, 279–319. Berlin: Mouton de Gruyter.
Panther, Klaus-Uwe and Linda Thornburg (eds.)
  2003a   *Metonymy and Pragmatic Inferencing*. Amsterdam/Philadelphia: John Benjamins.
Panther, Klaus-Uwe and Linda Thornburg
  2003b   Introduction: On the nature of conceptual metonymy. In: K.-U. Panther and L. Thornburg (eds.), *Metonymy and Pragmatic Inferencing*. 1–20. Amsterdam/Philadelphia: John Benjamins.
Panther, Klaus-Uwe and Linda Thornburg
  2007   Metonymy. In: D. Geeraerts and H. Cuyckens (eds.), *Handbook of Cognitive Linguistics*, 236–263. Oxford: Oxford University Press.
Panther, Klaus-Uwe, Linda Thornburg, and Antonio Barcelona (eds.)
  2009   *Metonymy and Metaphor in Grammar*. Amsterdam/Philadelphia: John Benjamins.
Papafragou, Anna
  1996   On metonymy *Lingua* 99: 169–195.
Paradis, Carita
  2004   Where does metonymy stop? Senses, facets and active zones. *Metaphor and Symbol* 19(4): 245–264.
Paradis, Carita
  2011   Metonymization. A key mechanism in semantic change. In: R. Benczes, A. Barcelona and F.-J. Ruiz de Mendoza Ibáñez, *Defining Metonymy in Cognitive Linguistics. Towards a Consensus View*, 62–87. Amsterdam: John Benjamins.
Peirsman, Yves and Dirk Geeraerts
  2006   Metonymy as a prototypical category. *Cognitive Linguistics* 17(3): 269–316.
Pérez Hernández, Lorena
  2007   High-level metonymies in the understanding of modality. In: K. Kosecki (ed.), *Perspectives on Metonymy. Proceedings of the International Conference "Perspectives on Metonymy"*, 133–146. Frankfurt a. M.: Peter Lang.
Pluciennik, Jaroslaw
  2007   Princess Antonomasia, individualism, and the quixotism of culture: A case of 'Tristram Shandy' by Laurence Stern. In: K. Kosecki (ed.), *Perspectives on Metonymy. Proceedings of the International Conference "Perspectives on Metonymy"*, 349–366. Frankfurt a. M.: Peter Lang.
Pragglejaz Group
  2007   MIP: A method for identifying metaphorically-used words in discourse. *Metaphor and Symbol* 22: 1–40.
Pustejovsky, James
  1995   *The Generative Lexicon*. Cambridge: MIT Press.
Radden, Günter
  2002   How metonymic are metaphors? In: R. Dirven and R. Pörings (eds.), *Metaphor and Metonymy in Comparison and Contrast*, 407–434. Berlin: Mouton de Gruyter.
Radden, Günter
  2005   The ubiquity of metonymy. In: J. L. Otal Campo, I. Navarro i Ferrando, and B. Bellés Fortuño (eds.), *Cognitive and Discourse Approaches to Metaphor and Metonymy*, 11–28. Castellón: Universitat Jaume I.

Radden, Günter
   2009   Generic reference in English: A metonymic and conceptual blending analysis. In: K.-U. Panther, L. Thornburg and A. Barcelona (eds.), *Metonymy and Metaphor in Grammar*, 199–228. Amsterdam/Philadelphia: John Benjamins.

Radden, Günter and René Dirven
   2007   *Cognitive English Grammar.* Amsterdam/Philadelphia: John Benjamins.

Radden, Günter and Zoltán Kövecses
   1999   Towards a theory of metonymy. In: K.-U. Panther and G. Radden (eds.), *Metonymy in Language and Thought*, 17–59. Amsterdam/Philadelphia: John Benjamins.

Radden, Günter and Klaus-Uwe Panther
   2004   Reflections on motivation. In: G. Radden and K.-U. Panther (eds.), *Studies in Linguistic Motivation*, 1–46. Berlin & New York: Mouton de Gruyter.

Rudzka-Ostyn, Brygida
   1995   Metaphor, schema, invariance. The case of verbs of answering. In: L. Goossens, P. Pauwels, B. Rudzka-Ostyn, A. Simon-Vanderbergen, and J. Vanparys (eds.) *By Word of Mouth. Metaphor, Metonymy and Linguistic Action in a Cognitive Perspective*, 205–243. Amsterdam/Philadelphia: John Benjamins.

Ruiz de Mendoza Ibáñez, Francisco José
   2000   The role of mappings and domains in understanding metonymy. In: A. Barcelona (ed.), *Metaphor and Metonymy at the Crossroads. A Cognitive Perspective*, 109–132. Berlin/New York: Mouton de Gruyter.

Ruiz de Mendoza Ibáñez, Francisco José
   2011   Metonymy and cognitive operations. In: R. Benczes, A. Barcelona and F.-J. Ruiz de Mendoza Ibáñez (eds.), *Defining Metonymy in Cognitive Linguistics. Towards a Consensus View*, 103–123. Amsterdam: John Benjamins.

Ruiz de Mendoza, Francisco José and Olga I. Díez Velasco
   2004   Metonymic motivation in anaphoric reference. In: G. Radden and K.-U. Panther (eds.), *Studies in Linguistic Motivation*, 293–320. Berlin/New York: Mouton de Gruyter

Ruiz de Mendoza Ibáñez, Francisco José and Ricardo Mairal Usón
   2007   High-level metaphor and metonymy in meaning construction. In: G. Radden, Günter, K.-M. Köpcke, T. Berg and P. Siemund (eds.), *Aspects of Meaning Construction*, 33–49. Amsterdam: John Benjamins.

Ruiz de Mendoza Ibáñez, Francisco José and José Luis Otal Campo
   2002   *Metonymy, Grammar and Communication.* Albolote: Comares.

Ruiz de Mendoza Ibáñez, Francisco José and Sandra Peña Cervel
   2005   Conceptual interaction, cognitive operations and projection spaces. In: F. J. Ruiz de Mendoza Ibáñez and S. Peña Cervel (eds.), *Cognitive Linguistics: Internal Dynamics and Interdisciplinary Interaction*, 249–280. Berlin/New York: Mouton de Gruyter.

Ruiz de Mendoza Ibáñez, Francisco José and Lorena Pérez Hernández
   2001   Metonymy and the grammar: motivation, constraints and interaction. *Language and Communication* 21(4): 321–357.

Ruiz de Mendoza Ibáñez, Francisco José and Lorena Pérez Hernández
   2003   Cognitive operations and pragmatic implication. In: K.-U. Panther and L. Thornburg (eds.), *Metonymy and Pragmatic Inferencing,* 23–49. Amsterdam/Philadelphia: John Benjamins.

Steen, Gerard, Aletta G. Dorst, J. Berenike Herrmann, Anna Kaal, Tina Krennmayr, and Trijintje Pasma
   2010   *A Method for Linguistic Metaphor Identification.* Amsterdam: John Benjamins.

Stefanowitsch, Anatol, and Stephan Th. Gries (eds.)
   2008   *Corpus-Based Approaches to Metaphor and Metonymy.* Berlin: Mouton De Gruyter.

Szawerna, Michal
  2007   Deverbal nominalization as a type of metonymic extension from processes to things. In: K. Kosecki (ed.), *Perspectives on Metonymy. Proceedings of the International Conference "Perspectives on Metonymy"*, 147–155.Frankfurt a. M.: Peter Lang.
Taylor, John
  [1989] 1995   *Linguistic Categorization. Prototypes in Linguistic Theory.* Oxford: Clarendon.
Thornburg, Linda and Klaus-Uwe Panther
  1997   Speech act metonymies. In: W.-A. Liebert, G. Redeker; and L. Waugh (eds.), *Discourse and Perspective in Cognitive Linguistics*, 205–219. Amsterdam/Philadelphia: Benjamins.
Traugott, Elizabeth Closs and Richard B. Dasher
  2002   *Regularity in Semantic Change.* Cambridge: Cambridge University Press.
Turner, Mark
  this volume   10. Blending in language and communication. Berlin/Boston: De Gruyter Mouton
Turner, Mark and Gilles Fauconnier
  2000   Metaphor, metonymy and binding. In: A. Barcelona (ed.), *Metaphor and Metonymy at the Crossroads. A Cognitive Perspective*, 133–145. Berlin/New York: Mouton de Gruyter.
Warren, Beatrice
  1999   Aspects of referential metonymy. In: K.-U. Panther and G. Radden (eds.), *Metonymy in Language and Thought*, 121–135. Amsterdam/Philadelphia: John Benjamins
Wilcox, Phyllis P.
  2004   A cognitive key: Metonymic and metaphorical mappings in ASL. *Cognitive Linguistics* 15(2): 197–222.
Wilcox, Sherman
  this volume   33. Signed languages. Berlin/Boston: De Gruyter Mouton
Zhang, Weiwei
  2013   Variation in metonymy. A Corpus-based cognitive-linguistic approach. Ph. D. Dissertation. University of Leuven.
Zhang, Weiwei, Dirk Speelman and Dirk Geeraerts
  2011   Variation in the (non)metonymic capital names in mainland Chinese and Taiwan Chinese. *Metaphor and the Social World* 1(1): 90–112.
Ziegeler, Debra
  2007   Arguing the case against coercion. In: G. Radden, Günter, K.-M. Köpcke, T. Berg and P. Siemund (eds.), *Aspects of Meaning Construction*, 99–123. Amsterdam: John Benjamins.

Antonio Barcelona, Córdoba (Spain)

8. Metaphor

1. Introduction
2. Cognitive linguistic findings
3. Finding metaphor in language and thought
4. Nonlinguistic evidence on conceptual metaphors
5. Verbal metaphor understanding
6. Conclusion
7. References

1. Introduction

Have you ever asked yourself the question, "Can a person who continually struggles with impure thoughts be genuinely saved?" Although this issue does not come to my mind very often, I stumbled across a website that gave a detailed answer to this challenging query. Part of the response included the following (http://questions.org/attq/can-a-person-who-continually-struggles-with-impure-thoughts-be-genuinely-saved/):

> "Although in this life we will never be completely freed from the taint of sin and impure thoughts, we can grow in our ability to control our response to them. ... By responding to our evil and impure thoughts with disciplined resistance, we can go a long way towards cleansing ourselves of habitual, willful sin. But we still live in a fallen world and will continue to struggle with our dark side."

We all roughly understand what is meant by the metaphoric phrases *taint of sin, impure thoughts*, as well as the idea that *with disciplined resistance, we can go a long way towards cleansing ourselves of habitual, willful sin*. Each of these refer, in part, to the common beliefs that good thoughts and behaviors are clean, while bad, or evil, thoughts and behaviors are dirty, contaminated, or polluted in some manner. Most historical approaches to metaphor see it as a special rhetorical tool that may reflect creative thinking and unique aesthetic abilities (Beardsley 1962; Ricoeur 1977). But what do metaphors like *impure thoughts* or *cleansing ... ourselves of sin* imply about people's cognitive and linguistic abilities?

Cognitive linguistic research on metaphor has explored how both conventional and novel metaphoric language reveals important insights into people's common metaphoric conceptions of various, mostly abstract, topics. Similar to research on other topics within cognitive linguistics, metaphoric structure and behavior has been studied not as if these are autonomous from ordinary cognition, but as reflections of general conceptual systems, psychological processing mechanisms, and specific patterns of bodily experience (Gibbs 1994; Lakoff and Johnson 1980, 1999). People speak metaphorically for communicative purposes, but metaphoric language emerges from systematic patterns of metaphoric thoughts known as "conceptual metaphors". Most importantly, perhaps, cognitive linguistic research on metaphor has advanced the idea that many conceptual metaphors emerge from recurring patterns of bodily experience, which offers compelling links between embodiment, metaphoric thought, and metaphoric language and action.

This chapter describes some of the empirical findings on metaphor within cognitive linguistics, and then considers several of the ongoing debates regarding the cognitive theory of metaphor. Cognitive linguistic approaches now dominate in the multi-disciplinary world of metaphor research. Yet cognitive metaphor theory has always evoked considerable controversy regarding its methods, data, and theoretical conclusions about language, minds, and bodies. My aim is to address some of these criticisms and suggest one way of advancing cognitive metaphor theory to better capture the complex realities of how people's metaphoric thought dynamically shapes their use and understanding of verbal metaphor.

2. Cognitive linguistic findings

The original evidence for conceptual metaphors comes from the systematic analysis of conventional expressions in different languages (Lakoff and Johnson 1980, 1999; Kövecses 2002). Consider the following ways that English speakers sometimes talk about their romantic relationships:

> *We're headed in opposite directions*
> *We're spinning our wheels*
> *Our relationship is at a crossroads*
> *Our marriage was on the rocks*

Cognitive linguistic analyses argue that these individual expressions are not clichéd idioms expressing literal meaning, but reflect, and are said to be partially motivated by, different aspects of the enduring conceptual metaphor LOVE RELATIONSHIPS ARE JOURNEYS. There is a tight mapping according to which entities in the domain of love (e.g., the lovers, their common goals, the love relationship) correspond systematically to entities in the domain of journeys (e.g., the traveler, the vehicle, destinations, etc.). Each linguistic expression above refers to a different correspondence that arises from the mapping of familiar, often embodied, understanding of journeys onto the more abstract idea of a love relationship (e.g., difficulties in the relationship are conceived of as obstacles on the physical journey). The hypothesis that some concepts may be metaphorically structured makes it possible to explain what until now has been seen as unrelated conventional expressions or even "dead metaphors".

Consider one other example of how metaphoric concepts may explain the systematicity among conventional phrases used to talk about abstract topics, related to the examples that opened this chapter (Stefanowitsch 2011: 301):

> the *stain* of guilt/sin/illegitimacy
> *impure* thoughts/soul/character
> a *dirty* mind/look/word/secret
> an *unclean* thought/spirit/mind
> to *contaminate* a relationship
> to *taint* someone's reputation
> to *pollute* someone's mind/thoughts

Each of these expressions may be motivated by the conceptual metaphor MORAL CORRUPTION IS UNCLEANLINESS, which is linked to the corresponding metaphor MORAL GOODNESS IS CLEANLINESS (Lizardo 2012). These conceptual metaphors, arising from bodily experiences related to cleanliness and health, give coherence to varying conventional phrases which otherwise might be seen as having arbitrary roots.

Most work within cognitive linguistics examines the systematicity of individual phrases and expressions, sometimes selected from dictionaries, or from specific corpora containing naturalistic discourse. Cognitive linguists typically do not analyze all the metaphoric words or expressions seen in a corpus, but select different examples from which the existence of particular conceptual metaphors may be inferred. The range of abstract conceptual domains motivated by conceptual metaphor is immense, and includes emotions, the self, morality, politics, science concepts, illness, mathematics, interpersonal relations, time, legal concepts, and many cultural ideologies, to name just a few of the many target domains motivated by conceptual metaphors. Conceptual metaphors have been found in virtually every contemporary language, both spoken and signed, as well as throughout history going back to ancient languages. For example, Cicero's speeches in ancient Rome give evidence of many dozens of conceptual metaphors still active in contemporary metaphor talk. Consider this brief comment, "Greek, which I have seized upon as eagerly as if I had been desirous of satisfying a long-continued thirst, with the result that I have acquired first-hand the information which you see me using in this discussion" (Sjoblad 2009: 59). It is partly structured around the conceptual metaphor DESIRE IS HUNGER/THIRST.

Cognitive linguistic research has also demonstrated that some of the meanings of polysemous words are motivated by conceptual metaphoric mappings (for an overview of polysemy, see Gries this volume). For example, the meaning of *see* referring to knowing or understanding as in *I can't see the point of your argument*, is motivated by an enduring conceptual metaphor UNDERSTANDING IS SEEING. Many instances of polysemy are historically derived from conceptual metaphors that are still active parts of human conceptual systems (Cuyckens and Zawada 2001; Sweetser 1990). Under this view, the lexical organization of polysemous words is not a repository of random, idiosyncratic information, but is structured by general cognitive principles, like conceptual metaphor, that are systematic and recurrent throughout the lexicon.

Conceptual metaphor has also been shown to play an important role in grammatical form and structure. Similar to characterizing polysemy relations, various approaches to construction grammar note that metaphor provides an essential link in constructional networks (Goldberg 1995; Langacker 1999). Metaphor has also been shown to be critical for explaining how motion verbs can be metaphorized to convey state of change as in *He went red* and *Here comes the beep*, which emerge from the mapping of the grammar of the source domain onto the grammar of the target domain (Lakoff and Johnson 1999; Panther and Thornburg 2009; Radden 1995). One cognitive theory, called the Lexical Constructional Model, gives metaphor, as well as metonymy, a central role in motivating various grammatical phenomena (Ruiz de Mendoza and Diez 2002). For example, high-level conceptual metaphors, such as EXPRIENTIAL ACTION IS EFFECTUAL ACTION, permit the sensible use of different caused motion constructions, like *John laughed Peter out of the office*. In this manner, high-level conceptual metaphors place external constraints on the ways that grammatical constructions may interact with lexical representations.

Another discovery within cognitive linguistics is that many novel metaphorical expressions do not express completely new source-to-target domain mappings, but are creative instantiations of conventional conceptual metaphors. For instance, the assertion, *Our marriage was a slow crawl through a long mud pit* presents a vivid perspective on how one's romantic relationship can be understood as a very specific physical journey (e.g., LOVE RELATIONSHIPS ARE JOURNEYS). Analyses of literary metaphors (Freeman 1995; Goatly 1997; Lakoff and Turner 1989) and novel metaphorical arguments in expository writing (Eubanks 2000; Koller 2004) demonstrate how many so-called "novel" metaphors are grounded in conventional mappings.

Of course, certain metaphors express "one-shot" metaphoric mappings as seen in resemblance or "A is B" expressions such as *Juliet is the sun*, *Man is wolf*, and *My surgeon is a butcher*. One cognitive linguistic approach to how people interpret "A is B" metaphors, "conceptual blending theory", assumes that multiple mental spaces can participate in a mapping, compared to the two-space or two-domain models in conceptual metaphor theory (Fauconnier and Turner 2002; Turner this volume). Metaphor meaning is captured by a blended space that inherits some structure from each of the input spaces. Consider the familiar metaphor *surgeons are butchers* (Grady et al. 1999). The mapping of information from the source domain of butchery to the target domain of surgery by itself does not provide a crucial element of our interpretation of this metaphorical statement, namely that the surgeon is incompetent. After all, butchers can indeed be as skilled at their job as surgeons are at theirs. Under a blending theory account, the target input space for surgery inherits elements from the corresponding frame for surgery such as of a person being operated upon, the identity of the person who is doing the operation, and the place where this all happens. The source domain butchery input space inherits information such as what a butcher does and his relevant activities such as using sharp instruments to slice up meat. Besides inheriting partial structure from each input space, the blend develops emergent content of its own, which arises from the juxtaposition of elements from the inputs. Specifically, the butchery space projects a means-end relationship that is incompatible with the means-end relationship in the surgery space. For instance, the goal of butchery is to kill the animal and sever the flesh from its bones. But surgeons aim to heal their patients. This incongruity of the butcher's means with the surgeon's end leads to an emergent inference that the surgeon is incompetent. Most generally, blending theory extends conceptual metaphor theory by allowing for mappings that are not unidirectional between multiple domains (see Fauconnier and Lakoff 2013; Tendahl 2008 for a discussion of the commonalities and differences existing between the two theories).

The rise of work in both conceptual metaphor theory and conceptual blending theory has led to significant advances in the study of metaphor in spoken and written discourse (Cameron 2011; Charteris-Black 2004; Hart this volume; Koller 2004; Mussolff 2004; Naciscione 2010; Oakley and Hougaard 2008; Semino 2009). This work is generally characterized by close attention to the presence and form of metaphorical ideas in discourse and what these reveal about the cognitive and socio-cultural grounding of metaphorical communication. Many of these discussions focus on the limitations of purely cognitive approaches to talk and text, as well as some of the methodological problems associated with clearly identifying specific conceptual metaphors, and different blending patterns, in naturalistic language. But the increased emphasis in examining situated metaphor use has gone far to illustrate how cognitive linguistic research can be applied to a wide range of discourse domains, which uncovers hidden metaphors in the ways people think about a vast range of abstract topics.

Metaphor is also well studied within corpus linguistics research (Deignan 2005; Gries and Stefanowitsch 2006). Although cognitive linguists often claim that their work is "usage-based", especially in comparison to traditional generative linguistics research, most classic cognitive linguistic studies typically examine isolated individual expressions outside of context. But the corpus linguistic research on metaphor enables scholars to examine specific hypotheses about real-world metaphor use by searching various small and large-scale corpora. The results of these studies demonstrate both important confirmation of facets of conceptual metaphor theory, for example, but also indicate cases where there may be far greater variation in the expression of metaphor than originally anticipated.

One reason why conceptual metaphors may be a prominent part of everyday language and thought is that they are often grounded in recurring patterns of bodily experience. For example, journeys frequently appear as source domains in different conceptual metaphors because of the regularity with which people take various journeys (i.e., starting from a source, moving along a path until reaching a goal). Similarly, people frequently describe good behavior in terms of cleanliness given the strong association between things that are clean and things that are good.

In fact, strong correlations in everyday embodied experience enable the creation of "primary metaphors", such as INTIMACY IS CLOSENESS (e.g., *We have a close relationship*), DIFFICULTIES ARE BURDENS (e.g., *She's weighed down by responsibilities*), and ORGANIZATION IS PHYSICAL STRUCTURE (e.g., *How do the pieces of the theory fit together*) (Grady 1997). In each case, the source domain of the metaphor comes from the body's sensorimotor system. A primary metaphor has a metaphorical mapping for which there is an independent and direct experiential basis and independent linguistic evidence. Blending primary metaphors into larger metaphorical wholes, on the other hand, create complex metaphors. For instance, the three primary metaphors PERSISTING IS REMAINING ERECT, STRUCTURE IS PHYSICAL STRUCTURE, and INTERRELATED IS INTERWOVEN can be combined in different ways to give rise to complex metaphors that have traditionally been seen as conceptual metaphors, such as the expression *The theory started to unravel and soon fell apart*.

There is continuing debate in cognitive linguistics over whether primary metaphors really represent metaphorical mappings as opposed to metonymic ones. For instance, "primary metaphors" may be conceptually possible due to either decontextualization of certain conventional metonymies (Radden 2002) or by a metonymic understanding of the domains connected by metaphor that leads to the recognition of a partial abstract similarity between source and target (e.g., *That is a loud color*) (Barcelona 2000, this volume). Kövecses (2013) argues that correlation metaphors, in particular, emerge from frame-like representations through a metonymic stage (e.g., KNOWING IS SEEING emerges from the logically prior metonymy SEEING SOMETHING PHYSICAL STANDS FOR KNOWING THE THING). These alternative accounts of primary metaphors, at the very least, suggest a greater role for metonymy in the development of metaphorical concepts.

Finally, the embodied nature of conceptual metaphors has led to the development of the neural theory of metaphor (Feldman 2006; Lakoff 2008). This perspective aims to characterize metaphoric mappings as being fundamentally grounded in neural activities, which provides the basis for the emergence of metaphoric concepts and how metaphoric language is used and interpreted. The neural theory of metaphor has frankly not, as yet, been widely influential within cognitive linguistics, although certain cognitive neuroscience evidence is consistent with the idea that sensorimotor brain processes are active when various conventional metaphors are understood (Desai et al. 2011).

Cognitive metaphor theory has done much to situate metaphor within central discussions of minds, bodies, and language within cognitive science, and in many people's view, is the dominant theory in the multidisciplinary world of metaphor research. But cognitive linguistic work on metaphor has evoked much criticism as scholars raise various methodological and theoretical questions about the very idea of conceptual metaphors. I now discuss some of these controversies.

3. Finding metaphor in language and thought

3.1. Identifying metaphoric language

A long-standing complaint about cognitive linguistic theories of metaphor is that many conventional expressions viewed as metaphoric by cognitive linguists are not metaphoric at all (Jackendoff and Aron 1991). Critics argue that expressions like *He was depressed* or *I'm off to a good start in graduate school* are entirely literal, and are not motivated by conceptual metaphors such as SAD IS DOWN or LIFE IS A JOURNEY. Some conventional expressions may have once been recognized as metaphoric, but are really seen by contemporary speakers as "literal" speech, instances of "dead" metaphors, or mere instances of polysemy (McGlone 2007; Murphy 1996).

How do we know if cognitive linguists' intuitions about the metaphoricity of conventional expressions in language are correct? A first step toward answering this question tries to determine which words are metaphorically used in discourse. One proposal, the "metaphor identification procedure" (MIP), suggests that an analyst may find metaphorically used words in context through the following process (Pragglejaz Group 2007):

1. Read the entire text (i.e., written text or talk transcript) to establish a general understanding of the discourse.
2. Determine the lexical units in the text.
3. For each lexical unit in the text, check metaphorical use: Establish the meaning of the lexical unit in context (i.e., how it applies to an entity, its relation in the situation evoked by the text [contextual meaning]). You should take into account what words are before and after the lexical unit. Determine if the lexical unit has a more basic current/contemporary meaning in other contexts than the one in the given context. For our purposes, basic meanings tend to be: more concrete; what they evoke is easier to imagine, see, hear, feel, smell and taste; related to bodily action; more precise (as opposed to vague); and historically older. Basic meanings are not necessarily the most frequent meaning of the lexical unit.
4. If the lexical unit has a more basic current/contemporary meaning in other contexts than the given context, decide whether the contextual meaning can be understood by comparison or contrast with the basic meaning. If yes, mark the lexical unit as metaphorical. Repeat steps 1–4 for each lexical unit.

Consider how MIP may be applied to analyze the first sentence of a newspaper story about former Indian Premier Sonia Gandhi. The lexical units in the sentence are marked by slashes as in the following /For/years/SoniaGandhi/has/struggled/to/convince/Indians/ that/she/is/fit/to/wear/the/mantle/of/the/political/dynasty/into/which/she/married/, let alone/ to/become/premier/

According to MIP, words such as *for*, *years*, *Sonia Gandhi*, and *has* are not metaphoric. However, *struggled* is deemed to be metaphoric because its contextual meaning, indicating effort, difficulty and lack of success in reaching a goal contrasts with its basic meaning referring to using one's physical strength against someone or something (e.g., *She picked up the child, but he struggled and kicked*). More importantly, the contrast between the contextual and basic meanings of *struggled* is based on comparison, such that we understand abstract effort, difficulty and opposition in terms of physical effort, difficulty, and conflict.[1]

Another word in the opening sentence with possible metaphoric meaning is *wear*. Its contextual meaning, given by the idiomatic *phrase wear the mantle*, refers to some person who has a leading role in a family whose members have occupied high political positions. The basic meaning of *wear* is defined as 'to have something on your body as clothing, decoration or protection', which is also historically prior to other meanings of *wear*. The difference between the contextual and basic meanings is understood by comparison such that we interpret the process of following family members in political positions in terms of physically adorning the clothing that symbolizes that process.

The Pragglejaz Group determined that six of the 27 lexical units in the first sentence of the Gandhi story were judged to convey metaphoric meaning. These decisions about metaphoric meaning are, of course, influenced by how the contextual and basic meanings are actually defined, and the possible differences between these meanings being due to comparison as opposed to some other relationship (e.g., contiguity, opposition) (see Barnden 2011 for a discussion of the problematic distinction metaphor and metonymy).

A variant of MIP, called MIP-VU, has been applied to the analysis of large segments of texts in several discourse genres (Steen et al. 2010). Across different genres, prepositions were determined to be most metaphorical (43 %), followed by verbs (29 %), and then adjectives (18 %). More interestingly, different genres indicate varying degrees of metaphoricity. Academic discourse contains the most metaphorically used words (18 %), followed by news stories (15 %), fiction (11 %), and finally conversation (7 %). Many scholars may suspect that fiction should contain the most metaphoric language, but academic discourse coveys the most metaphoricity given the frequent reference to abstract concepts in these writings.

Metaphor identification schemes like MIP and MIP-VU are now widely employed in metaphor research. These schemes, at the very least, enable researchers to state with greater confidence that some word or phrase really expressed metaphoric meaning. Moreover, the conventional phrases identified as metaphor by cognitive linguists are invariably judged to express metaphoric meanings when seen in realistic discourse contexts. Of course, metaphor exists in larger units than individual words, including longer stretches of text and discourse, and it not clear whether MIP or MIP-VU can be extended to identify metaphor beyond the word level.

It is also important to remember that analysts' conscious judgments about the metaphoricity of a word or utterance may not reflect how ordinary people understand the metaphoric meanings of speakers' utterances. Metaphoricity may really be a matter of cognitive activation for specific individuals in particular moments of speaking and listening (Gibbs and Santa Cruz 2012; Müller 2008). For example, people may use so-called dead metaphors, but still give evidence of having vital metaphorical knowledge motivating a word or phrase's use in context. Thus, a speaker may use the term *depressed* to talk of another individual. Some analysts would claim that the connection between *depressed* and being very sad or having negative affect is quite opaque or even dead. But examination of this same speaker's manual gestures during talk shows her moving her

---

[1] MIP does not necessarily embrace the classic idea that metaphor is simply a matter of abbreviated comparison.

hands in a slow, downward motion when saying *depressed*, which reflects her conceptual understanding of SAD IS DOWN even if her speech may be characterized, by some, as expressing, a dead metaphor (Müller 2008). Determining the degree to which any metaphor is dead, sleeping, or alive depends on assessing a person's communicative actions in the moment, involving analysis of the individual's entire repertoire of language, speech sounds, gestures, and other body movements. Most generally, judgments about whether some word or expression is metaphor or dead, or, in some people's view, "literal" cannot be reliably made by just looking at the language on the page alone.

3.2. Are some metaphors deliberate?

Skepticism about the metaphoric nature of many conventional expressions studied by cognitive linguists has most recently led to the proposal that a select few metaphors are special because they have been deliberately composed, and quite consciously employed for their unique, didactic, qualities and sometimes poetic beauty (Steen 2006). When Shakespeare wrote "Juliet is the sun" in *Romeo and Juliet*, for example, he uttered a falsehood as a deliberate invitation for listeners to understand Juliet from an unusual perspective. Conventional metaphors, on the other hand, are mostly produced and understood automatically without people having to draw any cross-domain mappings (i.e., drawing an inference from the domain of journeys to romantic relationships). People may employ certain "signaling" devices to highlight that a certain metaphor was deliberately composed and employed, such as using the words *metaphorically, actually, quite*, and *utterly*, or via phrases such as *one might say, so to speak*, and *as it were* (Goatly 1997).

Interest in the idea of deliberate metaphor stems from the concern that CMT does not pay sufficient attention to the special communicative role verbal metaphors have in discourse. But the idea that some metaphors, and not others, are deliberate in their composition and use suffers from several problems (Gibbs 2011). First, most of the signals and tuning devices discussed in the literature on "deliberate" metaphor are not at all specific to metaphor! Words and phrases such as *almost, just, and sort of* are found throughout spoken discourse and not just with metaphor. This observation implies that the so-called signaling devices used with deliberate metaphors will not really identify which metaphors are deliberate and which are not. Thankfully, Shakespeare was smart enough to resist signaling his metaphors in this way. (e.g., *Juliet is the sun, so to speak*).

A second problem with the deliberate metaphor proposal is that much cognitive linguistic research demonstrates that even conventional language implicitly conveys cross-domain mappings. Psycholinguistic research, discussed later, indicates that people infer underlying conceptual metaphors when using and understanding a range of conventional metaphoric language, including classic idioms, proverbs, and many so-called clichéd expressions, such as *We've come a long way*. Various conventional nonlinguistic actions, including gestures, music, art, and many human actions, are similarly motivated by cross-domain associations, as will be described later. Critics of cognitive linguistic work on metaphor must address the psychological research showing how conventional expressions typically evoke cross-domain mappings, exactly what is supposed to occur only for selective deliberate uses of metaphor.

Finally, psychological research shows that most creative acts are anything but conscious and deliberate (Gibbs 2011). Many cognitive unconscious forces shape the online production and understanding of metaphors, which are simply not accessible to our conscious intuitions, despite our strong beliefs to the contrary. Rather than envisioning Shakespeare, for example, as being highly conscious and deliberate in his choice of words, including his use of "Juliet is the sun", it may be more accurate to conceive of his writing as in the "flow" of experience where words and phrase cascade from his fingertips without significant conscious effort. Shakespeare may have had various aesthetic, communicative intentions in writing his poems and plays. But we should not assume that some special parts of what he wrote were deliberate, with all others being the automatic product of his unconscious mind.

3.3. Inferring conceptual metaphors

One of the most persistent criticisms of cognitive linguistic research on metaphor is that it has not provided a reliable method for inferring the existence of different conceptual metaphors. For example, Lakoff and Johnson (1980) originally stated that the conceptual metaphor ARGUMENT IS WAR motivates the existence of conventional expressions such as *He attacked my argument* and *He defended his position*. Cognitive linguistic research suggests that any expression about argument that did not fit the WAR theme is really evidence for another theme, such as WEIGHING, TESTING, or COMPARING. But this strategy implies that no linguistic statement can be brought forward as evidence against the ARGUMENT IS WAR metaphor, which makes the basic tenet of conceptual metaphor theory impossible to falsify (Vervaeke and Kennedy 1996). Furthermore, traditional cognitive linguistic analyses suggest that we understand arguments in terms of war because the source domain of war, or physical conflict is more directly related to our past and present experience. But the reverse is also true given that our experiences of arguments, which may occur daily, may be more personally salient than are wars or physical conflict (Howe 2008; Ritchie 2006).

The general question is whether cognitive linguistic analyses necessarily prove that certain conceptual metaphors, and not others, motivate the metaphoric meanings of different words and phrases. There has been fierce debate about this question both among cognitive linguists and from scholars in neighboring disciplines. Most obviously, there is no standard method for inferring the possible presence of conceptual metaphors within systematic clusters of conventional expressions, novel metaphors, polysemy, and nonlinguistic actions. Cognitive linguists learn how to do this from examples, but there is often inconsistency in the results obtained from any linguistic analysis given different analysts and different knowledge domains (Semino et al. 2004).

One possibility is that verbal metaphors have multiple, indeterminate roots which make it impossible to definitely link each verbal metaphor with a single underlying conceptual metaphor (Ritchie 2006). For example, conceptual metaphors such as ARGUMENT IS WAR arise from a large, complex, and densely interconnected set of schemes for competition and conflict, ranging from friendly, low ego-involvement games through highly competitive games, shouting matches, fisticuffs, brawls, all the way to full-scale war (Eubanks 2000). Different individuals may interpret the same expression, such as *He defended his argument*, according to varying implicit metaphors and derive different entailments. Conflict metaphors may originate with war, sports and game competitions, childhood rough and tumble play, or some other forms of interpersonal rivalry. But they all carry a set of potential meanings derived from these activities that are potentially useful to all speakers. Of course, speakers may not intend to communicate all of these, and listeners may infer only selected inferences depending on their motivations and the current discourse context. Determining the conceptual roots of any metaphoric word or phrase may ultimately be a psychological issue that is difficult to completely determine from analyzing the language alone.

A related debate in linguistic circles concerns whether conceptual metaphors are necessarily stored as pre-packaged conceptual entities in the private minds of individuals. One proposal along this line, called the "discourse dynamic approach", emphasizes the functions that metaphor has in "thinking and talking" rather than seeing verbal metaphors as mere linguistic manifestations of underlying conceptual metaphors (Cameron 2011). Cameron (2011) argues that the micro-level shifts and changes in the dynamics of linguistic metaphor in real discourse demonstrate the emergence of metaphor as an inherently social affair. Conventional metaphors do not have similar meanings in different contexts, but are dynamically re-created depending on the specific histories of the participants at the very points in which their talk unfolds, giving rise to in-the-moment "structural metaphors". For this reason, conceptual metaphors may be better characterized as emergent stabilities that become "actualized" as people solve different problems for themselves and coordinate their actions with others (Gibbs 2014).

4. Nonlinguistic evidence on conceptual metaphors

One longstanding complaint from psychologists about CMT is that it really requires nonlinguistic evidence to directly show that conceptual metaphors are part of thought and not just language (McGlone 2007; Murphy 1996). Finding conceptual metaphors in nonlinguistic experience is required to truly show that conceptual metaphors exist independently from language, as claimed by CMT. In fact, one of the most important applications of CMT is the emergence of studies showing the vast nonlinguistic domains that are partly structured by conceptual metaphoric knowledge (Forceville and Urios 2009; Gibbs 2008).

Take, for instance, cognitive linguistic studies on metaphoric gestures (Casasanto and Jasmin 2012; Cienki and Müller 2008). Several analyses of face-to-face conversations illustrate how metaphoric gestures support and extend information beyond that given by a speaker's words. Consider one exchange between Chinese speakers, presented in English translations (Chui 2011: 446):

> S1: "If you still had had contact with the guy."
> S2: "Right."
> S1: "Then, you had seen him again or whatever, that is, it would have been easy for you to be bogged down in a mess."

As S1 said *bogged down* her right hand, which had been held outward at chest level, was moved down to waist level. This going down movement suggests the metaphoric idea of BAD IS DOWN, referring to the girl getting *bogged down* in the complicated love affair.

Some metaphoric gestures express ideas not strictly communicated by speech alone. Consider the following exchange (Chui 2011: 449):

S1: "We called it 'dried tea'."
S2: "Dried tea."
S3: "What?"
S1: "Dried tea. Yesterday ... it was called 'dried tea' ... when the processing was finished at night."

When S1 produced the temporal adverbial *yesterday*, his left hand moved up from the stomach level, pointing back over his shoulder with an open-palm. This movement reveals how the speaker is not specifically talking about a specific point in time, but conceives herself to be moving through time (i.e., the past is behind the ego).

In general, metaphoric gestures "substantiate cross-domain cognitive mappings ... and they evidence the presence and the real-time activation of the source domain in the mind of the speaker" (Chui 2011: 454).

There is, however, another developing literature from experimental social psychology that offers some of the most exciting, and possibly persuasive, evidence on conceptual metaphors in nonlinguistic experience. These studies have explored how metaphoric thoughts shape various social perceptions, judgments, and bodily behaviors.

For example, there is the widespread set of metaphors suggesting that GOOD IS UP and BAD IS DOWN, concepts that arise from good experiences being upward (e.g., being alive and healthy) and bad ones being downward (e.g., sickness and death).[2] Experimental studies show that people evaluate positive words faster if these are presented in a higher vertical position on a computer screen and recognize negative words faster if they appear in the lower part of the screen (Meier and Robinson 2004). Spiritual concepts are also conceived along vertical spatial dimensions. Thus, people judged words related to God faster when these were presented in the top half of the computer screen, with the opposite occurring for Devil related words (Meier et al. 2007). When asked to guess which people, based on their pictures, were more likely to believe in God, participants chose people more often when their pictures were placed along the higher vertical axis on the computer screen. These findings are consistent with the idea that people conceive of good and bad as being spatially located along some vertical dimension.

People's immediate bodily experiences can also affect their metaphorical social judgments. For example, having people make judgments about strangers' behaviors in a dirty work area caused them to rate the behavior as more immoral than when the same judgments were made in a clean work area (Schnall et al. 2008). Asking people to recall an immoral deed, as opposed to an ethical one, made them more likely to choose an antiseptic wipe as a free gift after the experiment (Zhong and Liljenquist 2006). Both these findings are consistent with the conceptual metaphors GOOD IS CLEAN and BAD IS DIRTY. People also judge a fictitious person to be more important, and a better job candidate, when they made their evaluations while holding a heavy clipboard than when holding a lighter one (Ackerman et al. 2010), which surely reflects the common idea that IMPORTANCE IS WEIGHT. People judge others to be more affectionate interper-

---

[2] Once again, several linguists argue that these primary metaphors may have a metonymic basis (Barcelona 2000; Kövecses 2013; Radden 2002).

sonally after holding a warm, as opposed to a cold, cup of coffee (Williams and Bargh 2008), an expression of the basic correlation in experience of AFFECTION IS WARMTH. In general, people's immediate physical experiences have direct effects on the salience of different metaphorical, and possibly metonymic, ideas, which in turn influences their social judgments.

These studies reflect only some of the large number of experimental results showing how metaphoric concepts both emerge from correlations in bodily experience and influence people's social reasoning and actions. This line of research presents a powerful refutation to those scholars who claim that conceptual metaphors are only generalizations from language and have little to do with human thought.

5. Verbal metaphor understanding

Cognitive linguistic research on metaphor typically aims to detail the contents and structure of human conceptual systems, rather than on what specific individuals may be thinking on particular occasions. But, once more, many psychologists are skeptical of claims about human thought based solely on the analysis of linguistic patterns. They strongly argue that proposals about conceptual metaphor must be accompanied by evidence showing what people were thinking when they produced or understood verbal metaphors.

In fact, psycholinguistic studies have explored three related concerns: (a) do conceptual metaphors influence verbal problem solving and decision-making, (b) do conceptual metaphors influence people's tacit understandings of why various words and phrases express particular metaphoric meanings, and (c) do conceptual metaphors have an immediate role in people's online use and understanding of verbal metaphors. The experimental research generally suggests positive answers to all three of these questions.

5.1. Conceptual metaphors shape decision-making

Conceptual metaphor can have a significant role in people's verbal problem-solving behavior. In one set of studies, university students read a report about the crime rate in a fictitious city, named Addison (Thibodeau and Boroditsky 2011). Some of the students saw the report in which the crime was early on described as *a beast preying* on Addison, and the other students saw the crime report with a metaphor of *a virus infecting* Addison. Both stories contained identical information, presented after the metaphor, about crime statistics. After reading their respective stories, the students had to propose a solution to the Addison crime problem. The specific metaphor people read influenced their proposed crime solutions. The participants reading the *beast preying* metaphor suggested harsher enforcement always be applied to catching and jailing criminals. But participants who read the *virus infecting* metaphor proposed solutions that focused on finding the root causes of the crime and creating social programs to protect the community. Interestingly, people's problem-solving solutions was covert as students did not mention the metaphors when asked to state what influenced them the most in coming up with their crime solution (i.e., most people focused on the crime statistics). This study showed how simple metaphoric language can activate complex metaphoric knowledge that constrained people's subsequent decision-making abilities.

A different set of studies explored the ways English and Mandarin speakers solve time problems (Boroditsky 2001). Both English and Mandarin use horizontal front/back spatial terms to talk about time. For example, English speakers use expressions such as *We can look forward to the good times ahead* and *We are glad that the difficult times are behind us*, while Mandarin speakers also use vertical metaphors, so that earlier events are said to be *shàng* or 'up', and later events are described as *xià* or 'down'. About one-third of all time expressions in Mandarin use the vertical metaphor. Experimental studies show that when asked to arrange objects on a table in temporal order, one-third of Mandarins did so along vertical dimension, yet English speakers never used the vertical dimension in completing this time task. These results show how people's temporal judgments are influenced by their most salient conceptual metaphors.

5.2. Conceptual metaphors motivate metaphoric meanings

A major finding from cognitive linguistics is that conventional expressions with similar figurative meanings are sometimes motivated by different conceptual metaphors. For instance, the American conventional phrase *blow your top* expresses anger in terms of a pressurized container whose top blows off under high pressure (ANGER IS HEAT IN A PRESSURIZED CONTAINER), while *jump down your throat* reflects the metaphoric mapping ANGRY BEHAVIOR IS AGGRESSIVE ANIMAL BEHAVIOR by expressing anger in terms of an angry animal that attacks by jumping at someone's throat.

Do people tacitly understand that conventional phrases with roughly similar figurative meanings, such as *blow your top* and *jump down one's throat*, can be motivated by different conceptual metaphors? Nayak and Gibbs (1990) examined this question in a series of studies on people's intuitions about idioms and their relations to conceptual metaphors and their context-sensitive interpretations of idioms. Participants in a first study were quite good at linking idioms (e.g., *blow your stack*) with their underlying conceptual metaphors (e.g., ANGER IS HEATED FLUID IN THE BODILY CONTAINER), suggesting that they have tacit beliefs of conceptual metaphors that motivated their understanding of some idioms.

A later study asked people to read short scenarios that were constructed to prime different metaphorical mappings (e.g., ANGER IS HEAT IN A PRESSURIZED CONTAINER or ANGRY BEHAVIOR IS AGGRESSIVE ANIMAL BEHAVIOR). Participants were asked to rate the appropriateness of each idiom for the given scenario. If people access the metaphoric mappings underlying an idiom, they should choose one idiom as more appropriate given their metaphorical understanding of the story context. This is exactly what was found. These findings showed that idioms are not "dead metaphors" as traditionally assumed, because people can use the information about the conceptual metaphors underlying idiomatic phrases to make sense of why conventional metaphoric language conveys specific metaphoric meanings.

5.3. Conceptual metaphor in immediate verbal metaphor comprehension

Several psycholinguistic studies show that conceptual metaphors affect online processing of verbal metaphor. For example, people read euphemistic metaphors (e.g., *She's turning my crank* motivated by SEXUAL DESIRE IS AN ACTIVATED MACHINE) more quickly in contexts that depicted similar conceptual metaphors than in contexts that conveyed different conceptual metaphors (Pfaff et al. 1997). Similarly, novel metaphors were comprehended more quickly when they were read after a story containing conventional expressions motivated by the same conceptual metaphor than when they followed conventional expressions motivated by a different conceptual metaphor (Thibodeau and Durgin 2008). A different line of research showed that people's reading of idiomatic phrases (e.g., *John blew his stack*) primed their subsequent lexical decision judgments for word strings related to the conceptual metaphors motivating the figurative meanings of the idioms (e.g., "HEAT" for ANGER IS HEATED FLUID IN THE BODILY CONTAINER) (Gibbs et al. 1997). All these experimental studies are consistent with the idea that conceptual metaphors are actively recruited during online verbal metaphor comprehension.

One implication of cognitive linguistic analyses is that switching from one conceptual metaphor to another in discourse may require additional cognitive effort over that needed to understand metaphoric expressions motivated by the same conceptual metaphor. There have been several experimental tests of this idea. In one study, people at an airport (Chicago O'Hare) were presented a priming question about time in either the ego-moving form (e.g., *Is Boston ahead or behind in time?*) or the time-moving form (e.g., *Is it earlier or later in Boston than it is here?*) (Gentner et al. 2002). After answering, the participants were asked the target question *So should I turn my watch forward or back?* that was consistent with the ego-moving form. The experimenter measured response times to the target question with a stopwatch disguised as a wristwatch. Once again, response times for consistently primed questions were shorter than for inconsistently primed questions. Switching schemas caused an increase in processing time. These results again suggest that two distinct conceptual schemes are involved in sequencing events in time.

A different set of experiments examined people's understanding of TIME IS MOTION by first asking people to read fictive motion sentences, as in *The tattoo runs along his spine* (Matlock et al. 2005). Participants read each fictive motion statement or a sentence that did not imply fictive motion (e.g., *The tattoo is next to the spine*), and then answered the "move forward" question (e.g., *The meeting originally scheduled for next Wednesday has been moved forward two days.*). People gave significantly more Friday than Monday responses after reading the fictive motion expressions, but not the nonfictive motion statements. These results imply that people inferred TIME IS MOTION conceptual metaphor when reading the fictive motion expressions which primed their interpretation of the ambiguous "move forward" question (also see Matlock et al. 2011; Matlock and Bergmann this volume).

5.4. Embodied experience and verbal metaphor understanding

Many psycholinguistic studies have investigated cognitive linguistic ideas on the role of embodied experience in verbal metaphor understanding (Bergen this volume). For instance, in one series of studies on metaphorical talk about time, students waiting in line at a café were given the statement *Next Wednesday's meeting has been moved forward two days* and then asked *What day is the meeting that has been rescheduled?* (Boroditsky and Ramscar 2002). Students who were farther along in the line (i.e., who had thus very recently experienced more forward spatial motion) were more likely to say that the meeting had been moved to Friday, rather than to Monday. Similarly, people riding a train were presented the same ambiguous statement and question about the rescheduled meeting. Passengers who were at the end of their journeys reported that the meeting was moved to Friday significantly more than did people in the middle of their journeys. Although both groups of passengers were experiencing the same physical experience of sitting in a moving train, they thought differently about their journey and consequently responded differently to the rescheduled meeting question. These results suggest how ongoing sensorimotor experience has an influence on people's comprehension of metaphorical statements about time.

The idea that embodied simulations play some role in people's immediate processing of verbal metaphors, and language more generally, has received much attention in recent psycholinguistic research (Bergen 2012, this volume; Gibbs 2006). People may, for instance, be creating partial, but not necessarily complete, embodied simulations of speakers' metaphorical messages that involve moment-by-moment "what must it be like" processes as if they were immersed in the discourse situation. More dramatically, these simulation processes operate even when people encounter language that is abstract, or refers to actions that are physically impossible to perform. For example, Gibbs et al. (2006) demonstrated how people's mental imagery for metaphorical phrases, such as *tear apart the argument*, exhibit significant embodied qualities of the actions referred to by these phrases (e.g., people conceive of the *argument* as a physical object that when torn apart no longer persists). Wilson and Gibbs (2007) showed that people's speeded comprehension of metaphorical phrases like *grasp the concept* are facilitated when they first make, or imagine making, in this case, a grasping movement. These findings indicate that relevant bodily movement does not interfere with people's comprehension of abstract metaphoric meaning, a position advocated by traditional metaphor theorists. Instead, moving in certain ways enhances the embodied simulations people ordinary construct during their interpretation of metaphoric language (also see Johansson-Falck and Gibbs 2012).

My review of psycholinguistic studies suggests that there is much experimental evidence to support aspects of CMT as a psychological theory of verbal metaphor understanding. Of course, as many critics note, CMT is not a complete theory that explains all aspects of how people interpret metaphoric meanings. Much other social and cultural knowledge is relevant to people's context-sensitive understandings of metaphor. Furthermore, metaphor understanding relies on a variety of other linguistic factors, which linguists and psychologists have taken pains to show are very relevant, and yet ignored by CMT (e.g., Giora 2003, this volume; Svanlund 2007). There are also a few experimental studies whose findings appear to be contrary to the claims of CMT (Keysar and Bly 1995; Keysar et al. 2000). Some scholars criticize these contrary studies because of methodological and stimuli problems (Thibodeau and Boroditsky 2011). In general, though, the psycholinguistic evidence together presents an overwhelming body of work showing that conceptual metaphors are significant parts, yet not the only factors, in how people use and understand metaphoric language.

6. Conclusion

This chapter has touched on only some of the relevant linguistic and psycholinguistic work related to cognitive linguistic theories of metaphor. This collected body of research

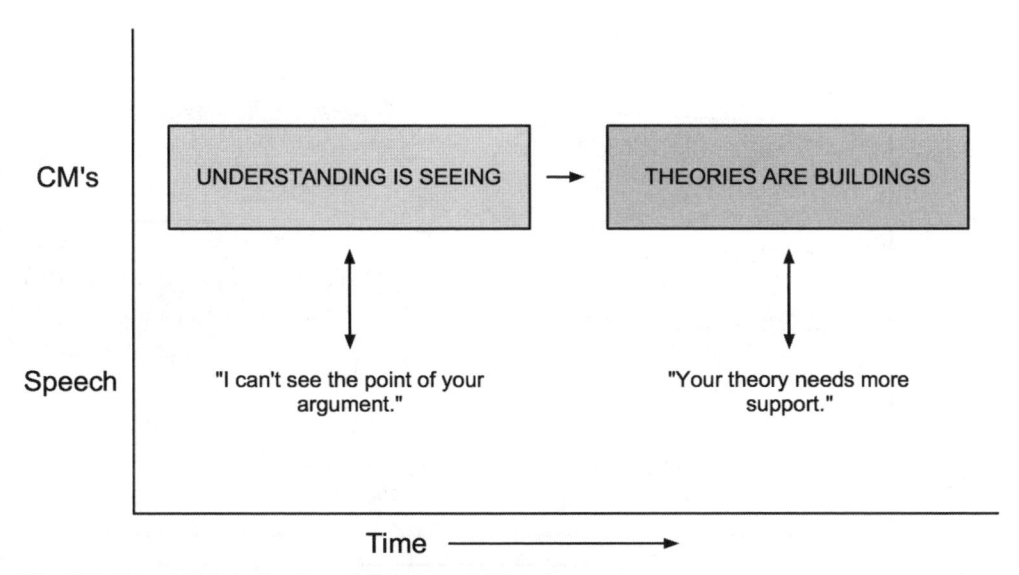

Fig. 8.1: Sequential Activation of Conceptual Metaphors

offers strong support for the major claim that enduring metaphoric thoughts have a primary role in verbal metaphor use and understanding. But cognitive linguists, and others, should articulate criteria for identifying metaphoric patterns in language and inferring specific conceptual metaphors from discourse. These procedures should be specified with sufficient detail so that other researchers can possibly replicate the analysis and emerge with similar conclusions (see Gibbs 2007). Adopting explicit procedures for metaphor identification in language and thought should help move cognitive linguistics closer to scientific practices within other fields in the cognitive sciences.

Finally, human cognition and language is always situated and influenced by the history of people's experiences up to that moment in time, as well as expectations about what is likely to occur next in human interaction. Consider a brief conversational exchange between two scientists discussing one of their theories in which one person states that, *I can't see the point of your argument. Your theory needs more support* (Gibbs and Santa Cruz, 2012). Figure 8.1 presents a schematic description of how a listener understands these conventional metaphoric expressions, according to a standard analysis within CMT.

Under this model, a listener hears an utterance and then automatically searches for relevant conceptual knowledge to understand what the speaker means. For the first expression, *I can't see the point of your argument*, people search for and then access the enduring metaphorical idea that UNDERSTANDING IS SEEING. Afterward, listeners apply this metaphoric concept to infer that the speaker meant he could not understand what his addressee was previously trying to say by his argument. Similarly, listeners next access the relevant metaphoric idea that THEORIES ARE BUILDINGS to interpret the following statement *Your theory needs more support*. In this manner, enduring conceptual metaphors are sequentially retrieved from long-term memory and then applied to create contextually-sensitive interpretations of speakers' metaphorical utterances.

But the complex reality of human interaction suggests that multiple forces simultaneously constrain people's understanding of verbal metaphors. People's interpretation of *Your*

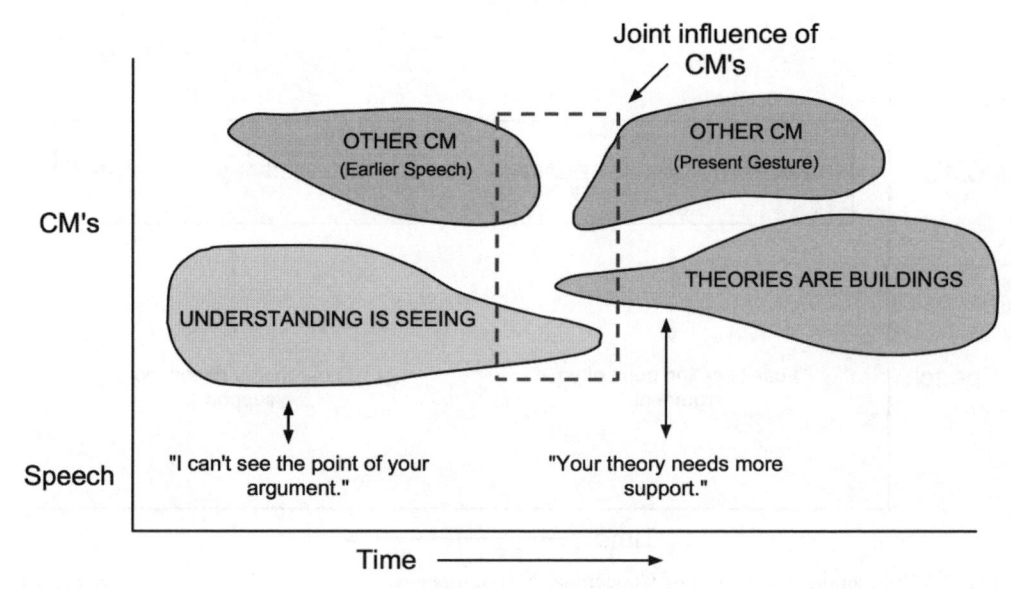

Fig. 8.2: Interacting Subsystem of Constraints

theory needs more support may be influenced by conceptual metaphors recruited during understanding of previous verbal metaphors and metaphorical gestures, as well as by conceptual metaphors that are most relevant to the particular utterance currently being processed (i.e., UNDERSTANDING IS SEEING), along with any other presently enacted metaphorical gestures (e.g., imagine the speaker placing a cupped hand outward signifying the foundation for THEORIES ARE BUILDINGS). Figure 8.2 presents a schematic representation of this account.

Under this theoretical model, conceptual metaphors are not necessarily accessed en bloc, with all their possible entailments spelled out, but can contribute partial constraints on people's metaphoric behaviors (i.e., similar to many "constraint satisfaction theories" of human cognition). This dynamical view does not deny that conceptual metaphors are an entrenched part of human cognition, yet sees the conventionalization of metaphoric thought and language as a continually emergent process, serving multiple adaptive purposes in everyday life (see MacWhinney this volume).

Cognitive linguists should study more of the complex temporal realities of human interaction to uncover the continuing presence of past conceptual metaphors in their analyses of verbal metaphor understanding. Moreover, we need to explore the ways different metaphoric concepts combine in probabilistic ways to shape any moment of metaphoric experience. The cognitive theory of metaphor has revolutionized the world of metaphor scholarship, but it is time to escape the traditional study of language on the page and see metaphor as something people do rather than something they tacitly know.

7. References

Ackerman, Joshua, Christopher Nocera, and John Bargh
   2010   Incidental haptic sensations influence social judgments and decisions. *Science* 328: 1712–1715.

Barnden, John
   2011   Metaphor and metonymy: Making their connections more slippery. *Cognitive Linguistics* 21: 1–34.
Barcelona, Antonio
   2000   On the plausibility of claiming a metonymic motivation for metaphorical mappings In: A. Barcelona (ed.), *Metaphor and Metonymy at the Crossroads. A Cognitive Perspective*, 31–58. Berlin: Mouton de Gruyter.
Barcelona, Antonio
   this volume   7. Metonymy. Berlin/Boston: De Gruyter Mouton.
Beardsley, Monroe
   1962   The metaphorical twist. *Philosophy and Phenomenological Research* 22: 293–307.
Bergen, Benjamin
   2012   *Louder than Words: The New Science of How the Mind Makes Meaning*. New York: Basic Books.
Bergen, Benjamin
   this volume   1. Embodiment. Berlin/Boston: De Gruyter Mouton.
Boroditsky, Lera
   2001   Does language shape thought? English and Mandarin speakers' conceptions of time. *Cognitive Psychology* 43: 1–22.
Boroditsky, Lera and Michael Ramscar
   2002   The roles of body and mind in abstract thought. *Psychological Science* 13: 185–189.
Cameron. Lynne
   2011   *Metaphor and Reconciliation: The Discourse Dynamics of Empathy in Post-Conflict Conversations*. London: Routledge.
Casasanto, Daniel and Kyle Jasmin
   2012   The hands of time: Temporal gestures in English speakers. *Cognitive Linguistics* 23: 653–674.
Charteris-Black, Jonathan
   2004   *Corpus Approaches to Critical Metaphor Analysis*. Basingstoke: Palgrave Macmillan.
Chui, Kawai
   2011   Conceptual metaphors in gesture. *Cognitive Linguistics* 22: 437–459.
Cienki, Alan and Cornelia Müller (eds.),
   2008   *Metaphor and Gesture*. Amsterdam: Benjamins.
Cuyckens, Hubert and Brigitte Zawada (eds.),
   2001   *Polysemy in Cognitive Linguistics*. Amsterdam: Benjamins.
Deignan, Alice
   2005   *Metaphor and Corpus Linguistics*. Amsterdam: Benjamins.
Desai, Rutvik, Jeffrey Binder, Lisa Conant, Quintano Mano and Mark Seidenberg
   2011   The neural career of sensory-motor metaphors. *Journal of Cognitive Neuroscience* 23: 2376–2386.
Eubanks, Philip
   2000   *A War of Words in the Discourse of Trade: The Rhetorical Constitution of Metaphor.* Carbondale: Southern Illinois University Press.
Fauconnier, Gilles and George Lakoff
   2013   On blending and metaphor. *Journal of Cognitive Semiotics* 5: 393–399.
Fauconnier, Gilles and Mark Turner
   2002   *The Way We Think: Conceptual Blending and the Mind's Hidden Complexities*. New York: Basic Books.
Feldman, Jerome
   2006   *From Molecule to Metaphor: A Neural Theory of Language*. Cambridge: MIT Press.
Forceville, Charles and Eduardo Urios-Aparisi (eds.),
   2009   *Multimodal Metaphor*. Berlin: Mouton De Gruyter.

Freeman, Dan
 1995 Catch(ing) the nearest way: Macbeth and cognitive metaphor. *Journal of Pragmatics* 24: 689–708.
Gentner, Dedre, Imai, D., and Lera Boroditsky
 2002 As time goes by: Understanding time as spatial metaphor. *Language and Cognitive Processes* 17: 537–565.
Gibbs, Raymond
 1994 *The Poetics of Mind: Figurative Thought, Language, and Understanding*. New York: Cambridge University Press.
Gibbs, Raymond
 2006 *Embodiment and Cognitive Science*. New York: Cambridge University Press.
Gibbs, Raymond
 2007 Why cognitive linguists should care about empirical methods? In: M. Gonzalez-Marquez, I. Mittelberg, S. Coulson, and M. Spivey (eds.), *Methods in Cognitive Linguistics*, 2–18. Amsterdam: Benjamins.
Gibbs, Raymond (ed.),
 2008 *The Cambridge Handbook of Metaphor and Thought*. New York: Cambridge University Press.
Gibbs, Raymond
 2011 Are deliberate metaphors really deliberate? A question of human consciousness and action. *Metaphor and the Social World*. 1: 26–52.
Gibbs, Raymond
 2014 Conceptual metaphor in thought and social action. In: M. Landau, M. Robinson, and B. Meier (eds.), *Metaphorical Thought in Social Life*. 17–50.Washington, DC: APA Books.
Gibbs, Raymond, Jody Bogdanovich, Jeffrey Sykes, and Dale Barr
 1997 Metaphor in idiom comprehension. *Journal of Memory and Language* 37: 141–154.
Gibbs, Raymond, Jessica Gould, and Michael Andric
 2006 Imagining metaphorical actions: Embodied simulations make the impossible plausible. *Imagination, Cognition, and Personality*, 25(3): 215–238.
Gibbs, Raymond and Malaika Santa Cruz
 2012 Temporal unfolding of conceptual metaphoric experience. *Metaphor and Symbol* 27: 299–311.
Giora, Rachel
 2003 *On our Minds: Salience, Context and Figurative Language*. New York: Oxford University Press.
Giora, Rachel
 this volume 29. Default nonliteral interpretations. Berlin/Boston: De Gruyter Mouton.
Goatly, Andrew
 1997 *The Language of Metaphors*. New York: Routledge.
Goldberg, Adele
 1995 *Constructions: A Construction Grammar Approach to Argument Structure*. Chicago: University of Chicago Press.
Grady, Joseph
 1997 Theories are buildings revisited. *Cognitive Linguistics* 8: 267–290.
Grady, Joseph, Todd Oakley, and Seana Coulson
 1999 Blending and metaphor. In: R. Gibbs and G. Steen (eds.), *Metaphor in Cognitive Linguistics*, 101–124. Amsterdam: Benjamins.
Gries, Stefan Th.
 this volume 22. Polysemy. Berlin/Boston: De Gruyter Mouton.
Gries, Stefan Th. and Anatol Stefanowitsch (eds.),
 2006 *Corpus Based Approaches to Metaphor and Metonymy*. Berlin/New York: Mouton de Gruyter.

Howe, James
   2008   Argument is argument: An essay on conceptual metaphor and verbal dispute. *Metaphor and Symbol* 23: 1–23.
Jackendoff, Ray and David Aaron
   1991   Review of Lakoff and Turner (1989). *Language* 67: 320–328.
Johansson-Falck, Marlene and Raymond Gibbs
   2012   Embodied motivations for metaphoric meanings. *Cognitive Linguistics* 23: 251–272.
Keysar, Boaz and Brigitte Bly
   1995   Intuitions of the transparency of idioms: Can one keep a secret by spilling the beans? *Journal of Memory and Language* 34: 89–109.
Keysar, Boaz, Yeshahayu Shen, Sam Glucksberg, and William s. Horton
   2000   Conventional language: How metaphoric is it? *Journal of Memory and Language* 43: 576–593.
Koller, Veronika
   2004   *Metaphor and Gender in Business Media Discourse: A Critical Cognitive Study.* Basingstoke: Palgrave.
Kövecses, Zoltán
   2002   *Metaphor: A Practical Introduction.* New York: Oxford University Press.
Kövecses, Zoltán
   2013   The metaphor-metonymy relationship: Correlation metaphors are based on metonymy. *Metaphor and Symbol* 28: 75–88.
Lakoff, George
   2008   The neural theory of metaphor. In: R. Gibbs (ed.), *Cambridge Handbook of Metaphor and Thought,* 17–38. New York: Cambridge University Press.
Lakoff, George and Mark Johnson
   1980   *Metaphors We Live By.* Chicago: University of Chicago Press.
Lakoff, George and Mark Johnson
   1999   *Philosophy in the Flesh.* New York: Basic Books.
Lakoff, George and Mark Turner
   1989   *More than Cool Reason: A Field Guide to Poetic Metaphor.* Chicago: University of Chicago Press.
Langacker, Ronald W.
   1999   *Grammar and Conceptualization.* Berlin: Mouton.
Lizardo, Omar
   2012   The conceptual bases of metaphors of dirt and cleanliness in moral and nonmoral reasoning. *Cognitive Linguistics* 23: 367–394.
MacWhinney, Brian
   this volume   34. Emergentism. Berlin/Boston: De Gruyter Mouton.
Matlock, Teenie, and Till Bergmann
   this volume   26. Fictive motion. Berlin/Boston: De Gruyter Mouton.
Matlock, Teenie, Kevin Holmes, Mahesh Srinivasan, and Michael Ramscar
   2011   Even abstract motion influences the understanding of time. *Metaphor and Symbol* 26: 260–271.
Matlock, Teenie, Michael Ramscar, and Lera Boroditsky
   2005   On the experiential link between spatial and temporal language. *Cognitive Science* 29: 655–664.
McGlone, Mathew
   2007   What is the explanatory value of a conceptual metaphor? *Language and Communication* 27: 109–126.
Meier, Brian and Michael Robinson
   2004   Why the sunny side is up. *Psychological Science* 15: 243–247.

Meier, Brian, Michael Robinson, Elizabeth Crawford and W. Ahlvers
    2007   When 'light' and 'dark' thoughts become light and dark responses: Affect biases brightness judgments. *Emotion* 7:366–376.

Müller, Cornelia
    2008   Metaphors Dead and Alive, *Sleeping and Waking: A Dynamic View*. Chicago: University of Chicago Press.

Murphy, Gregory
    1996   On metaphoric representations. *Cognition* 60: 173204

Mussolff, Andreas
    2004   *Metaphor and Political Discourse*. Basingstoke: Palgrave Macmillan.

Naciscione, Anita
    2010   *Stylistic Use of Phraseological Units in Discourse*. Amsterdam: Benjamins.

Nayak, Nandini and Raymond Gibbs
    1990   Conceptual knowledge in the interpretation of idioms. *Journal of Experimental Psychology: General* 119: 315–330.

Oakley, Todd and Anders Hougaard (eds.),
    2008   *Mental Spaces in Discourse and Interaction*. Amsterdam: Benjamins.

Panther, Klaus-Uwe, and LindaThornburg
    2009   On figuration in grammar. In: K.-U. Panther, L. Thornburg, and A. Barcelona (eds.), *Metonymy and Metaphor in Grammar*, 1–44. Amsterdam: Benjamins.

Pfaff, Kerry, Raymond Gibbs, and Michael Johnson
    1997   Metaphor in using and understanding euphemism and dysphemism. *Applied Psycholinguistics* 18: 59–83.

Pragglejaz Group
    2007   MIP: A method for identifying metaphorically-used words in discourse. *Metaphor and Symbol* 22: 1–40.

Radden, Gunther
    1995   Motion metaphorized. The case of coming and going. In: E. Casad (ed.), *Cognitive Linguistics in the Redwoods: The Expansion of a New Paradigm in Linguistics*, 423–458. New York: Mouton de Gruyter.

Radden, Gunther
    2002   How metonymic are metaphors. In: R. Dirven and R. Pörings (eds.), *Metaphor and Metonymy in Comparison and Contrast*, 407–424. Berlin/New York: Mouton de Gruyter.

Ricoeur, Paul
    1977   *The Rule of Metaphor*. Toronto: University of Toronto Press.

Ritchie, David
    2006   *Context and Communication in Metaphor*. Basingstoke: Palgrave.

Ruiz de Mendoza, Francisco and Olga Díez
    2002   Patterns of conceptual interaction. In: R. Dirven and R. Pörings (eds.), *Metaphor and Metonymy in Comparison and Contrast*, 489–532. Berlin/New York: Mouton de Gruyter.

Schnall, Simone, Jennifer Benton, and Sophie Harvey
    2008   With a clean conscience: Cleanliness reduces the severity of moral judgments. *Psychological Science 19:* 1219–122.

Semino, Elena
    2009   *Metaphor in Discourse*. New York: Cambridge University Press.

Semino, Elena, John Heywood, and Mick Short
    2004   Methodological problems in the analysis of a corpus of conversations about cancer. *Journal of Pragmatics* 36: 1271–1294.

Sjoblad, Aron
    2009   *Metaphors Cicero Lived By.* Lund: Center for Languages and Literature, Lund University.
Steen, Gerard
    2006   The paradox of metaphor: Why we need a three-dimensional model of metaphor. *Metaphor and Symbol* 23: 213–241.
Steen, Gerard, Dorst, Aletta, Berenike Herrmann, Anna Kaal, Tina Krennmayr, and Trijintje Pasma
    2010   *A Method for Linguistic Metaphor Identification.* Amsterdam: Benjamins.
Stefanowitsch, Anatol
    2011   Cognitive linguistics as cognitive science. In: M. Callies, W. Keller, and A. Lohofer (eds.), *Bi-directionality in the Cognitive Sciences*, 295–310. Amsterdam: Benjamins.
Svanlund, Jan
    2007   Metaphor and convention. *Cognitive Linguistics* 18: 47–89.
Sweetser, Eve
    1990   *From Etymology to Pragmatics: Metaphorical and Cultural Aspects of Semantic Structure.* New York: Cambridge University Press.
Tendahl, Markus
    2008   *A Hybrid Theory of Metaphor.* Basingstoke: Palgrave
Thibodeau Paul and Lera Boroditsky
    2011   Metaphors we think with: The role of metaphor in reasoning. PLoS ONE, 6 (2): e16782
Thibodeau, Paul and Frank Durgin
    2008   Productive figurative communication: Conventional metaphors facilitate the comprehension of related novel metaphors. *Journal of Memory and Language* 58: 521–540.
Turner, Mark
    this volume   10. Blending in language and communication. Berlin/Boston: De Gruyter Mouton.
Vervaeke, John and John Kennedy
    1996   Metaphors in language and thought: Disproof and multiple meanings. *Metaphor and Symbolic Activity* 11: 273–284.
Williams, Lawrence and John Bargh
    2008   Experiencing physical warm influences interpersonal warmth. *Science* 322: 606–607.
Wilson, Nicole and Raymond Gibbs
    2007   Real and imagined body movement primes metaphor comprehension. *Cognitive Science* 31: 721–731.
Zhong, Chen-Bo and Katie Liljenquist
    2006   Washing away your sins: Threatened morality and physical cleansing. *Science* 313: 1451–1452.

Raymond W. Gibbs, Santa Cruz (USA)

9. Representing Meaning

1. Introduction
2. Key issues in semantic representation
3. Theoretical perspectives
4. An integrated proposal: combining language-based and experiential information
5. Conclusion
6. References

1. Introduction

Understanding the meaning of words is crucial to our ability to communicate. To do so we must reliably map the arbitrary form of a spoken, written or signed word to the corresponding concept whether it is present in the environment, tangible or merely imagined (Meteyard et al. 2012: 2). In this chapter we review two current approaches to understanding word meaning from a psychological perspective: embodied and distributional theories. Embodied theories propose that understanding words' meanings requires mental simulation of entities being referred to (e.g., Barsalou 1999; see also Bergen this volume) using the same modality-specific systems involved in perceiving and acting upon such entities in the world. Distributional theories on the other hand typically describe meaning in terms of language use: something arising from statistical patterns that exist amongst words in a language. Instead of focusing on bodily experience, distributional theories focus upon linguistic data, using statistical techniques to describe words' meanings in terms of distributions across different linguistic contexts (e.g., Landauer and Dumais 1997; Griffiths et al. 2007). These two general approaches are traditionally used in opposition, although this does not need to be the case (Andrews et al. 2009) and in fact by integrating them we may have better semantic models (Vigliocco et al. 2009).

We will highlight some key issues in lexical representation and processing and describe historical predecessors for embodied theories (i.e., featural approaches) and distributional theories (i.e., holistic approaches). We conclude by proposing an integrated model of meaning where embodied and linguistic information are both considered vital to the representation of words' meanings.

2. Key issues in semantic representation

A theory of semantic representation must satisfactorily address two key issues: representation of words from different content domains and the relationship between semantics (word meaning) and conceptual knowledge.

2.1. Are words from different domains represented in the same way?

The vast majority of research investigating semantic representation has focused on concrete nouns. The past decade has seen increasing research into the representation of action verbs and a beginning of interest in the study of how abstract meaning is represented. A critical question is whether the same overarching principles can be used across these domains, or whether organisational principles must differ.

A fundamental difference between objects and actions is that objects can be thought of in isolation, as discrete entities, but actions are more complex, describing relations among multiple participants (Vigliocco et al. 2011). Connected to this are temporal differences: actions tend to be dynamic events with a particular duration while objects are stable with long-term states.

Because of the stable nature of objects, nouns' meanings tend to be relatively fixed. Verbs' meanings are less constrained and often more polysemous. These differences could underscore different representational principles for object-nouns and action-verbs, but do not preclude a semantic system in which objects and actions are represented in the same manner and differences in organisation arise from differences in representational content. Such an example is described by Vigliocco et al's (2004) FUSS model, in which representations for action and object words are modelled in the same lexico-semantic space, using the same principles and tools. Differences emerge from differences in the featural properties of the two domains rather than different principles of organisation.

When comparing concrete and abstract words, there is a stronger case for assuming different content and different organisational principles. It is well established that processing abstract words takes longer than processing concrete words (the "concreteness effect") for which Paivio's dual-coding theory provides a long-standing account (e.g., Paivio 1986). Under this view two separate systems contribute to word meaning: a word-based system and an image-based system. Whereas concrete words use both systems (with greater reliance on the latter), abstract words rely solely on word-based information. The concreteness effect would occur because concrete words use two systems instead of one, thus having richer and qualitatively different semantic representations than abstract words.

An alternative view, the context availability theory (Schwanenflugel and Shoben 1983), does not require multiple representational systems to account for the concreteness effect. Under this view, advantages for concrete words come from differences in associations between words and previous knowledge (i.e., differences in the number of links, rather than in content/organisation), with abstract concepts being associated with much less context. Here the concreteness effect results from the availability of sufficient context for processing concrete concepts in most language situations, but deficient context for processing abstract words (Schwanenflugel and Shoben 1983).

More recent proposals for the differences between concrete and abstract concepts and words include viewing abstract knowledge as arising out of metaphorical extension (Boroditsky 2000; Lakoff and Johnson 1980; Bergen this volume; Gibbs this volume), or differences in featural properties rather than different principles of organisation for abstract and concrete meaning: sensorimotor information underlying concrete meanings and affective and linguistic information underlying abstract meanings (Kousta et al. 2011).

To summarise, theories of semantic representation make different assumptions about semantic representations for different domains of knowledge, varying from a single, unitary semantic system to a much more fractionated system, where different principles of organisation are specified for different word types. However, there exists no strong evidence for assuming different principles, and following the argument of parsimony, we argue for a unitary system based on the same principles across domains. Instead of different organisational principles, differences across domains come about due to differences in content, namely differences in the extent to which a given type of content is most important for a given domain: sensory-motor information for the concrete domain and emotion and linguistic information for the abstract domain (Vigliocco et al. 2009).

2.2. How is conceptual knowledge linked to word meaning?

The fundamental goal of language is to talk about "stuff" such as objects, events, feelings, situations and imaginary worlds. Thus, there must be a strong mapping between our conceptual knowledge (the knowledge we use to categorise and understand the world) and the language we use. Since we begin life exploring and learning about our world, with language developing later, conceptual knowledge ultimately must develop before language. One important issue then is how words relate to conceptual knowledge. Should we think of word meanings and concepts interchangeably? This relationship has many important implications, for example, the extent of translation equivalency across languages.

One argument for treating words and concepts interchangeably is that many robust phenomena have been found to affect them both. If the same factors affect both and they behave similarly, then they must be closely linked, if not interchangeable. For example, feature type, feature correlations and distinguishing features have been shown to explain category-specific deficits in categorization of concepts (e.g., McRae and Cree 2002) and semantic priming effects for words (McRae and Boisvert 1998). Because characteristics of conceptual features seem to have comparable effects it would be parsimonious to consider conceptual representations the same as word meaning (consistent with Langacker 1982).

There are reasons, however to suggest that there is not a one-to-one mapping between the two. First, we possess far more concepts than words. There are often actions or situations that we know well and understand that are not lexicalized such as "the actions of two people manoeuvring for one armrest in a movie theatre or airplane seat" (Hall 1984 discussed in Murphy 2002). Further, one word can be used to refer to multiple meanings (e.g., polysemy) and so refers to a set of concepts instead of a single concept (see Gries this volume). This matter is further complicated when we look at cross-linguistic differences in links between conceptual knowledge and linguistic representations (see Vigliocco and Filipović 2004).

There are many examples of cross-linguistic differences in semantic representations that do not have any obvious explanations. For instance, although both English speakers and Italian speakers use different words to denote *foot* and *leg*, Japanese speakers use the same word *ashi* to describe both. One could hardly argue that conceptually, Japanese speakers do not know the difference between one's foot and one's leg. If linguistic categories are based on one-to-one mappings with conceptual structure, then cross-linguistic differences have clear implications for the assumption of universality of conceptual structure.

With the above issues in mind, below we present the two main perspectives on semantic representation, guided by the ideas that the same organising principles apply across word types and that meaning is distinct from but strongly linked to conceptual knowledge (e.g., Vigliocco and Filipović, 2004).

3. Theoretical perspectives

The main theoretical approaches to word meaning can be clustered into those that consider our sensorimotor experience as the building blocks of semantic representation and those that instead consider statistical patterns in language as the building blocks. This great divide corresponds to disciplinary boundaries between cognitive psychology and neuroscience on one side and computational linguistics and computer science on the other side. Within linguistics, both perspectives are represented as reflecting the distinction between sense and reference since Frege ([1892] 1952).

3.1. Embodiment

Embodied approaches posit that understanding words' meanings involves engagement of the systems used in perception, action and introspection (e.g., Barsalou 1999; Svesson 1999; Evans 2003; Lakoff and Johnson 1999; Bergen this volume). This approach focuses on content of semantic representations rather than relationships among them in semantic memory. Embodied theorists argue against "amodal" models of semantics (Figure 9.1a) because they are missing the vital link between meaning in language and experience in the real world. In other words, it is unclear how the meaning of a word is understood if language is simply made up of arbitrary symbols not linked to referents or experiences in the world (Harnad 1990). Here, to understand a word one simulates its meaning in the brain's sensorimotor systems, similarly to actually experiencing that concept. Instead of transducing information from experience into abstract symbols, the experience itself is, in a way, recreated (Barsalou 1999) (see Figure 9.1b). The distinction between conception and perception is blurred (Lakoff and Johnson 1999).

3.1.1. Featural theories as precursors to embodiment

Embodiment places emphasis on sensorimotor features as building blocks of meaning. This emphasis is shared with classic featural theories where a word's meaning is decomposable into a set of defining features (e.g., Collins and Quillian 1969; Rosch and Mervis 1975). Sets of conceptual features are bound together to form a lexical representation of the word's meaning. For example, the meaning of *chair* could be defined by features including *has legs, made of wood* and *is sat on*.

Featural properties of different word categories have been modeled to explain category-specific deficits in different forms of brain damage and to shed light on the organisation of the semantic system (e.g., Farah and McClelland 1991). By looking at the proportion of perceptual (e.g., *has fur*) and functional (e.g., *cuts food*) features for artifacts and natural kinds, Farah and McClelland (1991) described the topographic organisation of

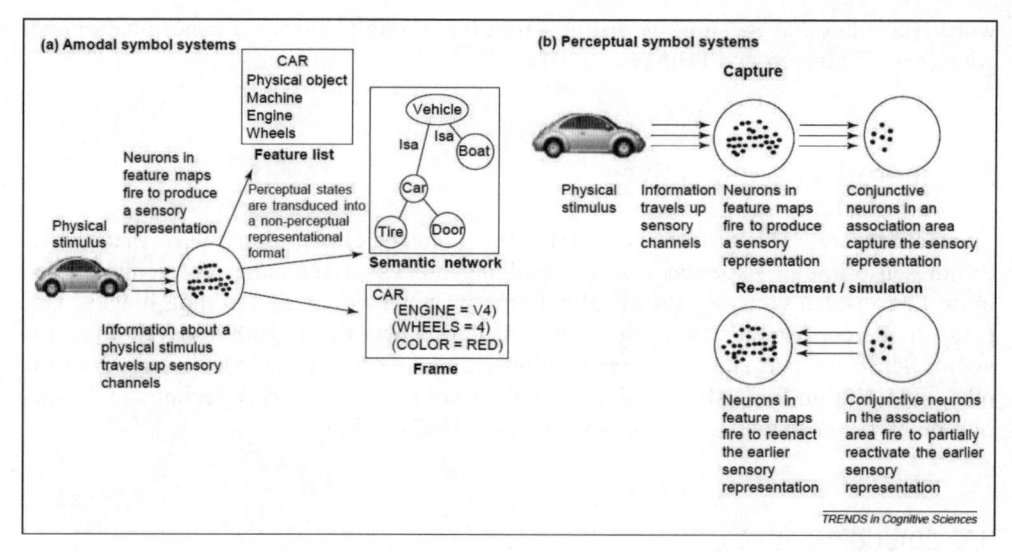

Fig. 9.1: Amodal vs. perceptual symbols. Taken from Barsalou, L. W., Simmons, W. K., Barbey, A., and Wilson, C. D. (2003). Grounding conceptual knowledge in modality-specific systems. *Trends in Cognitive Sciences*, 7, 84–91. (a) In amodal symbol systems neural representations from vision are transduced in an amodal representation such as a frame, semantic network or feature list. These amodal representations are used during word understanding. (b) In perceptual symbol systems neural representations from vision are partially captured by conjunctive neurons, which are later activated during word comprehension to re-enact the earlier state.

semantic memory in terms of modality rather than category. In their simulations, damage to perceptual features only caused selective deficits for processing of natural kinds, whereas conversely, damage to functional features only caused selective deficits for processing of artifacts. What was once seen as a category-specific deficit therefore emerged as a result of damage to specific feature types, suggesting that semantic memory is organised in terms of sensorimotor features and not categories.

In featural theories, semantic similarity between words can be described in terms of featural correlations and featural overlap. Both measures have been validated as indications of semantic similarity in behavioural tasks such as semantic priming (e.g., McRae and Boisvert 1998). Featural theories have been applied to explain differences between words referring to objects (nouns) and words referring to events (primarily verbs referring to actions) in terms of feature types and associations between features. Nouns' meanings appear to be more differentiated, with dense associations between features and properties (Tyler et al. 2001) across many different sensory domains (Damasio and Tranel 1993). They also have more specific features referring to narrow semantic fields, whereas verbs typically consist of features applying broadly across semantic fields and with less sensory associations (Vinson and Vigliocco 2002). In this sense, verbs could be considered to be more abstract than nouns (Bird et al. 2003). These differences have been invoked to account for patients with selective deficits in retrieving and producing nouns and those who had more problems with verbs (see Vigliocco et al. 2011). It is questionable whether these theories can be extended to account for differences between concrete and abstract words. However, a recently published collection of feature norms found that participants can generate features for abstract words with general agreement across subjects that could not be explained simply by associations (Buchanan et al. 2012).

Featural theories usually focus on concepts, not words (although concepts and words are often implicitly or explicitly assumed as the same). There are theories, however, that assume a separate semantic level where features are bound into a lexico-semantic representation (Vigliocco et al. 2004), and others that hypothesize "convergence zones" in the brain where information from multiple modalities is integrated (Damasio 1989, Simmons and Barsalou 2003; see Vigliocco et al. 2012).

Embodiment theories build upon these earlier accounts, as research that supports featural representations is necessarily compatible with embodied views. For example, semantic priming based on overlapping features (McRae and Boisvert 1998) could be explained by overlap in activation of the same sensorimotor area (e.g., Pecher et al. 2003).

3.1.2. Research supporting embodied theories

A large amount of behavioural evidence demonstrates the use of sensorimotor systems in language processing, typically with interactions between the processing of words' semantic content and sensory information (see Bergen this volume). For example, Meteyard et al. (2007) showed that visual discrimination of moving dots was hindered when processing direction verbs of the same direction (e.g., *dive*, *rise*). Conversely, lexical decisions to direction verbs were hindered when participants concurrently perceived motion of a matching direction at near-threshold levels (Meteyard et al. 2008). If processing semantic content involves shared sensory-motor systems, then combining word processing and sensory-motor processing should affect performance.

Numerous imaging studies provide support for embodied language processing, showing that areas of the brain involved in perception and action are engaged when processing words with similar content. For example, listening to verbs related to leg, face or arm action such as *kick*, *lick* and *pick* activates the motor cortex somatotopically (Hauk et al. 2004). This activation reflects action specificity, for example, a region within the bilateral inferior parietal lobule showed differential patterns of activation to words of different levels of specificity e.g., *to clean* versus *to wipe* (van Dam et al. 2010), and moreover is differentially lateralised depending upon participants' handedness indicating that the sensorimotor activation underlying word meaning is body-specific (Willems et al. 2010).

Strong evidence for the role of sensorimotor systems in word comprehension comes from studies in which deficits in motor or sensory processing result in a selective deficit in word processing of the same category. If sensorimotor systems play a critical role in semantic representation, damage to these areas should disrupt semantic processing of those word types. Research of this nature tends to look at patients with impairments in planning and executing actions, e.g., patients with motor neuron disease (e.g., Bak et al. 2001) or Parkinson's disease (e.g., Boulenger et al. 2008). Bak et al. (2001) found comprehension and production of verbs was significantly more impaired than nouns for patients with motor neuron disease but not for healthy controls or patients with Alzheimer's disease who have both semantic and syntactic language impairments. This selective deficit in patients with motor neuron disease suggests that the processes underlying verb representation is strongly related to those of the motor systems (see Vigliocco et al. 2011 for a review). In addition, transcranial magnetic simulation (TMS) over specific brain regions has been shown to influence processing of related word types, such as the motor strip and action verbs (e.g., Pulvermuller et al. 2005).

Critics have argued that embodied results may simply be epiphenomenal: the result of spreading activation from amodal representations to perceptual areas via indirect, associative routes due to the correlation between the two (e.g., Mahon and Caramazza 2008). Mahon and Caramazza (2008) argue that existing evidence can be explained by unembodied theories in which semantic information is independent of sensory-motor information. The observed interactions could come about indirectly; for example, semantic information may engage working memory systems which in turn recruit sensory-motor systems (Meteyard et al. 2012: 3). This argument however seems to fall short of explaining the observed lesion and TMS data. That is, if semantic processing is affected by disruption of the corresponding sensory-motor areas, then the affected areas must be a necessary part of semantic representation, and not epiphenomenal. Mahon and Caramazza's view is not completely disembodied, but rather falls along a continuum, as we will describe in the next section.

3.1.3. Different versions of embodiment

Theories of embodiment vary in terms of how strongly they define the role of the sensorimotor systems in semantic representation. Theories can be considered along a continuum from strongly embodied (full simulation), through weak embodiment and secondary embodiment, and then moving beyond embodiment to fully symbolic, disembodied theories (Meteyard et al. 2012; see Figure 9.2). Distributional approaches could be placed on the extreme, "disembodied" end of the continuum, assigning no role for sensory-motor information. Theories supporting secondary embodiment still see semantics as amodal and abstract but propose that semantic representation and sensory-motor information are directly associated, for example, amodal representations derived from sensory-motor input (Patterson et al. 2007). For weak embodiment, semantic representations are partly instantiated by sensory-motor information which does have a representational role, but some degree of abstraction still takes place. Areas adjacent to primary sensory-motor areas are involved in semantic representation and are reciprocally linked to primary areas. From a strong embodiment perspective, semantic processing necessarily activates sensory-motor information and is completely dependent upon it. Here, semantic processing takes place within primary sensory and motor areas and precisely the same systems are used for semantic processing and sensory-motor processing.

A fully symbolic theory is problematic because there is no link between language and world knowledge, which raises the grounding problem and the problem of referentiality: how do we understand what words refer to if they are not linked to the world

(Harnad 1990)? Based on the research evidence for sensory-motor activations during semantic processing (Meteyard et al. 2012), it is clear that sensory-motor systems play some role in semantic processing. Strong embodiment also appears to be unsatisfactory: some degree of abstraction must take place in order to extract and combine features into the correct conceptual conjunctions. Based on evidence from TMS and lesion studies, weak embodiment, where sensory-motor information plays an integral, representational role in semantic representation whilst maintaining some degree of abstraction seems the most plausible choice.

3.1.4. Key issues and embodied theories

Since word meanings appear to produce similar activation patterns to their real-world referents, different types of words will necessarily have different patterns of activation. Differences in semantic representations of objects and actions have clearly been demonstrated with neuropsychology (e.g., Damasio and Tranel 1993) and imaging data (e.g., Martin et al. 1995) (for review see Vigliocco et al. 2011). Here, it has generally been found that processing object-nouns involves activation of posterior sensory cortices while processing action-verbs involves activation of fronto-parietal motor areas.

Traditionally it has been argued that embodied theories have problems explaining how abstract concepts are represented. Abstract words pose a special problem to theories of embodied semantics because their content is not strongly perceptual or motoric, and as such, it is often argued that their meaning can only be represented in abstract propositional forms (e.g., Noppeney and Price 2004).

There are now a number of alternative (or complementary) hypotheses on embodiment of abstract concepts. One hypothesis is that the meaning of abstract words is understood through metaphorical mappings (Boroditsky 2000; Lakoff and Johnson 1980; see Gibbs this volume). For example one could conceptualize the mind as a container (Dove 2009) because it holds information. Metaphor allows abstract representations to be based on extensions of more concrete experience-based concepts grounded in perception and action. Boroditsky et al. (2001) showed how the abstract concept of time could be embodied using mental representations of the more concrete domain of space (see Evans this volume for greater discussion on the representation of time). The authors speculated that the link between the two concepts developed via correspondences between space and time in experience: moving in space correlates with time. Language then builds upon these simple correspondences.

Although metaphors highlight similarities between concepts, they do not define the differences (Dove, 2009): although the mind shares similarities with a container insofar as it *contains* information, it is much more than this and this information is not captured in the metaphor. Additionally, one can think of many aspects of abstract knowledge that cannot be accounted for by metaphor (Meteyard et al. 2012), such as scientific technical jargon (but see Glenberg 2011: 15). Although a role for metaphor could be acknowledged, the question is whether metaphorical mappings could really be the foundation of learning and representation of abstract concepts, or if they just provide structure for existing concepts (Barsalou 1999).

Label	Unembodied	Secondary embodiment	Weak embodiment	Strong embodiment
Semantic Content	Symbolic/Amodal	Amodal	Cross-modal integration/ Supramodal	Analogue/Multimodal
Neural Architecture	Semantic region(s) have no temporal or spatial overlap with sensory and motor areas	Region for amodal semantic content plus modality specific regions which code experiential attributes	Distributed network of areas which code integrated modal information, proximal to primary sensory and motor regions	Distributed network of areas within primary sensory and motor systems
Relationship to sensory-motor systems	Complete independence	Independent but associated	Partial dependence	Complete dependence
Explanation of interactions	Indirect activation	Secondary activation	Mediation	Modulation
Theories	Collins and Loftus (1975) Landauer and Dumais (1997) Lund, Burgess and Atchley (1995) Griffiths et al. (2007)	Mahon and Caramazza (2008) Patterson et al. (2007) Quillian (1968)	Barsalou (1999) Farah and McClelland (1991) Pulvermuller (1999) Simmons and Barsalou (2003) Vigliocco et al. (2004) Louwerse (2007) Vigliocco et al. (2009)	Glenberg and Gallese (2012) Pecher, Zeelenberg and Barsalou (2003)

Fig. 9.2: A continuum of embodiment. Adapted from Meteyard, L., Cuadrado, S. R., Bahrami, B. and Vigliocco, G. 2012, Coming of age: A review of embodiment and the neuroscience of semantics. *Cortex*, 48(7), 788–804.

The difference between concrete and abstract words may arise because of the number and type of simulations for each word type, similar to differences in context (cf. the context availability theory, Schwananflugel and Shoben 1983). Abstract words' meanings would be based on a wider range of simulations than concrete words, and tend to focus more on social, introspective and affective information than perceptual and motor (Barsalou and Wiemer-Hasting 2005; Kousta et al. 2011; Connell and Lynott 2012). Differences arise between the two word types because the type of information and situations relevant for abstract meaning is more difficult to access.

Kousta et al. (2011) and Vigliocco et al. (2009) described differences between abstract and concrete concepts as arising from the ecological statistical preponderance of sensory-motor features in concrete concepts compared to the statistical preponderance of linguistic and especially affective associations for abstract concepts. They argue that affect may be a critical factor in the learning and representation of abstract knowledge because abstract words tend to have emotional associations, and because emotional development precedes language development in children (Bloom 1998). Abstract words with greater affective associations are acquired earlier with the rate of acquisition rapidly increasing around age three (Bretherton and Beeghly 1982; Wellman et al. 1995), suggesting that affect affects abstract word acquisition. When all other factors are controlled, emotional associations of abstract words facilitate lexical decisions relative to concrete words, reversing the traditional concreteness advantage (Kousta et al. 2009). Unlike dual coding theory (e.g., Paivio 1986) where abstract words are disadvantaged due to their lack of imageability, emotional processing confers further benefits to abstract words (Vigliocco et al. 2013).

At present therefore a growing number of studies are attempting to describe embodiment of abstract concepts. Accounts based on metaphor and the range and nature of simulations successfully explain findings in a number of domains, yet there remain many more abstract and schematic elements of language which are not easily accounted for. For example, it is difficult to imagine how simulation can underlie the representation of abstract and schematic closed-class words such as prepositions and determiners (Meteyard et al. 2012), so a completely embodied semantic system seems unlikely.

Do embodied theories make a distinction between word meaning and conceptual knowledge? In terms of the continuum of embodied theories described above, as one moves further from abstract/symbolic theories to strong versions of embodiment, the content of semantic representation includes gradually more sensory-motor information (Meteyard et al. 2012), blurring the distinction between semantics and conceptual information.

3.1.5. Looking toward the future: Where should embodiment go?

Despite empirical support for embodiment many issues are still outstanding. First, research needs to go beyond simply showing effects of interaction between linguistic and sensory-motor stimuli and focus more on describing the nature of this relationship and the specific mechanisms responsible for these interactions. Simply accumulating evidence for *some* involvement of sensory-motor systems is unsatisfactory. Interaction effects between language and sensory-motor processes have been shown to cause both facilitation and interference effects; the processes underlying these differences need to be explored. For example, Glenberg and Kaschak (2002) found that semantic judgments were faster when direction of a physical response matched the direction described in the language (facilitation) but Kaschak et al. (2006) found slower responses when the direction of motion of an auditory stimulus matched the direction described in language (interference). Such opposing results might be explained by properties of the stimuli and presentation, such as the match in modality of the presented linguistic and perceptual stimuli, or the timing of presentation. To make progress on understanding the specific mechanisms underlying these effects, we need to clarify the influence of these variables.

A commonly raised question about simulation is its necessity. Do we need simulation in order to understand language or is it epiphenomenal (Mahon and Caramazza 2008), with activation in sensorimotor areas simply the result of spreading activation between dissociable systems? Looking carefully at the temporal dynamics of interactions between language and sensorimotor systems could address questions of epiphenomenalism. If language comprehension necessarily recruits sensorimotor systems, such effects should be observed very early in processing (Pavan and Baggio 2013).

Depth of processing is a related issue. It is unclear whether simulation occurs under all circumstances in all language tasks. Simulation may not be necessary for shallow language tasks, where a good-enough representation could be inferred simply from linguistic information alone, using statistical relations between words (Barsalou et al. 2008; Louwerse, 2011). Embodied simulations could instead be reserved for deeper processing.

One aspect of language awaiting future research from this perspective is the learning process. When and how are words linked with sensory systems? There have been some attempts to describe this process, for example via Hebbian learning mechanisms under the combined presence of object naming and the object's sensory affordances (Pulvermuller 1999; Glenberg and Gallese 2012) or by exploiting iconic mappings between linguistic form and meaning (Perniss et al. 2010).

It is clear that to move forward, embodied theories need to delve deeper into the mechanisms that underlie the wealth of empirical data and formulate a clear, precise and testable description of the specific nature of these processes and their temporal properties.

3.2. Distributional theories

Distributional theories, traditionally viewed in sharp contrast with embodied theories, are concerned with statistical patterns found in language itself, such as different types of texts or documents. Here a word's meaning is described by its distribution across the language environment and the mechanisms for learning are clear: words' meanings are inferred from the statistical patterns existent in language (see Gries; Geeraerts; and Divjak and Caldwell-Harris this volume). Distributional approaches have traditionally assigned no role to sensory-motor information, instead using only information present in linguistic data.

Dominant distributional approaches developed within cognitive science are latent semantic analysis (LSA, Landauer and Dumais 1997), hyperspace analogue to language (HAL, Lund et al. 1995) and more recently Griffiths et al.'s topic model (e.g., Griffiths

9. Representing Meaning

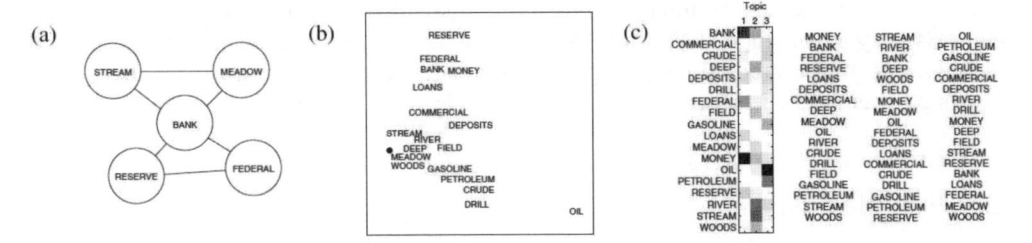

Fig. 9.3: Approaches to semantic representation. (a) In a semantic network, words are represented as nodes, and edges indicate semantic relationships. (b) In a semantic space, words are represented as points, and proximity indicates semantic association. These are the first two dimensions of a solution produced by latent semantic analysis (Landauer and Dumais, 1997). The black dot is the origin. (c) In the topic model, words are represented as belonging to a set of probabilistic topics. The matrix shown on the left indicates the probability of each word under each of three topics. The three columns on the right show the words that appear in those topics, ordered from highest to lowest probability. Taken from Griffiths, Steyvers and Tenenbaum (2007). Topics in semantic representation. *Psychological Review*, 114 (2), 211–244.

et al. 2007). All these approaches use large samples of text, evaluating properties of the contexts in which a word appears in order to estimate its relationship to other words, but differ in the way contexts are treated and the way relationships among words are assessed (see Riordan and Jones 2010 for a more in-depth review covering a broader range of distributional models). The topic model does consider words in terms of contexts from which they are sampled, but differs to LSA and HAL in its assumptions: contexts have themselves been sampled from a distribution of latent topics, each of which is represented as a probability distribution over words (e.g., Griffiths et al. 2007). The content of a topic is thus represented by those words that it assigned a high probability to, so the semantic representation of each word can be considered to be its distribution over latent topics; and the similarity between two words as similarity in distribution over topics.

These approaches have successfully simulated many aspects of human behaviour with the topic model as the most state-of-the-art as it provides a plausible solution to problems faced by LSA, namely ambiguity, polysemy and homonymy. Words are assigned to topics and can be represented across many topics with different probabilities so each sense or meaning of a word can be differentiated. Figure 9.3c shows how the different meanings of *bank* occur within two different topics. Words that share a high probability under the same topics tend to be similar and predictive of each other. A further benefit is that shared components of meaning are made explicit by providing a precise characterization of what "topics" are in terms of probability distributions. In comparison, for models like LSA or HAL it is presumed that words in similar contexts have related meanings but it is not specified how these may be defined or described.

While none of these models themselves are developmental in nature (i.e., modeling language acquisition), as they all compute representations based on a stable input corpus, they nonetheless can be explicitly applied to developmental processes simply by comparing the representations given different types of language corpora (e.g., comparing statistical patterns in corpora taken from children versus adults). Furthermore the probabilistic nature of topic models permits the possibility that distributions of topics, words and contexts may all change over time. As a result distributional models can be applied directly, and make predictions relevant to language development in a way that is not obvious for embodied theories.

3.2.1. Holistic theories

Distributional theories developed primarily from computational linguistics. Within psychology, however, these theories have as predecessors holistic theories, and within linguistics, theories of sense relations: concerned with the organisation, or structure of semantic representations rather than their content, and thus assume concepts are represented in a unitary fashion.

Holistic theories take a non-decompositional, relational view: the meaning of words should be evaluated as a whole, in terms of relations between words, rather than being decomposed into smaller components (such as features). Words take their meaning from relationships with other words, for example by associative links. In early theories of this type, meaning was described by semantic networks (e.g., Quillian 1968; Collins and Loftus 1975) where a word was denoted by a single node in a network and its meaning by connections to other nodes. The full meaning of a concept arises from the whole network, beginning from the concept node which alone is meaningless.

In holistic approaches, semantic similarity effects are explained in terms of spreading activation from an activated node (such as a prime or distractor word) to other concepts by connections between nodes (e.g., Quillian 1967). Response times in experimental tasks would be driven by the time it takes a semantically similar node to reach an activation threshold. As words that are semantically related will be closer together in the semantic space than semantically unrelated words, activation spreads more quickly from a related prime to the target word.

In some holistic models, differences between object-nouns and action-verbs have been modelled in terms of different relational links (e.g., Graesser et al. 1987; Huttenlocher and Lui 1979). In Wordnet (Miller and Fellbaum 1991) this is represented on a large scale with four distinct networks representing nouns, verbs, adjectives and adverbs. The representation of abstract words in Wordnet is no different to more concrete words of the same grammatical class, although abstract words tend to occur in shallower hierarchies.

Regarding the relationship between words and concepts, a strict one-to-one mapping is proposed. Each lexical concept is equal to a single, abstract representation in the conceptual system. This means that conceptual systems must contain representations of all concepts that are lexicalized in all languages. Any lexical differences that appear cross-linguistically must be due to conceptual differences. In order to defend the universality of conceptual structure, one must assume that not all concepts are lexicalized in each language (see Vigliocco and Filipović 2004).

3.2.2. Research supporting distributional theories

LSA (Landauer and Dumais 1997), topic model (Griffiths et al. 2007) and HAL (Lund et al. 1995) have successfully simulated a number of semantic effects including semantic similarity in semantic priming tasks. Using the word association norms of Nelson et al. (1998), the topic model successfully predicted associations between words greater than performance at chance level and outperformed LSA in this as well as a range of other semantic tasks.

LSA has successfully simulated a number of human cognitive behaviours. For example, simulated scores on a standard vocabulary test have been shown to overlap with human scores and simulations can mimic human word sorting behaviour (Landauer et al. 1998). If these theories can successfully approximate human language comprehension then they should be considered valid models of human language processing, reflecting processes to some extent analogous to human language processing (Landauer and Dumais 1997).

Attempts have been made to directly test distributional models and their power to predict neural activations. For example, Mitchell et al. (2008) found that voxel-level, item specific fMRI activations for concrete nouns could be predicted on the basis of distributional statistics based on a large text corpus, and similar data have been obtained using EEG data (Murphy et al. 2009). Such findings suggest that there is a close relationship between statistical co-occurrences of words in texts and neural activity related to understanding those words, further supporting the viability of distributional theories.

3.2.3. Key issues and distributional theories

In comparison to earlier relational approaches, relations between different word types here are not pre-specified; instead the same principles are used for all word types. Differences between word types such as noun-verb differences and concrete-abstract differences are captured in the relationships that result from these statistical models, patterns that exist in the source texts. Thus, distributional models have no problem defining all domains, as long as they are represented in the source texts.

The relationship between word meaning and conceptual knowledge is not explicitly discussed by these theories, and they are therefore implicitly assumed to be the same. The lack of connection between words and sensory-motor experience is a strong limitation of distributional models, as discussed below.

3.2.4. Looking toward the future: Where should distributional theories go?

Despite the power of distributional models in simulating human behaviour, some have argued that the statistical patterns that exist in language co-occurrences are merely epiphenomenal and play no role in semantic representation (Glenberg and Robertson 2000). That language-based models do not take into account information from other sources of meaning, such as perception and introspection, as embodied theories do, is a fundamental criticism that these approaches need to address. In addition the models cannot account for existing behavioural and neuroscientific evidence linking language to the brain's sensory-motor systems. One can use the famous "Chinese room" example (Searle 1980) to highlight the importance of this argument: how can meaning be inferred simply from the relationships that exist between amodal symbols that are themselves void of meaning?

Recently, distributional approaches have been developing in order to solve the "grounding" problem (Harnad 1990) by including experiential information as another type of distributional data, bringing together embodied and distributional ideas that have typically been considered independently. In the next section we will discuss this further.

4. An integrated proposal: Combining language-based and experiential information

Despite the apparent divide between embodied, experiential theories and amodal, distributional theories, these two types of information can be integrated to form a more general model of semantic representation. While maintaining a role for sensorimotor information in learning, linguistic information also plays a role. We have all used dictionaries to learn a word's meaning as well as inferring a new word's meaning from its linguistic context alone. The environment contains a rich source of both embodied and linguistic data: we experience words both in a physical environment and a language environment rather than one or the other. As Louwerse (2007) notes, the question should not be whether semantics is embodied or symbolic, but rather, to what extent is language comprehension embodied *and* symbolic?

Meaning in language could be both embodied and language-based, with the contribution of each system dependent on the language task at hand. Dove (2009) describes the conceptual system as divided into both modal and amodal representations with each responsible for different aspects of meaning. For example, it seems impossible that aspects of cognition such as logical reasoning or mathematics do not depend at all upon amodal symbols (Louwerse 2007).

The symbol interdependency theory (Louwerse 2007) describes meaning as composed of symbols that are dependent on other symbols and symbols that are dependent on embodied experiences. Here symbols are built upon embodied representations, but although they are grounded, language comprehension can proceed simply via interrelations amongst other symbols. Using linguistic representations allows for a more "quick and dirty" response, whereas embodied simulations develop more slowly, accessing a wide variety of detailed experiential information. Here, two predictions emerge. First, for shallow language tasks, involvement of linguistic representations should dominate over embodied representations. Second, for tasks that involve a deeper level of processing, embodied representations should dominate over linguistic. Barsalou et al. (2008) describe similar ideas with lexical processing incorporating two processes: an early activation of linguistic representations taking place in language areas of the brain and a later, situated simulation involving modal systems.

Vigliocco et al. (2009) describe language as another vital source of information, along with experiential information, from which semantic representations can be learnt. Statistical distributions of words within texts provide important information about meaning that can be integrated with sensory-motor experience. For example, a child could learn the meaning of the word *dog* via experience with dogs' perceptual features: having four legs, barking etc., as well as language experience of hearing "dog": it tends to occur with words such as *pet* and *animals*. Combining both distributions of information allows linguistic information to "hook up" to the world, thus grounding it.

Modern computational work is also beginning to model semantic meaning by integrating experiential and linguistic distributional data. It has been shown that models that combine both types of distributional data perform better in simulating semantic effects than either distributions alone (Andrews et al. 2009). The underlying principles employed in distributional models can also be applied to other domains of experience, not simply linguistic data. Johns and Jones (2012) proposed a model integrating both perceptual information (in the form of feature norms) and statistical information from language. Here, a word's full meaning is denoted by the concatenation of perceptual and linguistic vectors. Using a model of global lexical similarity with a simple associative mechanism, perceptual representations for words for which the model had no perceptual information could be inferred based on lexical similarity and the limited perceptual information of other words already existing in the model. Importantly, the inference can also go the other way, with the likely linguistic structure of a word estimated based on its perceptual information. Thus the model is able to infer the missing representation of a word based on either perceptual or linguistic information.

There are some potential shortcomings to current "integrated" models. Since concrete feature norms are generated by speakers verbally and via introspection, using them as "embodied information" means there are possible perceptual, sensorimotor and affective aspects of experiential information that may not be included, suggesting that we cannot generalize the findings to all word types. However, other methods for appropriately modelling experiential information are being explored. Recent methods are beginning to combine information from computer vision with text in distributional models; models including visual information outperform distributional models based on text only, at least when vision is relevant to words' meanings (Bruni et al. 2012a, 2012b). Future work will need to make use of more sophisticated types of perceptual information, as well as incorporating other aspects of bodily experience such as action and emotion.

5. Conclusion

The state of the art in cognitive science proposes that the learning and representation of word meanings involves the statistical combination of experiential information: sensorimotor and affective information gleaned from experience in the world (extralinguistic), and distributional linguistic information: statistical patterns occurring within a language itself (intralinguistic). Research suggests that sensory-motor and affective systems provide a central role in grounding word meaning in our worldly experiences. This grounding is thought crucial for the language system to learn word meanings from existent embodied word meanings. The associations between linguistic units allow learners to more quickly infer word meaning and locate the corresponding experiential information in the absence of any direct experience of the referent. By learning about word meaning from both distributions in parallel, ultimately a richer form of semantic information is gained.

6. References

Andrews, Mark, Gabriella Vigliocco and David P. Vinson
    2009   Integrating experiential and distributional data to learn semantic representations. *Psychological Review* 116(3): 463–498

Bak Thomas H., Dominic G. O'Donovan, John J. Xuereb, Simon Boniface and John R. Hodges
    2001   Selective impairment of verb processing associated with pathological changes in Brodmann areas 44 and 45 in the motor neuron disease-dementia-aphasia syndrome. *Brain* 124: 103–120.

Barsalou, Lawrence W.
    1999   Perceptual symbol systems. *Brain and Behavioural Sciences* 22: 577–660.

Barsalou, Lawrence W., Ava Santos, W. Kyle Simmons and Christine D. Wilson
    2008   Language and simulation in conceptual processing. In: M. de Vega, A. M. Glenberg, and A. C. Graesser (eds.), *Symbols, Embodiment and Meaning*, 245–283. Oxford: Oxford University Press.

Barsalou, Lawrence W. and Katja Wiemer-Hastings
    2005   Situating abstract concepts. In: D. Pecher and R. A. Zwaan (eds.), *Grounding Cognition: The Role of Perception and Action in Memory, Language, and Thought*, 129–163. New York: Cambridge University Press.

Bergen, Benjamin
    this volume   1. Embodiment. Berlin/Boston: De Gruyter Mouton.

Bird, Helen, David Howard and Sue Franklin
    2003   Verbs and nouns: The importance of being imageable. *Journal of Neurolinguistics* 16(2):113–149.

Bloom, Lois
    1998   Language acquisition in its developmental context. In: D. Kuhn and R. S. Siegler (eds.), *Handbook of Child Psychology* 2, 309–370. New York: Wiley

Boroditsky, Lera
    2000   Metaphoric structuring: Understanding time through spatial metaphors. *Cognition* 75(1): 1–28.

Boroditsky, Lera, Michael Ramscar and Michael Frank
    2001   The roles of body and mind in abstract thought. *Proceedings of the 23rd Annual Conference of the Cognitive Science Society.* University of Edinburgh.

Boulenger, Véronique, Laura Mechtouff, Stéphane Thobis, Emmaneul Broussolle, Marc Jeannerod and Tatjana A. Nazir
    2008   Word processing in Parkinson's disease is impaired for action verbs but not for concrete noun. *Neuropsychologia* 46: 743–756.

Bretherton, Inge, and Marjorie Beeghly
    1982   Talking about internal states: The acquisition of an explicit theory of mind. *Developmental Psychology* 18: 906–921.

Bruni, Elia, Marco Baroni, Jasper Uijlings and Nicu Sebe
    2012a   Distributional semantics with eyes: Using image analysis to improve computational representations of word meaning. *Proceedings of the 2th ACM International Conference on Multimedia*, 1219–1228.

Bruni, Elia, Gemma Boleda, Marco Baroni and Nam-Khanh Tran
    2012b   Distributional semantics in Technicolor. *Proceedings of the 50th Annual Meeting of the Association for Computational Linguistics*, 136–145.

Buchanan, Erin M., Jessica L. Holmes, Marilee L. Teasley and Keith A. Hutchinson
    2012   English semantic word-pair norms and a searchable Web portal for experimental stimulus creation. *Behavior Research Methods* 44(4): 746–757.

Collins, Allan M. and Elizabeth F. Loftus
 1975 A spreading-activation theory of semantic processing. *Psychological Review* 82: 407–428.
Collins, Allan M. and M. Ross Quillian
 1969 Retrieval time from semantic memory. *Journal of Verbal Learning and Verbal Behavior* 12: 240–247.
Connell, Louise and Dermot Lynott
 2012 Strength of perceptual experience predicts word processing performance better than concreteness or imageability. *Cognition* 125(3): 452–465
Damasio, Antonio R.
 1989 Time-locked multiregional retroactivation: A systems-level proposal for the neural substrates of recall and recognition. *Cognition* 33: 25–62.
Damasio, Antonio R. and Daniel Tranel
 1993 Nouns and verbs are retrieved with differently distributed neural systems. *Proceedings of the National Academy of Sciences Unites States of America*, 90: 4957–4960.
Divjak, Dagmar and Catherine Caldwell-Harris
 this volume 3. Frequency and entrenchment. Berlin/Boston: De Gruyter Mouton.
Dove, Guy
 2009 Beyond conceptual symbols. A call for representational pluralism. *Cognition* 110: 412–431.
Evans, Vyvyan
 2003 *The Structure of Time. Language, Meaning and Temporal Cognition.* Amsterdam: Benjamins
Farah, Martha J. and James L. McClelland
 1991 A computational model of semantic memory impairment: Modality-specificity and emergent category specificity. *Journal of Experimental Psychology: General* 120: 339–357.
Frege, Gottlob
 [1892] 1952 On sense and reference. In: P. T. Geach and M. Black (eds. and Trans.), *Philosophical Writings of Gottlob Frege.* Oxford: Basil Blackwell.
Geeraerts, Dirk
 this volume 13. Lexical semantics. Berlin/Boston: De Gruyter Mouton.
Glenberg, Arthur M.
 2011 How reading comprehension is embodied and why that matters. *International Electronic Journal of Elementary Education* 4(1): 5–18.
Glenberg, Arthur M. and Vittorio Gallese
 2012 Action-based language: a theory of language acquisition, comprehension and production. *Cortex* 48(7): 905–922.
Glenberg, Arthur M. and Michael P. Kaschak
 2002 Grounding language in action. *Psychonomic Bulletin and Review* 9: 558–565.
Glenberg, Arthur M. and David A. Robertson.
 2000 Symbol grounding and meaning: A comparison of high-dimensional and embodied theories of meaning. *Journal of Memory and Language* 43: 379–401.
Gibbs, Raymond W. Jr.
 this volume 8. Metaphor. Berlin/Boston: De Gruyter Mouton.
Graesser, Arthur C., Patricia L. Hopkinson and Cheryl Schmid
 1987 Differences in interconcept organization between nouns and verbs. *Journal of Memory and Language* 26: 242–253.
Gries, Stefan Th.
 this volume 22. Polysemy. Berlin/Boston: De Gruyter Mouton.
Griffiths, Thomas L., Mark Steyvers and Joshua B. Tenenbaum
 2007 Topics in semantic representation. *Psychological Review* 114(2): 211–244.

Hall, Richard
    1984   *Sniglets (snig'lit): Any Word That Doesn't Appear in the Dictionary, But Should.* Collier Books.
Harnad, Stevan
    1990   The symbol grounding problem. *Physica* 42: 335.
Hauk, Olaf, Ingrid Johnsrude and Friedemann Pulvermuller
    2004   Somatotopic representation of action words in human motor and premotor cortex. *Neuron* 41(2): 301–307.
Huttenlocher, Janellen and Felicia Lui
    1979   The semantic organization of some simple nouns and verbs. *Journal of Verbal Learning and Verbal Behavior* 18: 141–179.
Johns, Brendan T. and Michael N. Jones
    2012   Perceptual inference through global lexical similarity. *Topics in Cognitive Science* 4:103–120.
Kaschak, Michael P., Rolf A. Zwaan, Mark Aveyard and Richard H. Yaxley
    2006   Perception of auditory motion affects language processing. *Cognitive Science* 30: 733–744.
Kousta, Stavroula-Thaleia, Gabriella Vigliocco, David P. Vinson, Mark Andrews and Elena Del Campo
    2011   The representation of abstract words: why emotion matters. *Journal of Experimental Psychology General* 140: 14–34.
Kousta, Stavroula-Thaleia, David P. Vinson, and Gabriella Vigliocco
    2009   Emotion words, regardless of polarity, have a processing advantage over neutral words. *Cognition* 112(3): 473–481.
Lakoff, George and Mark Johnson
    1980   *Metaphors We Live By.* Chicago: University of Chicago Press.
Lakoff, George and Mark Johnson
    1999   *Philosophy in the Flesh: The Embodied Mind and its Challenge to Western Thought.* New York: Basic Books.
Landauer, Thomas K. and Susan T. Dumais
    1997   A solution to Plato's problem: The Latent Semantic Analysis theory of the acquisition, induction, and representation of knowledge. *Psychological Review* 104: 211–140.
Landauer, Thomas K., Peter W. Foltz and Darrell Laham
    1998   Introduction to Latent Semantic Analysis. *Discourse Processes* 25: 259–284.
Langacker, R. W.
    1982   *Foundations of Cognitive Grammar, Volume 1, Theoretical Prerequisites.* Stanford: Stanford University Press.
Louwerse, Max M.
    2007   Symbolic or embodied representations: A case for symbol interdependency. In: T. Landauer, D. McNamara, S. Dennis, and W. Kintsch (eds.), *Handbook of Latent Semantic Analysis,* 107–120. Mahwah: Erlbaum.
Louwerse, Max M.
    2011   Stormy seas and cloudy skies: conceptual processing is (still) linguistic and perceptual. *Frontiers in Psychology* 2(105): 1–4.
Lund, Kevin, Curt Burgess and Ruth A. Atchley
    1995   Semantic and associative priming in high-dimensional semantic space. In: J. D. Moore and J. F. Lehman (eds.), *Proceedings of the 17th Annual Meeting of the Cognitive Science Society,* 17: 660–665.
Mahon, Bradford Z. and Alfonso Caramazza
    2008   A critical look at the Embodied Cognition Hypothesis and a new proposal for grounding conceptual content. *Journal of Physiology – Paris* 102: 59–70.

Martin, Alex, James V. Haxby, Francoise M. Lalonde, Cheri L. Wiggs and Leslie G. Ungerleider
   1995   Discrete cortical regions associated with knowledge of color and knowledge of action. *Science* 270(5233): 102–105.
McRae, Ken and Stephen Boisvert
   1998   Automatic semantic similarity priming. *Journal of Experimental Psychology: Learning, Memory and Cognition* 24: 558–572a.
McRae, K., and George S. Cree
   2002   Factors underlying category-specific semantic deficits. In: E. M. E. Forde and G. W. Humphreys (eds.), *Category-Specificity in Brain and Mind*, 211–250. East Sussex, UK: Psychology Press.
Meteyard, Lotte, Bahador Bahrami and Gabriella Vigliocco
   2007   Motion detection and motion verbs. *Psychological Science* 18(11): 1007–1013.
Meteyard, Lotte, Sara. R. Rodriguez Cuadrado, Bahador Bahrami and Gabriella Vigliocco
   2012   Coming of age: A review of embodiment and the neuroscience of semantics. *Cortex* 48(7): 788–804.
Meteyard, Lotte, Nahid Zokaei, Bahador Bahrami and Gabriella Vigliocco
   2008   Visual motion interferes with lexical decision on motion words. *Current Biology* 18(17): 732–733.
Miller, George A. and Christiane Fellbaum
   1991   Semantic networks of English. *Cognition* 41: 197–229.
Mitchell, Tom M., Svletlana V. Shinkareva, Andrew Carlson, Kai-Min Chang, Vicente L. Malave, Robert A. Mason and Marcel A. Just
   2008   Predicting human brain activity associated with the meanings of nouns. *Science* 320: 1191.
Murphy, Gregory L.
   2002   *The Big Book of Concepts*. Cambridge: MIT Press.
Murphy, Brian, Marco Baroni and Massimo Poesio
   2009   EEG responds to conceptual stimuli and corpus semantics. *Proceedings of the Conference on Empirical Methods in Natural Language Processing (EMNLP 2009)*, 619–627. East Stroudsburg: ACL.
Nelson, Douglas L., Cathy L. McEvory and Thomas A. Schreiber
   1998   The University of South Florida word association, rhyme, and word fragment norms. http://www.usf.edu/FreeAssociation/
Noppeney, Uta and Cathy J. Price
   2004   Retrieval of abstract semantics. *Neuroimage* 22: 164–170.
Paivio, Allan
   1986   *Mental Representations: A Dual-Coding Approach*. Oxford: Oxford University Press.
Patterson, Karalyn, Peter J. Nestor and Timothy T. Rogers
   2007   Where do you know what you know? The representation of semantic knowledge in the human brain. *Nature Reviews Neuroscience* 8: 976–987.
Pavan, Andrea and Giosuè Baggio
   2013   Linguistic representations of motion do not depend on the visual motion system. *Psychological Science* 24: 181–188.
Pecher, Diane, René Zeelenberg and Lawrence W. Barsalou
   2003   Verifying different-modality properties for concepts produces switching costs. *Psychological Science* 14(2): 119–124.
Perniss, Pamela, Robin L. Thompson and Gabriella Vigliocco
   2010   Iconicity as a general property of language: Evidence from spoken and signed languages. *Frontiers in Psychology* 1: 227.
Pulvermuller, Friedemann
   1999   Words in the brain's language. *Behavioral and Brain Sciences* 22: 253–336.

Pulvermuller, Friedemann, Olaf Hauk, Vadim V. Nikulin and Risto J. Ilmoniemi
    2005   Functional links between motor and language systems, European Journal of Neuroscience 21(3): 793–797.

Quillian, M. Ross
    1967   Word concepts: A theory and simulation of some basic semantic capabilities. *Behavioural Science* 12: 410–430.

Quillian, M. Ross
    1968   Semantic memory. In: M. Minsky (ed.), *Semantic Information Processing*, 227–270. Cambridge: MIT Press.

Riordan, B., and M. N. Jones
    2010   Redundancy in linguistic and perceptual experience: Comparing distributional and feature-based models of semantic representation. *Topics in Cognitive Science* 3(2): 303–345.

Rosch, Eleanor and Carolyn B. Mervis
    1975   Family resemblance: Studies in the internal structure of categories. *Cognitive Psychology* 7: 573–605.

Santos, Ava, Sergio E. Chaigneau, W. Kyle Simmons, and Lawrence W. Barsalou
    2011   Property generation reflects word association and situated simulation. *Language and Cognition* 3: 83–119.

Schwanenflugel, Paula J. and Edward J. Shoben
    1983   Differential context effects in the comprehension of abstract and concrete verbal materials. *Journal of Experimental Psychology: Learning, Memory, and Cognition* 9(1): 82–102.

Searle, John
    1980   Minds, brains and programs. *Behavioral and Brain Sciences* 3(3): 417–457.

Simmons, W. Kyle, and Lawrence W. Barsalou
    2003   The similarity-in-topography principle: Reconciling theories of conceptual deficits. *Cognitive Neuropsychology* 20: 451–486.

Svensson, Patrik
    1999   *Number and Countability in English Nouns. An Embodied Model.* Uppsala: Swedish Science Press.

Tyler, Lorraine K., Richard Russell, Jalal Fadili and Helen E. Moss
    2001   The neural representation of nouns and verbs: PET studies. *Brain* 124: 1619–1634.

van Dam, Wessel O., Shirley-Ann Rueschemeyer and Harold Bekkering
    2010   How specifically are action verbs represented in the neural motor system: an fMRI study. *Neuroimage* 53: 1318–1325.

Vigliocco, Gabriella and Luna Filipović
    2004   From mind in the mouth to language in the mind. *Trends in Cognitive Sciences* 8: 5–7.

Vigliocco, Gabriella, Stavroula-Thaleia Kousta, David P. Vinson, Mark Andrews and Elena Del Campo
    2013   The representation of abstract words: What matters? A reply to Paivio. *Journal of Experimental Psychology: General* 142: 288–291.

Vigliocco, Gabriella, Lotte Meteyard, Mark Andrews and Stavroula-Thaleia Kousta
    2009   Toward a theory of semantic representation. *Language and Cognition* 1: 215–244.

Vigliocco, Gabriella, Daniel Tranel and Judit Druks
    2012   Language production: patient and imaging research. In: M. Spivey, K. McRae and M. Joanisse (eds.), *Cambridge Handbook of Psycholinguistics*, 443–464. Cambridge: Cambridge University Press.

Vigliocco, Gabriella, David Vinson, Judit Druks, Horacio Barber and Stefano F. Cappa
    2011   Nouns and verbs in the brain: A review of behavioural, electrophysiological, neuropsychological and imaging studies. *Neuroscience and Biobehavioural Reviews* 35: 407–426.

Vigliocco, Gabriella, David P. Vinson, William Lewis and Merrill F. Garrett
   2004   Representing the meaning of object and action words: The featural and unitary semantic space hypothesis. *Cognition* 48: 422–488.
Vinson, David P. and Gabriella Vigliocco
   2002   A semantic analysis of noun-verb dissociations in aphasia. *Journal of Neurolinguistics* 15: 317–351.
Wellman, Henry M., Paul L. Harris, Mita Banerjee and Anna Sinclair
   1995   Early understanding of emotion: Evidence from natural language. *Cognition and Emotion* 9: 117–149.
Willems, Roel M., Peter Hagoort and Daniel Casasanto
   2010   Body-specific representations of action verbs: Neural evidence from right- and left-handers. *Psychological Science* 21(1): 67–74.

Laura J. Speed, David P. Vinson and Gabriella Vigliocco, London (UK).

10. Blending in language and communication

1. Elements of blending
2. A classic example of blending
3. Challenges to blending theory
4. Words and morphemes
5. Syntax
6. Phrases, clauses, and sentences
7. Ground and viewpoint
8. Conclusion
9. References

1. Elements of blending

Cognitive linguistics analyzes how language derives from and interacts with basic mental operations not exclusive to language. Blending is a basic mental operation, interacting with other basic mental operations such as conceptual mapping, framing, and image-schematic structuring. It plays a pervasive role in language and communication. (See blending.stanford.edu and Turner 2014 for surveys of research).

Blending theory uses a number of new and old terms, presented below.

Mental frame: A frame (Fillmore 1976, 1982) is a small bundle of ideas, stereotypical for a community. We activate parts of frames mentally, often prompted by expressions. Think of a *stockbroker*. We have a mental frame for buying and selling, and a mental frame for the special case of buying and selling securities, particularly stocks and bonds. In it, there are roles for the buyer, the seller, what is sold, and the broker who arranges the transaction. When someone says, *I have to call my stockbroker*, everyone can activate the right mental *frame*.

Mental space: Following Gilles Fauconnier (1985), we use the term "mental space" to mean a small, bundled array of related mental elements that a person activates simultaneously. *Luke is a stockbroker* prompts us to activate a mental space with one element that we take to be a man (presumably) named "Luke", and another element, *stockbroker*, and a relation between them. The relation between them is obvious: Luke is a stockbroker, which is to say, we have a *role-value* relation, with *stockbroker* as the role and *Luke* as its value. If the next sentence is *He is my brother-in-law*, then we activate not just the mental space for *Luke is a stockbroker* but also another mental space, which contains *I*, the speaker. The relations between these mental spaces, and between elements within them, are complicated. For each of these two mental spaces, we need to draw on the kinship frame and its relation *brother-in-law*, which connects two people. In the *Luke* mental space, he is now a brother-in-law to the element *speaker* in the other mental space, so there is a relation connecting those two elements in two different mental spaces. In the *speaker* mental space, the speaker now has a brother-in-law, so there is a relation connecting that role *brother-in-law* in the *speaker* mental space to its value *Luke* in the *Luke* mental space. A network of such mental spaces might be called a *mental web*.

Mental web: A mental web is a set of mental spaces that are activated and connected as one is thinking about a topic. For example, *My brother-in-law, the stockbroker, and his family will travel from San Francisco to Cleveland for Thanksgiving, and we need to learn the time of their arrival so that I can drive down to pick them up* will prompt for many mental spaces, such as a mental space in which I drive my car through complicated holiday traffic, another in which I stop at the appropriate gate at the arrival deck of Cleveland Hopkins International Airport, and on and on. Typically, one cannot hold all these spaces equally active simultaneously in the mind. As we think, we focus on one or another mental space in the mental web. Recently activated mental spaces remain latent and are easier to activate.

Vital Relations: The mental web will have many conceptual connections. The most frequent and important mental connections are the "Vital Relations": *Time, Space, Identity, Change, Cause-Effect, Part-Whole, Analogy, Disanalogy, Representation, Property, Similarity, Category, Intentionality*, and *Uniqueness*. For example, in the mental web about my picking up my brother-in-law and family at the airport, there will be an element in several of those mental spaces corresponding to *I*, and all of those elements in all of those mental spaces will be connected by *Identity* relations. The pickup at the airport is connected by a *Time* connector to the Thanksgiving feast so that the pickup is suitably prior in time to the mental space in which we all have the feast. But the pickup is also connected by a *Time* connector to the mental space for the speaker in the moment of speaking, so that the pickup is suitably later in time than the moment of speaking. The mental space for that pickup at the airport is connected by a *Space* connector to the home where the feast is held, so that we understand that the airport is at a spatial remove from the home. And so on.

Blend. A *blend* is a mental space that results from *blending* mental spaces in a mental web. The blend is not an abstraction, or an analogy, or anything else already named and recognized in common sense, although blending is the basis of the cognitively modern human mind. A *blend* is a new mental space that contains some elements from different mental spaces in a mental web but that develops new meaning of its own that is not drawn from those spaces. This new meaning emerges in the blend. For example, suppose I say, *My brother-in-law, the stockbroker, lives in San Francisco. The stock market opens* *on the East Coast at 9:30 am, but at that moment, it is 6:30 am on the West Coast. So my brother-in-law must awaken every day at about 5 in the morning if he is going to be awake enough to start serious and risky work at 6:30 am. If I were my brother-in-law, I would be miserable.* This passage asks us to build a mental space that contains the brother-in-law and a mental space for me, and to connect many mental spaces, many small ideas. One of the spaces it asks us to build mentally is a mental space in which there is one man (*I*) who is imbued with some of what we think about the speaker and some of what we think about the brother-in-law, but only some in each case. This person in the blend has new ideas attached to it. In the blend, I am my brother-in-law, in a way: there is an element in the blend that has the personal identity of the speaker, but no longer has the speaker's job. It has the emotions of the speaker, but the competence and labor of the brother-in-law. This element is not available from any other space in the mental web. It is unique to the blend. There is a new idea here, one that emerges only in the blend. I-am-my-brother-in-law is a new idea, and a very complicated one.

The blend has many elements and properties that are not available from other spaces in the mental web. In the mental spaces that have the brother-in-law (living in San Francisco, arising at 5am, etc.), he is not miserable. In the mental space that has me, I am not miserable. But in the blend, there is a person who is miserable. This person emerges in the blend.

When a mental web contains a blended space, it is often called a "conceptual integration network", a "blending network", or a "blending web".

Projection. The elements and relations that come into the blend from the mental spaces that are blended are called *projections*. These projections to a blend are always *partial* or rather *selective*. For example, for *If I were my brother-in-law, I would be miserable*, we project to the blend the speaker but only a small part of what we know about the speaker. We do not project the speaker's current employment, for example, because then the speaker could not be a stockbroker. We do not project the speaker's currently living in Cleveland. We project from the mental space with the stockbroker brother-in-law the role *stockbroker* and perhaps even *living in San Francisco and accordingly rising every weekday at 5 am*, but not of course the physical appearance of the brother-in-law, or his family relations, and so on. (Otherwise, in the blend, I might have to be my own brother-in-law, which is taboo.)

Emergent structure in the blend and in the mental web: In the blend, there is a person who is a stockbroker and is miserable. In no other space is it true that anyone is miserable. The misery is *emergent* in the blend. Crucially, there is also new emergent structure in the mental web outside of the blend. Once we have constructed the mental blend, we realize that the speaker in his own actual reality has an aversion to rising early. This is new structure we build for the speaker. There is also emergent structure in the connection between the speaker in his input mental space and the stockbroker in his input mental space, namely a *disanalogy* connection between them having to do with disposition.

Human-scale: Some bundles of thought are tractable and manageable by the human mind. We call them *human-scale*. Other bundles of thought are not tractable, because we cannot grasp them mentally, or they go beyond our mental limits. Political cartoons specialize in providing such human-scale compressions of vast mental webs, as in a cartoon that shows the President of the United States, in a suit, snatching the rice bowl away from a starving child, and we use this human-scale compression to help us grasp the situation in which a presidential veto of legislation in the United States might affect food supply in far distant lands. Most mental webs laying out what we want to think about would be utterly intractable for us except that we can make a human-scale blend drawing on different mental spaces in the web. The blend then gives us a handy, tractable thing to think about. It helps us access, organize, manipulate, and adjust the mental web in which it now sits. For example, in the vast mental web of thinking about life and possibilities, I can have a compact blend in which I actually am a stockbroker – a simulation that arises through blending, going through the motions, and being miserable. The blend in this case is a human-scale mental simulation. I can now do my best to avoid it or anything like it.

Compression and Expansion: A blend is not a small abstraction of the mental spaces it blends and is not a partial cut-and-paste assembly, either, because it contains emergent ideas. It is a tight *compression*. It contains much less information than the full mental web it serves. From it, we can reach up to manage and work on the rest of the vast mental web in which it sits.

We use compressed, tight, tractable blends to help us think about larger mental webs. We might say that we carry small, compressed blends with us mentally, and *unpack* or *expand* them as needed to connect up to what we need to think about. For example, the pithy, compressed little blend with the miserable stockbroker can be used to help the speaker think about any job in a time zone other than the Eastern time zone (GMT −5) and lead him to be vigilant for downsides. He might now make specific inquiry to learn what demands any new job might impose upon him that arise because of events that take place in other time zones where people have sleep schedules that do not match his in universal time (UTC).

2. A Classic example of blending

Fauconnier and Turner (2002) give a quick illustration of these ideas – mental space, mental web, connectors between spaces, emergent structure, projection, compression, expansion, human-scale, blend:

> A Buddhist monk arrives at the foot of a mountain path a little while before dawn. At dawn, he begins walking up the mountain path, reaches the top at sunset, and meditates at the top overnight until, at dawn, he begins to walk back to the foot of the mountain, which he reaches at sunset. Make no assumptions about his starting or stopping or about his pace during the trips. Riddle: is there a place on the path that the monk occupies at the same hour of the day on the two separate journeys?

One way to solve this riddle is to blend the monk's ascent with the monk's descent, so that in the blend, at dawn, there are two monks, one at the foot of the mountain, the other at the top. They then take their journeys, each arriving at the opposite end of the path at sunset. They must meet somewhere, and where they meet is the spot on the path that they occupy at the same hour of the day on the two separate journeys. Again, this is a simulation constructed by blending.

The connected set of ideas for solving this riddle is a mental web. It contains at least three mental spaces. There are connectors between mental spaces, such as identity connectors between the path in the mental space for the ascent and the path in the mental space for the descent. Some but not all the information from those two mental spaces is projected to a blended mental space. We do not, for example, project the date of the ascent and the date of the descent, or the weather on those days, or the fact that the monk is aware of what is around him and would surely be shocked to find himself approaching himself on the path. We do not project the fact that a person cannot be in two places (foot and summit) at the same time. The blend is a compression of parts of its mental web, and it is at human-scale because it is a little vignette about two people approaching each other on a path; this is a simple and familiar scene of human walking. But this compressed blend also has emergent structure. It has two monks, and a meeting. We can use the compressed blend to think about and work on the mental web. We can expand or unpack the blend and connect it back up to elements in the larger mental web. Some of the emergent structure in the blend, namely, the fact that there is a meeting, leads us to project back to create new structure in the mental web itself: now, for example, there is an identity connection between some spot on the path in the ascent mental space and a spot on the path in the descent mental space such that the monk is located at that spot in his travel at the same time of day on the two separate days.

3. Challenges to blending theory

Challenge 1: Isn't blending just epiphenomenal, a kind of linear sum over many other processes (counterfactual thinking, metonymy, categorization, metaphor, other "rhetorical" forms of thought, etc.) that already have names? Why lump them together? Answer: Scientific generalization consists of locating substantive and systematic patterns that run across many apparently different products and effects. Words like "metonymy" and "counterfactual" are only labels, not siloed categories of thought, much less autonomous mental processes. Where there is commonality of mental process across activities, we should model it; where we find distinctions of process, we should model them. This is standard procedure in science: although there are many important differences between the apple's falling from the tree and the moon's orbiting the earth, there is a general pattern – gravitational attraction – governing the disparate events. Blending theory hypothesizes that blending is not epiphenomenal, although it operates at a fairly high level of organization; that there are fundamental patterns of process and intricate mechanics and patterns of compression that run over many different kinds of products. Blending interacts with the vast complexity of grammatical and conceptual operations; it does not replace them. It plays a surprisingly important role in human creative activity, but analyzing its mechanisms and power does not diminish the diversity of activities over which it operates or the differences between those activities. Indeed, blending research uncovers many generalizations about the way in which such diversity emerges (cf. Fauconnier and Turner 2008).

Challenge 2: Everyone has known about blending – the mental combination of old things to get new things – for a long time. So what is new? Answer: If we agree on the power of blending and the need to study it, then, united, we can plant the flag and turn to the minor parts of the challenge. Gilles Fauconnier and I have surveyed the work of invaluable thinkers dating from classical antiquity, including Aristotle, who analyzed particular products of blending quite insightfully, and who sometimes even commented on the general mental power of combining ideas. Yet, these excellent forerunners typically thought of blending as an exotic, exceptional, cognitively-expensive event, used exclusively in rare moments of high creativity, rather than as a basic mental operation, noncostly, constantly deployed in everyday cognition by every cognitively modern human being. Additionally, modern blending theory has proposed that there are overarching systematic principles of blending, generic integration templates, intricate mechanisms, and constraints that run across swaths of mental work whose products look quite different.

Challenge 3: If blending exists, shouldn't we be able to program it algorithmically? Isn't that how we specify a mental process in science? Answer: I have been lucky to participate in projects dedicated to exploring the ways in which blending theory might serve the valuable field of computational creativity and inference. Computational modeling has much to teach us. Yet, the mental process itself does not appear to me to be algorithmic. It is an important part of the flexibility of blending that outputs are not determined algorithmically from inputs, or, at a minimum, computer science, artificial intelligence, and psychology have not been able so far to characterize "inputs" to blending in such a way as to make computational models of blending more than suggestive and illustrative.

Challenge 4: Where are the quick psychological tests to show us how blending works? Why don't you put people into the fMRI machine so we can see where and when blending happens and how it works? Answer: The broad empirical evidence for blending comes from the classic scientific method of making generalizations over in-sample data (grammatical patterns, for example) and then testing those hypotheses against out-of-sample data to determine whether they in fact apply. Blending theory in this way predicts findings rather than effects, a scientific method used, e.g., throughout archeology, from the archeology of early hominins to the archeology of classical antiquity. Turner (2010) surveys possibilities for experiments directed at causal inference (treatment, control, validity) and the great obstacles to designing such experiments for advanced human cognition as opposed to, e.g., pharmaceuticals or visual physiology. McCubbins and Turner (2013) discusses a set of experiments we designed and ran to begin to locate which patterns of blending are more or less tractable for subjects. Turner (2014, Appendix, "The Academic Workbench") reviews possibilities for future experiments and tests, but cautions against hopes for simple models that assume simple consistency or simple linearity. Blending is often thought to have neural correlates. In Gilles Fauconnier's phrase, this is "hardly a surprising assumption. But the correlation is complex: blending creates networks of connected mental spaces, a 'higher level' of organization, if you like. It is presumably not itself a primitive neural process. It is however a capacity of some brains, and perhaps an exclusively human capacity in its double-scope form" (Coulson 2011: 414). As Fauconnier sums it up, "Neuroscience has made awesome progress in recent years, but does not provide direct observation of conceptual operations like mental space mapping" (Coulson 2011: 413).

Challenge 5: But we have no awareness except in rare moments that we are doing any blending, so what is the evidence that it is so? Answer: Awareness is immaterial. We have no awareness during vision that our brains are doing fabulous work and that 50% of neocortex is implicated in this work. In awareness, we just open our eyes and the visual field comes flooding in. In fact, of course, vision requires spectacular work, and the only moment in which we are likely to notice that anything is going on is when it fails, as when we have motion sickness and the visual field starts to "do" utterly inexplicable things. This makes the job of physiologists of vision quite difficult, since we cannot ask human beings to report their awareness of vision, much less rely on the answer if we could. It's just so with blending: the blending scientist must look far beyond what human beings are aware of for evidence of what is going on.

Challenge 6: But then, how do you know when a mental space, a network of mental spaces, or an integration (blending) network is active? For example, you say that to solve the riddle of the Buddhist Monk, we activate a mental space that selectively blends elements of the monk's ascent and descent. How do we know? Can we read minds? Answer: this is a fundamental question that goes to the heart of any research into human conceptualization. There are no methods for reading minds directly. Every method for detecting human conceptualization is indirect and inferential. Accordingly, cognitive science attempts to bring to bear as many methods as are suitable, and derives greater confidence according as more and more of them point to the same conclusion, the same inferences. One fundamental method, which has been in place at least as long as recorded history, and presumably further, is to check whether someone's behavior is consistent with the meaning we propose that they have constructed. We say, "Please pass the salt", and they pass the salt, or, if they do not, we have cause to seek some reason for their noncompliance. The reason might be physical inability, a disposition to the contrary, or, perhaps, a failure to have constructed the meaning we intended for them to construct. If we say, "Pass the salt", and they respond, "Say *please*", and we respond, "Please", and then they pass the salt, we derive some confidence that our idea of the meanings they have constructed is not fundamentally inaccurate. Looking for behavior consistent with the meaning we think they have constructed can mean looking for linguistic behavior. If we say something to them, and ask them to paraphrase what we have said, and they do, we check whether our understanding of the requirements and constraints of the grammatical constructions they have used in the paraphrase are consistent with our idea of the meaning they constructed. Asking for a paraphrase is an everyday kind of quiz, and science has developed many kinds of quiz to check on the meaning constructed. It quite commonly happens that people do not construct quite the meaning we intended. Consider the riddle of the Buddhist monk. If we ask the riddle, we may find that the addressees constructed none of the meaning we intended because they do not speak the language we used. The construction of meaning moreover depends upon learning many cultural frames and generic integration templates, and people from different cultures and subcultures often do not share the same frames and templates, so it is quite normal in these circumstances that an addressee does not construct the meaning we intended. But suppose we pose the riddle to two people who speak our language close to the way we do and share the same culture. It may easily turn out that one of them activates the blend and the other does not. Many people cannot solve the riddle, which we take as evidence that they have not activated a blended space containing the meeting of the ascending monk and the descending monk. But if they respond, "Yes, there must be a spot on the path that the monk occupies at the same hour of the day on the two successive days: it is the spot where the monk *meets himself*", then we take their use of the verb *meet* in this form and the reflexive personal pronoun as evidence for their having constructed a space in which there are indeed two agents, each corresponding to the monk, and that must be a blend, because in all the mental spaces for the journey, there is only one monk, and no meeting. We can quiz them further to check that they do not think this blended mental space refers to a mental space that is supposed to be actual for the journey. Often, blending researchers find that linguistic behavior leaves unexpressed some important part of the construction of meaning. For example, if we ask subjects to draw a cartoon corresponding to the sentence, "This surgeon is a butcher", we routinely find that the drawing represents the surgeon-butcher with slovenly, dirty, unkempt appearance, and often with an expression associated with some kind of mental deficiency. The drawing in this case is evidence of some covert mental space that is being used for constructing the identity of the surgeon-butcher, which we might otherwise not have detected. Similarly, linguistic paraphrases of "This surgeon is a butcher" frequently do not specify the scene in which the surgeon-butcher is working. But the cultural expectations of drawing usually lead the subject to be more specific about the scene: the surgeon-butcher is almost always drawn as working in an operating room rather than a butcher shop. When we say that someone has activated such-and-such mental spaces and such-and-such mappings, we of course mean that the reading we attribute to them requires such activations, and we may use every device known to science to check whether they have achieved that reading. Even then, attribution can be difficult, as when two different integration networks would both legitimate a particular expression. There is never a sure way to read another mind, and the researcher must always be open to the possibility that there are other constructions of meaning consistent with the subject's behavior and biological activity.

Challenge 7: Isn't blending theory incomplete? Answer: Absolutely. In fact, "blending theory" is more a framework for a research program on conceptual integration, compression, mapping, and so on than it is a theory. Many new insights have been generated inside this framework since its proposal. Its original architects look forward to future developments, which are sure to be considerable.

4. Words and morphemes

Perhaps the most natural beginning for a discussion of blending in language starts with lexical semantics. There are many lexical prompts for blending. *Safe*, for example, said of some situation, prompts us to activate a mental web corresponding to that situation, blend parts of it with the frame of *harm*, understand that the blend is counterfactual with respect to the original situation, and now blend the original situation and the counterfactual blend so that the counterfactual relation between them is compressed to *absence of harm* as emergent structure in the new blend. This compression involves conceiving of *absence of harm* as a property that can be signaled by the adjective *safe*. Other single words prompting for particular blending templates include *danger, lucky, accident, mistake, gap, dent, missing, detour*, and many others. A single sentence can contain many such words, calling for many such compressions, as in the National Public Radio warning a few days before Halloween, October 2000, "A halloween *costume* that *limits* sight or movement is an *accident lurking* in *disguise*."

The morphemes *over* and *under* in *overfish* and *undernourish* obviously call for blending networks. Turner (2007) analyzes the range of blending compressions involved in "We are eating the food off our children's plates. When we overfish, we eat not only today's fish but tomorrow's fish, too". Nili Mandelblit analyzes the use of morphological inflection of a main verb to prompt for blends of the frame of an action with the frame of causation (Mandelblit 2000, reviewed in Fauconnier and Turner 2002).

Fauconnier and Turner (2003) analyze polysemy as a consequence of blending. Through selective projection, expressions applied to an input can be projected to apply to counterparts in the blend. In this way, blends harness existing words in order to express the new meanings that arise in the blend. An example is the use of *here* in network news to mean roughly *present and active in the shared communicative scene of blended joint attention*. Combinations of expressions from the inputs may be appropriate for picking out structure in the blend even though those combinations are inappropriate for the inputs. In consequence, grammatical but meaningless phrases can become grammatical and meaningful for the blend. As an example, consider the news anchor's saying *Let me show you, here on my left*, as she points to her left, even though in the studio there is in fact nothing on her left to which she wishes to direct attention. Rather, the production crew has signaled to her that it will be insetting a clip into a window in the broadcast. The linguistic combination is fully grammatical for the blend but not for any of the individual input spaces. Similarly, one can say for the blend of same-sex marriage, *The brides married each other at noon*, even though this combination would have been infelicitous for a mental web of inputs that included only heterosexual marriage. Other examples include *computer virus* and *the square root of negative one*. Terminology that naturally applies to the blended space serves, through connections in the integration network, to pick out meaning that it could not have been used to pick out if the blend had not been built. As an example, consider the interactive, animated diagrams in (Kirk 2012), in which Olympians in an event over centuries "compete" against each other, in the sense that stick figures in compressed diagrams "race" against each other. All of the language for the frame of competition in an Olympic event applies naturally to the blend and picks out relationships across the mental spaces of the mental web containing all those individual Olympic events, even though one could not say that *Usain Bolt utterly defeated Thomas Burke* [the 1896 winner] of that mental web absent its blend. In all these ways, blending provides a continuum for polysemy effects. Polysemy is an inevitable and routine outcome of blending, but it is only rarely noticed. Some of the products of such blending strike hearers as "metaphoric" for reasons analyzed in Turner (1998).

"Change predicates" arise systematically through blending. For example, Fauconnier and Turner (2002) analyze a generic integration template according to which vital relations of analogy and disanalogy across mental spaces in a mental web are compressed in the blend to provide a human-scale concept. The analogical connections between input spaces are compressed to an identity or unity in the blend, and the disanalogical connections are compressed to change for that element in the blend. Grammar for expressing change can thereby be used of the blend. For example, we can say that "dinosaurs turned into birds" and rely on the hearer to expand from the structure in the blend and hence to recognize that we do not mean that any particular dinosaur changed at all or turned into a bird. In the blend, there is an identity, a group identity, consisting of *dinosaurs*, and this identity "changes" into a different group identity, *birds*. Such change predicates have been widely analyzed in the literature. Examples include *His girlfriend gets younger every year*, *My tax bill gets bigger every year*, and *Make this envelope disappear* [written on the back of an envelope, inviting the customer to sign up for electronic delivery of bills] (all from Fauconnier, personal communication); *The cars get three feet bigger when you enter Pacific Heights*, *The fences get taller as you move westward across the United States* (both from Sweetser 1997); *Your French has disappeared*, *You need to recover your tennis serve*, and *Kick the habit*. (See Tobin 2010 for a review of change predicates and blending.)

5. Syntax

Blends frequently have new emergent structure. Because linguistic constructions attached to the input spaces in the mental web can be projected down to be used of the blend to express that emergent structure, it is rare that new linguistic constructions are needed in order to express new meaning. But blending also provides a mechanism for creating emergent structure for the form part of a form-meaning pair.

Fillmore and Atkins (1992) presented the classic analysis of the verb *risk*, and the syntax of the verb *risk*, and its meaning. Fillmore and Atkins analyze the frame for *risk* as – in my words – not theirs, a blend of the frames for *chance* and *harm*. The frames for *chance* and *harm* are independent. If I say *There is a chance that it will be 30 degrees Celsius tomorrow and a chance that it will be 31 degrees Celsius tomorrow, but either one is fine*, it means that there is a possibility of one or the other, but no question of harm. Similarly, if harm is inevitable, then chance and possibility are not at issue. Accordingly, harm and chance are independent frames. But when we integrate the frames for *chance* and *harm*, we create one of the basic frames for *risk*, in particular, *running a risk*. Fillmore and Atkins offer the diagram I recreate here:

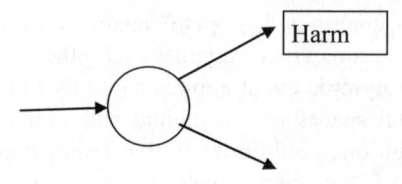

Fig. 10.1: Risk-running

In this diagram, a circle means *chance*. There is a chance of harm. There is also a chance of something else. This is the structure of the basic frame of running a risk. But Fillmore and Atkins point out that there is yet another blend, one that blends in an additional frame, namely the frame of *choice*. We can *choose* to place ourselves in a position where there is a *chance* of *harm*. Perhaps we are betting on a horse, for example, or we like the thrill of driving fast. Here is the diagram:

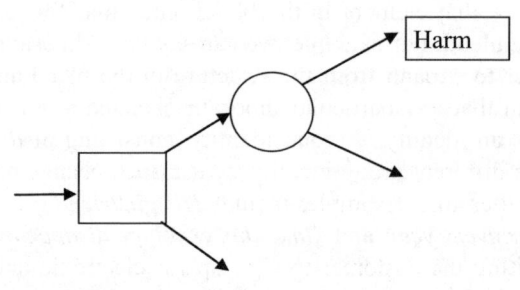

Fig. 10.2: Risk-taking

In this diagram, a circle means *chance*, and a square means *choice*.

In effect, Fillmore and Atkins have analyzed the lexical meaning of *risk* as a set of frame blends. Importantly, blending is selective: we do not take everything from the frame of *chance* and everything from the frame of *harm* and everything from the frame of *choice* and blend them compositionally. For example, the *harm* frame automatically brings in an evaluator. If there is harm, there must be harm to someone who evaluates it in that way. Think, for example, of a diamond and an owner. If the owner wants the diamond cut, then the cutting does not count as harm. But if the owner did not want the diamond cut, then the same cutting counts as harm. Of course, we might say that a connoisseur of fine diamonds, who is not the owner, might be caused aesthetic pain by the incompetent cutting of the diamond, even if the ignorant owner did not mind. In that case, the connoisseur is the evaluator who feels the harm.

Fillmore and Atkins talk about what they call "derivative syntax", which might instead be called "blended syntax". The syntax in such cases derives from the blending of conceptual frames. For example, Fillmore and Atkins consider the verb *smear*: when you smear something on a surface in such a way that the surface is covered by what you have smeared, then the verb *smear* acquires the syntax of *cover*, as in *I smeared the wall with mud*. In that case, the verb *smear* can be placed where *cover* would go. Similarly, when loading hay onto a truck results in the filling of the truck, then *load* can take on the syntax of *fill*, as in *I loaded the truck with hay*. We can always say that we *filled the truck with hay*, but when the loading results in filling, we can then say *I loaded the truck with hay*. Selective projection in the blending of these frames includes projection of some linguistic elements attached to those frames. Accordingly, blended syntax can result from frame blending.

Fillmore and Atkins observe that when *risk* means *expose to*, then *risk* can take on the syntax of *expose to*, as in "we must reinforce the boat before risking it to the waves". Similarly, "risk" can acquire through blending the syntax for *investing in* something, as in *Roosevelt risked more than $ 50,000 of his patrimony in ranch lands in Dakota Territory*. Emergent syntax for "risk" arises as part of the emergent structure of the blend.

Fauconnier and Turner (2002) present a common pattern of blending according to which a concept that is blended with other meaning projects to the blend its category; this is usually called "category extension". An example can be seen from the history of the concept of "number", which has taken on dramatically more complex structure as it has been blended with other structure to produce emergent structure in successive blends for fractions, zero, negative numbers, irrational numbers, real numbers, transcendental real numbers, and complex numbers, but the category *number* has been projected to each of these blends. This pattern in syntax results in nominal compounds, where one noun is taken from each of two blended spaces, and the blend is expressed by a syntactic structure, Noun + Noun, which still counts as something that can combine in the usual ways with constructions that call for a noun. Just as the category *number* was projected from one input to the new structure in the blend, so the category *Noun* is projected from the inputs to the new structure in the blend, except that we are more likely to call it a noun phrase.

Nominal compounds can themselves be composed into new syntactic forms. Consider the nominal compound *girl scout*. The Girl Scouts are an organization. Girl Scouts learn how to hike and camp and so on. *Girl* is a noun, *scout* is a noun, *Girl Scout* is a noun, in the sense that *Girl Scout* can go into the spots in the language that nouns can go. Now take *ballet school*. *School* is a noun and *ballet* is a noun. It prompts for a frame-compatible blend. People learn things in schools and ballet can be one of the things they learn, so the *ballet* frame is subordinated and nests in this case inside the *school* frame.

Now take *lace curtain*. Those are two nouns and they produce a nominal compound. It may seem strange to say, *She is a lace curtain ballet school girl scout*. But it is intelligible, and we understand what the grammar is prompting us to do. We see formal composition in the fact that *ballet school girl scout* is a nominal compound composed of two nominal compounds, and this can be again compounded with another nominal compound, *lace curtain*. What we might mean by *Oh, she is a lace curtain ballet school girl scout* could be that she receives a certain education (*ballet*) stereotypical for a certain demographic that is picked out by a style of decoration (*lace curtain*) and, as is stereotypical of these people in this social demographic, she belongs to a certain organization for children. We might even recognize this as a social stereotype if we live in certain parts of the United States.

Fauconnier and Turner (1996, 2002) analyze French double-verb causatives as an example of emergent syntax under blending. Part of the syntactic form comes from each of two input spaces, and part develops specifically for the blend. The blend has emergent syntax relative to the inputs. These causatives blend *faire* ("do") with a verb for the caused action, as in *Pierre fait manger Paul* 'Pierre makes eat Paul', *Pierre fait envoyer le paquet* 'Pierre makes send the package', and *Pierre fait mange la soupe à Paul* 'Pierre makes eat the soup to Paul'. These double-verb forms provide French speakers with ways to evoke a blending network that delivers a compressed, human-scale scene which integrates into one event at least two agents (Pierre and Paul), a causal action, a causal link, and a caused action (eat). The blend takes much of its clausal syntax from a compressed input that can be expressed via one of three single-verb forms (transitive, transfer, and optional transfer), but which does not quite serve the purpose for the causative meaning. French accordingly offers three complex blends for the compressed scene of causation and action. Each has as one input one of three compressed basic single-verb clausal constructions, and as the other input the diffuse chain of causal events with intermediate agents that we want to compress. The blend takes an additional verb from this chain of causal events, and the syntax in the blend thereby acquires two verbs.

6. Phrases, clauses, and sentences

Consider adjectives, such as those in *guilty pleasures*, *likely candidate*, and *red ball*. Notice that *likely candidate* (Eve Sweetser's example, personal communication) is usually used to refer to someone who is not (yet) a candidate. In that case, we are not composing the meaning of *candidate* and the meaning of *likely*. On the contrary, we are taking *candidate* from one mental space and *likely* from a mental space that includes a particular kind of frame. *Likely candidate* can be taken as prompting us to construct a blended frame in which there is someone who is likely *to become* a candidate. In *Allow yourself this guilty pleasure* and *Chocolate is a guilty pleasure*, it is not the pleasure itself that is guilty. Rather, it is the person who has the pleasure who feels guilty. In this case, there is a cause-effect vital relation between the input spaces – having the pleasure in one space causes the guilt in the other. But now, that outer-space cause-effect relationship is compressed in the blend into a feature of the pleasure. There are many similar examples, such as "grateful memories". The memories are not grateful. The person who has the memories is grateful for the events to which the memories refer. But in the blend that intentional relationship between the person and the person's memories and the events to which they refer is compressed into a feature of the memories.

Linguistic expressions for building "possibility" mental spaces (Fauconnier 1985) – e.g., *If I were a stockbroker, like my brother-in-law* – are routinely used to prompt for blending networks, as analyzed at length in Fauconnier and Turner (2002) and Dancygier and Sweetser (2005). "If-then" conditional constructions are one of the most obvious aspects of grammar used to prompt for blending, but there are many others, e.g. *I could be a stockbroker.*

Fauconnier and Turner (1996) build on Goldberg (1995) to analyze the ways in which basic clausal constructions like Caused-Motion, Resultative, and Ditransitive prompt for blending basic and familiar human-scale frames with sometimes large mental webs in order to produce compressed blends that can be expressed with the clausal form projected to the blend. The result is expressions that use verbs suited to other mental spaces in the web but not necessarily to caused-motion, resultative, or ditransitive frames. Goldberg presented Caused-Motion examples like *He sneezed the napkin under the table* and *She drank him under the table.* Others include *The officer waved the tanks into the compound, Junior sped the car around the Christmas tree* (where the verb comes from the manner of the caused motion), *I read him to sleep, I muscled the box into place,* and *Hunk choked the life out of him.* We can even say, *We blocked him from the door,* despite the fact that *block* is a verb for indicating the stopping of motion rather than the causing of motion. The frame of caused motion and the frame of blocked motion conflict directly, but through blending, we make a blend in which what is caused is absence of continued motion: an agent performs an action on an object that stops the motion of the object in a direction.

The case is similar for the Resultative construction. I can say, *No zucchini, tonight, honey. I boiled the pan dry.* The long causal chain that leads to a dry pan is compressed in the blend into a single action by the agent, although we do not actually know what that action was. Just as in the caused-motion construction, we achieve compressions in the blend. Consider *Roman imperialism made Latin universal. Latin* is not a thing and *universal* is not a feature. But in the blend, *Latin* becomes a thing and *universal* becomes a feature. Roman imperialism is not an agent, but in the blend Roman imperialism becomes an agent that works on an object, namely Latin, with the result that Latin becomes universal. This is the same general resultative network we see in *Catherine painted the wall white.* But now it runs over centuries, and hundreds of thousands of people, and vast causal connections: *Roman imperialism made Latin universal.*

The ditransitive construction uses as one of its input mental spaces transfer of an object from one person to another. When we blend that frame of transfer with a perhaps diffuse mental web not actually involving a hand-over, the ditransitive construction can be projected to the blend to express it, and various lexical items can come from the other input spaces, as in examples such as Goldberg provides: *She gave him that premise, She allowed him that privilege, She won him a prize, She showed him the view.* Consider *She gave him a headache.* She can give him a headache even though she does not have one. In the ditransitive scene, if I give her the eraser, it is because I have one. But now selective projection can create a blend in which the idea of giving has emergent structure. We might project to the blend only the reception, and the causal capacity to effect the result, not the initial possession.

We can use the ditransitive clause with a verb like *denied* or *refused*, which indicates stoppage. The ditransitive clause involves transfer and reception. We create a double-scope blend of two frames that conflict fundamentally, just as we did for *We blocked him from the door*. For *She denied him the job*, "she" did something that had a causal effect on the transfer of something to "him" and what she did was stop it. In the blend, now, the transfer is not completed. Blending is selective. In what Fauconnier and Turner (1996) call the "elaborate ditransitive", the benefit of the action on the object but not the object itself is "transferred" to the recipient, as in Goldberg's *Slay me a dragon*, or James Taylor's *Slide me a bass trombone* (in the song *Steamroller*). *Slide* comes in as the event action that the agent performs; what the speaker receives is not the bass trombone but the benefit of the sliding.

One of the most thoroughly analyzed clausal constructions whose meaning is an elaborate prompt for blending is the XYZ construction (e.g., *Paul is the father of Sally*, *These fire retardants are the asbestos of our time*). Turner's (1987) analysis of conceptual mappings used as its data kinship terms in patterns like "Death is the mother of beauty", an example of the "X is the Y of Z" construction (xyz). This xyz construction has routine everyday use, as in "Paul is the father of Sally". It has been analyzed by (Turner 1991, 1998; Fauconnier and Turner 2002). xyz contains the "y-of" construction. A "Y of" construction prompts us to perform an elaborate number of conceptual operations and can be composed repeatedly: "The doctor of the sister of the boss of Hieronymous Bosch". Such a composition of forms asks us to construct meanings, but the meanings are not compositions of the meanings in the various component expressions.

We understand an xyz construction as prompting us to find an unmentioned w in the mental space containing y, and to blend the x-z mental space with the y-w mental space. For example, an unmentioned w for "Death (x) is the mother (y) of beauty (z)" might be *daughter*. As (Steen and Turner 2014) discuss, there are two standard patterns for y, as follows: (1) y belongs to a standard frame commonly applied to the x-z scene; y is a role connecting at least two things in that frame; and x is the value of one of those roles and z is the value of the other. Examples are *archbishop* and *aunt*. (2) y is the anchor of an entrenched generic integration template used to blend together two conflicting frames. Examples are ancestor, anchor, architect, author, backbone, bane, birthplace, blood, blueprint, bottleneck, capital, cradle, ... as in phrases like "He is the architect of our business plan and that business plan is the backbone of our operation". But, impressively, one also easily finds very many data (Steen and Turner 2014) calling for blends of strongly conflicting frames where there is no already-entrenched y-based blending template. Examples are "The head of the C.D.C. told Congress MRSA is the cockroach of bacteria", "Bakersfield is the Alaska of California", and "These flame retardants are the asbestos of our time".

There are various constructions related to X is the Y of Z, as explained in (Turner 1991), such as the $xy_{adjective}z$ form. When the y in an xyz conceptual pattern is a commonplace transformation of one thing into another, its form may be $xy_{adjective}z$, so "Language is the fossil of poetry" may be expressed as "Language is fossil poetry". When the y-w conceptual relation is a part-whole frame relation, the form may be $xz_{adjective}y$, so "Las Vegas is the Monte Carlo of America" may be expressed as "Las Vegas is the American Monte Carlo." There are many other relations that permit the z-item to be expressed through a modifier for the y-item. The full form of the xyz figure has a corollary z-y compound noun form: "disc jockey", "road hog", "budget ceiling", "mall rat", "land yacht", "jail bait", "Westerns are back in the TV saddle", and "She is gymnastics royalty".

Eve Sweetser (personal communication) found an interesting example in a *New York Times* headline: "Now 80, George Washington will soon undergo the bridge equivalent of hip replacement" (*NYT* article headline, December 8, 2011, p A–22). This construction is z-equivalent-of-y. But as Gilles Fauconnier observes (personal communication), not all y-of-z constructions convert into z-equivalent-of-y. Although the sky is the daily bread of the eyes, we do not call the sky "the eyes-equivalent of daily bread". Although Paul is the father of Sally, we do not call him "the Sally-equivalent of father". It seems that the use of the z noun in the z-equivalent construction is easiest if z is already established as a common modifier in nominal compounds, e.g. "bridge repair", "bridge replacement", "bridge construction", "bridge span", "bridge jump".

7. Ground and viewpoint

The ground is a general conceptual frame (Fillmore 1976, 1982) for organizing specific communicative situations. It includes "the speech event, its setting, and its participants" (Langacker 1985: 113). Roles in this frame – such as the time and location of the communication – take on values in specific situations. Traditions of rhetoric, philology, semiotics, linguistics, and information theory have in one way or another considered the idea of the ground, and it has been treated by a range of cognitive linguists (Fillmore 1971; Rubba 1996; Talmy 1986).

The ground derives from a basic human frame, *joint attention*. Joint attention occurs in a human-scale scene in which people are attending to something and know they are all attending to it and know also that they are engaged with each other in attending to it (Tomasello 1995; Tobin 2008). In "communicative joint attention", these people are not only jointly attending but also communicating with each other about the focus of their attention. I use "classic joint attention" to refer to perhaps the most fundamental scene of communicative joint attention, in which two (or a few) people face-to-face are not only attending to something that is directly perceptible but are moreover communicating about it, e.g., *That blackbird in the hedge has red stripes on its wings*. The frame of *the ground* is tied to this idea of classic joint attention.

Inevitably, many constructions are specialized for classic joint attention. Deictics and, more broadly, indexicals – such as "I", "you", "here", and "now" – are form-meaning pairs tied to elements in the conceptual frame of *the ground*. Their utility depends on our ability for what Fauconnier and Turner (2002) call "simplex blending". In a simplex blending network, one input mental space is an established conceptual frame and the other input spaces contain elements of just the sort to which the conceptual frame is expected to apply. For example, if one mental space has the kinship frame *father-child*, and another mental space has two people, *Paul* and *Mary*, then the blended space can blend *Paul* with *father* and *Mary* with *child*, and we can prompt for this blend by saying *Paul is Mary's father*. In fact, given our idea that "Mary" is a female name, we are likely to infer that Mary is not just a *child* but a *daughter*.

Now I can help you look for something here in this uses the deictics "Now", "I", "you", "here" and "this" to invite the hearer to make a simplex blend in which the *ground* is activated and elements in it are blended with the particular speaker, hearer, time, and location. These deictics can prompt for meanings far from *the ground*. For example, Bolinger (1979) and Lansing (1989) discuss *impersonal you*, as in *Back in the pre-Cambrian, you couldn't see the sun because of all the steam*. "You" here cannot refer to the addressee, nor indeed to any generic *you* since there were no people in the pre-Cambrian. In the blend, there is a "focalizer", but the focalizer has no referent, individual or generic. The focalizer is a blended quasi-agent who has experience but no existence.

More familiarly, consider the way in which broadcast news anchors routinely use deictics, as in these attested examples:

1. Joining me now, [images of person 1 and person 2, both in studios far removed from the studio in which the anchor is being filmed, appear inset in rectangles on the screen]. All right, guys, thank you both so much for being here.
2. [The anchor looks at the camera] You've heard the news ...
3. This is the view from news-chopper 2. You saw this story unfolding live as breaking news on our CBS news between 5 and 7 am.
4. Welcome back. A quick update for you.
5. Hope to see you at 11 o'clock tonight. Until then, have a great evening.
6. And now you know the news of this Thursday, March the twentieth, 2008. Thanks for having us in.

One input to the broadcast news blend is *classic joint attention*, which provides tight, familiar, human-scale conceptual structure and linguistic constructions to the broadcast news scene of blended joint attention. There are many other potential inputs to the blend: the news reporting team in various places; recorded footage; "B-roll" stock footage; the broadcast studio; remote studios; reporters with a camera crew in the field; the studio production team; the corporation owning the network; a scene in which a particular viewer is viewing the news clip; computer browsers on which the clip can be played; YouTube and other archives of audiovisual clips; people on the street being interviewed, etc.

In the blend, there are roles for speaker, viewer, viewer's time and place, and so on, but those roles need not have any determinate value. That is, we need have no specific mental space with a specific viewer as an input to the blend. In the blended joint attention scene of network news, the roles are interacting even if there are no values for the roles. In this blend, "now" can signal the moment of viewing; "here" can signal the locus of the "object" of joint attention, which can be the blended scene of viewing. In particular, "you" can signal the role of the viewer, who usually is given certain features: the viewer is interested and present and loyal (not switching from channel to channel). Of course, the anchor can refer to any spaces in the mental web: *If you missed our broadcast last night*, *If you are just joining us*, etc. The anchor can say *Here comes a special report for you now* even when the show is recorded and the anchor cannot possibly know the actual location or moment of the viewing (given that the recording might be played many times by many people in many places) and need not even know the subject of the special report, which will be chosen by the production crew at a later time. The great variety of ways in which the roles in the scene of broadcast news blended joint attention can be filled can all be managed given the usual deictics from the input of classic joint attention, which are projected to the blend.

Such projection of deictic and indexical linguistic elements to serve a blend of joint attention that provides a very tight compression for a vast mental web is familiar from posters, such as "the face" of "Uncle Sam" "looking out" of the recruiting poster, and pointing his finger, saying "I want you for U. S. Army". We know that in the mental web that this blend serves, there is no single Uncle Sam, no particular "I", no particular "you", no utterance to a particular "you", and so on. We are not deluded, but blending provides us with a compressed, tractable mental conception and also provides us with the linguistic constructions for expressing that blend. Similarly, a U. S. World War II poster shows a man driving a convertible car with a chalk-sketch of Hitler in the passenger's seat. Its text reads, "When you ride alone, you ride with Hitler. Join a Car-Sharing Club Today!". The blend does not actually refer to a specific scene in the world; it is a compressed familiar scene of blended classic joint attention that receives all the language it needs from the inputs. We are not deluded: Hitler is not actually in our car. The person who reads the poster understands that the "you" applies to a role, an implied *you*, with certain features, which the person reading the poster might not possess: the viewer of these posters might be ineligible for recruitment to the army, might lack a driver's license or car, and so on. Scholars of literary and film representation routinely analyze the great complexities in the mental web for the implied roles in the blend, as when the character Huck Finn speaks in the first person to a reader referred to as "you", except that the reader knows that in the mental web there is an author, Mark Twain, and that Mark Twain's implied reader is rather different from Huck Finn's implied reader, or as when the voice of Jonathan Swift's *A Modest Proposal* constructs an implied speaker and an implied reader, who agree with the proposal for all its sound reasons, but Jonathan Swift also has an implied reader, one very different from the speaker's implied reader. *The 1001 Nights* is famously adept at keeping tight communicative blends for vast and cascading levels of mental webs of interacting stories (Turner 1996).

All of these *ground* phenomena are matters of *viewpoint*. Viewpoint arises inevitably from embodiment: participants in any scene of communicative joint attention are embodied, and blending projects selectively from viewpoint in the input mental spaces to the blend (see Sweetser 2012 for a review). Linguistic constructions suited to the expression of viewpoint in scenes of communicative joint attention are routinely projected to express new viewpoint phenomena that arise in blends based on joint attention.

Recanati (1995) analyzes the way in which what he calls "the epistolary present" expresses a blended temporal viewpoint belonging to the blended joint attention that arises for personal correspondence. In the blend, writer and reader are present in the moment and jointly attending, although they know that outside the blend in the mental web organized by the blend they are in different times and conditions. Recanati's attested examples include *J'ai devant moi ta lettre, et tu as devant toi ma reponse* 'I have before me your letter and you have before you my response.' The blend provides a human-scale compression. Of course, the writer is not prevented from expressing structure in mental spaces outside the blend. A letter containing a sentence like *I am so happy and know you are happy to hear it* can conclude with *By the time you receive this letter, I will already be on my way.*

Turner (1996) analyzes other temporal viewpoint blends, as when the wife, headed to the shower, says to her husband (who has asked how a certain task will be accomplished), *My husband took care of that while I was in the shower*. In the blend, the wife certainly has very much of her embodied viewpoint at the moment of utterance. But her blended viewpoint receives projections from the viewpoint of the wife (and husband) in a different, future mental space, after the shower. The wife's viewpoint from that future mental space focuses on a mental space in which the task is accomplished, and that mental space of accomplishment lies in the past, and the accomplishment accordingly has the certainty of the past. The blend provides a human-scale compression. The past tense from the viewpoint of the future space (where it is grammatical) is projected to the blend in order to prompt for new meaning in the blend, namely, that the accomplishment (by the husband) is certain. Projecting from this new structure in the blend back up to the mental space of his present communication, the husband creates not the factual existence of the accomplishment but rather the wife's absolute expectation of its impending accomplishment by him as she heads to the shower. The past tense construction demands a rationale; the husband achieves the rationale by taking the utterance as a prompt to build a mental web that includes this blended viewpoint; the wife used the past tense construction exactly to prompt the husband to build that mental network and to take it that the wife intended him to do so as the result of her using the past tense. The expression calls for a viewpoint blend, drawing on projections from both the viewpoint of the present and the viewpoint of the future.

Nikiforidou (2010, 2012) analyzes the role of blending in a construction she calls "Past tense + proximal deictic", with emphasis on the cases where the proximal deictic is "now". The preferred patterns are "was/were + now", as in *It was now possible ...* and, for a non-copula verb, "now + past tense", as in *He now saw that ...* Nikiforidou provides "a detailed blueprint of the blending mappings cued by the [past + proximal deictic] pattern" (2012). Essentially, the pattern calls for a blend of viewpoints, in which our overall understanding is stage-managed from the point of view of a narrator but some self or consciousness located in a previous time is contextually available and prominent, and the events experienced in that previous time are to be construed "from the point of view of that consciousness, as that character's thoughts, speech or perceptions" (2010). The blended viewpoint takes on elements of different perspectives and compresses a time relation. The mental space of the narrator's condition is still the mental space from which the narrated space is accessed and built up, but the experiential perspective comes from inside the narrated events. There is considerable emergent structure in the blend. In the blend, it is possible to have not only knowledge that is available only at a distance but also to have the experience, perception, and realization available only up close. In a study of the British National Corpus, Nikiforidou shows that this is a highly productive construction, even outside of literary genres.

Presciently, Nikiforidou writes that the grammatical pattern has the "effect of zooming in on the events" (Nikiforidou 2012). Steen and Turner (2014) report that a search in the Red Hen archive (http://redhenlab.org) reveals that documentaries often use the camera (and the blended joint attention scene in which the viewfinder of the camera is blended with the eye of the viewer) to "zoom in" on the "past consciousness" indicated by the *past* + now construction. The audiovisual zoom is a multimodal construction that supports *past* + now. There is a hitch in providing this *past* + *now* visual zoom, because the narrator speaks *at one time* about a consciousness *at a previous time*. That is a mismatch. The consciousness and its experiences are not available in the narrator's immediate environment, or indeed in any of the mental spaces we have for considering the production and broadcast of the narration. The news production team must provide some suitable prompt for that consciousness in the past. There are several ways to resolve the mismatch. The three most common appear to be (1) have the person who is coreferential with the consciousness we are narrating re-enact the events, with the appropriate setting and staging and so on, and film that scene; (2) find archival still photos of that person at the time and present them, perhaps, e.g., with a Kens Burns effect, as the narrator uses the *past + now* construction; (3) find historical film footage containing the person and run that footage as the narrator uses the *past + now* construction. One of the most interesting such cases arises when the narrator and the past consciousness are connected by an Identity relation, as in a PBS documentary on the Pentagon Papers, in which Daniel Ellsberg, who leaked the Pentagon Papers, is narrating in advanced age his exploits in the period 1967–1971. There is extraordinary emergent structure in this blend, including Ellsberg's ability to speak for his young self in a way that probably would not have been available to him at the time, and of course an enduring, manufactured, compressed character for "Ellsberg" the man: young Ellsberg and old Ellsberg are of course extremely different things, but the analogies between them, including analogies of viewpoint, can be compressed to a characterological unity in the blend.

Nikiforidou (2012: 179) writes of the linguistic construction, "In blending terms, ... resolution of (apparent) conflict is often achieved through the mechanism of compression, whereby elements that are conceptually separate in the input spaces are construed as one in the blended space. The construction at hand, I suggest, cues a particular kind of compression, namely compression of a time relation. The dynamic, continuously updated character of such blending networks renders them particularly suitable for representing meaning in a narrative, where formal clues may often give conflicting instructions even within the same sentence (as is the case with FIS [Free Indirect Style]).".

Sweetser (2012: 9–10) analyzes deictic displacement as a viewpoint blend:

> [A] clear example is that in English, the correct response to the invitation *Can you come to my party?* is *Sure, I'd love to come,* not *Sure, I'd love to go.* The invitation accepter might later say to a third party, *I'm going to Sandy's party on Friday.* and would be unlikely to say *come* in this context. The acceptance utterance thus participated in the inviter's deictic structure, displacing the accepter's deictic center to the inviter's ... .
>
> Note that the Speaker of *Can I come to your party?* has not completely recentered her deictic field on the Addressee – *I* still refers to the Speaker, and *you* to the Addressee ... But the spatial deictic coordinate space, which is most canonically centered on Ego (hence on the Speaker), in this blend is mapped onto the Addressee as center.
>
> The crucial point here is that our everyday construal of personal viewpoint is a blend. It is a blend that is so common that it is hard to notice it. We normally experience our own bodies simultaneously as loci of our conscious Selves or Egos, agents of our speech and action, spatial sources of our fields of perceptual access and manual reach, interfaces of social interaction, and more. But as stated above, we also naturally create such models for other individuals around us – aided, very possibly, by our mirror neurons, which respond to other humans' grasping actions (for example), as well as to our own. Once that is accomplished, a speaker can naturally describe motion away from herself with *come*, if she is profiling the deictic field structure relative to another participant (and leaving out mention of her own deictic field).

8. Conclusion

Blending is a mental operation constantly and widely deployed in human cognition, almost entirely below the horizon of observation. Far from costly or special, it is central and indispensable to language and multimodal human communication. Over time, groups of people establish generic integration templates, which other members of the group can learn, and which come to count as part of a group's abilities and even its identity. The form-meaning pairs of grammar often have as part of their meaning a set of hints and constraints on integration mapping. Communicative forms do not mean; instead, they prompt human beings to construct meaning. This chapter has been a topical introduction to some of the ways in which form-meaning patterns prompt for patterns of conceptual integration.

9. References

Bolinger, Dwight
   1979   To Catch a Metaphor: *You* As Norm. *American Speech* 54: 194–209.

Coulson, Seana
   2011   Constructing meaning: An interview with Gilles Fauconnier. *Review of Cognitive Linguistics* 9(2): 413–417.

Dancygier, Barbara and Eve Sweetser
   2005   *Mental Spaces in Grammar: Conditional Constructions*. Cambridge: Cambridge University Press.

Fauconnier, Gilles
   1985   *Mental Spaces: Aspects of Meaning Construction in Natural Language*. Cambridge: MIT Press.

Fauconnier, Gilles and Mark Turner
   1996   Blending as a Central Process of Grammar. In: A. Goldberg (ed.), *Conceptual Structure, Discourse, and Language*, 113–130. Stanford: Center for the Study of Language and Information. [Expanded web version 1998, available at http://markturner.org.]

Fauconnier, Gilles and Mark Turner
   2002   *The Way We Think: Conceptual Blending and the Mind's Hidden Complexities*. New York: Basic Books.

Fauconnier, Gilles and Mark Turner
   2003   Polysemy and Conceptual Blending. In: B. Nerlich, V. Herman, Z. Todd and D. Clarke (eds.), *Polysemy: Flexible Patterns of Meaning in Mind and Language*, 79–94. Berlin/New York: Mouton de Gruyter.

Fauconnier, Gilles and Mark Turner
   2008   Rethinking Metaphor. In: R. Gibbs (ed.), Cambridge Handbook of Metaphor and Thought, 53–66. New York: Cambridge University Press.

Fillmore, Charles
   1971   *Santa Cruz Lectures on Deixis*. Bloomington: Indiana University Linguistics Club.

Fillmore, Charles
   1976   Frame Semantics and the Nature of Language. *Annals of the New York Academy of Sciences* 280: 20–32. doi: 10.1111/j.1749–6632.1976.tb25467.x

Fillmore, Charles
   1982   Frame Semantics. In: Linguistic Society of Korea (ed.), *Linguistics in the Morning Calm*, 111–137. Seoul: Hanshin Publishing Company.

Fillmore, Charles J. and Beryl T. Atkins
   1992   Towards a frame-based organization of the lexicon: the semantics of RISK and its neighbors. In: A. Lehrer and E. Kittay (eds.), *Frames, Fields and Contrast: New Essays in Semantics and Lexical Organization*, 75–102. Hillsdale: Erlbaum.

Goldberg, Adele. E.
  1995   *Constructions: A Construction Grammar Approach to Argument Structure Constructions.* Chicago: University of Chicago Press.
Kirk, Chris
  2012   How Badly Would Usain Bolt Destroy the Best Sprinter of 1896? *Slate* 26 July 2012.
Langacker, Ronald W.
  1985   Observations and speculations on subjectivity. In: J. Haiman (ed.), *Iconicity* in *Syntax*, 109–150. Amsterdam/Philadelphia: John Benjamins
Lansing, Jeff
  1989   Impersonal you. Unpublished manuscript.
Mandelblit, Nili
  2000   The grammatical marking of conceptual integration: From syntax to morphology. *Cognitive Linguistics* 11(3/4): 197–252.
McCubbins, Mathew D. and Mark Turner
  2013   Concepts of Law. *Southern California Law Review* 86(3): 517–572.
Nikiforidou, Kiki
  2012   The constructional underpinnings of viewpoint blends: The *Past + now* in language and literature. In: B. Dancygier and E. Sweetser (eds.), *Viewpoint in Language: A Multimodal Perspective*, 177–197. Cambridge: Cambridge University Press.
Nikiforidou, Kiki
  2010   Viewpoint and construction grammar: The case of *past +* now. *Language and Literature* 19(2): 265–284.
Recanati, François
  1995   Le présent épistolaire: Une perspective cognitive. *L'Information Grammaticale* 66: 38–44.
Rubba, Jo
  1996   Alternate grounds in the interpretation of deictic expressions. In: G. Fauconnier and E. Sweetser (eds.), *Spaces, Worlds, and Grammar*, 227–261. Chicago: University of Chicago Press.
Steen, Francis and Mark Turner
  2014   Multimodal Construction Grammar. In: M. Borkent, B. Dancygier and J. Hinnell (eds.), *Language and the Creative Mind*, 255–274. Stanford: CSLI Publications.
Sweetser, Eve
  1997   Role and individual readings of change predicates. In: J. Nuyts and E. Pederson (eds.), *Language and Conceptualization*, 116–136. Oxford: Oxford University Press.
Sweetser, Eve
  2012   Introduction: Viewpoint and perspective in language and gesture from the Ground down. In: B. Dancygier and E. Sweetser (eds.), *Viewpoint in Language: A Multimodal Perspective*, 1–22. Cambridge: Cambridge University Press.
Talmy, Leonard
  1986   Decoupling in the semantics of attention and perspective. Presentation at the 12th Annual Meeting of the Berkeley Linguistics Society, University of California at Berkeley.
Tobin, Vera
  2008   Literary Joint Attention: Social Cognition and the Puzzles of Modernism. PhD dissertation, University of Maryland.
Tobin, Vera
  2010   Grammatical and rhetorical consequences of entrenchment in conceptual blending: Compressions involving change. In: F. Parrill, V. Tobin and M. Turner (eds.), *Meaning, Form, and Body*, 329–347. Stanford: Center for the Study of Language and Information.
Tomasello, Michael
  1995   Joint Attention as Social Cognition. In: C. Moore and P. Dunham (eds.), *Joint Attention: Its Origins and Role in Development*, 103–130. Mahwah: Lawrence Erlbaum Associates.

Turner, Mark
    1987   *Death is the Mother of Beauty: Mind, Metaphor, Criticism*. Chicago: University of Chicago Press.

Turner, Mark
    1991   *Reading Minds: The Study of English in the Age of Cognitive Science*. Princeton: Princeton University Press.

Turner, Mark
    1996   *The Literary Mind: The Origins of Thought and Language*. New York: Oxford University Press.

Turner, Mark
    1998   Figure. In: C. Cacciari, R. Gibbs, Jr., A. Katz and M. Turner (eds.), *Figurative Language and Thought*, 44–87. New York: Oxford University Press.

Turner, Mark
    2007   The way we imagine. In: I. Roth (ed.), *Imaginative Minds*, 213–236. London: Oxford University Press and The British Academy.

Turner, Mark
    2010   Blending Box Experiments, Build 1.0. [http://ssrn.com/author=1058129].

Turner, Mark
    2014   *The Origin of Ideas: Blending, Creativity, and the Human Spark*. New York: Oxford University Press.

Mark Turner, Case Western Reserve University (USA)

11. Grammar and cooperative communication

1. Meaning in animal and in human communication: managing versus sharing
2. Argumentative language use
3. Cooperative communication and joint cognition
4. Three types of common ground and three types of meaning
5. Hierarchy in joint projects: the niche for argumentation
6. Conclusion
7. References

1. Meaning in animal and in human communication: managing versus sharing[1]

Compared to animal communication, human language use appears to exhibit an exceptionally high degree of information sharing. Starting with Dawkins and Krebs (1978), behavioural biologists have come to the conclusion that animal signalling is best seen as

---

[1] I would like to thank the editors, Barend Beekhuizen, Ronny Boogaart, Max van Duijn and an anonymous reviewer for insightful comments on a first draft of this chapter.

an instrument for manipulation (both of conspecifics and members of other species), not for sharing information. Owings and Morton (1998) introduce the complementary notions of "management" (for the signaller's side) and "assessment" (for the interpreter's side) to characterize the nature of vocal communication among non-human animals as directly linked to the fundamental biological process of maximizing an organism's fitness; they contrast this with "exchanging information", which they associate with human communication. As they state at the very beginning of their book:

> This book provides a discussion of animal vocal communication that [...] links communication to fundamental biological processes. [...]. Animals use signals in self-interested efforts to manage the behavior of other individuals, and they do so by exploiting the active assessment processes of other individuals. [...] Communication reflects the fundamental processes of regulating and assessing the behavior of others, not of exchanging information. (Owings and Morton 1998: i)

Human communication, linguistic and otherwise, is the exception; as Tomasello (2008:5) remarks about a simple human pointing gesture to indicate something of interest to one's company: "Communicating information helpfully in this way is extremely rare in the animal kingdom, even in our closest primate relatives". Information is a potentially precious resource and sharing it does not obviously enhance fitness. Information sharing thus requires rather special conditions to be biologically adaptive, for example genetic relatedness ("kin-selection"). But humans also readily share information with non-kin. In the case of humans, the biological conditions consist in the special character of human sociality as exhibiting a level of cooperation that is unique in the animal kingdom (Enfield and Levinson 2006; Tomasello 2009, 2014), which is itself part of our adaptation to life in cultural environments: groups of collaborating individuals sharing a set of cultural practices and competing with other groups (Boyd and Richerson 2006; Richerson and Boyd 2005).

Another hallmark of human languages is that they are fundamentally conventional. A regular association between sound and meaning consists in a process of repeated use that is crucially based on – and at the same time (re)produces – mutually shared knowledge and expectations in a community, i.e., a convention. It is typical for a convention that it contains an element of arbitrariness, in the sense that another behavioural pattern could in principle work equally well. For example, I drive on the left side of the road in Great Britain just because I know that, in this community, everyone else does and that everyone expects everyone else (including me) to do so; I definitely switch to driving on the right when I find out, e.g., upon entering a country on the European continent, that is what everybody in that community does. In the same way, I use the sound *horse* for the concept HORSE just because I know that, in this community, everyone else uses it that way and everyone expects every other member of the community to use it that way. I would readily change my use of this sound if I were to find out that the members of the relevant community were using it in another way (which would amount to my finding out that I was wrong about the meaning of *horse* in this language). So conventionality is predicated on the basic willingness to cooperate in solving coordination problems (Lewis 1969). Thus, some "design features" (Hockett 1960) of language – referentiality, arbitrariness – are directly linked to distinctive characteristics of the human species. The same basic willingness to cooperate also underlies the universal property of language use that in actual utterances more is communicated than what is encoded in the conventional meanings of the signals used (first formulated in philosophy by Grice 1975, now more and more an empirical science, cf. Noveck and Sperber 2004), which in turn makes linguistic systems constantly subject to change (e.g., Keller 1998).

In this chapter, we will explore the connections between the overall structure of human cooperative communication and its cognitive "infrastructure" (Tomasello 2008; this work covers a wealth of empirical evidence concerning both) on the one hand, and distinct types of linguistic meaning on the other. The argument will be that a number of basic conceptual domains that are commonly encoded in the grammars of human languages – deixis ("grounding"), "descriptive" categorization ("frames"), "logical" operations like negation – pertain to particular features of human cooperative communication.

2. Argumentative language use

From the point of view of modern linguistic pragmatics, there is a certain irony in the emphasis on sharing information as a dominant feature of human communication in evolutionary approaches. Especially speech act theory started with the recognition that an important part of ordinary language use consists of all kinds of acts that *cannot* be properly characterized as descriptive statements about the world, i.e., as sharing information (Austin 1962; see Senft 2014, ch.1, for a concise overview). Undertaking commitments (*I promise*), transferring ownership (*It's yours*), issuing requests (*Please stay off the grass*) are ways of *doing* things in the (social) world, not of describing it. Specifically, issuing commands and asking questions – in general: directive speech acts – are attempts to influence the behaviour and mental states of addressees, and thus fit the biological processes of regulating and assessing that Owings and Morton identify as characteristic for animal communication. Indeed, connectives draw this parallel themselves:

> […] signals are not most usefully thought of as statements of fact that can be judged true or false; signals are more like human […] speech acts […] – outputs that serve to achieve some effect on targets. […] According to this approach, signals are not statements of fact, that can be judged to be true or false, but are efforts to produce certain effects. (Owings and Morton 1998: 211)

Focussing on the *effects* of using certain words and constructions, all kinds of language use that can be described as "argumentative" or "rhetorical" may be seen as serving basic and general biological functions of communicative behaviour. Clear cases are provided by situations in which the choice of words itself becomes an issue of controversy. For example, immediately after the attacks of September 11, 2001 on the New York World Trade Center and other prominent buildings in the USA, several commentators were searching for terminology to talk about the events; these events were felt to be unique, never experienced before, and thus lacking obvious words to describe them. Many people hit upon the notion of "crime" (usually accompanied by adjectives such as *horrendous* to indicate its extreme nature), while some (also) soon started to use the terminology of "war" ("This is an act of war", "America is at war", etc.). While the two terms are not incompatible (and were in fact sometimes used side by side), several commentaries clearly tended more to the use of one term rather than the other, and this became an issue of debate. The Dutch prime minister's initial reaction was in terms of "war", but he soon withdrew this term and apologized for having used it, after several members of parliament had criticized him for it. A few of the critics argued that the events lacked too many characteristics of "ordinary" acts of war (there was no conflict between states, the perpetrators were not an army, etc.), but the absolutely general point of the criticisms was that this terminology might easily lead to a kind of response that was bad or at least undesirable: retaliating with military force, possibly against people who had nothing to do with the terrorists.

So what was at stake was not so much whether the descriptive value of the terms *crime* or *war* fitted the situation better. Those who criticized the use of the term *war* certainly agreed that it was not an ordinary "crime" either. What was at stake was whether the situation at hand justified the *consequences* associated with the terms used: *crime* invites one to think that some kind of *police* force should be deployed, and that the *culprits* should be brought to *trial*, so that *justice* may be done, etc.; *war* on the other hand, invites one to think that the use of *military* force is called for, in order to *defeat* the *enemy*, in a large scale operation that will inevitably also affect others than the perpetrators themselves (*collateral damage*). That is to say, they differ systematically in the kind of *inferences* they invite, and in that sense they are clearly oriented towards specific effects on addressees.

These are phenomena known in cognitive linguistics under such labels as "frames", "(idealized) cognitive models", or "cultural models" (I will return to reasons for preferring the latter term later). Such concepts comprise both criteria for their application ("What features make a situation suitable to be labelled with this term?"), as well as a basis for inviting inferences (see Holleman and Pander Maat 2009; Thibodeau and Boroditsky 2011, for discussion and experimental evidence). It is interesting to notice that controversy easily arises over the applicability of the terms to a situation (what we may call "backward oriented meaning"), but hardly over the invited inferences ("forward oriented meaning"); precisely because of *agreement* over the inferences invited by the terms *crime* and *war*, people *dis*agree whether the 9/11 events are best called one or the other. Thus, we may say that knowing the meaning of category denoting terms like *war* and *crime* includes knowing culturally accepted inferences associated with them, i.e., their argumentative values.

A recent example from (Dutch) political language concerns the terms *religion* and *ideology*. The right-wing politician Geert Wilders, leader of the "Party for Freedom", claims that Islam is not a religion but an ideology, whereas other parties, including the Christian-Democrats, continue to call Islam a religion. In this case, it is especially clear that it would be hard, if not impossible, to specify objective criteria distinguishing a religion from an ideology, but nobody has the feeling that this implies that the meaning of the words is unclear or vague. On the contrary, everybody understands these meanings perfectly well, viz. as suggesting that the strict guarantees for the freedom of religion in The Netherlands, laid down in the country's constitution, should not apply to Islam according to Wilders, while they should according to others; by the same token, Wilders' opponents accuse him of undermining the constitutional state (as he proposes to withhold certain constitutional rights from the adherents of a religion), while Wilders himself uses his opinion[2] to refute this accusation – again: all clearly a matter of inferences being invited by the words, in a way that competent users of the language agree on.

---

[2] In the context of negotiations about a coalition government in 2010, the 'Party for Freedom' and two other parties had declared that they 'agree to disagree' in their views of the categorial

These cases demonstrate the need for taking argumentation into account as a component of the meaning of at least *some* linguistic expressions. Usually, analysts characterize a discourse as argumentative only if many of the utterances in it are presented and understood as reasons for and/or justifications of *another* explicitly stated opinion of which the addressee is to be persuaded, so if they appear in a context of a (real or virtual) dispute. This is the domain of (classical) rhetoric and (modern) argumentation theory (cf. Van Eemeren et al. 2014), as an approach to a presumably special type of language use. However, in a linguistic perspective, there are good reasons to adopt the position that the very same mechanisms operate in language use *in general*; the point is that both words and grammatical constructions work in the same way in "overt" argumentation in disputes and in everyday language use.

It was a profound insight of Ducrot (see Anscombre and Ducrot 1983; Ducrot 1996) that argumentativity does not constitute a special case of language use, but rather a common component of linguistic meaning. Ducrot's example (cf. Verhagen 2005: 11) involves a consideration of the seemingly purely informative statement *There are seats in this room*. He observes that this sentence can be felicitously followed by something like *But they are uncomfortable*, with a contrastive connective, but not by *And moreover, they are uncomfortable*, with an additive one. The use of the term *seats* is in itself sufficient to evoke a certain conclusion about the degree of comfort in the room: expectations about it are raised. But inferences cannot be licensed by a single proposition, so there must be another one functioning as the second premise in an implicit syllogism. This consists in the fact that for members of our culture, knowing what seats are (knowing the concept SEAT, denoted by *seat*) *includes* knowing that as a rule, they contribute positively to comfort (the "frame", or "cultural cognitive model"). As a consequence, mentioning the presence of seats intrinsically provides justification, an argument, for thinking that the room will provide more than a minimum of comfort. It is this invited inference that is countered by the subsequent assertion that the seats are uncomfortable; and it is this contrast that is marked by *But*, and that is incompatible with the use of *And moreover*. Schematically:

Tab. 11.1: Utterances as arguments: utterances provide specific premises which, together with an associated model providing a general premise, evoke inferences

Utterances	"There are seats in this room"	"But they are uncomfortable"
Cultural cognitive model	↓ ← NORMALLY, SEATS CONTRIBUTE POSITIVELY TO COMFORT →↓	
Inferences	a) Raise expectations about degree of room-comfort	b) Cancel a) (i.e., lower the expectations again)

The felicity or infelicity of discourse connectives (in particular *but*) in combination with relevant continuations can thus be used as diagnostics for the argumentative value of the

---

status of Islam (religion or ideology), clearly recognizing that the use of the terms is not a matter of facts. By the same token, though, this declaration makes it appear as if the use of terms then is a matter of choice (a kind of Humpty-Dumpty view of meaning), not recognizing the conventional, thus supra-individual and normative character of linguistic meaning (cf. Tomasello 2008: 290–292).

first utterance; *but* does not mark a contrast at the level of objective information (in fact, this seems inherent in the notion of contrast: uncomfortable seats are perfectly possible as part of reality; cf. Sweetser 1990: 103–4). Indeed, connectives function in exactly the same way in apparently innocent claims about seats (*There are seats in this room, but they are uncomfortable*) as in emotionally or politically charged claims about Islam (*There are adherents of Islam in this country, but they do not enjoy freedom of religion*). It may be harder to disagree about the applicability of some terms (like *seat*) than others (like *religion*), but this is not a difference in the structure and working of the semantic machinery: knowing a conceptual category denoted by a linguistic item involves knowing one or more cultural cognitive models that license conclusions of certain kinds. Linguistically, less and more controversial terms do not represent different types of meanings (say, descriptive versus argumentative); they are just less or more controversial.

The power of argumentativity as a systematic property of language was already demonstrated experimentally by Lundquist and Jarvella (1994), and is also highlighted by the fact that it turns out to be the unifying factor underlying the similarity in grammatical behaviour of a number of lexical items and grammatical patterns. The content of argumentation in the examples above comes from the lexical items, but the connective *but* has the very schematic role of countering the rhetorical force of the first conjunct, whatever its content: *The house is very nice but expensive* differs from *The house is expensive but very nice* precisely because the second conjunct rhetorically "wins" in both cases. Similarly, the feature that unifies the grammatical behaviour of different negation operators and perspectival predicates in a language is their effect on the argumentative character of the relevant utterances. The similarity in co-occurrence of *not* and *barely* with respect to the *let alone* construction, for example, reduces to the similarity of their roles as argumentative operators, and the same holds for the grammatical similarities of verbs of communication (*say, promise*) and cognition (*think, know*) with respect to complementation constructions across different person and tense markings and with respect to discourse connectives (cf. Verhagen 2005, 2008a; Fausey and Boroditsky 2010 and Fausey and Matlock 2010 are experimental studies of the argumentative force of different grammatical constructions).

So we now have both reasons to characterize language use as crucially different from animal communication (information sharing being normal) and as similar to it (efforts to produce effects being normal as well). The way to resolve this paradox is to undertake both a more thorough analysis of the types of meaning of the different linguistic expressions involved, and of the structure of communicative events.

3. Cooperative communication and joint cognition

Human cooperative communication involves a large amount of joint knowledge. Much of this functions as "common ground" (Clark 1996), and is a necessary condition for communication to succeed; at the same time, joint knowledge is also updated and expanded as communication proceeds. In section 4, we will look at the first dimension and its linguistic reflexes; section 5 will be concerned with the second dimension. As a basis for both, this section provides a conceptual analysis of what is involved in joint knowledge, in terms of a group of people acting as a cognitive unit.

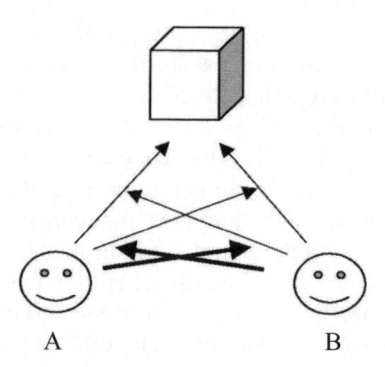

Fig. 11.1: Mutually shared attention

The role of common ground comes out clearly in the case of the – for humans – simple act of pointing. "Outside of any shared context, pointing means nothing. But if we are in the midst of a collaborative activity (say, gathering nuts), the pointing gesture is most often immediately and unambiguously meaningful ('there's a nut')" (Tomasello 2009: 73). It is because we both *know* that we are engaged in a joint activity – and moreover know that each of us knows – that establishing joint attention through a pointing gesture can provide the basis for a rich and specific inference, as well as the belief that this was precisely what the pointer intended. The point is that it must be obvious, transparent to all of us that we are engaged in a joint activity and what it consists in.

One way of thinking about this is in terms of the mental states of each participant about the mental states of others. According to Zlatev (2008: 227), joint attention, i.e., *mutually* shared attention rather than just shared attention, comprises an embedding of three levels of attention. Consider figure 11.1.

The idea is that both A and B (1) attend to the same object, (2) know that the other does, and (3) know that the other knows. Without the third level, they can be said to share their attention for some object, but not to *mutually* share it. However, what this way of thinking does not capture, is the insight that A and B form a *group*, are organized into a higher level entity that constrains and co-determines the roles and the mental states of the participants (figure 11.1 does not distinguish between competitive and cooperative situations). Humans have what philosophers call intentionality – ideas, goals, desires, etc.: mental states directed at objects and other individuals. They share this with other animals, certainly other primates. However, humans not only entertain such mental states as individual subjects, but also jointly, i.e., *inter*subjectively. They exhibit what Searle (1995) calls "*we*-intentionality". When two individuals are coordinating their activities in a collaborating group, they are not just two individuals engaged in their own projects (possibly including attention to others), but a "team" that is collectively engaged in a single project, part of which is joint attention for some entity. Recognizing this group-level is crucial for the proper characterization of certain forms of cognition. This becomes especially apparent in the light of tasks that are distributed over members of a group in such a way that coordination allows the group to produce results that no individual could produce on its own; from extensive empirical research into ship navigation (Hutchins 1995), Hutchins (2006: 377) concludes: "social groups can have cognitive properties that are distinct from the cognitive properties of the individuals who compose

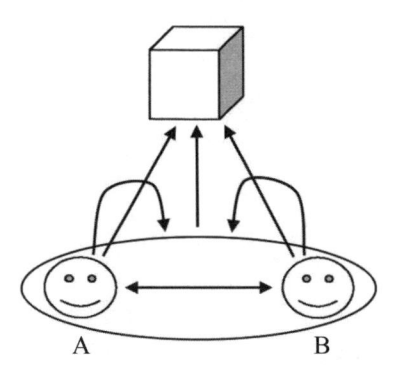

Fig. 11.2: Coordinated group cognition

the group" (Hull 1988 provides a lot of empirical evidence that the same holds for scientific research teams). So let us consider a "group-level" conception of joint cognition as represented in figure 11.2, the ellipse indicating the group of (in this case) two individuals that jointly attend to an object.

In this figure, the upward pointing arrows point to the object of attention, the horizontal bi-directional arrow represents the relationship of coordination, and the two bent arrows point from an individual to what the group is jointly attending to rather than to what each single other individual is attending to as in figure 11.1. The group of coordinating individuals is a cognitive unit, an information processing entity the boundaries of which happen not to coincide with a skull; the group is defined by a set of concepts and assumptions – common ground – which all members believe each other to have access to, allowing them to coordinate, which captures the idea of the "transparency" of mutual knowledge in the group. Indeed, this characterization not only applies to joint attention, but also to other joint mental states, like beliefs and goals. In particular, it also applies to the knowledge of conventions, including linguistic ones (Lewis 1969), and thus is in fact a general characterization of "joint cognition".

First of all, this idea provides an intuitively more direct representation of joint ("we", "you and I together") as opposed to shared ("you as well as I") attention, in a way that fits well with insights into conversation and other "joint projects" (Clark 1996, 2006 – below, I will return to Clark's proposals about the *structure* of joint projects), as well as with recently developed insights into specifically human forms of cooperation (Tomasello 2009, 2014).

Secondly, this way of conceptualizing joint cognition has interesting consequences when we realize that figure 11.2 represents an "outside" view. For a single member *inside* a group involved in joint cognition, it primarily looks as in figure 11.3.

Coordination comprises assigning to others the same mental capacities one has oneself (what Tomasello and Rakoczy 2003 eloquently call "self-other equivalence"); we can therefore allow projection from the group to individual members ("downward percolation"), i.e., deriving inferences about what an individual attends to, knows, believes, etc., from the assumption that s/he is a member of a group involved in attending to object X. Most elementary, it follows that B is attending to the same object and to the group, i.e., the "outside" view depicted in figure 11.2. It also follows that A may assume that B assumes that A is attending to X, and vice versa, i.e., configurations like the one

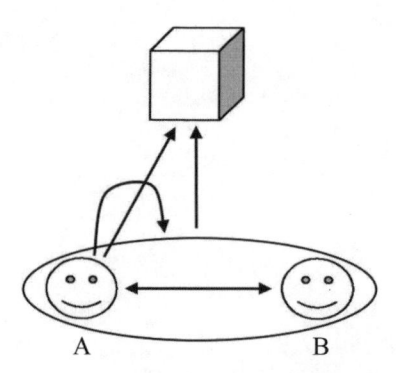

Fig. 11.3: Joint cognition, from individual point of view

depicted in figure 11.1, or ones with even more levels of embedding, applying the percolation rule over and over again. The same is true for meta-cognitive awareness: A may apply the rule to any group member, so also to ones involving A (e.g., "I know I am looking at X", "I believe that I understand why John thinks we have a problem"). Indeed, the ideas of "self" and subjectivity only make sense in the context of some awareness of *others* and their intentional stances – realizing that one can be the object of another's attention, and that there are different points of view, one of which is one's own (cf. Tomasello 1994). But processes of "recursive mind-reading", to use Tomasello's (2014) term, do not as such enter into the characterization of mutual knowledge, and since this is cognitively unrealistic (as recognized since Lewis 1969; cf. Campbell 2005), the group-level view of *we*-intentionality provides a better characterization than the multiple individuals view.

4. Three types of common ground and three types of meaning

A primary example of linguistic elements that can only be understood against the background of common ground, is constituted by so-called deictic elements. These are elements whose interpretation systematically and crucially is to be computed with knowledge of the communicative situation and its participants, what Langacker calls the "Ground" of an utterance (Langacker 1990, and various other publications). The reference of *I* and *you* is determined in terms of the roles defined by the communicative event: the producer of the utterance (more precisely: who is to be considered responsible for it; think of quotes, but also of a secretary typing a letter for the boss, the message box saying *I accept the conditions* that is to be clicked before installing software, etc.), and the addressee. The interpretation of third person pronouns cannot be determined positively in terms of elements of the common ground, but their semantics still makes crucial reference to it; they indicate that the referent is uniquely identifiable on the basis of joint knowledge of the ongoing communicative event. So it is for good reasons that Tomasello (2008: 5) invokes pronouns to illustrate his point about the special character of human communication:

11. Grammar and cooperative communication 241

> The ability to create common conceptual ground [...] is an absolutely critical dimension of all human communication, including linguistic communication with all of its *he*'s, *she*'s, and *it*'s.

Deictic meanings occur in all kinds of linguistic items. The present tense and expressions like *now* or *at this point in time* (due to the element *this*) denote situations that are co-extensive in time with some (first) person's speech act. Here too, we find "negative" deixis as in third person pronouns; although the time of a situation presented in a past tense clause cannot be positively determined, its semantics still makes crucial reference to the Ground: "a non-actual (e.g., remembered or imagined) situation, one that does not directly impinge on present issues". The exact characterization of different elements (in different languages) will differ, but the general point is that their conventional meaning makes essential reference to the Ground.

The consequence is that deictic elements can only be felicitously used when the relevant knowledge of the Ground (and its elements) is in fact mutually shared (at the very least: *made* shared by an additional communicative act, such as a pointing gesture); they *presuppose* sharedness. Suppose I say something like *Please hand me that screwdriver*. My use of the demonstrative *that* – a deictic element – indicates that you and I mutually agree on the same, single, specific exemplar of the category SCREWDRIVER in our present common environment that is the object of my request. This may be for a host of reasons: you may be holding one in your hand, there may be only one screwdriver in our common visual field, or only one that I used most recently (as you know), or there may be only one (mutually obvious to you and me) that is suited for the job I have to do, or whatever. But if the one you hand me turns out not to be the one I want, then something has gone wrong; we have to conclude (with hindsight) that the things co-present to us in the speech situation did not in fact make the same object uniquely salient to both of us – I may have mistakenly thought that you had one in your hand, for example, and then you hand me the one I had just been using myself. In general terms: When a deictic element is used and the relevant knowledge is in fact not mutually shared, communication fails.

Notice that this failure happens at a different level than that of conventional meanings. The problem is not that we do not share knowledge of the conventional function of the element *that*. Such situations occur too, e.g., in conversations between native and non-native speakers of English, such as speakers of Slavic languages, which do not have a system of definite and indefinite determiners like Western European languages. The latter kind of miscommunication is of the same type as when you say *Please hand me the pliers* and I hand you the pincers, resulting from us not sharing knowledge of the conventional rules for using the sound *pliers*. Here, the cause of the misunderstanding does exist at the level of conventional meaning, viz. the meaning of the sound *pliers*. The kind of misunderstanding described above (resulting from lack of joint knowledge of the speech event) cannot occur with a non-deictic term like *pliers*, as its meaning does not refer to, thus does not invoke, shared knowledge of the *present*, specific communicative situation.

This important distinction between levels is not always made fully explicit. For example, Tomasello and Rakoczy (2003: 128), discussing the emergence of a shared symbol when a child imitates an adult's use of some signal, write:

> [...] the child uses the new symbol to direct another person's attention precisely as they have used it to direct her attention (the role reversal comes out especially clearly in deictic terms such a[s] *I* and *you*, *here* and *there*). [...]. We may think of this bi-directionality or intersubjectivity of linguistic symbols as simply the quality of being socially "shared".

While this is not incorrect, it may suggest that deixis is just an extreme case of role reversal, as if this were a continuum on which linguistic items may take different positions. But that masks the categorical difference between these *types* of meanings:

a) all linguistic signals, consisting of (combinations of) conventional pairings of form and function, are understood on the basis of mutually shared knowledge, in a way that can in general be described in terms of role-reversal (I utter the form X to achieve the same effect in you as you achieve in me when you utter X);
b) *on top of that*, for *some* linguistic items, the very *content* of the effect being achieved by a form X is (partly) defined in terms of mutually shared mental states with respect to the specific communicative situation at hand, and may involve role reversal in that specific situation; for example: B utters the sound *I* to make A attend to B, which is the same effect – but only with role reversal – as when A uses the sound *I* to make B attend to A.

In other words: all linguistic items are being understood "intersubjectively" in the sense of being based on mutually shared knowledge of the connection between sound and meaning, but for only *some* of them, the meaning itself refers to mutually shared knowledge of the situation of use.[3] The latter are deictic terms, or more generally, in Langacker's terminology: "grounding predicates" (not all deictic terms have to involve true role reversal; recall the remarks on the past tense and third person pronouns above). The notion "intersubjectivity" is thus applied at different levels of linguistic analysis: generally ("All linguistic communication is based on mutually shared knowledge") and more specifically ("The meaning of some linguistic elements invokes mutually shared knowledge of the communicative situation"). We will see later that there is at least yet one more way to apply "intersubjectivity" in semantics.

Clark and Marshall (1981) relate the distinction between deictic elements and content elements, as well as their common basis in shared intentionality, to different types of *sources of evidence* for mutual knowledge. Based on their discussion, we can distinguish three major types. First, the most immediate source of evidence for mutual knowledge of participants in a communicative event is, of course, that event itself (Langacker's Ground). It is this source of evidence that is tapped by deictic elements.

The second type of evidence consists of the common personal history of interlocutors. In terms of linguistic categories, this is especially what allows the use of proper names to succeed in picking out unique referents. There may be many people by the name of *Andrew*, but if I use this name in a conversation with my wife, I can rely on her picking out a unique individual (not necessarily present in the speech situation) who is mutually

---

[3] This difference corresponds to the two types of signals in the evolutionary story of Tomasello (2008). On the one hand pointing, which may be seen as a precursor of linguistic deixis as it basically involves the same cognitive infrastructure not shared by apes; on the other hand pantomiming, i.e., iconic gesturing, which *is* shared with great apes, and can be seen as a precursor of descriptive terms.

the most salient one for us in our shared history (e.g., our son). And I can use exactly the same name to successfully refer to *another* individual in a conversation with *another* interlocutor, invoking the same mechanism of mutual knowledge of common personal history.

Finally, a third source of evidence for mutual knowledge is membership of the same community: a shared culture. Even before I start a conversation, even with someone I have never met before, I can and will assume all kinds of information to be mutually known to me and my interlocutor on the basis of the assumption that s/he is also Dutch, a linguist, an employee of the same company, etc. Shared knowledge of a language, i.e., of conventions for using certain vocal or visual signals, is another kind of community based mutual knowledge. For example, on the basis of some evidence that my interlocutor is a linguist, I will assume mutual knowledge of a specific meaning of the terms *subject* and *paradigm*. On the basis of evidence that he is Dutch, I assume mutual knowledge about a huge variety of things, such as the system of parliamentary elections in The Netherlands, the name of the Dutch king, the location (roughly) of the airport named *Schiphol*, the fact that the country's capital is not the seat of its government, and also such lexical items as *betekenis* (roughly: 'conventional meaning', as in *This word meant something totally different 200 years ago*) and *bedoeling* (roughly: 'intended meaning', as in *He meant something totally different than what you were thinking*), a conceptual distinction not conventionally associated with formally distinct lexical signals in English, for example. On the basis of evidence that my interlocutor is American, I will not be justified in assuming these pieces of information to be mutually known, but I will be in assigning some others that status, including the lexical items *commitment* and *obligation*, a conceptual distinction not conventionally associated with formally distinct lexical signals in Dutch.

So we have now established a distinction between three major types of meaning based on three major types of evidence for mutual knowledge: deictics invoke the most immediate evidence available to interlocutors, the speech event itself; proper names invoke a wider source of evidence: shared personal history; common nouns and verbs invoke the widest source: a shared culture.[4] The latter two types correspond to the episodic and semantic long term memory, respectively, while the first type corresponds to short term memory.

It is the third kind of meanings, conveyed by descriptive items denoting conceptual categories, which also provide access to knowledge about the kind of inferences conventionally licensed by the concepts involved. It is because of their basis in the shared culture of a community that the term "cultural models" is especially appropriate for knowledge of this kind. Deictic elements do not activate specific conceptual *content* licensing certain inferences. Proper names activate shared experience with the referents involved. This might in specific cases evoke certain inferences (the effect of uttering *Andrew gave me a pill for this problem* when Andrew is known to be a medical doctor may be different from when he is known to be an electronics engineer), but they do not

---

[4] Definite descriptions – the main topic of Clark and Marshall (1981) – do not invoke a specific source of evidence. The construction [*the* X] only indicates identifiability within *some* part of the common ground, be it the speech event (*Hand me the screwdriver*), shared personal history (*I went to see the doctor this morning*), or shared culture (*The king is coming to visit next week*).

do so conventionally, while common nouns do.[5] It is these culturally shared concepts that provide the implicit second premises underlying the *general* argumentative impact of "statements of fact" (cf. section 2).

5. Hierarchy in joint projects: the niche for argumentation

We have now seen how human communication in general is based on common ground, and how specific types of linguistic meaning are in turn grounded in different sources of evidence. Now how does argumentation relate to cooperative communication? The answer has to take into account that human activities exhibit a hierarchical structure, and that this has some special consequences when the project is a joint one (Clark 1996, 2006). Hierarchical structure is an elementary property of any goal-directed project. To use Clark's (2006) example, if I plan to construct the do-it-yourself TV-stand that I bought at the furniture store, that constitutes my main project; I then have to decide how to divide the job into subparts – What shall I build first: the top part or the lower part? And again, for the top part: which panels to attach first? And so on. Similarly, when Ann and Burton agree to construct the TV-stand *together*, they divide this entire project into smaller subprojects, each of which is split into smaller ones again, and so on.

With each step partitioning a project into subprojects, one is committed to the higher level project – the subproject is executed in order to achieve the goal of the project one-level higher in the hierarchy, and the latter is thus necessarily "on the agenda", presupposed. However, when this is a *joint* project, such commitments are much more strongly *binding* than when it is an individual project. In the latter case, it is no problem to drop a particular subproject midway and decide to change the order of execution of certain subprojects. But in the joint case, several serious risks are connected to such a course of action. The reason is that in a joint project, each participant's commitment is conditional upon *both* participants' commitment to the joint project: I commit myself to you to do my part so long as you commit yourself to do yours, and vice versa (Clark 2006: 130). My commitment therefore does not disappear when I conclude that another course of action would be better. If I abandon an ongoing subproject in the same way as I might in the case of an individual project, this is likely to cause serious harm, in the short run both to myself (because you will continue to do your part, and because it threatens the entire project) and to you (because you cannot do your part properly if I don't do mine, and again: because the entire project is put at risk), and also in the long run, because it threatens my relationship with you, and possibly my general reputation.

This provides additional support for the proposal in section 2 to view joint cognition as a group-level phenomenon rather than as just a phenomenon of a collection of individuals entertaining assumptions about the others and *their* individual cognition. But what is important for our purposes here, is the insight that the strongly binding commitments in joint projects, as long as a person is engaged in one, exist at the higher levels of the

---

[5] This also explains, at least partly, the referentially redundant use of descriptive lexical noun phrases in discourse, such as the use of *the president* where *he* would have been referentially sufficient in *Obama reformed the health insurance system; the president considered it his most important achievement* (cf. Maes 1990).

11. Grammar and cooperative communication 245

joint project but not (yet) at the lowest level that the participants are actually engaged in, because this is where a joint commitment for the further course of action has to be *established*.

It is here that argumentation is crucial for cooperation. Participants have to probe each other's conception of the current state of affairs (each other's mental model of the relevant part of the world), identify points of potential difference between them, and communicate ways of resolving such differences – if they are to achieve their joint goal of successfully executing this step, allowing them to go on to the next step. Consider the following partial exchange in one particular instance of a joint TV-stand-building project (Clark 2006: 128):

(1) A: So, you wanna stick the ((screws in)). Or wait is, is, are these these things, or?
  B: That's these things I bet. Because there's no screws.
  A: Yeah, you're right. Yeah, probably. If they'll stay in.
  B: I don't know how they'll stay in ((but))

At the point where A produces the utterance in the first line, the joint goal is to attach two pieces to each other. A starts with checking if her collaborator's plan is to use "the screws" (taken to be mutually salient). But before a response is forthcoming, A notices something else, within the joint field of attention (*these things*), that provide an alternative (*or*); so now there is an issue, a potential difference, which she puts on stage with her utterance.

B's response is a proposal for resolution, by picking one side of the alternatives presented (*these things*) and motivating it. The latter is done with the negative sentence *there's no screws*, so a proposal to A to change her mental model of the situation (THERE ARE SCREWS) and instead adopt B's; in the present context, given mutual knowledge about the joint project and its components, this also constitutes an argument for the proposal to use *these things*; the argument status is marked by the conjunction *because* (it does not mark the cause of *these things* being present).

A's acceptance (*you're right*) of the proposal to change her mental world model thus also constitutes acceptance of the argument status of the second part of B's utterance, and – again, given the joint commitment to the higher level project – of the conclusion as well. This constitutes reaching agreement on the course of action to be taken in the present subproject. Notice that the modal adverb *probably* does not count as a rejection of the conclusion (*We should use these things to attach the pieces*), but at most as a limitation of the personal responsibility of A for the choice of the course of action, and thus as at most an *opportunity* for B to provide more support or to reconsider; this "weakening" of the acceptance is motivated by A in the form of a conditional implying uncertainty about the functionality of *these things*. B expresses agreement with the uncertainty, but indicates that he is still in favour of the same course of action (*but*).

So what we can say is that the argumentative moves (marked by negation, several connectives (*or, because, but*), a modal adverb, conditionals) contribute to establishing coordination within the lowest subproject being executed, against the background of the joint commitments previously established on higher (sub)projects. It is the recognition of hierarchical structure of joint projects, which presupposes that joint commitments are in place at higher levels and at the same time have to be established for the present subproject, that provides us with the "niche" for argumentation *within* the general framework of human cooperative communication.

Argumentation definitely is a subtype of the kind of processes defining animal communication – "regulating" and "assessing" behaviour – but their character is crucially transformed by their being embedded in cooperative practices. In lexical semantic terms: Argumentation is not a synonym for regulating and assessing, it is a hyponym – a subordinate concept, a special case with special properties of its own, not inherited from its hyperonyms. It *is* directed at influencing an addressee, but the way it works is not by manipulating him or evoke the desired behavioural response directly, but by attempting to cause him to adopt a certain mental state: to be convinced himself, by the arguments provided, that a particular course of action is the optimal one in the given circumstances, to allow the present joint project to proceed. The benefits of that highly indirect way of influencing another person in the context of cooperation, are that it guarantees the most reliable execution of each participant's role, and also little loss of reputation or readiness to cooperate with each other in the future in case the course of action turns out not to work well after all, because responsibility is distributed and shared.

This is not to say that any argument is always a *good* argument, nor that manipulation is absent from human communication. People are most easily persuaded by arguments that they already believe, as these are least costly to introduce or to change.[6] Joint commitments, once established, may also be exploited by one participant to get the other to continue playing his part even if the latter would prefer not to (*You agreed that we were going to build this thing now, didn't you? So do your part!*).[7] But that does not alter the fact that argumentation constitutes an attempt to get the addressee to form the opinion, strengthened by the arguments provided, that X is the best thing to do and/or to believe, and to thereby make precisely this opinion – i.e., the addressee's own, not the sender's signalling behaviour – the *immediate* cause of the addressee's behaviour and/or belief.

If the chosen course of action in the present subproject fails, or the attempt to decide on a joint course of action fails, then this may be a reason to return to the higher level – which then by definition becomes the present subproject for which (new) agreement has to established (*Maybe it is a better idea to build the bottom part first, after all*),[8] and argumentation is relevant. But as Clark's analysis demonstrates, the higher the level of a joint project with respect to the one presently being executed (the "deeper" one gets into a joint project), the harder it becomes to renegotiate it. Joint commitments at very high levels may thus appear virtually impossible to (re)negotiate, as the risks of harm being done are simply too large to be considered (cf. the force of a threat of the type *You don't want to be excluded from the group, do you?*). Indeed, the fact that it is

---

[6] Drawing on a large body of empirical studies on inferential fallacies like confirmation bias, Mercier and Sperber (2011) use precisely this view of argumentation-in-service-of-human-cooperation to argue that it evolutionarily precedes and underlies human reasoning.

[7] This is one important risk of joint commitments that Clark (2006) discusses in connection with the "Milgram experiments" (designed as psychological experiments on obedience), where the experimenter, when refusing to renegotiate higher level joint commitments, may be said to perform such an exploitation.

[8] One of the conventional functions of an expression like *after all* is to mark such a return to a previously established higher subproject.

impossible to volitionally "choose" or change the meaning of linguistic expressions is a special case of this phenomenon; it would effectively result in all cooperation with other members of the community breaking down, i.e., abandoning the joint project of one's culture that makes all other, specific joint projects possible.[9]

Returning to the issue of linguistic meanings, the special role of negation (and other argumentative operators) and of connectives within a specific joint subproject, is to modify the argumentative value of an utterance and to relate such values of discourse segments to each other, respectively. In section 4, we established three types of linguistic meaning, all of which are characterizable as understood "intersubjectively", viz. as invoking the shared communicative situation, the shared personal histories, or the shared culture. The signs discussed here are not of one these "sharing" kinds of intersubjectivity, but they relate to intersubjectivity in yet another way: in order to establish cognitive coordination, participants have to explore, negotiate, and ultimately resolve potential differences, and it is this particular function that negation and other argumentative constructions are dedicated to.

But in service of this primary coordinating function, linguistic negation and other argumentative items invoke common ground as well. Marking an utterance as argumentative indicates a (potential) difference in epistemic stance or attitude towards some object of conceptualization; so there are always two distinct "mental spaces" involved. However, these mental spaces have to *share* an implicit background assumption for the argumentation to work. If I say to you *John didn't pass the first course* or *John barely passed the first course*, I can only thereby intentionally communicate to you that you should give up hope of John being successful in college, if the cultural model that passing a test normally strengthens the assumption that one will be successful is in our common ground. As we saw at the end of section 4, it is descriptive lexical items (*pass, course*) that provide access to such cultural models, and without these being jointly available, negation and other argumentative operators do not work in actual communication.

The projection of a mental space representing a stance different from the speaker's also makes this other stance *relevant* in the common ground; when saying *Mary is not happy*, the speaker presents "Mary is happy" as relevant.[10] As a consequence, utterances with (syntactic) negations may in a subtle way convey judgments about their topic; when someone says about a student *John did not give the right answer*, he presents "John gave

---

[9] Building on Mercier and Sperber (2011), Tomasello (2014: 110–112) develops a notion of "cooperative argumentation" that is conceptually quite similar to the one elaborated here, but he limits its applicability to the second major step in his account of the evolution of human thinking: that of collective on top of joint intentionality. In section 2 above however, I argued, in line with Verhagen (2005, 2008a, 2008b) that from a linguistic point of view, this limitation does not seem motivated. The structure and expression of overtly recognized justifications and implicit ones are the same; the two allegedly distinct domains do not differ in terms of grammatical properties. For instance, negation and contrast markers work in the same way across both domains. Another telling observation in this connection is, in my view, that negation is acquired very early – admittedly not immediately in all of its adult functions, but certainly with its modal force, about what "ought" not to happen (cf. Dimroth 2010).

[10] A recognition he is not committed to when using morphological negation (*Mary is unhappy*). Cf. Verhagen (2005: 70–75) for arguments and a discussion of some consequences, especially so-called double negations of the *not un*-Adjective type (*Mary is not unhappy*).

the right answer" as relevant, while he does not evoke that idea when saying *John gave a wrong answer*. In a series of experiments, Beukeboom et al (2010) show that readers of negative sentences of the first type actually get a more positive image of John's qualities as a student than readers of non-negated sentences of the second type; the sentence with negation implicitly conveys the idea that John normally gives correct answers, i.e., is a good student.

In short, two related systematic properties of natural language negation in usage – the necessity of a shared cultural background model and the joint relevance of a mental space representing a different epistemic stance – confirm that argumentative elements are adapted to cooperative communication just like deictic elements are, although their primary functions relate to different levels in the hierarchical structure of a joint project.

6. Conclusion

The fundamentally cooperative nature of human communication and the cognitive infrastructure associated with it underlie a typology of basic semantic dimensions of natural language expressions. First, the hierarchical nature of joint projects underlies the distinction between two types of expressions, each of which may be said to mark and presuppose intersubjectivity, in different ways. One type is exemplified by *deictics*, invoking mutual knowledge of the communication event to pick out objects for joint attention in agreed-upon subprojects. The other type consists of *argumentative* elements (negation, argumentative connectors, and the like) oriented towards coordination: establishing mutual agreement in the present subproject. These items presuppose possible differences (distinct mental spaces), but they also invoke mutual knowledge – of cultural models associated with "content words" – in order to allow such differences to be removed or resolved, and the project to proceed; the shared models provide the implicit premises necessary to allow conclusions to be drawn from the arguments that are presented explicitly. Although specific items of both types may well provide *some* information about the world they may relate to (think of male vs. female pronouns, for example), their distinctive deictic or argumentative character cannot be characterized in terms of features of objects of conceptualization, but has to be understood in terms of the structure of cooperative communication.

Second, mutual knowledge (common ground) is assumed on the basis of a number of systematically different *sources of evidence*, and these constitute another dimension of types of meanings, orthogonal to the first one. Co-presence in the communication event itself is the most direct source of evidence for what is mutually known, and it defines deictics. Shared personal histories constitute a wider source of evidence, and it especially underlies the use of proper names. The widest source of evidence for mutual knowledge is a shared culture; this underlies the argumentative value of, i.a., common nouns and verbs.

Further refinements and divisions may certainly be envisaged, and they are definitely necessary in studying the way this general conceptual space of cooperative communication is structured in different languages. The rich empirical study of items "attracted" or "repelled" by negative operators in Israel (2011), for example, reveals both detailed structure in the rhetoric of scalar argumentation, as well as intricate patterns of conventional associations between several expressions in English. Or take the difference between pronouns of "distance" and "solidarity", or the nature of honorifics in languages that have them; such markers operate in the dimension of intersubjective relations as well, but they pertain to these *without* a link to the object of conceptualization – the use of a second person pronoun of respect ("your$_{[+respect]}$ house") does not affect the construal of a clause's objective content, very much unlike negation, in particular.[11]

Apart from this, the point of this chapter is that generally recognized *major* types of meanings in human languages may insightfully be characterized in terms of their specific role with respect to the general structure of human cooperative communication. Sharing information and common ground have traditionally been recognized as distinctive characteristics of language use, and they underlie some of these types. When we take the hierarchical nature of joint projects into account as well, we find that the distinction between higher, agreed-upon levels and the current subproject where coordination has to be established, provides the niche where argumentation, and linguistic items structuring argumentation, play a specific role in the coordination process. Cooperation is generally recognized as a necessary condition for human communication, and human meaning, to evolve. The point is strongly reinforced by the close correspondence between major types of meaning and the basic structure of human cooperative communication. Detailed understanding of the structure of cooperation also allows us to see how, alongside sharing information, "managing others" – typical for animal communication – is also a component of human (linguistic) communication, transformed into argumentation for coordination in ongoing joint projects.

7. References

Anscombre, Jean-Claude and Oswald Ducrot
   1983   *L'argumentation dans la langue*. Liège/Bruxelles: Mardaga.
Austin, John L.
   1962   *How To Do Things With Words*. Oxford: Oxford University Press.
Beukeboom, Camiel J., Catrin Finkenauer and Daniël H. J. Wigboldus
   2010   The negation bias: When negations signal stereotypic expectancies. *Journal of Personality and Social Psychology* 99: 978–992.
Boyd, Robert and Peter J. Richerson
   2006   Culture and the evolution of the human social instincts. In: N. J. Enfield and S. C. Levinson (eds.), *Roots of Human Sociality. Culture, Cognition and Interaction*, 453–477. Oxford/New York: Berg.
Campbell, John
   2005   Joint attention and common knowledge. In: N. Eilan and J. Roessler (eds.), *Joint Attention: Communication and Other Minds*, 287–297. Oxford: Oxford University Press.
Clark, Herbert H.
   1996   *Using Language*. Cambridge: Cambridge University Press.

---

[11] We have seen before that the notion of "intersubjectivity" can be applied in semantic analyses in several ways, and this ("managing interpersonal relations totally independently of the object of conceptualization") is another one. This variability has sometimes caused confusion in the use of the term. Two insightful recent attempts to clarify these matters are Ghesquière et al (2012) and especially Nuyts (2012).

Clark, Herbert H.
2006   Social actions, social commitments. In: N. J. Enfield and S. C. Levinson (eds.), *Roots of Human Sociality. Culture, Cognition and Interaction*, 126–150. Oxford/New York: Berg.

Clark, Herbert H. and Catherine R. Marshall
1981   Definite reference and mutual knowledge. In: A. K. Joshi, B. L. Webber and I. A. Sag (eds.), *Elements of Discourse Understanding*, 10–63. Cambridge: Cambridge University Press.

Dawkins, Richard and John R. Krebs
1978   Animal signals: information or manipulation? In: J. R. Krebs and N. B. Davies (eds.), *Behavioural Ecology: An Evolutionary Approach*, 292–309. Oxford: Blackwell.

Dimroth, Christine
2010   The acquisition of negation. In: L. R. Horn (ed.), The Expression of Negation, 39–73. Berlin/New York: Mouton de Gruyter.

Ducrot, Oswald
1996   *Slovenian Lectures/Conférences Slovènes. Argumentative Semantics/Sémantique argumentative*. Ljubljana: ISH Inštitut za humanistične študije Ljubljana.

Eemeren, Frans H. van, Bart Garssen, Eric C. W. Krabbe, A. Francisca Snoeck Henkemans, Bart Verheij, Jean H. M. Wagemans
2014   *Handbook of Argumentation Theory*. Berlin: Springer.

Enfield, Nick J. and Stephen C. Levinson (eds.)
2006   *Roots of Human Sociality. Culture, Cognition, and Interaction*. Oxford/New York: Berg.

Fausey, Caitlin M. and Lera Boroditsky
2010   Subtle linguistic cues influence perceived blame and financial liability. *Psychonomic Bulletin and Review* 17: 644–650.

Fausey, Caitlin M. and Teenie Matlock
2010   Can grammar win elections? *Political Psychology* 32: 563–574.

Ghesquière, Lobke, Lieselotte Brems and Freek Van de Velde
2012   Intersubjectivity and intersubjectification. *English Text Construction* 5: 128–152.

Grice H. Paul
1975   Logic and conversation. In: P. Cole and J. L. Morgan (eds.), *Syntax and Semantics*, Vol. 3, *Speech Acts*, 41–58. New York: Academic Press.

Hockett, Charles F.
1960   The origin of speech. *Scientific American* 203: 88–111.

Holleman, Bregje C. and Henk L. W. Pander Maat
2009   The pragmatics of profiling: Framing effects in text interpretation and text production. *Journal of Pragmatics* 41: 2204–2221.

Hull, David L.
1988   *Science as a Process. An Evolutionary Account of the Social and Conceptual Development of Science*. Chicago: Chicago University Press.

Hutchins, Edwin
1995   *Cognition in the Wild*. Cambridge: MIT Press.

Hutchins, Edwin
2006   The distributed cognition perspective on human interaction. In: N. J. Enfield and S. C. Levinson (eds.), *Roots of Human Sociality. Culture, Cognition and Interaction*, 375–398. Oxford/New York: Berg.

Israel, Michael
2011   *The Grammar of Polarity. Pragmatics, Sensitivity, and the Logic of Scales*. Cambridge: Cambridge University Press.

Keller, Rudi
1998   *A Theory of Linguistic Signs*. Oxford: Oxford University Press.

Langacker, Ronald W.
   1990   Subjectification. *Cognitive Linguistics* 1: 5–38.
Lewis, David
   1969   *Convention. A Philosophical Study.* Cambridge: Harvard University Press.
Lundquist, Lita and Robert J. Jarvella
   1994   Ups and downs in scalar inferences. *Journal of Semantics* 11: 33–53.
Maes, Alfons A.
   1990   The interpretation and representation of coreferential lexical NPs in expository texts. *Journal of Semantics* 7: 143–174.
Mercier, Hugo and Dan Sperber
   2011   Why do humans reason? Arguments for an argumentative theory. *Behavioral and Brain Sciences* 34: 57–111.
Noveck, Ira A. and Dan Sperber (eds.)
   2004   *Experimental Pragmatics*. New York: Palgrave Macmillan.
Nuyts, Jan
   2012   Notions of (inter)subjectivity. *English Text Construction* 5: 53–76.
Owings, Donald H. and Eugene S. Morton
   1998   *Animal Vocal Communication. A New Approach.* Cambridge: Cambridge University Press.
Richerson, Peter J. and Robert Boyd
   2005   *Not by Genes Alone. How Culture Transformed Human Evolution.* London/Chicago: University of Chicago Press.
Searle, John R.
   1995   *The Construction of Social Reality.* New York: Free Press.
Senft, Gunter
   2014   *Understanding Pragmatics.* London/New York: Routledge.
Sweetser, Eve E.
   1990   *From Etymology to Pragmatics. Metaphorical and Cultural Aspects of Semantic Structure.* Cambridge: Cambridge University Press.
Thibodeau, Paul H. and Lera Boroditsky
   2011   Metaphors we think with: The role of Metaphor in Reasoning. *PLoS ONE*: 6 1–11.
Tomasello, Michael
   1994   On the interpersonal origins of self-concept. In: U. Neisser (ed.), *The Perceived Self. Ecological and Interpersonal Sources of Self Knowledge*, 174–184. Cambridge: Cambridge University Press.
Tomasello, Michael
   2008   *Origins of Human Communication*, Cambridge/London: MIT Press.
Tomasello, Michael
   2009   *Why We Cooperate.* Cambridge/London: MIT Press.
Tomasello, Michael
   2014   *A Natural History of Human Thinking.* Cambridge/London: Harvard University Press.
Tomasello, Michael and Hannes Rakoczy
   2003   What makes human cognition unique? From individual to shared to collective intentionality. *Mind and Language* 18: 121–147.
Verhagen, Arie
   2005   *Constructions of Intersubjectivity. Discourse, Syntax, and Cognition.* Oxford: Oxford University Press.
Verhagen, Arie
   2008a   Intersubjectivity and the architecture of the language system. In: J. Zlatev, T. P. Racine, C. Sinha and E. Itkonen (eds.), *The Shared Mind: Perspectives on Intersubjectivity*, 307–331. Amsterdam/Philadelphia: John Benjamins Publishing Company.

Verhagen, Arie
   2008b   Intersubjectivity and explanation in linguistics − a reply to Hinzen and Van Lambalgen. *Cognitive Linguistics* 19: 125−143.

Zlatev, Jordan
   2008   The co-evolution of intersubjectivity and bodily mimesis. In: J. Zlatev, T. P. Racine, C. Sinha and E. Itkonen (eds.), *The Shared Mind: Perspectives on Intersubjectivity*, 215−244. Amsterdam/Philadelphia: John Benjamins Publishing Company.

Arie Verhagen, Leiden (The Netherlands)

II. Overviews

12. Phonology

1. Introduction
2. Invariance, segmentation and storage of units: The fundamental issues
3. The invariance problem
4. The allophone question
5. Alternative views of categorization
6. The role of frequency in phonology
7. The nature of perception
8. Higher levels of structure
9. Conclusions
10. References

1. Introduction[1]

Phonology is a branch of Cognitive Linguistics which has developed more slowly than fields such as lexical semantics or morphology (Lakoff 1987; Brugman 1981; Lindner 1981; Langacker 1990; Rubba 1993). In the history of the journal *Cognitive Linguistics*, only eleven articles on the topic have been published, an average of fewer than one per year. This author made some preliminary suggestions in an early article (Nathan 1986), and has since expanded these explorations in various directions (Nathan 2007, 2008; Donegan and Nathan 2014). A number of others have also written Cognitive Linguistics-based works on phonology including Nesset (2008), Bybee (1999, 2001), and Pierrehumbert (2002), as well as the articles in Mompeán-González (2006).

The question of how speech sounds are stored, perceived and produced, which is the essence of phonology, is an old one. The earliest theorizing in what we would now call synchronic phonology can be traced back to the late nineteenth century, where two different strands emerged. One, originating with the work of Baudouin de Courtenay (1972), and to some extent Sapir ([1933] 1972), exemplifies the active processing, psychologically oriented view still current in Natural Phonology and in one version of Cognitive Phonology, while another, founded by Saussure ([1916] 1974) emphasizes the structuralist, oppositional/contrastive view of how speech sounds are stored, with little or no interest in how sounds are actually produced. Generative Phonology, classically defined in Chomsky and Halle (1968) constituted somewhat of a compromise between the contrast-only storage model introduced by Saussure and the active production model championed by Baudouin, and, to some extent, Sapir. In recent years generative phonology has mostly been succeeded by a computationally-based model, Optimality Theory (OT), that is somewhat neutral on the actual psychological mechanisms of production

---

[1] This paper has benefited from comments by Patricia Donegan, José Mompeán-González and three anonymous reviewers.

and perception and storage. OT, however, takes other aspects of how phonology works very seriously (particularly the tension between "naturalness" and minimization of divergence between underlying form and surface form – "faithfulness") (Prince and Smolensky 2004; Kager 1999; McCarthy 2008).

This chapter will examine the active theoretical issues that arise in trying to understand how phonology would work within a cognitive linguistics worldview. We will discuss the question of the nature of the entities stored (the "underlying form" or "phoneme" question), the nature of the production and perception mechanism (how psychologically real are "rules"?) and the extent to which physiology and perceptual mechanisms constrain or influence the answers to the preceding questions (the "naturalism" question).

I will focus my discussion primarily on the question of why there might be a field of "phonology". That is, why there might be general principles governing how the phonologies of individual languages are constrained, rather than being simply a massive list of individual variants of lexical items. The task, from a Cognitive Grammar (CG) point of view, is to find governing principles that are not attributable to an innate language organ, since CG has no analog to the generative notion of Universal Grammar to fall back on. Hence, every explanatory principle must be based on pre-existing cognitive principles. I will argue that such principles as categorization, embodied perception and motoric organization account for all that is "universal" in (phonological) grammar. I should briefly mention that I will not be discussing questions of "phonetics", which some earlier scholars did not distinguish from "phonology". I will assume that phonetics deals with "raw materials" (anatomy, physiology, acoustics, perceptual psychology) and can be a source of explanation for phonological facts, but is not itself part of "the structure of English (or any other language)". I consider it the same as the contrast between materials science and architecture – the former constrains the latter, but is not identical to it.

2. Invariance, segmentation and storage of units: The fundamental issues

2.1. The problem of invariance and variation

It has been known since the beginning of linguistics that the same *word* is pronounced differently every time it is uttered. To take a concrete example, the English word *banana* might be pronounced [bɔ̃.ˈnæ.nɔ̃] or it can be pronounced [ˈbnæ.nɔ̃], and there are a number of intermediate possibilities as well. And, of course, it can be pronounced by men, women, boys, girls, speakers from Detroit – [ˈbnẽɔ̃nɔ̃]) or RP – [bɔ̃ˈnɑ̃nə], and each one is different. Yet, to all intents and purposes, these variations are not even perceived by naive native speakers. Yes, anyone can recognize that Suzy or Daddy or Pierre said *banana*, but a child acquiring the language never thinks that the words refer to different objects, and it would be beyond imagination to try to spell each version differently – nobody (other than trained phoneticians) could perceive enough of a difference to know which spelling to use when.

It has also been known since very early in linguistics that the same *sound* is not the same either, but instead varies according to strict rules or principles based on such parameters as the nature of the preceding or following sound, or the prosodic status of the sound in question. The variation that has come to be known as "allophony" is classically illustrated by cases such as the American English phoneme /t/, which can be pronounced as a voiceless aspirated alveolar stop in *tall*, an unaspirated equivalent in *stall*, a voiced alveolar tap in *flatter*, a voiceless glottal stop in *flatten* and nothing at all in an allegro pronunciation of *Saturday*. Not only do native speakers not normally perceive this variation, it takes many months of phonetic training to get them to be able to transcribe it reliably. Similar facts pertain to Parisian French /e/, whose allophones [e] in open syllables and [ɛ] in closed syllables are completely opaque to most younger speakers (as noted by their inability to differentiate which way to spell the sound, among the traditional spellings for [e], namely <é> or <et> versus the traditional spellings for [ɛ]: <ais, ait, aient> etc.). To take one further example, Mandarin allophones [h] (as in *hao* 'good') and [x] (as in *heng* 'very') are indistinguishable to even moderately phonetically aware native speakers. The fact that speakers of a language are unable to hear the difference between sounds that are not only phonetically distinguishable, but are contrastive in other languages I consider to be significant evidence that phonemic perception is real.

2.2. The nature of units and storage

The vast majority of phonologists (of any stripe) accept that human beings segment the speech stream into roughly phoneme-sized segments. A few British phonologists in the nineteen-forties and fifties suggested that there might be some "segments" that were longer than a single phoneme (so that contrastive features such as nasalization might span a longer stretch of speech), but even contemporary autosegmental-based phonological models assume that the initial ("underlying", phonemic) string consists of segment-sized units (X-nodes or root-nodes), even if subsequent processing operates on larger stretches.[2] The fact that the vast majority of even minimally phonetically oriented writing systems are segment-based,[3] with a minority being syllable-based with segmental additions (Japanese Hiragana, Cuneiform Hittite) suggests that segment-sized entities are readily accessible to speakers of most languages.[4]

Some researchers over the years have suggested that the notion of speech as consisting of phoneme-sized units is an illusion brought on by the high level of literacy in (at least) the western world (see, e.g., Port 2010) and suggests that the existence of segments is not justified by the physically continuous nature of the speech signal, the absence of invariant cues for phonemes, and the fact that certain kinds of speech error do not seem

---

[2] Goldsmith discusses this issue in his seminal work (Goldsmith 1990), and even in his dissertation (Goldsmith 1976).
[3] Roman and Cyrillic-based writing systems, for example, and also Devanagari-based and most Semitic alphabets represent objects that are at least roughly segment-sized, although some Devanagari-derived alphabets are CV-based, but with diacritics to mark the non-default vowels, and additional segments to mark onset clusters (the coda symbols are diacritically-marked CV symbols).
[4] Note also that no orthography writes anything corresponding to what would be 'long segments' (in the Firthian sense). Even languages that mark tones orthographically mark them on individual segments or syllables.

to occur. Some of these issues will be dealt with below. Note however that storage of units larger than the segment does not preclude the notion that those units are *made up of smaller units*. The existence of puns, spoonerisms and taboo avoidance behaviors in some cultures suggest strongly that speakers have access to identities at the segmental level, and, as Stampe (1979) noted, this identity is not at the level of fine phonetic detail but rather at a more abstract, schematic level that is equivalent to the phoneme of the "psychological realist" school of phonology that includes Baudouin, Sapir and others. Just to take a simple case, *Batman* is an illustration of assonance, despite the fact that the two vowels are enormously different – one is short and oral, the other long and nasalized, yet this difference is a revelation to students in an introductory phonetics course.

The history of phonology has ranged widely over the possible answers to this question. Baudouin held that phonemes are mentally-stored sound images, but his colleague Saussure argued that they are systems of oppositions. European Structuralists such as Trubetzkoy ([1939] 1969) argued that phonemes were *defined* solely by their system of oppositions, so that if some sound was lacking in an opposition in some context, it wasn't even a real phoneme, but an *archiphoneme*. So, for example, English [ŋ] in *thank* was different from the [ŋ] in *thing* because there was an opposition *thing*:*thin* but none in *thank*:*thamk. So *think* would have been represented phonemically as /θɪNk/ but *thing* would be "spelled" /θɪŋ/.

Most American Structuralists were wary of archiphonemes. Hockett (1942: 10) for example, says they "confuse the facts without adding anything", but within various streams of Generative Phonology underspecified segments have become quite popular (there are various flavors of "underspecification theory" that go beyond the scope of the current chapter).

Natural Phonology has always agreed with Baudouin that phonemes are mental images of concrete sounds held in long-term storage, and thus are completely specified (i.e., all features are "filled in"). To the extent that cognitive linguists working within the usage-based model have considered the issue they have allowed for "schematic" sound storage, but with little exploration of how that concept would play out in a model of speech production or perception.

The question of whether phonological processes are psychologically real has been debated since at least the nineteen fifties (see, e.g, Hockett 1954; Baudouin de Courtenay 1972). Baudouin argued that physiophonetic "divergences" were calculated in the course of speaking, and Sapir ([1933] 1972), in his discussion of native speaker phonemic perception implied the same. Later Structuralists were either agnostic on the subject, or, in the case of Bloomfield's Behaviorist discussion (Bloomfield 1933) argued that the relationship among allophones was one of operant conditioning (as we would now say), thereby implying again that such "categorization" occurred in real time.

Generative phonologists have varied in their view of whether this kind of processing is or ought to be part of a model of linguistic performance (a competence model, of course, is agnostic on the subject). Because of an inherent bias against derivations (the essence of generative grammar) CG has assumed that there is no online "transformation" of linguistic structures. Langacker (1987: xxx) explicitly makes this claim, and virtually all subsequent work has continued to accept it.

The amount of detail stored for each phoneme (assuming sounds are stored as units) varies as well. Sounds are affected by their prosodic position, as well as proximity to neighboring sounds. If stress is predictable, are vowels stored as long if the language marks stress with length? If vowels are nasalized before nasal consonants, is that feature stored for each vowel in the lexicon that is so located?

In versions of Generative Phonology following closely on the classic Chomsky and Halle (1968) all morphophonemically related allomorphs were represented with a single form, so that *collide* and *collision* would be represented in the lexicon with a single underlying form, roughly /kolīd/. The alternations in the second syllable would be derived through the operation of several "rules" – Vowel Shift and/or Trisyllabic Laxing, which accounts for the two different vowels, and palatalization, which accounts for the /d ~ ʒ/ alternation. At the opposite extreme, many usage-based theorists have argued that each distinct pronunciation, whether "rule-governed" or governed by sociolinguistic or style-based factors, or perhaps even indexing individual speakers, is stored separately (Bybee 2010; Pierrehumbert 2002)

Again, this is a matter of the nature of phonological representations. Prague School linguists and generative phonologists argued that storage is not in actual sounds, but rather in lists of features. The set of features has, of course, varied over the seventy or so years since the concept was introduced, but this view continues to be popular among non-cognitive phonologists. Bybee argued that features are not relevant to phonological behavior (Bybee 2001; 2010). Natural phonologists have argued that features are not elements of storage but rather dimensions of categorization that govern the operation of processes (Donegan and Stampe 1979, 2009). For natural phonologists, as for usage-based theorists, representation is of real sounds (again, with the caveat that there is some question about the nature of sound schemas).

Finally, there is the question of what kind of mental unit a phoneme is. Structuralists generally did not deal with this question, with the exception of those experimenting with a behaviorist model, such as Bloomfield (1933: 33–41), for whom phonemes were behavioral units united by learned associations. Generative phonologists do not normally ask this question, because for most generative linguists linguistic units are sui generis, and thus not comparable to other units of cognition. This author proposed that phonemes were radial prototype categories (Nathan 1986), and the notion that phonemes are some kind of category has been considered fundamental for all cognitive linguists since then, although the issue of whether they are radial prototype categories or exemplar-based categories has remained contentious.

On a higher level of abstraction is the question of the nature of phoneme inventories. It has been known since at least Trubetzkoy ([1939] 1969) that there is much less variation among the phoneme inventories of the languages of the world than would be expected if they were randomly distributed. Greenberg (1966) was the first to investigate this statistically, and it has become a staple of phonological theorizing since then (a good source for relatively recent research is Ladefoged and Maddieson 1996). To illustrate with a few randomly-chosen examples: there are no phoneme inventories that consist solely of fricatives, nor any that have only low vowels. Although the overwhelmingly uniform nature of phonological inventories cannot be merely coincidence, there is disagreement among cognitively-oriented linguists on the reasons for the uniformity, with some, like the present author, arguing for physiological/perceptual pressures, while others, notably Blevins (2004) and Bybee (2001: 204) have argued that the influence of embodied processes is indirect, operating through sound change rather than synchronically. In addition, we should at least mention the fact that some have recently claimed that there are indeed no universals in phonology. The controversial paper by Evans and Levinson (2009: 431) argues that not even the existence of sounds is universal, since there are signed languages. This forces virtually all "universals" to contain "if-then" clauses. We would have to say "if languages have sounds, they have consonants and vowels", and similar contingent laws would have to obtain in the finer details of stop or vowel inventories.

Finally, phonology has long concerned itself with how (or whether) segments are grouped into larger units, particularly syllables, feet, prosodic phrases and so forth. The evidence for syllables is quite strong (although there have been serious questions raised about how universal they are [Hyman 2011]), and some evidence (albeit somewhat theory-dependent) for feet (McCarthy 1982) and perhaps phonological or intonational phrases. Finally, there is the somewhat contentious issue of whether there exist overall phonological typologies – traditionally syllable-timed, stress-timed and mora-timed. Although some phoneticians have, on the basis of measurements (or actually, the inability to find appropriate measurements [Dauer 1983, 1987]) questioned the essential typology, other researchers have found confirmation of at least some kind of division, using it to explain perception not only of speech but of music (Patel 2008).

3. The invariance problem

Much of the history of phonology consists of accounting for the fact that phonetic entities (however defined) that seem the same to native speakers (even linguistically-trained ones) are actually physically quite different. This first became evident with the nineteenth century development of phonetics, but after the invention of the sound spectrograph it became inescapable. As vowels succumbed to precise measurement it became obvious that no occurrence of any vowel was ever exactly the same. For consonants this is less strikingly obvious, but true nevertheless, as voice onset time, frication duration and similar parameters susceptible to precise measurement will demonstrate. The additional, linguistically significant detail is that much variation appears to be rule-governed. American English voiceless stops are aspirated at the beginning of words, except if preceded by /s/. Sanskrit and Thai stops are all voiceless unaspirated word-finally, even though there are minimal quadruples (triples for Thai) in word-onset position.

The consensus among most practicing phonologists in the first decade of the twenty-first century is that regular variation within phonemes is accounted for by some set of regularity principles. The more orthodox of the generative phonologists derive allophones from underlying phonemes through the operation of phonological rules, while Optimality Theory enthusiasts (McCarthy 2004; Kager 1999) prefer a set of ranked "markedness constraints" that permit deformation of target forms. Recent phonology texts (e.g, Hayes 2009; Gussenhoven and Jacobs 2005; Odden, 2005) tend to present both models, the former in the earlier chapters and the latter in the later ones.

The present author has argued, near the beginning of the development of CG, and in subsequent publications over the years (Nathan 1986, 2007, 2008; Donegan and Nathan 2014), that the systematic variants of target sounds represented members of a radial prototype category, with the "underlying form" itself being the prototype sound. Non-prototypical instantiations of the phoneme are generated online via "image schema transformations" (Nathan 1996), a cognitive operation explored first in semantic lexical representations by Lakoff (1987).

There is, however, another set of variants that raise far more complex questions, both of storage and of what and how much is computed online vs. what remains in long-term memory. The same word can be pronounced in many different ways, depending on social and individual speech-act factors. Casual speech variants, as well as socially-indexed variants (such as the Northern Cities Vowel Shift in the US, as well as variable consonant cluster simplification in African American Vernacular English) raise additional questions. This will be discussed below.

4. The allophone question

As was discussed above, the existence of large numbers of variants of "single sounds" is a crucial fact in our understanding phonemes, and the fact that this variation goes unremarked by native speakers is an important aspect of this variation. For example, in many dialects of American English there are (at least) two distinct lateral sonorants, a clear [l] and a dark [ɫ] in *leaf* and *feel*[5] respectively. While children acquiring English often have difficulty producing these sounds (frequently replacing the former with [j] and the latter with [w], or even both with [w]) there are no reported cases of children having difficulty *spelling* the two with the same letter. And, for those who have taught phonetics to native speakers of American English, it is clear that the difference between these two sounds is *very* hard for their students to hear. In fact, it has been my experience that students never end up being able to hear the difference, and just memorize the rules for when to use which example (and when the language, due to morphological differences, contrasts the two, as in *really* [rɪəɫi][6] vs. *freely* [frili], the difference is perceived as a vowel difference or as a morphological boundary).

Similarly, the four English words *bang* [bæ̃ɪŋ], *bad* [bæːd], *Hal* [hɛ̯əɫ] and *bat* [bæt] have four distinct vowels, each of which would be phonemically distinct in some other language, yet, again, children do not balk at spelling them with the same letter, and phonetics students have difficulty hearing the differences.[7] All of this leads to the inescapable conclusion that in some sense native speakers of a language do not "hear" allophonic differences, categorizing all instances of allophonically-related sounds as the same.

Stampe (1979) presented a number of pieces of evidence that phonemes are the units that are cognitively most active, including the well-documented fact that spoonerisms

---

5 Note also that there are actually more variants. /l/'s are voiceless after aspirated stops and voiceless fricatives (*please, floor* etc.). Again, this variation is largely unheard.

6 The phonetic transcriptions in this paper vary in degree of detail, depending on the particular point being made. For example, since it is not crucial to this point, the American English [ɹ] is represented in most examples as 'r'.

7 In fact, the mind boggles at attempting to teach second grade students to attend to these differences simply to learn how to spell. It is notable that no contemporary (and virtually no historical) orthographies mark allophones. Sanskrit Devanagari may be virtually unique in this respect.

and other speech errors appear to move phonemes, with allophones being expressed according to their new environments. Thus, a speaker I recently heard referred to *thynsesis* [θɪnsəsɪs] rather than *synthesis* [sɪn̪θsəsɪs] with a dental /n/. The assimilation of the /n/ to the /θ/ clearly "followed" the transposition of segments, a point that has been repeatedly documented since Fromkin (1973). Similarly, rhyme, even in folk poetry, is at the phonemic rather than allophonic level. For example, at a recent musical I attended, one of the singers "rhymed" *pretend,* pronounced as [priˈtɛnd], with *friend,* pronounced as [frɛntʰ]. This was possible because American English allophonically devoices final voiced consonants, but I am sure nobody in the audience, nor the singer himself was aware that these words did not have the same final codas, because, despite the physical realization, the codas are phonemically identical (/ɛnd/). Physically distinct sounds are perceived as identical, because rhyme is about phonemic rather than phonetic perception.

So, we have to do here with *categorization*, with speakers physically distinct objects into a single category. This forces us to consider the nature of human categorization behavior.

The structural phoneme was a traditional Aristotelian category, in which all members shared common characteristics, traditionally called *features*. This Aristotelian definition of phonemes led to problems first debated within the structuralist community and then during the phonological part of the "Linguistic Wars" in the late nineteen sixties and early seventies. There are several problems with an insistence on distinctive features and what came to be called "phonemic overlapping".

Classic cases in this debate included (for American English) the fact that both /t/ and /d/ seemed to have a common allophone [ɾ] (*betting:bedding*), and that sometimes there seemed to be predictable phonemes. The latter was particularly interesting. In American English vowels are longer before syllable final voiced stops than before voiceless ones (so Midwest *cot:cod* are [kʰɑt kʰɑːd], for example). But, on the other hand, there seem, at the same time, to be contrasts, such as *bomb:balm*. This led Bloch ([1941] 1966) to argue that the different vowels in *cot* and *cod* are distinct phonemes. "The words in the last pair, instead of exhibiting shorter and longer allophones of the same phoneme, have totally different phonemes" (Joos 1966: 96). While this permits the theory to maintain the Aristotelian character of the phoneme, it is challenged by the phonemic perception facts alluded to above.

Two distinct developments in categorization theory offered a way out. First, the development of fuzzy logic, which permitted objects to be members of some category to a measurable degree, allowed there to be overlap between categories. Secondly, the advent of the work of Rosch (1975, 1978 et seq.) permits us to understand how phonemic overlapping might be accommodated within a theory of phonemes as categories. Nathan (1986) proposed that phonemes were radial prototype categories, following the detailed notions developed in Lakoff (1987). There is a single, central sound which speakers perceive to be "the sound", and which in traditional phonological theory was identified as the principal allophone, or "underlying form". Each non-principal allophone constitutes a modification of the primary sound via the Lakoffian notion of *image schema transformation*. Each modification is phonetically-motivated (albeit sanctioned by the particular language and dialect), but a modification is subject to additional modification (as is found in all radial categories) such that long chains of extension in two distinct directions lead to sounds that share no common characteristics.

Just to take a hackneyed example, the American English phoneme /t/ can be instantiated by a glottal stop (as in *button*) and by a voiced alveolar tap (as in *butter*). These sounds share no distinctive features at all (other than being consonants). Furthermore, one of the allophones is identical to the allophone of a distinct phoneme – that in *rudder*. But, of course, this is not a theoretical problem in a non-Aristotelian category. What unites the members of the /t/ category is not that they have *features* in common, but that they are all traceable back to a common sound, via distinct routes. Just as the fact that a *cup* can be both a hole in the ground (the 18th hole) and a sports championship (the World Cup) is not a problem, because each can be traced back, via the undoing of mental transformations that are well understood (image schema rotations, metaphors, metonymies). This view explains accounts for the traditional phoneme as well as the anomalies that "killed" it, such as phonemic overlap and the lack of common "distinctive features". Allophones do not need to share common features, nor do they need to have an overarching "schema", as long as each one can be felt as an appropriate instantiation of the target, or of an instantiation of a substitute for the target. The fact that a chain of substitutes might run into a neighboring phoneme was further explored by Mompeán-González (2004) within this framework.

5. Alternative views of categorization

As mentioned above, there is a competing theory of how humans form categories, namely *exemplar theory*, extensively outlined (along with prototype theory) in Murphy (2002: 73–114) as well as Ramscar (this volume) and Baayen (this volume). Within phonology, Pierrehumbert proposes that people have detailed long-term memories of particular percepts and these are the "exemplars" of the theory. Exemplars are categorized using a label set, and each label is associated with a large set of remembered percepts. The label can be thought of as equivalent to a phoneme (Pierrehumbert 2002: 113).

Exemplar theory has become very popular in recent work in Cognitive Grammar, because it is inherently frequency-based, and seemingly requires no pre-existing linguistic apparatus, and hence no notion of innate linguistic categories, or of innate linguistic processing.

An additional facet of exemplar theory is that every percept is stored, in great phonetic detail. This has certain consequences that represent either an advantage or a disadvantage, depending on one's theoretical proclivities. What is stored is an image of each instance of an utterance, which would include both high-level information (what word was said) as well as low-level information such as the identity of the speaker, the rate of speaking, dialect and register information, and so on. The image, cited above, of instances continually superimposed on a perceptual map can be thought of as analogous to making a rubbing over a number of similar coins (or medieval etchings). Each additional coin adds detail, and some of the detail, that which is common to all the coins, will become progressively clearer, even as the differences will disappear into a blur. A particularly striking example of this notion is provided by the photographer Corinne Vionnet (Vionnet nd.), who collected hundreds of photographs of famous landmarks, both sent in by volunteers and collected from the web, then electronically superimposed them on top of each other. The results are somewhat blurry but clearly recognizable images of, for example, the Eiffel Tower and Tiananmen Square in Beijing.[8]

Another, related proposal for how sounds are stored is discussed in various works by Langacker (most extensively in Langacker 2007: 443–447). Langacker argues that allophones are nodes in a complex network of sounds, and that the contextually least restricted variant is the prototype. Langacker suggests that "higher-level nodes represent further abstractions capturing whatever is common to different sets of allophones" (Langacker 2007: 445). Features are "abstracted segments that are specific in regard to just a single property", while other higher-level schemas represent "syllables, words, prosodic patterns, and intonation contours". Further, "The phonotactic patterns of a language are thus embodied in schemas for phonologically complex clusters. As part of a dynamic processing system, such units function as templates (routinized packets of processing activity) with varying degrees of accessibility for the categorization of new expressions" (Langacker 2007: 445–6).

A similar argument (with considerably more detail) can be found in Kristiansen (2007). Kristiansen argues that a more generalized network model of speech sounds, rather than a specifically radial prototype structure can appropriately account for the fact that speakers of one dialect can, after relatively short exposure, understand speakers of different dialects, in which the allophones may not map in the same way.

For example, in some vernacular British dialects, glottal stops are exponents not only of /t/ but of all voiceless stops. Similarly, the same sound [ɑ] could represent, to a speaker of a Southern American dialect the vowel /ai/ as in *buy*, while to a speaker of the dialect of Boston or Maine it might represent /ɑr/ as in *bar*. What is crucial, for Kristiansen, is that speakers of both dialects may well be aware of what the other's dialect sounds like, and may have associated sociolinguistic and cultural reactions. Thus she argues that there is no reason to privilege a single dialect's array of variant forms with a single central prototype form, but rather have a loose network of related forms, over which a schematic generalization extracts some commonality.

6. The role of frequency in phonology

In Bybee's seminal works (Bybee 2001, 2010) she has argued that frequency of occurrence of forms has a powerful explanatory role in the acquisition, production and perception of phonology. In her view words are the fundamental unit of storage (Bybee 2001: 30), but schemas capture commonalities among words such as similar segments (allophones), and structural units such as syllables. One goal of her work is to argue against the structuralist/generative view of the phoneme as an abstract contrastive unit (her arguments are not quite as effective against the concrete, pronounceable storage unit proposed by non-structuralist phonologists such as Baudouin, Stampe and myself). She presents evidence of phonological variation that appears related to frequency of specific words. This includes distributionally predictable features that are lexically contrastive.

---

[8] I am grateful to Diane Larsen-Freeman for directing my attention to Vionnet's work, and pointing out the relevance to usage-based models.

In a widely cited work, Hooper [Bybee] (1978) examined "schwa-deletion" in English. As is exemplified by words such as *every*, *memory*, and *mammary*, word-internal schwas are optionally deleted (actually schwa-deletion is much more widespread than these cases, but deletions such as in the *banana* example discussed in section 1.1 and cases like *police* are not relevant to the current discussion). In the examples she discusses she reports that "high frequency words undergo the deletion to a greater extent than do low-frequency words" (Bybee 2001: 41). She notes that some words such as *every* are almost never pronounced with schwa, some variably with and without, such as *memory*, and some always have schwas, such as *mammary*. Since a structuralist analysis can be made that syllabic [ɚ] and non-syllabic [r] are allophones of a single phoneme, this would be an instance of allophony on a purely statistical basis. She notes that the non-syllabic version occurs post- and pre-consonantally (*trap*, *tarp*), while the syllabic version occurs elsewhere (*bird*). This, however, is not true, because the non-syllabic version also occurs intervocalically, in *arrange* and *berry*. In addition it is not a traditional view of allophones that the choice of allophones determines the syllable structure of a word – rather it is for most phonologists the reverse.

An alternative view would be that syllabic [ɚ] in *bird* is bi-phonemically /ər/, while its nonsyllabic equivalent [r] is a single phoneme /r/ which can occur intervocalically as in /bɛri/ or in codas as in /tɑrp/. Schwa-deletion, an optional process, is, like many other stylistic processes, sensitive to frequency. Put another way, speakers are aware of how common or rare are the words they are saying, and are more likely to choose a more "relaxed" (lenited) pronunciation when the word is more likely to be recognizable, while a rarer word is more likely to be pronounced closer to its underlying, prototypical pronunciation.

Gahl (2008), in a corpus-based study, presented evidence that speakers store fine phonetic detail, such as the small differences associated with differences in frequency of occurrence of words that might otherwise be identical, such as homonyms. Gahl found that the more frequent of pairs of English homonyms (such as *thyme* vs. *time*) are significantly shorter than the less frequent of the pair. This suggests that allophonic length might be determined by frequency in addition to the more usual conditions, such as word position, neighboring sounds and so on. On the other hand, the lower-frequency words were on average 7% longer than their higher frequency counterparts (396 vs. 368 ms.) (Gahl 2008: 481). A roughly 7% difference is enormously different from what is traditionally considered allophonic (say the English vowel length difference in *cot* vs. *cod*, which is roughly 100%) and much smaller than the differences that mark phonemic differences in various languages. A difference that small is within the normal range of error for the length of aspirated stops, for example. It would be interesting to see whether native speakers could identify the more frequent vs less frequent member of a homophone pair given these differences, out of context.

On the other hand, Cutler and her associates (Cutler et al. 2010; McQueen, et al. 2010) found what might be considered exactly the opposite conclusion – namely that short-term adjustments hearers make to small acoustic differences in phonemes among individual speakers immediately generalize to words that the hearers had not previously been exposed to. Cutler and her colleagues showed that speakers adjust their phonemic representations of all the words containing a particular phoneme if they are exposed to subtly adjusted renditions of that phoneme (analogous to hearing someone with a different accent or a speech defect). The adjustment (in this case of an ambiguous /f/ – /s/

stimulus) affected all words presented to the subjects, not only the ones that served as the initial "training" stimuli, arguing that perceptual adjustments apply "online" as the embodied perception discussed above suggests.

Notably, it is also clear that children must abstract and separate personally-identifiable information (such as gender or dialect) from lexical information, because no investigator has ever reported a child who has decided that *dog* spoken with a fundamental frequency of 200 Hz refers to a different object than the same word spoken by someone else with an F_0 of 100 Hz. There is evidence that children attend to and acquire different *languages* as spoken by different caretakers, but each individual *lexical* learning task does not appear to be linked in any way to gender, size or regional or social accent.

The other area where frequency is closely correlated with phonological variation involves processes that are sociolinguistically marked, such as the famous New York City /oh/-raising in words like *fourth*. For extensive discussion of this point, see Labov (2010: 282–286) who shows that there is a distinction between phonetically-conditioned variation, which is not socially sensitive, and socially-sensitive variation, which is not phonetically-conditioned. It may well be that this kind of variation is subject to a different kind of processing than the allophonic alternations we have been discussing above.

7. The nature of perception

One issue on which very little has been written is what it means, exactly, to perceive a speech sound. Following the fundamental tenets of CG, we are required to look outside linguistics proper to understand how human beings perceive and store speech, since we would expect that such perception and storage would not be modular, but rather work in the same fashion as perception and storage of other aspects of external reality. What makes speech perception "special", however, is that we are storing aspects of external reality that happen to correspond (for the most part) to aspects of "internal reality", because when we hear speech, we are hearing performances of objects that we ourselves also produce. To the extent that we are hearing speech of a language we speak, this kind of perception would be different from, say, the sound of an airplane, or the sight of an oak tree. And, in fact, to some extent we even treat the sound of an airplane as speech, because we can imitate the sound, and in so doing, we use our vocal tracts to do so.

Perception and production of external sounds produced by other animals, in fact, can even be conventionalized within our language, and, just as there are similarities within the phonologies of different languages, there are similarities in the imitation of animal sounds across related, and even unrelated languages.[9] Recent research shows that speakers are quite capable of exploiting the whole range of human vocal tract affordances in imitating the sound of percussive musical instruments. Proctor et al. (2013) show that artists can produce sounds from various places in the IPA chart that their native language does not possess while imitating snare drums and cymbals, for example.

---

[9] Comparison of words for 'bow-wow' across languages has been done both seriously and in various websites around the world, but goes beyond the scope of this paper. For an interesting take on how we perceive bird sounds, see Donegan and Stampe (1977).

One of the major tasks for a theory of perception of speech sounds is to deal with the connections that exist between the articulatory and auditory channels that are involved. Articulation is physiological (although, of course, we perceive our own productions). Conversely, perception of others' speech is, of course, primarily aural. Many have tried to develop theories of perception that bridge this gap. My own view has been strongly influenced by the work of the psychologist Gibson and his school (see Gibson 1982, 1986). More recent work within the Gibsonian framework is Spivey (2007). One of the mysteries surrounding how children acquire language (and how adults understand those around them, including those who speak different dialects or have non-native accents, or speech impediments, or even food in their mouths), is how they are able to recognize the words that they hear.

It is clear from the beginning of child language acquisition that children are engaged in considerable "pre-processing" of the sounds they hear and store. The speech of a prototypical father has a fundamental frequency in the realm of 120 Hz, while prototypical mother's speech has F_0's in the 210 Hz realm. (Grabe nd.) Children below the age of five are physically incapable of producing pitches in these ranges (their frequency ranges from 250–400 Hz), yet they have no trouble perceiving (and presumably acquiring) intonation contours, and, for tone languages, the tones of the language.

Even more puzzling, however, is children's ability to hear vowels and consonants. The raw waveforms that they hear have formants at very different values from those they can produce given the size of their vocal tracts. This makes any model based on reproduction of stored instances much more difficult to implement. For example, a study of contemporary American English vowels noted that average F1 and F2 values for /i/, /u/ and /ɑ/ were as follows:

Tab. 12.1: (from Hillenbrand et al. 1995: 3103)

Vowel	i		a		u	
	F1	F2	F1	F2	F1	F2
Men	342	2322	768	1333	469	1122
Women	437	2761	936	1551	519	1105
Children	452	3081	1002	1688	568	1490

In absolute terms, children's vowels are acoustically nowhere near the adult's, yet to adult ears (and presumably to the child), the vowel systems are not different at all.

Furthermore, information about point and manner of articulation is found in the transitions at the ends of formants, as well as some inherent pitches (for fricatives, for example). Although children may very well store this as a set of absolute values, they could not produce it themselves – their vocal tracts are incapable of it. Instead they must perform a complex transformation so that their vocal tracts can produce (what we call) the same vowels, stops and other consonants. This is also true, of course, for adults speaking with other adults, and, of course with children as well. If we assume a motor theory (see A. Liberman and Mattingly 1985 for the classic statement of this theory), or alternatively, an embodied theory of perception, this is no puzzle at all. Virtually speaking, perception of vowel values is perception of "what I would have to do to make that sound" – that is, perception of the interlocutor's intentions. It is likely that the human perceptual system is in fact designed to translate the sensory data of other's actions directly into percepts of our own actions. The fact that this complex transformation is accomplished automatically (and not limited to hearing, or to human beings[10]) suggests that perception of language is far more complex than an averaging of the storage of many individual instances, and that image schema transformations are part and parcel of our perceptual apparatus.

8. Higher levels of structure

Generally very little has been written on prosody within the CG framework. Although it might be tempting to argue that stress, for example, is simply part of the phonetic detail that is stored with each lexical item, there is strong evidence that overall sentence rhythm is part of the overall production computation system, primarily because it interacts with other aspects of human rhythmic behavior. In fact, I would argue, following (Donegan and Stampe 1983, 2009), that linguistic accent/stress simply is human rhythmic behavior to which strings of segments are mapped, much as hand-clapping and foot-tapping is mapped to internally generated or externally perceived rhythms.

Consider, for example the fact that speakers are able to map words to music without any training in either music or prosody. Children in English-speaking North America sing a playground song designed to embarrass two of their number by suggesting a romantic relationship between them. The first two lines are

(1)   X and Y, sitting in a tree
      K-I-S-S-I-N-G

where X and Y are first names. What is of interest is how Y is sung. M. Liberman (1979) provided an elegant analysis of the process of setting words to tunes (he used the taunting melody usually quoted as *Nyah nya nya NYAH NYA*, but the principle is the same).

Y is sung on two notes (descending third). If the name is monosyllabic the name is broken into two syllables with an inserted glottal stop:

(2)   Jo-ohn   [ˈdʒɔ ʔɔn]
                  | |
                  H   L

If the name is bisyllabic and has initial stress, the high tone (and accented syllable) falls on the first syllable and the low tone on the second syllable. However, if the name is iambic the first syllable is shortened and receives a slightly lower pitch and a "grace note", while the second syllable is broken in the same way as the previous example:

---

[10]   Gibson notes that spiders flinch if they see a pattern projected on a wall that suddenly expands – they perceive (as do humans in the same conditions) that something is rushing towards them. But spiders have eight eyes, and those eyes don't focus the way ours do.

(3) E-lai-aine [i 'le ʔeɪn]
               | | |
               M   H   L

As names get longer a similar principle is followed. The primary stressed syllable aligns with the high note, preceding syllables are reduced (even if secondarily stressed) and following syllables are mapped onto the low note:

(4) Alexan-dra [æ lɪg 'zæn drə]
                 \ / | |
                  M   H   L

The ability to do this (that is, to synchronize two aspects of temporally extended behavior, such as bodily movement and patterns of beats, or segmental and suprasegmental strings) is not a linguistic ability but simply an instance of entrainment (see London 2012: 32 and Repp 2005: 978 for extensive discussion). But it is possible to take this identity further and argue that stress systems in language are simply instantiations of this ability as well. Work by Goswami (2012: 58) argues that attention to syllable structure and attention to rhythmic beat in music are the same cognitive task. In addition, she notes that appropriately shaped onsets of rhythmic beats facilitate the ability to entrain (that is, to get the listener in sync with the music being heard). This fact underlies the claim made in Nathan (2008: 36) that the universal preference for CV syllables is driven by the perceptual preference for clearly demarcated beats with an audible onset. In addition, Goswami (2012: 60) has found evidence for a correlation between dyslexia and difficulty in perceiving speech prosody and syllable stress.

A brief comment here about the acquisition of constituents such as syllables. Although usage-based theorists have suggested that speakers extract information about the constituency and "relatedness" of pieces of (say) a syllable from statistically-based generalizations over multiple instances, this view of syllables as beats suggests that the acquisition of onset plus coda is more like the acquisition of how to hammer a nail. Hammering a nail requires a backstroke, the strike, and some kind of control over the rebound of the hammer, perhaps blending with the next hammer blow. While it is possible that the unit "hitting a nail with a hammer" is extracted from the statistical coincidence of backstroke–stroke–rebound in that order over numerous instances (both of the hammerer and others around the learner) it is more likely that hammering has an inherently "natural" structure based not on UG but on how hammers are best manipulated as users have learned through doing hammering. Exactly the same argumentation could be made for the near preference of CV structures over CVC, VC and more extreme cases.

Linguists have long puzzled over the nature of stress or accent. It is often easy to hear, but very difficult to measure in any simple way. The current consensus is that stress is a combination of length, amplitude and rapid pitch change (Ladefoged 2005; Rogers 2001; see also Lerdahl and Jackendoff 1983). However, as Stampe (p.c.) has pointed out, accent in the musical sense can easily be sensed in harpsichord music, which uses neither length nor amplitude (harpsichord strings are plucked by a mechanical device that does not respond to how hard the key is pressed, nor does the musician control how long the note lasts, unlike a piano). The only control a player has is the micro-timing of the pluck, but attention to that timing only makes sense against some internal representation of regular beats against which deviations could be perceived.

Given this, we can explore what is known about cognition of rhythm. London (2012) argues that there are universal parameters for the kinds of rhythms that human beings can perceive and entrain. It is notable that those rhythms align quite closely with normal speech delivery rates (London 2012: 27–30), and also with the natural periodicity for human jaw movement and perhaps also foot stomping and finger tapping.[11]

9. Conclusions

The status of phonology in CG is far from settled. One can identify at least three distinct strands – a usage-based, frequency-oriented view relying on exemplar theory, a related view in which the extraction of schemas from a network of instances permits the generation of higher-level abstract elements such as features, syllables and similar traditional linguistic units, and an active construction/realist view in which phonology is the immediate construction of physical action as a task to be accomplished, and the sympathetic reception of the results of others' similar constructions within the parameters set by each speaker's system. This appears to be a difference in vision about the fundamental nature of linguistic behavior that is represented in the tenor of the field in general. Work in lexical semantics and construction theory tends to emphasize the creative role of speakers in extending meanings and valence possibilities through well-known pathways such as metaphorical and metonymic extension, while work in grammaticalization theory and historical change has tended to focus more on the gradual change of units based on frequency. In addition, usage-based models tend to focus much more strongly on purely linguistic data (distributional factors, for example) while work in metaphor and metonymy looks at extralinguistic factors virtually by definition. My view has been that linguistic representations are embodied (i.e., that phonological storage is of images of sequences of vocal tract states) and that phonological processing is conventionalized adaptation of those states to each other. From this point of view, incidentally, phonological change is a change in which conventionalized adaptations have become more acceptable to the speech community, perhaps leading to a recoding of the target states over time (see Donegan and Nathan 2014 for details). Additionally, from this point of view, all phonological processing is conventionalization of independently-motivated facts about vocal tracts, auditory processing, categorization, rhythmic behavior, interpersonal activity (such as speaker/hearer estimation of recoverability of information during conversation, which determines degree of phonetic reduction) and so forth. By taking non-modularity of language seriously I believe we can get much closer to a truly explanatory view of the nature of phonology.

---

[11] Finger tapping proceeds at a faster pace than either head bobbing or foot stomping, and seems to correspond more to syllables, while the latter corresponds more to accentual feet. That is, finger rhythms correspond to subdivisions of larger limb movements. I am grateful to David Stampe for discussion of this isomorphism, but see also Tovey (1957: 175–176) and London (2012) for further discussion.

10. References

Baayen, Harald
   this volume   5. Analogy and schematization. Berlin/Boston: De Gruyter Mouton.

Baudouin de Courtenay, Jan
   1972   An attempt at a theory of phonetic Alternations. In: E. Stankiewicz (ed. and trans.), *A Baudouin de Courtenay Anthology: The Beginnings of Structural Linguistics*, 144–213. Bloomington/London: Indiana University Press.

Blevins, Juliette
   2004   *Evolutionary Phonology: The Emergence of Sound Patterns*. Cambridge and New York: Cambridge University Press.

Bloch, Bernard
   [1941] 1966   Phonemic overlapping. In: M. Joos (ed.), *Readings in Linguistics* I, 93–96. Chicago: University of Chicago Press.

Bloomfield, Leonard
   1933   *Language*. New York: Holt.

Brugman Claudia
   1981   *Story of Over*. Bloomington: Indiana Linguistics Club.

Bybee, Joan L.
   1999   Usage-based phonology. In: M. Darnell, E. A. Moravcsik, F. Newmeyer, M. Noonan and K. Wheatley(eds.), *Functionalism and Formalism in Linguistics*, Volume II: *Case Studies*, 211–242. Amsterdam: Benjamins.

Bybee, Joan L.
   2001   *Phonology and Language Use*. Cambridge/New York: Cambridge University Press.

Bybee, Joan L.
   2010   *Language, Usage, and Cognition*. Cambridge/New York: Cambridge University Press.

Chomsky, Noam, and Morris Halle
   1968   *The Sound Pattern of English*. New York: Harper and Row.

Cutler, Anne, Frank Eisner, James M. McQueen, and Dennis Norris
   2010   How abstract phonemic categories are necessary for coping with speaker-related variation. In: C. Fougeron, B. Kühnert, M. D'Imperio and N. Vallée (eds.), *Laboratory Phonology* 10, 91–111. Berlin: De Gruyter Mouton.

Dauer, R. M.
   1983   Stress-timing and syllable-timing reanalyzed. *Journal of Phonetics* 11: 51–62.

Dauer, R.M.
   1987   Phonetic and phonological components of language rhythm. *Proceedings of the 11th International Congress of Phonetic Sciences* 5: 447–450.

Donegan, Patricia J and Geoffrey S. Nathan
   2014   Natural phonology and sound change. In: J. Salmons and P. Honeybone (eds.), *The Oxford Handbook of Historical Phonology*. Oxford: Oxford University Press.

Donegan, Patricia J, and David Stampe
   1977   Old Sam Peabody Peabody Peabody: Verbal imitations of bird song. LSA Summer Meeting. Honolulu.

Donegan, Patricia J., and David Stampe
   1979   The study of natural phonology. In: D. Dinnsen (ed.), *Current Approaches to Phonological Theory*. Bloomington: Indiana University Press.

Donegan, Patricia J., and David Stampe
   1983   Rhythm and the holistic organization of language structure. In: J. F. Richardson, M. Marks, and A. Chukerman (eds.), *Papers from the Parasession on the Interplay of Phonology, Morphology, and Syntax*, 337–353. Chicago: Chicago Linguistic Society.

Donegan, Patricia J., and David Stampe
  2009   Hypotheses of natural phonology. *Poznań Studies in Contemporary Linguistics* 45(1): 1–31.
Evans, Nicholas, and Stephen Levinson
  2009   The myth of language universals: Language diversity and its importance for cognitive science. *Behavioral and Brain Sciences* 32(5): 429–492.
Fromkin, Victoria
  1973   Introduction. In: V. Fromkin (ed.), *Speech Errors as Linguistic Evidence*. The Hague: Mouton.
Gahl, Susanne
  2008   Time and thyme are not homophones: The effect of lemma frequency on word durations in spontaneous speech. *Language* 84(3): 474–496.
Gibson, James J.
  1982   *Reasons for Realism: Selected Essays of James J. Gibson*. Hillsdale: Lawrence Erlbaum.
Gibson, James J.
  1986   *The Ecological Approach to Visual Perception*. Hillsdale: Lawrence Erlbaum.
Goldsmith, John
  1976   *Autosegmental Phonology*. Bloomington: Indiana University Linguistics Club.
Goldsmith, John
  1990   *Autosegmental and Metrical Phonology*. Oxford: Blackwell.
Goswami, Usha
  2012   Entraining the brain: Applications to language research and links to musical entrainment. *Empirical Musicology Review* 7(1/2): 57–63.
Grabe, Esther and John Coleman
  n. d.   *Leaflet*. http://www.phon.ox.ac.uk/files/apps/IViE/leaflet.pdf
Greenberg, Joseph H.
  1966   *Language Universals: With Special Reference to Feature Hierarchies*. The Hague: Mouton.
Gussenhoven, Carlos, and Haike Jacobs
  2005   *Understanding Phonology*, Understanding Language Series. London: Hodder Arnold.
Hayes, Bruce
  2009   *Introductory Phonology*. Malden/Oxford: Wiley-Blackwell.
Hillenbrand, James, Laura Getty, Michael J. Clark, and Kimberlee Wheeler
  1995   Acoustic characteristics of American English vowels. *Journal of the Acoustical Society of America* 97(5): 3099–3111.
Hockett, Charles F.
  1942   A system of descriptive phonology. *Language* 18(1): 3–21.
Hockett, Charles F.
  1954   Two models of grammatical description. *Word* 10: 210–234.
Hooper [Bybee], Joan
  1978   Constraints on schwa-deletion in American English. In: J. Fisiak (ed.), *Recent Developments in Historical Phonology*, 183–207. Amsterdam: North Holland.
Hyman, Larry M.
  2011   Does Gokana really have no syllables? Or: What's so great about being universal? *Phonology* 28(1): 55–85.
Kager, René
  1999   *Optimality Theory*. Cambridge/New York: Cambridge University Press.
Kristiansen, Gitte
  2007   Towards a usage-based cognitive phonology. *International Journal of English Studies* 6(2): 107–140.

Labov, William
 2010 *Principles of Linguistic Change: Cognitive and Cultural Factors*. Oxford: Wiley-Blackwell.
Ladefoged, Peter
 2005 *Vowels and Consonants*. Malden/Oxford: Blackwell.
Ladefoged, Peter, and Ian Maddieson
 1996 *The Sounds of the World's Languages*. Oxford/Cambridge: Blackwell.
Lakoff, George
 1987 *Women, Fire and Dangerous Things – What Categories Reveal About the Mind*. Chicago: University of Chicago Press.
Langacker, Ronald W.
 1987 *Foundations of Cognitive Grammar*. Stanford: Stanford University Press.
Langacker, Ronald W.
 1990 *Concept, Image and Symbol*. Berlin: Mouton/de Gruyter.
Langacker, Ronald W.
 2007 Cognitive grammar. In: D. Geeraerts and H. Cuyckens (eds.), *The Oxford Handbook of Cognitive Linguistics*, 421–462. New York: Oxford University Press.
Lerdahl, Fred, and Ray S. Jackendoff
 1983 *A Generative Theory of Tonal Music*. Cambridge: MIT Press.
Liberman, A., and Ignatius Mattingly
 1985 The motor theory of speech perception revisited. *Cognition* 21: 1–36.
Liberman, Mark
 1979 *The Intonational System of English*. New York: Garland.
Lindner, Susan Jean
 1981 A lexico-semantic analysis of English verb particle constructions with *out* and *up*. Ph.D. Dissertation. University of California, San Diego.
London, Justin
 2012 *Hearing in Time: Psychological Aspects of Musical Meter*. New York: Oxford University Press.
McCarthy, John J.
 1982 Prosodic structure and expletive infixation. *Language* 58(3): 574–590.
McCarthy, John J.
 2004 *Optimality Theory in Phonology: A Reader*. Malden: Blackwell.
McCarthy, John J.,
 2008 *Doing Optimality Theory: Applying Theory to Data*. Malden/Oxford: Blackwell.
McQueen, James M., Anne Cutler, and Dennis Norris
 2010 Phonological abstraction in the mental lexicon. *Cognitive Science* 30(6): 1113–1126.
Mompeán-González, José A.
 2004 Category overlap and neutralization: The importance of speakers' classifications in phonology. *Cognitive Linguistics* 15(4): 429–469.
Mompeán-González, José A. (ed.)
 2006 Cognitive phonology issue. *International Journal of English Studies* 6(2).
Murphy, Gregory L.
 2002 *The Big Book of Concepts*. Cambridge: MIT Press.
Nathan, Geoffrey S.
 1986 Phonemes as mental categories. *Proceedings of the 12th Annual Meeting of the Berkeley Linguistics Society* 12, 212–224. Berkeley: Berkeley Linguistic Society.
Nathan, Geoffrey S.
 1996 Towards a cognitive phonology. In: B. Hurch and R. Rhodes (eds.), *Natural Phonology: The State of the Art*, 107–120, Berlin: Mouton de Gruyter.

Nathan, Geoffrey S.
   2007   Phonology. In: D. Geeraerts and H. Cuyckens (eds.), *The Oxford Handbook of Cognitive Linguistics*, 611–631. Oxford: Oxford University Press.
Nathan, Geoffrey S.
   2008   *Phonology: A Cognitive Grammar Introduction.* Amsterdam/Philadelphia: Benjamins.
Nesset, Tore
   2008   *Abstract Phonology in a Concrete Model: Cognitive Linguistics and the Morphology-Phonology Interface.* Berlin/New York: Mouton de Gruyter.
Odden, David
   2005   *Introducing Phonology.* Cambridge/New York: Cambridge University Press.
Patel, Aniruddh D.
   2008   *Music, Language, and the Brain.* New York: Oxford University Press.
Pierrehumbert, Janet
   2002   Word-specific phonetics. In: C. Gussenhoven and N. Warner (eds.), *Laboratory Phonology* 7, 101–139. Berlin/New York: Mouton de Gruyter.
Port, Robert F.
   2010   Language as a social institution: Why phonemes and words do not live in the brain. *Ecological Psychology* 22: 304–326.
Prince, Alan, and Paul Smolensky
   2004   *Constraint Interaction in Generative Grammar.* London: Blackwell.
Proctor, Michael, Erik Bresch, Dani Byrd, Krishna Nayak, and Shrikanth Narayanan
   2013   Paralinguistic mechanisms of production in human 'beatboxing': A real-time Magnetic Resonance Imaging study. *Journal of the Acoustical Society of America* 133(2): 1043–1054.
Ramscar, Michael
   this volume   4. Categorization. Berlin/Boston: De Gruyter Mouton.
Repp, Bruno
   2005   Sensorimotor synchronization: A review of the tapping literature. *Psychonomic Bulletin and Review* 12(6): 969–992.
Rogers, Henry
   2001   *The Sounds of Language: An Introduction to Phonetics.* Harlow: Pearson.
Rosch, Eleanor
   1975   Cognitive representations of semantic categories. *Journal of Experimental Psychology: General* 104: 192–233.
Rosch, Eleanor
   1978   Principles of categorization. In: E. Rosch and B. B. Lloyd (eds.), *Cognition and Categorization*, 27–48. Hillsdale: Lawrence Erlbaum.
Rubba, Jo
   1993   Discontinuous morphology in modern Aramaic. Ph.D. dissertation. University of California San Diego.
Sapir, Edward
   [1933] 1972   La réalité pschologique des phonemes [The psychological reality of phonemes]. In: V. Becker Makkai (ed.), *Phonological Theory: Evolution and Current Practice.* New York: Holt Rinehart and Winston.
Saussure, Ferdinand de
   [1916] 1974   *Course de Linguistique Générale.* Edition critique préparée par Tullio de Mauro. Paris: Payot.
Spivey, Michael
   2007   *The Continuity of Mind.* Oxford/New York: Oxford University Press.
Stampe, David
   1979   *A Dissertation on Natural Phonology.* New York: Garland.

Tovey, Donald Francis
   1957   *The Forms of Music: Musical Articles from the Encyclopedia Britannica*. Oxford: Oxford University Press.
Trubetzkoy, N. S
   [1939] 1969   *Gründzüge der Phonologie* [Principles of Phonology]. Translated by A. M. Baltaxe. Los Angeles: University of California Press.
Vionnet, Corinne
   n. d.   Corinnevionnet.Com. (retrieved 21 May 2014).

Geoffrey S. Nathan, Detroit (USA)

13. Lexical semantics

1. Contributions to semasiology
2. Contributions to onomasiology
3. Current developments
4. References

To the extent that linguistic categorization is a focal area for Cognitive Linguistics, lexical semantics provides a crucial source of inspiration for the cognitive approach: to a considerable degree (see Taylor, this volume), the research strategy of Cognitive Linguistics is characterized by an extrapolation to other areas of linguistics of theoretical insights and descriptive models initially developed in the study of word meaning. The present chapter provides a brief survey of the main lines of lexical semantic research in Cognitive Linguistics, organized in two groups: contributions to semasiology (the study of the internal semantic structure of words), and contributions to onomasiology (the study of the semantic structure of the vocabulary and the relations between words). The concluding section considers current methodological developments. For more details for the position of Cognitive Linguistics in the history of lexical semantics at large, see Geeraerts (2010), specifically chapter 5.

1. Contributions to semasiology

Cognitive Linguistics advances semasiology primarily by the development of a prototype-theoretical model of lexical-semantic structure. We will first introduce the prototype as such, and then discuss a related (but foundational) topic, viz. the mutual demarcation of meaning and vagueness, and the indeterminacy of polysemy. An overview of the development of prototype theory within Cognitive Linguistics may be found in Mangasser-Wahl (2000). Foundational monographs like Lakoff (1987) and Langacker (1987), and successful textbooks like Taylor (1989, third edition 2003b) and Aitchison (1987, third edition 2003) contributed considerably to the expansion of prototype-based descriptions. Testifying to the early adoption of prototype-based models in Cognitive Linguistics are collective volumes like Craig (1986), Rudzka-Ostyn (1988), Tsohatzidis (1989), and monographs like Kempton (1981), Geeraerts (1985), Sweetser (1990), Schmid (1993). Since then, a prototype-based form of semantic description has become a standard ingredient of a Cognitive Linguistic view of categorization.

1.1. Semantic salience: prototype effects and radial sets

Prototype models in linguistics were inspired by the psychological work of Eleanor Rosch. We will first present the original experimental results of Rosch and her colleagues, and then consider the general model of prototypicality effects that was developed in linguistic lexical semantics on the basis of the results obtained by Rosch. Characteristically, this model is applied on two different levels: within individual senses (in a monosemic context), and among different senses (in a polysemic context).

1.1.1. Prototypicality in a monosemic context

Rosch's results initially relate to perceptual categories, building on Berlin and Kay's anthropological study of colour terms (1969). Studying primary colour terms in a wide variety of languages, Berlin and Kay concluded that all languages select their primary colour terms from a set of eleven: black, white, red, yellow, green, blue, brown, purple, pink, orange and grey. There is a hierarchy among these terms, with five levels, in the sense that in a language with two colour terms, these terms will be *black* and *white*. A language with three terms invariably has *red* as the additional one. The fourth, fifth, and sixth term are chosen from among the colours on the third level (yellow, green, blue), and so on. Rosch inferred from these results that particular areas of the colour spectrum are more salient than others, and conjectured that these focal colours would be more easily encoded linguistically and more easily remembered than less salient colours. Both predictions were supported experimentally, and an extrapolation to other semantic domains turned out to be possible (see Rosch 1977: 15–18). Rosch concluded that the tendency to define categories in a rigid way clashes with the actual psychological situation. Perceptually based categories do not have sharply delimited borderlines, but instead of clear demarcations one finds marginal areas between categories that are only unambiguously defined in their focal points. Rosch developed this observation into a more general prototypical view of natural language categories, specifically, categories naming natural objects. The range of application of such categories is concentrated round focal points represented by prototypical members of the category. The attributes of these focal members are the structurally most salient properties of the concept in question, and conversely, a particular member of the category occupies a focal position because it exhibits the most salient features. This view of category structure is summarized in the statement that "much work in philosophy, psychology, linguistics, and anthropology assumes that categories are logical bounded entities, membership in which is defined by an item's possession of a simple set of criterial features, in which all instances possessing the

	extensional characterization (on the level of exemplars)	intensional characterization (on the level of definition)
non-equality (salience effects, core/periphery)	a) differences of typicality and membership salience	b) clustering into family resemblances
non-discreteness (demarcation problems, flexibility)	c) fuzziness at the edges, membership uncertainty	d) absence of necessary- and-sufficient definitions

Fig. 13.1: Prototype effects and their relations

criterial attributes have a full and equal degree of membership. In contrast, it has recently been argued ... that some natural categories are analog and must be represented logically in a manner which reflects their analog structure" (Rosch and Mervis 1975: 573–574).

Rosch's prototype results were introduced in linguistics in the early 1980s. In the course of the linguistic elaboration of the model, it became clear that prototypicality is itself, in the words of Posner (1986), a prototypical concept: the concept refers to various categorization phenomena that need not co-occur. The following four features in particular are important. First, prototypical categories exhibit degrees of typicality; not every member is equally representative for a category. Second, prototypical categories exhibit a family resemblance structure, or more generally, their semantic structure takes the form of a radial set of clustered and overlapping readings. Third, prototypical categories are blurred at the edges. Fourth, prototypical categories cannot be defined by means of a single set of criterial (necessary and sufficient) attributes.

These four features are systematically related along two dimensions. The first and the third characteristic take into account the referential, extensional structure of a category. In particular, they have a look at the members of a category; they observe that not all members of a category are equal in representativeness for that category, and that the referential boundaries of a category are not always determinate. These two aspects (non-equality and non-discreteness) recur on the intensional level, where the definitional rather than the referential structure of a category is envisaged: non-discreteness shows up in the fact that there is no single definition in terms of necessary and sufficient attributes for a prototypical concept, and the clustering of meanings that is typical of family resemblances and radial sets implies that not every reading is structurally equally important. The concept of prototypicality, in short, is itself a prototypically clustered one in which the concepts of non-discreteness and non-equality (either on the intensional or on the extensional level) play a major distinctive role. Non-discreteness involves the existence of demarcation problems and the flexible applicability of categories. Non-equality involves the fact that categories have internal structure: not all members or readings that fall within the boundaries of the category need have equal status, but some may be more central than others. Figure 13.1 schematically represents these relationships.

Going through Figure 13.1 in counter-clockwise fashion to illustrate the characteristics, we may have a look at the category *fruit*, which is also among the categories

	edible seed-bearing part	of wood-plant	juicy	sweet	used as dessert
apple	+	+	+	+	+
strawberry	+	−	+	+	+
banana	+	+	−	+	+
lemon	+	+	+	−	−

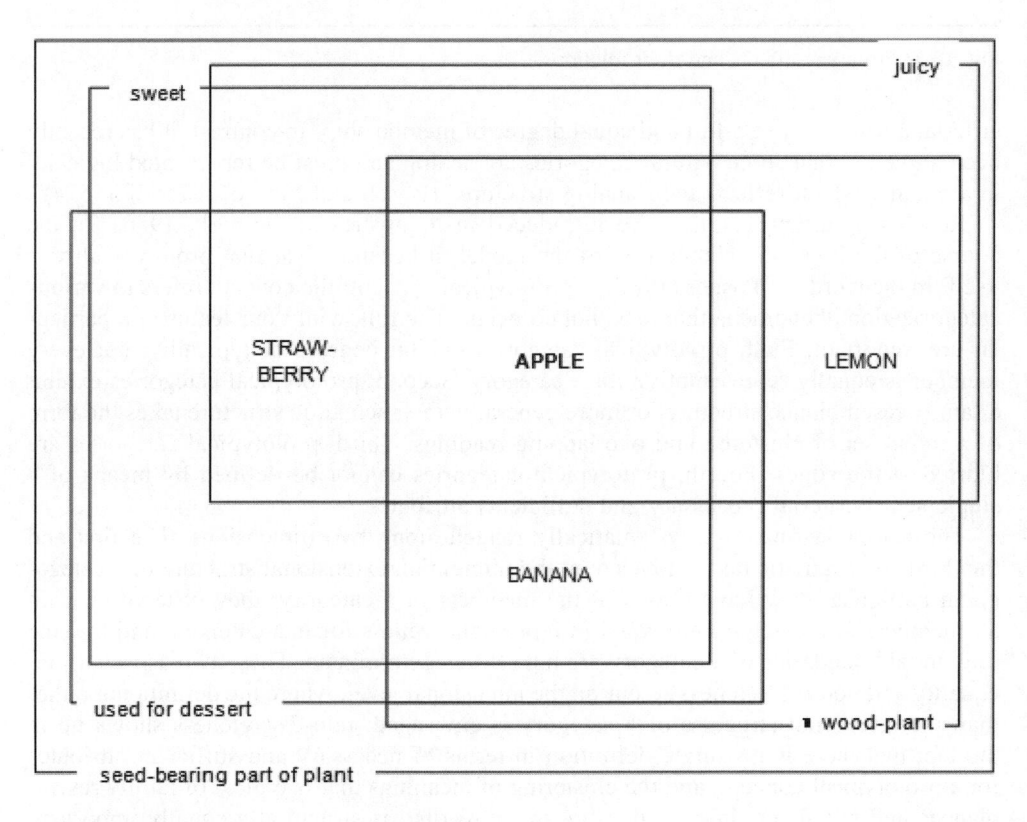

Fig. 13.2: The prototype structure of *fruit*

originally studied by Rosch. Her experimental results exemplify (a): for American subjects, oranges and apples and bananas are the most typical fruits, while watermelons and pomegranates receive lower typicality ratings. But is a coconut a fruit? We are not concerned here with the technical, biological reading of *fruit*, but with folk models of fruit as a certain category of edible things. Technically, any seed-containing part of a plant is the fruit of that plant; as such, nuts in general are fruit. In ordinary language, however, nuts and fruit are basically distinct categories: nuts are small, dry and hard, while fruits are typically somewhat bigger, soft, sweet, and juicy; also, the situations in which nuts and fruits are eaten are typically different. But coconuts are neither a typical nut nor a typical fruit, and so language users may hesitate how exactly to categorize coconuts – an indeterminacy about membership that establishes (c).

Intensionally, membership indeterminacy reflects on the definability of a category. If people hesitate about membership, evaluating the adequacy of a proposed definition may be difficult: should the definition cover coconuts or not? But even if we ignore the boundary problems and concentrate on bona fide cases of fruit, (d) emerges. A definition in a classical sense, in fact, would be one in which we can list a number of features that are shared by all fruits and that together distinguish fruits from other categories. The obvious candidates, however, do not apply to all fruit (not all fruits are sweet, they do not all grow on plants with a wooden structure, they are not all used for dessert …), and the ones that do are not collectively sufficient to distinguish fruit from nuts and vegetables. Assuming then that we cannot define the uncontroversial core members of *fruit* in a classical, necessary-and-sufficient fashion, we can appreciate the importance of (b). If *fruit* receives a classical definition in terms of necessary and sufficient attributes, all the definitional attributes have the same range of application (viz. the entire category). However, if such a classical definition cannot be given, the attributes that enter into the semantic description of *fruit* demarcate various subsets from within the entire range of application of *fruit*. The overall description of *fruit* then takes the form of a cluster of partially overlapping sets. Characteristics (d) and (b) are illustrated in Figure 13.2.

In the *fruit* example, all the relevant features of prototypicality are present, but as suggested before, that need not be the case for all categories. Armstrong et al. (1983), for instance, showed experimentally that even a mathematical concept like *odd number* exhibits representativity effects. This might seem remarkable, since *odd number* is a classical concept in all other respects: it receives a clear definition, does not take the form of a family resemblance or a radial set, does not have blurred edges. However, degrees of representativity among odd numbers are not surprising if the experiential nature of concepts is taken into account. For instance, because the even or uneven character of a large number can be determined easily by looking at the final digit, it is no wonder that uneven numbers below 10 carry more psychological weight: they are procedurally of primary importance. 'Odd number', then, is a peripheral case of prototypicality: it has one out of four features, whereas 'fruit' has all four.

1.1.2. Prototypicality in a polysemic context

The importance of family resemblance structures may be illustrated in yet another way, by looking at clusters of different senses rather than the structure of a single meaning. So far, we have been concerned only with the most common, everyday meaning of *fruit* (roughly, 'soft and sweet edible part of a tree or a bush'). There are other meanings to *fruit*, however. In its technical sense ('the seed-bearing part of a plant or tree'), the word also refers to things that lie outside the range of the basic reading, such as acorns and

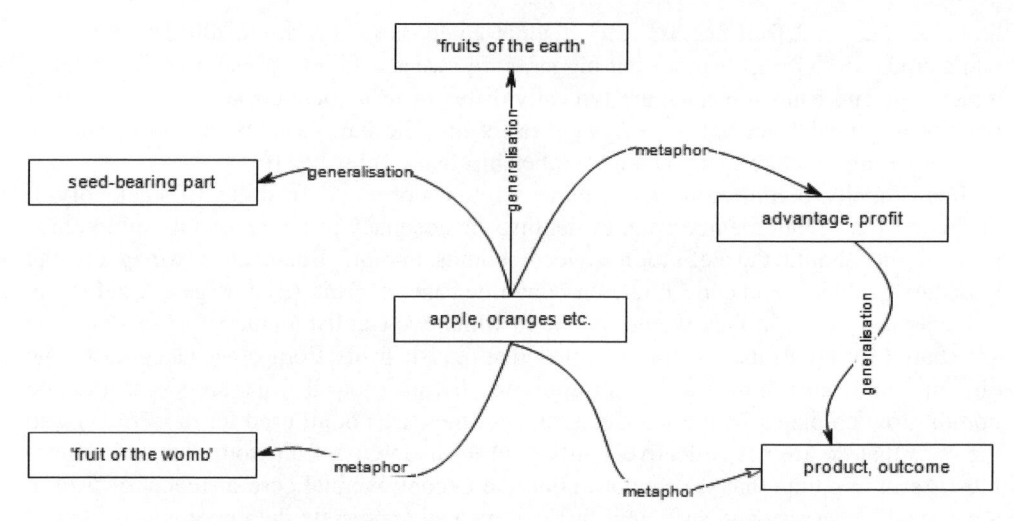

Fig. 13.3: The radial set structure of *fruit*

pea pods. In an expression like *the fruits of nature* the meaning is even more general, as the word refers to everything that grows and that can be eaten by people, including for instance grains and vegetables. Further, there is a range of figurative readings, including the abstract sense 'the result or outcome of an action' (*the fruits of his labour, his work bore fruit*), or the archaic reading 'offspring, progeny' (as in the biblical expressions *the fruit of the womb, the fruit of his loins*). Moreover, the 'result or outcome' sense often appears in a specialized form, as 'gain or profit'. These meanings do not exist in isolation, but they are related in various ways to the central sense and to each other. The technical reading ('seed-containing part') and the sense illustrated by *the fruits of nature* are both related to the central meaning by a process of generalisation. The technical reading generalizes over the biological function of the things covered by the central meaning, whereas the meaning 'everything that grows and that can be eaten by people' focuses on the function of those things for humans. The figurative uses in turn are linked to the others by metaphor. The overall picture, in short, is similar to that found within the single sense 'soft and sweet edible part of a tree or a bush': we find a cluster of mutually interrelated readings, concentrating round a core reading (the basic sense as analysed in the previous paragraph). Family resemblance effects, then, do not only apply *within* a single sense of a word like *fruit*, but also characterize the relationship *among* the various senses of a word.

A popular representational format for such prototype-based polysemous structure is the radial network model, first introduced by Brugman (1988, originally 1981) in her analysis of the English preposition *over*, and popularized through Lakoff's influential *Women, Fire, and Dangerous Things* (1987). In a radial network, senses are related to the prototype and to each other by means of individual links, possibly labelled with the appropriate semantic relation, as in Figure 13.3. Labelling of this type brings metonymy and metaphor into the picture: whereas all the examples of prototype-based category structure that we captured in Figure 13.2 involved relations of literal similarity, metaphor and metonymy need to be included in the description of polysemy.

But radial network representations as illustrated in Figure 13.3 have the disadvantage of representing the meanings as relatively isolated entities. The radial network representation suggests that the dynamism of a polysemous category primarily takes the form of individual extensions from one sense to another. This may hide from our view that the dimensions that shape the polysemous cluster may connect different senses at the same time. For a discussion and comparison of the various representational models of prototype effects, like radial sets in comparison to family resemblance models, see Lewandowska-Tomaszczyk (2007). More generally, the preposition *over*, with which Brugman introduced the radial network model, remained a rallying-point for discussions of semasiological structure in cognitive semantics, from Vandeloise (1990), over Cuyckens (1991), Geeraerts (1992), Dewell (1994), and Tyler and Evans (2003) to Deane (2005) – the list is not complete.

1.2. Flexibility and change: polysemy and contextual dynamics

Apart from representational questions, the transition from prototypicality within one meaning to salience effects among meanings raises a theoretical issue: is it acceptable to situate prototypicality both among senses and within senses (see Kleiber 1990)? Are the phenomena studied at the level of different senses really so theoretically similar to the phenomena studied at the level of a single sense, that they can be lumped together? One answer to this question could be purely practical. Even if it is not legitimate, in a theoretical sense, to equate the within-sense and the among-sense levels, the prototype-based phenomena that we discover on the level of polysemous clusters are worthy of description, and if a prototype model helps to describe them, so much the better. But a more principled answer is necessary too. It touches upon the possibility of systematically distinguishing between the within-sense and the among-sense levels: how stable is the distinction between the semantic level (that of senses) and the referential level (that of category members)? In other words, how stable is the distinction between polysemy and vagueness? This distinction involves the question whether a particular semantic specification is part of the stable semantic structure of the item, or is the result of a transient contextual specification. For instance, *neighbour* is not polysemous between the readings 'male dweller next door' and 'female dweller next door', in the sense that the utterance *my neighbour is a civil servant* will not be recognized as requiring disambiguation in the way that *this is rubbish* ('material waste' or 'worthless arguments and ideas'?) does. The semantic information associated with the item *neighbour* in the lexicon does not contain a specification regarding sex; *neighbour* is vague as to the dimension of sex.

Research in cognitive semantics suggests that the borderline between polysemy and vagueness (i.e. between variation at the levels of senses and variation at the level of membership within one sense) is not stable – and this, in turn, justifies the application of a prototype model to both levels. The synchronic instability of the borderline between the level of senses and the level of referents is discussed, among others, in Taylor (1992), Geeraerts (1993), Tuggy (1993). The common strategy of these articles is to show that different polysemy criteria (i.e. criteria that may be invoked to establish that a particular interpretation of a lexical item constitutes a separate sense rather than just being a case of vagueness or generality) may be mutually contradictory, or may each yield different results in different contexts.

To illustrate, let us consider one of various polysemy criteria that are discussed in the literature. So-called linguistic tests involve acceptability judgements about sentences that contain two related occurrences of the item under consideration (one of which may be implicit); if the grammatical relationship between both occurrences requires their semantic identity, the resulting sentence may be an indication for the polysemy of the item. For instance, the identity test described by Zwicky and Sadock (1975) involves 'identity-of-sense anaphora'. Thus, *at midnight the ship passed the port, and so did the bartender* is awkward if the two lexical meanings of *port* are at stake; disregarding puns, it can only mean that the ship and the bartender alike passed the harbour, or conversely that both moved a particular kind of wine from one place to another. A 'crossed' reading in which the first occurrence refers to the harbour, and the second to wine, is normally excluded. By contrast, the fact that the notions 'vintage sweet wine from Portugal' and 'blended sweet wine from Portugal' can be crossed in *Vintage Noval is a port, and so is blended Sandeman* indicates that *port* is vague rather than polysemous with regard to the distinction between blended and vintage wines. Similar arguments might involve coordination rather than anaphora. The case against a strict distinction between vagueness and polysemy then takes the form of showing that the test does not just rely on the words in question, but also on the specific context in which they are evaluated. For instance, Norrick (1981: 115) contrasted the odd sentence *Judy's dissertation is thought provoking and yellowed with age* with the perfectly natural construction *Judy's dissertation is still thought provoking though yellowed with age*. If the coordination generally requires that *dissertation* be used in the same sense with regard to both elements of the coordinated predicate, the sentences show that the distinction between the dissertation as a material product and its contents may or may not play a role: whether we need to postulate two senses or just one would seem to differ from one context to the other.

It now appears that the contextual flexibility of meaning, which is a natural component of a cognitive semantic conception of lexical semantics, may take radical forms: it does not just involve a context-driven choice between existing meanings, or the on-the-spot creation of new ones, but it blurs and dynamizes the very distinction between polysemy and vagueness. In the context of cognitive semantics, next to the papers already mentioned, discussions of the theoretical issues concerning prototypicality and polysemy include Wierzbicka (1985), Sweetser (1986, 1987), Geeraerts (1994), Cruse (1995), Schmid (2000), Janssen (2003), Taylor (2003a, 2006), Zlatev (2003), Allwood (2003), Riemer (2005), Evans (2006, 2009). These authors do not all take a radically maximalist approach, though: some pursue a more parsimonious position. The focus on the flexibility of language use has also sparked an interest in diachronic semantics. The prototype structure of semantic change in its various aspects is acknowledged and illustrated in one form or another in many studies, among them Dirven (1985), Dekeyser (1990), Casad (1992), Goossens (1992), Nerlich and Clarke (1992), Geeraerts (1997), Soares da Silva (1999, 2003), De Mulder and Vanderheyden (2001), Tissari (2003), Molina (2005). For a broader view of diachronic semantics in a cognitive context, see the collective volumes edited by Winters et al. Allan (2010) and Allan and Robinson (2011), and compare Hilpert (this volume).

2. Contributions to onomasiology

The contribution of Cognitive Linguistics to onomasiology is situated on two levels. On the first level, Cognitive Linguistics draws the attention to specific forms of onomasiological structure in the lexicon. On the second level, it introduces and develops the notion of salience in onomasiological research.

2.1. Structures in the lexicon: conceptual metaphor, conceptual metonymy, and frames

Structures in the lexicon above the level of the individual word are a traditional topic in lexicological research: structuralist theories (which dominated lexical semantics from roughly 1930 to 1970) focused on lexical fields or lexical relations like synonymy and antonymy, which link separate lexical items on the basis of their meaning. In the context of Cognitive Linguistics, the attention for supralexical structures in the lexicon focuses on three different types of structure: conceptual metaphor, conceptual metonymy, and frames. This does not imply, to be sure, that lexical relations are totally neglected, but they occupy a less central role than in structuralist approaches to the lexicon. Cognitive perspectives on lexical relations are explored in Cruse (1994) and Croft and Cruse (2004). More recently, the study of lexical relations is witnessing a renewal through the introduction of the experimental and corpus-based methods that will be discussed in section 3 below: see for instance Paradis, Willners and Jones (2009) for experimental approaches to antonymy, and Glynn (2010), Arppe (2008), Divjak (2010) for corpus-based approaches to synonymy.)

2.1.1. Conceptual metaphor

Metaphor constitutes a major area of investigation for Cognitive Semantics. The major impetus here came from Lakoff and Johnson's *Metaphors We Live By* (1980), a book that worked like an eye-opener for a new generation of linguists. In the linguistic climate of the 1970s, dominated by the formal framework of generative grammar, semantics seemed a peripheral issue, but *Metaphors We Live By*, more perhaps than the other foundational publications in Cognitive Semantics, was instrumental in putting semantics back on the research agenda. Conceptual Metaphor Theory, as introduced by Lakoff, includes two basic ideas: first, the view that metaphor is a cognitive phenomenon, rather than a purely lexical one; second, the view that metaphor should be analysed as a mapping between two domains. From an onomasiological point of view, the first feature is particularly important, because it now defines metaphor not primarily as a semasiological link between the sense of a single lexical item, but as a mechanism that pervades the lexicon (and, more broadly, non-linguistic systems of cognition and signification – but that lies beyond the scope of this chapter). In fact, metaphor seems to come in patterns that transcend the individual lexical item. A typical example is the following.

LOVE IS A JOURNEY
Look how *far* we've come. We are at a *crossroads*. We'll just have to go our separate *ways*. We cannot *turn back* now. We are *stuck*. This relationship is a *dead-end street*. I don't think this relationship is *going anywhere*. It's been a *long, bumpy road*. We have gotten *off the track*.

Groups of expressions such as these, tied together by a specific conceptual metaphor, constitute so to speak a metaphorical lexical field, an onomasiological structure of a type not envisaged by structuralist theorizing about onomasiological structures.

Metaphor studies within Cognitive Linguistics have developed explosively, specifically also if we take into account productive theoretical offshoots like the Conceptual Integration Theory developed by Fauconnier and Turner (2002; and see Turner, this volume). An indispensable handbook for metaphor research is Gibbs (2008), while Steen (2007) and Kövecses (2002) are excellent starting-points for getting acquainted with the literature. Edited volumes of specific interest include Paprotté and Dirven (1985), Ortony (1979, 1993), Gibbs and Steen (1999), Barcelona (2000), Dirven and Pörings (2002), Coulson and Lewandowska-Tomaszczyk (2005), Baicchi et al. (2005). Popular areas of application for metaphor theory (the domain is huge) include the study of emotion concepts (Kövecses 2000), literary and stylistic studies (Turner 1987; Lakoff and Turner 1989; Turner 1996), religious discourse (Feyaerts 2003), and cultural models (Kövecses 2005). For a more extensive treatment of relevant issues in metaphor studies, see Gibbs (this volume).

2.1.2. Conceptual metonymy

The emergence of Conceptual Metaphor Theory also led to a revival of the interest in metonymy. In Lakoff and Johnson (1980) already, metonymy figured next to metaphor as one of the conceptual mechanisms behind the semantic structure of language. That clearly should not come as a surprise: an approach that is interested in the semantic mechanisms behind language use and linguistic structures is likely to rediscover the traditional mechanisms of semantic extension. Lakoff and Johnson (1980: 38–39) list a number of metonymic patterns (like PART FOR WHOLE, LOCATION FOR LOCATED, or PRODUCER FOR PRODUCT) that might have been taken straightforwardly from a traditional pre-structuralist treatise on semantic change of the type that was dominant in lexical semantics before 1930. As in the case of conceptual metaphors, all expressions illustrating a particular metonymical pattern can be thought of as an onomasiological group.

Lakoff and Johnson emphasize that such metonymic patterns are conceptual and not purely linguistic, in much the same way that metaphorical concepts are. In the first place, metonymical concepts allow us to think of one thing in terms of its relation to something else. In that sense, we can distinguish a source and target in the description of metonymy just like we can for metaphors. In the second place, metonymies are systematic in the sense that they form patterns that apply to more than just an individual lexical item. In the third place, metonymic concepts structure not just the language, but also the language users' thoughts, attitudes and actions. From the late 1990s on (somewhat later than the rise in popularity of metaphor studies), the renewed interest in metonymy led to an upsurge of publications. Important collective volumes include Panther and Radden

(1999), Barcelona (2000), Dirven and Pörings (2002), Panther and Thornburg (2003), and Benczes et al. (2011). On the classification of metonymical patterns, see Peirsman and Geeraerts (2006).

Like conceptual metaphor studies, the interest in metonymy branches off in various directions. Without trying to be exhaustive (for more details on the scope of metonymy research in the framework of Cognitive Linguistics, see Barcelona, this volume), the following topics may be mentioned. First, a fair amount of attention is devoted to the mutual demarcation of metaphor and metonymy. Against the tradition in lexical semantics of defining the difference between both mechanisms in terms of similarity-based versus contiguity-based changes, a number of alternatives have been debated in Cognitive Linguistics: among other contributions, see Croft (1993), Peirsman and Geeraerts (2006), and Ruiz de Mendoza Ibáñez (2000). Second, Feyaerts (2000) and Panther (2005) explore the existence of metonymical hierarchies, in which more schematic and more specific metonymical patterns co-exist. Third, Paradis (2004) argues for a distinction between 'facets' and metonymy, building on Cruse (1995). Fourth, the function of metonymy in texts has not yet been studied as extensively as that of metaphors (for the latter, see Semino 2008), but see for instance Nunberg (1978) for pragmatic constraints on referential metonymy, Panther and Thornburg (1998, 2003) and Ruiz de Mendoza Ibáñez and Peña Cervel (2005) for the role of metonymy in inferences and speech acts, and Barcelona (2005) for an analysis of the functions of metonymies in discourse.

2.1.3. Frame semantics

The third type of onomasiological grouping that Cognitive Linguistics focuses on is the concept of frame as introduced by Charles Fillmore (Fillmore 1977, 1985; Fillmore and Atkins 1992, 1994, 2000). In contrast with metaphor and metonymy – traditional concepts that were part of linguistics long before the advent of Cognitive Linguistics – frame theory is an entirely original contribution to the field. Frame theory is specifically interested in the way in which language may be used to perspectivize an underlying conceptualization of the world: it's not just that we see the world in terms of conceptual models, but those models may be verbalized in different ways. Each different way of bringing a conceptual model to expression so to speak adds another layer of meaning: the models themselves are meaningful ways of thinking about the world, but the way we express the models while talking, adds perspective. This overall starting-point of Fillmorean frame theory leads to a description on two levels. On the one hand, a description of the referential situation or event consists of an identification of the relevant elements and entities and the conceptual role they play in the situation or event. On the other hand, the more purely linguistic part of the analysis indicates how certain expressions and grammatical patterns highlight aspects of that situation or event.

To illustrate, we may have a look at the standard example of frame theory, the COMMERCIAL TRANSACTION frame. The commercial transaction frame involves words like *buy* and *sell*. The commercial transaction frame can be characterised informally by a scenario in which one person gets control or possession of something from a second person, as a result of a mutual agreement through which the first person gives the second person a sum of money. Background knowledge involved in this scenario includes an understanding of ownership relations, a money economy, and commercial contracts. The categories that are needed for describing the lexical meanings of the verbs linked to the commercial transaction scene include Buyer, Seller, Goods and Money as basic categories. Verbs like *buy* and *sell* then each encode a certain perspective on the commercial transaction scene by highlighting specific elements of the scene. In the case of *buy*, for instance, the buyer appears as the subject of the sentence and the goods as the direct object; the seller and the money appear in prepositional phrases: *Paloma bought a book from Teresa for € 30*. In the case of *sell* on the other hand, it is the seller that appears as a subject: *Teresa sold a book to Paloma for € 30*.

In its further development, frame semantics was enriched, first, by the systematic use of corpus materials as the main source of empirical evidence for the frame-theoretical analyses, and second, the development of an electronic dictionary with frame-theoretical descriptions. These two developments go together in the Berkeley FrameNet project (Johnson et al. 2002; Ruppenhofer et al. 2006). The position of Fillmore's frame theory in comparison with structuralist field approaches is discussed in Post (1988) and Nerlich and Clarke (2000); more broadly, a comparison between different approaches to lexical structure (semantic fields, frames, prototypes, and lexical relations) is pursued in Lehrer and Kittay (1992), Lutzeier (1992). Examples of descriptive work in the frame approach include Dirven et al. (1982), Lawler (1989), Rojo and Valenzuela (1998), Martin (2001). The impact of the frame approach on applied lexicography may be measured in Atkins et al. (2003). Frame theory, incidentally, is not the only aspect of lexical semantics to have had an impact on lexicography: for the impact of prototype models on lexicography, see Geeraerts (1990, 2007) and Hanks (1994).

2.2. Onomasiological salience: basic levels, entrenchment, and sociolexicology

Possibly the major innovation of the prototype model of categorization is to give salience a place in the description of semasiological structure: next to the qualitative relations among the elements in a semasiological structure (like metaphor and metonymy), a quantifiable centre-periphery relationship is introduced as part of the architecture. But could the concept of salience not also be applied to the onomasiological domain?

The initial step in the introduction of onomasiological salience is the *basic level hypothesis*. The hypothesis is based on the ethno-linguistic observation that folk classifications of biological domains usually conform to a general organizational principle, in the sense that they consist of five or six taxonomical levels (Berlin et al. 1974; Berlin 1976, 1978). Figure 13.4 illustrates the idea with two sets of examples. The highest rank in the taxonomy is that of the 'unique beginner', which names a major domain like *plant* and *animal*. The domain of the unique beginner is subdivided by just a few general 'life forms', which are in turn specified by 'folk genera' like *pine, oak, beech, ash, elm, chestnut*. (The 'intermediate' level is an optional one.) A folk genus may be further specified by 'folk specifics' and 'varietal taxa'. To the extent that the generic level is the core of any folk biological taxonomy, it is the basic level: it is the most commonly used, everyday set of categories of folk biological knowledge. The generic level, in other words, is onomasiologically salient: given a particular referent, the most likely name for

	ethnobiological examples		clothing terms
kingdom	animal	plant	garment
life form	tree	fish	outer garment
intermediate	evergreen	freshwater fish	---
generic	pine	bass	trousers
specific	whitepine	black bass	ski pants
varietal	western whitepine	large-mouthed bass	stretch ski pants

Fig. 13.4: Taxonomical levels

that referent from among the alternatives provided by the taxonomy will be the name situated at the basic level.

As the basic level model was developed for the description of the folk classification of natural kinds; it is an open question to what extent it may be generalized to all kinds of taxonomies, like the taxonomical classification of artefacts. If we apply the basic level model to the lexical field of clothing terminology, items like *trousers*, *skirt*, *sweater*, *dress* are to be considered basic level categories: their overall frequency in actual language use is high, they are learned early in acquisition, and they typically have the mono-morphemic form of basic level categories. A further extrapolation yields the right-hand side of Figure 13.4, in which *garment* is considered a unique beginner in contrast with, say, *utensil* or *toy*.

Crucially, the basic level model contains a hypothesis about alternative categorizations of referents, i.e. it is a hypothesis about onomasiological salience: if a particular referent (a particular piece of clothing) can be alternatively categorized as a garment, a skirt, or a wrap-around skirt, the choice will be preferentially made for the basic level category 'skirt'. But differences of onomasiological preference also occur *among* categories on the same level in a taxonomical hierarchy. If a particular referent can be alternatively categorized as a wrap-around skirt or a miniskirt, there could just as well be a preferential choice: when you encounter something that is both a wrap-around skirt and a miniskirt, the most natural way of naming that referent in a neutral context would probably be 'miniskirt'. If, then, we have to reckon with intra-level differences of salience next to inter-level differences, the concept of onomasiological salience has to be generalized in such a way that it relates to individual categories at any level of the hierarchy (or what is left of it when all forms of hierarchical fuzziness are taken into account). Terminologically, this concept of *generalized onomasiological salience* can be seen as a specification of the notion of *entrenchment*, introduced by Langacker (1987: 59–60) in connection with the process of unit formation: a particular linguistic construct (such as a new compound, or the use of a word in a new reading) may gradually transcend its initial incidental status by being used more often, until it is so firmly entrenched in the grammar or the lexicon that it has become a regular well-established unit of the linguistic system. (Basic levels, entrenchment and salience in linguistics are discussed in Geeraerts (2000) and Schmid (2007); see also Divjak and Caldwell-Harris, this volume.)

The concept of generalized onomasiological entrenchment was studied and further developed in Geeraerts et al. (1994). Using corpus materials, this study established that the choice for one lexical item rather than the other as the name for a given referent is determined by the semasiological salience of the referent (i.e. the degree of prototypicality of the referent with regard to the semasiological structure of the category), by the onomasiological entrenchment of the category represented by the expression, and by contextual features of a classical sociolinguistic and geographical nature, involving the competition between different language varieties. By zooming in on the latter type of factor, a further refinement of the notion of onomasiological salience is introduced, in the form of the distinction between *conceptual* and *formal* onomasiological variation. Whereas conceptual onomasiological variation involves the choice of different conceptual categories for a referent (like the examples presented so far), formal onomasiological variation merely involves the use of different names for the same conceptual category. The names *jeans* and *trousers* for denim leisure wear trousers constitute an instance of conceptual variation, for they represent categories at different taxonomical levels. *Jeans* and *denims*, however, represent no more than different (but synonymous) names for the same denotational category. The addition of 'denotational' is not without importance here, because the assumption is not that the words are equivalent in *all* respects. They may have different stylistic values (which will show up in their distribution over different types of text), or they may belong to different lects (dialects, regiolects, sociolects, national varieties – whatever variety of a sociolinguistic nature that might be relevant).

The latter observation may be generalized: all forms of lexical variation considered so far may be subject to contextual, 'lectal' variation. Different dialects may use words in different meanings (semasiological variation). Experts are more likely to use specific, technical terms than laymen (conceptual onomasiological variation). And denotationally synonymous expressions may have different sociolinguistic distributions (formal onomasiological variation). This recognition then leads to an upsurge of socio-lexicological studies, as a practical consequence of the idea that all aspects of lexical variation (the semasiological, the conceptual onomasiological, and the formal onomasiological) are sensitive to lectal variation, and therefore require to be studied from a sociolinguistic point of view. Sample studies include Robinson (2010) for semasiological variation, Szelid and Geeraerts (2008) for conceptual onomasiological variation, and for formal onomasiological variation, the socio-lectometrical studies in which the distribution of denotational synonyms over language varieties is used as a measure of the distance between language varieties: see Speelman et al. (2003), Soares da Silva (2005), Zenner et al. (2012). More generally, the development of sociolexicological studies in Cognitive Linguistics is an element of a broader tendency towards variationist studies, often referred to as Cognitive Sociolinguistics: see Geeraerts and Kristiansen (this volume).

3. Current developments

The foregoing pages have highlighted the theoretical and descriptive contributions of Cognitive Linguistics to lexical semantics, either as a revival of traditional topics (the renewed interest in metaphor and metonymy as cognitive mechanisms), or as foundational innovations (the incorporation of salience effects in semasiological and onomasiological structure, and the recognition of the contextual instability of the distinction between polysemy and vagueness). Continuing these theoretical and descriptive lines of research, current developments in Cognitive Linguistic lexical semantics seem to be primarily of a methodological nature. Two trends may be mentioned.

First, a number of researchers enrich and support their linguistic analyses with data derived from psycho-experimental and neurobiological studies. This trend is perhaps most outspoken in metaphor studies, where a belief in the embodiment of metaphorical thinking leads to an active interest in psychological and neurophysiological evidence; see Gibbs (this volume) and Bergen (this volume). In the context of the developments sketched in the previous pages, this turn towards psycho-experimental and neurobiological data diminishes the gap between the psychological and the linguistic study of meaning and the lexicon. In fact, in spite of the psycholinguistic origins of linguistic prototype studies in the work of Rosch (see above), linguistics and psychology went remarkably separate ways in their development of that common starting-point. In contrast with the linguistic studies mentioned above, psychologically oriented prototype-based studies do not as a rule go beyond prototype effects in monosemic concepts, and at the same, they focus more than the linguistic studies on the formal modelling of the effects (see Murphy 2002 for an overview of the psychological developments, and compare Geeraerts 2010: 240–249 for a more extended discussion of the relationship between psychological and linguistic approaches in lexical semantics). A methodological rapprochement of the kind mentioned here will help to narrow the divide.

Second, we witness an increased emphasis on quantitative corpus analysis, specifically in the form of so-called distributional approaches that model meaning on the basis of the corpus contexts that a given word or expression occurs in: see Gries (this volume), and compare Geeraerts (2010: 165–178, 263–266) for a positioning of this trend in the history of lexical semantics. Such a corpus-based approach is attractive for any theoretical framework in lexical semantics, for the basic reason that it provides an unparalleled empirical basis for lexical research. The wealth of data contained in the corpora – regardless from what perspective they are analysed – will simply benefit any research endeavour in lexical semantics, Cognitive Linguistics no less so than other approaches. But more specifically and more importantly, there is a certain theoretical affinity between Cognitive Linguistics and the distributional analysis of corpus data, an affinity that rests on at least the following two features. First, both approaches are explicitly usage-based ones. In fact, it is difficult to see how Cognitive Linguistics can live up to its self-declared nature as a usage-based model if it does not start from actual usage data and a methodology that is suited to deal with such data. And second, the quantitative elaboration of a distributional corpus analysis provides a formal perspective on semantic data that is specifically congenial to Cognitive Linguistics. Quite a number of the phenomena that Cognitive Linguistics is interested in – fuzzy boundaries, graded category membership, differences of structural weight, onomasiological salience – are characteristics that are not optimally described by the discrete, all-or-none categories of classical linguistic formalization, but that require a quantitative perspective.

Both methodological developments mentioned here are emerging trends: in neither case have they reached a stable state – but that merely means that they testify to the continued dynamism of lexical semantics in the framework of Cognitive Linguistics.

4. References

Aitchison, Jean
   1987   *Words in the Mind. An Introduction to the Mental Lexicon.* Oxford: Blackwell.
Aitchison, Jean
   2003   *Words in the Mind. An Introduction to the Mental Lexicon.* 3rd edition. Oxford: Blackwell.
Allan, Kathryn and Justyna A. Robinson (eds.)
   2011   *Current Methods in Historical Semantics.* Berlin/New York: Mouton de Gruyter.
Allwood, Jens
   2003   Meaning potentials and context: Some consequences for the analysis of variation in meaning. In: H. Cuyckens, R. Dirven and J. Taylor (eds.), *Cognitive Linguistic Approaches to Lexical Semantics*, 29–66. Berlin: Mouton de Gruyter.
Armstrong, Sharon L., Lila R. Gleitman and Henry Gleitman
   1983   What some concepts might not be. *Cognition* 13: 263–308.
Arppe, Antti
   2008   *Univariate, Bivariate, and Multivariate Methods in Corpus-Based Lexicography. A study of synonymy.* PhD dissertation, University of Helsinki.
Atkins, B. T. Sue, Michael Rundell and Hiroaki Sato
   2003   The contribution of FrameNet to practical lexicography. *International Journal of Lexicography* 16: 333–357.
Baicchi, Annalisa, Cristiano Broccias and Andrea Sansò (eds.)
   2005   *Modelling Thought and Constructing Meaning. Cognitive Models in Interactions.* Milan: FrancoAngeli.
Barcelona, Antonio (ed.)
   2000   *Metaphor and Metonymy at the Crossroads: A Cognitive Perspective.* Berlin: Mouton de Gruyter.
Barcelona, Antonio
   2005   The multilevel operation of metonymy in grammar and discourse, with particular attention to metonymic chains. In: F. Ruiz de Mendoza Ibañez and S. Peña Cervel (eds.), *Cognitive Linguistics: Internal Dynamics and Interdisciplinary Interaction*, 313–352. Berlin: Mouton de Gruyter.
Barcelona, Antonio
   this volume   Metonymy. Berlin/Boston: De Gruyter Mouton.
Benczes, Réka, Antonio Barcelona and Francisco Ruiz de Mendoza Ibáñez (eds.)
   2011   *Defining Metonymy in Cognitive Linguistics: Towards a Consensus View.* Amsterdam: John Benjamins Publishing Company.
Bergen, Benjamin K.
   this volume   Embodiment.
Berlin, Brent
   1976   The concept of rank in ethnobiological classification: Some evidence from Aguarana folk botany. *American Ethnologist* 3: 381–400.
Berlin, Brent
   1978   Ethnobiological classification. In: E. Rosch and B. B. Lloyd (eds.), *Cognition and Categorization*, 9–26. Hillsdale: Lawrence Erlbaum Associates.
Berlin, Brent, Dennis E. Breedlove and Peter H. Raven
   1974   *Principles of Tzeltal Plant Classification: An Introduction to the Botanical Ethnography of a Mayan-speaking People of Highland Chiapas.* New York: Academic Press.
Berlin, Brent and Paul Kay
   1969   *Basic Color Terms: Their Universality and Evolution.* Berkeley: University of California Press.

Brugman, Claudia
  1988 *The Story of 'Over': Polysemy, Semantics and the Structure of the Lexicon*. New York: Garland.
Casad, Eugene H.
  1992 Cognition, history and Cora 'yee'. *Cognitive Linguistics* 3: 151–186.
Coulson, Seana and Barbara Lewandowska-Tomaszczyk (eds.)
  2005 *The Literal and Nonliteral in Language and Thought*. Frankfurt: Peter Lang.
Craig, Colette (ed.)
  1986 *Noun Classes and Categorization*. Amsterdam: John Benjamins Publishing Company.
Croft, William
  1993 The role of domains in the interpretation of metaphors and metonymies. *Cognitive Linguistics* 4: 335–370.
Croft, William and D. Alan Cruse
  2004 *Cognitive Linguistics*. Cambridge: Cambridge University Press.
Cruse, D. Alan
  1994 Prototype theory and lexical relations. *Rivista di Linguistica* 6: 167–188.
Cruse, D. Alan
  1995 Between polysemy and monosemy. In: H. Kardela and G. Persson (eds.), *New Trends in Semantics and Lexicography*, 25–34. Umeå: Swedish Science Press.
Cruse, D. Alan
  1995 Polysemy and related phenomena from a cognitive linguistic viewpoint. In: P. Saint-Dizier and E. Viegas (eds.), *Computational Lexical Semantics*, 33–49. Cambridge: Cambridge University Press.
Cuyckens, Hubert
  1991 *The Semantics of Spatial Prepositions in Dutch: A Cognitive Linguistics Exercise*. Ph.D. dissertation, University of Antwerp.
De Mulder, Walter and Anne Vanderheyden
  2001 L'histoire de centre et la sémantique prototypique. *Langue Française* 130: 108–125.
Deane, Paul D.
  2005 Multiple spatial representation: On the semantic unity of 'over'. In: B. Hampe (ed.), *From Perception to Meaning: Image Schemas in Cognitive Linguistics*, 235–282. Berlin: Mouton de Gruyter.
Dekeyser, Xavier
  1990 The prepositions 'with', 'mid' and 'again(st)' in Old and Middle English: A case study of historical lexical semantics. *Belgian Journal of Linguistics* 5: 35–48.
Dewell, Robert B.
  1994 'Over' again: On the role of image-schemas in semantic analysis. *Cognitive Linguistics* 5: 351–380.
Dirven, René
  1985 Metaphor as a basic means for extending the lexicon. In: W. Paprotté and R. Dirven (eds.), *The Ubiquity of Metaphor. Metaphor in Language and Thought*, 85–120. Amsterdam: John Benjamins.
Dirven, René, Louis Goossens, Yvan Putseys and Emma Vorlat
  1982 *The Scene of Linguistic Action and Its Perspectivization by 'Speak', 'Talk', 'Say' and 'Tell'*. Amsterdam: John Benjamins.
Dirven, René and Ralf Pörings (eds.)
  2002 *Metaphor and Metonymy in Comparison and Contrast*. Berlin: Mouton de Gruyter.
Divjak, Dagmar
  2010 *Structuring the Lexicon: A Clustered Model for Near-Synonymy*. Berlin: Mouton de Gruyter.
Divjak, Dagmar and Catherine Caldwell-Harris
  this volume Frequency and entrenchment.

Evans, Vyvyan
   2006   Lexical concepts, cognitive models and meaning-construction. *Cognitive Linguistics* 17: 491–534.
Evans, Vyvyan
   2009   *How Words Mean: Lexical Concepts, Cognitive Models, and Meaning Construction.* Oxford: Oxford University Press.
Fauconnier, Gilles and Mark Turner
   2002   *The Way We Think: Conceptual Blending and the Mind's Hidden Complexities.* New York: Basic Books.
Feyaerts, Kurt
   2000   Refining the Inheritance Hypothesis: Interaction between metaphorical and metonymic hierarchies. In: A. Barcelona (ed.), *Metaphor and Metonymy at the Crossroads: A Cognitive Perspective*, 59–78. Berlin: Mouton de Gruyter.
Feyaerts, Kurt (ed.)
   2003   *The Bible through Metaphor and Translation: A Cognitive Semantic Perspective.* Bern: Peter Lang.
Fillmore, Charles J.
   1977   Scenes-and-frames semantics. In: A. Zampolli (ed.), *Linguistic Structures Processing*, 55–81. Amsterdam: North-Holland Publishing Company.
Fillmore, Charles J.
   1985   Frames and the semantics of understanding. *Quaderni di Semantica* 6: 222–254.
Fillmore, Charles J. and B.T. Sue Atkins
   1992   Toward a frame-based lexicon: The semantics of 'risk' and its neighbors. In: A. Lehrer and E. Feder Kittay (eds.), *Frames, Fields and Contrasts. New Essays in Semantic and Lexical Organization*, 75–102. Hillsdale: Lawrence Erlbaum Associates.
Fillmore, Charles J. and B. T. Sue Atkins
   1994   Starting where dictionaries stop: The challenge of corpus lexicography. In: B.T. S. Atkins and A. Zampolli (eds.), *Computational Approaches to the Lexicon*, 349–393. Oxford: Oxford University Press.
Fillmore, Charles J. and B. T. Sue Atkins
   2000   Describing polysemy: The case of 'crawl'. In: Y. Ravin and C. Leacock (eds.), *Polysemy: Theoretical and Computational Approaches*, 91–110. Oxford: Oxford University Press.
Geeraerts, Dirk
   1985   *Paradigm and Paradox: Explorations into a Paradigmatic Theory of Meaning and its Epistemological Background.* Leuven: Leuven University Press.
Geeraerts, Dirk
   1990   The lexicographical treatment of prototypical polysemy. In: S. L. Tsohatzidis (ed.), *Meanings and Prototypes: Studies in Linguistic Categorization*, 195–210. London: Routledge. (Also in Geeraerts 2006, Words and Other Wonders 327–344.)
Geeraerts, Dirk
   1992   The semantic structure of Dutch 'over'. *Leuvense Bijdragen: Leuven Contributions in Linguistics and Philology* 81: 205–230. (Also in Geeraerts 2006, Words and Other Wonders 48–73.)
Geeraerts, Dirk
   1993   Vagueness's puzzles, polysemy's vagaries. *Cognitive Linguistics* 4: 223–272. (Also in Geeraerts 2006, Words and Other Wonders 99–148.)
Geeraerts, Dirk
   1994   Classical definability and the monosemic bias. *Rivista di Linguistica* 6: 189–207. (Also in Geeraerts 2006, Words and Other Wonders 149–172.)

Geeraerts, Dirk
  1997 *Diachronic Prototype Semantics: A Contribution to Historical Lexicology.* Oxford: Clarendon Press.
Geeraerts, Dirk
  2000 Salience phenomena in the lexicon: A typology. In: L. Albertazzi (ed.), *Meaning and Cognition*, 79–101. Amsterdam: John Benjamins. (Also in Geeraerts 2006, Words and Other Wonders 74–96.)
Geeraerts, Dirk
  2007 Lexicography. In: D. Geeraerts and H. Cuyckens (eds.), *The Oxford Handbook of Cognitive Linguistics*, 1160–1175. New York: Oxford University Press.
Geeraerts, Dirk
  2010 *Theories of Lexical Semantics.* Oxford: Oxford University Press.
Geeraerts, Dirk and Gitte Kristiansen
  this volume Variationist linguistics.
Geeraerts, Dirk, Stefan Grondelaers and Peter Bakema
  1994 *The Structure of Lexical Variation: Meaning, Naming, and Context.* Berlin: Mouton de Gruyter.
Gibbs, Raymond W. (ed.)
  2008 *The Cambridge Handbook of Metaphor and Thought.* Cambridge: Cambridge University Press.
Gibbs, Raymond W. Jr. and Gerard J. Steen (eds.)
  1999 *Metaphor in Cognitive Linguistics.* Amsterdam: John Benjamins.
Gibbs, Raymond W. Jr.
  this volume Metaphor.
Glynn, Dylan
  2010 Testing the hypothesis. Objectivity and verification in usage-based Cognitive Semantics. In: D. Glynn and K. Fischer (eds.), *Quantitative Methods in Cognitive Semantics: Corpus-Driven Approaches*, 239–269. Berlin: Mouton de Gruyter.
Gries, Stefan Th.
  this volume Polysemy. Berlin/Boston: De Gruyter Mouton.
Hanks, Patrick W.
  1994 Linguistic norms and pragmatic exploitations, or why lexicographers need prototype theory and vice versa. In: F. Kiefer, G. Kiss and J. Pajzs (eds.), *Papers in Computational Lexicography*, 89–113. Budapest: Hungarian Academy of Sciences.
Hilpert, Martin
  this volume Historical linguistics.
Janssen, Theo
  2003 Monosemy versus polysemy. In: H. Cuyckens, R. Dirven and J. Taylor (eds.), *Cognitive Approaches to Lexical Semantics*, 93–122. Berlin/New York: Mouton de Gruyter.
Johnson, Christopher R., Charles J. Fillmore, Esther J. Wood, Josef Ruppenhofer, Margaret Urban, Miriam R. L. Petruck and Collin F. Baker
  2002 *FrameNet: Theory and Practice.* Berkeley: International Computer Science Institute.
Kempton, Willett
  1981 *The Folk Classification of Ceramics: A Study in Cognitive Prototypes.* New York: Academic Press.
Kleiber, Georges
  1990 *La sémantique du prototype. Catégories et sens lexical.* Paris: Presses Universitaires de France.
Kövecses, Zoltán
  2000 *Metaphor and Emotion: Language, Culture and Body in Human Feeling.* Cambridge: Cambridge University Press

Kövecses, Zoltán
 2002 *Metaphor: A Practical Introduction.* Oxford: Oxford University Press.
Kövecses, Zoltán
 2005 *Metaphor in Culture: Universality and Variation.* Oxford: Oxford Uiversity Press.
Lakoff, George
 1987 *Women, Fire and Dangerous Things: What Categories Reveal about the Mind.* Chicago: University of Chicago Press.
Lakoff, George and Mark Johnson
 1980 *Metaphors We Live by.* Chicago: University of Chicago Press.
Langacker, Ronald W.
 1987 *Foundations of Cognitive Grammar,* Volume 1: *Theoretical Prerequisites.* Stanford: Stanford University Press.
Lawler, John M.
 1989 Lexical semantics in the commercial transaction frame: Value, worth, cost and price. *Studies in Language* 13: 381–404.
Lehrer, Adrienne and Eva Feder Kittay (eds.)
 1992 *Frames, Fields, and Contrasts: New Essays in Semantic and Lexical Organization.* Hillsdale: Lawrence Erlbaum Associates.
Lewandowka-Tomaszczyk, Barbara
 2007 Polysemy, prototyes, and radial categories. In: D. Geeraerts and H. Cuyckens (eds.), *The Oxford Handbook of Cognitive Linguistics,* 139–169. New York: Oxford University Press.
Lutzeier, Peter Rolf
 1992 Wortfeldtheorie und kognitive Linguistik. *Deutsche Sprache* 20: 62–81.
Mangasser-Wahl, Martina
 2000 *Von der Prototypentheorie zur empirischen Semantik.* Frankfurt: Peter Lang.
Martin, Willy
 2001 A frame-based approach to polysemy. In: H. Cuyckens and B. Zawada (eds.), *Polysemy in Cognitive Linguistics,* 57–81. Amsterdam: John Benjamins.
Molina, Clara
 2005 On the role of onomasiological profiles in merger discontinuations. In: N. Delbecque, J. Van der Auwera and D. Geeraerts (eds.), *Perspectives on Variation: Sociolinguistic, Historical, Comparative,* 177–194. Berlin: Mouton de Gruyter.
Murphy, Gregory L.
 2002 *The Big Book of Concepts.* Cambridge: MIT Press.
Nerlich, Brigitte and David D. Clarke
 1992 Outline of a model for semantic change. In: G. Kellermann and M. D. Morrissey (eds.), *Diachrony within Synchrony: Language History and Cognition,* 125–141. Frankfurt: Peter Lang.
Nerlich, Brigitte and David D. Clarke
 2000 Semantic fields and frames: Historical explorations of the interface between language, action and cognition. *Journal of Pragmatics* 32: 125–150.
Norrick, Neal R.
 1981 *Semiotic Principles in Semantic Theory.* Amsterdam: John Benjamins.
Nunberg, Geoffrey
 1978 *The Pragmatics of Reference.* Bloomington: Indiana University Linguistics Club.
Ortony, Andrew (ed.)
 1979 *Metaphor and Thought.* Cambridge: Cambridge University Press.
Ortony, Andrew (ed.)
 1993 *Metaphor and Thought.* 2nd edition. Cambridge: Cambridge University Press.

Panther, Klaus-Uwe
  2005   The role of conceptual metonymy in meaning construction. In: F. Ruiz de Mendoza Ibañez and S. Peña Cervel (eds.), *Cognitive Linguistics: Internal Dynamics and Interdisciplinary Interaction*, 353–386. Berlin: Mouton de Gruyter.
Panther, Klaus-Uwe and Günter Radden (eds.)
  1999   *Metonymy in Language and Thought*. Amsterdam: John Benjamins Publishing Company.
Panther, Klaus-Uwe and Linda Thornburg
  1998   A cognitive approach to inferencing in conversation. *Journal of Pragmatics* 30: 755–769.
Panther, Klaus-Uwe and Linda Thornburg (eds.)
  2003   *Metonymy and Pragmatic Inferencing*. Amsterdam: John Benjamins.
Paprotté, Wolf and René Dirven (eds.)
  1985   *The Ubiquity of Metaphor: Metaphor in Language and Thought*. Amsterdam: John Benjamins.
Paradis, Carita
  2004   Where does metonymy stop? Senses, facets, and active zones. *Metaphor and Symbol* 19: 245–264.
Paradis, Carita, Caroline Willners and Steven Jones
  2009   Good and bad opposites: Using textual and experimental techniques to measure antonym canonicity. *The Mental Lexicon* 4: 380–429.
Peirsman, Yves and Dirk Geeraerts
  2006   Metonymy as a prototypical category. *Cognitive Linguistics* 17: 269–316.
Posner, Michael
  1986   Empirical studies of prototypes. In: C. Craig (ed.), *Noun Classes and Categorization*, 53–61. Amsterdam: John Benjamins.
Post, Michael
  1988   Scenes-and-frames semantics as a neo-lexical field theory. In: W. Hüllen and R. Schulze (eds.), *Understanding the Lexicon. Meaning, Sense and World Knowledge in Lexical Semantics*, 36–47. Tübingen: Max Niemeyer Verlag.
Riemer, Nick
  2005   *The Semantics of Polysemy. Reading Meaning in English and Warlpiri*. Berlin: Mouton de Gruyter.
Robinson, Justyna A.
  2010   Awesome insights into semantic variation. In: D. Geeraerts, G. Kristiansen and Y. Peirsman (eds.), *Advances in Cognitive Sociolinguistics*, 85–110. Berlin/New York: Mouton de Gruyter.
Rojo, Ana and Javier Valenzuela
  1998   Frame semantics and lexical translation. *Babel* 44: 128–138.
Rosch, Eleanor
  1977   Human categorization. In: N. Warren (ed.), *Studies in Cross-cultural Psychology*, 1–49. New York: Academic Press.
Rosch, Eleanor and Carolyn B. Mervis
  1975   Family resemblances: Studies in the internal structure of categories. *Cognitive Psychology* 7: 573–605.
Rudzka-Ostyn, Brygida (ed.)
  1988   *Topics in Cognitive Linguistics*. Amsterdam: John Benjamins.
Ruiz de Mendoza Ibáñez, Francisco
  2000   The role of mappings and domains in understanding metonymy. In: A. Barcelona (ed.), *Metaphor and Metonymy at the Crossroads. A Cognitive Perspective*, 109–132. Berlin: Mouton de Gruyter.

Ruiz de Mendoza Ibáñez, Francisco and Sandra Peña Cervel
    2005   Conceptual interaction, cognitive operations and projection spaces. In: F. Ruiz de Mendoza Ibañez and S. Peña Cervel (eds.), *Cognitive Linguistics: Internal Dynamics and Interdisciplinary Interaction*, 249−279. Berlin: Mouton de Gruyter.

Ruppenhofer, Josef, Michael Ellsworth, Miriam R. L. Petruck, Christopher R. Johnson and Jan Scheffczyk
    2006   *FrameNet II*: *Extended Theory and Practice*. Berkeley: FrameNet.

Schmid, Hans-Jörg
    1993   *Cottage und Co., idea, start vs. begin. Die Kategorisierung als Grundprinzip einer differenzierten Bedeutungsbeschreibung*. Tübingen: Max Niemeyer Verlag.

Schmid, Hans-Jörg
    2000   *English Abstract Nouns as Conceptual Shells: From Corpus to Cognition*. Berlin: Mouton de Gruyter.

Schmid, Hans-Jörg
    2007   Entrenchment, salience, and basic levels. In: D. Geeraerts and H. Cuyckens (eds.), *The Oxford Handbook of Cognitive Linguistics*, 117−138. New York: Oxford University Press.

Semino, Elena
    2008   *Metaphor in Discourse*. Cambridge: Cambridge University Press.

Soares da Silva, Augusto
    1999   *A Semântica de 'deixar'. Uma Contribuição para a Abordagem Cognitiva em Semântica Lexical*. Lisboa: Fundação Calouste Gulbenkian.

Soares da Silva, Augusto
    2003   Image schemas and category coherence: The case of the Portuguese verb 'deixar'. In: H. Cuyckens, R. Dirven and J. Taylor (eds.), *Cognitive Approaches to Lexical Semantics*, 281−322. Berlin: Mouton de Gruyter.

Soares da Silva, Augusto
    2005   Para o estudo das relações lexicais entre o Português Europeu e o Português do Brasil: Elementos de sociolexicologia cognitiva e quantitativa do Português. In: I. Duarte and I. Leiria (eds.), *Actas do XX Encontro Nacional da Associação Portuguesa de Linguística*, 211−226. Lisboa: Associação Portuguesa de Linguística.

Speelman, Dirk, Stefan Grondelaers and Dirk Geeraerts
    2003   Profile-based linguistic uniformity as a generic method for comparing language varieties. *Computers and the Humanities* 37: 317−337.

Steen, Gerard J.
    2007   *Finding Metaphor in Grammar and Usage: A Methodological Analysis of Theory and Research*. Amsterdam: John Benjamins Publishing Company.

Sweetser, Eve E.
    1986   Polysemy vs. abstraction: Mutually exclusive or complementary? In V. Nikiforidou, M. Van Clay, M. Niepokuj and D. Feder (eds.), *Proceedings of the Twelfth Annual Meeting of the Berkeley Linguistics Society*, 528−538. Berkeley: Berkeley Linguistics Society.

Sweetser, Eve E.
    1987   The definition of 'lie': An examination of the folk models underlying a semantic prototype. In: D. Holland and N. Quinn (eds.), *Cultural Models in Language and Thought*, 43−66. Cambridge: Cambridge University Press.

Sweetser, Eve E.
    1990   *From Etymology to Pragmatics: Metaphorical and Cultural Aspects of Semantic Structure*. Cambridge: Cambridge University Press.

Szelid, Veronika and Dirk Geeraerts
    2008   Usage-based dialectology: Emotion concepts in the Southern Csango dialect. *Annual Review of Cognitive Linguistics* 6: 23−49.

Taylor, John R.
  1989   *Linguistic Categorization: Prototypes in Linguistic Theory.* Oxford: Clarendon Press.
Taylor, John R.
  1992   How many meanings does a word have? *Stellenbosch Papers in Linguistics* 25: 133–168.
Taylor, John R.
  2003a   Cognitive models of polysemy. In: B. Nerlich, Z. Todd, V. Herman and D. D. Clarke (eds.), *Polysemy: Flexible Patterns of Meaning in Mind and Language*, 31–47. Berlin: Mouton de Gruyter.
Taylor, John R.
  2003b   *Linguistic Categorization.* 3rd edition. Oxford: Oxford University Press.
Taylor, John R.
  2006   Polysemy and the lexicon. In: G. Kristiansen, M. Achard, R. Dirven and F. Ruiz de Mendoza Ibañez (eds.), *Cognitive Linguistics: Current Applications and Future Perspectives*, 51–80. Berlin: Mouton de Gruyter.
Tissari, Heli
  2003   *LOVEscapes. Changes in Prototypical Senses and Cognitive Metaphors since 1500.* Helsinki: Société Néophilologique de Helsinki.
Tsohatzidis, Savas L. (ed.)
  1989   *Meanings and Prototypes: Studies in Linguistic Categorization.* London: Routledge.
Tuggy, David
  1993   Ambiguity, polysemy, and vagueness. *Cognitive Linguistics* 4: 273–290.
Turner, Mark
  1987   *Death is the Mother of Beauty: Mind, Metaphor, Criticism.* Chicago: University of Chicago Press.
Turner, Mark
  1996   *The Literary Mind: The Origins of Thought and Language.* New York: Oxford University Press.
Turner, Mark
  this volume   Blending.
Tyler, Andrea and Vyvyan Evans
  2003   *The Semantics of English Prepositions: Spatial Scenes, Embodied Meaning and Cognition.* Cambridge: Cambridge University Press.
Vandeloise, Claude
  1990   Representation, prototypes, and centrality. In: S. L. Tsohatzidis (ed.), *Meanings and Prototypes: Studies in Linguistic Categorization*, 403–437. London: Routledge.
Wierzbicka, Anna
  1985   *Lexicography and Conceptual Analysis.* Ann Arbor: Karoma.
Winters, Margaret E., Heli Tissari and Kathryn Allan (eds.)
  2010   *Historical Cognitive Linguistics.* Berlin/New York: Mouton de Gruyter.
Zenner, Eline, Dirk Speelman and Dirk Geeraerts
  2012   Cognitive Sociolinguistics meets loanword research: Measuring variation in the success of anglicisms in Dutch. *Cognitive Linguistics* 23: 749–792.
Zlatev, Jordan
  2003   Polysemy or generality? Mu. In: H. Cuyckens, R. Dirven and J. Taylor (eds.), *Cognitive Approaches to Lexical Semantics*, 447–494. Berlin: Mouton de Gruyter.
Zwicky, Arnold and Jerry Sadock
  1975   Ambiguity tests and how to fail them. In: J. Kimball (ed.), *Syntax and Semantics*, Volume: 4, 1–36. New York: Academic Press.

Dirk Geeraerts, Leuven (Belgium)

14. Usage-based construction grammar

1. Introduction
2. Signs, constructions, and lexemes
3. Constructions at different levels of abstractness [taxonomic links]
4. Constructions at the same level of abstractness [horizontal links]
5. Constructions and syntactic categories [syntactic links]
6. Constructions and lexemes [lexical links]
7. Phrase structure
8. Conclusion
9. References

1. Introduction

The general goal of research on grammar in cognitive linguistics is to develop a framework for the analysis of linguistic structure that is grounded in general cognitive processes, i.e., processes that are not only involved in language, but also in other cognitive phenomena such as vision, attention, and abstract thought. The cognitive approach to the study of grammar contrasts sharply with the generative theory of grammar in which the core of the language users' grammatical knowledge (i.e., competence) is assigned to a particular faculty of the mind including innate categories and constraints that are exclusively needed for language (Pinker and Jackendoff 2005). In the cognitive approach there is no particular language faculty and grammatical knowledge is derived from linguistic experience. On this view, grammar is an "emergent phenomenon" (Hopper 1987) shaped by general psychological mechanisms such as categorization, analogy, and entrenchment (see Chapters 1 to 9 of this volume; see also Diessel 2011a for a review).

Early research in cognitive linguistics emphasized the importance of non-linguistic (spatial) concepts for the analysis of grammatical categories. Word classes, for instance, were described by means of conceptual primitives such as "boundedness" (e.g., count nouns and telic verbs are "bounded" vs. mass nouns and activity verbs are "unbounded"), and complex sentences were analyzed in terms of the figure-ground segregation, which gestalt psychologists proposed for the analysis of visual perception (Langacker 1982; Talmy 1978, 1988). In this early research, linguistic structure is immediately based on conceptual structure; but soon it became clear that an important aspect is missing in this approach, namely usage and development.

There is good evidence that linguistic structure and conceptual structure are related; but the relationship between them is indirect – it is mediated by language development, which in turn is driven by language use. This view of grammar underlies the "usage-based approach" – a term that Langacker (1988) proposed to emphasize the importance of usage and development for the analysis of linguistic structure. The general idea of this approach may be summarized as follows (cf. Hopper 1987; Langacker 2008; Bybee 2010):

> Grammar is a dynamic system of emergent categories and flexible constraints that are always changing under the influence of domain-general cognitive processes involved in language use.

The usage-based approach challenges central assumptions of linguistic analysis that have influenced grammatical research throughout the 20th century:

- It challenges the rigid division between the language system and language use, or competence (i.e., langue) and performance (i.e., parole).
- It abandons the structuralist dictum that the study of (synchronic) linguistic states must be separated from the study of (diachronic) language change.
- And it rejects the common assumption that syntactic analysis presupposes a set of primitive categories such as subject and noun phrase, which in other grammatical theories are often used as a "toolkit" for linguistic analysis (Jackendoff 2002: 75).

If we think of grammar as a dynamic system of emergent structures and flexible constraints, we cannot posit the existence of particular syntactic categories prior to grammatical analysis. On the contrary, what we need to explain is how linguistic structures evolve and change, both in history and acquisition. This explains why cognitive grammarians have turned to the study of language acquisition (e.g., Goldberg 2006) and why cognitive research on grammar has formed such a close liaison with research on grammaticalization (e.g., Bybee 2010; Hilpert 2013; Traugott and Trousdale 2013; see also Diessel 2007, 2011b, 2012 for some discussion of the parallels between L1 acquisition and language change). In the structuralist paradigm, grammatical theory seeks to provide formal representations of linguistic structure; but in the usage-based approach, grammatical research is primarily concerned with the dynamics of the grammatical system. This does not mean, however, that grammar is completely unconstrained in this approach. Like any other grammatical theory, the usage-based model rests on particular assumptions about the nature of grammatical elements and the overall organization of the grammatical system. As I see it, there are two general principles that underlie or constrain the analysis of linguistic structure in this approach:

- First, linguistic structure can be analyzed in terms of complex signs, i.e., constructions, combining a specific structural pattern with a particular function or meaning.
- Second, all linguistic signs (i.e., lexical signs and grammatical signs) are connected with each other by various types of links so that grammar (or language in general) can be seen as a dynamic network of interconnected signs.

The first principle has been discussed extensively. There is a large body of research on the symbolic nature of grammar and the importance of constructions in the usage-based approach (see Croft 2007 and Fried 2010 for two recent reviews of this research); but the second principle has not yet been sufficiently described and will be in the focus of this chapter. Section 2 provides a short discussion of the notion of construction and the nature of linguistic signs; and the rest of the chapter is concerned with the general architecture of grammar in the usage-based approach.

2. Signs, constructions, and lexemes

2.1. Some basic definitions

The ability to use signs or symbols is a fundamental capacity of the human mind providing a prerequisite for disembodied cognition and language (cf. Deacon 1997; Tomasello

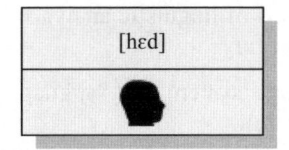

Fig. 14.1: Linguistic sign

1999). The classic example of a linguistic sign is the word (or lexeme). According to Saussure ([1916] 1994: 67), a word is a "two-sided psychological entity" that combines a particular form, i.e., the "signifier" (or "significant"), with a particular meaning, i.e., the "signified" (or 'signifié'). The English word *head*, for instance, consists of a specific sound pattern (i.e., [hɛd]) that is associated with a particular concept (or more specifically, with a network of related concepts, e.g., head as a body part, head of department, head of table; see Gries this volume).

Traditionally, the notion of sign is reserved for lexical expressions; but in cognitive linguistics it has been extended to grammatical entities, notably to constructions. A construction is as a grammatical unit in which a particular structural pattern is associated with a specific function or meaning. Construction grammar has played an important role in the development of the usage-based approach. In fact, in the literature construction grammar is often described as an integral part of the usage-based approach to the study of grammar (cf. Bybee 2010; Goldberg 2006; Hilpert 2014; Langacker 2008; Tomasello 2003; see also Diessel 2004: chapter 2); but the notion of construction grammar refers to a whole family of theories which are not all usage-based (see Hoffmann and Trousdale 2013 for a recent survey of different construction-based theories). Indeed, one of the earliest and most influential construction-based theories, i.e., the sign-based theory of construction grammar developed by Fillmore and Kay (1999), adopts the generative division between competence and performance and disregards usage and development (see also Michaelis 2013; Sag 2012). Other varieties of construction grammar, such as Cognitive Grammar (Langacker 2008) and Radical Construction Grammar (Croft 2001), take a dynamic perspective and have made important contributions to the usage-based approach (see also Bybee 2010; Goldberg 2006; Tomasello 2003; Steels 2011).

Constructions vary across a continuum of schematicity or abstractness. The term applies to both grammatical units that are associated with particular lexemes, e.g., idioms such as *kick the bucket* and prefabricated expressions such as *I don't know*, and grammatical units that are defined over abstract categories, or "slots", which can be filled by certain types of expressions. Consider, for instance, an imperative sentence such as *Open the door*, which is based on a "constructional schema" (Langacker 2008: 167) combing a particular syntactic configuration of linguistic elements with a particular function or meaning. In English, an imperative sentence includes an uninflected verb form at the beginning of the sentence, it usually lacks an overt subject, may include a postverbal element, e.g., a noun phrase or prepositional phrase, and functions as directive speech act. Imperative sentences can be analyzed as grammatical signs, i.e., constructions, that speakers use to express a particular illocutionary force (cf. Figure 14.2).

Like lexemes, constructions can be polysemous, i.e., they can have multiple functions or meanings. The imperative construction, for instance, can express a command, a re-

```
┌─────────────────────────────────┐
│     V_base [NP_non-subject]!    │
├─────────────────────────────────┤
│       DIRECTIVE SPEECH ACT      │
└─────────────────────────────────┘
```

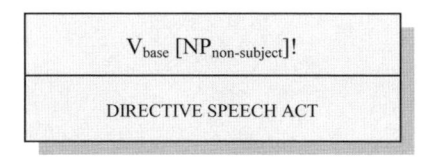

Fig. 14.2: The imperative construction

quest, an instruction, a warning, a permission, or good wishes (cf. 1–6) (cf. Stefanowitsch 2003; see also Searle 1979 for a general discussion of this point).

(1)	Open the door!	Command
(2)	Please pass me the salt.	Request
(3)	Melt the butter in the saucepan.	Instruction
(4)	Uh yeah go on there.	Permission
(5)	Just be careful!	Warning
(6)	Have a great birthday!	Good wishes

The notion of construction has a long history in linguistics. Traditionally, the term applies to particular clause types and phrases, e.g., imperative sentences, relative clauses, complex NPs including genitive attributes. However, in construction grammar the term has been extended to all grammatical patterns including highly productive clause types (e.g., transitive clauses) and phrases (e.g., ordinary PPs) (see below).

Note that in some of the usage-based literature, the notion of construction is not only used for grammatical patterns but also for lexical expressions (cf. Goldberg 1995; Croft and Cruse 2004: chapter 9). Both constructions and lexemes are signs, i.e., conventionalized form-function pairings; however, given that the parallels between lexemes and constructions are already captured by the notion of sign, there is no need to extend the notion of construction to lexical expressions. I will therefore restrict the notion of construction to grammatical units consisting of at least two elements (e.g., two lexemes or two categories) and will use the notion of sign as a cover term for both lexemes (i.e., lexical signs) and constructions (i.e., grammatical signs).[1]

2.2. Some general aspects of constructions

While construction grammarians have emphasized the importance of constructions for syntactic analysis, generative linguists have questioned the usefulness of this term. In fact, in Minimalism, i.e., the most recent versions of generative grammar, the notion of construction has been abandoned in favour of a fully compositional approach in which

---

[1] Morphologically complex words consisting of multiple morphemes (e.g., *armchair, untrue*) can be seen as particular types of constructions, i.e., as "morphological constructions" (cf. Langacker 1987: 83–85).

>   NP *be* V-*ed* [*by* NP]
>
>   X IS AFFECTED [BY Y]

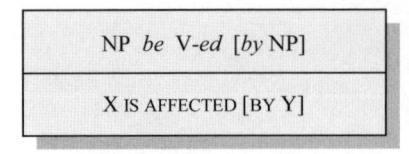

Fig. 14.3: The passive construction

all syntactic structures are derived from atomic primitives and combinatorial rules (cf. Chomsky 1995: 4). Cognitive linguists do not deny the compositionality of linguistic structure. In fact, if we restrict the notion of construction to grammatical patterns, i.e., if we exclude single lexemes from the notion of construction (see above), constructions are generally divisible into particular components that contribute to their meanings. However, compositionality is a matter of degree, and constructions are also associated with holistic properties, i.e., properties that are linked to the entire grammatical pattern rather than to particular components.

The best evidence for this comes perhaps from structures such as imperative sentences, which have always been analyzed as constructions. In traditional grammar (and early versions of generative grammar) these structures were described by means of construction-particular rules (or "transformations" in the "aspect model" of generative grammar; cf. Chomsky 1965), i.e., rules that are exclusively needed to derive a particular morphosyntactic pattern from atomic primitives. However, in Minimalism all construction-particular rules are eliminated and replaced by general syntactic operations such as "Move alpha" (Chomsky 1995). In contrast to Minimalism, usage-based construction grammar is a surface-oriented theory in which construction-particular properties are seen as an important aspect of grammar that cannot be explained by general rules (i.e., rules that are independent of particular constructions).

Take, for instance, a passive sentence such as *The door was opened by Peter*, which involves a particular configuration of grammatical elements: a clause-initial NP encoding the subject, a particular verb form consisting of the past participle of a transitive verb and the auxiliary *be*, and optionally a *by*-phrase denoting a semantic argument, i.e., the agent of the activity expressed by the verb. While passive sentences share important properties with other clause types (e.g., word order, subject-verb agreement), this configuration of syntactic elements is unique and associated with a particular meaning or function (i.e., a particular perspective on a causative event and a particular information structure, cf. Langacker 1991: 200–207). One way of analyzing this mixture of general and idiosyncratic properties is to assume that passive sentences are licensed by a constructional schema (cf. Figure 14.3).

The holistic properties of the passive are reminiscent of idiosyncratic properties of idiomatic expressions. In the generative approach, idioms are analyzed as irregular expressions that are stored together with words in the mental lexicon. But in the cognitive approach, idioms are analyzed in the same way as non-idiomatic grammatical expressions, i.e., constructions. On this view, there is no principled difference between a passive sentence such as *The door was opened by Peter* and an idiom such as *Where are you headed?* Like the passive, this idiom shares certain properties with other grammatical entities: It has the same word order as ordinary content questions and the auxiliary is inflected as in any other sentence type; but the meaning of the verb is of course idiosyncratic and cannot be derived by means of general (semantic) rules.

Idioms have played an important role in the development of construction grammar (cf. Fillmore et al. 1988; Nunberg et al. 1994). There is a wide range of idiomatic expressions that overlap to different degrees with regular grammatical patterns. Semantically, most idioms are unpredictable (e.g., *kick the bucket*); but some idiomatic expressions are semantically transparent in that their meaning can be derived by means of pragmatic principles (e.g., *answer the door*) (cf. Nunberg et al. 1994). Similarly, while some idiomatic expressions are syntactically irregular (e.g., *all of a sudden*), most idioms share some of their morphosyntactic properties with non-idiomatic grammatical expressions (e.g., *Curiosity killed the cat* has the same structure as an ordinary transitive clause) (cf. Fillmore et al. 1988). What is more, some idioms include "slots" like regular grammatical expressions. The comparative correlative construction (e.g., *The bigger, the better*), for instance, can be seen as a schematic idiom consisting of a lexically-specific frame, two comparative adjectives, and two slots that may or may not be filled by regular expressions (i.e., *The ADJ_{er} __ the ADJ_{er} __*).

Taken together, this research suggests that idiomaticity constitutes a continuum ranging from structures that are completely idiosyncratic and lexically particular to structures that share most of their semantic and syntactic properties with other grammatical patterns. On this view, there is no rigid division between idioms such as the comparative correlative construction, particular clause types such as the passive, and fully productive grammatical patterns such as basic declarative sentences. In fact, there is evidence that even the most productive and most variable clause types, e.g., the transitive SVO, have holistic properties, i.e., properties that are associated with the entire structural pattern.

2.3. The English transitive construction

In English, a (prototypical) transitive sentence consists of a clause-initial NP encoding the subject, a transitive verb denoting a causative event, and a postverbal NP encoding the object (e.g., *Peter closed the door*). In the syntactic literature, transitive sentences are commonly analyzed as fully compositional expressions formed from primitive categories by means of general rules; but research in psycholinguistics suggests that speakers of English conceive of the NP-V-NP sequence (or SVO) as a holistic entity that is associated with a particular scene involving an actor (or experiencer) and undergoer (or theme).

In a seminal study on sentence processing and language acquisition, Thomas Bever (1970) showed that English-speaking children often misinterpret passive sentences as active transitive clauses if the active interpretation is compatible with the meaning of the words in a (given) passive construction. For instance, a passive sentence such as *The girl was kissed by the boy* may be interpreted as an active sentence, meaning 'The girl kissed the boy', despite the fact that the structure occurs with passive morphology. There is evidence from psycholinguistic research that in English word order provides a stronger cue for grammatical relations than morphology so that English-speaking children often ignore the morphological marking of passive sentences and interpret them as active transitive clauses (cf. Slobin and Bever 1982). Since this type of mistake also occurs

```
┌─────────────────────┐
│      NP V NP        │
├─────────────────────┤
│     X ACTS ON Y     │
└─────────────────────┘
```

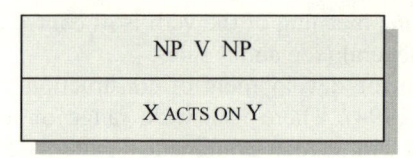

Fig. 14.4: The transitive construction

with several other clause types involving the order NP-V-NP (e.g., cleft sentences, reduced relative clauses), Bever suggested that children interpret these sentences based on a grammatical "template", which he called the "canonical sentence schema" of English. Subsequent research revealed that the same type of mistake occurs in comprehension experiments with adult speakers when they are put under time pressure while processing passive sentences or reduced relative clauses (cf. Ferreira 2003; see also Townsend and Bever 2001). Bever interpreted the canonical sentence schema as a "pseudosyntactic" device that children (and adults) use in lieu of true syntactic rules, as described in generative grammar; but from the perspective of construction grammar, the canonical sentence schema is a construction combining a particular structural pattern, i.e., NP-V-NP, with a particular meaning (cf. Figure 14.4).

2.4. The network architecture of language

In accordance with this view, cognitive research on grammar analyzes all clausal and phrasal patterns as constructions; i.e., as complex linguistic signs combining a particular structural pattern with a particular function or meaning. If grammar consists of grammatical signs, i.e., constructions, there is no principled difference between grammar and lexicon as in other theoretical approaches. This view of grammar has far-reaching implications for grammatical analysis. If linguistic structure consists of signs it is a plausible hypothesis that grammar is organized in the same way as the mental lexicon, which is commonly characterized as a network of related signs or symbols (cf. Figure 14.5).

In accordance with this view, cognitive linguists think of grammar as a network of interconnected signs, or a "structured inventory" of "symbolic units" (Langacker 1987: 57), that are related to each other by various types of links reflecting overlapping aspects of their structure, function, and meaning (cf. Goldberg 1995; Croft 2001; Bybee 2010; see also Diessel 1997). In generative linguistics, grammar and lexicon are two strictly distinguished components (or "modules"); but usage-based construction grammar has abandoned the division between lexicon and grammar in favour of a network model in which all linguistic elements are potentially connected with each other.

Network models have a long tradition in cognitive science. There are many different types of network models – some theoretical, some computational – that vary with regard to a wide range of parameters (see Elman 1995 for an overview); but what all network models have in common is that they are designed to "process" data and to "learn" from experience through data processing. Network models are thus usage-based models by definition.

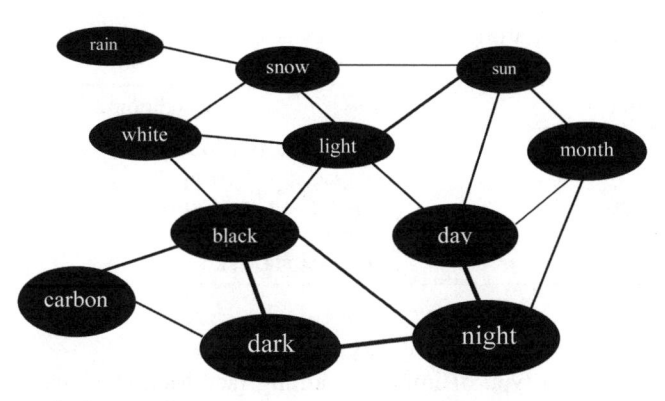

Fig. 14.5: Lexical network

In the remainder of this chapter, I will consider four different types of links between linguistic elements that are important to understand the network architecture of grammar in the usage-based approach, namely the links between ...

- constructions at different levels of abstractness [taxonomic links]
- constructions at the same level of abstractness [horizontal links]
- constructions and syntactic categories [syntactic links]
- constructions and lexical expressions [lexical links]

3. Constructions at different levels of abstractness [taxonomic links]

The first type of link concerns the hierarchical organization of grammar. As argued in section 2, constructions are schematic representations of linguistic structure that are instantiated in concrete utterances, sometimes referred to as "constructs" (cf. Fried 2010). The relationship between constructs and constructions is based on a process of schemati-

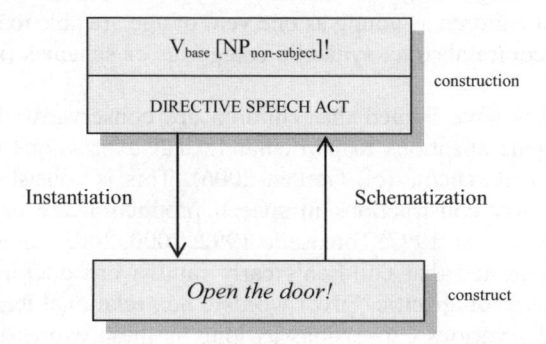

Fig. 14.6: Constructions and constructs

Tab. 14.1: Sample sentences of an artificial grammar, adopted from Gómez and Gerken (1999: 114)

Condition 1	Condition 2
VOT PEL JIC	PEL TAM RUD RUD
PEL TAM PEL JIC	VOT JIC RUD TAM JIC
PEL TAM JIC RUD TAM RUD	VOT JIC RUD TAM RUD
REL TAM JIC RUD TAM JIC	VOT PEL JIC RUD TAM
VOT PEL PEL JIC RUD TAM	PEL TAM PEL PEL PEL JIC

zation, which can be seen as a type of implicit learning (see Matthews and Krajewski and Baayen this volume) (cf. Figure 14.6).

Constructions emerge as generalizations over strings of concrete lexical expressions with similar forms and meanings. While this may happen at any time, most constructions are learned during childhood. The study of first language acquisition plays thus an important role in the usage-based analysis of linguistic structure (see Diessel 2013 for a recent review of usage-based research on the acquisition of constructions).

There is abundant evidence from psycholinguistic research that children are very good in detecting distributional regularities in strings of lexical expressions. For instance, in a series of studies Gómez and Gerken (1999) exposed 12-month-old infants to strings of monosyllabic nonce words (e.g., vot, pel, jic) that appeared in different structural patterns, or constructions, defined by linear order and the number of words they include. Each word the children learned occurred in one or more constructions in particular structural positions (e.g., after the first word, at the end of the construction). After training, i.e., after the infants had been exposed to the constructions for a few minutes, they were tested under two conditions (cf. Table 14.1).

In condition 1, they listened to the same constructions as the ones they had heard during training, but with different words; that is, each word the children had learned during training was replaced by a novel nonce word with the same distributional properties. And in condition 2, the infants were exposed to others constructions (i.e., constructions involving other word orders and including different numbers of words), but with the same novel nonce words as in condition 1. Using the head-turn preference procedure, Gómez and Gerken found that the infants recognized the constructions to which they were exposed during training although they had not heard any of the words of the test sentences before, suggesting that children as young as one year of age are able to abstract beyond specific words and to acquire abstract syntactic categories or schemas (see also Marcus et al. 1999).

However, a number of studies have argued that children are conservative learners who tend to restrict syntactic generalizations to particular lexical expressions that are commonly used in a constructional schema (cf. Gerken 2006). This is consistent with the hypothesis that children's early constructions in speech production are organized around particular words (cf. Lieven et al. 1997; Tomasello 1992, 2000, 2003). In a classic study, Martin Braine (1976) suggested that children's early multi-word utterances are "pivot schemas" that are composed of specific "pivot words", i.e., relational terms, and "open slots" that can be filled by various expressions as long as these expressions are semantically compatible with the pivot word (cf. Table 14.2).

Tab. 14.2: Pivot constructions (Braine 1976)

Pivot word	More __	All __	No __
Examples	More car More cereal More cookie More fish More juice More toast	All broke All clean All done All dressed All dry All shut	No bed No down No fix No home No mama No pee

Building on this research, Tomasello (1992) characterized children's early pivot schemas as "verb-island constructions" because most of them are based on pivot verbs; but there are also pivot schemas that revolve around other types of words (cf. Lieven et al. 1997; Dąbrowska 2004). Children's early questions, for instance, are usually organized around particular question words.

Like verb-argument constructions, questions originate from fixed expressions (e.g., *What-s-this?*) and formulaic frames (e.g., *Where-s __?*). As children grow older, their questions become increasingly more complex and variable. Consider, for instance, the sentences in (7) to (15), which illustrate the development of a particular type of question in the speech of a two-year-old child named Naomi (cf. Dąbrowska 2000).

(7) What doing? (many times)   1;11.11

(8) What's Mommy doing? (many times)   1;11.21

(9) What's donkey doing? (4 times)   2;0.18

(10) What's Nomi doing? (2 times)   2;0.18

(11) What's toy doing?   2;0.18

(12) What's Mommy holding?   2;0.26

(13) What's Georgie saying?   2;1.19

(14) What is the boy making?   2;11.17

(15) What is Andy doing?   2;11.18

As can be seen, the development originates from a pattern consisting of the question word *what* and the verb *doing*, which Naomi used many times before *what* appeared in any other context. Later, the child inserted the noun *Mommy* into this pattern; but it was only after the second birthday that she began to produce questions with different types of nouns and a bit later also with different types of verbs. At the end of the analyzed period, Naomi recognized that the question word *what* and the auxiliary *is* are separate words and abandoned the contracted form *what's*, which only recurred after a few months. Note that the overall structure of the question did not change throughout the entire period. In all of these examples the question word functions as patient (or object) of the activity expressed by the verb providing a lexical frame for the utterance (see also Dąbrowska and Lieven 2005).

```
                        ┌──────────────────┐
                        │ What AUX NP V?   │
                        └──────────────────┘
                         /                \
           ┌──────────────────┐      ┌──────────┐
           │ What's NP V-ing? │      │ WH ... ? │
           └──────────────────┘      └──────────┘
            /        |         \
┌──────────────────┐ ┌──────────────────┐ ┌───────────────────┐
│ What's Mommy doing?│ │What's donkey doing?│ │What's Mommy making?│
└──────────────────┘ └──────────────────┘ └───────────────────┘
```

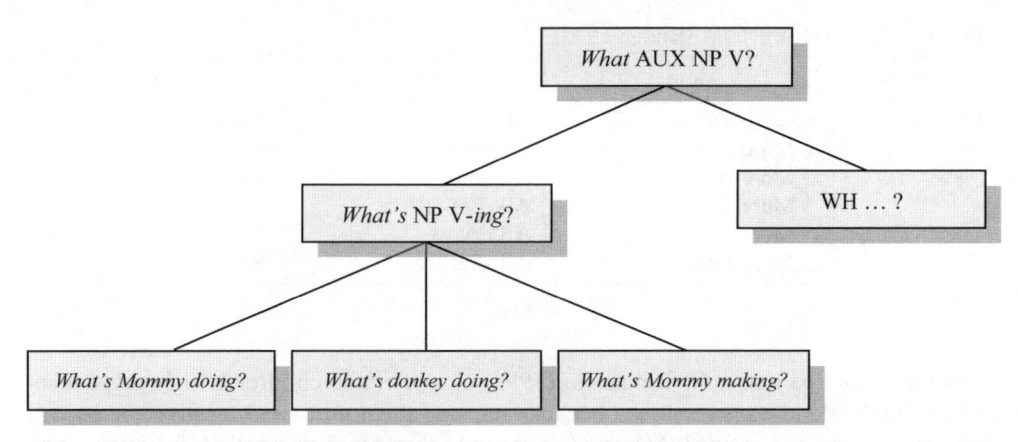

Fig. 14.7: Emerging taxonomy of WH-constructions in child speech

Such lexically particular constructions are characteristic of early child language (cf. Braine 1976; Lieven et al. 1997; Tomasello 1992, 2000, 2003); they provide a link between children's early holophrases and schematic representations of grammatical structure. The development involves a piecemeal, bottom-up process whereby children acquire increasingly more abstract syntactic patterns.

The emergence of grammatical schemas enriches the child's grammatical knowledge, but does not necessarily efface the memory of lower-level constructions and frequent strings of lexical expressions. In the generative approach, syntactic representations are maximally abstract and economical; but in the usage-based approach, linguistic information is often stored redundantly at different levels of abstractness (cf. Langacker 2000). What children eventually learn is a hierarchy of grammatical patterns reaching from prefabricated strings of lexical expressions to highly abstract constructional schemas. Figure 14.7 shows a simplified fragment of the taxonomy of WH-questions that one might extract from the analysis of Naomi's questions.

4. Constructions at the same level of abstractness [horizontal links]

The second type of link concerns the relationships between constructions at the same level of abstractness. These horizontal links are similar to the associative links between lexical expressions in the mental lexicon. There is abundant evidence from psycholinguistic research on speech errors and lexical priming that lexemes are related to each other by various types of links that influence language comprehension and production (cf. Harley 2001). For instance, research on lexical priming has demonstrated that words are more easily accessible if they follow a prime, i.e., a word that shares some of its semantic and/or phonetic features with the target item (McNamara 2005).

Priming effects have also been observed in research on grammatical constructions (see Tooley and Traxler 2010 for a recent review). The classic example of constructional priming in speech production involves passive sentences. As first noted by Weiner and Labov (1983), one factor favoring the use of a passive sentence in language production is the presence of another passive sentence in the preceding discourse, suggesting that priming does not only affect words but also constructions (cf. Gries 2005; Szmrecsanyi 2006).

This hypothesis has been confirmed by experimental evidence. For instance, in a seminal paper Kathryn Bock (1986) showed that speakers of English are much more likely to describe a ditransitive scene, i.e., a scene depicting an act of transfer, by the *to*-dative construction (rather than the ditransitive) if they had heard or used the *to*-dative construction prior to the experimental task. Parallel results were obtained for the active-passive alternation and other related clause types. Interestingly, while this type of priming is especially powerful if it involves the same sentence types (i.e., *to*-dative primes *to*-dative), Bock and Loebell (1990) showed that priming effects can also be observed between distinct grammatical patterns that share some of their structural properties. For instance, in one of their studies they found that an active sentence with a locative *by*-phrase can prime a passive sentence with an agentive *by*-phrase and vice versa (cf. 16–17).

(16) The 747 was landing by the airport's control tower. [locative *by*-phrase]

(17) The 747 was alerted by the airport's control tower. [passive *by*-phrase]

Since these priming effects occur even if prime and target have different meanings, Bock and colleagues dubbed this phenomenon "syntactic priming"; but later studies showed that priming also occurs with semantically related sentence types (e.g., Chang et al. 2003; Hare and Goldberg 2000). For instance, Hare and Goldberg (2000) showed that a sentence such *John provided Bill with news* primes a semantically related sentence such as *John gave the ball to Pete* although these sentences have very different structures. If there are priming effects between semantically or structurally related constructions, it is a plausible hypothesis that structures with similar forms and meanings are associated with each other like lexical expressions with similar phonetic and semantic features in the mental lexicon.

In accordance with this hypothesis, research on L1 acquisition has shown that grammatical development is crucially influenced by structural and semantic similarities between constructions (cf. Abott-Smith and Behrens 2006; Diessel 2004; Goldberg 2006). For instance, Diessel and Tomasello (2005) argued that the acquisition of relative clauses involves a piecemeal process whereby children gradually acquire various types of relative clauses based on their prior knowledge of simple sentences (i.e., main clauses). In English, the primary syntactic device to indicate the function of the head in the relative clause is word order. As can be seen in (18) to (21), the different structural types of relative clauses are differentiated by different word order patterns.

(18) The man who met Peter.   NP-*who*-V-NP   [subject RC]

(19) The man who Peter met.   NP-*who*-NP-V   [direct-object RC]

(20) The man who Peter sent the letter to.   NP-*who*-NP-V-NP-P   [indirect-object RC]

(21) The man who Peter went to.   NP-*who*-NP-V-P   [oblique RC]

German has the same range of relative clauses as English; but instead of word order, German uses relative pronouns to indicate the function of the head in the relative clause (cf. 22–25).

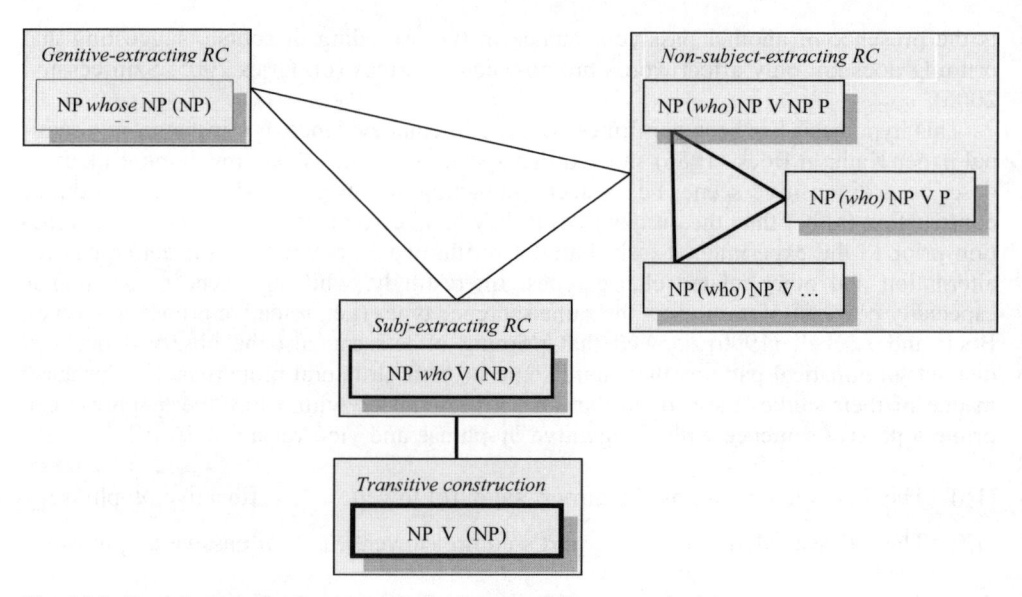

```
┌─────────────────────────┐                    ┌──────────────────────────────┐
│ Genitive-extracting RC  │                    │  Non-subject-extracting RC   │
│ ┌─────────────────────┐ │                    │  ┌────────────────────────┐  │
│ │  NP whose NP (NP)   │ │                    │  │  NP (who) NP V NP P    │  │
│ └─────────────────────┘ │                    │  └────────────────────────┘  │
└─────────────────────────┘                    │          ┌────────────────┐  │
                                               │          │ NP (who) NP V P│  │
                                               │          └────────────────┘  │
                                               │  ┌────────────────────────┐  │
                                               │  │   NP (who) NP V …      │  │
                                               │  └────────────────────────┘  │
                                               └──────────────────────────────┘
                    ┌─────────────────────────┐
                    │   Subj-extracting RC    │
                    │  ┌───────────────────┐  │
                    │  │  NP who V (NP)    │  │
                    │  └───────────────────┘  │
                    └─────────────────────────┘
                    ┌─────────────────────────┐
                    │  Transitive construction│
                    │  ┌───────────────────┐  │
                    │  │     NP V (NP)     │  │
                    │  └───────────────────┘  │
                    └─────────────────────────┘
```

Fig. 14.8: Partial network of grammatical relations and constructions.

(22) Der Mann, der Peter getroffen hat.   *der*-NP …   [subject RC]

(23) Der Mann, den Peter getroffen hat.   *den*-NP …   [direct-object RC]

(24) Der Mann, dem Peter den Brief   *dem*-NP …   [indirect-object RC]
      geschickt hat.

(25) Der Mann, zu dem Peter gegangen ist.   P-*dem*-NP …   [oblique RC]

Using a sentence repetition task, Diessel and Tomasello (2005) found (in accordance with much previous research) that subject relatives cause fewer difficulties for preschool children than non-subject relatives. However, while the children's responses to subject relatives were very similar in the two languages, English- and German-speaking children produced strikingly different responses to the various types of non-subject relative clauses. In German, direct-object relatives (cf. 23) caused fewer difficulties than indirect-object relatives (cf. 24) and oblique relatives (cf. 25), which is consistent with the fact that direct-object relatives are much more frequent in the ambient language than the two other types of non-subject relatives. However, in the English study all non-subject relatives caused the same amount of errors despite the fact that direct-object relatives are much more frequent than indirect-object relatives and oblique relatives. But how then do we account for the English results and the differences between the English and German studies?

Diessel and Tomasello argue that direct-object relatives, indirect-object relatives, and oblique relatives caused the same amount of errors in the English study because these relative clauses involve the same general word order pattern, i.e., NP (*who*) NP V, which the children of their English study frequently converted to the order NP (*who*) V NP, as in example (26):

(26) a. TEST ITEM: This is the girl [who the boy teased at school].

   b. Child: This is the girl [who teased the boy at school].

Since non-subject relatives in German do not have a particular property in common (the relative clauses in 23 to 25 are marked by different relative pronouns), they were *not* treated as members of a common class, as indicated by the fact that in the German study direct-object relatives caused significantly fewer errors than indirect-object relatives and oblique relatives. Diessel and Tomasello take this as evidence for their hypothesis that similarity between constructions plays an important role in grammatical development (see Diessel 2009 for additional data and discussion). What children eventually learn is a network of interconnected relative clause constructions. The development starts with subject relatives involving the same sequence of nouns and verbs as simple main clauses and it ends with genitive relatives (e.g., *the man whose dog was barking*), which are structurally and semantically distinct from all other types of relative clauses (cf. Figure 14.8).

5. Constructions and syntactic categories [syntactic links]

The third type of link concerns the relationship between constructions and syntactic categories (e.g., grammatical relations and word classes). Most grammatical theories presuppose a set of syntactic categories prior to syntactic analysis; but in the usage-based approach syntactic categories are emergent from the language users' experience with constructions. This is most forcefully expressed in Radical Construction Grammar, a usage-based variety of construction grammar developed by Croft (2001).

The starting point of Croft's analysis is the observation that syntactic categories vary across constructions and across languages. Let us consider grammatical relations to illustrate this point.[2] Grammatical relations define the syntactic functions of words and phrases in verb-argument constructions. In formal syntactic theories, grammatical relations are commonly defined as primitive categories; but Croft argues that grammatical relations are derived from particular constructions. Consider, for instance, the notion of subject.

In English, the subject is commonly defined as the nominal that immediately precedes the (finite) verb. However, while this may hold for basic declarative sentences, it does not generally hold for other sentence types. In (non-subject) questions, for instance, the subject occurs only after the auxiliary (cf. 27), and in sentences with preposed quotative clauses the (main clause) subject can follow the quotative verb (cf. 28).

(27) What did you say?

(28) "Good morning", said the young man with the red jacket.

---

[2] Traditionally, syntactic analysis involves two major types of categories: (i) grammatical relations (e.g., subject, object) and (ii) word classes (e.g., noun, verb). In addition, phrases (e.g., NP, VP) can be seen as syntactic categories (cf. Croft 2001); but in this chapter I treat phrases as constructions and keep them separate from syntactic categories because they evolve in different ways (see section 7).

In fact, even in simple declarative sentences, the subject does not always precede the verb. In the locative (inversion) construction, for instance, the position before the verb is occupied by an adverbial and the subject occurs only after the verb (cf. 29), and in constructions with negative inversion, the subject precedes the main verb and follows the auxiliary (cf. 30).

(29) Across the bridge lived an old man that was well-known in this region.

(30) Never would I talk to him about these things.

Another construction-particular property of grammatical relations is control. In complex sentences with non-finite complement clauses, for instance, the verb of the lower clause is usually controlled by the direct object of the higher clause (cf. 31); but if the main clause includes the verb *promise*, it is controlled by the matrix clause subject, i.e., the clause-initial NP (cf. 32).

(31) Peter convinced Sue to support his proposal.

(32) Peter promised Sue to support her proposal.

Similar construction-specific constraints have been observed in languages where grammatical relations are primarily expressed by morphological means, i.e., by case marking or agreement morphology (Croft 2001). In addition to such construction-particular properties, there are language-particular aspects of grammatical relations. Croft stresses that languages differ as to how they organize grammatical relations. There is an enormous amount of crosslinguistic variation in this domain, which typologists have analyzed in terms of three general semanto-syntactic roles: (i) the S role, which refers to the one participant that is entailed by an intransitive event, (ii) the A role, which refers to the most agent-like participant of a transitive event, and (iii) the P role, which refers to the most patient-like participant of a transitive event (e.g., Dixon 1994).

In English, the notion of subject subsumes the S and A roles, which are uniformly expressed by nominals that precede the finite verb (in basic declarative sentences); whereas the P role is encoded by a postverbal NP (cf. 33–34). Note, however, that in passive sentences the P role is promoted to subject and expressed by a preverbal nominal, whereas the A role is either omitted or demoted to an oblique (cf. 35).

(33) *The boy$_{AG}$ kicked the ball$_{PA}$.*

(34) *The man$_{AG}$ is running.*

(35) *The ball$_{PA}$ was kicked (by the boy$_{AG}$).*

Like English, many other languages encode S and A by the same word order or morphology; but this is not a universal strategy. It is well-known that in languages with ergative morphology, S and P are treated as a formal grammatical category (absolutive case) in contrast to A (ergative case), and that in languages with split-intransitive morphology the S role is divided into two categories: agent-like participants (e.g., *The man$_{AG}$ is running*) that are encoded in the same way as the A role of a transitive sentence, and patient-like participants (e.g., *The bomb$_{PA}$ exploded*) that are encoded in the same way

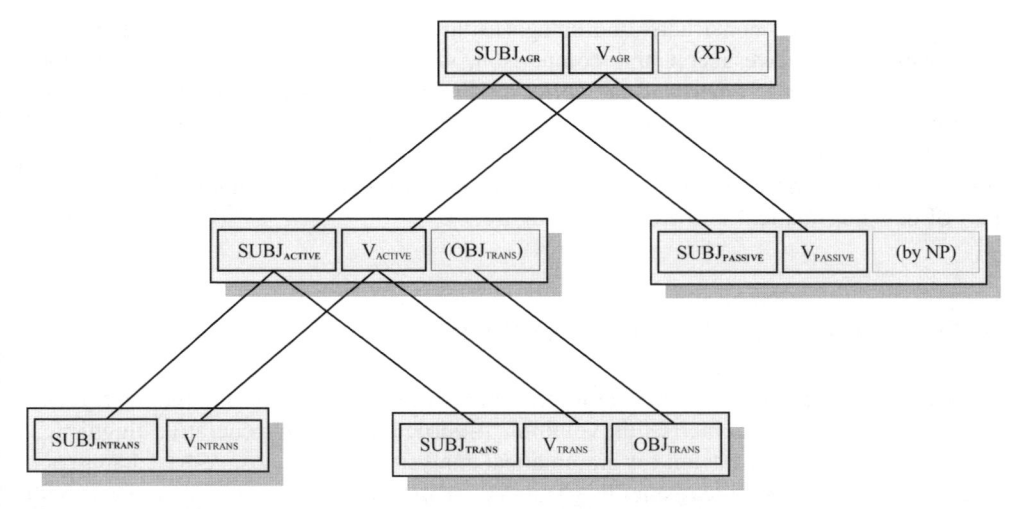

Fig. 14.9: Partial network of grammatical relations and constructions

as the P role. Moreover, there are languages in which the subject of a passive sentence occurs with the same case marker as the direct object (or an oblique), and there are other languages that differentiate between different P roles (see Bickel 2011 for a recent overview). Finally, the morphological marking of S, A and P does not always coincide with their syntactic functions. In fact, in most languages with ergative morphology, coordinate sentences and relative clauses are conjoined based on an S/A "pivot"; that is, most (morphological) ergative languages employ an S/A alignment pattern for the formation of complex sentences. Syntactic ergativity, i.e., occurrence of an S/P pivot, is a very rare phenomenon and always restricted to particular constructions (cf. Dixon 1994).

In general, there is an enormous amount of variation in the encoding of grammatical relations across languages and constructions. Most grammatical theories abstract away from this variation and define syntactic categories at a very high level of abstractness. In this approach, grammar includes a universal inventory of highly schematic categories that are defined prior to syntactic analysis. But this approach has been challenged by Croft (2001), who offers an alternative account in which syntactic categories are emergent from constructions:

> Constructions, not categories and relations, are the basic, primitive units of syntactic representation. (Croft 2001: 45–46)

Constructions are the basic units of grammar because in contrast to what is commonly assumed in linguistic theory, syntactic configurations are not derivable from atomic primitives. While Croft does not explicitly refer to usage and development, his analysis implies that syntactic categories are formed in the process of language acquisition and language change. On this view, syntactic categories are emergent from the language user's (unconscious) analysis of particular constructions and are therefore subject to change.

The relationship between constructions and categories is similar to that between constructions at different levels of abstractness. Constructions are generalizations over concrete utterances, i.e., constructs, and categories are generalizations over recurrent parts of constructions. If we accept this comparison, we can think of grammatical relations (and word classes) as emergent categories of linguistic structure that children acquire through the analysis of constructions and that continue to be reinforced and adjusted throughout speakers' lives as they interact with each other. Like constructs and constructions, categories and constructions are related to each other by taxonomic links that are part of our grammatical knowledge (cf. Figure 14.9).

6. Constructions and lexemes [lexical links]

Finally, there are associative links between (schematic) constructions and (concrete) lexical expressions (see Geeraerts this volume). In structuralist and generative linguistics, individual words are irrelevant for grammatical analysis; but in the usage-based approach linguistic structure is fundamentally grounded in the language user's experience with concrete lexical expressions. In fact, constructions are often immediately associated with particular words (see Diessel forthcoming for a review of the relevant literature). This is perhaps most obvious in the case of closed-class function words. The comparative correlative construction, for instance, includes two grammatical morphemes, i.e., two instances of *the*, which only occur in this particular pattern (cf. 36).

(36) The bigger the house, the smaller the garden.

Other constructions that are associated with particular function words are the passive construction (cf. 37), the nominal extraposition construction (cf. 38), the existential *there*-construction (cf. 39), the *way*-construction (cf. 40), and the hortative construction (cf. 41). In all of these sentence types, there are particular words that are so closely associated with the structural pattern that they can only be analyzed as an integral part of the construction.

(37) Peter was struck by lightening.
(38) It's unbelievable the amount of food that he can eat.
(39) There was an old man who lived in a house in the woods.
(40) John found his way out of business.
(41) Let's have a beer.

The relationship between constructions and content words is more variable. In fact, in the construction-based literature it is commonly assumed that construction include "open slots" for particular content words (see above); but these slots are usually associated with particular words by probabilistic links.

Stefanowitsch and Gries (2003) developed a corpus method, i.e., "collostructional analysis", to analyze the probabilistic links between lexemes and constructions. Let us consider the ditransitive construction to illustrate this approach. The ditransitive construction consists of a subject, a verb, and two noun phrases, which together denote an

```
┌──────┐                    ┌──────────────┐
│ give │────────────────────│  NP V NP NP  │
└──────┘       ╲        ╱   └──────────────┘
                ╲      ╱
                 ╲    ╱
                  ╲  ╱
                   ╳
                  ╱  ╲
                 ╱    ╲
                ╱      ╲
┌──────┐       ╱        ╲   ┌──────────────────┐
│ bring│────────────────────│  NP V to NP NP   │
└──────┘                    └──────────────────┘
```

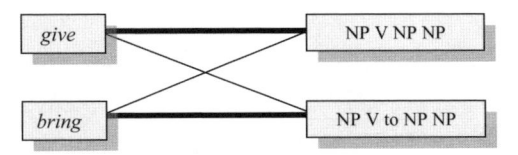

Fig. 14.10: The relationship between verbs and constructions

act of transfer between an actor and a recipient. The construction occurs with a wide range of verbs – *give, send, offer, show, teach,* to mention just a few. Most of these verbs can also appear in other grammatical contexts, in the *to*-dative, for instance, or in the transitive construction (cf. 42–44).

(42) Peter sent John a letter.

(43) Peter sent a letter to John.

(44) Peter sent a letter by mail.

What Stefanowitsch and Gries have shown is that individual lexemes are often more (or less) frequent in a particular construction than statistically expected if the relationships between lexemes and constructions were random. The verb *give*, for instance, is strongly attracted by the ditransitive construction and appears less frequently than expected in the *to*-dative; and for the verb *bring* it is the other way around (cf. Figure 14.10) (cf. Gries and Stefanowitsch 2004).

Both the ditransitive and the *to*-dative denote an act of transfer, but have slightly different meanings. The *to*-dative implies a greater distance between actor and recipient than the ditransitive and is therefore more strongly associated with activities involving motion (cf. Thompson and Koide 1987). This explains why the verbs *bring* and *take* are particularly frequent in the *to*-dative construction, whereas verbs such as *give* and *tell* are proportionally more frequent in the ditransitive (cf. Gries and Stefanowitsch 2004). In other words, verbs and constructions seem to "attract" (or "repel") each other based on their meanings: there is a tendency to use verbs that are semantically compatible with the constructional meaning (Goldberg [1995: 50] calls this the "Semantic Coherence Principle"); but the semantic fit is not the only factor influencing the relationships between lexemes and constructions.

Consider, for instance, the verb *donate*, which is semantically very similar to the verbs of transfer that are commonly used in the ditransitive and *to*-dative constructions; however, although *donate* is semantically compatible with both constructions, it is exclusively found in the *to*-dative (cf. 45) (in American English).[3] For most speakers, *donate* is unacceptable in the ditransitive construction (cf. 46); but not because *donate* would not fit the constructional meaning, but simply because *donate* has never been experienced in the ditransitive construction.

---

[3] In British English, *donate* is sometimes used in the ditransitive construction (Ewa Dąbrowska p.c.).

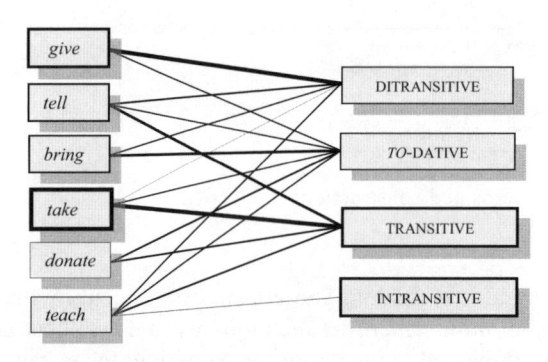

Fig. 14.11: Partial network of verbs and constructions

(45) Peter donated money to the Red Cross.
(46) *Peter donated the Red Cross money.

Similar semantically unmotivated restrictions have been observed for other verbs and other constructions, suggesting that the associations between verbs and constructions are not fully predictable from semantic criteria. In addition to the semantic fit, it is the language user's experience with an established pattern that influences the associative links between lexemes and constructions. Of course, the semantic fit affects the language users' linguistic behaviour, which in turn determines their experience, so that the two factors are likely to reinforce each other over time; but, as we have seen in the case of *donate*, the language users' linguistic experience does not always reflect the semantic fit between lexemes and constructions, suggesting that the two factors, i.e., semantic fit and frequency/entrenchment, are in principle independent of each other (see Diessel forthcoming for discussion of this point).

One can think of the relationship between lexemes and constructions as part of a probabilistic network shaped by language use. On this account, verbs (and other lexemes) and constructions are related to each other by connections with graded activation values that are determined by the combined effect of general semantic criteria and the language users' experience with particular lexical expressions and constructions (cf. Figure 14.11).

7. Phrase structure

To summarize the discussion thus far, we have looked at four different types of links between linguistic elements, namely the links between (i) constructions at different levels of abstractness (taxonomic links), (ii) constructions at the same level of abstractness (horizontal links), (iii) constructions and syntactic categories (syntactic links), and (iv) constructions and lexemes (lexical links). What we have not yet considered is constituent structure, i.e., the hierarchical organization of clauses and phrases, which provides perhaps the best evidence for a compositional approach. In generative grammar, constituent structure is derived from a small inventory of discrete categories, e.g., NP, VP, PP, and S, that are combined to larger syntactic units by general phrase-structure rules (e.g., PP

14. Usage-based construction grammar

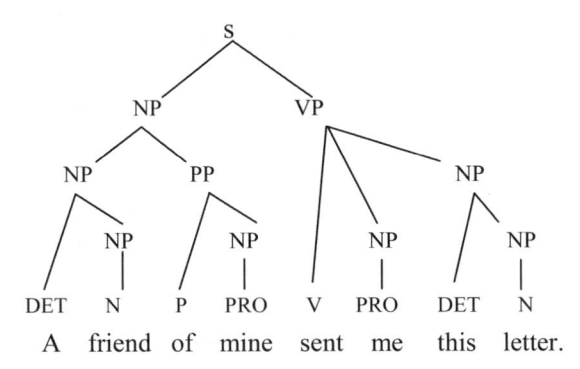

```
              S
          /      \
        NP        VP
       /  \      /|\
      NP   PP   / | \
      |   /  \ /  |  NP
      |  NP  NP NP /  \
      |   |   |  |   NP
     DET  N   P PRO V PRO DET N
      A friend of mine sent me this letter.
```

Fig. 14.12: Phrase structure graph

→ P-NP). The resulting structures are commonly represented in phrase-structure graphs, as exemplified in Figure 14.12.

Obviously, this analysis is not consistent with the dynamic nature of grammar in the usage-approach. If grammar is grounded in experience, we have to ask where do these structures come from and how do they change?

There is not much research on constituent structure in the usage-based approach; but Bybee (2002) and Langacker (2008) have made some interesting suggestions as to how constituency can be analyzed from a usage-based perspective. Specifically, Bybee argues that phrases, or phrasal constructions, are "processing units" that have evolved from frequent strings of linguistic elements. The development of these units is driven by two general aspects of language use, namely (i) semantic coherence and (ii) automatization or chunking.

In accordance with much previous research, Bybee argues that there is a general tendency to place semantically related elements next to each other. An early statement of this is Behaghel's 'first law':

> *Geistig eng Zusammengehöriges wird auch eng zusammengestellt.* 'Conceptually related entities are placed close to each other.' (Behaghel 1932)

The second factor that influences the emergence of constituency is frequency (see Divjak and Caldwell-Harris this volume). Specifically, Bybee argues that frequency is the driving force behind a cognitive mechanism which she calls "chunking", though "automatization" seems to be a better term, considering the way these terms, i.e., chunking and automatization, are used in cognitive psychology (see Diessel forthcoming for discussion).

Automatization is a general psychological mechanism whereby controlled processes are transformed into automatic processes. Almost all sequential activities start off as controlled processes, but are then often transformed into automatic processes through repetition or practice. This is a very common cognitive phenomenon involved in many everyday tasks. Automatization enables people to perform complex sequential activities with little effort, but is also a common source for certain types of mistakes, i.e., slips, that occur for lack of attention or lack of conscious control (cf. Logan 1988; Schneider and Chein 2003).

Lexical processing unit

```
[ I ] → [ don't ] → [ know ]
     ↑            ↑
  Transitional probabilities
```

Grammatical processing unit

```
[ NP ] → [ V ] → [ NP ]
      ↑       ↑
  Transitional probabilities
```

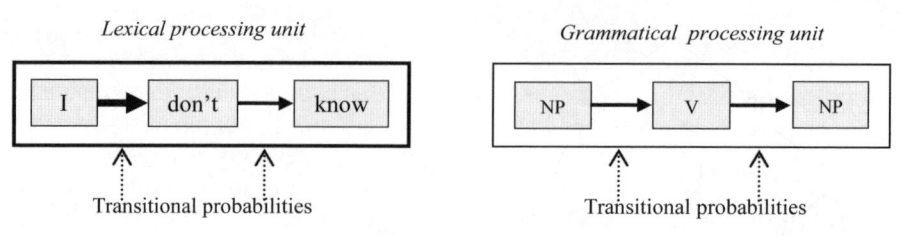

Fig. 14.13: Processing units

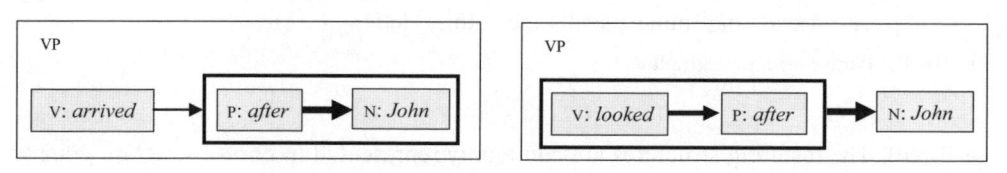

```
VP
[ V: arrived ] → [ P: after → N: John ]
```

```
VP
[ V: looked → P: after ] → [ N: John ]
```

Fig. 14.14: Processing units

Language is a sequential medium that is crucially influenced by automatization; but language unfolds in time. All linguistic elements, e.g., phonemes, morphemes, words, categories, and constructions, occur in sequence and are therefore subject to automatization. If we repeatedly process the same string of linguistic elements within a particular period of time, automatization creates associative links between them. This can involve either strings of (concrete) lexical expressions or strings of (abstract) categories. The strengths of the associative links can be expressed in terms of transitional probabilities or other statistical measures that have been explored in corpus and psycholinguistic studies (cf. Figure 14.13).

The cognitive result of this process is the emergence of an automated processing unit. Since automatization is a gradual process driven by frequency (or repetition) the units of speech vary on a continuum. Other things being equal, the more frequent a particular string of linguistic elements is processed, the stronger is the cohesion of the emerging processing unit; or as Bybee (2002: 220) put it: "the more often particular elements occur together, the tighter the constituent structure".

Since smaller units are usually more frequent than large ones, length and complexity vary with the degree of syntactic cohesion. As a consequence of this, more tightly organized processing units appear to be embedded in less automatized ones, creating a hierarchical organization of linguistic structure which one might analyze in terms of phrase structure trees. Note, however, that the resulting phrase structures are very different from traditional phrase structure representations. In generative grammar, syntactic phrase structure is analyzed by a set of discrete categories that are defined prior to syntactic analysis; but in the usage-based approach phrase structure is emergent and non-discrete. It is grounded in the language user's experience with strings of linguistic elements that are combined to fluid units. As a consequence of this, constituent structure is much more diverse and variable than in generative linguistics. Consider, for instance, a verb phrase such as *(She) arrived after John* (cf. Figure 14.14). In traditional phrase structure analysis, it is assumed that the VP consists of two immediate constituents, namely V and PP; but it is well-known that in a parallel structure such as *(She) looked after John* the preposition is more strongly associated with the verb than with the noun, creating a grouping of syntactic categories that is not consistent with general phrase-structure rules (i.e., [[V-P] NP]).

In the usage-based approach, this is readily explained by automatization or chunking. Since the sequence *look after* is much more frequent than *after John*, *look after* constitutes a chunk, i.e., an automated processing unit, that is largely independent of the general VP schema in which postverbal prepositions are associated with a subsequent noun, rather than with the verb. Other mismatches between traditional phrase structures and lexically specific chunks are described in Bybee and Scheibman (1999), Bybee (2002), and Beckner and Bybee (2009). Taken together these studies suggest that constituency is a gradient phenomenon emergent from concrete utterances of language use, just like any other aspect of grammar.

8. Conclusion

To conclude, this chapter has provided an overview of recent research on grammar in cognitive linguistics. The goal of this research is to develop a framework for the analysis of linguistic structure as it evolves from domain-general cognitive processes. In this approach, grammar is seen as a self-organizing system of emergent categories and fluid constructions that are in principle always changing, always in flux, under the influence of general cognitive mechanisms involved in language use such as analogy, categorization, and automatization (or chunking). There are two basic tenets that underlie the analysis of linguistic structure in this approach: First, linguistic structure consists of signs, i.e., constructions, and second constructions are associated with each other (and other linguistic signs) by various types of links creating an intricate system of interconnected elements that one might characterize as a dynamic network. The purpose of this chapter has been to elaborate the network metaphor of usage-based construction grammar, which had not yet been sufficiently described.

9. References

Abbott-Smith, Kirsten and Heike Behrens
   2006   How known constructions influence the acquisition of other constructions: The German passive and future constructions. *Cognitive Science* 30: 995–1026.

Baayen, Harald
   this volume   Analogy and schematization. Berlin/Boston: De Gruyter Mouton.

Beckner, Clay and Joan Bybee
   2009   A usage-based account of constituency and reanalysis. *Language Learning* 59: 27–46.

Behaghel, Otto
   1932   *Deutsche Syntax. Eine geschichtliche Darstellung*. Vol. IV. *Wortstellung, Periodenbau*. Heidelberg: Winter.

Bever, Thomas G.
   1970   The cognitive basis for linguistic structures. In: J. R. Hayes (ed.), *Cognition and Development of Language*, 279–352. New York: Wiley.

Bickel, Balthasar
   2011   Grammatical relations typology. In: J. J. Song (ed.), *The Oxford Handbook of Linguistic Typology*, 399–444. Oxford: Oxford University Press
Bock, Kathryn
   1986   Syntactic persistence in language production. *Cognitive Psychology* 18: 355–387.
Bock, Kathryn and Helga Loebell
   1990   Framing sentences. *Cognition* 35: 1–39.
Braine, Martin D. S.
   1976   Children's first word combinations, *Monographs of the Society for Research in Child Development* 41.
Bybee, Joan
   2002   Sequentiality as the basis of constituent structure. In: T. Givón and B. F. Malle (eds.) *The Evolution of Language out of Pre-Language*, 109–132. Amsterdam: John Benjamins.
Bybee, Joan
   2007   *Frequency and the Organization of Language*. Oxford: Oxford University Press.
Bybee, Joan
   2010   *Language, Usage, and Cognition*. Cambridge: Cambridge University Press.
Bybee, Joan and Joanne Scheibman
   1999   The effect of usage on degrees of constituency: The reduction of *don't* in English. *Linguistics* 37: 575–596.
Chang, Franklin, Kathryn Bock, and Adele E. Goldberg
   2003   Can thematic roles leave traces of their places? *Cognition* 90: 29–49.
Chomsky, Noam
   1965   *Aspects of the Theory of Syntax*. Cambridge: MIT Press.
Chomsky, Noam
   1995   *The Minimalist Program*. Cambridge: MIT Press.
Croft, William
   2001   *Radical Construction Grammar: Syntactic Theory in Typological Perspective*. Oxford: Oxford University Press.
Croft, William
   2007   Construction grammar. In: D. Geeraerts and H. Cuyckens. (eds.), *Handbook of Cognitive Linguistics*, 463–508. Oxford: Oxford University Press.
Croft, William and Alan Cruse
   2004   *Cognitive Linguistics*. Cambridge: Cambridge University Press.
Dąbrowska, Ewa
   2000   From formula to schema: the acquisition of English questions. *Cognitive Linguistics* 11: 83–102.
Dąbrowska, Ewa
   2004   *Language, Mind and Brain: Some Psychological and Neurological Constraints on Theories of Grammar*. Edinburgh: Edinburgh University Press.
Dąbrowska, Ewa and Elena Lieven
   2005   Towards a lexically-specific grammar of children's questions. *Cognitive Linguistics* 16: 437–474.
Deacon, Terrence
   1997   *The Symbolic Species. The Co-Evolution of Language and the Brain*. New York: W.W. Norton & Company.
Diessel, Holger
   1997   Verb-first constructions in German. In: M. Verspoor, L. K. Dong, and E. Sweetser (eds.), *Lexical and Syntactical Constructions and the Construction of Meaning*, 51–68. Amsterdam: John Benjamins.
Diessel, Holger
   2004   *The Acquisition of Complex Sentences*. Cambridge: Cambridge University Press.

Diessel, Holger
   2007   Frequency effects in language acquisition, language use, and diachronic change. *New Ideas in Psychology* 25: 108–127.

Diessel, Holger
   2009   On the role of frequency and similarity in the acquisition of subject and non-subject relative clauses. In: T. Givón and M. Shibatani (eds.), *Syntactic Complexity*, 251–276. Amsterdam: John Benjamins.

Diessel, Holger
   2011a   Review article of 'Language, Usage and Cognition' by Joan Bybee. *Language* 87: 830–844.

Diessel, Holger
   2011b   Grammaticalization and Language Acquisition. In: B. Heine and H. Narrog (eds.), *Handbook of Grammaticalization*, 130–141. Oxford: Oxford University Press.

Diessel, Holger
   2012   Language Change and Language Acquisition. In: A. Bergs and L. Brinton (eds.), *Historical Linguistics of English: An International Handbook*, Vol. 2, 1599–1613. Berlin: Mouton de Gruyter.

Diessel, Holger
   2013   Construction Grammar and First Language Acquisition. In: G. Trousdale and T. Hoffmann (eds.), *The Oxford Handbook of Construction Grammar*, 347–364. Oxford: Oxford University Press.

Diessel, Holger
   forthcoming   Frequency and lexical specificity. A critical review. In: H. Behrens and S. Pfänder (eds.), *Experience Counts: Frequency Effects in Language*. Berlin: Mouton de Gruyter.

Diessel, Holger and Michael Tomasello
   2005   A new look at the acquisition of relative clauses. *Language* 81: 1–25.

Divjak, Dagmar and Catherine Caldwell-Harris
   this volume   Frequency and entrenchment. Berlin/Boston: De Gruyter Mouton.

Dixon, R. M. W
   1994   *Ergativity*. Cambridge: Cambridge University Press.

Elman, Jeffrey L.
   1995   Language as a dynamical system. In: R. F. Port and T. van Gelder (eds.), *Minds as Motion, Explanations in the Dynamics of Cognition*, 195–225. Cambridge: MIT Press.

Ferreira, Fernanda
   2003   The misinterpretation of noncanonical sentences. *Cognitive Psychology* 47: 164–203.

Fillmore, Charles J. and Paul Kay
   1999   *Construction Grammar*. Berkeley: University of California.

Fillmore, Charles J., Paul Kay and Catherine O'Connor
   1988   Regularity and idiomaticity in grammatical constructions: The case of *let alone*. *Language* 64: 501–538.

Fried, Mirjam
   2010   *Construction Grammar*. In: A. Alexiadou and T. Kiss (eds.), *Handbook of Syntax*. Second edition. Berlin: Walter de Gruyter.

Geeraerts, Dirk
   this volume   Lexical semantics. Berlin/Boston: De Gruyter Mouton.

Gerken, LouAnn
   2006   Decisions, decisions: infant language learning when multiple generalizations are possible. *Cognition* 98: 67–74.

Goldberg, Adele E.
   1995   *Constructions: A Construction Grammar Approach to Argument Structure*. Chicago: University of Chicago Press.

Goldberg, Adele E.
   2006   *Constructions at Work. The Nature of Generalization in Language*. Oxford: Oxford University Press.

Gómez, Rebecca L. and Lou Ann Gerken
   1999   Artificial grammar learning by 1-year-olds leads to specific abstract knowledge. *Cognition* 70: 109–135.

Gries, Stefan Th.
   2005   Syntactic priming: A corpus-based approach. *Journal of Psycholinguistic Research* 34: 365–399.

Gries, Stefan Th.
   this volume   Polysemy. Berlin/Boston: De Gruyter Mouton.

Gries, Stefan Th. and Anatol Stefanowitsch
   2004   Extending collexeme analysis. *International Journal of Corpus Linguistics* 9: 97–129.

Hare, Mary and Adele E. Goldberg
   2000   Structural priming: purely syntactic? *Proceedings of the Twenty-first Annual Meeting of the Cognitive Science Society*, 208–211. Mahwah: Laurence Erlbaum.

Harley, Trevor
   2001   *The Psychology of Language. From Data to Theory*. Second edition. Hove: Taylor and Francis .

Hilpert, Martin
   2013   *Constructional Change in English: Developments in Allomorphy, Word-formation and Syntax*. Cambridge: Cambridge University Press.

Hilpert, Martin
   2014   *Construction Grammar and its Application to English*. Edinburgh: Edinburgh University Press.

Hoffmann, Thomas and Graeme Trousdale
   2013   *The Oxford Handbook of Construction Grammar*. Oxford: Oxford University Press.

Hopper, Paul
   1987   Emergent Grammar. *Proceedings of the Thirteenth Annual Meeting of the Berkeley Linguistics Society*, 139–157. Berkeley.

Jackendoff, Ray
   2002   *Foundations of Language. Brain, Meaning, Grammar, Evolution*. Oxford: Oxford University Press.

Langacker, Ronald W.
   1982   Space Grammar, analysability, and the English passive. *Language* 58: 22–80.

Langacker, Ronald W.
   1987   *Foundations of Cognitive Grammar, Vol. 1, Theoretical Prerequisites*. Stanford: Stanford University Press.

Langacker, Ronald W.
   1988   A usage-based model. In: B. Rudzka-Ostyn (ed.), *Topics in Cognitive Linguistics*, 127–161. Amsterdam: John Benjamins.

Langacker, Ronald W.
   1991   *Foundations of Cognitive Grammar, Vol. 2, Descriptive Application*. Stanford: Stanford University Press.

Langacker, Ronald W.
   2000   A dynamic usage-based model. In: M. Barlow and S. Kemmer (eds.), *Usage-based Models of Language*, 24–63. Stanford: Stanford University Press.

Langacker, Ronald W.
   2008   *Cognitive Grammar. A Basic Introduction*. Oxford: Oxford University Press.

Lieven, Elena V. M., Julian M. Pine and Gillian Baldwin
   1997   Lexically-based learning and early grammatical development. *Journal of Child Language* 24: 187–219.

Logan, Gordon D.
  1988 Toward an instance theory of automatization. *Psychological Review* 95: 492–527.
Marcus, Gary, S. Vijayan, S. B. Rao, P. M. Vishton
  1999 Rule learning by seven-month-old infants. *Science* 283: 77–80.
Matthews, Danielle and Grzegorz Krajewski
  this volume First language acquisition. Berlin/Boston: De Gruyter Mouton.
McNamara, Timothy P.
  2005 *Semantic Priming. Perspective from Memory and Word Recognition*. New York: Taylor & Francis.
Michaelis, Laura
  2013 Sign-based construction grammar. In: G. Trousdale and T. Hoffmann (eds.), *The Oxford Handbook of Construction Grammar*, 133–152. Oxford: Oxford University Press.
Nunberg, Geoffrey, Ivan A. Sag and Thomas Wasow
  1994 Idioms. *Language* 70: 491–538.
Pinker, Steven and Ray Jackendoff
  2005 The faculty of language: What's special about it? *Cognition* 95: 201–236.
Sag, Ivan A.
  2012 Sign-based construction grammar: An informal synopsis. In: H. C. Boas and I. A. Sag (eds.), *Sign-Based Construction Grammar*, 39–170. Stanford: CSLI Publications
Saussure, Ferdinand de
  [1916] 1996 *Course in General Linguistics*. La Salle, Illinois: Open Court.
Schneider, Walter and Jason M. Chein
  2003 Controlled and automatic processing: behavior, theory, and biological mechanisms. *Cognitive Science* 27: 525–559.
Searle, John R.
  1979 *Expression and Meaning: Studies in the Theory of Speech Acts*. Cambridge: Cambridge University Press.
Slobin, Dan I. and Thomas G. Bever
  1982 Children use canonical sentence schemas: A crosslinguistic study of word order and inflections. *Cognition* 12: 229–265.
Steels, Luc (ed.)
  2011 *Design Patterns in Fluid Construction Grammar*. Amsterdam: John Benjamins.
Stefanowitsch, Anatol
  2003 The English imperative. A construction-based approach. Unpublished manuscript. Universität Bremen.
Stefanowitsch, Anatol and Stefan Gries
  2003 Collostructions: Investigating the interaction of words and constructions. *International Journal of Corpus Linguistics* 8: 209–243.
Szmrecsanyi, Benedikt
  2006 *Morphosyntactic Persistence in Spoken English. A Corpus Study at the Intersection of Variationist Sociolinguistics, Psycholinguistics, and Discourse Analysis*. Berlin: Mouton de Gruyter.
Talmy, Leonard
  1978 Figure and ground in complex sentences. In: J. H. Greenberg (ed.), *Universals of Human Language*, Vol. 4, 625–649. Stanford: Stanford University Press.
Talmy, Leonard
  1988 The relation between grammar and cognition. In: B. Rudzka-Ostyn (ed.), *Topics in Cognitive Linguistics*, 165–205, Amsterdam: John Benjamins.
Thompson, Sandra A. and Yuka Koide
  1987 Iconicity and 'indirect objects' in English. *Journal of Pragmatics* 11: 399–406.

Tomasello, Michael
   1992   *First Verbs. A Case Study of Early Grammatical Development.* Cambridge: Cambridge University Press.
Tomasello, Michael
   1999   *The Cultural Origins of Human Cognition.* Cambridge: Harvard University Press.
Tomasello, Michael
   2000   Do young children have adult syntactic competence? *Cognition* 74: 209–253.
Tomasello, Michael
   2003   *Constructing a Language. A Usage-Based Approach.* Cambridge: Harvard University Press.
Tooley, Kristen M. and Matthew J. Traxler
   2010   Syntactic priming effects in comprehension: A critical review. *Language and Linguistics Compass* 4: 925–937.
Townsend, David J. and Thomas G. Bever
   2001   *Sentence Comprehension. The Integration of Habits and Rules.* Cambridge: MIT Press.
Traugott, Elizabteh Closs and Graeme Trousdale
   2013   *Constructionalization and Constructional Changes.* Oxford: Oxford University Press.
Weiner, Judith E. and William Labov
   1983   Constraints on agentless passive. *Journal of Linguistics* 19: 29–58.

Holger Diessel, Jena (Germany)

15. Discourse

1. Introduction
2. Cognitive Linguistics and Critical Discourse Analysis: A useful synergy?
3. The Cognitive Linguistic approach to CDA
4. Conceptual parameters for ideology
5. Conclusion

1. Introduction

In this chapter, I focus on discourse, understood as language in social practice. I focus specifically on media and political discourse to show how language can, through the patterns of conceptualisation it invokes, function ideologically. In doing so, I survey the most recent developments at the intersection between Cognitive Linguistics and Critical Discourse Analysis. This synergy represents both a social, or, more specifically, a critical, turn in Cognitive Linguistics as well as a cognitive turn in Critical Discourse Analysis, which has traditionally adopted more social science based methodologies. One site where these two perspectives have most successfully and most visibly converged is in the critical study of metaphor, which now constitutes one of the most productive and pervasive methodological approaches to ideological discourse research. More recently, however, the utility of combining Cognitive Linguistics and Critical Discourse Analysis has been expounded in relation to a wider range of linguistic and conceptual phenomena. In this chapter, then, I only very briefly touch up on critical metaphor studies and concentrate instead on some of the other ways in which Cognitive Linguistics and Critical Discourse Analysis can be usefully combined to shed light on the ideological properties of texts and conceptualisation. Rather than chronologically chart the development of this field, however, I offer an overview of the landscape from a contemporary vantage point which brings together several analytical strands inside a single, integrated framework.

2. Cognitive Linguistics and Critical Discourse Analysis: A useful synergy?

Critical Discourse Analysis (CDA) is a text-analytical tradition which studies the way language use encodes and enacts ideologies leading to social power abuse, dominance and inequality (Van Dijk 2001; Wodak 2001). Grounded in post-structuralist discourse analysis and Critical Theory, it comes with its own conceptualisation of the relationship between language and society in which language use, discourse, is seen as "socially constitutive as well as socially conditioned" (Fairclough and Wodak 1997: 258). That is, discourse exists in a dialectic with social situations and relations, both reflecting and reinforcing social structures. From a socio-cognitive rather than purely post-structuralist perspective, Van Dijk has argued that any cogent account of the relationship between discourse and social structure requires an explanation which first and foremost connects structures in text and talk with structures in the mind (e.g., Van Dijk 1998). The ideologies which support social action, he argues, consist in the socially shared "system of mental representations and processes of group members" (Van Dijk 1995: 18). To study the social action effects of language use, then, entails looking at the cognitive or conceptual effects of text and talk in social, economic and political contexts.

Cognitive Linguistics, of course, comes with its own explicitly theorised account of the relationship between language and conceptualisation (Langacker 1987, 1991; Talmy 2000). The incorporation of Cognitive Linguistics in CDA is therefore well motivated: Cognitive Linguistics offers CDA the "missing link" (cf. Chilton 2005) it needs to explain the relationship between discursive and social practices.[1] At the same time, CDA offers Cognitive Linguistics the opportunity to extend its analyses beyond linguistic and conceptual structure to include the constraints that these place on societal structure. This triangular relation is something which has always been alluded to in Cognitive Linguistics, as when, for example, Lakoff and Johnson (1980: 156) stated that "metaphors create realities for us, especially social realities. A metaphor may thus be a guide for future action, such actions will, of course, fit the metaphor". The body of work converging on a cognitive approach to language and ideology can therefore be seen to come from both cognitive linguists applying their theories in critical contexts and critical discourse ana-

---

[1] The mutual benefits that collaboration between CL and CDA brings and the extent to which they are compatible has been addressed in several works (including Dirven et al. 2007; Hart 2010, 2011b; Hart and Lukeš 2007; Koller 2014; Nuñez-Perucha 2011; Stockwell 1999).

lysts turning to Cognitive Linguistics for new methodologies.[2] Such work in the space between the two disciplines can, according to Dirven et al. (2003: 2), be seen as an invitation to CDA scholars not yet familiar with the tenets and analytic tools that Cognitive Linguistics has to offer to find out more about them as well as an invitation to cognitive linguists to look beyond the traditional areas of language structure to study the social belief and value systems (ideologies) that linguistic structures serve to maintain and perpetuate.[3]

The principle aim of CDA is to bring to the surface for inspection the otherwise clandestine ideological properties of text and talk and in so doing to correct a widespread underestimation of the influence of language in shaping thought and action (Fairclough 1989; Fowler 1991: 89). The claim in CDA is that representation in discourse is "always representation from some ideological point of view" (Fowler 1991: 85). Such perspectivised representations, however, may have become normalised within a given Discourse[4] so that they are no longer recognised as ideological but are rather taken for granted as common-sensical. Thus, language is seen, in line with Systemic Functional Linguistics, not only as "a resource for reflecting on the world" (Halliday and Matthiessen 1999: 7) but as a refracting force which "lends structure to ... experience and helps determine ... way[s] of looking at things" (Halliday 1973: 106).

This relativist position, of course, is also assumed in Cognitive Semantics which, in opposition to structuralist and generativist semantics, has shown that the cognitive models, in the form of categories, frames and conceptual metaphors, which underpin lexical relations, coherence and metaphor in language, are subjective and culturally specific (Lakoff 1987). Like CDA, then, Cognitive Linguistics has revealed that the knowledge structures we take for granted as corresponding with reality in fact mediate and organise reality for us in ways which accord with our language habits. This is most clear in the case of metaphor. One of the fundamental findings of Cognitive Linguistics has been the extent to which complex and abstract knowledge domains are structured, metaphorically, by more basic, familiar domains of experience (Lakoff and Johnson 1980; Gibbs this volume). Ontological correspondences in the source domain get mapped on to elements in the target domain to provide it with internal structure. This input, in turn, provides the basis for reason and inference within the target domain. These *conceptual metaphors* are evidenced by the systematic way that they are reflected in metaphorical *expressions*. Toward the more conventional end of the cline from novel to conventional

---

[2] It is unfortunate that a significant body of the American Cognitive Linguistic work on ideology (e.g., Lakoff 1996) does not pay heed to the more European and Australian work in CDA or European "critical" social theorists like Bakhtin, Bourdieu, Foucault and Habermas who present detailed treatments of the instrumentality of language within the social structure.

[3] The synergy between CL and CDA, then, which focuses more on functional variation in text and talk, is entirely in line with, and may be regarded as being part of, the movement toward a broader Cognitive Sociolinguistics (Dirven 2005; Kristiansen and Dirven 2008).

[4] Discourse in this more abstract sense is understood as a "regulated practice that accounts for a number of statements" (Foucault 1972: 80), including their lexical, grammatical, phonological, pragmatic and multimodal forms, within a given domain/genre. Discourses in this Foucauldian sense conceal ideology by "making what is social seem natural" (Kress 1989: 10). Following Gee (1990) we may use "(d)iscourse" to refer to language in use and "(D)iscourse" to refer to social practices that license and are licensed by language in use.

metaphor, however, language users are not aware that they are producing or processing metaphor.[5] Crucially, therefore, the "logic" in the target domain is not consciously experienced as derived and therefore mediated but is taken for granted as absolutely, objectively reflecting reality. There are obvious parallels here between conceptual metaphors and other forms of representation normalised inside a Discourse (see Hart 2010). More recently, experimental research on cross-linguistic differences has confirmed the effects of language on cognition in both basic and metaphorised domains of experience (Levinson 2003; Boroditsky 2001). The relativist argument is pursued in CDA, however, along the following lines: "differences of linguistic structure in the same variety of English (such as in different news reports) can cause readers to see the world being described in different ways" (O'Halloran 2003: 15). Metaphor is of particular significance here as alternative source domains are available to construe the same target domain in alternative terms, leading to different emotional reactions and "logical" conclusions. In so far as "ideology is made possible by the choices a language allows for representing the same material situation in different ways" (Haynes 1989: 119), then, metaphor in discourse is inherently ideological.[6] Consider a brief example:

(1) [A] largely peaceful demonstration **spilled over** into bloody violence in the centre of London ... Clashes later **erupted** at Mansion House Street and Queen Victoria Street near the Bank. (*Telegraph*, 1 April 2009)

(2) The G20 protests in central London turned violent today ahead of tomorrow's summit, with a **band of demonstrators** close to the Bank of England **storming** a Royal Bank of Scotland branch, and baton-wielding police **charging** a sit-down protest by students. (*Guardian*, 1 April 2009)

The contrast between (1) and (2) lies in the competing source domains recruited to conceptualise the same violent situation. In (1), the source domain is that of a VOLCANO. The image invoked is of a potentially dangerous liquid previously contained "boiling up" and escaping from the container. Such a conceptualisation suggests the need to control the liquid which in the target domain equates to the controversial crowd control technique known, presumably by no coincidence, as "kettling". The construal invoked by (1) thus seems to disempower the protesters, reducing their actions to natural phenomena and thus removing their agency, whilst at the same time sanctioning police practices. The source domain in (2), by contrast, is that of WAR. According to Semino (2008: 100), war metaphors in political discourse "tend to dramatize the opposition between different participants ... who are constructed as enemies". Crucially, however, the use of such militarising metaphors in relation to both sides serves to empower protesters, presenting

---

[5] As Shimko (1994: 657) states, "certain metaphors are so taken for granted that they usually slip into our thoughts and actions undetected and unrecognised".
[6] Ideology in discourse is defined most broadly here as "a systematically organised presentation of reality" (Hodge and Kress 1993: 15). In the Socio-Cognitive Approach to CDA, Van Dijk (e.g., 1998) has attempted to articulate at a finer level of detail the properties of ideologies. Most basically, for Van Dijk, ideologies involve an Us/Them polarisation and, typically, positive beliefs about and attitudes toward Us and negative beliefs about and attitudes toward Them. For a further, more detailed, discussion of the contents, structure and format of ideologies from a Cognitive Linguistic perspective see Koller (2014).

their actions as "fighting" for some cause. The use of *storm* in particular seems to have positive connotations of purpose and precision.

While metaphor is central in Cognitive Linguistic approaches to ideological discourse research, of equal importance is the relation between grammar and conceptualisation where, as Langacker puts it, "it is precisely because of their conceptual import – the contrasting images they impose – that alternative grammatical devices are commonly available to code the same situation" (1991: 295). Grammar, on this account, is inherently meaningful. Grammatical constructions impose a particular construal on the scene described. They guide attention along particular parameters where, analogous with visual processing, "what we actually see depends on how closely we examine it, what we choose to look at, which elements we pay most attention to, and where we view it from" (Langacker 2008: 55). Alongside what it has been able to reveal about semantic metaphor in discourse, then, another important contribution of Cognitive Linguistics in CDA has been to theorise in cognitively plausible terms the conceptual weight of grammatical metaphor (in the form of agentless passivisation and nominalisation), which, in specific discursive contexts, is also said to be ideologically load-bearing (Hart 2011b).

If linguistic (semantic or grammatical) structures have the facility, in specific contexts, to reproduce ideology, then language is not only an important instrument of power but, from a critical analytical perspective, it's operationalization in discourse is an important window on the ideologies of powerful speakers and the discourse communities over whom they have influence. It is in this sense that Cognitive Linguistics "offers analytic tools for the critical assessment of ideologies" (Dirven et al. 2007: 1236). It is a central tenet of Cognitive Linguistics that language reflects conceptual structures and processes, which are in turn grounded in more general cognitive abilities (Croft and Cruse 2004). And since "any ideology is a conceptual system of a particular kind" (Lakoff 1996: 37), it follows that language use affords access to ideologies. Linguistic analysis, and Cognitive Linguistic analysis in particular, is therefore an important tool in ideological research. Cognitive Linguistics addresses "the structuring within language of such basic conceptual categories as those of space and time, scenes and events, entities and processes, motion and location, and force and causation" (Talmy 2000: 3) – precisely the kind of transitivity phenomena that critical discourse analysts have been interested in. Cognitive Linguistics, then, is especially useful for CDA in so far as it can "lay bare the structuring of concepts and conceptions" (Dirven et al. 2003: 4) which constitute ideologies.[7] Cognitive Linguistics, in other words, can serve as an analytical lens through which the latent ideologies expressed in, and enacted through, discourse can be brought to critical consciousness.

In the following sections, I review some of the ways in which Cognitive Linguistics and CDA can be usefully combined in ideological discourse research.

3. The Cognitive Linguistic approach to CDA

Unsurprisingly given its centrality in the development of Cognitive Linguistics, the earliest and most influential combination of Cognitive Linguistics and CDA is in the guise

---

[7] On this account, ideology is seen as "a system of beliefs and values based on a set of cognitive models" (Dirven et al. 2003: 1) and may thus be analysed in terms of categories, frames,

of Critical Metaphor Analysis utilising Lakoff and Johnson's (1980) Conceptual Metaphor Theory (Chilton 1996; Santa Ana 2002; Wolf and Polzenhagen 2003; Musolff 2003, 2004; Charteris-Black 2004, 2006; Koller 2004; Maalej 2007; Goatly 2007). As readers of this handbook will know, however, there is much more to the Cognitive Linguistics bow than metaphor theory. Cognitive Linguistics offers a number of theories which have in common a specific set of assumptions including that linguistic (semantic and grammatical) structures are based on the same general cognitive abilities as other domains of cognition, that linguistic knowledge is conceptual in nature, that meaning is grounded in experience, and that words and constructions both construe experience. These theories address a range of linguistic/conceptual phenomena, including categorisation, schematisation, metaphor, salience, selection and perspectivisation (topics covered in this volume; see Ramscar; Baayen; Gibbs; Tomlin and Myachykov; and Langacker this volume), all of which can be seen, in certain discursive contexts, to function ideologically.[8] The broader synergy between Cognitive Linguistics and CDA aims to account for the reproduction of ideology in discourse in terms of these conceptual operations. This synergy thus offers an explanatory framework in which the ideological dimensions of language are related to general conceptual principles (Dirven et al. 2007: 1236). Indeed, it is a particular strength of the Cognitive Linguistic Approach to CDA that a wide array of ideological phenomena in discourse, which may appear to be diverse, can be accounted for against a common theoretical backdrop (Dirven et al. 2007). Whilst metaphor studies have dominated Cognitive Linguistic investigations of ideology in CDA, then, other theories in Cognitive Linguistics have been applied, including prototype theory (O'Halloran 2003), force-dynamics (Hart 2011a) and various aspects of Cognitive Grammar (Marín Arrese 2011a; Hart 2013a, 2013b). Cognitively motivated theories of linguistic description and conceptual modelling have also been developed to account for ideology in longer stretches of discourse, most notably Chilton's (2004) Discourse Space Theory.

Based on Croft and Cruse's (2004) classification of construal operations, Hart (2011b, 2013a, 2013b) offers a taxonomy which attempts to locate these analytical strands inside a single coherent framework.[9] Here, construal operations are classified as instantiations of four general cognitive systems: Gestalt, Comparison, Attention, and Perspective.[10] Similarly, the ideological functions of these construal operations can be analysed in terms of their realisation of four "discursive strategies": Structural configuration, framing, identification, and positioning (see Figure 15.1).[11] Discursive strategies are understood here, following Reisigl and Wodak (2001), as more or less intentional/institutionalised plans of practices whose realisation achieves particular cognitive, emotive and/or social action effects. Realisation, in its cognitive dimension, is understood as constituting hearers'

---

conceptual metaphors and image schemas as well as the "online" conceptualisations which may become idealised in more stable "offline" conceptual structures (Hart 2010).

[8] It should be noted that various labels and classifications have been applied to these "construal operations" (cf. Croft and Cruse 2004; Verhagen 2010).

[9] This is not to say that all authors in this field would necessarily situate their work with respect to this taxonomy or the broader Cognitive Linguistic Approach envisaged here.

[10] See Langacker (this volume) for an alternative classification.

[11] For alternative taxonomies of discursive strategies see Reisigl and Wodak (2001); Chilton and Schäffner (1997); Chilton (2004).

Strategy \ System	Gestalt	Comparison	Attention	Perspective
Structural Configuration	Schematization			
Framing		Categorization		
Framing		Metaphor		
Identification			Profiling	
Identification			Scanning	
Identification			Scalar adjustment	
Positioning				Point of view
Positioning				Deixis

Fig. 15.1: Construal operations and discursive strategies

conceptions of the situations/events described. Construal operations invoked in the hearer are the site of this realisation and thus ideological reproduction.[12]

In Figure 15.1 structural configuration strategies are realised through schematisation involving the imposition of a particular image-schematic representation which constitutes our most basic understanding of the object- or event-structure. Schematisation is based in the Gestalt system which enables conceptualisers to analyse complex scenes as holistic structures. Framing strategies concern the attribution of particular qualities to entities, actors, actions, relations and processes as alternative categories and metaphors are apprehended in their conceptualisation.[13] Identification strategies concern the salience with which social actors are represented in the conceptualisation and are realised through a number of construal operations including profiling, scanning and scalar adjustment. These construal operations are grounded in the system of attention. Positioning strategies can be spatial, temporal or modal. They relate to where, in space or time, we view a scene from and where we locate elements in the discourse relative to that "anchorage point". Modal positioning relates to where we locate propositions in the discourse rela-

---

[12] I stop short of suggesting that discursive strategies force particular conceptualisations and inferences on the grounds that speakers are never in total control of hearer's cognitive processes. However, they can construct contexts and guide interpretation in such a way that certain conceptualisations and inferences are at least likely to be entertained. The extent to which audiences are manipulated by language is a fundamental issue to CDA which has recently been revisited in light of developments in Cognitive Science (see Chilton 2005, 2011; Hart 2010, 2011c, 2013c; O'Halloran 2011; Oswald 2011; Maillat and Oswald 2011; Marín Arrese 2011b; de Saussure 2011).

[13] It should be noted that whilst structural configuration and framing strategies can be separated for purposes of analysis they are rarely, if ever, separable in the practice of discourse. For example, categorization and metaphor may involve the imposition of particular schemas.

tive to our own conceptions of reality (epistemic) and morality (deontic).[14] Positioning strategies are grounded in our ability to conceive of a scene from different perspectives. They are realised in point of view and deixis.

The ideological functions of these construal operations have been analysed across a range of specific contexts including, *inter alia,* immigration (El Refaie 2001; Santa Ana 2002; Charteris-Black 2006; Hart 2010), urban planning (Todolí 2007), business (Koller 2004), European politics (Musolff 2004; Sing 2011; Nasti 2012), war (Chilton 1996, 2004; Maalej 2007; Marín Arrese 2011a), and political protests (Hart 2013a, 2013b). In what follows, I try to demonstrate how Cognitive Linguistic analyses of some of these conceptual parameters allow a handle on the ideological properties of text and talk. Sections are organised around the discursive strategies given in Figure 15.1. I leave out framing strategies realised in categorisation and metaphor due to limits on space and the availability of a now significant body of research in this area (see references herein). I illustrate these strategies and construal operations with data from across various social and political Discourses and genres.

4. Conceptual parameters for ideology

4.1. Structural configuration (Gestalt)

Structural configuration is a strategy by means of which speakers impose on the scene a particular image-schematic representation which constitutes our most basic understanding of the topological and relational structure of the complex under conception. Grounded in the Gestalt system, it relies on our ability to analyse multifaceted entities and events in terms of particular, holistic structures – image schemas. Image schemas are abstract Gestalt structures many of which emerge pre-linguistically from repeated patterns in embodied experience (Johnson 1987; Mandler 2004). They later come to form the meaningful basis of many lexical concepts as well as grammatical constructions and are thus invoked in discourse to construe experience in particular ways.

Various image schemas have been identified in Cognitive Linguistics. These can be catalogued in various ways (see, for example, Evans and Green 2006: 190). However, let us here mention four broad domains of image schemata: SPACE, MOTION, FORCE, and ACTION. SPACE schemas include a CONTAINER schema, a VERTICALITY schema, a NEAR-FAR schema, and a CONTACT schema. MOTION schemas include a SOURCE-PATH-GOAL schema and a MOMENTUM schema. FORCE schemas incorporate the various force-dynamic schemas which, as described by Talmy (2000), constitute concepts of CAUSATION and LETTING. Finally, ACTION schemas would include the canonical ACTION-CHAIN as described by Langacker (1991, 2002) as well as 'transformations' of that schema. In structural configuration strategies, speakers select from the set of available schemas to construe entities and events as being of a particular type and internal structure. Schematisation is ideological, then, because image schemas "constrain and limit meaning as well as patterns of inference in our reasoning" (Johnson 1987: 42). And, since different sche-

---

[14] I would also be inclined to consider evaluations in the system of Appraisal as described by Martin and White (2007) as construal operations realising positioning strategies.

mas have different topological and relational properties, giving rise to different entailments – defined as functional "implications of the internal structure of image schemata" (Johnson 1987: 22) – their particular selection in discourse may achieve different ideological effects.

Hart (2011a) has shown how immigration discourse makes use of force-dynamic schemas to construe the physical, political and legal dimensions of immigration. Consider the contrast between (3) and (4).

(3)   It's estimated that between 1,000 and 1,200 asylum seekers are **coming into the country** every month. (*The Mirror*, 10 May 2002)

(4)   Downing Street acknowledge that illegal immigration was an issue because of growing frustrations over the stream of people **getting into Britain** from France through the Channel tunnel. (*Daily Telegraph*, 21 May 2000)

In (3), the speaker selects a MOTION schema to construe the physical process of migration. This schema consists of a Trajector (TR) (immigrants) moving along a path of motion into a Landmark (LM) (Britain). By contrast, (4), as a function of the lexical semantics for *getting* in this context, encodes a force-dynamic construal. Here, immigrants are cast in the role of an AGONIST (AGO), defined in Talmy's terminology like a Trajector as an entity whose circumstance or location is at issue. However, there is a second active participant, an ANTAGONIST (ANT), defined as an entity whose relation with the AGONIST determines its circumstance or location. The ANTAGONIST can be construed as engaging with the AGONIST in various force-dynamic relations, including impingement as in (4). Here the ANTAGONIST is left implicit but can be read as physical barriers to immigration. The two alternative schemas invoked by (3) and (4) can be modelled as in Figures 15.2 and 15.3 respectively. The arrow in Figure 15.2 designates "free" motion. In Figure 15.3, by contrast, it represents the resultant of a force-interaction between two entities in which the ANTAGONIST attempts to restrict the movement of the AGONIST but, as the stronger entity (+), the AGONIST is able to overcome or avoid the constraints placed upon it.

Schematising the movement of people in force-dynamic terms constructs a binary opposition in which ANT and AGO are pitted against one another and thus contributes to an Us versus Them ideological structure. There is then a further ideological dimension in which particular role participants are cast (Wolf and Polzenhagen 2003: 265). Casting immigrants in the role of AGONIST with an intrinsic tendency toward action as in (4)

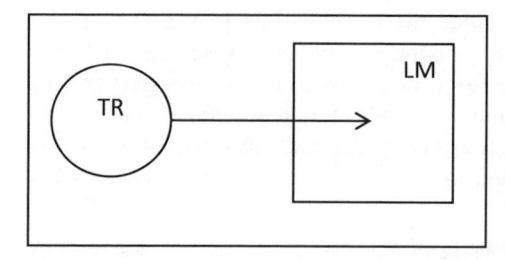

Fig. 15.2: MOTION schema

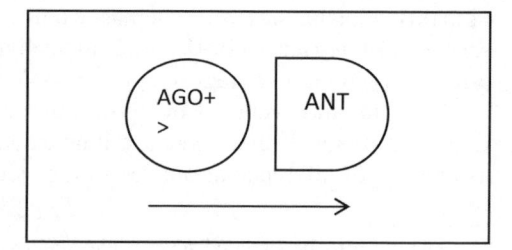

Fig. 15.3: FORCE schema

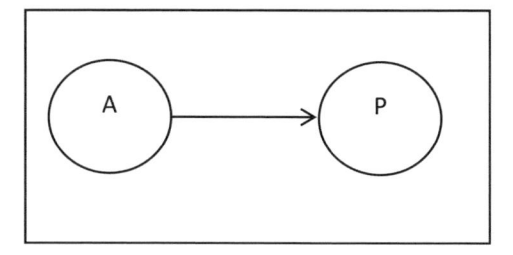

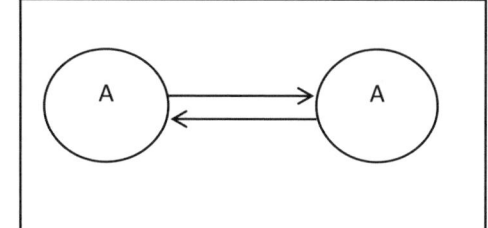

Fig. 15.4: ASYMMETRICAL ACTION schema   Fig. 15.5: RECIPROCAL ACTION schema

depicts them as instigators of force interactions. The ANTAGONIST, on the other hand, is seen as simply maintaining the status quo. More rhetorically, a force-dynamic construal seems to presuppose that immigration ought to be prevented and that in overcoming or avoiding the impinging force of the ANTAGONIST immigrants are acting wrongfully.

Hart (2013a, 2013b) has similarly shown the ideological effects of schematisation in media representations of political protests. Here he shows that the "cognitive discourse grammar" for representing interactions between police and protestors provides recourse to ACTION, FORCE or MOTION schemas. Ideologically, these schemas mitigate the role of participants in the events described to differing degrees. Consider, for example, the contrast between (5) and (6).

(5) A number of police officers were injured after they **came under attack from** youths, some wearing scarves to hide their faces. (*Times*, 10 November 2010)

(6) Activists who had masked their faces with scarves **traded punches with** police. (*Guardian*, 10 November 2010)

In (5), at a discourse level, the interaction between participants is construed in terms of a canonical action chain in which there is a transfer of energy from an AGENT (A) 'upstream' in the energy flow to a PATIENT (P) 'downstream' in the energy flow. As with force-dynamic construals, there is an ideological dimension to the roles that participants are assigned. In a case study of online press reports of the UK Student Fees protests in 2010, Hart (2013b) found that protestors were significantly more likely to be represented as agents in a canonical action chain and police as patients than the other way around. When police were construed as agentive in an ACTION event, it was found, as in (6), that this was more likely to be in a RECIPROCAL rather than the canonical ASYMMETRICAL action chain (Hart 2013b). The alternative construals invoked by (5) and (6) can be modelled as in Figures 15.4 and 15.5 respectively. The arrow in Figure 15.4 indicates the transfer of energy from an AGENT (the source of the energy flow) to a PATIENT (the target of the energy flow). In Figure 15.5, however, the energy flow is bidirectional. Each participant is both a source and a target and so both are assigned agency. Ideologically, construing interactions between police and protestors in terms of a reciprocal action chain serves to mutually apportion responsibility for the violent encounter. Thus, when police are attributed agency in violent interactions their part is mitigated as a consequence of shared accountability.

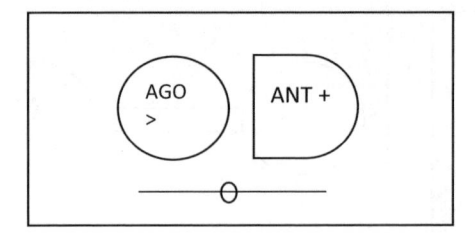

Fig. 15.6: FORCE schema

In the same case study, it was further found that police agency was most likely to be construed in terms of FORCE or MOTION schemas, thus further legitimating or mitigating their part in the violence. Consider (7) and (8).

(7) The 20 officers lining the route at Millbank faced an impossible task of trying to **hold back** thousands of demonstrators (*Daily Mail*, 10 November 2010)

(8) About 50 riot police **moved in** just after 5 pm (*Independent*, 10 November 2010)

In (7), the speaker selects a force-dynamic schema casting police in the role of ANTAGONIST and protestors in the role of AGONIST. Notice, then, that this sets up an oppositional relation in which protestors are seen as being on the wrong side of the law and presented as instigators of force or violence who, if not held back, will "take over". The police, by contrast, are presented in the valiant role of defenders of moral order. The schema invoked by (7) can be modelled as in Figures 15.6.

In this force-dynamic schema, the ANTAGONIST is the stronger entity (+) able to prevent the AGONIST from realising its intrinsic force tendency (>) resulting in a state of equilibrium (O). There is no transfer of energy from a source to a target but, rather, what is at stake is the balance of strength between the two participants. Compare this to (9) in which the police are agentive in a RETALIATORY ACTION schema:

(9) Rocks, wooden banners, eggs, rotten fruit and shards of glass were thrown at police officers trying to **beat back** the crowd with metal batons and riot shields. (*Telegraph*, 10 November 2010)

The schema invoked by (8) is the same as modelled in Figure 15.2. In this context, however, the construal serves euphemistically to present police action in terms of motion. The arrow denotes a path of motion rather than a transfer of energy with its terminus a location (GOAL) rather than a participant (PATIENT). The asymmetry in construal of agency between police and protestors contributes to a Discourse in which the current social order is legitimated and civil action is seen as deviant and therefore delegitimated.

Structural configuration strategies overlap with identification strategies as image schemata invoked in discourse are subject to various kinds of "focal adjustment" within the system of attention. We turn to identification strategies in the following section.

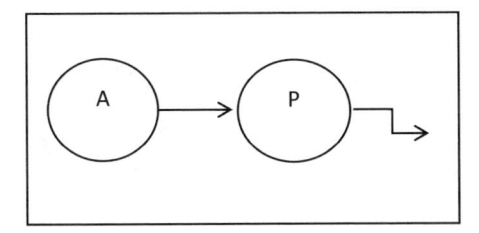

Fig. 15.7: ACTION schema (CHANGE OF STATE)

4.2 Identification (Attention)

Identification strategies concern the salience of social actors within the conceptual contents invoked by linguistic constructions. There is a significant amount of work in CDA on the ideological potential of particular types of grammatical construction, including agentless passives, which are said to "enable speakers to conjure away responsible, involved or affected actors (whether victims or perpetrators), or to keep them in the semantic background" (Reisigl and Wodak 2001: 58). In Cognitive Grammar, the conceptual reflex of such grammatical devices and the psychological reality of "the semantic background" are accounted for in terms of profile/base distinctions grounded in the system of attention (Langacker 2002).

It is a fundamental feature of cognition that in perceiving any scene one entity stands out relative to another. Cognitive Linguists (e.g., Talmy 2000; Langacker 2002) recognise this phenomenon in language too. Words and constructions bring to prominence particular facets of a given conceptual structure, such as a frame or schema. In Cognitive Grammar, this construal operation is called "profiling". According to this framework, transactive processes invoke an ACTION schema such as modelled in Figure 15.7.[15] The straight arrow represents the transfer of energy between participants. The stepped arrow represents the resultant of this interaction on the PATIENT.

Depending on the grammatical realisation, however, different constructions, by linguistically encoding particular aspects of the whole event-structure, distribute attention across the model in different ways. A full transactive clause, for example, profiles the whole schema, where the profiled portion of the schema is that stretch downstream of the participant encoded as Subject. This is modelled in Figure 15.8. An agentless passive construction, by contrast, profiles only that portion of the schema downstream of the PATIENT, leaving the AGENT in the 'scope of attention' but cognitively and experientially backgrounded. As Langacker (2008: 384) puts it, "when one participant is left unspecified, the other becomes more salient just through the absence of competition. On the other hand, augmenting the salience of one participant diminishes that of others (in relative terms)". Consider the following example.

---

[15] For present purposes, I am glossing over a third possible participant in the event-structure in the form of an INSTRUMENT or THEME.

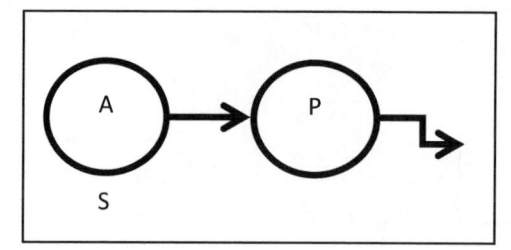

Fig. 15.8: Full profile

Fig. 15.9: Partial profile

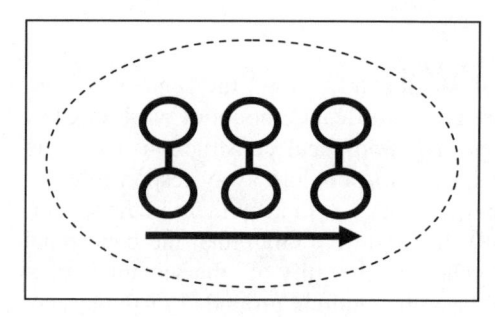

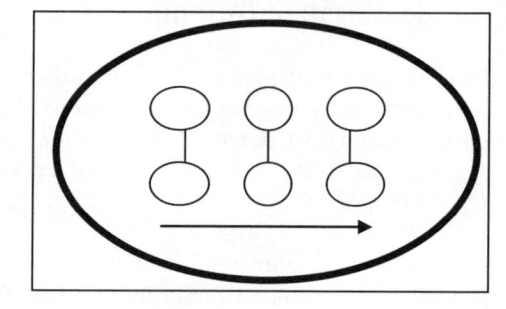

Fig. 15.10: Sequential scanning

Fig. 15.11: Summary scanning

(10) Seven **killed** in Afghanistan Koran burning protests [headline]
Seven people **were killed** today in clashes between Afghan security forces and protesters demonstrating against **the burning** of Muslim holy books at a NATO military base. (*Independent online,* 22 February 2012)

In (10), the agents of *killing* are not specified, either in the headline or the body of the article. The agentless passive construction invokes a conceptualisation as modelled in Figure 15.9. Such a construal, it would be argued in CDA, represents a "preferred model" (Van Dijk 1998) of the event in which agency in actions that are not consonant with dominant Discourses gets obfuscated (Toolan 1991). In this case, of course, the actions of Afghan security forces might be considered to destabilise the Discourse of democratization which sanctified intervention in Afghanistan.

Nominalisation can serve a similar ideological function in excluding agency from the lause (Fairclough 1989; Fowler 1991). The conceptual reflex of nominalisation is also grounded in the system of attention. In Cognitive Grammar it is said to involve a particular mode of "scanning". According to Cognitive Grammar we conceptualise events by mentally scanning the series of relations obtaining between participants at different (continuous) stages in the process that constitutes an event. There are two modes of scanning: sequential scanning and summary scanning. In sequential scanning, "the various phases of an evolving situation are examined serially, in noncumulative fashion" (Langacker 2002: 78–79). This is the mode of scanning invoked by a transactive clause where the relationships held between entities at different moments in the evolving event get profiled. However, as Langacker put is, "we nevertheless have the conceptual agility to construe an event by means of summary scanning" (2002: 79). In summary scanning, the various facets of an event are examined cumulatively so that the whole complex comes to cohere as a single gestalt (Langacker 2002). That is, we see an event as an OBJECT or THING rather than as a series of INTERACTIONS and PROCESSES. And since "things do not pertain to time, we do not scan their internal component states sequentially but see all of them accumulated" (Radden and Dirven 2007: 80). Through summary scanning, then, attention to internal event-structure, including participant roles, is occluded. In example (10) above, we see an instance of nominalisation in *the burning of Muslim holy books*. The nominalised verb profiles the reification and thus conceptually backgrounds agent-patient relations, again contributing to a preferred model of ideologically "awkward" events. The two modes of scanning are modelled in Figures 15.10 and 15.11.

The construal operations we have examined so far are semantically encoded. The final strategy we examine, in the next section, is positioning. Positioning strategies are more pragmatic in nature, directly anchored to the communicative context and more dependent on an intersubjective consensus of values.

4.3. Positioning (Perspective)

Positioning strategies in various (spatial, temporal and modal) guises have been studied from a broadly Cognitive Linguistic perspective (Bednarek 2006; Cap 2006, 2011; Marín Arrese 2011a). Positioning strategies pertain to the ontological relations between elements in a text, as well as epistemological/axiological relations between propositions and the speaker/hearer. They rely on our ability to "fix" conceptions relative to a particular perspective. Literally, this perspective is a VIEWPOINT (Langacker 1987) in space which is operationalised on two dimensions: the vertical or the horizontal. Langacker refers here to VANTAGE POINT and ORIENTATION respectively. The VIEWPOINT can, in turn, be construed at different DISTANCES from the scenes conceived. In Croft and Cruse's (2004) taxonomy of construal operations, deixis and Langacker's subjectivity/objectivity distinction are both also seen as instantiations of the PERSPECTIVE system. Grounded in Mental Spaces Theory (Fauconnier 1994) and geometrical approaches to conceptualisation (Gärdenfors 2004), Chilton (2004) proposes an inherently deictic cognitive model of discourse coherence in which spatial representations metaphorically extend to account for social, temporal and modal "positioning". This framework, which Chilton refers to as Discourse Space Theory, has become an increasingly popular approach to conceptually modelling the interpersonal and affective dimensions of political discourse (see, for example, Cap 2013; Kaal 2012; Filardo Llamas 2013).

Discourse Space Theory is specifically designed to account for the conceptual structures built in "discourse beyond the sentence".[16] The claim is that during discourse hearers open a mental space in which the world described in the discourse is conceptually represented. The mental space, or discourse space, consists of three intersecting axes around which the discourse world is constructed. These axes are a socio-spatial axis (S), a temporal axis (T) and a modal axis (M). Each axis represents a scale of remoteness from a "deictic centre", which corresponds with the deictic reference points for the communicative event. Crucially, for the theory, this extends beyond the spatiotemporal

---

[16] In this way, the theory has much in common with Text World Theory (Werth 1999) which is often applied in Cognitive Poetics (see Stockwell this volume).

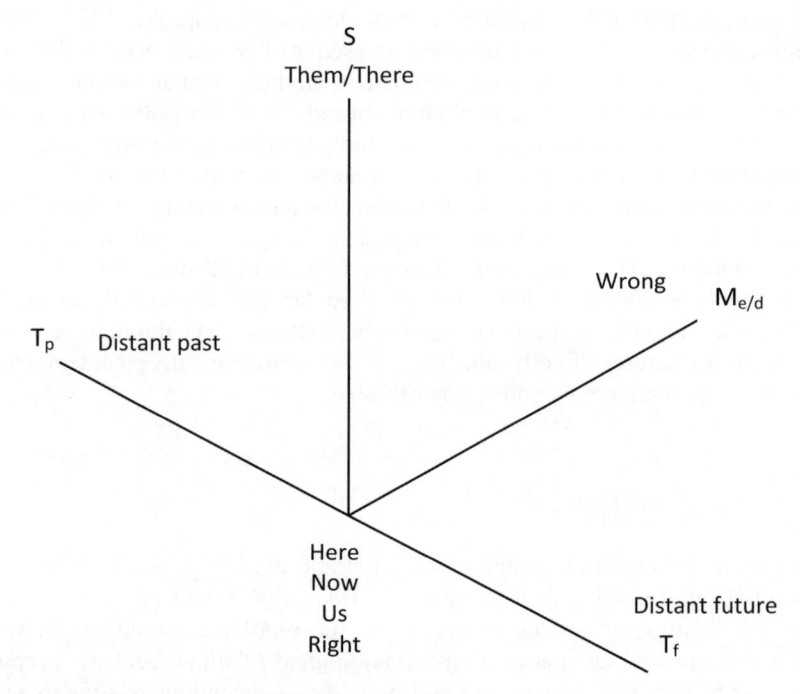

```
                    S
                Them/There
                    |
                    |
                    |
                            Wrong    M_{e/d}
   T_p   Distant past
                    |
                    |
                  Here
                  Now
                   Us          Distant future
                  Right              T_f
```

Fig. 15.12: Basic Discourse Space Model

"here" and "now" to include the social group "us" and shared evaluations of what is "right" both cognitively and morally. We can think of each axis as having polar reference points with various intermediate stations. For example, the S axis may be taken to represent an Us versus Them polarisation. The T axis represents a time line from "now" to "distant future" and "distant past". And the M axis represents a right-wrong scale.

The construction of discourse worlds involves the "plotting" of discourse elements within the three dimensional space relative to one and other and in relation to the topography of the basic model. The relative coordinates of these elements are indexed in text by linguistic representations and presupposed knowledge/value systems. Hearers are then invited to reconstruct this particular worldview. The basic architecture is seen in Figure 15.12.[17]

Crucially, the mapping out of elements inside the discourse space does not directly reflect reality but rather constructs it. The representation is thus subject to construal. Discourse elements can be proximised or distanced relative to the deictic centre. This deictic construal operation seems to be based on a CONTRACTION/PROTRACTION image schema. In the discourse space, this involves a shortening or lengthening of the distance between discourse elements and the deictic centre. Thus, as Chilton states, for many English speakers/hearers, Australia might be conceptualised as closer to the deictic centre along the socio-spatial axis than Albania. Evans (2004) shows that TIME too may be conceptualised as contracted or protracted.

---

[17] Note that the diagram is a two-dimensional representation of a three-dimensional space.

Cap (2006) presents an elaborated theory of "proximisation" – a rhetorical strategy which works by "alerting the addressee to the proximity or imminence of phenomena which can be a 'threat' to the addressee and thus require immediate reaction" (2006: 4). Within the taxonomy presented in Figure 1, we can characterise proximisation as a deictic construal operation realising spatio-temporal positioning strategies. To illustrate how all of this works, consider first the following extract from Tony Blair's (the then British Prime Minister) foreword to the 24 September 2002 dossier outlining the case for war against Iraq:

(11) I am in no doubt that the threat is serious and current, that he has made progress on WMD, and that he has to be stopped. Saddam has used chemical weapons, not only against an enemy state, but against his own people. Intelligence reports make clear that he sees the building up of his WMD capability, and the belief overseas that he would use these weapons, as vital to his 3 strategic interests, and in particular his goal of regional domination. And the document discloses that his military planning allows for some of the WMD to be ready within 45 minutes of an order to use them.
I am quite clear that Saddam will go to extreme lengths, indeed has already done so, to hide these weapons and avoid giving them up. In today's inter-dependent world, a major regional conflict does not stay confined to the region in question
...
The threat posed to international peace and security, when WMD are in the hands of a brutal and aggressive regime like Saddam's, is real. Unless we face up to the threat, not only do we risk undermining the authority of the UN, whose resolutions he defies, but more importantly and in the longer term, we place at risk the lives and prosperity of our own people.

The discourse world constructed by the text is (partially) modelled in Figure 15.13. Actors and locations are positioned along the S axis at relative distances from deictic centre, dependent on construed social distance. *Saddam Hussein* and his *regime* are constructed as Them and positioned at the extreme end of the S axis. Other participants are positioned between Them and the presupposed Us indexed in the text by *we*. The *United Nations* and the *international community* are construed as "closer" to Us than *Iraq* and the broader *region*.

The modal axis is simultaneously engaged in both a deontic and an epistemic capacity. In Figure 15.13 it is presented in its deontic guise where it stands as a scale of morality/immorality. Elements in the text like *brutal and aggressive, threat, WMD* and *regional domination*, based on an assumed shared value system, are associated with "immorality" and so positioned at the remote end of M_d. Elements along the different axes are linked by means of "connectors" which represent various kinds of relation including attribution, possession and intention. The zone around the deictic centre represents the extension of the conceptualiser's physical, social, moral and temporal ground.

The location of elements along S and M in the discourse space realise distancing positioning strategies. However, we can see both spatial and temporal proximisation where the *threat* posed by *Saddam Hussein* and his *WMD* is construed as (potentially) closer to or entering the conceptualiser's spatio-temporal ground. This construal operation is denoted in Figure 15.13 by the "vectors" pointing toward deictic centre along S and T_f. Spatial proximisation is indexed in the text by predicates which indicate (some-

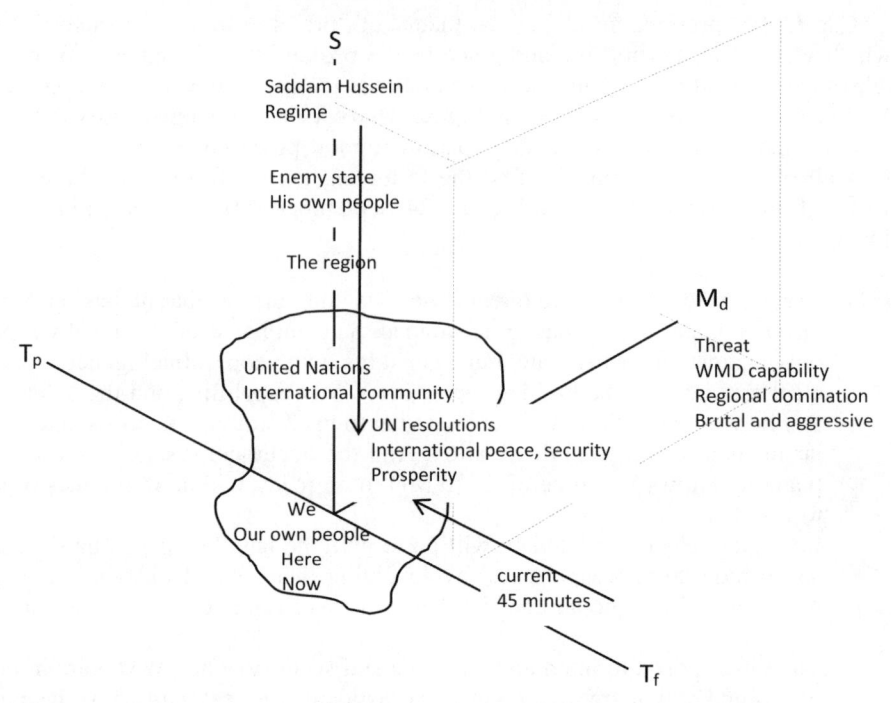

Fig. 15.13: Spatial and Temporal Proximisation

times indirectly) that the range of the threat may extend to the conceptualiser's physical ground. These include:

- has **used** chemical weapons, not only **against an enemy state**, but **against his own people**
- does not **stay confined to the region in question**
- **place at risk** the lives and prosperity of **our own people**

This proximisation, then, is built up in the text progressively as the threat is presented as extending from *enemy states* and *his own people* to the broader *region* and, finally, to *our own people*. Interestingly, this conceptual proximisation is also symbolically represented in the information sequence of the unfolding discourse. Temporal proximisation occurs where elements in the text position the reality of this threat as close to "now". Expressions of temporal proximisation include *current* and the now notorious *within 45 minutes*.

Operating over the other dimensions, we can identify epistemic proximisation as realising an epistemological positioning strategy (Hart 2014; see also Bednarek 2006). In the discourse space, the modal axis is also always engaged in an epistemic aspect representing a scale of reality/irreality. The discourse world for the text above, this time with the modal axis presented in its epistemic capacity, is shown in Figure 15.14. The zone around the deictic centre here represents the extension of the conceptualiser's epistemic ground, that is, what the conceptualiser takes to be "known reality" (Langacker 1991). Epistemic proximisation occurs as propositions embedded in the text, such as

15. Discourse

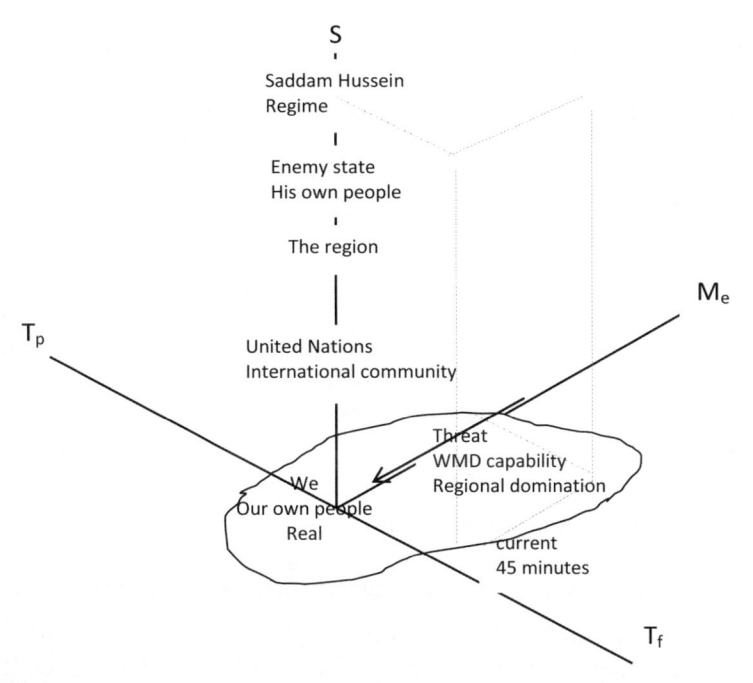

Fig. 15.14: Epistemic Proximisation

'Saddam Hussein possesses WMD and poses a threat to the world which may be realised within 45 minutes', represented in the discourse space by the connections between elements, are construed as part of known reality. Epistemic proximisation is indexed in text by expressions of epistemic modality and evidentiality, as well as existential presuppositions, which act as metaphorical "forces" (cf. Sweetser 1990; Talmy 2000) on the proposition propelling it toward the conceptutualiser's "right" at the deictic centre. In the text we find examples such as "I am in no doubt that", "is real", "intelligence reports make clear that" and *the document discloses that*.

One further, final, construal operation worth discussing in relation to modal positioning strategies is subjectivity/objectivity. This construal operation pertains to whether or not the speaker places themselves "onstage" as part of the object of conception (Langacker 1991) and, if so, whether this is alone or accompanied. According to Langacker, the speaker is objectified, made salient, if they are explicitly designated as the source of the predication. They are subjectified when they remain only implicitly the source of the predication. Since in both cases, the speaker rather than some third party is the source of the predication Langacker's subjectification and objectification both relate to notions of subjectivity as traditionally dealt with in the literature on stance and evaluation (e.g., Hunston and Thompson 2000; Englebretson 2007). Here, speakers may express either a subjective or an intersubjective stance on a given proposition. In Langacker's framework, a speaker may thus be subjectively or intersubjectively objectified.

Marín Arrese (2011a) discusses the ideological implications of subjectivity and, cutting across these notions, proposes a four-way classification of "epistemic stance-taking acts" as follows:

- Subjective Explicit (SE): the speaker is objectified as the sole evaluator
- Intersubjective Explicit (IE): the speaker and some other subject are together objectified as appraisers in agreement
- Subjective Implicit (SI): the speaker is subjectified but understood to be the sole evaluator
- Intersubjective Opaque (IO): the speaker is not identified as evaluator subjectively or objectively but rather evidence in favour of a particular evaluation is presented as (potentially) mutually accessible.

This "grammar" provides for ideologically motivated choices which depend on whether and to what extent of explicitness the speaker is prepared to claim sole responsibility for the assertion being made as in SE/SI, whether they wish to share in the evaluation either to stand behind an institution (*we the Government*) or to claim common ground with the audience (*we the speaker and addressee*) (IE), or whether the speaker needs to invoke external sources of support (IO). The expressions of epistemic proximisation in the text above are categorised in Marín Arrese's typology as follows:

- I am in no doubt that; I am clear that (SE)
- is real (SI)
- intelligence reports make clear that; the document discloses that (IO)

(SE) is a marked characteristic of Blair's rhetorical style (Marin Arrese 2011a). In effect, it asks the audience not just to believe the speaker but to believe *in* the speaker. It betrays a speaker confident in their own credibility. However, as Van Dijk (2011: 53) states, "speakers are more credible when they are able to attribute their knowledge or opinions to reliable sources, especially if some of the recipients may doubt whether they are well grounded". In order to convince audiences, therefore, political and media genres often require speakers to advance evidence for their assertions (Chilton 2004; Hart 2011c). Various types of evidence are available (see Bednarek 2006). However, particularly prominent in political discourse is the kind of "proof" invoked by Blair including "independent reports", "investigations", "studies" and "statistics".

5. Conclusion

In this chapter, I have tried to provide an overview of some of the ways in which Cognitive Linguistics and CDA can be combined to reveal ideological properties of text and conceptualisation. In doing so, I have surveyed a number of construal operations which, invoked by particular linguistic instantiations in discourse, may carry some ideological load. I have further attempted to systematise these inside a single, coherent theoretical framework relating construal operations to the domain-general cognitive systems on which they rely and to the discursive strategies which they potentially realise. Several construal operations have been identified as fulfilling an ideological potential in specific discursive contexts. Those discussed in this chapter should not be taken as an exhaustive set. Nearly all construal operations may be ideologically significant in certain contexts. They are, however, representative of those so far addressed within the body of work existing at the intersection between Cognitive Linguistics and CDA.

References

Baayen, Harald
  this volume 5. Analogy and schematization. Berlin/Boston: De Gruyter Mouton.
Bednarek, Monika
  2006 Epistemological positioning and evidentiality in English news discourse: A text-driven approach. *Text and Talk* 26(6): 635–660.
Boroditsky, Lera
  2001 Does language shape thought? English and Mandarin speakers' conceptions of time. *Cognitive Psychology* 43 (1): 1–22.
Cap, Piotr
  2006 *Legitimization in Political Discourse*. Newcastle: Cambridge Scholars Press.
Cap. Piotr
  2011 Axiological proximisation. In: C. Hart (ed.), *Critical Discourse Studies in Context and Cognition*, 81–96. Amsterdam: John Benjamins.
Cap, Piotr
  2013 *Proximization: The Pragmatics of Symbolic Distance Crossing*. Amsterdam: John Benjamins.
Charteris-Black, Jonathan
  2004 *Corpus Approaches to Critical Metaphor Analysis*. Basingstoke: Palgrave Macmillan.
Charteris-Black, Jonathan
  2006 Britain as a container: Immigration metaphors in the 2005 election campaign. *Discourse and Society* 17(6): 563–82.
Chilton, Paul A.
  1996 *Security Metaphors: Cold War Discourse from Containment to Common House*. New York: Peter Lang.
Chilton, Paul A.
  2004 *Analysing Political Discourse: Theory and Practice*. London: Routledge.
Chilton, Paul A.
  2005 Missing links in mainstream CDA: Modules, blends and the critical instinct. In R. Wodak and P. Chilton (eds.), *A New Research Agenda in Critical Discourse Analysis: Theory and Interdisciplinarity*, 19–52. Amsterdam: John Benjamins.
Chilton, Paul A.
  2011 Still something missing in CDA. *Discourse Studies* 13(6): 769–781.
Chilton, Paul A. and Christina. Schäffner
  1997 Discourse and politics. In: T. A. van Dijk (ed.), *Discourse as Social Interaction*, 206–230. London: Sage.
Croft, William and D. Alan Cruse
  2004 *Cognitive Linguistics*. Cambridge: Cambridge University Press.
de Saussure, Louis
  2011 Discourse analysis, cognition and evidentials. *Discourse Studies* 13(6): 781–788.
Dirven, René, Roslyn M. Frank and Martin Putz
  2003 Introduction: Categories, cognitive models and ideologies. In: R. Dirven, R. Frank and M. Putz (eds.), *Cognitive Models in Language and Thought: Ideology, Metaphors and Meanings*, 1–24. Berlin: Mouton de Gruyter.
Dirven, René, Frank Polzenhagen and Hanz-Georg Wolf
  2007 Cognitive linguistics, ideology and critical discourse analysis. In: D. Geeraerts and H. Cuyckens (eds.), *The Oxford Handbook of Cognitive Linguistics*, 1222–1240. Oxford: Oxford University Press.
El Refaie, Elisabeth
  2001 Metaphors we discriminate by: Naturalized themes in Austrian newspaper articles about asylum seekers. *Journal of Sociolinguistics* 5(3): 352–71.

Engelbretson, Robert (ed.)
  2007   *Stancetaking in Discourse: Subjectivity, Evaluation, Interaction.* Amsterdam: John Benjamins.
Evans, Vyvyan
  2004   *The Structure of Time: Language, Meaning and Temporal Cognition.* Amsterdam: John Benjamins.
Evans, Vyvyan and Melanie Green
  2006   *Cognitive Linguistics: An Introduction.* Edinburgh: Edinburgh University Press.
Fairclough, Norman
  1989   *Language and Power.* London: Longman.
Fairclough, Norman and Ruth Wodak
  1997   Critical discourse analysis. In: T. A. van Dijk (ed.), *Discourse as Social Interaction. Discourse Studies: A Multidisciplinary Introduction* Vol. 2, 258–284. London: Sage.
Fauconnier, Gilles
  1994   *Mental Spaces: Aspects of Meaning Construction in Natural Language* 2nd edn. Cambridge: Cambridge University Press.
Filardo Llamas, Laura
  2013   'Committed to the ideals of 1916': The language of paramilitary groups: the case of the Irish Republican Army. *Critical Discourse Studies* 10(1): 1–17.
Foucault, Michel
  1972   *Archaeology of Knowledge.* London: Routledge.
Fowler, Roger
  1991   *Language in the News: Discourse and Ideology in the Press.* London: Routledge.
Gärdenfors, Peter
  2004   *Conceptual Spaces: The Geometry of Thought* 2nd edn. Bradford: Bradford Books.
Gee, James P.
  1990   *Social Linguistics and Literacies: Ideology in Discourses.* London: Falmer Press
Gibbs, Raymond W Jr.
  this volume   8. Metaphor. Berlin/Boston: De Gruyter Mouton.
Goatly, Andrew
  2007   *Washing the Brain: Metaphor and Hidden Ideology.* Amsterdam: John Benjamins.
Halliday, Michael A. K.
  1973   *Explorations in the Functions of Language.* London: Edward Arnold.
Halliday, Michael A. K. and C. M. I. M. Matthiessen
  1999   *Construing Experience Through Meaning: A Language-Based Approach to Cognition.* London: Continuum.
Hart, Christopher
  2010   *Critical Discourse Analysis and Cognitive Science: New Perspectives on Immigration Discourse.* Basingstoke: Palgrave.
Hart, Christopher
  2011a   Force-interactive patterns in immigration discourse: A Cognitive Linguistic approach to CDA. *Discourse and Society* 22(3): 269–286.
Hart, Christopher
  2011b   Moving beyond metaphor in the Cognitive Linguistic approach to CDA: Construal operations in immigration discourse. In: C. Hart (ed.), *Critical Discourse Studies in Context and Cognition*, 171–192. Amsterdam: John Benjamins.
Hart, Christopher
  2011c   Legitimising assertions and the logico-rhetorical module: Evidence and epistemic vigilance in media discourse on immigration. *Discourse Studies* 13(6): 751–769.
Hart, Christopher
  2013a   Event-construal in press reports of violence in political protests: A Cognitive Linguistic Approach to CDA. *Journal of Language and Politics* 3: 159

Hart, Christopher
   2013b   Constructing contexts through grammar: Cognitive models and conceptualisation in British Newspaper reports of political protests. In: J. Flowerdew (ed.) *Discourse and Contexts,* 159–184. London: Continuum.
Hart, Christopher
   2013c   Argumentation meets adapted cognition: Manipulation in media discourse on immigration. *Journal of Pragmatics* 59: 200–209.
Hart, Christopher
   2014   *Discourse, Grammar and Ideology: Functional and Cognitive Perspectives.* London: Bloomsbury.
Hart, Christopher and Dominik Lukeš (eds.)
   2007   *Cognitive Linguistics in Critical Discourse Analysis: Application and Theory.* Newcastle: Cambridge Scholars Publishing.
Haynes, John
   1989   *Introducing Stylistics.* London: Hyman.
Hodge, Robert and Gunther Kress
   1993   *Language as Ideology* 2nd edn. London: Routledge.
Hunston, Susan and Geoff Thompson (eds.)
   2000   *Evaluation in Text: Authorial Stance and the Construction of Discourse.* Oxford: Oxford University Press.
Johnson, Mark
   1987   *The Body in the Mind: The Bodily Basis of Meaning, Imagination, and Reason.* Chicago: University of Chicago Press.
Kaal, Bertie
   2012   Worldviews: Spatial ground for political reasoning in Dutch Election manifestos. *Critical Approaches to Discourse Analysis across Disciplines* 6(1): 1–22.
Koller, Veronika
   2004   *Metaphor and Gender in Business Media Discourse: A Critical Cognitive Study.* Basingstoke: Palgrave.
Koller, Veronika
   2014   Cognitive Linguistics and ideology. In: J. R. Taylor and J. Littlemore (eds.), *Companion to Cognitive Linguistics*, 234–252. London: Continuum.
Kress, Gunther
   1989   *Linguistic Processes in Sociocultural Practice* 2nd edn. Oxford: Oxford University Press.
Lakoff, George
   1987   *Women, Fire, and Dangerous Things: What Categories Reveal about the Mind.* Chicago: University of Chicago Press.
Lakoff, George
   1996   *Moral Politics: How Liberals and Conservatives Think.* Chicago: University of Chicago Press.
Lakoff, George and Mark Johnson
   1980   *Metaphors We Live By.* Chicago: University of Chicago Press.
Langacker, Ronald W.
   1987   *Foundations of Cognitive Grammar,* vol. I: *Theoretical Prerequisites.* Stanford: Stanford University Press.
Langacker, Ronald W.
   1991   *Foundations of Cognitive Grammar,* vol. II: *Descriptive Application.* Stanford: Stanford University Press.
Langacker, Ronald W.
   2002   *Concept, Image, and Symbol: The Cognitive Basis of Grammar.* 2nd edn. Berlin: Mouton de Gruyter.

Langacker, Ronald W.
   2008   *Cognitive Grammar: A Basic Introduction.* Oxford: Oxford University Press.

Langacker, Ronald W.
   this volume   6. Construal. Berlin/Boston: De Gruyter Mouton.

Levinson, Stephen C.
   2003   *Space in Language and Cognition: Explorations in Cognitive Diversity.* Cambridge: Cambridge University Press.

Maalej, Zouhair
   2007   Doing critical discourse analysis with the contemporary theory of metaphor: Toward a discourse model of metaphor. In: C. Hart and D. Lukeš (eds.), *Cognitive Linguistics in Critical Discourse Analysis: Application and Theory*, 132–58. Newcastle: Cambridge Scholars Press.

Maillat, Didier and Steve Oswald
   2011   Constraining context: A pragmatic account of cognitive manipulation. In: C. Hart (ed.), *Critical Discourse Studies in Context and Cognition*, 65–80. Amsterdam: John Benjamins.

Mandler, Jean M.
   2004   *The Foundations of Mind: Origins of Conceptual Thought.* Oxford: Oxford University Press.

Marín Arrese, Juana
   2011a   Effective vs. epistemic stance and subjectivity in political discourse: Legitimising strategies and mystification of responsibility. In: C. Hart (ed.), *Critical Discourse Studies in Context and Cognition,* 193–224. Amsterdam: John Benjamins.

Marín Arrese, Juana
   2011b   Epistemic legitimizing strategies, commitment and accountability in discourse. *Discourse Studies* 13(6): 789–797.

Musolff, Andreas
   2003   Ideological functions of metaphor: The conceptual metaphors of *health* and *illness* in public discourse. In: R. Dirven, R. Frank and M. Putz (eds.), *Cognitive Models in Language and Thought: Ideology, Metaphors and Meanings*, 327–352. Berlin: Mouton de Gruyter.

Musolff, Andreas
   2004   *Metaphor and Political Discourse: Analogical Reasoning in Debates about Europe.* Basingstoke: Palgrave Macmillan.

Nasti, Chiara
   2012   *Images of the Lisbon Treaty Debate in the British Press: A Corpus-Based Approach to Metaphor Analysis.* Newcastle: Cambridge Scholars Publishing.

Nuñez-Perucha, Begoña
   2011   Critical Discourse Analysis and Cognitive Linguistics as tools for ideological research: A diachronic analysis of feminism. In: C. Hart (ed.), *Critical Discourse Studies in Context and Cognition* 97–118. Amsterdam: John Benjamins.

O'Halloran, Kieran
   2003   *Critical Discourse Analysis and Language Cognition.* Edinburgh: Edinburgh University Press.

O'Halloran, Kieran
   2011   Legitimations of the logico-rhetorical module: Inconsistency in argument, online discussion forums and electronic deconstruction. *Discourse Studies* 13(6): 797–806.

Oswald, Steve
   2011   From interpretation to consent: Arguments, beliefs and meaning. *Discourse Studies* 13(6): 806–814.

Radden, Gunter and Rene Dirven
   2007   *Cognitive English Grammar.* Amsterdam: John Benjamins.

Ramscar, Michael
   this volume   4. Categorization. Berlin/Boston: De Gruyter Mouton.
Reisigl, Martin and Ruth Wodak
   2001   *Discourse and Discrimination: Rhetorics of Racism and Anti-Semitism*. London: Routledge.
Santa Ana, Otto
   2002   *Brown Tide Rising: Metaphors of Latinos in Contemporary American Public Discourse*. Austin: University of Texas Press.
Semino, Elena
   2008   *Metaphor in Discourse*. Cambridge: Cambridge University Press.
Shimko, Keith L.
   1994   Metaphors and foreign policy decision making. *Political Psychology* 15(4): 655–671.
Sing, Christine
   2011   The ideological construction of European identities: A critical discourse analysis of the linguistic representation of the old vs. new Europe debate. In C. Hart (ed.), *Critical Discourse Studies in Context and Cognition*, 143–170. Amsterdam: John Benjamins.
Stockwell, Peter
   1999   Towards a critical cognitive linguistics. In: A. Combrink and I. Bierman (eds.), *Discourses of War and Conflict*, 510–528. Potchefstroom: Ptochefstroom University Press.
Stockwell, Peter
   this volume   20. Poetics. Berlin/Boston: De Gruyter Mouton.
Sweetser, Eve
   1990   *From Etymology to Pragmatics: Metaphorical and Cultural Aspects of Semantic Structure*. Cambridge: Cambridge University Press.
Talmy, Leonard
   2000   *Toward a Cognitive Semantics*. Cambridge: MIT Press.
Todolí, Júlia
   2007   Disease metaphors in urban planning. *Critical Approaches to Discourse Analysis across Disciplines* 1(2): 51–60.
Toolan, Michael J.
   1991   *Narrative: A Critical Linguistic Introduction*. London: Routledge.
Tomlin, Russell and Andriy Myachykov
   this volume   2. Attention and salience. Berlin/Boston: De Gruyter Mouton.
van Dijk, Teun A.
   1995   Discourse analysis as ideology analysis. In: C. Schäffner and A. I. Wenden (eds.), *Language and Peace*, 17–36. Amsterdam: Harwood Academic Publishers.
van Dijk, Teun A.
   1998   *Ideology: A Multidisciplinary Approach*. London: Sage.
van Dijk, Teun A.
   2001   Critical discourse analysis. In: D. Schiffrin, D. Tannen and H. E. Hamilton (eds.), *The Handbook of Discourse Analysis*, 352–371. Oxford: Blackwell.
van Dijk, Teun A.
   2011   Discourse, knowledge, power and politics: Towards critical epistemic discourse analysis. In: C. Hart (ed.), *Critical Discourse Studies in Context and Cognition*, 27–64. Amsterdam: John Benjamins.
Verhagen, Arie
   2010   Construal and perspectivisation. In D. Geeraerts and H. Cuyckens (eds.), *The Oxford Handbook of Cognitive Linguistics*, 48–81. Oxford: Oxford University Press.
Werth, Paul
   1999   *Text Worlds: Representing Conceptual Space in Discourse*. Harlow: Longman.

Wodak, Ruth
   2001   What is CDA about: A summary of its history, important concepts and its developments. In: R. Wodak and M. Meyer (eds.), *Methods of Critical Discourse Analysis*, 1–13. London: Sage.

Wolf, Hans-Georg and Frank Polzenhagen
   2003   Conceptual metaphor as ideological stylistic means: An exemplary analysis. In: R. Dirven, R. Frank and M. Putz (eds.), *Cognitive Models in Language and Thought: Ideology, Metaphors and Meanings*, 247–276. Berlin: Mouton de Gruyter.

Christopher Hart, Lancaster (United Kingdom)

16. Historical linguistics

1. Introduction
2. Language change and the usage-based model
3. Lexical semantic change
4. Grammaticalization
5. Historical sociolinguistics
6. Diachronic Construction Grammar
7. Concluding remarks
8. References

1. Introduction

At first blush it may seem odd that researchers in Cognitive Linguistics should have an interest in the historical development of language. After all, analyzing the relationship between language and cognition seems a much more feasible task if there are speakers whose behavior can be observed in the here-and-now. This of course is not possible with languages or language varieties that are no longer spoken. To give just two examples, one cannot conduct a lexical decision task with speakers of Old English, nor is it possible to study the metaphorical underpinnings of gestures that accompanied conversations in Hittite. How can a cognitive approach to language history be anything but utter speculation? This chapter will make the case that looking at language change is not only perfectly in line with the cognitive linguistic enterprise, but that furthermore an understanding of how language change works is a necessary prerequisite for an adequate theory of how language and cognition are related in synchrony. The key idea underpinning this argument is the usage-based approach to language, that is, the hypothesis that language use shapes speakers' cognitive representation of language.

    This argument will be made in five sections. The first section is a general presentation of the usage-based approach that Cognitive Linguistics brings to the study of language change (e.g., Langacker 1987; Bybee 2007, 2010). On this view, the major cause of language change is language use itself. Language change on a historical time-scale is viewed as the emergent outcome of speaker behavior in the here-and-now. This behavior, in turn, is governed by cognitive and social principles, which serve as explanations of why and how language changes. Grounding the study of language change in cognitively and socially motivated explanations can be seen as the main agenda of usage-based historical linguistics.

The introductory section sets the scene for four sections that illustrate different domains of language change. The first addresses lexical semantic change. The development of lexical meaning is inherently tied to the topics of conceptual metaphor and metonymy, polysemy, and prototype theory (Geeraerts 1997). The section will chart the semantic developments of selected lexical items and clarify the relation between historical change and synchronic polysemy. The next section discusses grammaticalization theory (Heine et al. 1991; Lehmann 1995; Hopper and Traugott 2003) and its relation to Cognitive Linguistics. The emergence of grammatical forms from lexical items yields evidence for conceptual and formal shifts that take place in highly similar ways across genetically unrelated languages; examples of such shifts will be presented. A third section will look at sociolinguistic change. A growing body of studies in Cognitive Linguistics acknowledges the importance of the social dimension of language and hence adopts a variationist framework (Geeraerts et al. 2010). It will be outlined how this work replaces the assumption of an idealized speaker-hearer with more realistic models of inter- and intraspeaker variation, and how it proceeds methodologically. The fourth section reports on work that applies the framework of Construction Grammar to the analysis of language change. Studies in Diachronic Construction Grammar (Noël 2007) analyze historical developments at the level of form-meaning pairings. This section discusses how such work differs from other approaches to the diachrony of language structure. A final section examines how these four domains of language change intersect and how they connect back to the usage-based approach of cognitive linguistics.

2. Language change and the usage-based model

There is ample theoretical motivation and empirical evidence that the synchronic structure of any human language is the emergent result of language use (Bybee and Hopper 2001; Barlow and Kemmer 2000). Grammatical structures are created through the social activity of human beings who engage in linguistic interaction, trying to "do things with words". As is discussed by Diessel (this volume), language use is dependent on several cognitive processes that are not in themselves linguistic. Amongst other things, the capacities for categorization, schematization, and analogy formation (cf. part I of this volume) are necessary cognitive prerequisites for language use. Similarly, language use is shaped by non-linguistic factors that are social in nature. These include the human inclination to co-operate (Grice 1975; Tomasello 2009), the ability to be polite, i.e., to respect the self-image of interlocutors in social interaction (Goffman 1955; Brown and Levinson 1987), and the disposition towards engaging in joint attention (Tomasello 1995), that is, "two people experiencing the same thing at the same time and knowing together that they are doing this" (Tomasello and Carpenter 2007: 121). A cornerstone of the usage-based model is hence the claim that language is grounded in domain-general socio-cognitive processes. The epithet domain-general indicates that these processes are active in basically all kinds of human cognition, not only cognition that relates to language.

A consequence of that claim is that it is impossible to separate the synchronic study of language from inherently dynamic issues, such as language acquisition and language change. Forming linguistic categories, constructional schemas, or analogies is not only what enables communication between human beings in the present, but these processes are also necessary for learning a first language (Matthews and Krajewski this volume), and the constant application of these processes by adult language users can be seen as the driving force behind language change: As particular forms of language are used again and again in linguistic interaction, routinization processes effectuate small steps of change in constructions' pronunciations, their meanings, their morpho-syntactic properties, etc. Frequency effects, together with the notion of entrenchment, are discussed in detail in Divjak and Caldwell-Harris (this volume). Some effects of this kind are seen a result of speech production. For example, certain frequency effects come about as the consequences of repeated, routinized events of language production (Bybee and Thompson 1997). For instance, in the phrase *I don't know what you mean* the negated auxiliary is often heavily reduced and the final stop of *what* shows palatization. By comparison, these phenomena do not occur to the same extent in the phonologically similar but much less frequent phrase *I don't notice the dot you mean*. Other types of change are believed to result from language processing. Frequent processing of a linguistic form leads to "chunking", in which a complex sequence of items comes to be mentally represented as a holistic unit (Bybee and Scheibman 1999). The more often a string of elements is processed in sequence, the more likely hearers are to process this string as a single unit. An example for this would be the chunk *sitting and waiting*, which in some respects behaves like a single verb: In the question *What are you sitting and waiting for?* it is the prepositional object of the verb *waiting* that is questioned. Usually however, it is not possible in English to question constituents that are part of a coordinated phrase (Ross 1967: 89). An utterance such as *What are you whistling and waiting for?* sounds unidiomatic if not ungrammatical to most speakers. This is evidence that speakers reanalyzed the string *sitting and waiting* as a chunk, i.e., as a single verbal constituent. The presence of such frequency effects suggests that speakers' mental grammars undergo gradual changes that are driven by repetition and that only eventually result in categorical changes. The idea that one's mental representation of grammar may change during adulthood is very much at odds with the theory that first language acquisition is the only place where grammar change can occur (Lightfoot 1979). Instead of viewing language change as the result of compromised transmission between generations of speakers, the usage-based model offers a perspective in which language change happens gradually, with every usage event.

A notion that is central for this perspective is that speakers retain a large number of usage events in memory (Bybee 2010: ch. 2). Each token of linguistic usage is stored in a highly detailed fashion, so that even minute aspects of sound and meaning are registered and remembered. To stay with the example of *sitting and waiting*, the mental bookkeeping of speakers will include the rate with which *sitting* is realized with a final alveolar nasal, the rate with which the verbal complex *sitting and waiting* is used intransitively, and the rate with which it is followed by a phrase referring to a time span, amongst many other details. Of course, speakers' memories of linguistic usage events do not form an unstructured collection, but rather, each usage event is categorized as being more or less similar to previously encountered tokens. Speakers thus form generalizations over "clouds" of exemplar tokens. When speakers repeatedly experience tokens that are peripheral to an established cloud, eventually the shape of that cloud may change. It may become more diffuse or it may drift into one particular direction, or it may indeed develop into two separate clouds. The acceptability of *What are you sitting and waiting for?* suggests that in current usage, the chunk *sitting and waiting* forms an exemplar cloud of its own that is autonomous from the clouds of the form *sitting* and the form *waiting* respectively. As time progresses, this kind of emancipation may, but need not, become ever stronger. For example, the emerging modal verb *gonna* is fully emancipated from lexical uses of *going to*, as in *going to the beach*. Emancipation can result in complete dissociation, such that for instance the indefinite article *an* is no longer recognized by present-day speakers as deriving from the numeral *one*. In all three cases though (*sitting and waiting*, *gonna*, *an*), the process that has been at work is essentially the same: A peripheral group of uses in the original exemplar cloud becomes frequent enough to develop its own center of gravity, so that eventually there are two exemplar clouds, which may be partly overlapping at first, but nonetheless distinct.

Two points fall out of this exemplar-based view. First, it follows that even instances of completely regular patterns are redundantly stored as holistic forms. Speakers of English know that the plural of /kæt/ is formed through the addition of a voiceless dental fricative, but this does not keep them from memorizing /kæts/ as a pattern of usage in its own right. The division of linguistic knowledge into productive rules on the one hand and exceptions on the other in the interest of representational parsimony has been criticized by Langacker (1987: 29) as the rule/list fallacy: It is not necessary to settle for either one or the other, speakers demonstrably do both (Dąbrowska 2008). Second, the exemplar-based view suggests that linguistic categories are fuzzy and gradient (Aarts 2007). Words, syntactic constructions, and also phonemes are represented as categories with substantial category-internal variation as well as overlap with other categories. In addition, exemplar-based categories may have one center of gravity, i.e., a single prototype (Rosch 1975), but they may also be pluricentric, so that there are several typical subcategories that are connected through family resemblances and together make up the structure of a superordinate category.

The exemplar-based view of variation that is built into the usage-based model of language holds a natural explanation for the fact that many linguistic forms develop multiple meanings over time, or may exhibit changes in their morphosyntactic behavior. What may start as a peripheral, context-dependent use of a form may eventually become a conventionalized pattern of usage. This insight is relevant for the study of lexical semantic change, where the development of polysemy can be observed. For instance, the English noun *paper* has, besides its sense of 'thin writing material', developed the senses of 'a piece of academic writing' and even 'an academic conference talk' (Nerlich and Clarke 2001). Hence, we find utterances such as *John gave an interesting paper*, which refer to the 'talk' sense, but not to any of the others.

Variation is furthermore important for the study of grammaticalization, where gradual changes in usage lead to what is called de-categorialization (Hopper 1991: 30), i.e., the development of discrete categorical differences between linguistic units. To illustrate, the English phrase *seeing as though* (Taylor and Pang 2008) has developed from a verbal complex into a clause connector in expressions such as *You should go and talk to him, seeing as though you're his only relative*. The meaning of the connector *seeing as though* can be circumscribed as 'considering that' or 'since'. It is clear enough that the clause connector goes back to a pattern that involves the lexical verb *seeing* in the sense of 'perceiving visually', but in several ways the form *seeing* that is part of the connector has become categorically different from its verbal source. First, unlike lexical *seeing*, the connector may not be used with a copula and an explicit subject (**I am seeing as though ...*). Second, lexical *seeing* can be negated or modified by an adverb, but this is not possible with the connector (**Clearly seeing as though ...*). Third, lexical *seeing* may be followed by a *that*-clause (*Seeing that John left ...*) or an accusative-cum-infinitive construction (*Seeing him leave ...*), but not by a canonical declarative clause *(*Seeing John is leaving...*), which is the default choice for *seeing as though*.

An area of language study that has long been concerned with variation in usage is of course sociolinguistics (Labov 1994, 2001, 2010). The growing awareness that sociolinguistic work is of tremendous importance for the usage-based research program has been termed the social turn in Cognitive Linguistics (Harder 2010). What this social turn boils down to is a more realistic notion of speakers' linguistic knowledge. The idea of an idealized speaker as a "brain in a vat" is no longer tenable if speakers are viewed as social agents that vary their language use according to the situational context. For instance, how speakers will formulate a request for someone to step aside will depend on a number of factors, including how well they know their interlocutor, how much the request interferes with their interlocutor's personal sphere, and how well the interlocutor can be assumed to anticipate the nature of the request (Brown and Levinson 1987). Likewise, in cases where there are different phonological realizations of a given form, such as for instance *running* with either a final [ŋ] or a final [n], speakers' choices will depend partly on their social allegiance with their interlocutor. Lastly, choices between alternative lexical expressions, such as *coat*, *jacket*, or *anorak*, are of course motivated by the prototypicality of the referent in question, but they also have a social dimension (Geeraerts et al. 1999; Grondelaers and Geeraerts 2003). Knowledge of language thus includes knowledge of how to say things in a certain situation, which is a conception of linguistic compentence that goes well beyond the ability to distinguish between sentences that are grammatical and ungrammatical respectively. As is pointed out by Geeraerts (2010: 238), a socially informed cognitive linguistics stands to gain a lot from engaging with the empirical methodologies of variationist sociolinguistics. These methods have been developed with the explicit goal of teasing apart which factors lead speakers to talk in a certain way in a certain situation, thus yielding small-scale models of what speakers must know in order to use a set of variant forms in appropriate ways. Thus far, most work in cognitive sociolinguistics has focused on issues in language synchrony (cf. Kristiansen and Dirven 2008; Geeraerts et al. 2010), but as language variation and change are inextricably interlinked, some research also has addressed cognitive aspects of variation in diachrony (Geeraerts et al. 1999; Gries and Hilpert 2010; Szmrecsanyi 2010, amongst others).

Finally, more and more studies that take a usage-based approach to language change adopt Construction Grammar (Goldberg 1995, 2006) as a theoretical framework (e.g., Israel 1996; Verhagen 2002; Bergs and Diewald 2008; Traugott and Trousdale 2010; Hilpert 2013; Traugott and Trousdale 2013). These studies investigate how the usage of symbolic form-meaning pairings shifts over time. Changes in usage patterns can be taken to reflect gradual differences in the corresponding generalizations that represent these constructions in speakers' minds. Present-day speakers of English thus cognitively represent a construction such as the *s*-genitive (*John's brother*) in a way that is different from how it used to be represented in the past (Szmrecsanyi 2010). Work in this area overlaps to a large extent with ongoing research into grammaticalization. However, the project of Diachronic Construction Grammar is broader in scope, as it not only comprises the development of grammaticalizing constructions, but also changes in constructions that are not readily defined as grammatical (Noël 2007). So while it might be a matter of debate whether or not a construction such as *What's X doing Y?* (Kay and Fillmore 1999) falls into the domain of grammatical markers, the emergence of this construction in English usage would definitely be a question of interest in Diachronic Construction Grammar. A second reason to treat the constructional perspective on language change as a subject of its own is that changes in constructions include processes that go beyond the kinds of developments that are recognized in grammaticalization. For instance, some definitions of grammaticalization exclude certain types of word order change (Hopper and Traugott 2003: 24) that would fall squarely into the domain of Diachronic Construction Grammar.

To sum up this section, the usage-based model of language is deeply interconnected with issues of language change that pertain to all levels of structure and meaning, i.e., everything from phonemes to syntactic constructions and further to discourse patterns, and everything from stable, conventionalized meanings to purely contextual and incidental meanings. The domain-general socio-cognitive processes that underlie language use in the present are also responsible for the fact that there is gradual change both in the patterns of usage and in the cognitive representations that speakers abstract away from those patterns. The following sections will return to the four aspects of language change that have been raised in this section, offering more examples and further motivating the claim that language change and human cognition are mutually interdependent.

3. Lexical semantic change

One of the key insights from work on cognitive lexical semantics (Geeraerts this volume; Gries this volume) is that word meanings are multifaceted and flexible. Depending on the context of use, a word such as for example *book* may mean quite different things.

(1)   a.   That book is slightly damaged.
       b.   That book is now a movie with Leonardo DiCaprio.
       c.   That book has been translated into over thirty languages.

The above examples make reference to a book as a physical object, as a story, and as a written text that can be translated. To come to terms with such flexibility, Croft and Cruse speak of the meaning potential of a word, which they define as "a region in conceptual space" (2004: 109) that outlines the range of possible interpretations that a word may have. Contained in that region are one or more areas that speakers will consider as central. These areas represent prototypical meanings, which are those that speakers will learn early during first language acquisition, verify swiftly as category members, offer as examples when asked, and rate as highly typical in experimental settings (Croft and Cruse 2004: 78). Importantly, the meaning potential of a lexical item may change over time. The conceptual space covered by a word may grow to include new meanings, or it may in fact shrink, so that some meanings fall out of use. In any event, the semantic changes that can be observed with a given lexical item reflect conceptual associations that speakers would have made between related meanings. Particularly important kinds of associations in this regard are metonymy (Barcelona this volume) and metaphor (Gibbs this volume). Over time, repeated meaning extensions give rise to the development of polysemy (Gries this volume), so that the meaning potential of a word is divided up into conceptual regions that are relatively distinct. Depending on how strong or weak the associations between these regions are, speakers may thus distinguish different word senses.

Nerlich and Clarke (2001: 261–263) discuss several examples of semantic change that involve metonymic reasoning, specifically conceptual associations between objects and related activities. The word *counter*, for instance, used to refer to an accountant's tool, an object made for counting. This meaning was extended to the accountant's desk, at which the counting was taking place. Eventually, the word *counter* was generalized to refer to any kind of desk in a commercial setting. As another example, the noun *toilet* entered the English language as a French loan word referring to a piece of cloth, which was used for wrapping clothes, and later also as a cover for one's shoulders while hairdressing, or for the covering of a dressing table. Through that association, *toilet* came to designate the things on the dressing table, the act of dressing itself, as well as the room in which the dressing took place. As dressing rooms were furnished with facilities for washing and performing bodily functions, *toilet* became a convenient euphemism for rooms of this kind, even when they did not have any dressing tables in them.

Whereas metonymic associations can go freely back and forth between objects, their parts and wholes, and related activities and persons, metaphorical association patterns are believed to be more constrained, insofar as changes tend to be unidirectional, going from a more concrete source domain to a more abstract target domain. For example, given that the word *fruit* synchronically has, amongst others, the senses 'edible product of a plant' and 'result', it would be a default assumption that the latter is a metaphorical extension of the former. It is however not always possible to exploit synchronic polysemy for the purpose of internal semantic reconstruction. Allan (2012: 32) presents the case of *dull*, which has the senses 'blunt', 'not clear or bright', 'stupid' and 'boring', amongst several others. Whereas it might be assumed that the senses denoting physical qualities are historically prior to the senses denoting mental and perceptual qualities, the historical record, in this particular case the Oxford English Dictionary, does not support that assumption. The historical sequence of metaphorically related word senses, though often in line with a development from more concrete to more abstract, can therefore not be inferred from general principles, but has to be determined on the basis of the empirical record. The hypothesis of unidirectionality in semantic change will be discussed further in the section on grammaticalization, where it is of central concern.

Besides metonymic and metaphorical shifts, lexical items also tend to undergo processes of narrowing and broadening. In such cases, the meaning of a word either comes to refer to only a subset of its erstwhile referents (e.g., English *deer* from Old English *dēor* 'animal') or, conversely, a word widens in its categorical scope (e.g., English *manage* from Early Modern English *manege* 'train/direct a horse'). Semantic shifts of this kind have sometimes been subsumed under the heading of metonymy (Seto 1999), but it may be useful to reserve separate labels for categorical relationships on the one hand, which concern the processes of narrowing and broadening, and contiguity relationships on the other, which concern metonymic extensions proper.

A final aspect of lexical semantic change to be discussed here is the fact that lexical items may undergo changes that do not affect their referential meaning, but rather their affective or evaluative meaning. A word that undergoes pejoration develops increasingly negative connotations, conversely, a word undergoing amelioration acquires more positive connotations. An example for the former would be the example of *toilet* that was already mentioned above. Initially, the word *toilet* functioned as a euphemism for 'a place where bodily functions are performed'. Over time however, euphemisms tend to wear out, so that they acquire the negative connotations that are associated with their referents. As a consequence, new euphemisms have to be invented to replace the old ones. Hence, present-day speakers prefer *bathroom* to *toilet* and *disabled* to *crippled*, and most nation states have a *ministry of defense* instead of a *ministry of war*. Keller (1994) explains the cyclic replacement of euphemisms in terms of an emergent process that he describes as the "invisible hand": Speakers aim to use socially acceptable expressions and thus will rather err on the side of caution, choosing a relatively more indirect term. As speech events of this kind repeat, an erstwhile euphemism comes to be regarded as the new default, whereas the old default term seems too direct and thus undergoes pejoration. The cognitive underpinnings of euphemistic speech include social awareness, i.e., speakers' ability to engage in mutual mind-reading, and an exemplar-based linguistic memory, which allows speakers to keep track of how often a phenomenon is labeled with one of several alternative expressions. Besides pejoration, there is also the converse development, amelioration. This process has been at work in examples such as *nice*, which used to mean 'ignorant, stupid', and *marshal*, which used to mean 'person who tends horses'. Both terms thus have meanings in Present-Day English that are more positive than their respective earlier meanings. Whereas pejoration is a process that can receive a principled socio-cognitive explanation, amelioration has to be seen as a relatively sporadic and circumstantial phenomenon.

Summing up this section, it can be stated that lexical semantic change reflects several domain-general socio-cognitive processes, such as reasoning in terms of metaphor and metonymy, categorization, social awareness, and exemplar-based memory. In their mutual combinations, these processes lead to different types of lexical semantic change. A typology of these kinds of change that further explains their respective cognitive motivations and thus expands on what is offered here can be found in Blank (1999).

4. Grammaticalization

Whereas the trajectories of change in the domain of lexis are relatively unconstrained and hence unpredictable, pervasive regularities have been documented in the domain of grammatical change. Studies in grammaticalization (Heine et al. 1991; Bybee et al. 1994; Heine and Kuteva 2002; Hopper and Traugott 2003; van der Auwera et al. this volume) have established that across languages, grammatical forms come into being and develop in strikingly similar ways. In order to elaborate on this point, it is necessary to clarify briefly what is meant by the terms grammar and grammaticalization.

Grammar (Diessel this volume) has in generative traditions been defined as a system of rules allowing speakers to produce well-formed utterances. Accompanying such a rule system would be a lexicon supplementing the words that can be put together into sentences by means of those rules. In Cognitive Linguistics, this dichotomy of a grammar and a lexicon is replaced by an integrated model. Knowledge of language is viewed as a 'constructicon' (Goldberg 2006: 64), that is, a network of symbolic units that contains exemplar-based representations of both highly abstract syntactic constructions, semi-fixed phrases, morphological constructions, and also simplex lexical items. Grammar, in that view, refers to the relatively more abstract parts of such a network. This would include syntactic schemas for questions, ditransitives, or cleft sentences, but also morphological schemas that serve as templates for the usage of verbs in the past tense, nouns in the plural, or adjectives in the comparative. Further, elements such as determiners, pronouns, or clause linkers, which have highly schematic meanings and commonly project an adjacent linguistic structure, would also be located towards the grammatical end of the constructicon. The question of what counts as grammar would thus primarily be answered on the basis of semantic and structural schematicity: A linguistic form is to be viewed as grammatical if it is schematic in form and if it conveys a relatively abstract meaning that can be characterized as a grammatical function, i.e., tense, aspect, modality, number, gender, case, definiteness, comparison, subordination, or topicality, to name just a few. Conceived of in this way, a terminological opposition of grammar and lexis can be maintained despite the fact that no crisp categorical distinction is made between the two. Towards the lexical end of the continuum, constructions are fully specified with regard to form and highly specific in meaning. Towards the grammatical end of the continuum, constructions tend to be schematic in form, more abstract in meaning, and internally complex (cf. Langacker 2005: 108, Figure 3). Importantly, they are also relatively more frequent in usage (Bybee 2007: ch. 16).

As was pointed out in the introduction, the usage-based perspective on language is inherently dynamic. Understanding what grammar is hence depends to a large extent on an understanding of how this grammar came into being. This question is addressed in research on grammaticalization. Grammaticalization refers to "the change whereby lexical items and constructions come in certain contexts to serve grammatical functions, and, once grammaticalized, continue to develop new grammatical functions" (Hopper and Traugott 2003: xv). With regard to the definition of grammar that was offered above, this means that when a word or construction grammaticalizes, a part of the constructicon is re-structured so that form and meaning of the grammaticalizing unit increases in schematicity as it acquires a grammatical function. Typically, the grammaticalizing unit simultaneously undergoes changes in its combinatorics.

Regarding these aspects of change, Traugott (2010) distinguishes two main pathways of grammaticalization. In the first of these, grammaticalizing forms reduce in phonological substance and become increasingly dependent on a morpho-syntactic host structure. This pathway produces markers of grammatical categories such as tense, person, case, or voice, which many languages express as obligatory inflections on the verb. One example of this would be the Germanic weak past tense marker found in forms such as English *walk-ed* or German *sag-te* 'said', which derives historically from a formerly independent verb *dōn* 'do' that was postposed to the main predicate (Kiparsky 2009). Another example is the inflectional passive in the North Germanic languages (Heltoft 2006). The final alveolar fricative in Swedish examples such as *Ingenting hörde-s* 'Nothing was heard' or *Dörren öppnade-s* 'The door was opened' derives from a full reflexive pronoun *sik* 'self' that became attached to its verbal host. The formal and combinatory changes that occur in these and other similar cases have been summarized by Lehmann

(1995) as parameters of increasing degrees of grammaticalization. As a form grammaticalizes, its relative placement becomes increasingly fixed, its presence is increasingly obligatory, its integrity as an independent word diminishes, it reduces its semantic scope to its host, it coalesces phonologically with the host, and it becomes part of a tightly organized paradigm of alternative forms, such as present vs. past or active vs. passive. Importantly, all of these changes can be interpreted as the result of increased frequency of usage. Through the repeated use of a certain sequence of linguistic units, routinization and chunking lead to fixation, semantic association, coalescence, reduction, and ultimately obligatorification. Whereas this pathway of morphologization arguably still represents the most widely shared definition of grammaticalization, inflectional morphology only comprises a subpart of the grammatical end of the constructicon. In particular, syntactic constructions and elements such as clause linkers or discourse markers are not accounted for in this pathway, and yet, their emergence would seem to constitute grammaticalization in a straight-forward interpretation of the term.

Traugott (2010: 274) therefore proposes a second pathway under the heading of grammaticalization as expansion. Expansion here refers to three separate processes that have been identified by Himmelmann (2004). The first of these is host-class expansion, which describes the fact that grammaticalizing units often do not reduce their combinatorial variability but conversely, are observed to expand the range of environments in which they can occur. An example of this would be the English *it*-cleft construction (Patten 2010). The construction initially just accommodated nominal elements in the focus phrase, as in *It was the butler that killed them*. In its later development, the construction expands to accommodate prepositional phrases (*It's in December that she's coming*) and even subordinate clauses (*It's because you cheated that you won*). The second type of expansion is syntactic expansion, which is the inverse process of Lehmann's parameter of scope decrease. Some grammaticalizing forms increase in syntactic scope. Notably, this applies to the development of discourse markers (Tabor and Traugott 1998) such as English *in fact*. As a discourse marker, it may take scope over an entire clause-level utterance (*In fact, why don't we ask John?*). As an adverbial, from which the discourse marker derives, it only takes scope over a phrase-level constituent (*If John in fact leaves the company, we'll hire Bob*). The third type of expansion is semantic and pragmatic expansion, which boils down to increasing schematicity in meaning of exactly the kind that was observed in the cases of morphologization that were discussed above. This third type of expansion hence works in parallel in both pathways of grammaticalization whereas the two other types of expansion are specific to the second pathway.

Grammaticalization as expansion shares a number of characteristics with lexical semantic change, in particular the processes of metonymic extension and semantic broadening. An example for this can be seen in the development of the degree modifier *a lot of* (Traugott 2008: 230). The lexical noun *lot* initially referred to a small wooden object that was used in the practice of selecting by chance. By metonymic extension, the noun came to refer to that which a person received if their lot was drawn, i.e., the allotment. Hence, the construction *a lot of* could develop a more general meaning equivalent to 'a certain quantity of something'. The meaning of 'a certain quantity' was then further extended to the present-day interpretation of 'a large quantity'. This change coincided with a syntactic reanalysis of the expression. Whereas in earlier usage, the noun *lot* constituted the head of an expression such as *a lot of books*, the copula in an utterance such as *A lot of books were on sale* agrees in number with *books*, indicating that reanalysis has taken place. As *a lot of* came to be conventionally associated with the meanings of 'many' and 'much', it became possible to use *a lot* as a degree modifier, as in *a lot faster* or *I enjoyed it a lot*. To summarize, this process of change shows host-class expansion, as *a lot* spreads to syntactic environments in which it was not found before; it shows syntactic expansion in examples such as *There was a lot of me and him not getting along*, with *a lot* taking scope over a clause rather than a nominal; and there is semantic and pragmatic expansion, which is evident in expressions such as *a lot faster*, in which *a lot* goes beyond specifying a quantity of physical things. It is especially the latter type of expansion that is also often found in lexical semantic change.

But despite such similarities with lexical semantic change, it was pointed out in the beginning of this section that processes of grammaticalization tend to be relatively more constrained and highly similar across genetically unrelated languages. Comparative research (Bybee et al. 1994; Heine and Kuteva 2002) has identified numerous semantic pathways that are cross-linguistically pervasive in the development of grammatical forms. For example, constructions with the grammatical function of future time reference tend to develop out of a small set of potential sources. Typologically common are lexical verbs of coming and going, verbs of obligation, and verbs of desiring. Another example can be seen in clause linkers with causal meaning, which often go back to elements that mean 'after' or 'since'. Yet another example would be markers of spatial relations, which in many languages exist in the form of adpositions or inflectional case affixes. Historically, these markers often derive from body part terms, so that there are etymological relations between expressions meaning 'face' and 'in front', 'back' and 'behind', or 'belly' and 'in'. These regularities in semantic change contrast sharply with the idiosyncratic trajectories in lexical semantic change. A semantic change such as the development of *nice* from 'stupid' to 'pleasant' is probably unique in the world's languages. By contrast, the development of *be going to* from 'movement' to 'future' represents a type of change that is highly common.

What explains the cross-linguistic regularities in grammaticalization is the fact that its semantic pathways are motivated by metonymic and metaphorical mappings that are widely shared across cultures. For instance, the grammaticalization of future markers from motion verbs draws on the conceptual metaphor TIME IS SPACE, which in turn is grounded in the repeated correlated experience of travelling through space and the passage of time. For the traveller, successive points in space correspond to successive points in time. Similarly, the development of causal meaning out of temporal meaning is grounded in the metonymic association of cause and effect. If two events are presented as happening in temporal sequence, as in *After Bob joined our team, things took a turn for the worse*, human conceptualizers have the tendency to view the two as causally related.

While developments in grammaticalization are arguably more strongly constrained than developments in lexical semantic change, it is disputed how regular grammaticalization really is. While grammaticalization is anything but deterministic – changes do not need to happen and may stop at any time – the claim has been made that when a form grammaticalizes, it undergoes a change that is in principle irreversible (Givón 1971; Lehmann 1995). This is the so-called unidirectionality hypothesis, which appears to hold true as a statistical tendency, but which also has to face a number of counterexamples (Janda 2001). While the validity of many such counterexamples is debated, one widely accepted case is the development of the enclitic *s*-genitive in English and the North

Germanic languages out of a case ending, which thus reverses several of Lehmann's parameters (Norde 2009). The strong tendency of unidirectionality in grammatical change can again be explained with reference to frequency of usage (Bybee 2011: 77). Repeated use of a form leads to schematization in form and meaning, but once this has happened, not even subsequent decreases in frequency can restore the semantic or formal details that characterized the lexical source of the grammaticalized form.

In summary then, cognitive factors such as the ability to form schemas from repeated tokens of experience and the ability to form metaphorical and metonymic associations go a long way towards explaining the regularities that are observed in grammaticalization, notably the presence of cross-linguistically attested semantic pathways and the tendency of unidirectional change in both morphologization and grammaticalization as expansion. A factor that might explain why grammatical change is more regular than lexical semantic change is frequency. Grammatical forms tend to be relatively more frequent in usage. The powerful shaping force of repetition is thus much more at work in the emergence of grammar than it is in the expansion of the lexicon.

5. Historical sociolinguistics

It was discussed in the introduction to this chapter that there is a growing trend in cognitive linguistics towards a view of language as a socially embedded phenomenon (Kristiansen and Dirven 2008; Geeraerts et al. 2010; Harder 2010). In the usage-based model of language, social factors stand on an equal footing with cognitive factors, and many important concepts, as for instance joint attention or face work, indeed resist a categorization as either one or the other. The introduction also mentioned that most research that has been done to date under the heading of cognitive sociolinguistics has addressed issues in language synchrony. Nonetheless, there are a number of studies that illustrate the approach of a cognitively oriented historical sociolinguistics, which borrows not only theoretical concepts from sociolinguistics, but crucially also many methodological tools.

Geeraerts et al. (1999) study diachronic variation in the lexicon of Belgian and Netherlandic Dutch. Their main research question is whether the two standard varieties of Dutch become more or less similar over time. This question is investigated on the basis of lexical units for items of clothing and for terms in football, which are retrieved from texts that were written in the 1950s, 1970s, and 1990s respectively. What is investigated is in what ratios a concept such as 'tight-fitting trousers made of stretch fabric' is expressed by words such as *legging, leggings,* or *caleçon*, and whether these ratios become more or less similar in Belgian and Netherlandic Dutch as time goes on. Geeraerts et al. (1999) analyze the usage of multiple lexical items in the domains of clothing and football, finding that in both domains there is increasing convergence between the two standard varieties, and that it is specifically Belgian Dutch that develops a normative orientation towards the Netherlandic standard. The general conclusion from the study is that when speakers label an object with a linguistic form, that process is influenced by cognitive factors, such as categorization and assessment of prototypicality, but also by social factors, such as orientation towards a certain standard variety. Geeraerts et al. (1999) thus show that social factors are at work in onomasiological change. Beyond that, they are also involved in semasiological change.

Robinson (2012) analyzes semasiological change in the English adjective *skinny*. In order to do so, she uses the socio-linguistic concept of apparent time, i.e., differences between speakers of different age brackets with regard to a linguistic variable. The study prompts respondents from different age groups and socioeconomic backgrounds for the meaning of *skinny*. While the sense 'thin' comfortably accounts for the majority of responses across all groups, the results indicate that certain senses of *skinny* are only used by older cohorts of speakers, as for instance 'mean, stingy' or 'showing skin'. The analysis also shows that the recently developed sense of 'low-fat', as in *skinny latte* 'coffee with low-fat steamed milk', is restricted to respondents between 19 and 60 years of age. Furthermore, it emerges that not only age but also other social factors account for the distribution of the different senses. For instance, the sense 'mean, stingy' is offered as a response mostly by old respondents from a relatively low socio-economic background. Robinson's study shows that lexical semantic change is not only a cognitive phenomenon that draws on processes such as metonymy and metaphor, but at the same time very much a social phenomenon, as new word senses propagate through networks of socially related speakers.

Of course, cognitive studies of sociolinguistic change have not been limited to developments in the lexicon. Socio-cognitive factors are also crucial for the study of grammatical change. Szmrecsanyi (2010) studies how the dynamics between the English *s*-genitive and the *of*-genitive has changed in recent British and American English across different text genres. As has been shown across many different studies, genitive choice in English depends on several factors relating to meaning and processing, such as the animacy of possessor and possessum and their length and thematicity. Several language-external factors have also been shown to matter to genitive choice. Specifically, the *s*-genitive is favored in informal genres, and it is more frequently used in American English. Given that a multitude of factors is at work, it is a non-trivial task to determine whether and how anything has changed in the ecology of factors that condition genitive choice in English. In order to analyze the interplay of cognitive and cultural factors as it unfolds over time, Szmrecsanyi (2010) compares how these factors govern genitive choice in ten different corpora, which differ with regard to modality (speech, writing), genre (conversation, reportage, editorial), variety (British, American), and time (1960s, 1990s). The main finding is that genitive choice is consistently governed by the same semantic and cognitive factors across the different corpora. For instance, speakers and writers of all corpora favor the *s*-genitive with animate possessors and when the possessum is long. However, the respective strengths of the factors are modulated by the language-external factors. The effect of priming for instance is more pronounced in the spoken corpora as compared to written corpora. Thematicity of the possessor favors the *s*-genitive, but only in writing, not in speech. The analysis also reveals several differences that concern the variable of time. For instance, genitive choice in British editorials becomes more colloquial between the 1960s and 1990s. The ecology of factors governing the choice between *s*-genitive and *of*-genitive thus increasingly resembles the pattern that is found in spoken data. Similarly, the gap between British and American press texts is widening over time, which is mainly due to American usage developing further away from older norms. On the whole then, the study shows that social factors are an indispensable complement to the cognitive factors that underlie probabilistic choices in grammar.

The examples of cognitively oriented historical sociolinguistics that this section has discussed present analyses of fairly recent and short-term changes. This reflects to a certain extent the focus on recent or on-going developments that characterizes the sociolinguistic mainstream. However, there are several strands of work that have established a wider temporal horizon in the sociolinguistic study of language change, addressing for instance Canadian French (Poplack and St-Amand 2007) or Early Modern English (Nevalainen and Raumolin-Brunberg 2003). Gries and Hilpert (2010) draw on the latter in a diachronic study of English present tense suffix *-(e)th*, which marks the third person singular. Between the early 15th century and the late 17th century, the interdental suffix that is seen in forms such as *giveth* gradually disappeared, and it was replaced with an alveolar fricative, as in *gives*. The overall phenomenon that is observed here is a case of variation in which one variant, in this case the Northern dialectal form *−(e)s*, gradually wins out over another one. This means that, similarly to the developments in genitive choice studied by Szmrecsanyi (2010), there are changes in the conditioning factors that govern the choice between *-(e)th* and *-(e)s*. In particular, it appears that those conditioning factors that once biased speakers towards the interdental variant are no longer at work: Speakers of Present-Day English invariably choose the alveolar variant. Among the factors that used to underlie the variation between the two variants, some concern language structure and some concern social factors. For instance, structural influences on the choice between the two include whether the verb stem ends in a sibilant, as in *wish*, or whether the following word begins with either an *s* or *th*. Social factors include the gender of author and intended recipient. Gries and Hilpert (2010) show that the observed variation is best explained by a dynamic interplay of structural and social factors. Crucially, some influences do not stay the same over time. For instance, verb-final sibilants matter, but only during one early period, after which the effect disappears. Similarly, the effect of writer gender is there, but it is transient. The study thus shows that there is not only a complex interplay of language-internal and language-external factors at work, but that this interplay is inherently dynamic and subject to change.

6. Diachronic Construction Grammar

The final avenue of research to be discussed in this chapter is the diachronic branch of Construction Grammar. Studies in Diachronic Construction Grammar focus on shifts in the usage of a particular conventionalized form-meaning pairing, i.e., a construction in the sense of Goldberg (2006: 5). These shifts may concern any aspect of a construction, notably its form and meaning, but also its text frequency, its productivity, or its dispersion across different types of writing or speech (Hilpert 2013: 16). In the well-worn example of English *be going to*, all of these aspects have undergone significant changes, but there are many cases of constructional change where only some of these aspects have been subject to change. For instance, the English *many a NOUN* construction, as exemplified by *many a day* or *many a mile*, has undergone recent changes in meaning and frequency, but not in form (Hilpert 2012).

Given that in Cognitive Linguistics knowledge of language is viewed as knowledge of constructions, it could be asked whether Diachronic Construction Grammar does not in fact subsume all phenomena of change that have been discussed in the previous three sections. In lexical semantic change, grammaticalization, as well as in sociolinguistic change, one can observe changes that pertain to individual form-meaning pairings, or to small sets of such symbolic units. It is certainly true that a constructional approach to language change largely converges in theory as well as in subject matter with the areas of research that were discussed above. The distinguishing mark of Diachronic Construction Grammar is that it maintains a focus on linguistic generalizations at the level of individual constructions. This is not necessarily so for the other approaches: Historical sociolinguistics might address issues such as systematic sound changes, which pertain to many lexical items at the same time. Similarly, research on lexical semantic change and grammaticalization aims to uncover the general pathways along which lexical items and grammatical formatives develop. The generalizations that come out of this kind of research span many constructions, often across many languages. The following paragraphs illustrate the approach of Diachronic Construction Grammar with a few examples.

A pioneering study of constructional change is Israel (1996). This study addresses the emergence of the English *way*-construction, as in *John cheated his way into law school*. The construction expresses the creation of a path through difficult terrain, often in a metaphorical interpretation. In accordance with this constructional meaning, the *way*-construction occurs in present-day usage with verbs denoting the manner of a movement, such as *crawl*, *wind*, or *stumble*, and with verbs such as *dig*, *cut*, or *force*, which can encode the means to create a path. Israel shows on the basis of data from the Oxford English Dictionary that both of these verb classes developed independently at first. Through repeated analogical formations, both the manner-thread and the means-thread occurred with an increasingly greater range of verbs, which eventually led to the formation of a single, overarching generalization, i.e., the modern *way*-construction. Israel observes that simultaneously to the increasing schematization of the constructional meaning, there is an increasing obligatorification of the path constituent of the construction. Whereas there are many examples without path constituents in earlier usage, such as *The moving legions speed their headlong way*, the modern *way*-construction requires the presence of a phrase such as *across the field* or *along the river*. In summary, the development of the *way*-construction is an example of a widening generalization: Speakers kept track of the verbs that they heard in the construction and kept producing analogical formations that widened the cloud of exemplar tokens that represented the construction in their minds.

Verhagen (2000) offers another early study of constructional change in which he analyzes the history of the Dutch analytic causative constructions with *doen* 'make' and *laten* 'let'. In Present-Day Dutch, the two constructions differ with regard to animacy and directness. Whereas *doen* primarily occurs with inanimate causers in contexts of direct causation, e.g., the sun causing temperatures to increase, *laten* favors animate causers and indirect causation, such as a writer causing a change of state in someone else's mind by means of written communication. Historically, Verhagen (2000) observes an apparent shift in usage. When speakers of Present-Day Dutch are confronted with some 18th century examples of causative *doen*, they can understand what is meant but would themselves use *laten* instead of *doen* in order not to sound old-fashioned. Verhagen (2000) goes on to show that the shift in usage has not been a mere replacement of *doen* with *laten*, the latter in fact does not increase in text frequency in the diachronic corpora that are consulted. Instead, what underlies the development is a more general change in the texts that are sampled. In earlier texts, causative *doen* is commonly used with causers that represent authorities such as kings, military officials, or doctors who prescribe treatments. Over time, the semantic category of authoritative causers drastically diminishes. This affects the usage of *doen*, whose meaning of direct causation is less and less suitable for the expression of causation between human beings. The usage of *laten*, on the other hand, is not affected much by this change. Verhagen (2000) further corroborates the idea of a cultural change with historical data of *doen* and *laten* that shows a gender asymmetry. Expectably, *doen* is used more often with male causers, whereas *laten* is more frequent with female causers. Typically, *doen* is used for the case of male causers acting on female causees. The intriguing idea of cultural change acting on usage is that the respective meanings and structures of constructions such as causative *doen* and *laten* may stay the same, and yet, there may be constructional change going on, insofar as there are changes in frequency and changes in the dispersion of the constructions across different text types.

Most studies in constructional change up to the present have addressed syntactic phenomena, but as Construction Grammar aims to be an all-encompassing theory of language, it stands to reason that also change at lower levels of linguistic organization should be of interest. Hilpert (2013) studies historical changes in the usage of the nominalizing morpheme *-ment*, which is found in nouns that encode actions (*development*), results (*settlement*), or means to an action (*refreshment*). The suffix tends to occur with verbal stems, but there are sporadic attestations of adjectival stems (*merriment*) and nominal stems (*scholarment*). Like Israel (1996), Hilpert (2013) uses data from the OED to analyze how the *ment*-construction developed over time. The dictionary entries suggest that an initial group of borrowed French forms served as a critical mass for the formation of a native productive schema. This schema is initially very closely modeled on existing loan words: Since the French loans typically involved transitive verbal stems and denoted actions (*punishment, judgment*, etc.), native formations followed this tendency. There are occasional departures from the mainstream, as is evidenced by forms such as *merriment* or *jolliment*, which are based on adjectives, but none of these departures gain enough momentum to become sustainably productive. In the 20th century, the construction is entirely unproductive, and the only forms with *-ment* that show up as new entries in the OED are in fact old formations with a new prefix, such as *malnourishment* or *noninvolvement*. The main result of the analysis is that the exemplar cloud of a construction may be pluricentric, such that there are particular subconstructions that can be productive at different points in time. Also, the analysis shows that Diachronic Construction Grammar is well-positioned to address issues of change in word formation.

7. Concluding remarks

The introduction of this chapter started with the question how issues of language change can possibly be relevant to Cognitive Linguistics. The preceding sections have tried to support the idea that the usage-based model that underlies synchronic research in Cognitive Linguistics is inherently dynamic, and hence not to be understood without reference to language change and language history. Any theory that aims to relate language and cognition thus needs to engage with issues of diachrony. By the same token, any theory of language change should be in accordance with what is known about language use and cognition in present-day speakers. Strengthening the on-going dialogue between historical linguistics and psycholinguistics will be a worthwhile challenge for Cognitive Linguistics in the coming years. A guiding question in this enterprise would be how the four areas of research that were discussed in this chapter can inform our understanding of how cognition and language change relate to one another. The existing research on lexical semantic change, grammaticalization, historical sociolinguistics, and Diachronic Construction Grammar needs to be mutually contextualized, and the usage-based model of Cognitive Linguistics provides the ideal conceptual bracket for this undertaking. If this path is followed, it just may turn out that the study of language change is not a marginal aspect of Cognitive Linguistics, but rather one of its central concerns.

8. References

Aarts, Bas
    2007   *Syntactic Gradience: The Nature of Grammatical Indeterminacy.* Oxford: Oxford University Press.

Allan, Kathryn
    2012   Using OED data as evidence. In: K. Allan and J. Robinson (eds.), *Current Methods in Historical Semantics* 17–40. Berlin: Mouton de Gruyter.

Barcelona, Antonio
    this volume   Metonymy. Berlin/Boston: De Gruyter Mouton.

Barlow, G. Michael and Suzanne E. Kemmer (eds.)
    2000   *Usage-Based Models of Language.* Stanford: CSLI.

Bergs, Alexander and Gabriele Diewald (eds.)
    2008   *Constructions and Language Change.* Berlin: Mouton de Gruyter.

Blank, Andreas
    1999   Why do new meanings occur? A cognitive typology of the motivations for lexical semantic change. In: A. Blank and P. Koch (eds.), *Historical Semantics and Cognition,* 61–90. Berlin: Mouton de Gruyter.

Brown, Penelope and Stephen C. Levinson
    1987   *Politeness: Some Universals in Language Usage.* Cambridge: Cambridge University Press.

Bybee, Joan
    2007   *Frequency of use and the Organization of Language.* Oxford: Oxford University Press.

Bybee, Joan
    2010   *Language, Usage and Cognition.* Cambridge: Cambridge University Press.

Bybee, Joan
    2011   Usage-based theory and Grammaticalization. In: H. Narrog and B. Heine (eds.), *The Oxford Handbook of Grammaticalization,* 69–78. Oxford: Oxford University Press.

Bybee, Joan L., Revere D. Perkins and William Pagliuca
    1994   *The Evolution of Grammar: Tense, Aspect and Mood in the Languages of the World.* Chicago: University of Chicago Press.

Bybee, Joan and Sandra Thompson
    1997   Three frequency effects in syntax. *Berkeley Linguistic Society* 23: 65–85.

Bybee, Joan and Joanne Scheibman
    1999   The effect of usage on degrees of constituency: The reduction of *don't* in American English. *Linguistics* 37(4): 575–596.

Bybee, Joan L. and Paul J. Hopper (eds.)
    2001   *Frequency and the Emergence of Language Structure.* Amsterdam: John Benjamins.

Croft, William and D. Alan Cruse
    2004   *Cognitive Linguistics.* Cambridge: Cambridge University Press.

Dąbrowska, Ewa
 2008 The effects of frequency and neighbourhood density on adult native speakers' productivity with Polish case inflections: An empirical test of usage-based approaches to morphology. *Journal of Memory and Language* 58: 931–951.
Diessel, Holger
 this volume Grammar. Berlin/Boston: De Gruyter Mouton.
Divjak, Dagmar and Catherine Cardwell-Harris
 this volume Frequency and entrenchment. Berlin/Boston: De Gruyter Mouton.
Geeraerts, Dirk
 1997 *Diachronic Prototype Semantics: A Contribution to Historical Lexicology*. Oxford: Clarendon Press.
Geeraerts, Dirk
 2010 Schmidt redux: How systematic is the linguistic system if variation is rampant? In K. Boye and E. Engberg-Pedersen (eds.), *Language Usage and Language Structure*, 237–262. Berlin: Mouton de Gruyter.
Geeraerts, Dirk
 this volume Lexical semantics. Berlin/Boston: De Gruyter Mouton.
Geeraerts, Dirk, Stefan Grondelaers and Dirk Speelman
 1999 *Convergentie en divergentie in de Nederlandse woordenschat. Een onderzoek naar kleding- en voetbaltermen*. Amsterdam: Meertens Instituut.
Geeraerts, Dirk, Gitte Kristiansen and Yves Peirsman (eds.)
 2010 *Advances in Cognitive Sociolinguistics*. Berlin: De Gruyter Mouton.
Gibbs, Raymond W., Jr.
 this volume Metaphor. Berlin/Boston: De Gruyter Mouton.
Givón, Talmy
 1971 Historical syntax and synchronic morphology: An archaeologist's field trip. *Chicago Linguistic Society* 7: 394–415.
Goffman, Erving
 1955 On Face-work: An analysis of ritual elements of social interaction. *Psychiatry: Journal for the Study of Interpersonal Processes* 18(3): 213–231.
Goldberg, Adele E.
 1995 *Constructions: A Construction Grammar Approach to Argument Structure*. Chicago: University of Chicago Press.
Goldberg, Adele E.
 2006 *Constructions at Work: The Nature of Generalization in Language*. Oxford: Oxford University Press.
Grice, H. Paul
 1975 Logic and conversation. In: P. Cole and J. L. Morgan (eds.), *Syntax and Semantics*, Volume 3: *Speech Acts*, 41–58. New York: Academic Press.
Gries, Stefan Th.
 this volume Polysemy. Berlin/Boston: De Gruyter Mouton.
Gries, Stefan Th. and Martin Hilpert
 2010 Modeling diachronic change in the third person singular: A multifactorial, verb- and author-specific exploratory approach. *English Language and Linguistics* 14(3): 293–320.
Grondelaers, Stefan and Dirk Geeraerts
 2003 Towards a pragmatic model of cognitive onomasiology. In: H. Cuyckens, R. Dirven & J. Taylor (eds.), *Cognitive Approaches to Lexical Semantics*, 67–92. Berlin: Mouton de Gruyter.
Harder, Peter
 2010 *Meaning in Mind and Society: A Functional Contribution to the Social Turn in Cognitive Linguistics*. Berlin: Mouton de Gruyter.

Heine, Bernd, Ulrike Claudi and Friederike Hünnemeyer
  1991   *Grammaticalization: A conceptual framework*. Chicago: University of Chicago Press.
Heine, Bernd and Tania Kuteva
  2002   *World Lexicon of Grammaticalization*. Cambridge: Cambridge University Press.
Heltoft, Lars
  2006   Grammaticalisation as content reanalysis: The modal character of the Danish S-passive. In: O. Thomsen (ed.), *Competing Models of Linguistic Change: Evolution and Beyond*, 268–288. Amsterdam: John Benjamins.
Hilpert, Martin
  2012   Diachronic collostructional analysis meets the noun phrase: Studying *many a noun* in COHA. In: T. Nevalainen & E. C. Traugott (eds.), *The Oxford Handbook of the History of English*, 233–244. Oxford: Oxford University Press.
Hilpert, Martin
  2013   *Constructional Change in English: Developments in Allomorphy, Word Formation, and Syntax*. Cambridge: Cambridge University Press.
Himmelmann, Nikolaus P.
  2004   Lexicalization and grammaticization: Opposite or orthogonal? In: W. Bisang, N. Himmelmann & B. Wiemer (eds.), *What makes Grammaticalization? A Look from Its Components and Its Fringes*, 21–42. Berlin: Mouton de Gruyter.
Hopper, Paul J.
  1991   On some principles of grammaticalization. In: E. C. Traugott & B. Heine (eds.), *Approaches to Grammaticalization*, Volume 1, 17–35. Amsterdam: John Benjamins.
Hopper, Paul J. & Elizabeth C. Traugott
  2003   *Grammaticalization*. 2nd edition. Cambridge: Cambridge University Press.
Israel, Michael
  1996   The way constructions grow. In: A. Goldberg (ed.), *Conceptual Structure, Discourse and Language*, 217–230. Stanford: CSLI.
Janda, Richard D.
  2001   Beyond 'pathways' and 'unidirectionality': On the discontinuity of language transmission and the counterability of grammaticalization. *Language Sciences* 23(2/3): 265–340.
Kay, Paul and Charles J. Fillmore
  1999   Grammatical constructions and linguistic generalizations: The What's X doing Y? construction. *Language* 75(1): 1–33.
Keller, Rudi
  1994   *On Language Change: The Invisible Hand in Language*. New York: Routledge.
Kiparsky, Paul
  2009   The Germanic weak preterite. In: P. O. Steinkrüger & M. Krifka (eds.), *On Inflection*, 107–124. Berlin: Mouton de Gruyter.
Kristiansen, Gitte and René Dirven (eds.)
  2008   *Cognitive Sociolinguistics: Language Variation, Cultural Models, Social Systems*. Berlin: Mouton de Gruyter.
Labov, William
  1994   *Principles of Linguistic Change*, Volume 1: *Internal Factors*. Oxford: Blackwell.
Labov, William
  2001   *Principles of Linguistic Change*, Volume 2: *Social Factors*. Oxford: Blackwell.
Labov, William
  2010   *Principles of Linguistic Change*, Volume 3: *Cognitive and Cultural Factors*. Oxford: Blackwell.
Langacker, Ronald W.
  1987   *Foundations of Cognitive Grammar*, Volume 1: *Theoretical Prerequisites*. Stanford: Stanford University Press.

Langacker, Ronald W.
 2005 Construction grammars: Cognitive, radical, and less so. In: F. J. Ruiz de Mendoza Ibáñez and M. Sandra Peña Cervel (eds.), *Cognitive Linguistics: Internal Dynamics and Interdisciplinary Interaction*, 101–159. Berlin: Mouton de Gruyter.

Lehmann, Christian
 1995 *Thoughts on Grammaticalization*. Munich: Lincom.

Lightfoot, David
 1979 *Principles of Diachronic Syntax*. Cambridge: Cambridge University Press.

Matthews, Danielle and Grzegorz Krajewski
 this volume First language acquisition. Berlin/Boston: De Gruyter Mouton.

Nerlich, Brigitte and David Clarke
 2001 Serial Metonymy: A study of reference based polysemisation. *Journal of Historical Pragmatics* 2(2): 245–272.

Nevalainen, Terttu and Helena Raumolin-Brunberg
 2003 *Historical Sociolinguistics: Language Change in Tudor and Stuart England*. London: Pearson.

Noël, Dirk
 2007 Diachronic construction grammar and grammaticalization theory. *Functions of Language* 14: 177–202.

Norde, Muriel
 2009 *Degrammaticalization*. Oxford: Oxford University Press.

Patten, Amanda L.
 2010 Grammaticalization and the *it*-cleft construction. In: E. C. Traugott and G. Trousdale (eds.), *Gradience, Gradualness and Grammaticalization*, 221–243. Amsterdam: John Benjamins.

Poplack, Shana and Anne St-Amand
 2007 A real-time window on 19th century vernacular French: The Récits du français québécois d'autrefois. *Language in Society* 36(5): 707–734.

Robinson, Justyna
 2012 A sociolinguistic perspective on semantic change. In: K. Allan and J. Robinson (eds.), *Current Methods in Historical Semantics*, 199–231. Berlin: Mouton de Gruyter.

Ross, John R.
 1967 Constraints on Variables in Syntax. PhD Dissertation, MIT.

Rosch, Eleanor
 1975 Cognitive Reference Points. *Cognitive Psychology* 7: 532–547.

Seto, Ken-ichi
 1999 Distinguishing metonymy from synecdoche. In: K. Panther and G. Radden (eds.), *Metonymy in Language and Thought*, 77–120. Amsterdam: John Benjamins.

Szmrecsanyi, Benedikt
 2010 The English genitive alternation in a cognitive sociolinguistics perspective. In: D. Geeraerts, G. Kristiansen and Y. Peirsman (eds), *Advances in Cognitive Sociolinguistics*, 141–166. Berlin: Mouton de Gruyter.

Tabor, Whitney and Elizabeth C. Traugott
 1998 Structural scope expansion and grammaticalization. In: A. G. Ramat and P. Hopper (eds.), *The Limits of Grammaticalization*, 227–270. Amsterdam: Benjamins.

Taylor, John R. and Kam-Yiu S. Pang
 2008 Seeing as though. *English Language and Linguistics* 12(1): 103–139.

Tomasello, Michael
 1995 Joint attention as social cognition. In: C. Moore and P. Dunham (eds.), *Joint Attention: Its Origins and Role in Development*, 103–130. Hillsdale: Lawrence Erlbaum.

Tomasello, Michael
 2009 *Why We Cooperate*. Cambridge: MIT Press.

Tomasello, Michael and Malinda Carpenter
   2007   Shared Intentionality. *Developmental Science* 10(1): 121–125.
Traugott, Elizabeth C.
   2008   Grammaticalization, constructions and the incremental development of language: Suggestions from the development of degree modifiers in English. In: R. Eckardt, G. Jäger, and T. Veenstra (eds.), *Variation, Selection, Development – Probing the Evolutionary Model of Language Change*, 219–250. Berlin: Mouton de Gruyter.
Traugott, Elizabeth C.
   2010   Grammaticalization. In: S. Luraghi and V. Bubenik (eds.), *Continuum Companion to Historical Linguistics*, 269–283. London: Continuum Press.
Traugott, Elizabeth C. and Graeme Trousdale (eds.)
   2010   *Gradience, Gradualness and Grammaticalization*. Amsterdam: John Benjamins.
Traugott, Elizabeth C. and Graeme Trousdale
   2013   *Constructionalization and Constructional Changes*. Oxford: Oxford University Press.
van der Auwera, Johan, Daniël van Olmen and Denies du Mon
   this volume   Grammaticalization. Berlin/Boston: De Gruyter Mouton
Verhagen, Arie
   2000   Interpreting usage: Construing the history of Dutch causal verbs. In: M. Barlow and S. Kemmer (eds.), *Usage-Based Models of Language*, 261–286. Stanford: CSLI.
Verhagen, Arie
   2002   From parts to wholes and back again. *Cognitive Linguistics* 13(4): 403–439.

Martin Hilpert, Neuchâtel (Switzerland)

17. Variationist linguistics

1. Introduction
2. Motivations for variationist Cognitive Linguistics
3. Domains of investigation
4. Challenges
5. References

1. Introduction

The past ten to fifteen years have witnessed a steady increase, within Cognitive Linguistics and other cognitively oriented approaches to language, of the interest in language variation in all its dimensions. Why is that and what type of studies fall within the scope of this development? In the present chapter (which is a revised and expanded version of Geeraerts and Kristiansen 2014), we will address these questions from a double perspective: what is the role of variationist linguistics within Cognitive Linguistics, and what does Cognitive Linguistics have to offer to variationist linguistics? As a first step, we will argue that studying cultural and lectal linguistic variation is an essential aspect of Cognitive Linguistics, for reasons relating to the historical position of Cognitive Linguistics in the development of contemporary linguistics. (We use the term *lectal* to refer to all types of language varieties or *lects*: dialects, regiolects, national varieties, registers, styles, idiolects etc.). Further, we will offer a brief survey of the state of the art in variationist Cognitive Linguistics, with a specific focus on the area of lectal variation (a field sometimes referred to as Cognitive Sociolinguistics). The chapter concludes with an overview of some of the challenges that a variationist approach to Cognitive Linguistics will have to meet.

To avoid misunderstandings about the scope of the chapter, three preliminary remarks are due. First, by "variationist approaches" in Cognitive Linguistics, we intend to refer to all kinds of research with an interest in the sociocultural aspects of linguistic variation, both from an intralingual and an interlingual perspective. To be sure, the interlingual, cross-linguistic perspective does not include the entire domain of linguistic typology: linguistic typology is interested in language variation, but not necessarily or predominantly from a social or cultural point of view. Second, a distinction needs to be made between variationist linguistics in the context of Cognitive Linguistics, and cognitive approaches to linguistic variation in a broader sense. In a general way, all approaches that combine psycholinguistic and sociolinguistic points of view are forms of "cognitive sociolinguistics", even if they do not specifically refer to theoretical concepts or descriptive practices that are typical for Cognitive Linguistics. In this sense, we will have to ask ourselves to what extent, to put it simplistically, Cognitive Sociolinguistics contributes to sociolinguistics. The distinction is, however, not an easy one, and we will come back to it in the final section. Third, applied studies are not taken into account in the following pages. Questions of language variation may play an important role in the classroom, or in the context of language policies, but that is an area that we will not attempt to cover here.

2. Motivations for variationist Cognitive Linguistics

When we try to understand why the study of linguistic variation might be of specific interest to Cognitive Linguistics, we need to take into account two perspectives: a theoretical one and a methodological one. The first is to some extent the more important of the two, because the methodological reasons for paying attention to linguistic variation derive from the theoretical ones, as we shall see.

2.1. Theoretical motivations for variationist Cognitive Linguistics

To arrive at a clear understanding of the theoretical reasons for looking at language variation, we first need to understand the position of Cognitive Linguistics in the history of linguistics. We will argue that Cognitive Linguistics embodies a far-reaching paradigm shift in linguistics, and that the interest in interlinguistic and intralinguistic language variation constitutes the cornerstone of that paradigm shift. This is a bold statement that undoubtedly requires a longer and more detailed argumentation than we can offer in these pages, but we believe that we can bring across the bottom line of the argument if we concentrate on a few essential features of the development of linguistics in the course of the 20th and the early 21st century. That development is broadly characterized by a succession of three stages of theory formation: the structuralist one, the generative one, and the cognitive-functional one. The structuralist era symbolically took off with the publication of De Saussure's *Cours de linguistique générale* in 1916, and if we stay within such a symbolical framework, we can situate the beginning of the generativist stage in 1957 with the publication of Chomsky's *Syntactic Structures*, and the emergence of Cognitive Linguistics in 1987, a year that saw the landmark publication of both Lakoff's *Women, Fire and Dangerous Things* and Langacker's 1987 *Foundations of Cognitive Grammar*. (We deliberately use the word 'emergence' to characterize the landmark year 1987, because the actual birth of Cognitive Linguistics should be situated about a decade earlier. See Geeraerts 2010a for details). Clearly, we are not suggesting that Cognitive Linguistics superseded generative grammar in the final quarter of the previous century in the same way in which the latter replaced structuralist linguistics in the third quarter: generative linguistics is still a strong tradition, but it now exists alongside a broad family of functional and cognitive approaches. That is a second point we have to emphasize: we focus on Cognitive Linguistics, but in the context of the history of linguistics, Cognitive Linguistics is just a member of a more extensive set of cognitive-functional approaches including approaches like Systemic Functional Grammar in the Hallidayan sense, the Amsterdam school of Functional Linguistics founded by Simon Dik, functional-typological approaches in the sense of Talmy Givón, and many others: see Nuyts (2007) for an insightful overview. Now, we do believe that Cognitive Linguistics is not just *a* member of that family of approaches, but that it actually is a *central* member – both in terms of the appeal that it exerts on large numbers of linguists and in terms of the quality and quantity of the conceptual and descriptive contributions that it renders. Again, this is a point that would have to be established at a more leisurely pace, but for now let us take it for granted that Cognitive Linguistics embodies, if not epitomizes, the post-generativist cognitive-functional approaches.

Crucially, these cognitive-functional approaches reverse the underlying drift of the development of linguistics in the two preceding stages of theory formation. As argued in Geeraerts (2010a), we may identify that trend as one of *decontextualization*: when linguistic theorizing reaches the generative stage, the core of linguistics (that subfield of linguistics that concentrates on what is considered essential to language) is conceived of as "autonomous syntax", i.e., the study of an innate and universal endowment for building formal syntactic structures. Disappearing from the centre of the attention are aspects of language like meaning and function (and the lexicon as a major repository of meaning), context of use, and social variation. In a more analytic fashion, we can identify three conceptual oppositions that were formulated in the successive stages of theory development, and that each contribute to the decontextualizing tendencies by the specific hierarchy of preferences that they are introduced with. First, structuralism introduces the distinction between language as system – *langue* – and language as usage – *parole*. *Langue* is defined as a social system, a set of collective conventions that constitutes a common code shared by a linguistic community. *Parole* on the other hand is an individual activity that takes the form of producing specific combinations from the elements that are present in the code. *Langue* is epistemologically prior to *parole*: the use of a semiotic code logically presupposes the existence of that code.

Second, generative grammar adds an emphasis on the universal aspects of language: in the opposition between the universal and the diverse, language variation is the losing party. Shifting the emphasis from language as a social code to language as a psychological phenomenon (and, in fact, largely ignoring the relevance of the social aspects of language), Chomsky emphasizes the innate, genetically given (and hence universal) aspects of language.

Third, generative grammar takes shape as a formal model of grammar, both in its adoption of symbolic formalization as the descriptive method of linguistics and its outspoken preference for form over function (or meaning) as the starting-point of linguistic analysis.

These three oppositions articulate the decontextualizing trend that leads from structuralism to generativism. The features of language that are deemed central to linguistic theorizing abstract away from meaning and function, from cultural and social diversity, from the actual contexts of language use in action and in interaction. We acknowledge that there might be other ways of spelling out the decontextualizing tendencies, but for our present purposes, these oppositions are particularly pertinent, because they help us to clarify how decontextualization implies a diminished relevance of – and focus on – the study of language variation. In particular, if the essence of language is genetically universal, the study of *interlinguistic* variation is not relevant per se, but only to the extent that it helps to determine what is typologically invariant in the diversity of languages. Similarly, when we think of languages as systems, such systems will have to be internally homogeneous, and *intralinguistic* variation takes the form of a network of dialects that are each (homogeneous) linguistic systems in their own right: the unit of variation, to the extent that variation is considered at all, is the homogeneous, self-contained linguistic system.

The three oppositions also help us to understand why we can think of Cognitive Linguistics as a recontextualizing approach to language. On each of the three counts, in fact, Cognitive Linguistics and functional approaches more generally take exactly the antithetical position from the structuralist and generativist tradition. Working through the three oppositions in reverse order, it hardly needs to be argued, first, that meaning and function take precedence over form in Cognitive Linguistics theorizing: if anything, Cognitive Linguistics is a systematic attempt to give meaning and function a central role in the description of natural language – by looking at language as a tool for categorization and cognitive construal. Second, Cognitive Linguistics embraces an experiential view of meaning. The meaning we construct in and through the language is not a separate and independent module of the mind, but it reflects our overall experience as human beings. There are at least two main aspects to this broader experiential grounding of linguistic meaning. On the one hand, we are embodied beings, not pure minds. Our organic nature influences our experience of the world, and this experience is reflected in the language we use. On the other hand, we are not just biological entities: we also have a cultural and social identity, and our language may reveal that identity (Kristiansen 2001, 2003), i.e., languages may embody the historical and cultural experience of groups of speakers (and individuals). What is interesting about language is then not just the universal features: the diversity of experience expressed in language matters at least as much.

Third, Cognitive Linguistics adopts a usage-based model of language, roughly in the sense that there is a dialectal relationship between structure and use: individual usage events are realizations of an existing systemic structure, but at the same time, it is only through the individual usage events that changes might be introduced into the structure.

"System", in fact, is primarily an observable commonality in the behavior of language users, and as such, it is the result of social interaction. People influence each other's linguistic behavior, basically by co-operative imitation and adaptation, and in some cases by opposition and a desire for distinctiveness.

It follows from this radical reversal of the decontextualizing mainstream positions that the study of language variation is a compelling field of research for Cognitive Linguistics. The interest in experiential diversity that comes with the second assumption translates into an interest in interlinguistic variation: to what extent do different cultures express a different construal of the world in their language use (cf. Koptjevskaja-Tamm this volume)? And the usage-based model certainly implies a concern with intralinguistic variation: "usage-based implies variational" (Geeraerts 2005). When we say that common linguistic behavior derives from the interaction between language users, it needs to be established just how common that behavior actually is, and how the existing variation is structured by social factors – precisely the kind of questions that are central within dialectology and sociolinguistics.

In other words, if Cognitive Linguistics is indeed a recontextualizing model of linguistics par excellence, and if that recontextualization involves reversing a number of preferences that seemed ingrained in mainstream 20th century linguistics – a preference for system over use, for universality over diversity, for form over function – then a thorough investigation of interlinguistic and intralinguistic variation is an integral part of the Cognitive Linguistics enterprise.

2.2. Methodological motivations for variationist Cognitive Linguistics

The usage-based nature of Cognitive Linguistics also implies that there are methodological reasons for taking into account variation (see also Tummers et al. 2005). If one believes in the existence of a homogeneous linguistic system, then there is at least some justification for the generativist preference for an introspective methodology: if all users of a given language have the same system in their heads, then any given language user constitutes a representative sample of the population – and which language user's internal grammar is more accessible than that of the linguists themselves? Condoning armchair linguistics, in other words, fits in with the assumptions of a "system before use" approach. As soon as that assumption is rejected, however, homogeneity can no longer be assumed, and armchair linguistics becomes anathema: there is no way in which the linguist could claim representativity for the linguistic population at large, and thus, data will have to be sampled in a way that ensures a broad coverage of the behavior in a linguistic community. This explains the rise of corpus linguistics in Cognitive Linguistics: as archives of non-elicited, spontaneous language behavior, text corpora constitute a suitable empirical basis for a usage-based linguistics. Similarly, there is a growing interest in experimental methods for studying the on-line aspects of language usage. Traditional variationist sociolinguistic methods such as surveys and ethnographic methods likewise aim to retrieve data that ultimately constitute a corpus.

More often than not, however, the corpus will not be internally homogeneous: because the texts collected for the corpus come from various sources, it will not be known in advance whether the variation that may be observed in the corpus is due to lectal factors or not. As such, determining the effects of such factors will be necessary for any cognitive linguistic attempt to analyse the usage data – even if the analysis is not a priori interested in lectal variation. That is to say, even if the analysis of lectal variation is not the primary concern of the investigation, filtering out lectal effects requires an analysis of variation. Methodologically speaking, an awareness of variation is thus indispensable for a data-oriented usage-based analysis.

3. Domains of investigation

Having established that an investigation of interlinguistic and intralinguistic variation should come naturally to Cognitive Linguistics, we may now address the question where the field actually stands. If we look back at the three oppositions with which we started, we may note that Cognitive Linguistics did not effectuate the reversal of the three perspectives at the same time. A shift from form to function and meaning has obviously been there all along; it was definitional for the Cognitive Linguistics theoretical framework from the very start. Rather, it is the other two oppositions that interest us more: we observe that the domain of interlinguistic and cultural variation is fairly well established, but that the study of intralinguistic and lectal variation has been slower to develop.

3.1. Interlinguistic and cultural variation

An interest in cultural effects at the level of interlinguistic variation existed from an early date in the history of Cognitive Linguistics. For instance, Rosch's research on prototype categorization (Rosch 1977), which had a major influence on theory formation in Cognitive Linguistics, is characterized by an anthropological background, just like Berlin's research on colour terms and ethnobiological classification from which it derived (Berlin and Kay 1969; Berlin et al. 1974). Questions of cultural relativity play a natural role in this kind of investigation, although the research endeavours are very much motivated by an interest in universal patterns of variation – we will come back to the point in a moment. The notion of "cultural model" (which invokes the notion of "frame" and "conceptual metaphor", that other pillar of semantics in Cognitive Linguistics, next to prototypicality) also made an early entrance: see Holland and Quinn (1987) for an influential early volume. Cross-cultural studies of metaphorical patterns and conceptual metaphors are by now an established line of research: for representative examples, see Dirven (1994), Yu (1998, 2009), Dirven, Frank and Ilie (2001), Dirven, Hawkins, and Sandikcioglu (2001), Dirven et al. (2003), Boers (2003), Littlemore and Low (2006), Sharifian et al. (2008). The existence of a book series entitled *Cognitive Linguistic Studies in Cultural Contexts* (with Sharifian 2011 as its first volume) points in the same direction. A broadly anthropological view on cultural linguistics has been developed by Palmer (1996) and Kronenfeld (1996).

Three additional remarks may help to represent the field with a little more detail. In particular, we would like to draw the attention to a number of shifts that occurred in the course of the development of culture-related research in Cognitive Linguistics.

In the first place, the traditional preference for universality ("traditional" from the point of view of mainstream 20th century linguistics as represented by generative theory, that is) seems to some extent to have influenced the interest in cultural variation in the framework of Cognitive Linguistics. As we noted earlier, the experiential nature of a Cognitive Linguistic conception of semantics involves both a physiological and a cultural kind of experience: embodiment and socialization, so to speak. But the physiological perspective suggests a universality that the cultural perspective lacks. In some domains of enquiry both perspectives opposed each other. This applies specifically to the study of conceptual metaphors for the emotions, a field which has always been one of the main areas of attention of Conceptual Metaphor Theory. In contrast with the predominantly physiological explanation for "anger" metaphors suggested by Kövecses (1986), Geeraerts and Grondelaers (1995) drew the attention to the culture-specific background of at least some of the anger expressions, which turn out to have a historical background in the theory of humours that dominated Western medical and psychological thinking from antiquity to the early modern period. Although Lakoff and Kövecses (1987; Kövecses 1995), in line with the tradition, at first opposed the cultural interpretation in favour of a physiological one, more recent work shows a wholehearted acceptance of the cultural perspective; in particular see Kövecses (2005), a book heralding a "cultural turn" of metaphor studies. As the "anger" studies suggest, a consequence of this growing cultural sensitivity of Conceptual Metaphor Theory could well be an increase in diachronic metaphor studies. Cultural models, i.e., the more or less coherent sets of concepts that cultures use to structure experience and make sense of the world are not reinvented afresh with every new period in the culture's development. But if it is by definition part of their cultural nature that they have a historical dimension, it is only by investigating their historical origins and their gradual transformation that their contemporary form can be properly understood. Diachronic research into the history of metaphors (as in the work of Gevaert 2005 or Allan 2009) is however still a relatively underdeveloped area of cross-cultural work in Cognitive Linguistics.

In the second place, the classificatory combination we are making in the title of this section between "interlinguistic" and "cultural" is one of convenience only. Surely, there can be cultural differences within one language: Lakoff's (1996) analysis of the distinction between a "stern father" and a "nurturing parent" model of political organization would be a case in point. Lakoff argues that the cluster of values and beliefs held by liberals on the one hand and by conservatives on the other, derive their internal coherence from the different metaphorical models that both political (sub)cultures in the US entertain with regard to the role of the state. Here as in other areas of Cognitive Linguistics, corpus linguistics provides the basis for new studies. Ahrens (2011), for instance, examines lexical frequency patterns in U.S. presidential speeches as a corroboration of the Lakovian hypothesis about underlying cultural models of liberals and conservatives. For another example of such a corpus-based study into intralinguistic cultural differences, see Speelman et al. (2008) on different preferences for evaluative adjectives in Netherlandic Dutch and Belgian Dutch. Intralinguistic cultural differences of this kind belong together with what we will refer to in the following section as "variation of meaning" studies, i.e., studies that look into the lectal distribution of meaningful phenomena within a given language.

In the third place, investigations into the relation between language diversity and thought exhibit an increasing methodological sophistication, as in the experimental approaches illustrated by the work of Boroditsky (2001), Lucy and Gaskins (2003), and Levinson (2003). A naïve approach might assume that the presence of certain expressions in a given language suffices to establish a difference of semantic outlook between that language and others that display a different set of expressions. However, from a usage-based perspective, it needs to be established on independent grounds whether language indeed influences thought at the level of actual usage. The essential methodological step that is taken in recent research into linguistic relativity is to define non-verbal tasks for a given conceptual domain, and then show that speakers of different languages perform differently on such tasks in a way that corresponds to the structural characteristics of their language. For instance, in Levinson's research on spatial reference, languages turn out to have different spatial systems: not all languages have a spatial system like English (in which things are located relative to the observer or to another landmark), but some of them use an "absolute" system of reference, in which the position of anything may be given in terms of the cardinal directions. Experimental data show that speakers of a language with such an absolute system of spatial reference are better at performing some kinds of non-verbal tasks, such as identifying positions in open terrain, whereas speakers of languages like English perform better in tasks involving locating objects relative to the speaker. For a further overview of recent research into linguistic relativity and the interface between language and thought, we refer to Everett (2013).

3.2. Intralinguistic and lectal variation

Within Cognitive Linguistics, the first decade of the present century has seen a growing interest for language-internal variation in all its dimensions, as witnessed by several publications referring to "Cognitive Sociolinguistics" or "social cognitive linguistics" as the study of lectal variation in the context of Cognitive Linguistics: Kristiansen and Dirven (2008), Croft (2009), Geeraerts et al. (2010), Pütz et al. (2012), and Kristiansen and Geeraerts (2013). Cognitive Sociolinguistics as demarcated by these publications strives towards a convergence of the usage-based traditions of language studies, as represented by pragmatics and sociolinguistics, and the post-generative theories of grammar illustrated by Cognitive Linguistics. The field of intralinguistic variation studies in Cognitive Linguistics may be broadly divided into three areas of research.

While the first area is concerned with general theoretical models of the role of social factors in language, the other two areas cover the descriptive contributions of Cognitive Linguistics to the study of linguistic variation. Theoretical and programmatic studies falling within that first area of research analyze the way in which the emergence of language as such and the presence of specific features in a language can only be adequately conceived of if one takes into account the socially interactive nature of linguistic communication. Important representatives of this strand of research include Croft (2000) on a socio-evolutionary view of language, Sinha (2007, 2009) on language as an epigenetic system, Zlatev (2005) on situated embodiment, Itkonen (2003) on the social nature of the linguistic system, Verhagen (2005) on the central role of intersubjectivity in language, Harder (2003, 2010) on the socio-functional background of language, and Beckner et al. (2009) on language as a complex adaptive system. Regardless of their differences, these approaches share a foundational perspective: they present high-level models of the principled role of social factors and usage-based phenomena in language and linguistic evolution. (It may be useful to add that the various approaches are mentioned here with just a few representative reference publications. For all of the models mentioned in this brief list, more literature can readily be found).

While all of these approaches emphasize the importance of language as a social phenomenon, they do not all pay equal attention to the existence of language-internal variation, i.e., to variation of the kind that constitutes the focus of sociolinguistics, dialectology, stylistics and related disciplines. There are basically two different types of reasons for this relative neglect. The theoretical position taken by Itkonen, for instance, relies heavily on a view of language systems as (largely implicit) social norms. Such a view, resembling a Saussurean conception of the linguistic system as a set of shared conventions, seems to assume the internal homogeneity of lects, in contrast with a more radical view that considers lects themselves to exhibit prototype structure. In methodological terms, this is reflected in Itkonen's adherence to intuition rather than observation as the basic method in linguistics. (For a more extended discussion of Itkonen's views, their relationship to variationist linguistics, and their methodological consequences, see Geeraerts 2005, and compare Geeraerts 2010b on the pervasiveness of variation).

Conversely, some of the theoretical approaches mentioned here simply focus on other aspects of the social nature of language than its lectal structure, without theoretical implications with regard to the latter. Verhagen's work on intersubjectivity, for instance, has an essentially grammatical focus: he argues that in many cases the meaning of grammatical constructions has more to do with the human capacity for taking other people's points of view than with providing referential descriptions of the world. Specific expressions and constructions (like negation, or complementation, or connectives) are shown to have an interactive function rather than just a descriptive meaning.

Similarly, theorists propagating a view of language as a complex adaptive system, like Croft and Sinha, tend to focus on the emergence and development of language from an evolutionary perspective. This is a perspective that links up directly with the interdisciplinary field of evolutionary linguistics, as represented a. o. by Kirby (1999; Christiansen and Kirby 2003) or Steels (2002, 2011). Steels for instance investigates experimentally how, in a setting with robots as artificial agents, languages with naturalistic properties arise through a process of self-organizing communication. Like the views formulated by Beckner et al., this kind of research is based on the hypothesis that language is a complex adaptive system that emerges through interactive coordination between agents, and that further linguistic evolutions occur in response to changes in the environment or the needs of the agents.

Approaches such as the intersubjectivity model or the complex adaptive system view far from exclude a more lectal approach; their current focus just lies elsewhere. But if Cognitive Linguistics aims to contribute to variationist linguistics, it should also produce studies with the empirical detail and the methodological rigor that is customary in sociolinguistics and dialectology. This entails the question what Cognitive Linguistics may specifically have to offer to variationist linguistics: we may be convinced of the relevance of a social perspective for Cognitive Linguistics, but can the latter convince variationist linguistics of its specific relevance? Two specific perspectives come to mind, which we may refer to in a lapidary way as studies in the *variation of meaning* and studies in the *meaning of variation*.

The basic question for the *variation of meaning* approach will be obvious: how does language-internal variation affect the occurrence of linguistic phenomena that have the specific attention of Cognitive Linguistics, notably meaning, and more generally, conceptual construal by linguistic means? The question is relevant for variationist linguistics at large because meaning is probably the least studied aspect of language in mainstream sociolinguistics (which, like mainstream grammar studies, favours formal variables). Variationist studies within Cognitive Linguistics, then, involve issues such as the social distribution of prototype-based meaning extensions (Robinson 2010), the lectal productivity of metonymical patterns (Zhang et al. 2011), the variable use of metaphor in discourse (Semino 2008), lexical variation in pluricentric languages (Soares da Silva 2005; Glynn 2008), usage-based approaches to borrowing (Zenner et al. 2012), spatial semantics at dialect level (Berthele 2006), and lectal variation of constructions and constructional semantics (Grondelaers et al. 2002; Speelman and Geeraerts 2009; Colleman 2010; Szmrecsanyi 2010; Hollmann and Siewierska 2011; Hollmann 2013; Schönefeld 2013; Gries 2013). Studies of intralingual cultural differences of the type that we mentioned in section 2.1 also fall in this category.

We should note that the importance of meaning for sociolinguistics goes well beyond descriptive comprehensiveness, because questions of meaning implicitly lie at the heart of the sociolinguistic enterprise. Consider the concept of a "sociolinguistic variable" as a cornerstone of the standard methodology of socio-variationist research. Simply put, a sociolinguistic variable in the sense of contemporary variationist sociolinguistics is a set of alternative ways of expressing the same linguistic function or realizing the same linguistic element, where each of the alternatives has social significance: "Social and stylistic variation presuppose the option of saying 'the same thing' in several different ways: that is, the variants are identical in reference or truth value, but opposed in their social and/or stylistic significance" (Labov 1972: 271). Thus, according to a variationist Labovian perspective, a sociolinguistic variable is a linguistic element that is sensitive to a number of extralinguistic independent variables like social class, age, sex, geographical group location, ethnic group, or contextual style and register. This automatically raises the question of semantic equivalence: if we are interested in the contextual choice between synonymous (functionally equivalent) expressions as a reflection of sociolinguistic factors, we first need to control for meaning – but how? Within the field of sociolinguistics, the methodological problem of semantic equivalence was recognized early on by Beatriz Lavandera. She argued that "it is inadequate at the current state of sociolinguistic research to extend to other levels of analysis of variation the notion of sociolinguistic variable originally developed on the basis of phonological data. The quantitative studies of variation which deal with morphological, syntactic, and lexical alternation suffer from the lack of an articulated theory of meanings" (Lavandera 1978: 171). In the mainstream development of sociolinguistics, however, the question of semantic equivalence, as a methodological prerequisite for the sociovariationist study of lexis and grammar, was not systematically explored. An important issue for Cognitive Sociolinguistics, then, is a renewed look at Lavandera's question and the interplay between semantic and formal variation. In practice, this research line is primarily being pursued by Geeraerts and his associates, with a focus on onomasiological variation within the lexicon: see the long-term development going from Geeraerts et al. (1994) over Geeraerts et al. (1999), Speelman et al. (2003), to Heylen et al. (2008) and Ruette et al. (2011).

The third main area of investigation for Cognitive Sociolinguistics is concerned with what we have called the *meaning of variation*, that is to say, with the way in which language variation is perceived and categorized by the language user. This is a field of research that links up with perceptual dialectology and folk linguistics in the sense of Preston and Niedzielski (2000) and related work. Relevant questions about the processing and representation of linguistic variation include the following: how do language users perceive lectal differences, and how do they evaluate them attitudinally? What models do they use to categorize linguistic diversity? How does linguistic stereotyping work: how do language users categorize other groups of speakers? What is the role of subjective and objective linguistic distances: is there a correlation between objective linguistic distances, perceived distances, and language attitudes? Are there any cultural models of language diversity: what models of lectal variation, standardization, and language change do people work with? To what extent do attitudinal and perceptual factors have an influence on language change? How do language users acquire lectal competence, how is it stored mentally, and how does it work in language production?

Again, in the context of this overview, we particularly need to ask ourselves what the specific contribution of Cognitive Linguistics to the field could be. In general, if the cognitive representation of language variation by the language user is of the same type as other types of categorization, then the categorization phenomena that Cognitive Linguistics typically focuses on should also be relevant for an analysis of the way in which language users mentally represent linguistic variation – in other words, we expect phenomena like prototypicality, metaphor and metonymy to play a role in the cognitive representation of variation. In practice, two strands of research so far stand out, concentrating on prototypicality effects and metaphorical conceptualization.

To begin with the latter, metaphorical models of lectal structure are concerned with the question to what extent metaphors frame people's perception of language varieties. Work in this direction covers both high-level cultural models of language variation and normativity in general (Geeraerts 2003; Polzenhagen and Dirven 2008), and attitudinal metaphors involving specific dialect and standard language environments (Berthele 2008, 2010).

Prototype-based models of lectal structure (Kristiansen 2003) emphasize that lects are not internally homogeneous, but are rather characterized by centrality effects: some aspects have a more central role than others, and will be more saliently represented in the mind of the language users. These central features can be linguistic phenomena: some pronunciation habits, or elements of lexis and grammar, are more typical than others. But the typical aspects can also be speakers of a variety: in Kristiansen's (2010) research into the acquisition of accent recognition in children, familiarity with iconic speakers appears to play a decisive role: when comparing the age groups of 6, 8 and 12, an increase in accent recognition correlated significantly with knowledge of social paragons and the ability to describe salient speech-related features. Clark and Trousdale (2010) in turn demonstrate how the cognitive identification with a specific social group correlates with the realization of linguistic features expressing that identity. In line with these thoughts, Guy (2013) observes that linguistic variants are indexical of social traits and social identities and that every speech community has many sociolinguistic variables, and asks the question whether multiple variables cohere in forming sociolects: if each variable has a variant considered "working class", do working class speakers use all such variants simultaneously? Soukup (2013) in turn examines identity projection in an

Austrian TV show and implements two empirical tests (a speech perception elicitation test and a speaker evaluation experiment) to derive evidence for the perception of linguistic cues associated with different social meanings.

This type of research opens up towards the interest that has been growing in sociolinguistics at large in the interactive and flexible use of social variables, as surveyed in Kristiansen (2008): whereas mainstream sociolinguistics of the Labovian type tends to focus on the more or less stable structural correspondences between social groups and linguistic variables, the so-called "third wave" of sociolinguistic studies (Eckert 2012) explores what individuals actively do with group-related variables in order to do meaningful things with variants. Traditional sociolinguistic variables such as gender, age, race, socio-economic status ultimately correspond to social identities, and when combined to multiple social identities that can be enacted through socially significant linguistic variables. Acts of identity (Le Page and Tabouret-Keller 1985) and proactive identity construal are key words in third wave sociolinguistics. Because this is a kind of variationist linguistics that is situated at usage level, interactional sociolinguistics is of specific interest to Cognitive Linguistics, all the more so since, up to a point, it combines the "variation of meaning" and "meaning of variation" perspectives: social variation of language that is perceived as meaningful by the language users is itself used in a situationally variable process of expressing and creating social meaning. In more technical terms, if lectal varieties and social identities form prototype categories that relate to one another through a metonymic link, perceptually salient group-related variants may be used to index existing identities or set up new, local schemas (Kristiansen 2003, 2006). The awareness and acquisition of socially related linguistic schemata is an experientially grounded process that emerges during the first ten years of life (Kristiansen 2010). These processes are crucial in the dialectic relationship of structure and use: if linguistic structure emerges from language use, socially structured language use will result in lectal subsystems – but once set up, these structured sets of choices become available to the individual user for imitation or for creative modulation. In spite of the overall relevance, though, the interactional perspective is not yet strongly represented in the actual descriptive practice of Cognitive Sociolinguistics. See Soukup (2013), Zenner et al. (2009) and Zenner et al. (2012) for a few representative examples.

The approaches described above are in consonance with the principles of frequency-based and exemplar-based approaches to language variation and change (Bybee 2006; Bod et al. 2003; Kretzschmar 2009). In exemplar-based models, as applied to e.g., phonetics, phonology, semantics or language acquisition, schematic mental representations emerge over usage-based events, defined by a rich inventory of tokens, or "exemplars", which are stored in long-term memory (cf. Ramscar this volume on categorization and Baayen this volume on analogy and schematization). By contrast, the generative conception of representation maintains that stored knowledge of a particular word consists of a minimal, abstract sequence of symbolic elements. In exemplar based-models, not only is language acquisition experientially grounded, but what children acquire are not a set of rules but a collection of fully specified examples that gradually result in generalisations and patterns (Abbot-Smith and Tomasello 2006; see also Matthews and Krajewski this volume). Thus, phonetic detail, for instance, is not discarded but plays an important role in the representation of lexical items (Bybee 2001; Pierrehumbert 2002), just as it does in the gradual acquisition of distinct lectal schemata. For a recent paper describing the importance of exemplar-based models for second dialect acquisition see Nycz (2013).

Nycz first defines the predictions of two prominent models of phonological representation (generative phonology and usage-based phonology) regarding how specific types of second dialect features are acquired, and then she evaluates these predictions against the results of a sociolinguistic study of native adult speakers of Canadian English who moved to the New York region. More information on the role of experience in the usage-based approach can be found in Divjak and Caldwell-Harris (this volume).

4. Challenges

We have shown that the study of cultural and lectal linguistic variation is an essential aspect of Cognitive Linguistics, for reasons deriving from the historical position of Cognitive Linguistics in the development of contemporary linguistics: as a usage-based, recontextualizing model of linguistics, interlinguistic and intralinguistic variation are a crucial element of the theory. With an emphasis on what the specific contribution of Cognitive Linguistics consists of, we have offered a survey of the field of variationist studies in Cognitive Linguistics by distinguishing four domains of enquiry: cross-cultural variation of meaning, general models of the socially mediated dialectic relationship between system and use, the study of "variation of meaning", and the study of the "meaning of variation".

The interest in variationist phenomena, specifically to the extent that they involve intralingual variation, is a relatively recent trend within Cognitive Linguistics, but as we have argued, this social turn is inextricably wound up with the very nature of Cognitive Linguistics as a usage-based approach. Given its recent character, the approach is not stabilized: it would be stretching the truth to claim that – beyond the shared interest in the social nature of language and language variation – a common framework of concepts and practices unites the approaches that we have presented in the previous pages. To complete the overview, it therefore seems fitting to attempt to identify the main challenges that the emerging field of variationist studies in Cognitive Linguistics will have to meet. We would like to suggest that there are fundamentally speaking two different types: a theoretical one, and a methodological one.

The theoretical challenge involves the relationship between variationist Cognitive Linguistics and the broader field of language variation studies. The approaches that we have introduced in these pages emerge, by and large, from cognitive linguists who recognize the importance of including social and lectal factors into the cognitive linguistic models. To be successful, then, these approaches will have to interact intensively with existing variationist linguistics, and defend the specific contribution of Cognitive (Socio)linguistics in that context. More specifically, as we mentioned in the introduction to this chapter, Cognitive Sociolinguistics will have to stake out its specific position within the context of cognitive sociolinguistics. The latter phrase may be used to identify any attempt to combine the traditionally distinct lines of variationist, sociolinguistic and cognitive, psycholinguistic research into the use of language. Cognitive Sociolinguistics is one such attempt, but it is important to observe that the convergence of perspectives is currently happening on a broader scale than what is happening within the confines of Cognitive Linguistics (and in fact, some of the authors that we referred to above would not necessarily consider themselves to be cognitive linguists). Without trying to be exhaustive, it may be useful to indicate and briefly illustrate the two main research lines that contribute to the convergence. They are, in a sense, each other's converse. On the one hand, starting from the psychological end, the question arises how sociolinguistic variation (and language variation at large) is cognitively represented and processed. On the other hand, starting from the sociolinguistic end, the question is how factors relating to cognitive processing and storage influence language variation.

To illustrate the first perspective, we can primarily refer to the well-established fields of perceptual dialectology and attitude research that were already mentioned. In addition, there is a somewhat younger line of research investigating how language variation influences speech perception (see Drager 2010 for a review) or lexical processing (see e.g., Clopper 2012), and a growing interest in individual differences in the mental representation of grammar (Dąbrowska 2012; see also Dąbrowska this volume). In language acquisition research as well there is a lively interest in sociophonetic variation, see Butler et al. (2011), Floccia et al. (2012), and Schmale et al. (2012) for a few examples of early accent recognition studies in infants. For the evolution of accent recognition across different age groups in early childhood see e.g., Floccia et al. (2009) and Kristiansen (2010).

To illustrate the second perspective, various types of work can be mentioned. In a very direct way, psycholinguistic factors can be among the features that describe the distribution of an expression or construction. A clear case in point is Szmrecsanyi (2009), who includes on-line processing factors next to structural and variational factors in a statistical model of morphosyntactic persistence. Similar "multivariate grammar" studies including psychological factors along variational ones among the explanatory variables are Grondelaers et al. (2008), and De Sutter et al. (2008). A second type of work links language variation to specific models of acquisition. Probably the best known example here is Labov's (2010) view that the transmission of speech patterns within a community is dependent on child language acquisition, whereas diffusion across communities is dependent on adult learning. A third type of work involves the different models that try to describe the mutual adaptation of interacting interlocutors, from older models like the accommodation theory of Giles and Powesland (1975), which sees linguistic convergence as reducing social distance, to newer models like the interactive alignment approach of Pickering and Garrod (2004), which assumes that persistent priming effects ensure an alignment of cognitive representations between interlocutors.

An important theoretical challenge for Cognitive Sociolinguistics, then, is to take into account the rich tradition of sociolinguistics, and specifically also those approaches that combine psycholinguistic and sociolinguistic perspectives, and to situate its specific contributions against that background. Interestingly, the double perspective that we displayed to introduce "cognitive sociolinguistics" in the broader sense is typical for the second major challenge that we would like to evoke. On the one hand, taking a psychological point of departure, we mentioned studies that introduce sociolinguistic variables into psychological research lines. On the other hand, taking a sociolinguistic point of departure, we found studies that introduce psycholinguistic variables into sociological research lines. When we cast the net a bit more widely, we can notice that that pattern occurs on a more systematic basis in the field that we are exploring here: sociolinguistic variation can be both the output and the input of the investigation. Consider what we said about semantics. On the one hand, Cognitive Sociolinguistics is interested in the way in which social factors influence the presence or emergence of meaning. On the other hand, when we try to define sociolinguistic variables, we try to keep meaning or function constant and see how social structure is present in or emerges from variation in the expression of that constant. Or think about the way in which constructions are studied. In "multivariate grammar" studies of the type referred to above, the occurrence of a construction α is modeled in terms of a variety of factors: semantic, structural, discursive, processing-related – and lectal, in the sense that the frequency of the construction in language variety A or language variety B, in the broadest possible reading of "language variety", plays a role in the analysis. According to this perspective, the existence of A or B is taken for granted in the analysis. But conversely, the very existence of A or B as separate varieties needs to be established – and that can be done by exploring, in aggregate studies, whether construction α systematically co-occurs with other linguistic phenomena in the context of external variables (geography for dialects, nations for natiolects, social features for sociolects etc.).

The Janus-headed nature of Cognitive Sociolinguistics also shows up on the methodological level. The incorporation of meaningfulness into variationist studies raises the methodological bar: what methods are most appropriate for throwing light on the interaction between language-internal linguistic variation, language-external social factors, and cognitive aspects of variation? It is testimonial to the dynamism of Cognitive Sociolinguistics that scholars working in that direction may often be found at the forefront of methodological innovation in linguistics. On an initial level, this may be illustrated by the various distributional methods for identifying meanings in corpus data, from collocational methods (Stefanowitsch and Gries 2003) over "behavioral profiles" (Gries 2010) to vector space models (Heylen et al. 2012). If we go beyond that initial level and look at the way lectal factors are incorporated into the analysis, we can discern two methodological lines that correspond neatly with the two perspectives that we pointed at. On the one hand, when social factors are part of the input, the preference is for regression analyses modelling the distribution of linguistic variables: see the dissertations of Grondelaers (2000) and Gries (2003) for pioneering examples, and Gries (2013) or Zenner et al. (2012) for the current state of development, involving mixed effects regression models. By way of example, Gries discusses three case studies which showcase how contextual as well as cognitive or psycholinguistic language-internal and sociolinguistic language-external factors interact. The many variables under scrutiny in the three case studies (the first two of which investigate syntactic priming effects in constructional alternations and the third diachronic morphological change) were successfully analysed by logistic regression and mixed-effects models that offer an "elegant treatment of interactions with and across internal and external factors" (Gries 2013: 14).

On the other hand, when social structure emerges from the analysis, the methodological focus lies on methods of aggregate analysis of the type illustrated by Geeraerts et al. (1999) and similar later work (see above). It will be appreciated that both methodological lines (both of which are young and in full development) mirror each other in the same way as the descriptive perspectives: either you investigate how lectal structure influences the behavior of linguistic variables, or you investigate how the joint behavior of linguistic variables establishes lectal structure.

The co-existence of these descriptive and methodological switches of perspective is typical for a usage-based view of language as a complex adaptive system. Common trends and patterns of linguistic behavior (the clusters of phenomena that we tend to refer to as dialects, natiolects, sociolects etc.) emerge from separate communicative events. But at the same time, once it has emerged, the transmission of such a lectal structure feeds the trends and patterns back to the level of usage. The two perspectives that we observed constitute the two sides of this complex adaptive coin, but then the methodological challenge will be to integrate the two viewpoints, which now mostly exist alongside each other, into a single comprehensive model. Thinking about language as a complex adaptive system has its own methodological complexities – but linguists will adapt ...

Acknowledgement

Financial support for the second author's contribution to this paper was provided by the Spanish Ministry of Science and Innovation (Research Project FFI2010-19395).

5. References

Abbot-Smith, Kirsten and Michael Tomasello
   2006   Exemplar-learning and schematization in a usage-based account of syntactic acquisition. *The Linguistic Review* 23: 275–290.

Ahrens, Kathleen
   2011   Examining conceptual metaphor models through lexical frequency patterns: A case study of U. S. presidential speeches. In: S. Handl and H.-J. Schmid (eds.), *Windows to the Mind. Metaphor, Metonymy and Conceptual Blending*, 167–184. Berlin: De Gruyter Mouton.

Allan, Kathryn
   2009   *Metaphor and Metonymy. A Diachronic Approach*. London: Wiley-Blackwell.

Baayen, Harald
   this volume   5. Analogy and schematization. Berlin/Boston: De Gruyter Mouton.

Beckner, Clay, Richard Blythe, Joan L. Bybee, Morten H. Christiansen, William Croft, Nick C. Ellis, John Holland, Jinyun Ke, Diane Larsen-Freeman and Tom Schoenemann
   2009   Language is a complex adaptive system. *Language Learning* 59: 1–26.

Berlin, Brent, Dennis E. Breedlove and Peter H. Raven
   1974   *Principles of Tzeltal Plant Classification: An Introduction to the Botanical Ethnography of a Mayan-speaking People of Highland Chiapas*. New York: Academic Press.

Berlin, Brent and Paul Kay
   1969   *Basic Color Terms. Their Universality and Evolution*. Berkeley: University of California Press.

Berthele, Raphael
   2006   *Ort und Weg. Die sprachliche Raumreferenz in Varietäten des Deutschen, Rätoromanischen und Französischen*. Berlin/New York: Walter de Gruyter.

Berthele, Raphael
   2008   A nation is a territory with one culture and one language: The role of metaphorical folk models in language policy debates. In: G. Kristiansen and R. Dirven (eds.), *Cognitive Sociolinguistics. Language Variation, Cultural Models, Social Systems*, 301–331. Berlin/New York: Mouton de Gruyter.

Berthele, Raphael
   2010   Investigations into the folk's mental models of linguistic varieties. In: D. Geeraerts, G. Kristiansen and Y. Peirsman (eds.), *Advances in Cognitive Sociolinguistics*, 265–290. Berlin/New York: De Gruyter Mouton.

Bod, Rens, Jennifer Hay and Stefanie Jannedy (eds.)
   2003   *Probabilistic Linguistics*. Cambridge: MIT Press.

Boers, Frank
   2003   Applied linguistics perspectives on cross-cultural variation in conceptual metaphor. *Metaphor and Symbol* 18: 231–238.

Boroditsky, Lera
   2001   Does language shape thought? Mandarin and English speakers' conceptions of time. *Cognitive Psychology* 43: 1–22.
Butler, Joseph, Caroline Floccia, Jeremy Goslin and Robin Panneton
   2011   Infants' discrimination of familiar and unfamiliar accents in speech. *Infancy* 16(4): 392–417.
Bybee, Joan L.
   2001   *Phonology and Language Use.* Cambridge: Cambridge University Press.
Bybee, Joan L.
   2006   *Frequency of Use and the Organization of Language.* Oxford: Oxford University Press.
Chomsky, Noam
   1957   *Syntactic Structures.* The Hague: Mouton.
Christiansen, Morten H. and Simon Kirby (eds.)
   2003   *Language Evolution.* Oxford: Oxford University Press.
Clark, Lynn and Graeme Trousdale
   2010   A cognitive approach to quantitative sociolinguistic variation: Evidence from th-fronting in Central Scotland. In: D. Geeraerts, G. Kristiansen and Y. Peirsman (eds.), *Advances in Cognitive Sociolinguistics*, 291–321. Berlin/New York: De Gruyter Mouton.
Clopper, Cynthia G.
   2012   Effects of dialect variation on the semantic predictability benefit. *Language and Cognitive Processes* 27: 1002–1020.
Colleman, Timothy
   2010   Lectal variation in constructional semantics: 'Benefactive' ditransitives in Dutch. In: D. Geeraerts, G. Kristiansen and Y. Peirsman (eds.), *Advances in Cognitive Sociolinguistics*, 191–221. Berlin/New York: De Gruyter Mouton.
Croft, William
   2000   *Explaining Language Change: An Evolutionary Approach.* Harlow: Longman.
Croft, William
   2009   Towards a social cognitive linguistics. In: V. Evans and S. Pourcel (eds.), *New Directions in Cognitive Linguistics*, 395–420. Amsterdam: John Benjamins.
Dąbrowska, Ewa
   2012   Different speakers, different grammars: Individual differences in native language attainment. *Linguistic Approaches to Bilingualism* 2: 219–253.
Dąbrowska, Ewa
   this volume   32. Individual differences. Berlin/Boston: De Gruyter Mouton.
De Saussure, Ferdinand
   1916   *Cours de linguistique générale.* Paris: Payot.
De Sutter, Gert, Dirk Speelman and Dirk Geeraerts
   2008   Prosodic and syntactic-pragmatic mechanisms of grammatical variation: the impact of a postverbal constituent on the word order in Dutch clause final verb clusters. *International Journal of Corpus Linguistics* 13: 194–224.
Dirven, René
   1994   *Metaphor and Nation: Metaphors Afrikaners Live by.* Frankfurt: Peter Lang.
Dirven, René, Roslyn Frank and Cornelia Ilie (eds.)
   2001   *Language and Ideology* 2. *Descriptive Cognitive Approaches.* Amsterdam: John Benjamins.
Dirven, René, Roslyn Frank and Martin Pütz (eds.)
   2003   *Cognitive Models in Language and Thought. Ideology, Metaphors and Meanings.* Berlin/New York: Mouton de Gruyter.
Dirven, René, Bruce Hawkins and Esra Sandikcioglu (eds.)
   2001   *Language and Ideology* 1. *Theoretical Cognitive Approaches.* Amsterdam: John Benjamins Publishing Company.

Divjak, Dagmar and Catherine Caldwell-Harris
  this volume 3. Frequency and entrenchment. Berlin/Boston: De Gruyter Mouton.
Drager, Katie
  2010 Sociophonetic variation in speech perception. *Language and Linguistics Compass* 4: 473–480.
Eckert, Penelope
  2012 Three waves of variation study: The emergence of meaning in the study of variation. *Annual Review of Anthropology* 41: 87–100.
Everett, Caleb
  2013 *Linguistic Relativity. Evidence Across Languages and Cognitive Domains*. Applications of Cognitive Linguistics 25. Berlin/New York: Mouton de Gruyter.
Floccia, Caroline, Joseph Butler, Frédérique Girard and Jeremy Goslin
  2009 Categorization of regional and foreign accent in 5- to 7-year-old British children. *International Journal of Behavioral Development* 33: 366–375.
Floccia, Caroline, Claire Delle Luche, Samantha Durrant, Joseph Butler and Jeremy Goslin
  2012 Parent or community: Where do 20-month-olds exposed to two accents acquire their representation of words? *Cognition* 124(1): 95–100.
Geeraerts, Dirk
  2003 Cultural models of linguistic standardization. In: R. Dirven, R. Frank and M. Pütz (eds.), *Cognitive Models in Language and Thought. Ideology, Metaphors and Meanings*, 25–68. Berlin/New York: Mouton de Gruyter.
Geeraerts, Dirk
  2005 Lectal variation and empirical data in Cognitive Linguistics. In: F. Ruiz de Mendoza Ibáñez and S. Peña Cervel (eds.), *Cognitive Linguistics. Internal Dynamics and Interdisciplinary Interactions*, 163–189. Berlin/New York: Mouton de Gruyter.
Geeraerts, Dirk
  2010a Recontextualizing grammar: Underlying trends in thirty years of Cognitive Linguistics. In: E. Tabakowska, M. Choinski and L. Wiraszka (eds.), *Cognitive Linguistics in Action: From Theory to Application and Back*, 71–102. Berlin/New York: De Gruyter Mouton.
Geeraerts, Dirk
  2010b Schmidt redux: How systematic is the linguistic system if variation is rampant? In: K. Boye and E. Engberg-Pedersen (eds.), *Language Usage and Language Structure*, 237–262. Berlin/New York: De Gruyter Mouton.
Geeraerts, Dirk and Stefan Grondelaers
  1995 Looking back at anger: Cultural traditions and looking back at anger: Cultural traditions and metaphorical patterns. In: J. R. Taylor and R. E. MacLaury (eds.), *Language and the Cognitive Construal of the World*, 153–179. Berlin/New York: Mouton de Gruyter.
Geeraerts, Dirk, Stefan Grondelaers and Peter Bakema
  1994 *The Structure of Lexical Variation. Meaning, Naming, and Context*. Berlin/New York: Mouton de Gruyter.
Geeraerts, Dirk, Stefan Grondelaers and Dirk Speelman
  1999 *Convergentie en divergentie in de Nederlandse woordenschat. Een onderzoek naar kleding- en voetbaltermen*. Amsterdam: Meertens Instituut.
Geeraerts, Dirk and Gitte Kristiansen
  2014 Cognitive linguistics and linguistic variation. In: J. Littlemore and J. Taylor (eds.), *The Bloomsbury Companion to Cognitive Linguistics*, 202–217. London: Continuum Publishing.
Geeraerts, Dirk, Gitte Kristiansen and Yves Peirsman (eds.)
  2010 *Advances in Cognitive Sociolinguistics*. Berlin/New York: De Gruyter Mouton.
Gevaert, Caroline
  2005 The anger is heat question: Detecting cultural influence on the conceptualisation of anger through diachronic corpus analysis. In: N. Delbecque, J. van der Auwera and D.

Geeraerts (eds.), *Perspectives on Variation. Sociolinguistic, Historical, Comparative*, 195–208. Berlin: Mouton de Gruyter.

Giles, Howard and Peter F. Powesland
1975 *Speech, Style and Social Evaluation*. London: Academic Press.

Glynn, Dylan
2008 *Mapping meaning. Towards a usage-based methodology in cognitive semantics*. PhD Thesis, University of Leuven.

Gries, Stefan Th.
2003 *Multifactorial Analysis in Corpus Linguistics: A Study of Particle Placement*. London/New York: Continuum Press.

Gries, Stefan Th.
2010 Behavioral profiles: A fine-grained and quantitative approach in corpus-based lexical semantics. *The Mental Lexicon* 5(3): 323–346.

Gries, Stefan Th.
2013 Sources of variability relevant to the cognitive sociolinguist, and corpus- as well as psycholinguistic methods and notions to handle them. In: G. Kristiansen and D. Geeraerts (eds.), *Contexts of Use in Cognitive Sociolinguistics*. Special Issue. *Journal of Pragmatics* 52: 5–16.

Grondelaers, Stefan
2000 *De distributie van niet-anaforisch er buiten de eerste zinplaats: Sociolexicologische, functionele en psycholinguïstische aspecten van er's status als presentatief signaal*. PhD dissertation, KU Leuven.

Grondelaers, Stefan, Marc Brysbaert, Dirk Speelman and Dirk Geeraerts
2002 'Er' als accessibility marker: on- en offline evidentie voor een procedurele interpretatie van presentatieve zinnen. *Gramma/TTT* 9: 1–22.

Grondelaers, Stefan, Dirk Speelman and Dirk Geeraerts
2008 National variation in the use of er "there". Regional and diachronic constraints on cognitive explanations. In: G. Kristiansen and R. Dirven (eds.), *Cognitive Sociolinguistics. Language Variation, Cultural Models, Social Systems*, 153–203. Berlin/New York: Mouton de Gruyter.

Guy, Gregory R.
2013 The cognitive coherence of sociolects: How do speakers handle multiple sociolinguistic variables? In: G. Kristiansen and D. Geeraerts (eds.), *Contexts of Use in Cognitive Sociolinguistics*. Special Issue. *Journal of Pragmatics* 52: 63–71.

Harder, Peter
2003 The status of linguistic facts: Rethinking the relation between cognition, social institution and utterance from a functional point of view. *Mind and Language* 18: 52–76.

Harder, Peter
2010 *Meaning in Mind and Society. A Functional Contribution to the Social Turn in Cognitive Linguistics*. Berlin/New York: De Gruyter Mouton.

Heylen, Kris, Yves Peirsman and Dirk Geeraerts
2008 Automatic synonymy extraction. In: S. Verberne, H. van Halteren and P.-A. Coppen (eds.), *Computational Linguistics in the Netherlands 2007*, 101–116. Amsterdam: Rodopi.

Heylen, Kris, Dirk Speelman and Dirk Geeraerts
2012 Looking at word meaning. An interactive visualization of Semantic Vector Spaces for Dutch synsets. In: M. Butt, S. Carpendale, G. Penn, J. Prokic and M. Cysouw (eds.), *Visualization of Language Patters and Uncovering Language History from Multilingual Resources. Proceedings of the EACL-2012 Joint Workshop of LINGVIS and UNCLH*, 16–24. Avignon: Association for Computational Linguistics.

Holland, Dorothy and Naomi Quinn (eds.)
1987 *Cultural Models in Language and Thought*. Cambridge: Cambridge University Press.

Hollmann, Willem
  2013 Constructions in cognitive sociolinguistics. In: T. Hoffmann and G. Trousdale (eds.), *The Oxford Handbook of Construction Grammar*, 491–509. Oxford: Oxford University Press.
Hollmann, Willem and Anna Siewierska
  2011 The status of frequency, schemas, and identity in Cognitive Sociolinguistics: A case study on definite article reduction. *Cognitive Linguistics* 22: 25–54.
Itkonen, Esa
  2003 *What is Language? A Study in the Philosophy of Linguistics.* Turku: Åbo Akademis tryckeri.
Kirby, Simon
  1999 *Function, Selection and Innateness: The Emergence of Language Universals.* Oxford: Oxford University Press.
Koptjevskaja-Tamm, Maria
  this volume 21. Semantic typology. Berlin/Boston: De Gruyter Mouton.
Kövecses, Zoltán
  1986 *Metaphors of Anger, Pride and Love: A Lexical Approach to the Structure of Concepts.* Amsterdam/Philadelphia: John Benjamins.
Kövecses, Zoltán
  1995 Anger: Its language, conceptualization, and physiology in the light of cross-cultural evidence. In: J. R. Taylor and R. E. MacLaury (eds.), *Language and the Cognitive Construal of the World*, 181–196. Berlin: Mouton de Gruyter
Kövecses, Zoltán
  2005 *Metaphor in Culture. Universality and Variation.* Oxford: Oxford University Press.
Kretzschmar, William A.
  2009 *The Linguistics of Speech.* Cambridge: Cambridge University Press.
Kristiansen, Gitte
  2001 Social and linguistic stereotyping: A cognitive approach to accents. *Estudios Ingleses de la Universidad Complutense* 9: 129–145.
Kristiansen, Gitte
  2003 How to do things with allophones: Linguistic stereotypes as cognitive reference points in social cognition. In: R. Dirven, R. Frank and M. Pütz (eds.), *Cognitive Models in Language and Thought: Ideologies, Metaphors, and Meanings*, 69–120. Berlin/New York: Mouton de Gruyter.
Kristiansen, Gitte
  2006 Towards a usage-based cognitive phonology. *International Journal of English Studies* 6(2): 107–140.
Kristiansen, Gitte
  2008 Style-shifting and shifting styles: A socio-cognitive approach to lectal variation. In: G. Kristiansen and R. Dirven (eds.), *Cognitive Sociolinguistics*, 45–88. Berlin/New York: Mouton de Gruyter.
Kristiansen, Gitte
  2010 Lectal acquisition and linguistic stereotype formation. In: D. Geeraerts, G. Kristiansen and Y. Peirsman (eds.), *Advances in Cognitive Sociolinguistics*, 225–264. Berlin/New York: De Gruyter Mouton.
Kristiansen, Gitte and René Dirven (eds.)
  2008 *Cognitive Sociolinguistics: Language Variation, Cultural Models, Social Systems.* Berlin/New York: Mouton de Gruyter.
Kristiansen, Gitte and Dirk Geeraerts (eds.)
  2013 *Contexts of Use in Cognitive Sociolinguistics.* Special issue. *Journal of Pragmatics* 52: 1–104.

Kronenfeld, David B.
　1996　*Plastic Glasses and Church Fathers. Semantic Extension from the Ethnoscience Tradition.* New York: Oxford University Press.

Labov, William
　1972　*Sociolinguistic Patterns.* Philadelphia: University of Pennsylvania Press.

Labov, William
　2010　*Principles of Linguistic Change* III. *Cognitive and Cultural Factors.* London: Wiley-Blackwell.

Lakoff, George
　1987　*Women, Fire and Dangerous Things. What Categories Reveal About the Mind.* Chicago: University of Chicago Press.

Lakoff, George
　1996　*Moral Politics: What Conservatives Know that Liberals Don't.* Chicago: University of Chicago Press.

Lakoff, George and Zoltán Kövecses
　1987　The cognitive model of anger inherent in American English. In: D. Holland and N. Quinn (eds.), *Cultural Models in Language and Thought*, 195–221. Cambridge: Cambridge University Press.

Langacker, Ronald W.
　1987　*Foundations of Cognitive Grammar* 1. *Theoretical Prerequisites.* Stanford: Stanford University Press.

Lavandera, Beatriz
　1978　Where does the sociolinguistic variable stop? *Language in Society* 7: 171–183.

Le Page, Robert Brock and Andrée Tabouret-Keller
　1985　*Acts of Identity: Creole-Based Approaches to Language and Ethnicity.* Cambridge: Cambridge University Press.

Levinson, Stephen C.
　2003　*Space in Language and Cognition. Explorations in Cognitive Diversity.* Cambridge: Cambridge University Press.

Littlemore, Jeannette and Graham Low
　2006　*Figurative Thinking and Foreign Language Learning.* Basingstoke: Palgrave MacMillan.

Lucy, John and Suzanne Gaskins
　2003　Interaction of language type and referent type in the development of nonverbal classification preferences. In: D. Gentner and S. Goldin-Meadow (eds.), *Language in Mind: Advances in the Study of Language and Thought*, 465–492. Cambridge: MIT Press.

Nycz, Jennifer
　2013　Changing words or changing rules? Second dialect acquisition and phonological representation. In: G. Kristiansen and D. Geeraerts (eds.), *Contexts of Use in Cognitive Sociolinguistics.* Special Issue. *Journal of Pragmatics* 52: 49–62.

Nuyts, Jan
　2007　Cognitive linguistics and functional linguistics. In: D. Geeraerts and H. Cuyckens (eds.), *The Oxford Handbook of Cognitive Linguistics*, 543–565. New York: Oxford University Press.

Palmer, Gary B.
　1996　*Toward a Theory of Cultural Linguistics.* Austin: University of Texas Press.

Pickering, Martin and Simon Garrod
　2004　Toward a mechanistic psychology of dialogue. *Behavioral and Brain Sciences* 27: 169–190.

Pierrehumbert, Janet
　2002　Word-specific phonetics. In: C. Gussenhoven and N. Warner (eds.), *Laboratory Phonology* VII, 101–140. Berlin/New York: Mouton de Gruyter.

Polzenhagen, Frank and René Dirven
2008   Rationalist and romantic models in globalisation. In: G. Kristiansen and R. Dirven (eds.), *Cognitive Sociolinguistics. Language Variation, Cultural Models, Social Systems*, 237–299. Berlin/New York: Mouton de Gruyter.

Preston, Dennis and Nancy Niedzielski
2000   *Folk Linguistics*. Berlin/New York: Mouton de Gruyter.

Pütz, Martin, Justyna A. Robinson and Monika Reif (eds.)
2012   *Cognitive Sociolinguistics: Social and Cultural Variation in Cognition and Language Use (Thematic issue of the Review of Cognitive Linguistics)*. Amsterdam: John Benjamins.

Ramscar, Michael
this volume   4. Categorization. Berlin/Boston: De Gruyter Mouton.

Robinson, Justyna A.
2010   Awesome insights into semantic variation. In: D. Geeraerts, G. Kristiansen and Y. Peirsman (eds.), *Advances in Cognitive Sociolinguistics*, 85–110. Berlin/New York: De Gruyter Mouton.

Rosch, Eleanor
1977   Human categorization. In: N. Warren (ed.), *Studies in Cross-Cultural Psychology*. 1–49. New York/London: Academic Press.

Ruette, Tom, Dirk Speelman and Dirk Geeraerts
2011   Measuring the lexical distance between registers in national varieties of Dutch. In: A. Soares da Silva, A. Torres and M. Gonçalves (eds.), *Línguas Pluricêntricas. Variação Linguística e Dimensões Sociocognitivas*, 541–554. Braga: Publicações da Faculdade de Filosofia, Universidade Católica Portuguesa.

Schmale, Rachel, Alejandrina Cristia and Amanda Seidl
2012   Toddlers recognize words in an unfamiliar accent after brief exposure. *Developmental Science* 15(6): 732–738.

Schönefeld, Doris
2013   It is ... quite common for theoretical predictions to go untested. A register-specific analysis of the English go un-V-en construction. *Contexts of Use in Cognitive Sociolinguistics*. Special issue. *Journal of Pragmatics* 52: 17–33.

Semino, Elena
2008   *Metaphor in Discourse*. Cambridge: Cambridge University Press.

Sharifian, Farzad
2011   *Cultural Conceptualisations and Language: Theoretical Framework and Applications*. Amsterdam: John Benjamins.

Sharifian, Farzad, René Dirven, Ning Yu and Susanne Niemeier (eds.)
2008   *Culture, Body, and Language. Conceptualizations of Internal Body Organs across Cultures and Languages*. Berlin/New York: Mouton de Gruyter.

Sinha, Chris
2007   Cognitive linguistics, psychology and cognitive science. In: D. Geeraerts and H. Cuyckens (eds.), *The Oxford Handbook of Cognitive Linguistics*, 1266–1294. New York: Oxford University Press.

Sinha, Chris
2009   Language as a biocultural niche and social institution. In: V. Evans and S. Pourcel (eds.), *New Directions in Cognitive Linguistics*, 289–309. Amsterdam: John Benjamins.

Soares da Silva, Augusto
2005   Para o estudo das relações lexicais entre o Português Europeu e o Português do Brasil: Elementos de sociolexicologia cognitiva e quantitativa do Português. In: I. Duarte and I. Leiria (eds.), *Actas do XX Encontro Nacional da Associação Portuguesa de Lingüística*, 211–226. Lisboa: Associação Portuguesa de Linguística.

Soukup, Barbara
  2013 Austrian dialect as a metonymic device: A cognitive sociolinguistic investigation of Speaker Design and its perceptual implications. In: G. Kristiansen and D. Geeraerts (eds.), *Contexts of Use in Cognitive Sociolinguistics*. Special Issue. *Journal of Pragmatics* 52: 72–82.

Speelman, Dirk and Dirk Geeraerts
  2009 Causes for causatives: the case of Dutch 'doen' and 'laten'. In: T. Sanders and E. Sweetser (eds.), *Causal Categories in Discourse and Cognition*, 173–204. Berlin: Mouton de Gruyter.

Speelman, Dirk, Stefan Grondelaers and Dirk Geeraerts
  2003 Profile-based linguistic uniformity as a generic method for comparing language varieties. *Computers and the Humanities* 37: 317–337.

Speelman, Dirk, Stefan Grondelaers and Dirk Geeraerts
  2008 Variation in the choice of adjectives in the two main national varieties of Dutch. In: G. Kristiansen and R. Dirven (eds.), *Cognitive Sociolinguistics. Language Variation, Cultural Models, Social Systems*, 205–233. Berlin/New York: Mouton de Gruyter.

Steels, Luc
  2002 Language as a complex adaptive system. In: F. Brisard and T. Mortelmans (eds.), *Language and Evolution*, 79–88. Antwerp: University of Antwerp.

Steels, Luc
  2011 *Design Patterns in Fluid Construction Grammar.* Amsterdam: John Benjamins Publishing Company.

Stefanowitsch, Anatol and Stefan Th. Gries
  2003 Collostructions: Investigating the interaction of words and constructions. *International Journal of Corpus Linguistics* 8(2): 209–243.

Szmrecsanyi, Benedikt
  2009 *Morphosyntactic Persistence in Spoken English. A Corpus Study at the Intersection of Variationist Sociolinguistics, Psycholinguistics, and Discourse Analysis.* Berlin/New York: Mouton de Gruyter.

Szmrecsanyi, Benedikt
  2010 The English genitive alternation in a cognitive sociolinguistics perspective. In: D. Geeraerts, G. Kristiansen and Y. Peirsman (eds.), *Advances in Cognitive Sociolinguistics*, 141–166. Berlin/New York: De Gruyter Mouton.

Tummers, José, Kris Heylen and Dirk Geeraerts
  2005 Usage-based approaches in Cognitive Linguistics: A technical state of the art. *Corpus Linguistics and Linguistic Theory* 1: 225–261.

Verhagen, Arie
  2005 *Constructions of Intersubjectivity: Discourse, Syntax, and Cognition.* Oxford: Oxford University Press.

Yu, Ning
  1998 *The Contemporary Theory of Metaphor. A Perspective from Chinese.* Amsterdam: John Benjamins Publishing Company.

Yu, Ning
  2009 *The Chinese Heart in a Cognitive Perspective. Culture, Body, and Language.* Berlin/ New York: Mouton De Gruyter.

Zenner, Eline, Dirk Geeraerts and Dirk Speelman
  2009 Expeditie tussentaal: leeftjd, identiteit en context in "Expeditie Robinson". *Nederlandse Taalkunde* 14(1): 26–44.

Zenner, Eline, Dirk Speelman and Dirk Geeraerts
  2012 Cognitive Sociolinguistics meets loanword research: Measuring variation in the success of anglicisms in Dutch. *Cognitive Linguistics* 23: 749–792.

Zhang, Weiwei, Dirk Speelman and Dirk Geeraerts
  2011 Variation in the (non)metonymic capital names in mainland Chinese and Taiwan Chinese. *Metaphor and the Social World* 1: 90–112.
Zlatev, Jordan
  2005 What's in a schema? Bodily mimesis and the grounding of language. In: B. Hampe (ed.), *From Perception to Meaning: Image Schemas in Cognitive Linguistics*, 313–342. Berlin/New York: Mouton de Gruyter.

Dirk Geeraerts, University of Leuven (Belgium)
Gitte Kristiansen, Universidad Complutense de Madrid (Spain)

18. First language acquisition

1. Introduction
2. Communication before words
3. Developing a lexicon
4. Grammar
5. Pragmatic skills: The case of reference
6. Summary
7. References

1. Introduction

With every year of a child's early life come remarkable bounds in language ability. In this chapter, we will cover some of the major linguistic abilities acquired by children under the age of five. Starting in infancy, we will consider how infants become able to direct others' attention and start to break into conventional language by learning first words. We will then discuss how children refine their word knowledge, building an ever more adult-like lexicon. Next, we briefly describe the transition to combinatorial speech, which brings with it the possibility of grammar. On this topic, we first consider syntax and then inflectional morphology. Finally, we consider some pragmatic skills by focussing on the ability to refer to things effectively. Where appropriate, we will link findings in developmental psycholinguistics to Cognitive Linguistics as a theoretical framework. This framework has been popular with child language researchers for a number of quite different reasons. First, it recognises that natural languages reflect the ways humans perceive and conceptualise their environment. By virtue of viewing the world through roughly the same cognitive lens, so to speak, infants are in a good position to start acquiring the linguistic conventions of their community. Second, it is a usage-based framework, which sees developing linguistic systems as shaped by the utterances children have actually heard or produced themselves. Seen this way, language is not a given but has formed historically to meet the communicative needs of a speech community. Children need to learn conventions that have evolved over historical time. Third, it proposes that usage events are stored "redundantly", even if they could, in principle, be decomposed and stored as separate words and rules. Learning and processing can take advantage of this redundancy. Fourth, it is non-reductionist (utterances are understood in terms of complex wholes, within which constituents are identified). Thus, the same processes that allow children to identify words in the speech stream could simultaneously help identify the structures into which the atomic elements of language can enter (Langacker 2000). All of these properties of Cognitive Linguistic theories have been called upon to explain a broad set of phenomena in first language acquisition. This chapter will review but a few illustrative cases of the kinds of things children learn as they become native speakers of their language(s). For broader reviews of child language acquisition, see Ambridge and Lieven (2011), Clark (2003), or Tomasello (2003).

2. Communication before words

Infants communicate with their caregivers from the word go. They love to make eye contact, to hear "motherese" and to engage in exquisitely timed dyadic exchanges of cooing and smiles, so much so that they will actively reengage a lapsing communicative partner (see Stephens and Matthews 2014 for a recent review). Over the first year of life, the ability to regulate interaction develops, so that infants become able to make the external world the topic of conversation with others. Thus, around 11 months, infants begin to point to things with the intention of directing their caregiver's attention to a referent. In doing so, they demonstrate some of the most fundamental psychological abilities and motivations that underpin all of language and communication (Bates 1976; Eilan 2005; Tomasello et al. 2007). Critically, around this point in development, infants are able to engage in *joint attention* (where the infant and caregiver both attend to the same thing and are mutually aware they are doing so) and they are motivated to share psychological states with others. Thus, they can both *follow* others' attention (e.g., they can follow an adults' gaze to an object located at a 90 degree angle to their line of vision) and *direct* the attention of others' (with pointing or with vocalisation and eye gaze). While all these social developments are taking place, infants are also getting to know more about the world and becoming adept in regulating their own attention to interesting new objects and events (Mandler 2004). Consequently, it comes naturally to them to communicate about things that have captured their attention, to set them as the topic to be talked about and commented on. Indeed, in her seminal 1976 book, Bates argued that it is the coming together of these two lines of development, contemplation of the external world and engaging of a caregiver, that sets the stage for the topic-comment structure of language (Bates 1976).

At the same time as discovering how to engage others in conversation, infants are tuning into the sounds of their language such that their perception, and to some degree their production, of speech sounds reflects the properties of the language(s) they have been exposed to (Jusczyk 2000; Vihman 1996). Whereas a new-born can perceive all the speech sounds of the entire world's languages (about 600 consonants and 200 vowels), a one-year-old will have lost the ability to tell apart many sounds that are not used contrastively in their native language. So, for example, a child exposed to English loses the ability to perceive the difference between a dental /t/ and a retroflex /t/, whereas a child exposed to Hindi or Urdu would retain this ability as the differences in sounds are used to mark differences in meaning in those languages (Werker and Lalonde 1988). When it comes to producing speech sounds, infants begin to engage in canonical babble (e.g., "dadada") around 6 months and by around 10 months the syllables infants produce reflect those most frequently found in the language the infant is learning (de Boysson-Bardies 1993; Oller and Eilers 1988). Indeed, this period of babble can be seen as an important precursor of language development, with the number of consonants an infant produces across this period having been found to correlate with their later ability to refer to things with words (McCune and Vihman 2001).

Another important process that infants engage involves segmenting the speech stream into units such as words. For an adult reader, it can be easy to forget that human speech does not come neatly separated into words by blanks in the way that written text is. Rather, listening to speech is rather like reading would be without spaces: onewordmergesintothenextwithonlytheoccasionalpauseatcertainboundaries. There has been substantial research into how children could break into continuous speech in order to be able to identify units (word forms), such that they could subsequently learn what these forms are used to mean (e.g., Monaghan and Christiansen 2010; Saffran et al. 1996). Infants could potentially use a variety of cues to segment the speech stream (e.g., statistical information about the transitional probabilities between syllables, prosodic cues, allophonic cues, and phonotactic constraints). Interestingly, when making use of these sources of information to segment speech, far more is likely to emerge from the process than simply a list of candidate words. Indeed, it has recently be proposed that the way children chunk the speech stream into units would also be helpful for the development of grammar (Bannard and Matthews 2008), which we will come to later in the chapter.

In sum, during the first year of life, infants set the foundations for language by learning how to engage others in conversation and by learning about the speech sounds of their language(s). They are also making first passes at the next critical steps: identifying linguistic units in the speech stream (words and constructions) and learning how they can be used as conventions to convey thoughts and intentions. Indeed, this transition to conventional language is predicted by an infant's earlier developmental achievements such that infants who are early to follow eye gaze, point and babble are generally also quick to learn words (R. Brooks and Meltzoff 2008; Colonnesi et al. 2010; McGillion et al. under review).

3. Developing a lexicon

Gauging when a child has first learnt to understand or say a word is a tricky business. It has recently been found that when infants between 6 and 9 months old are presented with a word they have heard frequently before and are shown two images, one corresponding to the word and another familiar distracter, they tend to look at the corresponding image slightly longer (Bergelson and Swingley 2012). Thus it seems that some aspects of word learning get going very early on in life, even while understanding of the sounds structure of language and its social function are still developing. However, associating a sound with an image is not all there is to word learning. As Tomasello argues, mere association "does not constitute an intersubjectively understood linguistic symbol used to direct and share attention with other persons – so it is not word learning" (Tomasello 2001: 1120). This difference between association and the awareness of the communicative function of words was illustrated in a recent study that compared the contexts in which infants were willing to use word knowledge gained in different settings (Bannard and Tomasello 2012 based on Baldwin et al. 1996). In the "coupled" setting, infants saw a novel object on a screen while sitting with an experimenter who labelled it with novel a name. In the "decoupled" setting, infants also saw a novel object while sitting with an experimenter, but this time another experimenter, who was on the other side of the room talking on the telephone (and completely unengaged with the infant), produced the novel names apparently as part of her phone conversation that was nothing to do with the images on the screen. In both conditions, infants came to associate the novel name with the novel image such that, when they heard the word, they would look preferentially to the correct image. However, when asked to point to the right object, infants only tended to do so if they had learnt the word in the coupled condition. Thus, making associations is one thing but understanding that and how a word can be used (with the goal of directing another's attention) is subtly but importantly different. Following Wittgenstein (1958), then, we can say that knowing the meaning of a word is knowing its use.

Social-pragmatic theories of word learning emphasise the idea that words are culturally created conventions and learning is all about figuring out how to use these conventions in the same way that everyone else does. On such accounts, children learn to talk by participating in interaction, often as part of familiar daily routines, using their skills of *joint attention* and *intention reading* (Tomasello 2003). A child and caregiver are in *joint attention* when they are attending to the same thing and are mutually aware that they are doing so. When in this attentional frame, it is especially easy for children to infer what a caregiver is talking about and to learn new words as a consequence. Early in development, an infant's ability to engage in joint attention is fragile and word learning tends to work best when the caregiver scaffolds learning by talking about what the infant is already attending to, a process called *following in* or *contingent talk* (Carpenter et al. 1998; McGillion et al. 2013). From around 18-months, infants become more adept at regulating joint attention themselves. For example, they can monitor a speaker's eye gaze and use this to infer what she must be talking about (Baldwin 1991; Nurmsoo and Bloom 2008). From about the first birthday infants also use their understanding of others intentions' to interpret communicative acts. For example, if an experimenter tells an 18-month-old that she is going to try to find *a toma* and then she proceeds to search through a number of buckets, looking at and rejecting the objects in them until one seems to meet her search (whereupon she stops searching with satisfaction) then the infant is likely to infer that the novel word refers to this final object (Tomasello 2003; Tomasello and Barton 1994).

Overall, there are a whole host of experiments that demonstrate how infants use pragmatic information about others' attention and intentions for word learning (see Grassmann 2014 for a review). It should be noted, however, that not all theories put pragmatics at the centre of word learning. Indeed, occasionally the same behaviour is assumed by some to be an illustration of a pragmatic inference and by others to demonstrate the application of a hard-wired lexical rule. Mutual exclusivity phenomena are perhaps the best example of this. In the standard mutual exclusivity test, a child is introduced to two objects, one that is familiar to them (e.g., an apple) and one that is not (i.e., a novel object). They are then asked to pick up something referred to with a novel word, e.g., *the modi*. Under such circumstances 18-month-olds will readily pick up the novel object (Markman and Wachtel 1988). By 24 months of age, children can succeed in a version of the test that controls for the possibility that children were simply drawn to the novel object. This time, the child is presented with two different novel objects. One is played with and labelled as, for example, *the toma* and the other is played with for the same length of time but not labelled. When the experimenter now asks for *the modi*, 24-month-olds will pick up the unlabelled novel object (Diesendruck and Markson 2001). On some accounts, these results demonstrate the application of a lexical principle that children bring with them to word learning (Markman 1991). On other, social-pragmatic accounts, these finding reflect children's application of the Principles of Contrast and Convention (Clark 1987, 2007), which state that children assume that speakers will use the same linguistic form to convey the same meaning across time and that any departure from this consistency marks a change in intended meaning. So, for this example, a child would reason along the following lines: "if the experimenter had wanted to refer to the object she just labelled as *a toma* then she should ask for *the toma*. But she asked for *the modi* and therefore she must mean the other object we played with". There has long been debate about which type of account, lexical principles or pragmatic inferences, can best explain mutual exclusivity and related findings. Recent observations of children with Autism seem to suggest there are multiple routes to mutual exclusivity inferences (de Marchena et al. 2011; Preissler and Carey 2005). Furthermore, work investigating the type of language children hear when they are young, suggests that children may *learn* a mutual exclusivity principle, since parents tend to stick to a one-word-one-meaning pattern in their speech to young children (Callanan and Sabbagh 2004; Callanan et al. 2007; Callanan and Siegel 2014). That assumptions of mutual exclusivity may be learned is supported by evidence that bilingual and trilingual children (who frequently hear more than one word for the same object) demonstrate these effects to a lesser degree than monolinguals (Byers-Heinlein and Werker 2009).

4. Grammar

Infants tend to produce their first words around their first birthdays and then spend several months producing single words or at least single unit expressions that are referred to as *holophrases* (e.g., *allgone* produced as if it were one word). Once children have about 100 single words in their lexicon, they generally start to combine these words into short phrases like *more juice* (Bates et al. 1995). In doing so, they take their first steps towards using grammar, i.e., organising words into larger structures. Interestingly, this 100 word transition point seems to hold regardless of the age of the child. In a study of adopted children, Snedeker et al. (2012) asked American parents to report the language abilities of children whom they had adopted from China/Russia either when they were infants or when they were pre-schoolers. The children had heard no English before arriving in the US and only English thereafter. Following adoption, the pre-schoolers learnt English words faster than the infants. However, no matter how fast they learnt single words, parental reports indicated that both the infants and the pre-schoolers began occasionally producing word combinations when they had about 80 words in their lexicon and they both began producing combinations regularly when they had learned about 230 words. This is a close match to non-adopted infants (Bates et al. 1995) and suggests a fundamental link between the development of the lexicon and grammar.

Traditionally, grammar has been seen as a system of abstract rules which govern the way whole sentences can be built from single words (much like algebraic formulas or programming language rules). This view of grammar has serious drawbacks though. First is that it does poorly with exceptions and anyone who has taken foreign language classes knows that most grammatical rules taught in the class is accompanied by a list of exceptions one has to memorise. Second is that conceptualising grammar as an abstract rule system makes the learning task very difficult for children. In fact, it has been claimed that the system is too complicated and the input children have available is not sufficient to figure it out and hence our linguistic competence must have some specific innate basis and language acquisition is more about maturation than about learning (Chomsky 1965, 1981, 1995). This is only an illusory solution, though, as it is not clear how the same innate basis could accommodate all the varied languages of the world and it is not clear how children could map what they hear and learn from the input onto this innate knowledge.

The Cognitive Linguistic approach offers an alternative solution to grammar and its learnability problem. The key concept of this solution is the *construction* (Croft 2001; Diessel this volume; Goldberg 1995). A construction can be any piece of linguistic material paired with its meaning. It can be a single word or a whole sentence, or just a fragment; it can be concrete (*The fox pushed the bear*) or somewhat schematic (*X pushed Y*), or even highly schematic (*Subject Verb Object*). There is no clear-cut distinction between the lexicon (the set of words) of a given language and the grammar of that language. Children start with learning whole concrete constructions that they have memorised verbatim (e.g., *more juice* or *a bowl of cornflakes*), just like they learn single words and their meanings. Once children have heard many similar sentences (e.g., *more cookies, more milk, a bowl of soup, a bowl of water*) and can draw analogies across them, they gradually build more schematic constructions (e.g., *more X, a bowl of X*). We will describe in greater detail what one such process of gradual schematisation might look like when we discuss inflections later in this chapter. For now, we can think of the language system as a structured inventory of constructions (Langacker 1987). This inventory is basically a representation of all the language children have ever heard, organised such that similar forms overlap and naturally form abstractions. A tiny corner of such an inventory is given by way of example in figure 18.1. The phrases at the bottom of the diagram are concrete examples of speech directed to young children learning English. The generalisations at each level above are possible abstractions a child could arrive at on the basis of what they've heard. Precisely how children make these generalisations, and how they constrain them so they do not over-generalise their grammar, is an empirical question that is hard to solve. In recent years substantial progress has been made by building computational models that simulate what kinds of grammars might emerge from the language children hear around them (Bannard et al. 2009; Freudenthal et al. 2010).

One assumption of a Cognitive Linguistic approach to first language acquisition is that the language children hear, the so called *Child Directed Speech* (CDS), or the "input", is repetitive and formulaic, offering ample opportunity to break into grammar. This has been shown to be the case with corpus studies, i.e., analyses of written transcripts

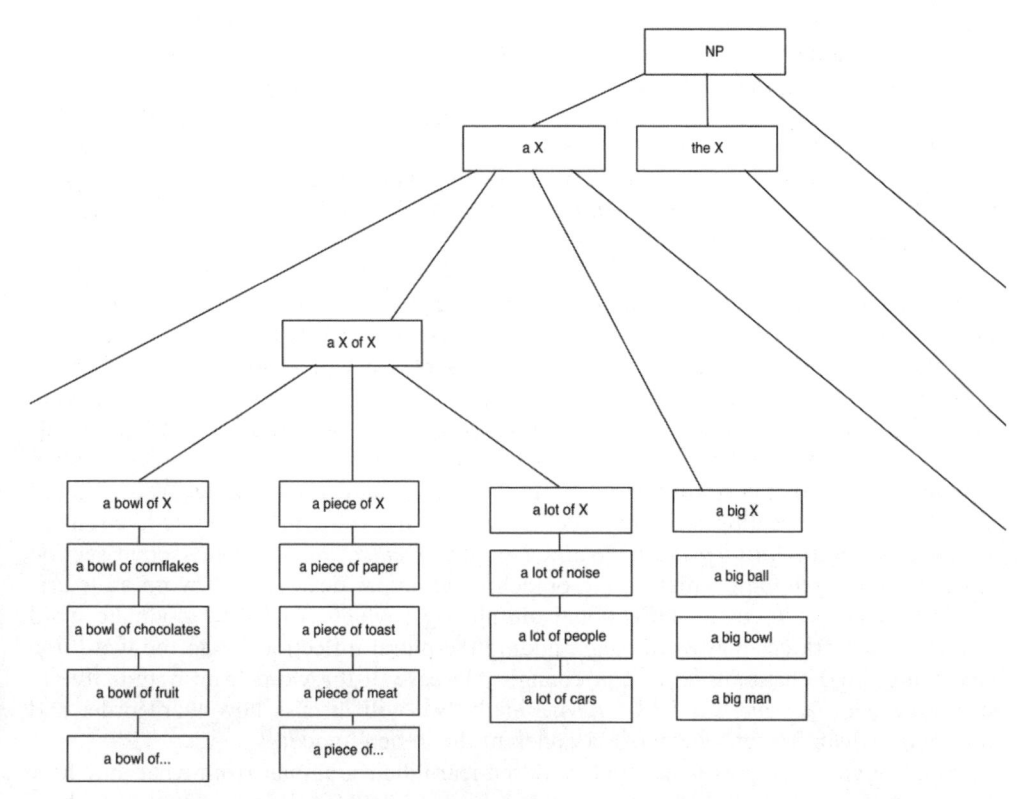

Fig. 18.1: Schematic diagram of part of a structured inventory of constructions. Concrete instances of child directed speech are presented at the bottom, with potential generalisations posited at higher levels.

of the spontaneous conversations that occur between young children and their caregivers. Indeed, Cameron-Faulkner et al. (2003) analysed the CDS addressed to 12 English speaking children (aged 2;0–3;0) and found out that 51% of all utterances in the corpus shared the first 1–3 words and that 45% of all utterances began with one of only 17 words! This means that the majority of utterances children hear can be accounted for by highly repetitive item-based frames. Stoll et al. (2009) report similar findings for other languages.

One prediction of this account of learning, then, would be that children's own utterances, even if they look fully mature and adult-like, should be highly repetitive themselves. Lieven et al. (2003) used corpus data to show that immediate repetitions and imitations of the mother as well as the exact repetitions of what the child had said in the previous six weeks of recording accounted for 63% of all the multi-word utterances in an hour-long recording session. 74% of the remaining utterances could be "traced back" to previous utterances by simple substitutions, deletions etc. (see also Bannard et al. 2009; Dąbrowska and Lieven 2005).

Another prediction is that we should be able to find evidence of children storing whole sequences of words. Bannard and Matthews (2008) used CDS corpora to identify frequent multi-word sequences (e.g., *sit in your chair*) and to match them to infrequent sequences differing only by the final word (e.g., *sit in your truck*). They then run an experiment showing that children were more accurate at repeating the frequent sequences. Since the final words of sequences were matched for frequency (e.g., the number of occurrences of *chair* and *truck* in the corpus was more or less the same), the results suggest that children do store whole chunks of linguistic material. A further study suggested that children are able to generalise abstract grammatical patterns from this learned material (Matthews and Bannard 2010).

While some usage-based accounts may assume specific learned word sequences to be at the heart of language use right up to adulthood, once the complexity of the generalisations being made reaches a certain degree, it is standard to talk about them in terms of more abstract grammatical "cues". These cues play a variety of functions. Perhaps most importantly, they are used to mark "who did what to whom" or agent-patient relations (for example in the sentence *the fox pushed the bear* the order of the words tells us that the fox did the pushing and the bear was pushed). There are two main grammatical cues that perform this function: word order and case marking. We will focus on each in separate sections. The first section will discuss word order in transitive sentences such as *The fox pushed the bear* and *The bear pushed the fox*. The second section will discuss *morphology*, which is the branch of grammar dealing with word structure. In this chapter, we focus on inflectional morphology, which is used to modulate word meaning and mark case on words (e.g., adding the plural inflection – s to the word *dog* makes *dogs*, and changing *he* to *him* changes the case of the word from nominative to accusative: *He likes me* but *I like him*). Finally, we will discuss how word order and case marking can be put together in a coherent theoretical model.

On a Cognitive Linguistic account, children learn their grammar from what they hear (and use themselves) without relying on some innate linguistic biases. Hence much of the research conducted within this framework, and the empirical studies we discuss in the following sections, has focused on one of two issues. One is the evidence of gradual (rather than instantaneous) development of abstract grammatical knowledge; the other one is the effect of characteristics of the language children hear (and cross-linguistic differences) on the acquisition process; and both are taken as evidence in favour of the hypothesis that children learn grammar from the input.

4.1. Word order

In many languages, including English, the ordering of words in larger structures, particularly sentences, plays an important role in marking *who did what to whom*, which usually is what children want to talk about with others when discovering the world around them and when engaging in their first joined communicative behaviours with other people. Although children tend to produce correct English word order from the start, it appears to take quite some time for them to learn its function. This is to say, it is some time before children know that in the sentence *The goat pushed the cow*, the goat is the *agent* (the pusher) since it comes before the verb and the cow is the *patient* (the pushee) since it comes after the verb. Since marking agent-patient relations is one of the key functions of grammar, considerable research has been dedicated to investigating how children make this discovery.

The main question of interest with respect to the development of word order has been how *productive* or abstract children's knowledge is. A child can be said to have fully productive knowledge of word order if they understand its function regardless of the particular words in the sentence. Whilst a child might know how to understand a transitive construction when it comes to sentences containing words they have frequently heard before (that is they may know that in the example *He pushed the cow* that the cow was pushed and not the pusher), they may not know that, in general, in transitive structures like this the first noun phrase typically corresponds to the agent. To test for truly productive knowledge, many studies have used novel (invented) verbs that the child could not possibly have heard before. So if, for example, children hear the sentence *Big bird chammed Cookie monster*, and assume that Big Bird did something (whatever that may be) to Cookie Monster, then they must be doing so on the basis a fairly abstract understanding of the function of word order.

Studies have used a variety of methods to test for productive knowledge of word order, with findings varying according to the precise test used. In a series of experiments, Tomasello and colleagues (Akhtar and Tomasello 1997; P. J. Brooks and Tomasello 1999) taught children novel verbs (e.g., by introducing the verb *chamming* while showing a familiar character, Big Bird, jumping on a curved platform and catapulting another familiar character, Cookie Monster). They then tested the children's comprehension of word order by asking them 1) to describe similar scenes with different characters (e.g., where Ernie chammed, Bert) and 2) to "act out" the appropriate actions, for example, to *make Kermit cham Elmo*. Their results suggest that only around the age of three do children start to show productive understanding of the transitive construction.

In contrast, experiments that use the preferential looking paradigm, a less demanding test of young children's comprehension than the "act-out" method, find sensitivity to word order at a younger age (e.g., Fisher 2002; Naigles 1990). In these experiments children hear an utterance, for example *the duck is gorping the bunny*, while simultaneously being presented with two video clips: one showing a duck doing something to the rabbit, and the other showing the duck and the rabbit each doing something alone. The length of the children's looking time to each video is compared, with the assumption that if a child understands the transitive sentence they should look more to the scene where the duck is doing something to the rabbit. Results of these studies suggest that two-year-old children can correctly interpret transitive sentences with novel verbs. There is thus some evidence of abstract knowledge at this stage, although it takes time before it can fully manifest itself in a wide variety of tasks. The question, of course, is whether it is plausible that one could learn this by the age of two based on hearing one's native language everyday.

4.2. Inflectional morphology

While in English, word order is the primary tool for marking who-did-what-to-whom, in many other languages, inflections (different endings on words) are more important. For example, in Polish the sentence *The goat pushed the cow* is *Koza pchnęła krowę*. Critically, although it would be more typical to have the words in SVO order, it is perfectly possible to change the order of the words in this language (*Krowę pchnęła koza*) and for the sentence to mean the same thing since word order is not marking who did what to whom. Instead this work is being done by the case markers (*-a* is in the nominative form on *koza* ['goat'] and *-ę* in the accusative form on *krowę* ['cow']). To change the meaning of the sentences such that the cow is the agent, one would need to change the case of the noun to the nominative (from *krowę* to *krowa*). In languages like Polish, then, the order of constituents is usually less important and adult speakers know that if the first noun phrase in a sentence is marked as accusative and the second as nominative they should follow case marking to arrive at the meaning of the sentence. Children learning such languages have to master their inflectional systems in order to become fully productive with their grammar.

Even in languages with relatively simple morphological systems, like English, inflections are used to modulate the meanings of words, for example, to mark plurality (dog + s > dogs), the past tense (walk + ed > walked) or person (1st person: *I sleep*; 3rd person: *She sleeps*). Inflectional systems in any language tend to form recurring, albeit not perfectly systematic, patterns which children have to notice and generalise. Clear evidence of a child having noticed an inflectional pattern comes when they *overgeneralise* the inflection and apply it to irregular words, saying things like *mouses* instead of *mice,* for example. When a child is able to add an inflection onto new words, we say that they can use it *productively.*

A classic experiment in the field of developmental psycholinguistics, the *wug test*, was developed to test children's productive knowledge of inflections (Berko 1958). In this test, a child is shown a drawing presenting a funny creature and given the novel name for that creature (*This is a wug*). The next drawing shows two such creatures and the child is encouraged to use the name in the plural form (*Now there is another one. There are two of them. There are two ...*). The use of novel words when performing such a test is critical: with familiar words (e.g., *One bird, two ...*) we could not be sure whether the child used the correct plural (*birds*) because they had already learnt the general pattern or simply because they remembered the plural form of that particular word. In the wug test, if the child says *wugs*, s/he necessarily has productive knowledge of the inflectional pattern. Indeed, as we have seen in the previous section on syntax, the use of novel words is a helpful tool when studying all sort of aspects of the development of grammar.

In the previous section we mentioned the great debate regarding the learnability of grammar. Those who think grammar is (at least to some extent) innate will posit a clear distinction between grammar and lexicon (since words are clearly something children have to learn from the input), and the grammar will be conceptualised as a set of abstract rules one has to apply to words in order to inflect and use them when building sentences. Such a *words and rules* approach to language (Pinker 1999) has been proposed to account for the acquisition and use of English inflections as well. In English, compared to most other languages, inflections are generally few and simple (e.g., adding *-s* to mark number). Whenever a single pattern cannot account for inflecting all words (e.g., *house > houses* but *mouse > mice*), there is nevertheless a fairly clear-cut distinction between the *regular* pattern and *irregular* exceptions. Seen from the words and rules perspective, children produce regular forms by applying a rule but they memorise irregular forms as separate words (just as they store any other words in the lexicon). In this approach, productive use of an inflection involves applying its rule to a given word and overgeneralisation indicates failure to retrieve a correct irregular from memory. As noted though, English is not the most typical language when it comes to morphology and the words

18. First language acquisition

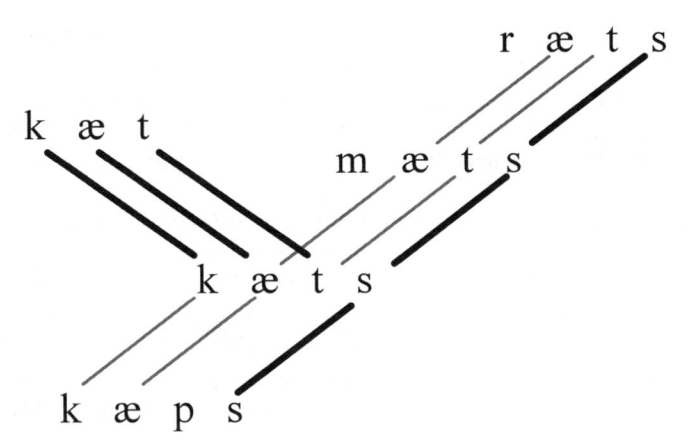

```
                    r æ t s
    k æ t
                  m æ t s

            k æ t s

     k æ p s
```

Fig. 18.2: An example of how word forms are stored in the mental lexicon according to the Network Model (from Bybee, 1995).

and rules approach struggles with more complex inflectional systems, where a single word can have many different forms, without there being a clear rule to tell which form is correct and when. Alternative accounts, routed in the tradition of Cognitive Linguistics, appear better able handle these cases where there is no clear cut between the grammar (rules) and the lexicon (words).

The most prominent model of inflectional morphology in this tradition is Bybee's Network Model (Bybee 1985, 1995), which offers a unified account of its acquisition, processing in adults, and diachronic change (i.e., language change over historical time). According to this model, all word forms, whether we call them regular or irregular, can be stored in your mental lexicon, as long as you have encountered them before (which seems sensible, since the mental lexicon is part of memory, and it does not seem reasonable that we keep some word forms in memory and discard others, based purely on some regularity criterion). Importantly, the mental lexicon is not just a loose bag of words. Rather, all words are stored in shared representational space such that they are interconnected based on their similarity: the more two items are similar to each other the stronger the connection between them. Words can be similar in their *phonological form* (what they sound like) and in their *meaning*. If the two types of similarity go together, a morphological *schema* can emerge (e.g., if a number of verb forms share the -ed ending and they are all associated with the meaning of "past" then we have the basis for a past tense schema).

At first sight, a fully emerged schema does not look very different from a traditional morphological rule. However, there are differences between the two and, crucially, these differences have implications for the acquisition process. Most importantly, the Network Model explains how schemas emerge in child language based on what a given child has heard (the *input*). There are two broadly defined input factors that affect the learning process. One is the above-mentioned similarity of form and meaning: the more similar lexical items are to each other, the faster a schema based on them will emerge, and the more similar an item is to an existing schema, the more likely the schema will be applied to it. The other factor is frequency, which can be further divided into two. The greater the number of different types of word types (e.g., *jumped, hopped, skipped, bounced* ...)

serving as a base for the schema generalisation (i.e., the greater its *type frequency*), the faster the schema will emerge and the easier it will be to apply it to novel items. On the other hand, the more often you hear a particular word form (i.e., the higher its *token frequency*), the stronger its representation, so the easier it will be to retrieve it from memory but at the same time the less "willing" it will be to participate in a schema generalisation.

Grounding the development of morphology in the actual language children hear, the model can explain some phenomena concerning English verbs that escape an easy explanation if one posits a clear-cut distinction between "regular" and "irregular" parts of the system. For example, there is some degree of productivity in children's use of "irregular" patterns on the one hand (e.g., *swung, clung, flung*) and there are effects of frequency and phonological similarity even for "regular" forms (Ambridge 2010; Bybee and Slobin 1982; Dąbrowska and Szczerbiński 2006; Köpcke 1998; Krajewski et al. 2011; Marchman 1997; Matthews and Theakston 2006).

Another important feature of inflectional schemas is their gradual development. Since children generalise schemas based on what they hear and already store in their memory, the learning process takes some time and, furthermore, early schemas will be limited in use (the more different word forms children know, the more open, i.e., easily applied to other items, their schemas will become). In fact, over-regularisation errors are not quite as common in morphological development as has been assumed. Even in English, a closer examination reveals that some words are far more prone to error than others and this difference is largely due to word frequency (Maslen et al. 2004). What turns out to be typical for the development of morphology across languages is the fact that early use of inflections is, at first, highly restricted in terms of different words an inflection will be used with. That is, children are actually quite conservative in the way they use their first inflections (Aguado-Orea 2004; Mueller Gathercole et al. 2002; Pine et al. 1998; Pizzuto and Caselli 1992).

This approach to morphological development receives further support from connectionist models, which are computational simulations of how people learn and represent knowledge (e.g., Cottrell and Plunkett 1994; Rumelhart and McClelland 1986; Westermann 1998). Connectionism became popular in cognitive psychology in the 1980's and one of the first things researchers tried their models on was the acquisition of English past tense. Results of these simulations replicate various experimental findings and strongly suggest that the learning is indeed possible without resorting to separate regular and irregular mechanisms.

In sum, Bybee's Network Model, as an example of the Cognitive Linguistics approach to grammar, radically rejects the traditional words and rules view of language. Instead it proposes that inflectional morphology develops gradually, without clear detachment from the lexicon, depends on input characteristics, and is prone to individual differences.

4.3. Combining word order and morphology to mark agent-patient relations: The cue competition model

While the above sections have illustrated how word order or inflectional morphology can be used to mark who did what to whom, it is worth noting that most languages actually use a combination of both types of marker. This can make learning grammar a little tricky for children and indeed some languages are easier to figure out in this respect than others. To account for all such cross-linguistic differences, Bates and MacWhinney (1989) proposed the Cue Competition Model. A cue can be any linguistic property (e.g., word order, inflections) that systematically co-occurs with a given function (e.g., marking agent-patient relations). The model makes predictions about the importance of a given cue in a given input language, taking into account how often a given cue is present when its function is present (*cue availability*; e.g., case marking is more available in Polish than in English) and how often a given function is present when the cue is present (*cue reliability*; word order is more reliable in English than in Polish). Many studies have tested this model and evidence suggests that the characteristics of the language children hear indeed affect how they learn various grammatical markers. The first studies of this type date back to the 1980's (MacWhinney et al. 1985; Sokolov 1988; Weist 1983) and in recent years new studies appeared, which use novel verbs and thus allow a better test of children's ability to use abstract transitive patterns (e.g., Dittmar et al. 2008). We know that in Turkish, which only minimally depends on word order for marking agent and patient, children do not pay much attention to it but are quick to learn to rely on inflections. In Serbo-Croatian, on the other hand, just like in Polish, younger children depend on word order heavily, even if it conflicts with inflections, perhaps because the latter form a complex and ambiguous system (Krajewski and Lieven 2014; Slobin and Bever 1982). We also know that children across languages find it more difficult to understand sentences with inanimate agents and animate patients (e.g., *The telephone meeks the horse* is more difficult than *The horse meeks the telephone*), which further confirms that learning is grounded in children's experience (Chan et al. 2009). All in all, studies on different languages and using different methods bring the same picture of development that is gradual and depends heavily on how easy it is for the learner to detect a grammatical marker and establish what it is used for.

5. Pragmatic skills: The case of reference

At the start of this chapter we noted how skilled infants are at engaging others in communicative exchanges. This can be considered a pragmatic skill, one which involves effective and appropriate use of language such that it is adapted to context and, particularly, the person we are speaking with. In this section, we will consider a number of other skills that are often described as pragmatic, although we should start by noting that this term is notoriously difficult to define (Ninio and Snow 1996). There are a whole host of pragmatic skills, such as engaging turn taking, using non-literal language (jokes, irony, metaphor), understanding implicatures (e.g., knowing that when I say *I ate some of the biscuits* it can be taken to mean I didn't eat them all) and being able to talk and write in an appropriate register (see Matthews 2014). We will focus here on a very restricted set of pragmatic skills, namely those required to refer to things effectively.

Learning how to refer to things is perhaps more difficult that one might initially expect since referring expressions (e.g., *my sister, she*, or *the girl over there with the blond hair*) convey meaning about how the speaker and addressee perceive the people and things they are talking about (Clark 1997). That is, they tell us about the perspective the speaker has or wants to confer upon the referent. Indeed, when speaking, even the apparently simple case of referring to tangible entities requires more than just matching up words to things. It requires choosing just those referring expressions that a co-operative listener could reasonably understand in a given context. For example, if a child in a crowded playground has her toy snatched from her and runs up to the teacher exclaiming *She took it off me!* then the teacher is unlikely to know who has taken what or to be able to do anything about it. This child has not yet learnt that you only use pronouns like *she* and *it* to refer to things the addressee already knows about or has direct perceptual access to.

The child in the playground is not alone in struggling to grapple with reference. The fact that different forms can refer to the same thing but to differing effect has long caused problems in the philosophy of language (Frege [1892] 1997) and has ultimately driven us to consider the meaning of an utterance as defined by use rather than the things words stand for (Wittgenstein 1958). In the field of linguistics, the differing functions of referring expressions have also been a major topic of discussion (Ariel 1988, 1990; Givón 1983; Gundel et al. 1993). When it comes to child language research, recent studies have shown that children gradually build up very detailed expectations regarding the expressions others will use, taking into account factors such as what can be seen in common ground, what has previously been talked about and the similarity of potential referents. Thus for example, children learn that it is fine to use pronouns (like *it*) if the thing being referred to is highly accessible to the interlocutor either because they are looking at it, or because it has recently been mentioned (Matthews et al. 2006). This view is compatible with Cognitive Linguistic accounts of pronoun use (van Hoek 1997; Matthews et al. 2009).

An important question concerns the type of experiences that are necessary for children to develop this knowledge of referring expressions. Although the many studies demonstrate some very early knowledge in this domain, it remains the case that fully mastering reference takes several years and children aged between 2 and 4 years have been shown to avoid linguistic reference altogether and to rely on pointing to refer to objects even in contexts where such gestures are extremely ambiguous (perhaps to spread the load of communication across the dyad). A recent series of training studies (Matthews et al. 2012; Matthews et al. 2006; Sarilar et al. 2013) demonstrated that actively engaging in conversations and needing to repair unsuccessful attempts at reference can help children to become more effective communicators. Indeed, by hearing specific options when being asked to clarify what they mean (e.g., *do you want the one who's skating or the one who's jumping*), they rapidly learn to use difficult-to-master constructions (such as relative clauses) very early on. Thus, when the pragmatic function of a given referring expression is made clear, young children readily learn to use this form in the future.

We assume, then, that over the course of countless conversations in the preschool years, children gradually build up very detailed expectations regarding how different types of referring expressions can be used, taking into account factors such as what can be seen in common ground and the similarity of potential referents. It appears that children play an active role in testing these expectations out, and propel along their learning in doing so (Morisseau et al. 2013).

6. Summary

We have seen that acquiring a language involves solving multiple interconnected challenges. In the first year of life, children discover that language can be used to regulate interaction and direct others' attention. They start to tune into the sounds of the ambient language and to segment the speech stream into meaningful units including words. In the second year, they learn the functions of hundreds of these words and start to understand how they can be combined to express a whole range of meanings. Over the following years, they develop a productive grasp on the grammar of their language, and gain all the expressive power this permits. In general, we can see the learning process as one of constant refinement: every experience of language leads to an ever more accurate grasp on the subtle differences that contrasting linguistic forms can mark. Sometimes these differences are important for marking semantic contrasts (e.g., the subtle difference in meaning between, *pull* and *tug*, for example) and other times they mark a pragmatic contrast (e.g., the difference between saying *she* or *my sister*). Children propel this process of refinement along themselves, actively seeking out information when their expectations about language use are not met.

7. References

Aguado-Orea, Javier
    2004   *The acquisition of morpho-syntax in Spanish: Implications for current theories of development.* Unpublished PhD, University of Nottingham.

Ambridge, Ben
    2010   Children's judgments of regular and irregular novel past tense forms: New data on the dual- versus single-route debate. *Developmental Psychology* 46(6): 1497–1504

Ambridge, Ben and Elena V. M. Lieven
    2011   *Child Language Acquisition: Contrasting Theoretical Approaches.* Cambridge: Cambridge University Press.

Akhtar, Nameera, and Michael Tomasello
    1997   Young children's productivity with word order and verb morphology. *Developmental Psychology* 33(6): 952–965.

Ariel, Mira
    1988   Referring and accessibility. *Journal of Linguistics* 24: 65–87.

Ariel, Mira
    1990   *Anaphoric Antecedents.* London: Croom Helm.

Baldwin, Dare A.
    1991   Infants' contribution to the achievement of joint reference. *Child Development* 62: 875–890.

Baldwin, Dare A., Ellen M. Markman, Brigitte Bill, Renee N. Desjardins, Jane M. Irwin, and Glynnis Tidball
    1996   Infants' reliance on a social criterion for establishing word-object relations. *Child Development* 67(6): 3135–3153.

Bannard, Colin, Elena V. M. Lieven, and Michael Tomasello
    2009   Modeling children's early grammatical knowledge. *Proceedings of the National Academy of Sciences* 106(41): 17284–17289.

Bannard, Colin, and Danielle E. Matthews
    2008   Stored word sequences in language learning: The effect of familiarity of children's repetition of four-word combinations. *Psychological Science, 19/*3, 241–248.

Bannard, Colin, and Michael Tomasello
    2012   Can we dissociate contingency learning from social learning in word acquisition by 24-month-olds? *PLoS ONE* 7(11): e49881.

Bates, Elizabeth
   1976   *Language and Context: The Acquisition of Pragmatics*. New York: Academic Press.
Bates, Elizabeth, Philip Dale, and Donna Thal
   1995   Individual differences and their implications for theories of language development. *The Handbook of Child Language*, 96–151. Oxford: Basil Blackwell.
Bates, Elizabeth, and Brian MacWhinney
   1989   *The Cross-Linguistic Study of Sentence Processing*. Cambridge: Cambridge University Press.
Bergelson, Elika, and Daniel Swingley
   2012   At 6–9 months, human infants know the meanings of many common nouns. *Proceedings of the National Academy of Sciences* 109(9): 3253–3258.
Berko, Jean
   1958   The child's learning of English morphology. *Word* 14: 150–177.
Brooks, Patricia J., and Michael Tomasello
   1999   How children constrain their argument structure constructions. *Language* 75: 720–738.
Brooks, Rechele, and Andrew N. Meltzoff
   2008   Infant gaze following and pointing predict accelerated vocabulary growth through two years of age: a longitudinal, growth curve modeling study. *Journal of Child Language* 35(1): 207–220.
Bybee, Joan
   1985   *Morphology: A Study of the Relation Between Meaning and Form*. Amsterdam: John Benjamins.
Bybee, Joan
   1995   egular morphology and the lexicon. *Language and Cognitive Processes* 10(5): 425–455.
Bybee, Joan, and Dan I. Slobin
   1982   Rules and schemas in the development and use of the English past tense. *Language* 58: 265–289.
Byers-Heinlein, Krista, and Janet F. Werker
   2009   Monolingual, bilingual, trilingual: Infants' language experience influences the development of a word-learning heuristic. *Developmental Science* 12: 815–823.
Callanan, Maureen A. and Mark A. Sabbagh
   2004   Multiple labels for objects in coversations with young children: Parents' language and children's developing expectations about word meanings. *Developmental Psychology* 40(5): 746–763.
Callanan, Maureen A., Deborah R. Siegel, and Megan R. Luce
   2007   Conventionality in family conversations about everyday objects. *New Directions for Child and Adolescent Development* 115: 83–97.
Callanan, Maureen A. and Deborah R. Siegel
   2014   Learning conventions and conventionality through conversation. In: D. Matthews (ed.), *Pragmatic Development in First Language Acquisition*. Amsterdam: John Benjamins.
Cameron-Faulkner, Thea, Elena V. M. Lieven, and Michael Tomasello
   2003   A construction based analysis of child directed speech. *Cognitive Science* 27(6): 843–873.
Carpenter, Malinda, Katherine Nagell, and Michael Tomasello
   1998   Social cognition, joint attention, and communicative competence from 9 to 15 months of age. *Monographs of the Society for Research in Child Development* 63(4): i–vi, 1–143.
Chan, Angel, Elena V. M. Lieven, and Michael Tomasello
   2009   Children's understanding of the agent-patient relations in the transitive construction: Cross-linguistic comparisons between Cantonese, German, and English. *Cognitive Linguistics* 20(2): 267–300.

Chomsky, Noam
   1965   *Aspects of the Theory of Syntax*. Cambridge: MIT Press.
Chomsky, Noam
   1981   *Lectures on Government and Binding*. Dordrecht: Forris.
Chomsky, Noam
   1995   *The Minimalist Program*. Cambridge: MIT Press.
Clark, Eve V.
   1987   The principle of contrast: A constraint on language acquisition. In: B. MacWhinney (ed.), *Mechanisms of Language Acquisition*, 1–33. Hillsdale: Erlbaum.
Clark, Eve V.
   1997   Conceptual perspective and lexical choice in acquisition. *Cognition* 64(1): 1–37.
Clark, Eve V.
   2003   *First Language Acquisition*. Cambridge: Cambridge University Press.
Clark, Eve V.
   2007   Conventionality and contrast in language and language acquisition. *New Directions for Child and Adolescent Development* 115: 11–23.
Colonnesi, Cristina, Geert J. J. M. Stams, Irene Koster and Marc J. Noom
   2010   The relation between pointing and language development: A meta-analysis. *Developmental Review* 30(4): 352–366.
Cottrell, Garrison W., and Kim Plunkett
   1994   Acquiring the mapping from meanings to sounds. *Connection Science* 6(4): 379–412.
Croft, William
   2001   *Radical Construction Grammar: Syntactic Theory in Typological Perspective*. Oxford: Oxford University Press.
Dąbrowska, Ewa and Elena V. M. Lieven
   2005   Towards a lexically specific grammar of children's question constructions. *Cognitive Linguistics* 16(3): 437–474.
Dąbrowska, Ewa and Marcin Szczerbiński
   2006   Polish children's productivity with case marking: the role of regularity, type frequency and phonological diversity. *Journal of Child Language* 33(3): 559–597.
de Boysson-Bardies, Bénédicte
   1993   *Ontogeny of Language-Specific Syllabic Productions*. Springer.
de Marchena, Ashley, Inge-Marie Eigsti, Amanda Worek, Kim E. Ono and Jesse Snedeker
   2011   Mutual exclusivity in autism spectrum disorders: Testing the pragmatic hypothesis. *Cognition* 119(1): 96–113.
Diesendruck, Gil, and Lori Markson
   2001   Children's avoidance of lexical overlap: a pragmatic account. *Developmental Psychology* 37(5): 630.
Diessel, Holger
   this volume   14. Usage-based construction grammar. Berlin/Boston: De Gruyter Mouton.
Dittmar, Miriam, Kirsten Abbot-Smith, Elena V. M. Lieven, and Michael Tomasello
   2008   Young German children's early syntactic competence: A preferential looking study. *Developmental Science* 11(4): 575–582.
Eilan, Naomi
   2005   Joint attention, communication and mind. In: N. Eilan, C. Hoerl, T. McCormack and J. Roessler (eds.), *Joint Attention: Communication and Other Minds,* 1–33. Oxford: Oxford University Press.
Fisher, Cynthia
   2002   The role of abstract syntactic knowlegde in language acquisition: a reply to Tomasello (2000). *Cognition* 82: 259–278.
Frege, Gottlob
   1997   On Sinn and Bedeutung. In: M. Beaney (ed.), *The Frege Reader*. Oxford: Blackwell.

Freudenthal, Daniel, Julian Pine and Fernand Gobet
2010   Explaining quantitative variation in the rate of Optional Infinitive errors across languages: A comparison of MOSAIC and the Variational Learning Model. *Journal of Child Language* 37(3): 643–669.

Givón, Talmy
1983   *Topic Continuity in Discourse: A Quantitative Crosslanguage Study.* Amsterdam: John Benjamins.

Goldberg, Adele E.
1995   *Constructions: A Construction Grammar Approach to Argument Structure.* Chicago: University of Chicago Press.

Grassmann, Susanne
2014   The pragmatics of word learning. In: D. Matthews (ed.), *Pragmatic Development in First Language Acquisition.* Amsterdam: John Benjamins.

Gundel, Jeanette K., Nancy Hedberg and Ron Zacharski
1993   Cognitive status and the form of referring expressions in discourse. *Language* 69: 274–307.

Jusczyk, Peter
2000   *The Discovery of Spoken Language.* Cambridge: MIT Press.

Köpcke, Klaus-Michael
1998   The acquisition of plural marking in English and German revisited: schemata versus rules. *Journal of Child Language* 25(2): 293–319.

Krajewski, Grzegorz and Elena V. M. Lieven
2014   Competing cues in early syntactic development. In: B. MacWhinney, A. Malchukov, and E. A. Moravcsik (eds.), *Competing Motivations in Grammar and Usage.* Oxford: Oxford University Press

Krajewski, Grzegorz, Anna L. Theakston, Elena V. M. Lieven and Michael Tomasello
2011   How Polish children switch from one case to another when using novel nouns: Challenges for models of inflectional morphology. *Language and Cognitive Processes* 26(4/6): 830–861.

Langacker, Ronald W.
1987   *Foundations of Cognitive Grammar* Vol. 1, *Theoretical Prerequisites.* Stanford: Stanford University Press.

Langacker, Ronald W.
2000   A dynamic usage-based model. In: S. Kemmer and M. Barlow (eds.), *Usage Based Models of Language.* Stanford: CSLI.

Lieven, Elena V. M., Heike Behrens, Jennifer Spears and Michael Tomasello
2003   Early syntactic creativity: A usage-based approach. *Journal of Child Language* 30(2): 333–370.

MacWhinney, Brian, Csaba Pleh and Elizabeth Bates
1985   The development of sentence interpretation in Hungarian. *Cognitive Psychology* 17(2): 178–209.

Mandler, Jean
2004   *The Foundations of Mind: Origins of Conceptual Thought.* Oxford: Oxford University Press.

Marchman, Virginia
1997   Children's productivity in the English past tense: The role of frequency, phonology and neighborhood structure. *Cognitive Science* 21(3): 283–304.

Markman, Ellen M.
1991   The whole-object, taxonomic and mutual exclusivity assumptions as initial constraints on word meanings. In: S. A. Gelman and J. P. Byrnes (eds.), *Perspectives on Language and Thought: Interrelations in Development*, 72–106. Cambridge: Cambridge University Press.

Markman, Ellen M. and Gwyn F. Wachtel
  1988   Children's use of mutual exclusivity to constrain the meanings of words. *Cognitive Psychology* 20(2): 121–157.
Maslen, Robert, Anna L. Theakston, Elena V. M. Lieven and Michael Tomasello
  2004   A dense corpus study of past tense and plural overgeneralization in English. *Journal of Speech Language and Hearing Research* 47: 1319–1333.
Matthews, Danielle E. (ed.).
  2014   *Pragmatic Development in First Language Acquisition*. Amsterdam: John Benjamins.
Matthews, Danielle E., and Colin Bannard
  2010   Children's production of unfamiliar word sequences is predicted by positional variability and latent classes in a large sample of child-directed speech. *Cognitive Science* 34(3): 465–488.
Matthews, Danielle E., Jessica Butcher, Elena V. M. Lieven, and Michael Tomasello
  2012   Two- and four-year-olds learn to adapt referring expressions to context: Effects of distracters and feedback on referential communication. *Topics in Cognitive Science* 4(2): 184–210.
Matthews, Danielle E. and Anna L. Theakston
  2006   Errors of omission in English-speaking children's production of plurals and the past tense: The effects of frequency, phonology and competition. *Cognitive Science* 30(6): 1027–1052.
Matthews, Danielle E., Anna L. Theakston, Elena V. M. Lieven and Michael Tomasello
  2006   The effect of perceptual availability and prior discourse on young children's use of referring expressions. *Applied Psycholinguistics* 27: 403–422.
Matthews, Danielle E., Elena V. M. Lieven, Anna L. Theakston and Michael Tomasello
  2009   Pronoun co-referencing errors: challenges for generativist and usage-based accounts. *Cognitive Linguistics* 20(3): 599–626.
McCune, Lorraine and Marilyn M. Vihman
  2001   Early phonetic and lexical development: A productivity approach. *Journal of Speech, Language and Hearing Research* 44(3): 670–684.
McGillion, Michelle L., Jane S. Herbert, Julian Pine, Tamar Keren-Portnoy, Marilyn Vihman and Danielle E. Matthews
  2013   Supporting early vocabulary development: What sort of responsiveness matters? *Autonomous Mental Development, IEEE Transactions on* 5(3): 240–248.
McGillion, Michelle L., Jane S. Herbert, Julian Pine. Marilyn Vihman, Tamar Keren-Portnoy and Danielle E. Matthews
  under review   Weighing up predictors of early word learning: The role of babble, pointing and maternal education.
Monaghan, Padraic and Morten H. Christiansen
  2010   Words in puddles of sound: modelling psycholinguistic effects in speech segmentation. *Journal of Child Language* 37(3): 545–564.
Morisseau, Tiffany, Catherine Davies and Danielle E. Matthews
  2013   How do 3-and 5-year-olds respond to under-and over-informative utterances? *Journal of Pragmatics* 59: 26–39.
Mueller Gathercole, Virginia. C., Eugenia Sebastián and Pilar Soto
  2002   The emergence of linguistic person in Spanish-speaking children. *Language Learning* 52(4): 679–722.
Naigles, Letitia
  1990   Children use syntax to learn verb meanings. *Journal of Child Language* 17: 357–374.
Ninio, Anat and Catherine E. Snow
  1996   *Pragmatic Development*. Boulder: Westview Press.

Nurmsoo, Erika and Paul Bloom
   2008   Preschoolers' perspective taking in word learning. *Psychological Science* 19(3): 211–215.

Oller, D. Kimbrough and Rebecca E. Eilers
   1988   The role of audition in infant babbling. *Child Development* 59(2): 441–449.

Pine, Julian M., Elena V. M. Lieven and Caroline F. Rowland
   1998   Comparing different models of the development of the English verb category. *Linguistics* 36: 807–830.

Pinker, Steven
   1999   *Words and Rules: The Ingredients of Language.* New York: Harper Collins.

Pizzuto, Elena and Maria C. Caselli
   1992   The acquisition of Italian morphology: Implications for models of language development. *Journal of Child Language* 19(3): 491–557.

Preissler, Melissa A. and Susan Carey
   2005   The role of inferences about referential intent in word learning: Evidence from autism. *Cognition* 97(1): B13–B23.

Rumelhart, David E. and James L. McClelland
   1986   On learning the past tenses of English verbs. In: D. Rumelhart, J. McClelland and T. P. Group (eds.), *Parallel Distributed Processing: Explorations in the Microstructure of Cognition.* Cambridge: MIT Press.

Saffran, Jenny R., Richard N. Aslin and Elissa L. Newport
   1996   Statistical learning by 8-month-old infants. *Science* 274(5294), 1926–1928.

Sarilar, Ayşe, Danielle E. Matthews, and Aylin C. Küntay
   2013   Hearing relative clauses boosts relative clause usage (and referential clarity) in young Turkish language learners. *Applied Psycholinguistics* FirstView, 1–28.

Slobin, Dan I. and Thomas G. Bever
   1982   Children use canonical sentence schemas: A cross-linguistic study of word order and inflections. *Cognition* 12: 229–265.

Snedeker, Jesse, Joy Geren and Carissa L. Shafto
   2012   Disentangling the effects of cognitive development and linguistic expertise: A longitudinal study of the acquisition of English in internationally-adopted children. *Cognitive Psychology* 65(1): 39–76.

Sokolov, Jeffrey L.
   1988   Cue validity in Hebrew sentence comprehension. *Journal of Child Language* 15(1): 129–155.

Stephens, Gemma and Matthews, D.
   2014   The communicative infant from 0–18 months: The social-cognitive foundations of pragmatic development. In: D. Matthews (ed.), *Pragmatic Development in First Language Acquisition.* Amsterdam: John Benjamins.

Stoll, Sabine, Kirsten Abbot-Smith and Elena V. M. Lieven
   2009   Lexically restricted utterances in Russian, German, and English child-directed speech. *Cognitive Science* 33(1): 75–103.

Tomasello, Michael
   2001   Could we please lose the mapping metaphor, please? *Behavioral and Brain Sciences* 24(6): 1119–1120.

Tomasello, Michael
   2003   *Constructing a Language: A Usage-Based Theory of Language Acquisition.* Cambridge: Harvard University Press.

Tomasello, Michael and Michelle Barton
   1994   Learning words in non-ostensive contexts. *Developmental Psychology* 30(5): 639–650.

Tomasello, Michael, Malinda Carpenter and Ulf Liszkowski
   2007   A new look at infant pointing. *Child Development* 78(3): 705–722.

Van Hoek, Karen
    1997   *Anaphora and Conceptual Structure*. Chicago: University of Chicago Press.
Vihman, Marilyn M.
    1996   *Phonological Development*. Oxford: Blackwells.
Weist, Richard M.
    1983   Prefix versus suffix information processing in the comprehension of tense and aspect. *Journal of Child Language* 10(1): 85–96.
Werker, Janet F. and Chris E. Lalonde
    1988   Cross-language speech perception: initial capabilities and developmental change. *Developmental Psychology* 24(5): 672.
Westermann, Gert
    1998   Emergent modularity and U-shaped learning in a constructivist neural network learning the English past tense. Paper presented at the Proceedings of the 20th Annual Meeting of the Cognitive Science Society.
Wittgenstein, Ludwig
    1958   *Philosophical Investigations.* (trans. G. E. M. Anscombe). Oxford: Blackwell.

Danielle Matthews, Sheffield (United Kingdom)
Grzegorz Krajewski, Warsaw (Poland)

19. Second language acquisition

1. Introduction
2. Constructions in first and second language acquisition
3. Components of a constructionist model of language learning
4. First vs. second language learning: (re-)constructing a language
5. Future priorities
6. References

1. Introduction

This chapter introduces a cognitive-linguistic perspective on second language acquisition (L2A).[1] Over the last 15 or so years, various aspects of L2 acquisition have been examined through a cognitive-linguistic lens, including phonology, morpho-syntax, lexis, syntax, and pragmatics. Likewise, various cognitive-linguistic frameworks including cognitive grammar, metaphor theory, and conceptual blending have been employed in L2 acquisition and teaching research. This chapter deliberately focuses on a construction grammar perspective on L2 acquisition. Robinson and Ellis (2008b), Littlemore (2009),

---

[1] Throughout this chapter, we use the terms *acquisition*, *learning*, and *development* interchangeably.

and Tyler (2012) give broader overviews of cognitive-linguistic L2 learning and teaching research.

In traditional generative approaches, language is understood as a modular system: phonology, morphology, syntax, and semantics (and, in some versions of generative grammar, also pragmatics) are distinct subsystems. These modules are largely independent in structure and functioning from other human cognitive processes, and largely uninfluenced by the ways in which humans interact with the world. This view of language as a largely autonomous system comprised of largely autonomous subsystems has stipulated the assumption of a *narrow language faculty* (or *Universal Grammar*) and a *broad language faculty* (Hauser et al. 2002). The broad language faculty comprises cognitive abilities that are required for and assist in, but are not exclusive to, language acquisition and processing, such as the human auditory, motor, and vocal systems, short- and long-term memory, and (joint) attention, among others (Jackendoff 2011).

Cognitive linguistics, in contrast, adopts a non-modular approach to language: language is seen as part of human cognition, with language and cognition being systematically intertwined. Consequently, the focus in cognitive linguistics is on how general human cognitive abilities are manifest in language, and how general cognitive abilities impact language form, change, processing, and acquisition. Similarly, cognitive linguistics is non-modular in the sense that the idea of distinct linguistic subsystems is discarded, including the long-standing distinction between words (the lexicon) and the rules that combine them (grammar). Instead, mastery of a language entails knowing constructions at different levels of complexity and schematization, as well as knowledge of the probabilistic (as opposed to rigid) tendencies underlying their combination. In the following, we outline the implications of these working assumptions of cognitive linguistics for L2A.

In section 2, we provide a summary of how research on multi-word units in language learning and processing calls for a revised understanding of linguistic competence, and how a construction grammar perspective answers that call by shifting the focus to constructions and how they are learnable by both L1 and L2 speakers. In section 3, we outline the components of a constructionist model of language learning. Section 4 briefly discusses the observable differences between first and second language learning, and how a constructionist perspective accounts for them. Section 5 closes with suggestions for future research.

2. Constructions in first and second language acquisition

There is copious evidence from psycholinguistics, corpus linguistics, and cognitive linguistics that language users have rich knowledge of the frequencies of forms and of their sequential dependencies in their native language. Ellis (2002) reviewed evidence that language processing is sensitive to the sequential probabilities of linguistic elements at all levels from phonemes to phrases, and in comprehension as well as in fluency and idiomaticity of speech production. He argued that this sensitivity to sequence information in language processing is evidence of learners' implicit knowledge of memorized sequences of language, and that this knowledge in itself serves as the basis for linguistic systematicity and creativity. The last ten years has seen substantial research confirming native language users' implicit knowledge of the constructions of their language and their probabilities of usage. This is not the place to review this research, instead see Rebuschat and Williams (2012), Ellis (2012a), Trousdale and Hoffman (2013), and chapters by Tremblay and by Divjak and Caldwell-Harris (this volume).

2.1. Do L2 learners have constructions too?

Such demonstrations of the psychological reality of constructions in native speakers' language raise the question if, and to what extent, constructions also underpin L2 learners' linguistic competence, and whether L2 learners implicitly "tally" and tune their constructional knowledge to construction-specific preferences in terms of the words that preferably occur in those constructions. There is mounting evidence that this is the case, as the following brief review of recent studies illustrates.

Jiang and Nekrasova (2007) examined the representation and processing of formulaic sequences using online grammaticality judgment tasks. L2 English and native English speakers were tested with formulaic and non-formulaic phrases matched for word length and frequency (e.g., *to tell the truth* vs. *to tell the price*). Both native and nonnative speakers responded to the formulaic sequences significantly faster and with fewer errors than they did to nonformulaic sequences. Similarly, Conklin and Schmitt (2007) measured reading times for formulaic sequences versus matched nonformulaic phrases in native and nonnative speakers. The formulaic sequences were read more quickly than the non-formulaic phrases by both groups of participants.

Ellis and Simpson-Vlach (2009) and Ellis et al. Maynard (2008) used four experimental procedures to determine how the corpus-linguistic metrics of frequency and mutual information (MI, a statistical measure of the coherence of strings) are represented implicitly in native and non-native speakers, thus to affect their accuracy and fluency of processing of the formulas of the Academic Formulas List (AFL; Simpson-Vlach and Ellis 2010). The language processing tasks in these experiments were selected to sample an ecologically valid range of language processing skills: spoken and written, production and comprehension, form-focused and meaning-focused. They were: (1) speed of reading and acceptance in a grammaticality judgment task, where half of the items were real phrases in English and half were not; (2) rate of reading and rate of spoken articulation; (3) binding and primed pronunciation – the degree to which reading the beginning of the formula primed recognition of its final word; and (4) speed of comprehension and acceptance of the formula as being appropriate in a meaningful context. Processing in all experiments was affected by various corpus-derived metrics: length, frequency, and mutual information (MI). Frequency was the major determinant for non-native speakers, whereas for native speakers it was predominantly the MI of the formula that determined processability.

Gries and Wulff (2005) showed that advanced German learners of English showed syntactic priming for ditransitive (e.g., *The racing driver showed the helpful mechanic* ...) and prepositional dative (e.g., *The racing driver showed the torn overall* ...) argument structure constructions in an English sentence completion task. Furthermore, they showed that learners' semantic knowledge of argument structure constructions affected their grouping of sentences in a sorting task. More specifically, learners' priming effects closely resembled those of native speakers of English in that they were highly correlated with native speakers' verbal subcategorization preferences whilst uncorrelated with the subcategorization preferences of the German translation equivalents of these verbs. Gries and Wulff (2009) found similar results for gerundial and infinitival complement constructions, and several other studies have demonstrated similar L2 syntactic priming effects (McDonough 2006; McDonough and Mackey 2006; McDonough and Trofimovich 2008). Liang (2002) replicated the semantic sorting experiment with three groups of Chinese learners of English at beginning, intermediate, and advanced proficiency levels, and found a significant positive correlation between the tendency to sort by construction and general proficiency.

Ellis and Ferreira-Junior (2009a, 2009b) analyzed longitudinal data for naturalistic L2 English learners in the *European Science Foundation* corpus (Klein and Perdue 1992; Perdue 1993) to show that naturalistic adult L2 learners used the same verbs in frequent verb argument constructions as are found in their input experience. Indeed, the relative ordering of the types in the input predicted uptake with correlations in excess of $r = 0.90$.

Taken together, these findings argue that grammatical and lexical knowledge are not stored or processed in different mental modules, but rather form a continuum from heavily entrenched and conventionalized formulaic units (unique patterns of high token frequency) to loosely connected but collaborative elements (patterns of high type frequency) (Bybee 2010; Ellis 2008c; Ellis and Larsen-Freeman 2009a, 2009b; Robinson and Ellis 2008a, 2008b). Accordingly, Wulff and Gries propose a constructionist definition of L2 accuracy as "the selection of a construction (in the Goldbergian sense of the term) in its preferred context within a particular target variety and genre" (2011: 70).

Thus, in both L1 and L2, learners are sensitive to the frequencies of occurrence of constructions and their transitional probabilities, and this suggests that they learn these statistics from usage, tallying them implicitly during each processing episode. Linguistic structure *emerges* from the conspiracy of these experiences (Ellis 1998, 2011). "The linguist's task is in fact to study the whole range of repetition in discourse, and in doing so to seek out those regularities which promise interest as incipient sub-systems. Structure, then, in this view is not an overarching set of abstract principles, but more a question of a spreading of systematicity from individual words, phrases, and small sets." (Hopper 1987: 143).

2.2. The role of formulaic language in L1 acquisition (L1A)

Demonstrating skilled language users' knowledge of formulaic language and other constructions is a separate but related matter from demonstrating that formulaic language plays a role in acquisition. It remains contentious in child language research whether children's early language (i) makes use of abstract categories and principles for composing sentences by combining those categories in ordered sequences, or whether it (ii) consists of a repertoire of more concrete constructions or formulas, many based on particular lexical items (e.g., *jump, put,* and *give*) rather than abstract syntactic categories like *Verb*. The corresponding theoretical positions are that (i) children don't need to learn grammar because the principles and categories of grammar are innate, requiring only minimal exposure to the language to be 'triggered', or that (ii) the process of syntactic development consists of acquiring a large repertoire of constructions and formulas by statistically inducing increasingly abstract categories on the basis of experience of the types of items that occupy their component parts. The last 20 years has seen considerable research that points to the second alternative. We have neither space nor remit here to dispute the case, and gladly defer to the chapters by Matthews and Krajewski (this volume) as well as other recent reviews (Ambridge and Lieven 2011; Behrens 2009; Dąbrowska 2004; Diessel 2013; Lieven et al. 2003; Tomasello 1992, 2003).

One important evidential source has been dense longitudinal corpora of naturalistic language development that capture perhaps 10% of children's speech and the input they are exposed to, collected from 2–4 years of age when children are undergoing maximal language development (Behrens 2008; Maslen et al. 2004). Without such dense sampling, it is difficult if not impossible to clearly identify sequences of development of linguistic items of relatively low frequency as they unfold over time (Tomasello and Stahl 2004).

Using dense corpora, Lieven and colleagues have used the 'traceback' method (Dąbrowska and Lieven 2005) of analyzing adult-child conversation to show that very often when a child produces what seems to be a novel utterance, the ingredients for that utterance are to be found earlier in the transcript. That is, the novel utterance has not been generated from scratch but rather a previous sentence has been manipulated, replacing one content word. Even when children are more productive than that, the data-dependent nature of children's underlying knowledge is evidenced in the relations between the frequency of structures in the input and the frequency of children's production of those structures. Children are initially conservative in their language in that their production is more formulaic than openly combinatorial. These are the essential observations for the developmental sequence from formula to limited-scope pattern to creative construction in L1A (Lieven et al. 2003; Tomasello 2000, 2003).

2.3. The role of formulaic language in L2 acquisition

2.3.1. A review of the research

What about when learners *re*construct an L2? The field of SLA showed early interest in multi-word sequences and their potential role in language development. Corder (1973) coined the term *holophrase*, and, in similar spirit, Brown (1973) defined prefabricated routines as unanalyzed multi-word sequences associated with a particular pragmatic function. One of the main research questions for SLA researchers at the time was: do prefabricated routines pose a challenge to the traditional view of language learning as a process by which children start out with small units (morphemes and words) and then gradually combine them into more complex structures? Do children alternatively and/or additionally start out from large(r) chunks of language which they then gradually break down into their component parts? Early studies did not yield conclusive results (a good discussion can be found in Krashen and Scarcella 1978). For example, Hatch (1972) found evidence for both learning strategies in the English production data of a 4-year old Chinese boy. Hakuta (1974, 1976), based on data from a 5-year-old Japanese learner of English, argued in favor of a more fine-grained distinction between prefabricated routines and prefabricated patterns, that is, low-scope patterns that have at least one variable slot. Wong-Fillmore's (1976) dissertation project was one of the first to track more than one child over a longer period of time; her analysis suggested that children do in fact start out with prefabricated patterns which they gradually break down into their component parts in search for the rules governing their L2, which, in turn, ultimately enables them to use language creatively.

There were only a few early studies on adult L2 learners (Wray 2002: 172–198 provides a detailed overview). The general consensus, however, was that while adult L2 learners may occasionally employ prefabricated language, there was less evidence than in children's data that knowledge of prefabricated language would foster grammatical development in adult L2A. Hanania and Gradman (1977), for instance, studied Fatmah, a native speaker of Arabic. Fatmah was 19 years old at the time of the study, and she had received only little formal education in her native language. When speaking English, Fatmah used several routines that were tied to specific pragmatic situations; however, the researchers found her largely unable to analyze these routines into their component parts. Similarly, Schumann (1978), who investigated data from several adult L2 learners with different native language backgrounds, found only little evidence in favor of prefabricated language use in the first place, or any positive effect of prefabricated language knowledge on language development for that matter. A slightly different picture emerged in Schmidt's (1983) well-known research on Wes, a native speaker of Japanese who immigrated to Hawaii in his early thirties. Wes seemed to make extensive use of prefabricated routines. However, while this significantly boosted Wes' fluency, his grammatical competence remained low. Ellis (1984), looking at the use of prefabricated language in an instructional setting, suggested that there is considerable individual variation in learners' ability to make the leap from prefabricated routines to the underlying grammatical rules they exemplify. Krashen and Scarcella (1978) were outright pessimistic regarding adult learners' ability to even retain prefabricated routines, and cautioned against focusing adult learners' attention on prefabricated language because "[t]he outside world for adults is nowhere near as predictable as the linguistic environment around Fillmore's children was" (Krashen and Scarcella 1978: 298).

In the light of developments in child language acquisition, Ellis (1996, 2002) revisited the issue, asking whether a common pattern of developmental sequence in both L1A and L2A might be from formulaic phrases to limited scope slot-and-frame patterns to fully productive schematic patterns. Ellis (2003) phrased the argument in terms of constructions rather than formulas. There are subsequent longitudinal studies in support of this sequence in L2A, though the available corpora are far from dense.

In an extensive study of secondary school pupils learning French as a foreign language in England, Myles (2004; Myles et al. 1999) analyzed longitudinal corpora of oral language in 16 beginning learners [(11–14 years old), tracked over the first 2 years, using 13 oral tasks] and 60 intermediate learners [20 classroom learners in each of years 9, 10 and 11 studied cross-sectionally using four oral tasks]. These data showed that multimorphemic sequences, which go well beyond learners' grammatical competence, are very common in early L2 production. Notwithstanding that these sequences contain such forms as finite verbs, wh-questions and clitics, Myles denied this as evidence for functional projections from the start of L2A because these properties are not initially present outside of chunks. Analyses of inflected verb forms suggested that early productions containing them were formulaic chunks. These structures, sometimes syntactically highly complex (e.g., in the case of interrogatives), cohabited for extended periods of time with very simple sentences, usually verbless, or when a verb was present, this was normally untensed. Likewise, clitics first appeared in chunks containing tensed verbs, suggesting that it is through these chunks that learners acquire them. Myles characterizes these early grammars as consisting of lexical projections and formulaic sequences, showing no evidence of functional categories. "Chunks do not become discarded; they remain grammatically advanced until the grammar catches up, and it is this process of resolving the tension between these grammatically advanced chunks and the current grammar which drives the learning process forward" (Myles 2004: 152). The study also investigated the development of chunks within individual learners over time, showing a clear correlation between chunk use and linguistic development:

> In the beginners' corpus, at one extreme, we had learners who failed to memorize chunks after the first round of elicitation; these were also the learners whose interlanguage remained primarily verbless, and who needed extensive help in carrying out the tasks. At the other extreme, we had learners whose linguistic development was most advanced by the end of the study. These were also the learners who, far from discarding chunks, were seen to be actively working on them throughout the data-collection period. These chunks seem to provide these learners with a databank of complex structures beyond their current grammar, which they keep working on until they can make their current generative grammar compatible with them. (Myles 2004: 153)

Eskildsen and Cadierno (2007) investigated the development of *do*-negation by a Mexican learner of English. *Do*-negation learning was found to be initially reliant on one specific instantiation of the pattern *I don't know*, which thereafter gradually expanded to be used with other verbs and pronouns as the underlying knowledge seemed to become increasingly abstract, as reflected in token and type frequencies.

Mellow (2008) describes a longitudinal case study of a 12-year-old Spanish learner of English, Ana, who wrote stories describing 15 different wordless picture books during a 201-day period. The findings indicate that Ana began by producing only a few types of complex constructions that were lexically-selected by a small set of verbs which gradually seeded a growing range of constructions.

Sugaya and Shirai (2009) describe the acquisition of Japanese tense-aspect morphology in L1 Russian learner Alla. In her ten-month longitudinal data, some verbs (e.g., *siru* 'come to know,' *tuku* 'be attached') were produced exclusively with the imperfective aspect marker *-te i-(ru)*, while other verbs (e.g., *iku* 'go,' *tigau* 'differ') were rarely used with *-te i-(ru)*. Even though these verbs can be used in any of the four basic forms, Alla demonstrated a very strong verb-specific preference. Sugaya and Shirai followed this up with a larger cross-sectional study of 61 intermediate and advanced learners (based on the ACTFL scale), who were divided into 34 lower and 27 higher proficiency groups using grammaticality judgment tasks. The lower proficiency learners used the individual verbs in verb-specific ways, and this tendency was stronger for the verbs denoting resultative state meaning with *-te i-(ru)* (e.g., achievement verbs) than the verbs denoting progressive meaning with *-te i-(ru)* (e.g., activity, accomplishment, and semelfactive verbs). Sugaya and Shirai concluded that the intermediate learners begin with item-based learning and low scope patterns and that these formulas allow them to gradually gain control over tense-aspect. Nevertheless, they also considered how memory-based and rule-based processes might co-exist for particular linguistic forms, and that linguistic knowledge should be considered a "formulaic-creative continuum".

On the other hand, there are studies of L2 that have set out to look for this sequence and found less compelling evidence.

Bardovi-Harlig (2002) studied the emergence of future expression involving *will* and *going to* in a longitudinal study of 16 adult L2 English learners (mean length of observation 11.5 months; 1,576 written texts, mainly journal entries, and 175 oral texts, either guided conversational interviews or elicited narratives based on silent films). The data showed that future *will* emerges first and greatly outnumbers the use of tokens of *going to*. Bardovi-Harlig described how the rapid spread of *will* to a variety of verbs suggests that, "for most learners, there is either little initial formulaic use of *will* or that it is so brief that it cannot be detected in this corpus" (Bardovi-Harlig 2002: 192). There was some evidence of formulaicity in early use of *going to*: "For 5 of the 16 learners, the use of *I am going to write* stands out. Their production over the months of observation show that the formula breaks down into smaller parts, from the full *I am going to write about* to the core *going to* where not only the verb but also person and number vary. This seems to be an example of learner production moving along the formulaic-creative continuum" (Bardovi-Harlig 2002: 197). But other learners showed greater variety of use of *going to*, with different verbs and different person-number forms, from its earliest appearance in the diary. Bardovi-Harlig concludes that "although the use of formulaic language seems to play a limited role in the expression of future, its influence is noteworthy" (Bardovi-Harlig 2002: 198).

Eskildsen (2009) analyzed longitudinal oral L2 classroom interaction for the use of *can* by one student, Carlo. *Can* first appeared in the data in the formula *I can write*. But Eskildsen noted how formulas are interactionally and locally contextualized, which means that they may possibly be transitory in nature, their deployment over time being occasioned by specific recurring usage events.

2.3.2. Methodological considerations

The outcome of such studies searching for developmental sequences seeded by use of formulaic patterns rests on a range of factors:

Firstly, regarding methodology, data has to be dense enough to identify repeated uses at the time of emergence (Tomasello and Stahl 2004). The use of formulas and constructions are determined by context, function, genre and register. If the elicitation tasks vary, the chance of sampling the same formula and its potential variants diminishes accordingly.

Secondly, they may vary as a function of L1A vs. L2A. L1A may indeed be more formulaic than L2 acquisition. When child learners are learning about language from formulaic frames (Ambridge and Lieven 2011; Mintz 2003; Tomasello 2003) and the analysis of sequences of words (Elman 1990; Kiss 1973; Redington and Chater 1998), they are learning from scratch about more abstract categories such as verb, pronoun, preposition, noun, transitive frame, etc. It is debatable whether the units of early L1A are words at all (Peters 1983). Adult L2 learners already know about the existence of these units, categories, and linguistic structures. They expect that there will be words and constructions in the L2 which correspond to such word classes and frames. Once they have identified them, or even, once they have searched them out and actively learned such key vocabulary, they are more likely therefore to attempt creative construction, swopping these elements into corresponding slots in frames.

Thirdly, as in all other areas of language processing, recognition of formulas is easier than production. As described in section 2.1, Ellis and Ferreira-Junior (2009a, 2009b) showed that naturalistic adult L2 learners used the same verbs in frequent verb argument constructions as are found in their input experience, with the relative ordering of the types in the input predicting uptake with correlations in excess of $r = 0.90$. Nevertheless, while they would accurately produce short simple formulaic sequences such as *come in* or *I went to the shop*, structurally more complex constructions were often produced in the simplified form of the Basic Variety (Klein and Perdue 1992; Perdue 1993) which involves a pragmatic topic-comment word ordering, where old information goes first and new information follows.

Fourthly, transfer from the L1 is also likely to affect the process (Granger 2001). The more learners attempt word-by-word translation from their L1, the more they deviate from L2 idiomaticity.

Finally, amount and type of exposure is bound to play a role. Children are naturalistic language learners from thousands of hours of interaction and input. While some adults learn naturalistically, others take grammar-rich courses. Dictionaries and grammar books do not provide naturalistic input, nor do they encourage fluent idiomatic expression of formulaic speech. Nevertheless, Myles (2004) demonstrates the viability of this sequence of acquisition even for classroom foreign language acquisition.

2.3.3. Caveat and conclusion

A common misunderstanding about the role of formulaic sequences in language acquisition warrants a caveat here. The fact that formulaic sequences play roles in the development of more creative competence does not imply that all apparently formulaic strings so serve. Far from it: Some formulaic sequences are readily learnable by dint of being highly frequent and prototypical in their functionality – *how are you?*, *it's lunch time*, *I don't know*, *I am going to write about*, and the like. These are likely candidates as construction seeds.

Other formulaic sequences are not readily learnable – these are of low frequency, often indeed rare, and many are non-transparent and idiomatic in their interpretation (e.g., *once in a blue moon*). As idioms they must be learned as such. However, learners require considerable language experience before they encounter these once, never mind sufficient times to commit them to memory (Ellis 2008b). This is why learners typically do not achieve nativelike idiomaticity (Granger 2001; Pawley and Syder 1983). These low frequency, low transparency formulas are targets for learning rather than seeds of learning. Hence the observations that learner language is often light in frequency of formulaic language compared to native norms (Granger 2001) and that acquisition of nativelike targets can be challenging (Pawley and Syder 1983).

Is the notion of language acquisition being seeded by formulaic phrases and yet learner language being formula-light 'having your cake and eating it too'? Pawley and Syder (1983) thought not. While much of their classic article concentrated on the difficulty L2 learners had in achieving nativelike formulaic selection and nativelike fluency, they nevertheless state "Indeed, we believe that memorized sentences are the normal building blocks of fluent spoken discourse, and at the same time, that they provide models for the creation of many (partly) new sequences which are memorable and in their turn enter into the stock of familiar uses" (1983: 208). Ellis (2012b) further examines this apparent paradox whereby large-scale analyses of learner corpora show that L2 learners typically do not achieve nativelike formulaicity and idiomaticity (Granger 2001; Pawley and Syder 1983) while, at the same time, formulas can provide learners with a databank of complex structures beyond their current grammar which can drive the learning process forward.

The most balanced conclusion is that linguistic knowledge is a formulaic-creative continuum. In this light, how are constructions acquired?

3. Components of a constructionist model of language learning

Constructionist accounts of language acquisition involve the distributional analysis of the language stream and the parallel analysis of contingent perceptual activity, with abstract constructions being learned from the conspiracy of concrete exemplars of usage following statistical learning mechanisms (Rebuschat and Williams 2012) relating input and learner cognition. Psychological analyses of this learning of constructions as form-meaning pairs is informed by the literature on the associative learning of cue-outcome contingencies where the usual determinants include: factors relating to the form such as frequency and salience; factors relating to the interpretation such as significance in the comprehension of the overall utterance, prototypicality, generality, redundancy, and surprise value; factors relating to the contingency of form and function; and factors relating to learner attention, such as automaticity, transfer, overshadowing, and blocking (Ellis, 2002, 2003, 2006, 2008a, 2008b). These various psycholinguistic factors conspire in the acquisition and use of any linguistic construction. This section briefly considers each in turn.

3.1. Frequency of construction in the input

According to usage-based approaches to language, frequency of exposure promotes learning and cognitive entrenchment. Type and token frequency play different roles. Token frequency is the frequency with which a particular construction (i.e., a particular phonotactic sequence, morpheme, or syntactic frame) occurs in the input. Type frequency, in contrast, refers to the number of distinct realizations of a given construction. For example, the English past tense morpheme – *ed* has a very high type frequency: in any sizeable data sample of English, it occurs with thousands of different verbs. Irregular past tense forms as in *blew*, *sang*, or *rode*, on the contrary, have low type frequency: they occur only with a comparatively restricted number of verbs. Type frequency is one indicator of the productivity of a construction because high type frequency allows the hearer to parse the construction in question and results in a stronger schematic representation of the form, which in turn renders it more available not only for reuse, but also novel uses (Bybee and Hopper 2001). Bybee (2006: 15) provides the following example:

If *happiness* is learned by someone who knows no related words, there is no way to infer that it has two morphemes. If *happy* is also learned, then the learner could hypothesize that – *ness* is a suffix, but only if it occurs on other adjectives would its status as a suffix become established. Thus a certain degree of type frequency is needed to uncover the structure of words and phrases.

High token frequency may in fact yield the opposite effect by promoting the conservation of specific realizations of a construction (see Bybee 2006 for a detailed discussion of the conserving, form-reducing, and autonomy-stipulating effects of high token frequency).

3.2. Distribution of construction in the input

In accordance with Goldberg et al. (2004), research suggests that acquisition benefits from initial exposure to massive, low-variance input that is centered around prototypical realizations (or exemplars) of the target construction (Elio and Anderson 1981, 1984). This focused and stereotypical input allows the learner to induce what accounts for the majority of the category members; continuing exposure to the full breadth of exemplar types later defines category boundaries (Nosofsky 1988). Both childrens' input and output in Goldberg et al. (2004) reflected a Zipfian distribution. According to Zipf's Law (Zipf 1935), in natural language, the frequency of a word is inversely proportional to its rank in a frequency table: the most frequent word occurs about twice as often as the second most frequent word, three times as often as the third most frequent word, and so on. Importantly, Goldberg et al. (2004) showed that Zipf's Law does not only hold when counting words in a given sample of naturalistic speech – it also seems to hold for verbs *within* a given construction. According to Goldberg et al., this Zipfian distribution of the childrens' input plays a significant role in acquisition: one specific typical verb is made salient by being extremely frequent in the input and serves as the "pathbreaking verb" in the process of category formation (see also Ninio 1999, 2006). Ellis and Ferreira-Junior (2009a, 2009b) examined a corpus of naturalistic L2A and likewise confirmed that the type/token ratio of the verbs in argument structure constructions is Zipfian. Furthermore, they were able to show that, as Tomasello (2003) has argued for L1A, the most frequent and prototypical verbs seem to act as "verb islands" around which the verb argument construction is gradually built up. Ellis and O'Donnell (2012) and Römer, O'Donnell, and Ellis (2015) confirm the Zipfian distribution of verb argument constructions in large-scale analyses of English language usage.

3.3. Recency of construction in the input

Research in cognitive psychology has taught us that three key factors influence the activation of memory schemata: frequency, recency, and context (Anderson 1989; Anderson and Schooler 2000). Recency, also referred to as priming or persistence, is an implicit memory effect: exposure to a stimulus affects a response to a later stimulus. Recency has been shown to impact processing at the level of phonology, conceptual representation, lexical choice, and syntax (McDonough 2006; McDonough and Mackey 2006; McDonough and Trofimovich 2008).

3.4. Salience, redundancy, and perception of form of the construction

The general perceived strength of a stimulus is referred to as its salience. As the Rescorla-Wagner (1972) model of associative learning encapsulates, the amount of learning induced from an experience of a cue-outcome association depends crucially upon the salience of the cue and the importance of the outcome: low salience cues are less readily learned. Many grammatical functors in English have low salience in the input, for example, inflections like the third person singular – *s* morpheme. It is not surprising, then, that it is these grammatical symbols in particular that L2 learners tend to have most difficulty with.

The Rescorla-Wagner (1972) model also accounts for the fact that redundant cues tend not to be acquired. Many grammatical constructions are not only low in salience, but also are redundant in the listener's understanding of an utterance in that they compete with more salient psychophysical forms. For example, third person singular – *s* marks present tense, but *today* is more salient in the input and effectively overshadows and blocks acquisition of the morpheme (Ellis 2006, 2008b; Ellis and Sagarra 2010b, Goldschneider and DeKeyser 2001). Generally, inflectional case markings such as tense are often accompanied by (more salient) adverbs that indicate temporal reference. Accordingly, L2 learners typically prefer adverbial over inflectional cues to tense, a phenomenon that has been well-documented in longitudinal studies of naturalistic L2A (Dietrich et al. 1995; Bardovi-Harlig 2000), training experiments (Ellis and Sagarra 2010b, 2011), and studies of L2 language processing (VanPatten 2006; Ellis and Sagarra 2010a).

3.5. Prototypicality of function

Categories have graded structure: some members are better exemplars of the category than others. In Prototype Theory (Rosch and Mervis 1975; Rosch et al. 1976), the prototype of a category is defined as an idealized mental representation of the best example of that category in the sense of encapsulating the most representative features of that category. The prototype serves as the gold standard against which exemplars are classified as more or less central members of the category. For example, people readily classify sparrows as birds: sparrows are good examples of the category BIRD because they incorporate various representative attributes (they are average in size, beak size, color, etc.). In contrast, people take considerably longer to confirm that albatrosses are birds too. Prototypical exemplars are judged faster and more accurately even upon first encounter (Posner and Keele 1970) – a sparrow will be instantly recognized as a bird even by a person who has never seen a sparrow before. Prototypicality and token frequency interact: the higher the token frequency of an exemplar, the higher the likelihood of this exemplar becoming the prototype. Accordingly, Goldberg et al. (2004) showed that in L1A, children's first uses of verbs, in particular verb-argument constructions, are often semantically typical generic verb types that are at the center of the construction meaning (*go* for verb-locative, *put* for verb-object-locative, and *give* for the ditransitive). Likewise for L2A, Ellis and Ferreira-Junior (2009a) showed that the verbs first used by L2 learners are prototypical and generic in function: *go* dominates in the verb-locative construction

(*She went home*), *put* in the verb-object-locative construction (*She put the groceries in the bag*), and *give* in the verb-object-object construction (*He gave her a flower*).

3.6. Contingency of form-function mapping

Psychological research on associative learning has long recognized that next to the form and the function of a given exemplar to be categorized and learned, the contingency of the form-function mapping plays a role as well (Shanks 1995). Let us return to the example of the category BIRD. All birds have eyes and wings, and so we encounter these features equally frequently. However, while many other animals have eyes, only birds have wings. That renders wings a much more reliable (or *distinctive*) cue to membership in the category BIRD than eyes. In other words, whether or not a given exemplar qualifies as a bird is much more contingent on its having the features "wings" than the feature "eyes". Such form-function mapping contingency is the driving force of all associative learning, which is often correspondingly referred to as *contingency learning*. One early powerful demonstration of contingency learning was Rescorla's (1968) classic conditioning study with rats. Rescorla found that if one removed the contingency between the conditioned stimulus and the unconditioned stimulus by preserving the temporal pairing between the two, yet adding trials where the unconditioned stimulus appeared on its own, the animals did not develop a conditioned response to the conditioned stimulus. Contingency, and its associated aspects of predictive value, information gain, and statistical association, have been at the core of learning theory ever since, including theories of L2A such as MacWhinney's *Competition Model* (MacWhinney 1987a, 1987b, 1997, 2001). Current research in cognitive and corpus linguistics focuses on the question which specific association measures are most predictive of linguistic representation, acquisition, and processing (Divjak and Gries 2012; Gries and Divjak 2012). Several studies have applied a Fisher Yates exact test as a measure of contingency of verb-complement construction pairings (Gries and Wulff 2009) and verb-tense/aspect morphology associations in learner data (Wulff et al. 2009); Ellis and Ferreira-Junior (2009b) used a directional association measure, DeltaP, to demonstrate effects of form-function contingency on the L2 acquisition of verb argument constructions (see Ellis 2006 for the use of this measure in research in human associative learning, Schmid 2010 supporting its use as a proxy for cognitive entrenchment, and Gries 2013 for its applications in collocation research); Boyd and Goldberg (2009) used conditional probabilities to analyze contingency effects in their L1A data of verb argument constructions. For a comprehensive contrastive analysis of corpus-based association measures and their correlation with behavioral data, see Wiechmann (2008).

4. First vs. second language learning: (re-)constructing a language

Countless studies in cognitive linguistics have demonstrated that language is grounded in our experience and our physical embodiment (Langacker 1987, 2000; Taylor 2002, Croft and Cruse 2004; Robinson and Ellis 2008b). The meaning of words in a given language, and how speakers combine them, depends on speakers' perception and categorization of, and interaction with, the real world around them. How speakers perceive, categorize, and interact with their environment is in turn a function of the human cognitive apparatus and bodily make-up. For example, the meaning of verbs like *push*, *poke*, *pull*, *hold* and so on, can only be fully distinguished if the sensori-motor features they encode, like hand posture, hand motions, force, aspect, and goals are taken into consideration (Bailey et al. 1997; Bergen and Chang 2005; Lakoff and Johnson 1999; Feldman 2006). Similarly, spatial language understanding is firmly grounded in our visual processing system as it relates to motor action (Regier and Carlson 2002; Conventry and Garrod 2004), multiple constraints relating to our knowledge about objects, dynamic-kinematic routines, and functional geometric analyses. What prepositions like *under*, *over*, *in*, or *on* mean is not fixed and steady, but dynamically construed on-line (Elman 2004; Spivey 2006; McRae et al. 2006). How exactly a given meaning is construed depends in large parts on where the language user's attention is being directed. Talmy (2000a, 2000b) describes the building blocks of the attentional system of language; each of around 50 building blocks, or factors, involves a particular linguistic mechanism that increases or decreases attention of a certain type of linguistic entity. Learning a language, then, means learning these various attention-directing mechanisms, which requires L1 learners to develop an attentional system in the first place, and L2 learners to reconfigure the attentional biases of having acquired their first language. In consequence, language cannot be taught through rules or rote-learning alone – ideally, it is learned in situated action.

Languages lead their speakers to experience different 'thinking for speaking' and thus to construe experience in different ways (Slobin 1996). Cross-linguistic research shows how different languages lead speakers to prioritize different aspects of events in narrative discourse (Berman and Slobin 1994). Because languages achieve these attention-directing outcomes in different ways, learning another language involves learning how to construe the world like natives of the L2, i.e., learning alternative ways of thinking for speaking (Cadierno 2008; Brown and Gullberg 2008, 2010) or 'rethinking for speaking' (Ellis and Cadierno 2009; Robinson and Ellis 2008a). Transfer theories such as the Contrastive Analysis Hypothesis (Lado 1957, 1964; James 1980, Gass and Selinker 1983) hold that L2A can be easier where languages use these attention-directing devices in the same way, and more difficult when they use them differently. To the extent that the constructions in L2 are similar to those of L1, L1 constructions can serve as the basis for the L2 constructions, but, because even similar constructions across languages differ in detail, the complete acquisition of the L2 pattern is hindered by the L1 pattern (Odlin 1989, 2008).

As Slobin (1993: 242) notes, "For the child, the construction of the grammar and the construction of semantic/pragmatic concepts go hand-in-hand. For the adult, construction of the grammar often requires a revision of semantic/pragmatic concepts, along with what may well be a more difficult task of perceptual identification of the relevant morphological elements". The human mind is built to integrate new information in a way that is maximally compatible with established knowledge – consequently, L1-attuned expectations and selective attention bias L2 acquisition.

5. Future priorities

Robinson and Ellis (2008b) provide a detailed list of issues in cognitive linguistics and L2 acquisition; we highlight just a few here.

A constructionist perspective, in particular, calls for thorough empirical analysis of language usage. This is the evidence from which learners induce how language works. We need to understand its latent structures. O'Donnell and Ellis (2010) and Römer et al. (2013) outline a proposal to describe a usage-based verbal grammar of English, to analyze the ways verb argument constructions map form and meaning, and to provide an inventory of the verbs that exemplify constructions, their lexical constituency, and their frequencies.

A constructionist perspective also calls for thorough empirical analysis of the syntactic and semantic bootstrapping of constructions. Given the demonstrated value of longitudinal corpus research in child language acquisition, corresponding corpora of L2A are needed that allow researchers to empirically investigate the adult L2A comprehensively, longitudinally, and cross-linguistically (Ortega and Iberri-Shea 2005; Collins and Ellis 2009).

The cognitive commitment we emphasize throughout this chapter demands converging evidence from corpus data and behavioral data (Ellis 2012a; Gries 2012). Only in combination will we be able to fully understand the interplay of input and cognition in shaping L2A. This holds in particular for recent discussions of the nature and relevance of frequency and form-function contingency effects in language acquisition.

Cognitive linguistics emphasizes how multiple factors at different scales jointly affect L2 acquisition: cognition, consciousness, experience, embodiment, brain, self, human interaction, society, culture, and history are all inextricably intertwined in rich, complex, and dynamic ways. Researching how these diverse factors interact dynamically in the emergence of linguistic structure will remain a priority and a challenge for some time to come. Ellis and Larsen-Freeman (2009a) provide an illustration of how computer simulations can inform this question for argument structure constructions. More generally, emergentism, complex adaptive systems theory, dynamic systems theory, exemplar theory, and related approaches provide means for modeling language development and language as a complex adaptive system (Ellis and Larsen-Freeman 2006a, 2006b, 2009b; Ellis 2008a; Beckner et al. 2009). Cognitive-linguistic and broader usage-based approaches have done much to inform our understanding of L2A. Nevertheless, the research agenda is long. Much remains to be done, both locally and within the still broader family of the cognitive sciences.

6. References

Ambridge, Ben and Elena Lieven
    2011   *Child Language Acquisition: Contrasting Theoretical Approaches.* Cambridge: Cambridge University Press.

Anderson, John R.
    1989   A rational analysis of human memory. In: E. Tulving, H. L. Roediger and F. I. M. Craik (eds.), *Varieties of Memory and Consciousness: Essays in Honour of Endel Tulving*, 195–210. Hillsdale: Lawrence Erlbaum.

Anderson, John R. and Lael J. Schooler
    2000   The adaptive nature of memory. In: E. Tulving and F. I. M. Craik (eds.), *The Oxford Handbook of Memory*, 557–570. London: Oxford University Press.

Bailey, David, Jerome Feldman, Srini Narayanan and George Lakoff
    1997   Modelling embodied lexical development. *Chicago Linguistics Society* 19: 19–24.

Bardovi-Harlig, Kathleen
   2000   *Tense and Aspect in Second Language Acquisition: Form, Meaning, and Use.* Oxford: Blackwell.

Bardovi-Harlig, Kathleen
   2002   A new starting point? *Studies in Second Language Acquisition* 24: 189−198.

Beckner, Clay, Richard Blythe, Joan Bybee, Morton H. Christiansen, William Croft, Nick C. Ellis, John Holland, Jinyun Ke, Diane Larsen-Freeman and Thomas Schoenemann
   2009   Language is a complex adaptive system. *Language Learning* 59: 1−26.

Behrens, Heike (ed.)
   2008   *Corpora in Language Acquisition Research: Finding Structure in Data.* Amsterdam: John Benjamins.

Behrens, Heike
   2009   Usage-based and emergentist approaches to language acquisition. *Linguistics* 47: 383−411.

Bergen, Benjamin and Nancy Chang
   2005   Embodied construction grammar in simulation-based language understanding. In: J. Östman and M. Fried (eds.), *Construction Grammars: Cognitive Grounding and Theoretical Extensions*, 147−190. Amsterdam: John Benjamins.

Berman, Ruth A. and Dan I. Slobin (eds.)
   1994   *Relating Events in Narrative: A Crosslinguistic Developmental Study.* Hillsdale: Lawrence Erlbaum.

Boyd, Jeremy K. and Adele E. Goldberg
   2009   Input effects within a constructionist framework. *Modern Language Journal* 93: 418−429.

Brown, Amanda and Marianne Gullberg
   2010   Changes in encoding of path of motion after acquisition of a second language. *Cognitive Linguistics* 21: 263−286.

Brown, Amanda and Marianne Gullberg
   2008   Bidirectional crosslinguistic influence in L1-L2 encoding of manner in speech and gesture. *Studies in Second Language Acquisition* 30: 225−251.

Brown, Roger
   1973   *A First Language.* Cambridge: Harvard University Press.

Bybee, Joan
   2006   *Frequency of Use and the Organization of Language.* Oxford: Oxford University Press.

Bybee, Joan and Paul Hopper (eds.)
   2001   *Frequency and the Emergence of Linguistic Structure.* Amsterdam: John Benjamins.

Bybee, Joan
   2010   *Language, Usage, and Cognition.* Cambridge: Cambridge University Press.

Cadierno, Teresa
   2008   Learning to talk about motion in a foreign language. In: P. Robinson and N. C. Ellis (eds.), *Handbook of Cognitive Linguistics and Second Language Acquisition*, 239−275. London: Routledge.

Collins, Laura and Nick. C. Ellis (eds.)
   2009   Input and second language construction learning: Frequency, form, and function. *Modern Language Journal* 93.

Conklin, Kathy and Norbert Schmitt
   2007   Formulaic sequences: Are they processed more quickly than nonformulaic language by native and nonnative speakers? *Applied Linguistics* 28: 1−18.

Corder, S. Pit
   1973   *Introducing Applied Linguistics.* New York: Penguin.

Coventry, Kenny R. and Simon C. Garrod
    2004   *Saying, Seeing and Acting: The Psychological Semantics of Spatial Prepositions.* Hove/ New York: Psychology Press.
Croft, William and Alan D. Cruse
    2004   *Cognitive Linguistics.* Cambridge: Cambridge University Press.
Dąbrowska, Ewa
    2004   *Language, Mind and Brain: Some Psychological and Neurological Constraints on Theories of Grammar.* Edinburgh: Edinburgh University Press.
Dąbrowska, Ewa and Elena Lieven
    2005   Towards a lexically specific grammar of children's question constructions. *Cognitive Linguistics* 16: 437–474.
Diessel, Holger
    2013   Construction grammar and first language acquisition. In G. Trousdale and T. Hoffmann (eds.), *The Oxford Handbook of Construction Grammar*, 347–364. Oxford: Oxford University Press.
Dietrich, Rainer, Wolfgang Klein and Colette Noyau (eds.)
    1995   *The Acquisition of Temporality in a Second Language.* Amsterdam: John Benjamins.
Divjak, Dagmar and Catherine Cardwell-Harris
    this volume   Frequency and entrenchment. Berlin/Boston: De Gruyter Mouton.
Divjak, Dagmar S. and Stefan Th. Gries (eds.)
    2012   *Frequency Effects in Language Representation.* Berlin/New York: Mouton de Gruyter.
Elio, Renee and John R. Anderson
    1981   The effects of category generalizations and instance similarity on schema abstraction. *Journal of Experimental Psychology: Human Learning and Memory* 7: 397–417.
Elio, Renee and John R. Anderson
    1984   The effects of information order and learning mode on schema abstraction. *Memory and Cognition* 12: 20–30.
Ellis, Nick C.
    1996   Sequencing in SLA: Phonological memory, chunking, and points of order. *Studies in Second Language Acquisition* 18: 91–126.
Ellis, Nick C.
    1998   Emergentism, connectionism and language learning. *Language Learning* 48: 631–664.
Ellis, Nick C.
    2002   Frequency effects in language processing: A review with implications for theories of implicit and explicit language acquisition. *Studies in Second Language Acquisition* 24: 143–188.
Ellis, Nick C.
    2003   Constructions, chunking, and connectionism: The emergence of second language structure. In: C. J. Doughty and M. H. Long (eds.), *Handbook of Second Language Acquisition*, 33–68. Oxford: Blackwell.
Ellis, Nick C.
    2006   Language acquisition as rational contingency learning. *Applied Linguistics* 27: 1–24.
Ellis, Nick C.
    2008a   Usage-based and form-focused language acquisition: The associative learning of constructions, learned-attention, and the limited L2 endstate. In: P. Robinson and N. C. Ellis (eds.), *Handbook of Cognitive Linguistics and Second Language Acquisition*, 372–405. London: Routledge.
Ellis, Nick C.
    2008b   Optimizing the input: Frequency and sampling in usage-based and form-focussed learning. In: M. H. Long and C. J. Doughty (eds.), *Handbook of Second and Foreign Language Teaching*, 139–158. Oxford: Blackwell.

Ellis, Nick C.
   2008c   Phraseology: The periphery and the heart of language. In: F. Meunier and S. Granger (eds.), *Phraseology in Language Learning and Teaching*, 1–13. Amsterdam: John Benjamins.

Ellis, Nick C.
   2011   The emergence of language as a complex adaptive system. In: J. Simpson (ed.), *Handbook of Applied Linguistics*, 666–679. London: Routledge/Taylor Francis.

Ellis, Nick C.
   2012a   Formulaic language and second language acquisition: Zipf and the phrasal teddy bear. *Annual Review of Applied Linguistics* 32: 17–44.

Ellis, Nick C.
   2012b   What can we count in language, and what counts in language acquisition, cognition, and use? In: S. Th. Gries and D. S. Divjak (eds.), *Frequency Effects in Language Learning and Processing*, 7–34. Berlin: Mouton de Gruyter.

Ellis, Nick C. and Diane Larsen Freeman (eds.)
   2006a   Language emergence: Implications for Applied Linguistics. *Applied Linguistics* 27.

Ellis, Nick C. and Diane Larsen Freeman
   2006b   Language emergence: Implications for Applied Linguistics (Introduction to the Special Issue). *Applied Linguistics* 27: 558–589.

Ellis, Nick C. and Diane Larsen-Freeman
   2009a   Constructing a second language: Analyses and computational simulations of the emergence of linguistic constructions from usage. *Language Learning* 59: 93–128.

Ellis, Nick C. and Diane Larsen Freeman (eds.)
   2009b   Language as a complex adaptive system. *Language Learning* 59.

Ellis, Nick C. and Fernando Ferreira-Junior
   2009a   Construction learning as a function of frequency, frequency distribution, and function. *Modern Language Journal* 93: 370–386.

Ellis, Nick C. and Fernando Ferreira-Junior
   2009b   Constructions and their acquisition: Islands and the distinctiveness of their occupancy. *Annual Review of Cognitive Linguistics* 7: 188–221.

Ellis, Nick C. and Matthew B. O'Donnell
   2012   Statistical construction learning: Does a Zipfian problem space ensure robust language learning? In P. Rebuschat and J. N. Williams (eds.), *Statistical Learning and Language Acquisition*, 265–304. Berlin: Mouton de Gruyter.

Ellis, Nick C. and Nuria Sagarra
   2010a   Learned attention effects in L2 temporal reference: The first hour and the next eight semesters. *Language Learning* 60: 85–108.

Ellis, Nick C. and Nuria Sagarra
   2010b   The bounds of adult language acquisition: Blocking and learned attention. *Studies in Second Language Acquisition* 32: 1–28.

Ellis, Nick C. and Nuria Sagarra
   2011   Blocking and learned attention in adult language acquisition: A replication and generalization study and meta-analysis. *Studies in Second Language Acquisition* 33: 589–624.

Ellis, Nick C. and Rita Simpson-Vlach
   2009   Formulaic language in native speakers: Triangulating psycholinguistics, corpus linguistics, and education. *Corpus Linguistics and Linguistic Theory* 5: 61–78.

Ellis, Nick C., Rita Simpson-Vlach and Carson Maynard
   2008   Formulaic language in native and second-language speakers: Psycholinguistics, corpus linguistics, and TESOL. *TESOL Quarterly* 42: 375–396.

Ellis, Nick C. and Teresa Cadierno (eds.)
   2009   Constructing a second language. Special section. *Annual Review of Cognitive Linguistics* 7: 111–290.

Ellis, Rod
1984 *Classroom Second Language Development*. Oxford: Pergamon.
Elman, Jeffrey L.
1990 Finding structure in time. *Cognitive Science* 14: 179–211.
Elman, Jeffrey L.
2004 An alternative view of the mental lexicon. *Trends in Cognitive Science* 8: 301–306.
Eskildsen, Søren W.
2009 Constructing another language – usage-based linguistics in second language acquisition. *Applied Linguistics* 30: 335–357.
Eskildsen, Søren W. and Teresa Cadierno
2007 Are recurring multi-word expressions really syntactic freezes? Second language acquisition from the perspective of usage-based linguistics. In: M. Nenonen and S. Niemi (eds.), *Collocations and Idioms 1: Papers from the First Nordic Conference on Syntactic Freezes*, 86–99. Joensuu: Joensuu University Press.
Feldman, Jerome A.
2006 *From Molecule to Metaphor: A Neural Theory of Language*. Boston: MIT Press.
Gass, Susan M. and Larry Selinker (eds.)
1983 *Language Transfer in Language Learning*. Rowley: Newbury House.
Goldberg, Adele E., Devin M. Casenhiser and Nitya Sethuraman
2004 Learning argument structure generalizations. *Cognitive Linguistics* 15: 289–316.
Goldschneider, Jennifer M. and Robert DeKeyser
2001 Explaining the "natural order of L2 morpheme acquisition" in English: A meta-analysis of multiple determinants. *Language Learning* 51: 1–50.
Granger, Sylviane
2001 Prefabricated patterns in Advanced EFL writing: Collocations and formulae. In: A. P. Cowie (ed.), *Phraseology: Theory, Analysis, and Applications*, 145–160. Oxford: Oxford University Press.
Gries, Stefan Th.
2012 Corpus linguistics, theoretical linguistics, and cognitive/psycholinguistics: Towards more and more fruitful exchanges. In: J. Mukherjee and M. Huber (eds.), *Corpus Linguistics and Variation in English: Theory and Description*, 41–63. Amsterdam: Rodopi.
Gries, Stefan Th.
2013 50-something years of work on collocations: What is or should be next. *International Journal of Corpus Linguistics* 18(1): 137–165.
Gries, Stefan Th. and Dagmar S. Divjak (eds.)
2012 *Frequency Effects in Language Learning and Processing*. Berlin/New York: Mouton de Gruyter.
Gries, Stefan Th. and Stefanie Wulff
2005 Do foreign language learners also have constructions? Evidence from priming, sorting, and corpora. *Annual Review of Cognitive Linguistics* 3: 182–200.
Gries, Stefan Th. and Stefanie Wulff
2009 Psycholinguistic and corpus linguistic evidence for L2 constructions. *Annual Review of Cognitive Linguistics* 7: 163–186.
Hakuta, Kenji
1974 Prefabricated patterns and the emergence of structure in second language acquisition. *Language Learning* 24: 287–97.
Hakuta, Kenji
1976 A case study of a Japanese child learning English. *Language Learning* 26: 321–51.
Hanania, Edith A. S. and Harry L. Gradman
1977 Acquisition of English structures: A case study of an adult native speaker of Arabic in an English-speaking environment. *Language Learning* 27: 75–91.

Hatch, Evelyn
  1972   Some studies in language learning. *UCLA Working Papers in Teaching English as a Second Language* 6: 29–36.
Hauser, Marc D., Noam A. Chomsky and W. Tecumseh Fitch
  2002   The faculty of language: What is it, who has it, and how did it evolve? *Science* 298: 1569–1579.
Hopper, Paul J.
  1987   Emergent grammar. *Berkeley Linguistics Society* 13: 139–157.
Jackendoff, Ray
  2011   What is the human language faculty? *Language* 87: 587–624.
James, Carl
  1980   *Contrastive Analysis*. London: Longman.
Jiang, Nan A. N., and Tatiana M. Nekrasova
  2007   The Processing of formulaic sequences by second language speakers. *The Modern Language Journal* 91: 433–445.
Kiss, George R.
  1973   Grammatical word classes: A learning process and its simulation. *The Psychology of Learning and Motivation* 7: 1–41.
Klein, Wolfgang and Clive Perdue
  1992   *Utterance Structure: Developing Grammars Again*. Amsterdam: John Benjamins.
Krashen, Stephen and Robin C. Scarcella
  1978   On routines and patterns in language acquisition and performance. *Language Learning* 28: 283–300.
Lado, Robert
  1957   *Linguistics Across Cultures: Applied Linguistics for Language Teachers*. Ann Arbor: University of Michigan Press.
Lado, Robert
  1964   *Language Teaching: A Scientific Approach*. New York: McGraw-Hill.
Lakoff, George and Mark Johnson
  1999   *Philosophy in the Flesh: The Embodied Mind and Its Challenge to Western Thought*. New York: Basic Books.
Langacker, Ronald W.
  1987   *Foundations of Cognitive Grammar*, Volume 1: *Theoretical Prerequisites*. Stanford: Stanford University Press.
Langacker, Ronald W.
  2000   A dynamic usage-based model. In: M. Barlow and S. Kemmer (eds.), *Usage-based Models of Language*, 1–63. Stanford: CSLI Publications.
Liang, John
  2002   Sentence comprehension by Chinese Learners of English: Verb centered or construction-based. M.A. dissertation, Guangdong University of Foreign Studies.
Lieven, Elena V. M., Heike Behrens, Jennifer Speares and Michael Tomasello
  2003   Early syntactic creativity: A usage based approach. *Journal of Child Language* 30: 333–370.
Littlemore, Jeanette
  2009   *Applying Cognitive Linguistics to Second Language Learning and Teaching*. Basingstoke/New York: Palgrave Macmillan.
MacWhinney, Brian
  1987a   Applying the Competition Model to bilingualism. *Applied Psycholinguistics* 8: 315–327.
MacWhinney, Brian
  1987b   The Competition Model. In: B. MacWhinney (ed.), *Mechanisms of Language Acquisition*, 249–308. Hillsdale: Lawrence Erlbaum.

MacWhinney, Brian
　1997　Second language acquisition and the Competition Model. In: A. M. B. de Groot and J. F. Kroll (eds.), *Tutorials in Bilingualism: Psycholinguistic Perspectives*, 113–142. Mahwah: Lawrence Erlbaum Associates.

MacWhinney, Brian
　2001　The competition model: The input, the context, and the brain. In: P. Robinson (ed.), *Cognition and Second language Instruction*, 69–90. New York: Cambridge University Press.

Maslen, Robert, Anna L. Theakston, Elena V. M. Lieven, and Michael Tomasello
　2004　A dense corpus study of past tense and plural overgeneralizations in English. *Journal of Speech, Language, and Hearing Research* 47: 1319–1333.

Matthews, Danielle and Grzegorz Krajewski
　this volume　First language acquisition.

McDonough, Kim
　2006　Interaction and syntactic priming: English L2 speakers' production of dative constructions. *Studies in Second Language Acquisition* 28: 179–207.

McDonough, Kim and Alison Mackey
　2006　Responses to recasts: Repetitions, primed production and linguistic development. *Language Learning* 56: 693–720.

McDonough, Kim and Pavel Trofimovich
　2008　*Using Priming Methods in Second Language Research*. London: Routledge.

McRae, Ken, Mary Hare, Jeffrey L. Elman and Todd Ferretti
　2006　A basis for generating expectancies for verbs from nouns. *Memory and Cognition* 33: 1174–1184.

Mellow, J. Dean
　2008　The emergence of complex syntax: A longitudinal case study of the ESL development of dependency resolution. *Lingua* 118: 499–521.

Mintz, Tobias
　2003　Frequent frames as a cue for grammatical categories in child directed speech. *Cognition* 90: 91–117.

Myles, Florence
　2004　From data to theory: The over-representation of linguistic knowledge in SLA. *Transactions of the Philological Society* 102: 139–168.

Myles, Florence, Mitchell, Rosamond, and Janet Hooper
　1999　Interrogative chunks in French L2: A basis for creative construction. *Studies in Second Language Acquisition* 21: 49–80.

Ninio, Anat
　1999　Pathbreaking verbs in syntactic development and the question of prototypical transitivity. *Journal of Child Language* 26: 619–653.

Ninio, Anat
　2006　*Language and the Learning Curve: A New Theory of Syntactic Development*. Oxford: Oxford University Press.

Nosofsky, Robert M.
　1988　Similarity, frequency, and category representations. *Journal of Experimental Psychology: Learning, Memory, and Cognition* 14: 54–65.

O'Donnell, Matt and Nick C. Ellis
　2010　Towards an inventory of English verb argument constructions. *Proceedings of the NAACL HLT Workshop on Extracting and Using Constructions in Computational Linguistics*: 9–16.

Odlin, Terence
　1989　*Language Transfer*. New York: Cambridge University Press.

Odlin, Terence
   2008   Conceptual transfer and meaning extensions. In: P. Robinson and N. C. Ellis (eds.), *Handbook of Cognitive Linguistics and Second Language Acquisition*, 306–340. Ellis. London: Routledge.

Ortega, Lourdes and Gina Iberri-Shea
   2005   Longitudinal research in second language acquisition: Recent trends and future directions. *Annual Review of Applied Linguistics* 25: 26–45.

Pawley, Andrew and Frances H. Syder
   1983   Two puzzles for linguistic theory: Native-like selection and native-like fluency. In: J. C. Richards and R. W. Schmidt (eds.), *Language and Communication*, 191–226. New York: Longman.

Perdue, Clive (ed.)
   1993   *Adult Language Acquisition*: *Cross-linguistic Perspectives*. Cambridge: Cambridge University Press.

Peters, Anne M.
   1983   *The Units of Language Acquisition*. New York: Cambridge University Press.

Posner, Michael I. and Steven W. Keele
   1970   Retention of abstract ideas. *Journal of Experimental Psychology* 83: 304–308.

Rebuschat, Patrick and John N. Williams (eds.)
   2012   *Statistical Learning and Language Acquisition*. Berlin: Mouton de Gruyter.

Redington, Martin and Nick Chater
   1998   Connectionist and statistical approaches to language acquisition: A distributional perspective. *Language and Cognitive Processes* 13: 129–192.

Regier, Terry and Laura Carlson
   2002   Spatial language: Perceptual constraints and linguistic variation. In: J. Matter Mandler, P. J. Bauer and M. Rabinowitz (eds.), *Representation, Memory, and Development*: *Essays in Honor of Jean Mandler*, 199–221. Mahwah, NJ: Lawrence Erlbaum.

Rescorla, Robert A.
   1968   Probability of shock in the presence and absence of CS in fear conditioning. *Journal of Comparative and Physiological Psychology* 66: 1–5.

Rescorla, Robert A. and Allen R. Wagner
   1972   A theory of Pavlovian conditioning: Variations in the effectiveness of reinforcement and nonreinforcement. In: A. H. Black and W. F. Prokasy (eds.), *Classical Conditioning II*: *Current Theory and Research*, 64–99. New York: Appleton-Century-Crofts.

Robinson, Peter and Nick C. Ellis
   2008a   Conclusion: Cognitive linguistics, second language acquisition and L2 instruction – issues for research. In: P. Robinson and N. C. Ellis (eds.), *Handbook of Cognitive Linguistics and Second Language Acquisition*, 489–546. London: Routledge.

Robinson, Peter and Nick C. Ellis (eds.)
   2008b   *Handbook of Cognitive Linguistics and Second Language Acquisition*. London: Routledge.

Römer, Ute, Matthew B. O'Donnell and Nick C. Ellis
   2015   Using COBUILD grammar patterns for a large-scale analysis of verb-argument constructions: Exploring corpus data and speaker knowledge. In: M. Charles, N. Groom and S. John (eds.), *Corpora, Grammar, Text and Discourse*: *In Honour of Susan Hunston*. Amsterdam: John Benjamins.

Rosch, Eleanor and Carolyn B. Mervis
   1975   Cognitive representations of semantic categories. *Journal of Experimental Psychology*: *General* 104: 192–233.

Rosch, Eleanor, Carolyn B. Mervis, Wayne D. Gray, David M. Johnson and Penny Boyes-Braem
   1976   Basic objects in natural categories. *Cognitive Psychology* 8: 382–439.

Schmid, Hans-Jörg
   2010   Does frequency in text instantiate entrenchment in the cognitive system? In: D. Glynn and K. Fischer (eds.), *Quantitative Methods in Cognitive Semantics*: *Corpus-Driven Approaches*, 101–133. Berlin/New York: Mouton de Gruyter.

Schmidt, Richard W.
   1983   Interaction, acculturation, and the acquisition of communicative competence: A case study of an adult. In: N. Wolfson and E. Judd (eds.), *Sociolinguistics and Language Acquisition*, 137–174. Rowley: Newbury House.

Schumann, John H.
   1978   Second language acquisition: the pidginization hypothesis. In: E. M. Hatch (ed.), *Second Language Acquisition*: *A Book of Readings*, 256–271. Rowley: Newbury House.

Shanks, David R.
   1995   *The Psychology of Associative Learning*. New York: Cambridge University Press.

Simpson-Vlach, Rita and Nick C. Ellis
   2010   An Academic Formulas List (AFL). *Applied Linguistics* 31: 487–512.

Slobin, Dan I.
   1993   Adult language acquisition: A view from child language study. In: C. Perdue (ed.), *Adult Language Acquisition*: *Cross-Linguistic Perspectives*, 239–252. Cambridge: Cambridge University Press.

Slobin, Dan I.
   1996   From "thought and language" to "thinking for speaking". In: J. J. Gumperz and S. C. Levinson (eds.), *Rethinking Linguistic Relativity*, 70–96. Cambridge: Cambridge University Press.

Spivey, Michael
   2006   *The Continuity of Mind*. Oxford: Oxford University Press.

Sugaya, N. and Yas Shirai
   2009   Can L2 learners productively use Japanese tense-aspect markers? A usage-based approach. In: R. Corrigan, E. A. Moravcsik, H. Ouali and K. M. Wheatley (eds.), *Formulaic language*, Volume 2: *Acquisition, Loss, Psychological Reality, Functional Applications*, 423–444. Amsterdam: John Benjamins.

Talmy, Leonard
   2000a   *Toward a Cognitive Semantics*: *Concept Structuring Systems*. Cambridge: MIT Press.

Talmy, Leonard
   2000b   *Toward a Cognitive Semantics*: *Typology and Process in Concept Structuring*. Cambridge: MIT Press.

Taylor, John. R.
   2002   *Cognitive Grammar*. Oxford: Oxford University Press.

Tomasello, Michael
   1992   *First Verbs*: *A Case Study of Early Grammatical Development*. New York: Cambridge University Press.

Tomasello, Michael
   2000   The item based nature of children's early syntactic development. *Trends in Cognitive Sciences* 4: 156–163.

Tomasello, Michael
   2003   *Constructing a Language*. Boston: Harvard University Press.

Tomasello, Michael and Daniel Stahl
   2004   Sampling children's spontaneous speech: How much is enough? *Journal of Child Language* 31: 101–121.

Trousdale, Graeme and Thomas Hoffmann (eds.)
   2013   *Oxford Handbook of Construction Grammar*. Oxford: Oxford University Press.

Tyler, Andrea
   2012   *Cognitive Linguistics and Second Language Learning*. London: Routledge.

VanPatten, Bill
   2006   Input processing in adult SLA. In: B. VanPatten and J. Williams (eds.), *Theories in Second Language Acquisition: An Introduction*, 115–135. Mahwah: Lawrence Erlbaum.

Wiechmann, Daniel
   2008   On the computation of collostruction strength. *Corpus Linguistics and Linguistic Theory* 4: 253–290.

Wong-Fillmore, Lilly
   1976   *The second time around*: Cognitive and social strategies in second language acquisition. PhD dissertation, Stanford University.

Wray, Alison
   2002   *Formulaic Language and the Lexicon*. Cambridge: Cambridge University Press.

Wulff, Stefanie and Stefan Th. Gries
   2011   Corpus-driven methods for assessing accuracy in learner production. In: P. Robinson (ed.), *Second Language Task Complexity: Researching the Cognition Hypothesis of Language Learning and Performance*, 61–88. Amsterdam/Philadelphia: John Benjamins.

Wulff, Stefanie, Nick C. Ellis, Ute Römer, Kathleen Bardovi-Harlig and Chelsea LeBlanc
   2009   The acquisition of tense-aspect: Converging evidence from corpora, cognition, and learner constructions. *Modern Language Journal* 93: 354–369.

Zipf, George K.
   1935   *The Psycho-Biology of Language: An Introduction to Dynamic Philology*. Cambridge: MIT Press.

Nick C. Ellis, Michigan (USA)
Stefanie Wulff, Florida (USA)

20. Poetics

1. Linguistics and literature
2. Precursors to a cognitive poetics
3. Cognition and literature
4. Developments in cognitive poetics
5. Futures
6. References

1. Linguistics and literature

The study of literature and culture has often proceeded in philosophical or thematic terms, influenced at different moments in history by an emphasis on sociology, anthropology or history itself. Currently in most university and college departments of literature across the world, the paradigm of discussion falls within a broad cultural studies, and we live in these early decades of the 21st century in one of the periodic moments in which the fact that literary texts are written in language is a relatively neglected notion. However, there has always been a thread running consistently through human intellectual development which has explored the workings of language both in its outward or recorded form (speech, writing, screen text) and in its inward manifestation (introspection, cognition and neuroscience). Most recently, this thread of interest in language has been finding expression once again in the study of literature, in a form variously known as *cognitive poetics, cognitive stylistics* or a generally *cognitive approach to literature*.

Literature is the most culturally highly valued form of language. It is usually regarded as being fixed in form as writing or public inscription, though there is a closely associated performative aspect that allows drama, theatre and readings aloud of poetry and prose to be encompassed within the notion of the literary. Hybrid forms blending poetry and graphic art, recitation and dance, and even quotation within architecture and horticulture can be regarded as even less prototypical examples. However, the normative historical perception of literature as writing on paper has encouraged a view of literary analysis in mainly formalist terms, whenever over time literature has been discussed for its language. The parameters of *language*, in other words, have been restricted to the boundaries of the physical text in most linguistic traditions of literary analysis. Aspects of language that a non-formalist might consider inherently part of the language system would include both the immediate and general social and ideological context, creative authorial perception and motivation, and the processes and predilections of a reader or reading community.

In the most famous statement of formalist literary analysis, Wimsatt and Beardsley (1954a, 1954b) set prescriptions against discussions of authorial intention on the one hand and against the psychology of the reader on the other. It must be borne in mind that Wimsatt and Beardsley and the whole New Critical movement of which they were a part were reacting to the worst sort of loose biographical musing and flowery speculation on readers and reading that served for much literary "debate" and "analysis" in those days. And the absurd and groundless treatments of literary authors in terms of their imagined psychoanalytical motivations or their assumed experiences and memories remain unfortunately a feature of the contemporary literary critical scene even today. However, the reaction against the extreme nonsense of the 1930s and '40s produced its own extremism: a bar on any consideration of psychology even when discussing readerly reactions; an assumption that aesthetic effects and meanings were purely the preserve of a text without reference to its reader; a literary work divorced from the integral culture of its language and the cognitive models and schemas that informed it.

Where much literary criticism in the latter part of the 20th century – especially in the US – headed off into abstraction and generalisation about language, other, more linguistically-focused traditions such as *stylistics* retained a formalist approach overall. Stylistics (arising mainly in France as *stylistique*, Germany as *stilistik*, and in Britain within applied linguistics) took a firmly delimited approach from linguistics to literary texts. It seems likely that this self-imposed constraint not to consider context alongside text was a contrastive reaction to literary critical theory's evasion of textuality altogether. The prohibitions of New Criticism still weighed heavily for stylisticians. And the nature of the linguistic toolkit available at the time led perhaps inevitably towards a focus on aspects of language up the rank-scale towards but not really including text linguistics and discourse analysis. For some, "linguistics" itself was a term that dealt only and single-mindedly with the rank-structure from phonology and phonetics and morphology and lexicology to semantics and syntax; even pragmatics, not to mention text and textuality, discourse and sociolinguistic matters, were regarded as extra-linguistic areas.

As stylistics evolved in the European tradition, the nature of its development has been a steady re-engagement with context, framed within a similarly rigorous and systematic methodology. Models from pragmatics, insights from sociolinguistics and discourse analysis, and the most recent advances in computerised corpus linguistics have enriched stylistics over the past few decades. The cognitive turn in the arts and humanities has been especially influential in stylistics, where there is no question it has been the main conduit for insights from cognitive science into literary studies. Today, the enrichment of literary studies by a cognitive poetics is a feature of literary research internationally. There are several different strands within this emerging but increasingly influential tradition, and several different angles on cognitive science that are taken by different areas of literary studies for different purposes, but it is becoming apparent that many of the concerns that literary critics and commentators have struggled to express inarticulately and in an ill-disciplined way are amenable to a rigorous cognitive poetics. In this chapter I will set out some of this variety, while also arguing for the sort of necessary focus on language textuality and texture that has served stylistics so well.

The study of literature is an important area within cognitive science. Literature is the most prestigious form of language in use. It is both highly culturally valued (as "Literature") and widely influential (as "literature" in all the demotic forms of popular lyrics and verses, formula fiction, trashy novels, soap operas, favourite good-reads and personal self-published stories and poetry blogs). Literary analysis reaches from the considered and disciplined work of professional literary critics and commentators in scholarly articles and the literary press right into the online reviews of books and reading groups, lists of favourites and all manner of informal observations on literature through the ages. Literary analysis, in short, has often been the territory on which more general discussions of language forms and effects have been conducted. Literary works themselves often incorporate particularly subtle features of everyday discourse, as well as features at the experimental edges of what is possible in language; the proper study of literary language – in all its fully contextualised diversity – offers the opportunity for cognitive scientists to understand human communication properly as well.

2. Precursors to a cognitive poetics

Poetics – the explicit statement and exploration of the theory of literary works – has an ancient history, and though some modern cognitive linguists point to the disjunctive revolutionary advances in the current discipline (see Lakoff and Johnson 1999), there are aspects of contemporary cognitive poetics that address directly concerns of human culture and expression that are centuries and millennia old. The earliest comprehensive theory of literary forms and effects was produced by Aristotle in around 330 BC as the *Poetics* (which mainly dealt with drama) and the *Rhetoric* (which, over three books, addressed poetry, persuasive speech and non-literary forms such as witness-statements, narrative accounts and the discourse of legal interrogation). While of course the ancient Greeks did not have access to neurological techniques nor what we might recognise as a modern scientific view of mind, their great innovation in intellectual human development was to bring an empirical sense to argumentation. Words of speech could be recorded in writing and examined for their forms; and the tangible effects of that language when performed could be observed in the audience, listener or court-room.

Crucially in Aristotle's work (and in that of other early theorists of poetics and rhetoric such as his precursors Plato and Isocrates, and later Roman writers such as Cicero and Quintilian, and for St Augustine in the 4th century AD), classical and early medieval Western rhetorical studies did not separate out the different facets of discourse: memory, knowledge, textual arrangement, word-choice and syntactic sequence, style of delivery, ideological intention, the immediate environment of the forum or culture of utterance, and the emotional, ethical and persuasive effects on the audience were all considered of a piece. The continuities between mind and body, embodiment and culture, and shared idealised cognitive models, frames and schemas that are at the heart of modern cognitive linguistics can all be discerned in these classical continuities.

For example, both classical poetics and rhetoric were concerned as much with performance and effect as with the structural content of the discourse. Aristotle (in the *Rhetoric*) arranges the nature of communication into three "appeals" rather than into formally-designated categories such as, perhaps, poetry, prose and drama, or fictional narrative and natural narrative, or political, romantic and pastoral topics, and so on. These "appeals" are meaning and informativity (*logos*), performative empathetic delivery (*pathos*), and the authority and moral credibility of the speaker (*ethos*). Cockcroft (2002) demonstrates how this Aristotelian scheme can be read through the lens of recent schema theory (from Schank and Abelson 1977 to G. Cook 1994), and he uses the cognitive scientific understanding of the classical scheme as an analytical tool for the exploration of writing in the English 16th century renaissance.

In the classical tradition, invention, text, and readerly effects were inextricably bound up with one another. However, as the study of rhetoric became instrumentalised by becoming a central part of European schooling in the later middle ages, the nature of human communication was partitioned. Informativity became the focus of study, for example in the five "canons" of rhetoric developed influentially by the 16th century writer Peter Ramus (also known as Pierre de la Ramée): *inventio, memoria, pronuntiatio, dispositio* and *elocutio*. These categories of invention, recall of facts, accuracy of pronunciation, the topical organisation of ideas and, lastly, lexicogrammatical style shift the focus onto meaningful content in a performative frame, with the relative demotion of explicit matters of emotion or ethics. Ong ([1958] 2004), writing in the 1950s, argues that the rise of print after 1500 and the spread of mass literacy across Europe and the US in the 19th century (see also Ong 1982) also served to diminish the emphasis on the performative aspects of discourse. We arrive in the middle of the 20th century with literary scholarship constrained by the New Critical formalism that was outlined at the beginning of this chapter.

More generally, it can be argued that the last five centuries encompassing the Enlightenment and the rise of analytical and empirical science have mainly founded our intellectual achievements on a necessary partitioning of human experience and the natural world. The principle within the scientific method of experimentally investigating a feature by observing a contrastive "control" requires the object under investigation to be delineated, isolated from other objects and defined exclusively. Crucially, the object and its interrelation with other objects needs to be detached from the observing consciousness. The central expression of this lies in the Cartesian dualities that separate mind from body, reason from perception, logical deduction from intuition, artificial from natural, and human consciousness and experience from the rest of the world and universe (see Descartes 1985).

All of this has created a good science that has led to advances in almost every aspect of human life, but we are now in a position of requiring a better science that remembers that objects and consciousnesses that have been artificially though necessarily separated are in actual fact part of a natural and holistic continuum. The 5th century BC precursor of the Aristotelian philosophers, Heraclitus (see 2001) originally characterised nature as flux, but contemporary cognitive science is establishing the demonstrable reality that mind is embodied, experience is situated, rational decisions are embedded within emotional decisions, and humans are connected by sharing common frames of knowledge and patterns of mind-modelling.

It is commonplace to mark the origins of recent cognitive poetics in the last two decades of the 20th century, with Tsur's (1992) coining of the phrase providing a home for several strands of work which brought together literary studies on the one hand and cognitive linguistics, cognitive psychology and neuroscience on the other. Pioneering studies of metaphor and conceptualisation (Lakoff and Johnson 1980; Lakoff 1987; Fauconnier and Turner 2003) often featured literary examples. Cognitively-informed accounts of narrative, such as Rumelhart's (1975, 1977) story-grammars and Schank and Abelson's (1977; Schank 1982) schema theory were adapted for application to literary narratives (for example by Cockcroft 2002; G. Cook 1994; and Culpeper 2001).

Cognitive poetics as a defined field and roughly common set of concerns and methods coalesced during the last decade of the 20th century. The polemical and demonstrative work of Turner (1991, 1996) in particular was instrumental in bringing the insights of cognitive science to the study of literature. Other key work from this period includes Spolsky (1993), Gerrig (1993), Fludernik (1996), Tsur (1992) and the work of Donald and Margaret Freeman (1995 and 2002, respectively). An influential textbook (Stockwell 2002) with companion volume (Gavins and Steen 2003), and a collection of papers (Semino and Culpeper 2002) served to bring the discipline to a wider and younger audience, and established it as a college and university course.

Though this work drew on the rapidly emerging insights from empirical cognitive science, West (2012) has recently pointed out that many of the concerns of modern cognitive poetics can also be discerned precursively in earlier work such as that of the English literary critic I. A. Richards. West argues that Richards was aiming at a science of criticism in much the same way as contemporary researchers in cognitive poetics. Of course, Richards did not have access to the recent insights into the mind that cognitive science is opening up today; he was scornful of the "monstrosities" of contemporary psychoanalysis (see West 2012: 8), but was enthusiastic about more empirical psychology such as that being developed at the time in Germany by the *gestalt* psychologists.

Similar arguments for precursors of modern cognitive poetics can be made for the work of Mikhail Bakhtin, Jan Mukařovský, and even F. R. Leavis. Though much of the writing of these scholars is cast in the register of their own times and can thus appear dogmatic and merely opinionated to our eyes, nevertheless Bakhtin was at pains to describe the inter-relations of textuality, culture and readerly cognition (see Keunen 2000); Mukařovský placed the effects of foregrounding at the centre of his understanding of literary reading (see van Peer 1986); and Leavis' notion of "enactment" in literature, whereby formal patterning is assigned a contextual significance by readers, is recognisable to modern cognitive poetics as literary iconicity (see Fischer 2014).

The main difference between these early precursors and modern cognitive poetics lies in the empirical basis of the disciplines of cognitive psychology and linguistics, which were not available in earlier ages. Modern practitioners of cognitive poetics are also conscious of the movements in literary theory which have swept across the field over the last few decades. While some of the positions argued and adopted in critical theory are proving to be at odds with the insights of cognitive science, other aspects of their thinking can be understood more clearly with reference to the rational evidence offered within cognitive poetics. In philosophical terms, cognitive poetics represents a form of experiential realism in the sense that most researchers assume a tangible set of data is available for investigation (authorial choices, textual patterns and readerly organisation), but that reality is only accessible through perceptual and cognitive mechanisms which represent it in particular though describable ways.

3. Cognition and literature

The study of literature comprises several different aspects, and the cognitive turn in arts and humanities affects all of them radically. The dominant paradigm in current literary scholarship is concerned with contextual matters of authorial creativity, the history of different edited versions of the literary work, the cultural environment at the text's initial publication, and the relationship of the literary work to parallel or similar philosophical or theoretical arguments. Historiography and critical theory, in other words, continue to dominate scholarly practice. While it is obvious that the close stylistic analysis of literary texts would be informed by cognitive linguistics, it is becoming apparent that cognitive scientific insights and methods can also inform historiography. Sotirova's (2013) work on manuscript versions of D. H. Lawrence's prose fiction is a case in point.

However, the current flight to historicism – or the "history of the book" – can be seen as the literary establishment's attempt to find something new "after Theory" (Eagleton 2003). Where it might be said that the literary work itself (its textuality and texture) was often overlooked in much recent critical-theoretical discussion, the new historicism placed the text at the centre of things once again, but mainly as an opportunity for exploring the culture of production. Textual versions and the history of editing became a prime concern, and so readerly reception and impact became relatively devalued once again. One of the key scholars of literary historicism, and also a highly influential literary-critical figure, Stephen Greenblatt (see 1992) has also argued for a refocus of attention in literary scholarship on the practice of teaching literature, as a means of reconnecting the profession of literary scholarship with public understanding.

All of these moves are interesting from the standpoint of anyone working in a stylistics, discourse analytical, or reception-theory tradition. Textual analysis in particular comes out of an applied linguistics field in which pedagogic practice was often the driving motivation behind the close attention to textual detail: stylistics has always been strongly teaching-focused. Much of the original drive towards atextual Theory and subsequent cultural poetics (Greenblatt 1989) originated in a desire to move away from the New Critical sense of a text integral to itself; so the focus (in historiography or text-editing theory) on the literary work as an artefact is ironic – where stylistic variation is not explored for its effect on meaning or aesthetic response but only for its value in what it tells us about its cultural origins.

In any case, the most recent work in cognitive poetics (see section 4 below) is in the process of demonstrating that even research into cultural production and reception, variants of editions, authorial choice and creativity are all amenable to and improvable by some attention to cognitive science.

All aspects of literary scholarship can (and should) be evaluated and defined with regard to the way they treat evidence. However, the definition and treatment of evidence when it comes to the practice of literary reading can have various aspects and outcomes. These are closely aligned with the methodology adopted in each case, as outlined below. The point I will emphasise throughout this brief survey is that the cognitive turn in poetics has affected each of these approaches.

3.1. Reader-control

In general, the "empirical approach to literature" has a strong German and Dutch tradition (see Schmidt 1982 and Ibsch et al. 1991), and has been promoted particularly by the journal *Poetics* and by the learned society *IGEL* (Internationale Gesellschaft für Empirische Literaturwissenschaft – Society for the Empirical Study of Literature and the Media). Here, the definition of empiricism is largely drawn from a social science perspective; where, in philosophy, rationalism and empiricism are regarded as being in dispute with each other (Morton 2004), in social science research, rational argument on extant phenomena and the experiential sense of those phenomena are regarded as complementary.

The core "IGEL" approach might be characterised as "hard empiricism", in which particular aspects of reading are controlled as rigorously as possible in order to discover measurable facts about the reading process and experience. This approach is very closely linked with the discipline of psychology, and indeed many of the studies in this tradition are undertaken by or in collaboration with psychologists (see, for example, Miall et al. 2004, or Bortolussi and Dixon 2003, or Louwerse and van Peer 2009). There is no question that this form of empirical investigation has yielded a host of valuable insights into literary reading, summarised most clearly by Miall (2012). Key questions concern the nature of literariness (what makes literary discourse singular), the nature of absorption (the extent to which readers feel themselves immersed in a literary work), and the nature of iconicity (the extent to which a literary text conveys patterns that also seem to embody or represent their meanings symbolically).

As mentioned, much of the methodology of this form of empirical poetics is drawn from psychology. So, typically, small groups of college students will be divided into a control and a variable group, given a task that corresponds to a literary reading experience, and then either observed for particular effects or questioned in the form of a variety of elicitation techniques. The advantage of this approach is that it isolates particular features of literary reading and renders largely measurable, statistically validatable results. The findings can be published with a high degree of confidence in their generalisability to the reading community at large.

Of course, there are also disadvantages to the approach. Often, groups which would be considered of an appropriate size for a psychological study (generally numbering in single-figures or tens) might be considered inadequately small from a sociolinguistic perspective. Often the objective of the approach is to discover generalisable facts about readers and the reading process, rather than particular facts or phenomena about the singular literary work that serves as a stimulus in the investigation. Many studies in this tradition therefore feature white middle-class young-adult college students as informants, which means at the very least that this socio-ethnic group is over-represented in the findings. Finally, of course, there is an inevitable privileging given to studies and phenomena that are easily (or even possibly) measurable, and less emphasis on those aspects of literary reading that are extremely subtle, transient or idiosyncratic, but which many might consider to be essential elements in the literary experience.

3.2. Reader-response

It should be said that many of the practitioners of "reader-control" empirical poetics are aware of these potential limitations, and often work hard to mitigate them. Miall (2005, 2006), in particular, blends the strongly quantitative psychology-leaning research with other, more qualitative techniques. Reader questionnaires, reading task protocols, thinking aloud techniques and other methods are designed to avoid the "lab-effect" of strongly reader-controlled experiments and aim more towards the exploration of a naturalistic reading experience. At the same time, experiments have been conducted in which readers are given real literary works instead of carefully controlled texts invented by the analysts, or complete texts rather than extracts and decontextualised sentences or "textoids" (Vipond and Hunt 1989; Gerrig 1993). Inevitably these sorts of approaches make it more difficult to control for precise textual or psychological features or effects, which is the cost of a more naturalistic and holistic set of data.

Moving even further away from the psychological method paradigm, several researchers within cognitive poetics have adopted more sociological methods in order to investigate the natural processes of reading. A common technique here is to use either the recorded notes and articulations of non-professional book-groups, blogs and discussions that are already available, or to engage in fieldwork data collection with these groups (see Whiteley 2011; Peplow 2011; Swann and Allington 2009). One advantage of these approaches is that the reading experiences that are being explored are not those of professional literary critics but often of a wider population of literary readers.

The results of the research might involve analytical frameworks that have a strong tradition in sociolinguistics (such as discourse analysis or accommodation theory) or alternatively the readers' responses can be analysed using models derived from cognitive linguistics or cognitive psychology (such as text worlds or schema theory). Often these sorts of studies are thoroughly qualitative, and are more particularly tied to the specific literary work in hand. This means of course that they gain as a democratic form of literary criticism, though there is perhaps less generalisability in terms of psychological process. And, of course, there are many examples of cognitive poetics (see section 3.5 below) in which a close cognitive poetic textual analysis is presented either to elaborate or interrogate a set of professional published literary critical responses. After all, literary critics are readers too, and their articulated responses are appropriate examples of data available for systematic analysis.

3.3. Computational and corpus stylistics

Both the quantitative and qualitative forms of readerly empiricism outlined above aim to avoid or mitigate the effects of the *reader's paradox* (Stockwell 2012a), a form of the *observer's paradox* familiar in sociolinguistic research. The latter recognises that investigators are likely to affect by their presence or intervention the data or informants they are researching. In the field of literary reading, the reader's paradox is even more intractable, because reading itself is a form of consciousness, and so even the slightest form of awareness or direct consideration will cause the experience to be different from the ordinary process of natural reading.

The great developments in computational corpus linguistics and concordance techniques over the last few decades offer possibilities for empirical poetics that minimise the effects of the reader's paradox in research. As Stubbs (2005, 2014) points out, features and effects that are distributed across a literary work can be explicitly apparent and measurable only by a software program, but they can reasonably be adduced as evidence for the generation of particular effects in literary readers. It may be that many literary effects operate at the level of sub-conscious processing, and their effects are only felt cumulatively or when several features are aligned for a particular thematic effect. In these cases, there is little point looking for the articulation of such effects with any degree of precision in the mainly intuitive and impressionistic discourse of literary criticism, nor in the discussions of non-professional readers. Nor is it useful to use the sort of quantitative empirical methods referenced in 3.1 and 3.2 above, because the effects that we are interested in might be too subtle or rarefied for accessible measurement. Instead, features that are distributed and diffused across a large expanse of literary text might cumulatively have a very subtle effect that is only measurable or even detectable objectively with the aid of a computer program and corpus stylistic technique.

Most corpus stylistics is not primarily cognitive poetic in design nor intention, but the method is adaptable enough to operate in the service of a cognitively-informed poetics. There have been explicit polemical arguments in this direction (O'Halloran 2007), and an increasing recognition that corpus linguistics has much empirical validation to offer cognitive linguistics (Gries and Stefanowitsch 2007; Arppe et al. 2010), and therefore to cognitive poetics (see 4.4 below).

3.4. Textual analysis

It has long been argued from within the discipline of stylistics that rigorous and systematic textual analysis itself is a form of empiricism. This argument rests on the assertion that textual and stylistic facts that are describable about a literary work are undeniably evidence for a particular reading or interpretation of that text. The commitment to clear description and openness of method in stylistic practice sets out the fruits of analysis for verification, adjustment or falsifiability by other readers. Aside from the reliance on textual evidence, this too represents a commitment to the empiricism of method.

Furthermore, there is a more indirect claim to evidential value in stylistic analysis, in the sense that the (usually) linguistic framework or insight that is deployed in the analysis at hand has almost always been tested and validated in another domain. So, for example, if a stylistician explores the effects of semantic prototypicality in a reading of a poem, the fact that there is a huge amount of evidence to suggest that semantic prototypicality is currently a reasonably safe hypothesis about language in general helps to underpin and validate indirectly the use of that model in the literary analysis. Of course, this indirect validation rests on the assumption that literary language is continuous with language in general, rather than being in itself formally different or special – most stylisticians today accept this fact: literary language is literary because of the deployment and framing, rather than for any inherent, essential properties of the text itself. It is this far that stylistics has moved from New Criticism.

Literary stylistics has been the discipline that has most enthusiastically embraced cognitive linguistics as a source for analytical frameworks. An early collection of articles (Semino and Culpeper 2002) was even entitled *cognitive stylistics*, and in general the most active part of literary analysis for the last couple of decades has been characterised by close textual attention. Sometimes this has involved radical reshaping of existing notions in stylistics; at other times, it might have seemed as if existing notions were simply being given a cognitivist gloss (see Tsur's 2008 criticism of Stockwell 2002 in this regard). However, it is important to recognise that both aspects of the revaluation were necessary, in order to establish a coherent single discipline and understand in a consistent terminology and mindset where stylistics could make its greatest contribution – as well as those areas in which it lacked adequate concepts.

The field of narratology has been a particularly vibrant area of revitalised research, with a postclassical or *cognitive narratology* now largely treated as mainstream in that field (see Bundgard et al. 2012, Herman 2000, 2003, 2009). Narratology draws more on cognitive psychology than linguistics, exploring such notions as the creation of storyworlds, the nature and representation of consciousness, and the literary deployment, codification and recreation of emotion, for example. It can be regarded as empirical in the same sense as stylistics above, though of course there are similar problems of definition. Sternberg (2003) has argued, for example, that cognitive narratology needs to decide whether to adopt a social science methodology and ethos or an approach more suited to the humanities. It seems to me, again, that the use and status of evidence is at the heart of this distinction, and in fact I have argued elsewhere (Stockwell 2012b) for a characterisation of the ethos of cognitive poetics as an "artful science". This is because in literary reading we are dealing not only with the quantifiable and measurable effects of textuality and cognition, but also with experiences that are delicate, difficult to articulate, subjective and perhaps only precisely accessible by introspection.

3.5. Introspection

Introspection is not a form of perception (nor even analogous to it); it is a form of peculiar (that is, particular) self-knowledge (Byrne 2005). It thus has more to do with belief than with perception, but this formulation makes it more, rather than less, amenable to a cognitive scientific account. With the rise of behaviourism through the 20th century, the use of introspection as a scientific method became devalued (Lyons 1986), since it is by definition subjective and idiosyncratic. However, even the most highly-controlled reader experiments in cognitive psychology have often relied on informants' self-report of their own reactions, and introspective report, for all its flaws, remains the only direct access to consciousness.

Most recently, Jack and Roepstorff (2003, 2004) argued for a revaluation of introspection in the scientific method. In relation to literary reading and literary analysis, I have argued (Stockwell 2013) that it is impossible to read and simultaneously to watch and reflect on your reading, for good psychological and perceptual reasons concerning figure and ground differentiation. It is of course possible to reflect backwards on a prior reading experience, so introspection is apparently retrospection, but as Overgaard (2006) points out, this means that you are having a memory of something that was at the time unconscious. Instead, introspection seems more like a rationalization of your consciousness. This is philosophically complex but in literary terms relatively simple: it means that the articulated recount of a reading experience equates to the reader's belief about that experience. This is a combination of both aware and sub-conscious factors, but since the introspective recount is the only product of the experience, then that is to all practical purposes the reading in hand. On this argument, introspection remains a valid form of evidence, perhaps in fact the only direct form of evidence of literary reading, and therefore introspection can be included in a list of types of empiricism.

In practice, several cognitive poetic analyses (including many of my own) rely on an introspective sense of a key effect or feature in a literary text and reading that is then pinpointed for systematic linguistic exploration. Furthermore, the analysis is presented in as transparent and principled a way as possible, and comparison with other readers' introspective experiences is invited. This procedure certainly relies on subjectivity and self-consciousness, but it also maintains contact with the sorts of external empiricism outlined in sections 3.1 to 3.4 above.

Finally, of course, the most common pattern of cognitive poetic analysis involves a combination of several of these empirical methods. The consequence is a sort of triangulation of approaches in order to arrive at an account of literary reading that would remain otherwise ineffable.

4. Developments in cognitive poetics

Over the last two decades, work that has fallen under the term "cognitive poetics" has diversified a great deal. As Louwerse and van Peer (2009) point out, surprisingly most examples of cognitive poetics over this period have drawn more on cognitive psychology rather than linguistics, though of course the two are not entirely distinct in cognitive literary analysis. Popular areas include explorations of conceptual metaphor, the worlds of literary fiction, schemas of contextual knowledge, how elements of literary texts are foregrounded and thematised, how genre is delineated, and how blending and compression work to create connections between literature and life.

The first of these – the exploration of conceptual metaphor – arises from the earliest work of Lakoff and Johnson (1980), and studies on this topic remain popular. Identifying conceptual metaphors that underlie literary works, especially plays and novels, can reveal extended tropes and themes across large bodies of text. Any particular idealised conceptual metaphor can be linguistically realised in a variety of ways, of course, and the most convincing work focused on this stylistic variation (see, for example, D. C. Freeman 1995, and the articles collected in Gavins and Steen 2003, and Semino and Culpeper 2002). The least convincing work simply listed the conceptual metaphors that featured in the text, falling into the old trap of neglecting to link the textual description to the interpretative level of significance. Another common flaw in some of these studies lies in analysing conceptual metaphors in a particular literary work that in fact are simply common conventional metaphors in the language system of English generally: so, for example, finding lots of LIFE IS A JOURNEY or IDEAS ARE CONTAINERS metaphors in a literary text is often not particularly significant for the text as literature. Mistakes such as this were often what motivated some literary critics to dismiss cognitive poetics as reductive or only interested in universals, rather than in the particularity or singularity of the literary work.

Many literary scholars have drawn with interest on the ways that cognitive psychology has accounted for mental representations, schemas, mental models and conceptual worlds. This tradition has become particularly strong in the area of cognitive narratology (see 3.4 above), which has essentially become paradigmatic in what Herman (2000) calls "post-classical narratology". Interest in the "storyworlds" that authors construct in texts for readers to re-imagine has drawn substantially on cognitive psychological frameworks. Again, though, much of this research is conceptual and thematic in nature. An exception is the work which has been undertaken in *text world theory* (Werth 1999, Gavins 2007), which marries up a contextualised model of world-building with a close linguistic analysis of discourse. The most useful aspect of the approach, for literary critical purposes, is the convincing way in which the model accounts for attentional and deictic "world-switches" caused by metaphor, temporal disjunctions, embedded beliefs, wishes and other modalisations, and other unrealised possibilities.

A third major trend within cognitive poetics has been the way in which scholars have revisited the key research questions of past literary theory with new tools from the cognitive revolution. So, for example, the defamiliarising or estranging effects of literature, or literariness itself, or the functioning of foregrounding as a literary mechanism, have all been freshly addressed with the benefit of the empirical grounding of cognitive science (see, for example, van Peer 1986, van Peer and Louwerse 2003).

Overall, the history of cognitive poetics over the last two decades has been to complete one of the main objectives of stylistics, which was to offer a persuasive rational account of the generation of meaningfulness in literary texts. Though this work is of course ongoing, the systematic account of context, framing and readerliness that recent advances have provided has been striking. Furthermore, we have witnessed a principled reintegration – thanks to cognitive poetics – of aesthetics and ethics (*pathos* and *ethos*, see section 2 above) into the analytical study of literature. Now in the second decade of the 21st century, it is becoming apparent that cognitive poetics is becoming prominent as an influence in literary studies in general. Under a more broad *cognitive literary studies* heading, literary scholars are increasingly turning their attention to insights appearing across the range of cognitive science disciplines. This includes not only cognitive psychology and cognitive linguistics, but neuroscience, consciousness studies, and evolutionary theory. While this is welcome in general, there is a risk (it seems to me) that once again the linguistic texture of the literary work is in danger of being overlooked. Literary scholars often do not seem to realise that cognitive poetics is not simply the latest critical theory, but is a scientific method with empirical roots.

4.1. The return to linguistics

Having said that cognitive literary studies risks neglecting the stylistic dimension, it is worth observing that one of the current emerging projects within cognitive poetics proper is a return to cognitive linguistics proper. For most of its history, stylistics has drawn on a systemic-functional linguistic tradition for its close textual analysis. Given the emphasis on meaning and its interpretative effects, this is not surprising. It is also perhaps to be expected that a grammatical model most popular outside the US would be preferred in the discipline of stylistics within its European and British Commonwealth context. Moreover, the various generative grammars emerging in the US at the time were not usable for the stylistic analysis of "surface structure" or actual linguistic surface realisation.

Most recently, however, several varieties of cognitive and construction grammars have emerged, perhaps most comprehensively Langacker's (2008) Cognitive Grammar. These provide a means of parsing and accounting for matters of transitivity and participant roles in a similar way as Halliday's (and Matthiessen 2004) systemic-functional grammar, and are at least as effective in this dimension. Additionally, of course, these cognitive grammars have the advantage of being rooted in psychological plausibility, either by empirical testing or indirectly by sharing a set of basic paradigmatic principles in cognitive science. This makes them potentially very attractive to stylisticians of literary works.

As yet, the number of applications of cognitive grammar to literature has been fairly limited. Hamilton (2003) offers an account of a Wilfred Owen war poem in order to explain the depth of its poignancy. There is an account of the shifting strength and weakness of characters in a battle scene in *The Lord of the Rings* (in Stockwell 2009), and an analysis of apocalyptic science-fiction narratives to focus on human helplessness (in Stockwell 2010). What is noticeable about these applications is that their main concern is not meaning but emotional effect. The collected analyses in Harrison et al. (2013) all draw on Cognitive Grammar to account for a range of effects across literary works.

4.2. Enactment and dramatisation

Another recent trend in cognitive poetics develops the fundamental cognitivist principle of embodiment in order to revisit the iconicity effect of literary enactment. So, for example, the prototypicality scaling of phonetic features is used to identify sounds in a 19th century seduction poem by Robert Bowning – sounds that make readers reading aloud form kisses with their mouths (Stockwell 2009). Many psychological studies report the empathetic effects on reading narratives of physical states: drinking from a warm cup makes you feel more warmly to a fictional character, sitting on a hard chair makes you feel less empathy, and so on (see Gibbs 2006, 2012), and readers report and are observed writhing uncomfortably in their own clothes while reading the passages in Dickens' *David Copperfield* that feature the slimy, squirming character Uriah Heep. Embodiment and readerly relationships with literary characters is a strongly emerging interest in research in the field (see Vermeule 2010).

Similarly of literary critical interest is the notion of *simulation* that appears in both Cognitive Grammar and in neurological research. In the former, Langacker (2008) points out that every linguistic utterance is a representation that is attenuated to a greater or lesser degree from the actual experience; every piece of language helps to create a simulation in the user's mind that operates as a heuristic for understanding. Simulation at a global level is also important in empathetic relationships, feelings and the creation of a "Theory of Mind" (see Zunshine 2006 and Keen 2007 for literary applications). These slightly different instantiations of the notion of simulation promise a great deal of insight into the ways in which readers feel they are transported, immersed or absorbed by a literary fictional world.

Prose fiction and dramatic monologue in poetry are obvious places for an application of simulation to be researched. However, this work also suggests new avenues for study in relation to dramatic performance (traditionally an area of complexity for a text-based stylistics): see McConachie and Hart (2006) and A. Cook (2010).

4.3. Singularity and situatedness

One of the accusations levelled traditionally at both stylistics and cognitive poetics has been that they are interested in general patterns of readerly behaviour, language universals and overall principles and patterns. While perhaps overstated in the best work, it is important to recognise that a particular literary text – while having generic connections with other works by the same author, in the same genre or mode, from the same period, or on the same theme – is unique to itself. Attridge (2004) calls this the *singularity* of the text, and it is a common feature of a sense of literariness. Reducing a literary work to patterns and generalities risks neglecting this centrally important feature for literature.

As an antidote to the universalising tendency, the cognitivist notion of *situatedness* offers a useful corrective (see Barsalou 2008, 2009). A concept is understood as a set of particular instantiations which might share some aspects but are fundamentally dependent on the uniquely experienced situation at hand. Instead of pulling down a schematic template or idealised model for a particular concept or experience, these concepts and linguistic articulations are "soft-assembled" (Gibbs 2006) for the case in hand. The notion of situatedness neatly captures both the singularity and genre-definitions of literature. This is a promising route for cognitive poetics research; what is less clear is how the notion of situatedness in literary reading can be operationalised to produce accounts that are recognisable as literary criticism.

Until these ideas are fully worked out, my contention remains the traditional stylistic position that the leaning towards universalising reductivism can be successfully mitigated by a constant emphasis that ties literary analysis down to the linguistic specifics of the text. Ultimately, the text that readers share remains the source of evidential value.

4.4. Subtlety

The greatest difficulty for a discipline founded on precise analysis and evidential value lies in those aspects of literary reading that are at or below the level of measurement. It is relatively easy to conduct a psychological or a cognitive poetic experiment to discover literary texts that generate empathetic grief, sadness, laugh-out-loud comedy, and so on. These effects are either easily physically observable or are clearcut examples that can be intuited and reported in a carefully designed protocol. But more subtle aesthetic reactions (wry melancholy, poignant nostalgia, perhaps?) are more difficult to articulate, define and explore systematically. And yet these are exactly the sort of rich effects that characterise literary reading, and that feature particularly in the writing of literary critics. It seems to me desirable and possible for cognitive poetics to address issues like these of subtlety, delicacy and bareness, where the experienced effect that is reported by readers is rarefied, barely conscious or so highly diffused in the experience that it is difficult to articulate in conventional descriptive terms.

For a simple, as yet unexplored example, I have recently been trying to account for the notion of *aura* in literary text (Stockwell 2014). This is the atmospheric or tonal sense of a vague association, often reported by readers and usually described by literary critics in poetic terms themselves. For example, in Philip Larkin's (1974) poem "The Explosion", a mining accident is described is highly subdued terms. The features of the industrial landscape and nature are given agency and animation, while the miners are described by their bodies and clothing, chasing rabbits, collecting lark's eggs. The underground explosion itself is narrated simply as "a tremor" that disturbed the cows grazing above. The poem ends with an imagined scene in which the wives of the men see them again, brightly walking towards them, still alive:

> for a second
> Wives saw men of the explosion
>
> Larger than in life they managed –
> Gold as on a coin, or walking
> Somehow from the sun towards them,
>
> One showing the eggs unbroken.
>
> Philip Larkin (1974: 42)

Almost all readers – both professional literary critics and others who have read the whole poem – report the poignancy in this closing passage. Part of this effect, it seems to me, arises from the echoic value of elements that recur throughout the text. These repetitions are not simply examples of lexical or semantic cohesion, but are more subtle and delicate. Features from domains that are not usually linked (clothing, faces, the natural landscape, and industry) are placed in close proximity, and weave between each other.

I have had some success in using Langacker's (2008) notion of *dominion* and Evans' (2009) work on *lexical concepts and conceptual models* to understand how words and phrases in the first part of the poem generate a set of expectations and associations in the minds of readers, only some of which are lexicalised again later on. The unrealised associations, it seems plausible to me, constitute a set of non-instantiated but fleeting meanings and feelings that pervade the rest of the text on the border of conscious awareness. This is where the subtle effects that readers report in the poem are located.

It would be very difficult to devise a controlled experiment to verify these ideas (though of course probably not impossible). However, triangulating a finding like this in any literary text can be effective. In corpus linguistics, the notion of *semantic prosody* (Louw and Milojkovic 2014) captures the shading or mood (in the non-linguistic, emotional sense) that is inherent in particular collocations and larger structures: certain phrases are always used negatively, for example, regardless of their semantic or dictionary content traditionally conceived – this is their semantic prosody characteristic. It strikes me that this sort of diffused semantic analysis (which in corpus linguistics can be measured) is a useful way of trying to pin down the same sorts of subtle effects that are captured in the cognitive grammatical account. This loose example is a preliminary illustration of the necessary triangulation that will be needed to catch such notions.

5. Futures

Cognitive poetics is inherently interdisciplinary, with researchers typically possessing a high awareness of both the scientific method and the state of current scholarship in social science. However, the natural home of cognitive poetics is clearly in arts and humanities, and an assertive emphasis on integrated linguistic form and effect offers discipline, rigour and insight where these have traditionally been rather neglected. A study of literature that is informed by cognitive linguistics seeks to broaden the potential of the cognitive revolution by encompassing the most culturally-valued form of language in use, and finally refuting the claim that cognitive linguistics is insufficiently social or critically aware in its practices.

On the other side, literary texts, literary readings, and poetics offer a great deal to cognitive science in general and cognitive linguistics in particular. Cognitive poetic analyses are always founded on whole texts in context, rather than isolated or invented fragments of language; the concerns that interest researchers in cognitive poetics serve as a reminder of the social world in which minds and bodies operate, and offer demonstrations in practice for how an extended embodied cognition works.

Finally, the field itself embodies a return to a time when a scholar could be interested professionally both in an engagement in the arts and a commitment to science and rational thinking. Cognitive poetics offers a practical means of achieving this integration.

References

Aristotle
   [1991]   *The Art of Rhetoric*. Harmondsworth: Penguin.
Aristotle
   [1996]   *Poetics*. Harmondsworth: Penguin.
Arppe, Antti, Gaëtanelle Gilquin, Dylan Glynn, Martin Hilpert and Arne Zeschel
   2010   Cognitive corpus linguistics: five points of debate on current theory and methodology. *Corpora* 5: 1–27.
Attridge, Derek
   2004   *The Singularity of Literature*. London: Routledge.
Barsalou, Lawrence
   2008   Grounded cognition. *Annual Review of Psychology* 59: 617–665.
Barsalou, Lawrence
   2009   Simulation, situated conceptualization and prediction. *Philosophical Transactions of the Royal Society* 364: 1281–1289.
Bortolussi, Marisa and Peter Dixon
   2003   *Psychonarratology: Foundations for the Empirical Study of Literary Response*. Cambridge: Cambridge University Press.
Bundgaard, Per, Frederik Stjernfelt and Henrik Skov Nielsen (eds.)
   2012   *Narrative Theories and Poetics: 5 Questions*. Copenhagen: Automatic Press.

Byrne, Alex
   2005   Introspection. *Philosophical Topics* 33(1): 79–104.
Cockcroft, Robert
   2002   *Renaissance Rhetoric: Reconsidered Passion – The Interpretation of Affect in Early Modern Writing*. London: Palgrave.
Cook, Amy
   2010   *Shakespearean Neuroplay: Reinvigorating the Study of Dramatic Texts and Performance Through Cognitive Science*. New York: Palgrave Macmillan.
Cook, Guy
   1994   *Discourse and Literature*. Oxford: Oxford University Press.
Culpeper, Jonathan
   2001   *Language and Characterisation: People in Plays and other Texts*. Harlow: Longman.
Descartes, René
   [1985]   *The Philosophical Writings of Descartes*: 2 volumes [trans. J. Cottingham, R. Stoothoff, D. Murdoch]. Cambridge: Cambridge University Press.
Eagleton, Terry
   2003   *After Theory*. New York: Basic Books.
Evans, Vyvyan
   2009   *How Words Mean: Lexical Concepts, Cognitive Models and Meaning Construction*. Oxford: Oxford University Press.
Fauconnier, Gilles and Mark Turner
   2003   *The Way We Think: Conceptual Blending and the Mind's Hidden Complexities*. New York: Basic Books.
Fischer, Olga
   2014   Iconicity. In: P. Stockwell and S. Whiteley (eds.), *The Handbook of Stylistics*, 377–392. Cambridge: Cambridge University Press.
Fludernik, Monika
   1996   *Towards a "Natural" Narratology*. London: Routledge.
Freeman, Donald C.
   1995   "Catch[ing] the nearest way": *Macbeth* and cognitive metaphor. *Journal of Pragmatics* 24: 689–708.
Freeman, Margaret H.
   2002   Cognitive mapping in literary analysis. *Style* 36: 466–483.
Gavins, Joanna
   2007   *Text World Theory*. Edinburgh: Edinburgh University Press.
Gavins, Joanna and Gerard Steen (eds.)
   2003   *Cognitive Poetics in Practice*. London: Routledge.
Gerrig, Richard J.
   1993   *Experiencing Narrative Worlds: On the Psychological Activities of Reading*. New Haven: Yale University Press.
Gibbs, Raymond W.
   2006   *Embodiment and Cognitive Science*. New York: Cambridge University Press.
Gibbs, Raymond W.
   2012   Walking the walk while thinking about the talk: embodied interpretation of metaphorical narratives. *Journal of Psycholinguistic Research* 42(4): 363–378.
Greenblatt, Stephen
   1989   Towards a poetics of culture. In: H. Aram Veeser (ed.) *The New Historicism*, 1–14. London: Routledge.
Greenblatt, Stephen (ed.)
   1992   *Redrawing the Boundaries: The Transformation of English and American Literary Studies*. New York: Modern Language Association of America.

Gries, Stephan Th. and Anatol Stefanowitsch (eds.)
  2007   *Corpora in Cognitive Linguistics: Corpus-Based Approaches to Syntax and Lexis*. Berlin: Mouton.
Halliday, Michael A.K. and Christian Matthiessen
  2004   *An Introduction to Functional Grammar*. London: Hodder.
Hamilton, Craig
  2003   A cognitive grammar of "Hospital Barge" by Wilfred Owen. In: J. Gavins and G. Steen (eds.), *Cognitive Poetics in Practice*, 55–65. London: Routledge.
Harrison, Chloe, Louise Nuttall, Peter Stockwell and Wenjuan Yuan (eds.)
  2013   *Cognitive Grammar in Literature*. Amsterdam: Benjamins.
Heraclitus
  [2001]   *Fragments: The Collected Wisdom of Heraclitus* [trans. B. Haxton]. New York: Viking.
Herman, David
  2000   Narratology as a cognitive science. *Image and Narrative* 1. http://www.imageandnarrative.be/inarchive/narratology/davidherman.htm
Herman, David (ed.)
  2003   *Narrative Theory and the Cognitive Sciences*. Stanford: CSLI.
Herman, David
  2009   Cognitive narratology. In: P. Hühn, J. Pier, W. Schmid and J. Schönert (eds.), *Handbook of Narratology*, 30–43. Berlin: de Gruyter.
Ibsch, Elrud, Dick Schram and Gerard Steen (eds.)
  1991   *Empirical Studies of Literature*. Amsterdam: Rodopi.
Jack, Anthony I. and Andreas Roepstorff
  2003   Trusting the subject I. *Journal of Consciousness Studies* 10: 9–10.
Jack, Anthony I. and Andreas Roepstorff
  2004   Trusting the subject II. *Journal of Consciousness Studies* 11: 7–8.
Keen, Suzanne
  2007   *Empathy and the Novel*. New York: Oxford University Press.
Keunen, Bart
  2000   Bakhtin, genre formation, and the cognitive turn: Chronotopes as memory schemata. *CLCWeb: Comparative Literature and Culture* 2(2) http://docs.lib.purdue.edu/clcweb/vol2/iss2/2
Lakoff, George
  1987   *Women, Fire and Dangerous Things: What Categories Reveal About the Mind*. Chicago: University of Chicago Press.
Lakoff, George and Mark Johnson
  1980   *Metaphors We Live By*. Chicago: University of Chicago Press.
Lakoff, George and Mark Johnson
  1999   *Philosophy in the Flesh*. Chicago: University of Chicago Press.
Langacker, Ronald
  2008   *Cognitive Grammar: A Basic Introduction*. New York: Oxford University Press.
Larkin, Philip
  1974   *High Windows*. London: Faber.
Louw, Bill and Marijka Milojkovic
  2014   Semantic prosody. In: P. Stockwell and S. Whiteley (eds.), *The Handbook of Stylistics*, 263–280. Cambridge: Cambridge University Press.
Louwerse, Max M. and Willie van Peer
  2009   How cognitive is cognitive poetics? The interaction between symbolic and embodied cognition. In: G. Brône and J. Vandaele (eds.), *Cognitive Poetics: Goals, Gains and Gaps*, 423–444. Berlin: de Gruyter.

Lyons, William
   1986   *The Disappearance of Introspection*. Cambridge: MIT Press.
McConachie, Bruce A. and F. Elizabeth Hart
   2006   *Performance and Cognition: Theatre Studies and the Cognitive Turn.* London: Taylor and Francis.
Miall, David S.
   2005   Beyond interpretation: the cognitive significance of reading. In: H. Veivo, B. Pettersson and M. Polvinen (eds.), *Cognition and Literary Interpretation in Practice*, 129–156. Helsinki: University of Helsinki Press.
Miall, David S.
   2006   *Literary Reading: Empirical and Theoretical Studies*. New York: Peter Lang.
Miall, David S.
   2012   In pursuit of literariness: emotional and empirical perspectives. Paper presented at PALA conference, University of Malta, 16–18 July 2012.
Miall, David S., Don Kuiken and Shelley Sikora
   2004   Forms of self-implication in literary reading. *Poetics Today* 25(2): 171–203.
Morton, Adam
   2004   *Philosophy in Practice: An Introduction to the Main Questions*. Oxford: Blackwell.
O'Halloran, Kieran A.
   2007   Critical discourse analysis and the corpus-informed interpretation of metaphor at the register level. *Applied Linguistics* 28(1): 1–24.
Ong, Walter J.
   1982   *Orality and Literacy: The Technologizing of the Word*. New York: Methuen.
Ong, Walter J.
   [1958] 2004   *Ramus, Method, and the Decay of Dialogue: From the Art of Discourse to the Art of Reason,* second edn. Cambridge: Harvard University Press.
Overgaard, Morten
   2006   Introspection in science. *Consciousness and Cognition* 15: 629–633.
Peplow, David
   2011   "Oh, I've known a lot of Irish people". Reading groups and the negotiation of literary interpretation. *Language and Literature* 20(4): 295–315.
Rumelhart, David E.
   1975   Notes on a schema for stories. In: D. G. Bobrow and A. Collins (eds.), *Representation and Understanding*, 211–236. New York: Academic Press.
Rumelhart, David E.
   1977   Understanding and summarizing brief stories. In: D. LaBerge and S. J. Samuels (eds.), *Basic Processes in Reading: Perception and Comprehension*, 265–303. Hillsdale: Lawrence Erlbaum.
Schank, Robert C.
   1982   *Dynamic Memory: A Theory of Reminding and Learning in Computers and People*. Cambridge: Cambridge University Press.
Schank, Robert C. and Roger Abelson
   1977   *Scripts, Plans, Goals and Understanding*, Hillsdale: Lawrence Erlbaum.
Schmidt, Siegfried J.
   1982   *Foundation for the Empirical Study of Literature: The Components of a Basic Theory* [trans. R. de Beaugrande]. Hamburg: Helmut Buske.
Semino, Elena and Jonathan Culpeper (eds.)
   2002   *Cognitive Stylistics*. Amsterdam: John Benjamins.
Sotirova, Violeta
   2013   *Consciousness in Modernist Fiction: A Stylistic Study.* London: Palgrave.
Spolsky, Ellen
   1993   *Gaps in Nature: Literary Interpretation and the Modular Mind*. New York: SUNY Press.

Sternberg, Meir (ed.)
   2003   *The Cognitive Turn?: A Debate on Interdisciplinarity.* Special issue of *Poetics Today* 24(2).

Stockwell, Peter
   2002   *Cognitive Poetics: An Introduction.* London: Routledge.

Stockwell, Peter
   2009   *Texture: A Cognitive Aesthetics of Reading.* Edinburgh: Edinburgh University Press.

Stockwell, Peter
   2010   The eleventh checksheet of the apocalypse. In: B. Busse and D. McIntyre (eds.) *Language and Style*, 419–432. London: Palgrave.

Stockwell, Peter
   2012a   The reader's paradox. In: M. Burke, S. Csabi, L. Week and J. Zerkowitz (eds.), *Pedagogical Stylistics*, 45–57. London: Continuum.

Stockwell, Peter
   2012b   The artful science of literary study [original in Chinese, translated by Juling Ma]. *Journal of Foreign Language and Literature* (Sichuan).

Stockwell, Peter
   2013   The positioned reader. *Language and Literature* 22(3): 263–277.

Stockwell, Peter
   2014   Atmosphere and tone. In: P. Stockwell and S. Whiteley (eds.) *The Handbook of Stylistics*, 360–374. Cambridge: Cambridge University Press.

Stubbs, Michael
   2005   Conrad in the computer: examples of quantitative stylistic methods. *Language and Literature* 14(1): 5–24.

Stubbs, Michael
   2014   Quantitative methods in literary linguistics. In: P. Stockwell and S. Whiteley (eds.), *The Handbook of Stylistics*, 46–62. Cambridge: Cambridge University Press.

Swann, Joan and Daniel Allington
   2009   Reading groups and the language of literary texts: a case study in social reading. *Language and Literature* 18(3): 247–264.

Tsur, Reuven
   1992   *Toward a Theory of Cognitive Poetics.* Amsterdam: Elsevier.

Tsur, Reuven
   2008   Deixis in literature – what *isn't* Cognitive Poetics? *Pragmatics and Cognition* 16(1): 123–154.

Turner, Mark
   1991   *Reading Minds: The Study of English in the Age of Cognitive Science.* Princeton: Princeton University Press.

Turner, Mark
   1996   *The Literary Mind.* New York: Oxford University Press.

van Peer, Willie
   1986   *Stylistics and Psychology: Investigations of Foregrounding.* London: Croom Helm.

van Peer, Willie and Max Louwerse (eds.)
   2003   *Thematics. Interdisciplinary Studies.* Amsterdam/Philadelphia: John Benjamins.

Vermeule, Blakey
   2010   *Why Do We Care about Literary Characters?* Baltimore: Johns Hopkins University Press.

Vipond, Doug and Russell A. Hunt
   1989   Literary processing and response as transaction: evidence for the contribution of readers, texts and situations. In: D. Meutsch and R. Viehoff (eds.), *Comprehension of Literary Discourse: Results and Problems of Interdisciplinary Approaches*, 155–174. Berlin: de Gruyter.

Werth, Paul
   1999   *Text Worlds*. Harlow: Longman.
West, David
   2012   *I. A. Richards and the Rise of Cognitive Stylistics*. London: Bloomsbury.
Whiteley, Sara
   2011   Text World Theory, real readers and emotional responses to *The Remains of the Day*. *Language and Literature* 20(1): 23–41.
Wimsatt, W. K. and Monroe C. Beardsley
   1954a   The intentional fallacy. In: *The Verbal Icon: Studies in the Meaning of Poetry*, 3–18. Lexington: University of Kentucky Press. First published in *Sewanee Review* 54: 468–488.
Wimsatt, W. K. and Monroe C. Beardsley
   1954b   The affective fallacy. In: *The Verbal Icon: Studies in the Meaning of Poetry,* 21–39. Lexington: University of Kentucky Press. First published in *Sewanee Review* 57(1): 31–p55.
Zunshine, Lisa
   2006   *Why We Read Fiction: Theory of Mind and the Novel*. Columbus: Ohio State University Press.

Peter Stockwell, Nottingham (United Kingdom)

III. Central topics

21. Semantic typology

1. Introducing semantic typology
2. Semantic typology: selected major examples
3. Methodological challenges in semantic typology
4. Lessons from semantic typology
5. Further research questions
6. References

Definitions of cognitive linguistics normally emphasize the interaction of language and cognition, cf. "[c]ognitive linguistics is the study of how language relates to the human mind" (Kibrik 2011: 15). As is customary, such programmatic statements operate with generic nouns, in this case "language" and "mind", and abstract away from the concrete manifestations of human languages and human minds. This is certainly justified for a research agenda, but it is important not to overlook the reality behind it. Leaving the issue of the diversity of minds to cognitive scientists, as a typologist I will focus here on language diversity: there are between 6,000 and 8,000 languages currently spoken in the world, and "[t]he crucial fact for understanding the place of language in human cognition is its diversity" (Evans and Levinson 2009: 431).

Linguistic diversity does not imply that any generalizations over language properties and the language-mind relations are meaningless or premature before these have been studied for all the world's languages, the majority of which still lack any decent description. It does imply, though, that such generalizations gain a lot from careful systematic cross-linguistic studies that may unveil cross-linguistic regularities behind diversity. This chapter focuses on the discipline for which cross-linguistic comparison is foundational, namely linguistic typology, and in particular on its semantically oriented direction, *semantic typology*. Section 1 introduces semantic typology, section 2 gives examples of central research within semantic typology. Section 3 discusses the major methodological challenges that semantic typologists face, section 4 summarizes the lessons to be drawn, and section 5 points out a few directions for further research. The chapter's overarching goal is to show the value of bringing linguistic diversity and semantic typology into research on "how language relates to mind".

1. Introducing semantic typology

Typology is "the study of linguistic patterns that are found cross-linguistically, in particular, patterns that can be discovered solely by cross-linguistic comparison" (Croft 2003: 1). Typological research takes linguistic diversity as its point of departure, assumes that the variation across languages is restricted, and aims at discovering the systematicity behind it.

The typological research angle that is probably most interesting for cognitive linguists is *semantic typology*, which comprises "the systematic cross-linguistic study of how languages express meaning by way of signs" (Evans 2011: 504). Semantic typology is orthogonal to the more traditional compartments of typology, such as phonetic/phonological, grammatical or lexical, since meanings are normally expressed by an intricate interplay among signs of various kinds – words, morphological markers, syntactic constructions, prosody, gestures, etc.

This chapter will focus on some of the linguistic domains where painstaking semantic comparison according to the standards of linguistic typology has demonstrated significant linguistic diversity coupled with regularities of great value for cognitive research. Purely grammatical phenomena (e.g., tense), as well as those that have mainly figured in grammatical discussions (e.g., word classes) are left out here. The majority of cases discussed will involve meanings expressed by lexical items, often in combination with particular constructions (*lexical semantic typology*, or just *lexical typology*). But even with these restrictions, it is not possible to do justice to all the semantic-typological research within the limited space of this chapter (for overviews and references cf. Brown 2001; Goddard 2001; Koptjevskaja-Tamm 2008; Koch 2001; Evans 2011).

The main emphasis will be on the *linguistic categorization* of different cognitive domains and/or on *different meanings* that can be expressed by one and the same word (often coupled with different constructions) or by words related to each other (either synchronically or historically), with somewhat different relative weight attached to these issues in different cases. Both categorization within cognitive domains (onomaseology) and questions of polysemy and semantic shifts, and in particular universal metaphoric and metonymic processes (semasiology) are, of course, central issues in cognitive semantics. The discussion will touch upon the following questions:

- How do speakers of different languages categorize a particular cognitive domain by means of words and other linguistic expressions?
- To what extent is linguistic categorization universal or language- and culture-specific?
- What semantic shifts are frequent across languages?
- What is the interplay among the various factors that shape linguistic categorization and patterns of semantic shifts?

2. Semantic typology: selected major examples

2.1. Colour

COLOUR has figured prominently in linguistic and anthropological research, in cognitive research in general and in cognitive linguistics in particular, among others, in discussion of prototypes (cf. Taylor this volume) and embodiment. It is a popular textbook example of striking cross-linguistic diversity in *linguistic categorization*, which has been claimed to be severely restricted, at least with respect to basic terms (allegedly present in all languages) and their foci. In the universalist view, stemming from Eleanor (Heider) Rosch's experiments on colour cognition among the Dugum Dani (Heider 1972) and the colour-naming survey by Berlin and Kay (1969), all languages choose their subsets of basic terms from a universal stock according to a universal hierarchy. Universality in linguistic colour categorisation is supposed to originate in the neurophysiology of vision (Kay and McDaniel 1978), and/or in the visual environment of humans (Shepard 1992).

This view has been strongly challenged by "relativists", such as Levinson (2001), Lucy (1997), or Wierzbicka (2005). They have, among other things, questioned the validity of the decontextualized denotation-based methodology (various tasks based on Munsell chips) underlying the lion's share of colour studies in the Berlin-Kay paradigm. It is, for instance, doubtful whether COLOUR constitutes a coherent semantic domain in many languages once their putative "basic" colour terms have undergone proper linguistic analysis (cf. Levinson 2000), not to mention the fact that the word 'colour' is absent from many (most?) of the world's languages. People use colour words (or words that come up as colour words in the Berlin-Kay paradigm) for communicating meanings that can hardly be reduced to the physiology of seeing but are most probably based on comparison with salient visual prototypes in the environments – universal (sky, fire or blood) or more local (such as local minerals) (Wierzbicka 2005). And surely, the word for 'red' in a language that only has 'black', 'white' and 'red' simply cannot *mean* the same as 'red' in a language with a richer repertoire of colour words.

Significantly, the distribution of the different colour systems across the languages of the world shows remarkable geographic differences (cf. Kay and Maffi 2005; Kay et al. 2009). For instance, many of the languages that do not distinguish 'blue' and 'green' (the "grue" languages, the majority of the 120 languages in Kay and Maffi 2005) are concentrated to the tropics. The inhabitants of these areas are exposed to sunlight with high proportions of ultraviolet-B, which, in turn, often leads to deficiency in colour vision (Lindsey and Brown 2002; Bornstein 2007). This casts additional doubts on the universality of the focal colour categories available to all (sighted) human beings.

COLOUR remains the most widely cross-linguistically studied domain in terms of the languages covered by systematic methodology and the intensity of theoretical discussions (cf. Malt and Wolff [eds.] 2010 for recent overviews; MacLaury et al. 2007 and references therein; and http://www.icsi.berkeley.edu/wcs/ for the World Color Survey Site).

2.2. From COGNITION to PERCEPTION

The well-known and putatively universal *metaphor* KNOWING IS SEEING (a special case of the THINKING IS PERCEIVING metaphor in the MIND-AS-BODY system) has been central in the discussions of embodiment (Sweetser 1990; Lakoff and Johnson 1999; Bergen this volume). In her influential study, Sweetser (1990) notices that in Indo-European languages, verbs of seeing often demonstrate metaphorical extensions to meanings of thinking and/or knowing. This contrasts them with verbs for other perception modalities. In particular, verbs of hearing often show semantic extensions to understanding and/or to obeying (social interaction). In Sweetser's (1990: 37) words, "[t]he objective, intellectual side of our mental life seems to be regularly linked with the sense of vision", because vision is our "primary source of data about the objective world", because it has "the ability to pick out one stimulus at will from many", and because it may be shared by different people in the same place. Hearing, on the other hand, is primarily connected to linguistic communication and is therefore a person's powerful means of intellectual and emotional power over other people. Sweetser hypothesizes that "[t]he link between physical hearing and obeying or heeding – between physical and internal receptivity or reception – may well, in fact, be universal, rather than merely Indo-European" (1990: 42) and that "[i]t would be a novelty for a verb meaning 'hear' to develop a usage meaning 'know' rather than 'understand', whereas such a usage is common for verbs meaning 'see'" (1990: 43).

However, as shown by Evans and Wilkins (2000) and contrary to Sweetser's hypotheses, the most recurrent semantic extension in Australian Aboriginal languages is between the auditory sense and cognition, whereas the visual sense mostly gives rise to social interaction readings such as desire and sexual attraction, aggression, etc. Also in Vanhove's (2008) sample of twenty-five languages from eight linguistic phyla, verbs of hearing normally have at least one extension to cognition, while the shift from vision to cognition is less common.

The discussion of these different patterns revolves in fact around the interaction between universal and cultural sides of embodiment. For Evans and Wilkins, the extensions from 'hear' to 'know' and 'think' in the Australian Aboriginal languages are rooted in social and cultural practices, among them the avoidance of literal face-to-face conversation and particular cultural scripts connecting learning to hearing stories and 'song lines'. In fact, the anthropology of senses suggests that the primacy of vision in modern societies is partly a social construct, possibly privileged by literacy, whereas oral traditions might privilege other senses, chiefly audition (Classen 1993). However, the straightforward connection between literacy vs. oral traditions and extensions from vision vs. hearing to cognition has not been confirmed (Vanhove 2008).

Vision does, however, appear to be primary within the linguistic domain of perception itself. Quite a few languages do not have dedicated verbs for the different sense modalities, but "conflate" several senses in one and the same verb. The Papuan language Kalam offers probably the most widely-quoted example, where "[i]n different contexts *nŋ*-, occurring as the lone content verb in a clause, may be glossed as 'know, be conscious, be aware, be awake, think, see, hear, smell, taste, feel, recognize, notice, understand, remember, learn, study'" (Pawley 1994: 392). There are, however, ways of making the intended "reading" more specific, e.g., by adding 'eye' vs. 'ear' for 'seeing' vs. 'hearing'. Would that mean that the Kalam speakers simply have one under-differentiated linguistic category for PERCEPTION and COGNITION? Or should *nŋ*- be analyzed as primarily meaning 'know' with extensions to perception, as primarily meaning 'perceive' with extensions to cognition, or as multiply polysemous and distinguishing between the senses of 'see', 'hear', and 'know' (cf. Goddard 2001 for an outline of the possible solutions)? In his influential work on perception verbs in fifty languages, Viberg (e.g., 2001) analyzes such cases as polysemy and shows that lexicalization of perception by verbs across languages and the patterns of sense conflation follow the sense-modality hierarchy

$$\text{sight} > \text{hearing} > \begin{matrix} \text{touch} \\ \text{taste} \\ \text{smell} \end{matrix}$$

That is, if a language has a dedicated verb for touching, tasting or smelling, it will distinguish between hearing and seeing verbs. Also 'see' or 'hear' may be used for the lower sense modalities (cf. *slyšat' zapax* 'lit. hear a smell' in Russian), but no languages will use tasting or smelling verbs for talking about vision. Later research has, by far and large, confirmed these cross-linguistic findings.

To conclude, the metaphor THINKING IS PERCEIVING seems to hold across languages, although its more concrete manifestation, KNOWING IS SEEING, is less universal than has been suggested in Sweetser (1990) and Lakoff and Johnson (1999), at least when it comes to verbs. Research on the semantics and grammar of perception and cognition is on the whole very active (cf. Aikhenvald and Storch 2013 for a recent addition).

2.3. MOTION events

For cognitively minded linguists and cognitive scientists, cross-linguistic research on MOTION is, most probably, firmly associated with the tradition stemming from Talmy's seminal chapter (1985) (cf. Filipović this volume), where much of the recent research focuses on Talmy's later distinction between verb-framed and satellite-framed languages.

However, the latest systematic investigations of languages that were not represented in Talmy's research and a closer attention to some of those that were have led to significant modifications of the Talmy typology. These involve both the addition of new types and the insight that languages make use of multiple constructional types depending on which particular motion event is involved (Croft et al. 2010: 233). Verkerk (2014) provides a statistical corroboration to the latter insight on the basis of a parallel corpus for sixteen Indo-European languages, which employ the different motion constructions to different extents. This is very much in line with the dominant position in modern typological research that classifications normally apply to particular phenomena rather than to whole languages. Languages as wholes are seldom purely isolating, agglutinating or flectional, exclusively nominative-accusative or ergative, etc., but normally have different mixtures of these properties.

The linguistic motion domain is, however, very complex and heterogeneous and lends itself to cross-linguistic research from different angles (e.g., the distinction between the 'DEICTIC' MOTION verb ['come'] and the 'non-deictic' verb ['go'] in Ricca 1993; Wilkins and Hill 1995; Wälchli and Cysouw 2012; or verbs of motion in a liquid Ground, AQUAMOTION, http://aquamotion.narod.ru/index-eng.html; Maisak and Rakhilina 2007; Koptjevskaja-Tamm et al. 2010).

2.4. BODY from different angles

BODY is one of the most crucial domains for cognitive linguistics and for cognitive research in general, given the strong commitment to embodiment (cf. Bergen this volume). A particularly interesting topic is the use of BODY-PART terms in conventionalised descriptions of EMOTIONS, MENTAL STATES and PERSONAL TRAITS, where languages differ significantly in which body-parts can be seats for which emotions and mental states (e.g., Enfield and Wierzbicka 2002; Sharifian et al. 2008; Maalej and Yu 2011).

Body-part terms also often develop into markers for SPATIAL RELATIONS (e.g., 'head' > 'on' or 'back' > 'behind'), numbers ('hand' > 'five'), etc., following cross-linguistically common grammaticalization patterns with interesting geographic variations (see Koptjevskaja-Tamm 2008: 27–31 for details).

However, the body itself, in its concrete physical manifestation, and consisting of seemingly self-evident parts, is also a fascinating object for cross-linguistic studies. The basic issue here is which parts of the body are labelled across languages, i.e., conceptualized as categories of their own, and what factors underlie this. There are some well-known "deviations" from what seems to be normal for speakers of English or French: Russian uses *ruka* for both hand and arm, *noga* for both 'foot 'and 'leg', and *palec* for both 'finger' (including the thumb) and 'toe'. But still, aren't there any clear partitions of the body? Aren't there universal linguistic body-part concepts?

Now, the Russian *ruka*, covering both 'hand' and 'arm', turns out not to be exotic against the background of the world's languages: 228 languages in Brown's (2005a) sample of 617 (i.e., 37%) languages show the same pattern. Even more strikingly, quite a few languages of the world (72 languages of the 593 languages, i.e., 12% in Brown 2005b) have the same word for 'hand' and 'finger'.

Research on the whole body covers only a handful of languages, but is an important example of cross-linguistic generalizations on linguistic categorization. For instance, Brown (1976) and Andersen (1978) suggest the following two *generalizations*:

– There will be distinct terms for BODY, HEAD, ARM, EYES, NOSE and MOUTH
– If there is a distinct term for FOOT (as opposed to LEG), then there will be a distinct term for HAND (as opposed to ARM).

'Body' has also been suggested to be a universally lexicalized concept within the Natural Semantic Metalanguage (cf. Goddard 2001; Wierzbicka 2007). However, many of the earlier generalizations have been challenged by the studies of ten lesser-known languages in Majid et al. (2006). For instance, Lavukaleve, a Papuan language isolate spoken on the Russell islands within the central Solomon Islands (Terrill 2006: 316), has one and the same word, *tau*, for both ARM and LEG, but none for ARM or LEG specifically, contradicting the claim that ARM is always lexicalized by a distinct term. Lavukaleve has also a distinct simple word, *fe*, for reference to FOOT, but nothing comparable for HAND – contradicting therefore the second claim above. Some of the languages in Majid et al. (2006) and elsewhere (e.g., Wilkins 1996) seem to lack the distinct label for BODY itself, as e.g., opposed to 'person', 'skin' or 'body', contradicting the first of the above-mentioned generalizations (and strongly contested in Wierzbicka 2007).

Majid (2010) gives an excellent summary of how a cross-linguistic categorization of the body challenges many of the current views on body parts in perception. Vision has been privileged over other senses in discussions about "natural" segments of the body, most of which use various versions of visual processing models such as the 3D theory by Marr (1982) whereby the different parts of human body are represented by a three-dimensional hierarchical model. However, "[t]here is now an emerging literature on how body parts are represented and organized in different perceptual modalities, as well as how these sensorial representations are pooled together to create an integrated and holistic representation of the body and its parts" (Majid 2010: 59–60). For instance, intentional actions may either disrupt or unify perception of body parts. Thus, two tactile stimuli applied to either the hand or to the arm are perceived closer than when one of them applies to the hand and the other to the arm. However, the perceptual distance between the hand and the arm decreases when the person has to move his/her hands (de Vignemont et al. 2009). Majid concludes that there are different body partonomies for different representational systems, but joints – and the concomitant perceptual discontinuities – appear to constitute landmarks for segmentation and provide limits on where languages may draw boundaries in their body-part nomenclature.

Some of the factors behind the cross-linguistic differences in how languages categorize the body may also be sought in the physical, socio-historical and cultural environment. Brown (2005a, 2005b) suggests that the significant statistical asymmetries in the distributions of the languages with the same word for FINGER and HAND, and of those with the same word for HAND and ARM are correlated either with geography/climate or with culture. Thus, languages without the HAND-ARM distinction tend to occur more frequently near the equator, which may be accounted for by the fact that people living in other parts of the world often need extensive clothing, which greatly increases the distinctiveness of arm parts. Languages without FINGER-HAND distinction tend to be spoken by traditional hunter-gatherers or by groups having a mixed economy of cultivation and foraging. These often lack the habit of carrying finger rings, which makes fingers salient as distinct hand parts (Brown 2005a, 2005b).

2.5. TEMPERATURE

Cross-l(inguistic research on temperature is a relatively new addition to semantic typology. The TEMPERATURE domain constitutes the focus of a recent collaborative project covering more than fifty genetically, areally and typologically diverse languages (Koptjevskaja-Tamm 2015). Significantly, where English has a fairly rich inventory of temperature words (*hot, warm, lukewarm, chilly, cool, cold*, etc.), many languages manage with a simple opposition between two, 'hot/warm' vs. 'cool/cold'. In addition, the temperature systems often consist of several subparts that behave differently. For instance, languages often single out personal-feeling temperatures ('I feel cold') by special words or by particular constructions, as compared to tactile temperatures ('The stones are cold') and to ambient temperature ('It is cold here'). On the other hand, the linguistic encoding of ambient temperature may share properties with those of either tactile or personal-feeling temperature. The motivation for this lies in the conceptual and perceptual affinities of ambient temperature with both of the other frames of temperature evaluation. Thus, ambient and personal-feeling temperature are rooted in the same type of experience, thermal comfort, whereas tactile temperature relates to evaluation of the temperature of other entities, based on perception received by the skin. However, both tactile and ambient temperatures are about temperatures that can be verified from "outside", whereas personal-feeling temperature is about a subjective "inner" experience of a living being. In addition some entities, for instance water, may require particularly elaborated subsystems of temperature expressions, with additional expressions for extreme temperature values, such as 'ice-cold' and 'boiling hot', or for in-between temperatures like 'tepid'. This is, in turn, linked to the omnipresence and importance of water in human life, where its functioning for different purposes requires a particular temperature. This questions the universality of TEMPERATURE as a coherent semantic domain in many languages, an assumption usually held in cognitive research and in cognitive linguistics (see Clausner and Croft 1999; cf. the discussion of colour in section 2.1).

The interest of cognitive linguists and cognitive researchers in temperature has so far been mainly related to metaphors underlying emotions, e.g., AFFECTION IS WARMTH (Lakoff and Johnson 1999: 50) and ANGER IS HEAT (Kövecses 1995). An important question raised in Geeraerts and Grondelaers (1995) is to what degree such extensions reflect universal metaphorical patterns or are based on common cultural traditions. The results in Koptjevskaja-Tamm (2015) show that while some languages demonstrate elaborated systems of such uses, quite a few languages lack them altogether. Languages also vary as to which temperature term has predominantly positive associations in its extended uses (e.g., 'cold' rather than 'warm'), partly due to the different climatic conditions.

Section 2 has hopefully demonstrated the value of bringing in linguistic diversity into research on "how language relates to mind". Due to the space limitations, much of the other important research has been left out here, e.g., the foundational work on space (Levinson and Wilkins 2006, Levinson and Meira 2003, Ameka and Levinson 2007) – some of which is reported on in Coventry (this volume) – or the abundant literature on KINSHIP and EMOTIONS across languages. Some of the new areas addressed in recent cross-linguistic studies include CUT and BREAK (Majid and Bowerman 2007), LOCATION (Ameka and Levinson 2007), PUT and TAKE (Narasimhan and Kopecka 2012) and PAIN (Reznikova et al. 2012). The rest of the chapter will present the methodological, theoretical and typological insights accumulated in all this research.

3. Methodological challenges in semantic typology

Semantic typology has to find its own way for balancing the methodological and theoretical ambitions of both theoretical semantics and general typology.

Serious work in semantics presupposes taking a stance on two major and partly interrelated problems: what can be meant by meaning and how to solve the issue of *polysemy/ semantic generality/vagueness*. For most semanticists, semantic analysis stands for understanding *descriptive meaning*, *sense*, or *intension*, rather than *denotation/extension*. This is especially true for cognitive semantics, for which linguistic meanings always imply a certain construal of a particular situation (cf. Langacker this volume) and are laden with particular associations, intimately related to the speakers' "world" knowledge. In line with the general usage-based view within cognitive linguistics, the meanings of linguistic expressions are consequences of their uses, and word meanings are always associated with certain constructions. Conversely, conventional meanings associated with linguistic expressions only partially sanction the senses evoked in particular contexts. As a consequence, there are different opinions on what counts as polysemy both within Cognitive Linguistics and also among different semantic theories, practices (such as dictionary entries) and language users (see Riemer 2005 and Gries this volume).

Typological and cross-linguistic research has its own methodological issues. First of all, it is dependent on comparable data from (many) different languages. Cross-linguistic identification of studied phenomena presupposes a procedure which ensures that we compare like with like. Crucially, it should involve theory-neutral or framework-neutral definitions and concern observable phenomena. Another big issue concerns language sampling: a large sample representing the world's languages is a preferred option if we want to say something general about cross-linguistic variation and its limits. Languages often share similarities because of common ancestry, but also because of direct and indirect contacts among them. Therefore something you find by comparing English, French, German, Czech, Hungarian and even Basque does *not* have to be a universal, but might be a result of combined genetic and prolonged contact factors: a "Standard Average European" property. In general, modern typological research is very cautious in declaring "universals", i.e., properties that are believed to be present in all or most languages. Most universals suggested by cross-linguistic comparison have either been falsified or have been shown to have many counter-examples (cf. The Universals Archive in Konstanz, http://typo.uni-konstanz.de/archive/intro/index.php). The World Atlas of Language Structures (Haspelmath et al. 2005; Dryer and Haspelmath 2011) is the currently most ambitious and most quoted collective achievement in linguistic typology, primarily devoted to grammatical and phonetic phenomena.

Most of the cross-linguistic research on semantics, and in particular, on lexicon is based on elicited data. The "Nijmegen method" of semantic typology uses standardized stimuli, such as sets of pictures, videoclips and films for collecting data on a number of cognitive domains directly in the field (cf. http://fieldmanuals.mpi.nl/). Each set covers a shared denotational grid allowing systematic comparisons of semantic distinctions potentially relevant for the domain and may be used under different elicitation conditions, including games. Data for many studies is collected by means of questionnaires, ranging from simple translational questionnaires (e.g., Viberg's 2001 research on perception verbs) to much more sophisticated questionnaires which elicit verbal descriptions of various situations (e.g., deictic verbs in Ricca 1993 and Wilkins and Hill 1995; pain descriptions in Reznikova et al. 2012; temperature descriptions in Koptjevskaja-Tamm 2015). Comparison of parallel texts (translations of one and the same text) is now gradually gaining ground as a relatively new and promising method for data collection in cross-linguistic work, where the number of translations vary from just a few to more than 100 (cf. Wälchli and Cysouw 2012). Cross-linguistic semantic studies based on secondary sources, like dictionaries, are quite limited (some of the exceptions include Andersen 1978; Brown 1976, 2005a, 2005b; Sweetser 1990 and François 2008).

Each data collection method has its merits and drawbacks. Elicitation techniques are designed as a systematic grid for targeting the key aspects of the relevant linguistic phenomena, but non-elicited data may disclose interesting and unexpected sides of the phenomena that the researcher was not aware of. Also many meanings hardly lend themselves to being investigated via stimuli: for instance, mental states such as *think*, or abstract domains such as POSSESSION and EXISTENCE (cf. also Evans and Sasse 2007).

Elicited data are most often decontextualized, although the degree of decontextualization varies significantly between different techniques and studies. Retelling a film for someone who has not seen it or exchanging verbal instructions during a game more closely reflect language in normal use than describing a series of disconnected videoclips or naming colour chips. Parallel texts have a clear advantage here as a source of context-embedded natural data that are semantically comparable across languages, even though translational equivalents across languages, in particular within a longer text, are never completely equivalent. The one text available in many languages are the various versions of the New Testament, which has severe limitations, but is a good source for studying motion events (cf. Wälchli and Cysouw 2012).

A successful study in semantic typology benefits from a combination of different types of data. Most of the recent enterprises with this orientation have been carried out as joint projects involving experts on particular languages. Because of this, studies in semantic typology usually operate with much more limited language samples (between ten and fifty languages) than is the norm in grammatical and phonetic typology.

A further issue is how the data are analyzed and how the results of the analysis are represented. Much of the current research in semantic typology sees the meanings of linguistic expressions as sets of uses, or as "etic definitions". To quote Levinson and Wilkins (2006: 8), "an 'etic' metalanguage (coined on the model of 'phonetic' by Pike) is some objective description of the domain which makes maximal discriminations, so that we can specify precisely how a language groups these discriminations within its own 'emic' (cf. 'phonemic') concepts". The step from "etic" to "emic" concepts is, however, far from trivial (cf. Evans 2011) and involves decisions as to which of the uses count as the same meaning viz. as instances of polysemy. Different decisions lead to different consequences, e.g., in conclusions about linguistic categories. For instance, Wierzbicka (2007) argues that it is far from clear to what extent the exclusively denotationally oriented research on body in Majid et al. (2006) gets to grips with the "real" meanings of the expressions under study and, consequently, with the categories perceived as different by those who use them. In other words, even though *ruka* in Russian covers both ARM and LEG, there might be reasons for distinguishing between the two meanings rather than lumping them into one. Only in the latter case is it legitimate to claim that the language does not conceptualize arm and leg as two distinct parts of the body.

The problem of a consistent meta-language for describing meaning across languages is enormous. This, in turn, relates to the general gap between theoretical semantics and actual lexicographic practices. Although cognitive semanticists oppose their "encyclopaedic" view on lexical meanings with the usual "dictionary view" (e.g., V. Evans and Green 2006: 207–222), there is little practical lexicographic work done in this tradition, with the notable exception of the FrameNet project (www.isci.berkeley.edu/framenet/). A growing praxis in semantic typology is to represent its findings by means of semantic maps, which are more or less explicitly agnostic about the distinction between polysemy and semantic generality. Standard "implicational" semantic maps, originally used for grammatical devices (Haspelmath 2003: 231), and further successfully extended to lexicon (François 2008) compete with "probabilistic" semantic maps, built automatically by means of statistical analysis techniques, e.g., multidimensional scaling (Cysouw and Wälchli 2012; Majid et al. 2007). Such maps are normally produced for the purpose of a particular study, which, unfortunately, creates obstacles for evaluating cross-linguistic connections even between studies of high semantic and lexicographic quality.

An important candidate for a consistent metalanguage for the purposes of cross-linguistic comparison is the Natural Semantic Metalanguage (NSM), originally advocated by Anna Wierzbicka. The proponents of the NSM strive to compare descriptive meanings rather than denotational ranges and aim at providing meaning definitions by means of reductive paraphrases based on a principled set of "universal semantic primitives" (e.g., Goddard and Wierzbicka 1994; Goddard 2001; Wierzbicka 2007). NSM linguists have recently proposed a systematic approach to lexical typology using the notions of semantic molecules and templates (e.g., Goddard 2012). The theory has both positive and negative sides, its strong basic assumption is debatable (cf., e.g., Riemer 2005 and

Evans 2011), but on the whole it deserves more attention in the typological enterprise and in cognitive linguistics than it has enjoyed so far.

4. Lessons from semantic typology

Cross-linguistic research on categorization (onomaseological semantic typology) starts from the basic assumption that experiences systematically encoded by one and the same linguistic label are perceived as representing one and the same category or categories closely related to each other. The question is then to what extent linguistic categorization is universal or language- and culture-specific. Some researchers consider categorization universal, at least when it comes to basic, universal and daily situations, so that lexical meanings "originate in non-linguistic cognition, and are shaped by perceptual and cognitive predispositions, environmental and biological constraints, and activities common to people everywhere" (Majid et al. 2007: 134). The radically relativistic view holds that the cross-linguistic variation in categorization is hardly limited at all and that meanings of linguistic expressions across languages are largely incommensurable.

The achievements of semantic typology provide evidence for an in-between position, i.e., that the cross-linguistic variation in how languages categorize one and the same domain operates within a constrained space, which in each case is defined in terms of cross-linguistically important dimensions. Some of these dimensions may, further, be explained by the human anatomy, and/or by general perceptual and cognitive predispositions. The examples of such explanations include neurophysiology of vision for colour (section 2.1) and its primacy within perception for categorization of perception by means of verbs (section 2.2), interaction of different perceptual modalities for the categorization of the body (section 2.3), or the structure of temperature perception (section 2.5). Perceptually salient topological features such as containment vs. support, properties of the figure (including animacy and agency) vs. ground are decisive for structuring various space- and motion-related domains (Levinson and Wilkins 2006; Ameka and Levinson 2007; Narasimhan and Kopecka 2012). The preferable attention to endpoints of motions rather than to sources may explain why the expression system for taking events in a language never displays a higher degree of elaboration than the one for putting events (cf. Narasimhan and Kopecka 2012 for the details and references).

Environmental factors, typical human activities (including communication), socio-cultural patterns, etc., are also often evoked as responsible for the shaping of linguistic categorization and for its instantiation in a particular language (cf. section 2.4 on TEMPERATURE and section 2.2 on the 'hand'/'arm', and 'hand'/'finger' distinctions).

Now, even though linguistic categorization of a particular domain normally operates within a constrained space, languages manifest an amazing cross-linguistic variation. First of all, there is an enormous diversity in the sheer number of lexical categories for carving up a certain domain. For instance, for describing 61 distinct cutting and breaking videoclips, the speakers of Yélî Dnye (Papuan) used only three verbs (Levinson 2007), whereas the Tzeltal (Mayan) speakers used more than fifty (Brown 2007).

In addition, even systems with comparable degrees of elaboration may differ in the details of the partitioning, e.g., in the placement of category boundaries. Categories, as they emerge in the course of cross-linguistic research, do not look like classical Aristotelian categories with necessary and sufficient meaning components, but have fuzzy boundaries and are rather organized in terms of prototypes, in the tradition of the mainstream cognitively oriented semantic research. One and the same situation may often be construed in different ways and may, consequently, be expressed by two different categories.

Much of what has been said above on onomaseological semantic typology applies, mutandis mutandis, to its semasiological counterpart, i.e., research on cross-linguistically recurrent metaphorical and metonymical patterns and other semantic associations. There are, however, unique methodological complications inherent in systematic cross-linguistic research on metaphor and metonymy. Conceptual Metaphor Theory emphasizes conceptual association that does not boil down to individual metaphorical uses or to linguistic convention. But to quote Gibbs (this volume), "cognitive linguists, and others, should articulate criteria for identifying metaphoric patterns in language and inferring specific conceptual metaphors from discourse. These procedures should be specified with sufficient detail so that other researchers can possibly replicate the analysis and emerge with similar conclusions". Translated into the methodology of systematic cross-linguistic research, this means that we can only test the extent to which some concrete manifestations of suggested metaphors hold (e.g., whether verbs for seeing are systematically extended to perception, or whether words for 'warm' are systematically extended to emotions), rather than whether the conceptual metaphors KNOWING IS SEEING or AFFECTION IS WARMTH as a whole are universal.

There are cross-linguistically recurrent patterns in semasiological typology, and the roots for them and for the cross-linguistic variation in their manifestations may again be found in human biology, perception, cognition, physical environment, typical human activities, history or socio-cultural patterns (cf. sections 2.4 and 2.5 on the use of body and temperature for talking about emotions and section 2.2 for the connection between perception and cognition). Pain is often described by means of cross-linguistically recurrent and conventionalized metaphors (Reznikova et al. 2012), and there are cross-linguistically recurrent metaphorical and metonymical patterns underlying body part nomenclature (Wilkins 1996; Koch 2008; Urban 2012).

A final reflection concerns the traditional separation between grammatical typology, focusing on the grammatical behaviour of words and on morphosyntactic patterns, and lexical typology, that has largely been restricted to domain-categorization by lexical means. This somewhat artificial distinction is coupled with fundamental problems. As Lucy (1997) points out, the mainstream tradition of research into colour terms across languages does not presuppose any deeper linguistic analysis of these terms. "Articles surveying terms in a dozen or more languages never mention anything about those languages, or even about the structural value of the terms. *You do not need to know anything about languages or linguistics at all to read this literature or even to conduct research within the tradition*" (1997: 330).

Fortunately, the recent developments within semantic typology witness an ambition to reconcile the lexical and grammatical interests and to engage in a dialogue with linguistic grammatical theory. Much of the research on space and motion explicitly transcends the lexicon-grammar distinction (Levinson and Wilkins 2006; Ameka and Levinson 2007.) Another example is the project on categorization of the CUT and BREAK domain (Majid and Bowerman 2007), where one of the leading issues has been the interface between syntax and lexical semantics, i.e., to what extent and how the argument structure properties of a verb are predictable from its meaning. An even more ambitious research agenda aiming at comparing wholesale verbal lexical profiles of different languages and their repercussions for the grammatical characteristics has been proposed by Kibrik (2012).

Cognitively minded linguists will certainly appreciate the rise of Construction Grammar (Casenhiser and Bencini this volume) as an appropriate framework for semantic-typological research, e.g., on PAIN predicates (Reznikova et al. 2012), on TEMPERATURE (Koptjevskaja-Tamm 2015), and on LOCATION−EXISTENCE−POSSESSION (Koch 2012). The Construction-Grammar inspired schemas are capable of covering linguistic phenomena on different levels (lexicon and grammar), are both sufficiently systematic for capturing cross-linguistic (dis)similarities and sufficiently flexible for leaving room for language- and phenomenon-specific details.

5. Further research questions

Systematic research in semantic typology has so far been carried out on rather limited language samples. These are often sufficient for falsifying some assumptions on the universality of a particular phenomenon and for unveiling major patterns in its cross-linguistic variation, but are hardly adequate for drawing reliable conclusions on the interplay among the various factors behind it and for clearly distinguishing between universal determinants and those due to historical relations among the languages. Systematic research in semantic typology needs, therefore, to be extended to more linguistic phenomena and to more languages. In particular, sign languages have been largely missing in most studies of semantic typology.

But there are further fascinating research issues that will benefit from taking into consideration linguistic diversity and findings in semantic typology, for instance

- How do linguistic and non-linguistic categories relate to each other? (See Malt et al. 1999 on a difference between linguistic and non-linguistic categorization of household storage containers among the speakers of American English, Argentinean Spanish and Mandarin Chinese.)
- How do linguistic and non-linguistic domains relate to each other? For instance, although COLOUR or TEMPERATURE languages are usually assumed to be coherent cognitive domains, languages do not necessarily treat them as such, cf. sections 2.1 and 2.5.
- Do semantic differences in the linguistic categorization systems and in the metaphorical/metonymical patterns affect cognition, perception and/or non-verbal behaviour in speakers of different languages? Compare here the revived interest for the issue of linguistic relativity (Li and Gleitman 2002; Levinson et al. 2002; Slobin 2003; Malt and Wolff [eds.] 2010).
- Will there be differences in linguistic categorization, cognition and perception in bilingual speakers as compared to monolingual ones and will these differences depend on the differences among the languages involved? (See Athanasopoulos et al. 2010 or A. Brown and Gullberg 2008 on the gradual conversion in the speakers' linguistic descriptions, cognitive processing, gestures and unconscious perception between the L1 and L2 systems.)

- Will there be substantial differences in how children acquire linguistic categories in different languages? (See Bowerman and Choi 2003 and Parish-Morris et al. 2010 on the gradual replacement of children's pre-language sensitivity to many different properties of specific spatial situations by selective sensitivity to the categories relevant in the language that the child is acquiring.)
- To what extent will semantic differences in the linguistic categorization systems and in the metaphorical/metonymical patterns find correlates in how these are represented in the brain (cf. Kemmerer 2010)?
- What is the division of labour across different sign modalities in expressing meaning? Can the semantic choices made in one subsystem affect the choices made in the other(s) (cf. "semiotic ecology" in Evans 2011)? We know very little about how information is distributed across different sign modalities, but some forms seem to be better for expressing certain things than others. For instance, in spite of all the rich lexical and grammatical resources for talking about space and emotions, precise spatial localization often requires deictic gestures, while emotion and emotional intensity is better captured by prosody, often together with gestures.

By pursuing these captivating questions, cross-linguistic diversity and semantic typology can make a substantial contribution to the study of how language relates to the human mind.

6. References

Aikhenvald, Alexandra Y. and Anne Storch (eds.)
  2013   *Perception and Cognition in Language and Culture*. Leiden: Brill.
Ameka, Felix K. and Stephen C. Levinson (eds.)
  2007   The typology and semantics of locative predication: Posturals, positionals and other beasts. *Linguistics* 45(5/6): 847–871.
Andersen, Elaine
  1978   Lexical universals of body-part terminology. In: J. H. Greenberg (ed.), *Universals of Human Language*, 335–368. Stanford: Stanford University Press.
Athanasopoulos, Panos, Benjamin Dering, Alison Wiggett, Jan-Rouke Kuipers and Guillaume Thierry
  2010   Perceptual shift in bilingualism: Brain potentials reveal plasticity in pre-attentive colour perception. *Cognition* 116(3): 437–443.
Bergen, Benjamin
  this volume   1. Embodiment. Berlin/Boston: De Gruyter Mouton.
Berlin, Brent and Paul Kay
  1969   *Basic Color Terms: Their Universality and Evolution*. Berkeley: University of California Press.
Bornstein, Marc H.
  2007   Hue categorization and color naming: Cognition to language to culture. In: R. MacLaury, G. V. Paramei and D. Dedrick (eds.), *Anthropology of Color: Interdisciplinary Multilevel Modeling*, 3–27. Amsterdam: John Benjamins.
Bowerman, Melissa and Soonja Choi
  2003   Space under construction: language-specific spatial categorization in first language acquisition. In: D. Gentner and S. Goldin-Meadow (eds.), *Language in Mind: Advances in the Study of Language and Thought*, 387–427. Cambridge: MIT Press

Brown, Amanda and Marianne Gullberg
  2008   Bidirectional crosslinguistic influence in L1-L2 encoding of manner in speech and gesture. *Studies in Second Language Acquisition* 30: 225–251.
Brown, Cecil H.
  1976   General principles of human anatomical partonomy and speculations on the growth of partonomic nomenclature. *American Ethnologist* 3: 400–424.
Brown, Cecil H.
  2001   Lexical typology from an anthropological point of view. In: M. Haspelmath, E. König, W. Oesterreicher and W. Raible (eds.), *Language Typology and Language Universals*, Volume 2, 1178–1190. Berlin: Walter de Gruyter.
Brown, Cecil H.
  2005a   Hand and arm. In: M. Haspelmath, M. Dryer, D. Gil and B. Comrie (eds.) *The World Atlas of Language Structures (WALS)*, 522–525. Oxford: Oxford University Press.
Brown, Cecil H.
  2005b   Finger and hand. In: M. Haspelmath, M. Dryer, D. Gil and B. Comrie (eds.) *The World Atlas of Language Structures (WALS)*, 526–529. Oxford: Oxford University Press.
Brown, Penelope
  2007   'She had just cut/broken off her head': Cutting and breaking verbs in Tzeltal. *Cognitive Linguistics* 18(2): 319–330
Casenhiser, Devin and Giulia Bencini
  this volume   28. Argument structure constructions. Berlin/Boston: De Gruyter Mouton.
Classen, Constance
  1993   *Worlds of Sense: Exploring the Senses in History and Across Cultures.* London: Routledge.
Clausner, Timothy C. and William Croft
  1999   Domains and image-schemas. *Cognitive Linguistics* 10: 1–31.
Coventry, Kenny
  this volume   23 Space. Berlin/Boston: De Gruyter Mouton.
Croft, William
  2003   *Typology and Universals* (Cambridge Textbooks in Linguistics). Cambridge: Cambridge University Press.
Croft, William, Jóhanna Barðdal, Willem Hollmann, Violeta Sotirova and Chiaki Taoka
  2010   Revising Talmy's typological classification of complex events. In: H. C. Boas (ed.), *Contrastive Construction Grammar*, 201–235. Amsterdam/Philadelphia: John Benjamins.
de Vignemont, Frédéreque, Asifa Majid, Corinne Jolla and Patrick Haggard
  2009   Segmenting the body into parts: evidence from biases in tactile perception. *Quarterly Journal of Experimental Psychology* 62: 500–512.
Dryer, Matthew S. and Martin Haspelmath (eds.)
  2011   *The World Atlas of Language Structures Online*. Max Planck Digital Library. http://wals.info/.
Enfield, N. J. and Anna Wierzbicka (eds.)
  2002   The body in description of emotion. *Pragmatics and cognition*, special issue 10(1–2).
Evans, Nicholas
  2011   Semantic typology. In J. J. Song (ed.), *The Oxford Handbook of Typology*, 504–533. Oxford: Oxford University Press.
Evans, Nicholas and Stephen Levinson.
  2009   The myth of language universals: Language diversity and its importance for cognitive science. *Behavioral and Brain Sciences* 32: 429 – 492.
Evans, Nicholas and Hans-Jürgen Sasse
  2007   Searching for meaning in the Library of Babel: Field semantics and problems of digital archiving. *Archives and Social Studies: A Journal of Interdisciplinary Research* 1.

(http://socialstudies.cartagena.es/index.php?option=com_contentandtask=viewandid=53andItemid=42)

Evans, Nicholas and David P. Wilkins
    2000   In the mind's ear: The semantic extensions of perception verbs in Australian languages. *Language* 76: 546–592.

Evans, Vyvyan and Melanie Green
    2006   *Cognitive Linguistics. An Introduction*. Mahwah/London: Lawrence Erlbaum

Filipović, Luna and Iraide Ibarretxe-Antuñano
    this volume   25. Motion. Berlin/Boston: De Gruyter Mouton.

François, Alexandre
    2008   Semantic maps and the typology of colexification: Intertwining polysemous networks across languages. In M. Vanhove (ed.), *From Polysemy to Semantic Change*, 163–215. Amsterdam/Philadelphia: John Benjamins.

Geeraerts, Dirk and Stef Grondelaers
    1995   Looking back at anger: Cultural traditions and metaphorical patterns. In J. R. Taylor & R. E. MacLaury (eds.), *Language and the Cognitive Construal of the World*. 153–179. Berlin: de Gruyter

Gibbs, Raymond W. Jr
    this volume   8. Metaphor. Berlin/Boston: De Gruyter Mouton.

Goddard, Cliff
    2001   Lexico-semantic universals: A critical overview. *Linguistic Typology* 5: 1–65.

Goddard, Cliff
    2012   Semantic primes, semantic molecules, semantic templates: Key concepts in the NSM approach to lexical typology. In: M. Koptjevskaja-Tamm and M. Vanhove (eds.), New directions in lexical typology. A special issue of *Linguistics* 50(3): 421–466.

Goddard, Cliff and Anna Wierzbicka (eds.)
    1994   *Semantic and Lexical Universals – Theory and Empirical Findings*. Amsterdam/Philadelphia: John Benjamins.

Gries, Stefan Th.
    this volume   22. Polysemy. Berlin/Boston: De Gruyter Mouton.

Haspelmath, Martin
    2003   The geometry of grammatical meaning: Semantic maps and cross-linguistic comparison. In: M. Tomasello (ed.), *The New Psychology of Language* 2. 211–242. Mahwah: Lawrence Erlbaum.

Haspelmath, Martin, Matthew Dryer, David Gil and Bernard Comrie
    2005   *The World Atlas of Language Structures (WALS)*. Oxford: Oxford University Press.

Haspelmath, Martin, Ekkehard König, Wulf Oesterreicher and Wolfgang Raible (eds.)
    2001   *Language Typology and Language Universals*, Volumes 1–2. Berlin: Walter de Gruyter.

Heider, Eleanor R.
    1972   Universals in color naming and memory. *Journal of Experimental Psychology* 93: 10–20.

Kay, Paul, Brent Berlin, Luisa Maffi, William R. Merrifield, and Richard Cook
    2009   *The World Color Survey*. Stanford: Center for the Study of Language and Information.

Kay, Paul and Lisa Maffi
    2005   Colour terms. In: M. Haspelmath, M. Dryer, D. Gil and B. Comrie (eds.), *The World Atlas of Language Structures (WALS)*, 534–545. Oxford: Oxford University Press.

Kay, Paul and Chad McDaniel
    1978   The linguistic significance of the meanings of basic color terms. *Language* 54: 610–46.

Kemmerer, David
    2010   How words capture visual experience: the perspective from cognitive neuroscience. In: B. C. Malt and P. Wolff (eds.), *Words and the Mind. How Words Capture Human Experience*, 287–327. Oxford: Oxford University Press.

Kibrik, Andrej
2011 *Reference in Discourse*. Oxford: Oxford University Press.
Kibrik, Andrej
2012 Toward a typology of verb lexical systems: A case study in Northern Athabaskan. In: M. Koptjevskaja-Tamm and M. Vanhove (eds.), New directions in lexical typology. A special issue of *Linguistics* 50(3): 495–532.
Koch, Peter
2001 Lexical typology from a cognitive and linguistic point of view. In: M. Haspelmath, E. König, W. Oesterreicher and W. Raible (eds.), *Language Typology and Language Universals*, Volume 2, 1142–1178. Berlin: Walter de Gruyter.
Koch, Peter
2008 Cognitive onomasiology and lexical change: around the eye. In: M. Vanhove (ed.), *From Polysemy to Semantic Change*, 107–137. Amsterdam/Philadelphia: John Benjamins.
Koch, Peter
2012 Location, existence, and possession: A constructional-typological exploration. In: M. Koptjevskaja-Tamm and M. Vanhove (eds.), New directions in lexical typology. A special issue of *Linguistics* 50(3): 533–604.
Koptjevskaja-Tamm, Maria
2008 Approaching lexical typology. In M. Vanhove (ed.), *From Polysemy to Semantic Change*, 3–52. Amsterdam/Philadelphia: John Benjamins.
Koptjevskaja-Tamm, Maria (ed.)
2015 *The Linguistics of Temperature*. Amsterdam/Philadelphia: John Benjamins.
Koptjevskaja-Tamm, Maria, Dagmar Divjak and Ekaterina Rakhilina
2010 Aquamotion verbs in Slavic and Germanic: A case study in lexical typology. In: V. Driagina-Hasko and R. Perelmutter (eds.), *New Approaches to Slavic Verbs of Motion*, 315–341. Amsterdam/Philadelphia: John Benjamins.
Koptjevskaja-Tamm, Maria and Martine Vanhove (eds.)
2012 New directions in lexical typology. A special issue of *Linguistics* 50(3).
Kövecses, Zoltan
1995 Anger: Its language, conceptualization, and physiology in the light of cross-cultural evidence. In: J. R. *Taylor* and R. E. *MacLaury* (eds.), *Language and the Cognitive Construal of the World*, 181–196. Berlin: Mouton de Gruyter.
Lakoff, George and Mark Johnson
1999 *Philosophy in the Flesh. The Embodied Mind and its Challenge to Western Thought*. New York: Basic books.
Langacker, Ronald W.
 this volume   6. Construal. Berlin/Boston: De Gruyter Mouton.
Levinson, Stephen
2001 Yélî Dnye and the theory of basic color terms. *Journal of Linguistic Anthropology* 10(1): 3–55.
Levinson, Stephen
2007 Cut and break verbs in Yélî Dnye, the Papuan language of Rossel Island. *Cognitive Linguistics* 18(2): 207–218.
Levinson, Stephen and Sergio Meira
2003 'Natural concepts' in the spatial topological domain – adpositional meanings in cross-linguistic perspective: an exercise in semantic typology. *Language* 79(3): 485–516.
Levinson, Stephen, Sotaro Kita, Daniel B. M. Hauna, and Björn H. Rasch.
2002 Returning the tables: Language affects spatial reasoning. *Cognition* 84: 155–188.
Levinson, Stephen and David Wilkins
2006 *Grammars of Space*. Cambridge: Cambridge University Press.
Li, Peggy and Lila Gleitman
2002 Turning the tables: language and spatial reasoning. *Cognition* 83: 265–294.

Lindsey, Delwin T. and Angela M. Brown
    2002   Color naming and the phototoxic effects of sunlight on the eye. *Psychological Science* 13(6): 506–512.
Lucy, John
    1997   The linguistics of 'color'. In C. L. Hardin and L. Maffi (eds.), *Color Categories in Thought and Language*, 320–346. Cambridge: Cambridge University Press.
Maalej, Zouheir A. and Ning Yu (eds.)
    2011   *Embodiment via Body Parts. Studies from Various Languages and Cultures.* Amsterdam/Philadelphia: John Benjamins Publishing Company.
MacLaury, Robert E., Galina V. Paramei and Don Dedrick (eds.)
    2007   *Anthropology of Color: Interdisciplinary Multilevel Modeling.* Amsterdam: John Benjamins.
Maisak, Timur and Ekaterina Rakhilina (eds.)
    2007   *Glagoly dviženija v vode: leksičeskaja tipologija.* [Verbs of motion and location in water: Lexical typology]. Moskva: Indrik.
Majid, Asifa
    2010   Words for parts of the body. In B. C. Malt and P. Wolff (eds.), *Words and the Mind. How Words Capture Human Experience*, 58–71. Oxford: Oxford University Press.
Majid, Asifa, and Melissa Bowerman
    2007   Cutting and breaking events: A crosslinguistic perspective. *Cognitive Linguistics* 18(2): 133–152.
Majid, Asifa, Nicholas J. Enfield and Miriam van Staden (eds.)
    2006   Parts of the body: Cross-linguistic categorisation. [Special issue] *Language Sciences*, 28(2–3).
Malt, Barbara C., Sloman, Steven A., Gennari, Silvia, Shi, Meiyi, and Wang, Yuan
    1999   Knowing versus naming: Similarity and the linguistic categorization of artifacts. *Journal of Memory and Language* 40: 230–262.
Malt, Barbara C. and Philipp Wolff (eds.)
    2010   *Words and the Mind. How Words Capture Human Experience.* Oxford: Oxford University Press.
Marr, David
    1982   *Vision: A Computational Investigation into the Human Representation and Processing of Visual Information.* New York: W.H. Freeman.
Narasimhan, Bhuvana and Anetta Kopecka (eds.)
    2012   *Events of 'Putting' and 'Taking': A Crosslinguistic Perspective.* Amsterdam/Philadelphia: John Benjamins.
Parish-Morris, Julia, Shannon M. Pruden, Weiyi Ma, Kathy Hirsh-Pasek and Roberta Michnick Golinkoff
    2010   A world of relations: relational words. In: B. C. Malt and P. Wolff (eds.), *Words and the Mind. How Words Capture Human Experience*, 219–242. Oxford: Oxford University Press.
Pawley, Andrew
    1994   Kalam exponents of lexical and semantic primitives. In: C. Goddard and A. Wierzbicka (eds.), *Semantic and Lexical Universals – Theory and Empirical Findings*, 387–422. Amsterdam/Philadelphia: John Benjamins.
Reznikova, Tatiana, Ekaterina Rakhilina and Anastasia Bonch-Osmolovskaya
    2012   Towards a typology of pain predicates. In: M. Koptjevskaja-Tamm and M. Vanhove (eds.), New directions in lexical typology. A special issue of *Linguistics*, 50(3): 421–466.
Ricca, Davide
    1993   *I verbi deittici di movimento in Europa: Una ricerca interlinguistica.* Firenze: La Nuova Italia Editrice.

Riemer, Nick
    2005   *The Semantics of Polysemy*. Berlin/New York: Mouton de Gruyter.
Sharifian, Farzad, René Dirven, Ning Yu, and Susanne Niemeier (eds.)
    2008   *Culture, Body and Language. Conceptualizations of Internal Body Organs Across Cultures and Languages*. Berlin: Mouton de Gruyter.
Shepard, Roger N.
    1992.   The perceptual organisation of colors: An adaptation to regularities of the terrestrial world? In: J. H. Barkow, L. Cosimedes, and J. Tooby (eds.), *The Adapted Mind: Evolutionary Psychology and the Generation of Culture*, 495–532. New York: Oxford University Press.
Slobin, Dan I.
    2003   Language and thought online: Cognitive consequences of linguistic relativity. In: D. Gentner and S. Goldin-Meadow (eds.), *Language in Mind: Advances in the Study of Language and Thought*, 157–191. Cambridge: MIT Press
Sweetser, Eve
    1990   *From Etymology to Pragmatics: Metaphorical and Cultural Aspects of Semantic Structure*. Cambridge: Cambridge University Press.
Talmy, Leonard
    1985   Lexicalization patterns. In T. Shopen (ed.), *Language Typology and Synchronic Description*, Volume 3, 47–159. Cambridge: Cambridge University Press.
Taylor, John R.
    this volume   27. Prototype effects in grammar. Berlin/Boston: De Gruyter Mouton.
Terrill, Angela
    2006   Body-part terms in Lavukaleve, a Papua language of the Solomon Islands. In: A. Majid, N. J. Enfield and M. van Staden (eds.), Parts of the Body: Cross-Linguistic Categorisation [Special issue] *Language Sciences*, 28(2–3): 304–322.
Urban, Matthias
    2012   *Analyzibility and Semantic Associations in Referring Expressions. A Study in Comparative Lexicology*. PhD Dissertation. Leiden University.
Vanhove, Martine
    2008   Semantic associations between sensory modalities, prehension and mental perceptions: A crosslinguistic perspective. In: M. Vanhove (ed.), *From Polysemy to Semantic Change*, 342–370. Amsterdam/Philadelphia: John Benjamins.
Verkerk, Annemarie
    2014   Where Alice fell into: Motion events from a parallel corpus. In B. Szmrecsanyi, and B. Wälchli (eds.), *Linguistic Variation in Text and Speech, Within and Across Languages*, 324–354. Berlin: de Gruyter.
Viberg, Åke
    2001   Verbs of perception. In: M. Haspelmath, E. König, W. Oesterreicher and W. Raible (eds.), *Language Typology and Language Universals*, Volume 2, 1294–1309. Berlin: Walter de Gruyter,
Wächli, Bernhard and Michael Cysouw
    2012   Lexical typology through similarity semantics: Toward a semantic map of motion verbs. In: M. Koptjevskaja-Tamm and M. Vanhove (eds.), New directions in lexical typology. A special issue of *Linguistics*, 50(3): 671–710.
Wierzbicka, Anna
    2005   There are no "color universals". But there are universals of visual semantics. *Anthropological Linguistics* 47(2): 217–244.
Wierzbicka, Anna
    2007   Bodies and their parts: an NSM approach to semantic typology. *Language Sciences* 29: 14–65.

Wilkins, David P.
　1996　Natural tendencies of semantic change and the search for cognates. In: M. Durie and M. Ross (eds.), *The Comparative Method Reviewed. Regularity and Irregularity in Language Change*, 264–304. New York/Oxford: Oxford University Press.

Wilkins, David P. and Deborah Hill
　1995　When GO means COME: Questioning the basicness of basic motion verbs. *Cognitive Linguistics* 6(2/3): 209–259.

Maria Koptjevskaja-Tamm, Stockholm (Sweden)

22. Polysemy

1. The notion of polysemy
2. Polysemy in cognitive linguistics
3. Polysemy in neighboring fields
4. Desiderata
5. References

1. The notion of polysemy

The probably most widely accepted definition of polysemy is as the form of ambiguity where 2+ related senses are associated with the same word; consider the meanings of *glass* in *I emptied the glass* ('container') and *I drank a glass* ('contents of the container'). Ever since this notion was proposed by Bréal (1897), it has been puzzling researchers from many disciplines: linguists, lexicographers, psycholinguists, psychologists, computer scientists, etc. In the componential Classical Theory of Meaning (Katz and Fodor 1963; Katz 1967), (i) meanings[1] of words were defined on the basis of necessary and sufficient conditions (or features/markers) without reference to contexts, (ii) therefore, a particular entity was either a full member of the category defined by a word or not, and (iii) the similarity of meanings of different words, or senses of the same word, could be quantified by counting the number of features/markers shared by meanings/senses. Thus, a word was ambiguous if it had more than one definition using such features (where no distinction between different kinds of ambiguity – homonymy and polysemy – was made).

Cognitive linguistics (CL), or cognitive semantics, drew on research in philosophy, anthropology, and cognitive psychology and adopted a perspective in which polysemy became an omnipresent property associated with lexical items but also morphemes, grammatical constructions, and whole grammatical classes. Section 2 sketches the devel-

---

[1] I use *meanings* for unrelated interpretations and *senses* for related interpretations.

opment of polysemy in CL. Section 3 explores how polysemy was addressed in neighboring fields (psycholinguistics and corpus linguistics), and section 4 points out desiderata for future CL research on polysemy.

2. Polysemy in cognitive linguistics

In this section, I will discuss the "history" of polysemy in CL; as in most of CL, I will mostly focus on lexical semantics.

The treatment of polysemy in CL involves (i) viewing meaning/sense as categorization, (ii) recognizing the importance of context for meaning/senses and that linguistic and encyclopedic knowledge are hard to keep separate, and (iii) incorporating prototype theory into linguistics. As for (i), meaning/sense is viewed as categorization such that, e.g., learning/recognizing that a sparrow is a bird amounts to establishing birds as a category of which sparrows are a member. That is, lexical items are the linguistically coded subset of all conceptual, mentally represented categories.

As for (ii), meanings of lexical items are difficult to pin down without considering both their *context* and *encyclopedic real-world knowledge*, an assumption from Fillmore's (1975, 1982) Frame Semantics. An early example involves what Cruse (1995: 44) calls cooperative readings: The presence of zeugma in (1a) appears to indicate that *dissertation* is polysemous with at least two senses ('intellectual content' vs. 'physical object'), but the slight change to (1b) results in an absence of zeugma, which does not support a similar polysemy (following Geeraerts 1993 and, ultimately, Norrick 1981):

(1) a. Judy's dissertation is thought-provoking and yellowed with age
    b. Judy's dissertation is still thought-provoking although yellowed with age

(2) the splinter in my hand

In fact, Taylor (2012: 220 ff.) points out it is often unclear where in an utterance polysemy resides – in a lexical item or its context. Is (2) polysemous because of the polysemy of *in* or of *hand* or do both senses co-select each other? Similarly, Taylor (2012: 226) illustrates how the meaning of *cut the lawn* changes from the prototypical one to the meaning of 'cut someone a piece of instant lawn (as *cut someone a piece of cake*)' that it may have in an instant lawn business. Finally, Labov (1973) has shown that speakers presented with something that looks like something between a bowl and a cup prefer to call it *bowl* when it contains potatoes, and *cup* when it contains coffee.

As for (iii), CL has drawn on research in cognitive psychology (much of it by Heider/Rosch, e.g., Rosch 1975, 1978) that showed subjects/speakers do not categorize objects using necessary/sufficient features but by comparing their similarity to the *prototype* (see Taylor this volume) of the candidate category/categories. Specifically, prototypical members of a category are listed more often/earlier in experiments where subjects are asked to list members of a category, their category membership is verified more quickly, and they give more rise to generalizations about the category. The notion of a prototype has been defined/operationalized in different ways (see Lakoff 1987): the prototypical sense of a word may be the most frequent and/or salient and/or most concrete one, the earliest attested one (historically or acquisitionally), the one from which most others can be derived best, but these criteria need not converge. I will consider a prototype (say, of *bird*) to be an abstract conceptual entity that combines attributes with a high cue validity for that category ('flies', 'has feathers', 'lays eggs', 'has a beak', etc.).

This perspective gave rise to the notions of (i) *radial categories* – categories with a central element combining many high-cue validity attributes and motivating the existence of less central members; the most-cited example is probably *mother* – and (ii) *family resemblance categories* – categories in which not all members share the same set of attributes but in which members are disjunctively related by sharing at least some attributes with each other; the usual example is Wittgenstein's ([1953] 2001) *game*. That means that prototype effects and category structure can be found on the level of the individual senses, on multiple levels of more schematic elements subsuming similar senses, and on the level of the whole category of interrelated senses of an element; thus, "the semantic value of a word need no longer be a single, unitary structure, but rather, [...] a set of interrelated senses" (Cuyckens and Zawada 2001: xiii). For example, Norvig and Lakoff (1986) discuss the structure of senses of the polysemous verb *take*. The prototype is exemplified by *John took the book from Mary* and different links are postulated to connect senses; for example,

- *profile shift*, relating the prototype to *John took the book to Mary*, which profiles the movement of the Agent$_i$ to the Recipient$_j$;
- metaphoric links (see Gibbs this volume): *John took the book to Mary* is connected to *John took the book at Mary* via the metaphor APPLYING FORCE IS TRANSFERRING AN OBJECT;
- metonymic links (see Barcelona this volume) and frame-addition links: *John took the book to Chicago* is connected to *John took Mary to the theater* via the metonymy GOING TO (public establishment) D STANDS FOR DOING C (activity conventionally done at D).

Additional important types of links connecting senses are generalizations, specializations, and image-schema transformations. The latter is exemplified by *John walked over the bridge* (involving a SOURCE schema) being related via an image-schema transformation to *John lives over the hill* (involving an ENDPOINT schema). This also means that, ultimately, some relations between senses of a word are motivated by speakers' conceptualizations of real-world events and concrete bodily/sensori-motor experience (cf. Lakoff and Brugman 1986, Gibbs and Matlock 2001).

2.1. Phase 1: extreme splitting

Considering studies of word senses on a continuum from extreme lumpers (strict monosemy analyses, e.g., Ruhl 1989) to extreme splitters (highly granular polysemy analyses), the initial phase of CL research on polysemy would be in the latter extreme. Beginning with Brugman's (1981) analysis of the preposition *over* (cf. also Lakoff 1987: 416 ff. and Brugman and Lakoff 1988) and Lindner (1981) on *up* and *out*, cognitive-semantic studies involved the above theoretical notions and many minimally different senses in the so-called *full-specification approach*. For instance, in Brugman's/Lakoff's account of *over*, (3) and (4) constitute different senses since they differ with regard to whether the trajectors (*Sam, the bird*) are in contact with the landmark (*the wall*) or not:

(3) The bird flew over the wall.
(4) Sam climbed over the wall.
(5) John walked over the bridge.
(6) John walked over the hill.

Similarly, (5) and (6) are considered different senses, because only (6) involves a landmark (*the hill*) that is vertically extended (Lakoff 1987: 422). Brugman's/Lakoff's analysis involves more than twenty senses arranged in a radial category around *over*'s prototypical sense, which they claim is exemplified by *The plane flew over*. Two crucial notions of such analyses are those of *cognitive/representational reality* and *motivation* (of links and senses). Regarding the former, many studies did not topicalize the ontological status of the lexical networks of polysemous items, but some literature assumed some cognitive reality: "a network-style mode of storage is cognitively real" (Brugman and Lakoff 1988: 477). Langacker offered less bold characterizations:

> It is not suggested that a strong claim of psychological reality can be made for any particular linguistic analysis as currently constituted. The description of a language is nevertheless a substantive hypothesis about its actual cognitive representation. (1987: 56, see also p. 382)

Regarding the latter, motivation is situated between unpredictable arbitrariness and perfect predictability. For instance, if one extended the analysis of *over* to non-prepositional cases – e.g., as a particle or prefix – one would encounter uses like *sleep overpowered him*. If one wanted to express the concept 'to overpower' but did not know the verb *overpower*, one might not *predict* there *must* be an English verb *overpower*. Nevertheless, once one considers the prototypical spatial meaning of *over* and the independently-postulated metaphor CONTROL IS UP, then a verb such as *overpower* "makes sense" (Lakoff 1987: 448).

For ten to fifteen years, this approach was extremely influential. In fact, since CL (i) viewed lexical items as categories, (ii) abandoned a strict separation between lexis and syntax, and (iii) therefore, viewed constructions as categories, too, polysemy analyses soon surfaced outside of lexical semantics: cf. Nikiforidou (1991) on genitives, Panther and Thornburg (2002) on *-er* nominalizations, Smith (2001) on Icelandic datives, Hendrikse (2001) on the Southern Bantu noun class system, Selvik (2001) on Setswana noun classes, etc. However, the most far-reaching extension was to the semantics of syntactic constructions. Goldberg's work (e.g., 1992, 1995) on argument structure constructions was particularly influential. First, it affected the decision where to localize polysemy: instead of assuming that different intransitive verbs such as *sneeze* or *cough* are polysemous in having a caused-motion sense (e.g., *Pat sneezed/coughed the napkin off the table*), she argued the syntactic pattern V-NP-PP itself has a meaning (here, 'caused-motion') and that, say, verbs in a constructional verb slot elaborate the construction's meaning; for instance, the prototypical transfer-of-possession sense of *give* elaborates the prototypical 'X causes Y to receive Z' meaning of the ditransitive construction V-NP-NP.

The second important extension was that constructions, just like words, were assumed to have multiple senses related by polysemy links. For instance, apart from the prototypical sense of the ditransitive, the ditransitive was argued to also have the senses listed in (7) (Goldberg 1995: section 3.3.3.2), and other analyses have posited constructional polysemy in other domains (cf. Michaelis and Lambrecht 1996 or Jackendoff 1997).

(7) a. Joe permitted Chris an apple.   'X enables Y to receive Z'
     b. Joe baked Bob a cake.   'X intends to cause Y to receive Z'
     c. Joe refused Bob a cake.   'X causes Y not to receive Z''

2.2. Phase 2: discussion and revision

While polysemy analyses became increasingly popular, scholars also began to discuss their shortcomings. One discussion was triggered by Sandra and Rice (1995); see also Rice (1996):

- how is the prototype defined? For *over*, Brugman/Lakoff postulated 'above-across' is the prototype, Tyler and Evans (2001) postulated 'above' to be central, Deane (2005) "characterized the preposition in terms of a trajector entity which intervenes between [an] observer and the landmark" (Taylor 2012: 236), etc.;
- how are different senses distinguished and is the fine level of resolution often adopted really warranted? Do (5) and (6) need to be distinguished as different senses or can they be conflated into one? (Are there even different word senses?)
- what motivates the different representational formats (cf. Lewandowska-Tomaszczyk 2007: section 4.2 for a comparison) and what is the ontological status of the proposed networks? Cognitive linguists often argued their analyses were compatible with, or stood for, some sort of cognitive reality, but how much do such linguistic analyses warrant psychological/psycholinguistic claims? (Cf. also Riemer (2005: Ch. 1)

Another discussion involved how much (cognitive) linguists can really say about mental representation (especially on the basis of something as volatile as introspection; cf. Nisbett and Wilson 1977). First, Croft (1998) argued that the typical introspective linguistic evidence – e.g., grammatical/semantic idiosyncrasies – can exclude more general models of mental representation (i.e., more schematic/monosemic models), but that, conversely, grammatical/semantic generality does not automatically support more general models – for that, additional experimental/observational evidence is required (e.g., sentence-sorting, sentence-similarity judgments, or [lack of] similar distributional behavior in corpora).

Sandra (1998) limited the purview of linguistic studies even more, arguing that "linguists have a very minor role to play when issues of mental representations are at stake [...] At most they can restrict the range of potential options" (1998: 361) Sandra also cautions CL to avoid the *polysemy fallacy* to automatically postulate very fine-grained sense distinctions (when more schematic sub-analyses might be sufficient) and to consider such analyses a rendering of the language user's mental representation of the linguistic data. This view, which appears to exhibit a slightly old-fashioned and non-interdisciplinary division of linguists vs. non-linguists/psycholinguists as well as a lack of recognition of, say, Tuggy's (1993) introduction of multiple levels of schematization, was addressed by Tuggy (1999). Tuggy points out shortcomings in Sandra's characterization of Croft's positions and the polysemy fallacy, but also argues that introspective data are "extremely important evidence" because "[w]hen such intuitions line up impressively, they acquire a degree of objectivity" (1999: 352). This argument actually reinforces Sandra's point since proper experimentation is a way to get intuitions by multiple speakers to "line up". Also, Tuggy proposes additional polysemy diagnostics such as direct intuitions about sense relations, perceptions of puns, evidence from speech errors, and "holes in the pattern", as when particular usages that should go with a particular form do not. (See Riemer 2005: Ch. 3 for discussion.)

Another point of critique involves the relation of the *polysemies of words and/in constructions*. One account discussed above with regard to (7) argued that constructions such as the ditransitive are polysemous just as the lexical items are. However, Croft (2003: 55) argued that the senses of, say, the ditransitive construction appear to be more due to the classes of verbs inserted into them: "It is not an accident that the verbs found with ditransitive sense E ['X enables Y to receive Z' from (7a)] are verbs of permission [...]. That is, it seems that the different 'senses' of the ditransitive construction are very closely tied to the verb classes that each 'sense' occurs with" (2003: 56). Croft proceeds to make a case for verb-class specific constructions and even verb-specific constructions (cf. also Boas 2008), which testifies to the many difficulties of locating at which level(s) polysemy is situated.

2.3. Phase 3: newer developments

As a result of the research mentioned above, research on polysemy went, simplistically speaking, two different ways. First, new theoretical approaches were developed, most notably Tyler and Evans's Principled Polysemy framework (but cf. also Kreitzer 1997); this approach will be discussed briefly in this section. Second, polysemy research turned to more diverse data, using psycholinguistic experimentation and corpus data, which is the topic of section 3.

The *Principled Polysemy approach* (cf. Tyler and Evans 2001; Evans 2005) targeted the first of the two problem areas. First, they proposed criteria to determine when two usages constitute different senses by doing more justice to the role of context and distinguishing polysemy from vagueness; second, they proposed criteria to identify the prototype, or sanctioning sense, of a polysemous category. As for the former, for some usage to count as a distinct sense of *x*, it must contain additional meaning not apparent in other senses associated with *x* (the meaning criterion) and it will feature unique or highly distinctive syntagmatic/collocational patterns (the concept elaboration criterion) and similarly distinctive structural dependencies (the grammatical criterion); the latter two criteria, thus, make an implicit reference to the study of corpus data. As for the latter, Evans (2005) lists four linguistic criteria (and mentions additional empirical evidence of the type discussed by Sandra and Rice [1995] or Croft [1998]): diachronic primacy, predominance in the lexical network, predictability regarding other senses, and – for *time* – a sense involving experience at the phenomenological level or – for *over* – relations to other prepositions.

This approach is promising as it is among the first to propose more rigorous "decision principles"; however, the concept elaboration and the grammatical criterion and many of the prototype criteria (which, curiously, do not feature acquisitional primacy) are gradable and may not converge. Nonetheless, these criteria help make decisions more replicable especially as more empirical evidence guiding linguists' decision is gathered.

3. Polysemy in neighboring fields

This section discusses how neighboring fields such as corpus linguistics and psycholinguistics have dealt with polysemy. This is essential because, as became apparent above, CL regularly points to findings/methods in neighboring fields (without, however, really integrating much of such work); cf. Cuyckens et al. (1997) for discussion. In general, one can make a coarse distinction between (i) corpus-linguistic work, which by its very nature is concerned more with *associative/co-occurrence relations* (cf. section 3.1) and psycholinguistic experimentation, which targets more *semantic/categorical relations* (cf. section 3.2).

3.1. Corpus linguistic approaches

Corpus-linguistic work on polysemy within CL comes in three kinds: first, there are studies where the corpus-linguistic component consists merely of using a corpus as a source of examples – ideally, examples are not just cherry-picked to support a particular point but also considered if they constitute counterexamples; given the limited role that corpus methods other than mere retrieval play in such work, this will not be discussed here. Second, there are analyses which involve the retrieval of, ideally, many examples of the element to be analyzed, which are then annotated for various characteristics, which are then analyzed statistically. Third, there are studies straddling the boundary between corpus linguistics and computational (psycho)linguistics, which differ from the previous kind of analyses in that many do not (i) involve (semi-)manual annotation and (ii) aim at uncovering something about human language *per se* but rather test/evaluate computational models of linguistic data (with no pretense of cognitive realism).

The main assumption underlying the latter two approaches is what Miller and Charles discuss as the *co-occurrence approach*, the assumption that distributional similarity is correlated with functional (semantic, pragmatic, etc.) similarity, as expressed in Harris's (1970: 785 f.) famous dictum that "difference of meaning correlates with difference of distribution". Miller and Charles (1991) contrast this with the *substitutability approach*, which essentially amounts to an experiment in which subjects fill gap in sentences with one of several words whose similarity is tested. From this they argue for the notion of a *contextual representation* of a word, which is

> a mental representation of the contexts in which the word occurs, a representation that includes all of the syntactic, semantic, pragmatic, and stylistic information required to use the word appropriately. (1991: 26)

Correspondingly, different levels of statistical complexity can be distinguished in this second approach. The earliest relevant corpus work is largely monofactorial in nature and does not yet include the more advanced statistics characteristic of much of contemporary corpus linguistics; relevant examples include Schmid (1993) and Kishner and Gibbs's (1996) work on how senses of *just* are correlated with different parts of speech in *just*'s environment.

More advanced analyses in "multidimensional corpus-based cognitive semantics" were then developed in particular in Gries's and Divjak's *Behavioral Profile* approach. This approach is similar in spirit to corpus-linguistic work such as Atkins (1987) and Hanks (1996, 2000) and has been applied to both polysemy and synonymy. It typically (i.e., not always) consists of four steps: (i) retrieving a sample of the expression(s) in question; (ii) annotating the concordance lines for a large number of features; (iii) converting these data into a table of percentage vectors that state how much of the data in percent exhibits a particular feature; (iv) statistically analyzing the data with exploratory tools (such as cluster analysis). Gries (2006) was the first to apply this approach in the study of polysemy, studying the verb *run* (cf. Glynn 2014 for a replication) and showing how the correlations of percentage vectors helps decide where to locate senses in a network, whether to lump or split senses, what the prototypical sense may be. Berez and Gries (2009) use cluster analysis as a corpus-based equivalent to psycholinguistic sense-sorting experiments to explore what senses of *get* exhibit high inter-sense similarity. Divjak and Gries (2009) extend this approach to the senses of near-synonymous phrasal verbs in English and Russian, and other work has targeted near synonymy (Divjak and Gries 2006; Divjak 2006; Gries and Otani 2010).[2] In addition, the BP approach has stimulated interesting extensions using different kinds of exploratory statistics and corpus data: Glynn (2010) applies what amounts to the BP approach to *bother* but instead of using cluster analysis he uses multiple correspondence analysis (MCA); Levshina (in prep.) uses an MCA to discover structure in the semantic field of seating furniture; Janda and Solovyev (2009) apply very similar methods to constructional similarities.

Finally, there are more computational approaches based on unannotated texts. Biber (1993) studies how the polysemy of the word *right* is reflected in the distribution of its collocates. More technical approaches involve NLP applications based on co-occurrence vectors in multi-dimensional space; cf. Schütze (2000) for a discussion of word, sense, and context vectors. However, much of this work is more concerned with ambiguity, not polysemy. Other similar work more concerned with psychological realism/applications is Burgess and Lund's (1997) HAL or Landauer and Dumais's (1997) LSA, which are both based on large co-occurrence matrices of words and have been used successfully in many domains, which may point to promising applications within cognitive semantics once the "symbol grounding problem" is addressed, possible via the notion of embodiment (cf. Traxler 2012: 89 f.).

Corpus data have been useful in cognitive semantics, but they usually do not allow researchers to make definitive statements about cause-effect relations or online processing. The studies discussed in the next section target these aspects.

3.2. Psycholinguistic approaches

Psycholinguistics was probably the field that CL related to first: Even when CL was still far from adopting experimental/observational approaches, there were attempts to inte-

---

[2] BP analyses were first presented independently by Gries and Divjak in 2003 at the ICLC; a similar but otherwise unrelated approach is Speelman et al. (2003).

grate the psycholinguistic models/findings regarding into CL. Deane (1988), for instance, is an attempt to unite the theory of image schemas, Relevance Theory, and Anderson's architecture of cognition. Geeraerts (1985) discusses how various characteristics of the human mind all motivate why the human mind should exhibit the type of conceptual organization around prototypes. But what about psycholinguistics proper?

Polysemy was not represented much in psycholinguistic research before the 1960s and some early work (Asch and Nerlove 1960 or Macnamara et al. 1972) was concerned with questions that may seem unrelated to CL work on polysemy. However, that is not entirely true. For instance, the former studied how children acquire and distinguish words denoting both a physical and a psychological quality, such as *hard*, *deep*, *bright*, etc., certainly a topic of current relevance. The latter study tests the hypotheses that speakers store meanings associated with a phonological form in a particular order, that this order is very similar across speakers, and that during comprehension speakers try meanings in that order. While this may seem far-fetched, given the lexical networks that have been developed, a usage-based approach that accords frequencies of words, senses etc. a primary role, implies at least some sort of rank-ordering of senses based on their frequencies. Indeed, the experimental results refuted that simplest rank-ordering hypothesis but also showed that (i) the first 1–2 senses named by subjects often coincided and (ii) context plays an important role in rapid online meaning disambiguation.

Such examples notwithstanding, most early work on the subject was concerned with ambiguity or homonymy and explored

- the *time course of activation* of word senses: are only relevant or relevant *and* irrelevant senses of words activated and how does the presence of multiple meanings or senses affect word recognition (cf. Hino and Lupker 1996 and Azuma and Van Orden 1997)?
- the importance of *context* for sense selection: does it have an effect at all, what exactly is it, and when does it kick in?
- the importance the *frequency/dominance of senses* plays for sense selection: less frequent meanings take longer to access (Hogaboam and Perfetti 1975);
- interactions of the above.

That is, most earlier studies on lexical access/disambiguation neither included any systematic distinction between homonymy and polysemy in their designs/explanations; in fact, some psychological/psycholinguistic studies use *polysemy* to refer to cases such as *ball* ('spherical object' vs. 'dance event'), which linguists would class as homonymy, others use *ambiguity* as meaning 'polysemy'. (In fact, some recent introductions to psycholinguistics – e.g., Byrd and Mintz (2010) or Menn (2011) – do not feature *polysemy* or *ambiguity* as index entries). Therefore, some early work speaks directly to many questions of CL, but much is 'only' indirectly related to CL since, e.g., it hardly explores the nature of the relations between senses or adopt the same fine degree of sense granularity; cf. Gibbs and Matlock (2001) or Klein and Murphy (2001). While the exact nature of lexical access is still debated, there is evidence that

- all meanings of a word are accessed even if they are contextually inappropriate (semantic or syntactic context cannot constrain initial access);
- context both before and after the word can help make subordinate but contextually appropriate meanings more available for selection; also, context helps suppress con-

textually inappropriate meanings of homonyms within approximately 200 ms and can make reactions to dominant senses as fast as to unambiguous controls;
- dominant and subordinate senses react differently to context (cf. Lupker 2007 for a detailed overview).

An early study that *does* speak to cognitive semanticists is Caramazza and Grober (1976). They first report results of three different tasks on the word *line* – acceptability judgments of concordance contexts, similarity judgments of such contexts, and a sentence production task – which produce highly interrelated results. Interestingly, they applied multidimensional scaling and cluster analysis to the similarity judgments and obtained a clear and interpretable 5-cluster/sense solution. On the whole, their model of how polysemy is represented in the mental lexicon, the Process Theory of Meaning, is similar to the monosemy approach and assumes a single or a small set of very general meanings. However, it also accords crucial roles to context and encyclopedic knowledge (cf. also Anderson and Ortony 1975 for similar conclusions): senses other than the central one are derived by extension/analogy, or "instruction rules", and an encyclopedic dictionary, which stores all factual information a speaker has about a word, constrains the application of the instruction rules.

Another relevant study is Durkin and Manning (1989). For nearly 200 words (11 % of them homonyms), they collected typical senses from subjects and relatedness ratings of all senses to central ones. They find that senses of polysemous words are rated as more similar to each other than senses of homonymous words, but also that, while contexts boosts senses' salience ratings, dominant senses enjoy a larger degree of salience even in contexts biasing subordinate senses. Also, the ease with which subordinate senses can be accessed differs considerably across words.

A classic study on the processing of homonymous meanings vs. polysemous sense is Frazier and Rayner (1990). Their eye-movement data indicate that, in the absence of a disambiguating context, fixation times for words with multiple meanings are longer while fixation times for words with multiple senses are not. They explain that as a consequence of having to immediately disambiguate such homonyms so as not to maintain inconsistent representations and selecting one meaning involves suppression of others, which requires extra processing time. Similarly, Pickering and Frisson (2001: 556) propose that, upon hearing a homonymous word in a non-disambiguating context, speakers make an early selection of a meaning whereas, upon hearing a polysemous word in such a context, the user "activates one underspecified meaning and uses context to home in on the appropriate sense".[3] Additional evidence in particular for the higher relatedness of senses of polysemous words (compared to the meanings of homonyms) comes from Williams (1992). He shows that senses of polysemous adjectives resulting in zeugma in the *do so* test prime contextually irrelevant related senses: "it does not appear to be possible to suppress the irrelevant meanings of a polysemous adjective in the same way as [those] of a homonym" (1992: 202). In addition, the time course of activation is similar to that of dominant properties of monosemous nouns. Finally, the direction of priming is significant, too: priming from non-central senses to central ones

---

[3] This approach is compatible with Frisson and Pickering's (1999) study, which shows that both literal and metonymic senses can be accessed immediately, "perhaps through a single underspecified representation" (1999: 1366).

was significant at all delays, but not the other way round, which Williams interprets as possibly related to category structure/similarity effects (e.g., prototype effects).

Similar differences were found in Brisard et al. (2001), who demonstrated significant priming effects for polysemous and vague adjectives, but not for homonymous adjectives. Also, consider Rodd et al. (2002, 2004). In the former study, they find that the unrelated senses of homonymous words (and their wider attractor basin) slow recognition down whereas the related senses and richer semantic representations (and deeper attractor basins) of polysemous words speed recognition up. In the latter, they propose a distributed-semantic-representation model of lexical knowledge that accommodates these effects by assuming that the related senses of polysemous words share overlapping regions in semantic space. Similarly, Beretta, et al. (2005) show that the meanings of homonymous words are accessed more slowly than senses of polysemous words; cf. also Azuma and Van Orden (1997).

On the other hand, in experiments similar to Light and Carter-Sobell's (1970) and Bainbridge et al.'s (1993), Klein and Murphy (2001, 2002) show that both memory performance and sensicality judgments suggest that senses of *paper* are related but not similar, stored separately or at least functionally distinct. In fact, senses of one word may be excited and inhibited at the same time. Also, Klein and Murphy (2001: exp. 3) find no performance difference between homonyms and polysemous words but, in Klein and Murphy (2002: exp. 1–3), conclude that the similarity of polysemous senses is graded, and that polysemous senses share more connections than homonymous meanings (not unlike what a family resemblance approach would predict).

In sum, there is some agreement on some issues, but most hypotheses implicit in CL polysemous analyses are far from as unambiguously supported as many in the CL mainstream would hope for – a great deal of work lies ahead.

4. Desiderata

Given the huge amount of research on polysemy and ambiguity, this overview was selective and much interesting work could not be discussed. While psycholinguistic work has yielded some robust findings, many of the central questions of CL regarding senses' distinctness, relatedness, representation, and their right level of granularity, remain largely unanswered. Across all three areas – CL, corpus linguistics, and psycholinguistics – a consensus is emerging to assume a multidimensional semantic space in which usages or senses are located such that their spatial proximity reflects distributional and/or semantic similarity; cf., e.g., Gries (2010) and Taylor (2012) for cognitive/corpus linguistics and, Rodd et al. (2004: 89) for psycholinguistics. Thus, while integral to early CL, the notion of distinct senses appears more of a descriptive device rather than a claim about psycholinguistic reality. This conception does justice to the fact that the same word/sense – i.e., region of semantic space – can be accessed or traversed at different levels of resolution and from different angles/trajectories. A simple example is shown in Figure 1, which represents the same usages (as dots) in semantic space from three different angles. The left panel suggests there is one group of relatively coherent usages, maybe corresponding to one sense. However, the other two panels show the same usages from different angles (e.g., from different semantic/discourse contexts), and these panels give rise to two or

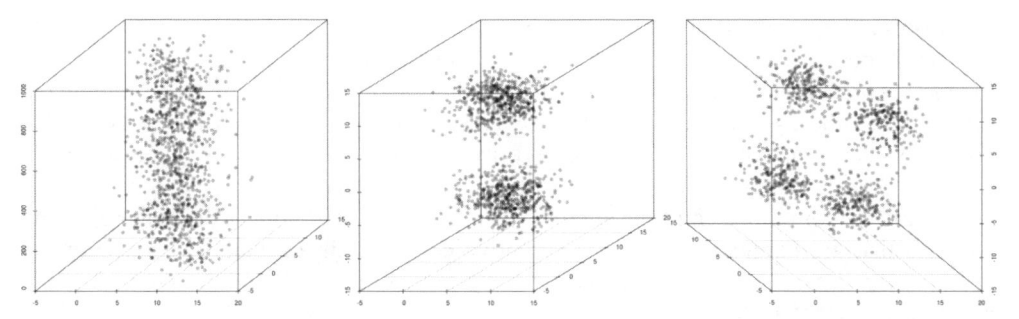

Fig. 22.1: A point cloud in three-dimensional 'semantic space', from three different angles

four senses. That is, context facilitates sense recognition by imposing a particular view on, or trajectory through, stored exemplars, and the possibility of creativity is afforded by the speaker's freedom to (i) approach the same region from different perspectives or (ii) see similarities between different point clouds in semantic space and exploit this linguistically by means of, say, analogy, or (iii) condense regions of space.

In what follows, I discuss a few areas for future research. First, corpus-based work needs to be developed further both in terms of scope (words, senses, and features included) and methodology. Current developments are promising and future work may evolve by including powerful new tools such as network models, fuzzy clustering, etc.

More importantly, CL must approach polysemy more interdisciplinarily. Many experimental studies in psycholinguistics on ambiguity should be replicated on the basis of CL analyses to shed more light on whether the fine-grained senses distinctions, the nature of links, etc. are supported. Similarly, we need better evidence on the role of prototypes in online processing and on how word senses interact with constructions and their senses.

With regard to language acquisition, there seem to be only few studies targeting polysemy from a CL perspective. The few studies that there are – e.g., Dowker (2003), Nerlich et al. (2003) on *get*, Rice (2003) on prepositional networks, Kidd and Cameron-Faulkner (2005) on *with* – have unfortunately not left enough of a mark on CL in spite of their relevance. Rice (2003: 275) makes the interesting suggestion that

> a lexical category for a young child does not start out as either monosemous or polysemous, but as potentially very homonymous. Additional senses do not emerge through extension. Rather, they *may* be integrated through some sort of schematization process at a much later date.

This is an area that needs more experimental/observational research, but also maybe computational modeling; cf., e.g., Parisien and Stevenson (2009) for a study of *get*.

Finally, neurolinguistics offers a completely new range of applications; cf. Coulson (2004) for an overview of EEG/ERP or Stringaris et al.'s (2006) fMRI study of semantic relatedness. Burgess and Simpson (1988) tested whether the brain's two hemispheres respond identically to target words more associated with the dominant or the subordinate meaning of an ambiguous word and found that "the two hemispheres have opposite responses to subordinate meanings. The left hemisphere deactivates subordinate meanings, but the right hemisphere increases them over time" (Traxler 2012: 528 f.). Mason and Just (2007) showed that the brain activity arising from processing lexically ambiguous words differs as a function of meaning dominance and working memory capacity (i.e., individual differences). Finally, CL has approached the polysemy of content and function words in the same way, but the two types of words seem to be lateralized differently (Bradley and Garrett 1983); in fact, Damasio and colleagues suggest that nouns vs. verbs and even different categories of concrete objects are represented in different neural regions, which has implications for polysemous words (cf. Lupker 2007: 169). Only by combining multiple approaches/tools will CL be able to develop polysemy analyses that are compatible with the cognitive commitment to make one's account of human language accord with what is generally known about the mind and brain from disciplines other than linguistics.

5. References

Anderson, Richard C. and Andrew Ortony
    1975   On putting apples into bottles. *Cognitive Psychology* 7(2): 167–180.

Asch, Solomon and Harriet Nerlove
    1960   The development of double function terms in children. In: B. Kaplan and S. Wapner (eds.), *Perspectives in Psychological Theory*, 47–60. New York: International Universities Press.

Atkins, Beryl T. Sue
    1987   Semantic ID tags: Corpus evidence for dictionary senses. In *Proceedings of the Third Annual Conference of the UW Centre for the New Oxford English Dictionary*, 17–36.

Azuma, Tamiko and Guy C. Van Orden
    1997   Why *safe* is better than *fast*: The relatedness of a word's meanings affects lexical decision times. *Journal of Memory and Language* 36(4): 484–504.

Bainbridge, J. Vivian, Stephan Lewandowsky, and Kim Kirsner
    1993   Context effects in repetition priming are sense effects. *Memory and Cognition* 21(5): 619–626.

Beretta, Alan, Robert Fiorentino, and David Poeppel
    2005   The effect of homonymy and polysemy on lexical access. *Cognitive Brain Research* 24(1): 57–65.

Berez, Andrea L. and Stefan Th. Gries
    2009   In defense of corpus-based methods: A behavioral profile analysis of polysemous *get* in English. In: S. Moran, D. S. Tanner, and M. Scanlon (eds.), *Proceedings of the 24th Northwest Linguistics Conference. University of Washington Working Papers in Linguistics* Vol. 27, 157–166. Seattle, WA: Department of Linguistics.

Biber, Douglas
    1993   Co-occurrence patterns among collocations: A tool for corpus-based lexical knowledge acquisition. *Computational Linguistics* 19(3): 531–538.

Boas, Hans C
    2008   Resolving form-meaning discrepancies in Construction Grammar. In: J. Leino (ed.), *Constructional Reorganization*, 11–36. Amsterdam/Philadelphia: John Benjamins.

Bradley, Dianne C. and Merrill F. Garrett
    1983   Hemisphere differences in the recognition of open and closed class words. *Neuropsychologia* 21(2): 155–159.

Bréal, Michel
    1897   The history of words. In: G. Wolf (ed./transl.), *The Beginnings of Semantics: Essays, Lectures and Reviews*, 152–175. London: Duckworth.

Brisard, Frank, Gert Van Rillaer, and Dominiek Sandra
2001   Processing polysemous, homonymous, and vague adjectives. In: H. Cuyckens and B. Zawada (eds.), *Polysemy in Cognitive Linguistics*, 261–284. Amsterdam/Philadelphia: John Benjamins.

Brugman, Claudia
1981   The story of *over*. M. A. thesis. University of California, Berkeley.

Brugman, Claudia and George Lakoff
1988   Cognitive topology and lexical networks. In: S. L. Small, G. W. Cottrell, and M. K. Tanenhaus (eds.), *Lexical Ambiguity Resolution*, 477–508. San Mateo, CA: Morgan Kaufman.

Burgess, Curt and Kevin Lund
1997   Modelling parsing constraints with high-dimensional context space. *Language and Cognitive Processes* 12(2/3): 177–210.

Byrd, Dani and Toben H. Mintz
2010   *Discovering Speech, Words, and Mind*. Chichester: John Wiley.

Caramazza Alfonso and Ellen Grober
1976   Polysemy and the structure of the subjective lexicon. In: C. Rameh (ed.), *Semantics: Theory and Application*, 181–206. Washington, DC: Georgetown University Press.

Coulson, Seana
2004   Electrophysiology and pragmatic language comprehension. In: I. Noveck and D. Sperber (eds.), *Experimental Pragmatics*, 187–206. Basingstoke: Palgrave MacMillan.

Croft, William
1998   Linguistic evidence and mental representation. *Cognitive Linguistics* 9(2): 151–173.

Croft, William
2003   Lexical rules vs. constructions: A false dichotomy. In: H. Cuyckens, T. Berg, R. Dirven, and K.-U. Panther (eds.), *Motivation in Language: Studies in Honour of Günter Radden*, 49–68. Amsterdam/Philadelphia: John Benjamins.

Cruse, D. Alan
1995   Polysemy and related phenomena from a cognitive linguistic viewpoint. In: P. Saint-Dizier and E. Viegas (eds.), *Computational Lexical Semantics*, 33–49. Cambridge: Cambridge University Press.

Cuyckens, Hubert, Dominiek Sandra, and Sally Rice
1997   Towards an empirical lexical semantics. In: B. Smieja and M. Tasch (eds.), *Human Contact through Language and Linguistics*, 35–54. Frankfurt a. M.: Peter Lang.

Cuyckens, Hubert and Britta Zawada
2001   Introduction. In: H. Cuyckens and B. Zawada (eds.), *Polysemy in Cognitive Linguistics*, ix–xxvii. Amsterdam/Philadelphia: John Benjamins.

Deane, Paul D.
1988   Polysemy and cognition. *Lingua* 75(4): 325–361.

Deane, Paul D.
2005   Multimodal spatial representation. In: B. Hampe (ed.), *From Perception to Meaning: Image Schemas in Cognitive Linguistics*, 235–282. Berlin/New York: Mouton de Gruyter.

Divjak, Dagmar S.
2006   Ways of intending: Delineating and structuring near synonyms. In: S. Th. Gries and A. Stefanowitsch (eds.), *Corpora in Cognitive Linguistics: Corpus-Based Approaches to Syntax and Lexis*, 19–56. Berlin/New York: Mouton de Gruyter.

Divjak, Dagmar S. and Stefan Th. Gries
2006   Ways of trying in Russian: Clustering behavioral profiles. *Corpus Linguistics and Linguistic Theory* 2(1): 23–60.

Divjak, Dagmar S. and Stefan Th. Gries
 2009 Corpus-based cognitive semantics: A contrastive study of phrasal verbs in English and Russian. In: K. Dziwirek and B. Lewandowska-Tomaszczyk (eds.), *Studies in Cognitive Corpus Linguistics*, 273–296. Frankfurt a.M.: Peter Lang.

Dowker, Ann
 2003 Young children's and adults' use of figurative language: How important are cultural and linguistic influences? In: B. Nerlich, Z. Todd, V. Herrman, and D. D. Clarke (eds.), *Polysemy: Flexible Patterns of Meaning in Mind and Language*, 317–332. Berlin/New York: Mouton de Gruyter.

Durkin, Kevin and Jocelyn Manning
 1989 Polysemy and the subjective lexicon: Semantic relatedness and the salience of intraword senses. *Journal of Psycholinguistic Research* 18(6): 577–612.

Evans, Vyvyan
 2005 The meaning of *time*: Polysemy, the lexicon and conceptual structure. *Journal of Linguistics* 41(1): 33–75.

Fillmore, Charles J.
 1975 An alternative to checklist theories of meaning. *Proceedings of the First Annual Meeting of the Berkeley Linguistics Society*, 123–131.

Fillmore, Charles J.
 1982 Frame semantics. In: The Linguistic Society of Korea (ed.), *Linguistics in the Morning Calm*, 111–137. Seoul: Hanshin Publishing Co.

Frazier, Lyn and Keith Rayner
 1990 Taking on semantic commitments: Processing multiple meanings vs. multiple senses. *Journal of Memory and Language* 29(2): 181–200.

Frisson, Steven and Martin J. Pickering
 1999 The processing of metonymy: Evidence from eye movements. *Journal of Experimental Psychology: Learning, Memory, and Cognition* 25(6): 1366–1383.

Geeraerts, Dirk
 1985 Cognitive restrictions on the structure of semantic change. In: J. Fisiak (ed.), *Historical Semantics. Historical Word-Formation*, 126–153. Berlin/New York: Mouton de Gruyter.

Geeraerts, Dirk
 1993 Vagueness's puzzles, polysemy's vagaries. *Cognitive Linguistics* 4(3): 223–272.

Gibbs, Raymond W. Jr. and Teenie Matlock
 2001 Psycholinguistic perspectives on polysemy. In: H. Cuyckens and B. Zawada (eds.), *Polysemy in Cognitive Linguistics*, 213–239. Amsterdam/Philadelphia: John Benjamins.

Glynn, Dylan
 2010 Testing the hypothesis: Objectivity and verification in usage-based Cognitive Semantics. In: D. Glynn and K. Fischer (eds.), *Quantitative Methods in Cognitive Semantics: Corpus-Driven Approaches*, 239–629. Berlin/New York: De Gruyter Mouton.

Glynn, Dylan
 2014 The many uses of *run*: Corpus methods and socio-cognitive semantics. In: D. Glynn and J. Robinson (eds.), *Corpus Methods for Semantics: Quantitative Studies in Polysemy and Synonymy,* 117–144. Amsterdam/Philadelphia: John Benjamins.

Goldberg, Adele E.
 1992 The inherent semantics of argument structure: The case of the English ditransitive construction. *Cognitive Linguistics* 3(1): 37–74.

Goldberg, Adele E.
 1995 *Constructions: A Construction Grammar Approach to Argument Structure*. Chicago: University of Chicago Press.

Gries, Stefan Th.
 2006 Corpus-based methods and cognitive semantics: The many meanings of *to run*. In: S. Th. Gries and A. Stefanowitsch (eds.), *Corpora in Cognitive Linguistics: Corpus-Based Approaches to Syntax and Lexis*, 57–99. Berlin/New York: Mouton de Gruyter.

Gries, Stefan Th.
2010   Behavioral Profiles: A fine-grained and quantitative approach in corpus-based lexical semantics. *The Mental Lexicon* 5(3): 323–346.

Gries, Stefan Th. and Naoki Otani
2010   Behavioral profiles: A corpus-based perspective on synonymy and antonymy. *ICAME Journal* 34: 121–150.

Hanks, Patrick
1996   Contextual dependency and lexical sets. *International Journal of Corpus Linguistics* 1(1): 75–98.

Hanks, Patrick
2000   Do word meanings exist? *Computers and the Humanities* 34(1/2): 205–215.

Harris, Zelig S.
1970   *Papers in Structural and Transformational Linguistics.* Dordrecht: Reidel.

Hendrikse, A.P.
2001   Systemic polysemy in the Southern Bantu noun class system. In: H. Cuyckens and B. Zawada (eds.), *Polysemy in Cognitive Linguistics*, 185–212. Amsterdam/Philadelphia: John Benjamins.

Hino, Yasushi and Stephen J. Lupker
1996   Effects of polysemy in lexical decision and naming: An alternative to lexical access accounts. *Journal of Experimental Psychology: Human Perception and Performance* 22(6): 1331–1356.

Hogaboam, Thomas W. and Charles A. Perfetti
1975   Lexical ambiguity and sentence comprehension: The common sense effect. *Journal of Verbal Learning and Verbal Behavior* 14(3): 265–275.

Jackendoff, Ray
1997   Twistin' the night away. *Language* 73(3): 534–559.

Janda, Laura A. and Valery D. Solovyev
2009   What constructional profiles reveal about synonymy: A case study of Russian words for *sadness* and *happiness*. *Cognitive Linguistics* 20(2): 367–393.

Katz, Jerrold J.
1967   Recent issues in semantic theory. *Foundations of Language* 3. 124–194.

Katz, Jerrold J. and Jerry A. Fodor
1963   The structure of a semantic theory. *Language* 39(2): 170–210.

Kidd, Evan and Thea Cameron-Faulkner
2005   Overcoming polysemy in first language acquisition: The case of *with*. *Proceedings of the 29th Annual Boston Conference on Language Development*, 341–352.

Kishner, Jeffrey M. and Raymond W. Gibbs Jr.
1996   How *just* gets its meanings: Polysemy and context in psychological semantics. *Language and Speech* 39(1): 19–36.

Klein, Deborah E. and Gregory L. Murphy
2001   The representation of polysemous words. *Journal of Memory and Language* 45(2): 259–282.

Klein, Deborah E. and Gregory L. Murphy
2002   Paper has been my ruin: Conceptual relations of polysemous senses. *Journal of Memory and Language* 47(4): 548–570.

Kreitzer, Anatol
1997   Multiple levels of schematization: A study in the conceptualization of space. *Cognitive Linguistics* 8(4): 291–326.

Labov, William
1973   The boundaries of words and their meanings. In: C.-J. Bailey and R. W. Shuy (eds.), *New Ways of Analyzing Variation in English*, 340–371. Washington, DC: Georgetown University Press.

Lakoff, George
  1987   *Women, Fire, and Dangerous Things: What Categories Reveal about the Mind*. Chicago: The University of Chicago Press.
Lakoff, George and Claudia Brugman
  1986   Argument forms in lexical semantics. In: V. Nikiforidou, M. van Clay, M. Niepokuj, and D. Feder, (eds.), *Proceedings of the Twelfth Annual Meeting of the Berkeley Linguistics Society*, 442–454. Berkeley: Berkeley Linguistics Society.
Landauer, Thomas K. and Susan T. Dumais
  1997   A solution to Plato's problem: The latent semantic analysis theory of acquisition, induction, and representation of knowledge. *Psychological Review* 104(2): 211–240.
Levshina, Natalia
  in prep.   Lexical fields and constructional spaces. A quantitative corpus-based model of semantics.
Lewandowska-Tomaszczyk, Barbara
  2007   Polysemy, prototypes, and radial categories. In: D. Geeraerts and H. Cuyckens (eds.), *The Oxford Handbook of Cognitive Linguistics*, 139–169. Oxford: Oxford University Press.
Light, Leah L. and Linda Carter-Sobell
  1970   Effects of changed semantic context on recognition behavior. *Journal of Verbal Learning and Verbal Behavior* 9(1): 1–11.
Lindner, Susan
  1981   A lexico-semantic analysis of English verb-particle constructions with *up* and *out*. Ph.D. dissertation. University of California, San Diego.
Lupker, Stephen J.
  2007   Representation and processing of lexically ambiguous words. In: M. G. Gaskell (ed.), *The Oxford Handbook of Psycholinguistics*, 159–174. Oxford: Oxford University Press.
Macnamara, John, Ann O'Cleirigh, and Thomas Kellaghan
  1972   The structure of the English lexicon: The simplest hypothesis. *Language and Speech* 15(2): 141–148.
Menn, Lise
  2011   *Psycholinguistics: Introduction and Applications*. San Diego: Plural.
Michaelis, Laura A. and Knud Lambrecht
  1996   Towards a construction-based theory of language function: The case of nominal extraposition. *Language* 72(2): 215–247.
Miller, George A. and Walter G. Charles
  1991   Contextual correlates of semantic similarity. *Language and Cognitive Processes* 6(1): 1–28.
Nerlich, Brigitte, Zazie Todd, and David D. Clarke
  2003   Emerging patterns and evolving polysemies: The acquisition of *get* between four and ten years. In: B. Nerlich, Z. Todd, V. Herrman, and D. D. Clarke (eds.), *Polysemy: Flexible Patterns of Meaning in Mind and Language*, 333–357. Berlin/New York: Mouton de Gruyter.
Nikiforidou, Kiki
  1991   The meanings of the genitive: A case study in semantic structure and semantic change. *Cognitive Linguistics* 2(2): 149–205.
Nisbett, Richard E. and Timothy DeCamp Wilson
  1977   Telling more than we know: Verbal reports on mental processes. *Psychological Review* 84(3): 231–259.
Norrick, Neal R.
  1981   *Semiotic Principles in Semantic Theory*. Amsterdam/Philadelphia: John Benjamins.

Norvig, Peter and George Lakoff
1986   Taking: a study in lexical network theory. In: J. Aske, N. Beery, L. A. Michaelis, and H. Filip (eds.), *Proceedings of the Thirteenth Annual Meeting of the Berkeley Linguistics Society*, 195–206. Berkeley: Berkeley Linguistics Society

Panther, Klaus-Uwe and Linda L. Thornburg
2002   The roles of metaphor and metonymy in English *-er* nominals. In: R. Dirven and R. Pörings (eds.), *Metaphor and Metonymy in Comparison and Contrast*, 279–319. Berlin/New York: Mouton de Gruyter.

Parisien, Christopher and Suzanne Stevenson
2009   Modelling the acquisition of verb polysemy in children. *Proceedings of the CogSci2009 Workshop on Distributional Semantics beyond Concrete Concepts*, 17–22.

Pickering, Martin J. and Steven Frisson
2001   Processing ambiguous verbs: Evidence from eye movements. *Journal of Experimental Psychology: Learning, Memory, and Cognition* 27(2): 556–573.

Rice, Sally
1996   Prepositional prototypes. In: M. Pütz and R. Dirven (eds.), *The Construal of Space in Language and Thought*, 135–165. Berlin/New York: Mouton de Gruyter.

Rice, Sally A.
2003   Growth of a lexical network: Nine English prepositions in acquisition. In: H. Cuyckens, R. Dirven, and J. Taylor (eds.), *Cognitive Approaches to Lexical Semantics*, 243–260. Berlin/New York: Mouton de Gruyter.

Riemer, Nick
2005   *The Semantics of Polysemy: Reading Meaning in English and Warlpiri*. Berlin/New York: Mouton de Gruyter.

Rodd, Jennifer M., Gareth Gaskell, and William D. Marlsen-Wilson
2002   Making sense of semantic ambiguity. *Journal of Memory and Language* 46(2): 245–266.

Rodd, Jennifer M., Gareth Gaskell, and William D. Marlsen-Wilson
2004   Modelling the effects of semantic ambiguity in word recognition. *Cognitive Science* 28(1): 89–104.

Rosch, Eleanor
1975   Cognitive reference points. *Cognitive Psychology* 7(4): 532–547.

Rosch, Eleanor
1978   Principles of categorization. In: E. Rosch and B. B. Lloyd (eds.), *Cognition and Categorization*, 27–48. Hillsdale: Lawrence Erlbaum.

Ruhl, Charles
1989   *On Monosemy: A Study in Linguistic Semantics*. Stony Brook: State University of New York Press.

Sandra, Dominiek
1998   What linguists can and can't tell you about the human mind: A reply to Croft. *Cognitive Linguistics* 9(4): 361–378.

Sandra, Dominiek and Sally A. Rice
1995   Network analyses of prepositional meaning: Mirroring whose mind – the linguist's or the language user's? *Cognitive Linguistics* 6(1): 89–130.

Schmid, Hans-Jörg
1993   *Cottage and Co., idea, start vs. begin*. Tübingen: Max Niemeyer.

Schütze, Hinrich
2000   Disambiguation and connectionism. In: Y. Ravin and C. Leacock (eds.), *Polysemy: Theoretical and Computational Approaches*, 205–219. Oxford: Oxford University Press.

Selvik, Kari-Anne
2001   When a dance resembles a tree. A polysemy analysis of three Setswana noun classes. In: H. Cuyckens and B. Zawada (eds.), *Polysemy in Cognitive Linguistics*, 161–184. Amsterdam/Philadelphia: John Benjamins.

Smith, Michael B.
   2001   Why Quirky Case really isn't quirky. Or how to treat dative sickness in Icelandic. In: H. Cuyckens and B. Zawada (eds.), *Polysemy in Cognitive Linguistics*, 115–160. Amsterdam/Philadelphia: John Benjamins.

Speelman, Dirk, Stefan Grondelaers, and Dirk Geeraerts
   2003   Profile-based linguistic uniformity as a generic method for comparing language varieties. Computers and the Humanities 37(3): 317–337.

Stringaris, Argyris, Nicholas Medford, Rachel Giora, Vincent C. Giampietro, Michael J. Brammer, and Anthony S. David
   2006   How metaphors influence semantic relatedness judgments: The role of the right frontal cortex. *NeuroImage* 33(2): 784–793.

Taylor, John R.
   2012   *The Mental Corpus.* Oxford: Oxford University Press.

Taylor, John R.
   this volume   27. Prototype effects in grammar. Berlin/Boston: De Gruyter Mouton.

Tuggy, David.
   1993   Ambiguity, polysemy, and vagueness. *Cognitive Linguistics* 4(3): 273–290.

Tuggy, David
   1999   Linguistic evidence for polysemy in the mind: A response to William Croft and Dominiek Sandra. *Cognitive Linguistics* 10(4): 343–368.

Traxler, Matthew J.
   2012   *Introduction to Psycholinguistics: Understanding Language Science.* Malden/Oxford: Wiley-Blackwell.

Tyler, Andrea and Vyvyan Evans
   2001   Reconsidering prepositional polysemy networks: the case of *over*. *Language* 77(4): 724–765.

Williams, John N.
   1992   Processing polysemous words in context: Evidence for interrelated meanings. *Journal of Psycholinguistic Research* 21(3): 193–218.

Wittgenstein, Ludwig
   (1953) 2001   *Philosophical Investigations.* Malden: Blackwell.

Stefan Th. Gries, Santa Barbara (USA)

23. Space

1. Introduction
2. Spatial language defined
3. Spatial adpositions
4. Spatial demonstratives
5. Cross-linguistic differences and 'linguistic relativity'
6. Conclusions
7. References

1. Introduction

Space has long been viewed as one of the fundamental building blocks in cognitive linguistics. For almost four decades it has been argued that both language and thought are grounded in more "basic" perceptual and experiential constructs, and the geometry of space has figured, arguably, as the most basic (Langacker 1986; Lakoff 1987; Talmy 1983). Candidate spatial relations that have been proposed as important underlying constructs for language and thought include containment, support, verticality, and contiguity, and (non-spatial) domains such as emotion, time, and metaphors in language are often assumed to be parasitic on these spatial concepts (Lakoff and Johnson 1980; Casasanto and Boroditsky 2008; see also chapters by Gibbs, Bergen, and Evans this volume). But what exactly are these spatial constructs, and how do they map onto language?

A useful starting point to get at these basic spatial building blocks for language is to focus on language that overtly relates to space – spatial language.

Several decades of research on spatial terms of various types reveals a series of findings that are illuminating regarding the nature of these basic primitives. Here I consider what we have learned about spatial language during this time, and what this tells us about the fundamental building blocks of language and thought. Two central themes will emerge; the importance of experimental approaches in cognitive linguistics (testing and complementing theoretical insights), and the importance of vision and **action** as underlying constraints on spatial language comprehension and production.

2. Spatial language defined

One can define spatial language as language that enables a hearer to narrow a search (usually visual) for the location of an object (Landau and Jackendoff 1993; Talmy 1983). Under this rubric come a range of types of term, including spatial adpositions (e.g., the spatial prepositions in English; such as *in, over, in front of*, etc.) and motion terms describing how an object is moving through space. Terms including spatial demonstratives (e.g., *this* and *that*) are also regarded as spatial, although the extent to which they define where an object is located is controversial (see for example Enfield 2003).

Word limits prevent me from surveying all areas of spatial language in this chapter (motion is covered by Filipović and Ibarretxe-Antunano this volume). Here my focus is on spatial adpositions and spatial demonstratives. The choice of the former is a reflection of the high frequency of these terms across languages as well as the versatility of these terms. The choice of the latter is motivated again by frequency concerns, but also by the universality of demonstratives, their philological importance, and the fact that they are among the first words children across cultures produce. Both categories also illustrate how experimental approaches are important for an understanding of the mapping between language and space.

3. Spatial adpositions

The spatial prepositions in English have received a lot of attention from linguists over many years, and indeed have formed a cornerstone of activity in cognitive linguistics. The so-called "locative/relational" prepositions in English have been categorized into simple "topological" terms, proximity terms, and "projective/dimensional" terms (Coventry and Garrod 2004). In many ways these distinctions are somewhat arbitrary – they all share features to some extent – but for our present purposes they will suffice. Here we do not review all the work done on spatial adpositions, but by necessity will be rather selective, focusing on the topological terms *in* and *on*, and the projective terms *over*, *under*, *above* and *below*. However, some general remarks are in order.

It has long been noted that spatial terms are highly polysemous, both in terms of the same words cropping up in spatial and non-spatial contexts (e.g., contrast *under the table* with *under the weather*), and also the same terms used spatially in different ways (contrast *the hand is over the table* with *the tablecloth is over the table*). One of the fundamental features of cognitive linguistic approaches to language is the notion that words are associated with a multitude of senses which are related, but do not all share exactly the same features. This idea can be traced backed to Wittgenstein (1953), and has been developed both theoretically and empirically as a kernel theme in cognitive linguistics (see for example the early data from Rosch and Mervis 1975; see Lakoff 1987 for review). Spatial adpositions can be regarded as "radial" categories, with central, "prototypical" image schemata, and more peripheral senses related to, and generated from, these schemata (Brugman 1988; Herskovits 1986). For example Brugman (1988) provides analyses of *over*, with three central image schemata representing the geometric relations underpinning dozens of senses, with more specific senses, both spatial and metaphorical, emerging from these central "prototypical" geometric conceptualizations. As we shall see, the range of parameters associated with spatial terms has moved away from the purely geometric, with empirical evidence for a wider range of relevant experiential constraints associated with the comprehension and production of these terms.

3.1. Topological terms – focus on *in* and *on*

Understanding of containment and support begins to emerge early in development, as do a range of spatial (binary) concepts (see Quinn 2005). Containers appear to exert a special fascination for children, revealed in their play (Bower 1982; Clark 1973), and several studies have shown knowledge of containment in infants of only a few months of age. For instance, when an object is shown lowered into a container, and the container is moved, 2.5 month olds are surprised when the object does not move with the container (e.g., Hespos and Baillargeon 2001; see also Casasola et al. 2003). Understanding of support is somewhat more protracted in development and emerges later than containment (Casasola and Cohen 2002). In terms of language acquisition, it has long been recognized that *in*, *on*, and *under* are among the earliest of all the prepositions across languages, appearing in the second and third years (Bowerman 1996; Johnson and Slobin 1979; Piaget and Inhelder 1956), building on the spatial concepts already well (but not fully) developed.

In and *on* can be used in a variety of ways. The spatial relation associated with *coffee in a cup* is different from the relations associated with *flowers in a vase*, and *a crack in a vase*. Moreover, one would say that a marble is *in a cup* when the cup is upright, but not when the cup is overturned with the marble *under* it, even though the marble is geometrically contained in both cases. Such examples have led to the view in cognitive linguistics that spatial terms are highly polysemous. But why are there so many different relations associated with these terms, and how best can one deal with the apparent polysemy? This is the first issue we wrestle with in this section.

Coventry and Garrod (2004) reviewed a body of empirical findings on the mapping between language and space, beginning with the basic question of how spatial language and the spatial world covary. In addition to examining how words co-occur/collocate with other words, such as the corpus linguistic work discussed elsewhere in this volume, it is equally important for spatial language to understand the real-world correlates of spatial language. To do so, an experimental approach to this question was pursued beginning in the 1980s, systematically manipulating visual scenes to examine how language comprehension and production is affected by changes in spatial relations and the objects those relations pertain to. Synthesizing the results from this experimental work, together with theoretical insights from both the perceptual sciences and linguistics, the "functional geometric framework" for spatial language was proposed by Coventry and Garrod involving three interconnected parameters that conjointly underpin the comprehension and production of spatial prepositions.

First, there are geometric relations or routines that capture the spatial relation between objects. In the case of *in*, the geometry of containment itself can account for many of the various uses/senses of *in*. Coventry and Garrod (2004) appealed to the region connection calculus (RCC) of Cohn and colleagues (Cohn et al. 1997) as a means of capturing the geometric constructs underlying *in* and *on* (moving a step beyond the somewhat abstract geometric constructs in image schemata). RCC is a qualitative geometry that defines containment and enclosure using just two primitives – connection and convexity – and these primitives have the attraction of being able to apply to a wide range of spatial relations that at first sight might appear to be different relations or senses or image schemata. For example, using the same essential formalism, RCC accounts for a range of ways in which one object can be in another object or objects. The strongest form of enclosure is when a region an object occupies is topologically inside (that is, completely surrounded by) the region the other object occupies, as in *a crack in a vase*, or *jam in a (sealed) jar*. However, this same basic notion allows for a range of weaker forms of enclosure as licensed in the calculus, dependent on the different ways in which an object has an inside. This includes subparts and overlaps in "convex hull" regions (e.g., *The flowers in a vase; tea in a cup*) and scattered insides (*The island in the archipelago*). The main point is that RCC (and later variants of qualitative geometry) give a formal and perceptually grounded account of the flexibility of spatial relations that allows a range of specific realizations of the same primitive spatial relations without the need for a multitude of separate senses of spatial relations (see also Tyler and Evans 2003, for a different approach to polysemy; see also Gries this volume). The way the geometry applies is dependent on the types of insides objects possess, thus accounting for enclosure in both 2D and more real-world 3D settings. Moreover, such an approach is also consistent with how spatial relations might be computed by the visual system (see for example Ullman 1996).

But geometric routines on their own are not enough to account for the myriad of uses of *in* and *on*. The second key component associated with *in* and *on* has to do with a second component of spatial relations – how objects interact with each other and how we interact with them. Coventry and Garrod (2004) coined the term "dynamic-kinematic routines" as a label for the types of routines – different from geometric routines – that are computed when looking at spatial scenes. For *in* and *on*, the specific dynamic-kinematic routine of "location control" was proposed originally in Garrod and Sanford (1989), and a similar notion was also suggested by Vandeloise (1991), and although not explicitly linked to containment and support, this is also related to the force dynamics proposed by Talmy (1988). Location control is the function of constraining the location of an object(s) over time, such that if one object moves, the contents will move with it. In a gravitational plane, containers afford constraining the location of contents, and this notion of location control is related to the geometry of enclosure, but is also empirically testable as being separate from it.

In a series of experiments we varied the geometry of spatial scenes and the degree of location control those scenes exhibited. For example, scenes with filmed (real) objects showed an apple perched on top of other fruit in a glass bowl at various heights, sometimes overhanging past the convex hull of the container. The scenes were static, or displayed various forms of movement. In the "strong location control" condition, the bowl plus fruit was shown moving from side-to-side at the same rate such that the bowl was controlling the location of the contents over time. In contrast, in a weak location control condition, the located object (e.g., the apple) was shown moving by itself, wiggling from side-to-side (but remaining in contact with the object immediately below it) while the rest of the objects (bowl and other fruit) remained stationary (see Figure 23.1 for examples). The consequences of these manipulations for spatial language have been examined using a range of measures, including free production studies where participants are asked "Where is the apple?" and rating studies where participants rate the appropriateness of sentences of the form *The apple is PREPOSITION the bowl* to accurately describe the pictures/videos. And the manipulations of geometry (i.e., height of pile) and

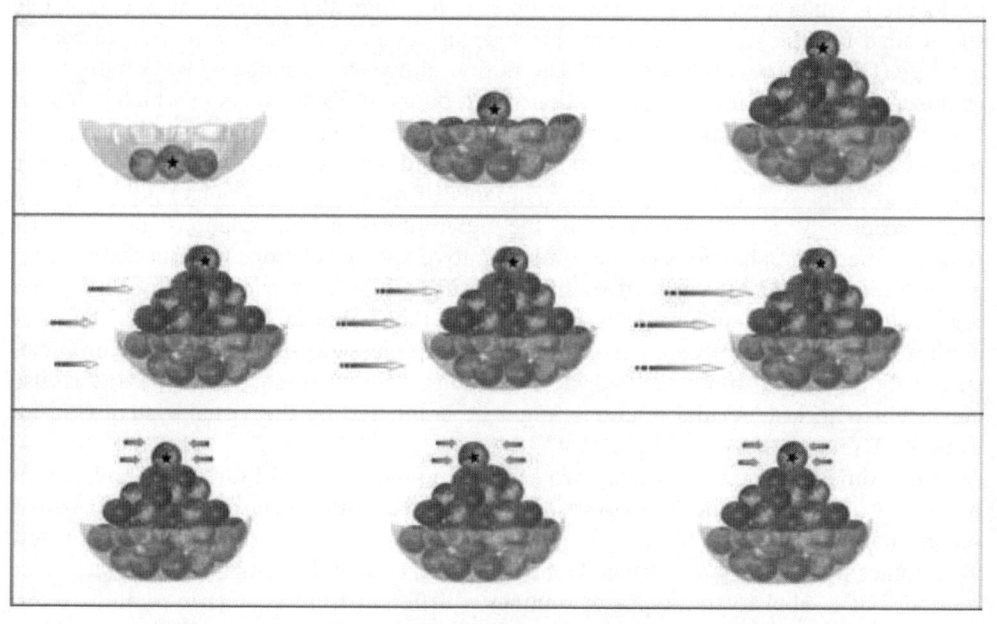

Fig. 23.1: Examples of scenes from Richards et al. (2004) showing geometry and location control manipulations. The top row shows manipulation of geometry. The middle row shows a schematic of strong location control; the bottom row, weak location control.

location control have been tested both with adults (Coventry 1998; Garrod et al. 1999) and children (Richards et al. 2004). The results of these studies show that both geometry **and** location control are important predictors of both the choice of *in* and *on* to describe object arrangements, and also the acceptability ratings given to sentences to describe spatial scenes. For example, Richards et al. (2004) found that children as young as four years of age preferred to describe the scenes using *in* as first or only mention in their spatial descriptions when the scenes showed strong location control, and in contrast used *in* as first or only mention least when the scenes showed weak location control. Garrod et al. (1999) have also shown that there is a direct relationship between independent judgments of location control and language to describe the same (static) spatial scenes. They had one group of participants rate the likelihood that the located object and reference objects would remain in the same relative positions were the reference object to be moved from side-to-side, and another group of participants rated the appropriateness of spatial expressions (e.g., *the ball is in the bowl*) to describe the same scenes. Significant correlations were found between the location control judgments and the language ratings for the same scenes, indicating that location control seems to systematically underpin the comprehension of *in* and *on*.

Location control may well be an important construct for non-spatial uses of prepositions also, as in the case of spatial metaphors such as *on the bottle* or in *a trance* (see Garrod and Sanford 1989 for discussion). However, while a combination of geometric routines and dynamic-kinematic routines is undoubtedly powerful, and can account for a wide range of uses of *in* and *on* (see also Tyler and Evans 2003, for discussion), on their own geometric and dynamic-kinematic routines do not account for the mapping between *in* and *on* and the spatial world. Particular objects have particular functions, and one learns about these through interaction with particular objects in particular situations and through the mapping words have with other words in a language.

In a series of studies (Coventry et al. 1994; Coventry and Prat-Sala 2001; Feist and Gentner 1998, 2003) the objects involved in a spatial relationship have been manipulated, showing consequences for spatial description across a range of methods. For example, Coventry et al. (1994) showed objects positioned at various heights in a bowl or in a jug (of similar dimensions). They found that *in* was judged to be a more appropriate description of a solid object (e.g., an apple) in *a bowl* compared to the same object in *a jug*. Moreover, adding liquid to the jug further diminished the appropriateness of *in* to describe the position of the apple with respect to the jug, but did not impact upon judgments for the apple in the bowl. These types of data suggest that objects come to have specific functions by virtue of the co-occurrence of objects together in particular configurations (more evidence of this is provided for vertical prepositions; see below).

Associating objects with particular functions does not only occur through perception – the collocation of prepositions and nouns in language is also important. For example in English two different nouns can be used for a receptacle with the same level of concavity – a *dish* versus a *plate*. In Figure 23.2, the coffee capsule can be described as *in the dish* or *on the plate*; *on the dish* or *in the plate* are less acceptable descriptions. In a series of studies manipulating labeling of the same objects (Coventry et al. 1994; Coventry and Prat-Sala 2001), we found that changing the name for the same viewed object affects the preposition chosen to refer to that spatial relation. The implications of this are that the situation-specific meaning of spatial language is a combination of differ-

Fig. 23.2: The coffee capsule is *in the dish* or *on the plate* (*on the dish/in the plate* are less preferable descriptions)

ent types of co-occurrence relations – the likelihood with which words co-occur with other words, the likelihood with which objects occur in particular spatial configurations and exhibit particular geometric and dynamic-kinematic relations, and how these constraints mesh together (see also Speed et al. this volume).

In summary, geometric routines, the dynamic-kinematic routine of location control, and rich situation knowledge about object associations, object-specific functions and collocations between nouns and prepositions are all necessary to give an account of the semantics of *in* and *on* (and equivalent terms in other languages: see Feist 2008 for discussion). Three points merit recapitulation. First, we have gone beyond drawing pictures of spatial relations in the form of image schemata to more grounded representations, both geometric and extrageometric, that are more plausibly computed by the vision and action systems. Second, such an account is able to deal with a wide range of senses of these prepositions using only a few parameters, thus avoiding the need for the explicit representation of extensive polysemy in some earlier cognitive linguistic accounts. Third, the empirical approach to spatial language gives good information regarding the mapping between language and space, using methods that go beyond relying on one's own intuitions about spatial relations (Sandra and Rice 1995).

3.2. Projective terms – focus on *over, under, above* and *below*

The projective prepositions in English include *left, right, in front of, behind, over, under, above*, and *below*. These terms require a reference frame from which a spatial direction is generated. For instance *above* is usually employed with respect to the gravitational axis (*above* an object is usually higher in the gravitational plane). However, one can also use *above* from the viewers' perspective (when performing a hand stand, viewing an object *above* can be lower in the gravitational plane). And when looking at someone else doing a handstand, one can also say that an object is *above her head* using her body as the axes rather than gravity. Levinson (1996, 2003) distinguishes between three classes of reference frame; the absolute reference frame (e.g., the gravitational plane, cardinal directions, and so on and so forth), the relative frame (determined by the changing position of the viewer), and the intrinsic frame (determined by the axes of the reference object).

There is a literature examining preferences for particular reference frames, as well as constraints on their use. Often reference frames are collapsed – for instance, *above* is usually used when the absolute (gravitational) and relative frames are aligned. Empirical work by Carlson and colleagues has played an important part in unpacking constraints on reference frames using experimental paradigms as well as event-related brain potentials that tease apart the use of individual frames (e.g., Carlson et al. 2002). Carlson-Radvansky and Irwin (1993) found that English projective terms display a distinct pattern of preferences on their use, with distinct preferences for the absolute frame for *above*, followed by the intrinsic frame, with less evidence for the use of a relative frame when the absolute and intrinsic frames do not coincide with relative use.

Once a reference frame has been selected for a projective term, the geometric routines for the vertical prepositions have been well articulated, with computational frameworks for these proposed and developed by Regier and Carlson (2001), and Regier (1996) building on earlier empirical results (e.g., Hayward and Tarr 1995; Logan and Sadler 1996). For example, the Attention Vector Sum model developed by Regier and Carlson (2001), partly inspired by population vector encoding in several neural subsystems (e.g., Georgopolous et al. 1986), elegantly computes acceptability ratings for *above* that map onto human judgments for varying positions of located objects in relation to various shapes of reference object.

In addition to geometric routines, evidence for dynamic kinematic routines for these terms has also been forthcoming. The comprehension and production of vertical prepositions is affected by the extent to which objects are shown to fulfill, or are expected to fulfill, their functions (e.g., Carlson-Radvansky et al. 1999; Coventry et al. 2001). For example, Coventry et al. (2001) presented participants with pictures of people holding objects with a protecting function, such as a person holding an umbrella (see Figure 23.3). The geometry of the scene was manipulated with the umbrella positioned either directly over the person, or at varying angles from the vertical. The scenes also manipulated the extent to which the protecting object was shown to protect the person from falling objects. In the functional condition, rain was shown falling on the umbrella, protecting the person. In the non-functional condition, rain was shown missing the protecting object, and making contact with the person. Participants rated the appropriateness of sentences containing the prepositions *over*, *under*, *above* and *below* to describe the relative positions of the objects (e.g., *The umbrella is over the man / The man is under the umbrella*). Several findings of interest emerged. First, both the relative positions of the located and reference objects and function affected ratings. For geometry, ratings were highest when the protecting object was directly over the person's head, and for function, ratings were highest when the protecting object was protecting and lowest when it was not. Second, there was an effect of function even when the protecting object was in the prototypical geometric position (i.e., directly above the person's head). Third, there were interactions between geometry and function and specific prepositions. While ratings for *above* and *below* were more affected by the relative positions of objects than those for *over* and *under*, the reverse was true for function. This latter finding suggests that English has two sets of vertical prepositions which are not synonyms, but rather pick out a differential focus on geometry (*above*, *below*) versus function (*over*, *under*).

Fig. 23.3: Examples of scenes used by Coventry et al. (2001)

Fig. 23.4: Examples of scenes used by Coventry et al. (2010)

Building on these earlier results, the dynamic-kinematic routine for vertical prepositions has been investigated using eye tracking and brain imaging methods. For example, in the scenes shown in Figure 23.4, the box and the bowl are in the same relative positions, but the objects falling from the box are not shown either directly reaching or missing the bowl. Coventry et al. (2010) posited that, if dynamic-kinematic routines are real, participants would have to project the path of falling objects in order to establish whether the box and bowl are interacting as one would typically expect when these objects occur together before they are able to give acceptability judgments. Eye tracking revealed that participants spent more time looking to the side of the bowl when the falling objects looked like they would miss the container (the right picture in Figure 23.4) than when the objects would be expected to end up in the container (middle picture) during a sentence-picture rating task.

This provides evidence that participants were indeed looking down the path of the falling objects prior to making their judgments about the suitability of spatial prepositions to describe the pictures. Moreover, in some recent brain imaging work (Coventry et al. 2013) we found that spatial language judgments when looking at similar pictures are associated with "mentally animating" the visual scene when viewing it. Using functional Magnetic Resonance Imaging, we localized the brain regions associated with motion processing (middle temporal and middle superior temporal regions). Participants performed a sentence picture verification task in the scanner; they first read sentences containing prepositions (e.g., *the box is over the bowl*) or comparative adjectives (*the box is bigger than the bowl*) followed by a picture (examples in Figure 23.4). Among the findings, we found that there was reliably more motion processing activation for the static images when they were preceded by sentences containing prepositions compared to sentences containing comparative adjectives. This shows that spatial language actually drives how a visual scene is processed when one is looking at it. Moreover, in whole brain analyses, we also found more premotor and motor activations during picture presentation when the pictures were again preceded by sentences containing prepositions as compared with comparative adjectives. This confirms that spatial language goes beyond geometric relations, pointing to the importance of the action system as well as the visual system as components associated with it.

Just as *in* and *on* require more than geometric and dynamic-kinematic routines to understanding the mapping with the spatial world, so too do the vertical prepositions. For example, in the protecting object experiments of Coventry et al. (2001), the influence of objects without a usual protecting function was also considered, but in situations where those objects could nevertheless afford protection. For instance, the umbrella in Figure 23.3 was substituted with a suitcase, which presumably does not have a lexicalized protecting function. Nevertheless, ratings of *the suitcase is over the man*, etc., were affected by the position of the falling rain. In another study, adding holes to an umbrella where the function is no longer afforded (i.e., when the rain a distance away from the object is expected to pass through the umbrella even though it is falling towards it) has been found to eliminate the influence of the position of the rain on spatial language ratings (Coventry et al., 2010). These examples (among others) show that consideration of situational and object knowledge is required for vertical spatial terms, just as it is for the prepositions *in* and *on*.

4. Spatial demonstratives

Spatial demonstratives, such as *this* and *that*, are particularly important to examine with respect to the mapping between language and space. These terms, like topological prepositions, are among the first words all children acquire (Clark 1973, 2003) but they are more closely associated with deictic gestures than other spatial terms, and other linguistic items in general (H. Clark 1996; Diessel 2006). They also occur in all languages, are high frequency terms within a language, and philologically emerge as the earliest traceable words in languages (Deutscher 2005; Diessel 2006). For these reasons spatial demonstratives should be one of the first ports of call when examining the mapping between language and space, but rather surprisingly they have received much less attention than spatial prepositions.

A useful starting point when considering demonstratives is the impressive cataloguing of demonstrative systems across languages by Diessel (1999, 2005). In a large-scale analysis of demonstrative systems across over 200 languages, Diessel found that the most basic distinction languages make is a binary distinction (54% of languages sampled; English among them). From this Diessel argues that a proximal-distal contrast underlies demonstrative systems across languages (Diessel 2005, 2006). As Enfield (2003) has argued, typologies are however not based on studies of real demonstrative use – and only recently have experimental studies begun to examine the mapping between demonstratives and perceptual space.

Using a methodology designed to elicit spatial demonstratives without speakers realizing that their language was being tested, Coventry et al. (2008) tested the mapping between spatial demonstrative use and perceptual space across two languages. English and Spanish-speaking participants were instructed to produce either *this* or *that* (or the Spanish equivalents: *este*, *ese*, *aquel*) to identify the position of coloured geometrical shapes/disks placed on a table at varying distances from them (whilst believing the experiment was about memory for object location; see Figure 23.5). First, an object was placed on a coloured dot various distances from the participant. Next, the participant had to point at the object saying either *this/that* colour shape (e.g., *this red triangle*). (Participants were told that they were in the 'language' condition in the memory experiment, and therefore it was important to stick to only three words in their descriptions [while pointing at the object] so that everyone in the language condition had the same amount of language.) When the object was placed within arm's reach, participants used *this* (*este* in Spanish) more often than *that*, with *that* used more than *this* when the object was positioned outside of arm's reach. Participants also used *this/este* more frequently

Fig. 23.5: The setup for the memory game experiments (Coventry et al., 2008), and some of the shaped used

when they had placed the object rather than when the experimenter had placed the object. Finally, an extension of the use of *this/este* to describe positions beyond arm's reach was found when participants pointed using a stick.

These data (and data from other studies; see for example Bonfiglioli et al. 2009; Maes and De Rooij 2007) map onto findings in neuroscience and neuropsychology that has identified two separate brain systems representing peripersonal (near) and extrapersonal (far) space (e.g., Berti and Rizzolatti 2002; Làdavas 2002). Indeed the extension of *this* using a stick and the manipulation of who places the object prior to description in Coventry et al. (2008) were motivated directly by findings on peripersonal space showing that peripersonal space can be extended through tool use and contact (e.g., Berti and Frassinetti 2000; Longo and Lourenco 2006).

So it appears that *where* an object is located is important for demonstrative choice, mapping into a basic distinction the perceptual system makes. But are demonstratives also affected by other extrageometric variables just as prepositions are?

Linguistic typological work across languages has shown that demonstrative systems vary quite considerably across languages, and some of the distinctions relate to the nature of the objects placed rather than their location. Some languages have three-term demonstrative systems, usually regarded as distance oriented (Spanish: Kemmerer 1999; Levinson 2003), or person oriented (e.g., Japanese: Diessel 2005), but other languages make distinctions such as whether an object is visible or not (e.g., Tiriyó: Meira 2003; Quileute: Diessel 1999), whether or not an object is owned by the speaker (e.g., Supyire: Diessel 1999), and whether the object is elevated on the vertical plan (e.g., Dyirbal, Lahu: Diessel 1999). Such cross-linguistic differences have led some to argue that demonstratives simply do not map onto perceptual space (see for example Enfield 2003; Kemmerer 1999, 2006 for discussion). However, an alternative possibility is that spatial demonstratives, just like adpositions, are associated with multiple constraints on their use. In a series of recent studies with English speakers using the memory game (Coventry et al. 2014) we varied whether the object placed was owned by the participant or not, whether the object was visible, and whether the object was familiar to the participant or not. For the visibility experiment, an object was placed and was then left uncovered, covered with a glass (so the object was still visible), or covered with a metal cover (so the object was occluded; see Figure 23.6). *This* was used least to describe the object when covered with the metal cover, with no difference between the glass cover and uncovered conditions. Although English does not make an explicit distinction in its binary demonstrative system between visible and hidden objects, English speakers nevertheless use that parameter to select demonstratives in their language.

For the ownership manipulation, participants at the start of the experiment were given participation payment in the form of coins, which were then used as stimuli in the experiment. Either the participant's coins were placed prior to description, or coins owned by the experimenter were placed. Participants used *this* significantly more than *that* to describe the location of their own coins compared to the coins owned by the experimenter.

If English demonstrative use is affected by object properties that are explicit in the demonstrative systems of some other languages, we wondered if further object properties might also be important, motivated by work we have conducted earlier on other types of spatial language. In the final experiment in this series, we examined familiarity of objects. The objects placed were either familiar colour-shape combinations (e.g., red

Fig. 23.6: The visibility manipulations in Coventry et al. (2014)

square) or less familiar combinations (e.g., vermillion ranunculoid). Participants in this experiment used *this* more frequently to describe the location of the familiar objects compared to the unfamiliar objects.

So the results of the memory game experiments in Coventry et al. (2014) show that demonstrative choice is affected by knowledge of the objects being described. And in all the experiments the object manipulations did not interact with distance (note that there was also an effect of peripersonal versus extrapersonal space on demonstrative choice in all experiments). But do these results also map onto the perception of space? To test this we ran further non-linguistic experiments. Objects were placed as in the memory game scenario, but this time participants had the task of remembering where an object had been placed immediately after its placement. We then compared estimated distance (participants instructed the experimenter to move a stick to where the object had been placed) to the actual object placement distance from the participant. The results directly mirrored the results of the language memory game experiments. Objects owned by the participant were remembered as being closer than objects owned by someone else; covered (invisible) objects were remembered as being further away than covered visible objects or uncovered objects; familiar objects were remembered as being nearer than unfamiliar objects. And just like the language data, the object effects did not interact with distance.

Overall demonstrative use in English appears to be affected by object properties that are explicitly distinguished in the demonstrative systems of some other languages. Moreover, it would appear that the factors that affect demonstrative choice mirror the factors that affect (non-linguistic) memory for object location. Thus demonstrative distinctions across languages as well as demonstrative choice within a language appear to be related to distinctions affecting the perception of space as reflected in memory for object location.

An important caveat is to note that the experimental approach we have briefly overviewed in this chapter should not be viewed as a substitute for other methods. For example, with respect to demonstratives, other parameters affecting their use have been documented in addition to the parameters we have investigated empirically, including joint attention (see Diessel 2006) and the shared knowledge states of interlocutors (e.g., Piwek et al. 2008), with insights from cross-linguistic and typological analyses. It is to the issue of cross-linguistic variation that I briefly turn.

5. Cross-linguistic differences and "linguistic relativity"

The fact that languages carve up space in different ways is challenging for the view that a set of basic universal primitive spatial concepts underlie all spatial language (Levinson and Meira 2003; Bowerman 1996; see also Koptjevskaja-Tamm this volume). For example, containment and support relations do not always cluster in the same way across languages when speakers of different languages are charged with sorting or describing spatial scenes. While English distinguishes between containment (*in*) and support (*on*) relations, Dutch is among a cluster of languages that more finely differentiates support relations, with a distinction between vertical attachment (*aan*: a picture on a wall, a handle on a door), and horizontal support (*op*: a cup on a table). In contrast, Spanish collapses containment and support relations with a single term, *en*, appropriate for containment and support (Bowerman 1996). Such differences lead to two questions that merit mention. First, does the language one learns affect how one structures space? Second, do speakers of different languages actually "think" spatially in different ways? I take each of these issues in turn.

It is tempting to think that the distinctions a language makes are revealing about the type of non-linguistic concepts and processes that speakers of that language employ. Indeed, with respect to *in* and *on*, differences in the way Korean and English languages carve up these relations has been the subject of a series of fascinating studies. While English distinguishes between containment and support events as the end points of motion actions, Korean distinguishes between tight-fit and loose-fit path events. In Korean the verb *kkita* is used for tight-fit path events (putting a video cassette in a video cassette box/putting a lid on a jar) while *nehta* is used for loose-fit containment paths and *nohta* for loose-fit support relations (Bowerman 1996). Choi et al. (1999), using a preferential looking method, showed that 1.5–2 year old Korean and English learning children already look at language-appropriate aspects of spatial relations when looking at visual scenes paired with words in their language. However, McDonough et al. (2003) and Hespos and Spelke (2004) found that younger infants learning Korean or English look at both geometric distinctions between containment and support and tight-fit loose-fit distinctions, suggesting that learning a language might focus on some perceptual distinctions more than others, rather than language structuring space uniquely for that language. Indeed, as I reviewed above, even English adults are sensitive to degrees of location control when using *in* and *on*, and therefore it might be mistaken to argue that language completely filters out distinctions. However, one has to be cautious; as Casasola (2008) notes, it is likely that the extent to which language structures spatial categories in development varies as a function of spatial category.

It has also been claimed that the language ones speaks affects performance on a range of non-linguistic tasks (i.e., a test of "linguistic relativity"; see Wolff and Holmes 2010 for discussion). A much-discussed example is that of Pederson and colleagues (1998), who found differences across a range of tasks between speakers of languages differing in their use of references frames. For example, Tzeltal speakers, who use the absolute frame of reference even in small-scale/table-top space, have a tendency, when they rotate 180 degrees, to rearrange objects absolutely, while Dutch and English speakers rotate the object arrangement in alignment with body rotation (i.e., they produce relative arrangements). The interpretation of these results as evidence for a strong form of the Whorfian hypotheses has been controversial (see Majid et al. 2004; Li and Gleitman 2002 for different views). What *is* clear is that speakers of languages can use their language a tool to aid performance on non-linguistic tasks (see Trueswell and Papafragou 2010). However, while speakers of a language may use the distinctions they have in their language when performing non-linguistic tasks, those distinctions may not capture how those terms are actually used within a language by speakers (cf. Coventry et al. 2014).

6. Conclusions

Spatial language is a natural place to start to examine the spatial constructs that are important for language. This brief (and highly selective) review of empirical research on spatial language has illustrated how experimental approaches to spatial language have helped to unpack the multiple constraints underpinning the mapping between language and space. Cross-linguistic data collected using multiple methods will continue to play an important role in understanding not only the extent of possible universal perceptual parameters underpinning spatial language across languages, but also the full range of constraints speakers may employ to use the spatial language they have within their own language.

7. References

Bergen, Benjamin
  this volume   1. Embodiment. Berlin/Boston: De Gruyter Mouton.
Berti, Anna and Francesca Frassinetti
    2000   When far becomes near: Remapping of space by tool use. *Journal of Cognitive Neuroscience* 12: 415–420.

Berti, Anna and Giacomo Rizzolatti
  2002   Coding near and far space. In: H.-O. Karnath, A. D. Milner, and G. Vallar (eds.), *The Cognitive and Neural Bases of Spatial Neglect*, 119–129. New York: Oxford University Press.
Bonfiglioli, Claudia, Chiara Finocchiaro, Beno Gesierich, Francesco Rositani, and Massimo Vescovi
  2009   A kinematic approach to the conceptual representations of *this* and *that*. *Cognition* 111: 270–274.
Bower, Thomas G. R.
  1982   *Development in Infancy* (2nd Edition). San Francisco: W. H. Freeman.
Bowerman, Melissa
  1996   Learning how to structure space for language: a cross-linguistic perspective. In: P. Bloom, M. A. Peterson, L. Nadel, and M. F. Garrett (eds.), *Language and Space*, 385–436. Cambridge: MIT Press.
Brugman, Claudia
  1988   *The Story of "over": Polysemy, Semantics and the Structure of the Lexicon*. New York: Garland.
Carlson, Laura A., Robert West, Holly A. Taylor, and Ryan S. Herndon
  2002   Neural correlates of spatial term use. *Journal of Experimental Psychology: Human Perception and Performance* 28(6): 1391–1407.
Carlson-Radvansky, Laura A., Eric S. Covey, and Kathleen M. Lattanzi
  1999   "What" effects on "where": Functional influences on spatial relations. *Psychological Science* 10: 516–521.
Carlson-Radvansky, Laura A., and David E. Irwin
  1993   Frames of reference in vision and language: where is above? *Cognition* 46: 223–244.
Casasanto, Daniel and Lera Boroditsky
  2008   Time in the mind: Using space to think about time. *Cognition* 106: 579–593.
Casasola, Marianella
  2008   The development of infants' spatial categories. *Current Directions in Psychological Science* 17: 21–25.
Casasola, Marianella and Leslie B. Cohen
  2002   Infant categorization of containment, support, and tight-fit spatial relationships. *Developmental Science* 5: 247–264.
Casasola, Marianella, Leslie B. Cohen, and Elizabeth Chiarello
  2003   Six-month-old infants' categorization of containment spatial relations. *Child Development* 74: 679–693.
Choi, Soonja, Laraine McDonough, Melissa Bowerman, and Jean M. Mandler
  1999   Early sensitivity to language-specific spatial categories in English and Korean. *Cognitive Development* 14: 241–268.
Clark, Eve V.
  1973   Nonlinguistic strategies and the acquisition of word meanings. *Cognition* 2: 161–182.
Clark, Eve V.
  2003   *First Language Acquisition*. Cambridge: Cambridge University Press.
Clark, Herbert H.
  1996   *Using Language*. Cambridge: Cambridge University Press.
Cohn, Anthony G., Brandon Bennett, John Gooday, and Nicholas M. Gotts
  1997   Qualitative spatial representation and reasoning with the region connection calculus. *Geoinformatica* 1: 1–42.
Coventry, Kenny R.
  1998   Spatial prepositions, functional relations and lexical specification. In: P. Oliver and K. Gapp (eds.), *The Representation and Processing of Spatial Expressions*, 247–262. Hillsdale: Lawrence Erlbaum Associates.

Coventry, Kenny R., Richard Carmichael, and Simon C. Garrod
   1994   Spatial prepositions, object-specific function and task requirements. *Journal of Semantics* 11: 289–309.

Coventry, Kenny R., Thomas Christophel, Thorsten Fehr, Berenice Valdés-Conroy, and Manfred Herrmann
   2013   Multiple routes to mental animation: Language and functional relations drive motion processing for static images. *Psychological Science* 24(8): 1379–1388.

Coventry, Kenny R., and Simon C. Garrod
   2004   *Saying, Seeing and Acting. The Psychological Semantics of Spatial Prepositions*. Hove and New York: Psychology Press, Taylor and Francis

Coventry, Kenny R., Debra Griffiths, and Colin J. Hamilton
   2014   Spatial demonstratives and perceptual space: Describing and remembering object location. *Cognitive Psychology* 69: 46–70.

Coventry, Kenny R., Dermot Lynott, Angelo Cangelosi, Lynn Monrouxe, Dan Joyce, and Daniel C. Richardson
   2010   Spatial language, visual attention, and perceptual simulation. *Brain and Language* 112(3): 202–213.

Coventry, Kenny R., and Merce Prat-Sala
   2001   Object-specific function, geometry and the comprehension of 'in' and 'on'. *European Journal of Cognitive Psychology* 13(4): 509–528.

Coventry, Kenny R., Merce Prat-Sala, and Lynn Richards
   2001   The interplay between geometry and function in the comprehension of 'over', 'under', 'above' and 'below'. *Journal of Memory and Language* 44: 376–398.

Coventry, Kenny R., Berenice Valdés, Alejandro Castillo, and Pedro Guijarro-Fuentes
   2008   Language within your reach: Near-far perceptual space and spatial demonstratives. *Cognition* 108: 889–898.

Deutscher, Guy
   2005   *The Unfolding of Language: An Evolutionary Tour of Mankind's Greatest Invention*. New York: Metropolitan Books.

Diessel, Holger
   1999   *Demonstratives. Form, Function, and Grammaticalization*. John Benjamins: Amsterdam.

Diessel, Holger
   2005   Distance contrasts in demonstratives. In: M. Haspelmath, M. Dryer, D. Gil, and B. Comrie (eds.), *World Atlas of Language Structures,* 170–173. Oxford: Oxford University Press.

Diessel, Holger
   2006   Demonstratives, joint attention, and the emergence of grammar. *Cognitive Linguistics* 17: 463–489.

Enfield, Nick J.
   2003   Demonstratives in space and interaction: data from Lao speakers and implications for semantic analysis. *Language* 79: 82–117.

Evans, Vyvyan
   this volume   24. Time. Berlin/Boston: De Gruyter Mouton.

Feist, Michele I.
   2008   Space between languages. *Cognitive Science* 32: 1177–1199.

Feist, Michele I. and Dedre Gentner
   1998   On plates, bowls and dishes: Factors in the use of English IN and ON. In: M. A. Gernsbacher and S. J. Derry (eds.), *Proceedings of the Twentieth Annual Meeting of the Cognitive Science Society,* 345–349. Hillsdale: Lawrence Erlbaum Associates.

Feist, Michele I. and Dedre Gentner
 2003 Factors involved in the use of in and on. In: R. Alterman and D. Kirsh (eds.), *Proceedings of the Twenty-fifth Annual Meeting of the Cognitive Science Society,* 390–395. Hillsdale: Lawrence Erlbaum Associates.
Filipović, Luna, and Iraide Ibarretxe-Antuñano
 this volume 25. Motion. Berlin/Boston: De Gruyter Mouton.
Garrod, Simon, Gillian Ferrier, and Siobhan Campbell
 1999 *In* and *on*: Investigating the functional geometry of spatial prepositions. *Cognition* 72(2): 167–189.
Garrod, Simon C., and Anthony J. Sanford
 1989 Discourse models as interfaces between language and the spatial world. *Journal of Semantics,* 6, 147–160.
Georgopolous, Apostolos P., Andrew B. Schwartz, and Ronald E. Kettner
 1986 Neuronal populating coding of movement direction. *Science* 233(4771): 1416–1419.
Gibbs, Raymond W.
 this volume 8. Metaphor. Berlin/Boston: De Gruyter Mouton.
Gries, Stefan Th.
 this volume 22. Polysemy. Berlin/Boston: De Gruyter Mouton.
Hayward, William G., and Michael J. Tarr
 1995 Spatial language and spatial representation. *Cognition* 55: 39–84.
Herskovits, Annette
 1986 *Language and Spatial Cognition: An Interdisciplinary Study of the Prepositions in English.* Cambridge: Cambridge University Press.
Hespos, Susan J., and Renée Baillargeon
 2001 Reasoning about containment events in very young infants. *Cognition* 78: 207–245.
Hespos, Susan J., and Elizabeth S. Spelke
 2004 Conceptual precursors to language. *Nature* 430(6998): 453–456.
Johnson, Judith, and Dan I. Slobin
 1979 The development of locative expressions in English, Italian, Serbo-Croatian and Turkish. *Journal of Child Language* 6: 529–546.
Kemmerer, David
 1999 "Near" and "far" in language and perception. *Cognition* 44: 1607–1621.
Kemmerer, David
 2006 The semantics of space: Integrating linguistic typology and cognitive neuroscience. *Neuropsychologia* 44: 1607–1621.
Koptjevskaja-Tamm, Maria
 this volume 21. Semantic typology. Berlin/Boston: De Gruyter Mouton.
Làdavas, Elisabetta
 2002 Functional and dynamic properties of visual peripersonal space. *Trends in Cognitive Science* 6: 17–22.
Lakoff, George
 1987 *Women, Fire, and Dangerous Things.* Chicago: Chicago University Press.
Lakoff, George, and Mark Johnson
 1980 *Metaphors We Live By.* Chicago: Chicago University Press.
Landau, Barbara, and Ray Jackendoff
 1993 'What' and 'where' in spatial language and cognition. *Behavioural and Brain Sciences* 16(2): 217–265.
Langacker, Ronald W.
 1986 *Foundations of Cognitive Grammar,* Vol. 1. Stanford: Stanford University Press.
Levinson, Stephen C.
 1996 Frames of reference and Molyneux's question. In: P. Bloom, M. A. Peterson, L. Nadel, and M. F. Garrett (eds.), *Language and Space,* 109–169. Cambridge: MIT Press.

Levinson, Stephen C.
    2003   *Space in Language and Cognition. Explorations in Cognitive Diversity*. Cambridge University press: Cambridge.

Levinson, Stephen C., and Sergio Meira
    2003   'Natural concepts' in the spatial topological domain – adpositional meanings in crosslinguistic perspective: An exercise in semantic typology. *Language* 79(3): 485–516.

Li, Peggy, and Lila Gleitman
    2002   Turning the tables: Language and spatial reasoning. *Cognition* 83: 265–294.

Logan, Gordon D., and Daniel D. Sadler
    1996   A computational analysis of the apprehension of spatial relations. In: P. Bloom, M. A. Peterson, L. Nadel, and M. F. Garrett (eds.), *Language and Space*, 494–530. Cambridge MIT Press.

Longo, Matthew R., and Stella F. Lourenco
    2006   On the nature of near space: Effects of tool use and the transition to far space. *Neuropsychologia* 44: 977–981.

Maes, Alfons, and C. De Rooij
    2007   How do demonstratives code distance? In: A. Branco, T. McEnery, R. Mitkov, and F. Silva (eds.), *Proceedings of the 6th Discourse Anaphora and Anaphor Resolution Colloquium DAARC 2007*, 83–89. Lagos, Pt: Centro Linguistica da Universidade do Porto.

Majid, Asifa, Melissa Bowerman, Sotara Kita, Daniel B. M. Haun, and Stephen C. Levinson
    2004   Can language restructure cognition? The case for space. *Trends in Cognitive Science* 8: 108–114.

McDonough, Laraine, Soonja Choi, and Jean M. Mandler
    2003   Understanding spatial relations: Flexible infants, lexical adults. *Cognitive Psychology* 46: 226–259.

Meira, Sergio
    2003   'Addressee effects' in demonstrative systems: The cases of Tiriyó and Brazilian Portuguese. In: F. Lenz (ed.), *Deictic Conceptualization of Space, Time and Person*. Amsterdam: John Benjamins.

Pederson, Eric, Eve Danziger, David Wilkins, Stephen Levinson, Sotaro Kita, and Gunter Senft
    1998   Semantic typology and spatial conceptualization. *Language* 74(3): 557–589.

Piaget, Jean, and Bärbel Inhelder, B.
    1956   *The Child's Conception of Space*. London: Routledge and Kegan Paul.

Piwek, Paul, Robbert-Jan Beun, and Anita Cremers
    2008   'Proximal' and 'distal' in language and cognition: Evidence from demonstratives in Dutch. *Journal of Pragmatics*, 40: 694–718.

Quinn, Paul C.
    2005   Developmental constraints on the representation of spatial relation information: Evidence from preverbal infants. In: L. A. Carlson and E. van der Zee (eds.), *Functional Features in Language and Space: Insights from Perception, Categorization, and Development*. New York: Oxford University Press.

Regier, Terry
    1996   *The Human Semantic Potential. Spatial Language and Constrained Connectionism*. Cambridge: MIT Press.

Regier, Terry and Laura A. Carlson
    2001   Grounding spatial language in perception: An empirical and computational investigation. *Journal of Experimental Psychology: General* 130(2): 273–298.

Richards, Lynn V., Kenny R. Coventry, and John Clibbens
    2004   Where's the orange? Geometric and extra-geometric factors in English children's talk of spatial locations. *Journal of Child Language* 31: 153–175.

Rosch, Eleanor, and Carolyn B. Mervis
  1975   Family resemblances: Studies in the internal structure of categories. *Cognitive Psychology* 7(4): 573–605.
Sandra, Dominiek, and Sally Rice
  1995   Network analyses of prepositional meaning. Mirroring whose mind – the linguist's or the language user's? *Cognitive Linguistics* 6: 8–130.
Speed, Laura, David P. Vinson and Gabriella Vigliocco
  this volume   9. Representing meaning. Berlin/Boston: De Gruyter Mouton.
Talmy, Leonard
  1983   How language structures space. In: H. Pick, and L. Acredolo (eds.), *Spatial Orientation: Theory, Research and Application*, 225–282. New York: Plenum Press.
Talmy, Leonard
  1988   Force dynamics in language and cognition. *Cognitive Science* 12: 49–100.
Trueswell, John, and Anna Papafragou
  2010   Perceiving and remembering events cross-linguistically: Evidence from dual-task paradigms. *Journal of Memory and Language* 63: 64–82.
Tyler, Andrea, and Vyvyan Evans
  2003   *The Semantics of English Prepositions: Spatial Scenes, Embodied Meaning and Cognition.* Cambridge: Cambridge University Press.
Ullman, Shimon
  1996   *High-level Vision. Object Recognition and Visual Cognition.* Cambridge: MIT Press.
Vandeloise, Claude
  1991   *Spatial Prepositions. A Case Study from French.* Chicago: University of Chicago Press.
Wittgenstein, Ludwig
  1953   *Philosophical Investigations.* Oxford: Blackwell.
Wolff, Phillip and Kevin J. Holmes
  2010   Linguistic relativity. *WIREs Cognitive Science* 2: 253–265.

Kenny R. Coventry, East Anglia (United Kingdom)

24. Time

1. Introduction
2. What is the nature and status of time?
3. What is the relationship between time and space?
4. What is the distinction between time and space?
5. Is time homogenous or multifaceted?
6. Are representations for time universal?
7. Why must time be represented in terms of sensory-motor experience at all?
8. Empirical research on time in cognitive science
9. References

1. Introduction

Research on time, in cognitive linguistics, is concerned with how time manifests itself in language and thought. Cognitive linguists study time as a cognitive phenomenon, which can be investigated, in part, from its linguistic reflexes. Being interdisciplinary in nature, cognitive linguistics has approached the study of time from various perspectives. In addition to linguistics, research on temporal cognition has been informed by findings from experimental psychology, philosophy, neuroscience, and (cognitive) anthropology. This chapter addresses the key questions that cognitive linguistics has raised and attempted to answer, with respect to time.

2. What is the nature and status of time?

Does time arise from an internal subjectively-real experience type? Or is it abstracted from external sensory-motor experiences arising in veridical reality – our experience of the world "out there"? Questions of this sort have been addressed, either directly or indirectly, by cognitive linguists working with sometimes different theoretical, analytic and descriptive goals.

Conceptual Metaphor Theory (see Gibbs this volume), for instance, has provided much of the impetus for exploring these specific questions. Lakoff and Johnson (1980, 1999) have argued that time is abstracted from veridical experiences, such as motion events: time is an abstract conceptual domain, while space is concrete. They put it as follows: "Very little of our understanding of time is purely temporal. Most of our understanding of time is a metaphorical version of our understanding of motion in space" (1999: 139). On this account time does not exist as a "thing-in-itself ... [w]hat we call the domain of time appears to be a conceptual domain that we use for asking certain questions about events through their comparison to other events." (Lakoff and Johnson 1999: 138). In short, time arises from the abstraction of relations between events that we perceive and experience in the world "out there". Once these relations have been abstracted, they are structured in terms of spatial correlates, allowing us to conceptualise time. And once time has been conceptualised we can then experience it. In short, "our concept of time is cognitively constructed ... events and motion are more basic than time." (Lakoff and Johnson 1999: 167).

Other conceptual metaphor theorists have taken a more nuanced view. Grady (1997) holds that time and space evince a qualitative distinction that, and contrary to Lakoff and Johnson, is not best captured in terms of relative abstractness versus concreteness. Grady proposes that time derives from phenomenologically real, albeit subjective experience types, while spatial concepts are grounded in sensory-motor experiences. Moore (e.g., 2006), in his work on space-to-time conceptual metaphors concurs. He argues that time is as basic as space. Hence, time antecedes the conceptual metaphors that serve to structure it. The utility of metaphor, Moore contends, is to make time more accessible for conceptualisation, rather than creating it.

Evans (2004; see also 2013b), focusing on lexical concepts for time – rather than conceptual metaphors – argues that time is in some ways more fundamental than space, at least at the neurological level: it facilitates and underpins our ability to perceive and interact in the world, to anticipate, and to predict. Based on neurological evidence, Evans argues that the distributed nature of temporal processing is critical to our ability to perceive events. Event-perception is therefore facilitated by temporal processing, an issue we return to later.

In large part, the view taken on the nature and status of time depends on whether we are addressing temporal representations (concepts), or neurological representations (experiences). Indeed, the issue resolves itself into the following bifurcation: time is a subjectively real experience – as Grady, Moore and Evans hold – yet it is also a mental achievement, not something in and of itself, but rather abstracted from our perception of events in the world – the position argued for by Lakoff and Johnson.

One way out of this conundrum is to conclude that time is in fact both: temporal concepts are grounded in experiences that are independent of space (and sensory-motor experience more generally), but, time is also reified as an ontological entity, abstracted from the experiences which ground it, giving rise to an abstract category which can be deployed for intersubjective reflection. And in terms of the latter, this abstract category that can be structured, in part via conceptual metaphors, derives from sensory-motor experience.

There is now a very large body of evidence which supports the former view: not only is time directly experienced, its manifestation is often independent of our experience of motion events in space. Moreover, the human experience of time is, in principle, distinct from sensory-motor experience. For instance, Flaherty (1999) has found that our perception of duration is a function of how familiar subjects happen to be with particular tasks: training can influence our experience of task duration. Ornstein ([1969] 1997) has demonstrated that the complexity of a given perceptual array influences perception of duration. And Zakay and Block (1997) found that temporal perception is influenced by how interesting a particular activity is judged to be, or whether we are paying attention to a particular activity.

Other research reveals that our ability to judge duration is a consequence of physiological mechanisms, which vary in inter-subjectively predictable ways. For instance, if vital functioning is accelerated by the consumption of stimulants such as amphetamines, or due to increased body temperature, this results in an overestimation of time amongst subjects (Hoagland 1933; Fraisse 1963, 1984). In contrast, reduced body temperature leads to an underestimation of time (Baddeley 1966). In general, an increase or decrease in vital function consistently leads to perceiving duration as elapsing more quickly or slowly respectively (see Wearden and Penton-Voak 1995 for review).

Flaherty (1999) has found that the nature of experience types can influence our experience of time. For instance, the phenomenon of *protracted duration* – the phenomenologically real and vivid experience that time is proceeding more slowly than usual appears to be a consequence of events including boredom and near death experiences. In contrast, routine tasks with which we are familiar can give rise to the opposite effect: *temporal compression* – the phenomenologically real experience that time is proceeding more quickly than usual.

While findings such as these suggest that time is directly perceived, and phenomenologically real, there are types of temporal representation that appear not to be directly grounded in phenomenologically real experiences of this kind. One example of this is the *matrix* conceptualisation of time (Evans 2004, 2013b), also referred to as *time-as-such* (Sinha et al. 2011). This relates to our understanding of time as a manifold which, metaphorically, is draped across, and constitutes the whole of history; from this perspective, time is *the* event within which all other events take place. This view of time is exemplified by the linguistic example in (1):

(1) Time flows on (forever)

From this perspective, it makes sense to talk of time as having a beginning, as if it were an entity that lies outside us, in some sense providing reality with structure. It is this Matrix conceptualisation that is implicit in the conception of time in the classical mechanics of Newton, and to some extent, in post-Einsteinian physics. And by virtue of time as a Matrix being conceived as an ontological category independent of events, we can discuss and study it, and describe its "history", as evidenced by Steven Hawking's book title: *A Brief History of Time*.

In sum, temporal representations include those grounded in directly perceived temporal experiences. But representations for time can also be abstracted away from these experiences and reified as an ontological category independent of such experiences. This gives rise to mental achievements that are then available for intersubjective reflection without regard to directly experienced time. Representations of this type presume the existence of an objectively-real substrate that can be physically measured or observed, in some sense. And this conceptualisation presumably facilitates our ability to construct and interpret time-measurement systems such as calendars and clocks (Evans 2013b).

3. What is the relationship between time and space?

The relationship between temporal and spatial representation is, in a profound sense, paradoxical. On the one hand, space and time are, for many cognitive linguists, equally basic conceptual domains (Langacker 1987). They are basic in the sense that, although involving distinct types of representations, relating to matter and action, all other domains would seem to assume both space and time. In terms of the experiential level, we must have evolved mechanisms for processing the properties associated with space and time.

Some cognitive linguists have assumed that the fundamental nature of space and time results from a common structural homology (e.g., Talmy 2000). Linguistic evidence for this comes from what Talmy refers to as *conceptual conversion operations*. Talmy (2000) points out, on the basis of linguistic evidence, that acts and activities (from the domain of time) can be converted into objects and mass (from the domain of space). When a temporal concept is *reified*, this is conveyed by expressions exemplified by *a wash* and *some help* in (2) and (3) respectively:

(2) An act   reified as an object   (discrete)
     John washed her.   John gave her a wash.

(3) Activity   reified as a mass   (continuous)
     John helped her.   John gave her some help.

In example (2), the expression *washed* encodes an act, while *a wash* conceives of the same act as if it were an object. It is precisely because lexical concepts relating to time and space can be quantified, Talmy argues, that they can exhibit the conceptual alternativity evident in (2).

In example (3), the expression *helped* encodes an activity, while *some help* encodes a mass lexical concept. When an act is reified as an object, it can be described in terms consistent with the properties of objects. For example, physical objects can be transferred: *to call (on the phone)* becomes: *he gave me a call*. Physical objects can also be quantified: *to slap* becomes: *She gave him two slaps*. As Talmy observes, however, there are constraints upon this process of reification. For example, a reified act or activity cannot be expressed in the same way that prototypical physical objects can. Example (4) illustrates that the reified act, *a call* is incompatible with verbal lexical concepts that are prototypically physical.

(4)   *John pushed/threw/thrust/slid Lily a call

The converse operation, which converts matter to action, is referred to as *actionalisation* (Talmy 2000). When units of matter are actionalised, they are expressed by lexical concepts encoded by verb phrase vehicles. This operation is illustrated by the following examples adapted from Talmy (2000: 45).

(5)   *An object*   actionalised as an act   (discrete)
      Jane removed the pit from the olive.   Jane pitted the olive.

(6)   *A mass*   actionalised as an activity   (continuous)
      Jane has a nosebleed.   Jane is bleeding from the nose.

In contrast, there are good reasons to think that, at the representational level, time and space are asymmetrically structured: time is supported by, and arguably parasitic on spatial representation: the position of Lakoff and Johnson (1980, 1999). Lakoff and Johnson argue that mappings recruit from the domain of space to provide structure for the domain of time, but not vice versa. Following seminal work by Clark (1973), Lakoff and Johnson have posited a "passage" conceptual metaphor, in which time recruits structure from (motion through) space. There are two versions of this conceptual metaphor, both based on linguistic evidence.

The first of these is the Moving Time Metaphor. In this conceptualisation there is a stationary Observer whose location corresponds to the present. The Observer faces the future, with the space behind corresponding to the past (Figure 24.1).

In Figure 24.1, events are represented by small circles. Motion is represented by the arrows. Events move from the future towards the Observer, and then behind into the past. The reason for thinking that speakers of English store this in their minds again comes from language:

Fig. 24.1: The Moving Time Metaphor

Tab. 24.1: Mappings for the Moving Time Metaphor

Source domain: MOTION OF OBJECTS	Mappings	Target domain: TIME
OBJECTS	→	TIMES
THE MOTION OF OBJECTS PAST THE OBSERVER	→	THE "PASSAGE" OF TIME
PROXIMITY OF OBJECT TO THE OBSERVER	→	TEMPORAL "PROXIMITY" OF THE EVENT
THE LOCATION OF THE OBSERVER	→	THE PRESENT
THE SPACE IN FRONT OF THE OBSERVER	→	THE FUTURE
THE SPACE BEHIND THE OBSERVER	→	THE PAST

(7) a. Christmas is *approaching*.
 b. The time for action *has arrived*.
 c. The end-of-summer sales *have passed*.

As these examples show, we employ the language of motion to refer to the passage of time. The regions of space in front of, co-located with, and behind the Observer correspond to future, present and past. In addition, we understand motion to relate to time's *passage*, as is clear by the use of *approaching*, in the first sentence. The series of mappings that allow us to understand these different aspects of the motion of objects in terms of TIME are captured in Table 24.2.

The second passage conceptual metaphor, which we can think of as being a reversal of the Moving Time Metaphor, is referred to as the Moving Ego, or Moving Observer metaphor. Here, time is conceived as a static "timescape" with events conceptualised as specific and static locations towards which the Observer moves and then passes (Figure 24.2).

As previously, events are represented by small circles in Figure 24.2, which are specific locations in the temporal landscape. Motion is represented by the arrows. In this case, it is the Observer, rather than the events, which is in motion. Here, we understand the passage of time *in terms of* the Observer's motion: the Observer moves across the temporal landscape towards and then past specific events, expressed as fixed locations in space. Lakoff and Johnson again point to evidence from language for this conceptualisation:

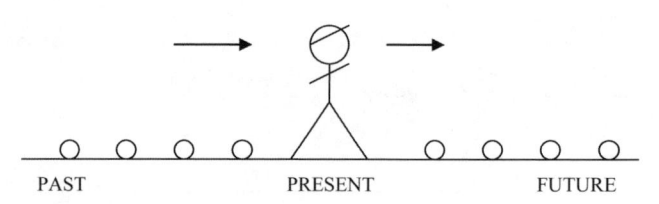

Fig. 24.2: The Moving Observer Metaphor

Tab. 24.2: Mappings for The Moving Observer metaphor

Source domain: MOTION OF OBSERVER	Mappings	Target domain: TIME
LOCATIONS ON OBSERVER'S PATH	→	TIMES
THE MOTION OF THE OBSERVER	→	THE "PASSAGE" OF TIME
THE LOCATION OF THE OBSERVER	→	THE PRESENT
THE SPACE IN FRONT OF THE OBSERVER	→	THE FUTURE
THE SPACE BEHIND THE OBSERVER	→	THE PAST
DISTANCE OF OBSERVER FROM LOCATION	→	TEMPORAL "DISTANCE" OF EVENT
RAPIDITY OF MOTION OF OBSERVER	→	IMMINENCE OF EVENT'S OCCURRENCE

(8) a. They're *approaching* crisis-point.
    b. The relationship *extended over* many years.
    c. He left *at* 10 o'clock.

Examples like these have been taken to reveal that, metaphorically, the Observer's motion is ascribed to time's passage. Time is being likened to a static landscape as we can see from expressions such as *extended over*. And the use of *at*, as in *He left at 10 o'clock* demonstrates that specific locations in the static landscape correspond to temporal events. See Table 24.2 for mappings that have been proposed for this metaphor.

In behavioural experiments, Boroditsky (2000; Boroditsky and Ramscar 2002) provided the first psycholinguistic support for Lakoff and Johnson's claim for asymmetric organisation between time and space. Boroditsky developed both spatial and temporal primes which she applied to temporal and spatial reasoning tasks. She reasoned that if spatial and temporal representations are structured symmetrically, which is to say, if temporal representation is just as useful for reasoning about space, as spatial representation is for time, then spatial cues should prime for temporal reasoning, while temporal cues should prime for spatial reasoning tasks. Boroditsky found evidence consistent with an asymmetric perspective: spatial cues appear to be useful for reasoning about time, but temporal primes appear not to be used when reasoning about space. More recently, Casasanto and Boroditsky (2008) have provided additional support for the asymmetric organisation of time in terms of space, making use of non-linguistic behavioural tasks.

One specific manifestation of the asymmetric organisation of space and time relates to *frames of reference* (FoRs). A FoR, in the domain of time, comprises three coordinates to locate or fix a temporal entity with respect to another (Zinken 2010). Early research focused on examining FoRs from the domain of space, investigating how they are recruited to structure temporal reference: the assumption being that FoRs from the domain of space are naturally mapped onto time. Two such taxonomies have been proposed (Bendner et al. 2010; Tenbrink 2011; see also Moore 2011). However, there is, as yet, little consensus on the nature of these taxonomies, or indeed whether spatial FoRs really do subserve temporal reference (see Bender et al. 2012 for critical evaluation). For instance, Evans (2013a, 2013b) has proposed that FoRs in the domain of time are qualitatively distinct from those in the domain of space. He has developed a time-based taxonomy of temporal FoRs deriving from the notion of *transience* (discussed below). Temporal FoRs is now one of the fastest developing areas of research in the study of temporal cognition.

At the neurological level, two proposals have been put forward to account for the relationship between time and space. Bonato et al. (2012) have proposed what they term the *Mental Time Line* (MTL) hypothesis. This hypothesis is consistent with the asymmetric organisation posited by Lakoff and Johnson's Conceptual Metaphor Theory. They posit that, at the neurological level, temporal experience is structured *in terms* of spatial characteristics.

A second possibility, one that would account for the data provided by Talmy, posits a single magnitude system. Such a system would provide a common metric allowing the different parameters associated with the domains of time and space to be quantified, and integrated. Such an approach has been proposed by Walsh (2003; Bueti and Walsh 2009) in *A Theory of Magnitude* (ATOM). Walsh proposes that there is a single generalised, neurologically-instantiated magnitude system, present at birth. This allows space and time to be quantified, in principle, in symmetrical ways.

Whichever of the two approaches, ATOM, or MTL, turns out to be correct – and there are arguments in favour of both – the only candidate brain region that might facilitate the interaction between spatial and temporal experience appears to be the inferior parietal cortex – this region of the brain is host to a series of closely-related sub-areas specialised for processing time, space and number (Bonato et al. 2012; Bueti and Walsh 2009; Walsh 2003).

4. What is the distinction between time and space?

If time does recruit structure from the domain of space, are the two domains distinct? In important work, Galton (2011) has proposed a number of parameters that allow representations for time and space to be compared and contrasted. This research demonstrates that time and space are qualitatively distinct conceptual domains. The relevant parameters enabling comparison of the two domains are: *magnitude*,[1] *dimensionality*,[2] and *directedness* (Galton 2011). I consider and nuance each of these parameters in turn.

The parameter of magnitude relates to the quantifiability of a given *substrate* – the stuff that makes up the domain. The substrate the makes up space is *matter*, of which two broad types can be distinguished: discrete entities (e.g., objects) and mass entities (e.g., fluids). This distinction, in types of matter, is reflected in the grammatical organisation of many languages, whereby a distinction between count versus mass nouns is encoded.

In addition, the substrate that makes up a domain exhibits a particular property allowing the substrate to be quantified: the way in which the substrate can be "cut up" into "amounts". The amounts, in the domain of space, relate to the property *extension*. Extension manifests itself in three distinct types – which is a function of the three-dimensional-

---

[1] Galton (2011) uses the term "extension".
[2] Galton (2011) uses the term "linearity".

Tab. 24.3: Comparing the parameter magnitude for space and time

Domain	Space	Time
Substrate	Matter	Action
Property	Extension	Duration
Distinction	Discrete vs. mass	Bounded vs. Unbounded

ity of space, discussed further below. Space's extension involves length (one dimension), area (two dimensions), and volume (three dimensions).

The substrate that makes up time is that of *action* (Talmy 2000). As with space, action can also be broadly subdivided, as reflected in language. This relates to whether action is *bounded* versus *unbounded*, analogous to the distinction between discrete versus mass for the substrate matter. This is illustrated by the grammatical distinction between perfective versus imperfective aspect in many languages.

In the domain of time, the property exhibited by action, and hence, the means of "cutting up" action into amounts is *duration*, rather than extension. While duration can, self-evidently, be quantified by using *measurement systems* involving material artefacts such as clocks, duration (of relatively shorts periods) can be estimated without the need for measurement systems such as these. The distinctions between space and time in terms of the parameter of magnitude are summarised in Table 24.3.

Dimensionality, in physical terms, relates to the *constituent structure* of matter. The constituent structure of matter involves three distinct planes with respect to which points can be located. These are the transversal (left/right), sagittal (front/back) and vertical (up/down) planes. Hence, our everyday representation of space can be said to be three-dimensional.

In contrast, in the domain of time the constituent structure of action involves *succession*: the sequential relationship that holds between distinct units and sub-units of action (cf. Moore 2006; Núñez et al. 2006). In other words, our representation for time involves a relationship between units of action in a sequence. This involves just one dimension.

Physical theories that incorporate time, such as in the Theory of General Relativity (Einstein 1916), treat time as the fourth dimension of space, forming a space-time continuum, or Minkowski space, after the celebrated 19th century mathematician who first proposed incorporating time into space. On this view, points can be "located" in time, where units of action are strung out, all at once, across time. Yet this view is at odds with the human phenomenological experience of time (see Evans 2004: Chapter 19). Insofar as time, from a phenomenological perspective, can be said to exhibit dimensionality, this relates to the sequential relationship between events, providing one-dimensional constituent structure.

The final parameter, directedness, relates to whether the substrate in a given domain is *symmetric* (i.e., isotropic) or *asymmetric* (i.e., anisotropic). Space is isotropic: it has no inherent asymmetry. Indeed, it is possible to proceed in any direction: forward or back, or from side to side. In contrast, time is anisotropic: it manifests asymmetric organisation. From a phenomenological perspective, time is experienced as anisotropic. This concerns the anticipation of a future event, the actual experience of the event, and finally, the recollection of the event as past.

In his work, Galton (2011) discusses an additional feature which he argues is exhibited by time, but not by space. This he refers to as *transience*: the fleeting quality associated with temporal experience. For Galton, transience is the hallmark of time, and hence part of its inalienable character.

5. Is time homogenous or multifaceted?

Linguistic evidence demonstrates that the conceptual domain of time is multifaceted (Evans 2004, 2013b; Grady 1997; Moore 2006). For instance, the English word *time* covers a range of quite different lexical concepts (Evans 2004). Consider the following examples:

(9) The time for action has arrived

(10) a. Time flies when you're having fun
 b. Time drags when you have nothing to do

(11) a. The young woman's time [= labour/childbirth] approached
 b. His time [= death] had come
 c. Arsenal saved face with an Ian Wright leveller five minutes from time [BNC]

(12) [T]ime, of itself, and from its own nature, flows equably without relation to anything external [Sir Isaac Newton]

In these examples, all involving the vehicle *time*, a different reading is obtained. In (9), a discrete temporal point or moment is designated, without reference to its duration. The examples in (10) provide a reading relating to what might be described as "magnitude of duration". (10a) relates to the phenomenologically real experience whereby time proceeds "more quickly" than usual – this constitutes the phenomenon of temporal compression (Flaherty 1999) discussed briefly above. The example in (10b) relates to the experience of time proceeding 'more slowly" than usual – the phenomenon of protracted duration, also discussed briefly above. In (11), the readings relating to *time* concern an event. In (11a) the event relates to the onset of childbirth, in (14b) the event designated relates to death, while in (11c) it concerns the referee blowing the whistle signalling the end of a game of soccer. In the sentences in (12) *time* prompts for an entity which is infinite, and hence unbounded in nature.

While English has one word for a range of (arguably) quite distinct experience types, other languages don't inevitably have a single word that covers the same semantic territory. For instance, recent research on the Amazonian language Amondawa reveals that there is no equivalent of the English word *time* in that language (Sinha et al. 2011). To give another example of a typologically and areally distinct language, it is also the case that Inuit languages don't have a single lexeme for *time*. Moreover, even genetically related languages utilise distinct lexical items to describe the semantic territory covered by the single lexical form, *time*, in English.

In sum, the English examples demonstrate that the form *time* relates to quite different types of representations – having a single word-form provides the illusion of semantic unity (Evans 2009), and gives rise to the myth that time relates to a homogenous set of experiences. The fact that other languages don't have a single word for the same set of experiences further underscores the cultural variability of cutting up the domain of time.

6. Are representations for time universal?

Some cognitive linguists have argued, or at least implied, that the motion-through-space conceptual metaphors for time are universal. For instance, Fauconnier and Turner put things as follows: "Time as [motion through] space is a deep metaphor for *all human beings*. It is common across cultures, psychologically real, productive and profoundly entrenched in thought and language" (2008: 54) [my emphasis]. But there are languages that appear not to have this conceptual metaphor. One example is the indigenous South American language Aymara; Aymara doesn't make use of motion on the sagittal plane to conceptualise time's passage (Núñez and Sweetser 2006).[3]

More strikingly, Sinha et al. (2011), based on their fieldwork of Amondawa, argue that motion-through-space metaphors for time are not transcultural universals. Amondawa is spoken by a small tribe of a little over 100 individuals located in remote western Amazonia. Official contact was not made until 1986. Based on their fieldwork, Sinha and colleagues make two claims. First, and in contrast to Indo-European languages, Amondawa does not make use of ascriptions from spatial language, and language relating to motion, to talk about time. Second, Amondawa does not make reference to time as an ontological category independent of events themselves: what Sinha et al. refer to as *time-as-such*. They maintain that there is no evidence from the Amondawa language or culture that the Amondawa have time available, per se, as an object of conscious (intersubjective) reflection.

If correct, what do these claims say about time? First off, they don't imply that all aspects of time are not universal. As we have seen, time is a complex and multifaceted domain. Moreover, it is, at least in part, grounded in specialised, albeit distributed, neurobiological processes and structures that are purely temporal (Kranjec and Chatterjee 2010). Our experience of time is variegated, directly perceived via interoception, and subjectively real. The basal ganglia and cerebellum are implicated in fundamental timekeeping operations upon which the coordination of motor control is dependent (Harrington et al. 1998). Other neuroscientists have argued that temporal processing is widely distributed across brain structures, being intrinsic to neural function (e.g., Mauk and Buonomana 2004), and is fundamental to cognitive function (Varela 1999). Distinct brain structures are implicated in the experience of duration, succession, our experience of the present, our recollection of the past and pre-experience of the future (see Evans 2013b for a review). Indeed, the emerging view from neuroscientific research is that the exquisitely sophisticated timing structures in the brain are key to a raft of fundamental cognitive functions such as motor control, and perception and may provide the cognitive "glue" that facilitates learning and memory, behaviour planning, awareness, imagination and creativity (Pouthas and Perbal 2004; Pöppel 2009; Rubia et al. 2009).

---

[3] However, Aymara does make use of motion on the transverse plane to conceptualise the succession of events.

Based on proposals in Evans (2013b), a taxonomy suggests itself for directly grounded temporal representations.[4] The most basic temporal concept is termed a *temporal element*. These are representations grounded in phenomenologically simple experience types that contribute to – or in some cases arise from – our experience of transience. Examples include felt experience types such as now, past, future, earlier and later, and are associated with the corresponding lexical forms (e.g., *now, past, future, earlier, later,* etc.).

The next type of temporal concept is grounded in the experience of transience, discussed earlier. Evans (2013b) suggests that there are three types of transience: *duration, succession,* and *anisotropicity*. Duration concerns the felt experience of the passage constituting an elapse – something greater than the *perceptual moment* – the smallest neurologically-instantiated unit of perceptual processing which is consciously accessible, and which is likely to constitute the basis for the human experience of now (Pöppel 1994, 2009). The perceptual moment has an outer limit of around 3 seconds (see Evans 2004, 2013b). Succession concerns the felt experience of the passage involving earlier and later experience types, which are sequenced with respect to each other. And anisotropicity concerns the felt experience that the passage exhibits inherent asymmetry – a felt distinction between future, present and past. Concepts associated with these transience types are encoded in language by lexical forms such as *duration, succession, passage,* and indeed *transience*. Table 24.4 summarises these transience types.

Transience logically supports more complex experience types: *temporal qualities*. Temporal qualities involve a comparison across events, with respect to transience. Examples include frequency, change and synchronicity. Change, for instance, involves a comparison, or awareness of a difference between two states at different temporal intervals, and hence, is processed with respect to transience. Frequency involves the identification of a number of iterations of experiences, or experience types at different temporal intervals. And synchronicity involves an awareness of two experiences or experience types occurring at the same temporal moment (see Table 24.5). Temporal qualities are more complex than either temporal elements or transience types as temporal qualities are presupposed by them.

While temporal elements, transience types and temporal qualities are all likely to be universal, there are representations for time that are not directly grounded in temporal experience. These can be thought of as mental achievements, in part supported (or constructed) by conceptual metaphors. A notable example concerns time conceptualised as

Tab. 24.4: Transience types

TRANSIENCE TYPE	DESCRIPTION
Duration	the felt experience of the passage constituting an elapse
Succession	the felt experience of the passage involving earlier and later experience types
Anisotropicity	the felt experience that the passage exhibits inherent asymmetry – a felt distinction between future, present and past

---

[4] Cf. Pöppel (1978) who argues for what he terms "elementary time experiences".

Tab. 24.5: Temporal qualities

TEMPORAL QUALITY	DESCRIPTION
Change	a comparison, or awareness of a difference between two states at different temporal intervals
Frequency	the identification of a number of iterations of experiences, or experience types at different temporal intervals
Synchronicity	an awareness of two experiences or experience types occurring at the same temporal moment

a valuable resource which can be bought and sold, just like physical merchandise (Lakoff and Johnson 1999). Many languages – especially those associated with pre-industrialised cultures – do not conceptualise time in terms of a commodity or a resource (Evans 2004). This suggests that some temporal representations are cultural constructs. In short, Sinha and colleagues appear to be correct that some temporal representations are culture-specific.

The second claim made by Sinha and colleagues, recall, is that Amondawa lacks the concept of time-as-such (aka the Matrix conception). This conceptualisation is a prerequisite for time-measurement systems, which the Amondawa also lack. The Matrix conception entails a reification of duration as an entity distinct from and external to our subjective, and phenomenologically real, experience of duration. This particular concept also appears to be a mental achievement; after all, conceiving of time as *the* event in which all else unfolds cannot be directly grounded in embodied experience. This would require an eternal lifespan! However, when the Amondawa acquire Portuguese, they seemingly have little difficulty in acquiring expertise in the language and the time-measurement artefacts of Brazilian Portuguese culture. This suggests that this mental achievement is accessible to the cognitively modern human mind, even if it is not native to the Amondawa culture.

7. Why must time be represented in terms of sensory-motor experience at all?

While it appears that time is grounded in interoceptive experience types that are purely temporal, many temporal concepts do, nevertheless, appear to be represented, at least in part, in terms of sensory-motor representations, especially relating to space and motion through space. A perennial question that has exercised research in cognitive linguistics concerns why this should be the case.

The answer often advanced is that of *experiential correlation* (Lakoff and Johnson 1980, 1999). Time inevitably and ubiquitously correlates with some salient aspects of spatial experience. The best worked out version is the notion of *grounding scenarios* which capture the details of the correlation (Moore 2006).

But a correlation account doesn't, in fact, provide a complete answer. After all, correlation can't account for the asymmetrical relationship between spatial and temporal representations as proposed by Lakoff and Johnson. While duration correlates with spatial length, the correlation doesn't, in and of itself, explain why time recruits structure from space, but space doesn't recruit structure from the domain of time. Experimental findings illustrate that duration and physical length are asymmetrically organised in just this way (Casasanto and Boroditsky 2008).

A more sophisticated correlation solution is provided by Grady (1997). Grady argues that for correlations to give rise to cross-domain mappings of a fundamental sort – *primary metaphors* in his parlance – the correlation must be accompanied by a qualitative distinction in the type of experiences being correlated. For Grady, temporal experiences, and the concepts that accrue, are responses to sensory-motor experiences: when we experience motion along a path we subjectively experience temporal passage, which is a response to our experience of motion. Hence, temporal concepts have what Grady terms *response content*, while sensory-motor concepts have *image content*. On this account, what makes something a source versus a target concept is contingent on whether it is a response or image concept, with target concepts involving response content (rather than whether it is concrete or abstract).

This analysis appears to be on the right track. It is plausible that temporal mechanisms and structures evolved in order to coordinate and thereby facilitate the perceptual process (Evans 2013b). Events are widely acknowledged to be the units of perception (Cutting 1981; Gibson 1979; Heider 1959; Johansson et al. 1980; Pittenger and Shaw 1975; Zacks et al. 2001). Indeed, Cutting (1981: 71) describes events as "our very units of existence". Events appear to be centred on object/action units that are goal directed (Zacks et al. 2001): they involve correlated aspects of both space and time. In seminal work modelling the provenance of conscious awareness, Crick and Koch (1990) argued that the so-called *binding problem* – how percepts are formed in the absence of a central association area for the integration of perceptual information in the brain – is achieved via the coordinated oscillation of neurons. Hence, perceptual binding may result from temporal activities which *bind* perceptual information; binding arises via temporally coordinated activity, rather than integrating information at a specific "association" site in the brain. In short, temporal processes appear to have a critical role in facilitating our perception of sensory-motor experience.

Our experience of the world comes to us via the perception of events, and events are temporally structured. Hence, it may be that it is this temporal structuring that facilitates the perception of our world of sensory experience. Hence, spatial awareness may be facilitated by the temporal mechanisms which control and facilitate perception. In short, not only is there an inevitable correlation between invariant aspects of sensory-motor experience, and time, but temporal experience appears to arise, in part (perhaps large part), so that the spatio-sensory world around us can be perceived in the first place.

But if correct, this implies that our experience of time is epiphenomenal: it arose in order to facilitate the perceptual process. Perception is about sensory-motor experience, but enabled by temporal processes. And as time is not the object of perception, but the manner whereby it is facilitated, our representational systems re-utilise the perceptually-correlated sensory-motor reflexes for purposes of re-presentation of time in the conceptual system. While our experience of time and space are distinct and distinguishable at the neurological level, at the representational level they appear to be largely asymmetrically organised.

8. Empirical research on time in cognitive science

Cross-cultural and experimental research on the nature and organisation of time is now a lively area of investigation in cognitive science, building in part on pioneering research in cognitive linguistics. Some of the key questions being addressed relate to the complex interplay between language, culture and mental representations for time, as well as the representation of time in modalities other than language, especially gesture. Other research addresses cultural and linguistic influences on temporal representation such as the nature of orthographic systems. This section provides a brief summary of some representative highlights of this body of research.

It has been discovered that the Yupno language in Papua New Guinea construes deictic time spatially in terms of allocentric topography: the past is construed as downhill, present as co-located with the speaker and future is construed as uphill (Núñez et al. 2012). Moreover, the Pormpuraawns – a grouping of aboriginal languages – arrange sequential time from east to west, whereby time flows from left to right when a person is facing south, from right to left when a person is facing north, towards the body when a person is facing east, and away from the body when a person is facing west (Boroditsky and Gaby 2010).

Other research has investigated the consequences of orthographic systems on temporal representation. It has been found that the left-to-right orientation of time in English stems from culturally specific spatial representations, i.e., the direction of orthography. As a result, the direction in which time flows along a person's lateral mental timeline has been shown to differ systematically across cultures (e.g., Boroditsky et al. 2010 for Mandarin; Casasanto and Bottini 2010 for Dutch; Bergen and Lau 2012 for Taiwanese; Fuhrman and Boroditsky 2010 for Hebrew; Tversky et al. 1991 for Arabic).

An increasingly important line of research concerns the concurrent use of gesture during spoken language use. English speakers have been found to have an implicit mental timeline that runs along the lateral axis, with earlier times on the left and later times on the right of body-centred space. When producing co-speech gestures spontaneously, English speakers tend to use the lateral axis, gesturing leftwards for earlier times and rightwards for later times. This left-right mapping of time is consistent with the flow of time on calendars and graphs in English-speaking cultures, but is completely absent from spoken metaphors (Casasanto and Jasmin 2012; see also Cooperrider and Núñez 2009).

In the final analysis, research on the nature of time, in both language and thought, is now a lively and rapidly accelerating arena of investigation. Experimental and cross-linguistic/cultural investigations in cognitive science have been informed by the major research questions, reviewed in this chapter, as developed within cognitive linguistics.

9. References

Baddeley, Alan
   1966   Time estimation at reduced body temperature. *American Journal of Psychology* 79(3): 475–479.

Bender, Andrea, Sieghard Beller and Giovanni Bennardo
   2010   Temporal frames of reference: Conceptual analysis and empirical evidence from German, English, Mandarin Chinese, and Tongan. *Journal of Cognition and Culture* 10: 283–307.

Bender, Andrea, Annelie Rothe-Wulf, Lisa Hüther and Sieghard Beller
   2012   Moving forward in space and time: How strong is the conceptual link between spatial and temporal frames of reference (FoRs)? *Frontiers in Psychology* 3: 486.

Bergen, Benjamin and Ting Ting Chan Lau
   2012   Writing direction affects how people map space onto time. *Frontiers in Cultural Psychology* 3: 109.

Bonato, Mario, Marco Zorzi and Carlo Umiltà
   2012   When time is space: Evidence for a mental time line. *Neuroscience and Biobehavioral Reviews* 36(10): 2257–2273.

Boroditsky, Lera
   2000   Metaphoric structuring: Understanding time through spatial metaphors. *Cognition* 75(1): 1–28.

Boroditsky, Lera, Orly Fuhrman and Kelly McCormick
   2010   Do English and Mandarin speakers think differently about time? *Cognition* 118(1): 123–129.

Boroditsky, Lera and Alice Gaby
   2010   Remembrances of times east: Absolute spatial representations of time in an Australian Aboriginal community. *Psychological Science* 21: 1635–1639.

Boroditsky, Lera and Michael Ramscar
   2002   The roles of body and mind in abstract thought. *Psychological Science* 13(2): 185–188.

Bueti, Domenica and Vincent Walsh
   2009   The parietal cortex and the representation of time, space, number and other magnitudes. *Philosophical Transactions of the Royal Society B* 364: 1831–1840.

Casasanto, Daniel and Lera Boroditsky
   2008   Time in the mind: Using space to think about time. *Cognition* 106: 579–593.

Casasanto, Daniel and Roberto Bottini
   2010   Can mirror-reading reverse the flow of time? In: C. Hölscher, T. F. Shipley, M. Olivetti Belardinelli, J. A. Bateman and N. S. Newcombe (eds.), *Spatial Cognition VII*, 335–345. Berlin Heidelberg: Springer.

Casasanto, Daniel and Kyle Jasmin
   2012   The hands of time: Temporal gestures in English speakers. *Cognitive Linguistics* 23(4): 643–674.

Clark, Herbert H.
   1973   Space, time, semantics, and the child. In: T. Moore (ed.) *Cognitive Development and the Acquisition of Language*, 27–63. New York: Academic Press.

Cooperrider, Kensy and Rafael Núñez
   2009   Across time, across the body: Transversal temporal gestures. *Gesture* 9(2): 181–206.

Crick, Francis and Christof Koch
   1990   Towards a neurobiological theory of consciousness. *Seminars in the Neurosciences* 2: 263–275.

Cutting, James E.
   1981   Six tenets for event perception. *Cognition* 10: 71–78.

Einstein, Albert
   1916   Die grundlage der allgemeinen relativitätstheorie. *Annalen der Physik* 7: 769–822

Evans, Vyvyan
   2004   *The Structure of Time: Language, Meaning and Temporal Cognition*. Amsterdam: John Benjamins.

Evans, Vyvyan
   2009   *How Words Mean: Lexical Concepts, Cognitive Models and Meaning Construction*. Oxford: Oxford University Press.

Evans, Vyvyan
   2013a   Temporal frames of reference. *Cognitive Linguistics* 24(3): 393–435.

Evans, Vyvyan
   2013b *Language and Time: A Cognitive Linguistics Approach*. Cambridge: Cambridge University Press.
Fauconnier, Gilles and Mark Turner
   2008 Rethinking metaphor. In: R. Gibbs (ed.), *Cambridge Handbook of Metaphor and Thought*, 53–66. Cambridge: Cambridge University Press.
Flaherty, Michael G.
   1999 *A Watched Pot: How We Experience Time*. New York: New York University Press.
Fraisse, Paul
   1963 *The Psychology of Time*. New York: Harper and Row.
Fraisse, Paul
   1984 Perception and estimation of time. *Annual Review of Psychology* 35: 1–36.
Fuhrman, Orly and Lera Boroditsky
   2010 Cross-cultural differences in mental representations of time: Evidence from an implicit nonlinguistic task. *Cognitive Science* 34: 1430–1451.
Galton, Antony
   2011 Time flies but space doesn't: Limits to the spatialization of time. *Journal of Pragmatics* 43: 695–703.
Gibbs, Raymond W. Jr.
   this volume 8. Metaphor. Berlin/Boston: De Gruyter Mouton.
Gibson, James J.
   1979 *The Ecological Approach to Visual Perception*. Boston: Houghton Mifflin.
Grady, Joseph E.
   1997 *Foundations of meaning: Primary metaphors and primary scenes*. Ph.D. Dissertation, University of California at Berkeley.
Harrington, Deborah, Kathleen Haaland and Robert T. Knight
   1998 Cortical networks underlying mechanisms of time perception. *Journal of Neuroscience* 18(3): 1085–1095.
Heider, Fritz
   1959 On perception, event structure and psychological environment. *Psychological Issues* 1(3): 1–123.
Hoagland, Hudson
   1933 The physiologic control of judgments of duration: Evidence for a chemical clock. *Journal of General Psychology* 9: 267–287.
Johansson, Gunnar, Claes von Hofsten and Gunnar Jansson
   1980 Event perception. *Annual Review of Psychology* 21: 27–66.
Kranjec, Alexander and Anjan Chatterjee
   2010 Are temporal concepts embodied? A challenge for cognitive neuroscience. *Frontiers in Psychology* 1(240): 1–9.
Lakoff, George and Mark Johnson
   1980 *Metaphors We Live By*. Chicago: University of Chicago Press.
Lakoff, George and Mark Johnson
   1999 *Philosophy in the Flesh*. New York: Basic Books.
Langacker, Ronald W.
   1987 *Foundations of Cognitive Grammar:* Vol. I. Stanford: Stanford University Press.
Mauk, Michael D. and Dean V. Buonomano
   2004 The neural basis of temporal processing. *The Annual Review of Neuroscience* 27: 307–40.
Moore, Kevin E.
   2006 Space-to-time mappings and temporal concepts. *Cognitive Linguistics* 17(2): 199–244.

Moore, Kevin E.
2011   Ego-perspective and field-based frames of reference: Temporal meanings of FRONT in Japanese, Wolof, and Aymara. *Journal of Pragmatics* 43: 759–776.

Núñez, Rafael, Kensy Cooperrider, D. Doan, and Jürg Wassmann
2012   Contours of time: Topographic construals of past, present, and future in the Yupno valley of Papua New Guinea. *Cognition* 124: 25–35.

Núñez, Rafael, Benjamin E. Motz and Ursina Teuscher
2006   Time after time: The psychological reality of the Ego-and Time-Reference-Point distinction in metaphorical construals of time. *Metaphor and Symbol* 21: 133–146.

Núñez, Rafael and Eve Sweetser
2006   With the future behind them: Convergent evidence from Aymara language and gesture in the crosslinguistic comparison of spatial construals of time. *Cognitive Science* 30: 401–450.

Ornstein, Robert E.
[1969] 1997   *On the Experience of Time*. Boulder: Westview Press.

Pittenger, John B., Robert E. Shaw
1975   Aging faces as viscal-elastic events: Implications for a theory of nonrigid shape perception. *Journal of Experimental Psychology: Human Perception Performance* 1: 374–382.

Pöppel, Ernst
1978   Time perception. In: R. Held, H. W. Leibowitz, and H.-L. Teuber (eds.), *Handbook of Sensory Physiology*, 713–729. Heidelberg: Springer.

Pöppel, Ernst
1994   Temporal mechanisms in perception. In: O. Sporns and G. Tononi (eds.), *Selectionism and the Brain: International Review of Neurobiology* 37:185–201.

Pöppel, Ernst
2009   Pre-semantically defined temporal windows for cognitive processing. *Philosophical Transactions of the Royal Society B* 364: 1887–1896.

Pouthas, Viviane and Séverine Perbal
2004   Time perception does not only depend on accurate clock mechanisms but also on unimpaired attention and memory processes. *Acta Neurobiologiae Experimentalis* 64: 367–385.

Rubia, Katya, Rozmin Halari, Anastasia Christakou and Eric Taylor
2009   Impulsiveness as a timing disturbance: Neurocognitive abnormalities in attention-deficit hyperactivity disorder during temporal processes and normalization with methylphenidate. *Philosophical Transactions of the Royal Society B: Biological Sciences* 364: 1919–1931.

Sinha, Chris, Vera da Silva Sinha, Jörg Zinken and Wany Sampaio
2011   When time is not space: The social and linguistic construction of time intervals in an Amazonian culture. *Language and Cognition,* 3(1): 137–169.

Talmy, Leonard
2000   *Toward a Cognitive Semantics* (2 volumes). Cambridge: MIT Press.

Tenbrink, Thora
2011   Reference frames of space and time in language. *Journal of Pragmatics* 43: 704–722.

Tversky, Barbara, Sol Kugelmass and Atalia Winter
1991   Cross-cultural and developmental trends in graphic productions. *Cognitive Psychology* 23: 515–557.

Varela, Francisco J.
1999   Present-time consciousness. *Journal of Consciousness Studies* 6(2/3): 111–140.

Walsh, Vincent
2003   A theory of magnitude: Common cortical metrics of time, space and quantity. *Trends in Cognitive Sciences* 7(11): 483–488.

Wearden, John H. and Ian S. Penton-Voak
  1995   Feeling the heat: Body temperature and the rate of subjective time, revisited. *Quarterly Journal of Experimental Psychology* 48B: 129–141.
Zacks, Jeffrey M., Barbara Tversky and Gowri Iyer
  2001   Perceiving, remembering, and communicating structure in events. *Journal of Experimental Psychology: General* 130: 29–58.
Zakay, Dan and Richard A. Block
  1997   Temporal cognition. *Current Directions in Psychological Science* 6: 12–16.
Zinken, Jörg
  2010   Temporal frames of reference. In: V. Evans and P. Chilton (eds.), *Language, Cognition and Space: The State of the Art and New Directions*, 479–498. London: Equinox Publishing.

Vyvyan Evans, Bangor (United Kingdom)

25. Motion[1]

1. Motion in linguistics
2. Lexicalization patterns and semantic typology
3. Motion in acquisition, translation and beyond
4. Motion in language and memory: Experimental psycholinguistic insights
5. Conclusions
6. References

1. Motion in linguistics

There are converging reasons why linguists in particular feel obliged to talk about motion. One reason is that motion expressions are considered basic and omnipresent; they are widely used not only to express spatial and non-spatial meanings (Heine and Kuteva 2002) but may be also employed as structural templates for any other linguistic structure (cf. "localist approaches", e.g., Jackendoff 1983). Another reason is that spatial organisation and expression are paramount to human cognition and generally considered to be fundamental for our thinking (Miller and Johnson-Laird 1976) and as such space and motion have been considered a crucial testing ground for linguistic behaviour (especially from the relativistic viewpoint, e.g., Levinson 2003).

---

[1] The preparation of this paper was financially supported by grants FFI2010-14903 and FFI2013-45553-C3-1-P from the Spanish Ministry of Economy and Competitiveness (MovEs project) and we are grateful for their generous support.

As a result, it is perhaps not too much of an exaggeration to say that every framework in linguistics has devoted some time and effort to describing how speakers think and talk about motion.[2]

In Cognitive Linguistics, motion is also a topic of special interest. Many cognitive linguists have devoted themselves to the study of motion, but the work of one scholar, Leonard Talmy, set the agenda for many subsequent studies in this area. We therefore start our discussion with a focus on his theory of lexicalization patterns (section 2) since this paradigm yielded the most prolific further research and novel theoretical and methodological developments in the field.

Motion is defined as change of location from a spatial position A to a different position B, whereby the moving figure was located at position A at time T1 and then located at position B at another time T2 (see Talmy 1985). Talmy distinguishes *motion* from *movement*, the latter being the state of motion at a location (e.g., wriggling at a single spot) rather than change of location, which is the defining feature of motion. The concept of *change*, which lies in the essence of motion events, is also relevant for distinctions among other events, such as change of state or change of posture. Part of the universality of human experience lies in the capability to perceive change, in the case of motion events, change of spatio-temporal location, and all languages of the world equip their speakers with means to talk about the change in spatial and temporal configurations that are the result of motion (see Filipović 2007a).

Much of the early research in this area was focused on prepositional meanings (static and dynamic; e.g., see Brugman 1988; Herskovits 1986; Vandeloise 1986) and subsequently expanded to the study of other spatial morphemes and to more complex constructions. The initial *localistic* approaches to spatial semantics, centered around one specific element of the sentence, have given way to more holistic approaches (*distributed spatial semantics*, Sinha and Kuteva 1995), with an addition of discourse analysis (see Hart this volume) to the sentence analysis.

2. Lexicalization patterns and semantic typology

Much of Talmy's (1985, 1991, 2000) work is devoted to the study of the variation that languages show in mapping morphosyntactic and lexical resources onto semantic domains. Talmy argues that any event can be analyzed into a set of *semantic elements* which are valid for any language and that each language has its own *surface elements* to codify those semantic components. Surface elements refer to linguistic forms such as verbs, adpositions, subordinate clauses and "satellites" – a coinage that refers to "the grammatical category of any constituent other than a noun-phrase or prepositional-phrase complement that is in a sister relation to the verb root" and that can be "either a bound affix or a free word" (2000: 102). Talmy examines different semantic domains in the context of semantic vs. surface elements, but motion is by far the most widely known and studied of all.

---

[2] A comprehensive database of references on motion linguistics from a variety of theoretical and empirical perspectives can be found at http://www.lit.kobe-u.ac.jp/~yomatsum/motionbiblio1.pdf.

Surface and semantic[3] components are useful to "dissect" motion events – in fact, these labels are now widespread and standard in motion event analysis – but they become much more interesting when one looks at these elements across languages. Talmy was not interested in providing details about every single possible codifying structure available in a given language, but just on those that are "characteristic" (2000: 27); that is, pervasive, frequent, colloquial and, we can also add, commonly employed by native speakers, young or adult.[4] In the case of motion events, Talmy (1985) considers the Path of motion to be the fundamental component of a motion event because without Path there is no motion (though there may be movement). The explicit presence of other components, such as Manner, though always present in reality, it is not obligatory for the verbalisation of a motion event.[5]

The result of his theoretical insights and exemplification from numerous genetically varied and geographically distant languages is a two-way language typology:[6]

- *Satellite-framed languages* (S-languages): Path is characteristically placed in the satellite. For instance, English *run **out***.
- *Verb-framed languages* (V-languages): Path is characteristically codified in the verb-root. For instance, French ***partir*** *en courant* 'leave running'.

Talmy's typological classification based on these lexicalization patterns is perhaps one of the most widely applied and well-known models in Cognitive Linguistics. As such it has generated positive as well as negative criticisms. We look at some empirical evidence from both camps.

2.1. Applications of the typology in linguistic research

Talmy's two-way typology has been applied now to a vast number of languages (see footnote 2 for references), and despite problems and caveats, it is safe to say that in the current motion literature, the distinction between satellite- and verb-framed languages, as well as his terminology for motion semantic components is just the springboard for

---

[3] For motion events, these components are: internal – Figure, Ground, Path, Motion, and co-event or secondary: Manner, Cause.
[4] This is a basic tenet in Talmy's proposal, which is only natural for a usage-based framework such as Cognitive Linguistics. Unfortunately, some critiques of the model (Croft et al. 2010; Kopecka 2006; Pourcel and Kopecka 2005) overlook this crucial premise, and consequently, insist on finding exceptions and problematic cases to the general framework. They focus their attention on all the possible motion structures a language may have available for the codification of motion instead of speakers' first/habitual/most frequent/preferred choices that Talmy talks about.
[5] Interestingly enough, Path and Manner do not come online at the same time; Path is acquired before Manner (see Mandler 2004; Pruden et al. 2004; also Pulverman et al. 2004 and Filipović 2007a, 2010 for the fundamental importance of Path in spatial and temporal conceptualisation).
[6] Talmy (1985) also proposed a previous three-way typology based on which semantic component was lexicalized in the verb root across languages (Manner-, Path-, and Figure-languages), but the crucial distinction still lies in the dichotomy based on whether the Path is lexicalized in the verb or out of the verb (see Filipović 2007a: 19).

most studies. There is one particular application of Talmy's insights that has gained equal importance in motion studies nowadays, namely Dan Slobin's (1991, 1996, 2004, 2006) *thinking-for-speaking* hypothesis.

Slobin proposes that the use of different lexicalization patterns has important, and easily observable, relativistic consequences in the online use of language. Speakers of satellite- and verb-framed languages have to describe motion events with the linguistic resources (that is, surface components) available in their languages, and as such, their descriptions of motion events are constrained by what is available in their languages. Slobin employs verbal elicitation methodology, using various visual stimuli, most prominently the illustrations depicting motion events from the *Frog Story* (see Berman and Slobin 1994; Strömqvist and Verhoeven 2004 for more details). He concludes that speakers, guided by their own lexicalization patterns, direct their attention to different aspects of the same motion event, the result of which is a different *rhetorical style* as well as difference in the quality and quantity of available information about a motion event.

The structure and resources of satellite-framed languages allow speakers to describe both Manner and Path very often and in detail since they have rich and expressive Manner of motion verb lexicon, the possibility to attach several Path segments to a single main verb, free main verb slots for Manner (since Path is in the satellite). Verb-framed speakers, on the other hand, follow the opposite pattern. They tend to mention Path in the main verb, add, at most, one extra Path segment, and hardly describe Manner unless it is crucial for the discourse flow. Verb-framed languages do not usually exhibit rich and expressive Manner of motion verb lexicons,[7] and since the Path verb occupies the main verb slot, the only possibility for Manner is to be expressed outside the verb, in a separate expression (adverbs, gerunds, adpositional phrases or subordinate clauses). This restrains information content with regard to Manner due to the added extra processing cost.

A wide range of crosslinguistic studies covering different complementary research areas have been carried out within this methodological framework in order to test how well different languages fit in the bipartite typology and differ in their rhetorical styles.

Some studies incorporate the role of gesture to verbal elicitation. McNeill and collaborators (Kita and Özyürek 2003; McNeill 1992, 2000, 2005; Özyürek et al. 2005; Stam 2006), for instance, found similar results to those of Slobin. Using data from the *Tweety Cartoon*, another widely-used elicitation tool[8] (see McNeill 1992, 2005 for further details), they find that motion gestures are ubiquitous in all narrations but that their function differs depending on the lexicalization pattern. For instance, whereas verb-framed speakers use Manner gestures to talk about information not mentioned in speech (the so-called *Manner fogs*), satellite-framed speakers gesture to reinforce what is already in the speech.

Some other studies take a step forward and test whether fictive motion (see Matlock and Bergmann this volume) and metaphorical motion (see Gibbs this volume) also match

---

[7] This is always in comparison to satellite-framed languages (see Cardini 2008; Cifuentes-Férez 2010). There are however other studies that point out that verb-framed languages rich in ideophones do possess equally rich Manner sources (Basque: Ibarretxe-Antuñano 2006, 2009a; Emai: Schaefer (2001); Japanese: Akita and Matsumoto ms.; Sugiyama 2005).

[8] Another elicitation tool for gesture and motion are *The Tomato Man* movies (see Özyürek, Kita and Allen 2001 for further details).

these lexicalization patterns and discourse tendencies. Özçalışkan (2004, 2005), for instance, examines English and Turkish texts only to find that the typological differences are kept in metaphorical motion. Based on English and Spanish data from three different genres (architecture, wine and sports), Caballero and Ibarretxe-Antuñano (forthcoming) refine Özçalışkan's findings. They argue that there are differences due to the genre specific discourse requirements; verb-framed metaphorical motion events are more expressive (i.e., a wider variety of Manner verbs are found more frequently) and dynamic (i.e., more details about Path and less about Ground) than their physical counterparts.

A significant amount of studies are produced from the applied perspective, especially examining the acquisition process of motion events in L1 and L2 across lexicalization patterns (see Cadierno forthcoming; Ellis and Cadierno 2009; Han and Cadierno 2010 for a review), and to a lesser extent translation (see Ibarretxe-Antuñano and Filipović 2013 for a review). Section 3 reports on some of these studies.

2.2. Problems and solutions

As just shown, many studies have confirmed the pervasive differences between Talmy's two contrasting lexicalization patterns. Over the years, however, some of its basic assumptions have also been challenged. The incorporation of new languages, the introduction of different tools and methodologies (e.g., electronic corpora and experimental design including response time and eye movement detection) and the growing number of very detailed empirically-based descriptions of motion events has revealed certain problems and caveats. Here, we review some of the most recurrent problems in the literature as well as some of the proposed solutions. In general, criticisms revolve around two main problematic issues: the theory fails (i) to account for all possible motion structures, including finely grained distinctions, and (ii) to provide explanations for variation between and within lexicalization patterns.

2.2.1. Challenging motion structures

Talmy (2000: 101–128) introduces the notion of satellite, a closed-class type of surface element, to encompass grammatical forms such as verb particles (e.g., English), verb prefixes (e.g., Russian), incorporated nouns (e.g., Caddo) and polysynthetic affixes (e.g., Atsugewi), among others. He argues that these elements, typical of satellite-framed languages, are mainly involved in the expression of Path, but that they could also express Path+Ground, Patient (Figure/Ground) in noun-incorporating languages, Cause (Instrument) and only very rarely Manner (e.g., as in Nez Perce). Some authors (Beavers et al. 2010; Croft et al. 2010; Filipović 2007a) have noted that the notion of satellite per se is confusing. They argue that the differentiation between particles and prepositions in English is not clear-cut and propose to extend the notion of satellite to cover these other cases. Another problem concerning satellites has to do with certain structures that turn up in verb-framed languages. For example, languages such as Chantyal (Noonan 2003) and Basque (Ibarretxe-Antuñano 2004) possess directionals or spatial case-inflected locative nouns whose function comes quite close to that of a satellite. Romance languages also keep some traces of their Latin (satellite-framed) ancestry.[9] French and Spanish, for instance, still keep some Path prefixes, and Italian uses Path particles that look like satellites too. It has been argued that these elements could be considered satellites (Porquier 2001; Iacobini and Masini 2007), but other authors (Hijazo-Gascón and Ibarretxe-Antuñano 2013) prefer to classify these elements as *pseudosatellites* since their productivity and combinability – two key factors in this usage-based approach – are far more scarce and restricted than that of satellites in satellite-framed languages.

An early caveat in Talmy's typology is the boundary-crossing constraint, a term coined in Slobin and Hoiting (1994) but initially pointed out by Aske (1989). It refers to those cases in verb-framed languages where the semantics of the verb-root constraints the type of aspectual directional phrase it goes with. If the main verb conflates Motion+Path (the characteristic verb-framed pattern), then the directional phrase can depict a situation where the Figure traverses a boundary. If the main verb, on the other hand, contains the semantic component of Manner, this kind of translational motion event expression is not permitted. In order to describe both Path and Manner, the latter should be lexicalized outside the verb (e.g., *Javier entró en la casa corriendo* 'Javier entered in the house running'). The boundary constraint[10] has become a distinctive feature of verb-framed languages.

Another criticism arises from the nature of semantic components. Categories such as Path and, especially, Manner are considered too broad to capture similarities and differences across languages. They are suitable for a general lexicalization pattern typology, but once a finer-grained analysis is in place, they are too wide and general. Several authors therefore have proposed further subdivisions of Path (Berthele 2006; Filipović 2010; Narasimham 2003; Slobin 2008; Talmy 2000; Vulchanova and van der Zee 2013; Wälchli 2001) and Manner (Filipović 2010; Ibarretxe-Antuñano 2006; Özçalıskan 2004; Slobin 2005).

2.2.2. Constraints and variation in lexicalization patterns

As mentioned above, the list of new languages that have been incorporated to the study of lexicalization patterns grows larger every day; accordingly, as does the risk of the model not being able to account for all the empirical data-driven observations. Many of these new studies reveal that the two-way typology may not be quite so clear-cut and may also fail to acknowledge variation between and within lexicalization patterns.

Two kinds of phenomena can be included under the general label of *intertypological variation*. First, it concerns what we could informally label as "mixed" languages. This includes: (i) languages which, despite their affiliation to one lexicalization pattern, show

---

[9] For more information on the evolution from satellite-framed Latin to verb-framed Romance, see Ferrari and Mosca (2010); Iacobini and Fagard (2011); Slotova (2008). See also Verkerk (2014) for Indo-European and Kutscher and Werning (2013) for information on space in Ancient languages.

[10] There are other restrictions on the type and complexity of directional information that a motion event clause can code. Bohnemeyer (2003), for instance, introduces the *Unique Vector Constraint* that states that all directional information in a single simple clause must keep the same direction vector.

patterns typical from the opposite lexicalization group. For instance, Aragonese (Hijazo-Gascón and Ibarretxe-Antuñano 2010) is a verb-framed language but (pseudo-)satellite constructions are widely used; and (ii) languages where speakers indistinctively use both satellite- and verb-framed constructions on a regular basis. For example, Modern Greek (Soroli 2012) is reported to be such a language. Talmy himself (2000) acknowledges this variation and calls it a *parallel conflation system*. Second, some languages cannot be classified either as satellite- or verb-framed because they use a third way of codifying motion events. Slobin (2004) calls this lexicalization pattern *equipollently-framed* since the semantic components Path and Manner are lexicalized in equivalent surface elements (e.g., Mandarin Chinese). In order to account for blurred lines of the division between and among different lexicalization patterns, some authors have opted to propose new typologies for motion events: Matsumoto's (2003) Head- and non-head framed languages, Bohnemeyer et al.'s (2007) Type I-II-III, Grinevald's (2011) "working typology", and Slobin's (2008) Path-in-non-verb vs. Path-in-verb, to name just a few, but none of those proposals have been widely implemented.

Intratypological variation refers to variation within the same lexicalization pattern. That is, languages within the same group show diversity with respect to the level of salience and granularity of motion semantic components (see Goschler and Stefanowitsch 2013). This occurs not only in genetically different languages (Basque and Spanish; see Ibarretxe-Antuñano 2004), but also in languages with the same genetic filiations (see Ragnarsdóttir and Strömqvist 2004 for the Germanic family; Hijazo-Gascón and Ibarretxe-Antuñano 2013 for the Romance; and Huang and Tanangkingsing 2005 for western Austronesian verb-framed languages). In fact, these intratypological differences have led some authors to propose *clines of salience* for motion semantic components. This suggests that the whole typology can be seen as a cline rather than a dichotomy (see Ibarretxe-Antuñano 2004, 2009b; Filipović 2007a; Slobin 2004).

Finally, there is also room for *diatopic variation*. This is an area that has not yet received the attention it deserves, but recently a number of authors (such as Berthele 2006 for Swiss German and Romansch; Ibarretxe-Antuñano and Hijazo-Gascón 2012 for Spanish and Aragonese; and Schwarze 1985 for Italian) have discovered that dialects from the same language do not necessarily behave in the same way. Berthele (2006), for instance, reports that Muotathal, a Swiss German dialect spoken in the Schwyz canton, hardly uses Manner verbs but frequently describes Path by means of syntactically and semantically complex structures. This behaviour evident in *Frog Story* narratives is different from other Swiss dialects and the standard language.

3. Motion in acquisition, translation and beyond

The study of both agentive and caused motion events was instrumental in determining what kind of information about motion events tends to be given in some languages more often and in more detail than in others. It was also important for the differences in the kinds of details that we can expect to be expressed and remembered better or worse based on language-specific narrative habits and preferred patterns for habitual inclusion or exclusion of information. This is of immense importance in numerous applied research and professional fields, such as language acquisition, translation and interpreting, as well as forensic linguistics, to name just a few.

3.1. Motion in acquisition

Developmental psychology has offered important insights into how we become capable of thinking and speaking about motion. Specifically, studies in child language development have provided new knowledge of how motion verbs and constructions are initially acquired by infants, as well as how these findings can help us understand the overall relationship between language and cognition and the role of language in cognitive development in general. The pioneering cross-linguistic work of Berman and Slobin (1994) showed that children as young as three-years-old already attended to the linguistic requirements of their own languages. Although children (ages: 3, 5, 7, 9) had to describe identical pictures (*Frog Story*), the resulting stories were different depending on the language they were learning (English, German, Hebrew, Spanish or Turkish). Pulverman et al. (2008) tested infants' ability to note changes in Path and Manner – the fundamental requirement for learning relational terms such as verbs regardless of the native language. They found that 14- to 17-month-old infants succeeded at this task regardless of gender or cultural and linguistic differences, which suggests that this may be a robust ability common to all normally developing children. Pulverman et al. (2004) demonstrated further that the introduction of a label differentially heightens attention to motion components. The conceptual foundation for the relationships expressed by verbs in languages appears to be universal, but verb learning is complicated by the fact that verbs package actions and events in different ways across languages (see Gentner and Boroditsky 2001). The effect of language-specific packaging of information on attention has been attested on numerous occasions. Infants' initial attention to motion components is further modulated by individual languages (see Bowerman and Choi 2003; Choi and Bowerman 1991; Hickmann and Hendriks 2010; Ji et al. 2011) after an apparent universal bias at the outset. Thus, the developmental process appears to initially involve the universal ability to note Path and Manner changes and form language-general nonlinguistic constructs, which are gradually refined and tuned to the requirements of the native language. In effect, infants are *trading spaces,* maintaining their sensitivity to some relational distinctions while dampening other distinctions, depending on how their native language expresses these constructs (see Göksun et al. 2010; Maguire et al. 2010).

Research on motion events within second language acquisition paradigm has also yielded novel and important findings with respect to cross-linguistic interactions in the mind of the speaker, while simultaneously being a fertile testing ground for many theoretical assumptions in SLA (see Cadierno forthcoming; Ellis and Cadierno 2009; Han and Cadierno 2010; Pavlenko 2011 for a review). The motion lexicalization domain proved to be prone to cross-linguistic influence (see Jarvis and Pavlenko 2007), and it is an area where not only the occurrence of L1–L2 transfer can be expected, but also the reverse transfer (Brown and Gullberg 2008). This represents an ideal opportunity for testing assumptions as to when, where and why transfer may occur. In general, L2 studies inspired by Talmy's typology agree that L2 speakers need to learn to *readjust* their L1 motion structures to the narrative style of the L2 (Cadierno 2004, 2008; Robinson and Ellis 2008). This readjustment is not an easy or straightforward procedure. Learners need to learn not only the lexicalization pattern of the L2 (that is, linguistic structures – speech and gesture – for codifying L2 language) but also which aspects of the motion event are to be mentioned in the L2 motion description and when (that is, the rhetorical style in L2). According to Cadierno (forthcoming), studies on L2 motion events have so far discovered that the learner's L1 influence is present in the L2 production (i) regardless of the type of L1 lexicalization pattern, satellite- or verb-framed (Cadierno 2004; Larrañaga et al. 2011; Negueruela et al. 2004); (ii) not only in speech but also in gesture (Brown and Gullberg 2008; Stam 2006), what Kellerman and van Hoof (2003) call *manual accent*; (iii) even in advanced learners (Choi and Lantolf 2008), and (iv) even in languages that belong to the same typological group. This applies to genetically-different (Hasko 2009) and genetically-similar languages (Hijazo-Gascón in press). In addition to L1 effects, there is also an overall tendency to resort to the (potentially) *universal, economy-of-form strategy* (Filipović and Vidaković 2010).

3.2. Motion in translation and interpreting

Translation studies is another area that has benefited from findings in motion event lexicalization. Early work in translation already paid attention to the typological differences across languages. Vinay and Darbelnet (1958), for instance, talk about the *chassé-croisé pattern* to refer to the interchange that occurs between English and French structures when translating motion (see also Snell-Hornby 1983). However, translating motion events is not just a question of exchanging grammatically correct structures from one language into another; it is also a question of preserving the rhetorical style of the target language while adapting the content.

Most of the studies devoted to the study of motion events have analyzed the translation product, that is, how motion events have been translated from the source into the target domain. One of the first studies in this area is Slobin's (1996) analysis of Spanish and English novels and their respective translations. The research results seem to confirm that translators do actually adapt the source texts to the rhetorical style and resources of the target language (e.g., translation into Spanish contain less Manner information than the English originals and translations into English contain added Manner information that is not present in the Spanish original). This line of research has been followed up by similar studies on different language combinations. Ibarretxe-Antuñano and Filipović (2013) provide a summary of all proposed translation strategies to date (twenty in total), which are not restricted to just omission or addition of Path/Manner information, but also include substitution of one semantic component for another as well as adaptation of partial information. Ibarretxe-Antuñano and Filipović (2013) also report on a translation experiment whereby bilingual speakers judged original witness reports in Spanish (which contained sparse or no information about Manner) less aggressive and they were less likely to imagine the events described as extremely violent, in contrast to the English Manner-rich translations of the same events, which elicited higher values on the violence judgement scale. Thus, the effects of the typological differences go beyond the expressions themselves, and they can affect speakers' judgments regarding events they hear or read about. Further, in the context of forensic linguistic research, Filipović (2007b, 2013) has demonstrated that the cross-linguistic differences that play a role in expression and memory of motion events (see the next section) also affect the quantity and quality of information given by witnesses in translation-mediated communication with the police or in court. Studies such as these can raise awareness of what kind of information is easy or hard to express in a particular language, and subsequently translate into another, so that more attention can be paid to these precise points of conflict in order to prevent it through focused education of language professionals. This would lead to practical applications, such as improved efficiency and accuracy of language-mediated interactions including investigative legal interviews, translation practice and training, language learning and language teaching.

4. Motion in language and memory: Experimental psycholinguistic insights

Studying cross-linguistic differences in motion lexicalization inspired re-examinations of some of the long-lasting empirical puzzles such as whether and, if yes, when and why, we may encounter language-specific effects on cognition, and how they can co-exist with certain universal features of language processing and cognitive functions (such as perception and memory). These Whorfian questions have recently been revisited in many cognitive domains and most recent studies converge on the idea that both universal and language-specific forces are involved in the perception and in the cognitive organisation of categories in the domain of colour (e.g., Regier and Kay 2009), space (Landau 2010), and motion (Filipović 2010).

The interest in thinking and speaking about motion events has been intense in the psycholinguistic community. Numerous cross-linguistic studies of event description and cognition have had a specific focus on motion events (e.g., Filipović 2010, 2011; Filipović and Geva 2012; Finkbeiner et al. 2002; Gennari et al. 2002; Malt et al. 2003; Papafragou et al. 2002; Slobin 2006; Trueswell and Papafragou 2010). Some of these studies report evidence for typological differences affecting certain aspects of information content and cognition (e.g., Finkbeiner et al. 2002; Filipović 2011; Filipović and Geva 2012), and some argue that such differences are found only on restricted occasions that encourage the use of *language as a strategy in organising information* (e.g., Malt et al. 2003). These different studies also use different experimental methodologies to elicit data, for example, static illustrations (Papafragou et al. 2002), video clips triads (Malt et al. 2003), and contrastive video clip pairs (Filipović 2011), which together with the variation in the experimental stimuli (e.g., simple motion events in Papafragou et al. 2002 and Malt et al. 2003, and complex motion events in Filipović 2011) may impact the experimental outcomes.

There is substantial evidence that language can be used as a system for organising experience under specific conditions, such as sorting out events (as well as objects, see for example Lucy and Gaskins 2003), especially after prior verbalization, which instantiates language as a stable and reliable classification system. Language can also be evoked in difficult tasks, namely when memory is explicitly required, whereby a reliable system for the organization of information is necessary and language-specific structuring of perceptual stimuli is resorted to (see Finkbeiner et al. 2002). However, simple events stimuli, like "one Manner + one Path" motion events do not necessarily activate "language as a strategy" automatically and universal strategies may be employed instead, for example when Spanish speakers remembered subtle manner distinctions as well as English speakers (Filipović 2010). Other strategies are also used to render Manner of motion instead of arbitrary phonological labels that manner verbs are, such as ideophones in Basque (see Ibarretxe-Antuñano 2006) or mimetic expressions that give clues to the nature of the referent in Japanese (Imai et al. 2008). An ability to attend to both Path and Manner thus appears to be universal and, in order to determine the conditions under which language may start to play the mediating role in the conceptual organisation of information and memory of events, we had to look for the reasons when and why speakers may resort to their languages as aids to memory.

One such occasion is an enhanced cognitive load. In general terms, any kind of circumstance of added memory load, or other kind of cognitive pressure, tends to *encourage stereotyping* (adherence to preferred, entrenched patterns of reasoning) in general cognition, and by analogy, in language (see Mendoza-Denton 2010). We revert to familiar conceptualizations under such pressures, and we tend to do the same when using language as an aid to problem-solving, opting for the most characteristic, familiar, and frequent lexicalization patterns. For English speakers, that process involves speaking about the Manner of motion; for Spanish speakers Manner is less of a priority.

This line of reasoning underlies a study of memory for motion events under enhanced cognitive load and language effect on memory of motion events that was first reported in Filipović (2011). This study has shown that monolingual speakers of English perform better in a recognition task than their Spanish peers, when describing details of the event that are relevant to the recognition task. Using *complex motion events* stimuli (three manners per event) which enhanced the cognitive load in the specific area where the two languages differ, Filipović found that it was the language used explicitly (or tacitly) that helped recognition memory in the case of the English speakers but not the Spanish speakers. This typological advantage does not seem to be of much assistance in some other tasks, namely when free encoding is disabled (see Filipović and Geva 2012) or when simple motion events stimuli are used (e.g., Malt et al. 2003). Therefore, we can say that language effects can be detected in on-line (but not off-line) processing and some languages can be more of aid than others in complex tasks resulting from enhanced cognitive pressures or information load (see also Lai et al. 2013). As a result of lexicalization preferences in their respective languages, English speakers remember complex motion events (Filipović 2011) and agents (Fausey and Boroditsky 2011) better, while Spanish speakers are better at recalling whether causation was intentional or non-intentional (see Filipović 2013).

In sum, since languages differ with respect to the means they make available to their speakers to talk about different aspects of motion events (such as Path, Manner, agentivity, causation), it is important to study those cross-linguistic contrasts in the domain of motion, and other domains alike, as they are indicative of the difficulties that may arise in different contexts of communication, and with respect to both linguistic expression and retrieval from memory. The studies briefly discussed here and similar ones provide central insights into both language-specific and universal factors in language processing. The fact that applied research into motion verbs and constructions leads to discoveries that shape our understanding of both domain-specific and general underlying principles of language use and language-mediated cognition is a testimony to the overall importance of the study of how we learn to think and speak about motion.

5. Conclusions

This chapter illustrated the current state of art in the domain of motion lexicalization research from a number of different linguistic and interdisciplinary perspectives. We can see that research in this domain is vibrant and multileveled, and that it brings about novel insights not just into how we speak and think about motion, but also how language processing mechanisms operate in different contexts such as acquisition or translation. Applied research in this area is developing rapidly and it is a testimony to the value of the insightful theoretical contributions made in the past that continue to inspire further research while at the same time informing the theory itself in return.

We saw that there is an interaction between both universal and language-specific factors, which co-exist when speakers use their language to relate their experience within their environments. Universal tendencies are moulded by language-specific preferences developmentally in first language acquisition, while in second language acquisition we seem to need to re-think-for-speaking, which is also a developmental process that moves along with L2 proficiency.

Finally, we witnessed an increasing number of current and future applications of this research in various practical and professional areas where language plays the central role. Language education and translation training stand to benefit immensely from raised awareness of the crucial cross-linguistic contrasts in motion lexicalization. Accuracy and efficiency of translation itself would be improved if we focused on the precise points of conflict between any two languages that can cause difficulties when framing the content of the message in two different systems respectively. The consequences of such conflicts may even go beyond the language itself and impact how we organize information for later judgment and for memory.

Studying the conditions under which we see the impact of linguistic habits beyond the text itself will lead to further understanding of the intimate relationship between language and the mind in this, as well as other, cognitive domains. It is not easy to capture the prolific output on motion research across the board, but we hope that this selective account depicts the multifaceted and dynamic field. The study of motion events in language and cognition has become a unifying platform for numerous disciplines, where empirically and methodologically diverse studies jointly afford new knowledge about a topic that can only be tackled in a truly interdisciplinary fashion. We hope that this account will inspire further research, especially in the domain that Filipović terms *applied linguistic typology* (see Filipović and Putz 2014; also Filipović forthcoming), namely where the academic scholarship both reflects upon and responds to the needs of users (i.e., learners or teachers of a language) by highlighting the phenomena that matter to their life and professional or personal involvement. Specifically, applied language typology studies the effects of typological contrasts that matter beyond the mere descriptions of languages and their typological groupings. Its focus is on how specific typological contrasts affect language practice. Applying linguistic typology in different contexts of use will further our knowledge not only about motion and other domains of experience but also about the impact of language on our increasingly multilingual personal and professional lives.

6. References

Akita, Kimi and Yo Matsumoto
    Ms.   Manner salience revisited: Evidence from two Japanese-English contrastive experiments. Osaka University and Kobe University.

Aske, Jon
 1989 Path predicates in English and Spanish: A closer look. *Proceedings of the Fifteenth Annual Meeting of the Berkeley Linguistics Society* 15: 1–14.
Beavers, John, Beth Levin and Shiao-Wei Tham
 2010 The typology of motion expressions revisited. *Journal of Linguistics* 44: 183–316.
Berman, Ruth and Dan I. Slobin (eds.)
 1994 *Relating Events in Narrative. A Cross Linguistic Developmental Study.* Hillsdale: Lawrence Erlbaum.
Berthele, Raphael
 2006 *Ort und Weg. Eine vergleichende Untersuchung der sprachlichen Raumreferenz in Varietäten des Deutschen, Rätorromanischen und Französichen.* Berlin: Mouton de Gruyter.
Bohnemeyer, Jürgen
 2003 The unique vector constraint. In: E. van der Zee and J. Slack (eds.), *Representing Direction in Language and Space*, 86–110. Oxford: Oxford University Press.
Bohnemeyer, Jürgen, Nick Enfield, James Essegbey, Iraide Ibarretxe-Antuñano, Sotaro Kita, Friederike Lüpke and Felix K. Ameka
 2007 Principles of event segmentation in language: The case of motion events. *Language* 83(3): 495–532.
Bowerman, Melissa and Soonja Choi
 2003 Space under construction: Language-specific spatial categorization in first language acquisition. In: D. Gentner and S. Goldin-Meadow (eds.), *Language in Mind: Advances in the Study of Language and Thought*, 387–427. Cambridge: MIT Press
Brown, Amanda and Marianne Gullberg
 2008 Bidirectional crosslinguistic influence in L1–L2 encoding of manner in speech and gesture: A study of Japanese speakers of English. *Studies in Second Language Acquisition* 30: 225–251.
Brugman, Claudia
 1988 *The Story of Over: Polysemy, Semantics, and the Structure of the Lexicon.* New York: Garland.
Caballero, Rosario and Iraide Ibarretxe-Antuñano
 forthcoming *And yet they DON'T move: A genre approach to metaphorical motion.* Berlin/New York: Mouton de Gruyter.
Cadierno, Teresa
 2004 Expressing motion events in a second language: A cognitive typological perspective. In: M. Achard and S. Niemeier (eds.), *Cognitive Linguistics, Second Language Acquisition, and Foreign Language Teaching*, 13–49. Berlin: Mouton de Gruyter.
Cadierno, Teresa
 2008 Learning to talk about motion in a foreign language. In P. Robinson and N. C. Ellis (eds.), *Handbook of Cognitive Linguistics and Second Language Acquisition*, 239–275. New York/London: Routledge.
Cadierno, Teresa
 Forthcoming Thinking for speaking about motion in a second language: Looking back and forword. In: I. Ibarretxe-Antuñano (ed.), *Motion and Space across Languages and Applications.* Amsterdam: John Benjamins.
Cardini, Filippo-Enrico
 2008 Manner of motion saliency: An inquiry into Italian. *Cognitive Linguistics* 19(4): 533–569.
Choi, Soonja and Melissa Bowerman
 1991 Learning to express motion events in English and Korean: The influence of language-specific lexicalization patterns. *Cognition* 41: 83–121.

Choi, Soojung and James P. Lantolf
  2008   Representation and embodiment of meaning in L2 communication: Motion Events in the Speech and Gesture of Advanced L2 Korean and L2 English Speakers. *Studies in Second Language Acquisition* 30(2): 191–224.
Cifuentes-Férez, Paula
  2010   The semantics of the English and the Spanish motion verb lexicons. *Review of Cognitive Linguistics* 8(2): 233–271.
Croft, William, Jóhanna Barðdal, Willem Hollmann, Violeta Sotirova and Chiaki Taoka
  2010   Revising Talmy's typological classification of complex constructions. In: H. C. Boas (ed.), *Contrastive Studies in Construction Grammar*, 201–236. Amsterdam: John Benjamins.
Ellis, Nick C. and Teresa Cadierno (eds.)
  2009   Constructing a second language. Special section of *Annual Review of Cognitive Linguistics* 7.
Fausey, Caitlin M. and Lera Boroditsky
  2011   Who dunnit? Cross-linguistic differences in eye-witness memory. *Psychonomic Bulletin and Review* 18(1): 150–157.
Ferrari, Giacomo and Monica Mosca
  2010   Some constructions of path: From Italian to some Classical languages. In: G. Marotta, A. Lenci, L. Meini and F. Roval (eds.), *Space in Language*, 317–338. Florence: Edizioni ETS.
Filipović, Luna
  2007a *Talking about Motion: A Crosslinguistic Investigation of Lexicalization Patterns*. Amsterdam: John Benjamins.
Filipović, Luna
  2007b Language as a witness: Insights from cognitive linguistics. *International Journal of Speech, Language and the Law* 14(2): 245–267.
Filipović, Luna
  2010   Thinking and speaking about motion: Universal vs. language- specific effects. In: G. Marotta, A. Lenci, L. Meini and F. Roval (eds.), *Space in Language*, 235–248. Florence: Edizioni ETS.
Filipović, Luna
  2011   Speaking and remembering in one or two languages: Bilingual vs. monolingual lexicalization and memory for motion events. *International Journal of Bilingualism* 15(4): 466–485.
Filipović, Luna
  2013   Constructing causation in language and memory: implications for access to justice in multilingual interactions. *International Journal of Speech, Language and the Law* 20(1): 1–19.
Filipović, Luna
  Forthcoming   Applied language typology: Practical applications of research on typological contrasts between languages. In: I. Ibarretxe-Antuñano (ed.), *Motion and Space across Languages and Applications*. Amsterdam: John Benjamins.
Filipović, Luna and Sharon Geva
  2012   Language-specific effects on lexicalization and memory of motion events. In: L. Filipović and K. M. Jaszczolt (eds.), *Space and Time across Languages and Cultures*: *Language Culture and Cognition*, 269–282. Amsterdam: John Benjamins.
Filipović, Luna and Martin Pütz (eds.)
  2014   *Multilingual Cognition and Language Use: Processing and Typological Perspectives*. Amsterdam/Philadelphia: Benjamins.

Filipović, Luna and Ivana Vidaković
2010   *Typology in the L2 classroom: Second language acquisition from a typological perspective* In: M. Pütz and L. Sicola (eds.), *Cognitive Processing in Second Language Acquisition. Inside the Learner's Mind*, 269–291. Amsterdam: John Benjamins.

Finkbeiner, Matthew, Janet Nicol, Delia Greth and Kumiko Nakamura
2002   The role of language in memory for actions. *Journal of Psycholinguistic Research* 31: 447–457.

Gennari, Silvia P., Steven A. Sloman, Barbara C. Malt and W. Tecumseh Fitch
2002   Motion events in language and cognition. *Cognition* 83(1): 49–79.

Gentner, Deidre and Lera Boroditsky
2001   Individualism, relativity, and early word learning. In: M. Bowerman and S. C. Levinson (eds.), *Language Acquisition and Conceptual Development*, 215–256. Cambridge: Cambridge University Press.

Gibbs, Raymond W.
this volume   8. Metaphor. Berlin/Boston: De Gruyter Mouton.

Göksun, Tilbe, Kathy Hirsh-Pasek and Roberta M. Golinkoff
2010   Trading spaces: Carving up events for language learning. *Perspectives on Psychological Science* 5: 33–42.

Goschler, Julianna and Anatol Stefanowitsch (eds.)
2013   *Variation and Change in the Encoding of Motion Events*. Amsterdam/Philadelphia: John Benjamins.

Grinevald, Colette
2011   On constructing a working typology of the expression of *path*. *Cahiers de Faits de Langue* 3: 43–70.

Han, Zhao-Hong and Teresa Cadierno (eds.)
2010   *Linguistic Relativity in SLA: Thinking for Speaking*. Clevedon: Multilingual Matters.

Hart, Christopher
this volume   15. Discourse. Berlin/Boston: De Gruyter Mouton.

Hasko, Victoria
2009   The locus of difficulties in the acquisition of Russian verbs of motion by highly proficient learners. *Slavic and East European Journal* 53(3): 360–385.

Heine, Bernd and Tania Kuteva
2002   *World Lexicon of Grammaticalization*. Cambridge: Cambridge University Press.

Herskovits, Annette
1986   *Language and Spatial Cognition. An Interdisciplinary Study of Prepositions in English*. Cambridge: Cambridge University Press.

Hickmann, Maya and Henriëtte Hendriks
2010   Typological constraints on the acquisition of spatial language. *Cognitive Linguistics* 21(2): 189–215.

Hijazo-Gascón, Alberto
In press   Acquisition of motion events in L2 Spanish by German, French and Italian speakers. *Language Learning Journal*.

Hijazo-Gascón, Alberto and Iraide Ibarretxe-Antuñano
2010   Tipología, lexicalización y dialectología aragonesa. *Archivo de Filología Aragonesa* 66: 181–215.

Hijazo-Gascón, Alberto and Iraide Ibarretxe-Antuñano
2013   Las lenguas románicas y la tipología de los eventos de movimiento. *Romanische Forschungen* 125: 467–494.

Huang, Shuanfan and Michael Tanangkingsing
2005   Reference to motion events in six western Austronesian languages: Toward a semantic typology. *Oceanic Linguistics* 44(2): 307–340.

Ibarretxe-Antuñano, Iraide
    2004   Language typologies in our language use: the case of Basque motion events in adult oral narratives. *Cognitive Linguistics* 15(3): 317–349.
Ibarretxe-Antuñano, Iraide
    2006   *Sound Symbolism and Motion in Basque*. Munich: Lincom Europa.
Ibarretxe-Antuñano, Iraide
    2009a   Lexicalization patterns and sound symbolism in Basque. In: J. Valenzuela, A. Rojo and C. Soriano (eds.), *Trends in Cognitive Linguistics: Theoretical and Applied Models*, 239–254. Hamburg: Peter Lang.
Ibarretxe-Antuñano, Iraide
    2009b   Path salience in motion events. In: J. Guo, E. Lieven, N. Budwig, S. Ervin-Tripp, K. Nakamura and S. Özçalışkan (eds.), *Crosslinguistic Approaches to the Psychology of Language: Research in the Tradition of Dan Isaac Slobin*, 403–414. New York: Psychology Press.
Ibarretxe-Antuñano, Iraide and Luna Filipović
    2013   Lexicalization patterns and translation. In: A. Rojo and I. Ibarretxe-Antuñano (eds.), *Cognitive Linguistics and Translation: Advances in Some Theoretical Models and Applications*, 253–283. Berlin/New York: Mouton de Gruyter.
Ibarretxe-Antuñano, Iraide and Alberto Hijazo-Gascón
    2012   Variation in motion events: Theory and applications. In: L. Filipović and K. M. Jaszczolt (eds), *Space and Time across Languages and Cultures*. Volume I: *Linguistic Diversity*, 349–371. Amsterdam: John Benjamins.
Imai, Mutsumi, Sotaro Kita, Miho Nagumo and Hiroyuki Okada
    2008   Sound symbolism facilitates early verb learning. *Cognition* 109: 5–65.
Iacobini, Claudio and Benjamin Fagard
    2011   A diachronic approach to variation and change in the typology of motion event expression. A case study: From Latin to Romance. *Cahiers de Faits de langue* 3: 151–172.
Iacobini, Claudio and Francesca Masini
    2007   The emergence of verb-particle constructions in Italian: locative and actional meanings. *Morphology* 16(2): 155–188.
Jackendoff, Ray
    1983   *Semantics and Cognition*. Cambridge: MIT Press.
Jarvis, Scott and Aneta. Pavlenko
    2007   *Crosslinguistic Influence in Language and Cognition*. New York/London: Routledge.
Ji, Yinglin, Henriëtte Hendriks and Maya Hickmann
    2011   How children express caused motion events in Chinese and English: Universal and language-specific influences. *Lingua* 121: 1796–1819.
Kellerman, Eric and Anne-Marie Van Hoof
    2003   Manual accents. *International Review of Applied Linguistics* 41: 251–269.
Kita, Sotaro and Aslı Özyürek
    2003   What does cross-linguistic variation in semantic coordination of speech and gesture reveal?: Evidence for an interface representation of spatial thinking and speaking. *Journal of Memory and Language* 48: 16–32.
Kopecka, Anetta
    2006   The semantic structure of motion verbs in French: Typological perspectives. In: M. Hickmann and S. Robert (eds.), *Space in Languages: Linguistic Systems and Cognitive Categories*, 83–101. Amsterdam: John Benjamins.
Kutscher, Silvia and Daniel A. Werning (eds.)
    2013   *On Ancient Grammars of Space. Linguistic Research on the Expression of Spatial Relations and Motion in Ancient Languages*. Berlin: Mouton De Gruyter.

Lai, Vicky Tzuyin, Gabriela Garrido-Rodriguez and Bhuvana Narasimhan
  2013   Thinking for speaking in early and late bilinguals. *Bilingualism: Language and Cognition* 17(1): 139–152.
Landau, Barbara
  2010   Paths in language and cognition: Universal asymmetries and their cause. In: G. Marotta, A. Lenci, L. Meini and F. Roval (eds.), *Space in Language*, 73–94. Florence: Edizioni ETS.
Larrañaga, Pilar, Jeanine Treffers-Daller, Françoise Tidball and Mari-Carmen Gil Ortega
  2011   L1 transfer in the acquisition of manner and path in Spanish by native speakers of English. *International Journal of Bilingualism* 16(1): 117–138.
Levinson, Stephen C.
  2003   *Space in Language and Cognition*. Cambridge: Cambridge University Press.
Lucy, John and Susan Gaskins
  2003   Interaction of language type and referent type in the development of nonverbal classification preferences. In: D. Gentner and S. Goldin- Meadow (eds.), *Language in Mind: Advances in the Study of Language and Thought*, 465–492. Cambridge: MIT Press.
Maguire, Mandy J., Kathy Hirsh-Pasek, Roberta M. Golinkoff, Mutsumi Imai, Etsuko Haryu, Sandra Vengas, Hiroyuki. Okada, Rachel Pulverman and Brenda Sanchez-Davis
  2010   A developmental shift from similar to language specific strategies in verb acquisition: A comparison of English, Spanish, and Japanese. *Cognition* 114(3): 299–319.
Malt, Barbara C., Steven A. Sloman and Silvia P. Gennari
  2003   Speaking versus thinking about objects and actions. In: D. Gentner and S. Goldin-Meadow (eds.), *Language in Mind*, 81–111. Cambridge: MIT Press.
Mandler, Jean M.
  2004   *The Foundations of Mind: Origins of Conceptual Thought*. New York: Oxford University Press.
Matlock, Teenie, and Till Bergmann
  this volume   26. Fictive motion. Berlin/Boston: De Gruyter Mouton.
Matsumoto, Yo
  2003   Typologies of lexicalization patterns and event integration: Clarifications and reformulations. In: S. Chiba et al. (eds.), *Empirical and Theoretical Investigations into Language: A Festschrift for Masaru Kajita*, 403–418. Tokyo: Kaitakusha.
McNeill, David
  1992   *Hand and Mind*. Chicago: University of Chicago Press.
McNeill, David
  2000   Analogic/analytic representations and cross-linguistic differences in thinking for speaking. *Cognitive Linguistics* 11: 43–60.
McNeill, David
  2005   *Gesture and Thought*. Chicago: University of Chicago Press.
Mendoza-Denton, Rodolfo
  2010   Are we born racist? Inside the science of stigma, prejudice and intergroup relations. (http://www.psychologytoday.com/blog/are-we-born-racist/201012/linguistic-forensics)
Miller, George A. and Philip N. Johnson-Laird
  1976   *Language and Perception*. Cambridge: Belknap Press of Harvard University Press.
Narasimham, Bhuvana
  2003   Motion events and the lexicon: a case study of Hindi. *Lingua* 113: 123–160.
Negueruela, Eduardo, James P. Lantolf, Stefanie R. Jordan and Jaime Gelabert
  2004   The "private function" of gesture in second language speaking activity: A study of motion verbs and gesturing in English and Spanish. *International Journal of Applied Linguistics* 14(1): 113–147.

Noonan, Michael
   2003   Motion events in Chantyal. In: E. Shay and U. Seibert (eds.), *Motion, Direction and Location in Languages − In Honor of Zygmunt Frajzyngier*, 211−234. Amsterdam: John Benjamins.

Papafragou, Anna, Christine Massey and Lila Gleitman
   2002   Shake, rattle, 'n' roll: The representation of motion in language and cognition. *Cognition* 84(2): 189−219.

Porquier, Rémy
   2001   'Il m'a sauté dessus', 'je lui ai couru après': un cas de postposition en français. *Journal of French Language Studies* 11: 123−134.

Pourcel, Stephanie and Anetta Kopecka
   2005   Motion expression in French: Typological diversity. *Durham and Newcastle Working Papers in Linguistics* 11: 139−153.

Pruden, Shannon M., Kathy Hirsh-Pasek, Mandy J. Maguire and Meredith A. Meyer
   2004   Foundations of verb learning: Infants form categories of path and manner in motion events. In: A. Brugos, L. Micciulla, and C. E. Smith (eds.), *Proceedings of the 28th Annual Boston University Conference on Language Development*, 461−472. Somerville: Cascadilla Press.

Pulverman, Rachel, Jennifer L. Sootsman, Roberta M. Golinkoff and Kathy Hirsh-Pasek
   2004   The role of lexical knowledge in nonlinguistic event processing: English-speaking infants' attention to manner and path. In: A. Brugos, L. Micciulla, and C. E. Smith (eds.), *Proceedings of the 28th Annual Boston University Conference on Language Development*, 662−673. Somerville: Cascadilla Press.

Pulverman, Rachel, Roberta M. Golinkoff, Kathy Hirsh-Pasek and Jennifer Sootsman Buresh
   2008   Infants discriminate manners and paths in non-linguistic dynamic events. *Cognition* 108: 825−830.

Özçalışkan, Şeyda
   2004   Encoding the manner, path, ground components of a metaphorical motion event. *Annual Review of Cognitive Linguistics* 2: 73−102.

Özçalışkan, Şeyda
   2005   Metaphor meets typology: Ways of moving metaphorically in English and Turkish. *Cognitive Linguistics* 16(1): 207−246.

Özyürek, Aslı, Sotaro Kita, and Shanley Allen
   2001   *Tomato Man* movies: Stimulus kit designed to elicit manner, path and causal constructions in motion events with regard to speech and gestures [Videotape]. Nijmegen: Max Planck Institute for Psycholinguistics.

Özyürek, Aslı, Sotaro Kita, Shanley Allen, Reyhan Furman and Amanda Brown
   2005   How does linguistic framing of events influence co-speech gestures? Insights from cross-linguistic variations and similarities. *Gesture* 5: 215−237.

Pavlenko, Aneta (eds.)
   2011   *Thinking and Speaking in Two Languages.* Bristol: Multilingual Matters.

Ragnarsdóttir, Hrafnhildur and Sven Strömqvist
   2004   Time, space, and manner in Swedish and Icelandic narrative construction in two closely related languages. In: S. Strömqvist and L. Verhoeven (eds.), *Relating Events in Narrative: Typological and Contextual Perspectives*, 113−141. Mahwah: Lawrence Erlbaum.

Regier, Terry and Paul Kay
   2009   Language, thought, and colour: Whorf was half right. *Trends in Cognitive Sciences* 13: 439−446.

Robinson, Peter and Nick C. Ellis (eds.)
   2008   *A Handbook of Cognitive Linguistics and Second Language Acquisition.* London: Routledge.

Schaefer, Ronald P.
  2001   Ideophonic adverbs and manner gaps in Emai. In: F. K. Erhard Voeltz and C. Kilian-Hatz (eds.), *Ideophones*, 339–354. Amsterdam/Philadelphia: John Benjamins.
Schwarze, Christoph
  1985   Uscire e andare fuori: struttura sintattica e semantica lessicale. In: A. Franchi De Bellis and L. M. Savoia (eds.), *Sintassi e morfologia della lingua italiana d'uso. Teoria ed applicazioni descrittive. SLI XXIV*, 355–371. Rome: Bulzoni.
Sinha, Chris and Tania Kuteva
  1995   Distributed spatial semantics. *Nordic Journal of Linguistics* 18: 167–199.
Slobin, Dan I.
  1991   Learning to think for speaking: Native language, cognition and rhetorical style. *Pragmatics* 1: 7–26.
Slobin, Dan I.
  1996   Two ways to travel: verbs of motion in English and Spanish. In: M. Shibatani and S. A. Thompson (eds.), *Grammatical Constructions: Their Form and Meaning*, 195–220. Oxford: Clarendon Press.
Slobin, Dan I.
  2004   The many ways to search for a frog: Linguistic typology and the expression of motion events. In: S. Strömqvist and L. Verhoeven (eds.), *Relating Events in Narrative. Typological and Contextual Perspectives*, 219–257. Mahwah: Lawrence Erlbaum.
Slobin, Dan I.
  2005   Relating narrative events in translation. In: D. D. Ravid and H. Bat-Zeev Shyldkrot (eds.), *Perspectives on Language and Language Development: Essays in Honor of Ruth A. Berman*, 115–129. Dordrecht: Kluwer.
Slobin, Dan I.
  2006   What makes manner of motion salient? Explorations in linguistic typology, discourse, and cognition. In: M. Hickmann and S. Robert (eds.), *Space in Languages: Linguistic Systems and Cognitive Categories*, 59–81. Philadelphia: John Benjamins.
Slobin, Dan I.
  2008   Typology and usage: Explorations of motion events across languages. Ms. University of California Berkeley.
Slobin, Dan I. and Nini Hoiting
  1994   Reference to movement in spoken and signed languages: Typological considerations. *Proceedings of the Twentieth Annual Meeting of the Berkeley Linguistics Society*, 487–503.
Slotova, Natalya
  2008   From satellite-framed Latin to verb-framed Romance. Late Latin as an intermediary stage. In: R. Wright (ed.), *Latin Vulgaire – Latin Tardif* VIII. *Actes du VIIIe Colloque International sur le Latin Vulgaire et Tardif*, 253–262. Zürich/New York: Olms-Weidmann.
Snell-Hornby, Mary
  1983   *Verb-Descriptivity in German and English: A Contrastive Study in Semantic Fields.* Heidelberg: Carl Winter Universitätsverlag.
Soroli, Eva
  2012   Variation in spatial language and cognition: Exploring visuo-spatial thinking and speaking cross-linguistically. *Cognitive Processing* 13: 333–337.
Stam, Gale
  2006   Thinking for speaking about motion: L1 and L2 speech and gesture. *International Review of Applied Linguistics* 44: 143–169.
Strömqvist, Sven and Ludo Verhoeven
  2004   *Relating Events in Narrative: Typological and Contextual Perspectives.* Mahwah: Lawrence Erlbaum.

Sugiyama, Yukiko
   2005   Not all verb-framed languages are created equal: The case of Japanese. *Proceedings of the Thirty-First Annual Meeting of the Berkeley Linguistics Society*, 299–310.
Talmy, Leonard
   1985   Lexicalization patterns: semantic structure in lexical form. In: T. Shopen (ed.), *Language Typology and Syntactic Description,* Vol. 3: *Grammatical Categories and the Lexicon*, 36–149. Cambridge: Cambridge University Press.
Talmy, Leonard
   1991   Path to realization: a typology of event conflation. *Proceedings of the Seventeenth Annual Meeting of the Berkeley Linguistics Society*, 480–520.
Talmy, Leonard
   2000   *Toward a Cognitive Semantics* (Vol. 2). Cambridge: MIT Press.
Trueswell, John and Anna Papafragou
   2010   Perceiving and remembering events cross-linguistically: Evidence from dual-task paradigms. *Journal of Memory and Language* 63: 64–82.
Vandeloise, Claude
   1986   *L'Espace en Français: Sémantique des Prépositions Spatiales*. Paris: Le Seuil.
Verkerk, Annemarie
   2014   Diachronic change in Indo-European motion event encoding. *Journal of Historical Linguistics* 4(1): 40–83.
Vinay, Jean Paul and Jean Darbelnet
   1958   *Stylistique Comparée du Français et de l'Anglais: Méthode de Traduction*. Paris: Didier.
Vulcanova, Mila and Emile Van der Zee
   2013   *Motion Encoding in Language and Space*. Oxford: Oxford University Press.
Wälchli, Bernhard
   2001   A typology of displacement (with special reference to Latvian). *Sprachtypologie und Universalienforschung* 54: 298–323.

Luna Filipović, East Anglia (United Kingdom)
Iraide Ibarretxe-Antuñano, Zaragoza (Spain)

26. Fictive motion

1. Introduction
2. Fictive motion: Where it started
3. Fictive motion: Where is has been lately
4. Fictive motion: Where it is going
5. Conclusion
6. References

1. Introduction

After returning from a road trip down the California coast, a friend asks which part of the drive was your favorite. You think about it for a moment and reply, "Santa Barbara."

In formulating your response, you mentally simulate portions of the drive down Highway 1. "Leaving" San Francisco, you "go" south, and "pass" through various coastal communities until you "get to" Los Angeles.[1] Before you embarked on your journey, you read a description of the route you would take:

> *Highway 1 runs along the coastline. It goes through Half Moon Bay, Santa Cruz, Monterey, and Carmel, and then enters the Big Sur region. Near Morro Bay, it ambles past the site of a prehistoric Chumash settlement and later it races past the Madonna Inn near San Luis Obispo. After leaving Santa Barbara, it crosses into Ventura County, and then it approaches Los Angeles.*

Sentences like these express no information about actual motion, yet they have been argued to include a fleeting, implied sense of motion. They fall under *fictive motion*, a broad conceptual category first characterized by Leonard Talmy (see Talmy 1983, 1996, 2000). The semantics of fictive motion has received much attention over the years, including theoretical and comparative work as well as experimental semantics work.

This chapter provides an overview of cognitive linguistics research on fictive motion. It starts with early foundational work before moving to recent experimental semantics work and ending with future directions.

2. Fictive motion: Where it started

People often use fictive motion expressions, such as *Highway 1 goes through Half Moon Bay* and *A scar runs down his back*. These expressions describe where objects are, and how they are configured in physical space. Fictive motion expressions occur in many spoken languages, including English (Talmy 1996), Spanish (Rojo and Valenzuela 2003), Hindi (Mishra and Singh 2010), Japanese (Matsumoto 1996a), Thai (Takahashi 2000), Ancient Hebrew (Dewey 2011), Finnish (Huumo 1999, 2005), as well as Serbian (Stosic and Sarda 2009). They are also common in signed languages (Liddell 2003).

Fictive motion sentences have interesting semantic properties that vary according to how the figure, or trajector (hereafter, TR), is conceptualized (Matlock 2004a; Talmy 2000). The TR in these sentences is stationary, for instance, *Highway 1* in *Highway 1 runs along the coastline*. The TR can be linearly extended in various directions, including vertically, as in *The ladder goes up the side of the building*, or horizontally, as in *The freeway runs along the edge of the city*. It can be large or small, as in *The mountain range goes from Mexico to Canada* and *The molecule runs along the hydrocarbon chain that links two benzene rings*. In some cases, the TR is a traversable path, as in *The highway races through the countryside* and *The trail climbs 1,000 meters*, and in others, a relatively long entity that is not ordinarily traversed, as in *The fence runs along the coastline* and *A cable runs underground*. In still other cases, the TR is neither linear nor

---

[1] Your mental journey is enabled by your capacity to create, update, and move through imagined spaces. Psychologists have shown that people mentally move through spatial mental models they create from memory and linguistic input (Bower and Morrow 1990; Franklin and Tversky 1990; Morrow et al. 1989; Tversky 1993; Zwaan and Radvansky 1998).

long, but, rather, it becomes lengthened through dynamic construal, as in *A table runs along the wall*, and *The pond runs along the hillside*.

Fictive motion sentences[2] are also inherently imperfective in that they emphasize the long term or permanent nature of a given situation or state (see Langacker 1987, Matlock 2010). For example, with *Highway 1 runs along the coastline*, it is assumed the highway will retain its position and structural integrity indefinitely. Because of their imperfective character, fictive motion sentences often avoid progressive forms. An exception is when new information about the current condition of the TR Is provided, as in *The highway is (now) running along the coastline*. Another exception is when the progressive is used to emphasize the temporary existence of a TR, as in *A heat rash is running down his leg*. And yet another exception is when the progressive is used to indicate that the conceptualizer is changing position. For instance, imagine you are driving down the road and telling your friend what you are observing moment to moment: *I'm on a road that was going down a long hill, and it's now meandering north* (see Langacker 2005 for discussion of perfective and imperfective versions of fictive motion).

In his pioneering work on fictive motion, cognitive linguist Leonard Talmy provided a rich taxonomy of fictive motion types, including *co-extension path* fictive motion, the focus of this chapter.[3] He claimed that, despite their static disposition, fictive motion expressions include schematic elements of actual motion. For instance, both *The highway runs along the coastline* and *The athlete runs along the coastline* include physical space and a path (or linear TR) (see Talmy 1975, 1983, 1996). Other cognitive linguists made similar claims, including Ronald Langacker and Yo Matsumoto, who focused on the subjective nature of fictive motion (Langacker 1986, 1987; Matsumoto 1996a, 1996b). Matsumoto also observed interesting differences between Japanese and English. He noted that English fictive motion expressions often have non-traversable TRs (e.g., *The fence goes along the coastline*), but Japanese fictive motion expressions rarely do (see Matsumoto 1996a).[4, 5] Other cognitive linguists, especially George Lakoff and Mark Turner, characterized fictive motion as a type of conceptual metaphor, in particular, FORM IS MOTION (see Lakoff and Turner 1989 for discussion).

Together, this work advanced our knowledge of the fictive motion. It was not until the 21st Century, however, that behavioral studies began testing claims about processing, especially whether they do indeed involve a fleeting sense of motion. Below is a summary of some of behavioral work on fictive motion.

3. Fictive motion: Where it has been lately

In recent years, cognitive linguists have begun using psychological methods to explore fictive motion processing. Much of this research has examined English fictive motion,

---

[2] The terms "fictive motion expression" and "fictive motion sentence" are used interchangeably.
[3] See Talmy (2000) for discussion of types of fictive motion, including co-extension path fictive motion, which is also called *linear path* extension fictive motion (see Talmy 1996).
[4] Ronald Langacker and Yo Matsumoto have referred to the type of fictive motion we are discussing here as "abstract motion" and "subjective motion", respectively (Langacker 1986; Matsumoto 1996a). Langacker has also discussed fictive motion in the context of virtual motion (Langacker 2000, 2005).
[5] Amagawa (1997) also discussed differences between English and Japanese fictive motion, focusing on the motion verb *run* and its counterpart *hashiru*.

but other languages are starting to be explored. This constellation of work, beginning with Matlock (2001, 2004b), seeks answers to the following questions: Does fictive motion include simulated motion, and if so, how is this realized? How does fictive motion vary under different conditions? Is it similar to actual motion? Methods used include surveys, drawing tasks, narrative understanding tasks, and eye movement tasks.

3.1. Narrative understanding tasks

The experiments reported in Matlock (2004b) explored fictive motion comprehension. Participants, university undergraduates with reported native or near native proficiency, were asked to read passages about motion through a spatial environment (e.g., a man driving through a desert), and then to quickly decide ("yes" or "no" response) whether a fictive motion target sentence (e.g., Road 49 crosses the desert) was related to what they had read. This required people to think about the motion they read about, and to re-experience how it unfolded along a path. Responses were measured in milliseconds and analyzed across participants and items.

In one experiment, people read passages that differed on velocity of travel. In some passages, the protagonist moved slowly, and in others, fast (e.g., driving 25 versus 100 miles per hour across a desert). People read a slow or fast travel passage, and decided whether a subsequent fictive motion sentence was related. In brief, the time it took people to make the decision about the target sentence varied according to travel velocity. On average people were quicker to make decisions about fictive motion target sentences after reading about fast travel than slow travel. In another experiment in Matlock (2004b), people read passages that differed on whether protagonists traveled short or long distances (e.g., 10 versus 100 miles), and then decided whether fictive motion target sentences were related. People made quicker decisions after reading about short distance travel than long distance travel on average. In yet another experiment, people read about travel through cluttered or uncluttered terrains (e.g., bumpy versus smooth). Their responses to fictive motion target sentences were quicker after reading about terrains that were uncluttered than those that were cluttered.

Together, the experiments in Matlock (2004b) showed that people were quicker to process fictive motion sentences in the context of travel with short distances (versus long), fast travel velocity (versus slow), and uncluttered terrains (versus cluttered). Control studies were also conducted using the same passages and target sentences that lacked fictive motion, such as *Road 49 is in the desert*, and no reliable processing differences emerged. Based on these results, it was concluded that fictive motion processing included mentally simulated motion.

3.2. Drawing studies

Drawing studies have also examined the conceptual structure of fictive motion sentences. In one experiment in Matlock (2006), people produced simple line drawings to depict their understanding of sentences that did or did not include fictive motion, for instance,

The highway runs along the coast and *The highway is next to the coast*. In this experiment, all TRs were inherently long, traversable paths, such as highways, and bike paths. In general, people drew relatively longer TRs in depictions of fictive motion sentences than in depictions of non-fictive motion sentences. In a second drawing experiment in Matlock (2006), people drew pictures of sentences that included TRs that could be construed as either short or long, such as tattoos, as in *The tattoo runs along his spine*, or *The tattoo is next to his spine*. None of these TRs were traversable. Once again, people drew relatively longer TRs in depictions of sentences that included fictive motion than in depictions of sentences that did not. The results were in line with the idea that fictive motion processing involves mentally simulated motion.

3.3. Eye movement studies

In Matlock and Richardson (2004), participants viewed scenes on a computer screen while listening to descriptions of those scenes. Each scene was a line drawing with both a vertical and a horizontal path or object (e.g., a line of trees running vertically, and a road running horizontally). Some sentences included fictive motion, and others did not, for instance, *The cord runs along the wall* and *The cord is on the wall*. While people viewed pictures and listened to sentences, their eye movements were tracked and recorded by an eye-tracking camera.[6] This approach allowed the researchers to pinpoint where and how people directed their visual attention across while processing linguistic information. The results showed that people spent more time viewing the region associated with the relevant path or linear object while listening to sentences with fictive motion. For example, they spent more time looking at the region of the scene that displayed a cord (than other parts of the scene) while listening to *The cord runs along the wall* than they did while listening to *The cord is on the wall*.

A follow-up study by Richardson and Matlock (2007) used similar visual and verbal stimuli. People listened to a sentence that did or did not include fictive motion, such as *The road runs through the valley* or *The road is in the valley*, after listening to a one-sentence terrain description, such as *The valley is covered with dust* or *The valley is covered with ruts*. In each case, the terrain description contained information that implied easy or difficult movement (e.g., *dust* versus *ruts*). Next, they viewed a scene (e.g., a valley). In this experiment, terrain information differentially influenced eye movement patterns with sentences with fictive motion, but not sentences without fictive motion. More visual attention was directed to paths or linear objects (e.g., roads) after listening to information about difficult terrains (e.g., ruts in a valley) than after listening to information about easy terrains (e.g., dust in a valley).

These eye-tracking studies provided evidence to support the hypothesis that fictive motion includes mentally simulated motion. Especially compelling was the second ex-

---

[6] Eye tracking allows researchers to measure where and when eye fixations occur in the time course of processing visual and linguistic information. For seminal research and comprehensive background, see Tanenhaus and Spivey-Knowlton (1996); Henderson and Ferreira (2004); Richardson and Dale (2005); and Richardson et al. (2007).

periment, where terrain information differentially influenced visual attention to the TR with fictive motion sentences only. These findings resonate to how we experience motion in the world; terrain affects how quickly and fluidly we move.

3.4. Time and motion surveys

Some fictive motion research has adapted experimental methods designed to examine the conceptual link between time and space. For decades, linguists and psychologists have argued that temporal reasoning is grounded in everyday thought about space (see, for instance, Clark 1973; Evans 2004, this volume; Lakoff and Johnson 1980; Radden 2011). A series of experiments in Boroditsky and Ramscar (2002) investigated how spatial thinking would influence temporal reasoning (see also McGlone and Harding 1998). People in one experiment were primed to imagine themselves moving toward a physical object, or about a physical object moving toward them, right before answering this question: *Next Wednesday's meeting has been moved forward two days. What day is the meeting now that it has been rescheduled?* A Monday response to this query suggests "moving" the meeting two days further into the past (relative to Wednesday), and a Friday response suggests "moving" two days further into the future. The results showed that the way people conceptualized motion influenced how they responded to the "move-forward" question. They were more likely to provide a Friday response after imagining themselves moving toward an object, and more likely to provide a Monday response after imagining the object moving toward them (see related work and alternative explanations in Núñez et al. 2006; Teuscher et al. 2008; Moore 2006).

Matlock et al. (2005) followed up on this work, and examined whether fictive motion would have a similar effect on temporal reasoning. In one experiment, people read a sentence that did or did not include fictive motion, such as *The bike path runs alongside the creek* or *The bike path is next to the creek*, and drew a picture to represent their understanding of that sentence. Next they answered the "move forward" time question used in Boroditsky and Ramscar (2002), *Next Wednesday's meeting has been moved forward two days. What day is the meeting now that it has been rescheduled?* The results of Matlock et al. (2005) showed that people who had read and depicted a sentence with fictive motion were more likely to provide a Friday response than a Monday response, and people who had read and depicted a sentence with no fictive motion, were no more likely to provide a Friday response than a Monday response. In addition, people were more likely to include motion elements (e.g., people jogging or riding bikes) in fictive motion depictions than in non-fictive motion depictions (see Matlock et al. 2004).

A second experiment in Matlock et al. (2005) further explored fictive motion and temporal reasoning. It investigated how people would conceptualize statements that implied a series of discrete scan points (i.e., a line of trees). Of interest was how fictive motion with increasingly more scan points (i.e., more and more trees along a driveway) would influence how people would respond to the subsequent "move forward" time question. People read about various numbers of trees along a driveway, specifically, *Four pine trees run along the edge of the driveway, Eight pine trees run along the edge of the driveway, Twenty pine trees run along the edge of the driveway,* or *Over eighty pine trees run along the edge of the driveway.* Next, they drew a picture to represent their understanding of the sentence, and then answered the "move forward" time question. People were more likely to give a Friday response than a Monday response overall, but the proportion of Friday responses varied according to number of pine trees. People were more likely to provide a Friday response with 8 pine trees and 20 pine trees, but not with 4 pine trees or over 80 pine trees. In brief, a "just right" number (i.e., easy to conceptualize as a path) primed people to "move" through time toward Friday. Four trees did not show the same effect because there were not enough trees to scan as a path. Over 80 trees meant too many trees to conceptualize in a linear fashion.[7]

A third experiment by Matlock et al. (2005) investigated direction. People read a fictive motion sentence that implied direction toward or away from the body: *The road goes all the way to New York* or *The road comes all the way from New York*. Next, they drew a picture and answered the "move forward" time question. The results revealed more Friday responses with the *goes to* fictive motion sentences, but more Monday responses with *comes from* fictive motion sentences, suggesting that fictive motion direction influenced temporal construal.

Similar effects were obtained in Matlock et al. (2011) in related research on the metaphorical construal of number lines.[8] That work explored the mental connection between number sequences (e.g., *5, 6, 7; 7, 6, 5*) and time. Numerical reasoning is known to be grounded in spatial reasoning, including thought about direction (Dehaene 1997; Lakoff and Núñez 2000). From this, it follows that reasoning about numbers would influence reasoning about time. In one experiment, before answering the "move forward" question, some people were given the numbers 5 and 17 with 11 blanks between, and asked to fill in the blanks. Others were given 17 and 5 with 11 blanks between and asked to fill in the numbers. The logic was that filling in the blanks in canonical counting direction would encourage people to take an ego-moving perspective and move forward through time toward a Friday response, and that counting backwards would not. People were more likely to provide a Friday response with 5 to 17, but not more likely to do so after filling in the blanks from 17 to 5. A second experiment with sequences of letters (e.g., *G, H, I* ... and *J, I, H* ...) led to similar results. These two studies showed that fictive motion need not involve physical space. Simply thinking about the direction of abstract entities in a point by point manner affected temporal reasoning.

Research on how fictive motion would influence time was expanded to include another type of fictive motion, *line of sight paths*, in Matlock (2010). Line of sight paths can use sensory and non-sensory verbs to create a sense of fictively moving, for example, *I slowly looked away from the window* or *I slowly turned my camera towards the door* (Talmy 2000). In the experiment, visual path length was modified in the following sentences: *I can see Fred across the table*, *I can see Fred across the room*, or *I can see Fred across the field* corresponding to short, medium, and long visual paths respectively. People read one of these sentences before answering the "move forward" question. The results revealed a greater likelihood of Friday responses with longer and longer visual

---

[7] Ramscar et al. (2010) did a follow-up study that omitted the drawing task and increased the numbers of scan points in their verbal stimuli, specifically, 10, 11, 12, 19, and 100 pine trees that ran along a driveway. The results were consistent overall with those of Matlock et al. (2005).

[8] Matlock et al. (2011) used the term "abstract motion", but the phenomena are essentially the same.

paths. The results provided further evidence to support the idea that visual paths are conceptually similar to motion paths (see Slobin 2008).

Together, this work contributes behavioral evidence to support the idea that our everyday understanding of language, including non-literal language, is grounded in our embodied experience (Barsalou 1999, 2008; Gibbs 2006; Glenberg 1999, 2010; Pecher and Zwaan 2005; Zwaan et al. 2004). We simulate motion along a path, linear object, or series of entities, including trees, numbers, or letters, and it has consequences for how we think about time in a way that is not unlike thought about actual motion through physical space. This body of work also provides evidence to support the idea that language involves dynamic construal (see Langacker, this volume).

4. Fictive motion: Where it is going

Many exciting theories about how people mentally "move" through spatial environments have been proposed over the years. Some researchers have argued that motion simulation is similar to engaging in or viewing actual motion (see Barsalou 1999, 2008; Gallese and Lakoff 2005; Gibbs 2006; Glenberg 1999). Such mental simulation is involved in the use and understanding of motion language, including figurative motion language (Bergen 2012; Feldman 2008; Gibbs and Matlock 2008; Matlock 2010; Narayanan 1997), such as discourse about political campaign races (Matlock 2012), romantic relationships (Gibbs 2012), and web use (Maglio and Matlock 1999; Matlock et al. 2014).

Many questions about fictive motion remain, including the following. How does the purported fleeting sense of motion unfold in real time? When do people mentally scan along the TR versus move along it, and is there any difference? Both involve motion. When and how do people extend a TR that is not necessarily long, for instance, while interpreting sentences such as *A table runs along the back wall* or *A scar goes down his back*? What neurological patterns emerge in processing fictive motion sentences, and to what extent do these patterns resemble those involved in processing perceiving or doing actual motion? Careful work is needed to get at processing details, and to clarify how simulation works in different contexts. It is also important to delve more deeply into the subjectivity of fictive motion. Insightful work by Jordan Zlatev and colleagues is beginning to explore this (see Blomberg and Zlatev 2014).

Neuroscientists have begun to study fictive motion processing. They have discovered that brain areas associated with processing actual motion are also activated when viewing scenes that merely suggest motion. In Kourtzi and Kanwisher (2000), people viewed static images that implied motion, for instance, a picture of a man about to hurl a discus. Their results showed that areas of the brain associated with motion perception were activated even though no actual motion was being perceived (see also Kourtzi 2004; Winawer et al. 2007). Such research provides strong evidence that we are biased to conceptualize or infer motion even at the mere suggestion of movement.

Saygin et al. (2010) used fMRI (functional magnetic resonance imaging) to investigate patterns of brain activation in fictive motion processing. People in their study were placed in the fMRI scanner and presented with three types of verbal stimuli: sentences with actual motion, such as *I drove from Modesto to Fresno*; sentences with no motion, such as *Modesto and Fresno are in California*; and sentences with fictive motion, such as *The highway runs from Modesto to Fresno*. The results showed that actual motion sentences activated brain areas associated with the processing of visual motion much more than did no-motion sentences did, and that fictive motion sentences elicited more activation than no-motion sentences (but less than actual motion sentences). These results suggested that fictive motion includes mentally simulated motion that mirrors actual motion. Similar results were obtained by Wallentin et al. (2005) in a study on the neurolinguistic processing of Danish fictive motion sentences. More work in this area is needed to gain a better understanding the dynamics of fictive motion processing.

Much research on fictive motion has focused on coextension path fictive motion. Other types include *access paths* (*The bakery is across the street from the bank*), in which fictive motion is expressed by path prepositions, and *demonstrative paths* (*The arrow on the signpost pointed towards the town*), in which the TR creates a line of sight path (see also Takahashi 2001). These fictive motion constructions do not use motion verbs, so the implicit sense of motion may be less salient than fictive motion constructions that do include motion verbs, but we will not know until this is empirically tested. Closer examination of a wide range of fictive motion sentences may lead to new insights about how spatial language is processed in general. For example, *The road leads to the north* may be processed quite differently from *The road goes to the north*.

It could be informative to apply some of the behavioral methods discussed in this chapter to linguistic constructions that have conceptual overlap with fictive motion, for example, instances of *fictive change* (Sweetser 1997), as in *His girlfriend gets taller every year* and *The windows keep getting cleaner as you walk towards the Bay*. This type of construction might elicit a similar fictive motion effect, with mental scanning proceeding from one window to another, or from one height to another. It might also be worthwhile to extend fictive motion behavioral research to cognitive linguistic work on other forms of spatial language associated with stasis, for instance, verbs of standing, sitting, and lying (see Newman 2002).

Though much behavioral work on fictive motion has focused on English, some experiments have examined other languages, including Spanish (Rojo and Valenzuela 2003), Hindi (Mishra and Singh 2010), and Danish (Wallentin et al. 2005). Large-scale cross-linguistic behavioral study on fictive motion processing would yield new insights about which aspects of fictive motion generalize, and provide valuable information about figurative language. Recent, careful cross-linguistic work has used behavioral methods to compare the interpretation of motion-emotion metaphors in Thai, Bulgarian, English, and Swedish (Zlatev et al. 2012). This approach could inform the design of future experiments that compare fictive motion processing across languages.

In this same vein, more behavioral work could examine manner of motion (see Filipovic and Ibarretxe's chapter on motion in this volume) in figurative language understanding. In English, manner verbs are not uncommon in fictive motion sentences that emphasize unusual or special properties of the TR, as seen in *The hiking trail zigzags up the side of the mountain* and *A bike path cruises through the park*. In some languages, such as English, manner is encoded in the motion verb itself. In other languages, including Spanish, manner is encoded with the help of additional lexical items. For example, to report that a boat rapidly entered a cave, an English speaker could use the manner verb *dart*, as in *The boat darted into the cave*. The verb *dart* would simultaneously express translational motion and speed. In contrast, a Spanish speaker could describe the situation by using a motion verb that conveys no speed along with an adjunct that does convey speed, as in *El barco entró en la cueva como una flecha*, literally *The boat entered the cave like an arrow*. So far, only one experiment (Matlock 2006) has explored people's conceptions of manner in fictive motion sentences. In a drawing study, people drew longer, straighter, and thinner lines while depicting fictive motion paths described with fast manner verbs (e.g., *race*) than those with slow manner verbs (e.g., *crawl*). Studying how manner is realized in various spatial descriptions across languages could shed some light on the issue of linguistic relativity. It is common, for instance, for speakers of Greek and Spanish to ignore or downplay manner information in language, at least in literal motion sentences (see Papafragou et al. 2002). What impact might this have on how they view linearly extended layouts?

It would be fruitful to look closely at grammatical aspect in processing fictive motion language. As mentioned earlier in this chapter, fictive motion has an imperfective quality, and therefore, it often appears without imperfective aspect. Studying when and how fictive motion interacts with progressive and non-progressive forms could tell us more about the role of aspect in language processing, especially in spatial descriptions and in figurative language (e.g., *The highway runs along the coastline*, *The highway is running along the coastline*). Some psychological work has begun to explore the role of aspect in language understanding and reasoning. Choice of aspect is known, for instance, to affect the inferences people make about magnitude of situations and states, including whether a political candidate seems suitable for office (Fausey and Matlock 2011).

Research on fictive motion in natural discourse would fill an important gap. It would tell us more about fictive motion use. Analyses of gestures in natural discourse, especially fictive motion depictions in face-to-face interactions, could also be informative. Gestures often occur in conversations about spatial configurations, for instance, route descriptions (see Bergmann and Matlock 2014). It would also be useful to investigate when and how children start producing fictive motion sentences in natural speech. We know that spatial relations play an important role in linguistic development (see Mandler 2012), but we do not know what role fictive motion plays.

Research on the explanatory power of fictive motion would be informative for learning abstract scientific concepts. Mathematics is rife with fictive motion (Lakoff and Núñez 2000; Núñez 2008). When discussing limits in calculus, for instance, people often use fictive motion expressions that imply motion and a limit, as in *The sum approaches 7 as n goes to infinity*. According to Núñez (2006), fictive motion (and other figurative language) facilitates the understanding of mathematical concepts (see also Keane 2007). Manual gestures also often occur while people are discussing mathematics, sometimes with fictive motion descriptions. In illustrating a rapidly increasing function, for instance, a person makes a quick, rightward manual gesture (Marghetis and Núñez 2013; Wittmann et al. 2012). Manual gestures are also useful for learning abstract geological concepts, such as relative sea level (see Herrera and Riggs 2013). Metaphorical motion language, including fictive motion language, is also common in learning physics (see Pulaczewska 1999). Much work has yet to be done on when and how fictive motion could be used to enhance learning abstract scientific material.

Finally, motion is a productive source domain in many basic, conceptual metaphors in human languages, such as TIME IS MOTION (Clark 1973; Radden 1996), LIFE IS A JOURNEY (Lakoff and Johnson 1980), RELATIONSHIPS ARE JOURNEYS (Gibbs 2012), and POLITICAL CAMPAIGNS ARE RACES (Matlock 2012), all of which are part of EVENT STRUC-

TURE (see Lakoff and Johnson 1999). Research on the dynamics of processing non-literal motion language, including how it interacts with grammatical systems, such as aspect, how it is used in everyday conversation, how it interacts with gesture, and how it varies across languages and situations, will help cognitive linguists come to a better understanding how figurative language and more generally, spatial language is processed. Until then, what we have learned about fictive motion research over the past 30 years will continue to take us in the right direction in the years to come.

5. Conclusion

This chapter reviewed cognitive linguistics research on fictive motion, including early theoretical and behavioral work. In sum, it appears that early claims about fictive motion processing were indeed correct: Fictive motion does involve a fleeting sense of motion. Like real motion, it can be modulated by environmental factors, such as how cluttered or uncluttered a terrain is. Like real motion, fictive motion also has magnitude and direction, and can thus influence how people metaphorically reason about time. More generally, the behavioral studies reported here provide good evidence to support claims that language representation and use is grounded in our embodied experience with motion in the physical world.

6. References

Amagawa, Toyoko
   1997   Subjective motion in English and Japanese: A case study of *run* and *hashiru*. *Tsukuba English Studies* 16: 33–50.
Barsalou, Lawrence W.
   1999   Perceptual symbol systems. *Behavioral and Brain Sciences* 22: 577–660.
Barsalou, Lawrence W.
   2008   Grounded cognition. *Annual Review of Psychology* 59: 617–645.
Bergmann, Till and Teenie Matlock
   2014   Fictive motion and gestures: Real discourse from the TV news archive. Presented at the 6th Annual Conference of the International Society for Gesture Studies. La Jolla, USA.
Bergen, Benjamin K.
   2012   *Louder Than Words: The New Science of How the Mind Makes Meaning*. New York: Basic Books.
Blomberg, Johan and Jordan Zlatev
   2014   Actual and non-actual motion: Why experientialist semantics needs phenomenology (and vice versa). *Phenomenology and the Cognitive Sciences* 13(3): 395–418.
Boroditsky, Lera and Michael Ramscar
   2002   The roles of body and mind in abstract thought. *Psychological Science* 13: 185–188.
Bower, Gordon H. and Daniel G. Morrow
   1990   Mental models in narrative comprehension. *Science* 247: 44–48.
Clark, Herbert H.
   1973   Space, time, semantics, and the child. In: T. E. Moore (ed.), *Cognitive Development and the Acquisition of Language*, 2–63. New York: Academic Press.

Dehaene, Stanislaus
   1997   *The Number Sense: How the Mind Creates Mathematics.* New York: Oxford University Press.

Dewey, Ryan
   2011   Fictive Motion in Ancient Hebrew Descriptions of Geographical Boundaries. Working Paper: Case Western Reserve University.

Evans, Vyvyan
   2004   *The Structure of Time: Language, Meaning and Temporal Cognition.* (Human Cognitive Processing 12.) Amsterdam/Philadelphia: John Benjamins.

Evans, Vyvyan
   this volume   Time. Berlin/Boston: De Gruyter Mouton.

Fausey, Caitlin M. and Teenie Matlock
   2011   Can grammar win elections? *Political Psychology* 32(4): 563–574.

Feldman, Jerome
   2008   *From Molecule to Metaphor: A Neural Theory of Language.* Cambridge: MIT Press.

Filipović, Luna and Iraide Ibarretxe-Antuñano
   this volume   Motion: Berlin/Boston: De Gruyter Mouton.

Franklin, Nancy and Barbara Tversky
   1990   Searching imagined environments. *Journal of Experimental Psychology: General* 119: 63–76.

Gallese, Vittorio and George Lakoff
   2005   The brain's concepts: The role of the sensory-motor system in reason and language. *Cognitive Neuropsychology* 22: 455–479.

Gibbs, Raymond W.
   2006   Embodiment and Cognitive Science. New York: Cambridge University Press.

Gibbs, Raymond W.
   2012   Walking the walk while thinking about the talk: Embodied interpretation of metaphorical narratives. *Journal of Psycholinguistic Research* 42: 363–378.

Gibbs, Raymond W. and Teenie Matlock
   2008   Metaphor, imagination, and simulation: Psycholinguistic evidence. In: R. W. Gibbs (ed.), *Cambridge Handbook of Metaphor and Thought*, 161–176. New York: Cambridge University Press.

Glenberg, Arthur M.
   1999   Why mental models must be embodied. In: G. Rickheit and C. Habel (eds.), *Mental Models in Discourse Processing and Reasoning*, 77–90. New York: Elsevier.

Glenberg, Arthur M.
   2010   Embodiment as a unifying perspective for psychology. *Wiley Interdisciplinary Reviews: Cognitive Science* 1: 586–596.

Henderson, John M. and Fernanda Ferreira
   2004   Scene perception for psycholinguists. In: J. M. Henderson and F. Ferreira (eds.), *The Interface of Language, Vision, and Action*, 1–58. New York: Psychology Press.

Herrera, Juan S. and Eric M. Riggs
   2013   Relating gestures and speech: An analysis of students' conceptions about geological sedimentary processes. *International Journal of Science Education* 35(12): 1979–2003.

Huumo, Tuomas
   1999   Path settings, subjective motion, and the Finnish partitive subject. In: S. J. J. Hwang and A. L. Lommel (eds.), *LACUS Forum XXV (The Linguistic Association of Canada and the United States)*, 363–374.

Huumo, Tuomas
   2005   How fictive dynamicity motivates aspect marking: The riddle of the Finnish quasi-resultative construction. *Cognitive Linguistics* 16: 113–144.

Keane, Karen A.
  2007   A characterization of dynamic reasoning: Reasoning with time as parameter. *Mathematical Reasoning* 26: 230–246.
Kourtzi, Zoe
  2004   "But still, it moves." *Trends in Cognitive Sciences* 8(2): 47–49.
Kourtzi, Zoe and Nancy Kanwisher
  2000   Activation in human MT/MST by static images with implied motion. *Journal of Cognitive Neuroscience* 12(1): 48–55.
Lakoff, George and Mark Johnson
  1980   *Metaphors We Live By.* Chicago: University of Chicago Press.
Lakoff, George and Mark Johnson
  1999   *Philosophy in the Flesh: The Embodied Mind and Its Challenge to Western Thought.* New York: Basic Books.
Lakoff, George and Rafael E. Nuñez
  2000   *Where Mathematics Comes From.* New York: Basic Books.
Lakoff, George and Mark Turner
  1989   *More than Cool Reason: A Field Guide to Poetic Metaphor.* Chicago: University of Chicago Press.
Langacker, Ronald W.
  1986   Abstract motion. In:V. Nikiforidou, M. van Clay, M. Niepokuj, and D. Feder (eds.), *Proceedings of the 12th Annual Meeting of the Berkeley Linguistics Society*, 455–471. Berkeley: Berkeley Linguistics Society.
Langacker, Ronald W.
  1987   *Foundations of Cognitive Grammar*, Volume 1: *Theoretical Prerequisites.* Stanford: Stanford University Press.
Langacker, Ronald W.
  2000   Virtual reality. *Studies in the Linguistic Sciences* 29: 77–103.
Langacker, Ronald W.
  2005   Dynamicity, fictivity, and scanning: The imaginative basis of logic and linguisticmeaning. In: D. Pecher, and R. A. Zwaan (eds.), *Grounding Cognition: The Role of Perception and Action in Memory, Language, and Thinking*, 164–197. Cambridge University Press.
Langacker, Ronald W.
  this volume   Construal. Berlin/Boston: De Gruyter Mouton.
Liddell, Scott K.
  2003   *Grammar, Gesture, and Meaning in American Sign Language.* New York: Cambridge University Press.
Maglio, Paul P. and Teenie Matlock
  1999   The conceptual structure of information spaces. In: A. Munro, D. Benyon, D. Hook and K. Hook (eds.), *Personal and Social Navigation of Information Space.* Berlin: Springer-Verlag.
Mandler, Jean M.
  2012   On the spatial foundations of the conceptual system and its enrichment. *Cognitive Science* 36(3): 421–451.
Marghetis, Tyler and Rafael Núñez
  2013   The motion behind the symbols: A vital role for dynamism in the conceptualization of limits and continuity in expert mathematics. *Topics in Cognitive Science* 5(2): 299–316.
Matlock, Teenie
  2001   How real is fictive motion? PhD dissertation, University of California, Santa Cruz.
Matlock, Teenie
  2004a   The conceptual motivation of fictive motion. In: G. Radden and R. Dirven (eds.), *Motivation in Grammar*, 221–248. Amsterdam: John Benjamins.

Matlock, Teenie
2004b   Fictive motion as cognitive simulation. *Memory and Cognition* 32: 1389–1400.
Matlock, Teenie
2006   Depicting fictive motion in drawings. In: J. Luchenbroers (ed.), *Cognitive Linguistics: Investigations Across Languages, Fields and Philosophical Boundaries*, 67–85. Amsterdam: John Benjamins.
Matlock, Teenie
2010   Abstract motion is no longer abstract. *Language and Cognition* 2(2): 243–260.
Matlock, Teenie
2012   Framing political messages with grammar and metaphor. *American Scientist* 100: 478–483.
Matlock, Teenie, Spencer C. Castro, Morgan Fleming, Timothy M. Gann and Paul P. Maglio
2014   Spatial metaphors in web use. *Spatial Cognition and Computation* 14. doi: 10.1080/13875868.2014.945587.
Matlock, Teenie, Kevin Holmes, Mahesh Srinivasan and Michael Ramscar
2011   Even abstract motion influences the understanding of time. *Metaphor and Symbol* 26(4): 260–271.
Matlock, Teenie, Michael Ramscar and Lera Boroditsky
2004   The experiential basis of motion language. In: A. S. da Silva, A. Torres and M. Gonçalves (eds.), *Linguagem, Cultura e Cognicao: Estudo de Linguistica Cognitiva*, 43–57.
Matlock, Teenie, Michael Ramscar and Lera Boroditsky
2005   The experiential link between spatial and temporal language. *Cognitive Science* 29: 655–664.
Matlock, Teenie and Daniel C. Richardson
2004   Do eye movements go with fictive motion? *Proceedings of the 26th Annual Conference of the Cognitive Science Society* 26: 909–914.
Matsumoto, Yo
1996a   Subjective motion and English and Japanese verbs. *Cognitive Linguistics* 7: 183–226.
Matsumoto, Yo
1996b   How abstract is subjective motion? A comparison of access path expressions and coverage path expressions. In: A. Goldberg (ed.), *Conceptual Structure, Discourse and Language*, 359–373. Stanford: CSLI Publications.
McGlone, Matthew S. and Jennifer L. Harding
1998   Back (or forward?) to the future: The role of perspective in temporal language comprehension. *Journal of Experimental Psychology: Learning Memory and Cognition* 24(5): 1211–1223.
Mishra, Ramesh K. and Niharika Singh
2010   Online fictive motion understanding: An eye-movement study with Hindi. *Metaphor and Symbol* 25(3): 144–161.
Moore, Kevin E.
2006   Space-to-time mappings and temporal concepts. *Cognitive Linguistics* 17: 199–244.
Morrow, Daniel G., Gordon H. Bower and Stephen L. Greenspan
1989   Updating situation models during narrative comprehension. *Journal of Memory and Language* 28: 292–312.
Narayanan, Srini
1997   Talking the talk is like walking the walk: A computational model of verbal aspect. *Proceedings of the Nineteenth Annual Conference of the Cognitive Science Society*, 548–553. Mahwah: Erlbaum.
Newman, John
2002   *The Linguistics of Sitting, Standing, and Lying*. Amsterdam: John Benjamins.

Núñez, Rafael
    2006   Do Real numbers really move? Language, thought, and gesture: The embodied cognitive foundations of mathematics. In: R. Hersh (ed.), *18 Unconventional Essays on the Nature of Mathematics*, 160–181. New York: Springer.

Núñez, Rafael
    2008   A fresh look at the foundations of mathematics: Gesture and the psychological reality of conceptual metaphor. In: A. Cienki and C. Müller (eds.), *Metaphor and Gesture*, 93–114. Amsterdam and Philadelphia: John Benjamins.

Núñez, Rafael, Benjamin A. Motz and Ursina Teuscher
    2006   Time after time: The psychological reality of the ego- and time-references-point distinction in metaphorical construals of time. *Metaphor and Symbol* 21: 133–146.

Papafragou, Anna, Christine Massey and Lila Gleitman
    2002   Shake, rattle, 'n' roll: the representation of motion in language and cognition. *Cognition* 84(2): 189–219.

Pecher, Diane and Rolf A. Zwaan (eds.)
    2005   *Grounding Cognition: The Role of Perception and Action in Memory, Language and Thinking*. New York: Cambridge University Press.

Pulaczewska, Hanna
    1999   *Aspects of Metaphor in Physics: Examples and Case Studies*. Tübingen: Max Niemeyer Verlag.

Radden, Günter
    1996   Motion metaphorized: The case of coming and going. In: E. H. Casad (ed.), *Cognitive Linguistics in the Redwoods: The Expansion of a New Paradigm in Linguistics*, 424–458. Berlin/New York: Mouton de Gruyter.

Radden, Günter
    2011   Spatial time in the West and the East. In: M. Brdar, M. Omazic, V. P. Takac, T. Erdeljic-Gradecak and G. Bulja (eds.), *Space and Time in Language*, 1–40. Frankfurt: Peter Lang.

Ramscar, Michael, Teenie Matlock and Melody Dye
    2010   Running down the clock: the role of expectation in our understanding of time and motion. *Language and Cognitive Processes* 25: 589–615.

Richardson, Daniel C. and Rick Dale
    2005   Looking to understand: The coupling between speakers' and listeners' eye movements and its relationship to discourse comprehension. *Cognitive Science* 29: 39–54.

Richardson, Daniel C., Rick Dale and Michael J. Spivey
    2007   Eye movements in language and cognition. In: M. Gonzalez-Marquez, I. Mittelberg, S. Coulson and M. J. Spivey (eds.), *Empirical Methods in Cognitive Linguistics*, 323–344. Amsterdam/Philadelphia: John Benjamins.

Richardson, Daniel C. and Teenie Matlock
    2007   The integration of figurative language and static depictions: an eye movement study of fictive motion. *Cognition* 102(1): 129–138.

Rojo, Ana and Javier Valenzuela
    2003   Fictive motion in English and Spanish. *International Journal of English Studies* 3: 123–150.

Saygin, Ayse P., Stephen McCullough, Morana Alac and Karen Emmorey
    2010   Modulation of BOLD response in motion-sensitive lateral temporal cortex by real and fictive motion sentences. *Journal of Cognitive Neuroscience* 22(11): 2480–2490.

Slobin, Dan I.
    2008   Relations between Paths of Motion and Paths of Vision: A Crosslinguistic and Developmental Exploration. In: V. C. Mueller Gathercole (ed.), *Routes to Language: Studies in Honor of Melissa Bowerman*, 197–221. Mahwah: Lawrence Erlbaum.

Stosic, Dejan and Laure Sarda
  2009   The many ways to be located in French and Serbian: the role of fictive motion in the expression of static location. In: M. Brala-Vukanović and L. Gruić-Grmuša (eds.), *Space and Time in Language and Literature*, 39–59. Newcastle: Cambridge Scholars Publishing.
Sweetser, Eve
  1997   Role and individual readings of change predicates. In: Jan Nuyts and E. Pederson (eds.), *Language and Conceptualization*. New York: Cambridge University Press.
Takahashi, Kiyoko
  2000   Expressions of emanation fictive motion events in Thai. PhD dissertation, Chulalonkorn University.
Takahashi, Kiyoko
  2001   Access path expressions in Thai. In: A. Cienki, B. Luka, and M. Smith (eds.), *Conceptual Structure in Discourse Factors in Linguistic Structure*, 237–252. Stanford: CSLI Publications.
Talmy, Leonard
  1975   Semantics and syntax of motion. In: J. P. Kimball (ed.), *Syntax and Semantics*, Volume I: *Conceptual Structuring Systems*, 181–238. New York: Academic Press.
Talmy, Leonard
  1983   How language structures space. In: H. L. Pick and L. P. Acredolo (eds.), *Spatial Orientation: Theory, Research, and Application*, 225–282. New York: Plenum.
Talmy, Leonard
  1996   Fictive motion in language and "ception." In: P. Bloom, M. A. Peterson, L. Nadel and M. F. Garrett (eds.), *Language and Space*, 211–276. Cambridge: MIT Press.
Talmy, Leonard
  2000   *Toward a Cognitive Semantics*. Cambridge: MIT Press.
Tanenhaus, Michael K. and Michael J. Spivey-Knowlton
  1996   Eye-tracking. *Language and Cognitive Processes* 11(6): 583–588.
Teuscher, Ursina, Marguerite McQuire, Jennifer Collins and Seana Coulson
  2008   Congruity effects in time and space: behavioral and ERP measures. *Cognitive Science* 32(3): 563–578.
Tversky, Barbara
  1993   Cognitive maps, cognitive collages, and spatial mental models. In: A. U. Frank and I. Campari (eds.), *Spatial Information Theory: A Theoretical Basis for GIS*, 14–24. Berlin: Springer-Verlag.
Wallentin, Mikkel, Torben E. Lund, Svend Østergaard, Leif Østergaard and Andreas Roepstorff
  2005   Motion verb sentences activate left posterior middle temporal cortex despite static context. *NeuroReport* 16: 649–652.
Winawer, Jonathan, Alex C. Huk and Lera Boroditsky
  2007   A motion aftereffect from still photographs depicting motion. *Psychological Science* 19: 276–283.
Wittmann, Michael C., Virginia J. Flood and Katrina E. Black
  2012   Algebraic manipulation as motion within a landscape. *Educational Studies in Mathematics* 82(2): 169–181.
Zlatev, Jordan, Johan Blomberg and Ulf Magnusson
  2012   Metaphors and subjective experience: motion-emotion metaphors in English, Swedish, Bulgarian and Thai. In: A. Foolen, U. Lüdtke, T. Racine and J. Zlatev (eds.), *Moving Ourselves – Moving Others: Motion and Emotion in Intersubjectivity, Consciousness, and Language*, 423–450. Amsterdam: John Benjamins.
Zwaan, Rolf A., Carol Madden, Richard H. Yaxley and Mark Aveyard
  2004   Moving words: Dynamic representations in language comprehension. *Cognitive Science* 28: 611–619.

Zwaan, Rolf. A. and Gabriel A. Radvansky
  1998 Situation models in language comprehension and memory. *Psychological Bulletin* 123(2): 162–185.

Teenie Matlock, Merced, (USA)
Till Bergmann, Merced, (USA)

27. Prototype effects in grammar

1. Introduction/Overview
2. Prototypes and prototype categories
3. Prototype effects
4. Application to grammar
5. Lexical categories
6. Word structure: derivation, compounding, and blending
7. Syntactic constructions
8. Conclusion

Keywords

Prototype, construction, polysemy, fuzziness, idiomaticity

1. Introduction/Overview

This chapter addresses the relevance of the prototype concept to the grammatical description of a language. It turns out that "prototype" is not a unified concept and can be understood in different ways with respect to different kinds of categories (section 2). The notion is, however, supported by a range of empirically founded prototype effects, the topic of section 3. The remainder of the chapter surveys the role of these effects in grammatical description, with a focus on lexical categories (section 5), word structure (section 6), and syntactic constructions (section 7). The latter are considered from the perspectives of their formal and semantic identification, and their productivity.

2. Prototypes and prototype categories

As Geeraerts (1987: 592), following Posner (1986), aptly remarked, prototype is itself a prototype concept. There is, namely, no set of necessary and sufficient conditions which are definitional of a prototype. This should not be surprising, given that prototypes can be understood in different ways according to the kind of category whose members are under discussion, the researcher's theoretical agenda, and the kinds of evidence which lead to the prototype's identification (Ramscar this volume).

The pioneering work of Eleanor Rosch, in the 1970s, is instructive in this respect. In her earliest work (Heider 1972, Rosch 1973) she addressed the categorization of colour, proposing that colour categories were structured around a focal colour (later to be dubbed the prototype). Colour samples could be called "red" to the extent that they resembled a focal red, with some samples being "better" examples of "red" than others. On this account, a category could be equated with its prototype. To "have" the category "red" is to know, quite simply, what constitutes a good red. Category membership is constrained only by the existence of neighbouring categories, such as orange, purple, or pink. Category boundaries are fuzzy, with samples near the fuzzy boundaries having ambiguous or uncertain status.

With a few exceptions, the colour model is not readily extendible to other categories. We could not, for example, define the bird category with respect to a good example – a sparrow, let us say – and propose that to have the category "bird" (alternatively, to know the meaning of the word *bird*) involves nothing more than to know what a sparrow is, with things being called birds to the extent that they resemble a sparrow. There are other differences vis-à-vis the colours. For example, the bird category does not gradually merge at its fuzzy boundaries with other categories of living creatures, such as reptiles or mammals. On the contrary, the set of things which are called birds is rather strictly circumscribed. The category does display degrees of representativity, however. Penguins, ostriches, and swans may not be particularly representative examples, but they are still birds, no less so than sparrows and crows.

Colour categories have some special properties which are not shared by categories such as "bird". Foremost amongst these is the fact that a colour sample may be uniquely characterized in terms its location on a number of continuous and independent dimensions, namely hue, brightness, and saturation. The focal colours may be thought of as points in this three-dimensional space. Any colour sample can be categorized as a function of its distance from one or more of these focal colours. Depending on the distance, the sample is considered to be a good, or less good member of the category in question.

For many of the categories named by the words in a language, a dimensional account would not be viable. What, for example, would be the dimensions which characterize "bird", "fruit", "vehicle", or "chair"? Whilst we might certainly refer to the attributes of these categories, the attributes do not constitute smoothly varying dimensions, with focal exemplars occupying distinctive locations on these dimensions. It is largely for this reason that we cannot equate the categories with a single, prototypical exemplar, neither do neighbouring categories gradually merge into each other. Having the category and knowing its boundaries requires familiarity with the range of its possible members.

It is worth mentioning, however, that some phonetic categories, especially those pertaining to vowel sounds and perhaps also the fricatives, do have a dimensional structure not unlike that of the colours. A vowel sound may be specified in terms of the location on a frequency scale of its lower formants, in association with the (again continuously variable) dimension of duration. Just as red merges gradually into orange or pink, we can have a range of vowel qualities ranging from [e] through [ɛ] to [æ]. Accordingly, the vowel categories of a language may be identified with prototypes, akin to the focal colours (Kuhl 1991).

A dimensional approach is of only limited applicability with respect to other linguistic categories (though some possible candidates will be discussed later in this chapter). Take the case of nouns and verbs. Givón (1979: 14) proposed that nouns and verbs are distinguished by the time stability of their referents, with nouns designating time-stable configurations, whilst verbs designate situations of rapid change. Whilst time stability certainly constitutes a smoothly varying dimension, nouns do not gradually shade into verbs. This is because categorization as noun or verb depends crucially on other attributes which are discrete in nature; for example, a word either inflects for past tense, or it does not. Though focussing mainly on their semantic aspects, Langacker (1987) also characterized nouns and verbs in terms of discrete properties, having to do with the nature of the entity that they profile, which in turn rests on notions of temporal scanning, domains, and regions.

Broadening the scope of her research in order to address the prototype structure of natural kinds and other categories, Rosch came to focus on the attributes of category members (Rosch 1978). A crucial notion was that of cue validity. An attribute has high cue validity if presence of the attribute is a good predictor of category membership. Ability to fly is a fairly good predictor of bird status (it is not 100% predictive, since some other kinds of creature can fly). Having a liver, on the other hand, is a very poor predictor. Whilst all birds do have a liver, so too do many other living creatures. The prototype was accordingly characterized as that member which maximized the cue validity of its attributes, the member, in other words, whose attributes, collectively, best predicted membership in the category and excluded membership in neighbouring categories.

In contrast to the category-as-prototype approach (exemplified by the colours), the weighted attribute approach was able to capture the full extent of a category, not just the specifics of its central member (Murphy 2002: 49). The approach was sufficiently flexible to allow for many different kinds of category structure. For one thing, it was consistent with the possibility that different category members might have few diagnostic features in common; all that is required for category membership is that the summed cue validity of the features exceeds some criterial value. Second, the approach allowed for the possibility of "virtual prototypes", not in fact instantiated by any actually occurring entity. Third, it envisaged the possibility that one or more of the attributes might be essential to category membership; in such a case, the boundary of the category will be clear-cut, as determined by the presence/absence of the criterial attribute(s), even though individual members might still display greater or lesser degrees of representativity, in accordance with the presence of other, non-criterial attributes.

Rosch's work had been concerned with the referential possibilities of linguistic terms, pre-eminently nouns which designate natural kinds (*bird, fruit, tree*) or cultural artefacts and activities (*furniture, vehicle, sport*). As her work became familiar to linguists (e.g., Lakoff 1987; Taylor 2003, 2008), an extension of the prototype notion saw the term applied to the semantic structure of linguistic items. The focus shifted from the range of entities that a word can designate (an extensional, referential, or onomasiological approach) to the range of senses exhibited by a word (an intensional, or conceptual perspective). An influential example of this shift was the Brugman/Lakoff account of the preposition *over* (Brugman and Lakoff [1988] 2006). It is not simply the fact that *over* can designate many different relations in the world. Rather, the word appears to manifest a cluster of related senses, each of which may constitute a prototype category in the extensional understanding of the term, characterized by a set of attributes of greater or lesser cue validity. A key claim of the intensional approach is that of the different senses, one can be identified as the prototype, that is, a central sense to which others are related in a radial, or network structure.

3. Prototype effects

In her 1978 paper *Principles of categorization*, Rosch was careful to emphasize that her empirical findings on the structure of categories did not constitute a theory of mental representation. What she did claim was that any cognitive theory of categorization had to be able to accommodate the range of prototype effects which she had discovered; these constituted a baseline for the viability of any theory of mental representation.

Prototype effects can be broadly divided into those which pertain to the (structural) centrality of the prototype and to its (cognitive) salience.

3.1. Centrality

The prototype is the "centre" of the category; things are assimilated to the category in accordance with their "distance" from the prototype. The metaphor is particularly apt with respect to colour categories. Centrality is also relevant to research on artificial categories, such as two-dimensional displays of dots, geometrical shapes, or configurations of numbers and letters (e.g., Posner and Keele 1968). The prototype in these studies constitutes a kind of category ideal (invented, of course, by the researchers), and displays can be ranked according to the extent to which they deviate from the ideal, or can be regarded as distortions of it. Although of little relevance to the study of word meanings (the primary focus of Rosch's research and its uptake in lexical semantics) a view of category structure as a function of the degree of distortion of an ideal configuration arguably does play a role in the study of the syntactic configurations of a language, a matter to which we return later in this chapter.

The notion of centrality needs to be understood in a somewhat looser sense with respect to the weighted attribute theory. The prototype constitutes the centre of gravity, as it were, of the category, in that it exhibits the maximum number of attributes which are diagnostic of category membership. The notion of centrality might also be applied to the attributes themselves. An attribute is central to the extent that it (a) has high cue validity, in the limiting case being essential to category membership, and (b) is exhibited by a large number (in the limiting case, by all) of the members of the category and by very few (in the limiting case, by none) of the members of contrasting categories.

Centrality is also at issue in the intensional view of polysemous categories, whereby the different senses of a polysemous word are thought of as radiating out, as it were, from the prototypical sense. A major issue with the intensional approach is methodological. Whereas Rosch's work on the referential aspects of prototype categories was supported by rigorous empirical research, the identification of the central, or "prototypical" sense of a polysemous word – not to mention the identification, enumeration, and characterization of the senses themselves – is largely a matter of introspection and theory-driven speculation. There are, in fact, several ways in which one sense of a polysemous word can be regarded as central, and the different approaches do not always converge on a unique solution.

a) The central sense is taken to be the historically oldest one, the progenitor, as it were, from which the others have been derived by processes of metaphor, metonymy, specialization, or generalization. Accordingly, the "literal" sense of a word is likely to be viewed as more central than its metaphorical uses, while concrete (often spatial) senses are taken as more central than abstract ones.

b) Taking a developmental perspective, the central sense is the one which children first learn and which, as it were, "seeds" the full acquisition of the word. Since children are likely to learn concrete and literal uses before abstract and metaphorical ones, the approach delivers outcomes which are largely consistent with historical development. Especially in the case of the prepositions, however, a fair number of the earliest uses tend to occur in a range of more or less fixed phrasal locutions (*on TV, over here*); these are uses which would probably be regarded as somewhat peripheral on most radial network accounts (e.g., Hallan 2001; Rice 2003).

b) The central sense is the one which enables semanticists and lexicographers to describe the polysemy most perspicaciously and economically. The central member is the one around which the others cluster, or from which they radiate, like spokes of a wheel.

Attempts have been made to ground network proposals in speakers' subjective estimates of the similarity of different uses of a word (Sandra and Rice 1995). Even so, there is sometimes little consensus on the identity of the central sense, especially with regard to highly polysemous words such as *over*. Brugman/Lakoff consider the central sense of *over* to be "above/across", as in *The bird flew over the field*. Tyler and Evans (2001), on the other hand, regard the "above" sense as central, as in *The bee is hovering over the flower*. Others, yet again, have seen the central sense as involving an up-down arc-like trajectory, as in *The cow jumped over the moon* (Dewell 1994).

3.2. Salience

A category prototype is cognitively more salient than other category members. Research by Rosch and others discovered a number of salience effects, including the following:

a) subjective judgements of goodness of membership. When presented with a category name, subjects are able to grade potential exemplars according to their goodness of membership. Results for a given population tend to be highly reliable, even though individual differences might be quite marked (Barsalou 1987).

b) listing. When presented with a category name, subjects are able to generate lists of exemplars, with more prototypical members being mentioned earlier, faster, and by a larger number of subjects than less central members (Battig and Montague 1969).

c) default member. The prototype is the category member that subjects invoke in the absence of contrary indications. Mention of a "grandmother" is likely to conjure up an image of a good-natured, grey-haired old lady. The default may be overridden once specific information is available about *this* grandmother (Fodor 1980).

d) reasoning. Inferences about a category may be based on the properties of prototypical members, not on properties characteristic of the category as a whole (Rips 1975).

e) asymmetrical similarity judgements. A prototype is a kind of cognitive reference point which tends to "draw in" outlying members, thereby reducing their subjective distance from the prototype. Thus, B (a marginal member) may be judged more similar to A (a more central member) than A is to B (Rips 1975; Rosch 1975).
f) imagability and embodiment. When asked to form a mental image of a category, subjects tend to imagine a prototypical instance. They are able to draw a picture of it, they are able to state its typical parts and their arrangement, and simulate how a person would typically interact with it (Rosch 1978).
g) contrastivity. Rosch's research on colour and the more complex categories studied in her subsequent work, points to the contrastive nature of prototypes. The weighted attributes approach, for example, leads to the identification of a prototype as a category member which is maximally distinct – in terms of its characteristic attributes – from the prototypes of neighbouring categories. The prototypical bird can fly; the prototypical mammal does not.

The salience of more central members is confirmed by other experimental techniques, such as priming and verification tasks. For example, in a lexical decision task, a category name is able to prime the names of more central members more effectively than the names of less central members, while sentences of the form *An A is an X* are judged to be true more quickly if A is a central member of category X than if it is a more marginal member.

3.3. Frequency

Centrality and salience effects need not (though they often do) coincide, and not all of these effects are relevant to all kinds of categories. This is especially true of grammatical categories, as we shall see. In this connection, one further effect needs to be mentioned: frequency.

Frequency – whether of non-linguistic experiences, linguistic forms, linguistic meanings, or form-meaning associations – will likely contribute to cognitive entrenchment, which in turn will map onto cognitive salience and thence onto degrees of prototypicality. We are inclined to suppose that apples, pears, and oranges are good examples of fruit because we encounter them more often than olives, papayas, and pineapples. For speakers of the 1890s the prototypical vehicle was no doubt a horse-drawn carriage, not a new-fangled motor-car. Neither is it surprising that rugby football should be a more salient kind of sport for New Zealanders than it is for North Americans (Marshall and Parr 1996).

Frequency effects are ubiquitous in language (Taylor 2012) and provide crucial input data to usage-based models of grammar and of linguistic knowledge more generally. It is not perhaps surprising that in studies of word usage, and of the interaction of words and the contexts in which they occur, frequency effects are often discussed in terms of prototypicality (e.g., Divjak and Arppe 2013; for a review, see Gries 2014). We need to be wary, however, of uncritically equating relative frequency with degrees of prototypicality, especially when other indications of prototypicality, of the kinds listed in the above sections, are not available or give conflicting results. For example, it is doubtful whether frequency plays a role in the prototype status of focal colours. Do we really encounter a "good red" more frequently than other shades of the colour? Experiments with artificial categories – such as displays of dots or configurations of numbers and letters – have shown that subjects are able to identify a prototype (understood as the configuration from which training exemplars have been derived by distortions of greater or lesser degrees), even though it has never been encountered in training sessions (Posner and Keele 1968).

An appeal to frequency is no doubt useful as a research heuristic, but as a pointer to prototypicality it needs to be supported by other considerations. We should probably not want to regard *be* as the prototypical member of the verb category, even though *be* (and its various forms) turns out to be the most frequent of the English verbs on most word counts. Or take the issue, raised above, of identifying the central sense of a polysemous word. Most linguists, as well as laypersons, I daresay, would want say that the "basic", or "central" uses of *eye*, *hand*, *head*, and *heart* refer to parts of a body, even though metaphorical and metonymic uses are equally frequent, if not more so (Deignan and Potter 2004; Hilpert 2006). Theoretical claims about the derived status of non-literal uses would take precedence over frequency data.

4. Application to grammar

Having looked at some different understandings of the notion of prototype and the range of effects which typically adhere to the prototype, let us now turn to the application of the notion, in its various guises, to the categories of linguistic description.

For some linguistic terms, the application of the prototype notion is (relatively) straightforward. In considering notions such as "dialect", "language", "native speaker", "bilingual speaker", and even "meaning", we can bring to bear the same kinds of considerations that are used to characterize "fruit", "vehicle", and "bird". We might, for example, list the attributes of these categories and assess their cue validity, in this way drawing up a profile of the category prototype. In the case of some terms, we might want to recognize a cluster of related senses, the terms, in other words, would need to be regarded as polysemous. *Meaning* is one such – consider the use of the word in expressions such as *word meaning, the meaning of life*, and *the meaning of Halloween*.

Many of the terms used in linguistic description, however, require a more sophisticated approach. This is especially true of those terms which refer to the symbolic resources of a language, that is, units of structure which associate a formal specification with a semantic characterization. At issue are categories such as word classes, patterns of word formation, syntactic constructions, and even such foundational concepts as word, morpheme, clause, and sentence. These categories are subject to both a formal and a semantic specification. The formal specification may refer to the internal make-up of category members, whether phonological, morphological, lexical, or syntactic. The formal specification may also make reference to the distribution of category members in the language, that is, the kinds of structures they are able to occur in and the kinds of items they are likely to co-occur with. Likewise, the semantic characterization may focus on the inherent content of the category as well as on its role in larger semantic structures. All of these aspects are liable to give rise to prototype effects, of one kind of another. Moreover, prototypicality from a formal perspective may not always correspond with semantic prototypicality. From the point of view of its distribution in the language, *explosion* is a pretty good example of the noun category. From the point of view of its semantics, however, it would have to be regarded as somewhat marginal.

5. Lexical categories

The sometimes conflicting results of a formal vs. semantic perspective are nowhere more evident than in the case of the lexical categories ("parts of speech"). Linguistics students learn very early in their career that you cannot identify the nouns in a sentence by looking for the names of persons, places, and things (the essence of the traditional semantic definition). The proper criteria, we teach our students, are distributional. *Explosion* is a noun, even though it seems to refer to an event. This is because the word behaves like a noun and has the internal structure of a noun: it terminates in a noun-forming affix *-ion*; it can pluralize; it can be quantified; it can be modified by an adjective; in combination with a determiner it can be part of a noun phrase, which in turn can function as the subject of a verb, the complement of a preposition, and so on.

These formal characteristics are akin to the attributes of semantic categories such as "bird" or "vehicle", and it is not surprising that they should give rise to similar kinds of representativity effects. *Music* would have to be regarded as a less representative noun than *explosion*, since it does not pluralize; a pluralia tantum noun such as *whereabouts* is even less representative, not only because there is no corresponding singular, but also because the word is virtually restricted to occurring in a possessive environment (*his whereabouts, the whereabouts of the suspect*). *Seem* is a less than prototypical verb because it does not readily occur in progressive and imperative environments, while *beware* is typically restricted to an imperative context or to use as an infinitive. There would, however, be no question about the status of the cited words as, respectively, nouns or verbs. Aarts (2007) discusses such matters in terms of what he calls "subsective gradience", that is, degree of representativity within a category.

The adjective category is notorious for the fact that there do not appear to be any formal attributes which uniquely identify its members. (Adverbs are even more heterogeneous). It is useful here to invoke the notion of cue validity. The fact that (many) adjectives can be used both attributively and predicatively (*a large box, the box is large*) loses some of its diagnostic value in light of the fact that nouns may be similarly distributed (attributive: *an apple pie*; predicative: *Jones is president*). Similarly, prefixation by *un-*, commonly cited as a characteristic of adjective status, has less than optimal cue validity, since quite a few verbs and adverbs can also take the prefix (*to undo, unwillingly*), as can derived nominals (*unimportance, untruth*) and even, occasionally, non-derived nouns (e.g., *unperson*, in Orwell's *1984*). The possibility of modification by an adverb is equally suspect, since verbs also display this property. Practically the only attribute uniquely associated with adjectives is the possibility of gradation (*big, bigger, biggest*), though not all adjectives display this property.

A particularly murky area concerns the differentiation of prepositions, particles, and subordinating conjunctions. We can, to be sure, easily cite prototypical examples of these categories, examples which betray no signs of ambiguous status. As noted earlier, prototypical examples tend to be cognitively salient: they are examples which immediately spring to mind when we are asked to list members of a category and they tend to be maximally contrastive vis-à-vis prototypical examples of neighbouring categories. There can be no question about the prepositional status of *on* in *on the bus*, of the participial status of *thinking* in *Thinking the matter over, I ...*, or about the status of *although* as a subordinating conjunction in *Although it was late, I ...* There are some words, however, which can easily be inserted into each of these three kinds of context; examples include *considering* and *regarding*. These words seem genuinely to blur the distinctiveness of the categories in question.

A notorious case, in English, concerns certain uses of gerundials (the literature is vast: see, however, Hudson 2007: Ch. 4 for a particular innovative solution). What is the lexical category of *saying* in *Without my saying a word*? Being construed with possessive *my*, with the resulting combination being the complement of a preposition, we should want to say that *saying* is a noun (or, more precisely, that *saying a word* has the status of a nominal). Yet *saying* takes a direct object – an unambiguous attribute of a verb. The criteria for classification shift somewhat with respect to the alternative (and semantically equivalent) wording *Without me saying a word*, raising the question whether the categorization of *saying* (and indeed the parsing of the whole expression) also undergoes a shift. And what about *Without her saying a word* – which neutralizes the above distinction?

In the above account of the formal attributes of a lexical category such as "noun", it was necessary to refer to other lexical categories, such as "adjective" and "determiner". How are these categories to be defined, from a formal point of view, if not in terms of their distribution with respect to other lexical categories? A certain degree of circularity enters into the discussion (Smith in press). If nouns are defined (in part) by their ability to be modified by adjectives, and if adjectives are defined (in part) by their ability to modify nouns, we need some independent means for identifying these categories. One approach is to re-admit a semantic characterization. Prototypical nouns and verbs designate things and events, as per the traditional account and as suggested by the acquisition literature (Clark in press). Conversely, if a word designates a thing, it will be, with a very high degree of probability, a noun. Semantic considerations thus permit a first and indispensable cut for the classification of word types. Words which do not match the semantic prototypes are then assimilated to the categories largely on the basis of their formal attributes (Taylor 2012). At the same time, the very fact of their membership in the formally defined categories may cause the semantic characteristics of the category prototype to adhere to the words. *Explosion* "reifies" the event, construing it as a thing, such that it can be quantified and can be referred to, and properties can be predicated of it (Langacker 1987).

Another way out of the vicious circle is define the categories with respect to larger containing constructions, themselves subject to both formal and semantic characterizations. Thus, determiners and nouns would be defined by their role in noun phrase constructions, whose semantic import is to refer to entities in the world (or, more generally, in a mental space). We address constructions below.

6. Word structure: derivation, compounding, and blending

Aarts (2007) maintained that between-category, or intersective gradience is virtually absent with respect to lexical categories. The situation is quite different when we turn to the structural aspects of words, namely, their status as morphologically simple vs. their status as derived forms, inflected forms, compounds, or blends.

Once again, one's first inclination is to regard these categories as clearly distinct, and it is not difficult to come up with good examples whose categorization is obvious and unambiguous: *farm* is simplex, *farmer* is a derived nominal, *deer-farm* is a compound, and *brunch* is a blend.

The notion of contrast, implicit in approaches to prototype categories, is also to the forefront when we consider the internal make-up of complex words (or, at least, prototypical examples of derivation, compounding, and blending) (Taylor in press). The constituent morphemes of a derived word like *farmer* are maximally contrastive on a number of dimensions. The *-er* of *farmer* (a) is semantically schematic (it merely characterizes a person in terms of what they do, the bulk of the semantic content of the word being supplied by the base form *farm*); (b) is phonologically dependent (unlike the stem, *-er* cannot stand alone as an independent form, but must attach to another item); and (c) determines the semantic type of the derived form, namely, as an agentive noun. Compounding is different, in that each component has the status of a phonologically independent and semantically contentful word. Note, however, that properties (a) and (b) are in principle continuous, and may thus be expected to give rise to category fuzziness. This is indeed the case. *Idealism* and *Darwinism* look like standard derivations; however, the fact that one can speak of intellectual *isms* suggests that the words have features of a compound (alternatively, that *ism* has some word-like properties).

Blends are something of an anomaly on standard views of word formation, in that the components are identified solely on the basis of their occurrence in the inputs to the blend and have no symbolic status outside the blend itself; there are, for example, no reasons to propose *br-* and *-unch* as morphemes whose meanings contribute to the meaning of *brunch*. Yet the distinction between blending, compounding, and derivation is fluid. *Infographic*, *infomercial*, and the like, occupy a space between compounds and blends. *Glitterati* no doubt first made its appearance as a blend (of *glitter* and *literati*); further examples such as *twitterati* suggest the emerging status of *-erati* as a derivational suffix (Kemmer 2003).

Neither is the distinction between compound and phrase immune to category blurring. In principle, the distinction is clear; it is based, amongst other things, on the semantic compositionality of phrases vs. the idiosyncratic meaning of compounds and final stress typical of phrases vs. initial stress characteristic of compounds. Problematic examples are legion (Bauer 1998): *stone wall*, *London University*, *High Church*, etc. Pursuing the matter further, we would find that the notion of "word" (namely, as a union of a stable phonologically autonomous form with a stable semantic content, relatively unrestricted in its co-occurrence possibilities) turns out to be less than clear-cut. There may be good reasons, for example, to regard *the* not so much as a word but as a clitic, or at least as a word-like clitic (or as a clitic-like word) (Taylor 2003). Although *the* happens to occupy top position in most frequency counts of English, it is unlikely to spring into people's minds as a good example of a word.

7. Syntactic constructions

As Croft (2001) has argued, the construction is the basic unit of linguistic description. As a matter of fact, there are different ways of defining a construction: as any internally complex form, as an association of a form with a meaning, or even as any linguistic unit (including phonological units) that speakers of a language have internalized (Taylor 2012). For present purposes, however, let us take construction to refer to any structural configuration, whether lexically specified or not, along with its associated semantics.

Given this very broad characterization, the number of constructions in a language is legion (and essentially open-ended). Inevitably, therefore, problems arise when we attempt to identify and enumerate the constructions of a language. Are constructions well-defined entities, clearly demarcated one from another? Or do they exhibit fuzzy boundaries, with some expressions having ambiguous status vis-à-vis more than one construction? Given the topic of this chapter, the question also arises whether constructions have a prototype structure, with some expressions being "better", or more representative instances of the construction than others. If this is the case, on what basis can the construction's prototype be identified?

I address these questions on the basis of a couple of examples. I make no claim that the discussion will be representative of the broad range of constructions in a language. I suspect, however, that many features of the examples will carry over, mutatis mutandis, to the study of other constructions in a language.

a) The middle construction

The middle construction in English (exemplified by *This book sells well*) features a verb which elsewhere in the language is transitive but which in the construction appears as intransitive; the verb takes as its subject a non-agentive, typically a patient entity; middles have a stative interpretation, in that they predicate a stable property of the subject entity (specifically, their propensity to participate in the kind of event designated by the verb) and hence typically appear in the simple present tense; the implied agent of the action may not be mentioned; finally, an adjunct phrase (*well*, *easily*, etc.), specifying the potentiality of the designated property to be manifested, is usually required (Yoshimura and Taylor 2004). It is the co-occurrence of these various features, both syntactic and semantic, which justifies the recognition of the middle as a distinct construction.

Middles contrast with a number of other constructions, which are themselves characterized by a cluster of distinctive semantic and syntactic features. With unaccusatives (*The window broke, The door opened*), a normally transitive verb is again used intransitively, with a patient entity as its subject, and again the implied agent remains unspecified. Unlike middles, however, unaccusatives have an event reading and an adjunct phrase is not usually required. Middles also contrast with unergatives, that is, intransitives whose subject performs the named activity (*John cried*).

While prototypical examples of the three constructions can easily be cited – prototypical in the sense that the expressions unambiguously exhibit each of the characteristic features – the violation or blurring of the criteria can lead to host of uncertain examples. *This knife cuts steak easily* would probably still be regarded as a middle, even though the subject is not a patient and the verb takes a direct object. *The door wouldn't open (when I tried to go in)* could refer to a stable property of the door, namely, its "non-open-ability", suggesting the status of the expression as a middle. The expression could also refer to the door's refusal to open on that particular occasion, suggesting its status as an unaccusative. Conceptually, it might be hard to differentiate the two readings; in fact, each seems to entail the other. Take, as another example (sourced from the Internet),

I cry easily over anything. The verb is intransitive, suggesting the status of an unergative. Yet the sentence also exhibits features of a middle, in that it predicates a stable property of the subject referent in association, moreover, with an adjunct (*easily*) which is often associated with the construction. The three constructions thus exemplify fuzzy boundaries, not unlike the colour categories with which we opened this chapter.

These brief remarks are not intended to cast doubt on the validity of the notion "middle construction" in a grammar of English. They do, however, suggest that the construction is by no means as clearly delineated as many scholars seem to presuppose. A more fruitful approach – one which cannot unfortunately be pursued here – would be to conceptualize the construction as a region in a multi-dimensional "transitivity space", defined by a range of formal and semantic/pragmatic aspects, including such matters as the inherent semantics of the verb, the semantic role of subject nominal, and the referential status of the expression.

b) prenominal possessives

From a formal point of view, prenominal possessives are noun phrases with the internal structure [NP]'s [N], exemplified by *the man's hat*. There is, however, a competing construction, the possessive compound, with the structure [N]'s [N], as exemplified by *(a) children's playground*. The distinction is likely to be blurred whenever the possessor is indefinite or generic, or can be interpreted as such (Rosenbach 2006; Taylor 1996). Consider examples such as *taxpayers' money* and *a man's skull* (in the sense "a human skull"). Possessive compounds, in turn, are in competition with non-possessive compounds, of the kind *passenger seat*. The differentiation is especially problematic in cases where the first component is able to be interpreted as a plural. In principle, orthography should be able to come to the rescue: *students union* vs. *students' union*. The use of the possessive apostrophe, however, is famously unstable, a fact which no doubt reflects the inherent fuzziness of the underlying structural and semantic distinction.

The prenominal possessive is compatible with a wide range of semantic relations between possessor and possessee. The same goes for yet another construction with which the prenominal possessive is in contrast, namely the binomial *of* construction, exemplified by *the woman of the year*, *a photograph of me*, *the end of the day*. The two constructions are not always interchangeable; *the year's woman* sounds odd, while *the car of me* is virtually unacceptable. The differences are partly due to the semantic-pragmatic properties of the nominals in a prenominal possessive. The possessor is preferentially high in animacy, has definite reference, and names an entity already introduced into the discourse. The possessed is interpreted as definite and tends to be an entity newly introduced in the discourse; there seems, however, to be no particularly strong constraint against inanimates and even abstracts appearing as possessees.

Interestingly, the semantic relation of possession – the supposedly prototypical value of the construction and the basis for its name – is not all that frequent in running text. The situation, however, is somewhat different for speech directed at infants; here, possession, kinship relations, and body part relations predominate (Stefanowitsch and Gries 2005). There is another reason why these relations might be especially associated with the construction. When it comes to designating a person's material possessions or their kin relations, the prenominal possessive is the default option, much preferred over a binomial *of* expression. In cases where the possessor is non-human or inanimate, however, the two constructions are more likely to be in competition. *By year's end* occurs 414 times in the 450 million words of the Corpus of Contemporary American English (COCA: Davies 2008), as against more than twice as many examples (925) of *by the end of the year*.

By all accounts, *year's end* would have to be regarded as a highly untypical possessive; it may even be disputed whether it is a prenominal possessive or a possessive compound. (It is worth noting, by the way, that even possessive compounds tend to favour, as their first element, nouns towards the top of the animacy scale). What is remarkable, however, is that *by year's end* appears to have something of the status of a fixed expression. While other nouns can replace *year*, they do so with rapidly decreasing frequency: *day* (107), *week* (100), *month* (98), *summer* (52), *season* (51), *war* (35), *decade* (31), *century* (26), and *game* (11). The same is true when we try to replace the preposition: *at year's end* (88 examples), *before* (52), *until* (10), *through* (6), *near* and *to* (4 each), *toward* (3), *till* and *from* (one each; data derived from COCA). When it comes to replacing the final nominal, *end*, we draw a complete blank. In spite of the semantic plausibility of the expressions, there are no examples in the corpus of *by year's start, by year's beginning, by year's middle*, and only one solitary instance of *at year's start* (vis-à-vis 60 examples of *at the start of the year*).

The prenominal possessive construction is highly productive; it is compatible with a wide range of semantic relations, in association with a wide choice of possessor and possessee nominals. Nevertheless, as we have seen, as expressions deviate from its prototypical values (such as animate and discourse-old possessor, discourse-new possessee) we encounter a certain degree of idiomaticity and some unexpected gaps in usage. The example suggests that the catalogue of prototype effects presented earlier in this chapter needs to be extended to include degree of productivity. As expressions deviate more and more from the prototypical value of a construction, they become increasingly subject to lexical and other kinds of idiosyncratic constraints.

c) For weeks on end

Constructions can be studied with an eye on the lexical items which can occur in them. The interaction has been insightfully studied by Stefanowitsch and Gries (2003) with their notion of collostruction. On the one hand, a construction tends to prefer certain lexical items, or items exhibiting certain semantic/pragmatic properties, in its various slots; on the other hand, a lexical item may occur preferentially in a certain construction. Combining the two perspectives makes it possible to identify preferred configurations, which Goldberg (2006) and Gries (2003) have no hesitation in referring to as a construction's prototype.

For my third example I look at one of the myriad phraseological constructions from this perspective. *For [NOUN$_{plural}$] on end* is lexically specified apart from one open slot, which in this case can be filled by a plural noun designating a period of time. Semantically, the construction suggests a subjective experience of the passing of time. It is as if a person is so involved in, or bored by, a situation that she is no longer aware of how many time units have elapsed. The most frequent instantiation in the BNC is *for hours on end*; other nouns, in decreasing order of frequency, which can occur in the construction include *days, weeks, months, minutes,* and *years* (see Fig. 27.1).

Whether we should regard the relative frequency of these nouns as prototype effects is moot. (Should we, for example, say that the prototypical use of the word *unmitigated*

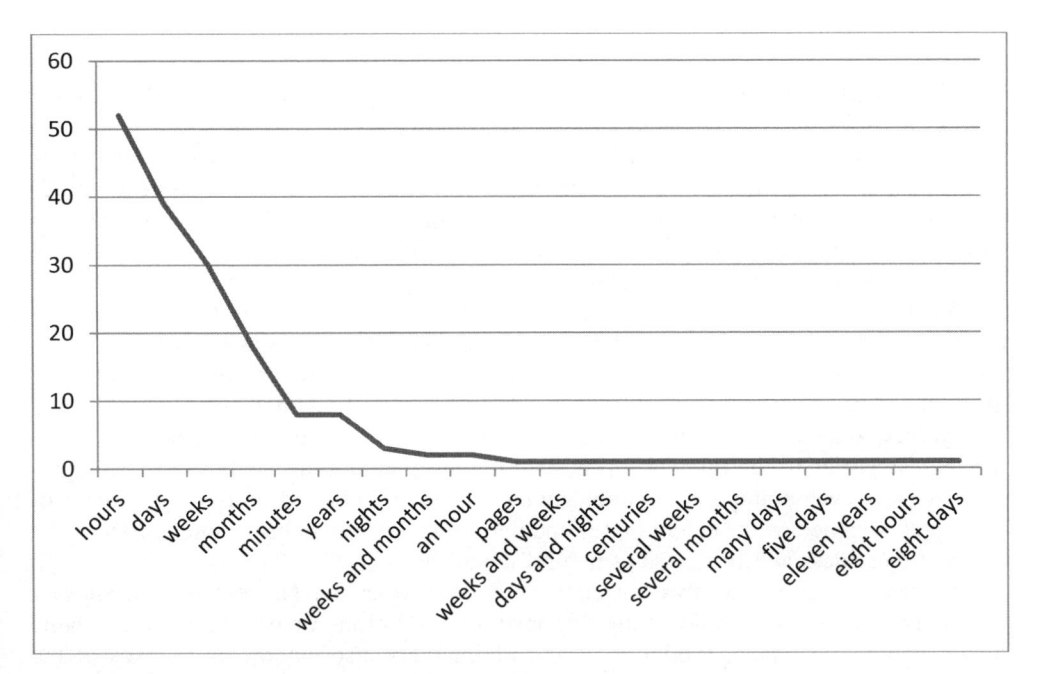

Fig. 27.1: Frequency of expressions of the form [for NP on end] in the BNC.

is in collocation with *disaster*? Or should we simply say that *unmitigated* typically collocates with *disaster*, and leave it at that?) What is of interest, however, is that we also encounter deviations from the canonical phraseology, albeit with much reduced frequencies. There are occasional examples of repeated and coordinated nominals (*for weeks and weeks on end, for weeks and months on end*), examples with a specific number of time units (*for five days on end*), and even sporadic examples where a single time unit is stated (*for an hour on end*) – the latter usage being somewhat at variance with the proposed semantic value of the construction. It is to be noted, however, that these deviations tend to make use of lexical items selected from the upper frequency range (*hour, month, day*), and in this respect are constrained by what may indeed be regarded as the construction's prototypical instances. *For one century on end* deviates too far from the construction's prototype; there are no corpus examples, and even a Google search failed to return any instances.

The reverse J-shaped distribution in Fig. 27.1 is Zipfian: a small number of types make up the lion's share of the construction's tokens, while a large number of types constitute only a tiny minority of the tokens. In this case, frequency stands out as the principal marker of prototypicality. The long tail of the distribution is largely made up of types which exemplify distortions, of various kinds, from the more prototypical (most frequent) types.

8. Conclusion

In the first part of the chapter I listed the various prototype effects that have been found in relation to the referential categories studied by Rosch and others. These cluster around centrality and salience effects. When the notion of prototype was extended to the study of the semantic structure of polysemous words (*over* being one of the earliest studied examples), a rather different understanding of prototype was needed, one which was based more firmly in the notion of structural centrality. The application of the notion to the grammatical categories of a language (especially those which associate a formal and a semantic specification) raises some further issues, in particular, the need to align prototypicality of form with prototypicality of meaning. Prototypes as the locus of structural and semantic contrast also came into focus. "Good" examples of noun and verb, of word and bound morpheme, of compound and phrase, of middles, unaccusatives, and unergatives, and so on, maximize the distinctiveness of the categories, thereby legitimizing the categories in the linguist's grammar, notwithstanding the plethora of less representative and even ambiguous examples which are easily attested. Indeed, the notion of prototype is valued to the extent that it enables the researcher to bring some order to the inherent messiness and fuzziness of natural language.

Frequency does not always correlate with prototypicality. Nevertheless, frequency does play a crucial role in the study of constructions and the items which are available to fill their various slots. Productivity and idiomaticity also emerge as reflexes of the structure of constructional categories.

9. References

Aarts, Bas
   2007   *Syntactic Gradience: The Nature of Grammatical Indeterminacy.* Oxford: Oxford University Press.

Barsalou, Laurence
   1987   The instability of graded structure: Implications for the nature of concepts. In: U. Neisser (ed.), *Concepts and Conceptual Development: Ecological and Intellectual Factors in Categorization,* 101–140. Cambridge: Cambridge University Press.

Battig, William F and William E. Montague
   1969   Category norms for verbal items in 56 categories. A replication and extension of the Connecticut category norms. *Journal of Experimental Psychology Monographs* 80: 1–46.

Bauer, Laurie
   1998   When is a sequence of two nouns a compound in English? *English Language and Linguistics* 2: 65–86.

Brugman, Claudia and George Lakoff
   [1988] 2006   Cognitive topology and lexical networks. In: D. Geeraerts (ed.), *Cognitive Linguistics: Basic Readings,* 109–139. Berlin: Mouton de Gruyter.

Clark, Eve
   In press   First words. In: J. R. Taylor (ed.), *The Oxford Handbook of the Word.* Oxford: Oxford University Press.

Croft, William
   2001   *Radical Construction Grammar: Syntactic Theory in Typological Perspective.* Oxford: Oxford University Press.

Davies, Mark
   2008   The Corpus of Contemporary American English (COCA). Available online at http://www.americancorpus.org
Deignan, Alice and L. Potter
   2004   A corpus study of metaphors and metonyms in English and Italian. *Journal of Pragmatics* 36: 1231–1252.
Dewell, Robert
   1994   *Over* again: Image-schema transformations in semantic analysis. *Cognitive Linguistics* 5: 351–380.
Divjak, Dagmar and Antti Arppe
   2013   Extracting prototypes from exemplars: What can corpus data tell us about concept representation? *Cognitive Linguistics* 24: 221–274.
Fodor, Jerry
   1980   The present status of the innateness controversy. In: *Representations: Philosophical Essays on the Foundations of Cognitive Science*, 257–316. Cambridge: MIT Press.
Geeraerts, Dirk
   1987   Introduction: Prospects and problems of prototype theory. *Linguistics* 27: 587–612.
Givón, Talmy
   1979   *On Understanding Grammar*. New York: Academic Press.
Goldberg, Adele
   2006   *Constructions at Work*. Oxford: Oxford University Press.
Gries, Stefan Th.
   2003   Towards a corpus-based identification of prototypical instances of constructions. *Annual Review of Cognitive Linguistics* 1: 1–27.
Gries, Stefan Th.
   2014   Corpus and quantitative methods. In: J. Littlemore and J. Taylor (eds.), *The Bloomsbury Companion to Cognitive Linguistics*, 279–300. London: Bloomsbury.
Hallan, Naomi
   2001   Paths to prepositions? A corpus-based study of the acquisition of a lexico-grammatical category. In: J. Bybee and P. Hopper (eds.), *Frequency and the Emergence of Linguistic Structure*, 91–120. Amsterdam: Benjamins.
Heider, Eleanor
   1972   Universals in color naming and memory. *Journal of Experimental Psychology* 93: 10–20.
Hilpert, Martin
   2006   Keeping an eye on the data? Metonymies and their patterns. In: A. Stefanowitsch and S. Th. Gries (eds.), *Corpus-based Approaches to Metaphor and Metonymy*, 123–152. Berlin: Mouton de Gruyter.
Hudson, Richard
   2007   *Language Networks: The New Word Grammar*. Oxford: Oxford University Press.
Kemmer, Suzanne
   2003   Schemas and lexical blends. In: H. Cuyckens, Th. Berg, R. Dirven, and K.-U. Panther (eds.), *Motivation in Language*, 69–97. Amsterdam: Benjamins.
Kuhl, Patricia
   1991   Human adults and human infants show a "perceptual magnet effect" for prototypes of speech categories, monkeys do not. *Perception and Psychophysics* 50: 93–107.
Lakoff, George
   1987   *Women, Fire, and Dangerous Things. What Categories Reveal about the Mind*. Chicago: Chicago University Press.
Langacker, Ronald. W.
   1987   Nouns and verbs. *Language* 63: 53–94.

Marshall, Caroline E. and Wendy V. Parr
　1996　New Zealand norms for a subset of Battig and Montague's (1969) categories. *New Zealand Journal of Psychology* 25: 24–29.
Murphy, Gregory
　2002　*The Big Book of Concepts*. Cambridge: MIT Press.
Posner, Michael
　1986　Empirical studies of prototypes. In: C. Craig (ed.), *Noun Classes and Categorization*, 53–61. Amsterdam: Benjamins.
Posner, Michael and Steven W. Keele
　1968　On the genesis of abstract ideas. *Journal of Experimental Psychology* 77: 353–363.
Ramscar, Michael
　this volume　4. Categorization. Berlin/Boston: De Gruyter Mouton.
Rice, Sally
　2003　Growth of a lexical network: Nine English prepositions in acquisition. In: H. Cuyckens, R. Dirven, and J. R. Taylor (eds.), *Cognitive Approaches to Lexical Semantics*, 243–280. Berlin: Mouton de Gruyter.
Rips, Lance J.
　1975　Inductive judgments about natural categories. *Journal of Verbal Learning and Verbal Behavior* 14: 665–81.
Rosch, Eleanor
　1973　On the internal structure of perceptual and semantic categories. In: T. E. Moore (ed.), *Cognitive Development and the Acquisition of Language*, 111–144. New York: Academic Press.
Rosch, Eleanor
　1975　Cognitive reference points. *Cognitive Psychology* 7: 532–547.
Rosch, Eleanor
　1978　Principles of categorization. In: E. Rosch and B. Lloyd (eds.), *Cognition and Categorization*, 27–48. Hillsdale, NJ: Lawrence Erlbaum.
Rosenbach, Anette
　2006　Descriptive genitives in English: a case study on constructional gradience. *English Language and Linguistics* 10: 77–118.
Sandra, Dominiek and Sally Rice
　1995　Network analyses of prepositional meaning: mirroring whose mind – the linguist's or the language user's? *Cognitive Linguistics* 6: 89–130.
Smith, Mark
　In press　Word categories. In: J. R. Taylor (ed.), *The Oxford Handbook of the Word*. Oxford: Oxford University Press.
Stefanowitsch, Anatol and Stefan Th. Gries
　2003　Collostructions: Investigating the interaction of words and constructions. *International Journal of Corpus Linguistics* 8: 209–243.
Stefanowitsch, Anatol and Stefan Th. Gries
　2005　Covarying collexemes. *Corpus Linguistics and Linguistic Theory* 1: 1–43
Taylor, John R.
　1996　*Possessives in English*. Oxford: Oxford University Press.
Taylor, John R.
　2003　*Linguistic Categorization*. Oxford: Oxford University Press.
Taylor, John R.
　2008　Prototypes in cognitive linguistics. In: P. Robinson and N. Ellis (eds.), *Handbook of Cognitive Linguistics and Second Language Acquisition*, 39–65. London: Routledge.
Taylor, John R.
　2012　*The Mental Corpus: How Language is Represented in the Mind*. Oxford: Oxford University Press.

Taylor, John R.
   In press   Word-formation in Cognitive Grammar. To appear in: P. Müller, I. Ohnheiser, S. Olsen, and F. Raine (eds.), *HSK Word-formation*. Berlin: de Gruyter.
Tyler, Andrea and Vyvyan Evans
   2001   Reconsidering prepositional polysemy networks: The case of over. *Language* 77: 724–765.
Yoshimura, Kimihiro and John R. Taylor
   2004   What makes a good middle? The role of qualia in the interpretation and acceptability of middle expressions in English. *English Language and Linguistics* 8: 293–321.

John R. Taylor, Christchurch (New Zealand)

28. Argument structure constructions

1. Introduction
2. Constructions are associated with meaning independent of the verb
3. Constructions mediate the mapping from "thought" to "talk" in language production
4. Learning argument structure construction
5. Conclusion
6. References

1. Introduction

Traditional Generativist (e.g., Chomsky 1957) theory approaches the notion of argument structure by identifying two components that are involved in specifying the meaning and form of an utterance. The first is a set of culturally determined strings (lexical items). The second is a set of universal and innate "linking rules" that map aspects of sentence meaning onto a structural representation of its form (syntax). Central to these approaches is the notion that aspects of sentence meaning, specifically relational meaning ("who does what to whom") as well as sentence form are assumed to be projections of the semantic and syntactic properties of the main verb (we refer to this as the projectionist account of argument structure). General linking rules plus a number of structural principles connect an underlying representation of the utterance to the surface ordering of words. Most traditional generativist theories also assume multi-stratal syntactic levels of representation intervening between meaning and surface structure. In generativist theory, then, the learning issue is simplified since the language learner only has to learn the meaning of lexical items (in particular of verbs), and then select the proper underlying form and linking rules that correspond to the spoken language.

More recently, however, a new approach to argument structure has appeared. This approach, called the constructional approach, eliminates the need for many of the traditional assumptions mentioned above. A number of variations of the constructional approach to argument structure exist (e.g., Birner and Ward 1998; Croft 2001; Fillmore et al. 1988; Lakoff 1987; Langacker 1987; Michaelis and Lambrecht 1996, among others;

cf. Goldberg 2013), but these approaches share a set of core assumptions that are sufficient to distinguish them sharply from traditional generative approaches, even when not every single assumption is adopted (Goldberg 2013). Following Goldberg (2013), key tenets of the constructional approach are that 1) knowledge of language consists of learned form-meaning pairings; 2) representations are surface-oriented and non-derivational; 3) constructions exist at different levels of generalization, from the more abstract to the more concrete and lexical.

The specific approach that has been best studied empirically is represented by Goldberg's (1995, 2006) work (though we stress that much of the work is applicable to other constructional approaches). Within a constructional approach to grammar, constructions may be morphemes, words, idioms, phrases or abstract linguistic patterns. Argument structure constructions are learned form-function pairings that are posited to exist independently of the specific verbs in the sentence (see also Diessel this volume). They are networks of features specifying mappings between syntactic form and semantic-pragmatic function. The patterns are typically specified in terms of semantic and or "functional" levels of processing (as in (1) below), though they may also be specified in terms of word order (as in the NP construction). In addition, constructions may be fully abstract as in the caused-motion construction in (1) or they may be partially lexically filled as in the What's X doing Y construction (Kay and Fillmore 1999) (2).

Example   **Construction Name: Pattern**
(1) Tom put the spoon into the drawer.   Caused-Motion Construction:
                                                 $<NP_{agent}> <verb_{motion}{}^{1}> <NP_{patient}> <PP_{path}>$
(2) What's that fly doing in my soup?   What's X doing Y:
                                                 What's X doing Y?

Constructions may be combined to form other constructions so long as their specifications do not conflict. The form or meaning of the containing construction, however, is not predictable by the sum of its parts, but is itself unique. Thus, although the caused-motion construction contains an NP and PP construction, its form and meaning are not predictable by the process of stringing NPs and PPs together with a verb.

If argument structure constructions (henceforth *constructions*) themselves are associated directly with relational meaning independent of the meaning of the verb, it should be possible to examine empirically the contribution of the construction to sentence meaning in various sentence comprehension tasks. Likewise, if constructions mediate the mapping between sentence meaning and form, constructions should also be detectable in sentence production tasks. In this chapter we first review evidence from comprehension and production studies that speakers access constructions in language use. Since constructions are *learned* form-meaning pairings, we then move on to examine the evidence that constructions are in fact learned and learnable.

2. Constructions are associated with meaning independent of the verb

The first study to examine the contribution of constructions to sentence meaning was Bencini and Goldberg (2000). The study compared the semantic contribution of the

---
[1] The motion may be real or implied.

construction with that of the verb in a categorization task where native speakers of English were asked to sort sentences based on meaning and to provide explanations for their sortings. The stimuli were obtained by crossing four verbs (two semantically light verbs: *get*, *take*, and two semantically rich verbs: *throw, slice*) with four different constructions (Transitive: Verb Object, e.g., *Michelle got the book*; Ditransitive: V Object1 Object2, e.g., *Chris threw Linda the pencil*; Resultative: Verb Object Result, e.g., *Nancy sliced the tire open*; Caused Motion: Verb Object Location, e.g., *Kim took the rose into the house*). Participants were instructed to sort the sixteen sentences by "overall sentence meaning" into groups of four. They were told that the purpose of the study was to understand how people sort sentences according to meaning and that there was no right or wrong answer. Non-linguistic categorization research has shown that there is a robust domain-general tendency towards "one-dimensional sorting" even with stimuli and categories that are by design created to induce multi-dimensional sorting (e.g., Medin et al. 1987). In Bencini and Goldberg's stimuli the one-dimensional sorting bias should be driven by the fact that the sentences shared a common verb. In spite of this bias, results showed that speakers categorized sentences based on overall meaning by taking into account the overall argument structure of sentences in addition to verbs. Participants' explanations for their sorting decisions, as judged by independent judges, showed that they were paying attention to sentence meaning rather than verb tokens. In some cases the explanations corresponded remarkably to the kinds of abstract relational meanings posited for constructions. For example, for a ditransitive sort, one protocol read: "In this pile there were two people, and one person was doing something for the other person" (cf. Ditransitive Meaning: X causes Y to receive Z). For a transitive sort, another protocol read: "In this pile a person is just doing something" (cf. Transitive Meaning: X acts on Y). Bencini and Goldberg took these results to indicate a contribution of sentence structure to sentence meaning, independent of the contribution made by the meaning of the verb. They hypothesized that participants overcame the one-dimensional sorting bias because constructions predict overall sentence meaning better than verbs.

Another series of studies that examined the semantics associated with sentence patterns was conducted by Kako (2006). Participants saw sentences composed of novel words appearing in various constructions, and were asked how likely each was to involve the semantic properties associated with the construction. For example, participants saw the sentence *The rom gorped the blick to the dax* and were asked "How likely is it that gorping involves someone or something changing location?". Results were consistent with the hypothesis that syntactic frames carry meaning independently of the meaning of verbs: likely properties for each construction received significantly higher ratings than did unlikely properties.

Additional comprehension studies that show the importance of constructions in determining aspects of sentence interpretation are the studies by Kaschak and Glenberg (2000) and Goldwater and Markman (2009). Both studies use novel verbs derived from nouns. In Kaschak and Glenberg's study, participants were given short passages that were designed to set up a transfer scenario. They were then asked to paraphrase sentences containing the novel verbs (e.g., *crutch*) and to answer questions related to the semantics of the event. Kaschack and Glenberg found that different constructions influenced speaker's interpretations of the novel verbs. If the verb occurred in the ditransitive construction (e.g., *She crutched him the apple*) they were more likely to say that sentence meant that she used the crutch to transfer him the apple. If the verb appeared in the transitive construction (e.g., *She crutched him*) they interpreted the sentence to mean that she hit him over the head with a crutch.

Goldwater and Markman (2009) used denominal verbs that required a change of state (e.g., the noun *sauce* used as a denominal verb *to sauce* suggesting a process of turning something into a sauce), and presented them either in a passive construction (*The ripe tomatoes were sauced expertly to compliment the pasta at the gala dinner*) or a middle construction (*The ripe tomatoes had sauced expertly to compliment the pasta at the gala dinner*). Speakers should have more difficulty making sense of sentences using the verb *sauce* in the middle construction than sentences in the passive because the event structure associated with the middle construction does not entail agency, while the event structure of the passive *does* entail agency. Indeed, participants judged middle constructions with novel denominal verbs more nonsensical than passive constructions containing the same novel verbs. Critically, agency could not be contributed by the verb because these verbs were novel.

The comprehension studies reviewed so far show that constructions play a role in speaker's interpretations of sentences. The studies, however, leave open the possibility of a strategic or meta-linguistic component to participants' responses. Johnson and Goldberg (2012) addressed this concern with an online study to determine whether abstract semantics is automatically associated with syntactic frames and whether this is also true of constructions instantiated with "Jabberwocky" sentences constructed entirely with nonsense open-class words. The paradigm was a lexical decision task requiring that participants rapidly decide whether a word presented on the computer screen is a real word or not. Before each lexical decision trial, participants read a Jabberwocky sentence instantiating one of four constructions (Ditransitive: *He daxed her the norp*; Resultative: *She jorped it miggy*; Caused-motion: *He lorped it on the molp*; Removal: *She vakoed it from her*). There were two semantic congruency conditions between the verb and the preceding construction: congruent and incongruent. For example, when *gave* was preceded by the ditransitive construction (e.g., *He jorped him the brap*), it is "congruent;" when *gave* is preceded by the removal construction it is incongruent. Verbs were high frequency associates of the construction or low frequency associates. High frequency associates are verbs that most frequently occur in the construction as determined by corpus studies. For example, *give* is the most frequent verb that occurs in the ditransitive. Low frequency associates are verbs that appear in the construction, but less frequently. For example, *hand* occurs in the ditransitive (e.g., *She handed him something*), but less frequently than *give* does. Results showed that when the construction and the verb were congruent, constructions elicited (*primed*) faster reaction times (RTs) compared to when they were incongruent. Moreover, constructions primed both high associate verbs, that is both verbs with which they regularly occur and verbs with which they occur less frequently. The results suggest that 1) constructions prime verb semantics during sentence comprehension, and 2) that syntactic patterns are associated with semantics even when they contain no open class lexical items.

3. Constructions mediate the mapping from "thought" to "talk" in language production

Evidence for verb-independent constructions as processing units at work in production comes from a particularly powerful experimental technique: structural priming. Structural priming refers to the tendency of speakers to produce previously experienced sentence patterns in their subsequent utterances. The priming logic allows us to draw inferences about the dimensions to which the cognitive architecture is sensitive. If processing of a prime stimulus influences the processing of a subsequent stimulus (the target), we can infer that the cognitive system is sensitive to the overlapping dimensions between the prime and the target. Priming has been used to investigate linguistic representations both in adults (Branigan 1995 et al.; Bencini 2002, 2013; Goldberg 2006) and children (e.g., Bencini and Valian 2008). In the classic implementation by Bock (1986), constructional priming was demonstrated with active vs. passive and double object vs. prepositional dative constructions. Speakers were more likely to describe two-participant transitive events (e.g., a picture of dog chasing a man) with a passive if they previously heard and repeated an unrelated passive sentence with different nouns and verbs (e.g., *The 747 was alerted by the airport control tower*). Whereas these results demonstrate the existence of verb-independent constructional priming in language production, what remains unclear is the nature of the semantic information supporting the priming. There are differences among authors with respect to whether they recognize semantic roles loosely corresponding to traditional thematic/event roles (or abstract relational meaning in constructional terms) such as AGENT, THEME, LOCATION, or whether the generalizations refer to more fine-grained semantic properties such as animacy and concreteness. Evidence against a thematic-role account is that structural priming appears not to depend on the identity of thematic roles in prime and target sentences. Bock and Loebell (1990, Experiment 1) found that prepositional locatives (e.g., *The wealthy widow drove the Mercedes to the church*) primed prepositional dative descriptions to the same degree as prepositional dative primes (e.g., *The wealthy widow gave the Mercedes to the church*). The prepositional locative and the prepositional dative have similar surface structural configurations (NP [V NP [P NP] PP] VP), but they differ in the event roles associated with the prepositional argument. In the prepositional locative, the prepositional phrase encodes the location of the action, while in the dative it encodes the recipient. A second experiment found stronger evidence against a purely thematic-role account of structural repetition (Bock and Loebell 1990, Experiment 2). Locative sentences like *The 747 was landing by the control tower* primed passive descriptions as much as did passives like *The 747 was alerted by the control tower*. The locatives and passives had similar surface structures (NP [AUX V [P NP] PP] VP), but the locatives had agents as subjects, while the passives had patients as subjects. Thematic role overlap per se did not increase structural priming: locatives and passives were equally effective primes for passive descriptions. The authors took these results to suggest that structural priming does not depend on thematic overlap between prime and target sentences. Instead of thematic roles, Bock et al. (1992) proposed that basic semantic features guide language production. Using once again a priming paradigm, they varied the animacy of the subjects of active and passive sentences, and found that an animate subject in the priming sentence increased the tendency to place animate entities as subjects in the target descriptions. Animacy priming was independent of structural priming, i.e., independent of the tendency to reuse the active or passive structure of priming sentences.

One problem in determining whether thematic roles play a role in structural priming is that in English, thematic role variations are typically accompanied by differences in sentence structure (e.g., active, passive) and/or animacy (e.g., ditransitive, prepositional dative). Chang et al. (2003), however, tested thematic-role priming without the confounding influences of animacy or structural changes, using locative constructions (the so called spray-load alternation) in which crucially 1) the order of constituents varies within the same syntactic structures and 2) both arguments are typically inanimate. In the locative alternation the order of the theme (the object that moves) and the location (the place that is moved to) vary within the same surface structure, traditionally NP [V NP [P NP] PP] VP. For example, in *The man sprayed wax on the car*, *wax* is the theme and *car* is its location. The alternative order puts the location before the theme, as in *The man sprayed the car with wax*. Priming of the structural configuration should not differ, but if the order of thematic roles matters, theme-location orders should prime other theme-location orders more than location-theme orders: i.e., *The man sprayed wax on the car* should prime *The workers scuffed dirt across the kitchen floor* more than *The workers scuffed the kitchen floor with dirt*. If thematic roles are not at work in production, no differences are expected between conditions with respect to priming. Consistent with a thematic role account of priming, results showed increased use of the location-theme orders after location-theme orders in the prime, and increased use of theme-location orders after theme-location orders in the prime.

The remaining inconsistent result that supports the notion that priming in production does not depend on thematic role overlap is Bock and Loebell (1990, Experiment 2) showing that Locative sentences like *The 747 was landing by the control tower* prime passives as much as passives like *The 747 was alerted by the control tower*.

We believe that part of the debate arises from the difference between defining constructions as static knowledge representations versus dealing with the processes of language production. The process of language production by definition is meaning driven, in that it starts out with a conceptual representation in the speaker's mind (the *message*) and ends with a grammatically encoded utterance. Therefore finding that at some point during the process of producing a sentence the processor is sensitive to form and less to meaning is not evidence against constructions. Moreover, two important features of the priming experiments using Bock's original paradigm (including Bock and Loebell 1990) are the nature of the priming task, and the nature of the stimuli. Unlike comprehension priming (which measures latencies), production priming examines how people describe pictures in front of them. In Bock and Loebell's Experiment 2, the fact that the surface similarity between locative sentences and passives equally primed participants to describe target pictures using a passive sentence is not surprising on a constructional account. First, construction grammar recognizes that sentences have both form and meaning, and that these are distinct types of information and can be independently accessed by the cognitive system. Second, in the classic production priming paradigm, the semantic support for using a passive is always present in the visual stimuli: target pictures for active/passive priming are events that lend themselves to passive descriptions even without priming. They are pictures of events in which the patient/theme is animate and or salient relative to the agent, e.g., "a bee stinging a man", "a truck hitting a nurse", "lightning striking a church".

The importance of the production priming studies with respect to constructions is that it points to representations that are in all respects "like" constructions in terms of their level of abstraction and in the non-derivational nature of the mapping (Bock et al. 1992). We therefore take the existence of verb-independent priming as strong converging evidence from the psycholinguistics of production for the cognitive reality of constructions.

4. Learning argument structure constructions

An important question and source of debate in acquisition research is whether and when children's early multi-word utterances reflect generalizations over verbs. Until recently, comprehension and production data in child language pointed to a "paradox" in which children appeared to rely on more abstract representations in comprehension than production (see Tomasello 2000, for a review).

Constructions, while being abstract in the sense that they contain open slots and generalizations over classes of words (e.g., verb, noun-phrase) and meanings (e.g., X causes Y to move to Z), are not so abstract that they cannot be learned on the basis of surface patterns in much the same way that other patterns perceived in the environment are learned – that is, through the use of general cognitive abilities. Early research on constructional learning was designed to show that constructions are learned on the basis of input rather than being innate. Like projectionist accounts, this research focused on the central role of the verb, and suggested that constructions are learned on a verb-by-verb basis. That is, while children are able to demonstrate the use of some verbs in a given construction, they are unable to use other verbs in the same construction (cf. Roberts 1983). So a given child might be able to act out *Big Bird tickled Cookie Monster* but be unable to act out *Big Bird hugged Cookie Monster*. Tomasello's (1992) verb island hypothesis makes a similar claim: children initially construct separate verb-specific schemas representing the verb's morphological and syntactic properties (e.g., <tickler> tickle <ticklee>). It is only after much exposure to similar patterns with other verbs (<hugger> hug <huggee>, and so forth) that the child forms an abstract schema, or construction: <agent> <verb> <patient>.

Subsequent research sought to corroborate this general pattern through experimental, rather than corpus-based results, and to develop a timeline for the shift from item-based constructions to abstract schemas. Akhtar and Tomasello (1997) conducted the first such study in which the authors crucially used novel verbs to eliminate the possibility that children were relying on previously learned verb-specific patterns during testing. The authors tested 2- and 3-year-olds' comprehension (via act-out tasks) and production of reversible transitive sentences. They found that as demonstrated by previous work (e.g., Olguin and Tomasello 1993), children could produce and comprehend the novel verbs with the same patients and agents that children heard during training. However, younger children generally did not produce the verbs in constructions with patients and agents different from the ones they heard the verbs used with during training. It was not until the age of about 3 (2;9–3;8) that children were able to comprehend reversible sentences using the novel verbs and agent/patient combinations different from the ones encountered during training (cf. also Abbot-Smith et al. 2001).

These studies mark an important departure from projectionist accounts. Because the projectionist account posits innate linking rules that dictate the form and meaning of an utterance by mapping syntactic positions on a formal template to the semantic positions of a verb's meaning, the template and linking rules need only be *identified*, not learned. Accordingly, children's productions are not predicted to show a pattern of initially conservative (i.e., verb-specific) usage. This notion has generated some controversy. Gertner et al. (2006), for example, found that children as young as 21 months are able to correctly identify scenes described using novel verbs in transitive sentences. The authors suggest that this is evidence that children's understanding of the transitive pattern is not tied to a particular lexical item, adding that children's performance does not seem to be influenced by their vocabularies since they failed to find any significant correlations between performance and vocabulary size and because 21-month-olds have rather small vocabularies to begin with. Moreover, 21 months is earlier than the age at which the previously mentioned studies suggest schema-based constructions develop. Dittmar and colleagues (Dittmar et al. 2008), however, argue that the results obtained by Gertner and colleagues were due largely to methodology. In particular, they suggest that the preferential looking paradigm used a practice phase (as is common) in which children were primed with several transitive sentences using the same nouns in the same syntactic roles and with the same syntactic marking as in the test sentences. Crucially, Dittmar and colleagues were only able to replicate the results of Gertner and colleagues when they also employed the target practice/training phase. Children, however, failed to show generalization when a more neutral training phase was used to expose children to the materials and methods of the study.

On the other hand, early construction-learning doesn't appear to be an all-or-nothing situation either (although early conservativism in construction use is well-established). Evidence that young children generalize to the level of constructions to some extent comes from structural priming studies similar to the adult language production studies reviewed in section 3. Bencini and Valian (2008) examined priming in young three-year-olds (ages 2;11–3;6) in the absence of verb overlap, and controlling for animacy. During priming, the experimenter described a picture (e.g., *The milk is stirred by the spoon*) and then the child repeated the utterance. This was followed by a "Your Turn" trial, in which the child described a different picture (e.g., a picture of a hammer cracking an egg). The results showed abstract priming of passive sentences, suggesting that 3-year-olds may produce at least some verb-independent constructions.

A crucial tenet of construction grammar is that learners are motivated to abstract to the level of the construction to determine the meanings of the sentences they hear. To examine whether constructional forms are predictive of sentence meaning in the naturally occurring input that children hear, Goldberg et al. (2005) examined a corpus of child directed speech to investigate how consistently the meaning of a construction was encoded by the meaning of the verb used in the construction on the one hand, and the meaning of the construction itself on the other.

The authors looked at two constructions: caused-motion, and ditransitive and examined verbs and constructions in terms of their cue validity and category validity. Cue validity is the probability that an entity belongs to a certain category given the occurrence of a certain cue or feature. Category validity is the inverse: the probability that an entity will have a certain cue or feature given that it is a member of a certain category. In the study, the authors investigated the cue validity of verbs for sentence meaning (e.g., the probability that a sentence [the object] has the meaning of "caused-motion" [the category] given that the verb is *put* [the cue]. Likewise, they investigated the category validity of verbs in sentences (i.e., the probability that a sentence with a caused-motion meaning would contain the verb *put*). Their analyses found that while some verbs had perfect cue validity – that is, they perfectly predicted the constructions that they would appear in (e.g., *put* in the caused-motion construction) – the cue validity of most other verbs was quite low. In fact, they found the cue validity of constructions to be at least as good as the cue validity of individual verbs. In contract, the authors found that constructions have much higher category validity than do verbs. That is, given a caused-motion meaning, for example, a sentence is much more likely to be framed in a caused-motion construction than it is to contain any particular verb (e.g., *put*). This is due to the fact that there is such a large number of different verbs that can appear in a given construction, and since only a few of the verbs – typically those called general purpose or light verbs – encode a meaning the same as the construction, the average category validity of verbs approaches zero as more verbs are considered in the analysis. This leads us to conclude that constructions are at least as useful for determining the meaning of an utterance as are verbs, but they occur with a given meaning more consistently than do verbs in general.

One might also ask whether the learner is able to use the distributional properties of the input to determine what *not* to say. That is, to determine that *She told her the news* is acceptable while *She explained her the news* sounds odd (examples from Goldberg 2011). Several researchers (e.g., Bowerman 1996; Goldberg 2006, 2011; Pinker 1989) have pointed out that the notion of entrenchment – the idea that we choose one way of expressing an idea simply because of the high frequency with which it occurs – is not an entirely sufficient explanation since it doesn't account for why some verbs, which occur with disproportionately high frequency in one argument structure construction are still acceptable when used in a different argument structure construction (i.e., one in which they rarely occur). *Sneeze*, for example, is entrenched in the intransitive construction, yet the utterance *I sneezed the ice cream cone into my lap*, in which *sneeze* occurs in the transitive and caused motion constructions, is acceptable in spite of the rarity of the use of *sneeze* with a direct object. To solve this problem, Goldberg (1993, 1995, 2006, 2011), building on Pinker's (1989) proposal for a preemptability marker in children's grammar, proposed a process of statistical preemption whereby construction A preempts construction B to the extent that a) both constructions ought to be equally appropriate in the given discourse context, and b) construction A occurs rather than construction B. Conducting an analysis of the dative and ditransitive constructions in the 450 million word Corpus of Contemporary American English, Goldberg (2011) shows that in discourse contexts in which the ditransitive might have been expected, the dative was used significantly more than would be expected by chance (83 % of the time on average, ranging from .53–1.0).

Experimental evidence also suggests that the notion of statistical preemption is correct. Brooks and Tomasello (1999), for example, modeled the description of a doll swinging a house on a rope by saying *The house is tamming* (intransitive) and *The doll is helping the house tam* (each repeated 44 times). A different group of children heard transitive and causative sentences: *The doll is tamming the house* and *The house is getting tammed*. When children were later asked to describe the scenes, children who heard the intransitive models used *tam* intransitively the vast majority of the time, while children who heard the transitive models had an overwhelming tendency to use it transitively.

Boyd and Goldberg's (2011) investigation of novel a-adjectives produced a similar experimental effect. A-adjectives like *asleep* and *alive* are dispreferred prenominally (*The asleep boy*, *The alive plant*). When adults were presented with two novel a-adjectives in relative clauses (e.g., *The fox that's adax*) just three times each, speakers treated those two novel a-adjectives in the same way as they treated known a-adjectives, producing them in relative clauses rather than in prenominal position. In fact, even when given two additional a-adjectives that they had not seem previously, participants still treated them as they did the known a-adjectives. Unlike these novel a-adjectives, novel adjectives not beginning with *a-* were freely used prenominally. Boyd and Goldberg's results suggest not only that statistical preemption is at work, but also that statistical preemption may be generalized across categories.

Children's ability to learn argument structure constructions themselves, that is to map novel constructional forms to novel meanings without being influenced (for better or worse) by patterns of language that the child already knows was recently investigated by Goldberg and colleagues in a number of studies that have produced evidence that children are in fact able to assign a novel meaning to a novel construction (e.g., Goldberg et al. 2005; Casenhiser and Goldberg 2005; Boyd et al. 2009).

The general paradigm used in each of the studies to date is reminiscent of the preferential looking paradigm used to test children's understanding of linguistic constructions (e.g., Fisher 1996; Naigles 1990). In it, a novel construction was employed whose meaning indicated that an NP theme appeared in an NP location in the manner specified by a nonsense verb. The form was as follows:

NP_{theme} $NP_{location}$ nonsense verb

The utterances generated with this construction were then paired with video-taped scenes depicting their meaning. For example, *the spot the king moopoed* indicated that the spot (NP_{theme}) appeared on the king ($NP_{location}$) in the manner indicated by the verb (in this case, "fading into existence"). The paradigm is rounded out by using a training phase in which participants are exposed to the utterances paired with the videotaped examples of the utterance's meaning. The intent is to simulate in a controlled manner the sorts of pairings between scenes and utterances that a learner would experience when exposed to a novel construction (cf. Hauser et al. 2002). In the testing phase of the experiment, two minimally different scenes are placed side-by-side while an utterance is played. The child is instructed to touch the scene that corresponds to the utterance. In this paradigm, only the meaning of the noun phrases is known. Thus participants had to determine from context, the meaning of the verb, the meaning of the construction, and the form of the construction. In fact, they also had to determine that the word order did in fact have a meaning rather than being haphazard.

The studies have demonstrated that children can generalize beyond the input they receive to distinguish between a simple transitive scene using transitive syntax (<agent> <verb> <patient>) and a scene of appearance using the novel appearance construction (with novel verbs), and that participants are able to use such newly acquired constructions productively – even when mappings run counter to specifications which are claimed to be universal (Pinker 1989).

4.1. Construction learning as category learning

Other work has investigated construction learning as an instance of category learning that is subject to the same sorts of facilitative and inhibitory effects as other types of category learning (see also Ramscar this volume). Goldberg and colleagues (Goldberg et al. 2007) present evidence that parallels evidence derived from non-linguistic category learning (Gentner and Medina 1998; Markman and Gentner 1993), suggesting that early presentation of stimuli with shared concrete similarity facilitates construction learning. Other work has demonstrated a facilitative effect on construction learning when exemplars follow a so-called Zipfian distribution (Zipf 1935) in which the frequency with which a verb occurs in a given construction accounts for the lion's share of tokens encountered by learners (Casenhiser and Goldberg 2005; Goldberg et al. 2004). A number of corpus-based studies (e.g., Gries et al. 2005; Gries and Wulff 2005; Cameron-Faulkner et al. 2003), have suggested that natural language input tends to mirror this effect (see also Divjak and Caldwell-Harris this volume for a discussion of frequency effects), and evidence from non-linguistic category learning (Elio and Anderson 1984) has shown a facilitative effect for such an input distribution.

This particular effect, however, is not to be overstated since the importance of type frequency (the frequency of occurrence of a pattern or category) in generalization may overshadow the effects of Zipfian distributions. In ESL studies (see also Ellis and Wulff this volume), McDonough and Kim (2009) found a facilitative effect of greater type frequency in priming *wh*-questions, and Collins and colleagues (Collins et al. 2009) also found type frequency (along with perceptual salience) to reliably distinguish early-learned L2 constructions from those that are learned later. Indeed, the facilitative effect of skewed input appears somewhat fragile and may well be limited to early learning, or may become washed out by extended training. In teaching the English ditransitive construction to Korean speakers, for example, Year and Gordon (2009) trained participants for a total of 200 minutes. Though participants did learn the construction, corroborating earlier results, the authors failed to find a facilitative effect for skewed input.

4.2. Neurolinguistic research on construction learning

Nonetheless, the notion of construction learning as an instance of category learning is an important one that suggests the learnability of syntax in the absence of innate categories. Moreover, there is now emerging neurophysiological evidence supporting the notion. Johnson and colleagues (in press) investigated the neural correlates of construction learning by presenting participants with the appearance construction used in Goldberg and colleagues' previous experiments. They compared fMRI activation during this condition with activation during a random condition in which participants encountered the same scenes, but the words were presented in random order (i.e., consistent meaning with no consistent constructional form). They found activation in neural areas related to statistical learning (specifically the left ventral striatum) during the patterned construction learning condition, but not during the condition in which participants were presented with scrambled words (i.e., when they were not learning a construction). This result presents the first evidence of the neurophysiological reality of construction learning. But more to the point of construction learning as an instance of category learning, they also found that the patterned condition showed increasing activation in areas associated with non-linguistic pattern learning (i.e., the posterior precuneus) over the course of the experiment, while no such activation was evident in the random condition. This pattern of activation suggests a neurocognitive kinship between construction learning and non-linguistic category learning.

In the only other neurolinguistic study of construction-learning, Allen and colleagues (2012) conducted an fMRI experiment designed to distinguish regions of neural activation during processing of the ditransitive (*Jessica sold Mike a hotdog*) and dative (*Jessica sold a hotdog to Mike*) constructions. Traditional projectionist theories suggest that such pairs of constructions have equivalent semantics owing to the premise that they are derived from the same underlying representation (e.g., Baker 1996; Hale et al. 1997). Others have argued that the two constructions have subtle but different meanings (e.g., Goldberg 2002) wherein the ditransitive connotes intended transfer and the dative indicates caused motion. Accordingly, if the two constructions are represented and/or processed differently by the brain, neurological differences ought to be able to be detected. This is, in fact, what Allen and colleagues found. Specifically, they found differences in processing for the two constructions with greater activation localized to the left anterior portion of Broadmann Area 22, which has been associated with the understanding and generation of words, and left Broadmann Area 47, which has been implicated in syntactic processing. This result holds in spite of the fact the lexical items in the sentences were identical (excepting the addition of *to* in the dative construction). Moreover, no such differences were found in controls in which the lexical items were presented in scrambled order.

5. Conclusion

In this chapter we have reviewed evidence for a constructional account of argument structure grounded in the empirical evidence for this approach in language use (comprehension and production) and language acquisition. We have reviewed evidence demonstrating that verb independent mappings from sentence level relational meanings to sentence forms are used by speakers to compute sentence meanings alongside verbs, that these mappings are learnable, and that they are at work in the process of language production both in adults and in children. Evidence for a constructional approach to argument structure within linguistics is now solidly convergent with evidence from disparate fields, making construction type units particularly useful to capture linguistic behaviors beyond the classic linguistic data.

6. References

Abbot-Smith, Kirsten, Elena Lieven, and Michael Tomasello
    2001   What preschool children do and do not do with ungrammatical word orders. *Cognitive Development* 16(2): 679–692.
Akhtar, Nameera, and Michael Tomasello
    1997   Young children's productivity with word order and verb morphology. *Developmental Psychology* 33(6): 952–965.
Allen, Kachina, Francisco Pereira, Matthew Botvinick and Adele E. Goldberg
    2012   Distinguishing grammatical constructions with fMRI pattern analysis. *Brain and Language* 123: 174–182.
Baker, Mark
    1996   On the structural positions of themes and goals. In: L. Zaring and J. Rooryck (eds.), *Phrase Structure and the Lexicon*, 7–34. Dordrecht: Kluwert.

Bencini Giulia M. L.
2002   The representation and processing of argument structure constructions. PhD Dissertation. University of Illinois.
Bencini Giulia M. L.
2013   Psycholinguistics. In: T. Hoffmann and G. Trousdale (eds.) *The Oxford Handbook of Construction Grammar* 379–398. Oxford: Oxford University Press.
Bencini, Giulia M. L., and Adele E. Goldberg
2000   The contribution of argument structure constructions to sentence meaning. *Journal of Memory and Language* 43(4): 640–651.
Bencini, Giulia M. L., and Virginia Valian
2008   Abstract sentence representations in 3-year-olds: Evidence from comprehension and production. *Journal of Memory and Language* 59: 97–113.
Birner, Betty, and Gregory Ward
1998   *Information Status and Noncanonical Word Order in English.* Philadelphia: John Benjamins.
Bock, Kathryn
1986   Syntactic persistence in language production. *Cognitive Psychology* 18: 355–87.
Bock, Kathryn, and Helga Loebell
1990   Framing sentences. *Cognition* 35: 1–39.
Bock, Kathryn J., Helga Loebell, and Randel Morey
1992   From conceptual roles to structural relations: Bridging the syntactic cleft. *Psychological Review* 99: 150–171.
Bowerman, Melissa.
1996   Argument structure and learnability: Is a solution in sight? *Proceedings of the Annual Meeting of the Berkeley Linguistics Society* 22(1): 454–468.
Boyd, Jeremy K. and Adele E. Goldberg
2011   Learning what not to say: categorization and preemption in a-adjective production. *Language* 81(1): 1–29.
Boyd, Jeremy K., Emily A. Gottschalk, and Adele E. Goldberg
2009   Linking rule acquisition in novel phrasal constructions. *Lingua* 59(Supplement 1): 64–89.
Branigan, Holly P., Martin J. Pickering, Simon P. Liversedge, Andrew J. Stewart, and Thomas P. - Urbach
1995   Syntactic priming: Investigating the mental representation of language. *Journal of Psycholinguistic Research* 24(6): 489–506.
Brooks, Patricia J., and Michael Tomasello
1999   How children constrain their argument structure constructions. *Language* 75(4): 720–738.
Cameron-Faulkner, Thea, Elena Lieven and Michael Tomasello
2003   A construction based analysis of child directed speech. *Cognitive Science* 27(6): 843–873.
Casenhiser, Devin M., and Adele E. Goldberg
2005   Fast mapping between a phrasal form and meaning. *Developmental Science* 8(6): 500–508.
Chang, Franklin, Kay Bock, and Adele E. Goldberg
2003   Do thematic roles leave traces in their places? *Cognition* 90(1): 29–49.
Chomsky, Noam
1957   *Syntactic Structures.* The Hague: Mouton.
Collins, Laura, Pavel, Trofimovich, Joanna White, Walcir Cardoso, and Marlise Horst
2009   Some input on the easy/difficult grammar question: An empirical study. *The Modern Language Journal* 93(3): 336–353.

Croft, William
   2001   *Radical Construction Grammar.* Oxford: Oxford University Press.
Diessel, Holger
   this volume   14. Usage-based Construction Grammar. Berlin/Boston: De Gruyter Mouton.
Dittmar, Miriam, Kirsten Abbot-Smith, Elena Lieven, and Michael Tomasello
   2008   Young German children's early syntactic competence: A preferential looking study. *Developmental Science* 11(4): 575–582.
Divjak, Dagmar and Catherine Caldwell-Harris
   this volume   3. Frequency and entrenchment. Berlin/Boston: De Gruyter Mouton.
Elio, Renee, and John R. Anderson
   1984   The effects of information order and learning mode on schema abstraction. *Memory and Cognition* 12(1): 20–30.
Ellis, Nick C. and Stefanie Wulff
   this volume   19. Second language acquisition. Berlin/Boston: De Gruyter Mouton.
Fillmore, Charles J., Paul Kay, Laura Michaelis, and Ivan Sag
   1988   *Construction Grammar.* Stanford: CSLI.
Fisher, Cynthia
   1996   Structural limits on verb mapping: The role of analogy in children's interpretations of sentences. *Cognitive Psychology* 31(1): 41–81.
Gertner, Yael, Cynthia Fisher, and Julie Eisengart
   2006   Learning words and rules: Abstract knowledge of word order in early sentence comprehension. *Psychological Science* 17(8): 684–691.
Gentner, Dedre, and Jose Medina
   1998   Similarity and the development of rules. *International Journal of Bilingualism* 65: 263–297.
Goldberg, Adele E.
   1993   Another look at some learnability paradoxes. *Proceedings of the 25th Annual Stanford Child Language Research Forum.* Stanford: CSLI Publications.
Goldberg, Adele E.
   1995   *Constructions: A Construction Grammar Approach to Argument Structure.* Chicago: Chicago University Press.
Goldberg, Adele E.
   2002   Surface generalizations: An alternative to alternations. *Cognitive Linguistics* 13(4): 327–356.
Goldberg, Adele E.
   2006   *Constructions at Work: The Nature of Generalization in Language.* Oxford: Oxford University Press
Goldberg, Adele E.
   2011   Corpus evidence of the viability of statistical preemption. *Cognitive Linguistics* 22(1): 131–154.
Goldberg, Adele E.
   2013   Constructional approaches. In: T. Hoffmann and G. Trousdale (eds.) *The Oxford Handbook of Construction Grammar* 15–31. Oxford: Oxford University Press.
Goldberg, Adele E., Devin M. Casenhiser, and Niya Sethuraman
   2004   Learning argument structure generalizations. *Cognitive Linguistics* 15(3): 289–316.
Goldberg, Adele E., Devin M. Casenhiser, and Niya Sethuraman
   2005   The role of prediction in construction-learning. *Journal of Child Language* 32(02): 407–426.
Goldberg, Adele E., Devin M. Casenhiser, and Tiffany R. White
   2007   Constructions as categories of language. *New Ideas in Psychology* 25(2): 70–86.

Goldwater, Micah B., and Arthur B. Markman
2009   Constructional sources of implicit agents in sentence comprehension. *Cognitive Linguistics* 20(4): 675–702.

Gries, Stefan Th., Beatte Hampe, and Doris Schönefeld
2005   Converging evidence: Bringing together experimental and corpus data on the association of verbs and constructions. *Cognitive Linguistics* 16(4): 635–676.

Gries, Stefan Th., and Stefanie Wulff
2005   Do foreign language learners also have constructions? Evidence from priming, sorting and corpora. *Annual Review of Cognitive Linguistics* 3: 182–200.

Hale, Kenneth, Jay Keyser, Miriam Butt, and Wilhelm Geuder
1997   On the complex nature of simple predicators. In: M. Butt and W. Geuder (eds.) *The Projection of Arguments*. Stanford, CA: CSLI.

Hauser, Marc D., Noam Chomsky, and W. Tecumseh Fitch
2002   The faculty of language: What is it, who has it, and how did it evolve? *Science* 298(5598): 1569–1579.

Johnson, Matthew A. and Adele E. Goldberg
2012   Evidence that constructional meaning is accessed automatically: Jabberwocky sentences prime associated verbs. *Language and Cognitive Processes* 28(10): 1439–1452.

Johnson, Matt A., Nick Turk-Browne, and Adele E. Goldberg
In press   Prediction is essential to language processing and development. Comment on Pickering and Garrod. *Brain and Behavioral Science*.

Kako, Edward
2006   The semantics of syntactic frames. *Language and Cognitive Processes* 21(5): 562–575.

Kaschak, Michael P., and Arthur M. Glenberg
2000   Constructing meaning: The role of affordances and grammatical constructions in sentence comprehension. *Journal of Memory and Language* 43: 508–529.

Kay, Paul. and Charles J. Fillmore
1999   Grammatical constructions and linguistic generalizations: The What's X doing Y? construction. *Language* 75: 1–34

Lakoff, George
1987   *Women, Fire, and Dangerous Things: What Categories Reveal about the Mind*. Chicago: University of Chicago Press.

Langacker, Ronald
1987   *Foundations of Cognitive Grammar* Volumes 1 and 2. Stanford: Stanford University Press.

Markman, Arthur B., and Dedre Gentner
1993   Structural alignment during similarity comparisons. *Cognitive Psychology* 25(4): 431–467.

McDonough, Kim M., and Youjin Kim
2009   Syntactic priming, type frequency, and EFL learners' production of wh-questions. *The Modern Language Journal* 93(3): 386–398.

Medin, Douglas L. and William D. Wattenmaker, and Sarah E. Hampson
1987   Family resemblance conceptual cohesiveness, and category construction. *Cognitive Psychology* 12: 242–279.

Michaelis, Laura A., and Knud Lambrecht
1996   Toward a construction-based model of language function: The case of nominal extraposition. *Language* 72: 215–247.

Naigles, Letitia
1990   Children use syntax to learn verb meanings. *Journal of Child Language* 17(2): 357–374.

Olguin, Rachel, and Michael Tomasello
   1993   Twenty-five-month-old children do not have a grammatical category of verb. *Cognitive Development* 8(3): 245–272.

Pinker, Stephen
   1989   *Learnability and Cognition: The Acquisition of Argument Structure.* Cambridge: MIT Press/Bradford Books.

Ramscar, Michael
   this volume   4. Categorization. Berlin/Boston: De Gruyter Mouton.

Roberts, Kenneth.
   1983   Comprehension and production of word order in stage I. *Child Development* 54(2): 443–449.

Tomasello, Michael
   1992   *First Verbs: A Case Study of Early Grammatical Development.* Cambridge: Cambridge University Press.

Tomasello, Michael
   2000   Do young children have adult syntactic competence? *Cognition* 74: 209–253.

Year, Jungeun, and Peter Gordon
   2009   Korean speakers. *Modern Language Journal* 93(3): 19.

Zipf, George K.
   1935   *The Psycho-Biology of Language.* Boston: Houghton Mifflin.

Devin M. Casenhiser, University of Tennessee Health Science Center (USA)
Giulia M. L. Bencini, The City University of New York (USA)

29. Default nonliteral interpretations
The case of negation as a low-salience marker

1. Introduction
2. Default nonliteral utterance-interpretation
3. General discussion
4. References

1. Introduction

This chapter looks into some emerging negative constructions in Hebrew.[1] It argues that such infrequent utterances convey *novel* nonliteral (e.g., metaphorical, sarcastic) interpretations by default. *Default nonliteral utterance-level interpretation* is a new notion, not yet (sufficiently) discussed in cognitive linguistics. It focuses both on "defaultness" and "nonliteralness", but importantly, also on the notion of "utterance-level *inter-*

---

[1] On emerging constructions in cognitive linguistics and construction grammar, see e.g., Bybee (2006); Divjak and Caldwell-Harris (this volume); Israel (2011).

pretation" and the cognitive representations involved in the process. *Default* utterance-level interpretations are singled out in that they differ from conventionalized coded meanings of lexicalized items (meanings listed in the mental lexicon) and from interpretations based on these coded (i.e., salient) meanings, termed here "salience-based interpretations" (Giora et al. 2007). Whereas coded meanings of words and collocations (whether sub- or supra-sentential) are retrieved directly from the mental lexicon (Giora 1997, 1999, 2003), utterance-level interpretations are novel, noncoded, and have to be construed on the fly (Gibbs 2002).

Novel noncoded interpretations are low on salience (Giora 1997, 2003). Albeit nonsalient, the novel nonliteral utterance interpretations to be discussed here are privileged in that they are favored over and processed faster than their noncoded but salience-based, here, literal alternatives. Such findings, attesting to the temporal priority of *nonsalient* nonliteral interpretations over their relatively available *salience-based* literal ones, cannot be accounted for by any contemporary processing model, including the Graded Salience Hypothesis (Giora 1997, 1999, 2003).

The aim of this chapter is to demonstrate, instead, that negation – a marker prompting low-salience interpretations by default – can account for the priority of nonsalient nonliteral interpretations over salience-based, literal ones (Giora 2006; Giora et al. 2005, 2010, 2013, 2015; Givoni et al. 2013). To allow an insight into the notion of default nonliteral interpretations induced by negation, consider the following natural examples (target utterances in bold, interpretations in italics):

(1) **I am not your wife, I am not your maid,** *I'm not someone that you can lay your demands [on] all of [the] time. I'm sick of this it's going to stop!* (Blige 2007).

(2) I will not use the word "*hater*" but **supportive she is not**. (Lady 2013).

(3) *Tom's wait is currently 3 years*, more-or-less. **Punctuality is not his forte** (Marzluf, 2011).

(4) sorry, my **French is not my best attribute**, in fact it is *awful*!! (Anonymous 2010).

In (1), the target constructions (*I am not your wife, I am not your maid*) are of the form "X is not Y". They convey a low-salience metaphorical interpretation (*I'm not someone that you can lay your demands [on] all of [the] time*), while rendering literal, defining features (*married, hired*) pragmatically irrelevant.[2] This interpretation is highlighted via the rejection of the concepts (*your wife, your maid*) by means of the negation marker. In (2), the target construction (*Supportive she is not*) is of the form "X s/he is not". It conveys a low-salience sarcastic interpretation which is brought to the fore via the rejection of the concept (*supportive*) within the scope of negation. It thus suggests a contrastive reading (similar to *hater*) of what is negated. In (3), the target construction (*Punctuality is not his forte*) is of the form "X is not his/her forte". It too conveys a low-salience sarcastic interpretation, suggesting the opposite of the negated concept (indicating a long

---

[2] The view of metaphor adopted here is similar to Glucksberg and Keysar's (1990) and to Carston's (1997, 2012) "broadening" and "narrowing" processes involved in metaphor interpretation.

delay of *3 years*, which makes the protagonist very late rather than punctual). In (4), the target construction (*French is not my best attribute*) is of the form "X is not his/her best attribute". It conveys a low-salience sarcastic interpretation by suggesting the opposite (*awful*) of what is negated (*best attribute*). As will be shown here, such nonliteral interpretations, albeit low on salience, are the preferred, default interpretations of such utterances.

Recall that the nonliteral interpretations of these emerging constructions are not lexicalized but need to be construed. No wonder they are often made explicit by their users. For instance, *I am not your wife* in (1) is used differently in (5). While metaphorical too, here, in (5), it is a protest, leveled by a wife against her husband who *didn't treat her with respect like one should treat one's wife* but instead shamed her by *cheating on her, deceiving her,* etc. Here too, negation invites low-salience features of "wife" (*should be treated with respect*), while rendering literal, defining features (*married*) pragmatically irrelevant (Giora et al. 2013):

(5) "**I am not your wife**. *You cheated me; you deceived me. You did not tell me that you were involved with Pakistanis. You did not tell me what were you up to,*" she said loudly (Singh 2002).

The notions of default, preferred, or privileged utterance-interpretation prevalent in the field are either agnostic with regard to degree of (non)literalness, or assume a literalness-based interpretation. Thus, the classical view (Aristotle 350 BCE; Beardsley 1958; Black 1954, 1962, 1979; Richards 1936), promoted by the Standard Pragmatic Model (Grice 1975; Searle 1979; see also Levinson 2000), assumes that an utterance default interpretation is literal, which, for the most part, is context independent. Literal utterance-level interpretations are, therefore, activated first, regardless of contextual information to the contrary (see discussions in Gibbs 1994, 2002; Hamblin and Gibbs 2003; Gibbs and Moise 1997; Récanati 1989, 1995).

The Graded Salience Hypothesis (Giora 1997, 1999, 2003) also assumes a context independent view of default utterance-interpretation, which, however, is not necessarily literal, but salience-based. A salience-based interpretation is an utterance-interpretation, based on the salient meanings of the utterance components. Salient meanings of linguistic (and nonlinguistic) components are coded in the mental lexicon, and enjoy prominence due to a number of factors, regardless of degree of (non)literalness. Factors contributing to salience might be cognitive, such as degree of prototypicality, or related to amount of exposure, such as degree of frequency, conventionality, and experiential familiarity (even if private, or related to the unspoken/unsaid that is often on our mind).

Given that utterance components might have either literal and/or nonliteral meanings high in salience, salience-based interpretations are agnostic with regard to degree of (non)literalness. Less-salient meanings – meanings low on prototypicality or degree of exposure – are also coded in the mental lexicon, regardless of degree of (non)literalness. However, they are low on prominence and might take a while to reach a threshold even in a supportive context. In contrast, novel, nonsalient meanings or interpretations are not coded, and are not considered default interpretations. Rather, they have to be learnt or constructed, often on the basis of contextual information. They can, however, be both, literal or nonliteral.

According to the Graded Salience Hypothesis, then, salience-based interpretations are default interpretations. They are, therefore, expected to be activated initially, regardless of contextual information. On the other hand, nonsalient meanings and interpretations are not derived by default and may therefore lag behind, even when contextual support is strong (Fein et al. 2015; Giora 2003, 2011; Giora et al. 2007; but see Peleg, Giora and Fein 2001 for the effects of predictive contexts).

In contrast to the Standard Pragmatic Model and the Graded Salience Hypothesis, most of the views of default utterance-interpretations postulate richer notions of defaultness, varying with respect to degree of context dependency. Some are more constrained such as "explicatures" (Carston 2002, 2012; Sperber and Wilson 1986/1995), and some are more flexible such as "privileged interactional interpretations" (Ariel 2002), or "primary meanings" (Jaszczolt 2005a, 2005b, 2009, 2010). However, these default interpretations too are indifferent to degree of nonliteralness (Ariel 2002, 2008, 2010; Bach 1994; Carston 2002; Gibbs and Moise 1997; Hamblin and Gibbs 2003; Jaszczolt 2005a, 2005b, 2009, 2010, 2011; Récanati 1989, 2001, 2004, 2005; Sperber and Wilson 1986/1995). This chapter, however, focuses on nonliteralness. It outlines the conditions for a novel notion termed here "default nonliteral utterance-interpretation".

2. Default nonliteral utterance-interpretation

The view of default nonliteral utterance-interpretation has been proposed, developed, and tested in our recent experimental studies, using contrived Hebrew stimuli, based, however, on natural instances, and read by native speakers of Hebrew. In addition, native speakers of Hebrew, English, German, and Russian were involved in corpora-based studies, which are not reported here (but see Giora 2006; Giora et al. 2010, 2013; Giora et al. 2014). In these studies we outlined the conditions for default nonliteral interpretations (specified in 6 below), which require that utterances be a priori potentially ambiguous between literal and nonliteral interpretations. These conditions, then, stipulate that cues, known to prompt nonliteralness, whether utterance external or internal, should be excluded, so that one interpretation may be favored over another *by default*:

(6) Conditions for default nonliteral interpretations
    a) Constituents (words, phrases, utterances) have to be *unfamiliar* so as to exclude salient/coded nonliteral *meanings* of expressions and collocations. For instance, salient nonliteral meanings of familiar idiomatic (*spill the beans*), metaphorical (*backseat*), sarcastic[3] (*you don't say*), or any conventional formulaic expressions (Bybee 2006; Fillmore et al. 1988; Gibbs 1980, 1981; Giora 2003), as well as prefabs (Erman and Warren 2000), or conventionalized, ritualistic utterances, (Kecskés 1999, 2000) should be excluded. If negative utterances are considered, they should not be negative polarity items (NPIs), but

---

[3] "Sarcasm" also relates to "sarcastic irony" and "verbal irony".

should, instead, have an acceptable affirmative counterpart, so that conventionality is avoided.[4]

b) *Semantic anomaly* (known to invite metaphoricalness, see Beardsley 1958) or any kind of opposition between the elements of a phrase or proposition (known to trigger a sarcastic reading, see Barbe 1993; Partington 2011) should be avoided so that both literal and nonliteral interpretations may be allowed. For this reason, "epitomizations" – negative object-subject-verb (OSV) constructions ("X s/he is not") – in which the fronted constituent is a proper noun, (*Einstein he is not*) – must be excluded. Such constructions are also metaphorical, not least in their affirmative version (Birner and Ward 1998; Ward 1983; Ward and Birner 2006; see also Prince 1981).

c) Specific and informative *contextual information* should not be involved so that pragmatic incongruity – a breach of pragmatic maxims or contextual misfit (Grice 1975) – on the one hand, and supportive biasing information, on the other, (Gibbs 1981, 1986a, 1986b, 1994, 2002; Katz 2009; Katz et al. 2004) may not invite or disinvite a nonliteral or a literal interpretation. Contextual or pragmatic cues such as *metaphorically speaking, sarcastically speaking, literally, pun intended* (see Givoni et al. 2013; Katz and Ferretti 2003), marked intonation/prosodic cues, whether nonliteral, such as sarcastic, effective even outside of a specific context (Bryant and Fox Tree 2002; Rockwell 2007; Voyer and Techentin 2010), corrective, such as assigned to metalinguistic negation (Carston 1996; Chapman 1996; Horn 1985, 1989), or nonverbal, such as gestures or facial expressions (Caucci and Kreuz 2012), should be avoided so that nonliteralness would neither be invited nor blocked.

The view of default nonliteral interpretation predicts that certain constructions, complying with the conditions for default nonliteral interpretations, will be perceived as such compared to an equivalent alternative (a) when presented outside of a specific context, (b) regardless of degree of structural markedness. Consequently, when embedded in a strongly biasing context, they (c) will be processed nonliterally initially, regardless of contextual information to the contrary. Given the preference and temporal priority of their nonliteral interpretation, (d) such utterances will convey a nonliteral interpretation when used by speakers and therefore (e) their contextual environment will resonate with and reflect this nonliteral albeit nonsalient interpretation. (For corpus-based evidence supporting predictions d–e, see Giora et al. 2010, 2013; Giora et al. 2014).

In the studies reported here, we tested predictions (a–c) using both offline and online measures (Giora 2006; Giora et al. 2010, 2013, 2015). We showed that negation is an operator generating novel nonliteral utterance-interpretation by default. Below I review our findings with regard to negative constructions such as "X is not Y" (*This is not Memorial Day*) which are primarily metaphorical (section 2.1), and "X s/he is not" (*Punctual he is not*), "X is not her/his forte" (*Punctuality is not her forte*), and "X is not her/his best feature" (*Punctuality is not her best feature*), which are primarily sarcastic (section 2.2).

---

[4] On NPIs exhibiting asymmetric behavior in minimal pairs of negative and affirmative sentences whereby, as a result of conventionalization, affirmatives are almost nonexistent (see Horn 1989; Israel 2006).

2.1. Default metaphorical utterance-interpretation: X is not Y constructions

Consider the following natural instances, exemplary of the kind of construction discussed in this section (target utterances in boldface, interpretations in italics):

(7) *I've heard about your needs/wants/desires/witnesses/mother's health a thousand times ...* **I am not your social worker**/*psychologist/person you vent to*. I am your lawyer. So, if I don't *speak to you every other day about your 'feelings'* ... (Seddiq, N.A., retrieved on August 28, 2012)

(8) My name is Mary K. Hill. *I am a Licensed Independent Social Worker.* **I am your Social Worker** at Hmong International Academy. (Hill 2012)

(9) There is such a *racket* going on downstairs, between *doors slamming and dogs barking*. – Makes me want to open the door and scream "**THIS IS NOT A DISCOTHEQUE!**" (Gordon 2011).

(10) Located in Walking Street up on the right hand side from Beach Road, upstairs from Candy Shop and opposite Soi Diamond, just find as it lights up Walking Street with a laser sign. **This is a Discotheque** *with live band, the music is House/Techno/Blip Blip*. Closed in Spring 2009. (http://www.pattayabarreview.com/tag/live-band/) [Accessed 28 August 2012].

In (7), the negative target utterance *I am not your social worker* is used metaphorically, getting across some non-defining features of the concept (*social worker*) via rejecting them (e.g., *heard about your needs/wants/desires/witnesses/mother's health, you vent to*, or *speak to you every other day about your 'feelings'*). This metaphor is further reinforced by similar figures of speech, such as *I am not your ... psychologist/person you vent to*. In contrast, in (8), the affirmative counterpart, *I am your Social Worker* gets across some defining features of the concept, such as "I am a Licensed Independent Social Worker". In (9), the target utterance *THIS IS NOT A DISCOTHEQUE*! focuses on a metaphorical nondefining feature of the negated concept *discotheque*, which here refers to disturbing noise (*racket, doors slamming and dogs barking*). Its affirmative counterpart in (10), however, highlights its defining features (*live band, the music is House/Techno/Blip Blip*).

Will such negative utterances be perceived as metaphorical, compared to their affirmative alternatives, when presented in isolation (section 2.1.1)? Will they be processed faster when embedded in metaphorically than in literally biasing context, as predicted by the view of negation as an operator inducing nonliteral interpretations by default (section 2.1.2)?

2.1.1. Evidence from offline measures

Our previous studies (Giora et al. 2010) show that some novel negative utterances (e.g., 7, 9), involving no semantic anomaly, were perceived as more metaphorical compared to their equally novel affirmative counterparts (e.g., 8, 10), when presented in isolation.

Items were followed by a 7-point metaphoricalness scale, which (randomly) instantiated either a literal or a metaphorical interpretation at the scale's end. Participants were asked to indicate the proximity of the utterance interpretation to any of those instantiations at the scale's ends (or otherwise propose an alternative).

Results showed that the metaphorical interpretation, albeit nonsalient, was the preferred interpretation of the novel negative items, scoring high on metaphoricalness (M = 5.50 SD = 0.96). In contrast, the preferred interpretation of their equally novel affirmative counterparts was the salience-based, literal one, scoring significantly lower on metaphoricalness (M = 3.48 SD = 1.27), $t1(47)$ = 10.17, p < .0001; $t2(14)$ = 4.36, p < .0005 (Giora et al. 2010).

2.1.2. Evidence from online measures

Given their preference for metaphoricalness, the view of negation as inducing nonliteral interpretations by default predicts that such negative utterances (as discussed in section 2.1.1) will be read faster when embedded in a context biasing them toward their metaphorical than toward their (equally strongly biased) literal interpretation. In Giora et al. (2013), we tested this prediction with regard to the utterances tested offline in Giora et al. (2010). Utterances were embedded in contexts controlled for equal strength of literal/nonliteral bias. They were followed by a two-word spillover segment, which allows testing whether difficulties in processing a target utterance spill over to the next utterance. The target utterances, followed by the spillover segment, were presented in context non-final position (to avoid wrap-up effects).

Participants were asked to read short paragraphs, which they advanced segment by segment by pressing a key, and answer the question that followed. Reading times of the target utterances and the spillover segments were measured by the computer. Results showed that, as predicted, the negative utterances were read faster when embedded in a context strongly biasing them toward their nonsalient metaphorical interpretation than toward their (equally strongly biased) salience-based literal interpretation, $t1(37)$ = 2.57, p < .01; $t2(11)$ = 1.51, p = .08 (see Figure 29.1). There were no spillover effects.

Such results support the view that negation generates nonliteral interpretations by default.

2.2. Default sarcastic utterance-interpretation: "X s/he is not" constructions

Consider the following natural instances, exemplary of the kind of constructions discussed in this section (target utterances in boldface, interpretations in italics):

(11) Katherine may be courageous, *but **smart she is not**. In fact, I wonder whether she has ever rubbed more than three brain cells together.* (http://www.drphil.com/messageboard/topic/2873/55/) [Accessed 16 October 2012]

(12) Meg is a *smart* girl, maybe she's not pretty, but **smart she is**" says Scott. (http://m.fanfiction.net/s/5142465/7/) [Accessed 16 October 2012]

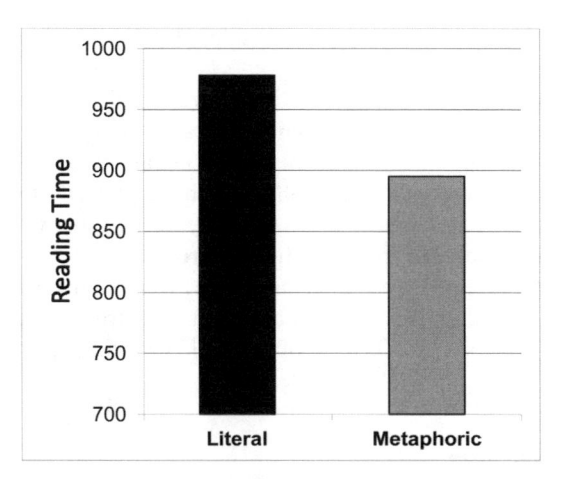

Fig. 29.1: Mean reading times (in ms) of metaphorically and literally biased targets

(13) **Smart he is not** ... Let it be said at once that Sharon may be as sharp as a whip, as cunning and elusive as an eel, but – as the Nahal Brigade troupe used to sing – "he's *not so smart*." Certainly *not so smart* as many, himself included, may think. (Rosenblum 2004).

The negative utterance in (11) (*smart she is not*) is used sarcastically, suggesting that the person in question is far from being smart and is in fact stupid, as the context clarifies (*wonder whether she has ever rubbed more than three brain cells together*). The alternative affirmative (*smart she is*) in (12) conveys a literal interpretation of the same concept (Meg is a *smart* girl). In (13), the negative construction (*Smart he is not*), does not convey the opposite of what is said but allows, instead, a mitigated version of the negated concept (Certainly *not so smart* as many, himself included, may think), which is a case of the construction being used literally.

Will such negative utterances be perceived as sarcastic compared to affirmative alternatives when presented in isolation (section 2.2.1)? Will they be processed faster when embedded in sarcastically than in literally biasing contexts (section 2.2.2)?

2.2.1. Evidence from offline measures

Our previous studies (Giora et al. 2013) show that some novel negative utterances of the form "X s/he is not" (*Ambitious she is not*; *Mesmerizing he is not*), involving no semantic anomaly or any internal incongruity, were interpreted sarcastically when presented in isolation. Items, controlled for novelty, were followed by a 7-point scale, instantiating either a literal or a sarcastic interpretation (randomly) displayed at the scale's ends. Participants were asked to indicate the proximity of the utterance interpretation to any of those instantiations at the scale's ends (or otherwise propose an alternative).

Results showed that the sarcastic interpretation, albeit nonsalient, was the preferred interpretation of the novel negative items, scoring high on sarcasm, ($M = 5.59$, $SD =$

0.87), significantly higher than 5 on a 7-point sarcasm scale, $t1(18) = 2.99$, $p < .005$; $t2(17) = 4.65$, $p < .0005$.

To verify that the interpretations of the negative items were indeed perceived as sarcastic (rather than only as the opposite of what is said), sarcasm ratings were collected. Participants were asked to rate degree of sarcasm of the negative items and their affirmative counterparts (all of similar novelty controlled for by a pretest). Items, presented in isolation, were followed by a 7-point sarcasm scale, ranging between 1 (not sarcastic at all) and 7 (highly sarcastic). No interpretations were provided.

Results showed that the negative items (*Ambitious she is not*) were significantly more sarcastic ($M = 5.92$, $SD = 0.94$) than their novel affirmative counterparts (*Ambitious she is yes*[5]) ($M = 2.67$, $SD = 1.33$); $t1(42) = 11.53$; $p < .0001$; $t2(17) = 45.55$, $p < .0001$.

2.2.2. Evidence from online measures

Given their default sarcastic interpretation, the view of negation as inducing nonliteral interpretations by default predicts that such negative utterance as discussed in section 2.2.1 will be read faster when embedded in a context biasing them toward their nonsalient sarcastic interpretation than toward their (equally strongly biased) salience-based literal interpretation. In Giora et al. (2013), such utterances were embedded in contexts controlled for equal strength of literal vs. nonliteral bias. They were followed by a two-word spillover segment. The target utterances, followed by the spillover segment, were presented in context non-final position and were followed by a Yes/No comprehension question.

As before, participants were asked to read the short paragraphs which they advanced segment by segment and answer a comprehension question. Reading times of the target

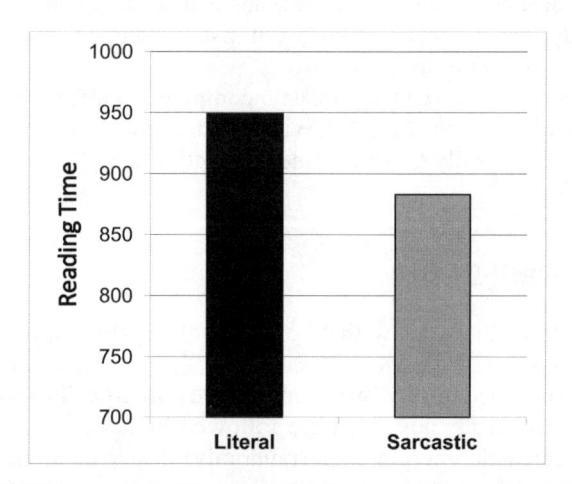

Fig. 29.2: Mean reading times (in ms) of sarcastically and literally biased targets

---

[5] In Hebrew the affirmative version is obligatorily marked for affirmation by an explicit marker.

utterances and the spillover segments were measured by the computer. Results showed that, as predicted, the negative utterances were read faster when embedded in a context strongly biasing them toward their nonsalient sarcastic interpretation than toward their (equally strongly biased) salience-based literal interpretation (see Figure 29.2), $t1(43) = 1.75$, $p < .05$; $t2(17) = 1.20$, $p = .12$. There were no spillover effects.

Such results support the view of negation as a low-salience marker generating novel nonliteral interpretations by default.

2.3. Default sarcastic utterance-interpretation: "X is not her forte" constructions

Consider the following natural instances, exemplary of the kind of constructions discussed in this section (target utterances in boldface, interpretations in italics):

(14) **Moderation is usually** *not my forte – I'm more of an all-or-none person*. (http://www.letsrun.com/forum/flat_read.php?thread=3020834andpage=4) [Accessed 27 July 2014]

(15) **Maintaining quality is our forte**, *so we ensure that every kind of business functions are monitored on each stage with best co-operation and co-ordination among various departments by a galaxy of supremely qualified and dedicated quality analysts ... The stringent quality control measures are strictly being implemented at each step ...* (http://www.phoenixbiologicals.net/company-information.html) [Accessed 25 October 2012]

(16) Piolo Pascual has admitted to having had *a bit of difficulty doing comedy*, acknowledging that **the genre is not his "forte"**. ... The 35-year old actor-singer maintained that the movie is quite *the change of pace for him* considering that his body of work consists mostly of romantic dramas ... the actor believes that people will find the movie quite *entertaining* since it's "more *relaxing*, hindi siya nakakapressure." (RAMOS 2012).

The negative utterance in (14) (*Moderation is usually not my forte*) is used sarcastically, suggesting that the speaker is far from being moderate but is, instead a person of extremes (*an all-or-none person*). The affirmative construction (*Maintaining quality is our forte*) in (15) conveys a literal interpretation (*The stringent quality control measures are strictly being implemented at each step ...*). In (16), however, the negative construction (*the genre [comedy] is not his "forte"*) is a case in which such utterances convey a mitigated, literal interpretation (the actor believes that people will find the movie quite entertaining) rather than the opposite of what is said.

Will such negative utterances (as in 14) be perceived as sarcastic when presented in isolation (section 2.3.1)? Will they be processed faster when embedded in sarcastically than in literally biasing contexts (section 2.3.2)?

2.3.1. Evidence from offline measures

Our recent studies (Giora et al. 2015) show that some novel negative utterances of the form "X is not her/his forte" (*Alertness is not his forte*), involving no semantic anomaly or any internal incongruity, were interpreted sarcastically when presented in isolation. Items, controlled for novelty, were followed by a 7-point scale, instantiating either a literal or a sarcastic interpretation, (randomly) displayed at the scale's ends. Participants were asked to indicate the proximity of the utterance interpretation to any of those instantiations at the scale's ends (or otherwise propose an alternative).

Results showed that the sarcastic interpretation, albeit nonsalient, was the preferred interpretation of the novel negative items, scoring high on sarcasm (M = 5.51, SD = 0.35), significantly higher than 5 on a 7-point sarcasm scale, $t(13) = 5.44$, $p < .0001$.

To verify that the interpretations of the negative items were perceived as sarcastic (rather than only as the opposite of what is said), sarcasm ratings were collected. Participants were asked to rate degree of sarcasm of the negative items and their affirmative counterparts (all controlled for novelty by a pretest). Items, presented in isolation, were followed by a 7-point sarcasm scale, ranging between 1 (not sarcastic at all) and 7 (highly sarcastic).

Results replicated previous findings, showing that the negative items (*Alertness is not his forte*) were significantly more sarcastic (M = 6.02, SD = 0.78) than their novel affirmative counterparts (*Alertness is his forte*) (M = 2.67, SD = 1.01), $t1(39) = 15.43$, $p < .0001$; $t2(13) = 22.07$, $p < .0001$.

Will these novel negative utterances be interpreted faster when embedded in contexts biasing them toward their nonsalient sarcastic interpretation than toward their salience-based literal interpretation?

2.3.2. Evidence from online measures

Given their preferred sarcastic interpretation, the view of negation as inducing nonsalient nonliteral interpretations by default predicts that such negative utterance, as discussed in section 2.3.1, will be read faster when embedded in a context biasing them toward their nonsalient sarcastic interpretation than toward their (equally strongly biased) salience-based literal interpretation. In Giora et al. (2015), we tested this prediction. Utterances were embedded in contexts controlled for equal strength of literal vs. nonliteral bias. They were presented in context non-final position and followed by a two-word spillover segment. Contexts were followed by a Yes/No comprehension question.

Participants were asked to read the short paragraphs which they advanced segment by segment and answer a comprehension question. Reading times of the target utterances and the spillover segments were measured by the computer. Results showed that, as predicted, the negative utterances were read faster when embedded in contexts strongly biasing them toward their nonsalient sarcastic interpretation (M = 1349 ms, SD = 401) than toward their (equally strongly biased) salience-based literal interpretation (M = 1790 ms, SD = 579), $t1(43) = 4.69$, $p < .0001$, $t2(13) = 4.48$, $p < .0005$ (see Figure 29.3). Additionally, there were spillover effects showing that, as predicted, following sarcastically biased targets, reading times of spillover segments were faster than those

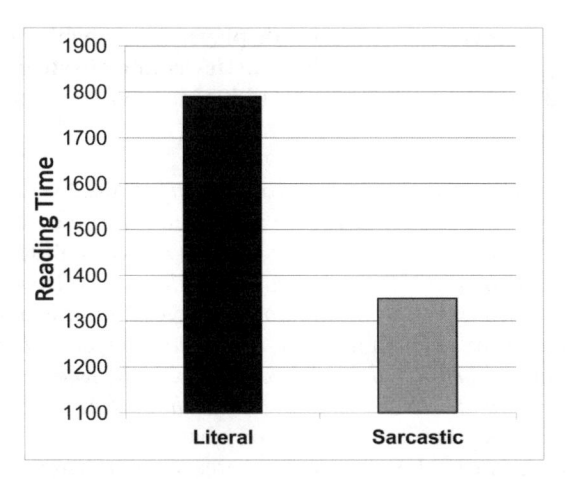

Fig. 29.3: Mean reading times (in ms) of sarcastically and literally biased targets

following literally biased targets, $t1(43) = 2.90$, $p < .0005$; $t2(13) = 1.94$, $p < .05$, suggesting processing difficulties in the literal but not in the sarcastic condition.

Such results support the view that negation is a low-salience marker, generating novel nonliteral interpretations by default.

2.4. Default sarcastic utterance-interpretation: "X is not her strong point" constructions

In this section we look at similar constructions to those studied in section 2.3, only short of their semantics (*not her/his forte*), which, despite their proven novelty, might already be associated with sarcasm. To replicate previous findings, the utterances tested here employ equivalent alternatives but keep the construction constant (*not her/his most distinctive feature, not her/his area of expertise/not what she excels at*). The following natural instances are exemplary of the kind of constructions discussed here (target utterances in boldface, interpretations in italics):

(17) The Baron of Hartlepool, Lord Mandelson, **humility is not his strong point**? This morning on The Andrew Marr show whilst being interviewed showed his inability to admit his wrongs and the *sheer arrogance* of his lordship(lol) was breathtaking to watch (Johnny D. 2008).

(18) ... **his deliverance of the stories is his strong point**. *His prose has been polished to the point that it sparkles and contains more than a good deal of poetry* (Voegele N.A.).

(19) ... if he is played in the lam/cam role on a consistent basis, he can arguably become *the best Asian player in football*. With the possible addition of RVP, I hope we see him used in the lam role rather than the central midfield role or benched in favor of a rooney /RVP partnership. Even without RVP, I hope SAF

knows *he is capable of playing in this role*, and wide players are capable of playing more centrally. However, I doubt that as ... erh ... **tactics is not his strong point**. (http://community.manutd.com/forums/p/244135/2145052.aspx) [Accessed 26 October 2012]

In (17), the negative construction (*humility is not his strong point*), is used sarcastically, conveying the opposite of what is said ("*sheer arrogance*"). In contrast, the affirmative version in (18) (*his deliverance of the stories is his strong point*) conveys a literal interpretation ("*His prose has been polished to the point that it sparkles ...* "). However, (in 19), the negative construction (*tactics is not his strong point*) conveys a mitigated, literal interpretation, given that he is good at other things (*the best Asian player in football*; *I hope we see him used in the lam role rather than the central midfield role or benched in favor of a rooney /RVP partnership. Even without RVP, I hope SAF knows he is capable of playing in this role*), rather than the opposite of what is said.

Will such negative utterances (as in 17) be perceived as sarcastic, compared to affirmative alternatives (19), when presented in isolation (section 2.4.1)? Will they be processed faster when embedded in sarcastically than in literally biasing context (section 2.4.2)?

2.4.1. Evidence from offline measures

Our recent studies (Giora et al. 2015) show that some novel negative utterances of the form "X is not her/his best attribute" (*Alertness is not her most pronounced characteristic*), involving no semantic anomaly or any internal incongruity, were interpreted sarcastically when presented in isolation. As before, items, controlled for novelty, were followed by a 7-point scale, instantiating either a literal or a sarcastic interpretation (randomly) displayed at the scale's ends.

Results showed that sarcastic interpretations, albeit nonsalient, were the preferred interpretation of the novel negative items, scoring high on sarcasm (M = 5.55, SD = 0.29), significantly higher than 5 on a 7-point sarcasm scale, $t(11) = 5.52$, $p < .0001$.

To verify that the interpretations of the negative items were perceived as sarcastic (rather than only as the opposite of what is said), sarcasm ratings were collected. Participants were asked to rate degree of sarcasm of the negative items and their affirmative counterparts, all controlled for novelty. Items, presented in isolation, were followed by a 7-point sarcasm scale, ranging between 1 (not sarcastic at all) and 7 (highly sarcastic). No interpretations were provided.

Results replicated previous findings, showing that the negative items (*Alertness is not her most pronounced characteristic*) were significantly more sarcastic (M = 5.96, SD = 0.76) than their novel affirmative counterparts (*Alertness is her most pronounced characteristic*) (M = 3.29, SD = 1.06), $t1(39) = 12.72$, $p < .0001$, $t2(11) = 13.95$, $p < .0001$.

2.4.2. Evidence from online measures

Given their preferred sarcastic interpretation, the view of negation as a low-salience marker, inducing novel nonliteral interpretations by default, predicts that such negative

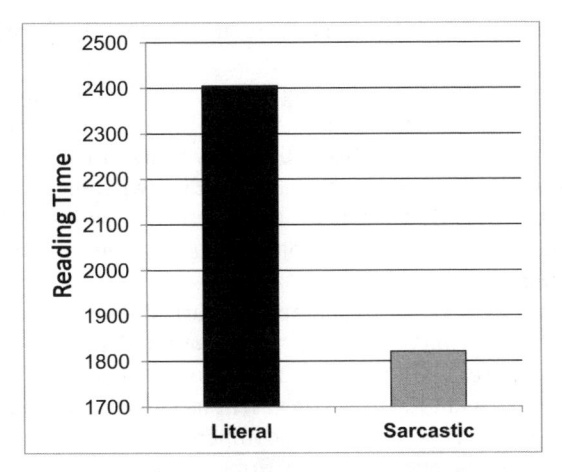

Fig. 29.4: Mean reading times (in ms) of sarcastically and literally biased targets

utterances (as discussed in section 2.4.1) will be read faster when embedded in a context biasing them toward their nonsalient sarcastic interpretation than toward their (equally strongly biased) salience-based literal interpretation. In Giora et al. (2015), we tested this prediction. Utterances, presented in context non-final position, followed by a two-word spillover segment, were embedded in contexts controlled for equal strength of literal vs. nonliteral bias.

As before, participants were asked to read the short paragraphs, which they advanced segment by segment, and answer a question that followed. Results showed that, as predicted, the negative utterances were read faster when embedded in a context strongly biasing them toward their nonsalient sarcastic interpretation (M = 1821 ms, SD = 588) than toward their (equally strongly biased) salience-based literal interpretation (M = 2405 ms, SD = 833), $t1(51)$ = 6.19, $p < .0001$; $t2(11)$ = 2.93, $p < .01$ (see Figure 29.4). Additionally, there were marginal spillover effects showing that, as predicted, following sarcastically biased targets, reading times of spillover segments were somewhat faster (M = 690 ms, SD = 208) than those following literally biased targets (M = 726 ms, SD = 275), disclosing processing difficulties in the latter condition, $t1(51)$ = 1.48, $p = .07$; $t2(11)$ = <1, n.s.

Such results support the view that negation is a low-salience marker generating novel nonliteral interpretations by default.

2.5. Default sarcastic utterance-interpretation: negation vs. structural markedness

Recall that the view of negation as inducing default nonliteral interpretation predicts that certain negative constructions, complying with the conditions for default nonliteral interpretations, will be perceived as nonliteral, regardless of degree of structural markedness (prediction b, section 2). Given that the sarcastic utterances tested here are structurally marked, involving a fronted constituent, it is necessary to tease apart negation from markedness effects. Which of the two plays a primary role in affecting nonliteralness by default?

Already at this stage, some of our findings argue against the markedness hypothesis. Recall that the constructions at hand are structurally marked both in the negative and the affirmative. In addition, some of them are also obligatorily marked (in Hebrew) for affirmation (*Ambitious she is **yes***). Regardless, results showed that, whereas the negative constructions were interpreted sarcastically by default, the affirmative counterparts were not, which renders the markedness hypothesis suspicious. Still, negation vs. markedness effects should be examined directly.

To weigh degree of negation (not/yes) against degree of markedness (+/-fronting) in a more systematic way, we ran 2 experiments. In one, we looked at "X s/he is not/yes" constructions (*Ambitious she is not/yes*) (Giora et al. 2013); in the other, we looked at "X is not/yes her/his forte/most prominent feature" constructions (*Alertness is not/yes his forte//most prominent feature*[6]) (Giora et al. 2015). We compared them with structurally unmarked alternatives differing only in negation vs. affirmation (*She is not/yes Ambitious*; *His forte//most prominent feature is not/yes alertness*). We predicted that the negative versions of the utterances will always be more sarcastic than their affirmative counterparts, regardless of degree of structural markedness. Structural markedness, however, may have an additive value.

In each experiment participants were presented 2 different constructions – marked and unmarked (20–23; 24–27), varying between whether they included a negative (not) or an affirmative (yes) marker. There were also 24 filler items, varying between sarcastic, literal, and metaphorical utterances. Four booklets were prepared so that participants saw only one version of a concept; the constructions were counterbalanced. In addition to the 24 filler items, each booklet then contained 8 structurally marked constructions, half negative and half affirmative, and 8 structurally unmarked constructions, half negative and half affirmative:

(20) Ambitious she is not

(21) Ambitious she is yes

(22) She is not ambitious

(23) She is yes ambitious

(24) Alertness is not her forte/most prominent feature

(25) Alertness is yes her forte/most prominent feature

(26) Her forte/most prominent feature is not alertness

(27) Her forte/most prominent feature is yes alertness

Participants were asked to rate the degree of sarcasm of each utterance on a 7-point sarcasm scale (where 1 = not sarcastic at all and 7 = highly sarcastic). Results for the first construction (*Ambitious she is not*) and its variations showed that the negative versions were always rated as more sarcastic than their affirmative counterparts. Marked-

---

[6] In Hebrew, such utterances may also be marked for the affirmative ("yes").

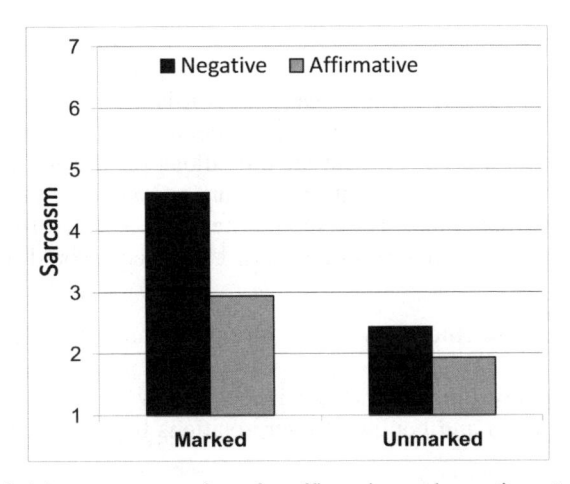

Fig. 29.5: Mean sarcasm ratings for affirmative and negative utterances

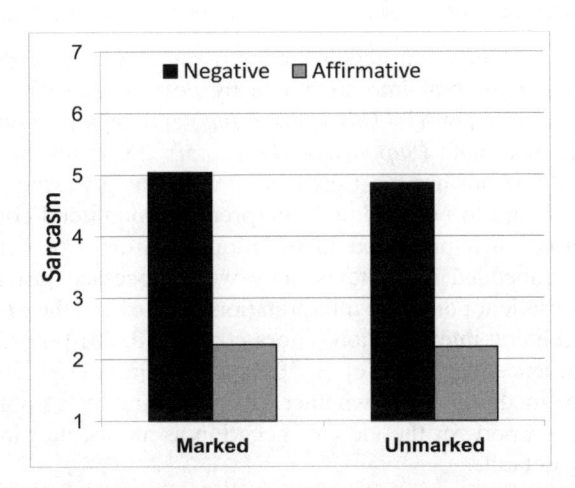

Fig. 29.6: Mean sarcasm ratings for affirmative and negative utterances

ness also played a role. However, as demonstrated by Figure 29.5, although the difference in sarcasm between negative and affirmative utterances was larger in the marked condition, it was significant in both the Marked ($F1(1, 47) = 26.22$, $p < .0001$; $F2(1, 15) = 55.07$, $p < .0001$) and Unmarked conditions ($F1(1, 47) = 4.25$, $p < .05$; $F2(1, 15) = 13.77$, $p < .005$):

Results for the second construction (*Alertness is not her forte/most prominent feature*) and its variations showed that markedness did not play any role in affecting sarcasm. Instead, it was only negation that played a crucial role in inducing sarcasm by default ($F_1(1,59) = 128.87$, $p < .0001$; $F_2(1,15) = 799.72$, $p < .0001$), as demonstrated by Figure 29.6:

These results support the view that negation, rather than structural markedness, plays a critical role in affecting novel nonliteralness by default.

3. General discussion

Findings in Giora et al. (2010, 2013, 2015) show that negation is an operator eliciting novel metaphorical and sarcastic utterance-interpretation by default. For an utterance to be interpreted nonliterally by default, it has to meet the conditions for default nonliteral interpretation. These conditions guarantee that utterances are *prima facie* ambiguous between literal and nonliteral interpretations. They should therefore be free of utterance external and internal hints known to prompt nonliteralness. Utterances should therefore be:

- *unfamiliar* so that salient/coded nonliteral *meanings* of expressions and collocations will not be involved;
- free of *semantic anomaly* or any kind of internal incongruency (known to trigger nonliteralness), so that both literal and nonliteral interpretations be permissible;

and

- presented outside of biasing *contextual information* so that any pragmatic incongruity or supportive information may neither invoke nor block a specific interpretation.

In this article, the focus is on a certain set of negative constructions, which, under such conditions, generated nonsalient nonliteral interpretations by default. Negative (metaphorical) utterances of the form "X is not Y" (*This is not a bus*) and negative (sarcastic) utterances of the form "X s/he/it is not" (*Supportive she is not*), "X is not her forte" (*Punctuality is not her forte*), "X is not her most distinctive attribute" (*Alertness is her most distinctive feature*), were found to be rated and interpreted as nonliteral compared to their affirmative counterparts when presented in isolation, regardless of degree of structural markedness. When embedded in contexts, they were processed faster when strongly biased toward their nonsalient nonliteral interpretation than toward their (equally strongly biased) salience-based literal interpretation (Giora et al. 2010, 2013, 2015). (For corroborating corpus-based evidence, see Giora et al. 2010, 2013; Giora et al. 2014).

Our studies use a variety of methodologies, whether offline, online, or corpus-based measures. They adduce robust support for the view of negation as an operator inducing low-salience nonliteralness by default.

These results are unprecedented and cannot be accounted for by existing processing models of nonliteral interpretations. For instance, the priority of nonsalient nonliteral interpretation cannot be explained by salience (Giora 1997, 1999, 2003); recall that according to the Graded Salience Hypothesis, nonsalient interpretations of utterances are not expected to be activated prior to their salience-based interpretations. Nor can semantic anomaly (Beardsley 1958), internal incongruity (Partington 2011), or pragmatic incongruity (Grice 1975) explain these results, given that these factors were excluded. Neither can contextual information (Campbell and Katz 2012; Gibbs 1986a, 1986b, 1994; Ortony et al. 1978; Katz 2009; Katz and Ferretti 2003) account for these findings, given that, when employed, contexts were equally strongly supportive of both the literal and nonliteral interpretations of the negative items.

Would construction grammar theories account for the results? Given that the interpretations of our stimuli, both in their negative and affirmative versions, are not coded, but have, instead, to be constructed (hence they are often spelled out or strengthened by similar examples, see examples 1, 5, 7), they might not be considered grammaticized.

They might therefore be hard to account for by e.g., Bybee's (2006), Fillmore et al.'s (1988), or Goldberg's (1995) views, according to which pairings of form and meaning are conventionalized in a way that is similar to the conventionalization of lexical items (Croft 2007). However, given that the items considered here show a strong association between specific negative constructions and nonliteral interpretations and specific affirmative constructions and literal interpretations (of whatever sort), this may be explained by Ariel's (2008) concept of "salient discourse profile". Salient discourse profile represents stored correlations between specific forms and their discourse functions. Such associations demonstrate a strong, though not necessarily coded, form/function association.

Given our focus here on the interpretations of novel negative constructions, we further propose that the view of negation as a low-salience marker may account for these results. As a low-salience marker, highlighting nonsalient interpretations via rejecting them, negation may account for the priority of novel nonliteral interpretations. (On negation and other low-salience markers bringing to the fore low-salience meanings and interpretations, see Giora et al. 2010, 2013, 2015; Givoni et al. 2013; On negation inducing sarcastic interpretation via rendering utterances into understatements or litotes, see Giora et al. 2005). And although a detailed analysis of the constraints of such negative constructions should await further research, the priority of nonsalient over salience-based interpretations challenges contemporary models of processing and interpretation.

Acknowledgements

This research was supported by THE ISRAEL SCIENCE FOUNDATION (grant no. 436/12).

4. References

Anonymous
   18. August   Default meanings, salient meanings, and automatic processing 2010http://anitas-ayer-hicksonsbrainpan.blogspot.co.il/2010/08/what-makes-good-father.html [Accessed 9 July 2012].
Ariel, Mira
   2002   Privileged interactional interpretations. *Journal of Pragmatics* 34(8): 1003–1044.
Ariel, Mira
   2008   Pragmatics and grammar. Cambridge: Cambridge University Press.
Ariel, Mira
   2010   *Defining Pragmatics*. Cambridge: Cambridge University Press.
Aristotle
   350 BCE   Poetics. Translated by Butcher S. H. The internet classic archive. http://classics.mit.edu/Aristotle/poetics.1.1.html.
Bach, Kent
   1994   Conversational impliciture. *Mind and Language* 9: 124–162.
Barbe, Katharina
   1993   "Isn't it ironic that …?": Explicit irony markers. *Journal of Pragmatics* 20: 578–590.
Beardsley, Monroe C.
   1958   *Aesthetics*. New York: Harcourt, Brace and World.

Birner, Betty J. and Gregory Ward
　1998　*Information Status and Noncanonical Word Order in English*. Amsterdam: John Benjamins.
Black, Max
　1954　Metaphor. *Proceedings of the Aristotelian Society* 55: 27.
Black, Max
　1962　*Models and Metaphors*: *Studies in Language and Philosophy*. Ithaca: Cornell University Press.
Black, Max
　1979　More about metaphor. In: A. Ortony (ed.), *Metaphor and Thought*, 19–43. Cambridge: Cambridge University Press.
Blige, Nellie
　2007　http://www.streetpoetry.net/id12.html [Accessed 3 May 2008].
Bryant, Greg A. and Jean E. Fox Tree
　2002　Recognizing verbal irony in spontaneous speech. *Metaphor and Symbol* 17: 99–117.
Bybee, Joan
　2006　From usage to grammar: The mind's response to repetition. *Language* 82(4): 711–733.
Campbell, John D. and Albert N. Katz
　2012　Are there necessary conditions for inducing a sense of sarcastic irony? *Discourse Processes* 49: 459–480.
Carston, Robyn
　1996　Metalinguistic negation and echoic use. *Journal of Pragmatics* 25(3): 309–330.
Carston, Robyn
　1997　Enrichment and loosening: Complementary processes in deriving the proposition expressed? *Linguistische Berichte* 8: 103–127.
Carston, Robyn
　2002　*Thoughts and Utterances*: *The Pragmatics of Explicit Communication*. Oxford: Blackwell.
Carston, Robyn
　2012　Metaphor and the literal-nonliteral distinction. In: K. Allan and K. Jaszczolt (eds.), *Cambridge Handbook of Pragmatics*, 469–492. Cambridge: Cambridge University Press.
Caucci, Gina M., and Roger J. Kreuz.
　2012　Social and paralinguistic cues to sarcasm. *Humor* 25: 1–22.
Chapman, Siobhan
　1996　Some observations on metalinguistic negation. *Journal of Linguistics* 32: 387–402.
Croft, William
　2007　Construction grammar. In: D. Geeraerts and H. Cuyckens (eds.), *The Oxford Handbook of Cognitive Linguistics*, 463–508. Oxford: Oxford University Press.
Divjak, Dagmar and Catherine Caldwell-Harris
　this volume　Frequency and entrenchment. Berlin/Boston: De Gruyter Mouton.
Erman, Britt and Beatrice Warren
　2000　The idiom principle and the open choice principle. *Text* 20: 29–62.
Fein, Ofer, Menahem Yeari and Rachel Giora
　2015　On the priority of salience-based interpretations: The case of irony. *Intercultural Pragmatics* 12(1): 1–32.
Fillmore, C. J., Paul Kay and Mary C. O'Connor
　1988　Regularity and idiomaticity in grammatical constructions: The case of let alone. *Language* 64(3): 501–538.
Gibbs, Raymond W. Jr.
　1980　Spilling the beans on understanding and memory for idioms in conversation. *Memory and Cognition* 8: 449–456.

Gibbs, Raymond W. Jr.
   1981   Your wish is my command: Convention and context in interpreting indirect requests. *Journal of Verbal Learning and Verbal Behavior* 20: 431–444.
Gibbs, Raymond W. Jr.
   1986a Comprehension and memory for nonliteral utterances: The problem of sarcastic indirect requests. *Acta Psychologica* 62: 41–57.
Gibbs, Raymond W. Jr.
   1986b On the psycholinguistics of sarcasm. *Journal of Experimental Psychology: General* 115: 3–15.
Gibbs, Raymond W. Jr.
   1994   *The Poetics of Mind: Figurative Thought, Language, and Understanding*. New York: Cambridge University Press.
Gibbs, Raymond W. Jr.
   2002   A new look at literal meaning in understanding what is said and implicated. *Journal of Pragmatics* 34: 457–486.
Gibbs, Raymond W. Jr. and Jessica F. Moise
   1997   Pragmatics in understanding what is said. *Cognition* 62: 51–74.
Giora, Rachel
   1997   Understanding figurative and literal language: The graded salience hypothesis. *Cognitive Linguistics* 7: 183–206.
Giora, Rachel
   1999   On the priority of salient meanings: Studies of literal and figurative language. *Journal of Pragmatics* 31: 919–929.
Giora, Rachel
   2003   *On our Mind: Salience, Context, and Figurative Language*. New York: Oxford University Press.
Giora, Rachel
   2006   Anything negatives can do affirmatives can do just as well, except for some metaphors. *Journal of Pragmatics* 38: 981–1014.
Giora, Rachel
   2011   Will anticipating irony facilitate it immediately? In: M. Dynel (ed.), *The Pragmatics of Humour across Discourse Domains*, 19–31. Amsterdam: John Benjamins.
Giora, Rachel, Ari Drucker and Ofer Fein
   2014   Resonating with default nonsalient interpretations: A corpus-based study of negative sarcasm. *Belgian Journal of Linguistics* 28: 3–18.
Giora, Rachel, Ari Drucker, Ofer Fein and Itamar Mendelson
   2015   Negation generates sarcastic interpretations by default: Nonsalient vs. salience-based interpretations. *Discourse Processes 52*.
Giora, Rachel, Ofer Fein, Jonathan Ganzi, Natalie Alkeslassy Levi and Hadas Sabah
   2005   On negation as mitigation: The case of irony. *Discourse Processes* 39: 81–100.
Giora, Rachel, Ofer Fein, Dafna Laadan, Joe Wolfson, Michal Zeituny, Ran Kidron, Ronie Kaufman and Ronit Shaham
   2007   Expecting irony: Context vs. salience-based effects. *Metaphor and Symbol* 22(2): 119–146.
Giora, Rachel, Ofer Fein, Nili Metuki and Pnina Stern
   2010   Negation as a metaphor-inducing operator. In: Laurence Horn (ed.), *The Expression of Negation*, 225–256. Berlin/New York: Mouton de Gruyter.
Giora, Rachel, Elad Livnat, Ofer Fein, Anat Barnea, Rakefet Zeiman and Ido Berger
   2013   Negation generates nonliteral interpretations by default. *Metaphor and Symbol* 28: 89–15.

Givoni, Shir, Rachel Giora and Dafna Bergerbest
  2013   How speakers alert addressees to multiple meanings. *Journal of Pragmatics* 48(1): 29–40.
Glucksberg, Sam and Boaz Keysar
  1990   Understanding metaphorical comparisons: Beyond similarity. *Psychological Review* 97: 3–18.
Goldberg, Adele E.
  1995   *Constructions*: *A Construction Grammar Approach to Argument Structure*. Chicago: University of Chicago Press
Gordon, David
  31 October 2011   David Gordon's Tumblr. http://mrdavidgordon.tumblr.com/post/12160981523/theres-such-a-racket-going-on-downstairs-between [Accessed 28 August 2012].
Grice, H. Paul
  1975   Logic and conversation. In P. Cole and J. Morgan (eds.), *Speech Acts*: *Syntax and Semantics*, Volume 3, 41–58. New York: Academic Press.
Hamblin, Jennifer L. and Raymond W. Gibbs Jr.
  2003   Processing the meanings of what speakers say and implicate. *Discourse Processes* 35: 59–80.
Hill, Mary
  19. June 2012   http://hia.mpls.k12.mn.us/hill_mary [Accessed 28 August 2012].
Horn, Laurence R.
  1985   Metalinguistic negation and pragmatic ambiguity. *Language* 61(1): 121–174.
Horn, Laurence R.
  1989/2001   *A Natural History of Negation*. Chicago: University of Chicago Press.
Israel, Michael
  2006   The pragmatics of polarity. In: L. Horn and G. Ward (eds.), *Handbook of Pragmatics*, 701–723. Oxford: Blackwell.
Israel, Michael
  2011   *The Grammar of Polarity*: *Pragmatics, Sensitivity, and the Logic of Scales*. Cambridge: Cambridge University Press.
Jaszczolt, Kasia M.
  2005a   *Semantics*: *Foundations of a Compositional Theory of Acts of Communication*. Oxford: Oxford University Press.
Jaszczolt, Kasia M.
  2005b   Prolegomena to default semantics. In: S. Marmaridou, K. Nikiforidou and E. Antonopoulou (eds.), *Reviewing Linguistic Thought*: *Converging Trends for the 21st Century*, 107–142. Berlin/New York: Mouton de Gruyter.
Jaszczolt, Kasia M.
  2009   Cancellability and the primary/secondary meaning distinction. *Intercultural Pragmatics* 6: 259–289.
Jaszczolt, Kasia M.
  2010   Default semantics. In: B. Heine and H. Narrog (eds). *The Oxford Handbook of Linguistic Analysis*, 193–221. Oxford: Oxford University Press.
Jaszczolt, Kasia M.
  2011   Default meanings, salient meanings, and automatic processing. In K. M. Jaszczolt and K. Allan (eds.), *Salience and Defaults in Utterance Processing*, 11–34. Berlin/New York: Mouton de Gruyter.
Johnny D.
  2008   The Baron of Hartlepool, Lord Mandelson, humility is not his strong point? http://uk.answers.yahoo.com/question/index?qid=20081019102454AAhMnSA [Accessed 25 October 25].

Katz, Albert
  2009   Commentary on "Does an ironic situation favor an ironic interpretation". In: G. Brône and J. Vandaele (eds.), *Cognitive Poetics: Goals, Gains and Gaps*, 401–406. Berlin/ New York: Mouton de Gruyter.
Katz, Albert, Dawn G. Blasko and Victoria A. Kazmerski
  2004   Saying what you don't mean: Social influences on sarcastic language processing. *Current Directions in Psychological Science* 13: 186–189.
Katz, Albert and Todd R. Ferretti
  2003   Reading proverbs in context: The role of explicit markers. *Discourse Processes* 36(1): 19–46.
Kecskés, István
  1999   The use of situation-bound utterances from an interlanguage perspective. In J. Verscheuren (ed.), *Pragmatics in 1998: Selected Papers from the 6th International Pragmatics Conference*, Volume 2, 299–310. Antwerp: International Pragmatics Association.
Kecskés, István
  2000   A cognitive-pragmatic approach to situation-bound utterances. *Journal of Pragmatics* 32: 605–625.
Lady
  3. May 2013   http://necolebitchie.com/2013/05/sneak-peek-tionna-smalls-lands-new-reality-show-girl-get-your-mind-right/ [Accessed 17 July 2014].
Levinson, Stephen C.
  2000   *Presumptive Meanings: The Theory of Generalized Conversational Implicature*. Cambridge: MIT Press.
Marzluf, Jonathan
  4. August 2011   http://test.woodwind.org/oboe/BBoard/read.html?f=10andi=18736andt=18711 [Accessed 9 July 2012].
Ortony, Andrew, Diane L. Schallert, Ralph E. Reynolds and Stephen J. Antos
  1978   Interpreting metaphors and idioms: Some effects of context on comprehension. *Journal of Verbal Learning and Verbal Behavior* 17: 465–478.
Partington, Alan
  2011   Phrasal irony: Its form, function and exploitation. *Journal of Pragmatics* 43(6): 1786–1800.
Peleg, Orna, Rachel Giora and Ofer Fein
  2001   Salience and context effects: Two are better than one. *Metaphor and Symbol* 16: 173–192.
Prince, Ellen F.
  1981   Topicalization, focus-movement, and Yiddish-movement: A pragmatic differentiation. *Berkeley Linguistics Society* 7: 249–264
RAMOS
  2012   Piolo Pascual admits comedy is not his forte http://mb.com.ph/node/358973/piolo-pa#.UIIeJMXR7-A [Accessed 25 October 2012].
Récanati, François
  1989   The pragmatics of what is said. *Mind and Behavior* 4: 295–329.
Récanati, François
  1995   The alleged priority of literal meaning. *Cognitive Science* 19: 207–232.
Récanati, François
  2001   What is said. *Synthese* 128: 75–91.
Récanati, François
  2004   *Literal Meaning*. Cambridge: Cambridge University Press.
Récanati, François
  2005   Literalism and contextualism: Some varieties. In: G. Preyer and G. Peter (eds.), *Contextualism in Philosophy: Knowledge, Meaning, and Truth*, 171–196. Oxford: Oxford University Press.

Richards, Ivor Armstrong
　1936　*The Philosophy of Rhetoric.* Oxford: Oxford University Press.
Rockwell, Patricia
　2007　Vocal features of conversational sarcasm: A comparison of methods. *Journal of Psycholinguistic Research* 36: 361–369.
Rosenblum, Doron
　5. March 2004　Smart he is not. http://www.haaretz.com/print-edition/opinion/smart-he-is-not-1.115908.
Searle, John
　1979　*Expression and Meaning.* Cambridge: Cambridge University Press.
Seddiq, Mirriam
　N. A.　Why I don't want to talk to you. http://notguiltynoway.com/2004/09/why-i-dont-want-to-talk-to-you.html.
Singh, Onkar
　17. December 2002　Parliament attack convicts fight in court. http://www.rediff.com/news/2002/dec/17parl2.htm [Accessed 24 July 2013].
Sperber, Dan and Deirdre Wilson
　1986/1995　*Relevance*: *Communication and Cognition.* Oxford: Blackwell.
Voegele, Jason
　N. A.　http://www.jvoegele.com/literarysf/cyberpunk.html
Voyer, Daniel and Cheryl Techentin
　2010　Subjective acoustic features of sarcasm: Lower, slower, and more. *Metaphor and Symbol* 25: 1–16.
Ward, Gregory
　1983　A pragmatic analysis of epitomization. *Papers in Linguistics* 17: 145–161.
Ward, Gregory and Betty J. Birner
　2006　Information structure. In: B. Aarts and A. McMahon (eds.), *Handbook of English Linguistics*, 291–317. Oxford: Basil Blackwell.

Rachel Giora, Tel Aviv (Israel)

30. Tense, aspect and mood

1. Introduction
2. Metaphor: EVENTS ARE (PHYSICAL) OBJECTS
3. Polysemy, construal, profiling, and coercion
4. Interactions of tense, aspect, and mood
5. Conclusion
6. References

1. Introduction

In the framework of cognitive linguistics we approach the grammatical categories of tense, aspect, and mood from the perspective of general cognitive strategies. Like most linguistic categories, the three grammatical categories of verbs discussed here display polysemy. The cognitive strategies relevant for polysemy are metaphor and metonymy, which help to structure radial categories by motivating extension from prototypical meanings (Lakoff 1987). Therefore metaphor and metonymy play an important role in the structure of tense, aspect, and mood categories. For verbal categories, reference to extralinguistic knowledge from domains like reasoning, probability, and hypothesis are particularly important, as are considerations of pragmatics. As a result, the same situation can be encoded differently in terms of tense, aspect, and mood in accordance with the speaker's construal of the situation. Cross-linguistically the categories of tense, aspect, and mood vary, though prototypes tend to be similar across languages.

The structure of grammatical categories of tense, aspect, and mood is motivated by a number of phenomena that are treated in more detail in other chapters in this volume. I refer in particular to Gries' chapter on Polysemy, Gibbs' chapter on Metaphor, Barcelona's chapter on Metonymy, and Taylor's chapter on Prototype effects. Although all three categories are dependent on how human beings conceptualize time, the topic of Evans' chapter in this volume, none of them merely encode parameters of reality, but instead are subject to the forces of construal, which is the topic of Langacker's chapter.

Tense reflects the speaker's experience of the sequencing of events. This alignment is inherently metaphorical, since tenses are conceived of in terms of regions along a timeline, which can be oriented and structured differently in different languages. In other words, tense is a metaphorical location of events with respect to a point of reference. Past and present are primary in that they are both available to the speaker; the past is relatively distant with respect to the present, while the future is both distant and unavailable. Tense is not rigidly defined by event time: many types of metaphoric shift are possible, as in (1), where present tense refers to a future event.

(1)   *I am flying to DC next week.*

Aspect is the grammatical expression of the experience of change (perfective) or lack thereof (imperfective), evaluated through the cognitive process of mental scanning. The speaker views the situation either in a summary fashion (perfective), or as a relationship that is extended in time (imperfective), and can construe the same situation differently in accordance with narrative and pragmatic intents. Aspect additionally includes the progressive and various types of Aktionsart (referring to modifications of the internal temporal constituency of an event). Verbs can have inherent (lexical) aspect, since some verbs, like *give*, are inherently more punctual or completive than others, like *love*. In addition, the arguments of the verb can contribute to the aspectual interpretation of an event, as we see in (2a) (with a definite subject, a singular object, and a perfective interpretation) vs. (2b) (with an indefinite subject, plural object, and an imperfective interpretation).

(2)   a.   *The writer wrote a book.*
       b.   *A writer writes books.*

Mood (and more generally modality) expresses the speaker's attitude toward the situation, most often in terms of force dynamics, where we see a force opposition between an agonist and an antagonist. Modal expressions are subjectively construed (offstage) grounding elements that refer to (potential) events beyond the bounds of the speaker's conceptualization of reality. While root (deontic) meanings of modals are motivated by the concrete experience of opposing forces (an embodied experience, cf. Bergen's chapter in this volume) and their extension to the domain of authority and permission as in (3a), modals are further metaphorically extended in epistemic uses to other domains such as reasoning as in (3b). The expression of modality is not limited to modal verbs, but includes imperatives, conditionals, subjunctives, counterfactuals, and a variety of impersonal constructions.

(3)   a.   *You must be home by midnight.*
       b.   *That must be John.*

This chapter first describes how core concepts of cognitive linguistics have shaped the analysis of tense, aspect, and mood, and then turns to interactions between the three categories. Sections 2 and 3 of this chapter take a thematic approach, exploring how studies in cognitive linguistics have used metaphor and construal to frame analyses of tense, aspect, and mood. Section 4 presents some studies of how tense, aspect, and mood interact with each other.

    This chapter presents only selected highlights from the study of tense, aspect, and mood from the perspective of cognitive linguistics. It does not discuss human conceptualization of time in any detail beyond that necessary to address tense, aspect, and mood. The reader is referred instead to Evans' chapter on Time in this volume. References to work on tense, aspect, and mood outside of cognitive linguistics are sparse and no attempt is made to compare achievements across linguistic traditions. This chapter also does not present a typological overview of tense, aspect, and mood phenomena in the world's languages, since such information can be found in other sources (e.g., Dahl 1985; Binnick 2012; Narrog 2012).

    I follow Croft (2012: 34) in using the term "event" to refer to all kinds of situations described by verbs. Following this tradition, I also use capitalized terms to refer to language-specific grammatical categories (like the Russian Perfective and the English Progressive), and lower-case terms to refer to categories in a more general sense (like perfective, progressive).

2. Metaphor: EVENTS ARE (PHYSICAL) OBJECTS

Implicitly or explicitly, tense, aspect, and mood rely upon a metaphorical understanding of events as "objects" in the domain of time. Thus reified, the situations described by verbs are placed in time, their properties are observed, and their relationship to reality is evaluated. The EVENTS ARE OBJECTS metaphor that underlies both the use of tense, aspect, and mood by speakers and its investigation by linguists is motivated as a special instance of the TIME IS SPACE conceptual metaphor that is probably universal in languages, although its concrete realizations are language-specific (Haspelmath 1997). Dahl (2013) takes a somewhat different perspective on the relationship between the domain of time and its "objects". He argues that it is our human ability to reify events as objects that makes it possible to understand not only their relationship to time, but time itself:

telic transitions between states are the cognitive constructs that themselves create the temporal dimension. One can thus view the timeline either as accompanied by a succession of events or as constituted by those events.

The comparison of events with objects makes it possible to treat verbs and nouns as parts of a single continuum. This continuum overlaps formally, of course, in the existence of deverbal nouns (such as *a look*) and noun-to-verb derivation or conversion (such as *to calve*). More importantly, this continuum reflects shared strategies in terms of the types of concepts that can be expressed grammatically, such as relative location, boundedness, multiplicity, definiteness, and force-dynamics.

The role of the EVENTS ARE OBJECTS metaphor in both language use and linguistic analysis is unsurprising because the mapping operation of metaphor is among the basic human cognitive mechanisms that motivate language and other cognitive behaviors. In this section, events are referred to as "event-objects" in order to highlight the metaphor that gives coherence to the various parallels observed in connection with the expression of tense, aspect, and mood.

2.1. Tense: event-objects in a timeline

The use of a timeline as a metaphorical "space" for locating event-objects relative to the moment of speech antedates cognitive linguistics (Reichenbach 1947; Comrie 1985). The presence of a mental timeline accounts for correlations between deictic spatial adverbials that can refer to proximal and distal locations and tenses with a similar range of distinctions. However, as Botne and Kershner (2008) show on the basis of Bantu data, the timeline itself can be quite complicated, including distinctions based on Moving Time vs. Moving Ego conceptualizations as well as various conceptual domains.

Time, grammatically realized as tense, is the most basic and first dimension in the linguistic system that connects tense, aspect, and mood. Aspect can be modeled as a second dimension orthogonal to time, dubbed the "qualitative state dimension" in which the contours of event-objects develop (Croft 2012; cf. Talmy 2000 v. II: 67–78; see 3.2 below). Some of the studies described in section 4 (Croft and Poole 2008; Croft 2012: 127–165; Eckhoff and Janda 2014) have yielded quantitative models in which tense and aspect emerge precisely as perpendicular axes in a two-dimensional space. A third dimension, also partly orthogonal to time, is mood, where event-objects directly experienced in the timeline serve to ground reality, against which the non-reality of possible and potential event-objects is judged as a deviation from the basic dimension of time (Langacker 2008: 300–302).

2.2. Aspect: observing the properties of event-objects

Whereas tense can be thought of as a system for investigating *where* event-objects are located on the timeline, aspect can be thought of as a system for investigating *what kinds of* event-objects there are. One can think of physical reality as comprised of two kinds of objects, often grammaticalized as the types of objects that are countable and the types that are not. The analogy between the count vs. mass distinction for nouns and the perfective vs. imperfective distinction for verbs has been observed often (Dahl 1985:

76). Janda (2004) works out this analogy in detail in an account of Russian aspect, with an inventory of fourteen properties of discrete solid objects as opposed to fluid substances that correlate to differences in aspectual usage. For example, discrete solid objects have inherent boundaries but fluid substances do not, and Perfective event-objects have temporal boundaries that Imperfective ones lack. Solid objects can exist as thin slices but fluid substances cannot, paralleled by the fact that punctual events are limited to Perfectives but Imperfectives require some duration. Fluid substances can be mixed together, whereas solid objects can only be adjacent to each other, though they can be embedded in fluid substances and these properties correspond to the various uses of aspect to express simultaneity and sequencing.

Huumo (2005, 2009) explores the properties of event-objects that are relevant for Finnish, which marks aspect by means of case in noun phrases instead of on its verbs. With transitive verbs there is a choice between Restrictive and Partitive case marking on the object. Restrictive case is associated with single, unique objects and with telic aspect. Partitive case is associated with mass nouns, plurals, and with atelic aspect. A conflict arises in so-called "quasi-resultative" sentences where verbs of position, sensory perception, and maintenance of a state, which would be expected to use the Partitive case, use instead the Restrictive case, thus representing the situation as the result of a change rather than as a neutral state (Huumo 2005). Another kind of interaction can arise with the case marking of predicate noun phrases with intransitive verbs. The general rule is that the Nominative case is associated with singular count nouns and represents the subject holistically, whereas the Partitive is associated with mass nouns or plurals and represents the subject incrementally. The aspectual interpretation of deverbal nouns, however, is directly affected by the case usage. Thus (4a) with the Nominative has a holistic interpretation, but (4b) with the Partitive has an atelic incremental interpretation (Huumo 2009).

(4)   a. *Tanssi   oli   kaunis.*
          Dance-NOM was beautiful-NOM
          'The dancing [a specific performance] was beautiful.'

     b. *Tanssi   oli   kaunista.*
          Dance-NOM was beautiful-PRT
          'The dancing [ongoing activity] was beautiful.'

Different languages will of course engage the event-object metaphor in their aspect systems in different ways. Even the closely related Slavic languages show differences in how their aspectual systems are focused. Dickey (2000) observes that two different versions of the event-object metaphor are relevant across the Slavic languages. In the west, Czech, Slovak, and Slovene focus on totality as the interpretation of Perfective as bounded and Gestalt-like. In the east, Russian, Ukrainian, and Bulgarian focus on definiteness as the relevant interpretation; Serbo-Croatian and Polish form transitional zones in this continuum. The distinction between totality in the west and definiteness in the east accounts for a number of differences in the use of aspect, most of which involve more use of the Perfective in the west, where Perfective can mark any action that is completed (including actions that are repeated or coincide with Present tense), whereas such contexts conflict with temporal definiteness in the east and are thus expressed with the Imperfective.

McGregor (2002) offers another perspective on the event-object metaphor by pointing out that in addition to having nominal classifiers, languages can also have verb classifiers. The most relevant type of nominal classifier system is that of numeral classifiers, where the nouns of a language refer to substances and classifiers serve to "unitize" the nouns into discrete objects, sorting the nouns into groups, usually according to the typical shapes of the objects they form. The use of such classifiers is associated with quantifiers and definiteness. McGregor's analogy links nouns to verbs, and quantifiers to aspect, and although he focuses on Australian languages, he argues that verb classifier systems are probably widespread among the world's languages, but have been overlooked because they have not been included in the inventory of features that typologists look for. Janda et al. (2013) present a series of statistical studies to support the hypothesis that Russian aspectual prefixes constitute a verb classifier system, which is likely valid for other Slavic languages as well. In addition to the connection between quantifiers and aspect, the verb classifier hypothesis examines distributional criteria and parallels between noun and verb classifier systems. Russian Imperfective verbs refer to unbounded states and activities (like the unformed substances referenced by nouns in numeral classifier languages), which are shaped into discrete Perfective events by aspectual prefixes, which also sort the verbal lexicon into different (though somewhat overlapping) groups. For example, Russian verbs that signal an APART meaning, like *bit'* 'break' and *krošit'* 'crumble' perfectivize with the prefix *raz-*, whereas verbs with an ARRIVE meaning like *blizit'sja* 'approach' and *celit'sja* 'aim at' perfectivize with the prefix *pri-*.

In addition to simple distinctions such as perfective, imperfective, and progressive, other types of event-objects can be identified, and a more detailed inventory is presented in section 3.2.

2.3. Mood and modality: force-dynamics of event-objects beyond reality

Langacker's model of modality emerges from the conception of reality, its subjective construal, and how these are reflected in the grounding of an event-object. Regardless of whether time is accompanied or constituted by the succession of event-objects, this succession yields a situation in which the past is defined, the present is being defined, and the future is yet to be defined. The human conceptualizer "C" has thus a personal history of experiences that make up immediate reality (along C's personal timeline), plus what is known to belong to reality but has not been directly experienced (parallel to C's immediate reality). Beyond reality lies non-reality, where we find event-objects that are suspected or hypothesized. Whereas mood can be thought of as a dimension that runs perpendicular to time in the past and present, both of which belong to reality, the distinction between mood and tense is less clear beyond that, and this is reflected in languages like English that have grammaticalized a modal verb such as *will* to mark future tense.

Modal elements like English modal verbs shift the grounding of the profiled event-object from the basic timeline of tense, such that it is offstage and subjectively construed. In other words, the force of the modal does not bear directly on the event-object itself, but on how it is viewed (in terms of its potential) from the perspective of the ground (Langacker 2008: 300–309). This model, with spaces corresponding to reality and non-reality, is of course a type of mental space model (Fauconnier 1985), in which modal elements serve to set up and structure the mental space that constitutes non-reality.

Mortelmans (2000) and Achard (2002) apply Langacker's model to verbal categories expressing mood, namely the German Past Subjunctive and the French Conditional respectively. These two grammatical categories are used to make a prediction about an event-object that is construed as alternative to reality. Based on knowledge of the structure of reality and its momentum, the speaker assumes that the event-object will not take place, as in (5) (Mortelmans 2007: 880–882).

(5)   *Wenn ich sie kennen würde, würde ich gleich zu ihr gehen*   German
      und mit ihr reden.
      Si je la connaissais, j'irais lui parler tout de suite.   French
      'If I knew her, I would go and talk to her right away.'

Talmy has investigated the role of force-dynamics in language, which are grammaticalized in the case of modals. An Agonist is an element that exerts a force, an Antagonist is an element that resists a force, and there are various force tendencies and results depending upon whether the force is directed from rest to action or the reverse. Modals like English *must, may* express grammatically similar situations of force or blockage that are also expressed lexically in verbs like *make* (*X happen*), *let* (*X happen*). However, the force tendencies of modals are contingent rather than intrinsic. In modal sentences like (6a) and (7a), the force is connected with the Agonist. Non-modal verbs present parallel situations in (6b) and (7b), where the force is connected instead to the Antagonist, which in this case removes a barrier. This model is elaborated to account for modal verbs, their negation, and also understanding of causation (Talmy 2000 v. I: 409–549).

(6)   a. *A flyball can sail out of the stadium.*
      b. *The lack of a dome makes it possible for a flyball to sail out of the stadium.*

(7)   a. *You may go to the playground.*
      b. *I permit you to go to the playground.*

Modal verbs tend to have peculiar syntax, as we see in (7a), where we have what looks like a collapsed two-clause structure. Pelyvás (2011) extends the force-dynamic model of modality to include counterforces and roles that motivate this trend. The "doer" (*you*) has a dual role, as both the passive obligee and the agentive of the potential action. The "imposer" (the speaker) is analyzed as a reference point, which is backgrounded, and this explains why it is unexpressed.

Takahashi (2012) offers a quantitative measure for force exertion according to six parameters (DESIRE, CAPABILITY, POWER, COST, BENEFIT, OBLIGATION) and demonstrates how this measure corresponds to prototypicality for English and Japanese imperatives, since a prototypical imperative like (8a) receives a high score, whereas (8b) receives a low one. A second factor in prototypicality is the subject of the imperative, which is individuated and agentive in a prototypical example, but generic (8c) or non-agentive (8d) in less prototypical uses.

(8)   a. *Do you have a problem? Tell me about it.*
      b. *So you find Tokyo expensive? Tell me about it! A cup of coffee can cost $ 10.*
      c. *Shake before using.*
      d. *Get well soon.*

3. Polysemy, construal, profiling, and coercion

Whereas the purpose of section 2 was to set up the basic framework for understanding tense, aspect, and mood, this section focuses on how the basic distinctions in each category are further elaborated. As we know, grammatical categories are typically polysemous, and the relations among the meanings of a category are usually motivated by extensions via metaphor and metonymy. In addition, we recognize the fact that language does not merely report the parameters of reality. The speaker selectively observes and construes both reality and non-reality, and this yields many more options than a mere report would allow. Construal is most often effected by means of differential profiling of event-objects. In addition, it is possible for conflicts between inherent and contextual values to extend the range of use of a category via coercion.

3.1. Tense: present as immediate vs. past as distal

Both the present and the past tense can be used to refer to event-objects that do not belong to the corresponding times. This is generally the result of construal or of coercion presenting a conflict between the tense and the context. Of course different languages conventionalize different construals of the timeline.

The present tense can be used to report event-objects that are associated with past, present, and future times. The historical present is a device that maps past event-objects to the present so that they can be metaphorically re-experienced as if they were immediate as in (9a). Langacker (2008: 303) attributes the use of the present tense in a statement lacking any real time reference like (9b) or to express a proximate future like (9c) to the fact that the speaker is reporting on things that are relevant for immediate reality. The proximate future is primarily used to describe event-objects that are scheduled to occur, so even though they are in the future, they are available to the speaker at the present. Gnomic statements about the inherent nature of the world are likewise available to the speaker at present, and can thus be reported as such. In both cases, the event-objects are construed as part of present experience.

(9) a. *Yesterday I met Sam. He says to me: What's up? I say: Not much. Then we go to lunch at our usual restaurant ...*
 b. *The earth revolves around the sun.*
 c. *We're flying home tomorrow.*

The past tense is also often found to have the capacity to express event-objects that did not take place in the past. Usually the result involves some kind of modal interpretation. In the case of (10a), *knew* does not refer to a past event-object, but rather to a hypothetical situation removed from immediate reality (Langacker 2008: 303). A similar effect is found in Dutch in (10b) (Janssen 1994: 122). The speaker exerts a modal force in both English (10c) and Russian (10d), trying to bring about a situation in the (near) future.

(10) a. *If I knew her, I would go and talk to her right away.* English

    b. *Nou, maar ik vertrok morgen!* Dutch
       Well but I left tomorrow
       'Well, but I was supposed to leave tomorrow!'

    c. *It's high time we left.* English

    d. *Pošli!* Russian
       Left-PAST-PLURAL
       'Let's go!'

Janssen (2002) invokes the deixis of demonstratives to account for these extensions of the present and past tenses. According to his analysis, the present tense signals 'THIS-context', which can include anything that the speaker has immediate access to. By contrast, the past tense signals 'THAT-context', which is more distal, making it amenable to interpretation as hypothetical, counterfactual, or even future.

3.2. Aspect

The standard baseline for aspectual distinctions are Vendler's (1967) four categories of lexical aspect (further elaborated below):

- States: *be hot, love*
- Activities: *walk, play*
- Achievements: *realize, reach the summit*
- Accomplishments: *write a letter, drown*

These lexical categories have typically been understood to correspond to grammatical aspect in that imperfective refers to states and activities, whereas perfective refers to achievements and accomplishments. Various tests for these categories have been proposed (cf. Mourelatos 1981), invoking features such as dynamicity, punctuality, and boundedness. However, neither the tests nor the categories themselves have proved adequate, largely due to the effects of construal and coercion. Indeed, most verbs can be shown to have multiple possible construals. The range of possibilities has been explored in detail by Talmy (2000 v. II) and Croft (2012) and are represented here in brief.

    Croft recognizes four types of states: transitory states, acquired permanent states, inherent permanent states, and point states. A given state can be distinguished according to whether it presupposes a prior state (as in 11a–b), is irreversible (as in 11b–c), or is construed as a point (as in 11d).

(11) a. transitory state *The door is open.*
     b. acquired permanent state *Princess Diana is dead.*
     c. inherent permanent state *Nicolas Sarkozy is French.*
     d. point state *It is five o'clock.*

Croft distinguishes two types of activities. Directed activities (cf. "gradient verbs" Talmy 2000 v. II: 68) like (12a) involve an incremental change, with continuous progress along a scale. Undirected activities (cf. Talmy's "multiplex verbs") like (12b) do not involve an incremental change and can often be construed as a series of cycles, like in the case of *chant*.

(12) a. directed activity   *The soup cooled.*
     b. undirected activity   *The girls chanted.*

Croft recognizes four types of achievements, plus a class of accomplishments. The first three types of achievements have the same contours as the corresponding states, differing only in profiling. Whereas the state is profiled for the former group, for the achievements, it is only the transition to the relevant state that is profiled. A reversible achievement (cf. Talmy's "one-way resettable") is (13a). An irreversible achievement (cf. Talmy's "one-way nonresettable") is (13b). Both reversible and irreversible achievements are directed changes, but a cyclic achievement (cf. Talmy's "full-cycle") like (13c), when interpreted to signal a single flash, is undirected. This is a common construal for verbs like *sneeze*, *wave*, *flash* which denote repeatable paired transitions between rest and action and the reverse. A runup achievement like (13d) includes an undirected activity (the presentation of various arguments which may or may not convince me), followed by a transition to the final phase (in which I believe Joe). The runup achievement type serves as a transition to accomplishments since it can also be understood as a nonincremental accomplishment, as opposed to a (neutral) accomplishment, which is incremental as in (13e).

(13) a. reversible achievement   *The door opened.*
     b. irreversible achievement   *Princess Diana died.*
     c. cyclic achievement   *The light flashed.*
     d. runup achievement   *Joe convinced me he was right.*
     e. accomplishment   *I wrote a letter.*

Croft observes that construal makes it possible for many verbs to have multiple aspectual interpretations. *Remember* signals a transitory state in (14a), but a directed achievement in (14b). Here different phases of the contour are profiled (the final state vs. the transition to it), and this can be understood as a metonymic relationship since different parts of the whole are selected. An utterance like (13c) can have different interpretations: if the light flashed once, it is a cyclic achievement; if it flashed for a while, it is an undirected activity. This is accounted for by Talmy's full-cycle vs. multiplex types. Croft invokes scalar adjustment for fine-grained (14c) vs. coarse-grained (14d) construals.

(14) a. *I remember how to do this.*
     b. *I remembered the answer.*
     c. *The bridge is collapsing.*
     d. *The bridge collapsed at 9:15 am.*

Croft (2012: 91–92) suggests that a usage-based approach would ideally treat the issues of default vs. alternative construals as an empirical question and investigate the relative frequencies and factors involved rather than making a priori assumptions about which construals exist and which ones are prototypical.

In support of his categories Croft presents a comparative study of English Present, Progressive, and Past constructions with Japanese Present, *te-iru*, and Past constructions. A multi-dimensional scaling analysis of this data yields a circular continuum of verbs, with clusters that correspond to transitory states (*be ill, be president*), directed achievements (*split, die*), directed activities (*cover, shrink*), undirected activities (*dance, run*), cyclic achievements (scratch, wave), and inactive actions (*touch, stand*). Thus the behavior of verbs (in terms of the constructions they appear in) supports Croft's categories for lexical aspect.

While Croft claims that his revision of the Vendlerian categories is universally applicable, the most valuable contribution of his model may be at a more abstract level. The combination of profiling and construal gives us a highly nuanced model and the use of aspectual contours makes it possible to visualize different aspectual types. Specific revisions and additions may be necessary in order to accommodate the facts of a given language (see Janda forthcoming, concerning adjustments needed for Russian), but this is possible if we accept the model as a flexible complex of components rather than as a fixed set of options.

3.3. Mood: root, epistemic, and speech-act modality

Whereas modals in their root (deontic) use refer to obligation, compulsion, and permission and belong primarily to the psychosocial domain, many of the same elements can be used to express epistemic modality. Instead of exposing an event-object to modal force outside the realm of reality, an epistemic modal assesses the likelihood that an event-object belongs to reality. Epistemic modals thus belong to the domain of knowledge and reasoning. A root modal is focused on realizing an event-object, but an epistemic modal, instead of influencing the realization of the event-object, focuses on deciding whether the event-object is likely to be realized. In (15a), *may* represents a root use and influences the outcome of the event-object *leave*, making it more likely to occur. The same modal in (15b) represents an epistemic use: it has no influence on the likelihood of rain, but instead reports the speaker's attitude toward the probability it will rain (Langacker 2008: 304–307). In addition to root and epistemic use, we observe speech-act modality in sentences like (15c). Here the modal is focused on the domain of conversation: *may* removes a barrier to accepting a statement (that John is a rocket scientist). In other words, the import of the modal is: "I accept the assertion that John is a rocket scientist and should be smart, but ..." Here modality applies to the conversational interaction rather than to any effect on an event-object or its evaluation as likely (Sweetser 1990: 69–73).

(15)   a.   root   *You may leave now.*
        b.   epistemic   *It may rain this afternoon.*
        c.   speech-act   *John may be a rocket scientist, but he sure is dumb.*

There is some controversy over the relationship between the types of modality, particularly between root and epistemic modality (see overview in Mortelmans 2007). Given that these different uses of modals pertain to different domains (reality vs. nonreality, reasoning, conversation), it is reasonable to interpret their relationship as a kind of mapping from the source domain of the root modals. It is not clear whether this mapping is metaphorical (Sweetser 1990) or metonymic (Bybee et al. 1994); additionally it has been suggested that epistemic uses result from increased subjectification (Traugott 1989). It is important to be aware that while Traugott and Langacker speak of subjectification and subjectivity in ways that may seem superficially similar, their notions differ; Mortelmans (2004) and Narrog (2012) explore these differences in detail. An alternative is to consider deontic and epistemic modality as equipollent components of modality rather than considering either one to be primary (Plungian 2011: 427). Narrog (2012) departs from the use of force dynamics and subjectivity in describing various types of modal expressions, relying instead on the parameters of speech-act orientation and volitivity. According to Narrog, modality refers primarily to a situation in which the factual status of a proposition is underdetermined.

4. Interactions of tense, aspect, and mood

In a previous overview article, Boogaart and Janssen (2007: 820–821) stated that it would be fruitful to explore interactions between the three categories of tense, aspect, and mood, but noted that such studies were sparse or lacking at the time. While there is still ample room for more research into such interactions, cognitive linguists have made considerable headway in filling this gap. Increasingly this involves empirical studies, usually of corpus data, to discover patterns of interaction. Most relevant studies focus on the interaction of only two of the categories, so the three logical pairings and recent studies pertaining to each are examined in turn.

4.1. Tense and aspect

Five studies are cited here to represent the current state of research on how tense and aspect interact. Langacker gives an analysis of how tense and lexical aspect can conflict in English. Croft and Poole present a major typological study, shedding new light on earlier data. The remaining studies focus on corpus analysis of data for Slavic languages, which are famous for their Perfective vs. Imperfective verbs: Russian (Janda and Lyashevskaya), Old Church Slavonic (Eckhoff and Janda), Croatian (Stanojević and Geld).

In an apparent paradox, Langacker (2011) asserts that despite the fact that the English Present cannot be used for present-time events, it does indicate coincidence with time of speaking. According to Langacker, an expression like (16a) is ungrammatical if used to express an ongoing action due a conflict between tense and aspect in English.

(16) a. *He mows the lawn.*
 b. *I order you to leave.*

If one presumes that English has a distinction between perfectives like *mow the lawn* vs. imperfectives like *know Italian*, one can state this restriction as a rule: English does not (usually) allow the use of the Present tense with perfectives. The conflict arises because in order to identify a perfective, one must observe the entire event-object, and usually this is not possible in the present, since a bounded event-object (a perfective) usually lasts longer than the present moment. Performatives like (16b) are a notable exception to this rule since they appear in the unusual situation in which a bounded event-object (ordering someone to leave) precisely coincides with the present moment (the utterance of the order). The performatives are the exceptions that prove the rule and solve the paradox, along with uses of the English Present for the historical present and proximate future with scheduled events (see 3.1 above): all of these represent event-objects that are available in their entirety at the present moment.

Croft and Poole (2008; see also Croft 2012) undertake a multi-dimensional scaling analysis for Dahl's (1985) data on the coding of tense-aspect markers in 250 contexts across 64 languages. The result is a two-dimensional map showing how various tense-aspect markers cluster; in other words, what kinds of groupings are attested cross-linguistically. The findings confirm the traditional division between tense and aspect, which emerge as perpendicular axes in the map. There is a central cluster consisting of hypothetical and gnomic situations as opposed to another cluster lying toward the future end of the continuum representing planned or expected future events. The separation between these two clusters is located in the future dimension, precisely where Langacker would predict an interaction between tense and mood (see 2.3 above). In terms of Croft's categories for lexical aspect, the contexts that fall on the imperfective end of the aspectual axis are all states or activities, but whereas the majority of contexts on the perfective end are achievements, we also find accomplishments, semelfactives, and even some activities and states. Although this result is not clear-cut, we acknowledge that construal can package activity and state verbs as bounded and therefore perfective event-objects (see 3.2 above).

Janda and Lyashevskaya (2011) present a corpus study of Russian verb forms across four subparadigms: Non-past, Past, Infinitive, and Imperative. The difference in distribution of these forms for Perfective vs. Imperfective verbs is statistically significant with a robust effect size. Furthermore, the difference in distribution between Perfective and Imperfective is the same regardless of whether it is marked by prefixes or suffixes, which shows that the aspectual categories have a consistent grammatical identity at a more abstract level. Janda and Lyashevskaya explore the verbs that are most attracted to various tense and aspect combinations. Despite the fact that grammars of Russian ascribe durative ongoing processes or repeated processes to the Imperfective Non-past, the verbs it attracts most all refer to gnomic event-objects, such as *javljaetsja* 'be' as in (17a). Perfective Non-past is associated in grammars with unique event-objects expected to be completed in the future. This study indeed finds verbs that signal promises (*upravitsja* 'will manage'), threats (*razterzaet* 'will tear to pieces'), and predictions (*vyzdoroveet* 'will get well'), but also performatives (*procitiruju* 'I quote'), and fixed expressions like (17b). Only among Imperfectives do we find verbs that are strongly attracted to the Past tense (the distribution for Perfective verbs is very wide), and these are associated with evidentials (*slyxal* 'heard'), habituals (*proxaživalsja* 'went for strolls'), and the narration of observations (*belel* 'showed white').

(17) a. *Koška   javljaetsja   mlekopitajuščim.*
    Cat-NOM is-3Sg-NONPAST mammal-INST
    'A cat is a mammal'

b. *vragu   ne poželaeš'*
   enemy-DAT not wish-2Sg-NONPAST
   'I wouldn't wish it on my worst enemy'

Ever since Dostál (1954) published his inventory of the aspectual types of Old Church Slavonic verbs, there has been controversy over whether the Perfective vs. Imperfective distinction was already in effect at that early stage of Slavic history. Eckhoff and Janda (2014) use corpus data to run a study similar to Janda and Lyashevskaya, but in reverse: with the distribution of verb forms as input, two different statistical models (correspondence analysis and divisive-clustering) test the structure of the data. The models do indeed separate the data according to aspect, with results that concur with Dostál's designations for 97% of verbs. Remarkably, while the first dimension that emerges from the correspondence analysis clearly aligns with Perfective vs. Imperfective aspect, the second dimension aligns with tense, yielding perpendicular aspect and tense axes similar to those found by Croft and Poole.

Stanojević and Geld (2011) examine the Croatian Aorist on the basis of both corpus and experimental data. The Croatian Aorist is a past tense formed only from Perfective verbs. Although standard grammars of Croatian state that the primary use of the Aorist is to mark past and often sequenced events, Stanojević and Geld observe that the Aorist is often used to signal recent past events with current relevance, as well as future events that are conceived of as (nearly) certain, as in (18a–b). Furthermore, as in these examples, the Aorist occurs predominantly in the first person singular form. As a Perfective form, the Aorist excludes the Present tense because it must view the event-object in its totality (cf. Langacker's analysis of the English Present above). Stanojević and Geld argue that the Aorist is epistemically immediate (as opposed to the Perfect which is epistemically distant), and this explains its reference to both immediate past and immediate future, as well as its association with the subjective experience of the speaker (first person).

(18) a. *Ljudi,   pogiboh!*
        People-NOM died-1Sg-AORIST
        'People, I'm dying!' (a call for help)

    b. *odoh   i   ja   sutra ...*
        left-1Sg-AORIST and I-NOM tomorrow
        'although I am leaving tomorrow ...'

4.2. Tense and mood

In the future, tense and mood overlap, since future events are necessarily beyond the established realm of reality (see 2.3 above). Additionally, Langacker (2008: 300–302) observes that the tensed forms of English modal verbs serve to indicate epistemic rather than temporal distance. For example, Present tense *can* refers to a potential in relation to reality, whereas Past tense *could* is usually interpreted not as potential, but counterfactual and thus even farther removed from reality. Patard (2011) takes a similar approach to the English Past and French Imperfect, and asserts that both express modality in utterances like (19a–b). In both types of examples, the past tense serves to mark epistemic distance, making such statements counterfactual.

(19) a. *If only I was rich.* English
 b. *Si j'étais riche.* French

4.3. Aspect and mood

There appears to be an association between aspect and modality in examples like (20a–b). Whereas the perfective in (20a) facilitates a deontic reading, exerting a force on the event-object itself, the imperfective in (20b) facilitates an epistemic reading, expressing an assessment of the likelihood that John is reading the book. Boogaart and Trnavac (2011) examine this connection across Germanic, Romance, and Slavic languages. They conclude that the motivation for this association is given by a more general connection between imperfective aspect and subjective information, however it seems that this option is exploited only in Germanic and Romance, but not in Slavic languages.

(20) a. *John must read that book.*
 b. *John must be reading that book.*

Russian lacks modal verbs (the only possible candidate being *moč'* 'be able'), but uses constructions containing modal words like *nado* 'have to' and *nel'zja* 'not allowed to' with Infinitives instead. In a quantitative study, Divjak (2009) showed that in such constructions Imperfectives are preferred to refer to generic obligations and possibilities, whereas Perfectives are preferred for specific event-objects. Janda and Lyashevskaya's (2011) results conformed with those in Divjak's study. In addition to aspect and tense (see 4.1), Janda and Lyashevskaya explore Russian verbs strongly attracted to Imperatives and Infinitives. In the Imperative mood it has traditionally been asserted that Imperfectives mark polite uses (21a) as opposed to Perfectives which mark rude uses (21b). However, Imperfective Imperatives are also associated with insistence (which can be rude), and there are many contexts in which a Perfective Imperative is neutral or polite.

(21) a. Imperfective *Sadites'*
  Sit-2Pl-IMPERATIVE
  'Please sit down'
 b. Perfective *Sjad'te*
  Sit-2Pl-IMPERATIVE
  'Sit!'

Šatunovskij (2009) suggests that the difference in aspect has to do with whether the hearer understands what is expected. If the hearer does understand what to do, the Imperfective is preferred (probably because it is gentler, like a fluid substance, cf. 2.2 above), whereas if the hearer needs to receive instructions, the Perfective is preferred (since the hearer needs access to the entire event-object that is expected). Note that Šatunovskij's model accounts for the complexity observed since in a polite situation usually the hearer knows what to do, and the Imperative just acknowledges when the action is to take place, but if the hearer is expected to do something and hesitates, the Imperative can express the speaker's frustration when the hearer fails when s/he should know better. Janda and Lyashevskaya's data confirm Šatunovskij's model, but also turn up some outliers that cannot be motivated, such as Imperfective requests for assistance (*vyručajte* 'help') and kind wishes (*vyzdoravlivajte* 'get well').

5. Conclusion

Despite a diversity of specific topics and languages, recent research on tense, aspect, and mood from a cognitive perspective presents a coherent story. Events are understood linguistically as objects and evaluated according to their location, properties, and relationship to reality or probability. Tense, aspect, and mood are confirmed both inductively and empirically as intersecting axes. All three grammatical categories can be manipulated to express speaker's construal, extending their scope beyond what would be needed to report on the objective reality of time. These three categories overlap and interact with each other in ways that we are only beginning to understand. In recent years, cognitive linguists have increasingly applied corpus-based empirical approaches to the study of these verbal categories. Future usage-based studies will hopefully expand our knowledge about the uses and patterns of tense, aspect, and mood both within given languages and cross-linguistically.

6. References

Achard, Michel
   2002   The meaning and distribution of French mood inflections. In: Frank Brisard (ed.), *Grounding: The Epistemic Footing of Deixis and Reference*, 197–249. Berlin: Mouton de Gruyter.

Binnick, Robert I. (ed.)
   2012   *The Oxford Handbook of Tense and Aspect.* Oxford: Oxford University Press.

Boogaart, Ronny and Theo Janssen
   2007   Tense and aspect. In: D. Geeraerts and H. Cuyckens (eds.), *The Oxford Handbook of Cognitive Linguistics*, 803–828. Oxford: Oxford University Press.

Botne, Robert and Tiffany L. Kershner
   2008   Tense and cognitive space: On the organization of tense/aspect systems in Bantu languages and beyond. *Cognitive Linguistics* 19: 145–218.

Bybee, Joan L., Revere D. Perkins and William Pagliuca
   1994   *The Evolution of Grammar: Tense, Aspect and Modality in the Languages of the World.* Chicago: University of Chicago Press.

Comrie, Bernard
   1985   *Tense.* Cambridge: Cambridge University Press.

Croft, William
   2012   *Verbs: Aspect and Causal Structure.* Oxford: Oxford University Press.

Croft, William and Keith T. Poole
   2008   Inferring universals from grammatical variation: Multidimensional scaling for typological analysis. *Theoretical Linguistics* 34: 1–37.

Dahl, Östen
  1985   *Tense and Aspect Systems*. Oxford: Basil Blackwell.
Dahl, Östen
  2013   How telicity creates time. *Journal of Slavic Linguistics* 21(1) (a special issue entitled *Aspect in Slavic: Creating Time, Creating Grammar*, ed. by Laura A. Janda): 45–76.
Dickey, Stephen M.
  2000   *Parameters of Slavic Aspect: A Cognitive Approach*. Stanford, CA: CSLI Publications.
Divjak, Dagmar
  2009   Mapping between domains: The aspect-modality interaction in Russian. *Russian Linguistics* 33: 249–269.
Dostál, Antonín
  1954   *Studie o vidovém systému v staroslověnštině* [A Study of the Aspectual System of Old Church Slavonic]. Prague: Státní pedagogické nakladatelství.
Eckhoff, Hanne M. and Laura A. Janda
  2014   Grammatical profiles and aspect in Old Church Slavonic. *Transactions of the Philological Society* 112, 231–258.
Fauconnier, Gilles
  1985   *Mental Spaces*. Cambridge: MIT Press.
Haspelmath, Martin
  1997   *From Space to Time: Temporal Adverbials in the World's Languages*. Munich: LINCOM Europa.
Huumo, Tuomas
  2005   How fictive dynamicity motivates aspect marking: The Riddle of the Finnish Quasi-resultative construction. *Cognitive Linguistics* 16: 113–144.
Huumo, Tuomas
  2009   Fictive dynamicity, nominal aspect, and the Finnish copulative construction. *Cognitive Linguistics* 20: 43–70.
Janda, Laura A.
  2004   A metaphor in search of a source domain: The categories of Slavic aspect. *Cognitive Linguistics* 15: 471–527.
Janda, Laura A.
  forthcoming   Russian Aspectual Types: Croft's Typology Revised. In: M. Shrager, G. Fowler, E. Andrews and S. Franks (eds.), *Festschrift for Ronald Feldstein*, Bloomington: Slavica Publishers. Preprint version at: http://ansatte.uit.no/laura.janda/mypubs/mypubs.html.
Janda, Laura A. and Olga Lyashevskaya
  2011   Grammatical profiles and the interaction of the lexicon with aspect, tense, and mood in Russian. *Cognitive Linguistics* 22: 719–763.
Janda, Laura A., Anna Endresen, Julia Kuznetsova, Olga Lyashevskaya, Anastasia Makarova, Tore Nesset and Svetlana Sokolova
  2013   *Why Russian Aspectual Prefixes aren't Empty: Prefixes as Verb Classifiers*. Bloomington: Slavica Publishers.
Janssen, Theo A. J. M.
  1994   Preterit and perfect in Dutch. In: C. Vet and C. Vetters (eds.), *Tense and Aspect in Discourse*, 115–146. Berlin: Mouton de Gruyter.
Janssen, Theo A. J. M.
  2002   Deictic principles of pronominals, demonstratives and tenses. In: Frank Brisard (ed.), *Grounding: The Epistemic Footing of Deixis and Reference*, 151–193. Berlin: Mouton de Gruyter.
Lakoff, George
  1987   *Women, Fire, and Dangerous Things*. Chicago: University of Chicago Press.
Langacker, Ronald W.
  2008   *Cognitive Grammar: A Basic Introduction*. Oxford: Oxford University Press.

Langacker, Ronald W.
2011 The English present: Temporal coincidence vs. epistemic immediacy. In: A. Patard and F. Brisard (eds.) *Cognitive Approaches to Tense, Aspect, and Epistemic Modality*, 45–86. Amsterdam/Philadelphia: John Benjamins.
McGregor, William B.
2002 *Verb Classification in Australian Languages*. Berlin: Mouton de Gruyter.
Mortelmans, Tanja
2000 Konjunktiv II and epistemic modals in German: A division of labour. In: A. Foolen and F. van der Leek (eds.), *Constructions in Cognitive Linguistics*, 191–215. Amsterdam: John Benjamins.
Mortelmans, Tanja
2004 Grammatikalisierung und Subjecktivierung: Traugott und Langacker revisited. *Zeitschrift für germanistische Linguistik* 2: 188–209.
Mortelmans, Tanja
2007 Modality in Cognitive Linguistics. In: D. Geeraerts and H. Cuyckens (eds.), *The Oxford Handbook of Cognitive Linguistics*, 869–889. Oxford: Oxford University Press.
Mourelatos, Alexander P. D.
1981 Events, processes and states. In: P. Tedeschi and A. Zaenen (eds.), *Tense and Aspect.* (Syntax and Semantics 14.), 191–212. New York: Academic Press.
Narrog, Heiko
2012 *Modality, Subjectivity, and Semantic Change: A Cross-Linguistic Perspective*. Oxford: Oxford University Press.
Patard, Adeline
2011 The epistemic uses of the English simple past and the French imparfait: When temporality conveys modality. In: A. Patard and F. Brisard (eds.), *Cognitive Approaches to Tense, Aspect, and Epistemic Modality*, 279–310. Amsterdam/Philadelphia: John Benjamins.
Pelyvás, Péter
2011 Motivation in English *must* and Hungarian *kell*. In: K. Panther and G. Radden (eds.), *Motivation in Grammar and the Lexicon*, 171–190. Amsterdam: John Benjamins.
Plungian, Vladimir A.
2011 *Vvedenie v grammatičeskuju semantiku: grammatičeskie značenija i grammatičeskie sistemy jazykov mira* [Introduction to the Semantics of Grammar: Grammatical Meanings and the Grammatical Systems of the World's Languages]. Moscow: RGGU.
Reichenbach, Hans
1947 *Elements of Symbolic Logic*. New York: The Free Press.
Šatunovskij, Il'ja B.
2009 *Problemy russkogo vida* [Problems of Russian Aspect]. Moscow: Jazyki slavjanskix kul'tur.
Stanojević, Mateusz-Milan and Renata Geld
2011 New current relevance in Croatian: Epistemic immediacy and the aorist. In: A. Patard and F. Brisard (eds.), *Cognitive Approaches to Tense, Aspect, and Epistemic Modality*, 159–180. Amsterdam/Philadelphia: John Benjamins.
Sweetser, Eve
1990 *From Etymology to Pragmatics: Metaphorical and Cultural Aspects of Semantic Structure*. Cambridge: Cambridge University Press.
Takahashi, Hidemitsu
2012 *A Cognitive Linguistic Analysis of the English Imperative: With Special Reference to Japanese Imperatives*. Amsterdam: John Benjamins.
Talmy, Leonard
2000 *Toward a Cognitive Semantics*. Cambridge: MIT Press.

Traugott, Elizabeth C.
　1989　On the rise of epistemic meanings in English: An example of subjectification in semantic change. *Language* 65: 31–55.

Vendler, Zeno
　1967　Verbs and times. In Z. Vendler (ed.), *Linguistics in Philosophy* 97–121. Ithaca: Cornell University Press.

Laura A. Janda, UiT, The Arctic University of Norway (Norway)

31. Grammaticalization

1. Introduction
2. Grammaticalization – 100 years and more
3. Cognition in grammaticalization theory
4. Grammaticalization in cognitive linguistic theory
5. Conclusion
6. References

1. Introduction

This chapter first provides a brief historical perspective on grammaticalization, in section 2: it gives a general definition of the process, examines the origin of both the term and the idea and describes how it rose to prominence in the 80s and has been problematized more and more since the late 90s. Some of the reasons for this recent development are raised in the next two sections, which look at the link between grammaticalization and cognitive linguistics from two different angles. Section 3, on the one hand, discusses what cognition – in the broadest sense of the word – there is in current grammaticalization work. The following issues in particular are addressed, though they are not necessarily unique to grammaticalization: language acquisition as the locus of change; grammatical innovation as the result of the principles of clarity and economy, the desire to be expressive or the ubiquitous variation in the construal of situations; the effects of frequency in grammaticalization and their cognitive basis; the role of reanalysis versus analogy; and, finally, the mechanisms underlying the semantic changes in grammaticalization. Section 4, on the other hand, looks at what grammaticalization there is in current cognitive approaches to grammar. The focus is on Construction Grammar and Cognitive Grammar, two theories whose original orientation was predominantly synchronic. It is discussed how the former's notion of (grammatical) constructionalization involves a drastic widening of the scope of investigation as compared to the linguistic phenomena traditionally subsumed under grammaticalization and how subjectification is central to the grammaticalization work within the latter framework. Section 5 is the conclusion.

2. Grammaticalization – 100 years and more

In general terms, grammaticalization is the process that creates grammar. Most of the work on grammaticalization has focused on the development of morphosyntactic categories such as 'perfect' and 'number', involving function words such as articles, auxiliaries, conjunctions and particles, and derivational and inflectional morphemes, out of lexical items or (multiword) constructions. Thus the English modal verb *ought* 'grammaticalized' from a verb that meant 'to owe', the French negative particle *pas* meaning 'not' derives from a noun meaning 'step', the Italian derivational adverb marker *-mente* (as in *rigorosamente* 'rigorously') comes from the noun *mens* 'mind', and the English dental preterite *-ed* as in *danced* probably originates from an ancestor of the verb *do*. It is taken for granted that grammaticalization is not a process affecting individual words only. Thus it is not really the word *pas* itself that grammaticalized from 'step' to 'not', but a specific construction containing *pas* as well as the negative particle *ne* also meaning 'not'. Outside of this kind of context *pas* retained its 'step' meaning. Another assumption is that the change from lexicon to grammar is gradual and that even within the realm of grammar formations can be more or less 'grammatical', with e.g. inflection being more grammatical than derivation. Furthermore, grammar is more than a system of function words, a crucial component being word order. If in any language the word order is strict, this strictness will have developed out of discourse habits, and this rigidification also constitutes grammaticalization.

It would thus seem that grammaticalization is central to the understanding of language. Nevertheless, at least the term if not also the concept of grammaticalization have been claimed to have outlived its usefulness. One recent 'death penalty' was pronounced in 2012, the very year of its one hundredth anniversary. The year of birth is 1912 and the place of birth is a frequently cited but much less frequently read[1] short French article, which appeared in an Italian journal with a Latin Italian name (*Scientia – Rivista di Scienza*), but which became more easily accessible through its inclusion in a 1921 edition of collected papers. The single parent is Antoine Meillet. To the extent that we can see, the term was indeed new, but the idea was not. Meillet was very explicit on this: he considered grammaticalization phenomena to be "well known, even by people that have never studied linguistics and everybody has the opportunity to study them or at least observe them" (Meillet 1912: 384, our translation). Meillet, did not, however, name any predecessors. Christian Lehmann (1995: 1) traces the study of *avant la lettre* grammaticalization back to the French philosopher Condillac (*Essai sur l'origine des connaissances humaines*, 1746) and Lehmann further assigns major roles to Wilhelm von Humboldt, Franz Bopp, and Georg von der Gabelentz and, in more general terms, to 19th century typology and Indo-European historical linguistics. In their introduction to a handbook

---

[1] A telling illustration of the way Meillet (1912) was not read with sufficient care comes from the study of negation. One of Meillet's illustrations of grammaticalization is the diachrony of negation as with French *ne* going to *ne pas* and then *pas*. The process became well known under the term 'Jespersen cycle', with reference to Jespersen (1917*)*. Jespersen (1917), however, came later than Meillet (1912), and Jespersen did not himself use the term 'cycle', whereas Meillet did use a 'cycle' type concept, viz. 'spiral' in good Gabelentzian tradition (von der Gabelentz 1891: 251; see van der Auwera 2009).

on grammaticalization, Heiko Narrog and Bernd Heine (2011: 1) even say that the study of grammaticalization is "almost as old as linguistics".

Despite this longevity, however, the days of grammaticalization might be numbered. At a conference on 'Refining Grammaticalization', organized in February 2012 by Ferdinand von Mengden and Horst Simon, Graeme Trousdale claimed that at least the term was no longer useful (see section 4 for his plea for 'constructionalization'). If we are allowed to read this as a death announcement, we could, of course, in good European royal tradition continue with the phrase 'Long live grammaticalization' and in a way Trousdale did exactly that, by organizing a conference on 'New perspectives on grammaticalization' in July in Edinburgh. Its goal was the same as the one in Berlin, viz. to refine current thinking on the topic. We can conclude that just like grammaticalization was not really born in 1912, it did not really die in 2012 either. Yet the existence of a concept of grammaticalization *avant la lettre* and the fact that even after a century *après la lettre* specialists are still in need of refining the concept show that grammaticalization is a problematic notion.

In the first seventy years following 1912, the topic was treated off and on but typically without using the term, e.g. Jespersen (1922: 367–395), Benveniste (1968), and Givón (1979) – one exception is Kuryłowicz (1965). At least a partial reason for the lack of interest in the topic was the synchronic preoccupation of both North American and European linguistics. This changed from 1982 on with the catalyst work by Christian Lehmann (1982), Elizabeth Closs Traugott (1982), and Bernd Heine and Mechtild Reh (1984), the latter two interacting with Lehmann at the University of Cologne. From the nineties on there was a veritable explosion of studies, important ones involving the ground breakers of the previous decade (e.g. Traugott and Heine 1991; Hopper and Traugott 2003; Heine et al. 1991). It is true that some linguists who entered the debate found the concept dubious or at least some of the by then standard assumptions about it, see especially Newmeyer (1998: 225–295) and a special issue of *Language Sciences* (Campbell 2001). It is also true that for the diachronic study of grammar other notions were proposed and increasingly more so. Of some it was claimed – and also contested – that they were more important, e.g. reanalysis (Roberts 1993 vs. Haspelmath 1998) or constructionalization (see section 4). Other notions referred to processes that were claimed to compete with grammaticalization, viz. analogical change (already in Meillet 1912), lexicalization (Lehmann 2002; Brinton and Traugott 2005; but already in Kuryłowicz 1965), degrammaticalization (Norde 2009; but already in Lehmann 1982), regrammaticalization (Greenberg 1991), exaptation (Lass 1990), pragmaticalization (special issue of *Linguistics* – Degand and Simon-Vandenbergen 2011; but already in Traugott 1982), and subjectification and intersubjectification (van der Auwera and Nuyts 2012). Meanwhile, 'grammaticalization' has seen contenders in 'auxilation' (Benveniste 1968), 'grammaticization' (Bybee, Perkins and Pagliuca 1994) and 'grammation' (Andersen 2006). In the literature confronting the various *-ation* terms, it is often difficult to decide to what extent the debate concerns important conceptual issues or only terminology. Hence the organizers of both the 2012 Berlin and Edinburgh conferences were correct: current thinking still needs refinement ... and this is also the case for the cognitive aspects of grammaticalization.

3. Cognition in grammaticalization theory

The question of which mental processes are at work in grammaticalization has been central to much of the work in the field of cognitive or functionalist linguistics. But generative linguists too have made certain claims about cognition in grammaticalization – especially with respect to the first of the two steps that Croft (2000: 4–5) distinguishes in language change, i.e., 'innovation' (the second one being 'propagation'). In their view, grammaticalization takes place during language acquisition (e.g. Roberts and Roussou 2003: 33–34). In essence, change is regarded as reanalysis by the learner of the language. Children are assumed to possess an innate set of principles (valid for all languages) and parameters (to be set), which allows the ambiguous output of an adult grammar to receive a representation in their grammars that differs from the 'original' one. The actual change is caused by considerations of least effort or economy within the linguistic system. According to Van Gelderen (2004), for instance, learners tend to posit a head rather than a phrase and to assume a position higher up in the tree in cases of ambiguity. In the minimalist framework, both tendencies can be argued to reduce the computational load: "full phrases have more features (to check) and they are more likely to be interpreted" and "the lower ... element in the tree has more semantic features whereas the grammatical/functional elements has uninterpretable features" (Van Gelderen 2011: 372).

Despite the increase in generative grammaticalization studies in the 21st century (e.g. Simpson and Wu 2002; Abraham 2004; and Fuß 2005), the model is problematic in at least two respects. Acquisition does not appear to be the primary locus of language change (see Croft 2000: 57–59 and Bybee 2010: 114–119). Moreover, it is highly doubtful from a typological as well as from an evolutionary perspective (see Croft 2001 and Christiansen and Chater 2008 respectively) that humans are born with a set of linguistic principles and parameters in any case. From a cognitive perspective (see Tomasello 2006) this assumption is unnecessary.

The dominant view, which is characteristic of the functionalist paradigm, is that grammaticalization does not happen during acquisition or is at least not restricted to it (see Bruyn 1995 on creoles and Singleton and Newport 2004 on sign language). Croft (2010: 6) distinguishes two models for the beginning of change in adult language. In the first model, innovation is triggered by the interaction of the conflicting principles of economy and clarity: first, economy motivates the formal reduction of grammatical items, then the desire to be clear prompts speakers to develop more substantial, typically periphrastic alternatives and the new forms may eventually be reduced as well. One of the exponents of this model is Langacker (1977: 128): "Language change reflects the pressure to achieve linguistic optimality". This goal subsumes the opposite tendencies toward simplicity on the one hand and perceptual optimality and transparency on the other hand (see also von der Gabelentz 1891 on *Bequemlichkeit* 'ease' and *Deutlichkeit* 'clearness').

The view that reduction comes first has been criticized by, among others, Haspelmath (1999, 2000), and this brings us to the second model. One of the arguments is that the first model "cannot explain why erosion does not stop at the point where it would threaten intelligibility" (Haspelmath 2000: 791). In Haspelmath's opinion, innovation is motivated by the desire to be expressive or, in his words, "extravagant". In an attempt to be noticed and achieve social success, speakers violate the so-called maxim of conformity and – within reason – draw on the lexicon to produce more 'creative' expressions. Lehmann (1985: 315) puts it as follows: "They do not want to express themselves the same way they did yesterday, and in particular not the same way as somebody else did yesterday. To some extent, language is comparable to fashion". The new forms then catch on, conventionalize and tend to become subject to formal reduction. This model is not unproblematic either, however. Croft (2010) is right in pointing to the pervasive nature of variation in speech. If new or different ways of saying things constitute expressiveness, every speaker can be said to be expressive almost all the time and no speaker will ever really be noticed. He argues that variation (and thus innovation) is inherent to ordinary speech and that it is cognitively motivated. As speakers experience and construe the same situation in various ways, it is only normal that their verbalizations differ too. According to Croft (2010: 42), who observes that the synchronic diversity of forms often reflects potential paths of grammaticalization, it is "this ubiquitous variation" on which "selection mechanisms [of a social type] operate" in language change (see Waltereit 2011: 415–416 for cursory criticism).

Most of the explanations discussed in the preceding paragraph are partially cognitive but primarily communicative in nature. But there are other factors. Frequency, for instance, has been shown to have a huge impact on the manner in which linguistic items are stored in the brain and, as such, on the manner in which they develop (see Bybee 2003, 2006 and Divjak and Caldwell-Harris, this volume). The fact that speaking is neuromotoric and that repetition correlates with increasing fluency accounts for the aforementioned phonetic erosion of high frequency (grammaticalizing) items. More significantly perhaps, the more a particular word sequence or construction occurs, the more it is 'saved' and uttered as a unit. As a consequence, it can disassociate itself from its components. At the formal level, this autonomy combines with repetition to result in fusion (e.g. *going to* turning into *gonna*). It also renders the word sequence or construction less analyzable and allows it to lose its internal structure and change categories (e.g. *be going to* becoming an auxiliary). At the functional level, autonomy makes it possible for a unit to get a new meaning (through repeated inferences, see below), which may not be reducible to the semantic sum of its subparts (e.g. *be going to* turning into a marker of futurity). On the whole, repetition can be regarded as an important driving force behind grammaticalization (but see e.g. Hundt 2001 on the low frequency of the *get*-passive). It is not the whole cognitive story, though.

One hotly debated issue is what happens mentally when, say, *be going to* develops into an auxiliary. The usual answer is reanalysis or a "change in the structure of an expression or class of expressions that does not involve any immediate or intrinsic modification of its surface structure" (Langacker 1977: 58) (see also Hopper and Traugott 2003: 50–63). In other words, speakers are said to restructure the sequence $[be + going]_{\text{MainVerbPhrase}} + [to + X]_{\text{Purpose}}$ as $[be + going + to]_{\text{Auxiliary}} + [X]_{\text{MainVerb}}$. Still, the role or even the existence of reanalysis has been called into question by some linguists (e.g. Haspelmath 1998). Fischer (2009: 7–8), for example, claims that "the very first time a historical speaker-listener identified *going-to* as an auxiliary, therefore, did not constitute an actual reanalysis of *going*(full verb)+*to*-infinitive but a category mistake that he could make because the *going-to* form fitted both the V-*to*-V as well as the Aux-V pattern". More fundamentally, reanalysis has been argued to be logically impossible: it suggests that new categories can come into being as the result of some structural ambiguity while this ambiguity "exists only in retrospect – that is, after the change has taken place" (De Smet 2009: 1729).

The alternative that most of the critics of reanalysis propose is analogy. In much of late 20th century and early 2000s work (e.g. Hopper and Traugott 2003: 63–68), analogy is regarded as interacting with reanalysis. The latter is responsible for rule changes and for creating forms, the former for widening a new rule's scope and for extending a new form's contexts of use (e.g. from activity verbs after *be going to* to all verbs). But especially in recent work within the usage-based framework which takes Antilla's (2003: 438) statement that "humans are simply analogical animals" to heart (e.g. Fischer 2008), analogy has taken center stage. Language – with no fundamental distinction between grammar and lexicon – is argued to be shaped by analogical connections in form and function between individual items or tokens, groups of tokens and/or types. In this model, analogy is considered not only a mechanism but also a cause for change. The grammaticalization of *a lot of* into a quantifier, for instance, can be said to be motivated by its similarity to the older construction *a heap of* (see Brems 2012).

It is not entirely clear, however, how strong an analogical link has to be to trigger change. The aforementioned 'match' between *be going to* and the Aux-V pattern can serve as an example: the auxiliaries followed by a *to*-infinitive that existed at the time of the change did not contain an *-ing* form (see Traugott 2011: 26). Relatedly, scholars have raised the question how the first auxiliary (or any new category) ever came into existence given the lack of a pattern to model it on. One tentative answer is that "the [first] 'auxiliary' would have been an under-analysed and grammatically isolated chunk" and that "only when another such chunk developed, language users could perceive a similarity between the two", at which "point a category 'auxiliary' arises" (De Smet 2009: 1751).

Another important question is how grammaticalizing items evolve semantically. Heine et al. (1991) look at the issue from a typological perspective and observe considerable similarities in the source and target meanings between languages. They argue that speakers "conceptualize abstract domains of cognition in terms of concrete domains" (Heine et al. 1991: 31) and try to capture this process of metaphorical extension in the following hierarchy: person > object > activity > space > time > quality. The semantic evolution of *be going to* can thus be said to involve the metaphor 'time is space'. One crucial aspect of the hierarchy is that the sources are typically anthropocentric (e.g. body parts, 'basic' activities such as 'say' and 'go') or, put differently, rooted in human experience. The metaphor approach has been criticized, however, for not explaining the gradual nature of the semantic evolution in grammaticalization. *Be going to* does not change from a marker of movement into one of futurity in one step but via a number of intermediate, metonymic steps – which, for clarity's sake, Heine et al. (1991) do acknowledge.

Several proposals have been made to account for these gradual changes (e.g. Nicolle 1998 within the framework of relevance theory), the most influential one being the invited inference theory by Traugott and Dasher (2002). The idea is that a form used by the speaker in a particular context (see Diewald 2002 and Heine 2002 on critical and bridging contexts respectively) encourages the addressee to draw a specific inference or, in other words, to see the conversational implicature as part of the message (but see Ariel 2002 on the role of explicatures in grammaticalization). Through repetition, this inference may generalize – i.e., it becomes typical but is still cancellable – and eventually conventionalize as the form's new meaning. According to Bybee, Perkins and Pagliuca

(1994: 268), markers of futurity such as *be going to* involve (at least) the following contiguous steps:

> The temporal meaning ... is already present as an inference from the spatial meaning. When one moves along a path toward a goal in space, one also moves in time ... The function of expressing intention comes into play. When a speaker announces that s/he is going somewhere to do something, s/he is also announcing the intention to do that thing ... The only change necessary is the generalization to contexts in which an intention is expressed, but the subject is not moving spatially to fulfill that intention.

On the whole, the metonymy of pragmatic inferencing seems to describe the semantic evolution of grammaticalizing items better than the metaphorical account, though the former could be argued to be motivated by the latter (see also Heine et al. 1991: 96).

Obviously, the mechanisms discussed in the present section are not restricted to grammaticalization. Analogy, inferences and the like belong to the general human mental faculty and also play a role in other processes of language change (see Hilpert, this volume) such as lexicalization as well as, if one accepts that it exists, pragmaticalization.

In the next section, we will turn things around. We will look at existing cognitive theories and describe how they deal with grammaticalization.

4. Grammaticalization in cognitive linguistic theory

Within the edifice of cognitive linguistics, several positions have been taken with regards to grammaticalization. This section deals with how two main strands in cognitive linguistics, viz. Cognitive Grammar (Langacker 1999, 2005, 2006, 2007, 2010) and (Diachronic) 'Construction Grammar' (Croft 2001; Noël 2007; Trousdale 2010; Hilpert, this volume).[2] Even though Construction Grammar (henceforth CxG) and Cognitive Grammar (henceforth CG) are very similar in that they are both usage-based, cognitive approaches, operating on the principle that language is built up of conventionalized form-meaning pairings ('symbolic units') that represent all grammatical knowledge, there are some important differences between the two. Exactly those differences have led to differing takes on grammaticalization.

CG and CxG conceive of the 'form' component of a construction differently. In CG, form solely refers to the phonological form (Langacker 2005: 104–107), whereas in CxG, form also captures grammatical form. The CG and CxG views on meaning are similar, but for CG meaning is the more important component and grammaticalization is seen as a primarily semantic phenomenon, to be described in terms of what is called 'construal' and 'profiling'. For CxG, grammaticalization concerns pairings of both meaning and form, i.e., the 'constructions', which come in different types and are related to each other in taxonomic networks. Traugott (2008a: 236) introduces a specific nomenclature to refer to four different types of constructions which can be distinguished in these

---

[2] The Traugott/Trousdale approach, which we will focus on below, is not strictly speaking a kind of (Diachronic) Construction Grammar, but since constructions and diachrony are crucial to them, we include it under this heading.

networks (although in some cases more or fewer levels can be distinguished (see also Hilpert 2013: 5). These types range from the lowest level or 'construct'-level, which are individual instantiations of language use. Higher up we find 'micro-constructions' or individual construction types. More abstract are 'meso-constructions', which represent sets of constructions. The highest level of abstraction are 'macro-constructions'; "meaning-form pairings that are defined by structure and function, e.g., Partitive, or Degree ModifierConstructions" (Traugott 2008a: 236).

4.1. (Diachronic) Construction Grammar

The CxG view on grammaticalization is different from that of CG, but there are in fact even different CxG views. Undoubtedly partly due to the characterization of grammaticalization as "the creation of constructions", it seems just one step away from conflating the term 'grammaticalization' with the framework-specific term 'constructionalization' or even with 'constructional change' (Wiemer and Bisang 2004: 4). There have been strong arguments, however, to maintain that 'grammaticalization' and 'constructionalization' should be kept apart (Noël 2007). Noël (2007: 195–196) argues that grammaticalization should still exist in diachronic construction grammar as a more advanced step in change, distinguishing it from constructionalization as an initial establishment of form-meaning pairings (see also Gisborne and Patten 2010). As a result, the term 'grammatical constructionalization' – as opposed to 'lexical constructionalization' – has found its way into the literature with only the former doing the grammaticalization work (Traugott 2008b; Trousdale 2008; Traugott and Trousdale 2010, 2013). However, grammatical constructionalization may still not be the same as grammaticalization. A true construction grammarian will adhere to a very wide conception of what is grammar, because all constructions are conceived of as the building blocks of grammar (e.g. Wiemer and Bisang 2004). Consequently, grammatical constructionalization may incorporate more conventionalized form-meaning pairings than traditional grammaticalization theorists will see apt in grammaticalization. In the following, we will go deeper into grammatical and lexical constructionalization as developed by both Traugott and Trousdale (individually or jointly).

For Traugott and Trousdale (Traugott 2008b; Trousdale 2008, 2010; Traugott and Trousdale 2010), constructionalization is the emergence of constructions at any level in the constructional taxonomy. Through conventionalization, it can result in what is traditionally known as the grammaticalization of a construction, now called "grammatical constructionalization" and also in what is traditionally known as the lexicalization of a construction. Put simply, through repeated language use grammaticalizing constructions emerge at an increasingly schematic level whereby they become more general, and whereby their schema becomes increasingly productive (Trousdale 2010: 52). Lexicalizing constructions, however, exhibit a smaller degree of schematicity and next to no syntactic productivity (Gisborne and Patten 2010: 102). Hilpert (2013: 18–19), amongst others, argues against the no productivity statement (giving the example of productive *-hood* and *-ness* words), and also Traugott and Trousdale (2013) take a new stance on this. Croft and Cruse (2004: 309) further explain that productivity, schematization and frequency are interdependent: the productivity of a construction is proportionate to the number of instances at any level of schematicity. Key features (or even prerequisites) for the gradual process of grammatical constructionalization at every level are an increase in productivity, semantic generality and non-compositionality (Langacker 2005; Gisborne and Patten 2010; Trousdale 2008). Compare, for instance, the lexical construction (or idiom) *kick the bucket*, which has no syntactic productivity nor semantic reduction to the extent that its internal components may be replaced by new ones (* *hit the bucket*, * *kick the pot*) and the grammatical aspectual construction (*GIVE N a V-ing*), exemplified by *he gave the dog a kicking*, which has become syntactically productive and semantically applicable to items previously not accepted in the constructional schema (*He gave her a thorough seeing to* > *He gave the shirt a good ironing*). In both processes features are not acquired in an abrupt fashion, rather the constructions undergo micro-steps towards constructionalization higher up the taxonomy.

Central to grammatical constructionalization (GCzn) accounts are two collaborating, yet seemingly opposite, forces. On the one hand, the GCzn of a construction/construct implies a bottom-up movement upward in the constructional taxonomy (Hudson 2007: 49). Change is only possible through language use. Construct-level ambiguity, supported by inherited schema knowledge[3] (or default inheritance, see below) is the first step towards change (see also Croft 2001: 126–129). Repeated use of related constructs may lead to the formation of a micro-construction. When this micro-construction becomes entrenched, a meso-construction may be formed on a higher level of abstraction. Through the ongoing, gradual conventionalization, the meso-construction can in turn affect new constructs and coerce them into forming a new micro-construction (Gisborne and Patten 2010: 103; Noël 2007: 184). This constitutes a feedback loop whereby a meso-construction becomes entrenched and more schematic and whereby it can, in itself, start to function as an analogical template for future innovations.

On the other hand, GCzn relies on the 'default inheritance' of constructional (idiosyncratic) properties from more schematic, higher-level constructions onto lower-level constructs. Default inheritance, here, represents all individual linguistic knowledge in a speaker. It also presents the basic mechanism of change in CxG accounts through which novel constructions may emerge. The macro- and meso-constructional schemas serve as templates with linguistically successful (conventional and productive) properties which may recruit new constructs and consequently project their internal properties onto them; this is a process of innovation by analogy. Gisborne and Patten (2010: 103) see these constructional schemas as coercion environments. In a way, then, we could say that language change is an innovation through coercion. This does not mean, however, that an emerging construction needs to inherit all the properties of the higher-level construction (see also Hudson 2007); otherwise it is not a newly recruited construction. Take for instance a subtype of the Composite Predicate Construction (Trousdale 2008) (1), which inherits from the Ditransitive Give Construction (*to give N to N*).

(1)   *He gave his employee a good grilling.*

The second noun in the Composite Predicate Construction is not retained but replaced by a verbal noun. In summary, the grammatical development of a construction should

---

[3]   It must be kept in mind that it is the schema (or construction *pattern*) that carries meaning, and that this meaningful pattern recruits new elements into it through analogy.

be seen in relation to the constructional taxonomy from which it inherits. If a chronological order needs to be assigned, this would happen after repeated use of a construct. The bidirectional construction strengthening can eventually lead to further entrenchment and abstraction as a macro-construction.

Even though the framework-specific term roughly captures the same changes traditionally associated with grammaticalization, it is considered better because it allows for a coherent account of the processes making up grammaticalization (Gisborne and Patten 2010; Trousdale 2010: 52, 55). In being able to map the specific steps inherent to constructionalization, grammatical change is unidirectional in a "non-trivial way" (Trousdale 2010: 55). Specifically, it tackles the seemingly contradictory accounts which have been appearing over the last three decades, where one conceives of the restriction and reduction of elements (in paradigmaticization, univerbation, semantic bleaching, etc.; Lehmann 1982) as well as of their expansion (semantic scope, complementation, etc.; Brinton 2006; Traugott 2010). The constructionalist approach mediates between these two initially contradictory views by allowing for both movements. A grammaticalizing construction shows stronger internal dependencies – restrictions and reductions such as morpho-phonological univerbation – and a scope flexibility of its environment (expansion).

All in all, we see the same processes in GCzn as we see in traditional grammaticalization theory, with the exception that they apply to more units than traditionally assumed. Also, subjectification can be part of GCzn (Trousdale 2008, 2010), but not to the extent that it defines the change, as in Cognitive Grammar.

4.2. Cognitive Grammar

If CxG can be referred to as the cognitive linguistic approach to syntax (Croft and Cruse 2004: 225), then CG – albeit "a kind of construction grammar" (Langacker 2010: 79) – could be referred to as the cognitive linguistic approach to semantics or meaning. With all grammatical items being meaningful and meaning being identified with conceptualization, it is taken as self-evident in CG that grammaticalization is primarily characterized in conceptual semantics. CG holds that the process of subjectification (which, as defined by Langacker, deals with construal and perspectivization) is central to grammaticalization. Grammaticalization itself is defined – quite simply – as "the evolution of grammatical elements from lexical sources" (Langacker 1999: 297). Grammatical status lies in the secondary, supplementing function of items to lexical, descriptive items. This secondary status (see Boye and Harder 2012) can be exhibited by conjunctions or case markers indicating how conceptual chunks fit together, they can be aspect or voice markers imposing a perspective for the object and they can point at external factors in the subjective realm through illocutionary force and deixis. Like most accounts, CG sees grammaticalization as a composite change with interrelated, mutually reinforcing aspects – although formal aspects are tended to more as a consequence of conceptual change (Langacker 2010: 83, 89; see also Trousdale and Norde 2013).

In the conceptual semantics advocated by CG, it is assumed that there is an 'object' and a 'subject' of conception. The object of conception is the content of the expression; the subject of conception is the conceptualizer, i.e., the speaker (and secondarily the hearer). Maximally objective is an expression with an implicit or 'off-stage' subject. When the subject is 'on-stage', it is objectified, i.e., in the object of conception as both the subject and object of conception, for example, by means of a subject pronoun *I*, *we*, *you*, ... The 'profile' is what most attention is directed at in the object of conception and is highly objectively construed. 'Construal' is the subject's particular selection of what is in the (profile of the) object of conception (Langacker 2006: 18, 2010: 80; see also Nuyts 2012: 67–69). Being in the object of conception means that an item is 'on-stage' and thus objectively construed. Construal always manifests itself 'on-stage'. Subjective construal is immanent in expressions, so most expressions have both subjectively and objectively construed elements, which can both only be 'on-stage' because they have been construed (Evans and Green 2006: 728).

The driving force behind grammatical change and grammaticalization in CG is subjectification (Evans and Green 2006: 728; Langacker 1999: 314). The term should not be confused with Traugott's use of this term, which refers to the subjective content of an entire expression (Langacker 2006: 17). In CG, subjectification is more complex. Subjectification as the main process moving just a single item on the continuum from lexical to grammatical is an umbrella term for a set of (reductive) changes affecting this item. It is the movement of an item from the objective to the subjective construal realm or, in other words, the attenuation of objectivity of an item whereby it goes from maximally specific to maximally schematic – schematization (Langacker 2006: 21; 2010: 81). In highly grammaticalized cases, this attenuation leads to transparency. The attenuation is characterized by at least four conceptual processes (Langacker 1999: 301–302): we can see a shift in the *locus of activity* or *potency* (from objectively construed (on-stage) to subjectively construed (off-stage), e.g. the English modals, see below), *status* (from actual to potential or from specific to generic) (e.g. the construction 'thing', see below), *focus* (from profiled to unprofiled), and *domain* (from physical interaction to a social or experiential one) of the item (e.g. the English modals). Additionally, grammaticalization and, by association, subjectification, is accompanied by other processes of attenuation, viz. phonological (i.e., formal) attenuation (*going to* > *gonna* > *gon/onna* > *a*) and a shift in salience from primary (lexical, i.e., descriptive) to secondary (grammatical, i.e., supplementary) *function*. See Figure 31.1.

```
    Lexicon ------------------------------------------------------Grammar
     on-stage-\----------------------Locus----------------------/----off-stage
       actual---|----------------------Status---------------------|-----generic
     profiled---|-----------------------Focus----------------------|----unprofiled
     physical---|----------------------Domain---------------------|----experiential
  descriptive--/---------------------Function--------------------\-supplementary
                           Phonological attenuation
          Objective ------------------------------------------------Subjective
        object of conception                                    subject of conception
```

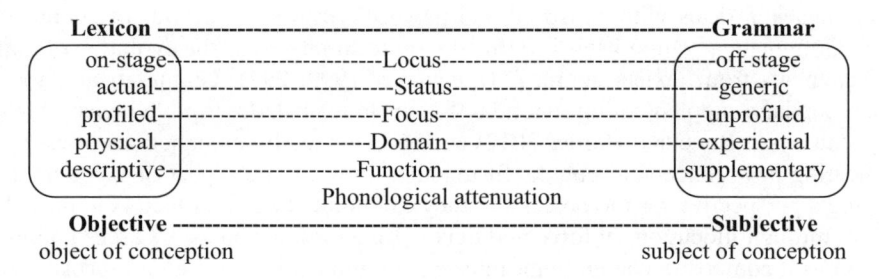

Fig. 31.1: Processes involved in subjectification

As such, grammaticalization is seen as a mainly reductive process. However, it can initially be seen as expansive when an item's reference starts to broaden from actual to generic, through which its meaning will be applicable to any content. This is what drives schematization and gradual loss of analyzability leading to the erosion of the original motivation for its spread (Langacker 2010: 83).

By means of illustration, a look at the word *thing* may be revealing. In its most specific meaning (2), it denotes an inanimate physical object. In its most schematic meaning (4), it can occur in the pronoun *something*, where it merely designates any product of grouping and reification (Langacker 2010: 81). An intermediate stage (3) shows that *thing* has abstract (discourse) reference.

(2) *What is that thing over there?*

(3) *Who said those awful things?*

(4) *You moaning is something I could really do without right now.*

In (4), the construction *thing* shows signatures of grammaticalization (and schematization) in the following ways: Being schematic, it has been subject to objective attenuation (i.e., subjectification). It is no longer profiled, and thus it can also occur in the pronoun *something*. It has moved from an actual to a generic domain, denoting any content labeled by a noun, any abstract or concrete product of grouping and reification. Another illustration (although highly simplified) is given by the present-day epistemic modal verbs, which have developed from objective (lexical) verbs to subjective (grammatical) markers of likelihood located in the subjective domain. As such, they have also become increasingly unprofiled, generic, experiential and even off-stage in that the likelihood is located in the subject's vantage point rather than in a grammatical subject or in the object of conception.

5. Conclusion

What does this overview teach us and what does it tell us about the future? First, we think that the sketch tells us that it does not matter too much what label one chooses to describe the phenomena at hand: grammaticalization by any other name would smell as sweet. Second, any term one settles for has to be defined or described as clearly as possible, and placed within a larger framework, where its role is to be delineated in relation to other factors and processes, cognitive, communicative and other. We briefly outlined two such frameworks, CcG and CG. Neither was originally designed for diachrony and both are coping with grammaticalization in promising ways.

6. References

Abraham, Werner
    2004   The grammaticalization of the infinitival preposition: Toward a theory of 'grammaticalizing reanalysis'. *Journal of Comparative Germanic Linguistics* 7: 111–170.

Andersen, Henning
    2006   Grammation, regrammation, and degrammation: Tense loss in Russian. *Diachronica* 23: 231–258.

Antilla, Raimo
    2003   Analogy: The warp and woof of cognition. In: B. D. Joseph and R. D. Janda (eds.), *The Handbook of Historical Linguistics*, 425–440. Oxford: Oxford University Press.
Ariel, Mira
    2002   Privileged interactional interpretations. *Journal of Pragmatics* 34: 1003–1044.
Benveniste, Émile
    1968   Mutations of linguistic categories. In: W. P. Lehmann and Y. Malkiel (eds.), *Directions for Historical Linguistics. A Symposium*, 85–94. Austin: University of Texas Press.
Boye, Kasper and Peter Harder
    2012   A usage-based theory of grammatical status and grammaticalization *Language* 88: 1–44.
Brems, Lieselotte
    2012   The establishment of quantifier constructions for size nouns: A diachronic study of heap(s) and lot(s). *Journal of Historical Pragmatics* 13: 202–231.
Brinton, Laurel J.
    2006   Pathways in the development of pragmatic markers in English. In: A. van Kemenade and B. Los (eds.), *The Handbook of the History of English*, 307–334. London: Blackwell.
Brinton, Laurel J. and Elizabeth C. Traugott
    2005   *Lexicalization and Language Change*. Cambridge: Cambridge University Press.
Bruyn, Adrienne
    1995   *Grammaticalization in Creoles: The Development of Determiners and Relative Clauses in Sranan*. Amsterdam: University of Amsterdam.
Bybee, Joan L.
    2003   Cognitive processes in grammaticalization. In: M. Tomasello (ed.), *The New Psychology of Language: Cognitive and Functional Approaches to Language Structure*, Volume 1, 145–167. Mahwah: Lawrence Erlbaum Associates.
Bybee, Joan L.
    2006   From usage to grammar: The mind's response to repetition. *Language* 82: 711–733.
Bybee, Joan L.
    2010   *Language, Usage and Cognition*. Cambridge: Cambridge University Press.
Bybee, Joan, Revere Perkins and William Pagliuca
    1994   *The Evolution of Grammar: Tense, Aspect and Modality in the Languages of the World*. Chicago: University of Chicago.
Campbell, Lyle (ed.)
    2001   *Grammaticalization: A Critical Assessment*, Special issue (2/3) *Language Sciences* 23.
Christiansen, Morten H. and Nick Chater
    2008   Language as shaped by the brain. *Behavioral and Brain Sciences* 31: 489–509.
Croft, William
    2000   *Explaining Language Change: An Evolutionary Approach*. London: Longman.
Croft, William
    2001   *Radical Construction Grammar: Syntactic Theory in Typological Perspective*. Oxford: Oxford University Press.
Croft, William
    2010   The origins of grammaticalization in the verbalization of experience. *Linguistics* 48: 1–48.
Croft, William and Alan Cruse
    2004   *Cognitive Linguistics*. Cambridge: Cambridge University Press.
de Condillac, Étienne Bonnot
    1746   *Essai sur l'Origine des Connaissances Humaines* [*Essay on the Origin of Human Knowledges*]. Paris.

Degand, Liesbeth and Anne-Marie Simon-Vandenbergen
  2011   *Grammaticalization, Pragmaticalization, and (Inter)Subjectification: Methodological Issues in the Study of Discourse Markers.* Special issue (3) *Linguistics* 49.
De Smet, Hendrik
  2009   Analysing reanalysis. *Lingua* 119: 1728–1755.
Diewald, Gabriele
  2002   A model for relevant types of contexts in grammaticalization. In: I. Wischer and G. Diewald (eds.), *New Reflections on Grammaticalization*, 103–120. Amsterdam: John Benjamins.
Divjak, Dagmar and Catherine Caldwell-Harris
  this volume   Frequency and entrenchment. Berlin/Boston: De Gruyter Mouton.
Evans, Vyvyan and Melanie Green
  2006   *Cognitive Linguistics: An Introduction.* Edinburgh: Edinburgh University Press.
Fischer, Olga
  2008   On analogy as the motivation for grammaticalization. *Studies in Language* 32: 336–382.
Fischer, Olga
  2009   Grammaticalization as analogically driven change? *Vienna English Working Papers* 18: 3–23.
Fuß, Eric
  2005   *The Rise of Agreement: A Formal Approach to the Syntax and Grammaticalization of Verbal Inflection.* Amsterdam: John Benjamins.
Gisborne, Nikolas and Amanda Patten
  2010   Construction grammar and grammaticalization. In: H. Narrog and B. Heine (eds.), *The Oxford Handbook of Grammaticalization*, 92–104. Oxford: Oxford University Press.
Givón, Talmy
  1979   From discourse to syntax: Grammar as a processing strategy. In: T. Givón (ed.), *Syntax and Semantics*, Volume 12: *Discourse and Syntax*, 81–112. New York: Academic Press.
Greenberg, Joseph H.
  1991   The last stages of grammatical elements: Contractive and expansive desemanticization. In: E. C. Traugott and B. Heine (eds.), *Approaches to Grammaticalization*, Volume 1, 301–314. Amsterdam: John Benjamins.
Haspelmath, Martin
  1998   Does grammaticalization need reanalysis? *Studies in Language* 22: 315–351.
Haspelmath, Martin
  1999   Why is grammaticalization irreversible? *Linguistics* 37: 1043–1068.
Haspelmath, Martin
  2000   The relevance of extravagance: A reply to Bart Geurts. *Linguistics* 38: 789–798.
Heine, Bernd
  2002   On the role of context in grammaticalization. In: I. Wischer and G. Diewald (eds.), *New Reflections on Grammaticalization*, 83–101. Amsterdam: John Benjamins.
Heine, Bernd, Ulrike Claudi and Friederike Hünnemeyer
  1991   *Grammaticalization: A Conceptual Framework.* Chicago: University of Chicago Press.
Heine, Bernd and Mechtild Reh
  1984   *Grammaticalization and Reanalysis in African Languages.* Hamburg: Buske.
Hilpert, Martin
  this volume   Historical Linguistics. Berlin/Boston: De Gruyter Mouton.
Hilpert, Martin
  2013   *Constructional Change in English: Developments in Allomorphy, Word Formation, and Syntax.* Cambridge: Cambridge University Press.
Hopper, Paul J. and Elizabeth C. Traugott
  2003   *Grammaticalization.* Cambridge: Cambridge University Press.

Hudson, Richard
  2007   *Language Networks: The New Word Grammar*. Oxford: Oxford University Press.
Hundt, Marianne
  2001   What corpora tell us about the grammaticalization of voice in *get*-constructions. *Studies in Language* 25: 49–88.
Jespersen, Otto
  1917   *Negation in English and Other Languages*. Copenhagen: A. F. Høst & Søn.
Jespersen, Otto
  1922   *Language: Its Nature, Development and Origin*. London: Georg Allen & Unwin.
Kuryłowicz, Jerzy
  1965   The evolution of grammatical categories. *Diogenes* 51: 55–71. [Reprinted in Kurylowiz, Jerzy. 1975. *Esquisses linguistiques II [Linguistic Sketches II]*, 38–54. Munich: Wilhelm Fink].
Lass, Roger
  1990   How to do things with junk: Exaptation in language evolution. *Journal of Linguistics* 26: 79–102.
Langacker, Ronald W.
  1977   Syntactic reanalysis. In: C. N. Li (ed.), *Mechanisms of Syntactic Change*, 57–139 Austin: University of Texas Press.
Langacker, Ronald W.
  1999   Grammar and Conceptualization. Berlin: Mouton de Gruyter.
Langacker, Ronald W.
  2005   Construction grammars: Cognitive, radical, and less so. In: F. J. Ruiz de Mendoza Ibáñez and S. Peña Cervel (eds.), *Cognitive Linguistics: Internal Dynamics and Interdisciplinary Interaction*, 101–159. Berlin: Mouton de Gruyter.
Langacker, Ronald W.
  2006   Subjectification, grammaticization, and conceptual archetypes. In: A. Athanasiadou, C. Canakis and B. Cornillie (eds.), *Subjectification: Various Paths to Subjectivity*, 17–40. Berlin: Mouton de Gruyter.
Langacker, Ronald W.
  2007   Cognitive Grammar. In: D. Geeraerts and H. Cuyckens (eds.), *The Oxford Handbook of Cognitive Linguistics*, 421–462. Oxford: Oxford University Press.
Langacker, Ronald W.
  2010   Grammaticalization and Cognitive Grammar. In: H. Narrog and B. Heine (eds.), *The Oxford Handbook of Grammaticalization*, 79–91. Oxford: Oxford University Press.
Lehmann, Christian
  1982   *Thoughts on Grammaticalization: A Programmatic Sketch*, Volume 1. Cologne: Institut für Sprachwissenschaft der Universität. (Revised in 1995 Munich: LINCOM EUROPA).
Lehmann, Christian
  1985   Grammaticalization: Synchronic variation and diachronic change. *Lingua e Stile* 20: 303–318.
Lehmann, Christian
  2002   New reflections on grammaticalization and lexicalization. In: I. Wischer and G. Diewald (eds.), *New Reflections on Grammaticalizations*, 1–18. Amsterdam: John Benjamins.
Meillet, Antoine
  1912   L'évolution des formes grammaticales [The evolution of grammatical forms]. *Scienti – Rivista di Scienza* 12: 384–400. [Reprinted in Meillet, Antoine. 1926. *Linguistique Historique et Linguistique Générale [Historical Linguistics and General Linguistics*, 130–148. Paris: H. Champion]
Narrog, Heiko and Bernd Heine
  2011   Introduction. In: H. Narrog and Bernd Heine (eds.), *The Oxford Handbook of Grammaticalization*, 1–16. Oxford: Oxford University Press.

Newmeyer, Frederick J.
   1998   *Language Form and Language Function*. Cambridge: MIT Press.
Nicolle, Steve
   1998   A relevance theory perspective on grammaticalization. *Cognitive Linguistics* 9: 1–35.
Noël, Dirk
   2007   Diachronic construction grammar and grammaticalization theory. *Functions of Language* 14: 177–202.
Norde, Muriel
   2009   *Degrammaticalization*. Oxford: Oxford University Press.
Nuyts, Jan
   2012   Notions of (inter)subjectivity. *English Text Construction* 5: 53–76.
Roberts, Ian
   1993   A formal account of grammaticalisation in the history of Romance futures. *Folia Linguistica Historica* 13: 219–251.
Roberts, Ian and Anna Roussou
   2003   *Syntactic Change: A Minimalist Approach to Grammaticalization*. Cambridge: Cambridge University Press.
Simpson, Andrew and Xiu-Zhi Zoe Wu
   2002   Agreement shells and focus. *Language* 78: 287–313.
Singleton, Jenny L. and Elissa L. Newport
   2004   When learners surpass their models: The acquisition of American Sign Language from inconsistent input. *Cognitive Psychology* 49: 370–407.
Tomasello, Michael
   2006   Construction grammar for kids. *Constructions*, Special issue 1. [http://elanguage.net/journals/constructions/article/view/26].
Traugott, Elizabeth C.
   1982   From propositional to textual to expressive meanings: Some semantic-pragmatic aspects of grammaticalization. In: W. P. Lehmann and Y. Malkiel (eds.), *Perspectives in Historical Linguistics*, 245–271. Amsterdam: John Benjamins.
Traugott, Elizabeth C.
   2008a Grammaticalization, constructions and the incremental development of language: Suggestions from the development of degree modifiers in English. In: R. Eckardt, G. Jäger and T. Veenstra (eds.), *Variation, Selection, Development: Probing the Evolutionary Model of Language Change*, 219–250. Berlin: Mouton de Gruyter.
Traugott, Elizabeth C.
   2008b The grammaticalization of NP of NP constructions. In: A. Bergs and G. Diewald (eds.), *Constructions and Language Change*, 23–45. Berlin: Mouton de Gruyter.
Traugott, Elizabeth C.
   2010   Grammaticalization. In: S. Luraghi and V. Bubenik (eds.), *A Companion to Historical Linguistics*, 269–283. London: Continuum Press.
Traugott, Elizabeth C.
   2011   Grammaticalization and mechanisms of change. In: H. Narrog and B. Heine (eds.), *The Handbook of Grammaticalization*, 19–30. Oxford: Oxford University Press.
Traugott, Elizabeth C. and Richard B. Dasher
   2002   *Regularity in Semantic Change*. Cambridge: Cambridge University Press.
Traugott, Elizabeth C. and Bernd Heine
   1991   *Approaches to Grammaticalization*, Volume 2. Amsterdam: John Benjamins.
Traugott, Elizabeth C. and Graeme Trousdale
   2010   *Gradience, Gradualness and Grammaticalization*. Amsterdam: John Benjamins.
Traugott, Elizabeth C. and Graeme Trousdale
   2013   *Constructionalization and Constructional Changes*. Oxford: Oxford University Press.

Trousdale, Graeme
  2008   Constructions in grammaticalization and lexicalization: Evidence from the history of a composite predicate construction in English. In: N. Gisborne and G. Trousdale (eds.), *Constructional Approaches to English Grammar*, 33−67. Berlin: Mouton de Gruyter.
Trousdale, Graeme
  2010   Issues in constructional approaches to grammaticalization in English. In: K. Stathi, E. Gehweiler and E. König (eds.), *Grammaticalization: Current Views and Issues*, 51−71. Amsterdam: John Benjamins.
Trousdale, Graeme and Muriel Norde.
  2013   Degrammaticalization and constructionalization: Two case studies. Language Sciences 36: 32−46.
van der Auwera, Johan
  2009   The Jespersen cycles. In: E. van Gelderen (ed.), *Cyclical Change*, 35−71. Amsterdam: John Benjamins.
van der Auwera, Johan and Jan Nuyt (eds.)
  2012   *Grammaticalization and (Inter)Subjectification*. Brussels: Koninklijke Vlaamse Academie van België voor Wetenschappen en Kunsten.
van Gelderen, Elly
  2004   *Grammaticalization as Economy*. Amsterdam: John Benjamins.
van Gelderen, Elly
  2011   *The Linguistic Cycle: Language Change and the Language Faculty*. Oxford: Oxford University Press.
von der Gabelentz, Georg
  1891   *Die Sprachwissenschaft. Ihre Aufgaben, Methoden und bisherigen Ergebnisse* [*Linguistics: Its Duties, Methods and Current Results*]. Leipzig: Weigel.
Waltereit, Richard
  2011   Grammaticalization and discourse. In: H. Narrog and B. Heine (eds.), *The Handbook of Grammaticalization*, 409−423. Oxford: Oxford University Press.
Wiemer, Björn and Walter Bisang
  2004   What makes grammaticalization? An appraisal of its components and fringes. In: W. Bisang, N. Himmelmann and B. Wiemer (eds.), *What Makes Grammaticalization? A Look From its Fringes and Its Components*, 3−20. Berlin: Mouton de Gruyter.

Johan van der Auwera, Antwerp (Belgium)
Daniël Van Olmen, Lancaster (United Kingdom)
Denies Du Mon, Antwerp (Belgium)

32. Individual differences in grammatical knowledge

1. Introduction
2. Irregular morphology: The Polish genitive singular
3. Regular morphology: The Polish dative
4. Complex syntax: Subordination
5. Simpler syntax: Quantifiers
6. Simpler syntax: Passives
7. Reasons for individual differences
8. Concluding remarks
9. References

1. Introduction

According to usage-based models, linguistic knowledge is built up from experience using domain-general cognitive abilities. Since speakers differ in general cognitive abilities and in their linguistic experience, we would expect considerable differences in their mental grammars as well. It is widely acknowledged that there are large differences between children in the rate and manner that they acquire language (Bates et al. 1988; Dąbrowska 2004; Peters and Menn 1993; Richards 1990) and between adult speakers in areas such as lexical knowledge, fluency, and processing speed (Clark 1997; Farmer et al. 2012; Mulder and Hulstijn 2011). Yet for several decades, generative linguists have confidently asserted (without providing any evidence) that " ... children in the same linguistic community all learn the same grammar" (Crain and Lillo-Martin 1999: 9; see also Bley-Vroman 2009: 179; Chomsky 1965: 11, 1975: 11; Crain et al. 2009: 124; Herschensohn 2009: 264; Lidz and Williams 2009: 177; Montrul 2008: 4; Nowak et al. 2001: 114; Smith 1999: 41), and this view continues to be widely espoused, even by cognitive and functional linguists.[1]

This chapter will show that the claim that all learners converge on the same grammar is a myth. It reviews a number of studies which demonstrate that speakers of the same language sometimes represent "the same" knowledge differently, and that some basic grammatical structures are not fully mastered by all native speakers. It will also explore some of reasons for individual differences in grammatical knowledge, and discuss their implications for linguistic theory.

2. Irregular morphology: The Polish genitive singular

As a first example, let us consider the Polish genitive. The genitive is the second most frequent case after the nominative, and the most frequent case in written language. It has several very general functions, including marking the possessor and the direct object of negated verbs, and is also used to mark the object of a number of frequent verbs and prepositions. The genitive of masculine nouns is signalled by two inflectional endings, *-a* and *-u*, whose distribution is determined by several factors (see Buttler et al. 1973: 158–172; Westfal 1956). Some of these are semantic: for instance, nearly all animate nouns, and a substantial majority of nouns designating body parts and small easily manipulable objects, take *-a*, while nouns designating substances, locations, collections of objects and abstract concepts usually take *-u*. Others are morphological and phonological: some derivational affixes and stem-final consonants or consonant clusters are associated with *-a*, others with *-u*. However, there are many exceptions to these tendencies, and they are sometimes in conflict. Thus, it is not clear what the 'correct' generalization, or generalizations, would be.

---

[1] There were, however, some dissenting voices: see, for example, Seuren (1982). It is also widely acknowledged that speakers of different dialects have different grammars; the discussion in this chapter concerns differences that are not attributable to systematic differences between linguistic communities or subcommunities.

Dąbrowska (2008a) describes a nonce word inflection experiment designed to reveal the generalizations underlying speakers' use of the two affixes with inanimate nouns.[2] Adult native speakers of Polish were taught nonce nouns referring to various unfamiliar objects and substances and asked to use them in grammatical contexts requiring the genitive. The results indicated that about 12% of the participants had a strong preference for -a, the most frequent ending overall: they used it with over 80% of inanimate referents. This suggests that they had acquired a simple general rule ("add -a to the stem if the noun is masculine") with a large number of exceptions. About 46% of the participants had a clear preference for -u (which is used with most inanimate nouns), also choosing it over 80% of time; these participants appear to have learned a somewhat more complex rule with fewer exceptions ("add -a if the noun is masculine and animate and -u if the noun is masculine and inanimate"). A further 8% had a narrow semantic rule and consistently used -a with nouns referring to objects and -u with nouns referring to substances. The remaining speakers either relied on phonological criteria or used the two endings more or less interchangeably. Thus, different speakers had extracted different rules from the input they had been exposed to.

3. Regular morphology: The Polish dative

The regularities found in the distribution of genitive endings are only partial and rather complex; it is not surprising, therefore, that different learners end up with different generalizations. The next example that we will consider, the Polish dative, is very different in that it is highly regular, with only a few exceptions, but rather infrequent with full nouns. There are four dative endings: -owi for masculines (with a few exceptions for high frequency nouns), -u for neuters, and -e and -i/y for feminines; the distribution of the feminine endings is determined by phonological properties of the last consonant of the stem.

Dąbrowska (2008b) investigated Polish speakers' productivity with dative endings. Adult native speakers of Polish were presented with nonce words in the nominative and asked to use them in grammatical contexts requiring the dative. It was hypothesized that speakers may rely on low-level schemas that apply to clusters of phonologically similar nouns rather than general rules which apply "across the board"; in order to determine whether this was the case, half of the nonce nouns came from densely populated phonological neighbourhoods (i.e., they resembled many real nouns) and half from sparsely populated neighbourhoods.

Mean scores on the task ranged from 38% target for low-density neuter neighbourhoods to 95% for high-density feminine neighbourhoods, with an overall mean of 74%. However, these figures hide vast individual differences. Individual scores ranged from 29% to 100%, and for words from low-density neuter neighbourhoods, from 0% to 100%. Interestingly, performance on the inflection task was strongly correlated ($r = 0.72$) with the number of years spent in formal education.

---

[2] Dąbrowska and Szczerbiński (2006) have shown that speakers consistently use -a with animate nouns.

Why should we see such a correlation? Since all participants reliably supplied the dative forms of some nouns, e.g. feminine nouns from densely populated neighbourhoods, we can rule out relatively uninteresting explanations such as failure to understand the experimental task, lack of familiarity with the testing situation, or unwillingness to cooperate. Follow-up studies revealed that even the less educated participants reliably inflected real nouns in the dative contexts used in the experiment and reliably selected the gender-appropriate form of a demonstrative adjective used in construction with the nonce nouns, showing that their failure to provide the correct dative inflection could not be attributed to lack of lexical knowledge about which verbs or prepositions require the dative case or problems with identifying the gender of the nonce noun. Thus their relatively low scores on the inflection task must be due to problems with the inflections themselves.

As argued in Dąbrowska (2008b), the education-related differences observed in the experiment can be most plausibly attributed to asymmetries in the distribution of dative nouns in spoken and written discourse, and differences in the amount of exposure to written discourse. In spoken language, the dative case is predominantly used to mark semantic functions such as experiencer, addressee and beneficiary, and the nouns used in these functions tend to be kinship terms, personal names or nicknames, and nouns referring to various occupations. Consequently, datives in spoken language occur with a fairly restricted range of nouns, resulting in relatively low type frequencies of the individual endings. In written language, the dative also occurs in a number of lexically-governed environments which allow a wider variety of nouns, including inanimate nouns. This can be seen by comparing the proportion of inanimate nouns used in the dative in various genres: 1.4% in child-directed speech, 14% in adult-directed speech, and 62% in written texts. Since more educated speakers have more experience with formal written language, they encounter a larger number of noun types in the dative, and since high type frequency leads to greater productivity, more educated speakers become more productive with dative inflections.

4. Complex syntax: Subordination

Both of the examples discussed so far involved knowledge of inflectional morphology. We now turn to studies examining adult native speakers' knowledge of syntax. Dąbrowska (1997) tested comprehension of four types of complex sentences in English, all based on examples from *Linguistic Inquiry*: complex NP sentences, which contained a subordinate clause with a noun complement clause in the subject position (e.g. *Paul noticed that the fact that the room was tidy surprised Shona*), 'tough movement' sentences (e.g. *John will be hard to get his wife to vouch for*), and two types of sentences with parasitic gaps (e.g. *It was King Louis who the general convinced that this slave might speak to*), as well as some sentences which slightly longer, but syntactically simpler; these served as control sentences. The participants (unskilled workers, undergraduates, postgraduates, and university lecturers) were asked simple questions about the sentences (e.g., *What did Paul notice?*, *Who will vouch?*).

The experiment revealed both individual and group differences in comprehension of the experimental sentences. As anticipated, the lecturers achieved the highest scores (mean 89 % correct), followed by postgraduates (68 %), undergraduates (59 %), and unskilled workers (42 %); all group differences were highly significant. Individual performance ranged from 0 % to 100 % on complex NP and tough movement sentences and from 25 % to 100 % on sentences with parasitic gaps. Performance on control sentences, in contrast, was much better: mean 91 % correct in the unskilled group and 100 % correct in the other groups (range 75–100 %).

The obvious question that arises at this point is whether the differences observed in the experiment are attributable to differences in linguistic knowledge, or whether they are due to linguistically irrelevant factors such as working memory limitations or failure to engage with the task. It should be noted that the participants were tested under ideal conditions: the sentences were presented to them in both spoken and written form, and they could re-read them, or have them repeated, as many times as they needed. Thus, there is a real sense in which some participants' inability to respond correctly can be regarded as a problem with linguistic knowledge, i.e. competence, rather than the ability to access that knowledge. On the other hand, it cannot be denied that the test sentences placed heavy demands on the processing system, and hence a performance explanation cannot be dismissed out of hand.

This issue was addressed by Chipere (2001), who conducted a more in-depth study of one of the structures used in the Dąbrowska (1997) study, namely, complex NP sentences. Chipere tested two groups of eighteen-year-olds from the same school. One group – the High Academic Attainment, or HAA group – obtained A's in at least 5 GCSE subjects, including English. The Low Academic Attainment (LAA) participants, in contrast, got a D or below in GCSE English. Chipere's participants were given two tasks: a comprehension task similar to that used in the Dąbrowska study, and recall task in which participants first read sentences and then had to recall them verbatim. The HAA group performed much better on both tasks. This finding is compatible with both explanations mentioned above, since both comprehension and recall would be affected if the participants had not acquired the construction (or its subcomponents) but also if they were unable to hold such complex sentences in working memory. To distinguish between these two interpretations, Chipere conducted a follow-up training experiment with the LAA participants only. The participants were randomly assigned to one of two training conditions: memory training, which involved learning to repeat complex NP sentences, and comprehension training, which involved a brief explanation of the target structure followed by practice with feedback. Both groups were trained on the pre-test sentences and then tested with a new set of complex NP sentences. The results were unequivocal. Memory training resulted in improved performance on the memory task, but had no effect on the comprehension task. Comprehension training, in contrast, improved performance on both tasks: the comprehension-trained LAA participants performed as well as the HAA group on the recall task, and even better than the HAA group on the comprehension task. Thus, it is clear that the low academic attainment participants' difficulties on the pre-test were attributable to lack of linguistic knowledge rather than limited working memory capacity.

5. Simpler syntax: Quantifiers

While Chipere's study provides strong evidence against explanations of individual differences in the comprehension of complex sentences that appeal only to processing capacity, there is no doubt that the structures tested in the studies described in the preceding section place heavy demands on working memory. Could comparable differences in performance be observed on simpler structures? Brooks and Sekerina's (2005/2006, 2006) work on comprehension of sentences with quantifiers shows that knowledge about quantifier scope is acquired late in the course of acquisition, and that even adults sometimes misinterpret sentences such as (1) and (2).[3]

(1)   *Every rabbit is in a hat.*

(2)   *Every hat has a rabbit in it.*

Brooks and Sekerina tested comprehension of sentences with quantifiers using a picture selection task (where participants heard one of the above sentences and had to select the matching picture from an array of two (see Figure 32.1) and a picture verification task (where the participants were shown one of the pictures and heard one of the sentences and had to decide whether the picture and the sentence matched). Their participants (undergraduate students) supplied the correct answer 79% of the time on the picture selection task and 87% of the time on the picture verification task. Although this is well above chance (50%), their performance was far from perfect, and many individuals in both studies were in fact performing at chance.

To determine whether the individual differences observed in these studies were related to educational attainment, Street and Dąbrowska (2010) compared the performance of high and low academic achievement participants (postgraduate students and unskilled workers respectively) using a picture-selection task similar to that employed by Brooks

Fig. 32.1: Examples of pictures used by Street and Dąbrowska (2010) to test comprehension of sentences with the universal quantifier *every*

---

[3]   Note that these sentences, and the pictures in Figure 32.1, come from a later study by Street and Dąbrowska (2010); however, the pictures and sentences used by Brooks and Sekerina were similar.

and Sekerina. The experiment also tested comprehension of passive sentences (discussed in the next section) and actives, which were used as a control condition. As expected, all HAA participants performed at ceiling (100% correct) in all conditions. The LAA participants performed very well (97% correct) on actives, but had problems with the quantifier sentences, scoring 78% on simple locatives with *every* such as (1), and 43% (i.e., at chance) on *have*-locatives such as (2). Individual scores in the LAA group ranged from 0 to 100% on both types of quantifier sentences, with the majority of participants performing at or even below chance.

In a second experiment, LAA participants were pretested on comprehension of the same structures. The results were very similar to those obtained in the first study. Those participants who scored no more than 4 out of 6 in each of the experimental conditions (the two types of quantifier sentences and passives) were randomly assigned to either a quantifier training condition or a passive training condition. In both cases, training involved a short explanation of the kind that one might give to second language learners followed by practice with feedback using the sentences from the pre-test; the whole training session lasted about 5 minutes. Participants were then given three post-tests, one administered immediately after training, one a week later, and the last one twelve weeks later. Finally, all participants, including those who did not participate in the training phase, were given a questionnaire investigating their reading habits and the short version of the need for cognition questionnaire (Cacioppo et al. 1984), which measures how much people enjoy effortful cognitive activities.

The results for the quantifier training group are shown in Figure 32.2. As can be seen from the figure, training resulted in a dramatic increase in performance on the trained construction (i.e., quantifiers). Moreover, the improvement was long-lasting: even 12 weeks after training, the LAA participants performed close to ceiling. Performance on the passive (the untrained construction), on the other hand, remained unchanged. Thus, participants were clearly able to perform the task, and able to learn the construction with a minimal amount of exposure (and hence were not language impaired).

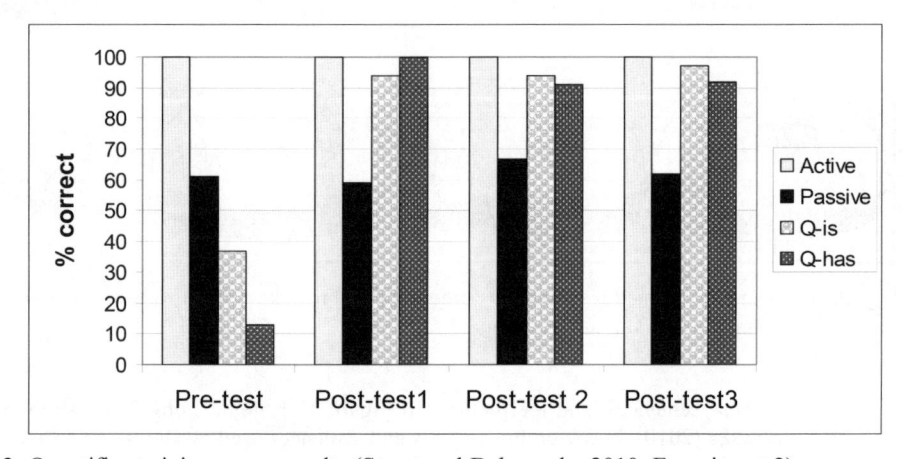

Fig. 32.2: Quantifier training group results (Street and Dąbrowska 2010, Experiment 2)

6. Simpler syntax: Passives

Three studies (Dąbrowska and Street 2006; Street and Dąbrowska 2010, 2014) examined individual and education-related differences in the comprehension of another relatively simple structure, namely passives. Earlier research by Ferreira (2003) demonstrated that even university students sometimes misinterpreted passive sentences, particularly semantically implausible ones. Since passives occur predominantly in formal written texts, one would predict that less educated speakers, who typically have relatively little exposure to such texts, will make even more errors.

Dąbrowska and Street (2006) tested comprehension of plausible and implausible passives (*The man was bitten by the dog* v. *The dog was bitten by the man*); the corresponding actives were used as controls. The task was to identify the "do-er" (i.e., the agent) in each sentence. As in the studies discussed earlier, two groups of participants were tested: a high academic attainment group (postgraduate students) and a low academic attainment group (manual workers who had no more than secondary-school education). The HAA group performed at ceiling on all sentence types. The LAA group were at ceiling on plausible sentences, 64% correct on implausible actives, and 36% correct on implausible passives. The high error rates on active sentences suggest that some of the LAA participants may have misunderstood the task, perhaps thinking that they were being asked what a person who uttered a sentence like *The dog was bitten by the man* probably meant, rather than what the sentence meant, and thus chose the more plausible (though syntactically impossible) interpretation. However, such pragmatic normalization cannot explain all the results, since performance on implausible passives was much worse than on the corresponding actives. Thus, in addition to a possible problem with the task itself, the LAA participants also had difficulty with the passive construction.

This was confirmed by a second study (Street and Dąbrowska 2010), which tested unbiased passives such as *The boy kissed the girl* using a different methodology, namely, picture selection – a less demanding task which can be used even with very young children. In this study, the HAA participants were again at ceiling, while the LAA group scored 88% correct (range: 33–100%) in experiment 1 and 79% (range: 17–100%) on the pre-test in experiment 2. In spite of the relatively low group averages, a significant proportion of the LAA participants (59% in experiment 1 and 43% in experiment 2) performed at ceiling.

As indicated earlier, the second experiment described in Street and Dąbrowska (2010) was a training study. The results for the passive training group are presented in Figure 32.3, and mirror those for the quantifier training group: there was a substantial improvement in performance on the trained construction, but not on the other sentences, and the effects were long-lasting.

Note that in the last two experiments, which used unbiased passives, the LAA participants' performance, though relatively poor, was still above chance, suggesting that they had some knowledge. The last study that will be discussed here, Street and Dąbrowska (2014), examined the nature of their knowledge in more detail. The study was designed to explore two possible explanations for this above-chance-but-below-ceiling pattern of performance.

Usage-based models of language acquisition claim that early in development, learners acquire lexically specific templates which are gradually generalized to more abstract schemas as they experience type variation in various positions in the construction (see

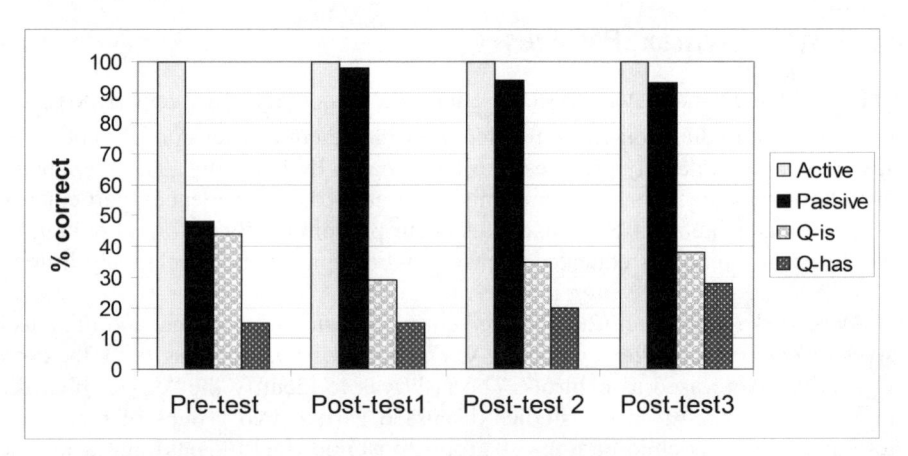

Fig. 32.3: Passive training group results (Street and Dąbrowska 2010)

Matthews and Krajewski this volume). If this is the case, then it is possible that speakers who don't read very much never progress beyond lexically specific templates for constructions which are relatively infrequent in spoken language – such as the passive: in other words, such speakers may acquire lexically specific passive templates such as *NP1 BE injured by NP2*, containing verbs that frequently occur in the passive, but not a fully general passive construction (*NP1 BE VERB-ed by NP2*). Such speakers would perform relatively well on verbs that occur frequently in the passive voice, but would be at chance on verbs which are used predominantly in the active.

Ferreira (2003) offers a different explanation for the less-then-perfect performance on passives that she observed in her experiment. She adopts a two-stage model of processing, according to which speakers first perform a "quick and dirty" parse which relies on simple processing heuristics (such as NVN = Agent-Verb-Patient) to arrive at a preliminary interpretation of a sentence, which is then verified through a full parse. Processing heuristics are faster and less effortful than a full syntactic analysis, and the representations they produce are 'good enough' for most everyday purposes; consequently, speakers don't always complete the full parse, particularly when they are under time pressure, or when their processing resources are limited. Ferreira's approach could explain the education-related differences observed in the studies discussed here if we assume that LAA participants' processing resources are more limited, and hence they are more likely to abandon processing after the first stage. If this were the case, we would expect a negative relationship between passive processing speed and accuracy: in other words, participants who responded quickly (after the first stage of processing) would make more errors on passives.

To test these hypotheses, Street and Dąbrowska (2014) presented HAA and LAA participants with active and passive sentences and asked them to decide whether a particular person mentioned in the sentence was the "do-er", i.e., agent, or the "acted-on", i.e., patient. Half of the sentences contained 'passive-attracting' verbs such as *injure* and *attach*, i.e., verbs which are relatively frequent in the passive; the other half contained 'active-attracting' verbs like *touch* or *shake*. All the sentences used in the study were semantically reversible. The dependent variables were decision accuracy and reaction time.

The experiment confirmed earlier findings on individual and education-related differences in comprehension of passive sentences. The HAA participants were at ceiling on both constructions. The LAA participants were also at ceiling on actives (98 % correct), but performed significantly worse on passives (only 86 % correct). Moreover, there were considerable individual differences within the LAA group: while 31 % of the participants were at ceiling (100 % correct), 22 % were at chance, and one participant performed significantly *below* chance;[4] the remaining participants were above chance but below ceiling.

The results are broadly compatible with usage-based models. Participants were faster and more accurate with active sentences than with passives, which is likely to be an entrenchment effect; and they processed passives with passive-attracting verbs faster than passives with active-attracting verbs, suggesting that they have lexical templates for verbs which frequently occur in the passive. However, there was no difference in accuracy on passives with the two verb types, and the reaction time data indicated that both groups showed the same advantage for passives with passive-attracting verbs: in other words, there was no interaction between verb type and group for either accuracy or reaction time. Thus, the group differences cannot be attributed to the LAA participants relying more on lexical templates.

The results also do not support a processing heuristics account of individual differences, which predicts a positive correlation between speed and accuracy (speakers who do not conduct a full parse should respond faster but less accurately). Instead, the results revealed a moderately significant *negative* correlation between reaction time and accuracy ($r = .-41$ for LAA group; $r = .-42$ for all participants): in other words, participants who responded faster were also more accurate. The most plausible interpretation of these findings is that all of the HAA, and the majority of the LAA participants, had lexical templates *as well as* a more general passive construction, but for the LAA group, these were less well entrenched, presumably because they had less experience with written texts. Moreover, a small but significant minority of the LAA group showed no evidence of having mastered the passive.

7. Reasons for individual differences

The research described in this chapter indicates that there are individual differences in performance on tasks tapping knowledge of various linguistic constructions, including case marking, "tough movement", various types of subordination, quantifiers, and passives. These differences cannot be explained by appealing to working memory capacity, test-taking skills, or willingness to cooperate with the experimenter (see Dąbrowska 2012). How do these differences come about? Logically, they could be attributed to individual differences in language learning abilities, cognitive style, etc., to differences in language experience, or, most likely, to some combination of the two.

There is some evidence that underlying cognitive differences play a significant role. It is well known that individual differences in sentence processing skill correlate with

---

[4] This participant reliably supplied the target answer with active sentences, suggesting that s/he consistently applied the first NP = Agent strategy.

working memory capacity (Daneman and Menkle 1996; Farmer et al. 2012; Just and Carpenter 1992). There are also moderately strong relationships between grammatical comprehension and nonverbal IQ and need for cognition, i.e., the extent to which people enjoy, and hence seek, effortful cognitive activities (Brooks and Sekerina 2006; Street and Dąbrowska 2010). More recent research (Dąbrowska in preparation) suggests a close link between grammatical comprehension and metalinguistic awareness. Of course, correlation is not the same as causation, so we must be careful in interpreting these results; however, given that there are substantial individual differences in almost every area of human cognition (Gruszka et al. 2010) and that language development depends on general cognitive abilities, there are good theoretical grounds for postulating a causal link.

It is also likely that differences in linguistic knowledge are at least partially attributable to differences in experience. The linguistic experience of individual speakers varies considerably both in amount and quality, and these differences are correlated with education and occupational status. University students and professionals rely on language more in their daily lives than individuals who do menial jobs, in that most of their working day is spent in some kind of linguistic activity. They also tend to read more, and are more likely to be skilled readers. This means that they are exposed to more language (since skilled readers absorb more words per unit of time than skilled conversationalists – see Dąbrowska 2004: 19) and also more varied language (since many complex constructions are considerably more frequent in written language than in speech – see Biber 1986; Miller 1994; Roland et al. 2007). Highly educated speakers will also have experienced more complex language in various educational settings. Furthermore, they often come from middle class backgrounds, which means that they are likely to have been spoken to (Ginsborg 2006; Hart and Risley 1995, 1999) and read to (Hartas 2011) more as children, and there is some evidence that early childhood experience may be particularly important for ultimate language attainment (Pakulak and Neville 2010). This is yet another example of the accumulation of advantage, or what Stanovich (1986) called the "Matthew effect" (the rich get richer and the poor get poorer, metaphorically speaking: for instance, children who are good readers read more, which makes them even better readers, while poor readers usually read less, which causes them to fall even further behind their peers.) Note, however, that exposure to reading has an effect on performance that is independent of educational experience: Street and Dąbrowska (2010) found a significant correlation between amount of reading and grammatical comprehension in a group of LAA speakers of very similar educational backgrounds.

Perhaps the most convincing evidence that differences in grammatical attainment are at least partly attributable to differences in linguistic experience comes from the two training studies discussed earlier (Chipere 2001; Street and Dąbrowska 2010). As we have seen, Chipere demonstrated that additional experience with a construction improves comprehension as well as memory for that construction, while Street and Dąbrowska found that training results in improvement on the trained construction (but not the untrained one), and, moreover, that the effects are long lasting. In both studies, the number of exemplars presented during training was quite small (10 the Chipere experiment and just 6 in Street and Dąbrowska's study). This raises an interesting question: if such a minimal amount of exposure is enough for learning to occur, why hadn't the participants acquired the construction earlier? After all, they are likely to have experienced much more than 10 exemplars of the trained constructions prior to their participation in the experiment, and yet they had not acquired the relevant knowledge.

The training provided during the two studies differs from normal experience in two ways: the participants were presented with a number of exemplars in a very short time (whereas in normal experience, individual exemplars are usually more spaced), and it involved explicit explanation and feedback as well as exposure to relevant data. Research on learning in general, and construction learning in particular, suggests that 'spaced' exposure, where individual learning episodes are distributed over a number of sessions, is more effective than 'massed' exposure, where the same number of learning opportunities is presented in a single session (Ambridge et al. 2006; Childers and Tomasello 2002; Divjak and Cardwell-Harris this volume). This suggests that the fact that the training session provided more intensive exposure is unlikely to be primarily responsible for the dramatic improvement in performance observed in the experiments.

It is important to note that not every instance of exposure to the relevant structure is necessarily a learning episode. In order for construction learning to take place, there must be enough contextual information to allow the learner to infer the meaning of the utterance exemplifying the construction, and the learner must be attending to the linguistic form and the relevant the contextual information. In the training phase of both studies, the experimenter explicitly directed the participants' attention to the relevant aspects of both form and meaning, thus maximising the chances of learning taking place. It is likely that some language learners are not exposed to this kind of input often enough, and as a result, do not acquire these constructions. Importantly, the HAA participants were more likely to have had parents (or teachers) who provided this kind of experience, and hence more opportunities for learning.[5]

The dramatic improvement in performance in the training study raises some interesting questions. One may wonder, for instance, whether the knowledge that the participants acquired during the training session will generalize to ordinary language use outside the lab, and, if it does, whether it is of the same kind as the knowledge possessed by participants who were already performing at ceiling at pre-test. It could be argued that the trained participants' knowledge is likely to be explicit, and hence differs fundamentally from the implicit knowledge of "normal" native speakers, and is more like the kind of knowledge acquired by second language learners. It must be pointed out, however, that it also possible that at least some of those who performed well at pre-test were also relying on explicit knowledge. Clearly, further research will be necessary to answer these questions. In particular, we may need to re-examine the widely-held assumption that first language acquisition is almost entirely implicit. While it is undeniable that implicit learning plays an important role in acquisition, the results reported here suggest that explicit processes, at least at the level of attending to the relevant information, may also be involved (for further discussion, see Dąbrowska 2009).

To sum up: the results summarized here suggest that individual differences in native language attainment are partly attributable to individual cognitive differences and partly to environmental differences. It should be stressed that these factors interact in complex ways. Children of university-educated parents often get more input than their peers (Hart

---

[5] I am not suggesting that parents or teachers provide true grammar lessons, i.e., that they actually explain the structure and meaning of the construction, but simply that they ensure that the language learner attends to both structure and meaning at the same time – for instance, by emphasizing particular phrases in the utterance while pointing to the critical elements in the scene, by explicitly contrasting two utterances, etc.

and Risley 1995, 1999), and their input tends to be of higher quality (e.g., more one-on-one interaction, more book reading, etc.). This leads to better language skills, and better language skills lead to educational success. As a result, they become better readers, and hence read more, and thus get more varied input; they are also more likely to go on to higher education, and so on – the Matthew effect all over. In other words, we have a virtuous circle: better language skills lead to educational success which leads to better language skills, while the opposite often happens in children from less privileged backgrounds (Hoff 2006, 2013).

Finally, it is worth noting that different factors may contribute in different ways to knowledge of different constructions. Street and Dąbrowska (2010) provide some suggestive evidence that this might be the case: in their study, reading was the best predictor of performance on passives, while need for cognition was a better predictor of performance on quantifier constructions. This may be due to the fact that full passives are much more frequent in written texts than in informal spoken discourse; hence, people who read more get more exposure to this construction. Conversely, the relationship between comprehension of sentences with quantifiers and need for cognition may be attributable to the fact that quantifiers play an important role in logical reasoning.

8. Concluding remarks

The existence of individual differences in native language attainment raises some interesting questions. First, if speakers have different grammars, how can they understand each other? This can be partly explained by the fact that the same expressions can be produced using different grammars (see Dąbrowska 2014). Consider, for example, the Polish dative neuter inflection discussed earlier. While some speakers have a fully general rule for the dative neuter, most speakers appear to have a number of low-level schemas, and some may only have memorized a few exemplars. However, the forms that they actually produce are identical. One may also observe that speakers do not need to have exactly the same grammar to be able to communicate. We are very good at reading people's minds (Tomasello 2008), and we are usually able to construct a reasonable approximation of a speakers' communicative intention on the basis of relatively little evidence.

Secondly, if different speakers have different grammars, in what sense can they be said to speak the same language? In one of his famous analogies, Saussure suggests that speakers belonging to a particular speech community have copies of the same dictionary in their heads:

> A language, as a collective phenomenon, takes the form of a totality of imprints in everyone's brain, rather like a dictionary of which each individual has an identical copy ... Thus it is something which is in each individual, but is none the less common to all. (Saussure [1972] 1986: 19)

This is clearly an oversimplification: while some words, such as *head*, *give*, and *good* are presumably shared by all English speakers, others (*mumble*, *haunted*, *declare*) may not be, and some (*cataphoric*, *amygdala*) are known only by a relatively small number of specialists. So different speakers have different dictionaries in their heads – although, of course, there is considerable overlap between them. The same is true of grammar. A linguistic convention, be it a lexical item or a grammatical construction, will survive in the language as long as it is shared by some speakers; it needn't be shared by everyone. As Millikan (2008: 88) argues,

> Speakers and hearers may have quite different sets of linguistic conventions in their repertoires, so long as there is some overlap ... all that is required for a ... convention to survive, to be repeated and passed on, is to succeed in coordinating the interests of speakers and hearers some critical proportion of the time.

Languages belong to communities, not to individual speakers: an individual speaker "owns" only a part of his/her language. However, since speakers approximate each other's behaviour, collective grammars tend to be more systematic than individual grammars (see Dąbrowska 2013; Hurford 2000: 342).

The existence of individual differences also has important methodological implications. We cannot simply assume that what is true of one native speaker of a language will also be true of others: to make general statements about a particular language or language variety, we need to collect data from a range of speakers. Related to this, we need to be aware that data from highly educated participants is not representative: as we have seen earlier, their responses tend to be much more homogenous than those of less educated speakers. This is not surprising, given that their linguistic competence has been shaped by years of schooling in the standard language – which itself was to some extent shaped by language planners (Deumert and Vandenbussche 2003; Garvin 1993).

That variation is ubiquitous in language is widely acknowledged in sociolinguistics (Henry 2002). On the other hand, theoretical linguists steeped in the nativist tradition are committed to the idea that speakers' mental grammars are strongly constrained by a shared Universal Grammar and find it hard to accept that individual grammars differ substantially. This, however, should not come as a surprise to cognitive linguists: after all, there are large individual differences in almost every area of human cognition, and different individuals experience different subsamples of language, so we expect considerable variation. Yet many cognitive linguists implicitly accept the Chomskyan idealization that all speakers in the same community share the same grammar, thus neglecting the study of individual differences in linguistic knowledge.

The research described here shows that differences between speakers run even deeper than the previous sociolinguistic research suggests, in that they involve knowledge of linguistic constructions, i.e. competence, rather than just frequency of use of particular variants. As we have seen, even when two speakers' overt production is identical, the underlying grammatical system may not be: in other words, the differences may be invisible to the naked eye (or rather inaudible to the naked ear) and only revealed by a specially designed experimental procedure (see, for example, the earlier discussion of Polish speakers' ability to produce dative forms of real and nonce nouns).

This is not surprising, given that most aspects of linguistic structure, and virtually all aspects of meaning, are not directly observable, and hence must be inferred by the learner from indirect cues, and hence – as many linguists have pointed out – a given corpus of data is compatible with many descriptions. Thus, grammar viewed as a mental phenomenon is necessarily private, andso to speak, is counterbalanc this fact necessarily leads to variation. This "centrifugal" force, so to speak, is counterbalanced by the fact that in actual language use, speakers tend to align, or accommodate to each other's speech. They do this not just in order to communicate successfully, although communication is obviously an important motive: speaker alignment is also a major mechanism for maintaining social cohesion (Dediu et al. 2013), and acts as a centripetal force which prevents individual grammars from becoming too different. The tension between the centrifugal force of individual grammars and the centripetal norms that evolve in the speech community is a central factor shaping language (Croft 2000), and we cannot hope to understand language in either its individual or its social dimension without considering their interaction (cf. Geeraerts 2010). Let us hope that future research in cognitive linguistics will give this question the attention that it deserves.

9. References

Ambridge, Ben, Anna L. Theakston, Elena Lieven and Michael Tomasello
    2006   The distributed learning effect for children's acquisition of an abstract grammatical construction. *Cognitive Development* 21: 74–193.

Bates, Elizabeth, Inge Bretherton and Lynn Snyder
    1988   *From First Words to Grammar: Individual Differences and Dissociable Mechanisms*. Cambridge: Cambridge University Press.

Biber, Douglas
    1986   Spoken and written textual dimensions in English: Resolving the contradictory findings. *Language* 62: 384–414.

Bley-Vroman, Robert
    2009   The evolving context of the fundamental difference hypothesis. *Studies in Second Language Acquisition* 31: 175–198.

Brooks, Patricia J. and Irina A. Sekerina
    2005/2006   Shortcuts to quantifier interpretation in children and adults. *Language Acquisition* 13: 177–206.

Brooks, Patricia J. and Irina A. Sekerina
    2006   Shallow processing of universal quantification: A comparison of monolingual and bilingual adults. In: K. Forbus, D. Gentner and T. Regier (eds.), *Proceedings of the 28th Annual Conference of the Cognitive Science Society*, 2450. Mahwah: Lawrence Erlbaum Associates.

Buttler, Danuta, Halina Kurkowska and Halina Satkiewicz
    1973   *Kultura języka polskiego [A Guide to Polish Usage]*. Warszawa: PWN.

Cacioppo, John T., Richard E. Petty and Chaun Feng Kao
    1984   The efficient assessment of need for cognition. *Journal of Personality Assessment* 48: 306–307.

Childers, Jane B. and Michael Tomasello
    2002   Two-year-olds learn novel nouns, verbs and conventional actions from massed or distributed exposures. *Developmental Psychology* 38: 967–978.

Chipere, Ngoni
    2001   Native speaker variations in syntactic competence: Implications for first language teaching. *Language Awareness* 10: 107–124.

Chomsky, Noam
    1965   *Aspects of the Theory of Syntax*. Cambridge: MIT Press.

Chomsky, Noam
  1975   *Reflections on Language.* New York: Pantheon.
Clark, Herbert H.
  1997   Communal lexicons. In: K. Malmkjær and J. Williams (eds.), *Context in Language Learning and Language Understanding*, 63–87. Cambridge: Cambridge University Press.
Crain, Stephen, Rosalind Thornton and Keiko Murasugi
  2009   Capturing the evasive passive. *Language Acquisition* 16: 123–133.
Croft, William
  2000   *Explaining Language Change: An Evolutionary Approach.* London: Longman.
Dąbrowska, Ewa
  1997   The LAD goes to school: A cautionary tale for nativists. *Linguistics* 35: 735–766.
Dąbrowska, Ewa
  2004   *Language, Mind and Brain: Some Psychological and Neurological Constraints on Theories of Grammar.* Edinburgh: Edinburgh University Press.
Dąbrowska, Ewa
  2008a   The later development of an early-emerging system: The curious case of the Polish genitive. *Linguistics* 46: 629–650.
Dąbrowska, Ewa
  2008b   The effects of frequency and neighbourhood density on adult speakers' productivity with Polish case inflections: An empirical test of usage-based approaches to morphology. *Journal of Memory and Language* 58: 931–951.
Dąbrowska, Ewa
  2009   Constructing a second language: Some final thoughts. *Annual Review of Cognitive Linguistics* 7: 277–290.
Dąbrowska, Ewa
  2012   Different speakers, different grammars: Individual differences in native language attainment. *Linguistic Approaches to Bilingualism* 2: 219–253.
Dąbrowska, Ewa
  2013   Functional constraints, usage, and mental grammars: A study of speakers' intuitions about questions with long-distance dependencies. *Cognitive Linguistics* 24: 633–665.
Dąbrowska, Ewa
  in preparation   Grammar, vocabulary and collocations.
Dąbrowska, Ewa
  2014   Recycling utterances: A speaker's guide to sentence processing. *Cognitive Linguistics* 25: 617–653
Dąbrowska, Ewa and James A. Street
  2006   Individual differences in language attainment: Comprehension of passive sentences by native and non-native English speakers. *Language Sciences* 28: 604–615.
Dąbrowska, Ewa and Marcin Szczerbiński
  2006   Polish children's productivity with case marking: the role of regularity, type frequency, and phonological coherence. *Journal of Child Language* 33: 559–597.
Daneman, Meredith and Philip M. Merikle
  1996   Working Memory and Language Comprehension: A Meta-Analysis. *Psychonomic Bulletin and Review* 3: 422–433.
Dediu, Dan, Michael Cysouw, Stephen C. Levinson, Andrea Baronchelli, Morten H. Christiansen, William Croft, Nicholas Evans, Simon Garrod, Russell D. Gray, Anne Kandler and Elena Lieven
  2013   Cultural evolution of language. In: P. J. Richerson and M. H. Christiansen (eds.), *Cultural Evolution: Society, Technology, Language, and Religion*, 303–332. Cambridge: Cambridge University Press.

Deumert, Ana and Wim Vandenbussche
    2003   Standard languages: Taxonomies and Histories. In: A. Deumert and W. Vandenbussche (eds.), *Germanic Standardizations: Past and Present*, 1–14. Amsterdam/New York: John Benjamins.

Divjak, Dagmar and Catherine Cardwell-Harris
    this volume   Frequency and entrenchment. Berin/Boston: De Gruyter Mouton.

Farmer, Thomas A., Jennifer B. Misyak and Morten H. Christiansen
    2012   Individual differences in sentence processing. In: M. Spivey, K. McRae and M. Joannisse (eds.), *Cambridge Handbook of Psycholinguistics*, 353–364. Cambridge: Cambridge University Press.

Ferreira, Fernanda
    2003   The misinterpretation of noncanonical sentences. *Cognitive Psychology* 47: 164–203.

Garvin, Paul L.
    1993   A conceptual framework for the study of language standardization. *International Journal of the Sociology of Language* 100/101: 37–54.

Geeraerts, Dirk
    2010   Schmidt redux: How systematic is language if variation is rampant? In: K. Boye and E. Engeberg-Pedersen (eds.), *Language Usage and Language Structure*, 237–262. Berlin/New York: De Gruyter Mouton.

Ginsborg, Jane
    2006   The effects of socio-economic status on children's language acquisition and use. In: J. Clegg and J. Ginsborg (eds.), *Language and Social Disadvantage*, 9–27. Chichester: John Wiley and Sons.

Gruszka, Aleksandra, Gerald Matthews and Błażej Szymura (eds.)
    2010   *Handbook of Individual Differences in Cognition: Attention, Memory, and Executive Control*. New York: Springer.

Hart, Betty and Todd R. Risley
    1995   *Meaningful Differences in the Everyday Experience of Young American Children*. Baltimore: Paul Brooks.

Hart, Betty and Todd R. Risley
    1999   *The Social World of Children Learning to Talk*. Baltimore: Paul Brookes.

Hartas, Dimitra
    2011   Families' social backgrounds matter: Socio-economic factors, home learning and young children's language, literacy and social outcomes. *British Educational Research Journal* 37: 893–914.

Henry, Alison
    2002   Variation and syntactic theory. In: J. K. Chambers, P. Trudgill and N. Shilling-Estes (eds.), *The Handbook of Language Variation and Change*, 267–282. Oxford: Blackwell.

Herschensohn, Julia
    2009   Fundamental and gradient differences in language development. *Studies in Second Language Acquisition* 31: 259–289.

Hoff, Erika
    2006   How social contexts support and shape language development. *Developmental Review* 26: 55–88.

Hoff, Erika
    2013   Interpreting the early language trajectories of children from low-SES and language minority homes: Implications for closing achievement gaps. *Developmental Psychology* 49: 4–14.

Hurford, James R.
    2000   Social transmission favours linguistic generalisation. In: C. Knight, M. Studdert-Kennedy and J. R. Hurford (eds.), *The Evolutionary Emergence of Language: Social Function and the Origins of Linguistic Form*, 324–352. Cambridge: Cambridge University Press.

Just, Marcel A. and Patricia A. Carpenter
 1992   A capacity theory of comprehension: Individual differences in working memory. *Psychological Review* 99: 122–149.
Lidz, Jeffrey and Alexander Williams
 2009   Constructions on holiday. *Cognitive Linguistics* 20: 177–189.
Matthews, Danielle and Grzegorz Krajewski
 this volume   First language acquisition. Berlin/Boston: De Gruyter Mouton.
Miller, Jim E.
 1994   Speech and writing. In: R. E. Asher and J. M. Y. Simpson (eds.), *The Encyclopaedia of Language and Linguistics*, Volume 8, 4301–4306. Oxford: Pergamon Press.
Millikan, Ruth G.
 2008   A difference of some consequence between conventions and rules. *Topoi* 27: 87–99.
Montrul, Silvina
 2008   *Incomplete Acquisition in Bilingualism: Re-Examining the Age Factor*. Amsterdam: John Benjamins.
Mulder, Kimberley and Jan H. Hulstijn
 2011   Linguistic skills of adult native speakers, as a function of age and level of education. *Applied Linguistics* 32: 475–494.
Nowak, Martin A., Natalia Komarova and Partha Niyogi
 2001   Evolution of Universal Grammar. *Science* 291: 114–118.
Pakulak, Eric and Helen Neville
 2010   Proficiency differences in syntactic processing of monolingual native speakers indexed by event-related potentials. *Journal of Cognitive Neuroscience* 22: 2728–2744.
Peters, Ann M. and Lise Menn
 1993   False starts and filler syllables: Ways to learn grammatical morphemes. *Language* 69: 742–777.
Richards, Brian J.
 1990   *Language Development and Individual Differences: A Study of Auxiliary Verb Learning*. Cambridge: Cambridge University Press.
Roland, Douglas, Frederic Dick and Jeffrey L. Elman
 2007   Frequency of basic English grammatical structures: A corpus analysis. *Journal of Memory and Language* 57: 348–379.
Saussure, Ferdinand de
 [1972] 1986   *Course in General Linguistics* (R. Harris, Trans.). Peru: Open Court Publishing Company.
Seuren, Pieter
 1982   Internal variability in competence. *Linguistische Berichte* 77: 1–31.
Smith, Neil
 1999   *Chomsky: Ideas and Ideals*. Cambridge: Cambridge University Press.
Stanovich, Keith E.
 1986   Matthew effects in reading: Some consequences of individual differences in the acquisition of literacy. *Reading Research Quarterly* 21: 360–407.
Street, James A. and Ewa Dąbrowska
 2010   More individual differences in language attainment: How much do adult native speakers of English know about passives and quantifiers? *Lingua* 120: 2080–2094.
Street, James A. and Ewa Dąbrowska
 2014   Lexically specific knowledge and individual differences in adult native speakers' processing of the English passive. *Applied Psycholinguistics* 35: 97–118.
Tomasello, Michael
 2008   *Origins of Human Communication*. Cambridge: MIT Press.

Westfal, Stanisław
  1956   *A Study in Polish Morphology: The Genitive Singular Masculine.* The Hague: Mouton.

Ewa Dąbrowska, Northumbria University (UK)

33. Signed languages

1. Introduction
2. Signed language structure
3. Cognitive linguistics and signed languages
4. Signed language and gesture
5. Dynamic systems theory
6. Conclusions
7. References

1. Introduction

For centuries, signed languages were not considered to be language. Rather, they were regarded as depictive gestures lacking features of language such as phonology, word formation, and syntax. The Roman rhetorician Quintilian made passing reference to the use of gestures by deaf people in his Institutes of Oratory, saying that for them gestures are a substitute for speech. The view that signed languages are merely pantomimic gestures culminated in the debate over the use of speech versus signing in the education of deaf children that took place during the Milan Conference of 1880. Supporters of speech maintained that signed languages lacked any features of language and thus were not suited for developing the minds of deaf children. One of the proponents of speech proclaimed that children who are taught to sign are defiant and corruptible. He attributed this to the disadvantages of signed language, claiming that they cannot convey number, gender, person, time, nouns, verbs, adverbs, adjectives (Lane 1984). Because of this, educators maintained that signed languages cannot elicit reasoning, reflection, generalization, and abstraction. These views persisted into the 20th century, with psychologists, educators, and linguists continuing to deny the linguistic status of signed languages, maintaining that they are harmful for intellectual and educational development.

A similarly contentious picture describes the relation between language and gesture. While some early philosophers believed the origin of language lay in gesture, for the most part gesture was placed in an either/or relation with language. Whorf and Caroll (1956), for example, proposed a dualistic mode of thinking in the Western mind characterized by such either/or thinking: either a word, or, in the absence of adequate vocabulary, a gesture.

Although Pike (1967) offered a unified model of language and gesture, most linguists held views such as Chomsky's (1972: 70), who grouped human gesture with animal communication and considered both to be categorically distinct from human language: "The examples of animal communication that have been examined to date do share many of the properties of human gestural systems, and it might be reasonable to explore the possibility of direct connection in this case. But human language, it appears, is based on entirely different principles." Many scholars however have argued to the contrary, that non-human primate gestural communication is more similar to human language than primate vocalizations (Liebal et al. 2007). It has only been within the last several decades that psycholinguists (Bates and Dick 2002; McNeill 1992, 2005), gesture researchers (Kendon 2004; Müller 2007), neuroscientists (Gentilucci 2006; Husain et al. 2009; Rizzolatti and Arbib 1998) and others (Capirci et al. 2002; Corballis 2003; Skipper et al. 2009; Xu et al. 2009) have discovered cognitive and neural links between language and gesture.

There is a need to establish an overarching framework that can encompass spoken language, signed language, and gesture as a manifestation of the human expressive ability (Wilcox and Xavier 2013). Currently, two approaches attack the problem: an abstractionist solution and an embodied solution. The abstractionist solution accomplishes unification across the distinct modalities in which spoken and signed languages are manifest by viewing language as a system of abstract rules independent of physical manifestation. This solution strips away the performance of language by means of vocal tracts, hands, faces, and the anatomy and musculature that controls these articulators. Likewise, perceptual systems play no part in the cognitive organization of language from this perspective. In more traditional formalist terminology, the abstractionist solution maintains a distinction between competence and performance. The abstractionist solution is best represented by structuralist and formalist approaches (Aronoff et al. 2005; Brentari 1998; Lillo Martin 1986; Neidle et al. 2000; Petronio and Lillo Martin 1997; Pfau and Quer 2003, 2007; Sandler and Lillo Martin 2006; Stokoe 1960).

The embodied solution claims that all language, and indeed all communication, is made possible because we have physical bodies that we move to produce signals (Bergen this volume; Wilcox 2013). What unites language across different modalities from this perspective is that both spoken and signed languages, and gestures, are the performance of physical systems in actual usage events.

Thus, the abstractionist solution maintains that while the physical embodiment of language may have an impact on production, it has no impact on the cognitive organization of grammar. The embodied solution argues instead that physical embodiment has direct influence on the nature of cognition, which is manifest in all aspects of language.[1]

2. Signed language structure

Phonology

The view that signed languages lacked linguistic structure was most powerfully manifest in the claim that they lack duality of patterning, that the meaningful elements of

---

[1] See Thelen and Smith (1994) for a similar claim about two approaches to the development of cognition and action systems. Rączaszek-Leonardi and Kelso (2007) also make the case against what is here called the abstractionist solution and in favor of a more embodied approach, also incorporating dynamic systems theory into their model.

these languages are not formed from a finite set of meaningless elements – that is, that signed languages lack a phonology. Stokoe (1960) dispelled this view with his pioneering description of the phonology of American Sign Language (ASL). Stokoe demonstrated that signs consist of analyzable units of sublexical structure. Stokoe coined the term 'chereme' for these units, the structural equivalent of the phonemes of spoken languages.

Stokoe analyzed the phonology of signs into three major classes: handshape (the configuration that the hand makes when producing the sign), location (the place where the sign is produced, for example on the head, or in the neutral space in front of the signer's body), and movement (the motion made by the signer in producing the sign, for example upward or towards the signer's body). Battison (1978) added a fourth class, orientation (the direction the hand faces when producing the sign). Since Stokoe's discovery, a multitude of phonological theories of signed languages have been proposed (Brentari 1998; Liddell 1984; Padden and Perlmutter 1987; Sandler 1999; Uyechi 1996).

Use of space

One unique characteristic of signed languages is that they are produced in visible space. This "signing space" plays a critical role in the grammar of signed languages. For example the arguments of certain verbs are marked by locations in space (Meier 2002). In ASL, the agent and recipient of GIVE-TO "X gives the book to Y" are indicated by points in the signing space.

Time is often marked by spatial location. The present is in the plane of the signer's body, the future is indicated by the space in front of the signer, and the past is marked by spatial locations behind and over the signer's shoulder. Time may also be indicated by side-to-side spatial locations and movements (Engberg-Pedersen 1993).

Topics may be indicated by location in space as well. For example, if a signer is discussing two competing linguistic theories, she may place one in the signing space on her left, and another on her right. Pointing to these spatial locations, or even orienting her upper torso in the direction of these locations, may be used to direct the addressee's attention to the corresponding topic.

Facial grammar

In addition to the hands, the signer's face, including the eyes, eyebrows, cheeks, and mouth, is an important articulator in signed languages. In many signed languages, the face predominantly functions as grammatical or discourse markers. In ASL, for example, the face may be used to mark polar questions, content questions, topics, and conditionals. The mouth has a variety of functions, marking adverbial meaning (e.g., the distinction between "work carelessly" and "work carefully" is marked in ASL by different mouth gestures), and intensification (Bridges and Metzger 1996).

Eye gaze is another important aspect of facial grammar. It may be used to mark pronominal reference (Metzer 1998) and as a syntactic agreement marker in ASL (Thompson et al. 2006). Eye gaze also marks role shift in narratives; for example, a change from the narrator's perspective to that of a character in the story may be marked by a change in eye gaze.

Lexicalization and grammaticization

Lexicalization is the process by which words (signs) are formed in a language. One common lexicalization process in signed languages is compounding. In ASL, for example, many compounds have become lexicalized: 'bruise' from BLUE_SPOT; 'brother' and 'sister' from BOY_SAME and GIRL_SAME; 'husband' and 'wife' from MAN_MARRY and WOMAN_MARRY. Lexicalization has been described in detail for Australian Sign Language (Johnston and Schembri 2007); British Sign Language (Sutton-Spence and Woll 1999), and American Sign Language (Janzen 2012).

Grammaticization refers to the process by which lexical morphemes, or grammatical morphemes, take on grammatical or more grammatical function (Bybee et al. 1994). Grammaticization operates in signed languages in two ways. In the first, certain lexical morphemes take on grammatical meaning. Janzen (2012) shows that the ASL lexical item FINISH, for example, has developed from a full verb to a more grammatical form used to mark completives and perfectives, eventually forming an affix. Another example from ASL is the lexical verb 'leave', meaning movement in physical space, which takes on grammatical function as a future marker. Janzen (2012) also claims that topic marking has developed along the following grammaticization path:

generalized questioning gesture > yes/no question marking > topic marking

This grammaticization path also demonstrates the second way in which grammaticization appears in signed languages: gestural forms may become incorporated into a signed language, often first as lexical forms, which take on more grammatical function. The future marker described above, which grammaticized from a lexical verb, seems to have originated as a gesture meaning 'leave'. The grammaticization of gesture is described in more detail in the section *Gesture is incorporated into signed languages*.

3. Cognitive linguistics and signed languages

Linguists have found cognitive linguistic theory especially revealing when applied to the study of signed languages. Wilcox and colleagues (Wilcox 2007; Wilcox and Morford 2007; Wilcox and P. Wilcox 2009) have documented the application of cognitive linguistics to signed languages. Janzen and colleagues (Janzen 2006, 2012; Janzen et al. 2001) examined the linguistic use of space, the construal of events, and the cognitive factors at work in lexicalization and grammaticalization in signed languages. Working with Danish Sign Language, Engberg-Pedersen (1993, 1996a, 1996b, 1999) has also contributed to our understanding of the role of space. Shaffer (2002, 2004) applied force dynamics to the study of modality in ASL. Liddell (1995, 1998, 2000, 2003a) pioneered the application of conceptual blending theory to ASL. Expanding on this work, Dudis (2004; Wulf and Dudis 2005) described body partitioning, a construction unique to signed languages, and investigated its role in conceptual blends. In body partitioning, one part of a signer's body is used to represent one character in a story, while another part depicts a second character. For example, in telling about the reaction of a person being punched in the face by another person, the signer's face will represent the person getting hit, and the signer's arm and fist will represent the arm and fist of the person who is hitting.

Metaphor
    Wilbur (1987) was one of the first scholars to systematically explore metaphor in ASL. She noted that many ASL signs exhibit spatialization metaphors. The metaphor

HAPPY IS UP is exemplified in signs such as HAPPY, CHEERFUL, and LAUGH, which are produced with upward movements. The metaphor NEGATIVE IS DOWN shows up in signs such as LOUSY, IGNORE, and FAIL, which are produced with downward movements.

P. Wilcox (2000) expanded the analysis of metaphor in ASL by demonstrating systematic relationships among the signs used to convey the metaphor IDEAS ARE OBJECTS. P. Wilcox noted that this metaphor is expressed in ASL by distinct lexical signs. IDEAS ARE OBJECTS TO BE GRASPED may be expressed using the S-handshape (Figure 33.1). The S-handshape in ASL is used to express the concept of grasping. It would be used to sign 'grasp a bicycle handlebar' and is seen in ASL signs meaning 'broom' and 'to sweep' where it depicts holding a broom handle. The S-handshape is also used to 'hold' or 'grasp' ideas as metaphorical objects.

Fig. 33.1: S-handshape

Handshapes which are used to represent grasping a flat object can also be used metaphorically to represent IDEAS ARE OBJECTS TO BE MANIPULATED (Figure 33.2). This handshape appears in signs used to express the manipulation of objects: moving an object from one location to another (for example, 'to give') or removing a paper from a shelf. When ideas are metaphorically understood to be objects to be manipulated, moved, or placed, this handshape is used. For example, a signer would use this handshape to talk about moving ideas around various locations in her mind to convey the concept of organizing her thoughts.

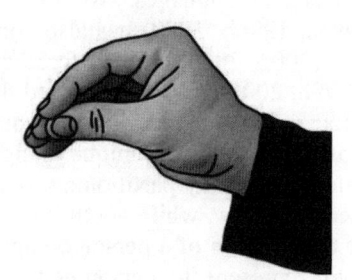

Fig. 33.2: Grasping flat-O handshape

When an idea is metaphorically discriminated, carefully selected, or extracted from some location, the F-handshape is used (Figure 33.3). This handshape is used in ASL to convey the notion of selecting or picking up small physical objects such as seeds, small buttons, or a sewing needle. When used metaphorically with the concept of ideas, it suggests that the idea is being carefully selected. It also implies limited quantity; whereas the S-handshape may represent the grasping of many ideas, when the F-handshape is used metaphorically in connection with ideas it suggests that only a single idea has been selected.

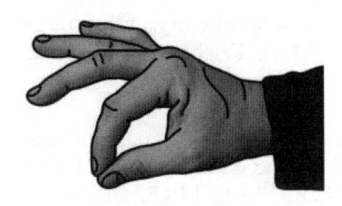

Fig. 33.3: F-handshape

While the congruent metaphors MIND IS A CONTAINER and IDEAS ARE OBJECTS (that are contained within the mind) are pervasive in signed languages, including ASL, British Sign Language (BSL), Catalan Sign Language (LSC), French Sign Language (LSF), and Italian Sign Language (LIS), they are not universal (P. Wilcox 2007). Signed languages exhibit cultural variability in metaphorical expression. In Japanese Sign language (JSL) the metaphor TORSO IS A CONTAINER interacts with IDEAS ARE OBJECTS and UNDERSTANDING IS CONSUMING FOOD. In JSL, the torso is understood as the container for ideas; the body, the same cavity where food is digested, instead of the forehead, provides a container where understanding takes place. The JSL sign meaning 'to comprehend' is DRINK-QUICK.

Metonymy

Wilcox and colleagues (Wilcox et al. 2003) reported several types of lexical metonymies in ASL and LSC. The metonymy PROTOTYPICAL CHARACTERISTIC FOR WHOLE ENTITY appears in both ASL and LSC, in which the signs for 'bird', 'horse', and 'cow' depict prototypical physical properties of these animals: the beak, the ears, and horns, respectively. In ACTION FOR INSTRUMENT metonymies, the action of the hands in interaction with some object represents the instrument. In the ASL sign TYPEWRITER, for example, the hands and fingers are moved in a way representing the action of typing. In the metonymy PROTOTYPICAL ACTION FOR ACTIVITY the hands and their movement represent prototypical action taken with an object; this in turn may come to metonymically express the general activity. The ASL and LSC signs DRIVE-CAR, EAT, and BATHE exemplify this. The ASL sign DRIVE-CAR, for example, represents the prototypical action of the hands holding onto a car's steering wheel. In LSC, the signs DRINK-BEER, DRINK-BRANDY, DRINK-RUM-AND-COKE use specific handshapes representing interaction with a container of a specific, prototypical shape, as well as movements characteristic of drinking from these containers.

A number of signs in LSC rely on a metonymy in which a salient characteristic of a well-known person is extended to stand for a more general quality. These metonymies also typically involve metonymic chains. The LSC sign CHARLIE-CHAPLIN is a compound that iconically depicts Chaplin's moustache and the movement of holding the cane and moving it in circles as Chaplin did, thus relying on a physical characteristic for person (in this case two characteristics) metonymy. The sign is also used to mean 'person moving fast', which extends the first metonymy to a more abstract characteristic of person for general quality metonymy.

Wilcox and P. Wilcox (2013) describe the role that metaphor and metonymy play in the semantic extension and grammaticization of perception signs. ASL has a family of tactile perception signs related phonologically and semantically. Phonologically, the signs are made with the open-8 handshape (Figure 33.4). Frishberg and Gough ([1973] 2000: 111) described this family of signs:

> The meaning this handshape carries relates to feelings, both sensation and emotion, with some interesting extensions along those lines. Along the chest we find DISCOURAGED, DEPRESSED, THRILLED, EXCITED, SENSITIVE, FEEL, LIKE, DISLIKE, HAVE-A-HUNCH, and INTERESTING. In some cases both hands use the configuration and in other cases just one hand does. On the forehead we find SICK, SICKLY ('habitually sick'), differing only in that the second has characteristic slow repetition, which is used quite productively to show habitual, repeated action or plurality. Other signs which use this handshape include DELICIOUS, TASTE (at the mouth), TOUCH (on the back of the hand), FAVORITE (on the chin). GLORY and SHINING are variants of one another which both occur on a palm up base hand. BRILLIANT shows the same movement and handshape as shining except that it is made on the forehead, like many other words having to do with thought processes.

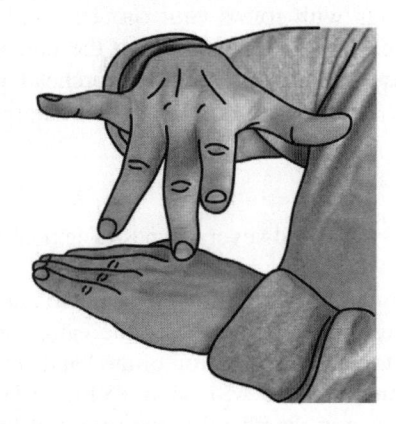

Fig. 33.4: ASL sign TOUCH.

The phonological parameter of location is a source of metaphorical meanings using the TOUCH sign. SHINING is produced in a neutral space in front of the signer, in a location where bright, shining light would most prototypically be viewed. BRILLIANT (in the mental sense) uses the same handshape and movement as SHINING, but it is produced at the forehead, thus evoking a metaphorical connection with the head as the place where cognitive activities take place. The signs DISCOURAGED, DEPRESSED, THRILLED, EXCITED, SENSITIVE, FEEL, LIKE, DISLIKE, HAVE-A-HUNCH, and INTERESTING are produced on the chest, suggesting a metaphorical connection between the heart and emotions or intuitive feelings. DELICIOUS, TASTE, and FAVORITE are produced on the mouth or chin. TOUCH is produced on the back of the hand in citation form, but can be produced on other locations as well to indicate touching some specific location.

In many languages the verb meaning 'feel' in the tactile sense is also used to indicate general sensory perception (Sweetser 1990). Sweetser notes that "the sense of touch is not only linked with general sense perception, but is also closely tied to emotional 'feeling'" (Sweetser 1990: 37). She also points out that there is a metonymic link between touch and emotion: physical pain, for example, makes us unhappy, while physical pleasure makes us cheerful. Metaphor and metonymy play a role in semantic extension and grammaticalization of TOUCH and FEEL forms in ASL (Figures 33.4 and 33.5). A metonymic path of semantic extension leads from TOUCH and FEEL referring to the perception of external sensations, to the perception of internal sensation, to emotion, to emotion tied to cognitive action, and finally to the use of TOUCH/FEEL forms to refer primarily to cognitive activity with little or no emotional content such as planning, considering, or deciding (Wilcox and P. Wilcox 2013).

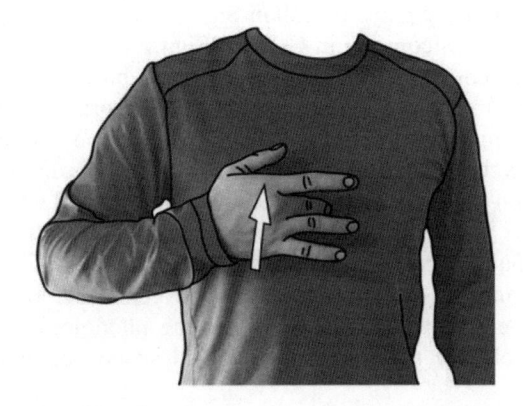

Fig. 33.5: ASL sign FEEL.

Iconicity

Signed languages are particularly intriguing for linguists interested in the study of iconicity. Early on, linguists recognized the pervasive iconicity of signed languages. Stokoe et al. (1965) noted metaphorical, metonymic, and iconic aspects of ASL. Mandel (1977) described several iconic devices that he argued play a role in the grammar of ASL. Following this period of interest in iconicity, linguists began to document constraints on iconicity. Frishberg (1975) studied the erosion of iconicity in historical change. While acknowledging the two faces of signs – the iconic face and the encoded, arbitrary face – Klima and Bellugi (1979: 34) argued that grammatical processes in ASL work to diminish lexical iconicity:

> Grammatical operations that signs undergo can further submerge iconicity. Thus many signs, while having their roots deeply embedded in mimetic representation, have lost their original transparency as they have been constrained more tightly by the linguistic system.

The example they offer is the morphological marking of intensification in ASL, expressed phonologically as an initial hold of the sign's movement followed by sudden, rapid release. When this grammatical marker appears on the ASL root sign SLOW the resulting sign means 'very slow'. Klima and Bellugi pointed out that the sign VERY-SLOW is made with a faster movement than that used in the sign SLOW, and thus they argued that the form of VERY-SLOW is non-iconic with its meaning: VERY-SLOW is articulated very fast. Wilcox (2004a) proposed a metaphorical analysis of the intensification marker on VERY-SLOW as the build up and sudden of release of pressure. Since the sign is produced with an initial hold followed by a sudden release movement, he argued that rather than demonstrating how grammar diminishes iconicity, this example instead is a case of iconicity emerging in grammatical morphology.

Recently, research on iconicity has seen a resurgence, with linguists documenting its role in the grammars of signed languages. Meir and colleagues (Meir et al. 2007) have shown that iconic signs denoting states of affairs manifests an inherent pattern of iconicity in which the signer's body represents one argument of the verb, the subject, and the hands, moving in relation to the body, represent other arguments. Taub (2001) and Meir (2010) have documented the complex relation between iconicity and metaphor. Russo and colleagues explored the role iconicity plays in Italian Sign Language poetry (Russo et al. 2001). Perniss (2007) reported on iconicity in German Sign Language.

Wilcox (2004a) introduced the concept of cognitive iconicity, based on cognitive grammar (Langacker 1987, 2008). In the cognitive grammar framework, semantic and phonological structures reside within conceptual space. Similarities among concepts are regarded as distance relations between structures in conceptual space (Gärdenfors 2000, 2014). Cognitive iconicity builds on these concepts by defining iconicity not as a relation between the form of a sign and its real world referent, but as a distance relation within a multidimensional conceptual space between the phonological and semantic poles of symbolic structures. Greater distance in conceptual space between a symbolic unit's semantic and phonological poles creates arbitrariness. When the phonological and semantic poles of a sign lie more closely together in conceptual space, iconicity is increased.

Cognitive iconicity is a manifestation of the cognitive abilities that structure both the phonological and semantic poles of language. A key claim of cognitive grammar is that grammar and language are structured by an embodied conceptual system with certain basic abilities. One cognitive ability is schematization, "the process of extracting the commonality inherent in multiple experiences to arrive at a conception representing a higher level of abstraction" (Langacker 2008: 17). One class of schemas is conceptual archetypes; examples include "a physical object, an object in a location, an object moving through space, the human face and its parts, a physical container and its contents, seeing something, holding something, handing something to someone, exerting force to effect a desired change, a face-to-face encounter" (Langacker 2008: 33).

Cognitive iconicity captures the fact that conceptual archetypes derive not only from our experience with general events in the world, but also from a distinct class of visible events: hands, faces, and their movements. Hands are arguably the physical objects with which we have the most experience. They are certainly the most common way that we interact with the world. Signing or gesturing hands are located in and move through space. Facial gestures are used in every known signed language. Hands are containers, both for real contents and for metaphorical contents such as ideas or emotions. Hands are visually perceived. Hands exert force on other objects to effect change, making the phonological pole of signs describable in terms of transitivity (Wilcox and P. Wilcox

1995). For signed languages these articulators have rich conceptual import. Hands and faces are not only the means by which semantic structures are phonologically expressed, they are themselves a significant source of our embodied conceptual system. In other words, signing hands have rich semantic properties, a feature described by Stokoe (1991) as semantic phonology.

4. Signed language and gesture

Unburdened by the need to defend the status of signed languages as nothing more than gesture, sign linguists have begun to explore the complex relationship between the two systems. Gesture and sign may co-occur in signer's utterances, either simultaneously or in alternation. Gestures also become incorporated over time into the linguistic systems of signed languages through lexicalization and grammaticalization.

Gesture and sign co-occur
   A growing body of research examines how gesture and sign co-occur within an utterance. Vermeergen and Demey (2007) offer a comprehensive review with data from Flemish Sign Language, showing how sign and gesture co-occur in utterances both simultaneously and in alternation. McCleary and Viotti (2009) provide an overview of the interaction of gesture and sign and demonstrate such co-occurrence in Língua Brasileira de Sinais (Libras). Duncan (2005) has suggested that Taiwanese Sign Language signers incorporate manual gestures into signs at the point in narratives where hearing narrators using spoken language also make manual gestures.
   One proposal for the interaction of gesture and sign is offered by Liddell (2003a, 2003b), who suggests that sign and gesture co-occur simultaneously in several ways, including aspects of spatialized syntax, pointing or indexical signs, and classifier predicates. Liddell argues that location in pointing signs cannot be morphemic because the number of possible locations is uncountable. He applies the same analysis to classifier signs, arguing that while parts of these signs (e.g., handshape and movement) are linguistic, other parts (locations) are variable, gradient elements and should be classified as gesture (see also Schembri et al. 2005: 287, who suggest that classifier verbs may be analyzed as blends of linguistic and gestural elements).
   For example, Liddell (2003b: 212) argues that in ASL constructions such as UP-RIGHT-PERSON-WALK-ALONG, meaning 'person walks along (in an unhurried manner and in a normal forward orientation)', the handshape and movement are formally stable and linguistic, but the initial and end locations are gradient and thus gesture. Wilbur (2013) makes a cogent, non-cognitive argument against this analysis.
   A cognitive linguistic rebuttal would point out first that what Liddell analyzes as a sign is actually a complex symbolic construction, and, more importantly, that what he characterizes as gestural elements (the initial and end locations) are more appropriately analyzed as schematic components in this complex, composite construction. English constructions can serve as an example. Adjectives such as *moonless* and *hopeless* lead to the abstraction of a schematic template *N+less*, which sanctions *senseless* and *thoughtless* and is itself a component of a more complex construction $N_1+less\ N_2$ (Langacker 2008: 24). Parts of this complex construction are more specific (*-less*), and parts are more schematic (N_1 and N_2).

Similarly, signers extract schematic constructional templates from usage events. The ASL expression UPRIGHT-PERSON-WALK-ALONG may lead to the abstraction of a schematic template in which the frequently occurring handshape and movement are more specific (specifying a person walking normally), while the variable initial and end locations are more schematic (until they are actually articulated). In the complex English construction, the more schematic elements will sanction limitless conventional as well as novel instantiations (in Langacker's discussion, even the unlikely novel expression *ireless dwarf* is sanctioned by the schematic assembly N_1+*less* N_2). The same is true for the novel instantiations of the initial and end locations of the ASL construction, which, as Liddell points out, also appear to be uncountable. The mistake we should not make is categorizing the schematic elements as gesture.

Gesture is incorporated into signed languages

Gestures may become lexicalized and grammaticalized into the linguistic system of signed languages (Janzen 2012). Wilcox and Xavier (2013) offer data demonstrating lexicalization of gesture in Libras. The thumb-up gesture performed with one hand is a gestural emblem[2] for Brazilian hearing people (Sherzer 1991), as well as for deaf Brazilian users of Libras. The gesture also appears to be the source for several lexical signs in Libras, which fall along a continuum from more gesture-like (emblems incorporating some Libras morphology) to more linguistic (fully lexicalized signs incorporating Libras morphology).

Once lexicalized, gesture may undergo grammaticalization. Several researchers have documented the process by which lexicalized gestures grammaticalize (Janzen and Shaffer 2002; Pfau and Steinbach 2007; Wilcox 2004b, 2005; Wilcox and P. Wilcox 1995). In general, the process starts with a manually produced gesture which enters a signed language as a lexical morpheme. That lexical sign then acquires grammatical meaning. For example, it has been proposed (Janzen and Shaffer 2002) that a departure gesture used in the Mediterranean region entered French Sign Language (LSF) as the lexical sign PARTIR 'leave'. Because ASL is historically related to French Sign Language (LSF), the sign also appeared in ASL at the turn of the 20th century with the lexical meaning 'to depart'. It also occurs with a more grammatical function marking future.

In addition to manual gestures becoming grammaticalized, a second route leads from gesture to language (Wilcox 2004b, 2005; Wilcox et al. 2010). This route begins as facial gestures or manner of movement gestures. These gestures do not enter the linguistic system as lexical signs; rather, they first appear as prosody or intonation. As they grammaticalize, they take on grammatical function as, for example, markers of interrogatives, topics, conditionals, verb aspect, and intensification.

What is language and what is gesture?

Examining the relation between gesture and language raises the question of how to determine what is gesture and what is language. Distinguishing between gesture and language within the diachronic approach is relatively straightforward: gestures are those behaviors that can be shown to be in use outside of the signed language community. In

---

[2] Emblems are conventionalized gestures that have a spoken equivalent, such as the V gesture representing 'victory'.

the example discussed above, the departure gesture used by non-signers that is the source for PARTIR is well-documented by gesture scholars (de Jorio and Kendon [1832] 2001; Morris et al. 1979). Facial gestures that may serve as the non-linguistic source of prosody and intonation have been studied and documented as well (Darwin 1872) and arguably have a language external, biological origin (see also Bolinger 1986). Manner of movement of gesture has a long history of description. According to Aldrete (1999: 36–37), Quintilian taught that "by altering the speed with which a gesture was made and its range of motion, the same gesture could have multiple meanings or purposes."

The proposal that gesture and signed language co-occur poses a more serious problem, since they are both produced with the same articulators. Often, sign linguists who make the claim for the distinction of language and gesture adopt criterial models of language and gesture as classical categories, assuming that linguistic material is categorical, discrete, and conventional, while gestural material is gradient, analog, and idiosyncratic (Liddell 2003a; Sandler 2009).

These assumptions contradict cognitive linguistic research findings in three ways. First, cognitive linguists have soundly rejected criterial and shared properties models in favor of prototype models (Lakoff 1987; Langacker 2008). Second, linguists working within usage-based and cognitive linguistic theories have convincingly demonstrated that gradience pervades language at all levels (Bybee 2010; Langacker 2008). Whereas some sign linguists classify gradience in morphology as non-linguistic gesture, spoken language linguists come to quite a different conclusion. Hay and Baayen (2005: 346) ask whether morphological structure is inherently graded and reply, "The issue is controversial, but the evidence that is currently accumulating in the literature suggests that the answer is yes." This leads them to conclude that gradedness is part and parcel of the grammar (Hay and Baayen 2005).

The third way these assumptions are at odds with usage-based and cognitive linguistic findings is that they implicitly accept the formalist distinction between competence and performance. The formalist approach assumes that linguistic competence consists of "well-defined discrete categories and categorical grammaticality criteria. Performance may be full of fuzziness, gradience, and continua, but linguistic competence is not" (Bod et al. 2003: 1). Fuzziness, gradience, and continua characterize the grammars of spoken language; a cognitive linguistic approach recognizes them as properties of the grammars of signed languages as well.

Looking towards the future of cognitive linguistic research on signed languages, linguists should recognize that language and gesture are not classical categories based on objective properties. A solution to the problem of what is language and what is gesture more compatible with the cognitive linguistic framework would be to recognize that language and gesture are culturally and linguistically constructed prototype categories. As Lakoff (1987: 8) long ago explained, categories are "a matter of both human experience and imagination – of perception, motor activity, and culture on the one hand, and of metaphor, metonymy, and mental imagery on the other." We should expect that deaf and hearing people will have different notions of what is language and what is gesture, if only because they have different perceptual, motor, and cultural experiences. We also should predict that, just as for any category, the boundaries of language and gesture will be fuzzy and gradient, varying by individual, by context, and subject to change over time (see also Bybee 2010 on the nature of categories).

5. Dynamic systems theory

A foundational assumption of cognitive linguistics and the usage-based approach is that language is a dynamic, emergent system (Barlow and Kemmer 2000; Bybee 2000; Langacker 2000; MacWhinney this volume). Dynamic systems theory (DST) strives to account for how emergent systems arise. Looking to the future of cognitive linguistics, a unified framework will require, as one step, the integration of cognitive linguistics with dynamic systems theory.

One of the first applications of dynamic systems theory to language was an approach called articulatory phonology or gestural phonology (Browman and Goldstein 1985). In this model, the basic units of speech are articulatory gestures, where gesture is defined as "a functional unit, an equivalence class of coordinated movements that achieve some end" (Studdert Kennedy 1987: 77). These functionally-defined ends, or tasks, are modeled in terms of task dynamics (Hawkins 1992).

The significance of DST for cognitive linguistics, and for an embodied solution that seeks to unify the relationship between signed language, spoken language, and gesture, is that it applies not only to the production of language as articulatory gesture but to the emergence and cognitive organization of grammar (Bybee 2010). Rather than viewing the units of language – whether they are phonemes, syllables, morphemes, words or formalist structural descriptions – as timeless and non-physical (i.e., mental) units which must be passed to and implemented in a performance system, the dynamic view defines language "in a unitary way across both abstract 'planning' and concrete articulatory 'production' levels" (Kelso et al. 1986: 31). Thus, the distinction between competence and performance, between language as knowledge and language as action, is replaced by a single system described not in the machine vocabulary of mental programs and computational systems, but in terms of a "fluid, organic system with certain thermodynamic properties" (Thelen and Smith 1994: xix).

Several other linguists and cognitive scientists also have explored a dynamic systems approach to language (Elman 1998; Port and van Gelder 1995; Spivey 2007). To date, however, there has been no systematic exploration of how DST can be integrated with cognitive linguistics. Key principles of DST are clearly mirrored in cognitive linguistic theory. One example is entrenchment, the process by which a complex structure becomes automatized through repetition or rehearsal, eventually becoming established as a unit (Divjak and Caldwell-Harris this volume; Langacker 2008). Entrenchment is the cognitive linguistic equivalent of the DST concept of entrainment, a process by which two or more independent systems become functionally coupled, resulting in a structure with fewer degrees of freedom. In cognitive grammar terminology, the complex structure acquires unit status.

One of the first efforts to apply DST to signed languages was a study of the articulatory phonetics of fingerspelling (Wilcox 1992). Using motion tracking equipment to measure the trajectories of the hand and fingers, Wilcox found that fluent fingerspelling exhibits synchronicity across multiple articulators. In producing letters and letter combinations, the articulators are harnessed to produce task-specific patterns of coordinated motion. This functional entrenchment or entrainment results in a reduction of degrees of freedom characteristic of dynamic systems.

Dynamic systems theory also has been used to analyze signed language production. Tyrone and her colleagues (Tyrone and Mauk 2010; Tyrone et al. 2010) examined prosodic lengthening at phrase boundaries, and sign lowering and phonetic reduction, in ASL. Their findings are consistent with the predictions of a task-dynamic model. Advances in motion tracking technology, and the relative ease with which visible sign articulators can be tracked compared to vocal articulators, makes research on DST approaches to signed language a field ripe for future research.

The application of DST to speech and language suggests a theoretical basis for describing language as a dynamic, real-time, physical process (Bybee 2001; Fowler 2004, 2010; Fowler et al. 1980; Kelso 1995). When we consider the theoretical problems posed in developing an embodied theory of spoken language, signed language, and gesture, it becomes clear that a unified solution will require "compatible dynamics so that perception, action, and cognition can be mutually and flexibly coupled" (Iverson and Thelen 1999: 37) across different perceptual and motor systems.

6. Conclusions

Cognitive linguistics has greatly advanced our understanding of signed languages. In turn, discoveries from the analysis of signed languages challenge linguists to rethink our basic ideas about language and gesture as semiotic systems, and how a modality-free theory may be developed within a usage-based approach in which grammar is directly constructed from experience.

Signed languages presented two problems for linguists. The first problem was to ensure that linguistic theory could account for languages in two modalities. One solution to this problem is offered by formalist or generative theories that posit modality-free grammars independent of physical implementation. In a usage-based theory, grammar emerges from form-meaning pairings of actual utterances. Still, this leaves open the question of how to unify spoken utterances and signed utterances, how to cross the acoustic-optical perceptual divide. The embodied solution, which couples cognitive linguistics with dynamic systems theory, provides an answer.

The second problem was to understand the relationship between language and gesture. This problem was long overlooked by spoken language linguists, who regarded the two as entirely distinct systems. The issue has proved to be challenging for signed language linguists. First, the field had to overcome the widespread perception that signs are nothing more than gestures. Then, unable to apply a simple rubric classifying gestures as behavior that is produced by the hands and face (because signs are produced with the same articulators), sign linguists sought to distinguish the two by viewing them as classical categories definable by objective properties. These proposals, however, contradict two of the most robust findings of cognitive linguistics: that criterial models cannot account for linguistic data, and that gradience pervades language. Relying on criterial models and classical categories to distinguish language from gesture by characterizing language as the domain of the discrete and categorical, and gesture as the realm of gradience and variability, is certain to prove futile. As Bybee (2010: 2) observes, "All types of units proposed by linguists show gradience, in the sense that there is a lot of variation within the domain of the unit (different types of words, morphemes, syllables) and difficulty in setting the boundaries of the unit."

Spoken language, signed language, and gesture are gradient, variable, and emergent systems. The most important contribution that cognitive linguistics can make to future research on signed languages will be to take the usage-based perspective (Bybee 2010; Croft 2001; Langacker 2008) seriously and explore the implications fully. The results of such research are also likely to transform our understanding of language and human communication.

Acknowledgement

Figures designed by Kip Fletcher, Riverlight Studios, Oregon City, OR.

7. References

Aldrete, Gregory S.
   1999   *Gestures and Acclamations in Ancient Rome*. Baltimore: Johns Hopkins University Press.

Aronoff, Mark, Irit Meir and Wendy Sandler
   2005   The paradox of sign language morphology. *Language* 81(2): 301–344.

Barlow, Michael and Suzanne Kemmer
   2000   *Usage-based models of language*. Stanford: CSLI Publications Center for the Study of Language and Information.

Bates, Elizabeth and Frederic Dick
   2002   Language, gesture, and the developing brain. *Developmental Psychobiology* 40(3): 293–310.

Battison, Robbin
   1978   *Lexical borrowing in American Sign Language*. Silver Spring: Linkstok Press.

Bergen, Benjamin
   this volume   1. Embodiment. Berlin/Boston: De Gruyter Mouton.

Bod, Rens, Jennifer Hay and Stefanie Jannedy
   2003   *Probabilistic Linguistics*. Cambridge: MIT Press.

Bolinger, Dwight
   1986   *Intonation and its Parts: Melody in Spoken English*. Stanford: Stanford University Press.

Brentari, Diane
   1998   *A Prosodic Model of Sign Language Phonology*. Cambridge: MIT Press.

Bridges, Byron and Melanie Metzger
   1996   *Deaf Tend Your: Non-Manual Signals in American Sign Language*. Silver Spring: Caliope Press.

Browman, Catherine P. and Louis M. Goldstein
   1985   Dynamic modeling of phonetic structure. In: V. A. Fromkin (ed.), *Phonetic Linguistics*. New York: Academic Press.

Bybee, Joan
   2000   The phonology of the lexicon: Evidence from lexical diffusion. In: M. Barlow and S. Kemmer (eds.), *Usage-Based Models of Language*, 65–85. Stanford: CSLI.

Bybee, Joan
   2001   *Phonology and Language Use*. Cambridge: Cambridge University Press.

Bybee, Joan
   2010   *Language, Usage and Cognition*. Cambridge/New York: Cambridge University Press.

Bybee, Joan, Revere Perkins and William Pagliuca
   1994   *The Evolution of Grammar: Tense, Aspect, and Modality in the Languages of the World*. Chicago: University of Chicago Press.

Capirci, Olga, Cristina Caselli, Jana Iverson, Elena Pizzuto and Virginia Volterra
    2002   Gesture and the nature of language in infancy: The role of gesture as a transitional device en route to two-word speech. In: D. F. Armstrong, M. A. Karchmer and J. V. Van Cleve (eds.), *The Study of Signed Languages: Essays in Honor of William C. Stokoe*, 213–246. Washington, DC: Gallaudet University Press.

Chomsky, Noam
    1972   *Language and Mind*. New York: Harcourt Brace Jovanovich.

Corballis, Michael C.
    2003   From mouth to hand: Gesture, speech, and the evolution of language. *Behavioral and Brain Sciences* 26(2): 199.

Croft, William
    2001   *Radical Construction Grammar: Syntactic Theory in Typological Perspective*. Oxford: Oxford University Press.

Darwin, Charles
    1872   *The Expression of the Emotions in Man and Animals*. London: J. Murray.

de Jorio, Andrea and Adam Kendon
    [1832] 2001   *Gesture in Naples and Gesture in Classical Antiquity: A Translation of La Mimica degli Antichi Investigata nel Gestire Napoletano, Gestural Expression of the Ancients in the Light of Neapolitan Gesturing*. Bloomington: Indiana University Press.

Divjak, Dagmar and Catherine Caldwell-Harris
    this volume   3. Frequency and entrenchment. Berlin/Boston: De Gruyter Mouton.

Dudis, Paul G.
    2004   Body partitioning and real-space blends. *Cognitive Linguistics* 15(2): 223–238.

Duncan, Susan
    2005   Gesture in signing: A case study in Taiwan Sign Language. *Language and Linguistics* 6: 279–318.

Elman, Jeffrey L.
    1998   Language as a dynamical system. In: R. F. Port and T. van Gelder (eds.), *Mind as Motion: Explorations in the Dynamics of Cognition,* 195–225. Cambridge: MIT Press.

Engberg-Pedersen, Elisabeth
    1993   *Space in Danish Sign Language: The Semantics and Morphosyntax of the Use of Space in a Visual Language*. Hamburg: SIGNUM-Verlag.

Engberg-Pedersen, Elisabeth
    1996a   Iconic motivations in conflict: Language-specific structure and influence from the medium. In: E. Engberg-Pedersen, M. Fortescue, P. Harder, L. Heltoft, and L. F. Jakobsen (eds.), *Content, Expression and Structure: Studies in Danish Functional Grammar*, 39–64. Amsterdam: John Benjamins Publishing Company.

Engberg-Pedersen, Elisabeth
    1996b   Iconicity and arbitrariness. In: E. Engberg-Pedersen, M. Fortescue, P. Harder, L. Heltoft, and L. F. Jakobsen (eds.), *Content, Expression and Structure: Studies in Danish Functional Grammar*, 453–468. Amsterdam: John Benjamins Publishing Company.

Engberg-Pedersen, Elisabeth
    1999   Space and time. In: J. Allwood & P. Gärdenfors (eds.), *Cognitive Semantics: Meaning and Cognition*, 131–152. Amsterdam: John Benjamins Publishing Company.

Fowler, Carol A.
    2004   Listeners do hear sounds, not tongues. *The Journal of the Acoustical Society of America* 99(3): 1730–1741.

Fowler, Carol A.
    2010   Embodied, embedded language use. *Ecological Psychology* 22(4): 286–303.

Fowler, Carol A., Philip Rubin, Richard E. Remez and Michael Turvey
    1980   Implications for speech production of a general theory of action. In: B. Butterworth (ed.), *Language Production*, 373–420. New York: Academic Press.

Frishberg, Nancy
   1975   Arbitrariness and iconicity: Historical change in American Sign Language. *Language* 51: 676–710.

Frishberg, Nancy and Bonnie Gough
   [1973] 2000   Morphology in American Sign Language. *Sign Language and Linguistics* 3(1): 103–131.

Gärdenfors, Peter
   2000   *Conceptual Spaces: The Geometry of Thought*. Cambridge: MIT Press.

Gärdenfors, Peter
   2014   *The Geometry of Meaning: Semantics Based on Conceptual Spaces*. Cambridge: MIT Press.

Gentilucci, Maurizio
   2006   From manual gesture to speech: A gradual transition. *Neuroscience and Biobehavioral Reviews* 30(7): 949–960.

Hawkins, Sarah
   1992   An introduction to task dynamics. *Papers in Laboratory Phonology: Gesture, Segment, Prosody* 2: 9–25.

Hay, Jennifer B. and R. Harald Baayen
   2005   Shifting paradigms: gradient structure in morphology. *Trends in Cognitive Science* 9(7): 342–348.

Husain, Fatima T., Debra J. Patkin, Hung Thai-Van, Allen R. Braun and Barry Horwitz
   2009   Distinguishing the processing of gestures from signs in deaf individuals: An FMRI study. *Brain Research* 1276: 140–150.

Iverson, Jana and Esther Thelen
   1999   Hand, mouth and brain. The dynamic emergence of speech and gesture. *Journal of Consciousness Studies* 6(11): 19–40.

Janzen, Terry
   2006   Visual communication: Signed language and cognition. In: G. Kristiansen, M. Achard, R. Dirven, and F. R. M. de Ibáñez (eds.), *Cognitive Linguistics: Current Applications and Future Perspectives*, 359–377. Berlin/New York: Mouton de Gruyter.

Janzen, Terry
   2012   Lexicalization and grammaticalization. In: M. Steinbach, R. Pfau and B. Woll (eds.), *Handbook of Sign Languages,* 1–23. Berlin: Mouton de Gruyter.

Janzen, Terry and Barbara Shaffer
   2002   Gesture as the substrate in the process of ASL grammaticization. In: R. Meier, D. Quinto and K. Cormier (eds.), *Modality and Structure in Signed and Spoken Languages*, 199–223. Cambridge: Cambridge University Press.

Janzen, Terry, Barbara O'Dea and Barbara Shaffer
   2001   The construal of events: Passives in American Sign Language. *Sign Language Studies* 1(3): 281–310.

Johnston, Trevor and Adam Schembri
   2007   *Australian Sign Language (Auslan): An Introduction to Sign Language Linguistics*. Cambridge: Cambridge University Press.

Kelso, J. A. Scott
   1995   *Dynamic Patterns: The Self-Organization of Brain and Behavior*. Cambridge: The MIT Press.

Kelso, J. A. Scott, Elliot Saltzman and Betty Tuller
   1986   The dynamical perspective on speech production: Data and theory. *Journal of Phonetics* 14: 29–59.

Kendon, Adam
   2004   *Gesture: Visible Action as Utterance*. Cambridge/New York: Cambridge University Press.

Klima, Edward and Ursula Bellugi
　1979　*The Signs of Language.* Cambridge: Harvard University Press.
Lakoff, George
　1987　*Women, Fire, and Dangerous Things: What Categories Reveal About the Mind.* Chicago: University of Chicago Press.
Lane, Harlan
　1984　*When the Mind Hears: A History of the Deaf.* New York: Random House.
Langacker, Ronald W.
　1987　*Foundations of Cognitive Grammar,* Volume 1: *Theoretical Foundations.* Stanford: Stanford University Press.
Langacker, Ronald W.
　2000　A dynamic usage-based model. In: M. Barlow and S. Kemmer (eds.), *Usage-Based Models of Language,* 1–63. Stanford: CSLI Publications Center for the Study of Language and Information.
Langacker, Ronald W.
　2008　*Cognitive Grammar: A Basic Introduction.* Oxford: Oxford University Press.
Liddell, Scott K.
　1984　Think and believe: Sequentiality in American Sign Language. *Language* 60(2): 372–399.
Liddell, Scott K.
　1995　Real, surrogate, and token space: Grammatical consequences in ASL. In: K. Emmorey and J. Riley (eds.), *Language, Gesture, and Space,* 19–41. Hillsdale: Lawrence Erlbaum Associates, Inc.
Liddell, Scott K.
　1998　Grounded blends, gestures, and conceptual shifts. *Cognitive Linguistics,* 9(3): 283–314.
Liddell, Scott K.
　2000　Blended spaces and deixis in sign language discourse. In: D. McNeill (ed.), *Language and Gesture,* 331–357. Cambridge: Cambridge University Press.
Liddell, Scott K.
　2003a　*Grammar, Gesture, and Meaning in American Sign Language.* New York: Cambridge University Press.
Liddell, Scott K.
　2003b　Sources of meaning in ASL classifier predicates. In: K. Emmorey (ed.), *Perspectives on Classifier Constructions in Sign Languages,* 199–220. Mahwah: Lawrence Erlbaum Associates.
Liebal, Katja, Cornelia Müller and Simone Pika (eds.)
　2007　*Gestural Communication in Nonhuman and Human Primates.* (Benjamins Current Topics 10.) Amsterdam/Philadelphia: John Benjamins Publishing.
Lillo Martin, Diane
　1986　Two kinds of null arguments in American Sign Language. *Natural Language and Linguistic Theory* 4(4): 415–444.
MacWhinney, Brian
　this volume　34. Emergentism. Berlin/Boston: De Gruyter Mouton.
Mandel, Mark A.
　1977　Iconic devices in American Sign Language. In: L. A. Friedman (ed.), *On the Other Hand: New Perspectives on American Sign Language,* 57–108. New York: Academic Press.
McCleary, Leland and Evani Viotti
　2009　Sign-gesture symbiosis in Brazilian Sign Language narrative. In: F. Parrill, V. Tobin and M. Turner (eds.), *Meaning, Form, and Body,* 181–201. Stanford: CSLI Publications.

McNeill, David
   1992   *Hand and Mind: What Gestures Reveal about Thought.* Chicago: University of Chicago Press.

McNeill, David
   2005   *Gesture and Thought.* Chicago: University of Chicago Press.

Meier, Richard
   2002   The acquisition of verb agreement: Pointing out arguments for the linguistic status of agreement in signed languages. In: G. Morgan and B. Woll (eds.), *Directions in Sign Language Acquisition*, 115–141. Amsterdam: John Benjamins.

Meir, Irit
   2010   Iconicity and metaphor: Constraints on metaphorical extension of iconic forms. *Language* 86(4): 865–896.

Meir, Irit, Carol Padden, Mark Aronoff and Wendy Sandler
   2007   Body as subject. *Journal of Linguistics* 43(03): 531–563.

Metzger, Melanie
   1998   Eye gaze and pronominal reference in American Sign Language. In: C. Lucas (ed.), *Pinky Extension and Eye Gaze: Language Use in Deaf Communities*, 170–182. Washington, DC: Gallaudet University Press.

Morris, Desmond, Peter Collett, Peter Marsh and Marie O'Shaughnessy
   1979   *Gestures: Their Origin and Distribution.* New York: Stein and Day.

Müller, Cornelia
   2007   A dynamic view of metaphor, gesture, and thought. In: S. D. Duncan, J. Cassell and E. T. Levy (eds.), *Gesture and the Dynamic Dimension of Language. Essays in Honor of David McNeill*, 109–116. Amsterdam/Philadelphia: John Benjamins.

Neidle, Carol, Judy Kegl, Dawn MacLaughlin, Benjamin Bahan and Robert Lee
   2000   *American Sign Language: Functional Categories and Hierarchical Structure.* Cambridge: MIT Press.

Padden, Carol A. and David M. Perlmutter
   1987   American Sign Language and the architecture of phonological theory. *Natural Language and Linguistic Theory* 5(3): 335–375.

Perniss, Pamela M.
   2007   *Space and Iconicity in German Sign Language (DGS).* MPI Series in Psycholinguistics 45, Radboud University Nijmegen.

Petronio, Karen and Diane Lillo Martin
   1997   Wh-movement and the position of spec-CP: Evidence from American Sign Language. *Language* 73(1): 18–57.

Pfau, Roland and Josep Quer
   2003   V-to-neg raising and negative concord in three sign languages. Paper presented at the XXIX Incontro di Grammatica Generativa, Urbino, February.

Pfau, Roland and Josep Quer
   2007   On the syntax of negation and modals in Catalan Sign Language and German Sign Language. *Trends in Linguistics Studies and Monographs* 188: 129.

Pfau, Roland and Martin Steinbach
   2007   Modality independent and modality specific aspects of grammaticalization in sign languages. *Linguistics in Potsdam* 24: 3–98.

Pike, Kenneth L.
   1967   *Language in Relation to a Unified Theory of the Structure of Human Behavior.* The Hague: Mouton.

Port, Robert F. and Timothy van Gelder
   1995   *Mind as Motion: Explorations in the Dynamics of Cognition.* Cambridge: The MIT Press.

Rączaszek-Leonardi, Joanna and J. A. Scott Kelso
 2008   Reconciling symbolic and dynamic aspects of language: Toward a dynamic psycholinguistics. *New Ideas in Psychology* 26(2): 193–207.
Rizzolatti, Giacomo and Michael A. Arbib
 1998   Language within our grasp. *Trends in Neurosciences* 21(5): 188–194.
Russo, Tommaso, Rosaria Giurana and Elena Pizzuto
 2001   Italian Sign Language (LIS) poetry: Iconic properties and structural regularities. *Sign Language Studies* 2(1): 85–112.
Sandler, Wendy
 1999   A prosodic model of sign language phonology. *Phonology* 16(3): 443–447.
Sandler, Wendy
 2009   Symbiotic symbolization by hand and mouth in sign language. *Semiotica* 2009(174): 241–275.
Sandler, Wendy and Diane Lillo Martin
 2006   *Sign Language and Linguistic Universals.* Cambridge: Cambridge University Press.
Schembri, Adam, Caroline Jones, and Denis Burnham
 2005   Comparing action gestures and classifier verbs of motion: Evidence from Australian Sign Language, Taiwan Sign Language, and nonsigners' gestures without speech. *Journal of Deaf Studies and Deaf Education* 10(3): 272–290.
Shaffer, Barbara
 2002   CAN'T: The negation of modal notions in ASL. *Sign Language Studies*, 3(1): 34–53.
Shaffer, Barbara
 2004   Information ordering and speaker subjectivity: Modality in ASL. *Cognitive Linguistics* 15(2): 175–195.
Sherzer, Joel
 1991   The Brazilian thumbs-up gesture. *Journal of Linguistic Anthropology* 1(2): 189–197.
Skipper, Jeremy I., Susan Goldin-Meadow, Howard C. Nusbaum and Steven L. Small
 2009   Gestures orchestrate brain networks for language understanding. *Current Biology* 19(8): 661–667.
Spivey, Michael
 2007   *The Continuity of Mind.* Oxford/New York: Oxford University Press.
Stokoe, William C.
 1960   Sign language structure. *Studies in Linguistics, Occasional Papers* 8. Buffalo: Department of Anthropology and Linguistics, University of Buffalo.
Stokoe, William C.
 1991   Semantic phonology. *Sign Language Studies* 71: 107–114.
Stokoe, William C., Dorothy Casterline and Carl Croneberg
 1965   *A Dictionary of American Sign Language on Linguistic Principles.* Washington, DC: Gallaudet College Press.
Studdert-Kennedy, Michael
 1987   The phoneme as a perceptuomotor structure. In: D. Allport (ed.), *Language Perception and Production: Relationships between Listening, Speaking, Reading, and Writing*, 67–84. London: Academic Press.
Sutton-Spence, Rachel and Bencie Woll
 1999   *The Linguistics of British Sign Language: An Introduction.* Cambridge: Cambridge University Press.
Sweetser, Eve E.
 1990   *From Etymology to Pragmatics: Metaphorical and Cultural Aspects of Semantic Structure.* Cambridge: Cambridge University Press.
Taub, Sarah
 2001   *Language from the Body: Iconicity and Metaphor in American Sign Language.* Cambridge: Cambridge University Press.

Thelen, Esther and Linda B. Smith
  1994   *A Dynamic Systems Approach to the Development of Cognition and Action*. Cambridge: The MIT Press.
Thompson, Robin, Karen Emmorey and Robert Kluender
  2006   The relationship between eye gaze and verb agreement in American Sign Language: An eye-tracking study. *Natural Language & Linguistic Theory* 24(2): 571–604.
Tyrone, Martha E. and Claude Mauk
  2010   Sign lowering and phonetic reduction in American Sign Language. *Journal of Phonetics* 38(2): 317–328.
Tyrone, Martha E., Housung Nam, Elliot Saltzman, Gaurav Mathur and Louis M. Goldstein
  2010   Prosody and movement in American Sign Language: A task-dynamics approach. *Speech Prosody*, 100957: 1–4.
Uyechi, Linda
  1996   *The Geometry of Visual Phonology*. Stanford: CSLI Publications Center for the Study of Language and Information.
Vermeerbergen, Miriam and Eline Demey
  2007   Sign + gesture = speech + gesture? In: M. Vermeerbergen, L. Leeson and O. Crasborn (eds.), *Simultaneity in Signed Languages: Form and Function*, 257–282. Amsterdam/Philadelphia: John Benjamins Publishing Company.
Whorf, Benjamin L. and John B. Caroll
  1956   *Language, Thought, and Reality*. Cambridge: MIT Press.
Wilbur, Ronnie B
  1987   *American Sign Language: Linguistic and Applied Dimensions*. Boston: College-Hill Press.
Wilbur, Ronnie B.
  2013   The point of agreement: Changing how we think about sign language, gesture, and agreement. *Sign Language and Linguistics* 16(2): 221–258.
Wilcox, Phyllis Perrin
  2000   *Metaphor in American Sign Language*. Washington, DC: Gallaudet University Press.
Wilcox, Phyllis Perrin
  2007   Constructs of the mind: Cross-linguistic contrast of metaphor in verbal and signed languages. In: E. Pizzuto, P. Pietrandrea and R. Simone (eds.), *Verbal and Signed Languages: Comparing Structures, Constructs and Methodologies*, 251–274. Berlin/New York: Mouton de Gruyter.
Wilcox, Sherman
  1992   *The Phonetics of Fingerspelling*. Amsterdam/Philadelphia: John Benjamins Publishing Company.
Wilcox, Sherman
  2004a Cognitive iconicity: Conceptual spaces, meaning, and gesture in signed language. *Cognitive Linguistics* 15(2): 119–147.
Wilcox, Sherman
  2004b Gesture and language: Cross-linguistic and historical data from signed languages. *Gesture* 4(1): 43–75.
Wilcox, Sherman
  2005   Routes from gesture to language. *Revista Da ABRALIN – Associação Brasileira De Lingüística* 4(1/2): 11–45.
Wilcox, Sherman
  2007   Signed languages. In: D. Geeraerts and H. Cuyckens (eds.), *The Oxford Handbook of Cognitive Linguistics*, 1113–1136. Oxford: Oxford University Press.
Wilcox, Sherman
  2013   Language in motion: A framework for unifying spoken language, signed language, and gesture. *Anuari de Filologia Estudis de Lingüística* 2: 49–57.

Wilcox, Sherman and Jill P. Morford
    2007   Empirical methods in signed language research. In: M. Gonzalez-Marquez, S. Coulson, M. Spivey and I. Mittelberg (eds.), *Methods in Cognitive Linguistics*, 171–200. Amsterdam: John Benjamins Publishing Company.
Wilcox, Sherman, Paulo Rossini and Elena Antinoro Pizzuto
    2010   Grammaticalization in sign languages. In: D. Brentari (ed.), *Sign Languages*, 332–354. Cambridge: Cambridge University Press.
Wilcox, Sherman and Phyllis Perrin Wilcox
    1995   The gestural expression of modality in American Sign Language. In: J. Bybee and S. Fleischman (eds.), *Modality in Grammar and Discourse*, 135–162. Amsterdam: John Benjamins Publishing Company.
Wilcox, Sherman and Phyllis Perrin Wilcox
    2009   The analysis of signed languages. In: B. Heine and H. Narrog (eds.), *The Oxford Handbook of Linguistic Analysis*, 739–760. Oxford: Oxford University Press.
Wilcox, Sherman and Phyllis Perrin Wilcox
    2013   Cognitive linguistics and signed languages. *International Journal of Cognitive Linguistics* 3(2): 127–151.
Wilcox, Sherman, Phyllis Perrin Wilcox, and Maria Josep Jarque
    2003   Mappings in conceptual space: Metonymy, metaphor, and iconicity in two signed languages. *Jezikoslovlje* 4(1): 139–156.
Wilcox, Sherman and André Xavier
    2013   A framework for unifying spoken language, signed language, and gesture. *Revista Todas as Letras* 15(1): 88–110.
Wulf, Alyssa and Paul Dudis
    2005   Body partitioning in ASL metaphorical blends. *Sign Language Studies* 5(3): 317–332.
Xu, Jiang, Patrick J. Gannon, Karen Emmorey, Jason F. Smith and Allen R. Braun
    2009   Symbolic gestures and spoken language are processed by a common neural system. *Proceedings of the National Academy of Sciences* 106(49): 20664–20669

Sherman Wilcox, University of New Mexico (USA)

34. Emergentism

1. The three frameworks supporting Emergentism
2. Emergentist approaches
3. Mechanisms
4. Methods
5. Ten core issues
6. Conclusion
7. References

The modern study of language can be viewed as the tale of two competing paradigms: Universal Grammar (UG) and Emergentism. These two paradigms assume fundamentally different positions on ten core issues: the scope of language, the uniqueness of recursion, rules vs. cues, the relevance of E-Language, the suddenness of the evolution of language, the genetic control of language, the idea that speech is special, critical periods for language learning, neurological modules for language, and the poverty of the stimulus during the language learning.

UG analyses emphasize explanations of language structure grounded on inborn principles specific to human language (Hauser et al. 2002), as expressed in recursive function theory (Chomsky 1963, 1976, 2010). In contrast, emergentist analyses are grounded on three core frameworks deriving from adaptive systems theory. The first is the Darwinian theory of evolution based on proliferation, competition, and selection. The second is the analysis of complex systems as structured hierarchically into levels, such that higher levels of complexity emerge from lower levels in ways not fully predictable from lower level properties. The third is the theory of timeframes that holds that processes on different levels are linked to very different timescales that mesh together through competition in the present. These three frameworks are not unique to linguistic analysis. In fact, they are fundamental to scientific investigation of all physical, biological, and social processes. In this paper, we will first describe how these frameworks apply to the study of language. Second, we will consider the relation between Emergentism and more specific linguistic frameworks, such as functionalism, cognitive linguistics, connectionism, embodied cognition, usage-based linguistics, and competition theory. Third, we will examine some of the specific mechanisms and structures involved in emergentist models. Fourth, we will survey the methods required for elaborating the theory of language emergence. Finally, we will contrast the Emergentist Program with the Minimalist Program of Universal Grammar in terms of their positions on the ten core issues mentioned above.

1. The three frameworks supporting Emergentism

In this section we will explain and illustrate the ways in which Emergentism relies on the theories of natural selection, complexity, and timeframes.

1.1. Natural selection and competition

Competition is fundamental to biological processes. Darwin (1859) showed how the evolution of the species emerges from the competition between organisms for survival and reproduction. The three basic principles Darwin identified are proliferation, competition, and selection. Proliferation generates variation through mutation and sexual recombination. Organisms with different compositions then compete for resources or rewards such as food, shelter, and the opportunity to reproduce. The outcome of competition is selection through which more adaptive organisms survive and less adaptive ones disappear.

The emergence of structures from proliferation, competition, and selection represents the basic source of change in all biological and social systems, including language. Economic analysis (Friedman 1953) has shown that free markets generate a wide variety of products, sellers, and buyers who then compete and cooperate to achieve optimal pricing and efficiency. In social systems, we can characterize the emergence and spread of new fashions, trends, and ideas through the theory of memetics (Mesoudi et al. 2006), which is closely modelled on evolutionary theory (D. Campbell 1960). In multicellular organisms, the immune system proliferates a multitude of antigens to compete with and defeat invading antibodies. Those antigens that match actual threats are replicated and those that do not are winnowed out. In all of these systems, from economics to the brain, development emerges from the mindless interaction of proliferation and competition without relying on any external master plan.

Emergentist approaches to language (MacWhinney 1999) also view language shape and language change as arising from the processes of proliferation and competition. For the organism as a whole, the fundamental functional pressure is to reproduce. For language, the overall functional pressure is to communicate. However, just as the genes are the basic units of biological proliferation and competition, the actual units of linguistic competition are the constructions, which are mappings between forms and functions. Functions include motives as diverse as identifying a referent (Silverstein 1976), expressing politeness (Helmbrecht 2013), expressing derision through imitation (Haiman 2014), setting a temporal reference point (Smith 1991), coding exclusive disjunction (Ariel 2014), placing presentational focus (Francis and Michaelis 2014), shifting agential perspective (MacWhinney 2008c), inserting parenthetical material (Kaltenboeck and Heine, 2014), and scores of others. All of these many functions are mapped onto forms using overlapping vocal, gestural, and prosodic constructions in a process of continual competition (MacWhinney 1987) during language use, learning, and change.

As MacWhinney et al. (1984: 128) noted, "the forms of natural languages are created, governed, constrained, acquired and used in the service of communicative functions". Bates and MacWhinney (1982) noted that this functionalist position can be dissected into three separate claims. The first is that language change across generations is determined by communicative function; the second is that language acquisition in the child is shaped by communicative function; and the third is that language form in real time conversations is controlled by communicative function. On all three levels, the facilitation of communicative function is viewed as depending on the availability of supporting neural mechanisms.

The handmaiden of competition is cooperation. As Bates and MacWhinney (1982) noted, humans have a great many ideas that they would love to express all at once. But language only allows us to say one thing at a time. One way in which language addresses this problem is by allowing motives to form coalitions. Bates and MacWhinney (1982) analysed the possible solutions to competition as: (1) peaceful coexistence, (2) divide-the-spoils, and (3) winner-take-all.

We can illustrate these solutions by looking at subject marking in English. In the unmarked active transitive clause, such as *the car hit the pole*, the subject (*the car*) expresses a coalition of motives including agency, perspective, givenness, and topicality. This construction represents peaceful coexistence or coalition between the motives, because they all point in the same direction. In the vast majority of cases, these motives do in fact co-occur yielding the active clause as the dominant form for transitive verbs. Peaceful coexistence depends on natural patterns of co-occurence in the real world. For example, the properties of solidity, boundary, and firmness tend to co-occur for objects. Similarly, in animals, properties such agency, movement, warmth, and directed attention all tend to cooccur.

When speakers of a language choose to emphasize one of the features in a peaceful coalition over others, the coalition can break down, precipitating a divide-the-spoils solution. For example, English uses the passive construction, as in *the pole was hit by a car*, as a way of dividing the spoils between the topic/perspective (*the pole*) and the agent (*a car*). In this case, the topic receives the prizes of subject position and agreement and the agent receives the "consolation prize" of placement in a by-clause. An alternative to this divide-the-spoils approach is the winner-take-all solution in which one motivation overrides the others. For English transitive verbs, this solution gives rise to the truncated passive, as in *the pole was hit*. In that solution, the agent is not expressed at all.

1.2. Complexity

Complexity arises from the hierarchical recombination of small parts into larger structures. For biological evolution, the parts are the genes. For the brain, the parts are neuronal structures working to generate competing ideas (D. Campbell 1960). For language, the parts are articulatory gestures. In a seminal article entitled *The Architecture of Complexity*, Simon (1962) analyzed higher-level cognitive processes as hierarchically-structured combinations of elementary information processes or modules into which they could be partially decomposed. The basic principles involved can be illustrated by the four levels of structure that emerge during protein folding (N. A. Campbell et al. 1999). In this process, the primary structure of the protein is determined by the sequence of amino acids in the chain of RNA used by the ribosome as the template for protein synthesis. This chain then folds into a secondary structure of coils and folds created by hydrogen bonding across the amino acid chain. These forces can only impact the geometry of the protein once the primary structure is released from the ribosome and begins to contract. Next, a tertiary structure emerges from hydrophobic reactions and disulfide bridges across the folds and coils of the secondary structures. Finally, the quaternary structure derives from the aggregation of polypeptide subunits based on the ternary structures. It is this final structure that allows each protein to serve its unique role, be it oxygen transport for hemoglobin or antigen detection for antibodies. In this partially decomposable emergent system, each level involves a configuration of components from lower levels, but the physical and biochemical constraints operative on each level are unique to that level and only operate once that level has emerged during the process of folding. If a given protein operates successfully, it promotes the adaptation of the whole organism, eventually leading to positive evolutionary selection for the DNA sequence from which it derives. This can be viewed as a type of backwards or downwards causality between levels (Andersen et al. 2000). These principles of partial decomposability, level-specific constraints, and backwards causality apply with even greater force to the study of language, where the interactions between levels and timeframes are so intense. For language studies, the level of analysis achieved in the study of proteomics is clearly not yet possible. However, we can use these principles is to guide our analysis of linguistic levels, cue strength, and the ways in which levels mesh (Labov 1972).

1.3. Timeframes

To understand how cues combine in real time, we must examine inputs from processes that are sensitive to inputs across very different timeframes. This integration is particularly important for understanding the connections between psycholinguistic processes and historical change. The usual assumption here is that adaptive changes in the moment lead to long-term typological shifts (Bybee 2010). However, to elaborate these models we will need rich longitudinal corpora that can allow us to study changing patterns over time. In the area of child language acquisition, the CHILDES corpus (MacWhinney 1991) has begun to fill this need. However, the fields of second language acquisition, sociolinguistics, neurolinguistics, or language typology will need much greater amounts of publically available longitudinal data to understand the details of timeframe linkages.

Integration across levels occurs at the moment of speaking as we activate patterns in motor cortex that then lead to articulatory gestures and phonation. Before this final volley of excitation, our brains have integrated competing information from a wide variety of stored lexical, prosodic, constructional, and conceptual patterns. Although these patterns reveal their interactions in the moment, their relative strength and scope has been shaped by hours, days, or even decades of usage. Across these various timescales, patterns have come to adjust their input to the ways in which they can be expressed in the moment. For example, the WXDY construction found in *what is this fly doing in my soup* (Kay and Fillmore 1999) only surfaces rarely. When it occurs, it expresses a unique configuration of shock or pretended shock regarding some untoward condition, and either enough social solidarity to withstand the intended irony or else a power differential that allows for expression of some level of approbation or even accusation. These various sociolinguistic and affective assignments depend on the computation of the status of personal relations as they have developed across days, months, and years. These computations must then be linked to more immediate practical judgments regarding the unexpected nature of the condition (i.e., the fly in the soup). If the relevant preconditions are not fulfilled, we may select a more neutral statement, such as *Oh goodness, there is a fly in my soup*.

In order to understand how the brain links such inputs across diverse timeframes, it will help to take a detour into the simpler world of the honeybee. Menzel (1999) explains how honeybee cognition relies on five memory phases, each involving different cellular processes, different timeframes, and different environmental challenges. The first phase is early short-term memory (eSTM). When foraging within a single patch of flowers of the same type, bees are able to concentrate on a pollen source by resonant activation of a particular neural ensemble (Edelman 1987; Pulvermüller 2003). In the second phase of late short-term memory (lSTM), synthesis of the PKA protein kinase begins to solidify the currently active circuit. The third phase of middle-term memory (MTM) spans a timeframe of hours and involves the formation of covalent modifications in the synapses between neurons. During these first three timeframes, bees have not yet returned to the hive, but are still processing flowers encountered during a single foraging bout. The fourth phase of memory consolidation relies on the formation of early long-term memories (eLTM) through the action of nitrous oxide (NO) and PKC1. This type of consolidation is important, because it allows the bee to return to remembered pollen sources even after a trip back to the hive. The fifth phase of consolidation in late long-term memory (lLTM) operates across a timeframe of over three days, using PKC2 protein synthesis for even more permanent memories. Thus, each of the five phases of memory consolidation is responsive to the nature of the memory that must be retained to allow the bee to continue successful foraging.

When the bee is trying to decide where to fly, her decision is impacted by an array of wheels that mesh in the current moment. Some of the wheels derive from the memories for pollen sources described above. Others derive from activities in the hive, including the dances of other bees. Still others relate to the season, the need to defend the hive, and so on. Bees have an neural module for evaluation that meshes information from all of these sources, much as our language production device serves to evaluate and mesh inputs from all sorts of memories and motives. For both the bee and the human speaker, this meshing of inputs from contrasting timeframes all occurs at the moment of deciding either where to fly or what to say.

This linkage between environmental tasks, timeframes, and neuronal processes is not unique to bees. However, these relations are particularly transparent in the honeybee, because of the way in which the distribution of flowers structures the bee's environment. We find the same five memory mechanisms operating across these timeframes in humans. However, for humans, there are additional mechanisms that support even more complex consolidation over longer timeframes for integrating increasingly complex memories. Many of these additional mechanisms rely on links between the hippocampus and the cortex (McClelland et al. 1995; Wittenberg et al. 2002), including episodic storage in the medial temporal lobes (Daselaar et al. 2004). In addition, the frontal lobes provide a hierarchical system of executive control involving increasingly complex and longer-term structures as one moves from the posterior to anterior frontal areas (Koechlin and Summerfield 2007).

For both bees and humans, behavior is often organized into sequences of repetitive actions. Flying in bees and walking and breathing in humans is based on an iterative closed loop that includes methods for monitoring and stabilizing the iterative process (Feldman 2006). In speech, the basic iterative loop involves the repetitive production of syllables lasting about 150 ms each (Massaro 1975). MacNeilage and Davis (1998) argue that the basic syllable gesture has a CV (consonant-vowel) structure that is homologous to the lip-smacking gesture in other primates. In their frame-content theory, the positioning of the jaw and articulatory closures for the consonant constitutes the "frame" and the positioning of the tongue for the vowel constitutes the "content". The generation of these gestures is controlled by the pars opercularis (Bookheimer 2007) which is the segment of the inferior frontal gyrus nearest to the motor area, which places it next to the motor map for the tongue and lips. In a syllable-timed language like Spanish, this circuit produces a clear periodicity of syllabic gestures. We can think of this process as a wheel revolving with a periodicity of 150 milliseconds. The output of this wheel is then further modified by a second wheel that imposes syllabic stress at the slightly longer timeframe of the metrical foot. The imposition of stress on the syllabic chain can be based either on lexical signals or on conversational emphases.

Short-term processes must mesh with long-term processes. Some of these long-term processes reside not just in neural memories, but also in the memes of social symbolism as they spread through the community (Hruschka et al. 2009). Language is essentially a collection of social memes that becomes internalized within group members. The memes controlling conventions for conversational sequencing, alignment, and focusing also mesh with physical systems for maintaining gaze contact, proxemics, and postural alignment. The analysis of meshing across timeframes can help us understand exactly how motivations compete. In this way, we can better evaluate the claims of the strong functionalist position.

Online meshing takes in motives or pressures from across at least ten major functional domains, each sensitive to inputs from different timeframes. These ten domains include: word production, word comprehension, sentence production, sentence comprehension, language acquisition, diachronic change, interactional maintenance, encounter structure, group membership, and phylogenetic change. Example analyses of how meshing occurs can be found in MacWhinney (2014), Toscano and McMurray (2010), Goodwin (2002), and Poplack and Cacoullos (2014).

2. Emergentist approaches

Recent work in linguistics has produced a variety of theoretical frameworks with overlapping goals and assumptions. Among these are functionalism (Givón 1979), Systemic Functional Grammar (Halliday and Matthiessen 2004), Cognitive Grammar (Langacker 1987), Usage-based Linguistics (Bybee and Hopper 2001), Sociolinguistic Variable Rule Analysis (Kay 1978), the Competition Model (MacWhinney 1987), Construction Grammar (Goldberg 2006), Conceptual Metaphor Theory (Lakoff and Johnson 1980), Blending Theory (Fauconnier and Turner 1996), Optimality Theory (Bresnan et al. 2001; Kager 1999), and the Neural Theory of Language (Feldman 2006). In psychology, theories such as Parallel Distributed Processing (Rumelhart and McClelland 1986), self-organizing maps (Kohonen 2001), Bayesian modeling (Kemp et al. 2007), Information Integration Theory (Massaro 1987), and Dynamic Systems Theory (Thelen and Smith 1994) provide quantifiable predictions regarding the outcomes of competition. In addition, formulations from neurolinguistics such as mirror neurons (Arbib 2010), Embodied Cognition (Pecher and Zwaan 2005), and Common Coding (Schütz-Bosbach and Prinz 2007) link up well with many aspects of functionalist linguistics.

Faced with this embarrassment of theoretical riches, students often ask what is the relation between Emergentism and all these other approaches. The answer is that all of these approaches fall under the general category of Emergentism, because all recognize the importance of the principles of proliferation, competition, selection, and complexity. However, within this general framework, there is a great diversity of contrasting emphases on specific mechanisms of emergence. We will discuss some of these alternative approaches in the next section. It is also true that, although these approaches utilize the basic concepts of competition and complexity, many of them provide no clear role for the processes that mesh inputs across timeframes. There are some exceptions to this. First, there are sociolinguistic analyses, such as those presented by Poplack and Cacoullos (2014) that have succeeded in tracing changes and continuities in grammar and lexicon over centuries, based on indirect accounts from spoken language data. Second, researchers such as Goodwin (2000), Sfard and McClain (2002), and Lemke (2000) have shown how the use of artifacts (tools, maps, books, color chips, computers) during interaction can provide links to long-term timeframes. Third, researchers in child language (Bates and Goodman 1999) and second language (Verspoor et al. 2011) have developed longitudinal corpora to trace the ways in which competing processes interact across several years. MacWhinney (2005a, 2014) provides further analysis of this issue.

3. Mechanisms

Emergentist approaches to language can be characterized most clearly in terms of the emphases they place on alternative mechanisms for language use, learning, and change. In some cases, similar approaches differ only in the detailed computational algorithms they utilize. For example, Parallel Distributed Processing (Rumelhart and McClelland 1986), Self-Organizing Feature Maps (Kohonen 2001), and Dynamic Systems Theory (Thelen and Smith 1994) all represent networks of connections, but differ in the algorithms that operate on these connections. Sometimes there is overlap in terms of both concepts and mechanisms. For example, Construction Grammar (Goldberg 2006) is a direct outgrowth of work in Cognitive Grammar (Langacker 1987), differing largely in terms of the detail with which it analyses competitions between constructions. All emergentist theories recognize the importance of embodied cognition, but they may differ in terms of how they see these effects operating in detail. To understand some of these contrasts, it is helpful to survey some of the most important emergentist mechanisms that have been proposed.

1. Generalization. Many emergentist theories emphasize the basic cognitive mechanism of generalization, often pointing to its basis in neuronal connectivity and spreading activation. Generalization plays a major role as a further support for theories of coercion (MacWhinney 1989), polysemy (Gries this volume), metaphor (Gibbs this volume), prototype application (Taylor this volume), constructions (Perfors et al. 2010), and learning (McDonald and MacWhinney 1991).
2. Error correction. Some learning theories emphasize the importance of corrective feedback, although this feedback can also involve failure to match self-imposed targets, as in the DIVA model of phonological learning (Guenther and Perkell 2003).
3. Self-organization. Mechanisms such as the self-organizing feature map (Kohonen 2001) provide alternatives to mechanisms based on error propagation. An important assumption of these models is that the brain prefers to establish connections between local units, rather than between distant units (Jacobs and Jordan 1992).
4. Structure mapping. Theories of metaphor, metonymy, and analogy in Cognitive Linguistics often assume some method of mapping from the structure of a source domain to a target domain (Gentner and Markman 1997). Mechanisms of this type can also be used to account for convergence between cognitive systems (Goldstone et al. 2004).
5. Embodied representations. The representations and schemata used in Cognitive Linguistics align well with neurolinguistic theories of body image (Knoblich 2008), embodied perspective-taking (MacWhinney 2008c), empathy (Meltzoff and Decety 2003), situated spatial processing (Coventry this volume), and motion processing (Filipović this volume). For further discussion of embodiment, see Bergen (this volume) and Speed et al. (this volume).
6. Item-based patterns. The theory of item-based patterns (MacWhinney 1975, 1982; Tomasello 2000) provides a solid underpinning for Construction Grammar (Goldberg 2006), as well as a systematic answer to the logical problem of language acquisition (MacWhinney 2004).
7. Composition. All syntactic theories must deal with the ways in which words cluster into phrases. Emergentist models of comprehension such as O'Grady (2005) show

how this can be done in an incremental fashion. In this area, the emphasis in UG Minimalism on the Merge process (Chomsky 2007) is compatible with emergentist accounts.
8. Conversational emergence. Linguistic structures adapt to frequent conversational patterns. For example, Du Bois (1987) has argued that ergative marking emerges from the tendency to delete the actor in transitive sentences, because it is already given or known.
9. Perceptual recording. Studies of infant auditory perception have revealed that, even in the first few months, infants apply general-purpose mechanisms to record and learn sequential patterns from both visual and auditory input (Thiessen and Erickson 2014).
10. Imitation. Human children display a strong propensity to imitate gestures (Meltzoff and Decety 2003), actions (Ratner and Bruner 1978), and vocal productions (Whitehurst and Vasta 1975). Imitation in both children and adults is the fundamental mechanism postulated by usage-based linguistics.
11. Plasticity. Children with early left focal lesions are able to recover language function by reorganizing language to the right hemisphere. This plasticity in development is a general mechanism that supports a wide variety of emergent responses to injury or sensory disability (MacWhinney et al. 2000).
12. Physical structures. Phonologists have shown that the shape of the vocal mechanism has a wide-ranging impact on phonological processes (Ohala 1974). Rather than stipulating phonological rules or constraints (Bernhardt and Stemberger 1998), we can view them as emergent responses to these underlying pressures.

This is just a sampling of the many mechanisms and pressures that shape the emergence of language. Understanding how these mechanisms interact to produce language structures is the major task facing emergentist approaches to language.

4. Methods

The growth of emergentist approaches to language has depended heavily on the introduction of new scientific methods and the improvement of old methods through technological advances. In particular, we can point to advances in these six methodologies:

1. Corpora. The development of usage-based linguistics has relied heavily on the creation of web-accessible corpora of language interactions, such as those distributed through the CHILDES (Child Language Data Exchange System at http://childes.talkbank.org), TalkBank (http://talkbank.org), and LDC (Linguistic Data Consortium at http://www.ldc.upenn.edu) systems. These databases include transcripts of learners' written productions, as well as spoken productions linked to audio and/or video. As these databases grow, we are developing increasingly powerful analytic and computational linguistic methods, including automatic part of speech tagging (Parisse and Le Normand 2000), dependency parsing (Sagae et al. 2007), lexical diversity analysis (Malvern et al. 2004), and other analytic routines (MacWhinney 2008b).
2. Multimedia Analysis. The construction of an emergentist account of language usage also requires careful attention to gestural and proxemic aspects of conversational

interactions (Goldman et al. 2007). The last few years have seen a rapid proliferation of technology for linking transcripts to video and analysing these transcripts for conversational and linguistic structures (MacWhinney 2007). Longitudinal video corpora are particularly useful for studying the meshing of competing motivations across timeframes.
3. Neural Network Modelling. Neural network modelling has allowed researchers to examine how complex systems can emerge from the processing of input patterns. Increasingly, these systems are linked to benchmark data sets that can be used to compare and test alternative emergentist models (MacWhinney 2010)
4. Neuroimaging. Before the recent period, our understanding of neurolinguistics was dependent primarily on data obtained from brain lesions that produced aphasia. This type of data led researchers to focus on localizing language in specific modules (MacWhinney and Li 2008). However, with the advent of fine-grained localization through fMRI imaging, researchers have been able to formulate emergentist accounts of neural functioning based on the dynamic interactions of functional neural circuits. In addition, it has been possible to use ERP methodology to study competition between languages in second language and bilingual processing (Tolentino and Tokowicz 2011).
5. Neuroscience. Advances in neuroscience have also begun to extend our understanding of cognitive function down to the level of individual cells and local cell assemblies. Although this level of detail is not yet available for imaging methods such as fMRI, ERP, or MEG, we are learning a great deal from the study of single cell recordings in animals (Rizzolatti et al. 1996) and humans undergoing surgery for epilepsy (Bookheimer 2007). This work has emphasized the ways in which the brain encodes a full map of the body, thereby providing support for the theory of embodied cognition (Klatzky et al. 2008).
6. In vivo learning. Until very recently, it has been difficult to study the learning of second languages in realistic contexts. However, we can now use web-based methods (http://talkbank.org/SLA) to study students' learning of second languages on a trial-by-trial basis as they engage in exercises over the web, providing further tests and elaborations of emergentist theories.

5. Ten core issues

Over the last three decades, the dialog between Emergentism and UG has revolved around ten core issues.
1. What is Language? UG focuses its attention on the recursive application of rules in the modules of the syntactic component. This emphasis leaves large areas of lexicon, phonology, dialog, meaning, and interpretation outside of the domain of the language faculty. In contrast, Emergentism treats all of the components of human language, including those controlling communication, as parts of an interlocking, unified system.
2. E-Language vs I-Language. UG bases limits linguistic inquiry to the study of the internalized I-Language of the ideal speaker-hearer. Emergentism views language as

arising dynamically from the ways in which speakers reach conceptual consensus (Goldstone et al. 2004; Wittgenstein 1953).
3. The Uniqueness of Recursion. UG views recursion as the crucial defining feature of human language (Hauser et al. 2002). Emergentism views recursion as emerging in contrasting linguistic structures from the combined activities of memory, lexicon, discourse, and role activation (MacWhinney 2009).
4. Rules vs. Cues. Emergentism holds that linguistic structures are not the deterministic rules of UG, but cue-based patterns that arise from usage, generalization, and self-organization (MacWhinney, Malchukov, and Moravcsik 2014).
5. Evolution. UG holds that language evolved recently as a way of supporting more elaborate cognition. Emergentism views language as deriving from a gradual adaptation of the human species to the niche of upright posture, communication in large social groups, and support for late infant maturation (MacWhinney 2008a).
6. Genetics. UG accounts seek to link the supposed recent emergence of language to specific genetic changes (Fisher and Scharff 2009) in the last 70,000 years. Emergentism views language as grounded on a wide-ranging set of genetic adaptations across millions of years.
7. Speech is special. Generative theory has often been associated with the idea that, "speech is special." Emergentist approaches to speech and phonological development emphasize the role of physiological mechanisms in controlling articulation (Oller 2000). They also view auditory learning as governed by basic aspects of the auditory system and temporal processing constraints (Holt and Lotto 2010).
8. Critical Periods. Many UG formulations hold that there is an expiration date on the Special Gift underlying language learning and use (Lenneberg 1967). Emergentist accounts attribute the gradual decline in language learning abilities to loss of plasticity through entrenchment of the first language, parasitic transfer of first language abilities, and social isolation (MacWhinney 2012).
9. Modularity. UG emphasizes the encapsulated, modular composition of grammar (Fodor 1983). Emergentist accounts emphasize interactivity between permeable, emergent modules (McClelland et al. 2006).
10. Poverty of the stimulus. UG holds that there is insufficient information in the input to the language learner to properly determine the shape of the native language (Piattelli-Palmarini 1980). As a result, language learning is guided by a rich set of innate hypotheses regarding the shape of Universal Grammar. Emergentist accounts emphasize the richness of the input to the learner and the role of item-based learning strategies in achieving effective learning of complex structures (MacWhinney 2005b).

6. Conclusion

This dialog between Emergentism and UG has stimulated three decades of useful empirical and theoretical work. However, Emergentism must now move beyond the confines of this debate. Because Emergentism views language as a meshing of inputs from at least seven structural levels (MacWhinney 2014), these accounts will necessarily be more complex. Fortunately, we can use powerful new methods for qualitative and quantitative analysis of longitudinal multimedia corpora to track the effects of inputs from the many contrasting processes and inputs that shape the totality of human language. Models as diverse as variable rule analysis, dynamic systems theory, and neural networks can be translated into a core language (Farmer 1990) of cue strength and interactive activation. We will need to move ahead on six fronts simultaneously: (1) neurolinguistics and neuroimaging, (2) longitudinal collection of naturalistic and structured corpora, (3) linkage of typology and diachrony to synchronic processes, (4) psycholinguistic experimentation, (5) computational linguistic analysis, and (6) computational modelling. Finally, we must work to interpret the results from each of these six efforts in the context of advances from the other five. We definitely have our work cut out for us.

7. References

Andersen, Peter, Claus Emmeche, Niels Finnemann and Peder Christiansen (eds.)
    2000   *Downward causation: Minds, Bodies, and Matter.* Aarhus: Aarhus University Press.

Arbib, Michael
    2010   *Beyond the Mirror: Evolving Language and our Social Selves.* New York: Oxford University Press.

Ariel, Mira
    2014   Or-constructions: monosemy versus polysemy. In: B. MacWhinney, A. Malchukov and E. Moravcsik (eds.), *Competing Motivations in Grammar and Usage* 333–347. New York: Oxford University Press.

Bates, Elizabeth and Judith Goodman
    1999   On the emergence of grammar from the lexicon. In: B. MacWhinney (ed.), *The Emergence of Language,* 29–80. Mahwah: Lawrence Erlbaum Associates.

Bates, Elizabeth and Brian MacWhinney
    1982   Functionalist approaches to grammar. In: E. Wanner and L. Gleitman (eds.), *Language Acquisition: The State of the Art,* 173–218. New York: Cambridge University Press.

Bergen, Benjamin
    this volume   1. Embodiment. Berlin/Boston: De Gruyter Mouton.

Bernhardt, Barbara and Joseph Stemberger
    1998   *Handbook of Phonological Development from the Perspective of Constraint-based Nonlinear Phonology.* San Diego: Academic Press.

Bookheimer, Susan
    2007   Pre-surgical language mapping with functional magnetic resonance imaging. *Neuropsychological Review* 17, 145–155.

Bresnan, Joan, Shipra Dingare and Christopher Manning
    2001   Soft constraints mirror hard constraints: Voice and person in English and Lummi. Paper presented at the LFG01, Hong Kong.

Bybee, Joan
    2010   *Language, Usage, and Cognition.* New York: Cambridge University Press.

Bybee, Joan and Paul Hopper
    2001   *Frequency and the Emergence of Linguistic Structure.* Amsterdam: John Benjamins.

Campbell, Donald
    1960   Blind variation and selective retention in creative thought as in other knowledge processes. *Psychological Review* 67, 380–400.

Campbell, Neil A., Jane B. Reece and Larry G. Mitchell
    1999   *Biology* Fifth Edition. Menlo Park: Addison Wesley.

Chomsky, Noam
1963   Formal properties of grammars. In: R. Bush, R. Luce and E. Galanter (eds.), *Handbook of Mathematical Psychology*, Volume 2. New York: Wiley.
Chomsky, Noam
1976   Conditions on rules of grammar. *Linguistic Analysis* 2: 163–210.
Chomsky, Noam
2007   Approaching UG from below. In: U. Sauerland and M. Gaertner (eds.), *Interfaces + Recursion = Language?*, 1–30. New York: Mouton de Gruyter.
Chomsky, Noam
2010   Some simple evo devo theses: How true might they be for language. In: R. Larson, V. Déprez and H. Yamakido (eds.), *The Evolution of Language: Biolinguistic Perspectives*, 45–62. Cambridge: Cambridge University Press.
Coventry, Kenny
this volume   23. Space. Berlin/Boston: De Gruyter Mouton
Darwin, Charles
1859   *On the Origin of Species*. London: John Murray.
Daselaar, Sander, Dick Veltman and Menno Witter
2004   Common pathway in the medial temporal lobe for storage and recovery of words as revealed by event-related functional MRI. *Hippocampus* 14: 163–169.
Davis, Barbara L., and Peter F. MacNeilage
(1995)   The articulatory basis of babbling. *Journal of Speech and Hearing Research* 38: 1199–1211.
Du Bois, John
1987   The discourse basis of ergativity. *Language*, 63: 805–856.
Edelman, Gerald
1987   *Neural Darwinism: The Theory of Neuronal Group Selection*. New York: Basic Books.
Farmer, J. Doyne
1990   A Rosetta Stone for connectionism. *Physica* 42: 153–187.
Fauconnier, Gilles and Mark Turner
1996   Blending as a central process of grammar. In: A. Goldberg (ed.), *Conceptual Structure, Discourse, and Language*, 113–130. Stanford: CSLI.
Feldman, Jerome
2006   *From Molecule to Metaphor: A Neural Theory of Language*. Cambridge: MIT Press.
Filipović, Luna
this volume   25. Motion. Berlin/Boston: De Gruyter Mouton
Fisher, Simon and Constance Scharff
2009   FOXP2 as a molecular window into speech and language. *Trends in Genetics* 25: 166–177.
Francis, Elaine and Laura Michaelis
2014   Why move? How weight and discourse factors combine to predict relative clause extraposition in English. In: B. MacWhinney, A. Malchukov and E. Moravcsik (eds.), *Competing Motivations in Grammar and Usage* 70–87. New York: Oxford University Press.
Friedman, Milton
1953   *Essays in Positive Economics*. Chicago: University of Chicago Press.
Gentner, D. and A. Markman
1997   Structure mapping in analogy and similarity. *American Psychologist* 52: 45–56.
Gibbs Jr., Raymond W.
this volume   8. Metaphor. Berlin/Boston: De Gruyter Mouton
Givón, T.
1979   *On Understanding Grammar*. New York: Academic Press.

Goldberg, Adele
    2006   *Constructions at Work: The Nature of Generalization in Language.* Oxford: Oxford University Press.
Goldman, Ricki, Roy Pea, Brigid Barron and Sharon Derry (eds.)
    2007   *Video Research in the Learning Sciences.* Mahwah: Lawrence Erlbaum Associates.
Goldstone, Robert, Ying Feng and Brian Rogosky
    2004   Connecting concepts to each other and the world. In: Rolf Zwaan and Diane Pecher (eds.), *The Grounding of Cognition: The Role of Perception and Action in Memory, Language, and Thinking.* Cambridge: Cambridge University Press.
Goodwin, Charles
    2000   Gesture, aphasia, and interaction. In: D. McNeill (ed.), *Language and Gesture*, 84–98. Cambridge: Cambridge University Press.
Goodwin, Charles
    2002   Time in action. *Current Anthropology* 43: 19–35.
Gries, Stefan Th.
    this volume   22. Polysemy. Berlin/Boston: De Gruyter Mouton
Guenther, Frank and Joseph Perkell
    2003   A neural model of speech production and its application to studies of the role of auditory feedback in speech. In: B. Maasen, R. D. Kent, H. Peters, P. van Lieshout and W. Hulstijn (eds.), *Speech Motor Control in Normal and Disordered Speech,* 29–50. Oxford: Oxford University Press.
Haiman, John
    2014   On competing motives for repetition. In: B. MacWhinney, A. Malchukov and E. Moravcsik (eds.), *Competing Motivations in Grammar and Usage* 348–363. New York: Oxford University Press.
Halliday, Michael and Christian Matthiessen
    2004   *An Introduction to Functional Grammar.* 3rd revised edition. London: Hodder Arnold.
Hauser, M., Noam Chomsky and T. Fitch
    2002   The faculty of language: What is it, who has it, and how did it evolve? *Science* 298: 1569–1579.
Helmbrecht, Johannes
    2013   Politeness distinctions in personal pronouns – a case study of competing motivations. In: B. MacWhinney, A. Malchukov and E. Moravcsik (eds.), *Competing Motivations in Grammar and Usage.* New York: Oxford University Press.
Holt, Lori, and Andrew Lotto
    (2010)   Speech perception as categorization. *Perception and Psychophysics* 72(5): 1218–1227.
Hruschka, Daniel, Morten Christiansen, Richard Blythe, William Croft, Paul Heggarty, Salikoko Mufwene, Janet B. Pierrehumbert and Shana Poplack
    2009   Building social cognitive models of language change. *Trends in Cognitive Sciences* 13: 464–469.
Jacobs, Robert and Michael Jordan
    1992   Computational consequences of a bias toward short connections. *Journal of Cognitive Neuroscience* 4: 323–336.
Kager, René
    1999   *Optimality Theory.* New York: Cambridge University Press.
Kaltenboeck, Gunther and Bernd Heine
    2014   Sentence grammar vs. thetical grammar: two competing domains. In: B. MacWhinney, A. Malchukov and E. Moravcsik (eds.), *Competing Motivations in Grammar and Usage,* 348–363. New York: Oxford University Press.
Kay, Paul
    1978   Variable rules, community grammar, and linguistic change. In: D. Sankoff (ed.), *Linguistic Variation: Models and Methods.* New York: Academic Press.

Kay, Paul and Charles Fillmore
  1999   Grammatical constructions and linguistic generalization: The "what's X doing Y?" construction. *Language* 75: 1–33.
Kemp, Charles, Amy Perfors and Joshua Tenenbaum
  2007   Learning overhypotheses with hierarchical Bayesian models. *Developmental Science* 10: 307–321.
Klatzky, Roberta, Brian MacWhinney and Marlene Behrmann (eds.)
  2008   *Embodiment, Ego-Space, and Action*. New York: Psychology Press.
Knoblich, Guenther
  2008   Bodily and motor contributions to action perception. In: R. Klatzky, B. MacWhinney and M. Behrmann (eds.), *Embodied Cognition*. Mahwah: Lawrence Erlbaum.
Koechlin, Etienne and Christopher Summerfield
  2007   An information theoretical approach to prefrontal executive function. *Trends in Cognitive Sciences* 11: 229–235.
Kohonen, Teuvo
  2001   *Self-organizing Maps* Third edition. Berlin: Springer.
Labov, William
  1972   *Sociolinguistic Patterns*. Philadelphia: University of Pennsylvania Press.
Lakoff, George and Mark Johnson
  1980   *Metaphors We Live By*. Chicago: Chicago University Press.
Langacker, Ronald
  1987   *Foundations of Cognitive Grammar:* Vol. 1: *Theory*. Stanford: Stanford University Press.
Lemke, Jay
  2000   Across the scales of time: Artifacts, activities, and meanings in ecosocial systems. *Mind, Culture, and Activity* 7: 273–290.
Lenneberg, Eric
  (1967) *Biological Foundations of Language*. New York: Wiley.
MacWhinney, Brian
  1975   Pragmatic patterns in child syntax. *Stanford Papers And Reports on Child Language Development* 10: 153–165.
MacWhinney, Brian
  1982   Basic syntactic processes. In: S. Kuczaj (ed.), *Language Acquisition:* Vol. 1. *Syntax and Semantics,* 73–136. Hillsdale: Lawrence Erlbaum.
MacWhinney, Brian
  1987   The Competition Model. In: B. MacWhinney (ed.), *Mechanisms of Language Acquisition,* 249–308. Hillsdale: Lawrence Erlbaum.
MacWhinney, Brian
  1989   Competition and lexical categorization. In: R. Corrigan, F. Eckman and M. Noonan (eds.), *Linguistic Categorization*, 195–242. Philadelphia: Benjamins.
MacWhinney, Brian
  1991   *The CHILDES Project: Tools for Analyzing Talk*. Hillsdale: Erlbaum.
MacWhinney, Brian
  2004   A multiple process solution to the logical problem of language acquisition. *Journal of Child Language* 31: 883–914.
MacWhinney, Brian
  2005a   The emergence of linguistic form in time. *Connection Science* 17: 191–211.
MacWhinney, Brian
  2005b   Item-based constructions and the logical problem. *Proceedings of the Workshop on Psychocomputational Models of Human Language Acquisition,* 46–54. Association for Computational Linguistics

MacWhinney, Brian
   2007   A transcript-video database for collaborative commentary in the Learning Sciences. In: R. Goldman, R. Pea, B. Barron and S. Derry (eds.), *Video Research in the Learning Sciences*, 537–546. Mahwah: Lawrence Erlbaum Associates.

MacWhinney, Brian
   2008a   Cognitive precursors to language. In: K. Oller and U. Griebel (eds.), *The Evolution of Communicative Flexibility*, 193–214. Cambridge: MIT Press.

MacWhinney, Brian
   2008b   Enriching CHILDES for morphosyntactic analysis. In: H. Behrens (ed.), *Trends in Corpus Research: Finding Structure in Data*, 165–198. Amsterdam: John Benjamins.

MacWhinney, Brian
   2008c   How mental models encode embodied linguistic perspectives. In: R. Klatzky, B. MacWhinney and M. Behrmann (eds.), *Embodiment, Ego-Space, and Action*, 369–410. Mahwah: Lawrence Erlbaum.

MacWhinney, Brian
   2009   The emergence of linguistic complexity. In: T. Givon and M. Shibatani (eds.), *Linguistic Complexity*, 405–432. New York: Benjamins.

MacWhinney, Brian
   2010   Computational models of child language learning. *Journal of Child Language* 37: 477–485.

MacWhinney, Brian
   2012   The logic of the Unified Model. In: S. Gass and A. Mackey (eds.), *The Routledge Handbook of Second Language Acquisition*, 211–227. New York: Routledge.

MacWhinney, Brian
   2014   Competition across time. In: B. MacWhinney, A. Malchukov and E. Moravcsik (eds.), *Competing Motivations in Grammar and Usage*. New York: Oxford University Press.

MacWhinney, Brian (ed.)
   1999   *The Emergence of Language*. Mahwah, NJ: Lawrence Erlbaum Associates.

MacWhinney, Brian, Elizabeth Bates and Reinhold Kliegl
   1984   Cue validity and sentence interpretation in English, German, and Italian. *Journal of Verbal Learning and Verbal Behavior* 23: 127–150.

MacWhinney, Brian, Heidi Feldman, Kelly Sacco and Raul Valdes-Perez
   2000   Online measures of basic language skills in children with early focal brain lesions. *Brain and Language* 71: 400–431.

MacWhinney, Brian and Ping Li
   2008   Neurolinguistic computational models. In: B. Stemmer and H. Whitaker (eds.), *Handbook of the Neuroscience of Language*, 229–236. Mahwah: Lawrence Erlbaum Associates.

MacWhinney, Brian, Andrej Malchukov, and Edith Moravcsik (eds.)
   2014   *Competing Motivations in Grammar and Usage*. New York: Oxford University Press.

Malvern, David, Brian Richards, Ngoni Chipere and Pilar Purán
   2004   *Lexical Diversity and Language Development*. New York: Palgrave Macmillan.

Massaro, Dominic
   1987   *Speech Perception by Ear and Eye*. Hillsdale: Lawrence Erlbaum.

Massaro, Dominic (ed.)
   1975   *Understanding Language: An Introduction-Processing Analysis of Speech Perception, Reading, and Psycholinguistics*. New York: Academic Press.

McClelland, James L., Bruce McNaughton and Randy O'Reilly
   1995   Why there are complementary learning systems in the hippocampus and neocortex: Insights from the successes and failures of connectionist models of learning and memory. *Psychological Review* 102: 419–457.

McClelland, James, Daniel Mirman, and Lori Holt
(2006) Are there interactive processes in speech perception? *Trends in Cognitive Sciences* 10: 363–369.
McDonald, Janet and Brian MacWhinney
1991 Levels of learning: A microdevelopmental study of concept formation. *Journal of Memory and Language* 30: 407–430.
Meltzoff, Andrew and Jean Decety
2003 What imitation tells us about social cognition: A rapprochement between developmental psychology and cognitive neuroscience. *Philosophical Transactions of the Royal Society of London B* 358: 491–500.
Menzel, Randolf
1999 Memory dynamics in the honeybee. *Journal of Comparative Physiology A* 185: 323–340.
Mesoudi, Alex, Andrew Whiten and Kevin Laland
2006 Towards a unified science of cultural evolution. *Behavioral and Brain Sciences* 29: 329–383.
O'Grady, William
2005 *Syntactic Carpentry*. Mahwah: Lawrence Erlbaum Associates.
Ohala, John
1974 Phonetic explanation in phonology. In: A. Bruck, R. Fox and M. La Galy (eds.), *Papers from the Parassession on Natural Phonology*, 251–274. Chicago: Chicago Linguistic Society.
Oller, D. Kimbrough
(2000) *The Emergence of the Speech Capacity*. Mahwah: Lawrence Erlbaum Associates.
Parisse, Christophe and Marie-Thérèse Le Normand
2000 Automatic disambiguation of the morphosyntax in spoken language corpora. *Behavior Research Methods, Instruments, and Computers* 32: 468–481.
Pecher, Diane and Rolf Zwaan (eds.)
2005 *Grounding Cognition*. Cambridge: Cambridge University Press.
Perfors, Amy, Joshua Tenenbaum and Elizabeth Wonnacott
2010 Variability, negative evidence, and the acquisition of verb argument constructions. *Journal of Child Language* 37: 607–642.
Poplack, Shana and Rena Cacoullos
2014 A variationist paradigm for linguistic emergence. In: B. MacWhinney and W. O'Grady (eds.), *Handbook of Language Emergence*. New York: Wiley.
Pulvermüller, Friedemann
2003 *The Neuroscience of Language*. Cambridge: Cambridge University Press.
Ratner, Nancy and Jerome Bruner
1978 Games, social exchange and the acquisition of language. *Journal of Child Language* 5: 391–401.
Rizzolatti, Giacomo, Luciano Fadiga, Vittorio Gallese and Leonardi Fogassi
(1996) Premotor cortex and the recognition of motor actions. *Cognitive Brain Research* 3: 131–141.
Rumelhart, David and James McClelland
1986 *Parallel Distributed Processing*. Cambridge: MIT Press.
Sagae, Kenji, Eric Davis, Alon Lavie, Brian MacWhinney and Shuly Wintner
2007 High-accuracy annotation and parsing of CHILDES transcripts *Proceedings of the 45th Meeting of the Association for Computational Linguistics*, 1044–1050. Prague: ACL.
Schütz-Bosbach, Simone and Wolfgang Prinz
2007 Perceptual resonance: Action-induced modulation of perception. *Trends in Cognitive Sciences* 11: 349–355.

Sfard, Anna and Kay McClain
    2002   Special Issue: Analyzing tools: Perspective on the role of designed artifacts in mathematics learning. *Journal of the Learning Sciences* 11: 153–388.

Silverstein, Michael
    1976   Shifters, linguistic categories and cultural description. In: K. H. Basso and H. A. Selby (eds.), *Meaning in Anthropology* 11–55. Albuquerque: University of New Mexico Press.

Simon, Herbert
    1962   The architecture of complexity. *Proceedings of the American Philosophical Society* 106: 467–482.

Smith, Carlota
    1991   *The Parameter of Aspect*. Dordrecht: Kluwer.

Speed, Laura, David P. Vinson and Gabriella Vigliocco
    this volume   9. Representing meaning. Berlin/Boston: De Gruyter Mouton

Thelen, Esther and Linda Smith
    1994   *A Dynamic Systems Approach to the Development of Cognition and Action*. Cambridge: MIT Press.

Thiessen, Erik and Lucy Erickson
    2014   Perceptual development and statistical learning. In: B. MacWhinney and W. O'Grady (eds.), *Handbook of Language Emergence*. New York: Wiley.

Tolentino, Leida and Natasha Tokowicz
    2011   Across languages, space, and time: A review of the role of cross-language similarity in L2 (morpho)syntactic processing as revealed by fMRI and ERP. *Studies in Second Language Acquisition* 33: 1–34.

Tomasello, Michael
    2000   The item-based nature of children's early syntactic development. *Trends in Cognitive Sciences* 4: 156–163.

Toscano, Joseph C. and Bob McMurray
    2010   Cue integration with categories: Weighting acoustic cues in speech using unsupervised learning and distributional statistics. *Cognitive Science* 34: 434–464.

Taylor, John R.
    this volume   27. Prototype effects in grammar. Berlin/Boston: De Gruyter Mouton.

Verspoor, Marjolijn, Kees de Bot and Wander Lowie
    2011   *A Dynamic Approach to Second Language Development*. New York: John Benjamins.

Whitehurst, G. and R. Vasta
    1975   Is language acquired through imitation? *Journal of Psycholinguistic Research* 4: 37–59.

Wittenberg, Gayle, Megan Sullivan and Joe Tsien
    2002   Synaptic reentry reinforcement based network model for long-term memory consolidation. *Hippocampus* 12: 637–647.

Wittgenstein, Ludwig
    1953   *Philosophical Investigations*. Oxford: Blackwell.

Brian MacWhinney, Carnegie Mellon University (USA)

Indexes

Authors index

A

Albright, Adam 102
Ariel, Mira 404, 597, 611, 639, 691
Aristotle 215, 434–435, 596
Atkins, Beryl T. 220–221, 283–284, 479

B

Baayen, Harald 3, 57, 59, 63, 65–67, 89, 92–93, 103, 105–106, 108, 110, 112–113, 115–116, 261, 304, 327, 377, 379
Barcelona, Antonio 3, 18, 136, 144n, 145–148, 151–158, 172, 178n, 282- 283, 352, 474, 617
Barnden, John 147n, 174
Barsalou, Lawrence W. 5, 21, 23, 82, 190, 193–195, 197, 199, 200, 204, 445, 553, 566
Bates, Elizabeth 33, 43, 390, 393–394, 401, 651, 669, 691, 695
Bencini, Giulia M. L. 4, 62, 465, 580, 581, 583, 586
Bergen, Benjamin 1, 3, 4, 6, 18, 21, 22–23, 137, 139, 181–182, 190, 191, 193, 195, 287, 422, 455, 457, 491, 523, 553, 618, 669, 696
Bergmann, Till 3, 134, 139, 181, 530, 555
Berko, Jean 406
Berthele, Raphael 375–376, 532–533
Bierwiaczonek, Bogusław 153–154
Bock, Kathryn 32, 36, 38–39, 43–44, 307, 583–584
Bod, Rens 108, 679
Boroditsky, Lera 19, 82, 179–182, 191, 197, 373, 491, 515, 522–523, 533, 537, 551
Bowerman, Melissa 6, 460, 464, 466, 492, 503, 534, 587
Braine, Martin 61–62, 304–306
Brdar, Mario 153, 155–157
Brooks, Patricia 61–62, 80, 391, 397, 587, 655, 660
Brown, Cecil H. 350, 459, 463, 534–535
Bybee, Joan 24, 54–55, 60–61, 253, 257, 262–263, 297–298, 302, 315–316, 347–348, 353–354, 356–357, 377, 399–400, 412, 418–419, 594n, 597, 611, 627, 636–639, 671, 679–681, 693, 695

C

Caldwell-Harris, Catherine 3, 16, 54, 56–57, 63, 200, 285, 315, 348, 378, 411, 589, 594n, 645, 680
Carlson, Laura 422, 497
Casasanto, Daniel 177, 491, 515, 522–523
Casenhiser, Devin M. 3, 62, 465, 587–589
Chafe, Wallace 33, 40
Chilton, Paul 323, 327–329, 335–336
Chipere, Ngoni 654, 660
Chomsky, Noam 14, 300, 394, 690, 697
Clark, Eve V. 36, 390, 393, 401, 492, 499, 570, 651
Clark, Herbert H. 237, 239, 244–246, 499, 513, 551, 555
Coulson, Seana 216, 282, 483
Coventry, Kenny R. 3, 460, 491, 493, 495, 497–502, 698
Croft, Bill (William) 61, 145–146, 150, 152, 281, 283, 297–299, 302, 309n, 309–311, 326–327, 335, 351, 373–374, 395, 421, 435–436, 453, 457–458, 476–477, 529, 532, 571, 579, 611, 618–619, 624–630, 637–638, 640–643, 665, 682
Cruse, Alan 61, 147, 280–281, 283, 299, 326–327, 335, 351, 421, 473, 641, 643
Cutler, Anne 57, 263

D

Dąbrowska, Ewa 3, 4, 6, 16, 104, 108, 114–115, 305, 349, 379, 395, 400, 413, 651–663
Daelemans, Walter 223
Dancygier, Barbara 63–64, 66, 107–108
Darwin, Charles 679, 690
Dasher, Richard 157, 639
Deignan, Alice 171, 568
Descartes, René 435
Diessel, Holger 3, 53, 55, 296–298, 302, 304, 307–309, 312, 314–315, 347, 353, 394, 413, 499, 501, 503, 580
Dirven, René 146–148, 151, 155, 158–159, 280, 282–284, 323n, 324, 324n, 326n, 326–327, 335, 350, 357, 371, 373, 376

Divjak, Dagmar   3, 5, 16, 55–56, 59, 63, 67, 200, 281, 285, 315, 348, 378, 411, 423, 479, 567, 589, 594n, 630, 638, 661, 680
Donegan, Patrica   254n, 257–258, 264, 266, 268
Du Mon, Denies   3
Ducrot, Oswald   236

E

Ellis, Nick. C   16, 55, 412, 417–418, 420, 422–423
Elman, Jeff   57–58, 62, 64–65, 67, 104, 286, 302, 355, 372, 375, 416, 420, 479n, 622, 626–627, 680, 693
Evans, Nicholas   258, 453–454, 456, 461–463, 466
Evans, Vyvyan   3, 18, 53, 82, 132, 193, 197, 279–280, 329, 336, 446, 462, 476, 477, 491, 493, 495, 510–512, 515, 517–522
Evert, Stefan   58

F

Fauconnier, Gilles   135, 149, 153, 170–171, 212, 214–216, 218–219, 221–225, 282, 335, 436, 519, 621, 695
Fein, Ofer   597
Feldman, Jerome   21, 140, 172, 422, 553, 694–695
Filipović, Luna   3, 192, 193, 202, 457, 491, 528, 529n, 531–533, 535–538
Fillmore, Charles   82, 147, 211, 220–221, 225, 283–284, 298, 301, 351, 414, 473, 579–580, 597, 611, 693
Fischer, Olga   37, 158, 436, 638–639
Fowler, Carol   324, 334, 681

G

Galton, Anthony   516, 518
Gavins, Joanna   436, 442–443
Geeraerts, Dirk   3, 5–6, 104, 146, 148, 151n, 151–152, 154, 156, 200, 273–274, 279–280, 283–287, 312, 347, 350–351, 368, 370, 372–376, 380, 460, 473, 480, 562, 664
Gentner, Derdre   136, 181, 495, 534, 589, 696
Gibbs, Raymond G.   3–4, 6, 10, 18–19, 22, 136, 139, 144, 153, 157–158, 168, 174–175, 177, 180–183, 191, 198, 282, 287, 324, 327, 352, 444–445, 464, 474, 479–480, 491, 510, 530, 553, 555, 595–598, 610, 617, 696
Giora, Rachel   3, 6, 182, 595–602, 604, 606–608, 610–611
Givoni, Shir   595, 598, 611
Glenberg, Arthur M.   21–22, 25, 197, 200, 203, 553, 581
Goatly, Andrew   170, 175, 327
Goldberg, Adele. E.   3–4, 14–15, 62, 154, 170, 223–224, 297–299, 302, 307, 313, 350, 354, 359, 394, 412, 419–421, 475–476, 574, 580–583, 586–589, 611, 695–696
Goossens, Louis   153, 280
Goswami, Usha   267
Gries, Stefan Th.   3, 5, 16, 18, 55, 59, 67, 127, 158, 170–171, 192, 200, 287, 298, 307, 312–313,350–352, 359, 375, 380, 411–412, 421, 423, 440, 460, 479n 479, 482, 495, 567, 573–574, 589, 617, 696

H

Hart, Christopher   3, 326–327, 329, 331, 338, 660–661
Haspelmath, Martin   461–462, 618,636–638
Heine, Bernd   150, 157, 347, 353, 356, 327, 635, 639–640, 691
Herman, David   441, 443
Hilpert, Martin   3, 5, 55, 154, 157, 280, 297–298, 350, 359, 361, 568, 640–641
Hopper, Paul   55, 157, 226, 296, 347, 349, 351, 353–354, 412, 418, 636, 638–639, 695
Huumo, Tuomas   3, 491, 530n, 531–533, 535–536

I

Ibarretxe-Antuñano, Iraide   3, 5, 153, 356, 479, 619–621, 626–631

J

Janda, Laura   671, 678
Janzen, Terry   10, 12, 17, 19–21, 82, 135, 140, 144–145, 154, 168n, 168, 170, 178, 191, 193, 197, 281–282, 284, 323–324, 327, 329–330, 422, 434, 436, 442, 454, 457, 460, 491–492, 510–511, 513–516, 521–522, 527, 551, 555–5565, 582, 589, 695
Johnson, Mark   55, 59
Jurafsky, Dan   41, 42

K

Kaiser, Elsi   591
Kako, Edward   373, 457, 461, 463–464, 468, 506
Koptjevskaja-Tamm, Maria   19, 126, 144, 146, 148–151, 154–155, 172, 178n, 282, 372, 460
Kövecses, Zoltán   3, 6, 36, 53, 307, 351, 380, 403–404, 416, 669
Krajewski, Grzegorz   3, 263, 289, 327, 353, 360, 369, 372, 376, 379–380, 382
Kristiansen, Gitte   1–3, 6, 12, 15, 18–21, 76, 82, 135–136, 138, 140, 143–147, 153–154, 157, 168, 170–172, 176, 191, 193, 197, 253, 260, 261, 276, 281, 284–285, 326–327, 329–330, 371, 375, 425, 437, 439, 445, 458, 460, 463, 476–479, 494–495, 513–514, 516–519, 526–527, 557, 560–562, 564, 573, 575, 588, 627, 690, 706

L

Lakoff, George   1–4, 15, 32–33, 36, 60–61, 104, 106–108, 121–125, 127, 129–130, 133–134, 137–138, 143, 146, 148, 150–154, 156–157, 170, 192, 225, 240, 242, 253, 257, 263, 276, 288, 299, 301, 303, 305, 309, 318, 326, 329–330, 332, 336–338, 341–342, 349, 352, 357, 371, 397, 424, 447, 449, 463, 478, 494, 515, 557, 562, 573, 579, 588, 627, 629, 631–633, 637–639, 648–649, 651, 653–656, 687–680, 689–691, 693, 706–707
Landauer, Thomas   190–202
Langacker, Ronald   1–4, 15, 32–33, 36, 60–61, 104, 106–108, 121–125, 127, 129, 130, 133–134, 137–138, 143, 146, 148, 150, 152–154, 156–157, 170, 192, 225, 240, 242, 253, 256, 262, 273, 285, 296, 298, 300, 302, 306, 315, 323, 326–327, 329, 333–335, 338–339, 346, 349, 354, 368, 390, 394, 421, 444, 446, 460, 475, 491, 521, 548, 553, 564, 570, 579, 617, 619, 621–623, 626–629, 637–638, 640, 642–645, 676–680, 682, 695–696
Lehmann, Christian   6, 233, 249, 259, 350, 353, 376, 456, 458, 463, 465–470, 499, 504, 506, 532, 606
Levinson, Stephen C.   556, 681–682, 688–690
Liddell, Scott   6, 53, 62, 114, 307–309, 393, 398, 404, 416, 419, 556
Lieven, Elena V. M.   271
London, Justin   200, 204, 441, 445–446
Louwerse, Max M.   3, 33, 38, 53, 62, 184, 404, 424, 691, 702, 704, 706–710

M

MacWhinney, Brian   461–463, 465–467, 507
Majid, Asifa   3, 134, 139, 181, 237, 477, 483, 536, 556–562, 564
Matlock, Teenie   134, 536, 539, 546, 556, 557
Matsumoto, Yo   3, 6, 16, 36, 53, 56, 66, 103, 106, 114, 307, 351, 380, 393–394, 398–399, 403–405, 416, 669
Matthews, Danielle   56–57, 63–64, 193, 403, 705–707, 710
McClelland, James   81, 193, 278, 423, 495
Mervis, Carolyn B.   190, 195–199
Meteyard, Lotte   5, 173, 177, 192, 203, 262, 290, 483, 485, 573
Murphy, Gregory   38, 41–45, 127, 330
Myachykov, Andriy   417–418, 420
Myles, Florence   598

N

Naigles, Letitia   3, 94, 227, 253, 258–261, 270–271
Nathan, Geoff S.   5, 80, 85, 422
Nosofsky, Robert   707

O

O'Grady, William   126, 146, 153–155, 156–157, 160, 170, 285–286, 478

P

Panther, Klaus-Uwe   253, 257, 261, 377
Pierrehumbert, Janet   299, 401, 597–598
Pinker, Steven   77, 106, 107
Port, Robert   35, 37, 39, 45, 80, 278, 423, 571, 574, 577
Posner, Michael   126, 143–144, 146–156, 170, 172, 178, 285, 338, 560, 564

R

Radden, Günter   3, 5, 77, 81–82, 85, 87–88, 90–92, 103, 106–110, 113–114, 116, 120, 181, 262, 330, 380, 518, 560–561, 572, 598
Ramscar, Michael   90, 92, 109–110, 112–114, 423–424

Rescorla, Robert   65, 153, 197, 213, 234, 350, 352, 364, 378, 414, 479–480, 482, 486, 499, 575, 606, 608, 620
Rice, Sally   5, 113–114, 81–82, 91, 193, 261, 277–279, 290, 352, 374, 423, 457, 476, 495, 572–576, 585
Rosch, Eleanor   146. 151–153, 155–157, 170, 286
Ruiz de Mendoza, Francisco   575

S

Sandra, Dominiek   53, 59, 61, 67, 277, 283, 288, 417, 424, 441, 482
Schmid, Hans-Jörg   171, 176, 286, 328, 378, 439, 444–445
Semino, Elena   692
Simon, Herbert   28, 376, 377, 514, 523–524, 526, 533
Sinha, Chris   106
Skousen, Royal   114, 304, 403–404, 425, 468, 495, 536, 538–541, 543, 562
Slobin, Dan I.   3, 25
Speed, Laura   289, 375, 378, 482
Speelman, Dirk   234, 246–247, 607
Sperber, Dan   59, 158, 169, 171, 299, 312–313, 380, 440, 533, 573, 574
Stafanowitsch, Anatol   257–258, 260, 263, 265, 267, 270–271
Stampe, David   158, 166, 174–175, 224, 228, 285, 439, 445
Steen, Gerard   326, 338, 439, 442, 444–445, 447, 449
Stockwell, Peter   667–669
Street, James   20, 170, 219, 222–223, 225, 227, 229–230, 237, 277, 283, 342, 458, 459–460, 464, 524, 563, 636–637, 686
Sweetser, Eve   2–3, 6, 32–33, 121, 126, 134, 139, 143, 225, 296, 323, 326, 329–330, 333, 339, 368, 422, 457, 491, 494, 509, 512–513, 516–517, 528–534, 547–548, 552, 619, 622, 624–625

T

Talmy, Leonard   3, 76, 139, 146, 153, 224, 273, 279, 280, 349, 421, 454, 473, 476, 482, 564, 567, 570–573, 617, 696

Taylor, John R.   190, 200–203, 479
Thomas L. Griffiths   6, 16–17, 92, 114, 120, 225, 233–234, 236, 238–242, 247, 297–298, 304–309, 322, 347, 377, 390–392, 397, 413, 416, 419, 585, 587, 637, 661–662, 664, 696
Tomasello, Michael   3, 32–34, 38–39, 41–42, 44, 127, 139, 143, 327
Tomlin, Russell   157, 167, 297, 347, 350–351, 353–355, 627, 634, 636, 638–641, 643–644
Traugott, Elizabeth C.   297–298, 350, 376, 411, 636, 640–63
Trousdale, Graeme   436, 441
Tsur, Reuven   547, 620
Turner, Mark   3, 32, 104, 120, 135, 145–147, 153, 170, 211, 214–216, 218–219, 221–225, 227–228, 282, 436, 519, 548, 695
Tyler, Andrea   18, 194, 279, 410, 476–477, 493, 495, 566, 579

V

van der Auwera, Johan   3, 353, 366, 635–636
Van Gelderen, Elly   637
Van Olmen, Daniël   3
Verhagen, Arie   3–4, 6, 236–237, 247, 327n, 350, 360–361, 366, 373–374
Viberg, Åke   456, 461
Vigliocco, Gabriella   3, 190–199, 202, 204
Vinson, David P.   1, 3, 194

W

Werth, Paul   335, 443
Wierzbicka, Anna   280, 455, 457–458, 462
Wilcox, Phyllis   157, 669, 671–676, 678, 680
Wilcox, Sherman   3, 23, 157, 669, 671–676, 678, 680
Wilkins, David P.   456–458, 460–464
Wulff, Stefanie   3, 411–4122, 421, 589

Z

Zlatev, Jordan   238, 280, 373, 389, 553–554

Subject index

A

abstract motion   548n, 552n
abstraction   1, 64, 80–81, 85, 88, 90, 100–101, 103–105, 107–111, 113–116, 122, 135–137, 196–197, 257, 262, 394, 433, 510, 584, 641–643, 668–669, 676–678
acquisition of language   2, 3, 6, 20, 61, 80, 109, 114, 122, 199, 201, 262, 265, 267, 297, 301, 304, 307, 311, 348, 351, 377, 379, 389–403, 409–423, 483, 492, 531, 533, 534, 538, 566, 570, 585, 590, 634, 637, 655, 657, 661, 691, 693, 695, 696
action chain   329, 331
allophone   253, 255–256, 259–263
analogy   3, 106, 212, 219, 296, 317, 347, 377, 481, 483, 537, 634, 639–640, 642, 642n, 696
animal communication   232, 234, 237, 249, 669
argument structure   3, 16, 62, 411, 423, 475, 579- 581, 585, 587–588, 590
argumentation   236, 244–249
association measures   59, 67–68, 421
associative learning   24, 90, 190, 418, 420–421
attention   3, 6, 31–42, 44–45, 121, 123–124, 126–128, 130, 132, 139, 153–154, 219, 225–228, 238–240, 242, 245, 248–249, 326–238, 33–335, 347, 357, 390, 392, 422
automatization   60–61, 61n, 115, 315–317

B

basic level category   2, 104, 135–136, 153, 159, 170–172, 211–225, 227–229, 409, 570–571, 671
blending   10–11, 12, 14–16, 18–19, 22–23, 25–26, 125, 172, 174–175, 195, 356, 435, 457–459, 462–464, 496, 523, 568, 573, 639, 670, 671, 673, 676, 696, 698
body (see also embodiment)   18, 22, 26, 124–125, 144–145, 149–151, 298, 356, 457–459, 462, 464, 568, 573, 639, 651, 671, 673
body parts   5, 11–12, 14–15, 19, 21–26, 35–36, 54, 56, 60–62, 64–65, 76, 86–89, 103, 105, 115, 120, 144n, 150–152 172, 193, 195–196, 203–204, 216, 350, 423, 466, 483–484, 498–499, 501, 516, 519, 522, 553–554, 590, 638, 662, 691–693, 696, 698
brain   1, 3, 13–14, 32, 54, 55, 61, 76–91, 93, 110, 127, 129–131, 139, 148n, 152, 156, 192–195, 221, 234, 237, 241–243, 256–261, 273–279, 284–287, 296–299, 301, 304, 309–312, 314, 316–317, 324, 326–329, 347–354, 357, 369, 371, 376–377, 412–413, 416, 419, 420–422, 454–456, 458–459, 462–466, 473–475, 477–478, 482–484, 491–492, 504, 511–512, 519, 528, 532, 536, 562–571, 576, 581, 586–589, 617–618, 622–624, 626–628, 631, 635, 638–639, 679

C

categorization/category   1–3, 5, 13–14, 16, 32, 55, 75–93, 110, 127, 129–131, 139, 146, 150–152, 154–156, 192–195, 212, 221, 234, 237, 241–243, 254, 256–262, 268, 273–279, 284–287, 296–299, 309–312, 314, 316–317, 324, 327, 347–349, 351, 353, 357, 369, 371, 376–377, 412–413, 416, 419, 420–422, 454–456, 458–459, 462–466, 472–475, 478, 482–484, 492, 504, 536, 562–571, 576, 581, 586–589, 617–618, 623–624, 626–628, 631, 638–639, 679, 681
cline   156, 623–624, 642, 696
coercion   6, 11–13, 104, 114–116, 121, 135, 139, 143, 144n, 153, 168, 183–184, 204, 216, 229, 234, 237–240, 244–245, 257, 268, 281, 297, 325, 327, 333, 346–347, 351, 361–362, 410–411, 417–418, 423, 432–433, 436–437, 441, 447, 453–457, 463–465, 480, 510, 516, 527, 534, 536–538, 634, 637, 639, 656, 660, 662–664, 669, 669n, 681, 690, 693, 696, 698–699
cognition   2, 15, 60, 114–115, 128–130, 133, 137, 151n, 254, 261, 297–298, 327, 333–334, 368, 444, 634, 640, 643, 676, 695–696
Cognitive Grammar   13, 21, 26, 259
cognitive operation   93, 379, 465
cognitive processing   2, 6, 10–11, 19, 62, 66, 68, 93, 172, 183, 194, 200, 205, 302, 328n, 423, 434, 436–438, 443–444, 447, 523
cognitive science   279–281, 324, 460, 472, 479

cognitive semantics 286, 324n, 357, 367, 373, 376–380
cognitive sociolinguistics 237–40, 243–244, 247–249
common ground 16, 213, 256, 296–298, 394, 410–411, 414, 417, 654, 663, 669, 679–680
competence 108, 176, 219, 333, 400–401, 421, 690–691, 695–696, 698
competition 692, 695
complexity 131–143, 137
conceived time 563, 576
concept 135–136, 218, 230
conceptual integration 143, 168–172, 175–184, 281–283, 324–325, 327, 347, 356, 371–372, 442–443, 464, 510–511, 513–514, 516, 519–520, 548, 555, 618, 695
conceptual metaphor 120–122, 124-, 126–127, 130, 132–135, 138–140, 143, 325–337, 339–340369–370, 375, 548, 552–553, 616–618, 621, 623–626, 628, 631, 634, 640, 643–644, 671
construal 9,11,23–24,43,49,63,67,69–70,75–76, 98–100, 111, 114, 121–122, 134, 140, 147, 160, 162, 164–165, 178, 225–226, 228–237, 242, 245, 251, 276, 288, 304–309, 311–325, 334, 337, 341–342, 344, 355–360, 362–364, 367–370, 382–383, 387–388, 399, 402–403, 405, 410, 417–421, 423, 425–431, 452, 456, 465, 467–468, 480–485, 491, 541–542, 545, 562, 570, 576, 578–584, 587–598, 602n -604, 606–609, 611–619, 626, 634, 638, 642–644, 646–651, 653, 661–662, 664–671, 679, 685–686, 699–701, 704–705
construction 2, 3, 21, 101, 120, 140, 170, 298–302, 347, 350–351, 359–362, 409–410, 584, 586, 594, 610, 634, 640n, 640–641, 643, 696
construction grammar 153, 172, 368–370
contextualization 234, 237, 244, 246, 248–249
cooperative communication 4, 58, 68, 171, 370, 372, 410, 421, 434, 440, 446, 473, 478–479, 482
corpus linguistics 32, 34, 138, 156, 159, 192, 202, 310, 325, 356–357, 367, 396, 401, 422–423, 453–455, 457–466, 501, 503–504, 530, 534–538, 554, 617, 631
cross-linguistic/crosslinguistic (comparisons, research) 159, 439, 461

D

data collection 11
default non-salient interpretations 26, 234, 241–242, 329, 335, 624, 643
deixis 491, 499–503, 554, 624
demonstrative 347, 359–362, 641
diachronic construction grammar 3, 33–35, 41, 44, 128, 131, 144n, 153–154, 157–160, 171, 173–175, 177, 283, 322–340, 351, 355, 433–435, 437–440, 443, 482, 528, 530–531, 553, 555, 611, 635, 653, 662, 670
discourse 327, 335
discourse space theory 3, 100, 115
discriminative learning 201, 203, 205
distributional models 423, 669n, 680–681, 695–696, 700
dynamic systems 624
dynamicity 65n, 653, 655, 657–660, 662, 668

E

education 21, 23, 182, 200, 204
embodied simulation 3, 10–16, 18–26, 153, 168, 193, 195–200, 227, 287, 372–373, 421, 423, 435, 444, 454–457, 567, 669, 696
embodiment (see also body) 3, 690, 695, 697, 699
emergence 3, 53, 55, 57, 60–63, 65–68, 284–286, 296, 314, 348, 418, 421, 567, 587, 643, 659, 680, 699
entrenchment 65, 77, 234, 242n, 246n, 247n, 373–374, 379, 637, 639–640, 643, 689–692, 699
evolution 87–88, 90 92–94, 96–97, 114–116, 121–122, 124, 249, 265, 269, 276, 356–357, 361–362, 368–369, 385, 426–429, 431, 491, 571, 574, 576, 607–608, 611, 613, 668- 670
exemplar 85–86, 106–108
exemplar models 12, 14–19, 24, 63, 65, 110–116, 122–124, 126–129, 135, 137, 139–140, 145, 147, 148n, 156, 168–169, 171–172, 176–179, 181–184, 193, 197, 203–205 226, 228–229, 243, 301–302, 309, 312–316, 324–325, 327, 329, 357, 369, 372, 378, 401–403, 412–413, 417, 420–423, 433, 435–436, 438–442, 444–446, 459, 463, 474, 477, 510–512, 516–522, 528, 536, 538, 549, 551, 553, 556, 567, 618, 621, 623, 629, 638–639, 651, 653, 657, 659–660, 661, 663, 676, 681
experience 193–195

F

featural theories 3, 82, 134, 137–139, 181, 530, 546–556
fictive motion 135, 137
fictivity (see also fictive motion) 327, 494, 617, 619, 621–622, 627, 671
force dynamics/force-dynamics 533
forensic linguistics 412–413, 416–417
formulaic language 40, 43–44, 90–91, 148–149, 171, 211–212, 218–219, 220–225, 283–284, 305, 333, 376, 414, 473, 496–497, 504, 618, 693–694
frame 143, 328n, 329, 443
framing 3, 16, 18, 53–54n, 54–60, 62–63, 66–68, 262–265, 315–316, 348, 400, 418, 420, 423, 567–568, 571, 574–576, 589
frequency 493
functional geometric framework 562, 571, 573, 576, 679
fuzziness 491, 493–495, 497

G

geometry 3, 23, 90, 223, 238, 523, 530, 530n, 534–535, 555, 668–669, 671, 677–681, 694
gesture 569–570, 679, 681
gradience 2–4, 14–16, 21, 31n, 31–35, 44–45, 53, 60, 67, 101–102, 105–106, 108, 111–116, 121, 124, 126–130, 133, 137–138, 140, 144n, 151, 153, 156–157, 159, 170, 219, 222–223, 232, 234, 254, 256, 261, 281, 285, 296–304, 309, 311, 314–317, 326–327, 331, 333–334, 340, 347–348, 350–351, 353–354, 357–361, 368–370, 373, 375–376, 379–380, 389, 391, 393–394, 396, 398, 400, 403, 409–410, 412, 415, 417–418, 422–423, 436, 444, 457, 464–465, 567–568, 573, 576, 580, 584, 586–587, 594n, 610, 628–629, 634–637, 639–641, 643–644, 651, 661–664, 669–670, 675–676, 679–681, 689–690, 695–696, 699
grammar 347, 349, 351–357, 359, 458, 634–641, 643–645, 671, 675, 677–678
grammaticalization 32, 124–125, 128, 132, 139, 225–227, 238–241, 245, 247–249, 296, 442, 463
ground 357–358, 362

H

historical sociolinguistics 202
holistic theories 201, 472, 480
homonymy 107–108, 116
hybrid models 131, 157, 436, 438, 444, 675–676

I

iconicity 332–333, 376, 442, 460, 520–521, 563, 565–567
identification 301, 410, 417–418, 574, 576
idiomaticity 17, 36, 82, 90–91, 258, 260–261, 266, 327n, 329–330, 332, 336, 389, 480, 492–493, 496
image schema 266
image schema transformation 135, 519, 679
imaginative phenomena/imagination 115, 304
implicit learning 3, 12, 379, 400, 484, 566, 650–652, 655, 659–663
individual differences 19, 23, 62, 79–80, 86, 132, 154, 171, 175, 177, 205, 216–217, 235–236, 238–239, 243, 283, 324, 328–329, 392–393, 555, 566, 583, 638–639, 640
inference 4, 13, 17, 377, 416, 597, 695
interactional 242, 247–249n, 373–374
intersubjectivity 533
intratypological variation 158, 193, 203, 205, 433, 441–442, 476, 565
introspection 696
item-based (patterns) 6, 219, 225–228, 238–239, 248, 347, 357, 390, 392, 503

J

joint attention 237, 239–240, 244
joint cognition 239, 244, 245, 247–249, 462
joint projects 36, 199, 202, 296, 391, 413–414, 660

L

language development 55, 92, 103, 410, 413, 659, 690, 699
language learning 33, 56, 59, 62, 64, 67, 92, 103, 105, 116, 134, 139, 195, 203, 348, 410–411, 417, 420, 536–538, 555
language processing/processing 3, 24, 26, 36, 53, 55, 58, 60, 62–66, 76, 78–83, 85–93,

100, 102–103, 106–110, 114–116, 192, 197, 199–200, 205, 304, 389–394, 398–402, 410, 413–418, 420–422, 503–504, 519, 534, 536, 555, 585–586, 588–589, 659–661, 696, 698, 699
learning (see also associative learnaning, discriminative learning) 286, 375
lectal variation 347, 349, 353, 356–360, 362
lexical semantic change 3, 154, 218, 253, 268, 273–274, 280–282, 284, 286–287, 330, 351, 464, 473, 475, 565
lexical semantics 301, 317, 657, 658
lexical specificity 456, 528–538
lexicalization pattern 33, 35, 58, 78, 103, 105–107, 113, 124, 126–127, 170, 257, 279, 281, 285, 287, 300, 302, 306–307, 353–354, 357–358, 375, 389, 391, 393–394, 398–400, 410, 461, 464–465, 481, 530, 595–596, 621, 635, 637, 639, 644, 698–69
lexicon 3, 373, 465, 503–504, 509
linguistic relativity 432–434, 437–438, 442, 444, 447
literature 462, 474
lumping v. splitting 146, 148n, 201, 310, 511–512, 521

M

meaning 61–66, 80, 83, 85–87, 101, 103, 106–107, 112, 115, 149, 183, 194, 196, 306, 348, 377, 399–400, 417, 419, 482, 500–503, 535–537, 547n, 654, 659, 660, 693–694
memory (see also working memory) 128, 133, 137, 139, 190, 214, 553
mental simulation 2, 135–137, 170, 212–219, 222–228, 247–248, 335, 570, 621
mental space(s) 458, 462
metalanguage 2, 3, 18–22, 104, 113, 122, 135–136, 139, 143–148, 153–154, 158–159, 167–184, 191, 197, 199, 215, 219, 261, 268, 278, 281–283, 286–287, 322–329, 346–347, 352–353, 356–358, 360, 371–372, 375–376, 401, 409, 436 442–443, 454–455, 457, 460, 464–466, 474–475, 491–492, 495, 510–516, 519–523, 530–531, 548, 552, 554–556, 565–566, 568, 594–601, 608, 610, 617–621, 623, 627, 639–640, 660, 671–676, 679, 695–696
metaphor 530–531

metaphorical motion 4–5, 85, 159, 287, 370, 375, 416, 434, 438, 441, 455, 464, 483, 500, 530, 586, 657, 698
methodology 3, 18, 19, 20, 126, 143–159, 170, 172, 174, 215, 278, 281–284, 286, 347, 352, 353, 358, 376, 464, 474, 566, 617, 623, 640, 673–675, 679, 689, 696
metonymy 3, 17, 157, 190, 194, 200, 354, 358, 456, 617, 618, 621, 622, 626, 627, 629, 630, 671, 681
modality 329, 337, 618, 626–7
modality, deontic 329, 337, 339, 626–627, 630
modality, epistemic 155
morphosyntactic processes 3, 15, 21, 23–25, 82, 131, 134, 137–139, 155, 170, 175, 181–182, 200, 214, 215, 216, 223, 229, 313, 326, 329–323, 356, 422, 457, 461, 463, 464, 475, 491, 499, 510, 511, 513–515, 519, 521–522, 527–538, 546–556, 580–582, 586–587, 590, 670, 674–676, 680–681
motion 134, 170, 356, 457, 530, 534, 537, 548, 554–555
motion verb 239–245, 248
mutual knowledge 234, 237, 245, 247–249, 374, 415, 594–600, 602–611, 622, 635

N

negation 652–3
neighbourhood effects 302, 483
network models 596, 597, 610
non-literal meaning 594, 597–598, 608–610
nonliteralness 335, 339, 477, 644

O

objectivity 273, 281
onomasiology 121, 136, 178, 193, 195, 197, 203, 228, 254–258, 260, 264–266, 296, 376–379, 390, 420–421, 433, 435, 441, 455–461, 463–468, 477, 502–503, 510–511, 519, 522, 536, 553, 620, 674–675, 679, 681, 697

P

perception 520
perceptual moment 16, 21, 22, 25, 32, 35, 55, 68, 87, 107, 116, 195, 203, 256, 264,

Subject index

297, 298, 445, 482, 504, 586, 620, 652, 654, 655, 654–662, 669, 679–680
performance   6, 16, 39, 53, 58, 62, 63, 65, 66, 76–77, 88–89, 92–93, 100, 103, 109, 113–116, 121, 139, 145, 170, 172, 175, 190, 192–193, 196, 200, 228, 236, 281, 283–284, 287, 298,, 300, 302, 315, 322–329, 335, 348, 351, 354, 367, 372–380, 398, 401, 409–410, 423, 438, 472, 474, 483, 496, 510, 512, 515, 517, 528, 531, 537, 552, 562, 566, 568, 569, 574, 616, 618, 621, 631, 634, 636, 637, 639, 643, 669, 670, 682, 691–692, 696
perspective   16, 54, 101, 255–263, 316, 349, 351, 410, 670, 680
phoneme   255–256, 260
phonemic perception   432–447
poetics   3, 5, 18–20, 127, 153–154, 170, 173, 176, 192, 201, 218–219, 273, 278–280, 287, 347, 349, 352, 454, 456, 460, 462, 472–484, 492–493, 496, 566, 617, 623, 696
polysemy   38, 40, 45, 287, 327, 328, 329, 335–338, 694
positioning   34, 234, 373, 392, 409–410, 433–434, 617
pragmatics   17, 36, 105, 111, 129, 130, 199, 278, 279, 284, 298, 317, 348, 355, 411, 416, 422, 474, 475–477, 483, 491–501, 528, 531, 554, 566, 569, 570, 574, 583, 653
preposition   54, 108, 131, 133–134, 181, 481, 516
processing time   4, 105, 123–132, 139, 146, 155, 229, 328, 333–335, 465, 474, 479, 564, 568, 611, 616, 621, 623, 625–626, 640, 644–645
profiling, profile   4, 121, 126, 127, 128, 130, 333, 596, 634
prominence   511, 518
protracted duration   2,16, 20, 21, 54, 59, 301, 361, 389, 398, 410, 473, 479, 480, 482, 483, 584
psycholinguistics   2, 257–258, 260, 262, 274–279, 474–5, 492, 565, 566, 617

R

radial category/set/structure   56, 65, 227, 248, 325, 327, 391, 433, 435, 436–446, 660, 662
reader   355, 634, 636–639

reanalysis   13, 16–17, 23, 31–36, 44–45, 53, 55, 60–69, 76–93, 100, 103–108, 111–115, 121, 135–137, 148–149, 172, 190–205, 212, 227, 239, 257, 263, 268, 278–279, 297, 303, 306, 316, 323–325, 328–331, 335–336, 346, 348–351, 354. 376–377, 379, 394, 399–400, 411, 420–421, 441, 443–444, 458–459, 475–476, 478, 481–482, 496, 511–515, 517–523, 565, 579, 580, 583–585, 590, 595, 637, 675, 696
representation   144, 151, 154, 168, 225, 234, 236–237, 248, 331, 337, 340, 434–435, 530, 534–535, 668
rhetoric   3, 6, 31–45, 69, 122, 127–128, 131, 143, 156, 179, 274, 279, 281, 284–287, 327–328, 333, 418, 420, 533, 565–567, 576, 589, 594–597, 600, 602–607, 610–611, 644

S

salience   457, 529–532
satellite-frame   20, 132–134, 137–328, 334–335
scanning   3, 15, 55, 61, 66, 104, 107–108, 113–114, 116, 126, 130–131, 134, 137–139, 147, 152, 159, 181, 183–184, 199, 236–237, 256–257, 261–262, 268, 275, 283, 298, 300–306, 311–312, 317, 327–333, 347–348, 354–355, 357, 360–361, 377, 394–395, 399–400, 410, 414, 418–419, 433, 435–436, 439, 442–443, 445, 465, 474, 476, 483, 492, 494, 548, 571, 585–586, 641, 642, 644–645, 652, 657, 676–678, 696
schema   2, 3, 55, 153, 159, 409–423, 531, 534, 538, 661, 693, 695, 698
second language acquisition (SLA)   462
semantic map   34–36, 76, 115, 120, 151, 154, 190, 193, 196, 198, 199, 204, 240, 241–242, 280–281, 283–284, 324, 371–372, 375, 377, 379, 410, 433, 457, 460–462, 473, 475, 496, 528, 532, 547, 569, 572–573, 581–582, 590, 605, 643
semantics   273, 454
semasiology   12, 17–20, 23, 54, 59, 76–77, 85, 91, 104, 110, 126, 134, 147, 152, 154–156, 193, 201–202, 267, 274, 277–281, 324, 349, 352, 358, 368, 438, 442, 445–446, 455–457, 460, 472–484, 492–493,

496, 547–548, 552, 554, 556, 564–566, 568, 573–675
sense   32, 33, 38, 41, 42, 43, 44, 45, 68, 580, 695
sentence production   3, 258, 547, 668- 682
signed language   23, 83, 115, 123, 182, 194, 196, 199–200, 203–204, 214, 400, 423, 444–445, 553
simulation   350, 357, 367, 370, 373, 374, 375, 377, 379, 434, 439
sociolinguistics   3, 82, 90–91, 123, 127, 132, 137, 197, 326, 328,-329, 335–336, 356, 460, 463–464, 466, 479, 490–504–523, 527, 532, 536, 547–548, 551–553, 563, 618–619, 621, 639–640, 670–671, 676
space   422, 490–491, 493–496, 49- 499, 501, 503–504, 519, 554, 556
spatial language   327–329, 332, 572, 583, 584
structural configuration   374, 433, 434, 437, 439, 440, 441, 443, 44, 445
stylistics   548n
subjective motion   240, 242, 247–249n, 335, 339, 373–374, 442, 553, 627
subjectivity   4, 151, 221, 246, 354–355, 480, 481, 483, 528, 530, 650, 653, 659
subordinate/subordination   59
surprisal   67, 90, 113, 135, 255, 257, 258, 260, 262, 263, 266, 267, 268, 391, 680, 681, 694
syllable   368, 389, 398, 409–410, 419, 433, 464, 475, 579, 588–589, 622, 643, 650, 653–654, 657, 668, 677
syntax   360, 459- 461, 463- 465, 511

T

temperature   551
temporal compression   335n, 443
text world theory   3, 5, 13, 21, 25, 35, 54n, 58, 68, 81–82, 108, 123, 125, 129, 131–137, 169, 178, 180–183, 197, 202, 212, 214.225–228, 241, 258, 263, 302, 316, 326, 328, 335–336, 356, 358, 361, 389, 393, 397, 399, 411, 415, 477, 481, 491, 509–523, 531, 551–553, 555–556, 564, 574–575, 582, 585, 600–602, 604–605, 607, 617–619, 621, 623, 627, 631, 639–640, 658, 660, 668, 670, 690, 692–700
time   519, 527
time-as-such   690, 692–695, 698
timeframe   54–55, 66, 400, 418–420
token frequency   516, 518, 520
transience   3, 177, 192, 412, 417, 461, 527, 531–533, 535–536, 538, 635, 461, 535–536, 538
translation   55, 400, 418–419, 589, 653, 665
type frequency   144, 149, 151, 159, 248, 258, 340, 353, 367, 460–464, 529,-530, 532–534, 538, 635, 693, 700
typology   464
typology, grammatical   454, 462
typology, lexical   3, 453–454, 460–466, 468
typology, semantic   262, 275, 418, 671, 697, 698, 705, 706, 707

U

Universal Grammar (UG)   69, 378, 383, 426, 698, 703, 705
usage-based approaches   374, 375, 382, 383, 385, 386

V

variationist linguistics   358, 383
variationist sociolinguistics   465, 537, 538, 539, 540, 541, 543
verb-frame   225, 227–229, 335
viewpoint   44, 45, 52, 558, 559
visual attention   95, 204, 492, 662,667, 668

W

working memory   427, 597

Z

Zipfian distribution   293